GUN TRADER'S GUIDE

FOURTEENTH EDITION

Revision by: John E. Traister
Managing Editor: Charlene Cruson Step

STOEGER PUBLISHING COMPANY

Published by Stoeger Publishing Company
55 Ruta Court
South Hackensack, New Jersey 07606

ISBN: 0-88317-153-8
Manufactured in the United States of America

Distributed to the book trade and to the sporting goods trade by Stoeger Industries, 55 Ruta Court, South Hackensack, New Jersey 07606

In Canada, distributed to the book trade and to the sporting goods trade by Stoeger Canada, Ltd., Unit 16, 1801 Wentworth Street, Whitby, Ontario L1N 5S4

COVER DESIGN AND PHOTOGRAPHS: Ray Wells

FRONT COVER: Remington No. 7 Target Rifle (left) with rolling-block army pistol frame, made 1903-1911. Remington Model 89 double-barreled shotgun (center), made 1889-1908. Remington Model 8A Autoloading Rifle (right), made 1906 to 1936. From the Remington Museum Collection, courtesy Remington Arms Company, Inc.

INTRODUCTION

Gun trading is an old American custom. It dates back to Colonial days when the family muzzleloader was "purchased" by trading home-grown goods. Since then, the basic uses of the firearm have remained virtually unchanged: self-protection, food gathering, target practice, games, sport. What has revolutionized over the almost four centuries since the early settlers arrived are 1) the prices, and 2) the mammoth variety of styles and models that have evolved through the help of improved technology. Since 1900 alone, the numbers of manufacturers and firearms products have skyrocketed.

This is where a book like GUN TRADER'S GUIDE is of infinite value. For anyone interested or involved in firearms in any capacity—gun dealer, manufacturer, gunsmith, collector, military personnel, law enforcement/security police, shooting editor/writer, museum curator, auctioneer, appraiser or insurance adjuster—the GUN TRADER'S GUIDE details thousands of modern 20th-century firearms.

This new 14th edition in its more than 500 pages encompasses descriptions of over 4,400 firearms dating from 1900, plus about 2,200 illustrations. Each listing includes complete specifications, such as caliber/gauge, barrel length, overall length, weight, distinguishing features and variations, plus the dates of production. And, of course, a price that indicates current value in the used-gun market. (For more about gun values, see "How To Use This Book" on page 5). In addition, black and white photos or illustrations accompany the text so you can, if necessary, accurately identify a particular gun with a visual image. What's different from the 13th edition is the addition of a number of manufacturers, such as Action Arms, Auto-Ordnance, Glock, Kimber, Targa, Texas Longhorn Arms, Wichita Arms, Wilkinson Arms, and others, plus an expanded Luger handgun section in response to reader requests.

The first edition of GUN TRADER'S GUIDE, a triumph in reporting, so to speak, for the firearms industry, was published in 1953 with about 1,360 listings supplemented by 100 photos. In that edition and many subsequent revisions, guns were organized chronologically by date of production within alphabetical manufacturer groupings. As the number of firearms and variations multiplied through the years, it became increasingly difficult to track the models. It also became a challenge to find a specific model in the book, if all you knew was the name or model number and not the date it was manufactured. So, to make it easier for those who use this book, the 12th edition, offered in 1986, revamped the organization of the listings. That arrangement was, and continues in this edition, that guns are grouped by category first: Handguns, Rifles, Shotguns. They are then arranged alphabetically by name of manufacturer. Within each manufacturer's entries, *Model Numbers* appear first in consecutive numerical order, followed by *Model Names* in alphabetical order.

Most of the major gunmakers that initially appeared—the Brownings, Colts, Marlins, Remingtons, Smith & Wessons, Winchesters, etc.—have remained in operation over the past 37 years. Some of them, however, like Iver Johnson and Winchester, have changed ownership, but are still producing firearms under the original brand name. Other manufacturers—Kessler, Harrington & Richardson, High Standard, to name a few—have fallen by the wayside. This is another area in which GUN TRADER'S GUIDE is particularly helpful. . . in identifying and establishing values for discontinued firearms. For example, Winchester Repeating Arms Co. has discontinued no less than two dozen different models. If all the variations of these guns were taken into account, the number would jump to nearly 100. Remington and Colt each report about the same count of discontinued models. Travel back to the turn of the century, include all the smaller companies, and this figure soars to over 5,000 discontinued models in the United States alone. Consider also that GUN TRADER'S GUIDE describes the firearms of dozens of foreign manufacturers, as well as "private label" brands.

No book can include every firearm ever produced or discontinued. You'd need a set of encyclopedias for that. GUN TRADER'S GUIDE tries to reflect those guns most-often traded or inquired about by readers, in a practical, one-volume size that is easy to use. We apologize for any oversights, and encourage readers to write to us with their impressions and reactions to the book, or for suggestions for improvement.

During its many years of publication, GUN TRADER'S GUIDE has met with great success and acceptance. The editors hope that by providing essential firearms data in an easy-to-use format that it will continue to be a meaningful reference to all who are involved with firearms.

ACKNOWLEDGMENTS

The Publisher wishes to express special thanks to Kenneth D. Green, Manager of Product Service at the Remington Arms Company, Inc., for his help in coordinating the photo shooting for this edition's front cover, and to Mr. Robert Fisch, curator of the West Point Museum, for new photographs of Luger handguns, which have helped enhance that revised section. A grateful bow is made in the direction of the numerous collectors, dealers, shooting editors and others whose suggestions and advice have contributed to making this a better book over the years. Thank you to Triple K Manufacturing Co. for permission to use the pistol illustrations (indicated by *) from their catalog. And to all the firearms firms—their public relations and product personnel, and all the research people the Stoeger editors work with throughout the year—we are particularly thankful to all of you for your assistance and cooperation in compiling information for GUN TRADER'S GUIDE and for allowing us to reproduce photographs and illustrations of your firearms.

HOW TO USE THIS BOOK

To use this book effectively, it is important to understand how the prices in GUN TRADER'S GUIDE were obtained, and how they should be used. Consequently, this section of the book explains the derivation of the prices to ensure that you understand how the firearms are priced.

Please bear in mind that the prices contained in this book are "retail"; that is, the price that the consumer may be expected to pay for a similar item. However, many variables must be considered when buying or selling any gun. In general, scarcity, demand, geographical location, the buyer's position and the gun's condition will govern the selling price of a particular gun. Sentiment also enters into the value of an individual's gun, but cannot be logically cataloged.

To illustrate how the price of a particular gun may fluctuate, let's assume that you have a standard Model 12 Winchester pump shotgun with plain barrel, in 12 gauge. You find the gun listed in this book, and see a price of $550. Since you really have no use for the gun, you decide to sell it, and therefore take it to your closest gun dealer, asking him to purchase it for $550. Here are some possible reactions from the dealer:

1. If the shotgun is in excellent condition; that is, if it contains at least 95 percent of the original finish on both the metal and wood, has a perfect bore and contains a modified choke, then the gun does have a retail value of about $550. However, the dealer is in business to make some profit. If he pays you $550 for the gun, he will have to charge more than this when he sells it. If more is charged than the fair market value, then either the gun will not sell, or someone will pay more than the gun is worth. Therefore, the dealer will have to offer you less than the retail price for the gun to make a fair profit. However, the exact amount will vary from dealer to dealer and from situation to situation. For example, if this dealer already has a dozen or so of the same model on his shelf and they have been slow moving, the dealer's offer will probably be rather low. OR, if the dealer has only one or two Model 12s left and most have been selling reasonably well, chances are he may slightly increase his offer.

2. You may not have considered the condition of your shotgun. Perhaps the inside bore is badly pitted, or a replacement stock has been fitted, or most of the bluing has worn off the gun. Since this will dramatically affect the resale value of the gun, the dealer's offering to you would be minimal.

3. Perhaps the shotgun has most of its original finish, but at one time a choke attachment was added to the end of the barrel. Since this is a modification or a deviation from the factory original, the value of the gun could decrease by as much as 50 percent or more.

4. So your Winchester Model 12 looks nearly new . . . just out of the box; you have no choke attachment, and the gun seems to work perfectly. Therefore, you are convinced that the dealer is going to pay you full value, less a reasonable profit. However, when the dealer offers you about half what you expected, you are shocked! Is the dealer trying to beat you? Perhaps you were not aware that the gun had recently been refinished, and although the finish looks new to you, you did not notice the rounding of the formerly sharp edges of the receiver, or the slight funneling of some screw holes that were a dead giveaway that the gun had at one time been refinished. Therefore, your gun has less than "book" value.

Now if you are somewhat of an "expert" and know for certain that your shotgun has never been refinished or otherwise tampered with, and there is still at least 95 percent of its original finish, and believe you have a firearm that is worth full book value, you may possibly obtain the full value by advertising in a local newspaper—selling the firearm directly to a private individual. However, this approach may prove both frustrating and expensive, for many reasons. Chances are, the next time you have a firearm to sell, you will be more than happy to sell it to a dealer and let him make his fair share of profit.

The above examples present some of the factors that can affect the value of a firearm. However, there are countless others, and the brief examples given are meant only to provide a basic understanding of the process.

CONDITION

Condition, without any doubt, is a prime factor in determining the value of a used gun. Several sets of "standards" have been available over the years with the National Rifle Association Standards of Condition for Modern Firearms probably being the most popular. However, in recent years, condition has been specified by percentage of original finish remaining on the firearm—both on the wood and metal. For example, a firearm that appears factory new with the exception of some bluing worn around the muzzle and on some very sharp edges on the receiver may be considered to be in excellent condition with from 95 to 98 percent original finish; the bore will have been cleaned out after each firing, so the bore should be in excellent shape; the only exception to this would be with ultra high-velocity rounds such as the .220 Swift and the .264 Win., in which case the bores can be completely shot out in less than 200 rounds if fired rapidly.

For the purpose of assigning comparative values as a basis for trading, firearms listed in this book are assumed to be in excellent condition with 95 percent or better remaining overall finish; no noticeable marring of wood or metal, and bores excellent with no pits. To the novice, this means a practically new gun, almost as though you had removed it from the factory carton. The trained eye, however, will know the difference between new or mint condition, and excellent.

From the above paragraph, any other defects, regardless of how minor, lower the value from those listed in this book. For example, if more than five percent of the original finish is gone, and there are minor surface dents or scratches—regardless of how small—the gun is no longer in excellent condition; rather, it takes on the condition of "very good," provided the gun is in perfect working order. Even in this state, other than for the minor defects, the gun will still look relatively new to the uninitiated gun buyer.

If the gun is in perfect working condition—functions properly, does not jam, and is accurate—but has minor wear on working surfaces, perhaps some bad scratches on the wood or metal, etc., then the gun takes on the condition of "good"—one grade below very good—according to the NRA Standards. Again, the price in this book for that particular firearm must be lowered more to obtain its true value.

The two remaining NRA conditions fall under the headings of "fair" and "poor," respectively.

Previous editions of GUN TRADER'S GUIDE gave multiplication factors to use for firearms in other than excellent condition. While these factors are still present in this edition, please be aware that these factors are not infallible, depending upon the model and brand of firearm.

TABLE OF MULTIPLICATION FACTORS FOR GUNS IN OTHER THAN EXCELLENT CONDITION

For guns in other than excellent condition, multiply the price in this book for the model in question by the following appropriate factors:

Condition	Multiplication Factor
Mint or New	1.25
Excellent	1.00
Very Good	0.85
Good	0.68
Fair	0.35
Poor	0.15

NATIONAL RIFLE ASSOCIATION STANDARDS OF CONDITION OF MODERN FIREARMS

New: Not previously sold at retail, in same condition as current factory production.

New, Discontinued: Same as New, but discontinued model.

Perfect: In new condition in every respect; sometimes referred to as "mint."

Excellent: New condition, used very little, no noticeable marring of wood or metal, bluing perfect (except at muzzle or sharp edges). This is the condition used to price firearms in GUN TRADER'S GUIDE.

Very Good: In perfect working condition, no appreciable wear on working surfaces, no corrosion or pitting, only minor surface dents or scratches.

Good: In safe working condition, minor wear on working surfaces, no broken parts, no corrosion or pitting that will interfere with proper functioning.

Fair: In safe working condition, but well worn, perhaps requiring replacement of minor parts or adjustments which should be indicated in advertisement; no rust but may have corrosion pits which do not render the article unsafe or inoperable.

Poor: Badly worn, rusty and battered, perhaps requiring major adjustment or repairs to place in operating condition.

When a collector firearm has been expertly refinished to excellent condition, a rule of thumb is to deduct fifty (50) percent from the value indicated in this book. If poorly done, deduct ninety (90) percent.

Note: All prices shown in this book are for guns in excellent condition (almost new) and the prices are retail (what a dealer would normally charge for them). A dealer will seldom pay the full value shown in this book. If a gun is in any condition other than excellent, the price in this book must be multiplied by the appropriate factor to obtain a true value of the gun in question.

CONTENTS

Section II
RIFLES

Section III
SHOTGUNS

Section I

HANDGUNS

ACTION ARMS
Philadelphia, Pennsylvania

Action Arms AT-84
Double Action Pistol

Action Arms AT-84 DA Automatic Pistol $375
Caliber: 9mm Parabellum. 15-shot magazine. 4¾-inch barrel. 8 inches overall. Weight: 35 oz. Fixed front sight; drift adjustable rear. Checkered walnut stocks. Blued finish. Made in Switzerland from 1987 to 1989.

ADVANTAGE ARMS
St. Paul, Minnesota

Advantage Arms Model 6 Double Derringer $225
Calibers: .410 and 45 Colt. 6-inch barrel. 8.2 inches overall. Weight: 21 oz. Satin or high-polished stainless steel.

Advantage Arms Model 7 Ultra Lightweight
Calibers: 38 S&W, 380 Auto, 32 S&W Long, 32 Mag. 38 Special, 22 LR and 44 Mag. Same general specifications as Model 6, except weighs 7½ oz. and chambered for different calibers.

38 S&W, 380 Auto and 32 S&W	**$125**
32 Magnum	**130**
38 Special	**140**
22 Long Rifle	**140**
44 Special	**345**

Advantage Arms Model 11 Lightweight. $140
Same general specifications as Model 7, except weighs 11 oz. and chambered for 38 Special only.

Advantage Arms
Model 422

Advantage Arms Model 422 . . . . $105
Calibers: 22 LR and 22 Mag. 4-cartridge capacity. Barrel: 2½ inches. 4½ inches overall. Weight: 15 oz. Fixed sights. Walnut grips. Blued or nickel finish. Discontinued 1986.

Advantage Arms Semmerling LM-4 Vest Pocket
Caliber: 45 ACP or 9mm. 5-shot capacity. 5 inches overall.

Blued Finish	**$ 995**
Stainless Finish	**1250**

S. A. ALKARTASUNA FABRICA DE ARMAS
Guernica, Spain

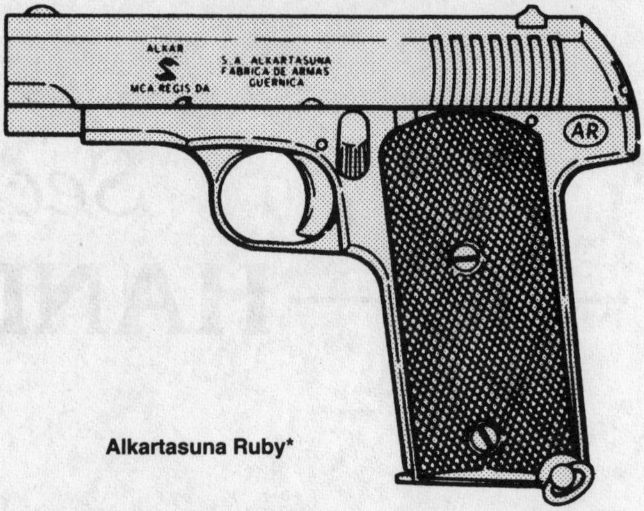

Alkartasuna Ruby*

Alkartasuna "Ruby" Automatic Pistol $225
Caliber: 32 Automatic (7.65mm). 9-shot magazine. 3⅝-inch barrel. 6⅜ inches overall. Weight: about 34 oz. Fixed sights. Blued finish. Checkered wood or hard rubber stocks. Made from 1917 to 1922. *Note:* Mfd. by a number of Spanish firms, the Ruby was a secondary standard service pistol of the French Army in World Wars I and II. Specimens made by Alkartasuna bear the "Alkar" trademark.

AMERICAN DERRINGER CORPORATION
Waco, Texas

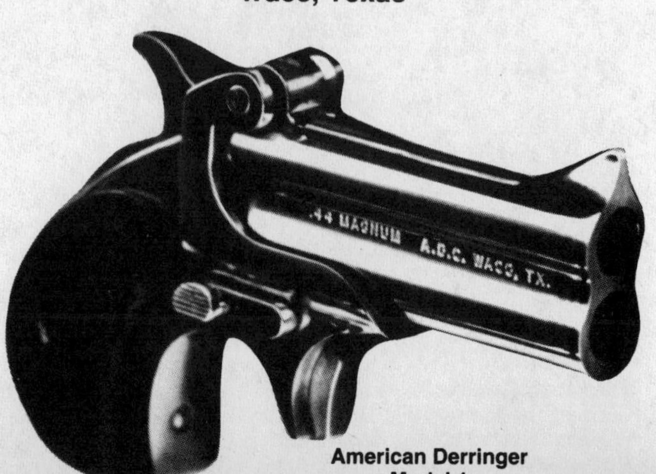

American Derringer
Model 1

HANDGUNS

American Derringer Model 1, Stainless
Single-action pocket pistol. 2-shot capacity. Barrel: 3 inches. 4.82 inches overall. Weight: 15 oz. Automatic barrel selection. Satin or high-polished stainless steel. Rosewood grips. Made from 1985 to date.

45 Colt, 44-40 Win., 44 Special	**$205**
45 Colt or 2½" .410, .410 × 2½" or 45 Colt	**235**
45 Win. Mag., 357 Max.	**185**
45 Win. Mag., 45-70, 44 Mag., 41 Mag., 30-30 Win., 223 Rem.	**275**
357 Max.	**185**
357 Mag.	**165**
38 Special, 32 Mag., 22 LR, 22 Rim. Mag.	**160**
38 Super, 380 Auto, 9mm Luger, 30 Luger	**150**

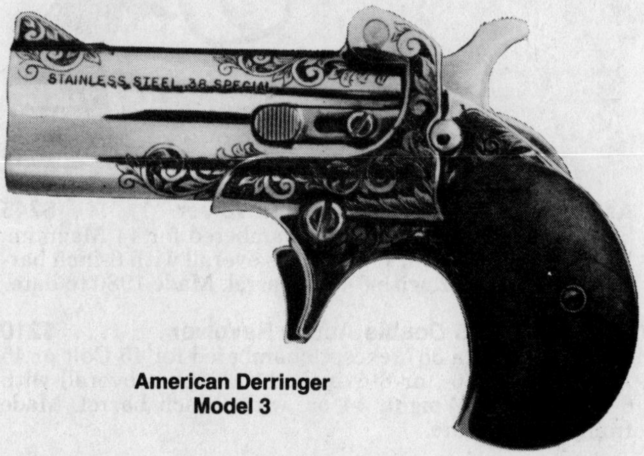

American Derringer Model 3

American Derringer Model 3 Stainless Steel Single Shot **$80**
Caliber: 38 Special. Barrel: 2½ inches. 4.9 inches overall. Weight: 8.5 oz. Rosewood grips. Made from 1984 to date.

American Derringer Model 4 Stainless Steel Double Derringer **$280**
Calibers: 3-inch .410 shotshell or 45 Colt. Barrel: 4.1 inches. 6 inches overall. Weight: 16½ oz. Stag horn grips. Made from 1984 to date.

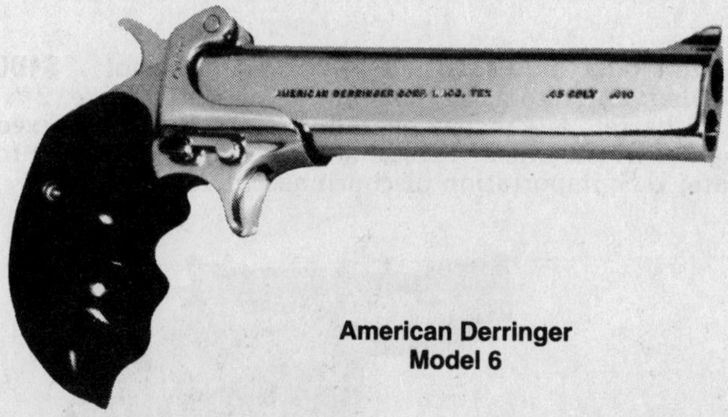
American Derringer Model 6

American Derringer Model 6 .... **$280**
Caliber: .410 or 45 Colt. Barrel: 6 inches. 8.2 inches overall. Weight: 1 lb. 6 oz. Satin or high-polished stainless steel with rosewood grips. Made from 1986 to date.

American Derringer Model 7
Same general specifications as the Model 1, except high-strength aircraft aluminum is used to replace some of the stainless steel parts, which reduces its weight to 7½ oz. Made from 1986 to date.

38 Special	**$150**
38 S&W, 380 Auto, 22 LR	**140**
44 Special	**325**

American Derringer Model 11 .... **$140**
Same general specifications as Model 1 except chambered for .38 Special only, and weighs 11 oz. Made 1980 to date.

American Derringer 25 Automatic Pistol **$150**
Calibers: 25 ACP or 250 Mag. Barrel: 2.1 inches. 4.4 inches overall. Weight: 15½ oz. Smooth rosewood grips. Made from 1984 to date.

American Derringer Alaskan Survival Model **$270**
Same general specifications as the Model 4, except upper barrel comes in 45-70 or 3-inch .410 and 45 Colt lower barrel. Also available in 45 Auto, 45 Colt, 44 Special, 357 Mag. and .357 Max. Made from 1985 to date.

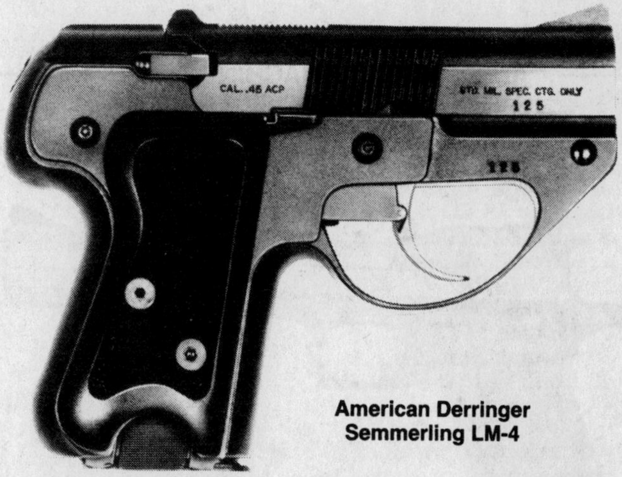

American Derringer Semmerling LM-4

American Derringer Semmerling LM-4
Double action. Calibers: 45 ACP or 9 mm. 5-round capacity. Weight: 24 oz. Overall length: 5.2 inches. Made from 1986 to date.

Blued Finish	**$2200**
Stainless Steel	**2500**

— AMERICAN FIREARMS MFG. CO., INC. — San Antonio, Texas

American 25 Auto Pistol
Caliber: 25 Automatic. 8-shot magazine. 2.1-inch barrel. 4.4 inches overall. Weight: 14½ oz. Fixed sights. Stainless steel or blued ordnance steel. Smooth walnut stocks. Made from 1966 to 1974.

Stainless Steel Model	**$180**
Blued Steel Model	**150**

American 380 Automatic

American 380 Auto Pistol **$225**
Stainless steel. Caliber: 380 Automatic. 8-shot magazine. 3½-inch barrel. 5½ inches overall. Weight: 20 oz. Smooth walnut stocks. Made from 1972 to 1974.

AMT (ARCADIA MACHINE & TOOL)
Irwindale, California

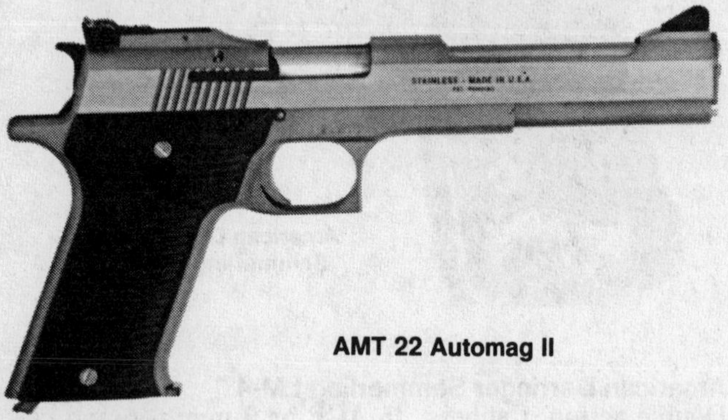

AMT 22 Automag II

AMT Automag II Automatic Pistol **$225**
Caliber: 22 WRF. 9-shot magazine. Barrel lengths: 3⅜-, 4½-, 6-inch. Weight: 32 oz. Fully adjustable Millett sights. Stainless finish. Smooth black composition stocks. Made from 1986 to date.

AMT Lightning Auto Pistol
Caliber: 22 Long Rifle. 10-shot magazine. 5-, 6½-, 8½-, 10-inch barrels. 10¾ inches overall w/6½-inch barrel. Weight: 45 oz. w/6½-inch barrel. Fully adjustable Millett sights. Stainless finish. Checkered rubber stocks. Made from 1984 to date.
Standard Model **$215**
Bull's-Eye Model **330**

ASTRA PISTOLS
Guernica, Spain
Manufactured by Unceta y Compania

Astra Model 41 Double Action Revolver **$225**
Same general specifications as Model 44 except chambered for 41 Magnum.

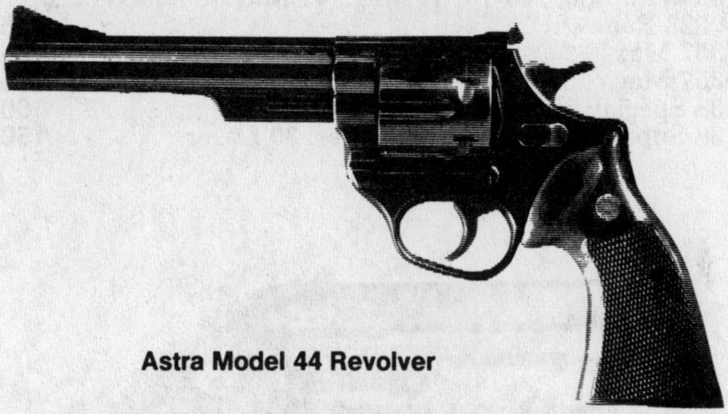

Astra Model 44 Revolver

Astra Model 44 Double Action Revolver **$245**
Similar to Astra 357, except chambered for 44 Magnum. Barrels: 6-, 8½-inch. 11½ inches overall with 6-inch barrel. Weight: 44 oz. with 6-inch barrel. Made 1980 to date.

Astra Model 45 Double Action Revolver **$210**
Similar to Astra 357, except chambered for 45 Colt or 45 ACP. Barrels: 6-, or 8½-inch. 11½ inches overall with 6-inch barrel. Weight: 44 oz. with 6-inch barrel. Made from 1980 to date.

Astra Model 200 Firecat

Astra Model 200 Firecat Vest Pocket Auto Pistol . **$160**
Caliber: 25 Automatic (6.35mm). 6-shot magazine. 2¼-inch barrel. 4⅜ inches overall. Weight: 11¾ oz. Fixed sights. Blued finish. Plastic stocks. Made from 1920 to date; U.S. importation discontinued in 1968.

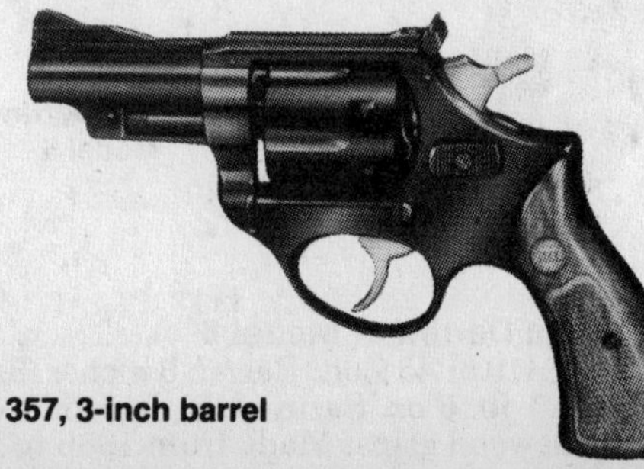

Astra 357, 3-inch barrel

Astra 357 Double Action Revolver $195
Caliber: 357 Magnum. 6-shot cylinder. Barrels: 3-, 4-, 6-, 8½-inch. 11¼ inches overall with 6-inch barrel. Weight: 42 oz. with 6-inch barrel. Ramp front sight, adjustable rear sight. Blued finish. Checkered wood stocks. Made from 1972 to date.

Astra Model 400

Astra Model 600

Astra Model 400 Auto Pistol $295
Caliber: 9mm Bayard Long (38 ACP, 9mm Browning Long, 9mm Glisenti, 9mm Luger and 9mm Steyr cartridges may be used interchangeably in this pistol because of its chamber design). 9-shot magazine. 6-inch barrel. 10 inches overall. Weight: 35 oz. Fixed sights. Blued finish. Plastic stocks. *Note:* This pistol, as well as Astra Models 600 and 3000, is a modification of the Browning Model 1912. Made from 1922 to 1945.

Astra Model 600 Military/Police Type Auto Pistol . . $285
Calibers: 32 Automatic (7.65mm), 9mm Luger. 10-shot magazine (32 cal.), 8-shot (9mm). 5¼-inch barrel. 8 inches overall. Weight: about 33 oz. Fixed sights. Blued finish. Plastic stocks. Made from 1944 to 1945.

Astra Model 800 Condor

Astra Model 800 Condor Military Auto Pistol . . . $325
Similar to Models 400 and 600, except has an external hammer. Caliber: 9mm Luger. 8-shot magazine. 5¼-inch barrel. 8¼ inches overall. Weight: 32½ oz. Fixed sights. Blued finish. Plastic stocks. Made from 1958 to 1965.

Astra Model 2000 Camper

Astra Model 2000 Camper Automatic Pistol $215
Same as Model 2000 Cub, except chambered for 22 Short only, has 4-inch barrel; overall length, 6¼ inches; weight, 11½ oz. Made from 1955 to 1960.

Astra Model 2000 Cub

Astra Model 2000 Cub Pocket Auto Pistol $175
Calibers: 22 Short, 25 Auto. 6-shot magazine. 2¼-inch barrel. 4½ inches overall. Weight: about 11 oz. Fixed sights. Blued or chromed finish. Plastic stocks. Made from 1954 to date; U.S. importation discontinued in 1968.

Astra Model 3000

Astra Model 3000 Pocket Auto Pistol $210
Calibers: 22 Long Rifle, 32 Automatic (7.65mm), 380 Automatic (9mm Short). 10-shot magazine (22 cal.), 7-shot (32 cal.), 6-shot (380 cal.). 4-inch barrel. 6⅜ inches overall. Weight: about 22 oz. Fixed sights. Blued finish. Plastic stocks. Made from 1947 to 1956.

Astra Model 4000 Falcon

Astra Model A-90

Astra Model 4000 Falcon Auto Pistol $225
Similar to Model 3000, except has an external hammer. Calibers: 22 Long Rifle, 32 Automatic (7.65mm), 380 Automatic (9mm Short). 10-shot magazine in 22 caliber, 8-shot in 32 caliber, 7-shot in 380 caliber. $3\frac{2}{3}$-inch barrel. $6\frac{1}{2}$ inches overall. Weight: 20 oz. in 22 caliber, $24\frac{3}{4}$ oz. in 32 and 380 caliber. Fixed sights. Blued finish. Plastic stocks. Made from 1956 to 1971.

Astra Model A-60 DA Automatic Pistol $280
Similar to the Constable, except in 380 only, with 13-shot magazine and slide-mounted ambidextrous safety. Blued finish only. Made from 1980 to date.

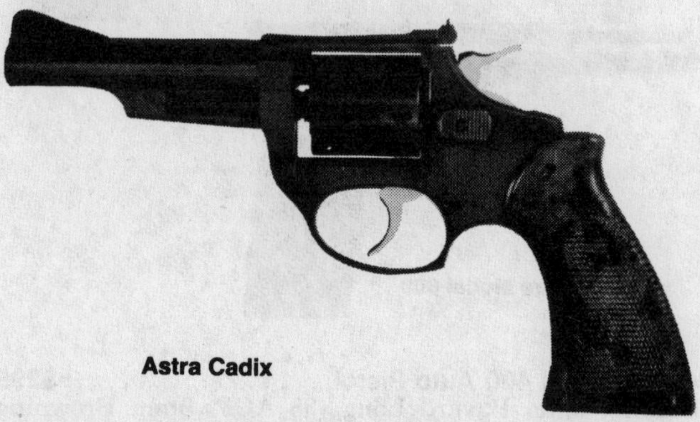

Astra Cadix

Astra Cadix Double Action Revolver $145
Calibers: 22 Long Rifle, 38 Special. 9-shot cylinder in 22 caliber, 5-shot in 38 caliber. Barrels: 4-, 6-inch. Weight: about 27 oz. with 6-inch barrel. Ramp front sight, adjustable rear sight. Blued finish. Plastic stocks. Made from 1960 to 1968.

Astra Model A-80

Astra Model A-80 Auto Pistol $300
Calibers: 9mm Parabellum, 38 Super, 45 ACP. 15-shot magazine (9 shot for 45 ACP). Barrel: $3\frac{3}{4}$ inches. 7 inches overall. Weight: 36 oz. Made from 1982 to date.

Astra Model A-90 DA Automatic Pistol $320
Calibers: 9mm Parabellum, 45 ACP. 15-shot (9mm) or 9-shot (45 ACP) magazine. 3.75-inch barrel. 7 inches overall. Weight: about 40 oz. Fixed sights. Blued finish. Checkered plastic stocks. Made from 1985 to date.

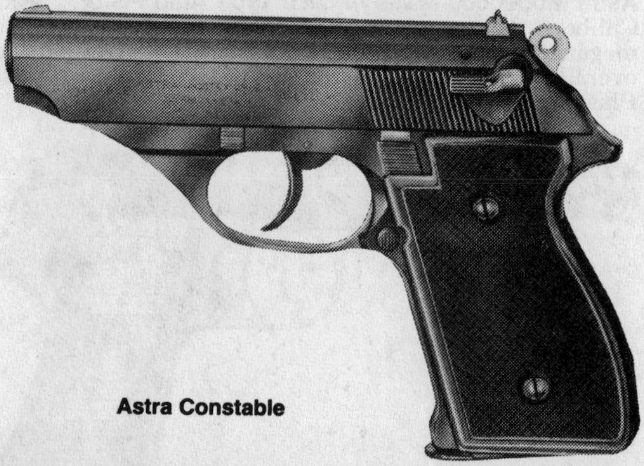

Astra Constable

Astra Constable Double Action Auto Pistol
Calibers: 22 Long Rifle, 32 Automatic (7.65mm), 380 Automatic (9mm Short). 10-shot magazine in 22 caliber, 8-shot in 32 caliber, 7-shot in 380 caliber. $3\frac{1}{2}$-inch barrel. $6\frac{1}{2}$ inches overall. Weight: about 24 oz. Blade front sight, windage adjustable rear sight. Blued or chromed finish. Made from 1965 to date.
Stainless Finish **$250**
Blued or Chrome **235**

AUTO-ORDNANCE CORPORATION
West Hurley, New York

Auto-Ordnance 1911 A1
Gov't. Automatic Pistol

Auto-Ordnance 1911A1 Government Auto Pistol
Calibers: 9mm Parabellum, 38 Super, 45 ACP. 9-shot (9mm, 38 Super) or 7-shot (45 ACP)) magazine. 5-inch barrel. $8\frac{1}{2}$ inches overall. Weight: 39 oz. Fixed blade front sight; rear adjustable. Blued finish. Checkered plastic stocks.
45 Caliber **$265**
9mm, 38 Super **290**

BAUER FIREARMS CORPORATION
Fraser, Michigan

Bauer 25 Automatic

Bauer 25 Automatic Pistol $115
Stainless steel. Caliber: 25 Automatic. 6-shot magazine. $2\frac{1}{8}$-inch barrel. 4 inches overall. Weight: 10 oz. Fixed sights. Checkered walnut or simulated pearl stocks. Made from 1972 to date.

BAYARD PISTOLS
Herstal, Belgium
Mfd. by Anciens Etablissements Pieper

Bayard Model 1908*

Bayard Model 1908 Pocket Automatic Pistol . . . $180
Calibers: 25 Automatic (6.35mm), 32 Automatic (7.65mm), 380 Automatic (9mm Short). 6-shot magazine. $2\frac{1}{4}$-inch barrel. $4\frac{7}{8}$ inches overall. Weight: about 16 oz. Fixed sights. Blued finish. Hard rubber stocks.

Bayard Model 1923 Pocket Automatic Pistol . . . $185
Caliber: 25 Automatic (6.35mm). $2\frac{1}{8}$-inch barrel. $4\frac{5}{16}$ inches overall. Weight: 12 oz. Fixed sights. Blued finish. Checkered hard rubber stocks.

Bayard Model 1923 Pocket Automatic Pistol . . . $170
Calibers: 32 Automatic (7.65mm), 380 Automatic (9mm Short). 6-shot magazine. $3\frac{5}{16}$-inch barrel. $5\frac{1}{2}$ inches overall. Weight: about 19 oz. Fixed sights. Blued finish. Checkered hard rubber stocks.

Bayard Model 1930

Bayard Model 1930 Pocket 25 Automatic Pistol . . $160
This is a modification of the Model 1923, which it closely resembles.

BEEMAN PRECISION ARMS, INC.
Santa Rosa, California

Beeman FAS 601 Semiautomatic
Caliber: 22 Short. 9¼-inch sight radius. Weight: about 41 oz. Top loading magazine. Ventilated with gas vents. Adjustable, removable trigger.
Right **$510**
Left **525**

Beeman/FAS 602 Semiautomatic
Caliber: 22 LR. 8½-inch sight radius. Weight: 40 oz.
Right **$560**
Left **575**

Beeman/Korth . . . . $750 to 1500
Calibers: 357 Mag. or 22 LR with interchangeable combo cylinders of 357 Mag./9mm Para or 22 LR/22 WMR. Barrel: 6-inch target; 3-, 4-inch combat. Walnut grips.

Beeman SP Deluxe Metallic Silhouette
Caliber: 22 LR. Single shot. Barrel: 6, 8, 10 or 15 inches. Adjustable rear sight; receiver ground for scope mount. Walnut target grips with adjustable palm rest.
With 8-or 10-inch bbl. **$210**
With 12-inch bbl. **220**
With 15-inch bbl. **225**

Beeman/Unique 69 Target Pistol

Beeman/Unique 69 Target Pistol
Caliber: 22 LR. 5-shot magazine. 8.7-inch sight radius. Adjustable grips. Trigger adjusts for position and pull weight. Weight: about 35 oz.
Right **$420**
Left **435**

BEHOLLA PISTOL
Suhl, Germany
Mfd. both by Becker and Holländer and Stenda-Werke GmbH

Beholla Pocket Automatic Pistol $165
Caliber: 32 Automatic (7.65mm). 7-shot magazine. 2.9-inch barrel. 5½ inches overall. Weight: 22 oz. Fixed sights. Blued finish. Serrated wood or hard rubber stocks. Made from 1915 to 1920 by Becker and Holländer, circa 1920-1925 by Stenda-Werke. *Note:* Essentially the same pistol was manufactured concurrently with the Stenda version as the "Leonhardt" by H. M. Gering and as the "Menta" by August Menz.

Beholla Pocket Pistol*

BERETTA USA CORP.
Accokeek, Maryland

Beretta pistols are manufactured by Fabbrica D'Armi Pietro Beretta S.p.A. in the Gardone Valtrompia (Brescia), Italy. This prestigious gunmaking firm has been in business for over 300 years.

Beretta Model 20 Double Action Auto Pistol $155
Caliber: 25 ACP. 8-shot magazine. 2.5-inch barrel. 4.9 inches overall. Weight: 10.9 oz. Plastic or walnut grips. Fixed sights. Made from 1984 to 1985.

Beretta Model 21

Beretta Model 21 Double Action Auto Pistol
Calibers: 22 LR and 25 ACP. 7-shot (22 LR) or 8-shot (25 ACP) magazine. 2½-inch barrel. 4.9 inches overall. Weight: about 12 oz. Blade front sight; V-notch rear. Walnut grips. Made from 1985 to date.
Blued Finish **$160**
Nickel Finish (22 LR only) **180**
Model 21EL Engraved Model **190**

Beretta Model 70

Beretta Model 71

Beretta Model 71 Automatic Pistol **$195**
Same general specifications as lightweight alloy Model 70. Caliber: 22 Long Rifle. 6-inch barrel. 8-round magazine. Adjustable rear sight. Medium frame. Single action. Made from 1959 to date. *Note:* Formerly marketed in U.S. as the "Jaguar Plinker."

Beretta Model 70 Automatic Pistol **$205**
Improved version of Model 1935. Steel or lightweight alloy. Calibers: 32 Auto (7.65mm), 380 Auto (9mm Short). 8-shot magazine in 32, 7-shot in 380 caliber. 3½-inch barrel. 6½ inches overall. Weight: steel, 22¼ oz.; alloy, 16 oz. Fixed sights. Blued finish. Checkered plastic stocks. Made from 1959 to 1985. *Note:* Formerly marketed in U.S. as "Puma" for alloy model in 32 and "Cougar" for steel model in 380.

Beretta Model 70S **$190**
Similar to Model 70T, except chambered for 22 Auto and 380 Auto. Longer barrel guide, safety lever blocking hammer; sight and rear sight blade fixed on breech block. Weight: 1 lb. 7 oz. Made from 1977 to date.

Beretta Model 72

Beretta Model 72 .... **$210**
Same as Model 71, except has 6-inch barrel, weighs 18 oz. Made from 1959 to date. *Note:* Formerly marketed in U.S. as "Jaguar Plinker."

Beretta Model 70T

Beretta Model 76

Beretta Model 70T Automatic Pistol **$215**
Similar to Model 70. Caliber: 32 Automatic (7.65mm). 9-shot magazine. 6-inch barrel. 9½ inches overall. Weight: 19 oz. Adjustable rear sight, blade front sight. Blued finish. Checkered plastic stocks. Introduced in 1959. Discont.

Beretta Model 76 Auto Target Pistol **$285**
Caliber: 22 Long Rifle. 10-shot magazine. 6-inch barrel. 8.8 inches overall. Weight: 33 oz. Adjustable rear sight, front sight with interchangeable blades. Blued finish. Checkered plastic stocks. Made from 1966 to date. *Note:* Formerly marketed in the U.S. as the "Sable." Made from 1966 to 1985.

Beretta Model 76W Auto Pistol **$295**
Same general specifications as Model 76 except has wood grips.

Beretta Model 81

Beretta Model 81 Double Action Auto Pistol $255
Caliber: 32 Automatic (7.65mm). 12-shot magazine. 3.8-inch barrel. 6.8 inches overall. Weight: 23.5 oz. Fixed sights. Blued finish. Plastic stocks. Made principally for the European market from 1975 to date, with similar variations to the Model 84.

Beretta Model 84 Double Action Auto Pistol $275
Same as Model 81, except made in caliber 380 Automatic with 13-shot magazine. 3.82-inch barrel. 6.8 inches overall. Weight: 23 oz. Fixed front and rear sights. Made from 1975 to about 1982.

Beretta Model 84B
Double Action Pistol

Beretta Model 84B DA Auto Pistol $345
Improved version of Model 84 with strengthened frame and slide, and firing pin block safety added. Ambidextrous, reversible magazine release. Blued or nickel finish. Checkered black plastic or wood grips. Other specifications same. Made from about 1982 to about 1984.

Beretta Model 84BB Double Action Auto Pistol
Improved version of Model 84B, with further strengthened slide and frame and recoil spring. Caliber: 380 ACP. 13-shot magazine. Barrel: 3.82 inches. 6.8 inches overall. Weight: 23 oz. Checkered black plastic or wood grips. Blued or nickel finish. Fixed sights. Made from about 1984 to date.
Blued Finish **$340**
Blued w/Wood Grips **360**
Nickel Finish **385**

Beretta Model 85 Double Action Auto Pistol $275
This is basically the same gun as the Model 84 and has seen a similar evolution. However, this 8-shot version has no ambidextrous magazine release, has a slightly narrower grip and weighs 21.8 oz. It was introduced a little later than the Model 84.

Beretta Model 85B DA Auto Pistol $280
Improved version of the Model 85. Made from about 1982 to 1985.

Beretta Model 85BB
Double Action Pistol

Beretta Model 85BB Double Action Pistol
Improved version of the Model 85B, with strenthened frame and slide. Caliber: 380 ACP. 8-shot magazine. 3.82-inch barrel. 6.8 inches overall. Weight: 21.8 oz. Blued or nickel finish. Checkered black plastic or wood grips. Made from 1985 to date.
Blued Finish w/Plastic Grips **$285**
Blued Finish w/Wood Grips **295**
Nickel Finish **305**

Beretta Model 86

Beretta Model 86 Double Action Auto Pistol $300
Caliber: 380 auto. 8-shot magazine. Barrel: 4.33 inches. 7.33 inches overall. Weight: 23 oz. Made 1986 to date.

Beretta Model 87BB

Beretta Model 87BB Auto Pistol
Similar to the Model 85, except in 22 LR with 8-shot magazine and optional extended 6-inch barrel (in single action). Overall length: 6.8 inches; 8.9 w/6-inch bbl. Weight: 20.8 oz.; 23 oz. w/6-inch bbl. Checkered wood grips. Made from 1977 to date.
Blued Finish (Double Action) **$310**
Long Barrel (Single Action) **320**

Beretta Model 90

Beretta Model 90 Double Action Auto Pistol $240
Caliber: 32 Automatic (7.65mm). 8-shot magazine. $3\frac{5}{8}$-inch barrel. $6\frac{5}{8}$ inches overall. Weight: $19\frac{1}{2}$ oz. Fixed sights. Blued finish. Checkered plastic stocks. Made from 1969 to 1975.

Beretta Model 92

Beretta Model 92 Double Action Auto Pistol $385
Caliber: 9mm Luger. 15-shot magazine. 4.9-inch barrel. 8.5 inches overall. Weight: 33.5 oz. Fixed sights. Blued finish. Plastic stocks. Made from 1976 to date.

Beretta Model 92F Compact Double Action Auto Pistol $465
Caliber: 7.65 Parabellum. 13-shot magazine. Barrel: 4.3 inches. 7.8 inches overall. Weight: 31.5 oz. Wood grips. Square-notched bar rear sight; blade front sight, integral with slide. Made from 1986 to date.

Beretta Model 92SB Double Action Auto Pistol . . $435
Same general specifications as standard Model 92 except has 16-shot magazine capacity. Discontinued 1985.

Beretta Model 92 SB-F

Beretta Model 92 SB-F Double Action Auto Pistol $445
Caliber: 9mm Parabellum. 15-shot magazine. Barrel: 4.9 inches. $8\frac{1}{2}$ inches overall. Weight: 34 oz. Plastic or wood grips. Square-notched bar rear sight; blade front sight, integral with slide. This model has been selected to be the standard issue sidearm for the U.S. Armed Forces. Made from 1985 to date.

Beretta Model 101 .... $215
Same as Model 70T, except caliber 22 Long Rifle, has 10-shot magazine. Introduced in 1959. Discontinued.

Beretta Model 318 (1934)*

Beretta Model 318 (1934) Auto Pistol $215
Caliber: 25 Automatic (6.35mm). 8-shot magazine. 2½-inch barrel. 4½ inches overall. Weight: 14 oz. Fixed sights. Blued finish. Plastic stocks. Made from 1934 to c. 1939.

Beretta Model 949 Olimpionico

Beretta Model 949 Olimpionico Auto Pistol $500
Calibers: 22 Short, 22 Long Rifle. 5-shot magazine. 8¾-inch barrel. 12½ inches overall. Weight: 38 oz. Target sights. Adjustable barrel weight. Muzzle brake. Checkered walnut stocks with thumb-rest. Made from 1959 to 1964.

Beretta Model 950B

Beretta Model 950B Auto Pistol $115
Same general specifications as Model 950CC, except caliber 25 Auto, has 7-shot magazine. Made from 1959 to date. *Note:* Formerly marketed in U.S. as "Jetfire."

Beretta 950BS

Beretta Model 950 BS Single Action Semiautomatic
Calibers: 25 ACP or 22 Short. Magazine capacity: 7 rounds (22 short); 8 rounds (25 ACP). 2½- or 4-inch barrel. 4½ inches overall (2½-inch bbl.) Weight: about 10 oz. Blade front sight; V-notch in rear. Checkered black plastic grips. Made from 1987 to date.

Blued Finish	$135
Nickel Finish	155
With 4-inch bbl. (22 short)	145
Model 950 EL gold-etched version	165

Beretta Model 950CC

Beretta Model 950CC Auto Pistol $125
Caliber: 22 Short. 6-shot magazine. Hinged, 2⅜-inch barrel. 4¾ inches overall. Weight: 11 oz. Fixed sights. Blued finish. Plastic stocks. Made from 1959 to date. *Note:* Formerly marketed in the U.S. as "Minx M2."

Beretta Model 950CC Special

Beretta Model 950CC Special Auto Pistol $135
Same general specifications as Model 950CC Auto, except has 4-inch barrel. Made from 1959 to date. *Note:* Formerly marketed in U.S. as "Minx M4."

Beretta Model 951 (1951)

Beretta Model 951 (1951) Military Auto Pistol . . . $325
Caliber: 9mm Luger. 8-shot magazine. $4\frac{1}{2}$-inch barrel. 8 inches overall. Weight: 31 oz. Fixed sights. Blued finish. Plastic stocks. Made from 1952 to date. *Note:* This is the standard pistol of the Italian Armed Forces; also used by Egyptian and Israeli armies and by the police in Nigeria. Egyptian and Israeli models usually command a higher premium. Formerly marketed in the U.S. as the "Brigadier."

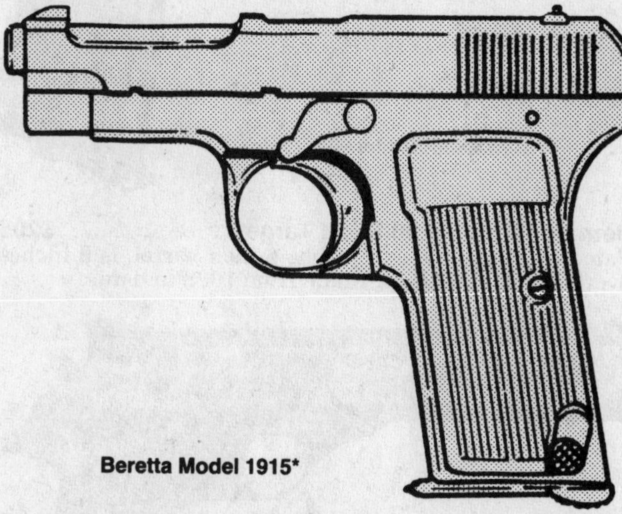

Beretta Model 1915*

Beretta Model 1915 Auto Pistol $325
Caliber: 32 Automatic (7.65mm). 8-shot magazine. 3.3-inch barrel. 5.9 inches overall. Weight: 20 oz. Fixed sights. Blued finish. Wood stocks. Made from 1915 to 1930. *Note:* Specifications and illustration are of the 1919 modification; the earlier type is seven-shot. From 1915 to 1919, Beretta also made an enlarged version of Model 1915 chambered for the 9mm Luger cartridge.

Beretta Model 1923*

Beretta Model 1923 Auto Pistol $355
Caliber: 9mm Luger. 8-shot magazine. 4-inch barrel. $6\frac{1}{2}$ inches overall. Weight: 30 oz. Fixed sights. Blued finish. Plastic stocks. Made from 1923 to c. 1936.

Beretta Model 1934

Beretta Model 1934 Auto Pistol
Caliber: 380 Automatic (9mm Short). 7-shot magazine. $3\frac{3}{8}$-inch barrel. $5\frac{7}{8}$ inches overall. Weight: 24 oz. Fixed sights. Blued finish. Plastic stocks. Official pistol of the Italian Armed Forces. Wartime production is not as well made and finished as commercial models. Made from 1934 to 1959.
Commercial Model **$320**
War Model **255**

Beretta Model 1935*

Beretta Model 1935 Auto Pistol
Caliber: 32 Automatic (7.65mm). 8-shot magazine. $3\frac{1}{2}$-inch barrel. $5\frac{3}{4}$ inches overall. Weight: 24 oz. Fixed sights. Blued finish. Plastic stocks. A roughly finished version of this pistol was produced during World War II. Made from 1935 to 1959.
Commercial Model **$245**
War Model **205**

VINCENZO BERNARDELLI, S.P.A.
Gardone V. T. (Brescia), Italy

Bernardelli Model 60

Bernardelli Model 60 Pocket Automatic Pistol . . $155
Calibers: 22 Long Rifle, 32 Auto (7.65mm), 380 Auto (9mm Short). 8-shot magazine in 22 and 32, 7-shot in 380. 3 1/2-inch barrel. 6 1/2 inches overall. Weight: about 25 oz. Fixed sights. Blued finish. Bakelite stocks. Made 1959 to date.

Bernardelli Model 69 Automatic Target Pistol . . . $220
Caliber: 22 Long Rifle. 10-shot magazine. 5.9-inch barrel. 9 inches overall. Weight: 2.2 lbs. Fully adjustable target sights. Blued finish. Stippled right- or left-hand wrap-around walnut grips. Made from 1987 to date. *Note:* This was previously Model 100.

Bernardelli Model 80

Bernardelli Model 80 Automatic Pistol $170
Calibers: 22 Long Rifle, 32 Automatic (7.65mm), 380 Automatic (9mm Short). Magazine capacity: 10-shot in 22, 8-shot in 32, 7-shot in 380 caliber. 3 1/2-inch barrel. 6 1/2 inches overall. Weight: 25.6 oz. Adjustable rear sight, white dot front sight. Blued finish. Plastic thumb-rest stocks. Made from 1968 to date. *Note:* Model 80 is a modification of Model 60 designed to conform with U.S. import regulations.

Bernardelli Model 90

Bernardelli Model 90 Sport Target $205
Same as Model 80, except has 6-inch barrel, is 9 inches overall, weighs 26.8 oz. Made from 1968 to date.

Bernardelli Model 100

Bernardelli Model 100 Target Automatic Pistol . . $270
Caliber: 22 Long Rifle. 10-shot magazine. 5.9-inch barrel. 9 inches overall. Weight: 37 3/4 oz. Adjustable rear sight, interchangeable front sight. Blued finish. Checkered walnut thumb-rest stocks. Made from 1969 to 1986: *Note:* Formerly Model 69.

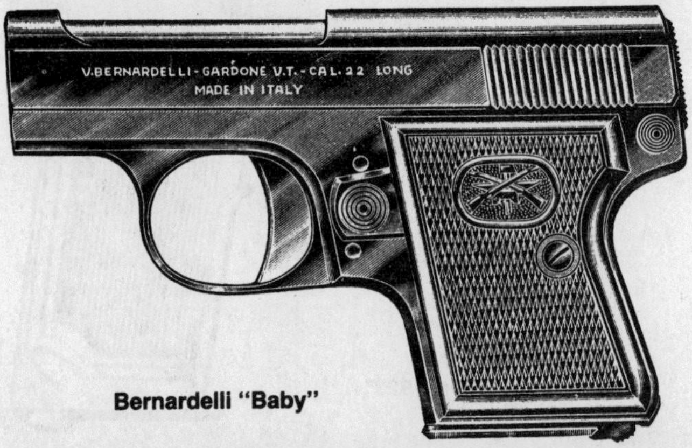

Bernardelli "Baby"

Bernardelli "Baby" Automatic Pistol $200
Calibers: 22 Short, 22 Long. 5-shot magazine. 2 1/8-inch barrel. 4 1/8 inches overall. Weight: 9 oz. Fixed sights. Blued finish. Bakelite stocks. Made from 1949 to 1968.

Bernardelli P018 Compact Model **$320**
Slightly smaller version of the Model P018 standard DA automatic, except has 14-shot magazine and 4-inch barrel. 7.68 inches overall. Weight: 33 oz. Walnut grips only. Made from 1987 to date.

Bernardelli P018 Double Action Automatic Pistol
Caliber: 9mm Parabellum. 16-shot magazine. $4\frac{3}{4}$-inch barrel. $8\frac{1}{2}$ inches overall. Weight: 36 oz. Fixed combat sights. Blued finish. Checkered plastic or walnut stocks. Made from 1987 to date.
With Plastic Grips **$300**
With Walnut Grips **330**

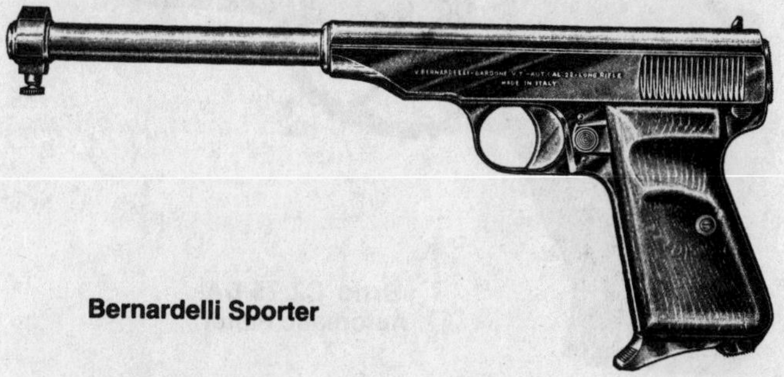

Bernardelli Sporter

Bernardelli Sporter Automatic Pistol **$245**
Caliber: 22 Long Rifle. 8-shot magazine. Barrel lengths: 6-, 8-, and 10-inch. 13 inches overall with 10-inch barrel. Weight: about 30 oz. with 10-inch barrel. Target sights. Blued finish. Walnut stocks. Made from 1949 to 1968.

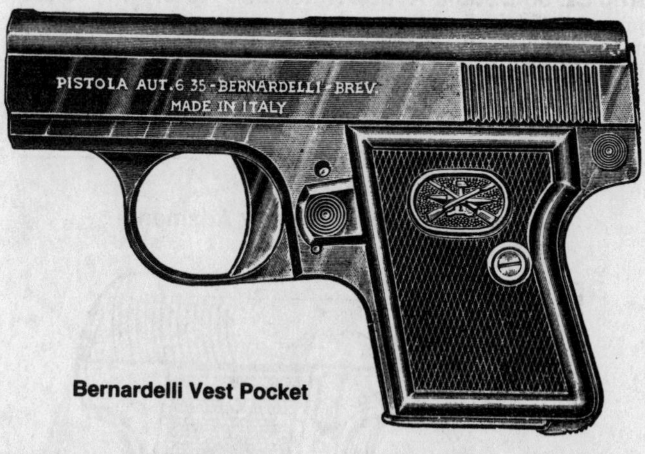

Bernardelli Vest Pocket

Bernardelli Vest Pocket Automatic Pistol **$175**
Caliber: 25 Automatic (6.35mm). 5-shot or 8-shot magazine. $2\frac{1}{8}$-inch barrel. $4\frac{1}{8}$ inches overall. Weight: 9 oz. Fixed sights. Blued finish. Bakelite stocks. Made from 1945 to 1968.

BERSA PISTOLS
Imported from Argentina by Interarms

Bersa Model 97

Bersa Model 97 Auto Pistol **$150**
Caliber: 380 ACP. 7-shot magazine. $3\frac{1}{2}$-inch barrel. $6\frac{1}{2}$ inches overall. Weight: $1\frac{3}{4}$ pounds. Made 1982 to date.

Bersa Model 223
Same general specifications as Model 383, except comes in 22 LR caliber with 10-round magazine capacity.
Double Action **$135**
Single Action **120**

Bersa Model 224
Caliber: 22 LR. 10-shot magazine. 4-inch barrel. Front blade sight; square-notched rear sight adjustable for windage. Blued finish. Custom wood grips. Discontinued 1986.
Double Action **$135**
Single Action **120**

Bersa Model 226
Same general specifications as Model 224, but with 6-inch barrel.
Double Action **$135**
Single Action **120**

Bersa Model 383
Double Action

Bersa Model 383
Single Action

Bersa Model 383
Caliber: 380 Auto. 7-shot magazine. 3½-inch barrel. Front blade sight integral on slide; square-notched rear sight adjustable for windage. Custom wood grips on double action; nylon grips on single action. Blued finish.
Double Action $165
Single Action 125

Bersa Model 622

Bersa Model 622 Auto Pistol $115
Caliber: 22 Long Rifle. 7-shot magazine. 4- or 6-inch barrel. 7-, 9-inch overall length respectively. Weight: 2¼ pounds. Made from 1982 to date.

Bersa Model 644

Bersa Model 644 Auto Pistol $100
Caliber: 22 Long Rifle. 10-shot magazine. 3.5-inch barrel. Weight: 26½ oz. 6½ inches overall. Adjustable rear sight, blade front sight. Contoured black nylon grips. Made from 1980 to date.

BRNO PISTOLS
Rocky River, Ohio
Manufactured in Czechoslovakia

Brno CZ 75 DA
Automatic Pistol

Brno CZ 75 Double Action Automatic Pistol . . . $450
Caliber: 9mm Parabellum. 15-shot magazine. 4¾-inch barrel. 8 inches overall. Weight: 35 oz. Fixed sights. Blued finish. Checkered wood stocks.

Brno CZ 83 Double Action Automatic Pistol . . . $320
Calibers: 32 ACP, 380 ACP. 15-shot (32 ACP) or 13-shot (380 ACP) magazine. 3¾-inch barrel. 6¾ inches overall. Weight: 26½ oz. Fixed sights. Blued finish. Checkered black plastic stocks.

Brno CZ 85 Double Action Automatic Pistol . . . $490
Same as CZ 75, except with ambidextrous slide release and safety. Calibers: 9mm Parabellum, 7.65mm. Made from 1986 to date.

BRONCO PISTOL
Eibar, Spain
Manufactured by Echave y Arizmendi

Bronco Model 1918*

Bronco Model 1918 Pocket Automatic Pistol . . . $140
Caliber: 32 Automatic (7.65mm). 6-shot magazine. 2½-inch barrel. 5 inches overall. Weight: 20 oz. Fixed sights. Blued finish. Hard rubber stocks. Made circa 1918-1925.

BROWNING PISTOLS
Morgan, Utah

The following Browning pistols have been manufactured by Fabrique Nationale d'Armes de Guerre (now Fabrique Nationale Herstal) of Herstal, Belgium; by Arms Technology Inc. of Salt Lake City; and by J. P. Sauer & Sohn of Eckernförde, W. Germany. (*See* also FN Browning and J.P. Sauer & Sohn listings.)

Browning 9mm Gold Classic

Browning 9mm Classic
Same general specifications as 9mm Auto, except for high-grade engraving, finely checkered walnut grips with double border, and limited to 5000 production. Gold Classic limited to 500 production. Made in 1985.

Gold Classic	$1200
Standard Classic	650

Browning 9mm Double Action Automatic Pistol . $325
Caliber: 9mm Luger. 13-shot magazine. Barrel: about 5 inches. 7¾ inches overall. Weight: 32 oz. Checkered walnut grips. Adjustable rear sight. Made from 1985 to date.

Browning 9mm Hi-Power Ambidextrous Safety

Browning 9mm Hi-Power Ambidextrous Safety . $425
Same general specifications as regular 9mm Hi-Power, except matte blued model with ambidextrous safety. Made from 1987 to date.

Browning Hi-Power 9mm Standard Model

Browning 9mm Hi-Power Automatic Pistol
Same general specifications as FN Browning Model 1935. 13-shot. Fixed sights; also available with rear sight adjustable for windage and elevation and ramp front sight. Standard Model, blued finish, checkered walnut stocks. Renaissance Engraved Model, chrome-plated, Nacrolac pearl stocks. Made by FN from 1955 to date.

Standard Model, fixed sights	$ 380
Standard Model, adjustable sights	425
Renaissance Model, fixed sights	1125
Renaissance Model, adjustable sights	1225
Single Action Model	325

Browning 25 Automatic Standard Model

Browning 25 Automatic Pistol
Same general specifications as FN Browning Baby. Standard Model, blued finish, hard rubber grips. Lightweight Model, nickel-plated, Nacrolac pearl grips. Renaissance Engraved Model, nickel-plated, Nacrolac pearl grips. Made by FN from 1955 to 1969.

Standard Model	$230
Lightweight Model	365
Renaissance Model	775

Browning 380 Automatic Standard Model (1955-Type)

Browning 380 Automatic Pistol, 1955 Type
Same general specifications as FN Browning 380 Pocket Auto. Standard Model, Renaissance Engraved Model, as furnished in 25 Automatic. Made by FN from 1955 to 1969.
Standard Model **$305**
Renaissance Model **895**

Browning BDA-380

Browning 380 Automatic Standard Model (1971-Type)

Browning 380 Automatic Pistol, 1971 Type
Same as 380 Automatic, 1955 Type, except has longer slide, $4^{7}/_{16}$-inch barrel, is $7^{1}/_{16}$ inches overall, weighs 23 oz. Rear sight adjustable for windage and elevation, plastic thumb-rest stocks. Made 1971 to 1975.
Standard Model **$325**
Renaissance Model **950**

Browning BDA-380 Nickel

Browning BDA Automatic

Browning BDA Double Action Automatic Pistol . . $365
Similar to SIG-Sauer P220. Calibers: 9mm Luger, 38 Super Auto, 45 Automatic. 9-shot magazine in 9mm and 38, 7-shot in 45. 4.4-inch barrel. 7.8 inches overall. Weight: 29.3 oz. Fixed sights. Blued finish. Plastic stocks. Made from 1977-79 by Sauer.

Browning BDA-380 Double Action Automatic Pistol
Caliber: 380 Auto. 13-shot magazine. Barrel length: $3^{13}/_{16}$ inches. $6^{3}/_{4}$ inches overall. Weight: 23 oz. Fixed blade front sight, square notch drift adjustable rear sight. Made from 1982 to date.
Blue finish **$300**
Nickel finish **355**

Browning Buck Mark 22 Automatic Pistol $150
Caliber: 22RF. 10-shot magazine. Barrel: $5^{1}/_{2}$ inches. $9^{1}/_{2}$ inches overall. Weight: 32 oz. Black molded grips. Adjustable rear sight. Made from 1985 to date.

Browning Buck Mark 22 Plus $155
Same general specifications as standard Buck Mark 22, except for black molded, impregnated hardwood grips. Made from 1987 to date.

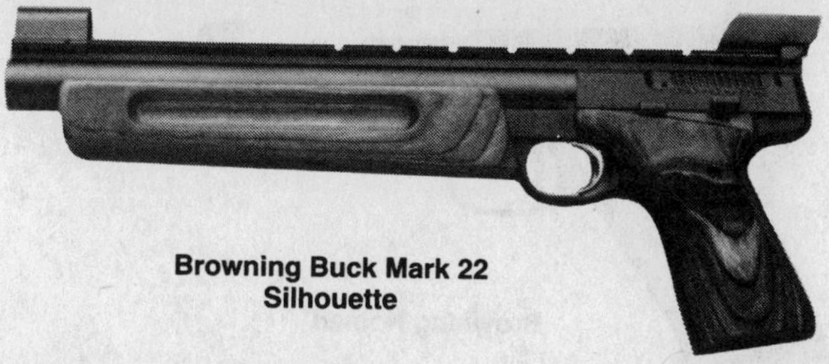

Browning Buck Mark 22 Silhouette

Browning Buck Mark 22 Silhouette $225
Same general specifications as standard Buck Mark 22, except for 9⅞-inch barrel, 53-oz. weight, and laminated hardwood grips and forend. Made from 1987 to date.

Browning Buck Mark 22 Varmint Auto Pistol $200
Same general specifications as standard Buck Mark 22, except for 9⅞-inch barrel, 48-oz. weight, and laminated hardwood grips. Made from 1987 to date.

Browning Challenger Gold Model

Browning Challenger Renaissance Model

Browning Challenger Standard Model

Browning Challenger Automatic Pistol
Caliber: 22 Long Rifle. 10-shot magazine. Barrel lengths: 4½- and 6¾-inch. 11⁷⁄₁₆ inches overall with 6¾-inch barrel. Weight: 38 oz. with 6¾-inch barrel. Removable blade front sight, screw adjustable rear sight. Standard

Browning Challenger (cont.)
finish, blue; also furnished gold-inlaid (Gold Model) and engraved and chrome-plated (Renaissance Model). Checkered walnut stocks; finely figured and carved stocks on Gold and Renaissance Models. Standard made by FN from 1962 to 1975, higher grades introduced in 1971.

Standard Model	$350
Gold Model	625
Renaissance Model	950

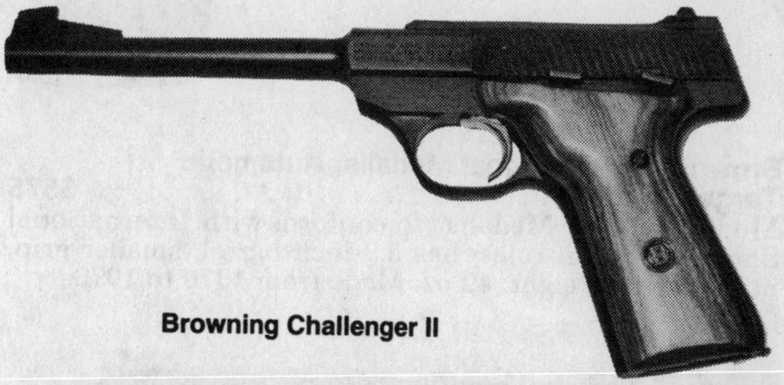

Browning Challenger II

Browning Challenger II Automatic Pistol $180
Same general specifications as Challenger Standard Model with 6¾-inch barrel. Aside from changed grip angle and impregnated hardwood stocks, appearance is similar. Original Challenger design was modified for lower production costs. Made by ATI from 1976 to 1983.

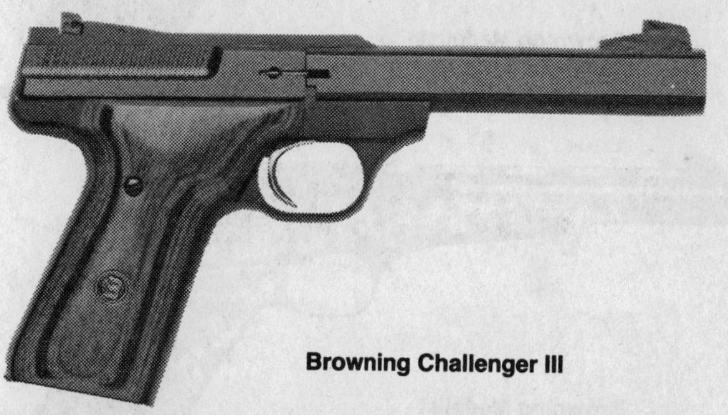

Browning Challenger III

Browning Challenger III Sporter 22

Browning Challenger III Automatic Pistol $195
Same general description as Challenger II, except has 5½-inch bull barrel, alloy frame, and new sight system. Weight: 35 oz. Made from 1982 to 1984.

Browning Challenger III Sporter Automatic $180
Same general specifications as regular Challenger III except 6¾-inch barrel. Made from 1984 to 1986.

Browning International Medalist

Browning International Medalist Automatic Target Pistol **$575**
Modification of Medalist to conform with International Shooting Union rules; has 5.9-inch barrel, smaller grip, no forearm. Weight: 42 oz. Made from 1970 to 1973.

Browning Medalist Renaissance Model

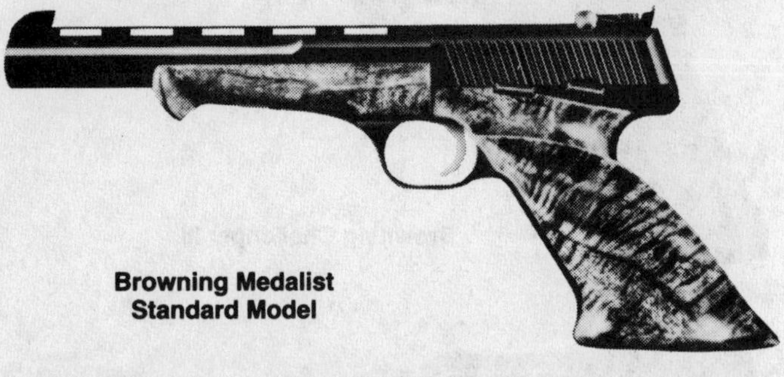

Browning Medalist Standard Model

Browning Medalist Automatic Target Pistol
Caliber: 22 Long Rifle. 10-shot magazine. $6\frac{3}{4}$-inch barrel with vent rib. $11\frac{15}{16}$ inches overall. Weight: 46 oz. Removable blade front sight, click-adjustable micrometer rear sight. Standard finish, blue; also furnished gold-inlaid (Gold Model) and engraved and chrome-plated (Renaissance Model). Checkered walnut stocks with thumb rest (for right- or left-handed shooter); finely figured and carved stocks on Gold and Renaissance Models. Made by FN from 1962 to 1975, higher grades introduced in 1971.

Standard Model . . . . **$ 595**
Gold Model **1195**
Renaissance Model **2000**

Browning Nomad Automatic Pistol **$250**
Caliber: 22 Long Rifle. 10-shot magazine. Barrel lengths: $4\frac{1}{2}$- and $6\frac{3}{4}$-inch. $8\frac{15}{16}$ inches overall with $4\frac{1}{2}$-inch barrel. Weight: 34 oz., $4\frac{1}{2}$-inch barrel. Removable blade front sight, screw adjustable rear sight. Blued finish. Plastic stocks. Made by FN from 1962 to 1974.

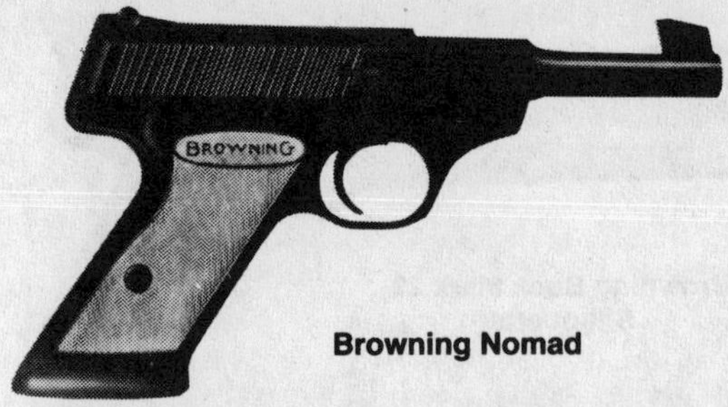

Browning Nomad

Browning Renaissance Cased Set

Browning Renaissance 9mm, 25 Auto and 380 Auto (1955) Engraved Models, Cased Set **$3450**
One pistol of each of the three models in a special walnut carrying case; all chrome-plated with Nacrolac pearl stocks. Made by FN from 1955 to 1969.

BUDISCHOWSKY PISTOL
Mt. Clemens, Michigan
Mfd. by Norton Armament Corporation

Budischowsky TP-70

Budischowsky TP-70 Double Action Automatic Pistol
Calibers: 22 Long Rifle, 25 Automatic. 6-shot magazine. 2.6-inch barrel. 4.65 inches overall. Weight: 12.3 oz. Fixed sights. Stainless steel. Plastic stocks. Made 1973 to 1977.

22 Long Rifle **$375**
25 Automatic **295**

CHARTER ARMS CORPORATION
Stratford, Connecticut

Charter Arms Model 40 Automatic Pistol $285
Caliber: 22RF. 8-shot magazine. 3.3-inch barrel. 6.3 inches overall. Weight: 21½ oz. Fixed sights. Checkered walnut grips. Stainless steel finish. Made from 1985 to 1986.

Charter Arms Model 79K Automatic Pistol $280
Calibers: 380 or 32 Auto. 7-shot magazine. 3.6-inch barrel. 6.5 inches overall. Weight: 24½ oz. Fixed sights. Checkered walnut grips. Stainless steel finish. Made from 1985 to 1986.

Charter Arms Bulldog 44

Charter Arms Bulldog 44 Double Action Revolver
Caliber: 44 Special. 5-shot cylinder. 3-inch barrel. 7½ inches overall. Weight: 19 oz. Fixed sights. Blued or nickel-plated finish. Checkered walnut Bulldog or square buttstocks. Made from 1973 to date.

Blued Finish/Pocket Hammer (2½″)	$165
Blued Finish/Bulldog Grips (3″)	160
Stainless Steel/Bulldog Grips	195
Neoprene Grips/Pocket Hammer	200

Charter Arms Bulldog 357

Charter Arms Bulldog 357 Double Action Revolver $175
Caliber: 357 Magnum. 5-shot cylinder. 6-inch barrel. 11 inches overall. Weight: 25 oz. Fixed sights. Blued finish. Checkered walnut square buttstocks. Introduced in 1977. Discontinued.

Charter Arms Police Bulldog
32 H&R Magnum

Charter Arms Bulldog Police, 32 H&R Magnum Double Action Revolver $150
Same general specifications as standard Bulldog Police, except chambered for 32 H&R Magnum.

Charter Arms Police Bulldog
New Model

Charter Arms Police Bulldog
Old Model

Charter Arms Bulldog Police DA Revolver
Caliber: 38 Special. 6-shot cylinder. 4-inch barrel. 8½ inches overall. Weight: 20½ oz. Adjustable rear sight, ramp front sight. Blued or stainless finish. Checkered walnut square buttstocks. Made from 1976 to date. Shroud dropped on new model.

Blued Finish	$150
Stainless Finish	175

Charter Arms Bulldog Pug

Charter Arms Bulldog Pug Stainless Double Action Revolver **$200**
Caliber: 44 Special. 5-shot cylinder. $2^1/_2$-inch barrel. $7^1/_4$ inches overall. Weight: 20 oz. All stainless steel frame. Fixed ramp front sight; fixed square-notch rear. Checkered neoprene or walnut grips. Made from 1988 to date.

Charter Arms Target Bulldog

Charter Arms Bulldog Target Double Action Revolver **$190**
Calibers: 357 Magnum, 44 Special (latter introduced in 1977). 4-inch barrel. $8^1/_2$ inches overall. Weight: in 357, $20^1/_2$ oz. Adjustable rear sight, ramp front sight. Blued finish. Checkered walnut square buttstocks. Intro. 1976. Discontinued.

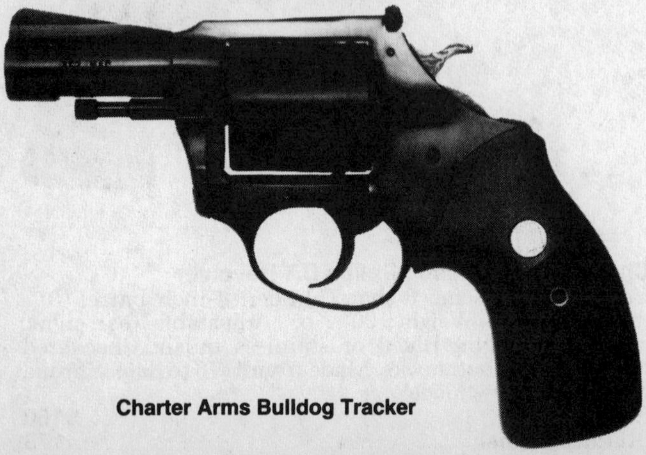

Charter Arms Bulldog Tracker

Charter Arms Bulldog Tracker Double Action Revolver **$165**
Caliber: 357 Mag. 5-shot cylinder. $2^1/_2$-, 4- or 6-inch barrel. 11 inches overall with 6-inch barrel. Weight: 21 oz., $2^1/_2$-inch barrel. Adjustable rear sight, ramp front sight. Checkered walnut grips. Blued finish. 4- and 6-inch barrels discontinued 1986.

Charter Arms Explorer II

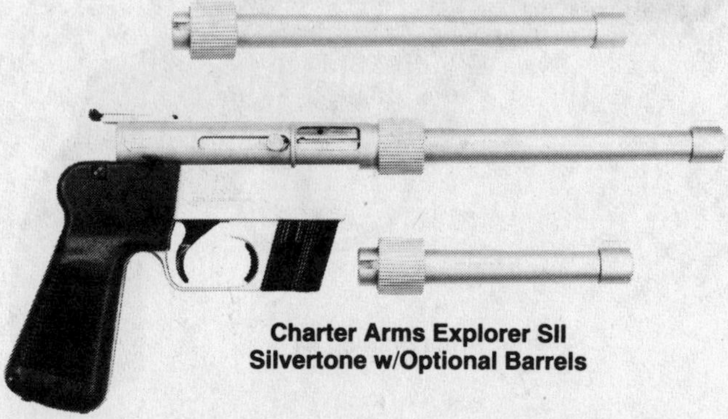

Charter Arms Explorer SII
Silvertone w/Optional Barrels

Charter Arms Explorer II Semiautomatic Survival Pistol **$95**
Caliber: 22RF. 8-shot magazine. 6-, 8- or 10-inch barrel. $13^1/_2$ inches overall with 6-inch barrel. Weight: 28 oz. Finishes: black, heat cured, semigloss textured enamel or silvertone anticorrosion. Silvertone with optional 6- and 10-inch barrels, $85. Discontinued 1987.

Charter Arms Off-Duty Double Action Revolver
Caliber: 38 Special. 5-shot cylinder. 2-inch barrel. $6^1/_4$ inches overall. Weight: 16 oz. Fixed rear sight, Patridge-type front sight. Plain walnut grips. Matte black or stainless steel finish.
Matte Black Finish **$130**
Stainless Steel **165**

Charter Arms Pathfinder
Old Model

Charter Arms Pathfinder
New Model

Charter Arms Pathfinder Double Action Revolver **$165**
Calibers: 22 Long Rifle, 22 Win. Mag. R.F. 6-shot cylinder. Barrel lengths: 2-, 3-, 6-inch. 7$^{1}/_{8}$ inches overall with 3-inch barrel and regular stocks. Weight: with 3-inch barrel, 18$^{1}/_{2}$ oz. Adjustable rear sight, ramp front sight. Blued finish. Plain walnut regular, checkered Bulldog or square buttstocks. Made from 1970 to date. *Note:* Originally designated "Pocket Target." Name changed to "Pathfinder" in 1971. Grips changed in 1984.

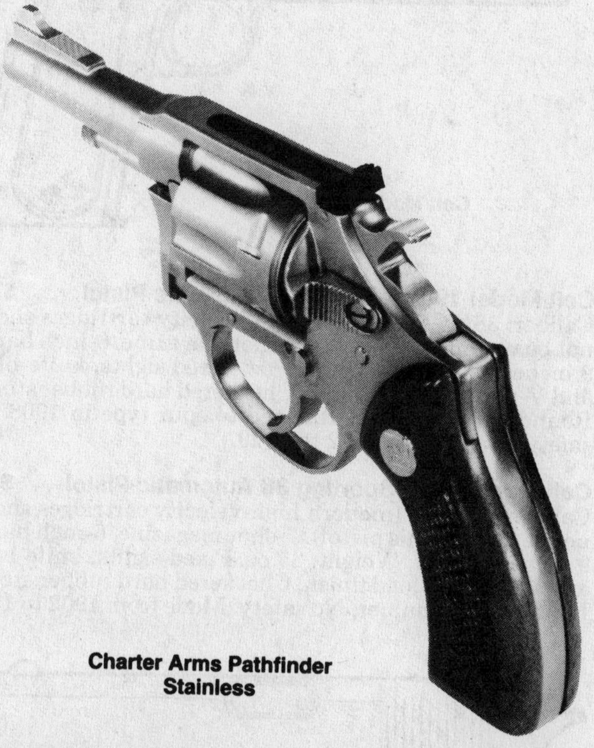

Charter Arms Pathfinder
Stainless

Charter Arms Pathfinder Stainless Double Action Revolver **$190**
Same general specifications as standard Pathfinder, except has stainless steel finish.

Charter Arms Undercover 32 H&R Magnum Double Action Revolver
Same general specifications as standard Undercover, except chambered for 32 H&R Magnum, and has 6-shot cylinder.
Blued Finish **$150**
Stainless Steel **190**

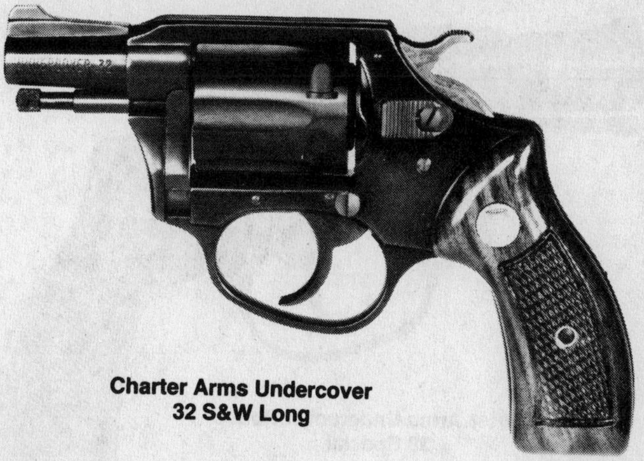

Charter Arms Undercover
32 S&W Long

Charter Arms Undercover 32 S&W Long Double Action Revolver **$150**
Same general specifications as standard Undercover, except chambered for 32 S&W Long and has 6-shot cylinder.

Charter Arms Undercover Double Action Revolver **$155**
Caliber: 38 Special. 5-shot cylinder. Barrel lengths: 2-, 3-, 4-inch. 6$^{1}/_{4}$ inches overall with 2-inch barrel and regular grips. Weight: 16 oz., with 2-inch barrel. Fixed sights. Blued or nickel-plated finish. Plain walnut regular stocks, checkered Bulldog or square buttstocks. Made from 1965 to date.

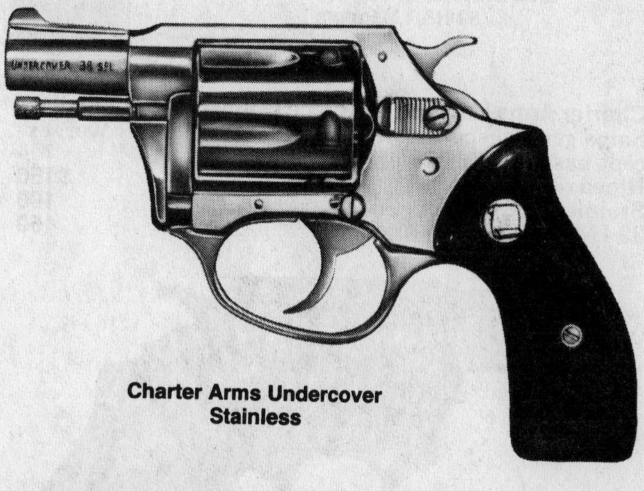

Charter Arms Undercover
Stainless

Charter Arms Undercover Double Action Stainless Revolver **$185**
Same general specifications as standard Undercover, except has stainless steel finish.

Charter Arms Undercover Pocket Police Double Action Revolver
Same general specifications as standard Undercover, except has 6-shot cylinder and pocket-type hammer. Blued or stainless steel finish.
Blued Finish **$150**
Stainless Steel **190**

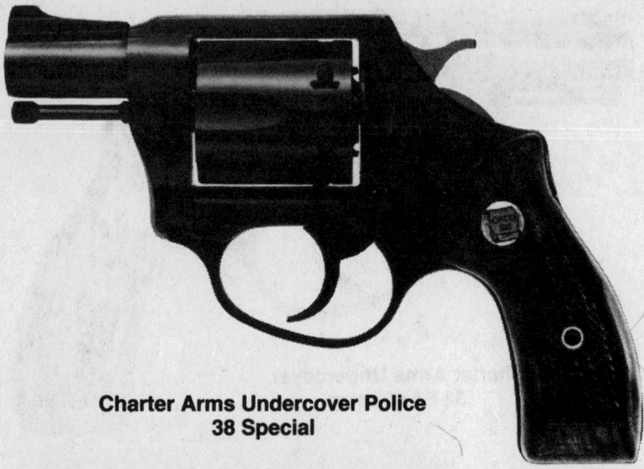

Charter Arms Undercover Police
38 Special

Charter Arms Undercover Police
32 H&R Magnum

Charter Arms Undercover Police Double Action Revolver
Same general specifications as standard Undercover, except has 6-shot cylinder.

Blued, 38 Special	$150
Stainless, 38 Special	190
32 H&R Magnum	150

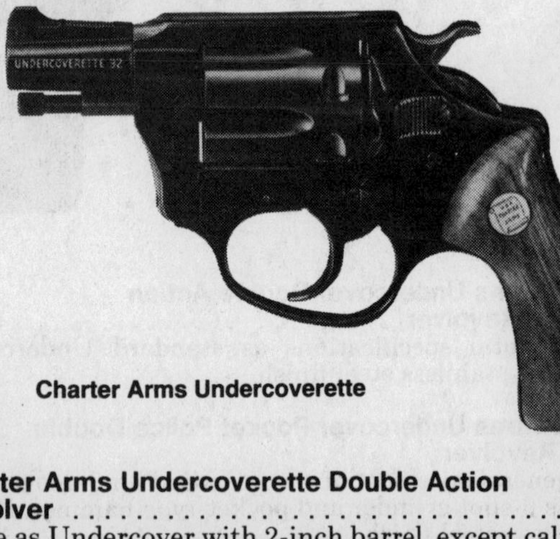

Charter Arms Undercoverette

Charter Arms Undercoverette Double Action Revolver $145
Same as Undercover with 2-inch barrel, except caliber 32 S&W Long, 6-shot cylinder, blued finish only; weighs 16½ oz. Made from 1972 to 1983.

COLT INDUSTRIES, FIREARMS DIV.
Hartford, Connecticut

Production of some Colt handguns spans the period from before World War II to the postwar years. Values shown for these models are for earlier production. Those manufactured c. 1946 and later generally are less desirable to collectors, and values are approximately 30 percent lower. Data on commemorative Colts supplied by Mr. Robert E. P. Cherry, Cherry's Sporting Goods, Greensboro, N.C.

COLT AUTOMATIC PISTOLS

Colt Model 1900 38 Automatic Pistol $795
Caliber: 38 ACP (modern high-velocity cartridges should not be used in this pistol). 7-shot magazine. 6-inch barrel. 9 inches overall. Weight: 35 oz. Fixed sights. Blued finish. Plain walnut stocks. Sharp-spur hammer. Combination rear sight and safety. Made from 1900 to 1903.

Colt Model 1902 Military*

Colt Model 1902 Military 38 Automatic Pistol . . . $795
Caliber: 38 ACP (modern high-velocity cartridges should not be used in this pistol). 8-shot magazine. 6-inch barrel. 9 inches overall. Weight: 37 oz. Fixed sights, knife-blade and V-notch. Blued finish. Checkered hard rubber stocks. Round back hammer, changed to spur type in 1908. No safety. Made from 1902 to 1929.

Colt Model 1902 Sporting 38 Automatic Pistol . . $695
Caliber: 38 ACP (modern high-velocity cartridges should not be used in this pistol). 7-shot magazine. 6-inch barrel. 9 inches overall. Weight: 35 oz. Fixed sights, knife-blade and V-notch. Blued finish. Checkered hard rubber stocks. Round back hammer. No safety. Made from 1902 to 1908.

Colt Model 1903 Pocket*

Colt Model 1903 Pocket 38 Automatic Pistol . . . $395
Caliber: 38 ACP (modern high-velocity cartridges should not be used in this pistol). Similar to Model 1902 Sporting 38, but with 4$^1/_2$-inch barrel. 7$^1/_2$ inches overall. Weight: 31 oz. Fixed sights, knife-blade and V-notch. Blued finish. Checkered hard rubber stocks. Round back hammer, changed to spur type in 1908. No safety. Made from 1903 to 1929.

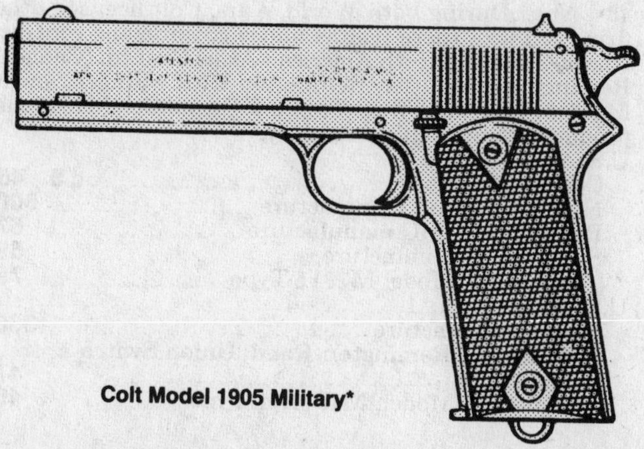

Colt Model 1905 Military*

Colt Model 1905 Military 45 Automatic Pistol . . . $835
Caliber: 45 Automatic. 7-shot magazine. 5-inch barrel. 8 inches overall. Weight: 32$^1/_2$ oz. Fixed sights, knife-blade and V-notch. Blued finish. Checkered walnut stocks. Similar to Model 1902 38 Automatic Pistol. Made from 1905 to 1911.

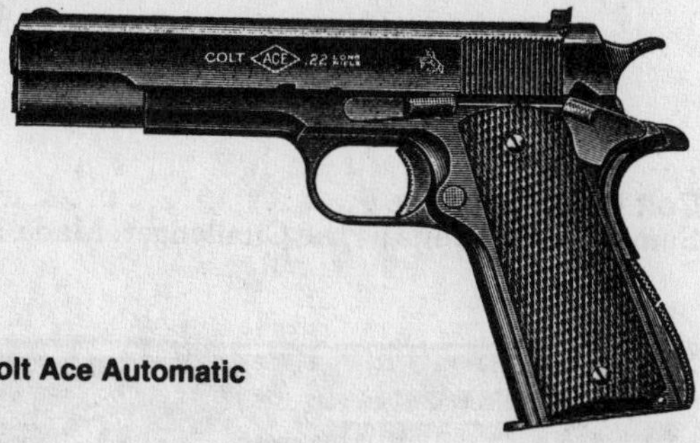

Colt Ace Automatic

Colt Ace Automatic Pistol $800
Caliber: 22 Long Rifle (regular or high speed). 10-shot magazine. Built on the same frame as the Government Model 45 Auto, with same safety features, etc. Hand-honed action, target barrel, adjustable rear sight. 4$^3/_4$-inch barrel. 8$^1/_4$ inches overall. Weight: 38 oz. Made from 1930 to 1940.

Colt Challenger Automatic Pistol $225
Same basic design as Woodsman Target, Third Issue, but lacks some of the refinements. Fixed sights. Magazine catch on butt as in old Woodsman. Does not stay open on last shot. Lacks magazine safety. 4$^1/_2$- or 6-inch barrel. 9 or 10$^1/_2$ inches overall depending upon barrel length. Weight: 30 oz., 4$^1/_2$-inch bbl.; 31$^1/_2$ oz., 6-inch bbl. Blued finish. Checkered plastic stocks. Made from 1950 to 1955.

Colt Combat Commander

Colt Combat Commander Automatic Pistol $330
Same as lightweight Commander, except has steel frame, available in blued or nickel-plated finish, weighs 36 oz. Made from 1970 to date.

Colt Commander

Colt Commander Lightweight Automatic Pistol . . $360
Same basic design as Government Model, but shorter and lighter in weight; receiver and mainspring housing are forged from a special lightweight metal, "Coltalloy." Calibers: 45 Auto, 38 Super Auto, 9mm Luger. 7-shot magazine in 45 cal., 9-shot in 38 Auto and 9mm Luger. 4$^1/_4$-inch barrel. 8 inches overall. Weight: 26$^1/_2$ oz. Fixed sights. Round spur hammer. Improved safety lock. Blued finish. Checkered plastic or walnut stocks. Made from 1951 to date.

Colt Conversion Unit—22-45 . . . . $175
Converts Government Model 45 Auto to a 22 L.R. target pistol. Unit consists of slide assembly, barrel, floating chamber (as in Service Ace), bushing, ejector, recoil spring, recoil spring guide and plug, magazine and slide stop. Made from 1938 to date. *Note:* Now designated "22 Conversion Unit," postwar model of this unit is also adaptable to the Super 38 pistols.

Colt Conversion Unit—45-22 . . . . $400
Converts Service Ace 22 to National Match 45 Auto. Unit consists of match grade slide assembly and barrel, bushing, recoil spring, recoil spring guide and plug, magazine and slide stop. Made from 1938 to 1942.

Colt Delta Elite

Colt Delta Elite Semiauto Pistol
Caliber: 10 mm. 5-inch barrel. 8½ inches overall. 8-round cylinder. Weight: 38 oz., empty. Checkered rubber combat grips with Delta medallion. 3-dot, high-profile front and rear combat sights. Blued or stainless finish.
Blued Finish **$475**
Stainless Finish **525**

Colt Gold Cup Mark III National Match, 38 Spl. . . . $610
Similar to Gold Cup National Match 45 Auto, except chambered for 38 Special mid-range. 5-shot magazine. Made from 1961 to 1974.

Colt Gold Cup National Match 45

Colt Gold Cup National Match 45 Auto $575
Match version of Government Model 45 Auto with same general specifications, except: match grade barrel with new design bushing, flat mainspring housing, long wide trigger with adjustable stop, hand-fitted slide with improved ejection port, adjustable rear sight, target front sight, checkered walnut grips with gold medallions. Weight: 37 oz. Made 1957 to 1970.

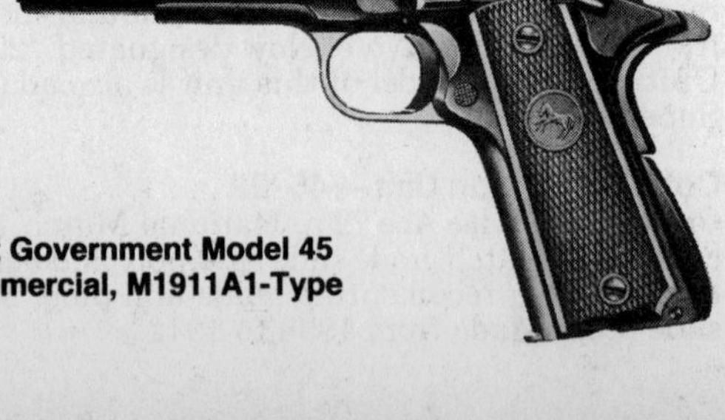

Colt Government Model 45 Commercial, M1911A1-Type

Colt Government Model 45 Automatic Pistol
U.S. Models 1911 and 1911A1. Caliber: 45 Auto. 7-shot magazine. 5-inch barrel. 8½ inches overall. Weight: 39 oz. Fixed sights. Blued finish on Commercial Model, Parkerized or similar finish on most military pistols. Checkered walnut stocks formerly furnished, plastic grips on later production. Checkered, arched mainspring housing and longer grip safety spur adopted in 1923. (M1911A1 has these features.) Made from 1911 to 1970. Letter "C" precedes or follows serial number on Commercial Model 45s. *Note:* During both World Wars, Colt licensed other firms to make these pistols under government contract: Ithaca Gun Co., North American Arms Co. Ltd. (Canada), Remington-Rand Co., Remington-UMC, Singer Sewing Machine Co., and Union Switch & Signal Co.; M1911 also produced at Springfield Armory.

U.S. Model 1911

Colt manufacture	**$ 450**
North American manufacture	**6000**
Remington-UMC manufacture	**675**
Springfield manufacture	**595**
Commercial Model M1911 Type	**795**

U.S. Model 1911A1

Singer manufacture	**3500**
Colt, Ithaca, Remington-Rand, Union Switch manufacture	**475**
Commercial Model, M1911A1 Type	**450**

Colt Huntsman

Colt Huntsman $230
Same specifications as the Challenger. Made 1955 to 1976.

Colt Match Target, Second Issue

Colt Match Target Automatic Pistol, Second Issue $425
Same basic design as Woodsman Target, Third Issue. Caliber: 22 Long Rifle (regular or high speed). 10-shot magazine. 6-inch flat-sided heavy barrel. 10½ inches overall. Weight: 40 oz. Click adjustable rear sight, ramp front sight. Blued finish. Checkered plastic or walnut stocks. Made from 1948 to 1976.

Colt Match Target "4½" Automatic Pistol $375
Same as Match Target, Second Issue, except has a 4½-inch barrel. 9 inches overall. Weight: 36 oz. Made 1950 to 1976.

Colt's MK IV/Series '70
Gold Cup National Match 45

Colt MK IV/Series '70 Gold Cup National Match 45 Auto $495
Match version of MK IV/Series '70 Government Model. Caliber: 45 Automatic only. Flat mainspring housing. Accurizor barrel and bushing. Solid rib, Colt-Elliason adjustable rear sight, undercut front sight. Adjustable trigger, target hammer. 8¾ inches overall. Weight: 38½ oz. Blued finish. Checkered walnut stocks. Made from 1970 to date.

Colt's MK IV/Series '70
Government Model 45

Colt MK IV/Series '70 Government Model Automatic Pistol $365
Calibers: 45 Auto, 38 Super Auto, 9mm Luger. 7-shot magazine in 45, 9-shot in 38 and 9mm. 5-inch barrel. 8⅜ inches overall. Weight: 38 oz., 45; 39 oz., 38 and 9mm. Fixed rear sight and ramp front sight. Blued or nickel-plated finish. Checkered walnut stocks. Made from 1970 to date.

Colt MK IV/Series '80 Combat Commander $385
Updated version of the MK IV/Series '70. Same general specifications.

Colt MK IV/Series '80 Gold Cup National Match $520
Same general specifications as Match '70 version.

Colt MK IV Series '80
Government Model, Blue

Colt MK IV/Series '80 Government Model $365
Same general specifications as Government Model Series '70.

Colt MK IV/Series '80
380 Govt., Bright Nickel

Colt MK IV/Series '80 380 Automatic Pistol
Caliber: 380 ACP. 3.29-inch barrel. 6.15 inches overall. Weight: 21.8 oz. Composition grips. Fixed sights. Made from 1984 to date.

Blued Finish $235
Bright Nickel 245

Colt MK IV/Series '80 Lightweight Commander . $380
Updated version of the MK IV/Series '70. Same general specifications as Series '70 counterpart.

Colt MK IV/Series '80
Mustang 380 Auto

Colt MK IV/Series '80 Mustang 380 Automatic
Caliber: 380 ACP. 5-round magazine. $2\frac{3}{4}$-inch barrel. 5.5 inches overall. Weight: $18\frac{1}{2}$ oz. Black composition grips. Currently in production.

Blued Finish	$250
Nickel Finish	275

Colt MK IV/Series '80 Mustang Plus II $275
Caliber: 380 ACP. 7-round magazine. $2\frac{3}{4}$-inch barrel. 5.5 inches overall. Weight: 20 oz. Blued finish with checkered, black composition grips, full-length as the 380 Government Model. Made from 1988 to date.

Colt MK IV/Series '80 Mustang Pocketlite

Colt MK IV/Series '80 Mustang Pocketlite $275
Same general specifications as the Mustang 380 Automatic, except weighs only $12\frac{1}{2}$ oz. with aluminum alloy receiver. Blued finish. Optional wood grain grips. Made from 1988 to date.

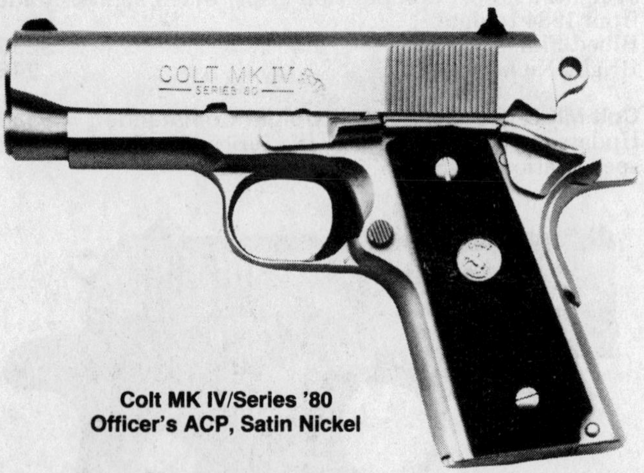

Colt MK IV/Series '80 Officer's ACP, Satin Nickel

Colt MK IV/Series '80 Officer's ACP Automatic Pistol
Caliber: 45 ACP. $3\frac{5}{8}$-inch barrel. $7\frac{1}{4}$ inches overall. Weight: 34 oz. Made from 1984 to date.

Matte Finish	$380
Satin Nickel Finish	425

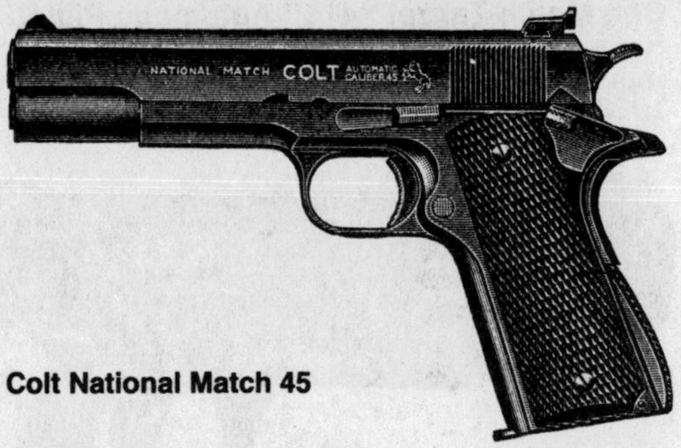

Colt National Match 45

Colt National Match Automatic Pistol
Identical with the Government Model 45 Auto, but with hand-honed action, match grade barrel, adjustable rear sight and ramp front sight or fixed sights. Made from 1932 to 1940.

With adjustable sights	$750
With fixed sights	500

Colt NRA Centennial 45 Gold Cup National Match $485
2500 produced in 1971.

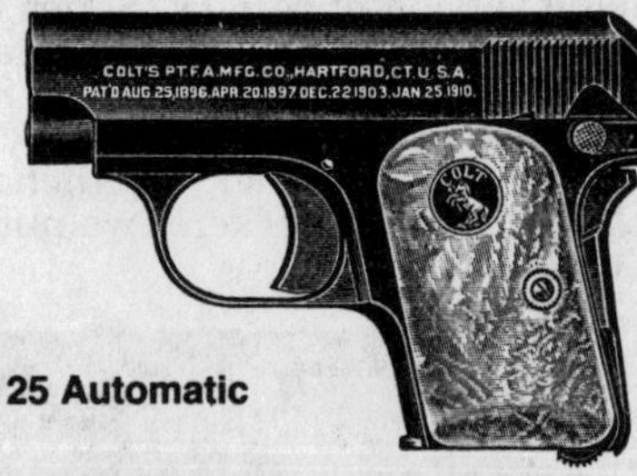

Colt Pocket 25 Automatic

Colt Pocket Model 25 Automatic Pistol $365
Caliber: 25 Automatic. 6-shot magazine. 2-inch barrel. $4\frac{1}{2}$ inches overall. Weight: 13 oz. Flat top front, square notch, rear sight in groove. Blued or nickel finish. Checkered hard rubber stocks on early models, checkered walnut on later type; special pearl stocks illustrated. Disconnector added in 1916 at pistol No. 141000. Made from 1908 to 1941.

Colt Pocket Model 32 Automatic Pistol First Issue $475
Caliber: 32 Auto. 8-shot magazine. 4-inch barrel. 7 inches overall. Weight: 23 oz. Fixed sights. Blued finish. Checkered hard rubber stocks. Hammerless. Slide lock and grip safeties. Barrel-lock bushing similar to that on Government Model 45 Auto. Made from 1903 to 1911.

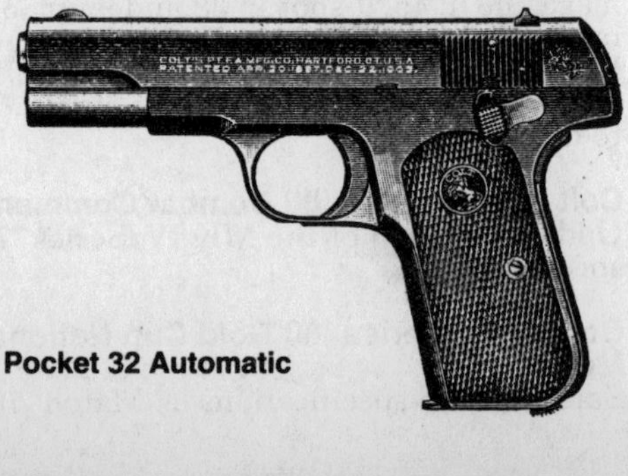
Colt Pocket 32 Automatic

Colt Pocket Model 32 Automatic Pistol Second Issue $350
Same as First Issue but without barrel-lock bushing. Made from 1911 to 1926.

Colt Pocket Model 32 Automatic Pistol Third Issue $360
Caliber: 32 Auto. Similar to First and Second Issues, but has safety disconnector on all pistols above No. 468097 which prevents firing of cartridge in chamber if magazine is removed. 3³/₄-inch barrel. 6³/₄ inches overall. Weight: 24 oz. Fixed sights. Blued or nickel finish. Checkered walnut stocks. Made from 1926 to 1945.

Colt Pocket Model 380 Automatic Pistol First Issue $425
Same as Pocket 32 Auto, First Issue, except chambered for caliber 380 Auto, 7-shot magazine. Made from 1908 to 1911.

Colt Pocket Model 380 Automatic Pistol Second Issue $320
Same as Pocket 32 Auto, Second Issue, except chambered for 380 Auto, 7-shot magazine. Made from 1911 to 1926.

Colt Pocket Model 380 Auto Pistol, Third Issue . $395
Same as Pocket 32 Auto, Third Issue, except chambered for 380 Auto, 7-shot magazine. Safety disconnector on all pistols above No. 92,894. Made from 1926 to 1945.

Colt Pocket Junior

Colt Pocket Junior Model Automatic Pistol $185
Made in Spain by Unceta y Cia (Astra). Calibers: 22 Short, 25 Auto. 6-shot magazine. 2¹/₄-inch barrel. 4³/₄ inches overall. Weight: 12 oz. Fixed sights. Checkered walnut grips. Made from 1958 to 1968.

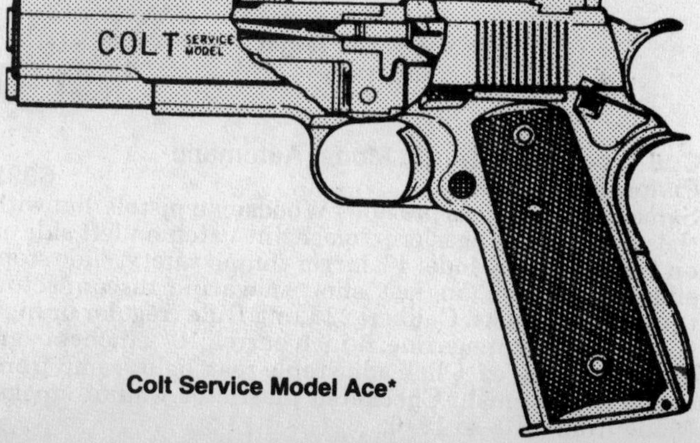

Colt Service Model Ace*

Colt Service Model Ace Automatic Pistol $1295
Identical to National Match Model 45 Auto, except for caliber, magazine capacity and weight; has "floating chamber" amplifying recoil to four times that normal in a 22. Caliber: 22 Long Rifle (regular or high speed). 10-shot magazine. Weight: 42 oz. Made from 1938 to 1942.

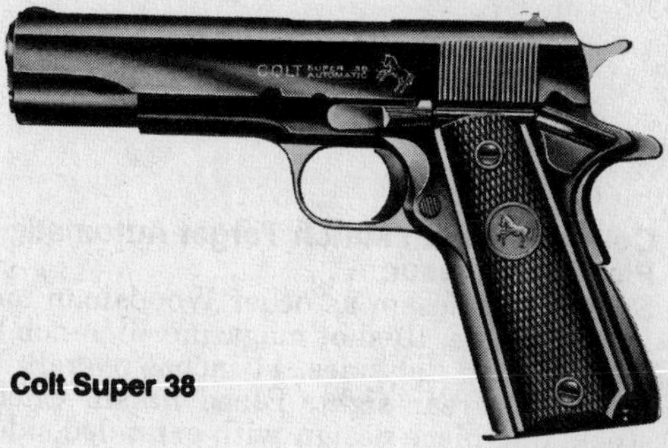

Colt Super 38

Colt Super 38 Automatic Pistol
Identical with Government Model 45 Auto, except for caliber and magazine capacity. Caliber: 38 Automatic. 9-shot magazine. Made from 1928 to 1970.
Pre-war $795
Post-war 425

Colt Super Match 38 Automatic Pistol
Identical to Super 38 Auto, but with hand-honed action, match grade barrel, adjustable rear sight and ramp front sight or fixed sights. Made from 1933 to 1940.
With adjustable sights $895
With fixed sights 625

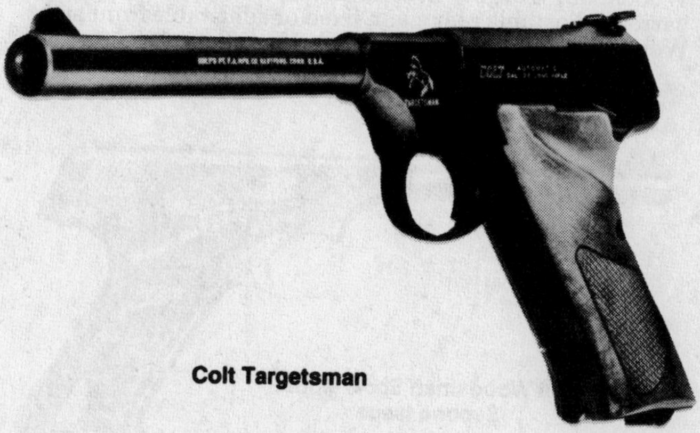

Colt Targetsman

Colt Targetsman $225
Similar to Woodsman Target but has "economy" adjustable rear sight, lacks automatic slide stop. Made from 1959 to 1976.

Colt Woodsman Match Target
First Issue

Colt Woodsman Match Target Automatic Pistol, First Issue $595

Same basic design as other Woodsman models. Caliber: 22 Long Rifle. 10-shot magazine. 6½-inch barrel, slightly tapered with flat sides. 11 inches overall. Weight: 36 oz. Adjustable rear sight. Blued finish. Checkered walnut stock, one-piece design with extended sides. Made from 1938 to 1942.

Colt Woodsman Sport Model
First Issue

Colt Woodsman Sport Model Automatic Pistol, First Issue $365

Caliber: 22 Long Rifle (regular or high speed). Same as Woodsman Target, Second Issue, except has 4½-inch barrel. Adjustable rear sight, fixed or adjustable front sight. Weight: 27 oz. 8½ inches overall. Made from 1933 to 1948.

Colt Woodsman Sport Model
Second Issue

Colt Woodsman Sport Model Automatic Pistol, Second Issue $425

Same as Woodsman Target, Third Issue, but with 4½-inch barrel. 9 inches overall. Weight: 30 oz. Made 1948 to 1976.

Colt Woodsman Target
First Issue

Colt Woodsman Target Model Automatic Pistol, First Issue $400

Caliber: 22 Long Rifle (regular velocity). 10-shot magazine. 6½-inch barrel. 10½ inches overall. Weight: 28 oz. Adjustable sights. Blued finish. Checkered walnut stocks. Made from 1915 to 1932. *Note:* The mainspring housing of this model is not strong enough to permit safe use of high-speed cartridges. Change to a new heat-treated mainspring housing was made at pistol No. 83,790. Many of the old models were converted by installation of new housings. The new housing may be distinguished from the earlier type by the checkering in the curve under the breech; new housing is grooved straight across, while the old type bears a diagonally checkered oval.

Colt Woodsman Target
Second Issue

Colt Woodsman Target Model Automatic Pistol, Second Issue $425

Caliber: 22 Long Rifle (regular or high speed). Same as original model, except has heavier barrel and high-speed mainspring housing. See note under Woodsman, First Issue. Weight: 29 oz. Made from 1932 to 1948.

Colt Woodsman Target
Third Issue

Colt Woodsman Target Model Automatic Pistol, Third Issue $395

Same basic design as previous Woodsman pistols, but with these changes: longer grip, magazine catch on left side as on Government Model 45, larger thumb safety, slide stop, slide stays open on last shot, magazine disconnector, thumb-rest stocks. Caliber: 22 Long Rifle (regular or high speed). 10-shot magazine. 6-inch barrel. 10½ inches overall. Weight: 32 oz. Click adjustable rear sight, ramp front sight. Blued finish. Checkered plastic or walnut stocks. Made from 1948 to 1976.

Colt WWI Commemorative
Deluxe Grade, Meuse Argonne

Colt WWI Commemorative
Standard, Second Battle of the Marne

Colt World War I 50th Anniversary Commemorative Series 45 Auto
Limited production replica of Model 1911 45 Auto engraved with battle scenes, commemorating Battles at Chateau Thierry, Belleau Wood, Second Battle of the Marne, Meuse Argonne. In special presentation display cases. Production: 7400 standard model, 75 deluxe, 25 special deluxe grade. Match numbered sets offered. Made in 1967, 1968, 1969. Values indicated are for commemoratives in new condition.

Standard Grade	$ 550
Deluxe Grade	1295
Special Deluxe Grade	2595

Colt WWII Commemorative
European Theater

Colt WWII Commemorative
Pacific Theater

Colt World War II Commemorative 45 Auto $595
Limited production replica of Model 1911A1 45 Auto engraved with respective names of locations where historic engagements occurred during World War II, as well as specific issue and theater identification. European model has oak leaf motif on slide; palm leaf design frames the Pacific issue. Cased. 11,500 of each model were produced. Made in 1970. Value listed is for gun in new condition.

SINGLE SHOT PISTOLS AND DERINGERS

Values indicated for commemoratives are for those in new condition.

Colt Camp Perry, First Issue

Colt Camp Perry Model Single Shot Pistol, First Issue $725
Built on Officers' Model frame. Caliber: 22 Long Rifle (embedded head chamber for high-speed cartridges after 1930). 10-inch barrel. 13¾ inches overall. Weight: 34½ oz. Adjustable target sights. Hand-finished action. Blued finish. Checkered walnut stocks. Made from 1926 to 1934.

Colt Camp Perry, Second Issue

Colt Camp Perry Model, Second Issue $1050
General specifications same as First Issue, except this model has shorter hammer fall and 8-inch barrel. 12 inches overall. Weight: 34 oz. Made from 1934 to 1941 (about 440 produced).

Colt Civil War Centennial (Cased Pair)

Colt Civil War Centennial Model Pistol

Single shot replica, $^{7}/_{8}$ scale, of Colt Model 1860 Army Revolver. Caliber: 22 Short. 6-inch barrel. Weight: 22 oz. Blued finish with gold-plated frame, grip frame, and trigger guard, walnut grips. Cased. 24,114 were produced. Made in 1961.

Single Pistol **$150**
Pair with consecutive serial numbers **350**

Colt Deringer No. 4 (Cased Pair)

Colt Deringer No. 4

Replica of Deringer No. 3 (1872). Single shot with side-swing barrel. Caliber: 22 Short. $2^{1}/_{2}$-inch barrel. $4^{15}/_{16}$ inches overall. Weight: $7^{3}/_{4}$ oz. Fixed sights. Gold-finished frame, blued barrel, walnut grips; also available nickel-plated with simulated ivory grips. Cased. Made from 1959 to 1963.

Single Pistol **$125**
Pair with consecutive serial numbers **250**

Colt Deringer No. 4 Commemorative Models

Limited production version of 22 Deringer issued, with appropriate inscription, to commemorate historical events.

1961 Issue

Geneseo, Illinois, 125th Anniversary (104 produced) **$600**

1962 Issue

Fort McPherson, Nebraska, Centennial (300 produced) **$300**

Colt Lord and Lady Deringers

Same as Deringer No. 4. Lord model is blued with gold-plated frame and walnut stocks. Lady model is gold-plated with simulated pearl stocks. Furnished in cased pairs. Made from 1970 to 1972.

Lord Deringer, pair in case **$180**
Lady Deringer, pair in case **210**
Lord and Lady Deringers, one each, in case **200**

Colt Rock Island Arsenal Centennial Pistol $200

Limited production (550 pieces) version of Civil War Centennial Model single shot 22 pistol, made exclusively for Cherry's Sporting Goods, Geneseo, Illinois, to commemorate the centennial of the Rock Island Arsenal in Illinois. Cased. Made in 1962.

COLT REVOLVERS

Colt Agent, First Issue

Colt Agent, Second Issue

Colt Agent Double Action Revolver, First Issue . $225

Same as Cobra, First Issue, except has short-grip frame, 38 Special only, weighs 14 oz. Made from 1962 to 1973.

Colt Agent Double Action Revolver, Second Issue $160

Same as Cobra, Second Issue, except has short service stocks, is $6^{5}/_{8}$ inches overall, weighs 16 oz. Made from 1973 to 1981.

Colt Army Special Double Action Revolver $295

41-caliber frame. Calibers: 32-20, 38 Special (41 Colt). 6-shot cylinder, right revolution. Barrel lengths: 4-, $4^{1}/_{2}$-, 5- and 6-inch. $9^{1}/_{4}$ inches overall with 4-inch bbl. Weight: 32 oz. with 4-inch bbl. Fixed sights. Blued or nickel-plated finish. Hard rubber stocks. Made from 1908 to 1927. *Note:* This model has a somewhat heavier frame than the New Navy, which it replaced. Serial numbers begin with 300,000. The heavy 38 Special High Velocity loads should not be used in 38 Special arms of this model.

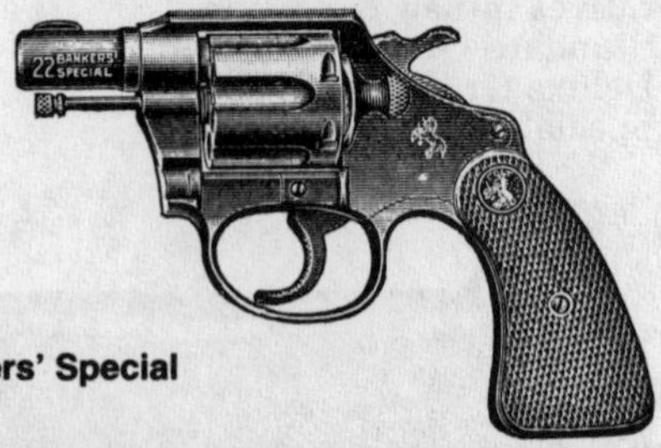

Colt Bankers' Special

Colt Bankers' Special Double Action Revolver

This is the Police Positive with a 2-inch barrel, otherwise specifications same as that model; rounded butt introduced in 1933. Calibers: 22 Long Rifle (embedded head-cylinder for high speed cartridges introduced 1933), 38 New Police. $6^{1}/_{2}$ inches overall. Weight: 23 oz., 22 cal.; 19 oz., 38 cal. Made from 1926 to 1940.

38 Caliber **$395**
22 Caliber **640**

Colt Bisley Model Single Action Revolver
Variation of the Single Action Army, developed for target shooting; grips, trigger and hammer changed. Calibers: general specifications same as Single Action Army. Also made in Target Model with flat-topped frame and target sights. Made from 1894 to 1915.
Standard Model **$1295**
Target Model **2595**

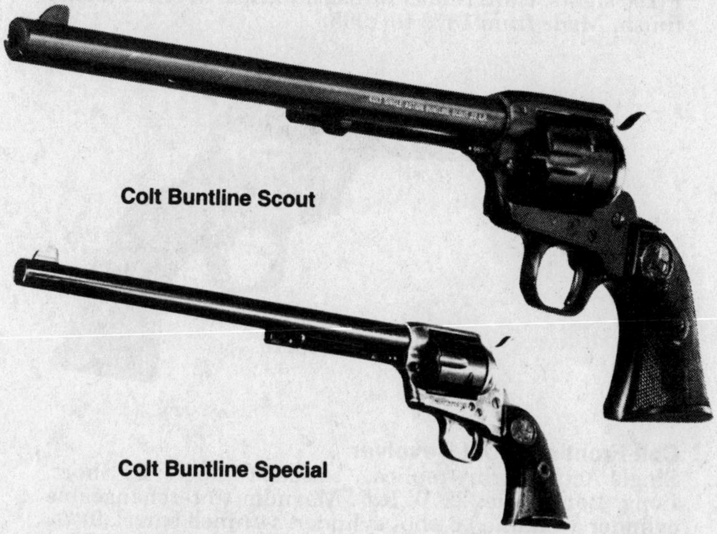

Colt Buntline Scout

Colt Buntline Special

Colt Buntline Scout **$180**
Same as Frontier Scout, except has 9½-inch barrel. Made from 1959 to 1971.

Colt Buntline Special 45 . . . . **$695**
Same as standard Single Action Army, except has 12-inch barrel, caliber 45 Long Colt. Made from 1957 to 1975.

Colt Cobra, Round Butt First Issue

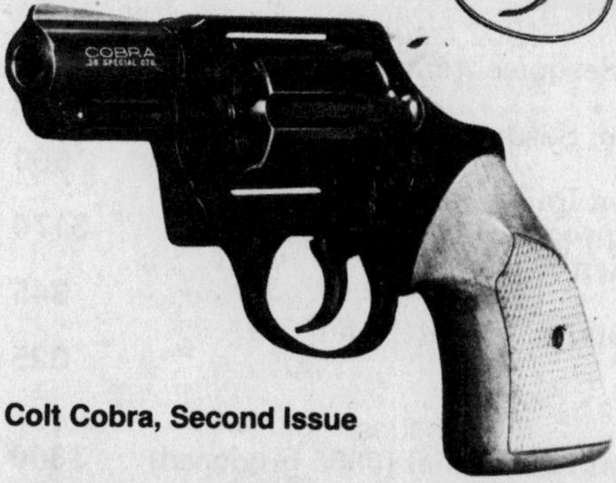

Colt Cobra, Second Issue

Colt Cobra Double Action Revolver, Round Butt First Issue **$285**
Lightweight Detective Special with same general specifications as that model, except with Colt-alloy frame. 2-inch barrel. Calibers: 38 Special, 38 New Police, 32 New Police. Weight: 15 oz., 38 cal. Blued finish. Checkered plastic or walnut stocks. Made from 1951 to 1973.

Colt Cobra Double Action Revolver, Second Issue **$255**
Lightweight version of Detective Special, Second Issue; has aluminum alloy frame, weighs 16½ oz. Made from 1973 to 1981.

Colt Cobra Double Action Revolver Square Butt **$285**
Lightweight Police Positive Special with same general specifications, except has Colt-alloy frame. 4-inch barrel. Calibers: 38 Special, 38 New Police, 32 New Police. Weight: 17 oz. in 38 caliber. Blued finish. Checkered plastic or walnut stocks. Made from 1951 to 1973.

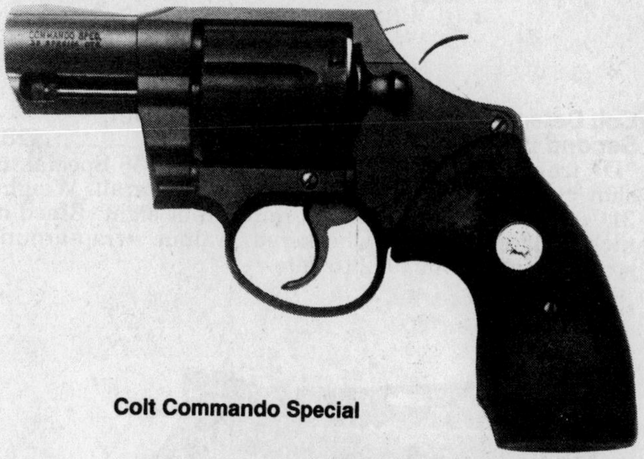

Colt Commando Special

Colt Commando Special Double Action Revolver **$185**
Caliber: 38 Special. 6-shot cylinder. 2-inch barrel; 6⅞ inches overall. Weight: 21½ oz. Fixed sights. Low-luster blue finish. Made from 1982 to 1986.

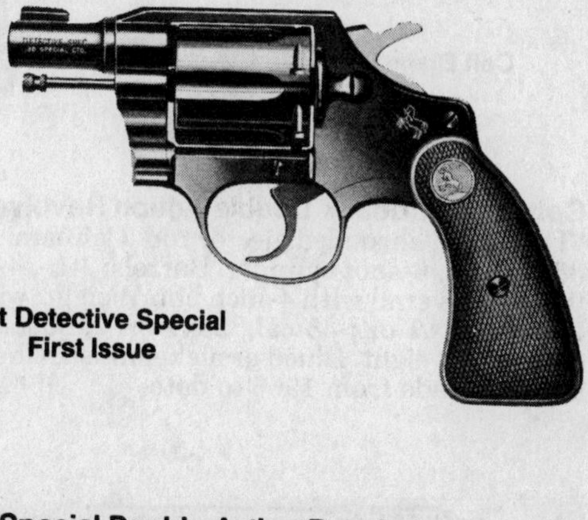

Colt Detective Special First Issue

Colt Detective Special Double Action Revolver, First Issue **$265**
This is the Police Positive Special with a 2-inch barrel, otherwise specifications same as that model; rounded butt introduced in 1933. Originally supplied in 38 Special only, it was also made in calibers 32 New Police, 38 New Police. Weight: 17 oz. in 38 cal. 6¾ inches overall. Made from 1926 to 1972.

Colt Detective Special, Second Issue

Colt Detective Special Double Action Revolver, Second Issue **$285**
"D" frame, shrouded ejector rod. Caliber: 38 Special. 6-shot cylinder. 2-inch barrel. $6\frac{7}{8}$ inches overall. Weight: $21\frac{1}{2}$ oz. Fixed rear sight and ramp front sight. Blued or nickel-plated finish. Checkered walnut wrap-around stocks. Made from 1972 to date.

Colt Diamondback

Colt Diamondback Double Action Revolver **$325**
"D" frame, shrouded ejector rod. Calibers: 22 Long Rifle, 38 Special. 6-shot cylinder. Barrels: $2\frac{1}{2}$-, 4-inch; vent rib. 9 inches overall with 4-inch bbl. Weight: with 4-inch bbl., 22 cal., $31\frac{3}{4}$ oz.; 38 cal., $28\frac{1}{2}$ oz. Adjustable rear sight, ramp front sight. Blued or nickel finish. Checkered walnut stocks. Made from 1966 to date.

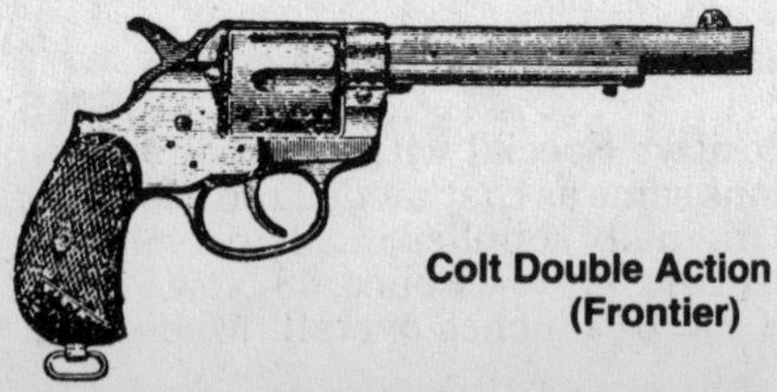

Colt Double Action Army (Frontier)

Colt Double Action Army Revolver **$895**
Also called Double Action Frontier. Similar in appearance to the smaller Lightning Model, but has heavier frame of different shape, round disc on left side of frame, lanyard loop in butt. Calibers: 38-40, 44-40, 45 Colt. 6-shot cylinder. Barrel lengths: $3\frac{1}{2}$- and 4-inch without ejector; $4\frac{3}{4}$-, $5\frac{1}{2}$- and $7\frac{1}{2}$-inch with ejector. $12\frac{1}{2}$ inches overall with $7\frac{1}{2}$-inch bbl. Weight: 45 cal. with $7\frac{1}{2}$-inch bbl., 39 oz. Fixed sights. Hard rubber birdshead grips. Blued or nickel finish. Made from 1878 to 1905.

Colt Frontier Scout

Colt Frontier Scout Revolver
Single Action Army replica, $\frac{7}{8}$ scale. Calibers: 22 Short, Long, Long Rifle; 22 W.R.F. Magnum (interchangeable cylinder available.) 6-shot cylinder. $4\frac{3}{4}$-inch barrel. $9\frac{15}{16}$ inches overall. Weight: 24 oz. Fixed sights. Plastic stocks. Originally made with bright alloy frame; since 1959 with steel frame, blue finish, also in all nickel finish with wood stocks. Made from 1958 to 1971.

Blue finish, plastic stocks	**$215**
Nickel finish, wood stocks	**220**
Extra interchangeable cylinder	**25**

Colt Frontier Scout Revolver Commemorative Models
Limited production versions of Frontier Scout issued, with appropriate inscription, to commemorate historical events. Cased. *Note:* Values indicated are for commemoratives in new condition.

1961 Issues

Kansas Statehood Centennial (6201 produced)	**$300**
Pony Express Centennial (1007 produced)	**510**

1962 Issues

Columbus, Ohio, Sesquicentennial (200 produced)	**$600**
Fort Findlay, Ohio, Sesquicentennial (130 produced)	**650**
Fort Findlay Cased Pair, 22 Long Rifle and 22 Magnum (20 produced)	**3170**
New Mexico Golden Anniversary (1000 produced)	**345**
West Virginia Statehood Centennial (3452 produced)	**325**

1963 Issues

Arizona Territorial Centennial (5355 produced)	**$300**
Battle of Gettysburg Centennial (1019 produced)	**300**
Carolina Charter Tercentenary (300 produced)	**395**
Fort Stephenson, Ohio, Sesquicentennial (200 produced)	**700**
General John Hunt Morgan Indiana Raid (100 produced)	**900**
Idaho Territorial Centennial (902 produced)	**360**

Colt Frontier Scout Commemoratives (cont.)

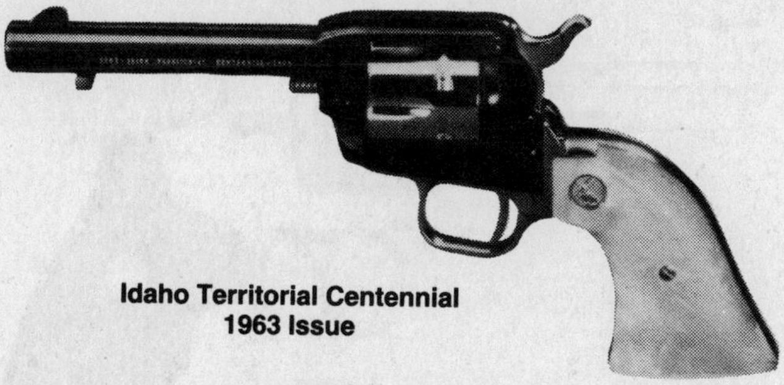

Idaho Territorial Centennial
1963 Issue

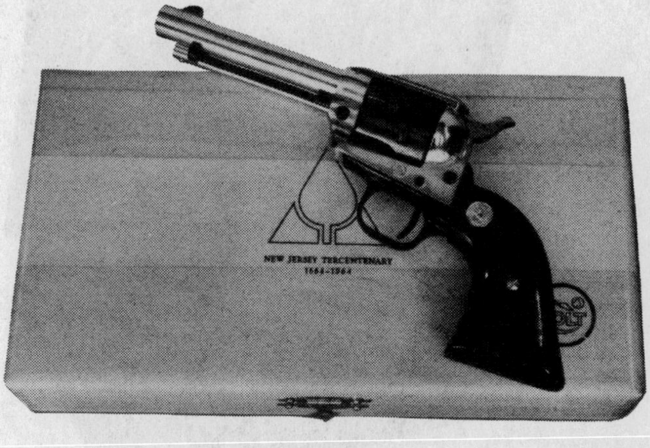

New Jersey Tercentenary
1964 Issue

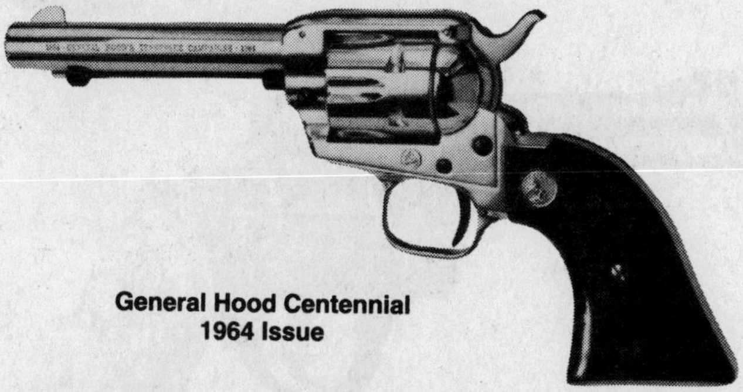

General Hood Centennial
1964 Issue

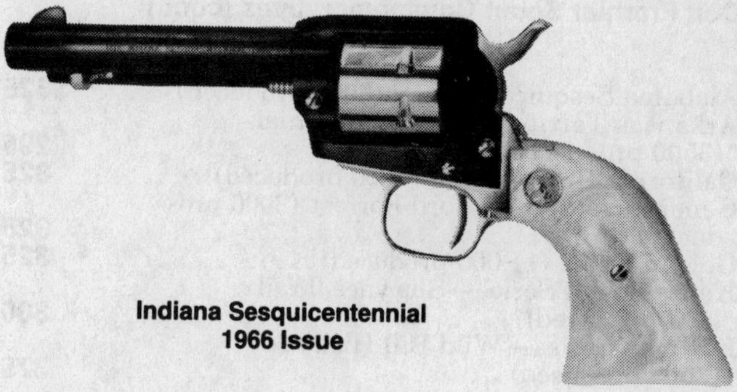

Indiana Sesquicentennial
1966 Issue

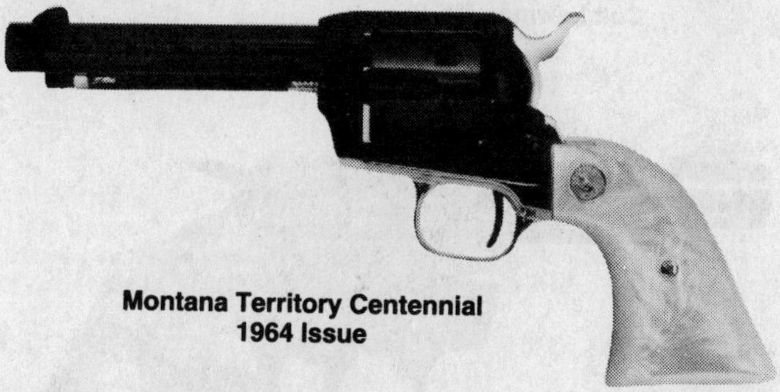

Montana Territory Centennial
1964 Issue

1964 Issues

California Gold Rush (500 produced)	**$350**
Chamizal Treaty (450 produced)	**350**
General Hood Centennial (1503 produced)	**300**
Montana Territorial Centennial (2300 produced)	**300**
Nevada "Battle Born" (981 produced)	**300**
Nevada Statehood Centennial (3984 produced)	**300**
New Jersey Tercentenary (1001 produced)	**300**
St. Louis Bicentennial (802 produced)	**300**
Wyoming Diamond Jubilee (2357 produced)	**300**

1965 Issues

Appomattox Centennial (1001 produced)	**$300**
Forty-Niner Miner (500 produced)	**300**
General Meade Campaign (1197 produced)	**300**
Kansas Cowtown Series—Wichita (500 produced)	**345**
Old Fort Des Moines Reconstruction (700 produced)	**340**
Oregon Trail (1995 produced)	**300**
St. Augustine Quadricentennial (500 produced)	**350**

1966 Issues

Colorado Gold Rush (1350 produced)	**$300**
Dakota Territory (1000 produced)	**300**
Indiana Sesquicentennial (1500 produced)	**295**
Kansas Cowtown Series—Abilene (500 produced)	**360**
Kansas Cowtown Series—Dodge City (500 produced)	**375**
Oklahoma Territory (1343 produced)	**300**

1967 Issues

Alamo (4500 produced)	**$325**
Kansas Cowtown Series—Coffeyville (500 produced)	**350**
Kansas Trail Series—Chisholm Trail (500 produced)	**300**
Lawman Series—Bat Masterson (3000 produced)	**395**

1968 Issues

Kansas Trail Series—Santa Fe Trail (501 produced)	**$395**
Kansas Trail Series—Pawnee Trail (501 produced)	**395**
Lawman Series—Pat Garrett (3000 produced)	**360**
Nebraska Centennial (7001 produced)	**350**

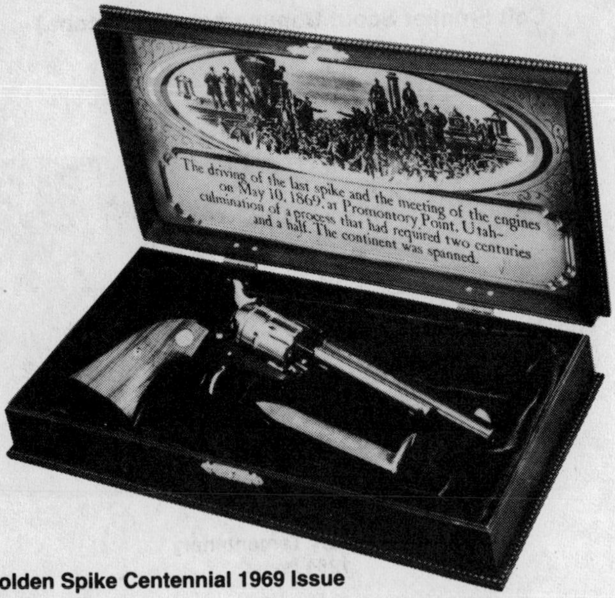

Golden Spike Centennial 1969 Issue

Colt Frontier Scout Commemoratives (cont.)

1969 Issues

Alabama Sesquicentennial (3001 produced)	**$325**
Arkansas Territory Sesquicentennial (3500 produced)	**295**
California Bicentennial (5000 produced)	**325**
General Nathan Bedford Forrest (3000 produced)	**325**
Golden Spike (11,000 produced)	**325**
Kansas Trail Series—Shawnee Trail (501 produced)	**300**
Lawman Series—Wild Bill Hickock (3000 produced)	**375**

1970 Issues

Kansas Fort Series—Fort Larned (500 produced)	**$325**
Kansas Fort Series—Fort Hays (500 produced)	**325**
Kansas Fort Series—Fort Riley (500 produced)	**325**
Lawman Series—Wyatt Earp (3000 produced)	**410**
Maine Sesquicentennial (3000 produced)	**325**
Missouri Sesquicentennial (3000 produced)	**325**

1971 Issues

Kansas Fort Series—Fort Scott (500 produced)	**$300**

1972 Issues

Florida Territory Sesquicentennial (2001 produced)	**$350**

1973 Issues

Arizona Ranger (3001 produced)	**$300**

Colt King Cobra Revolvers

Caliber: 357 Mag. Barrel lengths: 2½-, 4- or 6-inch. 9 inches overall w/4-inch barrel. Weight: 42 oz., average. Matte stainless steel finish. Black neoprene combat grips. Made from 1986 to date. 2½-inch barrel, and "Ultimate" bright or blued finish made from 1988 to date.

Matte Stainless	**$310**
Ultimate Bright Stainless, 2½″ or 4″	**340**
Blued, 4″ or 6″	**290**

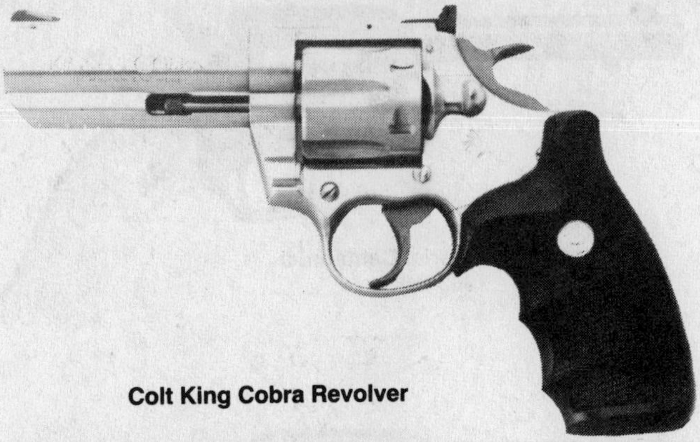
Colt King Cobra Revolver

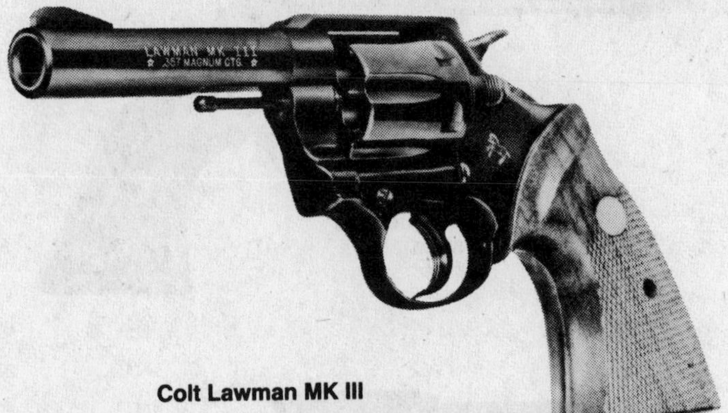

Colt Lawman MK III

Colt Lawman MK V

Colt Lawman MK III Double Action Revolver $200

"J" frame, shrouded ejector rod on 2-inch barrel only. Caliber: 357 Magnum. 6-shot cylinder. Barrel lengths: 2-, 4-inch. 9⅜ inches overall with 4-inch barrel. Weight: with 4-inch bbl., 35 oz. Fixed rear sight and ramp front sight. Service trigger and hammer or target trigger and wide-spur hammer. Blued or nickel-plated finish. Checkered walnut service or target stocks. Made from 1969 to date.

Colt Lawman MK V DA Revolver $240

Similar to Trooper MK V. Caliber: 357 Mag. 6-shot cylinder. 2- or 4-inch barrel; 9⅜ inches overall with 4-inch barrel. Weight: 35 oz. with 4-inch barrel. Fixed sights. Checkered walnut grips. Made from 1983 to 1985.

Colt Marine Corps Model Double Action Revolver $775
General specifications same as New Navy, Second Issue, except this has round butt, was supplied only in 38 caliber (38 Short & Long Colt, 38 Special) with 6-inch barrel. Made from 1905 to 1909.

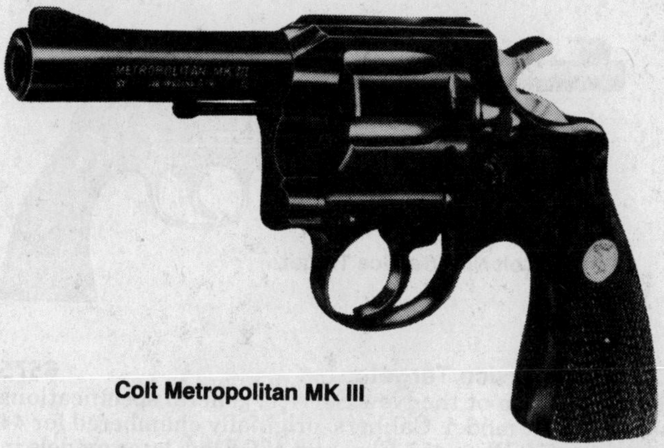

Colt Metropolitan MK III

Colt Metropolitan MK III Double Action Revolver $195
Same as Official Police MK III, except has 4-inch barrel, option of service or target stocks; weighs 36 oz. Made from 1969 to 1972.

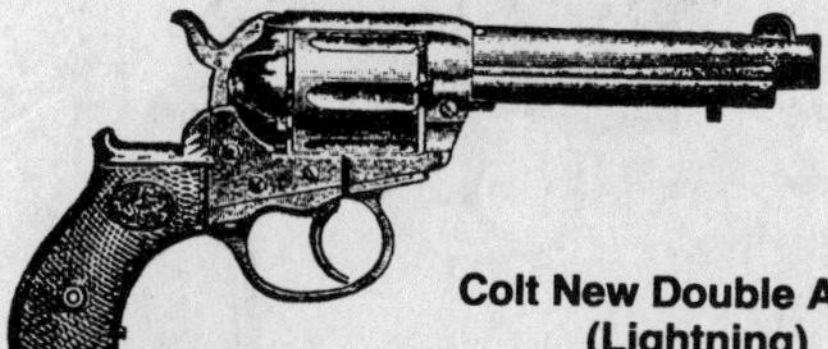

Colt New Double Action (Lightning)

Colt New Double Action Central Fire Revolver . . $625
Also called Lightning Model. Calibers: 38 and 41 Centerfire. 6-shot cylinder. Barrel lengths: $2\frac{1}{2}$-, $3\frac{1}{2}$-, $4\frac{1}{2}$- and 6-inch without ejector, $4\frac{1}{2}$- and 6-inch with ejector. $8\frac{1}{2}$ inches overall with $3\frac{1}{2}$-inch barrel. Weight: 38 cal. with $3\frac{1}{2}$-inch bbl., 23 oz. Fixed sights. Blued or nickel finish. Hard rubber birdshead grips. Made from 1877 to 1909.

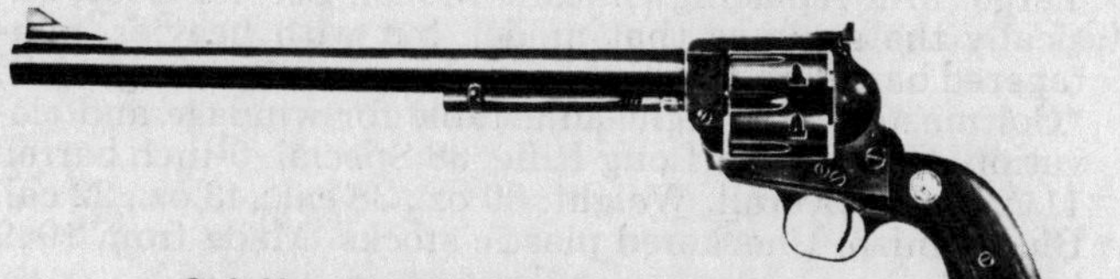

Colt New Frontier Buntline Special

Colt New Frontier Buntline Special $550
Same as New Frontier Single Action Army, except has 12-inch barrel. Made from 1962 to 1966.

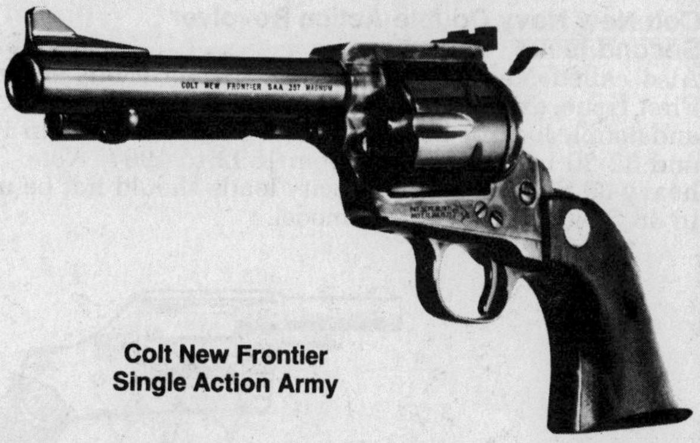

Colt New Frontier Single Action Army

Colt New Frontier Single Action Army Revolver . $495
Same as Single Action Army, except has flat-top frame, adjustable target rear sight, ramp front sight, smooth walnut grips. $5\frac{1}{2}$- or $7\frac{1}{2}$-inch barrel. Calibers: 357 Magnum, 44 Special, 45 Colt. Made from 1961 to date.

Colt New Frontier 22

Colt New Navy

Colt New Frontier Single Action 22 Revolver . . . $225
Same as Peacemaker 22, except has flat-top frame, adjustable rear sight, ramp front sight. Made from 1971 to 1976.

Colt New Navy Double Action Revolver First Issue $325
Also called New Army. Calibers: 38 Short & Long Colt, 41 Short & Long Colt. 6-shot cylinder, left revolution. Barrel lengths: 3-, $4\frac{1}{2}$- and 6-inch. $11\frac{1}{4}$ inches overall with 6-inch bbl. Weight: 32 oz., 6-inch bbl. Fixed sights, knife-blade and V-notch. Blued or nickel-plated finish. Walnut or hard rubber grips. Made from 1889 to 1894. *Note:* This model, which was adopted by both the Army and Navy, was Colt's first revolver of the solid frame, swing-out cylinder type. It lacks the cylinder-locking notches found on later models made on this 41 frame; ratchet on the back of the cylinder is held in place by a double projection on the hand.

Colt New Navy Double Action Revolver Second Issue **$295**
Also called New Army. General specifications same as First Issue, except this model has double cylinder notches and double locking bolt. Calibers: 38 Special added in 1904 and 32-20 in 1905. Made from 1892 to 1907. *Note:* The heavy 38 Special High Velocity loads should not be used in 38 Special arms of this model.

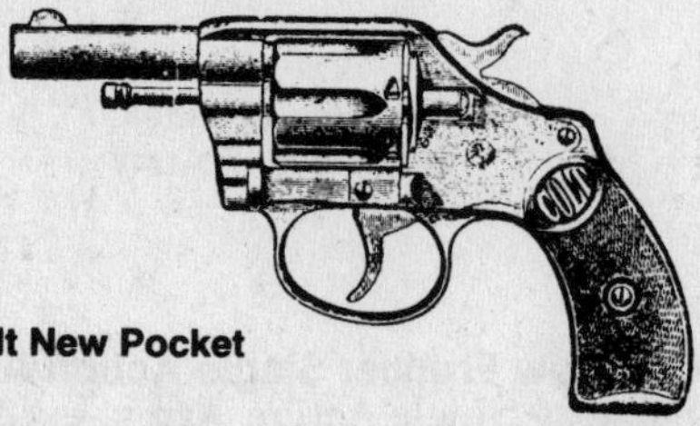

Colt New Pocket

Colt New Pocket Double Action Revolver **$300**
Caliber: 32 Short & Long Colt. 6-shot cylinder. Barrel lengths: $2\frac{1}{2}$-, $3\frac{1}{2}$- and 6-inch. $7\frac{1}{2}$ inches overall with $3\frac{1}{2}$-inch barrel. Weight: 16 oz., $3\frac{1}{2}$-inch bbl. Fixed sights, knife-blade and V-notch. Blued or nickel finish. Rubber stocks. Made from 1893 to 1905.

Colt New Police Double Action Revolver **$265**
Built on New Pocket frame, but with larger grip. Calibers: 32 Colt New Police, 32 Short & Long Colt. Barrel lengths: $2\frac{1}{2}$-, 4- and 6-inch. $8\frac{1}{2}$ inches overall with 4-inch barrel. Weight: 17 oz., 4-inch bbl. Fixed sights, knife-blade and V-notch. Blued or nickel finish. Rubber stocks. Made from 1896 to 1905.

Colt New Police Target Double Action Revolver **$285**
Target version of the New Police with same general specifications. Target sights. 6-inch barrel. Blued finish only. Made from 1896 to 1905.

Colt New Service

Colt New Service Double Action Revolver
Calibers: 38 Special, 357 Magnum (intro. 1936), 38-40, 44-40, 44 Russian, 44 Special, 45 Auto, 45 Colt, 450 Eley, 455 Eley, 476 Eley. 6-shot cylinder. Barrel lengths: 4-, 5- and 6-inch in 38 Special and 357 Magnum; $4\frac{1}{2}$-, $5\frac{1}{2}$- and $7\frac{1}{2}$-inch in other calibers. $9\frac{3}{4}$ inches overall with $4\frac{1}{2}$-inch bbl. Weight: 39 oz., 45 cal. with $4\frac{1}{2}$-inch bbl. Fixed sights. Blued or nickel finish. Checkered walnut stocks. Made from 1898 to 1942. *Note:* More than 500,000 of this model in caliber 45 Auto (designated "Model 1917 Revolver") were purchased by the U.S. Government during World War I. These arms were later sold as surplus to National Rifle Association members through the Director of Civilian Marksmanship. Price was $16.15 plus packing charge. Supply exhausted during the early 1930s.

Commercial Model	**$495**
Magnum	**460**
1917 Army	**450**

Colt New Service Target

Colt New Service Target **$575**
Target version of the New Service; general specifications same as that model. Calibers: originally chambered for 44 Russian, 450 Eley, 455 Eley and 476 Eley; later models in 44 Special, 45 Colt and 45 Auto. Barrel lengths: 6- and $7\frac{1}{2}$-inch. $12\frac{3}{4}$ inches overall with $7\frac{1}{2}$-inch bbl. Adjustable target sights. Hand-finished action. Blued finish. Checkered walnut stocks. Made from 1900 to 1940.

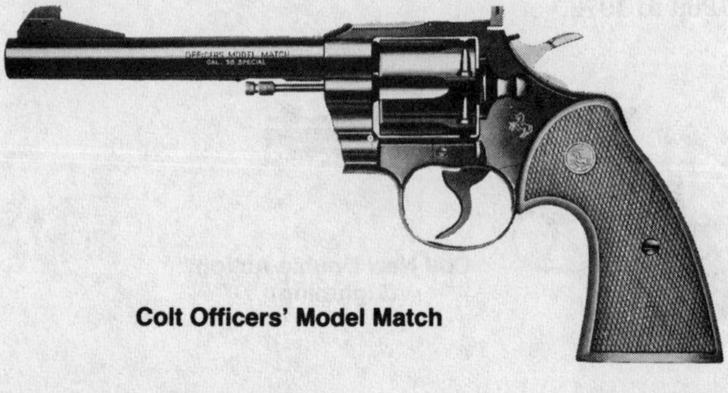

Colt Officers' Model Match

Colt Officers' Model Match **$335**
Same general design as Officers' Model revolvers. Has tapered heavy barrel, wide hammer spur, Accro rear sight, ramp front sight, large target stocks of checkered walnut. Calibers: 22 Long Rifle, 38 Special. 6-inch barrel. $11\frac{1}{4}$ inches overall. Weight: 43 oz., 22 cal.; 39 oz., 38 cal. Blued finish. Made from 1953 to 1970.

Colt Officers' Model Special **$295**
Target arm replacing Officers' Model, Second Issue; basically the same as that model, but with heavier, non-tapered barrel, redesigned hammer, ramp front sight and "Coltmaster" rear sight adjustable for windage and elevation. Calibers: 22 Long Rifle, 38 Special. 6-inch barrel. $11\frac{1}{4}$ inches overall. Weight: 39 oz., 38 cal.; 43 oz., 22 cal. Blued finish. Checkered plastic stocks. Made from 1949 to 1953.

Colt Officers' Model Target Double Action Revolver, First Issue **$600**
Caliber: 38 Special. 6-inch barrel. Hand-finished action. Adjustable target sights. Checkered walnut stocks. General specifications same as New Navy, Second Issue. Made from 1904 to 1908.

Colt Officers' Model Target
Second Issue

Colt Officers' Model Target, Second Issue $395
Calibers: 22 Long Rifle (introduced 1930, embedded head-cylinder for high speed cartridges after 1932), 32 Police Positive (introduced 1932, discontinued 1942), 38 Special. 6-shot cylinder. Barrel lengths: 4-, 4½-, 5-, 6- and 7½-inch in 38 Special; 6-inch only in 22 L.R. and 32 P.P. 11¼ inches overall with 6-inch bbl. in 38 Special. Adjustable target sights. Blued finish. Checkered walnut stocks. Hand-finished action. General features same as Army Special and Official Police of same date. Made from 1908 to 1949 (with exceptions noted).

Colt Official Police

Colt Official Police Double Action Revolver
Calibers: 22 Long Rifle (introduced 1930, embedded head-cylinder for high speed cartridges after 1932), 32-20 (discontinued 1942), 38 Special, 41 Long Colt (discontinued 1930). 6-shot cylinder. Barrel lengths: 4-, 5-, and 6-inch; 2-inch barrel and 6-inch heavy barrel in 38 Special only, 22 L.R. with 4- and 6-inch barrels only. 11¼ inches overall. Weight: 36 oz. with standard 6-inch bbl. in 38 Special. Fixed sights. Blued or nickel-plated finish. Checkered walnut stocks on all revolvers of this model, except some of postwar production had checkered plastic stocks. Made from 1927 to 1969. *Note:* This model is a refined version of the Army Special, which it replaced in 1928 at about serial number 520,000. The Commando 38 Special was a wartime adaptation of the Official Police made to Government specifications. Commando can be identified by its sandblasted blued finish; serial numbers start with number 1 (1942).
Commercial Model **$295**
Commando Model **250**

Colt Official Police MK III

Colt Official Police MK III Double Action Revolver $175
"J" frame, without shrouded ejector rod. Caliber: 38 Special. 6-shot cylinder. Barrel lengths: 4-, 5-, 6-inch. 9¼ inches overall with 4-inch bbl. Weight: with 4-inch bbl., 34 oz. Fixed rear sight and ramp front sight. Service trigger and hammer or target trigger and wide-spur hammer. Blued or nickel-plated finish. Checkered walnut service stocks. Made from 1969 to 1975.

Colt Peacekeeper

Colt Peacekeeper Double Action Revolver $240
Caliber: 357 Mag. 6-shot cylinder. 4- and 6-inch barrels; 11⅛ inches overall with 6-inch barrel. Weight: 46 oz. with 6-inch barrel. Adjustable white outline rear sight; red insert ramp-style front. Non-reflective matte blued finish. Made from 1985 to date.

Colt Peacemaker 22
Second Amendment Commemorative

Colt Peacemaker 22 Second Amendment Commemorative $350
Peacemaker 22 Single Action Revolver with $7\frac{1}{2}$-inch barrel. Nickel-plated frame, barrel, ejector rod assembly, hammer and trigger; blued cylinder, backstrap and trigger guard. Black pearlite stocks. Barrel inscribed "The Right to Keep and Bear Arms." Presentation case. Limited edition of 3000 issued in 1977. Value is for revolver in new condition.

Colt Peacemaker 22

Colt Peacemaker 22 Single Action Revolver $225
Calibers: 22 Long Rifle and 22 Win. Mag. R.F. Furnished with cylinder for each caliber. 6-shot. Barrels: $4\frac{3}{8}$-, 6- or $7\frac{1}{2}$-inch. $11\frac{1}{4}$ inches overall with 6-inch bbl. Weight: with 6-inch bbl., $30\frac{1}{2}$ oz. Fixed sights. Black composite stocks. Made from 1971 to 1976.

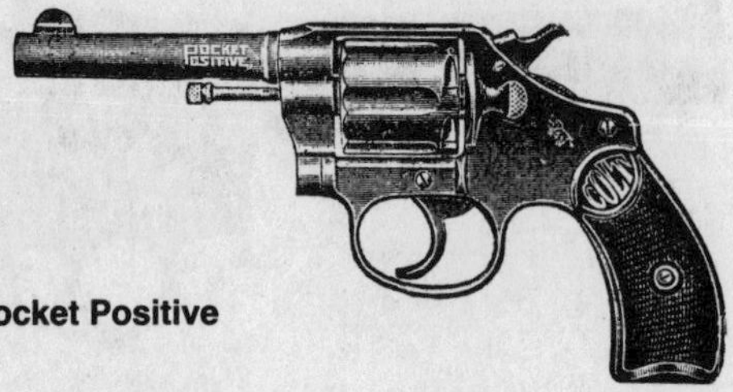
Colt Pocket Positive

Colt Pocket Positive Double Action Revolver . . . $295
General specifications same as New Pocket, except this model has positive lock feature (see Police Positive). Calibers: 32 Short & Long Colt (discontinued 1914), 32 Colt New Police (32 S&W Short & Long). Fixed sights, flat top and square notch. Made from 1905 to 1940.

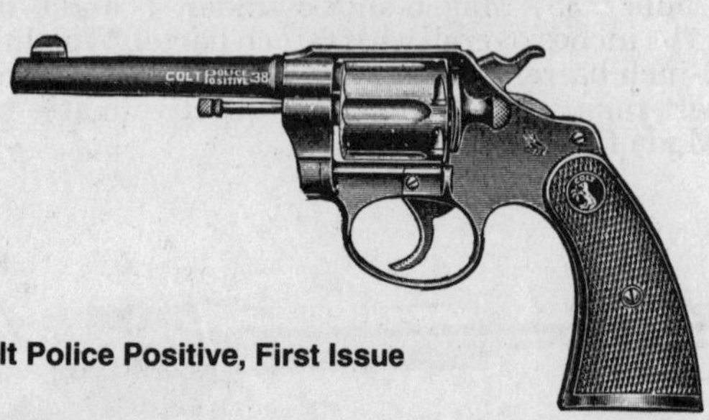
Colt Police Positive, First Issue

Colt Police Positive Double Action Revolver, First Issue $295
Improved version of the New Police with the "Positive Lock," which prevents the firing pin from coming in contact with the cartridge except when the trigger is pulled. Calibers: 32 Short & Long Colt (discontinued 1915), 32

Colt Police Positive Double Action Revolver, First Issue (cont.)
Colt New Police (32 S&W Short & Long), 38 New Police (38 S&W). 6-shot cylinder. Barrel lengths: $2\frac{1}{2}$- (32 cal. only), 4-, 5- and 6-inch. $8\frac{1}{2}$ inches overall with 4-inch bbl. Weight: 20 oz. with 4-inch bbl. Fixed sights. Blued or nickel finish. Rubber or checkered walnut stocks. Made from 1905 to 1947.

Colt Police Positive, Second Issue

Colt Police Positive Double Action Revolver, Second Issue $185
Same as Detective Special, Second Issue, except has 4-inch barrel, is 9 inches overall, weighs $26\frac{1}{2}$ oz. Introduced in 1977. *Note:* Original Police Positive (First Issue) has a shorter frame, is not chambered for 38 Special.

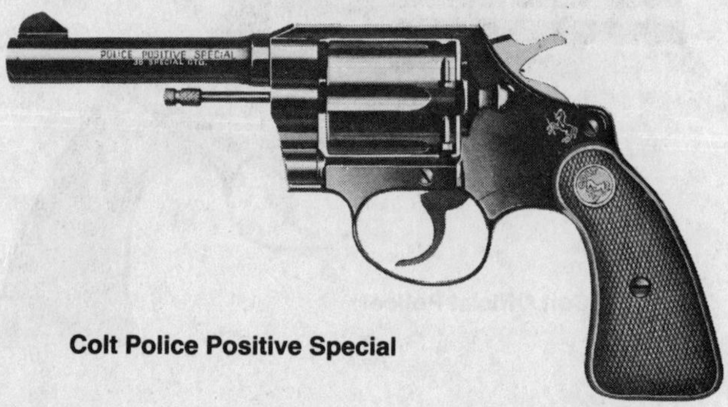
Colt Police Positive Special

Colt Police Positive Special Double Action Revolver $235
Based on the Police Positive with frame lengthened to permit longer cylinder. Calibers: 32—-20 (discontinued 1942), 38 Special, 32 New Police and 38 New Police (introduced 1946). 6-shot cylinder. Barrel lengths: 4- (only length in current production), 5- and 6-inch. $8\frac{3}{4}$ inches overall with 4-inch bbl. Weight: 23 oz. in 38 Special with 4-inch bbl. Fixed sights. Checkered stocks of hard rubber, plastic or walnut. Made from 1907 to 1973.

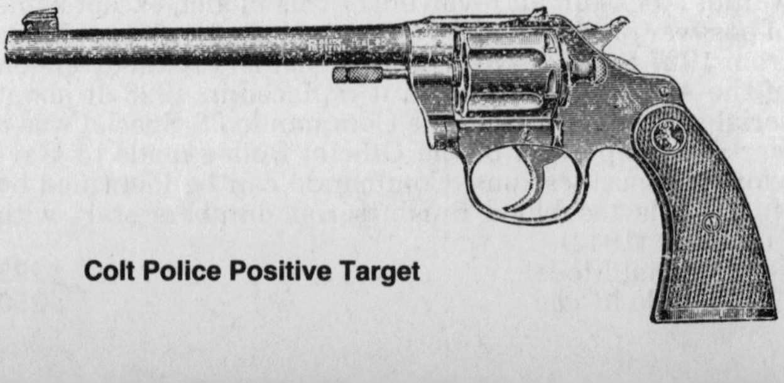
Colt Police Positive Target

Colt Police Positive Target Double Action Revolver **$450**
Target version of the Police Positive. Calibers: 22 Long Rifle (introduced 1910, embedded head-cylinder for high speed cartridges after 1932), 22 W.R.F. (introduced 1910, discontinued 1935), 32 Short & Long Colt (discontinued 1915), 32 New Police (32 S&W Short & Long). 6-inch barrel, blued finish only. 10½ inches overall. Weight: 26 oz. in 22 cal. Adjustable target sights. Checkered walnut stocks. Made from 1905 to 1940.

Colt Shooting Master

Colt Python–Early Model

Colt Python Ultimate Stainless

Colt Shooting Master Double Action Revolver . . **$640**
Deluxe target arm based on the New Service model. Calibers: originally made only in 38 Special; 44 Special, 45 Auto and 45 Colt added in 1933 and 357 Magnum in 1936. 6-inch barrel. 11¼ inches overall. Weight: 44 oz., 38 cal. Adjustable target sights. Hand-finished action. Blued finish. Checkered walnut stocks. Rounded butt. Made from 1932 to 1941.

Colt Single Action Army Revolver
Also called Frontier Six-Shooter and Peacemaker. Calibers: 22 Rimfire (Short, Long, Long Rifle), 22 W.R.F., 32 Rimfire, 32 Colt, 32 S&W, 32-20, 38 Colt, 38 S&W, 38 Special, 357 Magnum, 38-40, 41 Colt, 44 Rimfire, 44 Russian, 44 Special, 44-40, 45 Colt, 45 Auto, 450 Boxer, 450 Eley, 455 Eley, 476 Eley. 6-shot cylinder. Barrel lengths: 4¾, 5½ and 7½ inches with ejector; 3 and 4 inches w/o ejector. 10¼ inches overall with 4¾-inch barrel. Weight: 36 oz., 45 cal. with 4¾-inch barrel. Fixed sights. Also made in Target Model with flat top-strap and target sights. Blued finish with casehardened frame or nickel-plated. One-piece smooth walnut or checkered black rubber stocks.

Colt Single Action Army

Colt Python Double Action Revolver
"I" frame, shrouded ejector rod. Caliber: 357 Magnum. 6-shot cylinder. Barrels: 2½-, 4-, 6-, 8-inch; vent rib. 11¼ inches overall with 6-inch bbl. Weight: 44 oz. with 6-inch bbl. Adjustable rear sight, ramp front sight. Blued, nickel-plated or stainless. Checkered walnut target stocks. Made from 1955 to date. Ultimate stainless finish made from 1985 to date.
Blued Finish **$385**
Stainless Finish **545**

Colt Sheriff's Model 45
Limited edition of replica of Storekeeper's Model in caliber 45 Colt, made exclusively for Centennial Arms Corp., Chicago, Illinois. Numbered from "1SM." Blued finish with casehardened frame or nickel-plated. Walnut stocks. 478 were produced in blue, 25 in nickel. Made in 1961.
Blued Finish **$1395**
Nickel Finish **3350**

S.A. Army Revolvers with serial numbers above 165,000 (circa 1896) are adapted to smokeless powder; cylinder pin screw was changed to spring catch at about the same time. Made from 1873 to 1942; production resumed in 1955 with serial number 1001SA. Current calibers: 357 Magnum, 44 Special, 45 Long Colt.
Frontier Six-Shooter, 44-40 . . . . **$2300**
Storekeeper's Model, 3-inch/4-inch bbl., w/o ejector **2700**
Target Model, flat top-strap, target sights **5000**
U.S. Artillery Model, 45 Colt, 5½-inch bbl. **2195**
U.S. Cavalry Model, 45, 7½-inch bbl. **2250**
(Above values apply only to original models, not to similar S.A.A. revolvers of recent manufacture.)
Standard Model, pre-1942 . . . . **$950**
Standard Model, current. Discontinued 1982 . . . . **550**

Colt Single Action Army—125th Anniversary . . . $695
Limited production deluxe version of Single Action Army issued in commemoration of Colt's 125th Anniversary. Caliber: 45 Long Colt. $7\frac{1}{2}$-inch barrel. Gold-plated frame, trigger, hammer, cylinder pin, ejector rod tip, and stock medallion. Presentation case with anniversary medallion. Serial numbers from "50AM." 7368 were produced. Made in 1961.

Colt Single Action Army Commemorative Models
Limited production versions of Single Action Army 45 issued, with appropriate inscription to commemorate historical events. Cased. *Note:* Values indicated are for commemorative revolvers in new condition.

1963 Issues

Arizona Territorial Centennial (1280 produced) . . . . . **$ 750**
West Virginia Statehood Centennial (600 produced) **795**

1964 Issues:

Chamizal Treaty (50 produced) **$1795**
Colonel Sam Colt Sesquicentennial
Presentation (4750 produced) **900**
Deluxe Presentation (200 produced) **2000**
Special Deluxe Presentation (50 produced) . . . **2960**
Montana Territorial Centennial (851 produced) **750**
Nevada "Battle Born" (100 produced) **2250**
Nevada Statehood Centennial (1877 produced) **750**
New Jersey Tercentenary (250 produced) **875**
Pony Express Presentation (1004 produced) . . **925**
St. Louis Bicentennial (450 produced) **795**
Wyatt Earp Buntline (150 produced) **1795**

1965 Issues

Appomattox Centennial (500 produced) . . . . . **$ 750**
Old Fort Des Moines Reconstruction (200 produced) **825**

Peacemaker Centennial 45
1975 Issue

Peacemaker Centennial 44-40
1975 Issue

Colt Single Action Army Commemoratives (cont.)

1966 Issues

Abercrombie & Fitch Trailblazer—Chicago (100 produced) **$1750**
Abercrombie & Fitch Trailblazer—New York (200 produced) **1625**
Abercrombie & Fitch Trailblazer—San Francisco (100 produced) **1750**
California Gold Rush (130 produced) **1650**
General Meade (200 produced) **925**
Pony Express Four Square (4 guns) **3925**

1967 Issues

Alamo (1000 produced) . . . . . **$ 825**
Lawman Series—Bat Masterson (500 produced) **895**

1968 Issues

Lawman Series—Pat Garrett (500 produced) . . . **$ 895**

1969 Issues

Lawman Series—Wild Bill Hickok (500 produced) . . . . . **$ 850**

1970 Issues

Lawman Series—Wyatt Earp (501 produced) . . . **$1395**
Missouri Sesquicentennial (501 produced) **725**
Texas Ranger (1000 produced) **1395**

1971 Issues

NRA Centennial, 357 or 45 (5001 produced) . . . . **$ 725**

1975 Issues

Peacemaker Centennial 45 (1501 produced) . . . . . **$ 850**
Peacemaker Centennial 44-40 (1501 produced) **850**
Peacemaker Centennial Cased Pair (501 produced) **1850**

1979 Issues

Ned Buntline 45 (3000 produced) . . . . . **$ 895**

Colt Three-Fifty-Seven Double Action Revolver
Heavy frame. Caliber: 357 Magnum. 6-shot cylinder. 4- or 6-inch barrel. Quick-draw ramp front sight, Accro rear sight. Blued finish. Checkered walnut stocks. $9\frac{1}{4}$ or $11\frac{1}{4}$ inches overall. Weight: 36 oz., 4-inch bbl.; 39 oz., 6-inch bbl. Made from 1953 to 1961.
With standard hammer and service stocks **$275**
With wide-spur hammer and target stocks **300**

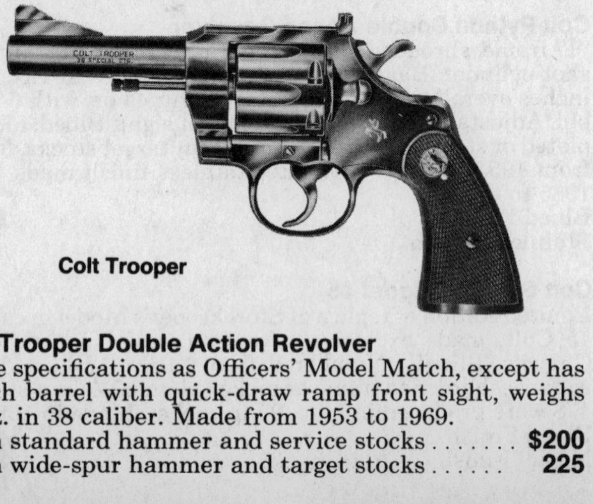

Colt Trooper

Colt Trooper Double Action Revolver
Same specifications as Officers' Model Match, except has 4-inch barrel with quick-draw ramp front sight, weighs 34 oz. in 38 caliber. Made from 1953 to 1969.
With standard hammer and service stocks **$200**
With wide-spur hammer and target stocks **225**

Colt Trooper MK III

Colt Trooper MK III Double Action Revolver $235
"J" frame, shrouded ejector rod. Caliber: 357 Magnum. 6-shot cylinder. Barrel lengths: 4-, 6-inch. 9½ inches overall with 4-inch barrel. Weight: with 4-inch bbl., 39 oz. Adjustable rear sight, ramp front sight. Target trigger and hammer. Blued or nickel-plated finish. Checkered walnut target stocks. Made from 1969 to date.

Colt Trooper MK V

Colt Trooper MK V Revolver $240
Re-engineered Mark III for smoother, faster action. Caliber: 357 Magnum. 6-shot cylinder. Barrel lengths: 4-, 6-, 8-inch. Adjustable rear sight, ramp front sight, red insert and vent rib. Checkered walnut stocks. Made 1982 to 1986.

Colt U.S. Bicentennial Commemorative Set . . . $2100
Replica Colt 3rd Model Dragoon Revolver with accessories, Colt Single Action Army Revolver, and Colt Python Revolver. Matching roll-engraved unfluted cylinders, blued finish, and rosewood stocks with Great Seal of the United States silver medallion. Dragoon revolver has silver grip frame. Serial numbers 0001 to 1776; all revolvers in set have same number. Deluxe drawer style presentation case of walnut, with book compartment containing a reproduction of "Armsmear." Issued in 1976. Value is for revolvers in new condition.

Colt U.S. Bicentennial Commemorative Set

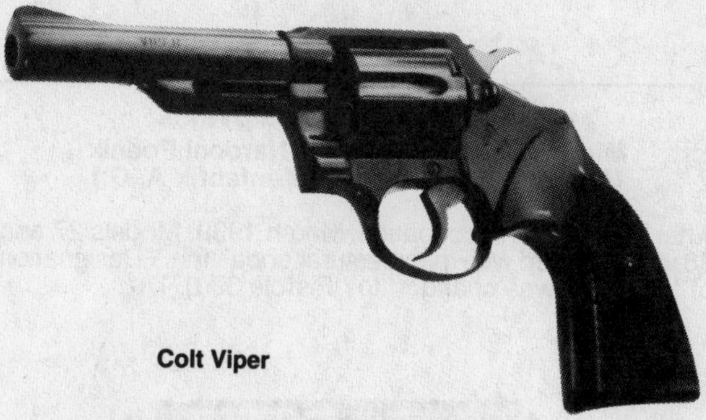

Colt Viper

Colt Viper Double Action Revolver $175
Same as Cobra, Second Issue, except has 4-inch barrel, is 9 inches overall, weighs 20 oz. Introduced in 1977.

COONAN ARMS, INC.
St. Paul, Minnesota

Coonan Arms Model B

Coonan Arms Model B
Caliber: 357 Mag. 7-round magazine. 5-inch barrel. 8.3 inches overall. Weight: 42 oz. Front ramp interchangeable sight; fixed rear sight, adjustable for windage. Black walnut grips.
Competition Grade **$950**
Standard Grade **495**

CZ PISTOLS
Strakonice, Czechoslovakia
Mfd. by Ceska Zbrojovka-Nardoni Podnik (formerly Böhmische Waffenfabrik A. G.)

After the German occupation, March 1939, Models 27 and 38 were marked with manufacturer code "fnh." Designation of Model 38 was changed to "Pistole 39(t)."

CZ Model 27 Automatic Pistol

CZ Model 27 Auto Pistol $190
Caliber: 32 Automatic (7.65mm). 8-shot magazine. 4-inch barrel. 6 inches overall. Weight: 23½ oz. Fixed sights. Blued finish. Plastic stocks. Made from 1927 to 1951.

CZ Model 38 Double Action Automatic Pistol

CZ Model 38 Double Action Auto Pistol $225
Caliber: 380 Automatic (9mm). 9-shot magazine. 3¾-inch barrel. 7 inches overall. Weight: 26 oz. Fixed sights. Blued finish. Plastic stocks. Made from 1939 to 1945.

CZ Model 1945 Pocket Auto

CZ Model 1945 DA Pocket Auto Pistol $195
Caliber: 25 Automatic (6.35mm). 8-shot magazine. 2½-inch barrel. 5 inches overall. Weight: 15 oz. Fixed sights. Blued finish. Plastic stocks. Introduced 1945, production now discontinued.

CZ Duo Pocket Auto

CZ Duo Pocket Auto Pistol $150
Caliber: 25 Automatic (6.35mm). 6-shot magazine. 2⅛-inch barrel. 4½ inches overall. Weight: 14½ oz. Fixed sights. Blued or nickel finish. Plastic stocks. Made from 1926 to c. 1960.

CZ New Model .006

CZ New Model .006 Double Action Auto Pistol . . $295
Caliber: 32 Automatic (7.65mm). 8-shot magazine. $3\frac{1}{8}$-inch barrel. $6\frac{1}{2}$ inches overall. Weight: 24 oz. Fixed sights. Blued finish. Plastic stocks. Introduced 1951. Discont. *Note:* Official designation of this pistol, used by the Czech National Police, is "VZ50." "New Model .006" is export designation.

DAKOTA/E.M.F. CO.
Santa Ana, California

Dakota Model 1873

Dakota Model 1873 Single Action Revolver
Calibers: 22 LR, 22 Mag., 357 Mag., 45 Long Colt, 30 M1 carbine, 38-40, 32-20, 44-40. Barrel lengths: $3\frac{1}{2}$, $4\frac{3}{4}$, $5\frac{1}{2}$, $7\frac{1}{2}$ inches. Blue or nickel finish. Engraved models available.

Standard Model	**$275**
With Extra Cylinder	**325**

Dakota Model 1875 Outlaw

Dakota Model 1875 Outlaw SA Revolver $295
Calibers: 45 Long Colt, 357 Mag., 44-40. $7\frac{1}{2}$-inch barrel. Case-hardened frame, blued finish. Walnut grips. This is an exact replica of the Remington #3 revolver produced from 1875 to 1889.

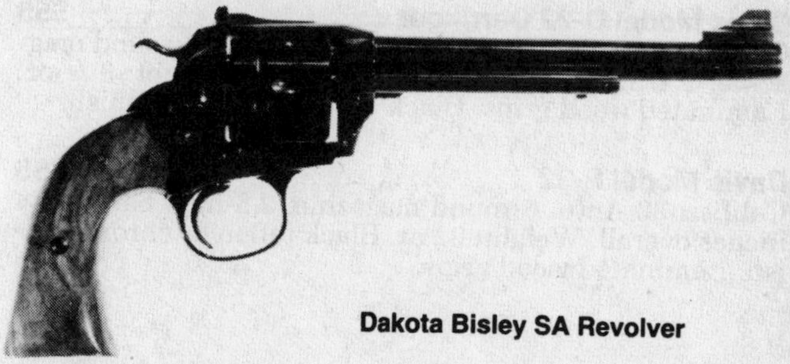

Dakota Bisley SA Revolver

Dakota Bisley Single Action Revolver $370
Calibers: 44-40, 45 Long Colt, 357 Mag. $5\frac{1}{2}$- or $7\frac{1}{2}$-inch barrel.

Dakota Bisley Target Model $395
Same general specifications as Bisley Single Action model, except in target version.

Dakota Target Revolver

Dakota Target Single Action Revolver $320
Calibers: 45 Long Colt, 357 Mag., 22 LR. $5\frac{1}{2}$- or $7\frac{1}{2}$-inch barrel. Polished, blued finish, case-hardened frame. Walnut grips. Ramp front, blade target sight, adjustable rear sight.

DAVIS INDUSTRIES
Chino, California

Davis Model P-32

Davis Model D-22 Derringer **$55**
Calibers: 25 Auto, 22 LR, 32 Auto, 22 Mag. 2-round magazine. 2.4-inch barrel. 4 inches overall. Weight: 9½ oz. Laminated wood grips. Black teflon or chrome finish.

Davis Model P-32 .... **$55**
Caliber: 32 Auto. 6-round magazine. 2.8-inch barrel. 5.4 inches overall. Weight: 22 oz. Black teflon or chrome finish. Laminated wood grips.

DETONICS FIREARMS INDUSTRIES
Bellevue, Washington

Detonics Combat Master
Calibers: 45 ACP, 451 Detonics Mag. 6-round magazine. 3½-inch barrel. 6¾ inches overall. Combat-type with fixed or adjustable sights. Checkered walnut stock. Stainless steel construction.

MK I matte blue, fixed sights. Discontinued	**$450**
MK I stainless steel finish	**485**
MK IV polished blue, adjustable sights. Discontinued	**460**
MK V matte stainless steel, fixed sights. Discontinued	**475**
MK VI polished stainless steel, adjustable sights	**490**
MK VI in 451 Magnum	**525**
MK VII matte stainless steel, no sights	**455**
MK VII in 451 Magnum	**550**

Detonics Pocket 9 .... **$370**
Calibers: 9mm Parabellum, 380. 6-round magazine. 3-inch barrel. 5⅞ inches overall. Fixed sights. Double- and single-action trigger mechanism. Discontinued 1986.

Detonics Scoremaster **$795**
Calibers: 45 ACP, 451 Detonics Mag. 7-round magazine. 5- or 6-inch heavyweight match barrel. 8¾ inches overall. Weight: 47 oz. Stainless steel construction, self-centering barrel system.

Detonics Service Master **$550**
Caliber: 45 ACP. 7-round magazine. 4¼-inch barrel. Weight: 39 oz. Interchangeable front sight, millett rear sight.

Detonics Service Master II **$600**
Same general specifications as standard Service Master, except comes in polished stainless steel with self-centering barrel system.

DREYSE PISTOLS
Sommerda, Germany
Mfd. by Rheinische Metallwaren und Maschinenfabrik ("Rheinmetall")

Dreyse Model 1907*

Dreyse Model 1907 Automatic Pistol **$310**
Caliber: 32 Automatic (7.65mm). 8-shot magazine. 3½-inch barrel. 6¼ inches overall. Weight: about 24 oz. Fixed sights. Blued finish. Hard rubber stocks. Made from 1907-c. 1914.

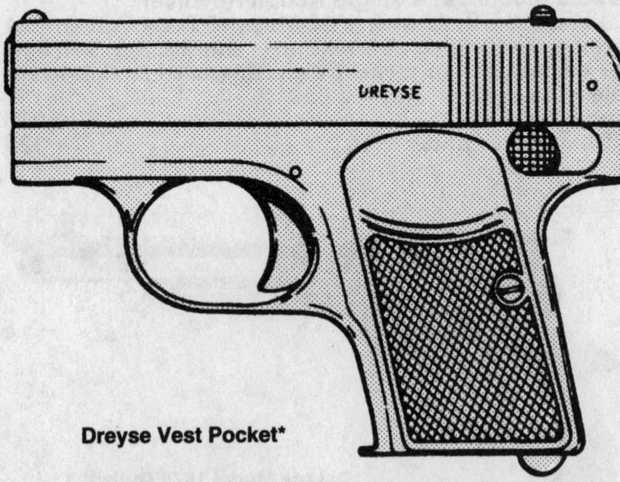

Dreyse Vest Pocket*

Dreyse Vest Pocket Automatic Pistol **$230**
Conventional Browning type. Caliber: 25 Automatic (6.35mm). 6-shot magazine. 2-inch barrel. 4½ inches overall. Weight: about 14 oz. Fixed sights. Blued finish. Hard rubber stocks. Made from c. 1909-1914.

HANDGUNS

DWM PISTOL
Berlin, Germany
Mfd. by Deutsche Waffen-und-Munitionsfabriken

DWM Pocket*

DWM Pocket Automatic Pistol **$395**
Similar to the FN Browning Model 1910. Caliber: 32 Automatic (7.65mm). 3½-inch barrel. 6 inches overall. Weight: about 21 oz. Blued finish. Hard rubber stocks. Made from c. 1921-1931.

ENFIELD REVOLVER
Enfield Lock, Middlesex, England
Manufactured by Royal Small Arms Factory

Enfield (British Service) No. 2 MK 1 Revolver . . . **$165**
Webley pattern. Hinged frame. Double action. Caliber: 380 British Service (38 S&W with 200-grain bullet). 6-shot cylinder. 5-inch barrel. 10½ inches overall. Weight: about 27½ oz. Fixed sights. Blued finish. Vulcanite stocks. First issued in 1932, this was the standard revolver of the British Army in World War II. Now obsolete. *Note:* This model was also produced with spurless hammer as No. 2 Mk 1* and Mk 1**.

ERMA-WERKE
Dachau, West Germany

Erma-Werke Model KGP68

Erma-Werke Model KGP68 Automatic Pistol **$195**
Luger type. Calibers: 32 Automatic (7.65mm), 380 Automatic (9mm Short). 6-shot magazine in 32, 5-shot in 380. 4-inch barrel. 7⅜ inches overall. Weight: 22½ oz. Fixed sights. Blued finish. Checkered walnut stocks. Made from 1968 to date.

Erma-Werke Model KGP69

Erma-Werke Model KGP69 Automatic Pistol **$175**
Luger type. Caliber: 22 Long Rifle. 8-shot magazine. 4-inch barrel. 7¾ inches overall. Weight: 29 oz. Fixed sights. Blued finish. Checkered walnut stocks. Made 1969 to date.

FIALA OUTFITTERS, INC.
New York, New York

Fiala Repeating Pistol **$395**
Despite its appearance, which closely resembles that of the early Colt Woodsman and High-Standard, this arm is not an automatic pistol. It is hand-operated by moving the slide to eject, cock and load. Caliber: 22 Long Rifle. 10-shot magazine. Barrel lengths: 3-, 7½- and 20-inch. 11¼ inches overall with 7½-inch barrel. Weight: 31 oz. with 7½-inch barrel. Target sights. Blued finish. Plain wood stocks. Shoulder stock was originally supplied for use with 20-inch barrel. Made from 1920 to 1923. Value shown is for pistol with one barrel and no shoulder stock.

F.I.E. CORPORATION
Hialeah, Florida

F.I.E. Model A27BW

F.I.E. Model A27BW "The Best" Semiauto $125
Caliber: 25 ACP. 6-round magazine. $2\frac{1}{2}$-inch barrel. $6\frac{3}{4}$ inches overall. Weight: 13 oz. Fixed sights. Checkered walnut stock.

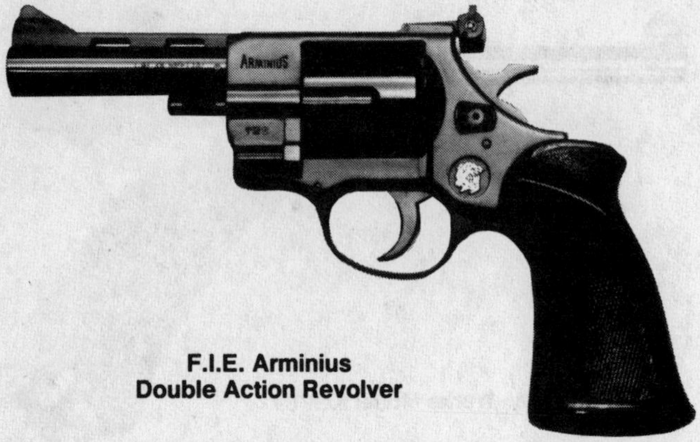

F.I.E. Arminius Double Action Revolver

F.I.E. Arminius Double Action Revolver
Calibers: 22 Long Rifle; 22 combo w/interchangeable cylinder; 32 S&W, 38 Special, 357 Magnum. 6, 7 or 8 rounds depending on caliber. Swingout cylinder. Barrel lengths: 2-, 3-, 4-, 6-inch. Vent rib on calibers other than 22. 11 inches overall w/6-inch barrel. Weight: 26 to 30 oz. Fixed or micro-adjustable sights. Checkered plastic or walnut stocks. Blued finish. Made in West Germany.
22 LR **$105**
22 Combo **120**
32 S&W **125**
38 Special **130**
357 Magnum **175**

F.I.E. Buffalo Scout Single Action Revolver
Calibers: 22 Long Rifle, 22 WRF; 22 combo w/interchangeable cylinder. $4\frac{3}{4}$-inch barrel. 10 inches overall. Weight: 32 oz. Adjustable sights. Blued or chrome finish. Smooth walnut or black checkered nylon grips. Made in Italy.
Blued Standard . . . . **$ 60**
Blued Convertible **75**
Chrome Standard **70**
Chrome Convertible **85**

F.I.E. Hombre Single Action Revolver $190
Calibers: 357 Magnum, 44 Magnum, 45 Colt. 6-shot cylinder. Barrel lengths: 6 or $7\frac{1}{2}$ inches. 11 inches overall w/6-inch barrel. Weight: 45 oz. w/6-inch barrel. Fixed sights. Blued barrel with color casehardened receiver. Smooth walnut stocks. Made from 1979 to date.

F.I.E. Little Ranger Single Action Revolver
Same as the Texas Ranger, except with $3\frac{1}{4}$-inch barrel and bird's-head grips. Made from 1986 to date.
Standard **$75**
Convertible **85**

F.I.E. Super Titan II
Caliber: 32 ACP or 380 ACP. $3\frac{1}{4}$-inch barrel. Weight: 28 oz. Blued or chrome finish.
32 ACP in Blue **$125**
32 ACP in Chrome **140**
380 ACP in Blue **155**
380 ACP in Chrome **170**

F.I.E. Texas Ranger Single Action Revolver
Calibers: 22 Long Rifle, 22 WRF; 22 combo w/interchangeable cylinder. Barrel lengths: $4\frac{3}{4}$-, $6\frac{1}{2}$-, 9-inch. 10 inches overall w/$4\frac{3}{4}$-inch barrel. Weight: 32 oz. w/$4\frac{3}{4}$-inch barrel. Fixed sights. Blued finish. Smooth walnut stocks. Made from 1983 to date.
Standard **$75**
Convertible **85**

F.I.E. Titan Tiger

F.I.E. Titan Tiger Double Action Revolver $115
Caliber: 38 Special. 6-shot cylinder. 2- or 4-inch barrel. $8\frac{1}{4}$ inches overall w/4-inch barrel. Weight: 30 oz. w/4-inch barrel. Fixed sights. Blued finish. Checkered plastic or walnut stocks. Made in the U.S.

F.I.E. Titan II

F.I.E. Titan II Semiautomatic
Calibers: 22 LR, 32 ACP, 380 ACP. 10-round magazine. Integral tapered post front sight, windage-adjustable rear sight. European walnut grips. Blued or chrome finish.
22 LR in Blue **$115**
32 ACP in Blue **125**
32 ACP in Chrome **135**
380 ACP in Blue **155**
380 ACP in Chrome **160**

F.I.E. Model TZ75
Satin Chrome

Firearms International
Regent Revolver

F.I.E. Model TZ75 DA Semiautomatic
Double action. Caliber: 9mm. 15-round magazine. 4½-inch barrel. 8¼ inches overall. Weight: 35 oz. Ramp front sight, windage-adjustable rear sight. European walnut or black rubber grips.
Blued Finish **$280**
Satin Chrome **295**

F.I.E. Yellow Rose Single Action Revolver
Same general specifications as the Buffalo Scout, except in 22 combo w/interchangeable cylinder and plated in 24 karat gold. Limited Edition with scrimshawed ivory polymer grips and American walnut presentation case. Introduced in 1987.
Yellow Rose 22 Combo **$110**
Yellow Rose Ltd. Edition **285**

FIREARMS INTERNATIONAL CORP.
Washington, D.C.

Firearms International Model D

Firearms Int'l. Model D Automatic Pistol $175
Caliber: 380 Automatic. 6-shot magazine. 3⅛-inch barrel. 6⅛ inches overall. Weight: 19½ oz. Blade front sight, windage-adjustable rear sight. Blued, chromed, or military finish. Checkered walnut stocks. Made from 1974 to 1977.

Firearms Int'l. Regent Double Action Revolver ... $75
Calibers: 22 Long Rifle, 32 S&W Long. 8-shot cylinder in 22 caliber, 7-shot in 32 caliber. Barrels: 3-, 4-, 6-inch in 22 caliber; 2½-, 4-inch in 32 caliber. Weight: with 4-inch barrel, 28 oz. Fixed sights. Blue finish. Plastic stocks. Made from 1966 to 1972.

FN BROWNING PISTOLS
Liege, Belgium
Mfd. by Fabrique Nationale Herstal

See also Browning Pistols.

FN Browning 6.35mm

FN Browning 6.35mm Pocket Model Auto Pistol $350
Same specifications as Colt Pocket Model 25 Automatic Pistol.

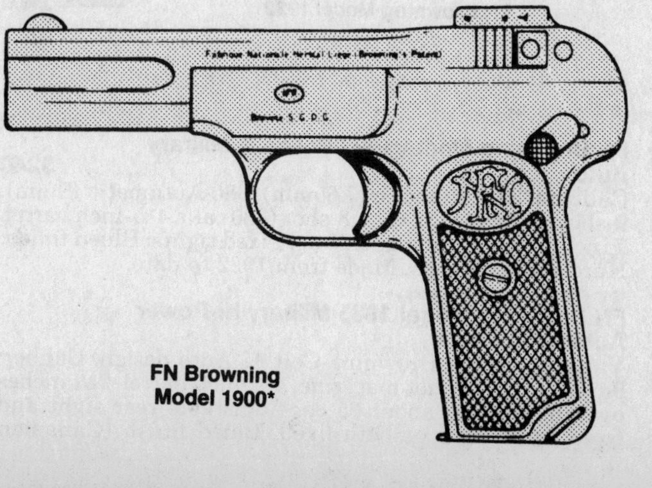

FN Browning
Model 1900*

FN Browning Model 1900 Pocket Auto Pistol . . . $390
Caliber: 32 Automatic (7.65mm). 7-shot magazine. 4-inch barrel. $6\frac{3}{4}$ inches overall. Weight: 22 oz. Fixed sights. Blued finish. Hard rubber stocks. Made from 1899 to 1910.

FN Browning Model 1903 Military Auto Pistol . . . $375
Caliber: 9mm Browning Long. 7-shot magazine. 5-inch barrel. 8 inches overall. Weight: 32 oz. Fixed sights. Blued finish. Hard rubber stocks. *Note:* Aside from size, this pistol is of the same basic design as the Colt Pocket 32 and 380 Automatic pistols. Made from 1903 to 1939.

FN Browning Model 1910

FN Browning Model 1910 Pocket Auto Pistol . . . $395
Calibers: 32 Automatic (7.65mm), 380 Automatic (9mm). 7-shot magazine (32 cal.), 6-shot (380 cal.). $3\frac{1}{2}$-inch barrel. 6 inches overall. Weight: $20\frac{1}{2}$ oz. Fixed sights. Blued finish. Hard rubber stocks. Made from 1910 to date.

FN Browning Model 1922

FN Browning Model 1922 Police & Military Auto $240
Calibers: 32 Automatic (7.65mm), 380 Automatic (9mm). 9-shot magazine (32 cal.), 8-shot (380 cal.). $4\frac{1}{2}$-inch barrel. 7 inches overall. Weight: 25 oz. Fixed sights. Blued finish. Hard rubber stocks. Made from 1922 to date.

FN Browning Model 1935 Military Hi-Power Automatic Pistol
Variation of the Browning-Colt 45 Auto design. Caliber: 9mm Luger. 13-shot magazine. $4\frac{5}{8}$-inch barrel. $7\frac{3}{4}$ inches overall. Weight: about 35 oz. Adjustable rear sight and fixed front sight or both fixed. Blued finish (Canadian

FN Browning Model 1935 Hi-Power

FN Browning Model 1935 Military Hi-Power Automatic Pistol (cont.)
manufacture Parkerized). Checkered walnut or plastic stocks. *Note:* Above specifications in general apply to both the original FN production and the pistols made by John Inglis Company of Canada for the Chinese Government. A smaller version, with shorter barrel and slide and 10-shot magazine, was made by FN for the Belgian and Rumanian Governments from about 1937 to 1940. Both types were made at the FN plant during the German Occupation of Belgium.

With adjustable rear sight	**$695**
FN manufacture, with fixed rear sight	**595**
Inglis manufacture, with fixed rear sight	**650**

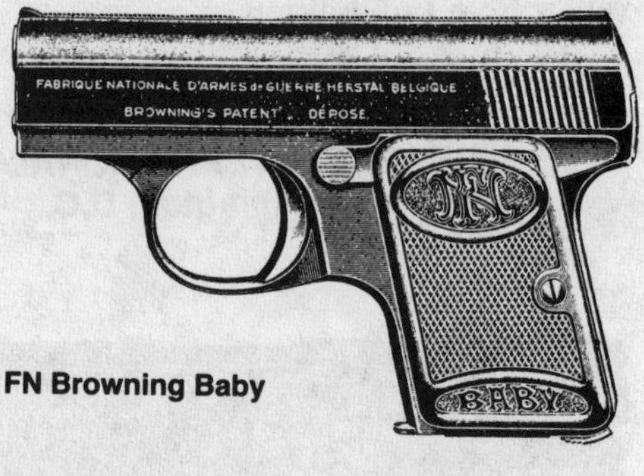

FN Browning Baby

FN Browning Baby Auto Pistol $405
Caliber: 25 Automatic (6.35mm). 6-shot magazine. $2\frac{1}{8}$-inch barrel. 4 inches overall. Weight: 10 oz. Fixed sights. Blued finish. Hard rubber stocks. Made from 1940 to date.

FOREHAND & WADSWORTH
Worcester, Massachusetts

Forehand & Wadsworth Revolvers
See listings of comparable Harrington & Richardson and Iver Johnson revolvers for values.

LE FRANCAIS PISTOLS
St. Etienne, France
Produced by Manufacture Francaise d'Armes et Cycles

Le Francais Army Model Automatic Pistol $130
Similar in operation to the Le Francais 25 Automatics. Caliber: 9mm Browning Long. 8-shot magazine. 5-inch barrel. 7¾ inches overall. Weight: about 34 oz. Fixed sights. Blued finish. Checkered walnut stocks. Made from 1928 to 1938.

Le Francais Policeman*

Le Francais Policeman Model Automatic Pistol . $125
Double action. Hinged barrel. Caliber: 25 Automatic (6.35mm). 7-shot magazine. 3½-inch barrel. 6 inches overall. Weight: about 12 oz. Fixed sights. Blued finish. Hard rubber stocks. Made from 1914 to date.

Le Francais Staff Officer*

Le Francais Staff Officer Model Automatic Pistol . $125
Caliber: 25 Automatic. Similar to the "Policeman" Model, except does not have cocking-piece head, barrel is about an inch shorter and weight is an oz. less. Made 1914 to date.

FREEDOM ARMS
Freedom, Wyoming

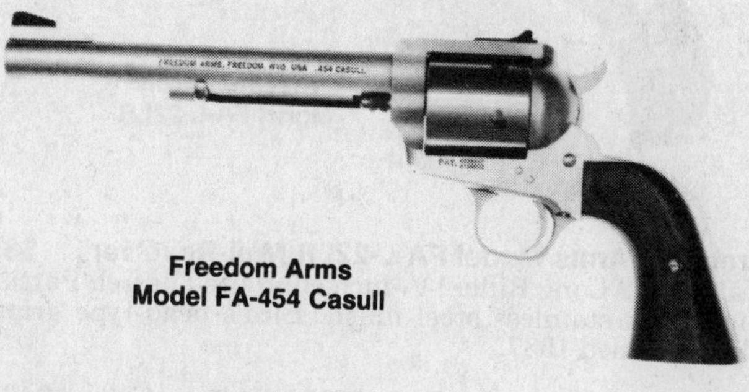
Freedom Arms
Model FA-454 Casull

Freedom Arms Model FA-454AS Casull Revolver $995
Caliber: 454 Casull. Barrel lengths: 4¾, 6, 7½, 10, 12 inches. Adjustable sight. Hardwood grips. Brush stainless steel finish.

Freedom Arms Model FA-454FS Revolver $950
Same general specifications as Model FA-454AS, except with fixed sight.

Freedom Arms FA-454GAS
Field Grade

Freedom Arms Model FA-454GAS Revolver $595
Field Grade version of Model FA-454AS, except not made with 12-inch barrel. Matte stainless finish, Pachmayr presentation grips. Adjustable sights; fixed sight on 4¾-inch barrel.

Freedom Arms Model FA-BG-22LR Mini-Revolver $95
Caliber: 22 Long Rifle. 3-inch tapered barrel. Partial high-gloss stainless steel finish. Discontinued 1987.

Freedom Arms Model FA-BG-22M Mini-Revolver $120
Same general specifications as model FA-BG-22LR, except in caliber 22 Win. Mag.

Freedom Arms Model FA-BG-22P Mini-Revolver $120
Same general specifications as Model FA-BG-22LR, except in 22 percussion. Discontinued 1987.

Freedom Arms Model FA-L-22LR

Freedom Arms Model FA-L-22LR Mini-Revolver . . $85
Caliber: 22 Long Rifle. $1^3/_4$-inch contoured barrel. Partial high-gloss stainless steel finish. Bird's-head-type grips. Discontinued 1987.

Freedom Arms Model FA-L-22M Mini-Revolver . $120
Same general specifications as Model FA-L-22LR, except in caliber 22 Win. Mag. Discontinued 1987.

Freedom Arms Model FA-L-22P Mini-Revolver . . . $95
Same general specifications as Model FA-L-22LR, except in 22 percussion. Discontinued 1987.

Freedom Arms Model FA-S-22LR Mini-Revolver . $85
Caliber: 22 Long Rifle. 1-inch contoured barrel. Partial high-gloss stainless steel finish.

Freedom Arms Model FA-S-22M Mini-Revolver . $120
Same general specifications as Model FA-S-22LR, except in caliber 22 Win. Mag.

Freedom Arms Model FA-S-22P Mini-Revolver . . . $95
Same general specifications as Model FA-S-22LR, except in percussion.

FRENCH MILITARY PISTOL
Cholet, France
Mfd. by Société Alsacienne de Constructions Mécaniques (S.A.C.M.)

French Model 1935A

French Model 1935A Automatic Pistol $225
Caliber: 7.65mm Long. 8-shot magazine. 4.3-inch barrel. 7.6 inches overall. Weight: 26 oz. Fixed sights. Blued finish. Checkered stocks. Made from 1935 to 1945. *Note:* This pistol was used by French troops during World War II and in Indo-China 1945-54.

FROMMER PISTOLS
Budapest, Hungary
Mfd. by Fémáru-Fegyver-és Gépgyár R.T.

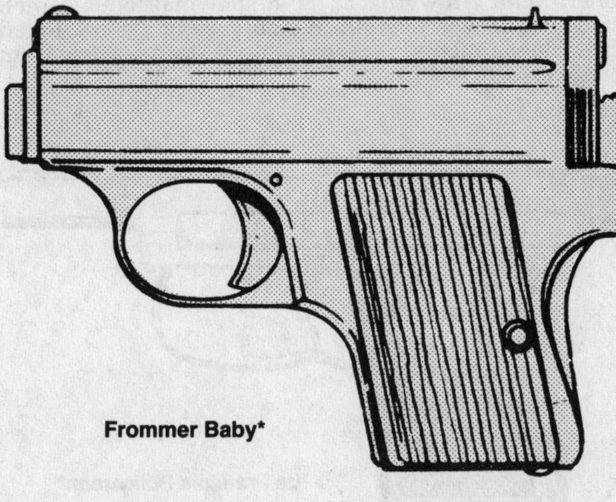

Frommer Baby*

Frommer Baby Pocket Automatic Pistol $290
Similar to Stop model, except has 2-inch barrel, is about $4^3/_4$ inches overall, weighs about $17^1/_2$ oz. Magazine capacity is one round less. Introduced shortly after World War I.

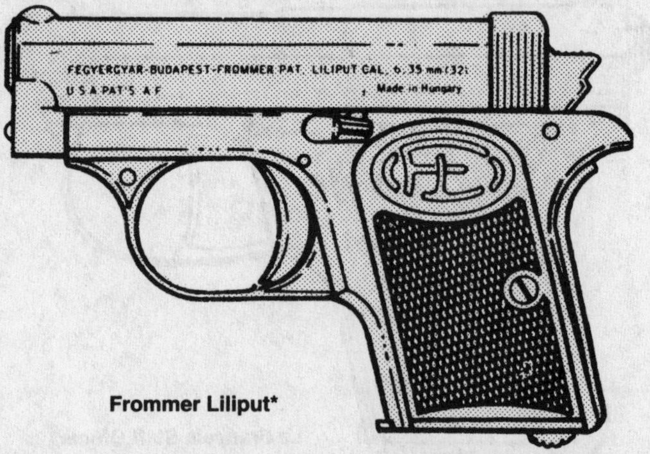

Frommer Liliput*

Frommer Liliput Pocket Automatic Pistol $300
Caliber: 25 Automatic (6.35mm). 6-shot magazine. 2.14-inch barrel. 4.33 inches overall. Weight: $10^1/_2$ oz. Fixed sights. Blued finish. Hard rubber stocks. Made during early 1920s. *Note:* Although similar in appearance to the Stop and Baby, this pistol is blowback operated.

Frommer Stop*

Galesi Model 9*

Frommer Stop Pocket Automatic Pistol $275
Locked-breech action, outside hammer. Calibers: 32 Automatic (7.65mm), 380 Automatic (9mm short). 7-shot magazine (32 cal.), 6-shot (380 cal.). 3⅞-inch barrel. 6½ inches overall. Weight: about 21 oz. Fixed sights. Blued finish. Hard rubber stocks. Made from 1912 to 1920.

GALESI PISTOLS
Collebeato (Brescia), Italy
Mfd. by Industria Armi Galesi

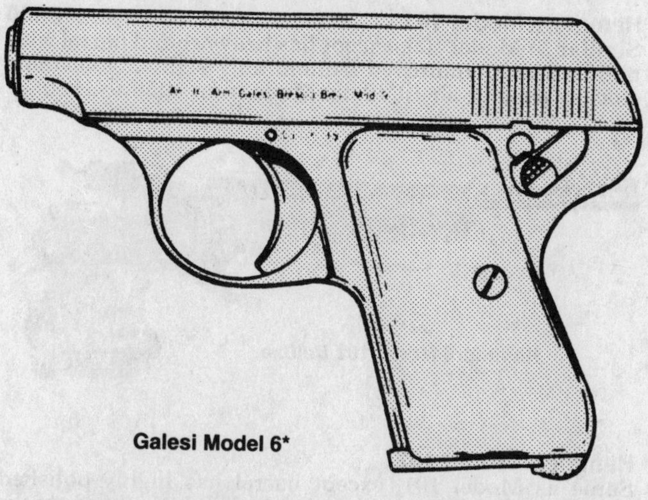

Galesi Model 6*

Galesi Model 6 Pocket Automatic Pistol $120
Calibers: 22 Long, 25 Automatic (6.35mm). 6-shot magazine. 2¼-inch barrel. 4⅜ inches overall. Weight: about 11 oz. Fixed sights. Blued finish. Plastic stocks. Made from 1930 to date.

Galesi Model 9 Pocket Automatic Pistol
Calibers: 22 Long Rifle, 32 Automatic (7.65mm), 380 Automatic (9mm Short). 8-shot magazine. 3¼-inch barrel. 5⅞ inches overall. Weight: about 21 oz. Fixed sights. Blued finish. Plastic stocks. Made from 1930 to date. *Note:* Specifications vary; those shown are for 32 Automatic of common type.

Galesi Model 9 Pocket Automatic Pistol (cont.)
22 Long Rifle or 380 Automatic **$140**
32 Automatic **135**

GLISENTI PISTOL
Carcina (Brescia), Italy
Mfd. by Societa Siderurgica Glisenti

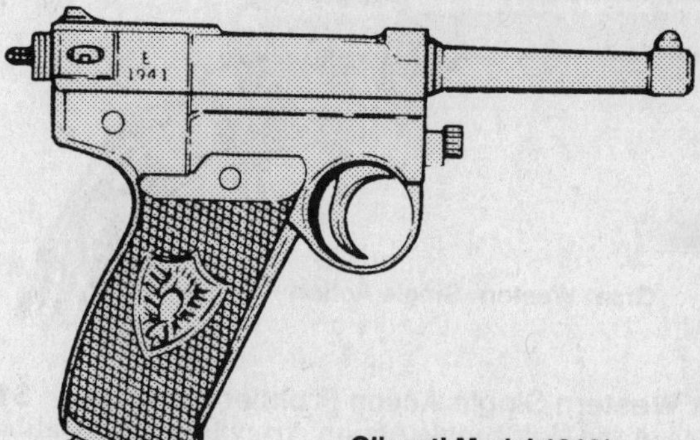

Glisenti Model 1910*

Glisenti Model 1910 Italian Service Automatic . . $295
Caliber: 9mm, Glisenti. 7-shot magazine. 4-inch barrel. 8½ inches overall. Weight: about 32 oz. Fixed sights. Blued finish. Checkered wood. Hard rubber or plastic stocks. Adopted 1910 and used through World War II.

GLOCK, INC.
Smyrna, Georgia

Glock Model 17 Automatic Pistol $355
Caliber: 9mm Parabellum. Double action. 17-shot magazine. 4½-inch barrel. 7.2 inches overall. Weight: about 22 oz., empty. Hi-tech polymer frame and receiver; steel barrel, slide and springs. Fixed or adjustable rear sights. Composed of only 33 different components, including 3 internal safety devices. This gun received the "Best Pistol

Glock Model 17
Automatic Pistol

Glock Model 17 Automatic Pistol (cont.)
Award of Merit" in 1987 by the American Firearms Industry. Made in Austria from 1983 to date.

GREAT WESTERN ARMS CO.
North Hollywood, California

Great Western Double Barrel Derringer **$75**
Replica of Remington Double Derringer. Caliber: 38 S&W. Double barrels (superposed), 3-inch. Overall length: 5 inches. Fixed sights. Blued finish. Checkered black plastic grips. Made from 1953 to 1962.

Great Western Single Action

Great Western Single Action Frontier Revolver . **$175**
Replica of the Colt Single Action Army Revolver. Calibers: 22 Long Rifle, 357 Magnum, 38 Special, 44 Special, 44 Magnum, 45 Colt. 6-shot cylinder. Barrel lengths: $4\frac{3}{4}$-, $5\frac{1}{2}$- and $7\frac{1}{2}$-inch. Weight: 22 cal. with $5\frac{1}{2}$-inch bbl., 40 oz. Overall length: with $5\frac{1}{2}$-inch bbl., $11\frac{1}{8}$ inches. Fixed sights. Blued finish. Imitation stag grips. Made from 1951 to 1962. *Note:* Value shown is for improved late model revolvers; early Great Westerns are variable in quality and should be evaluated accordingly. It should also be noted that, beginning about July 1956, these revolvers were also offered in "do-it-yourself" kit form; values of guns assembled from these kits will, in general, be lower than for factory-completed weapons.

HÄMMERLI AG JAGD-UND SPORTWAFFENFABRIK
Lenzburg, Switzerland

Hämmerli Model 33MP Free Pistol **$800**
System Martini single-shot action, set trigger. Caliber: 22 Long Rifle. $11\frac{1}{2}$-inch octagon barrel. $16\frac{1}{2}$ inches overall. Weight: 46 oz. Micrometer rear sight, interchangeable front sights. Blued finish. Walnut stocks and forearm. Made from 1933 to 1949.

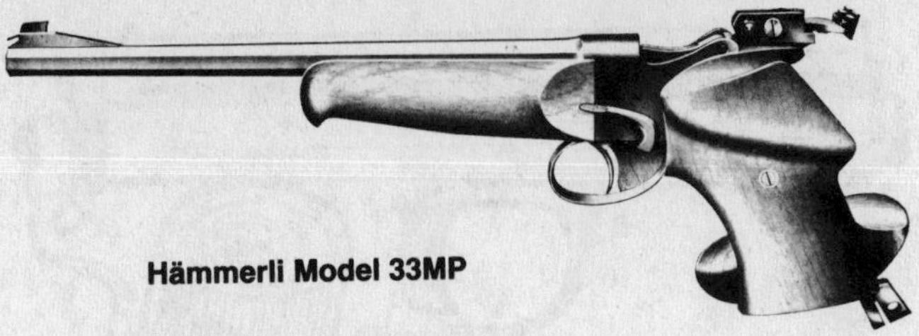

Hämmerli Model 33MP

Hämmerli Model 100 Free Pistol
Same general specifications as Model 33MP. Improved action and sights, redesigned stock. Standard model has plain stocks and forearm; deluxe model has carved stocks and forearm. Made from 1950 to 1956.
Standard Model **$805**
Deluxe Model **960**

Hämmerli Model 101

Hämmerli Model 101 . . . . **$800**
Similar to Model 100, except has heavy round barrel with matte finish, improved action and sights, adjustable stocks. Weight: about 49 oz. Made from 1956 to 1960.

Hämmerli Model 102 Deluxe

Hämmerli Model 102
Same as Model 101, except barrel has highly polished blued finish. Deluxe model (illustrated) has carved stocks and forearm. Made from 1956 to 1960.
Standard Model . . . . **$ 650**
Deluxe Model **1000**

Hämmerli Model 103 . . . . **$880**
Same as Model 101, except has lighter octagon barrel (as in Model 100) with highly polished blued finish, stocks and forearm of select French walnut. Weight: about 46 oz. Made from 1956 to 1960.

Hämmerli Model 104 . . . . **$800**
Similar to Model 102, except has lighter round barrel, improved action, redesigned stocks and forearm. Weight: 46 oz. Made from 1961 to 1965.

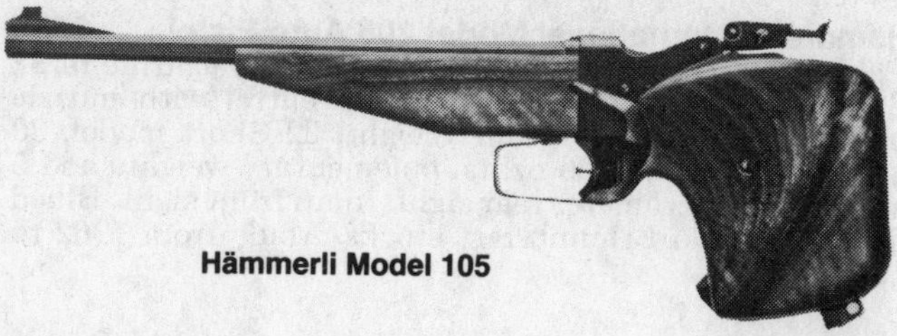

Hämmerli Model 105

Hämmerli Model 105 .... **$875**
Similar to Model 103, except has improved action, redesigned stocks and forearm. Made from 1961 to 1965.

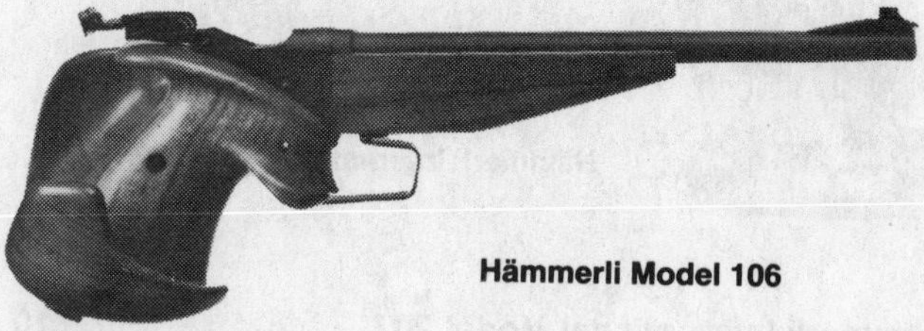

Hämmerli Model 106

Hämmerli Model 106 .... **$845**
Similar to Model 104, except has improved trigger and stocks. Made from 1966 to 1971.

Hämmerli Model 107 Deluxe

Hämmerli Model 107
Similar to Model 105, except has improved trigger and stock. Deluxe model (illustrated) has engraved receiver and barrel, carved stocks and forearm. Made from 1966 to 1971.
Standard Model .... **$ 925**
Deluxe Model **1360**

Hämmerli Model 120 Heavy Barrel
Adjustable Stocks

Hämmerli Model 120 Heavy Barrel
Same as Models 120-1 and 120-2, except has 5.7-inch heavy barrel. Weight: 41 oz. Available with standard or adjustable stocks. Made from 1972 to date.
With standard stocks **$515**
With adjustable stocks **590**

Hämmerli Model 120-1

Hämmerli Model 120-1 Single Shot Free Pistol .. **$520**
Side lever-operated bolt action. Adjustable single-stage or two-stage trigger. Caliber: 22 Long Rifle. 9.999-inch barrel. 14³/₄ inches overall. Weight: 44 oz. Micrometer rear sight, front sight on high ramp. Blued finish barrel and receiver, lever and grip frame anodized aluminum. Checkered walnut thumb-rest stocks. Made from 1972 to date.

Hämmerli Model 120-2 .... **$540**
Same as Model 120-1, except has hand-contoured stocks with adjustable palm rest (available for right or left hand). Made from 1972 to date.

Hämmerli Model 150 Free Pistol

Hämmerli Model 150 Free Pistol **$970**
Improved Martini-type action with lateral-action cocking lever. Set trigger adjustable for weight, length and angle of pull. Caliber: 22 Long Rifle. 11.3-inch round barrel, free-floating. 15.4 inches overall. Weight: 43 oz. (with extra weights, 49¹/₂ oz.). Micrometer rear sight, front sight on high ramp. Blued finish. Select walnut forearm and stocks with adjustable palm-shelf. Made from 1972 to date.

Hämmerli Model 208

Hämmerli Model 208 Standard Auto Pistol $840
Caliber: 22 Long Rifle. 3-shot magazine. 5.9-inch barrel. 10 inches overall. Weight: 35 oz. (barrel weight adds 3 oz.). Micrometer rear sight, ramp front sight. Blued finish. Checkered walnut stocks with adjustable heel plate. Made from 1966 to date.

Hämmerli Model 211 . . . . $780
Same as Model 208, except has standard thumb-rest stocks. Made from 1966 to date.

Hämmerli Model 212 Hunter's Pistol $750
Caliber: 22 Long Rifle. $4\frac{7}{8}$-inch barrel. $8\frac{1}{2}$ inches overall. Weight: 31 oz. Fully adjustable sights. Blued finish. Checkered walnut stocks. Made from 1984 to date.

Hämmerli Model 230-1 Rapid Fire Auto Pistol . . . $730
Caliber: 22 Short. 5-shot magazine. 6.3-inch barrel. 11.6 inches overall. Weight: 44 oz. Micrometer rear sight, post front sight. Blued finish. Smooth walnut thumb-rest stocks. Made from 1970 to date.

Hämmerli Model 230-2

Hämmerli Model 230-2 . . . . $740
Same as Model 230-1, except has checkered walnut stocks with adjustable heel plate. Made from 1970 to date.

Hammerli Model 232
Rapid Fire Pistol

Hämmerli Model 232 Rapid Fire Auto Pistol $735
Caliber: 22 Long Rifle. 5-shot magazine. 5.2-inch barrel. $10\frac{3}{8}$ inches overall. Weight: 44 oz. Fully adjustable target sights. Blued finish. Stippled walnut wraparound target stocks. Made from 1984 to date.

Hämmerli International Model 206

Hämmerli International Model 206 Auto Pistol . . $550
Calibers: 22 Short, 22 Long Rifle. 6-shot magazine in 22 Short, 8-shot in 22 L.R. $7\frac{1}{16}$-inch barrel with muzzle brake. $12\frac{1}{2}$ inches overall. Weight: 22 Short model, 33 oz.; 22 L.R. model, 39 oz. (supplementary weights add 5 and 8 oz.). Micrometer rear sight, ramp front sight. Blued finish. Standard thumb-rest stocks. Made from 1962 to 1969.

Hämmerli International Model 207

Hämmerli International Model 207 . . . . $710
Same as Model 206, except has stocks with adjustable heel plate, weighs 2 oz. more. Made from 1962 to 1969.

Hämmerli International Model 209 Auto Pistol . . $800
Caliber: 22 Short. 5-shot magazine. $4\frac{3}{4}$-inch barrel with muzzle brake and gas-escape holes. 11 inches overall. Weight: 39 oz. (interchangeable front weight adds 4 oz.). Micrometer rear sight, post front sight. Blued finish. Standard thumb-rest stocks of checkered walnut. Made from 1966 to 1970.

Hämmerli International Model 210

Hämmerli International Model 210 . . . . $830
Same as Model 209, except has stocks with adjustable heel plate; is 0.8-inch longer and weighs one ounce more. Made from 1966 to 1970.

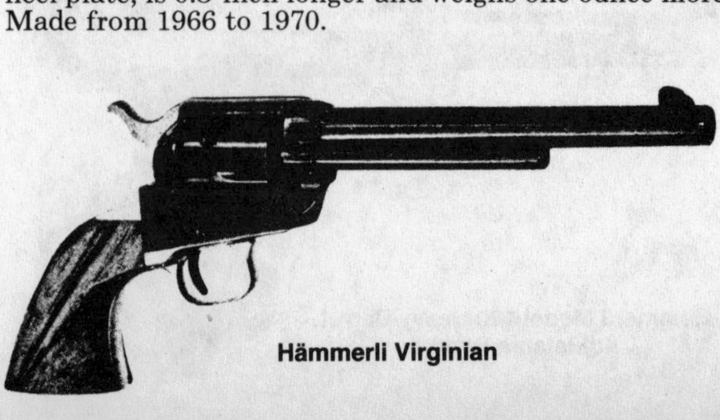
Hämmerli Virginian

Hämmerli Virginian Single Action Revolver **$240**
Similar to Colt Single Action Army, except has base pin safety system (SWISSAFE). Calibers: 357 Magnum, 45 Colt. 6-shot cylinder. Barrels: 4⁵/₈-, 5¹/₂-, 7¹/₂-inch. 11 inches overall with 5¹/₂-inch barrel. Weight: with 5¹/₂-inch barrel, 40 oz. Fixed sights. Blued barrel and cylinder, casehardened frame, chrome-plated grip frame and trigger guard. One-piece smooth walnut stock. Made from 1973 to 1976 for Interarms, Alexandria, Va.

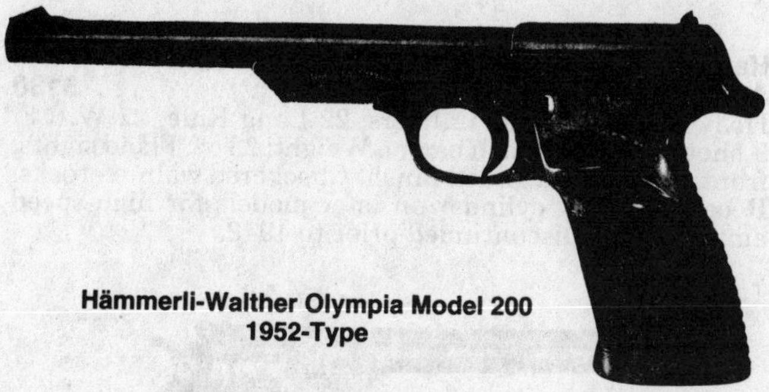

Hämmerli-Walther Olympia Model 200
1952-Type

Hämmerli-Walther Olympia Model 200 Automatic Pistol, 1952-Type **$640**
Similar to 1936 Walther Olympia Funfkampf Model. Calibers: 22 Short, 22 Long Rifle. 6-shot magazine in 22 Short, 10-shot in 22 L.R. 7.5-inch barrel. 10.7 inches overall. Weight: 22 Short model (light alloy breechblock), 27.7 oz.; 22 L.R. model, 30.3 oz.; supplementary weights provided. Adjustable target sights. Blued finish. Checkered walnut thumb-rest stocks. Made from 1952 to 1958.

Hämmerli-Walther Olympia Model 200
1958-Type, Standard Stocks

Hämmerli-Walther Olympia Model 200, 1958-Type **$725**
Same as Model 200, 1952 Type, except has muzzle brake, 8-shot magazine in 22 Long Rifle model. 11.6 inches overall. Weight: 22 Short model, 30 oz.; 22 Long Rifle model, 33 oz. Made from 1958 to 1963.

Hämmerli-Walther Olympia Model 201 . . . . **$645**
Same as Model 200, 1952 Type, except has 9¹/₂-inch barrel. Made from 1955 to 1957.

Hämmerli-Walther Olympia Model 202 . . . . **$695**
Same as Model 201, except has stocks with adjustable heel plate. Made from 1955 to 1957.

Hämmerli-Walther Olympia
Model 203, 1958-Type

Hämmerli-Walther Olympia Model 203
Same as corresponding Model 200 (1955 Type lacks muzzle brake), except has stocks with adjustable heel plate. Made from 1955 to 1963.
1955 Type **$725**
1958 Type **800**

Hämmerli-Walther Olympia Model 204
American Model. Same as corresponding Model 200 (1956 Type lacks muzzle brake), except chambered for 22 Long Rifle only, has slide stop and micrometer rear sight. Made from 1956 to 1963.
1956 Type **$765**
1958 Type **845**

Hämmerli-Walther Olympia
Model 205

Hämmerli-Walther Olympia Model 205
American Model. Same as Model 204, except has stocks with adjustable heel plate. Made from 1956 to 1963.
1956 Type **$830**
1958 Type **800**

SIG-Hämmerli Model P240

SIG-Hämmerli Model P240 Automatic Pistol
Caliber: 38 Special (wadcutter). 5-shot magazine. 6-inch barrel. 10 inches overall. Weight: 41 oz. Micrometer rear sight, post front sight. Blued finish. Smooth walnut thumb-rest stocks. Accessory 22 Long Rifle conversion unit available. Made from 1975 to date.
Model P240 . . . . **$735**
22 Conversion Unit **370**

SIG-Hämmerli Model P240 Target Auto Pistol . . $1035
Same general specifications as Model P240 Automatic, except with fully adjustable target sights and stippled walnut wraparound target stocks. Weight: 49 oz.

HARRINGTON & RICHARDSON, INC.
Gardner, Massachusetts

Formerly Harrington & Richardson Arms Co. of Worcester, Mass. One of the oldest and most distinguished manufacturers of handguns, rifles and shotguns, H & R suspended all operations in 1986.

H&R Model 4 (1904)
Double Action Revolver

Harrington & Richardson Model 4 (1904) Double Action Revolver $75
Solid frame. Calibers: 32 S&W Long, 38 S&W. 6-shot cylinder (32 cal.), 5-shot (38 cal.). Barrel lengths: 2½-, 4½- and 6-inch. Weight: about 16 oz., 32 cal. Fixed sights. Blued or nickel finish. Hard rubber stocks. Discontinued prior to 1942.

H&R Model 5

Harrington & Richardson Model 5 (1905) Double Action Revolver $80
Solid frame. Caliber: 32 S&W. 5-shot cylinder. Barrel lengths: 2½-, 4½- and 6-inch. Weight: about 11 oz. Fixed sights. Blued or nickel finish. Hard rubber stocks. Discontinued prior to 1942.

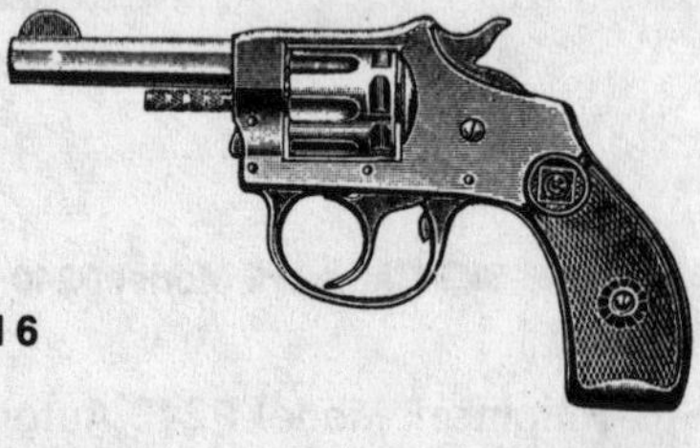
H&R Model 6

Harrington & Richardson Model 6 (1906) Double Action Revolver $75
Solid frame. Caliber: 22 Long Rifle. 7-shot cylinder. Barrel lengths: 2½-, 4½- and 6-inch. Weight: about 10 oz. Fixed sights. Blued or nickel finish. Hard rubber stocks. Discontinued prior to 1942.

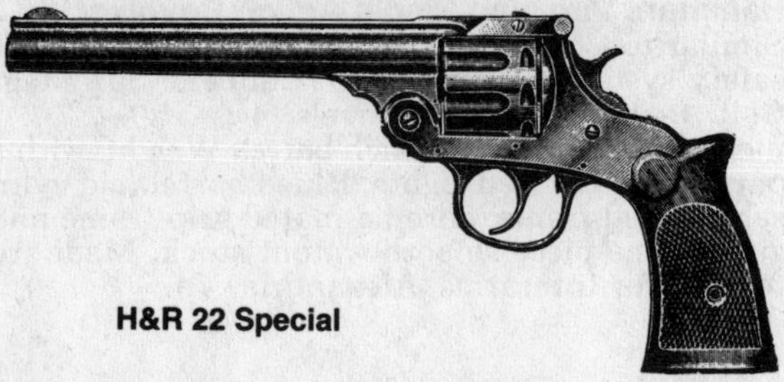
H&R 22 Special

Harrington & Richardson 22 Special Double Action Revolver $130
Heavy hinged frame. Calibers: 22 Long Rifle, 22 W.R.F. 9-shot cylinder. 6-inch barrel. Weight: 23 oz. Fixed sights, front gold-plated. Blued finish. Checkered walnut stocks. Recessed safety cylinder on later models for high-speed ammunition. Discontinued prior to 1942.

H&R Model 199 Sportsman

Harrington & Richardson Model 199 Sportsman SA Revolver $190
Hinged frame. Caliber: 22 Long Rifle. 9-shot cylinder. 6-inch barrel. 11 inches overall. Weight: 30 oz. Adjustable target sights. Blued finish. Checkered walnut stocks. Discontinued 1951.

Harrington & Richardson Model 504 Double Action Revolver $140
Caliber: 32 H&R Magnum. 5-shot cylinder. 4- or 6-inch barrel, square butt; 3- or 4-inch barrel, round butt. Made from 1984 to 1986.

Harrington & Richardson Model 532 Double Action Revolver $80
Caliber: 32 H&R Magnum. 5-shot cylinder. 2½- or 4-inch barrel. Weight: approx. 20 and 25 oz. respectively. Fixed sights. American walnut grips. Lustre blue finish. Made from 1984 to 1986.

Harrington & Richardson Model 586 Double Action Revolver $150
Caliber: 32 H&R Magnum. 5-shot cylinder. Barrel lengths: 4½, 5½, 7½, 10 inches. Weight: 30 oz. average. Adjustable rear sight, blade front sight. Walnut finished hardwood grips. Made from 1984 to 1986.

Harrington & Richardson Model 603 Target Revolver $105
Similar to Model 903, except in 22 Win. Mag. R.F. 6-shot capacity with unfluted cylinder. Made from 1980 to 1983.

Harrington & Richardson Model 604 Target Revolver $105
Similar to Model 603, except with 6-inch bull barrel. Weight: 38 oz. Made from 1980 to 1983.

H&R Model 622

Harrington & Richardson Model 622 Double Action Revolver **$70**

Solid frame. Caliber: 22 Short, Long, Long Rifle. 6-shot cylinder. Barrel lengths: 2$^1/_2$-, 4-, 6-inch. Weight: with 4-inch bbl., 26 oz. Fixed sights. Blued finish. Plastic stocks. Made from 1957 to 1986. *Note:* **Model 623** is same, except chrome or nickel finish.

H&R Model 632 Guardsman

Harrington & Richardson Model 632 Guardsman Double Action Revolver **$70**

Solid frame. Caliber: 32 S&W Long. 6-shot cylinder. Barrel lengths: 2$^1/_2$- or 4-inch. Weight: with 2$^1/_2$-inch barrel, 19 oz. Fixed sights. Blued or chrome finish. Checkered Tenite stocks (round butt on 2$^1/_2$-inch, square butt on 4-inch). Made from 1953 to 1986. *Note:* **Model 633** is same, except chrome or nickel finish.

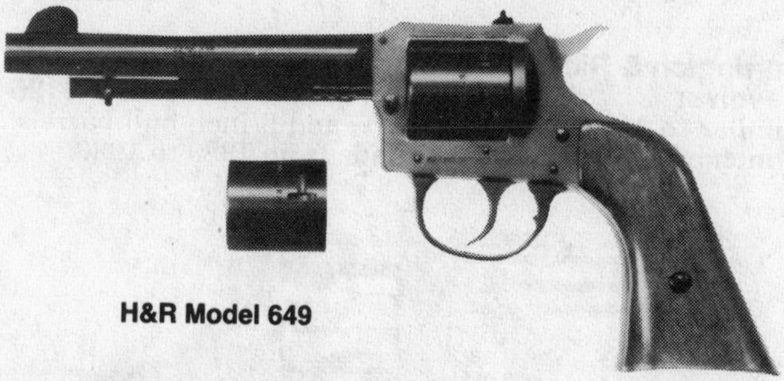

H&R Model 649

H&R Model 650, Nickel Finish

Harrington & Richardson Model 649 Double Action Revolver **$110**

Solid frame. Side loading and ejection. Convertible model with two cylinders. Calibers: 22 Long Rifle, 22 Win. Mag. R.F. 6-shot cylinders. 5$^1/_2$-inch barrel. Weight: 32 oz. Adjustable rear sight, blade front sight. Blued finish. One-piece, Western-style walnut stock. Made from 1976 to 1986. *Note:* **Model 650** is same, except nickel finish.

H&R Model 666

Harrington & Richardson Model 666 Double Action Revolver **$75**

Solid frame. Convertible model with two cylinders. Calibers: 22 Long Rifle, 22 Win. Mag. R.F. 6-shot cylinders. 6-inch barrel. Weight: 28 oz. Fixed sights. Blued finish. Plastic stocks. Made from 1976 to 1978.

H&R Model 676

Harrington & Richardson Model 676 Double Action Revolver **$110**

Solid frame. Side loading and ejection. Convertible model with two cylinders. Calibers: 22 Long Rifle, 22 Win. Mag. R.F. 6-shot cylinders. Barrel lengths: 4$^1/_2$-, 5$^1/_2$-, 7$^1/_2$-, 12-inch. Weight: with 5$^1/_2$-inch bbl., 32 oz. Adjustable rear sight, blade front sight. Blued finish, color-casehardened frame. One-piece, Western-style walnut stock. Made from 1976 to 1980.

H&R Model 686

Harrington & Richardson Model 686 Double Action Revolver **$140**

Caliber: 22 Long Rifle and 22 Win. Mag. R.F. Barrels: 4$^1/_2$-, 5$^1/_2$-, 7$^1/_2$-, 10- and 12-inches. 6-shot magazine. Adjustable rear sight, ramp and blade front sight. Blued with color casehardened frame. Weight: 31 oz., 4$^1/_2$-inch bbl. Made from 1980 to 1986.

H&R Model 733, Nickel Finish

Harrington & Richardson Model 732 Double Action Revolver **$90**
Solid frame, swing-out cylinder. Calibers: 32 S&W, 32 S&W Long. 6-shot cylinder. Barrel lengths: 2½-, 4-inch. Weight: with 4-inch bbl., 26 oz. Fixed sights (windage adjustable rear on 4-inch bbl. model). Blue finish. Plastic stocks. Made from 1958 to 1986. *Note:* **Model 733** is same, except nickel finish.

Harrington & Richardson Model 826 Double Action Revolver **$100**
Caliber: 22 Win. Mag. R.F. 6-shot magazine. 3-inch bull barrel. Ramp and blade front sight, adjustable rear sight. American walnut grips. Weight: 28 oz. Made 1981-83.

H&R Model 830, Nickel Finish

Harrington & Richardson Model 829 Double Action Revolver **$115**
Same as Model 826, except in 22 Long Rifle caliber. 9-shot capacity. Made from 1981 to 1983. **Model 830** in nickel finish, $120.

Harrington & Richardson Model 832 Double Action Revolver **$115**
Same as Model 826, except in 32 S&W Long. Made 1981 to 1983. **Model 833** in nickel finish, $120.

H&R Model 900

Harrington & Richardson Model 900 Double Action Revolver **$75**
Solid frame, snap-out cylinder. Calibers: 22 Short, Long, Long Rifle. 9-shot cylinder. Barrel lengths: 2½-, 4-, 6-inch. Weight: with 6-inch bbl., 26 oz. Fixed sights. Blued finish. Blade Cycolac stocks. Made from 1962 to 1973. *Note:* **Model 901** (discontinued in 1963) is the same, except chrome finish, has white Tenite stocks.

H&R Model 903

Harrington & Richardson Model 903 Target Revolver **$125**
Caliber: 22 Long Rifle. 6-inch target weight flat side barrel. 9-shot capacity. Single and double action, swing-out cylinder. Blade front sight, adjustable rear sight. American walnut grips. Weight: 35 oz. Made from 1980 to 1983.

H&R Model 904

Harrington & Richardson Model 904 Target Revolver **$125**
Similar to Model 903, except 4- and 6-inch bull barrels. 4-inch barrel weighs 32 oz. Made from 1980 to 1986.

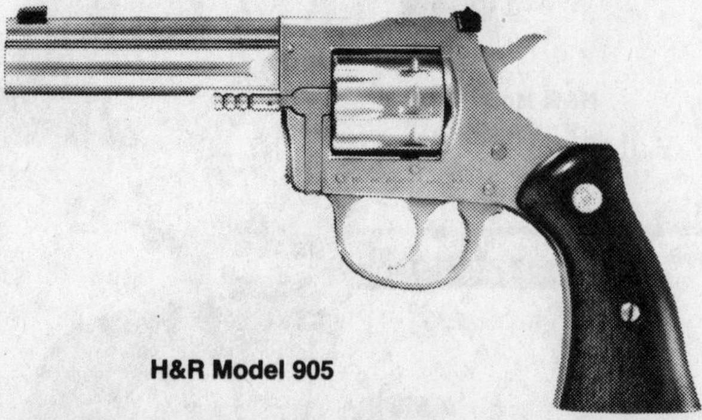

H&R Model 905

Harrington & Richardson Model 905 Target Revolver **$125**
Same as Model 904, except with 4-inch barrel only. Nickel finish. Made from 1981 to 1983.

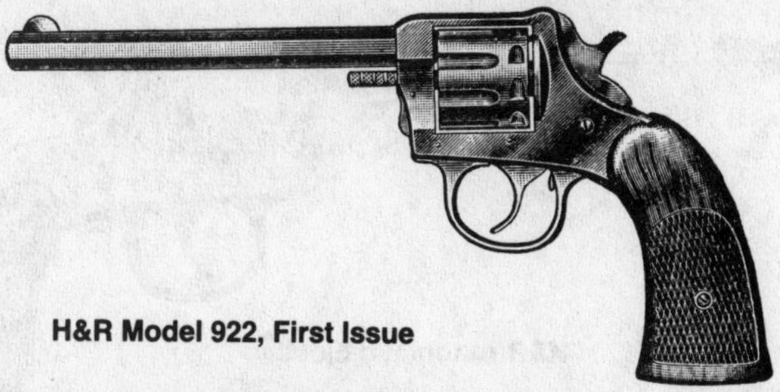

H&R Model 922, First Issue

Harrington & Richardson Model 922 Double Action Revolver, First Issue **$125**
Solid frame. Caliber: 22 Long Rifle. 9-shot cylinder. Barrel lengths: 6-inch on later production; early model, 10-inch barrel. Weight: with 6-inch bbl., 26 oz. Fixed sights. Blued finish. Checkered walnut stocks. Safety cylinder and round barrel on later models, earlier production had octagon barrel. Discontinued prior to 1942.

H&R Model 922, Second Issue

Harrington & Richardson Model 922 Double Action Revolver, Second Issue **$70**
Solid frame. Caliber: 22 Long Rifle. 9-shot cylinder. Barrel lengths: 2½-, 4-, 6-inch. Weight: with 4-inch bbl., 24 oz. Fixed sights. Blued finish. Plastic stocks. Made from 1950 to 1986. *Note:* Current Model 922 has a different frame from that of the First Issue. **Model 923** is same as Model 922, Second Issue, except nickel finish.

H&R Model 925

Harrington & Richardson Model 925 Defender Double Action Revolver **$105**
Hinged frame. Caliber: 38 S&W. 5-shot cylinder. 2½-inch barrel. Weight: 22 oz. Adjustable rear sight, fixed front sight. Blued finish. One-piece wrap-around grip. Made from 1964 to 1978.

H&R Model 926

Harrington & Richardson Model 926 Double Action Revolver **$115**
Hinged frame. Calibers: 22 Long Rifle, 38 S&W. 9-shot cylinder in 22, 5-shot in 38. 4-inch barrel. Weight: 31 oz. Adjustable rear sight, fixed front sight. Blued finish. Checkered walnut stocks. Made from 1968 to 1978.

H&R Model 929

Harrington & Richardson Model 929 Sidekick Double Action Revolver **$90**
Solid frame, swing-out cylinder. Caliber: 22 Long Rifle. 9-shot cylinder. Barrel lengths: 2½-, 4-, 6-inch. Weight: with 4-inch bbl., 24 oz. Fixed sights. Blued finish. Checkered plastic stocks. Made from 1956 to 1986. *Note:* **Model 930** is same, except nickel finish.

H&R Model 939

Harrington & Richardson Model 939 Ultra Sidekick Double Action Revolver **$90**
Solid frame, swing-out cylinder. Safety lock. Calibers: 22 Short, Long, Long Rifle. 9-shot cylinder. 6-inch barrel with flat sides, ventilated rib. Weight: 33 oz. Adjustable rear sight, ramp front sight. Blued finish. Checkered walnut stocks. Made from 1958 to 1986. *Note:* **Model 940** is same, except has round barrel.

H&R Model 949

H&R Model 950

Harrington & Richardson Model 949 Forty-Niner Double Action Revolver $90
Solid frame. Side loading and ejection. Calibers: 22 Short, Long, Long Rifle. 9-shot cylinder. $5\frac{1}{2}$-inch barrel. Weight: 31 oz. Adjustable rear sight, blade front sight. Blue or nickel finish. One-piece, Western-style walnut grip. Made from 1960 to 1986. *Note:* **Model 950** is same, except nickel finish.

Harrington & Richardson Model 976 Double Action Revolver $80
Same as Model 949, except has color-casehardened frame, $7\frac{1}{2}$-inch barrel, weighs 36 ounces. Introduced in 1977.

H&R Model 999 Sportsman First Issue

Harrington & Richardson Model 999 Sportsman Double Action Revolver, First Issue $125
Hinged frame. Calibers: 22 Long Rifle, 22 W.R.F. Same specifications as Model 199 Sportsman Single Action. Discontinued prior to 1942.

Harrington & Richardson Model 999 Sportsman Double Action Revolver, Second Issue $100
Hinged frame. Caliber: 22 Long Rifle. 9-shot cylinder. 6-inch barrel with ventilated rib. Weight: 30 oz. Adjustable sights. Blued finish. Checkered walnut stocks. Made from 1950 to 1986.

Harrington & Richardson American Double Action Revolver $75
Solid frame. Calibers: 32 S&W Long, 38 S&W. 6-shot cylinder (32 cal.), 5-shot (38 cal.). Barrel lengths: $2\frac{1}{2}$-, $4\frac{1}{2}$- and 6-inch. Weight: about 16 oz. Fixed sights. Blued or nickel finish. Hard rubber stocks. Discont. prior to 1942.

H&R Automatic Ejecting

Harrington & Richardson Automatic Ejecting Double Action Revolver $125
Hinged frame. Calibers: 32 S&W Long, 38 S&W. 6-shot cylinder (32 cal.), 5-shot (38 cal.). Barrel lengths: $3\frac{1}{4}$-, 4-, 5- and 6-inch. Weight: about 16 oz., 32 cal.; 15 oz., 38 cal. Fixed sights. Blued or nickel finish. Black hard rubber stocks. Discontinued prior to 1942.

H&R Bobby

Harrington & Richardson Bobby Double Action Revolver $125
Hinged frame. Calibers: 32 S&W, 38 S&W. 6-shot cylinder (32 cal.), 5-shot (38 cal.). 4-inch barrel. 9 inches overall. Weight: 23 oz. Fixed sights. Blued finish. Checkered walnut stocks. Discontinued 1946. *Note:* This revolver was originally designed and produced for use by London's bobbies.

H&R Defender 38

Harrington & Richardson Defender 38 Double Action Revolver $145
Hinged frame. Based on the Sportsman design. Caliber: 38 S&W. Barrel lengths: 4- and 6-inch. 9 inches overall with 4-inch barrel. Weight: 25 oz., 4-inch bbl. Fixed sights. Blued finish. Black plastic stocks. Discontinued 1946. *Note:* This model was manufactured during World War II as an arm for plant guards, auxiliary police, etc.

Harrington & Richardson Expert Model Double Action Revolver $150
Same specifications as 22 Special, except has 10-inch barrel. Weight: 28 oz. Discontinued prior to 1942.

Harrington & Richardson Hammerless Double Action Revolver, Large Frame $100
Hinged frame. Calibers: 32 S&W Long, 38 S&W. 6-shot cylinder (32 cal.), 5-shot (38 cal.). Barrel lengths: 3¼-, 4-, 5- and 6-inch. Weight: about 17 oz. Fixed sights. Blued or nickel finish. Hard rubber stocks. Discont. prior to 1942.

H&R Hammerless Small Frame

Harrington & Richardson Hammerless Double Action Revolver, Small Frame $90
Hinged frame. Calibers: 22 Long Rifle, 32 S&W. 7-shot cylinder (22 cal.), 5-shot (32 cal.). Barrel lengths: 2-, 3-, 4-, 5- and 6-inch. Weight: about 13 oz. Fixed sights. Blued or nickel finish. Hard rubber stocks. Discont. prior to 1942.

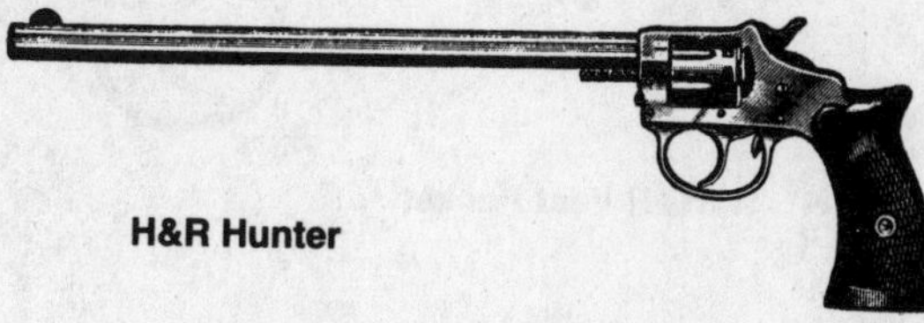
H&R Hunter

Harrington & Richardson Hunter Model Double Action Revolver $125
Solid frame. Caliber: 22 Long Rifle. 9-shot cylinder. 10-inch octagon barrel. Weight: 26 oz. Fixed sights. Blued finish. Checkered walnut stocks. Safety cylinder on later models. *Note:* An earlier Hunter Model was built on the smaller 7-shot frame. Discontinued prior to 1942.

H&R New Defender

Harrington & Richardson New Defender Double Action Revolver $180
Hinged frame. Caliber: 22 Long Rifle. 9-shot cylinder. 2-inch barrel. 6¼ inches overall. Weight: 23 oz. Adjustable sights. Blued finish. Checkered walnut stocks, round butt. *Note:* Basically, this is the Sportsman D.A. with a short barrel. Discontinued prior to 1942.

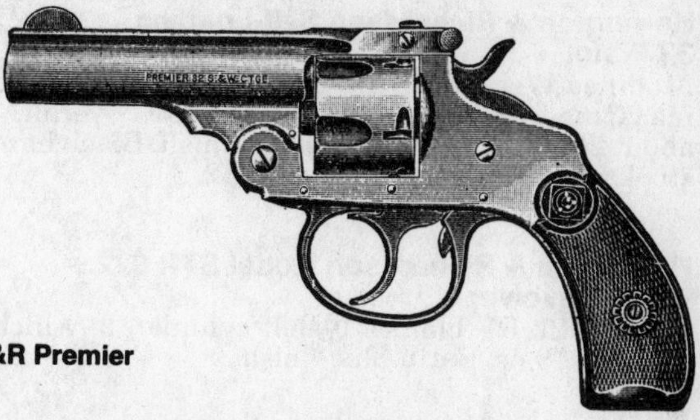
H&R Premier

Harrington & Richardson Premier Double Action Revolver $80
Small hinged frame. Calibers: 22 Long Rifle, 32 S&W. 7-shot cylinder (22 cal.), 5-shot (32 cal.). Barrel lengths: 2-, 3-, 4-, 5- and 6-inch. Weight: 13 oz., 22 cal.; 12 oz., 32 cal. Fixed sights. Blued or nickel finish. Black hard rubber stocks. Discontinued prior to 1942.

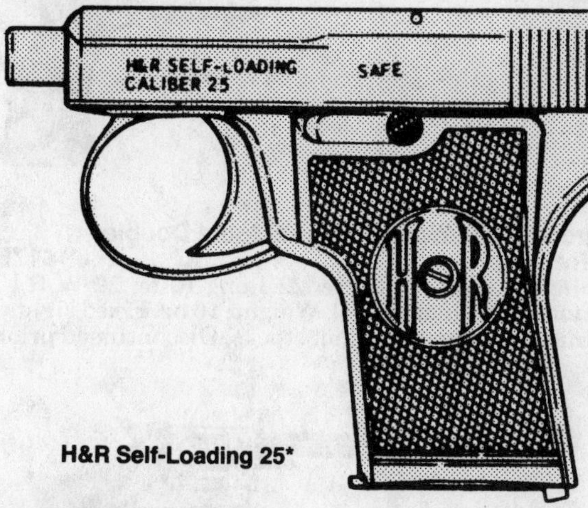

H&R Self-Loading 25*

Harrington & Richardson Self-Loading 25 Pistol . . $275
Modified Webley & Scott design. Caliber: 25 Auto. 6-shot magazine. 2-inch barrel. 4½ inches overall. Weight: 12 oz. Fixed sights. Blued finish. Black hard rubber stocks. Discontinued prior to 1942.

H&R Self-Loading 32*

Harrington & Richardson Self-Loading 32 Pistol $250
Modified Webley & Scott design. Caliber: 32 Auto. 8-shot magazine. 3½-inch barrel. 6½ inches overall. Weight: about 20 oz. Fixed sights. Blued finish. Black hard rubber stocks. Discontinued prior to 1942.

Harrington & Richardson Model STR 022 Blank Revolver $65
Caliber: 22 RF blanks. 9-shot cylinder. 2½-inch barrel. Weight: 19 oz. Satin blue finish.

Harrington & Richardson Model STR 032 Blank Revolver $65
Same general specifications as STR 022 except chambered for 32 S&W blank cartridges.

H&R Target Model

Harrington & Richardson Target Model Double Action Revolver $175
Small hinged frame. Calibers: 22 Long Rifle, 22 W.R.F. 7-shot cylinder. 6-inch barrel. Weight: 16 oz. Fixed sights. Blued finish. Checkered walnut stocks. Discontinued prior to 1942.

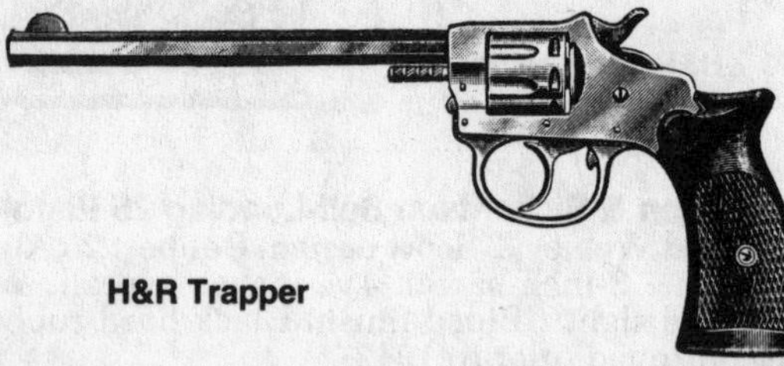

H&R Trapper

Harrington & Richardson Trapper Model Double Action Revolver $125
Solid frame. Caliber: 22 Long Rifle. 7-shot cylinder. 6-inch octagon barrel. Weight: 12¼ oz. Fixed sights. Blued finish. Checkered walnut stocks. Safety cylinder on later models. Discontinued prior to 1942.

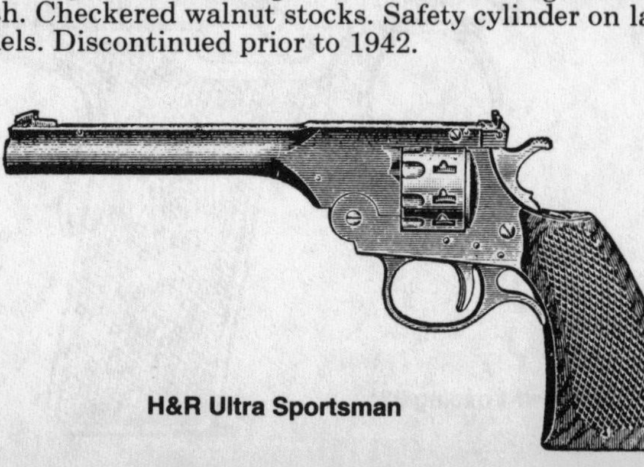

H&R Ultra Sportsman

Harrington & Richardson Ultra Sportsman Revolver $195
Single action. Hinged frame. Caliber: 22 Long Rifle. 9-shot cylinder. 6-inch barrel. Weight: 30 oz. Adjustable target sights. Blued finish. Checkered walnut stocks. This model has short action, wide hammer spur; cylinder is length of a 22 Long Rifle cartridge. Discont. prior to 1942.

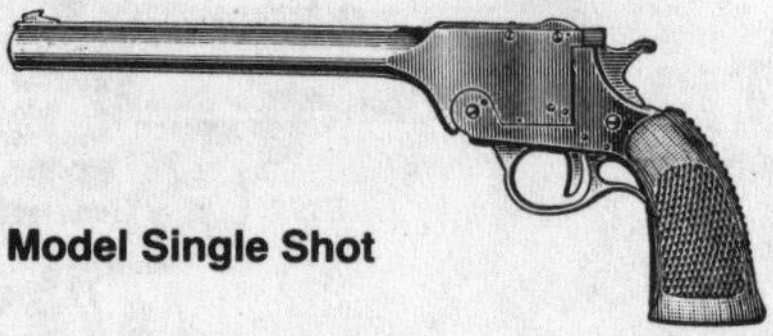

H&R USRA Model Single Shot

Harrington & Richardson USRA Model Single Shot Target Pistol $425
Hinged frame. Caliber: 22 Long Rifle. Barrel lengths: 7-, 8- and 10-inch. Weight: 31 oz. with 10-inch bbl. Adjustable target sights. Blued finish. Checkered walnut stocks. Made from 1928 to 1941.

H&R Vest Pocket

Harrington & Richardson Vest Pocket Double Action Revolver $75
Solid frame. Spurless hammer. Calibers: 22 Rimfire, 32 S&W. 7-shot cylinder (22 cal.), 5-shot (32 cal.). 1⅛-inch barrel. Weight: about 9 oz. Blued or nickel finish. Hard rubber stocks. Discontinued prior to 1942.

H&R Young America

Harrington & Richardson Young America Double Action Revolver $85
Solid frame. Calibers: 22 Long, 32 S&W. 7-shot cylinder (22 cal.), 5-shot (32 cal.). Barrel lengths: 2-, 4½- and 6-inch. Weight: about 9 oz. Fixed sights. Blued or nickel finish. Hard rubber stocks. Discont. prior to 1942.

HARTFORD ARMS & EQUIPMENT CO.
Hartford, Connecticut

Hartford pistols were the forebears of the original High Standard line, since High Standard Mfg. Corp. acquired Hartford Arms & Equipment Co. in 1932. The High Standard Model B is essentially the same as the Hartford Automatic.

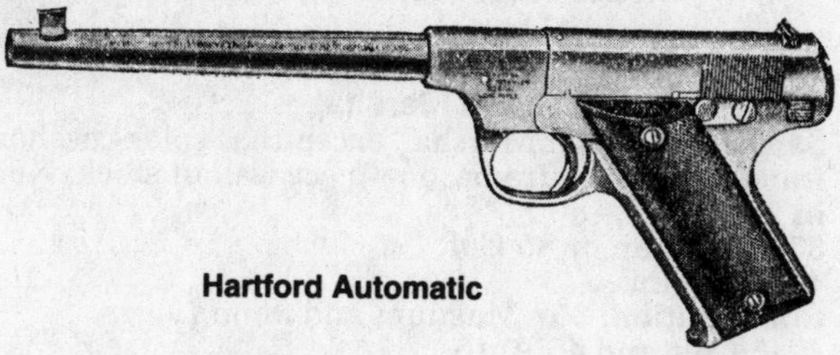

Hartford Automatic

Hartford Automatic Target Pistol **$455**
Caliber: 22 Long Rifle. 10-shot magazine. 6³/₄-inch barrel. 10³/₄ inches overall. Weight: 31 oz. Target sights. Blued finish. Black rubber stocks. This arm closely resembles the early Colt Woodsman and High Standard pistols. Made from 1929 to 1930.

Hartford Repeating Pistol **$495**
Same general design as the automatic pistol of this manufacture, but this model is a hand-operated repeating pistol on the order of the Fiala. Made from 1929 to 1930.

Hartford Single Shot Target Pistol **$510**
Similar in appearance to the Hartford Automatic. Caliber: 22 Long Rifle. 6³/₄-inch barrel. 10³/₄ inches overall. Weight: 38 oz. Target sights. Mottled frame and slide, blued barrel. Black rubber or walnut stocks. Made from 1929 to 1930.

HAWES FIREARMS
Van Nuys, California

Hawes Deputy Denver Marshal

Hawes Deputy Denver Marshal
Same as Deputy Marshal SA, except has brass frame.
22 Long Rifle, plastic stocks **$75**
Combination, 22 Long Rifle and 22 Win. Mag. R.F., plastic stocks **85**
Extra for walnut stocks **5**

Hawes Deputy Marshal

Hawes Deputy Marshal Single Action Revolver
Caliber: 22 Long Rifle; also 22 Win. Mag. R.F. in two cylinder combination. 6-shot cylinder. 5¹/₂-inch barrel. 11 inches overall. Weight: 34 oz. Adjustable rear sight, blade front sight. Blued finish. Plastic or walnut stocks. Made from 1973 to date.
22 Long Rifle, plastic stocks **$65**
Combination, 22 Long Rifle and 22 Win. Mag. R.F., plastic stocks **75**
Extra for walnut stocks **5**

Hawes Deputy Montana Marshal

Hawes Deputy Montana Marshal
Same as Deputy Marshal, except has brass grip frame, walnut stocks only.
22 Long Rifle **$75**
Combination, 22 L.R. and 22 Win. Mag. R.F. **85**

Hawes Deputy Silver City Marshal

Hawes Deputy Silver City Marshal
Same as Deputy Marshal, except has chrome-plated frame, brass grip frame, blued cylinder and barrel.
22 Long Rifle, plastic stocks **$70**
Combination, 22 Long Rifle and 22 Win. Mag. R.F., plastic stocks **80**
Extra for walnut stocks **5**

Hawes Deputy Texas Marshal

Hawes Deputy Texas Marshal

Same as Deputy Marshal, except has chrome finish.

22 Long Rifle, plastic stocks **$70**

Combination, 22 Long Rifle and 22 Win. Mag. R.F., plastic stocks **85**

Extra for walnut stocks **5**

Hawes Favorite

Hawes Favorite Single Shot Target Pistol **$100**

Replica of Stevens No. 35. Tip-up action. Caliber: 22 Long Rifle. 8-inch barrel. 12 inches overall. Weight: 24 oz. Target sights. Chrome-plated frame. Blued barrel. Plastic or rosewood stocks (add $5 for the latter). Made 1968 to 1976.

Hawes Sauer Chief Marshal

Hawes Sauer Chief Marshal SA Target Revolver

Same as Western Marshal, except has adjustable rear sight and front sight, oversized rosewood stocks. Not made in 22 caliber.

357 Magnum or 45 Colt **$165**

44 Magnum **175**

Combination, 357 Magnum and 9mm Luger, 45 Colt and 45 Auto **200**

Combination, 44 Magnum and 44-40 .... **210**

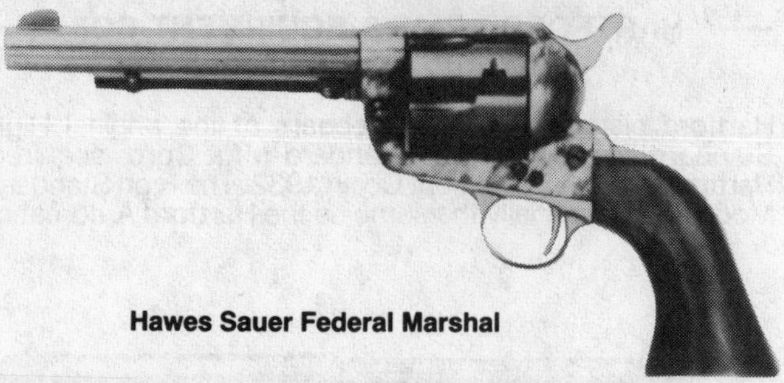

Hawes Sauer Federal Marshal

Hawes Sauer Federal Marshal

Same as Western Marshal, except has color-casehardened frame, brass grip frame, one-piece walnut stock. Not made in 22 caliber.

357 Magnum or 45 Colt **$165**

44 Magnum **170**

Combination, 357 Magnum and 9mm Luger, 45 Colt and 45 Auto **200**

Combination, 44 Magnum and 44-40 .... **210**

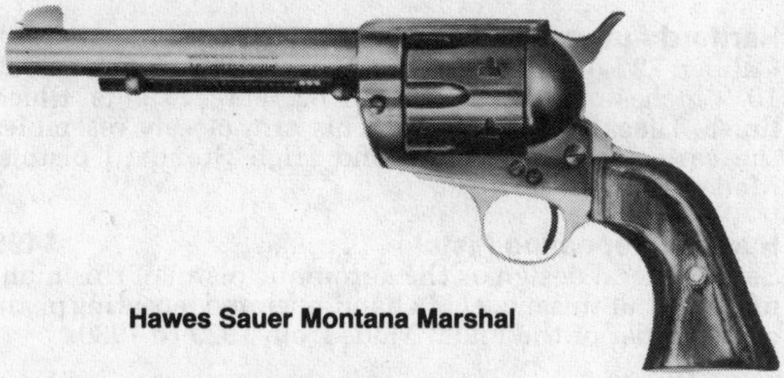

Hawes Sauer Montana Marshal

Hawes Sauer Montana Marshal

Same as Western Marshal, except has brass grip frame. 22 caliber discontinued.

357 Magnum or 45 Colt **$155**

44 Magnum **160**

Combination, 357 Magnum and 9mm Luger, 45 Colt and 45 Auto **185**

Combination, 44 Magnum and 44-40 .... **195**

22 Long Rifle **140**

Combination, 22 Long Rifle and 22 Win. Mag. R.F. **165**

Hawes Sauer Silver City Marshal

Hawes Sauer Silver City Marshal

Same as Western Marshal, except has nickel-plated frame, brass grip frame, blued cylinder and barrel, pearlite stocks.

44 Magnum **$175**

Combination, 357 Magnum and 9mm Luger, 45 Colt and 45 Auto **200**

Combination, 44 Magnum and 44-40 .... **210**

Hawes Sauer Texas Marshal

Hawes Sauer Texas Marshal

Same as Western Marshal, except nickel-plated, has pearlite stocks. 22 caliber discontinued.

357 Magnum or 45 Colt	**$160**
44 Magnum	**170**
Combination, 357 Magnum and 9mm Luger, 45 Colt and 45 Auto	**195**
Combination, 44 Magnum and 44-40	**200**
22 Long Rifle	**145**
Combination, 22 Long Rifle and 22 Win. Mag. R.F.	**175**

Hawes Sauer Western Marshal

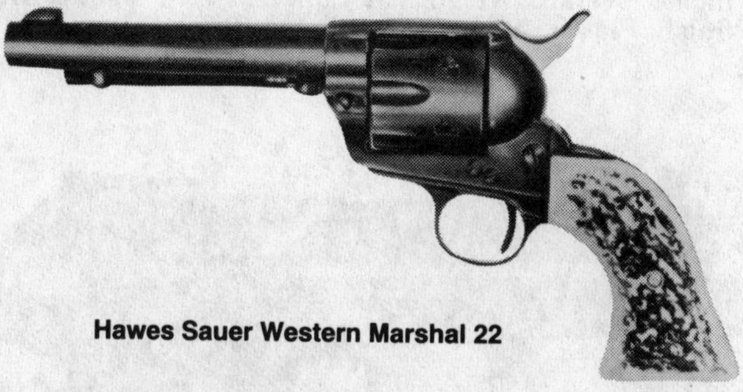

Hawes Sauer Western Marshal 22

Hawes Sauer Western Marshal Single Action Revolver

Calibers: 22 Long Rifle (discont.), 357 Magnum, 44 Magnum, 45 Auto. Also in two-cylinder combinations: 22 Win. Mag. R.F. (discont.), 9mm Luger, 44-40, 45 Auto. 6-shot cylinder. Barrel lengths: 5½-inch (discont.), 6-inch. 11¾ inches overall with 6-inch bbl. Weight: 46 oz. Fixed sights. Blued finish. Originally furnished with simulated stag plastic stocks; recent production has smooth rosewood stocks. Made from 1968 to date by J. P. Sauer & Sohn, Eckernforde, West Germany.

357 Magnum or 45 Colt	**$140**
44 Magnum	**145**
Combination, 357 Magnum and 9mm Luger, 45 Colt and 45 Auto	**165**
Combination, 44 Magnum and 44-40	**175**
22 Long Rifle	**115**
Combination, 22 Long Rifle and 22 Win. Mag. R.F.	**145**

HECKLER & KOCH GMBH
Oberndorf/Neckar, West Germany, and Chantilly, Virginia

Heckler & Koch HK4

Heckler & Koch Model HK4 Double Action Automatic Pistol

Calibers: 380 Automatic (9mm Short); also 22 Long Rifle, 25 Automatic (6.35mm), 32 Automatic (7.65mm) with conversion kits. 7-shot magazine in 380; 8-shot in other calibers. 3 11/32-inch barrel. 6 3/16 inches overall. Weight: 18 oz. Fixed sights. Blued finish. Plastic stock. Discontinued 1984.

380 Automatic	**$295**
380 Automatic with 22 conversion unit	**350**
380 Automatic with 22, 25, 32 conversion units	**450**

Heckler & Koch Model P7K3

Heckler & Koch Model P7K3 DA Auto Pistol

Caliber: 380 ACP. 8-round magazine. 3.8 inch-barrel. 6.3 inches overall. Weight: about 26 oz. Adjustable rear sight. Made from 1988 to date.

P7K3 in 380 Cal.	**$660**
22 LR Conversion Kit	**320**

Heckler & Koch P7 M8

Heckler & Koch Model P7 M8 . . . . **$495**
Caliber: 9mm. 8-shot magazine. 4.13-inch barrel. 6.73 inches overall. Weight: 29.9 oz. Matte black finish. Adjustable rear sight. Made 1985 to date.

Heckler & Koch P7 M13

Heckler & Koch Model P7 M13 . . . . **$575**
Caliber: 9mm. 13-shot magazine. 4.13-inch barrel. 6.65 inches overall. Weight: 34.42 oz. Matte black finish. Adjustable rear sight. Made 1985 to date.

Heckler & Koch Model P7 (PSP)

Heckler & Koch Model P7(PSP) Double Action Automatic Pistol **$475**
Caliber: 9mm Parabellum/Luger. 8-shot magazine. 4.13-inch barrel. 6.54 inches overall. Weight: about 33.5 oz. Blue finish. Made from 1983 to 1985.

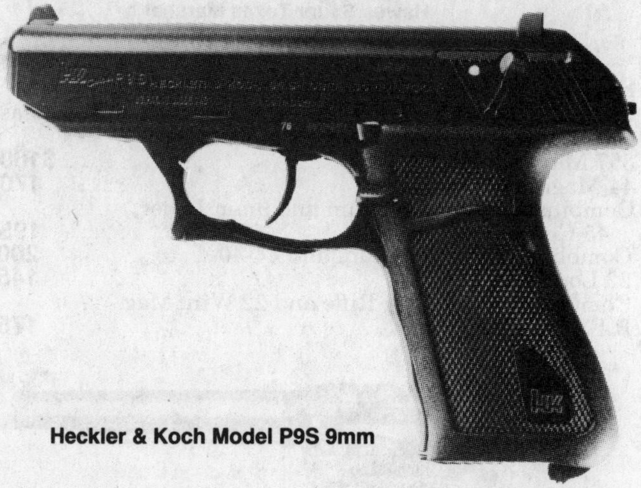
Heckler & Koch Model P9S 9mm

Heckler & Koch Model P9S 9mm Double Action Automatic Pistol **$550**
Caliber: 9mm Luger. 9-shot magazine. 4-inch barrel. 7⅝ inches overall. Weight: 32 ounces. Fixed sights. Blued finish. Plastic stock. Discontinued 1986.

Heckler & Koch
Model P9S 9mm Target

Heckler & Koch Model P9S 9mm Target **$630**
Same as standard Model P9S 9mm, except has adjustable trigger, trigger stop, adjustable rear sight.

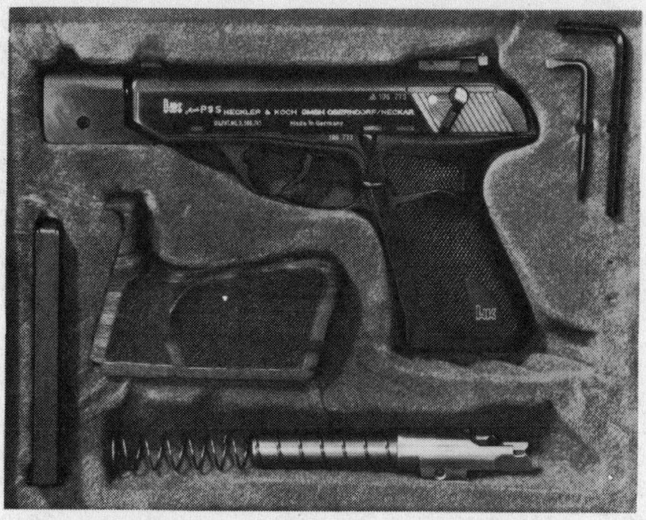

Heckler & Koch Model P9S 9mm Competition Kit

Heckler & Koch Model P9S 9mm Target Competition Kit
Same as Model P9S 9mm Target, except comes with extra 5½-inch barrel and barrel weight. Also available with walnut competition stock.
With standard stock **$625**
With competition stock **695**

Heckler & Koch Model P9S 45

Heckler & Koch Model P9S 45 .... $525
Same as standard Model P9S 9mm, except caliber 45 Automatic; has 7-shot magazine.

Heckler & Koch Model VP'70Z Double Action Automatic Pistol $295
Caliber: 9mm Luger. 18-shot magazine. 4½-inch barrel. 8 inches overall. Weight: 32½ oz. Fixed sights. Blued slide, plastic receiver and stock. Discontinued; availability limited.

Heckler & Koch Model VP'70Z

J. C. HIGGINS HANDGUNS

See Sears, Roebuck & Company.

HIGH STANDARD SPORTING FIREARMS
East Hartford, Connecticut
Formerly High Standard Mfg. Co., Hamden, Conn.

High Standard Model A

HIGH STANDARD AUTOMATIC PISTOLS

High Standard Model A Automatic Pistol $275
Hammerless. Caliber: 22 Long Rifle. 10-shot magazine. Barrel lengths: 4½ and 6¾ inch. 11½ inches overall with 6¾-inch barrel. Weight: 36 oz. with 6¾-inch bbl. Adjustable target sights. Blued finish. Checkered walnut stocks. Made from 1938 to 1942.

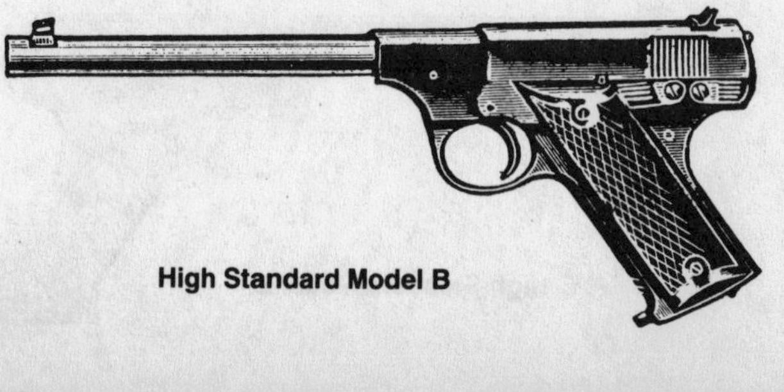

High Standard Model B

High Standard Model B Automatic Pistol $300
Original Standard pistol. Hammerless. Caliber: 22 Long Rifle. 10-shot magazine. Barrel lengths: $4\frac{1}{2}$- and $6\frac{3}{4}$-inch. $10\frac{3}{4}$ inches overall with $6\frac{3}{4}$-inch bbl. Weight: 33 oz. with $6\frac{3}{4}$-inch bbl. Fixed sights. Blued finish. Hard rubber stocks. Made from 1932 to 1942.

High Standard Model C Automatic Pistol $285
Same as Model B except chambered for 22 Short. Made from 1935 to 1942.

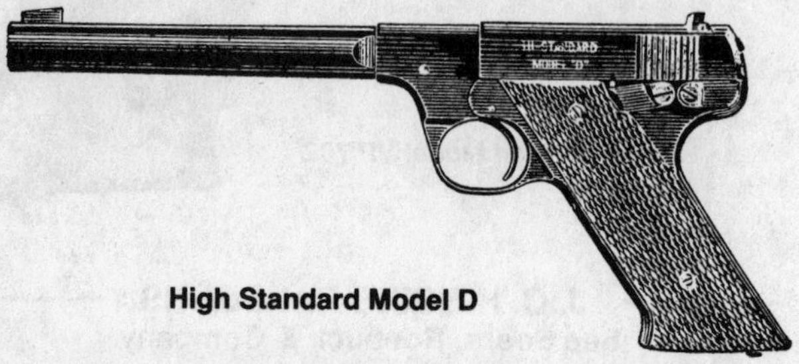

High Standard Model D

High Standard Model D Automatic Pistol $315
Same general specifications as Model A, but with heavier barrel. Weight: 40 oz. with $6\frac{3}{4}$-inch barrel. Made from 1937 to 1942.

High Standard Dura-Matic

High Standard Dura-Matic Automatic Pistol $195
Takedown. Caliber: 22 Long Rifle. 10-shot magazine. Barrels: $4\frac{1}{2}$- or $6\frac{1}{2}$-inch, interchangeable. Overall length: with $6\frac{1}{2}$-inch bbl., $10\frac{7}{8}$-inches. Weight: with $6\frac{1}{2}$-inch bbl., 35 oz. Fixed sights. Blued finish. Checkered grips. Made from 1952 to 1970.

High Standard Model E

High Standard Model E Automatic Pistol $375
Same general specifications as Model A, but with extra heavy barrel and thumb-rest stocks. Weight: 42 oz. with $6\frac{3}{4}$-inch bbl. Made from 1937 to 1942.

High Standard Field-King Automatic Pistol
Same general specifications as Sport-King, but with heavier barrel and target sights. Late model $6\frac{3}{4}$-inch barrels have recoil stabilizer feature. Weight: 43 oz. with $6\frac{3}{4}$-inch barrel. Made from 1951 to 1958.
With one barrel **$205**
With both barrels **275**

High Standard Flite-King Automatic Pistol—First Model
Same general specifications as Sport-King, except caliber 22 Short, has aluminum alloy frame and slide, weighs 26 oz. with $6\frac{1}{2}$-inch bbl. Made from 1953 to 1958.
With one barrel **$200**
With both barrels **250**

High Standard Flite-King Automatic Pistol Second Model $210
Same as Sport-King—Second Model, except caliber 22 Short and weighs 2 oz. lighter. Made from 1958 to 1966.

High Standard Model G-380

High Standard Model G-380 Automatic Pistol . . . $350
Lever takedown. Visible hammer. Thumb safety. Caliber: 380 Automatic. 6-shot magazine. 5-inch barrel. Weight: 40 oz. Fixed sights. Blued finish. Checkered plastic stocks. Made from 1943 to 1950.

High Standard Model G-B

High Standard Model G-B Automatic Pistol
Lever takedown. Hammerless. Interchangeable barrels. Caliber: 22 Long Rifle. 10-shot magazine. Barrel lengths: $4\frac{1}{2}$- and $6\frac{3}{4}$-inch. $10\frac{3}{4}$ inches overall with $6\frac{3}{4}$-inch bbl. Weight: 36 oz. with $6\frac{3}{4}$-inch bbl. Fixed sights. Blued finish. Checkered plastic stocks. Made from 1948 to 1951.
With one barrel **$295**
With both barrels **350**

High Standard Model G-D Automatic Pistol
Lever takedown. Hammerless. Interchangeable barrels. Caliber: 22 Long Rifle. 10-shot magazine. Barrel lengths: $4\frac{1}{2}$- and $6\frac{3}{4}$-inch. $11\frac{1}{2}$ inches overall with $6\frac{3}{4}$-inch bbl. Weight: 41 oz. with $6\frac{3}{4}$-inch bbl. Target sights. Blued finish. Checkered walnut stocks. Made from 1948 to 1951.
With one barrel **$305**
With both barrels **360**

High Standard Model G-E

High Standard Model G-E Automatic Pistol
Same general specifications as Model G-D, but with extra heavy barrel and thumb-rest stocks. Weight: 44 oz. with $6\frac{3}{4}$-inch barrel. Made from 1949 to 1951.
With one barrel **$350**
With both barrels **425**

High Standard Model H-A

High Standard Model H-A Automatic Pistol **$315**
Same as Model A, but with visible hammer, no thumb safety. Made from 1939 to 1942.

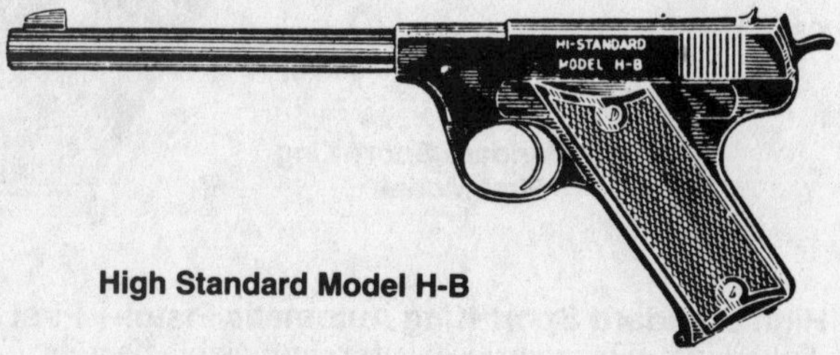

High Standard Model H-B

High Standard Model H-B Automatic Pistol **$300**
Same as Model B, but with visible hammer, no thumb safety. Made from 1940 to 1942.

High Standard Model H-D Automatic Pistol **$315**
Same as Model D, but with visible hammer, no thumb safety. Made from 1939 to 1942.

High Standard Model H-DM Automatic Pistol ... **$300**
Also called H-D Military. Same as Model H-D, but with thumb safety. Made from 1941 to 1951.

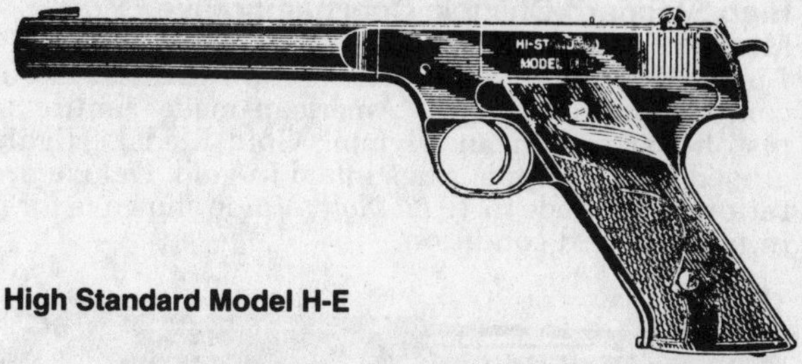

High Standard Model H-E

High Standard Model H-E Automatic Pistol **$345**
Same as Model E, but with visible hammer, no thumb safety. Made from 1939 to 1942.

High Standard Olympic, First Model

High Standard Olympic Automatic Pistol—First Model
Same general specifications as Model G-E, but chambered for 22 Short, has light alloy slide. Made from 1950 to 1951.
With one barrel **$475**
With both barrels **525**

High Standard Olympic Second Model

High Standard Olympic Automatic Pistol—Second Model
Same general specifications as Supermatic, but chambered for 22 Short, has light alloy slide. Weight: 39 oz. with $6\frac{3}{4}$-inch barrel. Made from 1951 to 1958.
With one barrel **$335**
With both barrels **360**

High Standard Olympic Automatic Pistol Third Model **$300**
Same as Supermatic Trophy with bull barrel, except caliber 22 Short. Made from 1963 to 1966.

High Standard Olympic Commemorative Model **$895**
Limited edition of Supermatic Trophy Military issued to commemorate the only American-made rimfire target pistol ever to win an Olympic Gold Medal. Highly engraved with Olympic rings inlaid in gold. Deluxe presentation case. Made in 1972. *Note:* Value shown is for pistol in new, unfired condition.

High Standard Olympic I.S.U.

High Standard Olympic I.S.U. **$300**
Same as Supermatic Citation, except caliber 22 Short, 6³/₄- and 8-inch tapered barrels with stabilizer, detachable weights. Made from 1958 to date; 8-inch barrel discontinued in 1964.

High Standard Olympic I.S.U. Military

High Standard Olympic I.S.U. Military **$310**
Same as Olympic I.S.U., except has military grip and bracket rear sight. Introduced in 1965. Discontinued.

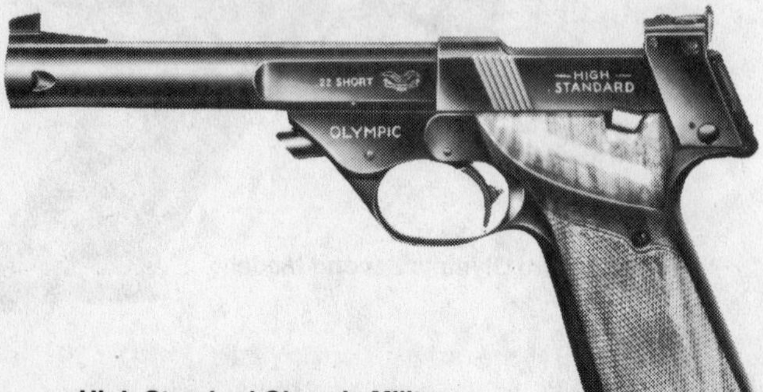

High Standard Olympic Military

High Standard Olympic Military **$295**
Same as Olympic—Third Model, except has military grip and bracket rear sight. Made in 1965.

High Standard Plinker

High Standard Plinker **$195**
Similar to Dura-Matic with same general specifications. Made from 1971 to 1973.

High Standard Sharpshooter

High Standard Sharpshooter Automatic Pistol . . **$215**
Takedown. Hammerless. Caliber: 22 Long Rifle. 10-shot magazine. 5¹/₂-inch bull barrel. 9 inches overall. Weight: 42 oz. Micrometer rear sight, blade front sight. Blued finish. Plastic stocks. Made from 1971 to 1983.

High Standard Sport-King First Model

High Standard Sport-King Automatic Pistol—First Model
Takedown. Hammerless. Interchangeable barrels. Caliber: 22 Long Rifle. 10-shot magazine. Barrel lengths: 4¹/₂- and 6³/₄-inch. 11¹/₂ inches overall with 6³/₄-inch bbl. Weight: 39 oz. with 6³/₄-inch bbl. Fixed sights. Blued finish. Checkered plastic thumb-rest stocks. Made from 1951 to 1958. *Note:* 1951-54 production has lever takedown as in "G" series; later version illustrated has push-button takedown.

With one barrel	$210
With both barrels	250

High Standard Sport-King Third Model

High Standard Sport-King Second Model

High Standard Sport-King Automatic Pistol Second Model **$215**
Caliber: 22 Long Rifle. 10-shot magazine. Barrels: 4½- or 6¾-inch, interchangeable. 11¼ inches overall with 6¾-inch bbl. Weight: with 6¾-inch bbl., 42 oz. Fixed sights. Blued finish. Checkered grips. Made from 1958 to 1970.

High Standard Sport-King Automatic Pistol Third Model **$200**
Similar to Sport-King—Second Model, with same general specifications. Available in blued or nickel finish. Introduced in 1974. Discontinued.

High Standard Sport-King Lightweight
Same as standard Sport-King, except has forged aluminum alloy frame, weighs 30 oz. with 6¾-inch barrel. Made from 1954 to 1965.
With one barrel **$215**
With both barrels 255

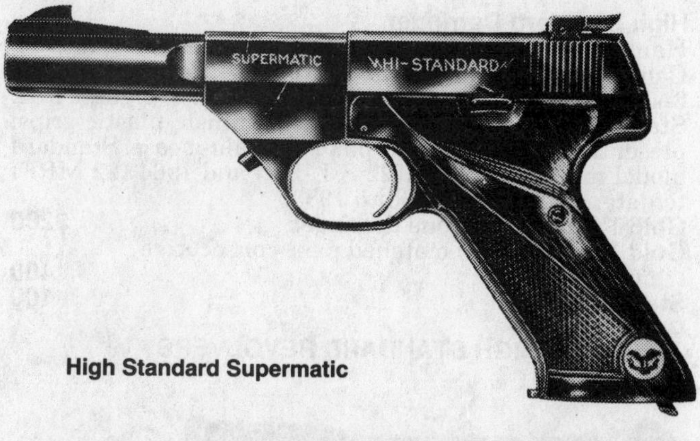

High Standard Supermatic

High Standard Supermatic Automatic Pistol
Takedown. Hammerless. Interchangeable barrels. Caliber: 22 Long Rifle. 10-shot magazine. Barrel lengths: 4½- and 6¾-inch. Late model 6¾-inch barrels have recoil stabilizer feature. Weight: with 6¾-inch bbl., 43 oz. 11½ inches overall with 6¾-inch bbl. Target sights. Elevated serrated rib between sights. Adjustable barrel weights add 2 or 3 oz. Blued finish. Checkered plastic thumb-rest stocks. Made from 1951 to 1958.
With one barrel **$320**
With both barrels 375

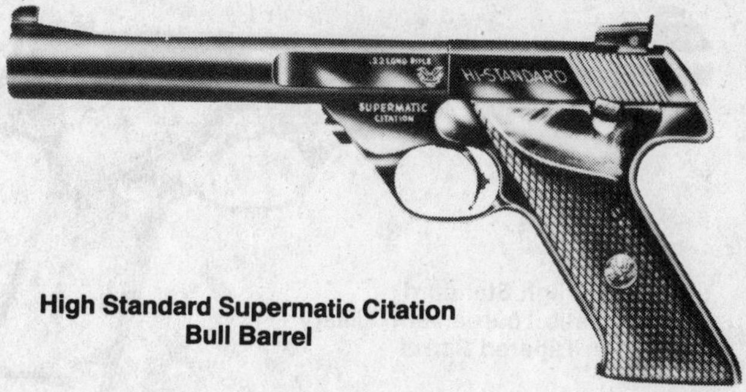

High Standard Supermatic Citation Bull Barrel

High Standard Supermatic Citation
Same as Supermatic Tournament, except 6¾-, 8-, 10-inch barrels, tapered, with stabilizer and two removable weights. Also furnished with Tournament's 5½-inch bull barrel, adjustable trigger pull, recoil-proof click adjustable rear sight (barrel-mounted on 8- and 10-inch barrels), checkered walnut thumb-rest grips on bull barrel model. Currently mfd. with only bull barrel. Made 1958 to date.
With bull barrel **$300**
With tapered barrel 325

High Standard Supermatic Citation Military Fluted Barrel

High Standard Supermatic Citation Military
Same as Supermatic Citation, except has military grip and bracket rear sight, barrels as in Supermatic Trophy. Made from 1965 to date.
With bull barrel **$285**
With fluted barrel 325

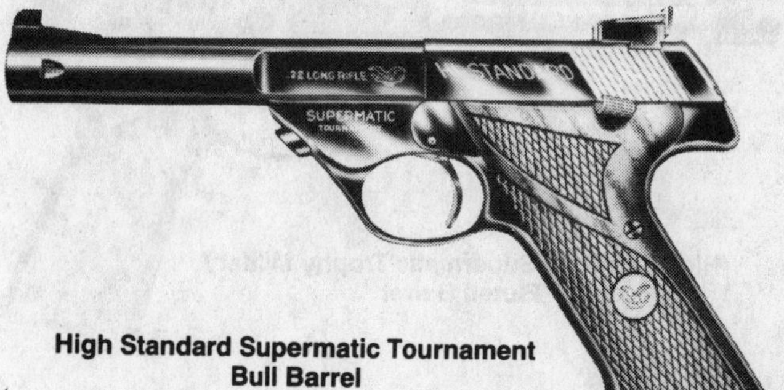

High Standard Supermatic Tournament Bull Barrel

High Standard Supermatic Tournament Automatic **$335**
Takedown. Caliber: 22 Long Rifle. 10-shot magazine. Barrels (interchangeable): 5½-inch bull, 6¾-inch heavy tapered, notched and drilled for stabilizer and weights. 10 inches overall with 5½-inch bbl. Weight: with 5½-inch bbl., 44 oz. Click adjustable rear sight, undercut ramp front sight. Blued finish. Checkered grips. Made 1958 to 1966.

High Standard
Supermatic Tournament Military
Tapered Barrel

High Standard Supermatic Tournament Military **$315**
Same as Supermatic Tournament, except has military grip. Made from 1965 to 1971.

High Standard Supermatic Trophy
Bull Barrel

High Standard Supermatic Trophy
Same as Supermatic Citation, except $5^{1}/_{2}$-inch bull barrel or $7^{1}/_{4}$-inch fluted barrel with detachable stabilizer and weights, extra magazine. High-luster blued finish, checkered walnut thumb-rest grips. Made from 1963 to 1966.
With bull barrel **$295**
With fluted barrel **345**

High Standard Supermatic Trophy Military
Fluted Barrel

High Standard Supermatic Trophy Military
Same as Supermatic Trophy, except has military grip and bracket rear sight. Made from 1965 to date.
With bull barrel **$305**
With fluted barrel **375**

High Standard Victor Automatic Pistol **$315**
Takedown. Caliber: 22 Long Rifle. 10-shot magazine. Barrels: $4^{1}/_{2}$-inch solid or vent rib, $5^{1}/_{2}$-inch vent rib; interchangeable. $9^{3}/_{4}$ inches overall with $5^{1}/_{2}$-inch barrel.

High Standard Victor
Solid Rib Barrel

High Standard Victor Automatic Pistol (cont.)
Weight: with $5^{1}/_{2}$-inch bbl., 52 oz. Rib-mounted target sights. Blued finish. Checkered walnut thumb-rest stocks. Standard or military grip configuration. Made from 1972 to date (standard-grip model, 1974-75).

HIGH STANDARD DERRINGER

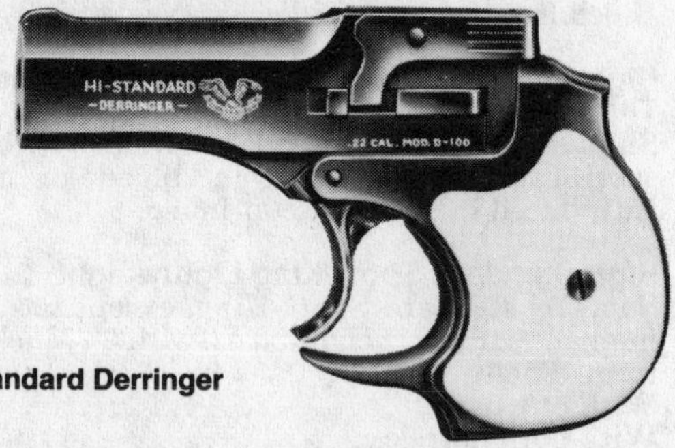

High Standard Derringer

High Standard Derringer
Hammerless, double action, double barrel (over/under). Calibers: 22 Short, Long, Long Rifle; 22 Magnum Rimfire. 2-shot. $3^{1}/_{2}$-inch barrels. 5 inches overall. Weight: 11 oz. Standard model has blued or nickel finish, plastic grips; presentation model is gold-plated in walnut case. Standard model made from 1963 (22 S-L-LR) and 1964 (22 MRF) to date; gold model, 1965 to 1983.
Gold Presentation, one derringer **$200**
Gold Presentation, matched pair, consecutive numbers **400**
Standard Model **100**

HIGH STANDARD REVOLVERS

High Standard Camp Gun

High Standard Camp Gun **$145**
Same as Sentinel Mark I/Mark IV, except has 6-inch barrel, adjustable rear sight, target-style checkered walnut stocks. Caliber: 22 Long Rifle or 22 Win. Mag. R.F. Made from 1976 to 1983.

High Standard Double-Nine Double Action Revolver—Aluminum Frame **$115**
Western-style version of Sentinel. Blued or nickel finish with simulated ivory, ebony or stag grips. 5½-inch barrel. 11 inches overall. Weight: 27¼ oz. Made from 1959 to 1971.

High Standard Double-Nine Deluxe **$140**
Same as Double-Nine—Steel Frame, except has adjustable target rear sight. Introduced in 1971. Discont.

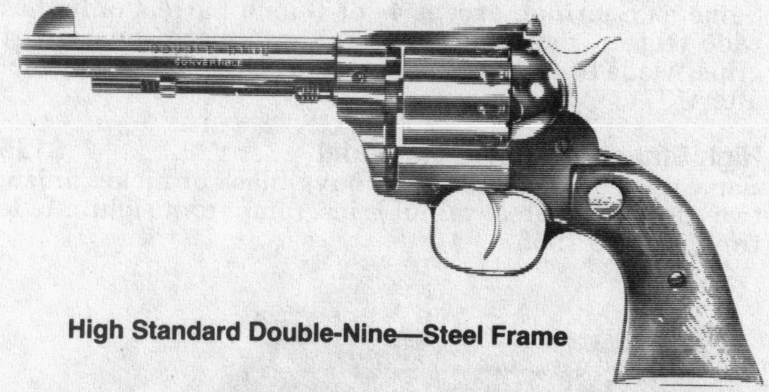
High Standard Double-Nine—Steel Frame

High Standard Double-Nine—Steel Frame **$130**
Similar to Double-Nine—Aluminum Frame, with same general specifications, except has extra cylinder for 22 Win. Mag. R.F., walnut stocks. Introduced in 1971. Discont.

High Standard Durango

High Standard Durango **$125**
Similar to Double-Nine—Steel Frame, except 22 Long Rifle only, available with 4½-, as well as 5½-inch barrel. Made from 1971 to 1973.

High Standard High Sierra

High Standard High Sierra Double Action Revolver
Similar to Double-Nine—Steel Frame, except has 7-inch octagon barrel, gold-plated grip frame; available with either fixed or adjustable sights. Made from 1973 to 1983.
With fixed sights **$135**
With adjustable sights **155**

High Standard Hombre **$115**
Similar to Double-Nine—Steel Frame, except 22 Long Rifle only, lacks single-action type ejector rod and tube, has 4½-inch barrel. Made from 1971 to 1973.

High Standard Kit Gun

High Standard Kit Gun Double Action Revolver . **$145**
Solid frame, swing-out cylinder. Caliber: 22 Long Rifle. 9-shot cylinder. 4-inch barrel. 9 inches overall. Weight: 19 oz. Adjustable rear sight, ramp front sight. Blued finish. Checkered walnut stocks. Made from 1970 to 1973.

High Standard Longhorn—Aluminum Frame

High Standard Longhorn—Aluminum Frame
Similar to Double-Nine—Aluminum Frame. Longhorn hammer spur. Blued finish 4½-inch barrel with simulated pearl grips; 5½-inch, simulated stag grips; 9½-inch, walnut grips. Latter model made from 1960 to 1971, others made from 1961 to 1966.
With 4½- or 5½-inch barrel **$125**
With 9½-inch barrel **140**

High Standard Longhorn—Steel Frame

High Standard Longhorn—Steel Frame
Similar to Double-Nine—Steel Frame, except has $9\frac{1}{2}$-inch barrel; available with either fixed or adjustable sights. Made from 1971 to 1983.
With fixed sights **$140**
With adjustable sights **150**

High Standard Natchez

High Standard Natchez **$125**
Similar to Double-Nine—Aluminum Frame, except $4\frac{1}{2}$-inch barrel (10 inches overall, weighs $25\frac{1}{4}$ oz.), blued finish, simulated ivory birdshead grips. Made 1961-66.

High Standard Posse

High Standard Posse **$110**
Similar to Double-Nine—Aluminum Frame, except $3\frac{1}{2}$-inch barrel (9 inches overall, weighs $23\frac{1}{4}$ oz.), blued finish, brass-grip frame and trigger guard, walnut grips. Made from 1961 to 1966.

High Standard Sentinel

High Standard Sentinel Double Action Revolver **$100**
Solid frame, swing-out cylinder. Caliber: 22 Long Rifle. 9-shot cylinder. Barrels: 3-, 4- or 6-inch. Overall length, with 4-inch bbl., 9 inches. Weight: with 4-inch bbl., 19 oz. Fixed sights. Aluminum frame. Blued or nickel finish. Checkered grips. Made from 1955 to 1956.

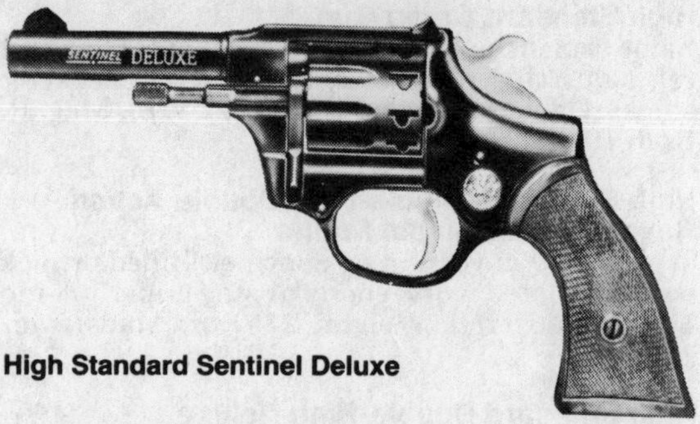

High Standard Sentinel Deluxe

High Standard Sentinel Deluxe **$120**
Same as Sentinel, except 4- or 6-inch barrels only; has wide trigger, movable rear sight, two-piece square-butt grips. Made from 1957 to 1974. *Note:* Designated Sentinel after 1971.

High Standard Sentinel Imperial **$125**
Same as Sentinel, except has onyx-black or nickel finish, two-piece checkered walnut grips, ramp front sight. Made from 1962 to 1965.

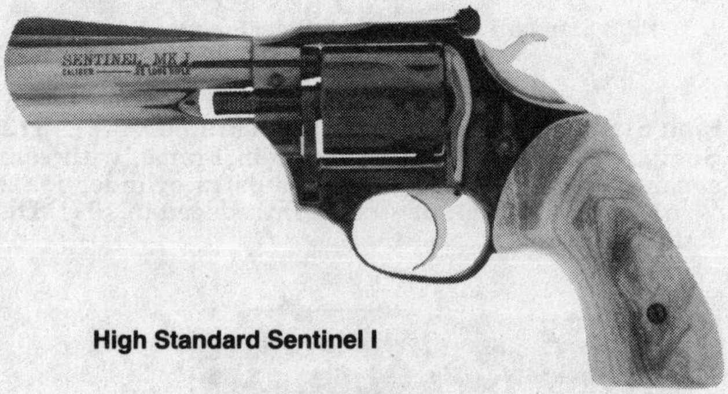

High Standard Sentinel I

High Standard Sentinel I Double Action Revolver
Steel frame. Caliber: 22 Long Rifle. 9-shot cylinder. Barrel lengths: 2-, 3-, 4-inch. $6\frac{7}{8}$ inches overall with 2-inch bbl. Weight: with 2-inch bbl., $21\frac{1}{2}$ oz. Ramp front sight, fixed or adjustable rear sight. Blued or nickel finish. Smooth walnut stocks. Made from 1974 to 1983.
With fixed sights **$135**
With adjustable sights **150**

High Standard Sentinel Mark II

High Standard Sentinel Mark II Double Action Revolver **$165**
Caliber: 357 Magnum. 6-shot cylinder. Barrel lengths: $2\frac{1}{2}$-, 4-, 6-inch. 9 inches overall with 4-inch bbl. Weight: with 4-inch bbl., 38 oz. Fixed sights. Blued finish. Walnut service or combat-style stocks. Made from 1974 to 1976.

High Standard Sentinel Mark III

High Standard Sentinel Mark III **$180**
Same as Sentinel Mark II, except has ramp front sight and adjustable rear sight. Made from 1974 to 1976.

High Standard Sentinel Mark IV
Same as Sentinel Mark I, except chambered for 22 Winchester Magnum Rimfire. Made from 1974 to 1983.

With fixed sights **$130**
With adjustable sights **145**

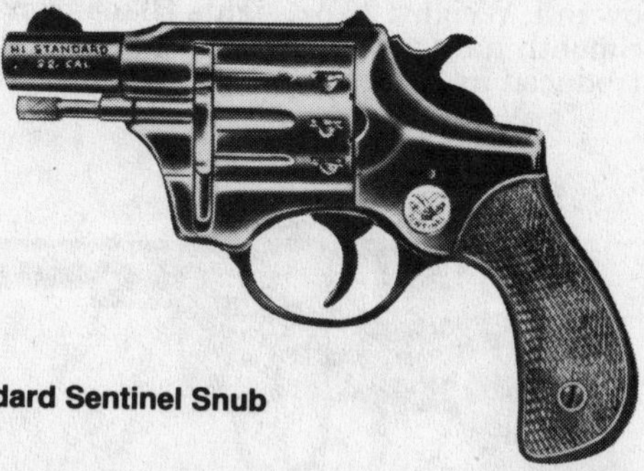

High Standard Sentinel Snub

High Standard Sentinel Snub **$135**
Same as Sentinel Deluxe, except $2\frac{3}{8}$-inch barrel ($7\frac{1}{4}$ inches overall, weighs 15 oz.), checkered birdshead-type grips. Made from 1957 to 1974.

HOPKINS & ALLEN ARMS CO.
Norwich, Connecticut

Hopkins & Allen Revolvers
See listings of comparable Harrington & Richardson and Iver Johnson models for values.

INTERARMS
Alexandria, Virginia

See also Bersa Pistol.

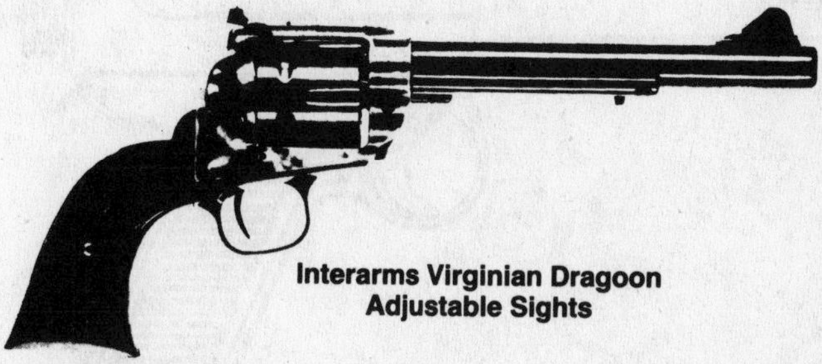

Interarms Virginian Dragoon Adjustable Sights

Interarms Virginian Dragoon Single Action Revolver
Calibers: 357 Magnum, 44 Magnum, 45 Colt. 6-shot cylinder. Barrels: 5- (not available in 44 Magnum), 6-, $7\frac{1}{2}$-, $8\frac{3}{8}$-inch (latter only in 44 Magnum model with adjustable sights). $11\frac{7}{8}$ inches overall with 6-inch barrel. Weight: with 6-inch bbl., 48 oz. Fixed sights or micrometer rear sight and ramp front sight. Blued finish with color-case-treated frame. Smooth walnut stocks. SWISSAFE base pin safety system. Manufactured by Interarms Industries Inc., Midland, Virginia. Introduced in 1977.

Standard Dragoon **$235**
Engraved Dragoon **460**
Deputy Model **220**

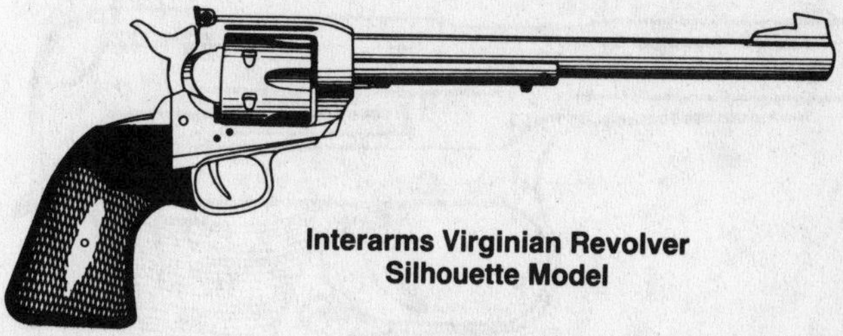

Interarms Virginian Revolver Silhouette Model

Interarms Virginian Revolver Silhouette Model . . **$325**
Same general specifications as regular model except designed in stainless steel with untapered bull barrel lengths of $7\frac{1}{2}$, $8\frac{3}{8}$ and $10\frac{1}{2}$ inches. Made from 1985 to 1986.

Interarms Virginian Single Action Revolver **$240**
See listing under Hämmerli (manufacturer).

INTRATEC U.S.A. INC.
Miami, Florida

Intratec Model TEC-9 Semiautomatic **$195**
Caliber: 9mm Luger/Parabellum. 20- or 36-round magazine. 5-inch barrel. Weight: 50 oz. Open fixed front sight, adjustable rear. Military non-glare blue finish.

Intratec Model TEC-9S Semiautomatic **$215**
Caliber: 9mm Luger/Parabellum. 36-round magazine. 5-inch threaded barrel. Weight: 51 oz. Stainless steel non-glare finish. Open, fixed front sights, adjustable rear sights. Firing-pin block safety.

JAPANESE MILITARY PISTOLS
Tokyo, Japan
Manufactured by Government plant

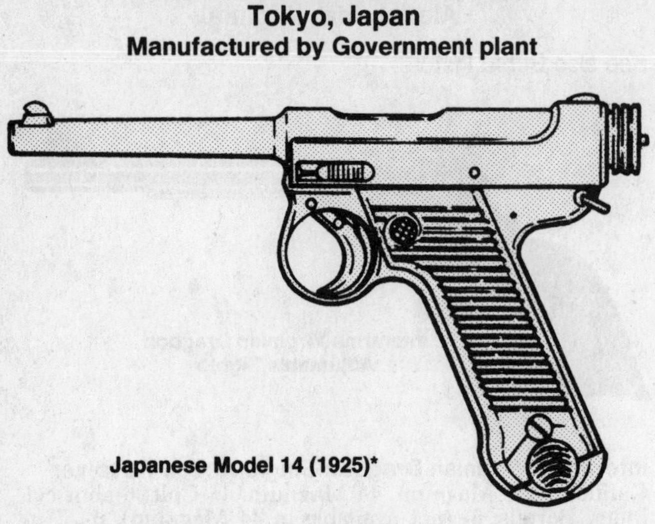

Japanese Model 14 (1925)*

Japanese Model 14 (1925) Automatic Pistol $225
Modification of the Nambu Model 1914, changes chiefly intended to simplify mass production. Either standard round trigger guard or oversized guard to permit firing while wearing glove. Caliber: 8mm Nambu. 8-shot magazine. 4¾-inch barrel. 9 inches overall. Weight: about 29 oz. Fixed sights. Blued finish. Grooved wood stocks. Introduced 1925; mfd. through WWII.

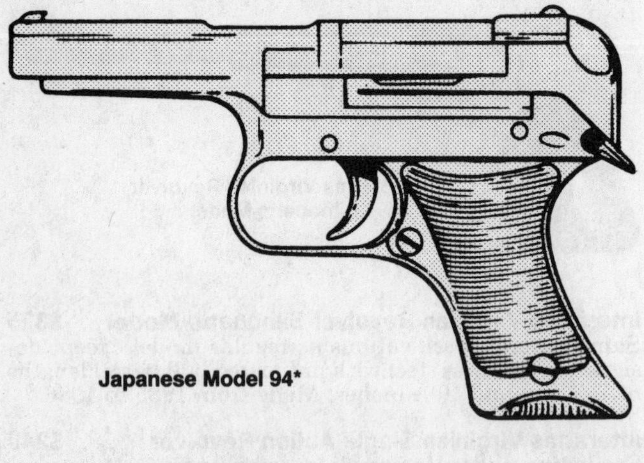

Japanese Model 94*

Japanese Model 94 (1934) Automatic Pistol $200
This weapon is of extremely poor design and construction; the sear is exposed on the left side, and the pistol can be fired by pressure on this part. Caliber: 8mm Nambu. 6-shot magazine. 3⅛-inch barrel. 7⅛ inches overall. Weight: about 27 oz. Fixed sights. Blued finish. Hard rubber or wood stocks. Introduced in 1934, principally for export to Latin American countries, production continued through WWII.

Japanese Nambu Model 1914 Automatic Pistol . $250
Original Japanese service pistol, resembles Luger in appearance and Glisenti in operation. Caliber: 8mm Nambu. 7-shot magazine. 4½-inch barrel. 9 inches overall. Weight: about 30 oz. Fixed front sight, adjustable rear sight. Blued finish. Checkered wood stocks. Made from 1914 to 1925.

IVER JOHNSON'S ARMS
Jacksonville, Arkansas

Operation of this company dates back to 1871, when Iver Johnson and Martin Bye partnered to manufacturer metallic cartridge revolvers. Johnson became the sole owner and changed the name to Iver Johnson's Arms & Cycle Works, which it was known as for almost 100 years. Modern management shortened the name, and after several owner changes, the firm was moved from Massachusetts, its original base, to Jacksonville, Arkansas. It is now a division of the American Military Arms Corporation (AMAC).

Iver Johnson 9mm DA Automatic

Iver Johnson 9mm Double Action Automatic ... $225
Caliber: 9mm. 6-round magazine. 3-inch barrel. 6.5 inches overall. Weight: 26 oz. sights Blade front, adjustable rear. Smooth hardwood grip. Blued or matte blued finish. Introduced in 1986.

Iver Johnson Model 55A

Iver Johnson Model 55A Target Double Action Revolver $75
Solid frame. Caliber: 22 Long Rifle. 8-shot cylinder. Barrel lengths: 4½-, 6-inch. 10¾ inches overall (6-inch bbl.). Weight: 30½ oz. (6-inch bbl.). Fixed sights. Blued finish. Walnut stocks. Made from 1955 to 1977. *Note:* Original model designation was 55, changed to 55A when loading gate was added in 1961.

Iver Johnson Model 57A Target

Iver Johnson Model 57A Target Double Action Revolver **$90**

Solid frame. Caliber: 22 Long Rifle. 8-shot cylinder. Barrel lengths: $4\frac{1}{2}$-, 6-inch. $10\frac{3}{4}$ inches overall (6-inch bbl.). Weight: $30\frac{1}{2}$ oz., 6-inch bbl. Adjustable sights. Blued finish. Walnut stocks. Made from 1956 to 1975. *Note:* Original model designation was 57, changed to 57A when loading gate was added in 1961.

Iver Johnson Model 66 Trailsman

Iver Johnson Model 66 Trailsman Double Action Revolver **$105**

Hinged frame. Rebounding hammer. Caliber: 22 Long Rifle. 8-shot cylinder. 6-inch barrel. 11 inches overall. Weight: 34 oz. Adjustable sights. Blued finish. Walnut stocks. Made from 1958 to 1975.

Iver Johnson Model 67 Viking

Iver Johnson Model 67 Viking Double Action Revolver **$120**

Hinged frame. Caliber: 22 Long Rifle. 8-shot cylinder. Barrel lengths: $4\frac{1}{2}$- and 6-inch. 11 inches overall with 6-inch bbl. Weight: with 6-inch bbl., 34 oz. Adjustable sights. Walnut stocks with thumb rest. Made from 1964 to 1975.

Iver Johnson Model 67S Viking Snub

Iver Johnson Model 67S Viking Snub Double Action Revolver **$125**

Hinged frame. Calibers: 22 Long Rifle, 32 S&W Short and Long, 38 S&W. 8-shot cylinder in 22; 5-shot in 32 and 38 calibers. $2\frac{3}{4}$-inch barrel. Weight: 25 oz. Adjustable sights. Tenite grips. Made from 1964 to 1975.

Iver Johnson Model 1900 Double Action Revolver

Iver Johnson Model 1900 Double Action Revolver **$100**

Solid frame. Calibers: 22 Long Rifle, 32 S&W, 32 S&W Long, 38 S&W. 7-shot cylinder (22 cal.), 6-shot (32 S&W), 5-shot (32 S&W Long, 38 S&W). Barrel lengths: $2\frac{1}{2}$-, $4\frac{1}{2}$- and 6-inch. Weight: 12 oz., 32 S&W with $2\frac{1}{2}$-inch bbl. Fixed sights. Blued or nickel finish. Hard rubber stocks. Made from 1900 to 1947.

Iver Johnson Model 1900 Target Double Action Revolver **$125**

Solid frame. Caliber: 22 Long Rifle, 7-shot cylinder. Barrel lengths: 6- and $9\frac{1}{2}$-inch. Fixed sights. Blued finish. Checkered walnut stocks. This earlier model does not have counterbored chambers as in the Target Sealed 8. Made from 1925 to 1942.

Iver Johnson American Bulldog

Iver Johnson American Bulldog Double Action Revolver
Solid frame. Calibers: 22 Long Rifle, 22 Win. Mag. R.F., 38 Special. 6-shot cylinder in 22, 5-shot in 38. Barrel lengths: $2\frac{1}{2}$-, 4-inch. 9 inches overall with 4-inch bbl. Weight: with 4-inch bbl., 30 oz. Adjustable sights. Blued or nickel finish. Plastic stocks. Made from 1974 to 1976.
38 Special **$85**
Other calibers **75**

Iver Johnson Armsworth Model 855 Single Action Revolver $125
Hinged frame. Caliber: 22 Long Rifle. 8-shot cylinder. Barrel length: 6 inches. Overall length: $10\frac{3}{4}$ inches. Weight: 30 oz. Adjustable sights. Blued finish. Checkered walnut one-piece grip. Adjustable finger rest. Made from 1955 to 1957.

Iver Johnson Cadet Double Action Revolver
Solid frame. Calibers: 22 Long Rifle, 22 Win. Mag. R.F., 32 S&W Long, 38 S&W, 38 Special. 6- or 8-shot cylinder in 22, 5-shot in other calibers. $2\frac{1}{2}$-inch barrel. 7 inches overall. Weight: 22 oz. Fixed sights. Blued finish; nickel finish also available in 32 and 38 Special models. Plastic stocks. Made from 1955 to 1977. *Note:* Loading gate added in 1961; 22 cylinder capacity changed from 8 to 6 rounds in 1975.
38 Special **$110**
Other calibers **90**

Iver Johnson Cattleman Single Action Revolver
Calibers: 357 Magnum, 44 Magnum, 45 Colt. 6-shot cylinder. Barrel lengths: $4\frac{3}{4}$-, $5\frac{1}{2}$- (not available in 44), 6- (44 only), $7\frac{1}{4}$-inch. Weight: about 41 oz. Fixed sights. Blued barrel and cylinder, color-casehardened frame, brass grip frame. One-piece walnut stock. Made by Aldo Uberti, Brescia, Italy, from 1973 to 1978.
44 Magnum **$180**
Other calibers **170**

Iver Johnson Cattleman Buckhorn SA Revolver
Same as standard Cattleman, except has adjustable rear sight and ramp front sight. Barrels: $4\frac{3}{4}$- (44 only), $5\frac{3}{4}$- (not available in 44), 6- (44 only), $7\frac{1}{2}$-, 12-inch. Weight: almost 44 oz. Made from 1973 to 1978.
357 Magnum or 45 Colt, 12-inch barrel **$195**
357 Magnum or 45 Colt, other barrels **150**
44 Magnum, 12-inch barrel **225**
44 Magnum, other barrels **200**

Iver Johnson Cattleman Buntline SA Revolver
Same as Cattleman Buckhorn, except has 18-inch barrel, walnut shoulder stock with brass fittings. Weight: about 56 oz. Made from 1973 to 1978.
44 Magnum **$375**
Other calibers **345**

Iver Johnson Cattleman

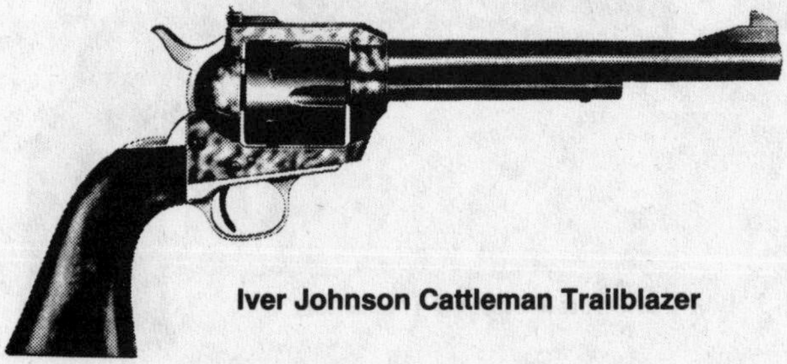

Iver Johnson Cattleman Trailblazer

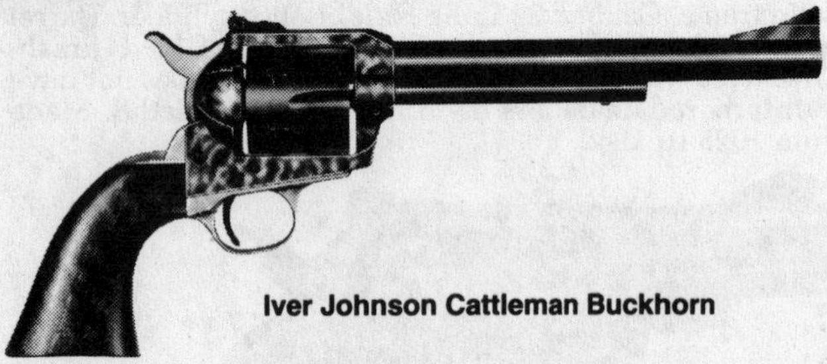

Iver Johnson Cattleman Buckhorn

Iver Johnson Cattleman Buntline

> *Note:* For engraved Cattleman revolvers, add $450 to values indicated.

Iver Johnson Cattleman Trailblazer $175
Similar to Cattleman Buckhorn, except 22 caliber; has interchangeable 22 Long Rifle and 22 Win. Mag. R.F. cylinders, $5\frac{1}{2}$- or $6\frac{1}{2}$-inch barrel. Weight: about 40 oz. Made from 1973 to 1978.

Iver Johnson Champion

Iver Johnson Champion 22 Target Single Action Revolver $140
Hinged frame. Caliber: 22 Long Rifle. 8-shot cylinder. Counterbored chambers as in Sealed 8 models. 6-inch barrel. $10\frac{3}{4}$ inches overall. Weight: 28 oz. Adjustable target sights. Blued finish. Checkered walnut stocks, adjustable finger rest. Made from 1938 to 1948.

Iver Johnson Deluxe Target

Iver Johnson Deluxe Target **$90**
Same as Sportsman, except has adjustable sights. Made from 1975 to 1976.

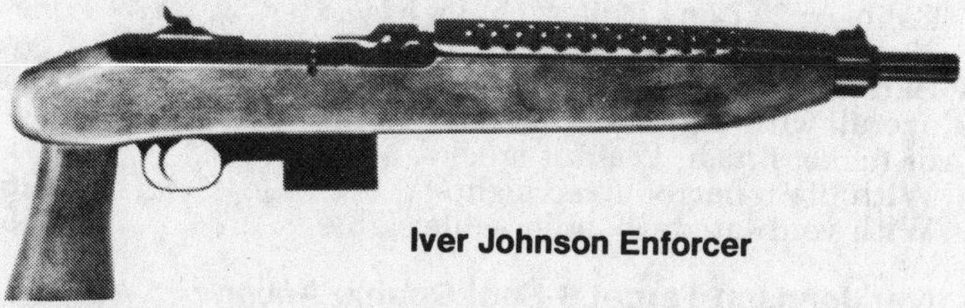

Iver Johnson Enforcer

Iver Johnson Enforcer **$250**
Caliber: 30. 5-, 15-, or 30-round magazine. Semiautomatic. $9\frac{1}{2}$ inch barrel. Weight: $5\frac{1}{2}$ pounds. Adjustable sights. Walnut stock. Made mid-1980's to date.

Iver Johnson PP30 Super Enforcer Automatic Pistol **$210**
Caliber: 30 US Carbine. 15- or 30-shot magazine. $9\frac{1}{2}$-inch barrel. 17 inches overall. Weight: 4 pounds. Adjustable peer rear sight, blade front. American walnut stock. Introduced 1984.

Iver Johnson Pony

Iver Johnson Pony Automatic Pistol **$195**
Caliber: 380 Automatic. 6-shot magazine. 3.1-inch barrel. 6.1 inches overall. Blue, matte or nickel finish. Weight: 20 oz. Wooden grips. Smallest of the locked breech automatics. Introduced in 1982. Discontinued.

Iver Johnson Protector Sealed 8

Iver Johnson Protector Sealed 8 Double Action Revolver **$125**
Hinged frame. Caliber: 22 Long Rifle. 8-shot cylinder. $2\frac{1}{2}$-inch barrel. $7\frac{1}{4}$ inches overall. Weight: 20 oz. Fixed sights. Blued finish. Checkered walnut stocks. Made from 1933 to 1949.

Iver Johnson Rookie

Iver Johnson Rookie Double Action Revolver **$75**
Solid frame. Caliber: 38 Special. 5-shot cylinder. 4-inch barrel. 9-inches overall. Weight: 30 oz. Fixed sights. Blued or nickel finish. Plastic stocks. Made from 1975 to 1977.

Iver Johnson Safety Hammer

Iver Johnson Safety Hammer Double Action Revolver **$100**
Hinged frame. Calibers: 22 Long Rifle, 32 S&W, 32 S&W Long, 38 S&W. 7-shot cylinder (22 cal.), 6-shot (32 S&W Long), 5-shot (32 S&W, 38 S&W). Barrel lengths: 2, 3, $3\frac{1}{4}$, 4, 5 or 6 inches. Weight with 4-inch bbl.: 15 oz., 22, 32 S&W; $19\frac{1}{2}$ oz., 32 S&W Long; 19 oz., 38 S&W. Fixed sights. Blued or nickel finish. Hard rubber stocks, round butt; square butt, rubber and walnut stocks available. *Note:* 32 S&W Long and 38 S&W models built on heavy frame. Made from 1892 to 1950.

Iver Johnson Safety Hammerless

Iver Johnson Safety Hammerless Double Action Revolver **$115**
Hinged frame. Calibers: 22 Long Rifle, 32 S&W, 32 S&W Long, 38 S&W. 7-shot cylinder (22 cal.), 6-shot (32 S&W Long), 5-shot (32 S&W, 38 S&W). Barrel lengths: 2, 3, $3\frac{1}{4}$, 4, 5 or 6 inches. Weight with 4-inch bbl.: 15 oz., 22, 32 S&W; $20\frac{1}{2}$ oz., 32 S&W Long; 20 oz., 38 S&W. Fixed sights. Blued or nickel finish. Hard rubber stocks, round butt. Square butt, rubber and walnut stocks available. *Note:* 32 S&W Long & 38 S&W models built on heavy frame. Made from 1895 to 1950.

Iver Johnson Sidewinder Double Action Revolver **$105**
Solid frame. Caliber: 22 Long Rifle. 6- or 8-shot cylinder. Barrel lengths: $4\frac{3}{4}$-, 6-inch. $11\frac{1}{4}$ inches overall with 6-inch bbl. Weight: with 6-inch bbl., 31 oz. Fixed sights. Blued or nickel finish; also available with color-casehardened frame. Plastic "staghorn" stocks; model with casehardened frame has walnut stocks. Made from 1961 to date. *Note:* Cylinder capacity changed from 8 to 6 rounds in 1975.

Iver Johnson Sidewinder "S" **$115**
Same as Sidewinder, except has interchangeable cylinders in 22 Long Rifle and 22 Win. Mag. R.F., adjustable sights. Made from 1974 to date.

Iver Johnson Sportsman Double Action Revolver **$90**
Solid frame. Caliber: 22 Long Rifle. 6-shot cylinder. Barrel lengths: $4\frac{3}{4}$-, 6-inch. $10\frac{3}{4}$ inches overall with 6-inch bbl. Weight: with 6-inch bbl., $30\frac{1}{2}$ oz. Fixed sights. Blued finish. Plastic stocks. Made from 1974 to 1976.

Iver Johnson Supershot 9-Shot Double Action Revolver **$115**
Same as Supershot Sealed 8, except this model has nine chambers, not counterbored. Made from 1929 to 1949.

Iver Johnson Supershot 22 Double Action Revolver **$120**
Hinged frame. Caliber: 22 Long Rifle. 7-shot cylinder. 6-inch barrel. Fixed sights. Blued finish. Checkered walnut stocks. This earlier model does not have counterbored chambers as in the Supershot Sealed 8. Made from 1929 to 1949.

Iver Johnson Supershot Model 844 Double Action Revolver **$95**
Hinged frame. Caliber: 22 Long Rifle. 8-shot cylinder. Barrel lengths: $4\frac{1}{2}$- or 6-inch. Overall length, with $4\frac{1}{2}$-inch bbl., $9\frac{1}{4}$ inches. Weight: with $4\frac{1}{2}$-inch bbl., 27 oz. Adjustable sights. Blued finish. Checkered walnut one-piece grip. Made from 1955 to 1956.

Iver Johnson Supershot Sealed 8

Iver Johnson Supershot Sealed 8 Double Action Revolver **$150**
Hinged frame. Caliber: 22 Long Rifle. 8-shot cylinder. 6-inch barrel. $10\frac{3}{4}$ inches overall. Weight: 24 oz. Adjustable target sights. Blued finish. Checkered walnut stocks. Postwar model does not have adjustable finger rest as earlier version. Made from 1931 to 1957.

Iver Johnson Swing Out

Iver Johnson Swing Out Double Action Revolver
Calibers: 22 Long Rifle, 22 Win. Mag. R.F., 32 S&W Long, 38 Special. 6-shot cylinder in 22, 5-shot in 32 and 38. Barrels: plain, 2-, 3-, 4-inch; vent rib, 4-, 6-inch. $8\frac{3}{4}$ inches overall with 4-inch bbl. Fixed or adjustable sights. Blued or nickel finish. Walnut stocks. Made in 1977.
With plain barrel, fixed sights **$125**
With ventilated rib, adjustable sights **155**

Iver Johnson Target 9-Shot Double Action Revolver **$105**
Same as Target Sealed 8, except this model has nine chambers, not counterbored. Made from 1929 to 1946.

Iver Johnson Target Sealed 8

Iver Johnson Target Sealed 8 Double Action Revolver **$125**
Solid frame. Caliber: 22 Long Rifle. 8-shot cylinder. Barrel lengths: 6- and 10-inch. $10\frac{3}{4}$ inches overall with 6-inch barrel. Weight: 24 oz. with 6-inch bbl. Fixed sights. Blued finish. Checkered walnut stocks. Made from 1931 to 1957.

Iver Johnson Model TP

Iver Johnson Model TP Double Action Automatic Pistol **$135**
Calibers: 22 Long Rifle, 25 ACP. 7-shot magazine. 2.85-inch barrel. 5.39 inches overall. Blue finish. Weight: 14.46 oz. Introduced in 1982. Discontinued.

Iver Johnson Model TP22 Double Action Automatic Pocket Pistol **$125**
Caliber: 22 LR. 7-round magazine. 3-inch barrel. $5\frac{1}{2}$ inches overall. Weight: 12 oz. Black plastic grips and blued finish. Currently in production.

Iver Johnson Model TP25 Double Action Automatic Pocket Pistol **$130**
Same general specifications as the Model TP22, except made in 25 ACP caliber. Currently in production.

Iver Johnson Trailsman Automatic Pistol
Caliber: 22 LR. 10-shot magazine. $4\frac{1}{2}$- or 6-inch barrel. $8\frac{3}{4}$ inches overall with $4\frac{1}{2}$-inch barrel. Weight: 46 oz. Fixed target-type sights. Checkered composition grips. Made from 1984 to date.

Standard Model **$140**
Deluxe Model **160**

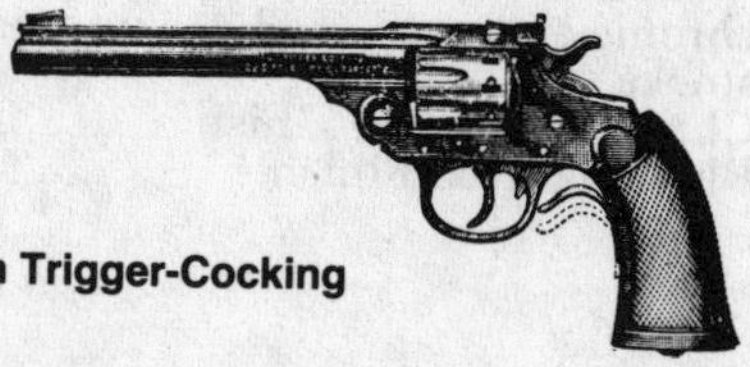
Iver Johnson Trigger-Cocking

Iver Johnson Trigger-Cocking Single Action Target Revolver **$145**
Hinged frame. First pull on trigger cocks hammer, second pull releases hammer. Caliber: 22 Long Rifle. 8-shot cylinder, counterbored chambers. 6-inch barrel. $10\frac{3}{4}$ inches overall. Weight: 24 oz. Adjustable target sights. Blued finish. Checkered walnut stocks. Made from 1940 to 1947.

LAHTI PISTOLS

Mfd. by Husqvarna Vapenfabriks A. B. Huskvarna, Sweden, and Valtion Kivaar Tedhas ("VKT") Jyväskyla, Finland

Lahti, Swedish Model

Lahti Automatic Pistol
Caliber: 9mm Luger. 8-shot magazine. $4\frac{3}{4}$-inch barrel. Weight: about 46 oz. Fixed sights. Blued finish. Plastic stocks. Specifications given are those of the Swedish Model 40 but also apply in general to the Finnish Model L-35 which differs only slightly. A considerable number of

Lahti Automatic Pistol (cont.)
Swedish Lahti pistols were imported and sold in the U.S. a few years ago; the Finnish Model, which is somewhat better made, is a rather rare modern pistol. Finnish Model L-35 adopted in 1935. Swedish Model 40 adopted in 1940, manufactured through 1944.

Finnish Model **$575**
Swedish Model **245**

L.A.R. MANUFACTURING, INC.

West Jordan, Utah

L.A.R. Mark I Grizzly Win. Mag.

L.A.R. Mark I Grizzly Win. Mag. Automatic Pistol
Calibers: 357 Mag., 45 ACP, 45 Win. Mag. 7-shot magazine. $6\frac{1}{2}$-inch barrel. $10\frac{1}{2}$ inches overall. Weight: 48 oz. Fully adjustable sights. Checkered rubber combat-style grips. Blued finish. Made from 1983 to date. 8-inch and 10-inch barrels made from 1987 to date.

357 Mag. ($6\frac{1}{2}''$ barrel) **$525**
45 Win. Mag.($6\frac{1}{2}''$ barrel) **505**
8-inch barrel **940**
10-inch barrel **975**

LIGNOSE PISTOLS

Suhl, Germany

Aktien-Gesellschaft "Lignose" Abteilung

The following Lignose pistols were manufactured from 1920 to the mid-1930s. They were also marketed under the Bergmann name.

Lignose Model 2 Pocket Auto Pistol **$300**
Conventional Browning type. Same general specifications as Einhand Model 2A, but lacks the one-hand operation feature.

Lignose Einhand Model 2A*

Lignose Einhand Model 2A Pocket Auto Pistol . . $200
As the name implies, this pistol is designed for one-hand operation; pressure on a "trigger" at the front of the guard retracts the slide. Caliber: 25 Automatic (6.35mm). 6-shot magazine. 2-inch barrel. 4$^{3}/_{4}$ inches overall. Weight: about 14 oz. Blued finish. Hard rubber stocks.

Lignose Einhand Model 3A

Lignose Einhand Model 3A Pocket Auto Pistol . . $225
Same as the Model 2A except has longer grip, 9-shot magazine, weighs about 16 oz.

LLAMA HANDGUNS
Vitoria, Spain
Manufactured by Gabilondo y Cia

Llama Model IIIA

Llama Model IIIA Automatic Pistol $190
Caliber: 380 Automatic. 7-shot magazine. 3$^{11}/_{16}$-inch barrel. 6$^{1}/_{2}$ inches overall. Weight: 23 oz. Adjustable target sights. Blued finish. Plastic stocks. Made 1951 to date.

Llama Model IIIA Deluxe
Blue Engraved

Llama Model IIIA Deluxe
Chrome Engraved

Llama Models IIIA, XA, XV Deluxe
Same as standard Model IIIA, XA and XV, except finish—chrome engraved or blue engraved—and simulated pearl stocks.
Chrome-engraved Finish **$290**
Blue-engraved Finish **275**

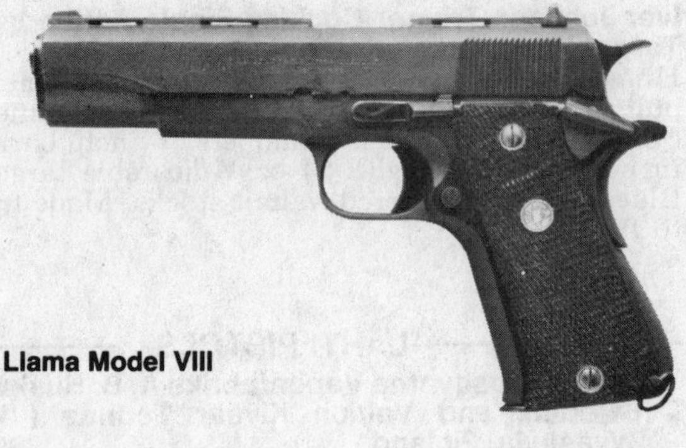
Llama Model VIII

Llama Model VIII Automatic Pistol $230
Caliber: 38 Super. 9-shot magazine. 5-inch barrel. 8$^{1}/_{2}$ inches overall. Weight: 40 oz. Fixed sights. Blued finish. Wood stocks. Made from 1952 to date.

Llama Models VIII, IXA, XI Deluxe
Same as standard Models VIII, IXA and XI, except finish—chrome engraved or blue engraved—and simulated pearl stocks.
Chrome-engraved Finish **$270**
Blue-engraved Finish **240**

Llama Model IXA Automatic Pistol $230
Same as Model VIII, except caliber 45 Automatic, 7-shot magazine.

Llama Model XA Automatic Pistol $225
Same as Model IIIA, except caliber 32 Automatic, 8-shot magazine.

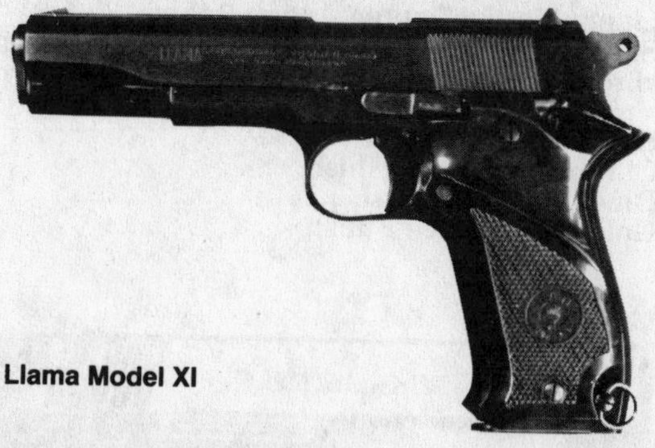

Llama Model XI

Llama Model XI Automatic Pistol **$230**
Same as Model VIII, except caliber 9mm Luger.

Llama Model XV Automatic Pistol **$190**
Same as Model XA, except caliber 22 Long Rifle.

Llama Models BE-IIIA, BE-XA, BE-XV **$290**
Same as Models IIIA, XA and XV, except blue-engraved finish. Introduced in 1977.

Llama Models BE-VIII, BE-IXA, BE-XI Deluxe . . . **$290**
Same as Models VIII, IXA and XI, except blue-engraved finish. Introduced in 1977.

Llama Models C-IIIA, C-XA, C-XV **$200**
Same as Models IIIA, XA and XV, except in satin-chrome.

Llama Model C-XI

Llama Models C-VIII, C-IXA, C-XI **$275**
Same as Models VIII, IXA and XI, except in satin-chrome.

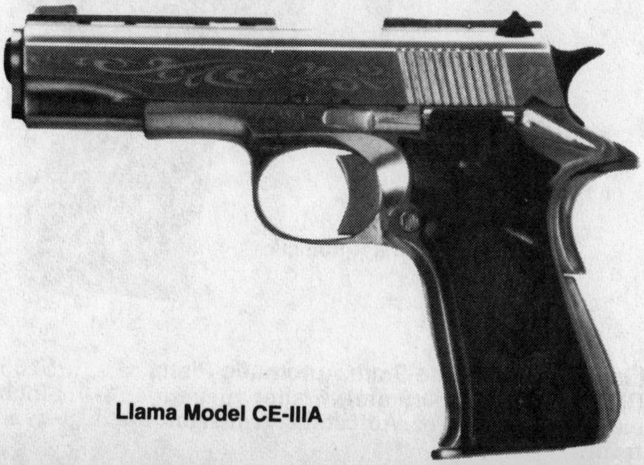

Llama Model CE-IIIA

Llama Models CE-IIIA, CE-XA, CE-XV **$300**
Same as Models IIIA, XA and XV, except chrome-engraved finish. Introduced in 1977.

Llama Models CE-VIII, CE-IXA, CE-XI **$290**
Same as Models VIII, IXA and XI, except chrome-engraved finish. Introduced in 1977.

Llama Comanche I

Llama Comanche I Double Action Revolver **$185**
Same general specifications as Martial 22. Introduced in 1977.

Llama Comanche II **$190**
Same general specifications as Martial 38. Introduced in 1977.

Llama Comanche III Double Action Revolver . . . **$200**
Caliber: 357 Magnum. 6-shot cylinder. 4-inch barrel. 9¼ inches overall. Weight: 36 oz. Adjustable rear sight, ramp front sight. Blued finish. Checkered walnut stocks. Made from 1975 to date. *Note:* Prior to 1977, this model was designated "Comanche."

Llama Comanche III Chrome

Llama Comanche III Chrome **$255**
Same general specifications as Comanche III, except has satin chrome finish. 4- or 6-inch barrels. Made from 1979 to date.

Llama Model G-IIIA Deluxe **$975**
Same as Model IIIA, except gold damascened, has simulated pearl stocks.

Llama Large-Frame 45

Llama Large-Frame Automatic Pistol $225
Caliber: 45 Auto. 7-shot magazine. 5-inch barrel. Weight: 2 lbs. 8 oz. Adjustable rear sight, Patridge-type front. Blued finish. Walnut grips. Made from 1984 to date.

Llama Large-Frame Satin Chrome Finish Automatic Pistol $235
Same general specifications as standard model except satin chrome finish and teakwood grips.

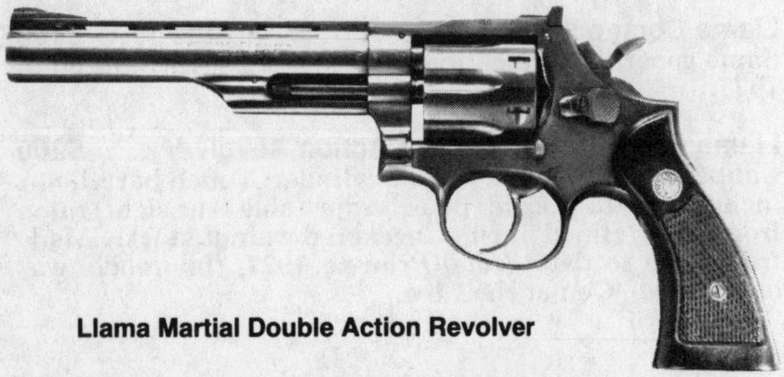

Llama Martial Double Action Revolver

Llama Martial Deluxe, Gold Damascened

Llama Martial Double Action Revolver. $175
Calibers: 22 Long Rifle, 38 Special. 6-shot cylinder. Barrel lengths: 4-inch (38 Special only), 6-inch. 11¼ inches overall with 6-inch barrel. Weight: with 6-inch bbl., about 36 oz. Target sights. Blued finish. Checkered walnut stocks. Made from 1969 to 1976.

Llama Martial Double Action Deluxe
Same as standard Martial, except finish—satin chrome, chrome engraved, blue engraved, gold damascened; has simulated pearl stocks.

Satin-chrome Finish	$ 250
Chrome-engraved Finish	275
Blue-engraved Finish	265
Gold-damascened Finish	1250

Llama Omni

Llama Omni 9mm Double Action Automatic $325
Same general specifications as 45 Omni except chambered for 9mm, with 13-shot magazine. Discontinued 1986.

Llama Omni 45 Double Action Automatic Pistol . $350
Caliber: 45 Auto. 7-shot magazine. 4¼-inch barrel. 7¾ inches overall. Weight: 40 oz. Adjustable rear sight, ramp front sight. Highly polished deep blue finish. Made from 1984 to 1986.

Llama Single Action Automatic Pistol $325
Calibers: 38 Super, 9mm, 45 Auto. 9-shot magazine (7-shot for 45 Auto). 5-inch barrel. 8½ inches overall. Weight: 2 lbs. 8 oz. Introduced in 1981.

Llama Small-Frame Automatic

Llama Small-Frame 9mm Automatic Pistol $185
Caliber: 380 Auto (9mm). 7-shot magazine. 3$^{11}/_{16}$-inch barrel. Weight: 23 oz. Adjustable rear sight, Patridge-type front.

Llama Small-Frame Automatic Pistol **$165**
Same general specifications as 9mm Small-Frame, except chambered for 22 RF and has 8-shot magazine.

Llama Small-Frame Satin Chrome Finish Automatic Pistol **$200**
Same general specifications as above small-frame automatics except finished in satin chrome.

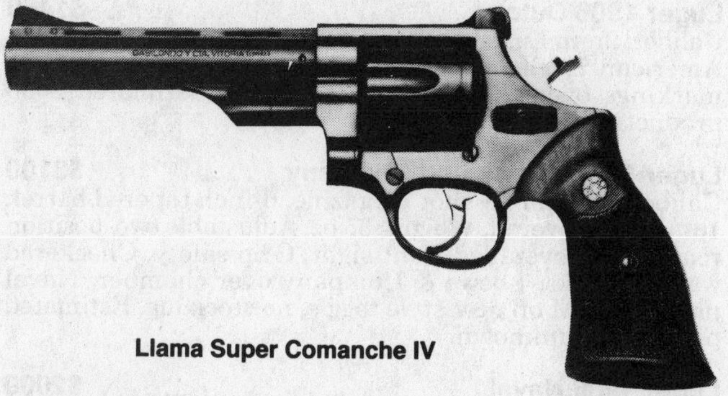

Llama Super Comanche IV

Llama Super Comanche IV Double Action Revolver **$260**
Caliber: 44 Magnum. 6-shot cylinder. 6-inch barrel. $11\frac{3}{4}$ inches overall. Weight: 3 lbs. 2 oz. Adjustable rear sight, ramp front sight. Polished deep blue finish. Checkered walnut grips. Made from 1980 to date.

Llama Super Comanche V DA Revolver **$250**
Caliber: 357 Mag. 6-shot cylinder. 4-, 6- or $8\frac{1}{2}$-inch barrel. Weight: 3 pounds. Rear click adjustable sight, ramped blade front sight.

LUGER PISTOLS

GERMANY and SWITZERLAND

Mfd. by Deutsche Waffenund Munitionsfabriken (DWM), Berlin, Germany; also by Königlich Gewehrfabrik Erfurt, Heinrich Krieghoff Waffenfabrik, Mauser-Werke, Simson & Co., Vickers Ltd., Waffenfabrik, Bern.

Luger (Parabellum) Automatic Pistol
Lugers were made in two calibers: 7.65 mm and 9 mm. Generally, Lugers manufactured prior to 1908 have a flat mainspring, and a number of other parts differ from later models. Early pistols have grip safety (not found on later production, except for export to Switzerland), some pre-World War I models lack the shoulder stock lug found on most Lugers. German Service Lugers bear a year stamp on the receiver, not found on the commercial models, which are also better finished. Pistols made for export to the U.S. were generally stamped with an American Eagle on receiver or breechblock; those imported by A. F. Stoeger, Inc. after World War I bear that firm's name. Other variations are as detailed in the listings below. Made from 1900 to 1942; production resumed in 1970 by Mauser. *See also* Mauser and Stoeger listings.

Luger 1900
U.S. Army Pistol

Luger 1900 American Eagle **$995**
Caliber: 7.65mm. 8-shot magazine. Thin, $4\frac{3}{4}$-inch long, tapered barrel. $9\frac{1}{2}$ inches overall . Weight: 32 oz. Fixed rear sight, dovetailed front sight. Grip safety. Checkered walnut grips. Early-style toggle, narrow trigger, wide guard, no stock lug. American Eagle over chamber. Estimated 8000 production.

Luger 1900 Commercial **$1395**
Same specifications as Luger 1900 American Eagle, except DWM on early-style toggle, no chamber markings. Estimated 8000 production.

Luger 1900 Swiss **$1150**
Same specifications as Luger 1900 American Eagle, except Swiss cross in sunburst over chamber. Estimated 9000 production.

Luger 1902 American Eagle **$2800**
Caliber: 9mm Luger. 8-shot magazine. 4-inch, heavy tapered barrel. $8\frac{3}{4}$ inches overall. Weight: 30 oz. Fixed rear sight, dovetailed front sight. Grip safety. Checkered walnut stocks. American Eagle over chamber, DWM on early-style toggle, narrow trigger, wide guard, no stock lug. Estimated 700 production.

Luger 1902 Carbine **$6100**
Caliber: 7.65mm. 8-shot magazine. $11\frac{3}{4}$-inch tapered barrel. $16\frac{1}{2}$ inches overall. Weight: 46 oz. Adjustable 4-position rear sight, long ramp front sight. Grip safety. Checkered walnut stocks and forearm. DWM on early-style toggle, narrow trigger, wide guard, no chamber markings, stock lug. Estimated 3200 production.

Luger 1902 Cartridge Counter **$7500**
Caliber: 9mm Luger. 8-shot magazine. Heavy, tapered 4-inch barrel. $8\frac{3}{4}$ inches overall. Weight: 30 oz. Fixed rear sight, dovetailed front sight. Grip safety. Checkered walnut stocks. DWM on dished toggle with lock, American Eagle over chamber when marked; no stock lug. Estimated production unknown.

Luger 1902 Commercial **$3000**
Same basic specifications as Luger 1902 Cartridge Counter, except DWM on early-style toggle, narrow trigger, wide guard, no chamber markings, no stock lug. Estimated 400 production.

Luger 1903 American Eagle **$5500**
Same basic specifications as Luger 1902 Cartridge Counter, except American Eagle over chamber, DWM on early-style toggle, narrow trigger, wide guard, no stock lug. Estimated 700 production.

Luger 1904 Naval (Reworked) **$6500**
Caliber: 9mm Luger. 8-shot magazine. Barrel length altered to 4 inches. 8³/₄ inches overall. Weight: 30 oz. Adjustable two-position rear sight, dovetailed front sight. Thumb lever safety. Checkered walnut stocks. Heavy tapered barrel. DWM on new-style toggle with lock, 1902 over chamber. With or without grip safety and stock lug. Estimated 800 production.

Luger 1904 GL "Baby"

Luger 1904 GL "Baby" **$125,000**
Caliber: 9mm Luger. 7-shot magazine. 3¹/₄-inch barrel. 7³/₄ inches overall. Weight: approx. 20 oz. Serial number 10077B. "GL" marked on rear of toggle. Georg Luger's personal sidearm. Only one made in 1904.

Luger 1906 (11.35) **$45,000**
Caliber: 45 ACP. 6-shot magazine. 5-inch barrel. 9³/₄ inches overall. Weight: 36 oz. Fixed rear sight, dovetailed front sight. Grip safety. Checkered walnut stocks. GL monogram on rear toggle link, larger frame with altered trigger guard and trigger, no proofs, no markings over chamber. No stock lug. Estimated production 2.

Luger 1906 American Eagle (7.65) **$1400**
Caliber: 7.65mm. 8-shot magazine. Thin, 4³/₄-inch, tapered barrel. 9¹/₂ inches overall. Weight: 32 oz. Fixed rear sight, dovetailed front sight. Grip safety. Checkered walnut stocks. DWM on new-style toggle, American Eagle over chamber; no stock lug. Estimated 8000 production.

Luger 1906 American Eagle (9mm) **$2100**
Same basic specifications as the 7.65mm 1906, except in 9mm Luger with 4-inch barrel, 8³/₄ inches overall and weight of 30 ounces. Estimated 3500 production.

Luger 1906 Bern (7.65mm) **$750**
Same basic specifications as the 7.65mm 1906 American Eagle, except checkered walnut stocks with 3/8-inch borders, Swiss Cross on new-style toggle, Swiss proofs, no markings over chamber, no stock lug. Estimated 17,874 production.

Luger 1906 Brazilian (7.65mm) **$1200**
Same general specifications as the 7.65mm 1906 American Eagle, except with Brazilian proofs, no markings over chamber, no stock lug. Estimated 4500 production.

Luger 1906 Brazilian (9mm) **$1750**
Same basic specifications as the 9mm 1906 American Eagle, except with Brazilian proofs, no markings over chamber, no stock lug. Estimated production unknown.

Luger 1906 Commercial
Calibers: 7.65mm, 9mm. Same specifications as the 1906 American Eagle versions, above, except no chamber markings, no stock lug. Estimated production: 6000 (7.65mm); 3500 (9mm).
7.65mm **$1200**
9mm **1350**

Luger 1906 Dutch **$1450**
Caliber: 9mm Luger. Same specifications as the 9mm 1906 American Eagle, except tapered barrel with proofs, no markings over chamber, no stock lug. Estimated 3000 production.

Luger 1906 Loewe and Company **$3100**
Caliber: 7.65mm. 8-shot magazine. 6-inch tapered barrel. 10³/₄ inches overall. Weight: 35 oz. Adjustable two-position rear sight, dovetailed front sight. Grip safety. Checkered walnut stocks. Loewe & Company over chamber, Naval proofs, DWM on new-style toggle, no stock lug. Estimated production unknown.

Luger 1906 Naval **$2000**
Caliber: 9mm Luger. 8-shot magazine. 6-inch tapered barrel. 10³/₄ inches overall. Weight: 35 oz. Adjustable two-position rear sight, dovetailed front sight. Grip safety and thumb safety with lower marking (1st issue), higher marking (2nd issue). Checkered walnut stocks. No chamber markings, DWM on new-style toggle without lock; with stock lug. Estimated production: 8000 (1st issue); 12,000 (2nd issue).

Luger 1906 Naval Commercial **$2500**
Same basic specifications as the 1906 Naval, except lower marking on thumb safety, no chamber markings, DWM on new-style toggle, with stock lug and commercial proofs. Estimated 3000 production.

Luger 1906 Portuguese Army **$950**
Same specifications as the 7.65mm 1906 American Eagle, except with Portuguese proofs, crown and crest over chamber; no stock lug. Estimated 3500 production.

Luger 1906 Portuguese Naval **$7500**
Same specifications as the 9mm 1906 American Eagle, except with Portuguese proofs, crown and anchor over chamber; no stock lug. Estimated production unknown.

Luger 1906 Russian **$10,000**
Same general specifications as the 9mm 1906 American Eagle, except thumb safety has markings concealed in up position, DWM on new-style toggle, DWM barrel proofs, crossed rifles over chamber. Est. prod. unknown.

Luger 1906 Swiss **$2400**
Same general specifications as the 7.65mm 1906 American Eagle Luger, except Swiss Cross in sunburst over chamber, no stock lug. Estimated 10,300 production.

Luger 1906 Swiss (Rework) **$3000**
Same basic specifications as the 7.65mm 1906 Swiss, except in barrel lengths of 3⁵/₈, 4 and 4³/₄ inches, overall length 8³/₈ inches and up, weight 32 oz. and up. DWM on new-style toggle, barrel with serial number and proof marks, Swiss Cross in sunburst or shield over chamber, no stock lug. Estimated production unknown.

Luger 1906 Swiss Police **$2400**
Same general specifications as the 7.65mm 1906 Swiss, except DWM on new-style toggle, Swiss Cross in matted field over chamber, no stock lug. Estimated 10,300 production.

Luger 1908 Bulgarian **$2000**
Caliber: 9mm Luger. 8-shot magazine. 4-inch tapered barrel. 8¾ inches overall. Weight: 30 oz. Fixed rear sight, dovetailed front sight. Thumb safety with lower marking concealed. Checkered walnut stocks. DWM chamber marking, no proofs, crown over shield on new-style toggle, lanyard loop, no stock lug. Estimated production unknown.

Luger 1908 Commercial **$1250**
Same basic specifications as the 1908 Bulgarian, except higher marking on thumb safety. No chamber markings, commercial proofs, DWM on new-style toggle; no stock lug. Estimated 4000 production.

Luger 1908 Erfurt Military **$900**
Caliber: 9mm Luger. 8-shot magazine. 4-inch tapered barrel. 8¾ inches overall. Weight: 30 oz. Fixed rear sight, dovetailed front sight. Thumb safety with higher marking concealed. Checkered walnut stocks. Serial number and proof marks on barrel, crown and Erfurt on new-style toggle, dated chamber; no stock lug. Estimated production unknown.

Luger 1908 Military
Same general specifications as the 9mm 1908 Erfurt Military Luger, except *1st and 2nd Issue* have thumb safety with higher marking concealed, serial number on barrel, no chamber markings, proofs on frame, DWM on new-style toggle; no stock lug. Estimated production: 10,000 (1st issue); 5000 (2nd issue). *3rd Issue* has serial number and proof marks on barrel, dates over chamber, DWM on new-style toggle; no stock lug. Estimated 3000 production.
1st Issue **$1200**
2nd Issue **1400**
3rd Issue **900**

Luger 1908 Naval **$2800**
Same basic specifications as the 9mm 1908 Military Lugers, except with 6-inch barrel, adjustable two-position rear sight, no chamber markings, DWM on new-style toggle; with stock lug. Estimated 26,000 production.

Luger 1908 Naval (Commercial) **$3600**
Same specifications as the 1908 Naval Luger, except no chamber markings or date. Commercial proofs, DWM on new-style toggle; with stock lug. Est. 1900 produced.

Luger 1914 Erfurt Artillery **$1400**
Caliber: 9mm Luger. 8-shot magazine. 8-inch tapered barrel. 12¾ inches overall. Weight: 40 oz. Artillery rear sight, dovetailed front sight. Thumb safety with higher marking concealed. Checkered walnut stocks. Serial number and proof marks on barrel, crown and Erfurt on new-style toggle, dated chamber, with stock lug. Estimated production unknown.

Luger 1914 Erfurt Military **$850**
Same specifications as the 1914 Erfurt Artillery, except with 4-inch barrel and corresponding length, weight, etc., and fixed rear sight. Estimated 3000 production.

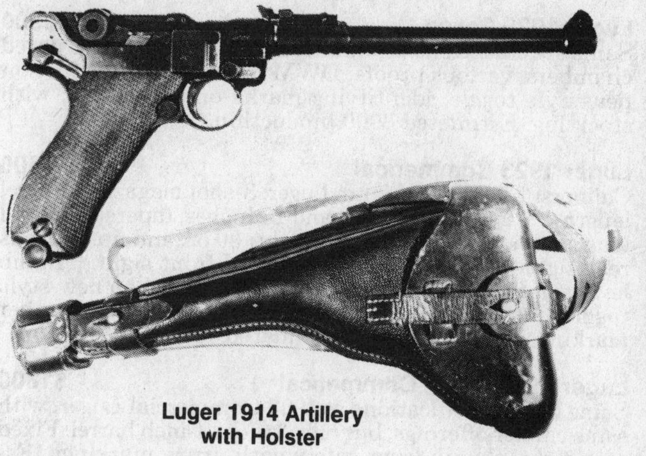

Luger 1914 Artillery with Holster

Luger 1914 Naval **$1750**
Same specifications as 9mm 1914 Lugers, except has 6-inch barrel with corresponding length and weight, and adjustable two-position rear sight. Dated chamber, DWM on new-style toggle; with stock lug. Estimated 40,000 production.

Luger 1914-1918 DWM Artillery **$1450**
Caliber: 9mm Luger. 8-shot magazine. 8-inch tapered barrel. 12¾ inches overall. Weight: 40 oz. Artillery rear sight, dovetailed front sight. Thumb safety with higher marking concealed. Checkered walnut stocks. Serial number and proof marks on barrel, DWM on new-style toggle, dated chamber; with stock lug. Estimated 3000 production.

Luger 1914-1918 DWM Military **$800**
Same specifications as the 9mm 1914-1918 DWM Artillery, except with 4-inch tapered barrel and corresponding length, weight, etc., and fixed rear sight. Estimated production unknown.

Luger 1920 Carbine
Caliber: 7.65mm. 8-shot magazine. 11¾-inch tapered barrel. 15¾ inches overall. Weight: 44 oz. Four-position rear sight, long ramp front sight. Grip (or thumb) safety. Checkered walnut stocks and forearm. Serial numbers and proof marks on barrel, no chamber markings, various proofs, DWM on new-style toggle; with stock lug. Estimated production unknown.
Carbine With Forearm **$6500**
Carbine Less Forearm **2750**

Luger 1920 Commercial **$750**
Calibers: 7.65mm, 9mm Luger. 8-shot magazine. Barrel lengths: 3⅝, 3¾, 4, 4¾, 6, 8, 10, 12, 16, 18, 20 inches; tapered. Overall length: 8⅜ to 24¾ inches. Weight: 30 oz. and up. Varying rear sight configurations, dovetailed front sight. Thumb safety. Checkered walnut stocks. Serial numbers and proof marks on barrel, no chamber markings, various proofs, DWM or crown over Erfurt on new-style toggle; with stock lug. Estimated production not documented.

Luger 1920 DWM and Erfurt Military **$750**
Caliber: 9mm Luger. 8-shot magazine. 4-inch tapered barrel. 8¾ inches overall. Weight: 30 oz. Fixed rear sight, dovetailed front sight. Thumb safety. Checkered walnut stocks. Serial numbers and proof marks on barrel, dated chamber, various proofs, DWM or crown over Erfurt on new-style toggle; with stock lug. Est. 3000 production.

Luger 1920 Police **$900**
Same specifications as 9mm 1920 DWM with some dated chambers, various proofs, DWM or crown over Erfurt on new-style toggle, identifying marks on grip frame; with stock lug. Estimated 3000 production.

Luger 1923 Commerical **$600**
Calibers: 7.65mm and 9mm Luger. 8-shot magazine. Barrel lengths: 3⁵/₈, 3³/₄, 4, 6, 8, 12 and 16 inches; tapered. Overall length: 8³/₈ inches and up. Weight: 30 oz. and up. Various rear sight configurations, dovetailed front sight. Thumb lever safety. Checkered walnut stocks. DWM on new-style toggle, serial number and proofs on barrel, no chamber markings, with stock lug. Estimated 15,000 production.

Luger 1923 Dutch Commerical **$1800**
Same basic specifications as 1923 Commercial Luger, with same caliber offerings, but only 3⁵/₈- or 4-inch barrel. Fixed rear sight, thumb lever safety with arrow markings. Estimated production unknown.

Luger 1923 Krieghoff Commercial **$1750**
Same specifications as 1923 Commercial Luger, with same caliber offerings but barrel lengths of 3⁵/₈, 4, 6, and 8 inches. "K" marked on new-style toggle; serial number, proofs and Germany on barrel; no chamber markings; with stock lug. Estimated production unknown.

Luger 1923 Safe and Loaded **$900**
Same caliber offerings, barrel lengths and specifications as the 1923 Commercial, except thumb lever safety with safe markings. Other markings the same; with stock lug. Estimated 10,000 production.

Luger 1923 Stoeger **$2750**
Same general specifications as the 1923 Commercial Luger, with the same caliber offerings and barrel lengths of 3³/₄, 4, 6, and 8 inches. Thumb lever safety. DWM on new-style toggle, serial number and/or proof marks on barrel, American Eagle over chamber usually; no stock lug. Estimated production unknown.

Luger 1926 "Baby" Prototype **$75,000**
Calibers: 7.65mm Browning and 9mm Browning (short). 5-shot magazine. 2¹⁵/₁₆-inch barrel. About 6¹/₄ inches overall. Small-sized frame and toggle assembly. Prototype for a Luger "pocket pistol," but never manufactured commercially. Checkered walnut grips, slotted for safety. Only four known to exist, but possibly as many as a dozen could have been made.

Luger 1929 Swiss **$1200**
Caliber: 7.65mm. 8-shot magazine. 4³/₄-inch tapered barrel. 9¹/₂ inches overall. Weight: 32 oz. Fixed rear sight, dovetailed front sight. Long grip safety and thumb lever with S markings. Stepped receiver and straight grip frame. Checkered plastic stocks. Swiss Cross in shield on new-style toggle, serial numbers and proofs on barrel, no markings over chamber; no stock lug. Est. 1900 prod.

Luger 1934 Krieghoff Commercial (Side Frame) **$6550**
Caliber: 7.65mm and 9mm Luger. 8-shot magazine. Barrel lengths: 4, 6, and 8 inches. Overall length: 8³/₄ inch and up. Weight: 30 oz. and up. Various rear sight configurations, dovetailed front sight. Thumb lever safety. Checkered brown plastic stocks. Anchor with H K Krieghoff Suhl on new-style toggle, no chamber markings, tapered barrel with serial number and proofs; with stock lug. Estimated 1700 production.

Luger 1934 Krieghoff S
Caliber: 9mm Luger. 8-shot magazine. 4-inch tapered barrel. 8³/₄ inches overall. Weight: 30 oz. Fixed rear sight, dovetailed front sight. Thumb lever safety. Anchor with H K Krieghoff Suhl on new-style toggle, S dated chamber, barrel proofs; stock lug. *Early Model:* Checkered walnut or plastic stocks. Estimated 2500 production. *Late Model:* Checkered brown plastic stocks. Estimated 1200 production.
Early Model **$1450**
Late Model **1250**

Luger 1934 byf **$800**
Caliber: 9mm Luger. 8-shot magazine. 4-inch tapered barrel. 8³/₄ inches overall. Weight: 30 oz. Fixed rear sight, dovetailed front sight. Thumb lever safety. Checkered walnut or plastic stocks. byf on new-style toggle, serial number and proofs on barrel, 41-42 dated chamber; stock lug. Estimated 3000 production.

Luger 1934 Mauser 42 . . . . **$1450**
Caliber: 9mm Luger. 8-shot magazine. 4-inch tapered barrel. 8³/₄ inches overall. Weight: 30 oz. Fixed rear sight, dovetailed front sight. Thumb lever safety. Checkered walnut or plastic stocks. 42 on new-style toggle, serial number and proofs on barrel, 1939-40 dated chamber markings; stock lug. Estimated 3000 production.

Luger 1934 Mauser 42 (Dated) **$2000**
Same specifications as Luger 1934 Mauser 42, above, except 41 dated chamber markings; stock lug. Estimated production unknown.

Luger 1934 Mauser Banner (Military) **$1750**
Same specifications as Luger 1934 Mauser 42, except Mauser in banner on new-style toggle, tapered barrel with serial number and proofs usually, dated chamber markings; stock lug. Estimated production unknown.

Luger 1934 Mauser Commercial **$2800**
Same specifications as Luger 1934 Mauser 42, except checkered walnut stocks. Mauser in banner on new-style toggle, tapered barrel with serial number and proofs usually, no chamber markings; stock lug. Estimated production unknown.

Luger 1934 Mauser Dutch **$1250**
Same specifications as Luger 1934 Mauser 42, except checkered walnut stocks. Mauser in banner on new-style toggle, tapered barrel with caliber, 1940 dated chamber markings; stock lug. Estimated production unknown.

Luger 1934 Mauser Latvian **$3000**
Caliber: 7.65mm. 8-shot magazine. 4-inch tapered barrel. 8³/₄ inches overall. Weight: 30 oz. Fixed, square-notched rear sight, dovetailed Patridge front sight. Thumb lever safety. Checkered walnut stocks. Mauser in banner on new-style toggle, 1937 dated chamber markings; stock lug. Estimated production unknown.

Luger 1934 Mauser (Oberndorf) **$2100**
Same specifications as Luger 1934 Mauser 42, except checkered walnut stocks. Oberndorf 1934 on new-style toggle, tapered barrel with proofs and caliber, Mauser in banner over chamber; stock lug. Est. 6000 produced.

Luger 1934 Simson-S Toggle **$1800**
Same specifications as Luger 1934 Mauser 42, except checkered walnut stocks. S on new-style toggle, tapered barrel with serial number and proofs, no chamber markings; stock lug. Estimated 10,000 production.

Luger 42 Mauser Banner **$1200**
Same specifications as Luger 1934 Mauser 42, except weight 32 oz.; Mauser in banner on new-style toggle, tapered barrel with serial number and proofs usually, dated chamber markings; stock lug. Estimated production unknown.

Luger Abercrombie and Fitch **$4500**
Calibers: 7.65mm and 9mm Luger. 8-shot magazine. 4 3/4-inch tapered barrel. 9 1/2 inches overall. Weight: 32 oz. Fixed rear sight, dovetailed front sight. Grip safety. Checkered walnut stocks. DWM on new-style toggle, Abercrombie & Fitch markings on barrel, Swiss Cross in sunburst over chamber; no stock lug. Estimated 100 production.

Luger Dutch Royal Air Force **$1150**
Caliber: 9mm Luger. 8-shot magazine. 4-inch tapered barrel. 8 3/4 inches overall. Weight: 30 oz. Fixed rear sight, dovetailed front sight. Grip safety and thumb safety with markings and arrow. Checkered walnut stocks. DWM on new-style toggle, barrel dated with serial number and proofs, no markings over chamber, no stock lug. Estimated 4000 production.

Luger DWM (G Date) **$750**
Caliber: 9mm Luger. 8-shot magazine. 4-inch tapered barrel. 8 3/4 inches overall. Weight: 30 oz. Fixed rear sight, dovetailed front sight. Thumb lever safety. Checkered walnut stocks. DWM on new-style toggle, serial number and proofs on barrel, G (1935 date) over chamber; with stock lug. Estimated production unknown.

Luger DWM and Erfurt **$850**
Caliber: 9mm Luger. 8-shot magazine. Barrel length: 4 or 6 inches, tapered. Overall length: 8 3/4, 10 3/4 inches. Weight: 30 or 38 oz. Fixed rear sight, dovetailed front sight. Thumb safety. Checkered walnut stocks. Serial numbers and proof marks on barrel, double dated chamber, various proofs, DWM or crown over Erfurt on new-style toggle; with stock lug. Estimated production unknown.

Luger Krieghoff 36 . . . . **$1800**
Caliber: 9mm Luger. 8-shot magazine. 4-inch tapered barrel. 8 3/4 inches overall. Weight: 30 oz. Fixed rear sight, dovetailed front sight. Thumb lever safety. Checkered brown plastic stocks. Anchor with H K Krieghoff Suhl on new-style toggle, 36 dated chamber, serial number and proofs on barrel; stock lug. Estimated 700 production.

Luger Krieghoff–Dated 1936-1945 . . . . **$1800**
Same specifications as Luger Krieghoff 36, except 1936-1945 dated chamber, barrel proofs. Estimated 8600 production.

Luger Krieghoff (Grip Safety) **$3500**
Same specifications as Luger Krieghoff 36, except grip safety and thumb lever safety. No chamber markings, tapered barrel with serial number, proofs and caliber; no stock lug. Estimated production unknown.

Luger Mauser Banner (Grip Safety) **$3000**
Caliber: 7.65mm. 8-shot magazine. 4 3/4-inch tapered barrel. 9 1/2 inches overall. Weight: 30 oz. Fixed rear sight, dovetailed front sight. Grip safety and thumb lever safety. Checkered walnut stocks. Mauser in banner on new-style toggle, serial number and proofs on barrel, 1939 dated chamber markings; no stock lug. Estimated production unknown.

Luger Mauser Banner 42 (Dated) **$1250**
Caliber: 9mm Luger. 8-shot magazine. 4-inch tapered barrel. 8 3/4 inches overall. Weight: 30 oz. Fixed rear sight, dovetailed front sight. Thumb lever safety. Checkered walnut or plastic stocks. Mauser in banner on new-style toggle, serial number and proofs on barrel usually, 42 dated chamber markings; stock lug. Estimated production unknown.

Luger Mauser Banner (Swiss Proof) **$1600**
Same specifications as Luger Mauser Banner 42, above, except checkered walnut stocks and 1939 dated chamber.

Luger Mauser Freise **$3000**
Same specifications as Mauser Banner 42, except checkered walnut stocks, tapered barrel with proofs on sight block and Freise above chamber. Estimated production unknown.

German Luger S/42
Dated 1936

Luger S/42
Caliber: 9mm Luger. 8-shot magazine. 4-inch tapered barrel. 8 3/4 inches overall. Weight: 30 oz. Fixed rear sight, dovetailed front sight. Thumb lever safety. Checkered walnut stocks. S/42 on new-style toggle, serial number and proofs on barrel; stock lug. *Dated Model:* has dated chamber; estimated 3000 production. *G Date:* has G (1935 date) over chamber; estimated 3000 production. *K Date:* has K (1934 date) over chamber; production figures unknown.

Dated Model	$ 850
G Date Model	600
K Date Model	1500

Luger Russian Commercial **$1800**
Caliber: 7.65mm. 8-shot magazine. 3 5/8-inch tapered barrel. 8 3/8 inches overall. Weight: 30 oz. Fixed rear sight, dovetailed front sight. Thumb lever safety. Checkered walnut stocks. DWM on new-style toggle, Russian proofs on barrel, no chamber markings; with stock lug. Estimated production unknown.

Luger Simson and Company **$1100**
Calibers: 7.65mm and 9mm Luger. 8-shot magazine. Weight: 32 oz. Fixed rear sight, dovetailed front sight. Thumb lever safety. Checkered walnut stocks. Simson & Company Suhl on new-style toggle, serial number and proofs on barrel, date over chamber usually; with stock lug. Estimated 10,000 production.

Luger Vickers-Dutch **$2250**
Caliber: 9mm Luger. 8-shot magazine. 4-inch tapered barrel. 8¾ inches overall. Weight: 30 oz. Fixed rear sight, dovetailed front sight. Grip safety and thumb lever with arrow markings. Checkered walnut stocks (coarse). Vickers LTD on new-style toggle, no chamber markings, dated barrel; no stock lug. Estimated 10,000 production.

LUNA FREE PISTOL
Zella-Mehlis, Germany
Originally mfd. by Ernst Friedr. Büchel and later by Udo Anschütz

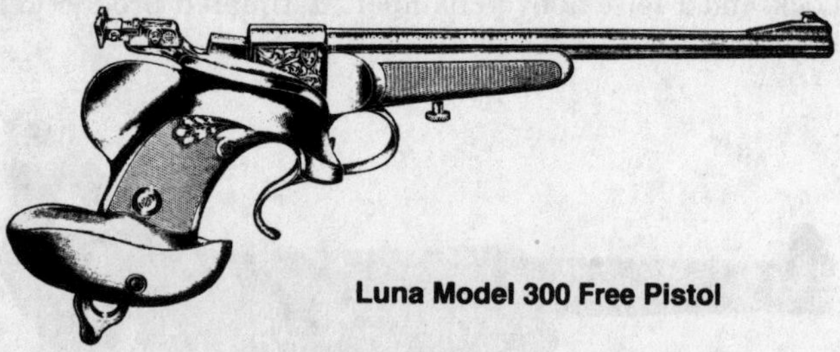

Luna Model 300 Free Pistol

Luna Model 300 Free Pistol **$920**
Single shot. System Aydt action. Set trigger. Caliber: 22 Long Rifle. 11-inch barrel. Weight: 40 oz. Target sights. Blued finish. Checkered and carved walnut stock and forearm; improved design with adjustable hand base on later models of Udo Anschütz manufacture. Made prior to World War II.

M.A.C./DEFENSE SYSTEMS INTL.
Marietta, Georgia

M.A.C. Ingram Model 10A1S

M.A.C. Ingram Model 10A1S Semiautomatic **$235**
Caliber: 9mm or 45 ACP. 30- or 32-round magazine. 5¾-inch barrel. 10½ inches overall. Weight: 6¼ pounds. Front protected post sight, fixed aperture sight in rear. Manually operated Garand-type safety located in trigger guard. Based on Military Armament Corporation's Ingram 10 design.

MAGNUM RESEARCH INC.
Minneapolis, Minnesota

Magnum Research Desert Eagle

Magnum Research Desert Eagle Semiautomatic
Calibers: 357 Mag., 41 Mag., 44 Mag. 8- or 9-shot magazine. Gas-operated. Barrel lengths: 6 (standard), 10 (44 Mag. only) and 14 inches; polygonal. 10.6 inches overall w/6-inch barrel. Weight (w/6-inch bbl.): 357 Mag.—52 oz. w/alum. alloy frame, 62 oz. w/steel frame; 41/44 Mag.—56 oz. w/alloy; 67 oz. w/steel. Fixed or adjustable combat sights. Combat-type trigger guard. Finishes: Military black oxide, nickel, chrome, stainless and blued. Wraparound rubber stocks. Made by Israel Military Industries from 1984 to date.
357 Standard (steel) and Alloy **$442**
357 Stainless Steel **475**
41/44 Mag. **525**

MAUSER PISTOLS
Oberndorf, Germany
Waffenfabrik Mauser of Mauser-Werke A.G.

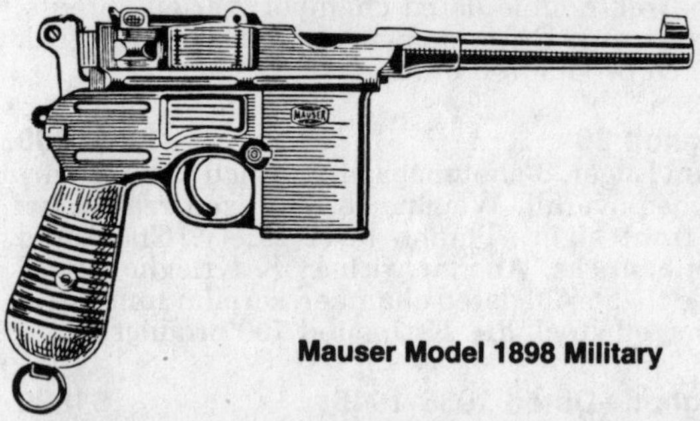

Mauser Model 1898 Military

Mauser Model HSc

Mauser Model 1898 Military Auto Pistol $1500
Caliber: 7.63mm Mauser; also chambered for 9mm Mauser and 9mm Luger; the latter is identified by a large red "9" in the stocks. Box magazine, 10-shot. 5¼-inch barrel. 12 inches overall. Weight: 45 oz. Adjustable rear sight. Blued finish. Walnut stocks. Made from 1898 to 1945. *Note:* Specialist collectors recognize a number of varieties of this pistol at higher values. Price here is for more common type.

Mauser Model HSc Double Action Auto Pistol . . $325
Calibers: 32 Automatic (7.65mm), 380 Automatic (9mm Short). 8-shot magazine in 32, 7-shot in 380. 3.4-inch barrel. 6.4 inches overall. Weight: 23.6 oz. Fixed sights. Blued or nickel finish. Checkered walnut stocks. Made from 1938 to 1945, from 1968 to date.

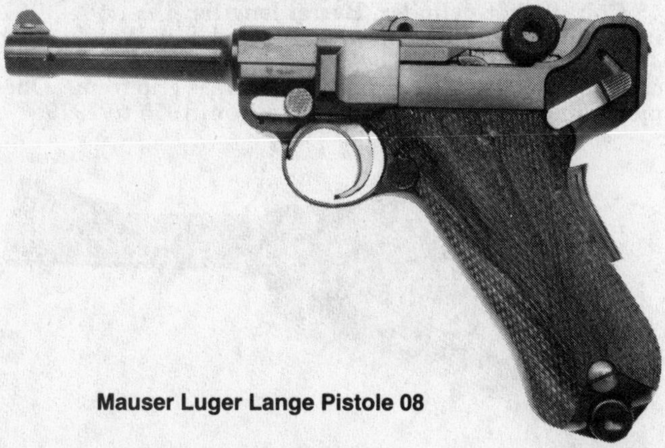

Mauser Luger Lange Pistole 08

Mauser Luger Lange Pistole 08 . . . . $1150
Caliber: 9mm Parabellum. 8-inch barrel. Checkered grips. Blued finish. Accessorized with walnut shoulder stock, front sight tool, spare magazine, leather case. Currently in production. Also made in commemorative version in limited quantities with ivory grips and 14-carat gold monogram plate.

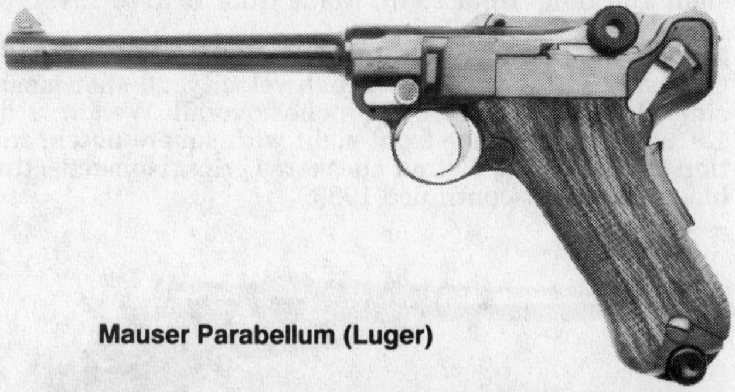

Mauser Parabellum (Luger)

Mauser Parabellum (Luger) Auto Pistol $1200
Current commercial model. Swiss pattern with grip safety. Calibers: 7.65mm Luger, 9mm Luger. 8-shot magazine. Barrel lengths: 4-, 6-inch. 8¾ inches overall with 4-inch bbl. Weight: with 4-inch bbl., 30 oz. Fixed sights. Blued finish. Checkered walnut stocks. Made from 1970 to date. *Note:* Pistols of this model sold in the U.S. have the American Eagle stamped on the receiver.

Mauser Pocket Model 1910 Auto Pistol $215
Caliber: 25 Automatic (6.35mm). 9-shot magazine. 3.1-inch barrel. 5.4 inches overall. Weight: 15 oz. Fixed sights. Blued finish. Checkered walnut or hard rubber stocks. Made from 1910 to 1934.

Mauser Pocket Model 1914 . . . . $220
Similar to Pocket Model 1910. Caliber: 32 Automatic (7.65mm). 8-shot magazine. 3.4-inch bbl. 6 inches overall. Weight: 21 oz. Fixed sights. Blued finish. Checkered walnut or hard rubber stocks. Made from 1914 to 1934.

Mauser Pocket Model 1934 . . . . $250
Similar to Pocket Models 1910 and 1914 in the respective calibers. Chief difference is in the more streamlined one-piece stocks. Made from 1934 to c. 1939.

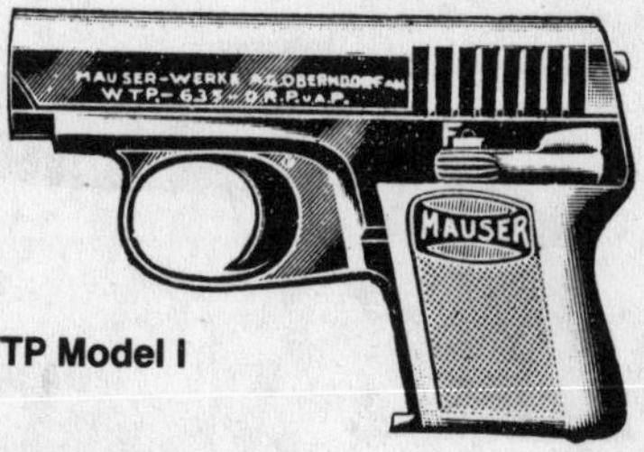

Mauser WTP Model I

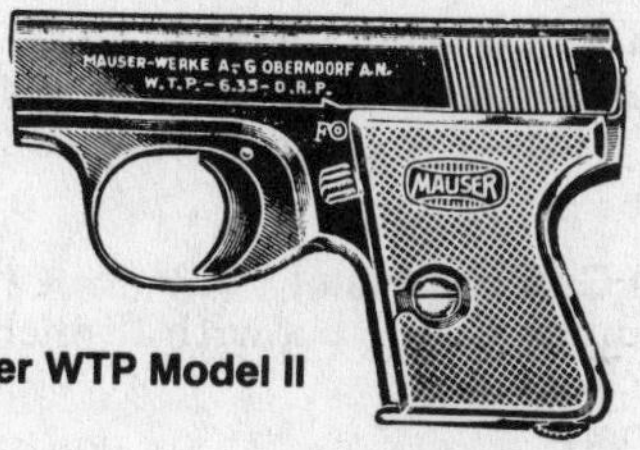

Mauser WTP Model II

Mauser WTP Model I Auto Pistol $250
"Westentaschen-Pistole" (Vest Pocket Pistol). Caliber: 25 Automatic (6.35mm). 6-shot magazine. 2½-inch barrel. 4½ inches overall. Weight: 11½ oz. Blued finish. Hard rubber stocks. Made from c. 1922 to 1937.

Mauser WTP Model II Auto Pistol $275
Similar to Model I, but smaller and lighter. Caliber: 25 Automatic (6.35mm). 6-shot magazine. 2-inch barrel. 4 inches overall. Weight: 9½ oz. Blued finish. Hard rubber stocks. Made from 1938 to 1940.

MKE PISTOL
Ankara, Turkey
Mfd. by Makina ve Kimya Endüstrisi Kurumu

MKE Kirikkale
Double Action Automatic*

MKE Kirikkale Double Action Automatic Pistol . . $150
Similar to Walther PP. Calibers: 32 Automatic (7.65mm), 380 Automatic (9mm Short). 7-shot magazine. 3.9-inch barrel. 6.7 inches overall. Weight: 24 oz. Fixed sights. Blued finish. Checkered plastic stocks. Made 1948 to date. *Note:* This is a Turkish Army standard service pistol.

MOA CORPORATION
Dayton, Ohio

MOA Maximum Pistol

MOA Maximum Single Shot Pistol $375
Calibers: 22 Hornet to 358 Win. 10- or 14-inch Douglas barrel. Weight: 3 lbs. 13 oz. to 4 lbs. 3 oz. Smooth walnut grips. Currently in production.

MOA Maximum Carbine Pistol $450
Similar to Maximum Pistol, but with 18-inch barrel. Currently in production.

NAVY ARMS COMPANY
Ridgefield, New Jersey

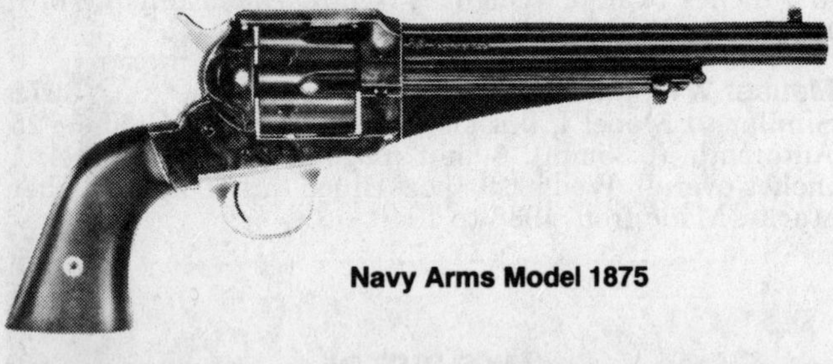

Navy Arms Model 1875

Navy Arms Model 1875 Single Action Revolver . $175
Replica of Remington Model 1875. Calibers: 357 Magnum, 44-40, 45 Colt. 6-shot cylinder. $7\frac{1}{2}$-inch barrel. $13\frac{1}{2}$ inches overall. Weight: about 48 oz. Fixed sights. Blued or nickel finish. Smooth walnut stocks. Made in Italy from c. 1955 to 1980. *Note:* Originally marketed in the U.S. as Replica Arms Model 1875; that firm was acquired by Navy Arms Company.

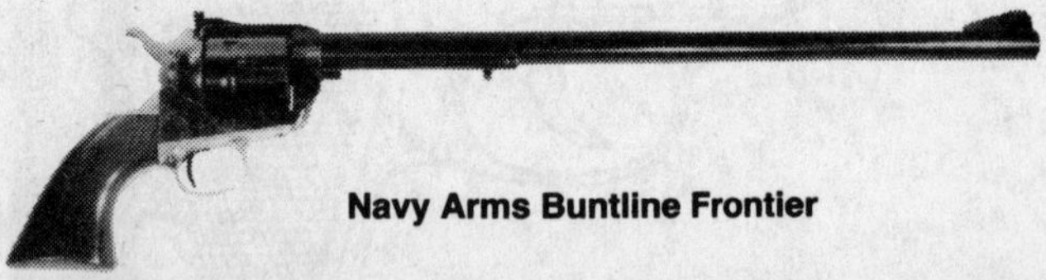

Navy Arms Buntline Frontier

Navy Arms Buntline Frontier $250
Same as Target Frontier, except has detachable shoulder stock and $16\frac{1}{2}$-inch barrel. Calibers: 357 Magnum and 45 Colt only. Made from 1975 to 1979.

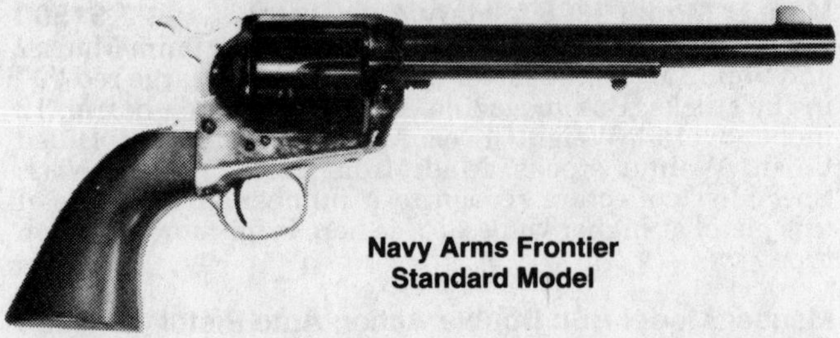

Navy Arms Frontier Standard Model

Navy Arms Frontier Single Action Revolver, Standard Model $160
Calibers: 22 Long Rifle, 22 Win. Mag. R.F., 357 Magnum, 45 Colt. 6-shot cylinder. Barrel lengths: $4\frac{1}{2}$-, $5\frac{1}{2}$-, $7\frac{1}{2}$-inch. $10\frac{1}{4}$ inches overall with $4\frac{1}{2}$-inch bbl. Weight: with $4\frac{1}{2}$-inch bbl., about 36 oz. Fixed sights. Blued barrel and cylinder, color-casehardened frame, brass grip frame. One-piece smooth walnut stock. Made from 1975 to 1979.

Navy Arms Frontier Target Model

Navy Arms Frontier Target Model $175
Same as Standard Frontier, except has adjustable rear sight and ramp front sight. Made from 1975 to 1979.

Navy Arms Luger (Standard) Automatic $165
Caliber: 22 LR, standard or high velocity. 10-shot magazine. Barrel: 4.5 inches. 8.9 inches overall. Weight: 1 lb. $13\frac{1}{2}$ oz. Square blade front sight with square notch, stationary rear sight. Walnut checkered grips. Non-reflecting black finish. Discontinued 1983.

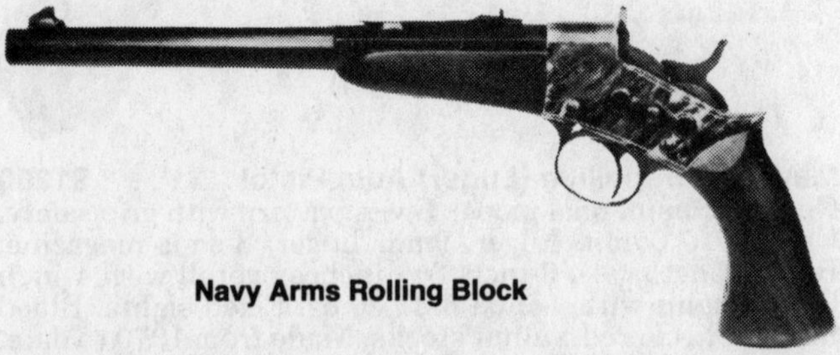

Navy Arms Rolling Block

Navy Arms Rolling Block Single Shot Pistol $135
Calibers: 22 Long Rifle, 22 Hornet, 357 Magnum. 8-inch barrel. 12 inches overall. Weight: about 40 oz. Adjustable sights. Blued barrel, color-casehardened frame, brass trigger guard. Smooth walnut stock and forearm. Made from 1965 to 1980.

NORTH AMERICAN ARMS
Freedom, Wyoming

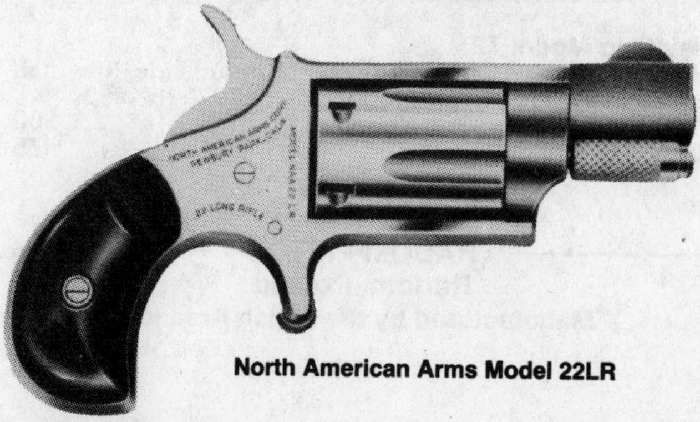

North American Arms Model 22LR

North American Arms Model 22LR $95
Same as Model 22S, except chambered for 22 Long Rifle, is 3⁷/₈ inches overall, weighs 4¹/₂ oz. Made from 1976 to date.

North American Arms Model 22S

North American Arms Model 22S Mini Revolver $110
Single action. Caliber: 22 Short. 5-shot cylinder. 1¹/₈-inch barrel. 3¹/₂ inches overall. Weight: 4 oz. Fixed sights. Stainless steel. Plastic stocks. Made from 1975 to date.

North American Arms 450 Magnum Express . . . $595
Single action. Calibers: 450 Magnum Express, 45 Win. Mag. 7¹/₂-inch barrel. Matte stainless steel finish. Cased. Discontinued 1986.

North American Arms Model 454C

North American Arms Model 454C Single Action Revolver $595
Caliber: 454 Casull. 5-shot cylinder. 7¹/₂-inch barrel. 14 inches overall. Weight: 50 oz. Fixed sights. Stainless steel. Smooth hardwood stocks. Introduced in 1977.

NORWEGIAN MILITARY PISTOLS
Mfd. by Kongsberg Vaapenfabrikk, the government arsenal at Kongsberg, Norway

Norwegian Model 1914

Norwegian Model 1914 Automatic Pistol $240
Similar to Colt Model 1911 45 Automatic with same general specifications, except has lengthened slide stop. Made from 1919 to 1946.

Norwegian Model 1912 is same except has conventional slide stop; only 500 were made and this is a very rare collector's item.

ORTGIES PISTOLS
Erfurt, Germany
Manufactured by Deutsche Werke A.G.

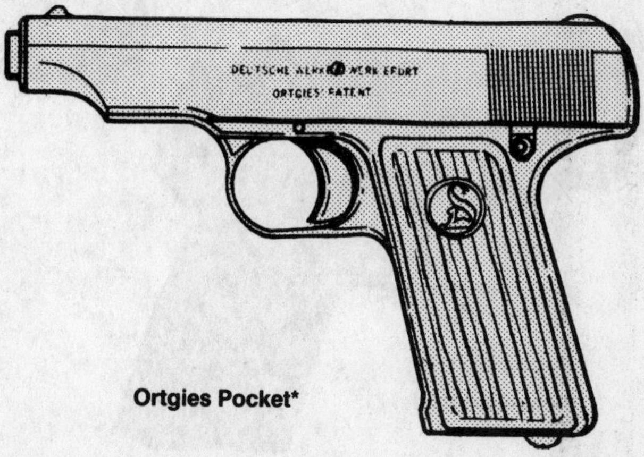

Ortgies Pocket*

Ortgies Pocket Automatic Pistol $195
Calibers: 32 Automatic (7.65mm), 380 Automatic (9mm). 7-shot magazine (380 cal.), 8-shot (32 cal.). 3¹/₄-inch barrel. 6¹/₂ inches overall. Weight: 22 oz. Fixed sights. Blued finish. Plain walnut stocks. Made in 1920s.

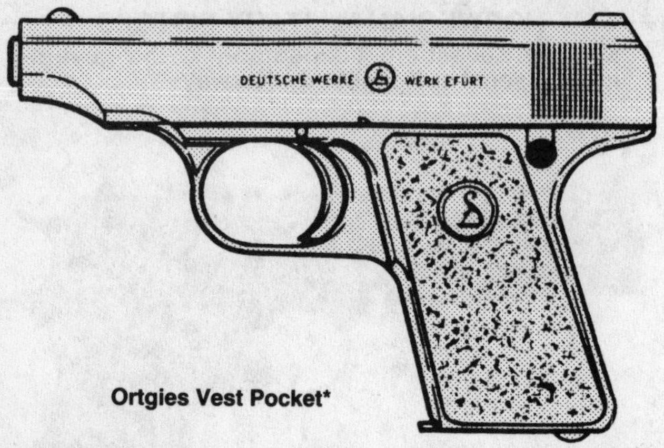

Ortgies Vest Pocket*

Ortgies Vest Pocket Automatic Pistol $180
Caliber: 25 Automatic (6.35mm). 6-shot magazine. $2^{3}/_{4}$-inch barrel. $5^{3}/_{16}$ inches overall. Weight: $13^{1}/_{2}$ oz. Fixed sights. Blued finish. Plain walnut stocks. Made in 1920s.

PLAINFIELD MACHINE COMPANY
Dunellen, New Jersey

The operation of this firm was discontinued about 1982.

Plainfield Model 72

Plainfield Model 71

Plainfield Model 71 Automatic Pistol
Calibers: 22 Long Rifle, 25 Automatic; conversion kit available. 10-shot magazine in 22, 8-shot in 25. $2^{1}/_{2}$-inch barrel. $5^{1}/_{8}$ inches overall. Weight: 25 oz. Fixed sights. Stainless steel frame and slide. Checkered walnut stocks. Made from 1970 to 1982.

Plainfield Model 71 Automatic Pistol (cont.)
22 Long Rifle or 25 Auto only **$60**
With Conversion Kit **75**

Plainfield Model 72
Same as Model 71, except has aluminum slide, $3^{1}/_{2}$-inch barrel, is 6 inches overall. Made from 1970 to 1982.
22 Long Rifle or 25 Auto only **$60**
With Conversion Kit **75**

RADOM PISTOL
Radom, Poland
Manufactured by the Polish Arsenal

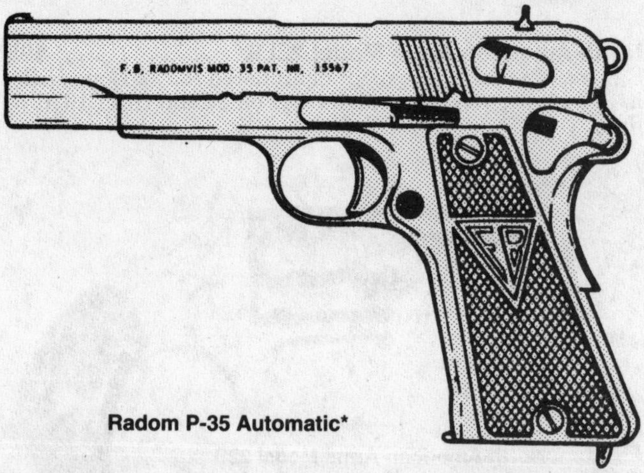

Radom P-35 Automatic*

Radom P-35 Automatic Pistol $290
Variation of the Colt Government Model 45 Auto. Caliber: 9mm Luger. 8-shot magazine. $4^{3}/_{4}$-inch barrel. $7^{3}/_{4}$ inches overall. Weight: 29 oz. Fixed sights. Blued finish. Plastic stocks. Made from 1935 through World War II.

RECORD-MATCH PISTOLS
Zella-Mehlis, Germany
Manufactured by Udo Anschütz

Record-Match Model 200

Record-Match Model 200 Free Pistol $875
Basically the same as Model 210 except plainer, with different stock design and conventional set trigger, spur trigger guard. Made prior to WW II.

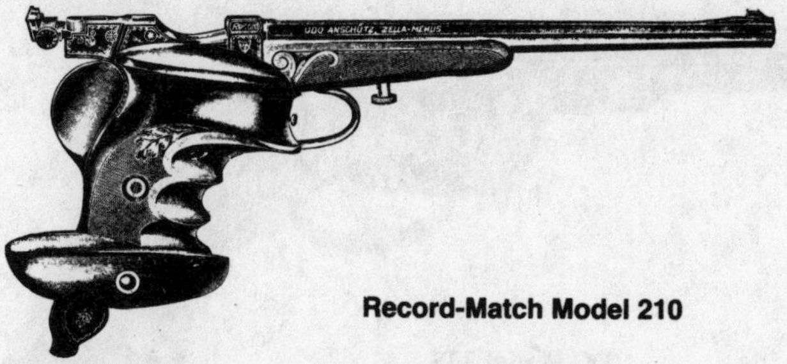
Record-Match Model 210

Record-Match Model 210 Free Pistol **$1150**
System Martini action, set trigger with button release. Caliber: 22 Long Rifle. Single shot. 11-inch barrel. Weight: 46 oz. Target sights, micrometer rear. Blued finish. Carved and checkered walnut stock and forearm, adjustable hand base. Also made with dural action (Model 210A); weight of this model, 35 oz. Made prior to WW II.

REISING ARMS CO.
Hartford, Connecticut

Reising Target Automatic*

Reising Target Automatic Pistol **$350**
Hinged frame. Outside hammer. Caliber: 22 Long Rifle. 12-shot magazine. $6\frac{1}{2}$-inch barrel. Fixed sights. Blued finish. Hard rubber stocks. Made from 1921 to 1924.

REMINGTON ARMS COMPANY
Ilion, New York

Remington Model 51

Remington Model 51 Automatic Pistol **$350**
Calibers: 32 Auto, 380 Auto. 7-shot magazine. $3\frac{1}{2}$-inch barrel. $6\frac{5}{8}$ inches overall. Weight: 21 oz. Fixed sights. Blued finish. Hard rubber stocks. Made from 1918 to 1934.

Remington Model 95 Double Derringer
Engraved Model

Remington Model 95 Double Derringer
Single action. Caliber: 41 Short Rimfire. Double barrels (superposed), 3-inch, $4\frac{7}{8}$ inches overall. Early models have long hammer spur and two-armed extractor; later production have short hammer spur and sliding extractor (a few have no extractor). Fixed sights: front blade integral with barrels, rear groove. Finishes: all blued, blued with nickel-plated frame, fully nickel-plated; also furnished with factory engraving. Grips: walnut, checkered hard rubber, pearl, ivory. Weight: 11 oz. Made from 1866 to 1935. Approximately 150,000 were manufactured. *Note:* During the 70 years of its production, serial numbering of this model was repeated two or three times. Therefore aside from hammer and extractor differences between the earlier model and the later type, the best clue to the age of a Double Derringer is the stamping of the company's name on the top of the barrel or side rib. Prior to 1888, derringers were stamped "E. Remington & Sons"; from 1888 to 1910, "Remington Arms Co."; from 1910 to 1935, "Remington Arms-U.M.C. Co."

Plain model **$450**
Factory-engraved model with ivory or pearl grips **995**

Remington New Model Single Shot Target Pistol **$1250**
Also called Model 1901 Target. Rolling-block action. Calibers: 22 Short, 22 Long Rifle, 44 S&W Russian. 10-inch bbl., half-octagon. 14 inches overall. Weight: 45 oz., 22 cal. Target sights. Blued finish. Checkered walnut grips and forearm. Made from 1901 to 1909.

Remington Model XP-100
Custom Pistol

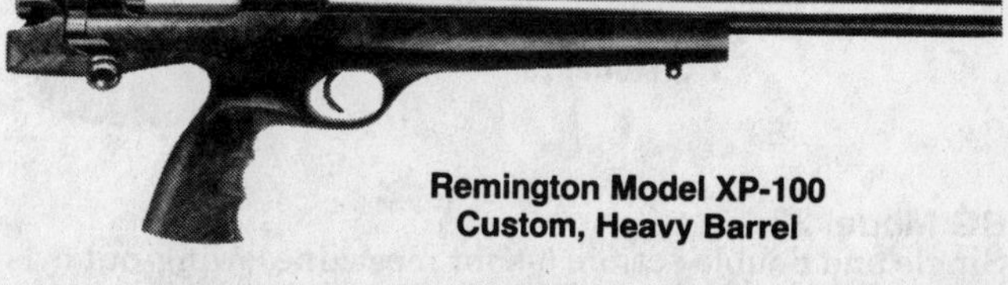
Remington Model XP-100
Custom, Heavy Barrel

Remington Model XP-100 Custom Pistol **$665**
Bolt-action, single-shot, long-range pistol. Calibers: 223 Rem., 7mm-08 or 35 Rem. $14\frac{1}{2}$-inch barrel, standard contour or heavy. Weight: about $4\frac{1}{4}$ pounds. Currently in production.

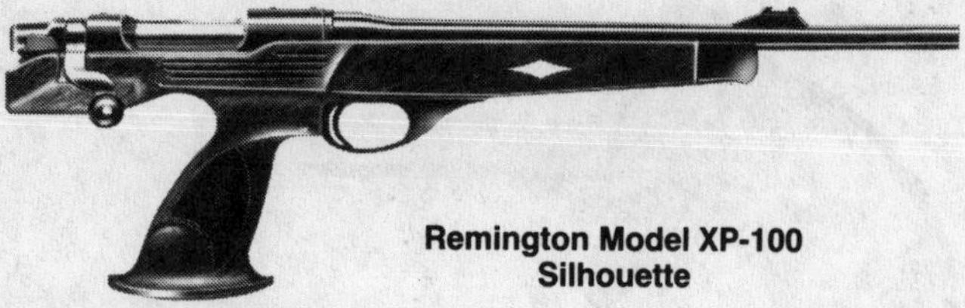

Remington Model XP-100 Silhouette

Remington Model XP-100 Silhouette $280
Same general specifications as Model XP-100, except chambered for 7mm BR Rem. cartridge, $14\frac{3}{4}$-inch barrel and weighs $4\frac{1}{8}$ pounds.

Remington Model XP-100 Single Shot Pistol $250
Bolt action. Caliber: 221 Remington "Fire Ball." $10\frac{1}{2}$-inch bbl. with vent rib. $16\frac{3}{4}$ inches overall. Weight: $3\frac{3}{4}$ pounds. Adjustable rear sight, blade front sight; receiver drilled and tapped for scope mounts. Blued finish. One-piece brown nylon stock. Made from 1963 to date.

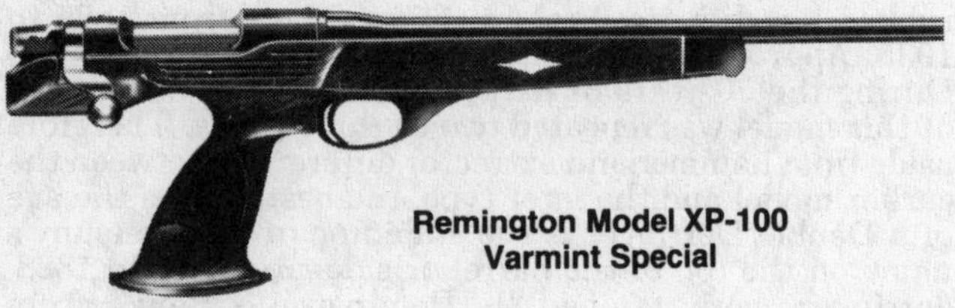

Remington Model XP-100 Varmint Special

Remington Model XP-100 Varmint Special $325
Bolt-action, single-shot, long-range pistol. Calibers: 223 Rem., 7mm BR. $14\frac{1}{2}$-inch barrel. $21\frac{1}{4}$ inches overall. Weight: about $4\frac{1}{4}$ pounds. One-piece Du Pont nylon stock with universal grips. Currently in production.

RG REVOLVERS
Miami, Florida

RG Model 23

RG Model 23
Single and double action. 6-shot magazine, swing-out cylinder. Caliber: 22 Long Rifle. $1\frac{3}{4}$- and $3\frac{3}{8}$-inch barrels. Overall length: $5\frac{1}{8}$ and $7\frac{1}{2}$ inches. Weight 16 to 17 oz. Fixed sights. Blued or nickel finish. Currently in production.
Blued Finish $60
Nickel Finish 70

RG Model 38S

RG Model 38S
Single and double action. 6-shot magazine, swing-out cylinder. Caliber: 38 Special. 3- and 4-inch barrels. Overall length: $8\frac{1}{4}$ and $9\frac{1}{4}$ inches. Weight: 32 to 34 oz. Windage-adjustable rear sight. Blued finish. Currently in production.
With Plastic Grips . . . . $ 95
With Wood Grips 105

ROSSI REVOLVERS
Sáo Leopoldo, Brazil
Manufactured by Amadeo Rossi S.A.

Rossi Model 31 Double Action Revolver $100
Caliber: 38 Special. 5-shot cylinder. 4-inch barrel. Weight: 20 oz. Blue or nickel finish.

Rossi Model 51 Double Action Revolver $110
Caliber: 22 LR. 6-shot cylinder. 6-inch barrel. Weight: 28 oz. Blued finish.

Rossi Model 68 . . . . $115
Caliber: 38 Special. 5-round magazine. 2- or 3-inch barrel. Overall length: $6\frac{1}{2}$ and $7\frac{1}{2}$ inches. Weight: 21 to 23 oz. Blued finish. Nickel finish available with 3-inch barrel.

Rossi Model 84 Revolver

Rossi Model 84 Double Action Revolver $150
Caliber: 38 Special. 6-shot cylinder. 3-inch barrel. 8 inches overall. Weight: $27\frac{1}{2}$ oz. Stainless steel finish. Made from 1984 to 1986.

Rossi Model 85 Double Action Revolver $160
Same as Model 84 except has ventilated rib.

Rossi Model 88 Double Action Revolver $130
Caliber: 38 Special. 5-shot cylinder. 2- or 3-inch barrel. Weight: 21 oz. Stainless steel finish.

Rossi Model 88/2 Double Action Revolver $130
Caliber: 38 Special. 6-shot cylinder. 2-inch barrel. 6½ inches overall. Weight: 21 oz. Stainless steel finish. Made in 1985.

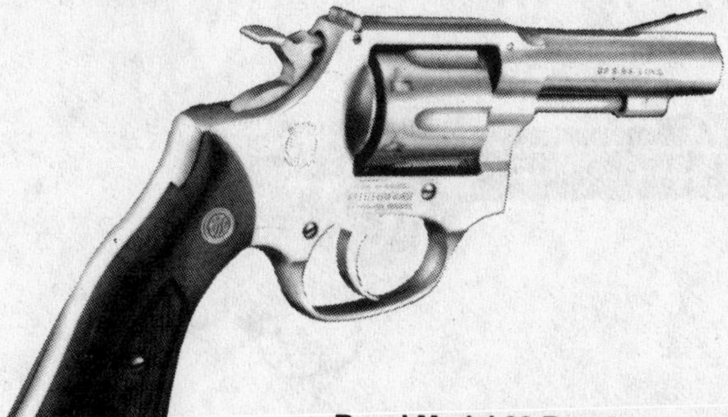

Rossi Model 89 Revolver

Rossi Model 89 Double Action Revolver $120
Caliber: 32 S&W. 6-shot cylinder. 3-inch barrel. 7½ inches overall. Weight: 17 oz. Stainless steel finish.

Rossi Model 94 Double Action Revolver $145
Caliber: 38 Special. 6-shot cylinder. 3-inch barrel. 8 inches overall. Weight: 29 oz.

Rossi Model 95 Revolver $150
Caliber: 38 Special. 6-round magazine. 3-inch barrel. 8 inches overall. Weight: 27½ oz. Ventilated rib. Blued finish.

Rossi Model 841 Revolver

Rossi Model 841 Double Action Revolver $150
Same general specifications as Model 84 except has 4-inch barrel, 9-inch overall length, and weighs 30 oz. Made from 1985 to 1986.

Rossi Model 941 Double Action Revolver $140
Caliber: 38 Special. 6-shot cylinder. 4-inch barrel. 9 inches overall. Weight: 30 oz. Blue finish. Made from 1985 to 1986.

Rossi Model 951 Double Action Revolver $150
Same general specifications as Model 941 except has ventilated rib.

Rossi Double Action Revolver

Rossi Double Action Revolver $95
Calibers: 22 Long Rifle, 32 S&W Long, 38 Special. 5-shot cylinder in 38, 6-shot in other calibers. Barrel lengths: 3-, 6-inch. Weight: with 3-inch bbl., 22 oz. Adjustable rear sight, ramp front sight. Blued or nickel finish. Wood or plastic stocks. Made from 1965 to date.

Rossi Sportsman's 22

Rossi Sportsman's 22 .... $155
Caliber: 22 Long Rifle. 6-round magazine. 4-inch barrel. 9 inches overall. Weight: 30 oz. Stainless steel finish.

RUBY PISTOL

Manufactured by Gabilondo y Urresti, Eibar, Spain, and others

Ruby 7.65mm Automatic*

Ruby 7.65mm Automatic Pistol $75
Secondary standard service pistol of the French Army in World Wars I and II. Essentially the same as the Alkartasuna; see listing of that pistol for specifications. Other manufacturers: Armenia Elgoibarresa y Cia., Eceolaza y Vicinai y Cia., Hijos de Angel Echeverria y Cia., Bruno Salaverria y Cia., Zulaika y Cia., all of Eibar, Spain; Gabilondo y Cia., Elgoibar, Spain; Ruby Arms Company, Guernica, Spain. Made from 1914 to 1922.

RUGER HANDGUNS
Southport, Connecticut
Manufactured by Sturm, Ruger & Co.

Rugers made in 1976 are designated "Liberty" in honor of the U.S. Bicentennial and bring a premium of approximately 25 percent in value over regular models.

Ruger Bearcat

Ruger Bearcat Single Action Revolver $240
Aluminum frame. Caliber: 22 Long Rifle. 6-shot cylinder. 4-inch barrel. $8\frac{7}{8}$ inches overall. Weight: 17 oz. Fixed sights. Blued finish. Smooth walnut stocks. Made from 1958 to 1973.

Ruger Bisley, Large Frame

Ruger Bisley, Small Frame

Ruger Bisley SA Revolver, Large Frame $230
Calibers: 357 Mag., 41 Mag., 44 Mag., 45 Long Colt. $7\frac{1}{2}$-inch barrel. 13 inches overall. Weight: 48 oz. offered with either a non-fluted cylinder; or a fluted cylinder, no engraving. Adjustable rear sight, ramp front sight. Blued satin finish. Made from 1986 to date.

Ruger Bisley Single-Six Revolver, Small Frame . $190
Calibers: 22LR rimfire and 32 Mag. 6-shot cylinder. $6\frac{1}{2}$-inch barrel. $11\frac{1}{2}$ inches overall. Weight: 41 oz. Fixed rear sight; blade front sight. Made from 1986 to date.

Ruger Blackhawk

Ruger Blackhawk Single Action Convertible $275
Same as Blackhawk, except has extra cylinder. Caliber combinations: 357 Magnum and 9mm Luger, 45 Colt and 45 Automatic. Made from 1967 to 1972.

Ruger Blackhawk Single Action Revolver $250
Calibers: 30 Carbine, 357 Magnum, 41 Magnum, 45 Colt. 6-shot cylinder. Barrel lengths: $4\frac{5}{8}$-inch (357, 41, 45 caliber), $6\frac{1}{2}$-inch (357, 41 caliber), $7\frac{1}{2}$-inch (30, 45 caliber). $10\frac{1}{8}$ inches overall in 357 model with $4\frac{5}{8}$-inch bbl. Weight: 357 with $4\frac{5}{8}$-inch bbl., 38 oz. Adjustable rear sight, ramp front sight. Blued finish. Checkered hard rubber or smooth walnut stocks. Made from 1956 to 1973.

Ruger Blackhawk 44

Ruger Blackhawk SA 44 Magnum Revolver
Single action with heavy frame and cylinder. Caliber: 44 Magnum. 6-shot cylinder. $6\frac{1}{2}$-inch barrel. Overall length: $12\frac{1}{8}$ inches. Weight: 40 oz. Adjustable rear sight, ramp front sight. Blued finish. Smooth walnut stocks. Made from 1956 to 1973.
Standard **$295**
Flat Top **425**

Ruger GP-100 Double Action Revolver
Caliber: 357 Magnum. 4-inch heavy barrel, or 6-inch standard or heavy barrel. Overall length: $9\frac{3}{8}$ or $11\frac{3}{8}$ inches. Cushioned grip panels. Made from 1986 to date.
Blued Finish **$240**
Stainless Steel Finish **260**

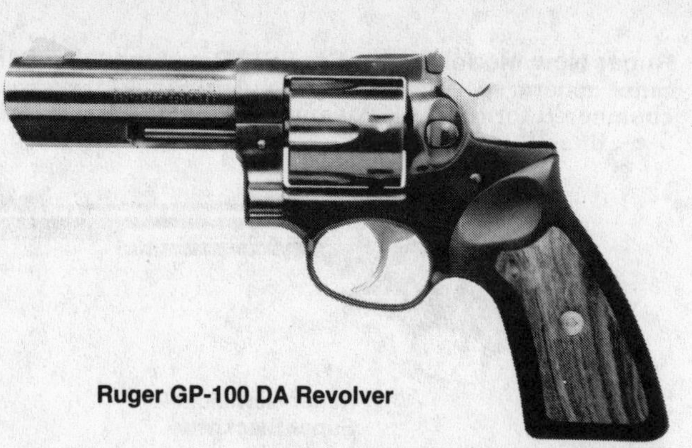

Ruger GP-100 DA Revolver

Ruger Hawkeye

Ruger Hawkeye Single Shot Pistol **$1000**
Single action; cylinder replaced by rotating breechblock; chamber is in barrel. Caliber: 256 Magnum. $8\frac{1}{2}$-inch barrel. $14\frac{1}{2}$ inches overall. Weight: 45 oz. Blued finish. Click adjustable rear sight, ramp front sight. Smooth walnut stocks. Made from 1963 to 1965.

Ruger Mark I Target

Ruger Mark I Target Model Automatic Pistol ... **$160**
Caliber: 22 Long Rifle. 9-shot magazine. Barrels: $5\frac{1}{4}$- or $6\frac{7}{8}$-inch heavy tapered, $5\frac{1}{2}$-inch untapered bull barrel. $10\frac{7}{8}$ inches overall with $6\frac{6}{8}$-inch bbl. Weight: with $5\frac{1}{2}$- or $6\frac{7}{8}$-inch bbl., 42 oz. Adjustable rear sight, under-cut target front sight. Blued finish. Hard rubber stocks or checkered walnut thumb-rest stocks (add $10 to value for latter). Made 1951 to 1981.

Ruger Mark II Automatic Pistol **$150**
Caliber: 22 Long Rifle. $4\frac{3}{4}$- or 6-inch barrel. 10-shot magazine. Blued finish. Similar in appearance to Standard Model. Intro. 1982; stainless steel models intro. 1983.

Ruger Mark II Stainless
22 Long Rifle

Ruger Mark II Automatic Stainless **$475**
Same as standard Mark II, except in stainless steel. Production limited to 5000. Made in 1982.

Ruger Mark II Bull Barrel

Ruger Mark II Bull Barrel Automatic Pistol
Same as standard Mark II, except for bull barrel ($5\frac{1}{2}$- or 10-inch). Weight: about $2\frac{3}{4}$ pounds.

Blued Finish	**$160**
Stainless Model, intro. 1985	**180**

Ruger Mark II Government
Target Automatic

Ruger Mark II Government Target Automatic Pistol **$195**
Civilian version of the Mark II used by U.S. Armed Forces. Caliber: 22 Long Rifle rimfire. 10-shot magazine. $6\frac{7}{8}$-inch bull barrel. $11\frac{1}{8}$ inches overall. Weight: 44 oz., empty. Made from 1986 to date.

Ruger Mark II Target Pistol
Same as standard Mark II, except has $6\frac{7}{8}$-inch tapered barrel. Made from 1982 to date.

Blued Finish	**$150**
Stainless Steel Finish	**185**

Ruger Mark II Target Model
22 LR Stainless

Ruger New Model Blackhawk Convertible **$230**
Same as New Model Blackhawk, except has extra cylinder; blued finish only. Caliber combinations: 357 Magnum and 9mm Luger, 45 Colt and 45 Automatic. 45 Colt and 45 Automatic discontinued 1983.

Ruger New Model Blackhawk

Ruger New Model Blackhawk
Stainless, 357 Magnum

Ruger New Model Blackhawk Single Action Revolver
Interlocked mechanism. Calibers: 30 Carbine, 357 Magnum, 41 Magnum, 44 Magnum, 44 Special, 45 Colt. 6-shot cylinder. Barrel lengths: $4\frac{5}{8}$-inch (357, 41, 45 caliber), $5\frac{1}{2}$-inch (44 Mag., 44, Spec.), $6\frac{1}{2}$-inch (357, 41, 45 long Colt calibers), $7\frac{1}{2}$-inch (30, 45, 44 Special, 44 Mag. calibers). $10\frac{3}{8}$ inches overall in 357 with $4\frac{5}{8}$-inch bbl.; $10\frac{1}{2}$-inch bbl. in 44 Mag. Weight: 357 with $4\frac{5}{8}$-inch bbl., 40 oz. Adjustable rear sight, ramp front sight. Blued finish or stainless steel; latter only in 357. Smooth walnut stocks. Made from 1973 to date.
Blued finish **$180**
Stainless steel **195**
357 Maximum **215**
44 Magnum, intro. 1987 .... **240**

Ruger New Model Single-Six SSM
32 Magnum

Ruger New Model Single-Six SSM Revolver **$165**
Same general specifications as standard Single-Six, except chambered for 32 H&R Magnum cartridge. Barrel: $4\frac{5}{8}$-, $5\frac{1}{2}$-, $6\frac{1}{2}$-, $9\frac{1}{2}$-inch.

Ruger New Model
Super Blackhawk

Ruger New Model Super Blackhawk Single Action Revolver **$240**
Interlocked mechanism. Caliber: 44 Magnum. 6-shot cylinder. $5\frac{1}{2}$-inch, $7\frac{1}{2}$-inch and $10\frac{1}{2}$-inch bull barrel. $13\frac{3}{8}$ inches overall. Weight: 48 oz. Adjustable rear sight, ramp front sight. Blued and stainless steel finish. Smooth walnut stocks. Made from 1973 to date. $5\frac{1}{2}$-inch barrel made from 1987 to date.

Ruger New Model Super
Single-Six Convertible

Ruger New Model Super Single-Six Convertible Revolver
Single action with interlocked mechanism. Calibers: 22 Long Rifle and 22 Win. Mag. R.F. Interchangeable 6-shot cylinders. Barrel lengths: $4\frac{5}{8}$, $5\frac{1}{2}$, $6\frac{1}{2}$, $9\frac{1}{2}$ inches. $10\frac{13}{16}$ inches overall with $4\frac{5}{8}$-inch bbl. Weight: with $4\frac{5}{8}$-inch bbl., 33 oz. Adjustable rear sight, ramp front sight. Blued finish or stainless steel; latter only with $5\frac{1}{2}$- or $6\frac{1}{2}$-inch bbl. Smooth walnut stocks. Made from 1972 to date.
Blued finish **$150**
Stainless steel **180**

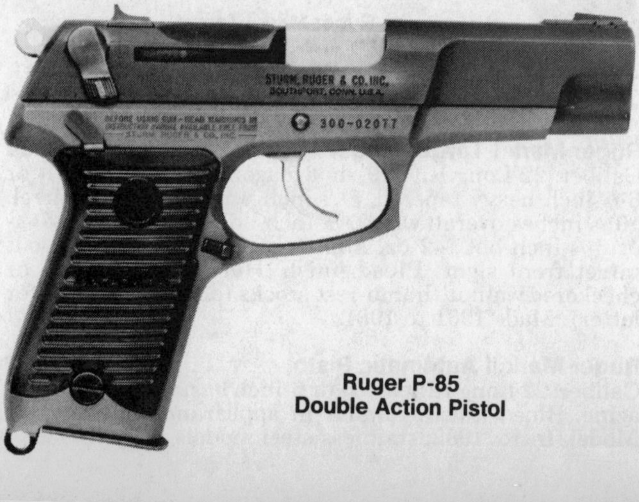

Ruger P-85
Double Action Pistol

Ruger Model P-85 Automatic Pistol **$220**
Caliber: 9mm. Double action, recoil-operated. 15-shot capacity. $4\frac{1}{2}$-inch barrel. 7.84 inches overall. Weight: 32 oz. Fixed rear sight, square-post front. Made from 1987 to date.

Ruger Police Service-Six Stainless Steel

Ruger Police Service-Six
Same general specifications as Speed-Six, except has square butt. Stainless steel models and 9mm Luger caliber available with only 4-inch barrel. Made from 1971 to date.

38 Special, blued finish	**$180**
38 Special, stainless steel	**200**
357 Magnum or 9mm Luger, blued finish	**200**
357 Magnum, stainless steel	**260**

Ruger Redhawk Alloy Steel, Blued

Ruger Redhawk Double Action Revolver **$300**
Calibers: 357 Mag., 41 Mag., 44 Mag. 6-shot cylinder. $5\frac{1}{2}$- and $7\frac{1}{2}$-inch barrel. 11 and 13 inches overall, respectively. Weight: about 52 oz. Adjustable rear sight, interchangeable front sights. Stainless finish. Made 1979 to date; 357 Mag. discontinued 1986. Alloy steel model with blued finish introduced in 1986 in 41 Mag. and 44 Mag. calibers.

Ruger Redhawk w/Integral Scope Mounting System

Ruger Redhawk Stainless Double Action Revolver Scope Ring Model **$350**
Same general specifications as standard Redhawk except chambered for 44 Mag. only, and has integral scope mounting system.

Ruger Security-Six

Ruger Security-Six Double Action Revolver
Caliber: 357 Magnum; handles 38 Special. 6-shot cylinder. Barrel lengths: $2\frac{3}{4}$-, 4-, 6-inch. $9\frac{1}{4}$ inches overall with 4-inch bbl. Weight: with 4-inch bbl., $33\frac{1}{2}$ oz. Adjustable rear sight, ramp front sight. Blued finish or stainless steel. Square butt. Checkered walnut stocks. Made from 1971 to 1985.

Blued finish	**$185**
Stainless steel	**215**

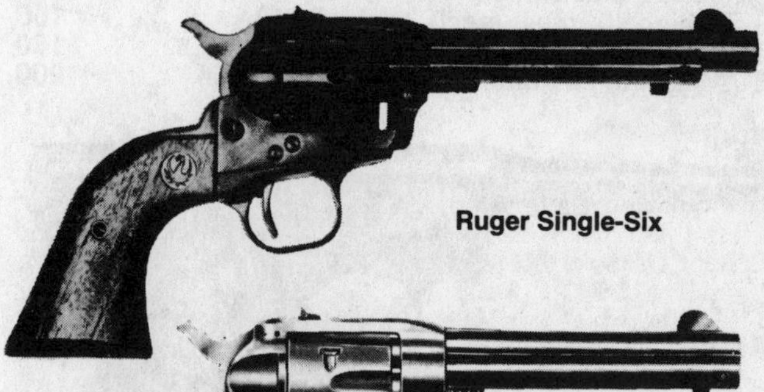

Ruger Single-Six

Ruger Single-Six Lightweight

Ruger Single-Six **$210**
Single action. Calibers: 22 Long Rifle, 22 Win. Magnum Rimfire. 6-shot cylinder. Barrel lengths: $4\frac{5}{8}$, $5\frac{1}{2}$, $6\frac{1}{2}$, $9\frac{1}{2}$ inches. Overall length with $5\frac{1}{2}$-inch bbl., $10\frac{7}{8}$ inches. Weight: about 35 oz. Fixed sights. Blued finish. Checkered hard rubber or smooth walnut grips. Made from 1953 to 1973. *Note:* Pre-1956 model has flat loading gate, is worth about twice as much as later version.

Ruger Single-Six—Convertible **$200**
Same as Single-Six, except has two cylinders for 22 Long Rifle and 22 Win. Mag. R.F.

Ruger Single-Six—Lightweight **$300**
Same general specifications as Single-Six, except has $4^{5}/_{8}$-inch barrel, 10 inches overall length, weighs 23 oz.; cylinder, cylinder frame and grip frame of lightweight alloy. Made in 1956.

Ruger Speed-Six

Ruger Speed-Six Double Action Revolver
Calibers: 38 Special, 357 Magnum, 9mm Luger. 6-shot cylinder. Barrel lengths: $2^{3}/_{4}$-, 4-inch; 9mm available only with $2^{3}/_{4}$-inch bbl. $7^{3}/_{4}$ inches overall with $2^{3}/_{4}$-inch bbl. Weight: with $2^{3}/_{4}$-inch bbl., 31 oz. Fixed sights. Blued finish or stainless steel; latter available in 38 Special with $2^{3}/_{4}$-inch bbl., 357 Magnum and 9mm with either barrel. Round butt. Checkered walnut stocks. Made 1973-1987.
38 Special, blued finish **$140**
38 Special, stainless steel **160**
357 Magnum or 9mm Luger, blued finish **160**
357 Magnum or 9mm Luger, stainless steel **200**

Ruger Standard Model

Ruger Standard Model Automatic Pistol
Caliber: 22 Long Rifle. 9-shot magazine. $4^{3}/_{4}$- or 6-inch barrel. $8^{3}/_{4}$ inches overall with $4^{3}/_{4}$-inch bbl. Weight: with $4^{3}/_{4}$-inch bbl., 36 oz. Fixed sights. Blued finish. Hard rubber or checkered walnut stocks. Made from 1949 to date. *Note:* In 1951, after the death of Alexander Sturm, the color of the eagle on the stock medallion was changed from red to black as a memorial. Known as the "Red Eagle Automatic," this early type is now a collector's item. Discontinued in 1981.
With red eagle medallion **$425**
With black eagle medallion **125**
Extra for walnut stocks **10**

Ruger Super Bearcat

Ruger Super Bearcat **$290**
Same general specifications as Bearcat, except has steel frame. Weight: 25 oz. Made from 1971 to 1973.

Ruger Super Blackhawk

Ruger Super Blackhawk Single Action Revolver **$295**
Caliber: 44 Magnum. 6-shot cylinder. $7^{1}/_{2}$-inch barrel. $13^{3}/_{8}$ inches overall. Weight: 48 oz. Click adjustable rear sight, ramp front sight. Blued finish. Steel or brass grip frame. Smooth walnut stocks. Made from 1959 to 1973.

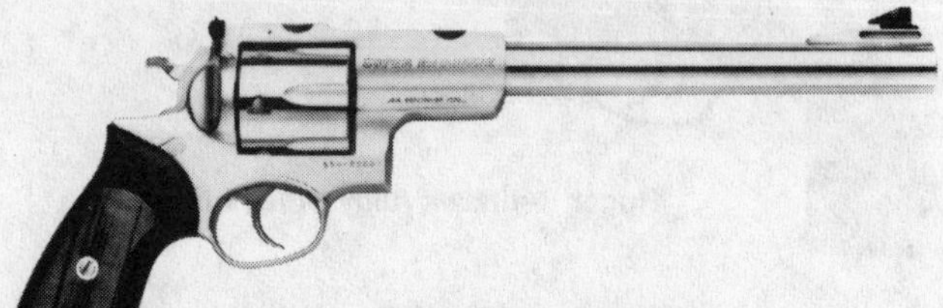

Ruger Super Redhawk

Ruger Super Redhawk Revolver **$400**
Caliber: 44 Magnum. $7^{1}/_{2}$- or $9^{1}/_{2}$-inch barrel. 13 or 15 inches overall. Weight: 53 to 58 oz. Cushioned grips. Satin polished stainless steel finish. Introduced in 1987.

Ruger Super Single-Six Convertible

Ruger Super Single-Six Convertible Revolver ... **$200**
Same general specifications as Single-Six, except has ramp front sight, click-adjustable rear sight with protective ribs

Ruger Super Single-Six Convertible Revolver (cont.)
integral with frame; 5½- or 6½-inch barrel only; two interchangeable cylinders, 22 LR and 22 WMR. Made from 1973 to date.

RUSSIAN SERVICE PISTOL

Mfd. by Government plants at Tula and elsewhere

Tokarev-type pistols also have been made in Hungary, Poland, Yugoslavia, People's Republic of China and North Korea.

Russian Tokarev*

Russian Model 30 Tokarev Service Automatic Pistol **$250**
Modified Colt-Browning type. Caliber: 7.62mm Russian Automatic (also uses 7.63mm Mauser Automatic cartridge). 8-shot magazine. 4½-inch barrel. 7¾ inches overall. Weight: about 29 oz. Fixed sights. Made from 1930 to mid-1950s. *Note:* A slightly modified version with improved locking system and different disconnector was adopted in 1933.

SAKO HANDGUNS

Riihimaki, Finland
Manufactured by Oy Sako Ab

Sako 22-32 Olympic Pistol

Sako 22-32 Olympic Pistol
Calibers: 22 Long Rifle, 22 Short, 32 S&W Long. 5-round magazine. Barrels: 6 or 8.85 (22 Short) inches. Weight: about 46 oz. (22 LR); 44 oz. (22 Short); about 48 oz. (32). Steel frame. ABS plastic, anatomically designed grip. Nonreflecting matte black upper surface and chromium-plated slide. Equipped with carrying case and tool set. Made from 1983 to 1989.
Sako 22-32 Single Pistol **$1045**
Sako Triace, triple-barrel set w/wooden grip . . . **1840**

SAUER HANDGUNS

Mfd. through WW II by J. P. Sauer & Sohn, Suhl, Germany. Now mfd. by J. P. Sauer & Sohn, GmbH, Eckernförde, West Germany

Sauer Model 1913*

Sauer Model 1913 Pocket Automatic Pistol **$260**
Caliber: 32 Automatic (7.65mm). 7-shot magazine. 3-inch barrel. 5⅞ inches overall. Weight: 22 oz. Fixed sights. Blue finish. Black hard rubber stocks. Made 1913 to 1930.

Sauer Model 1930

Sauer Model 1930 Pocket Automatic Pistol **$260**
Authority Model (Behorden Modell). Successor to Model 1913, has improved grip and safety. Caliber: 32 Automatic (7.65mm). 7-shot magazine. 3-inch barrel. 5¾ inches overall. Weight: 22 oz. Fixed sights. Blued finish. Black hard rubber stocks. Made from 1930 to 1938. *Note:* Some pistols of this model have indicator pin showing when cocked. Also mfd. with dural slide and receiver; this type weighs about ⅓ less than the standard model.

Sauer Model H Automatic

Sauer Model H Double Action Automatic Pistol . $350
Calibers: 25 Auto (6.35mm), 32 Auto (7.65mm), 380 Auto (9mm). Specifications shown are for 32 Auto model. 7-shot magazine. $3\frac{1}{4}$-inch barrel. $6\frac{1}{4}$ inches overall. Weight: 20 oz. Fixed sights. Blued finish. Black plastic stocks. Also made in dural model weighing about $\frac{1}{3}$ less. Made from 1938 to 1945. *Note:* This pistol, designated Model 38, was mfd. during WWII for military use. Wartime models are inferior to earlier production, as some lack safety lever.

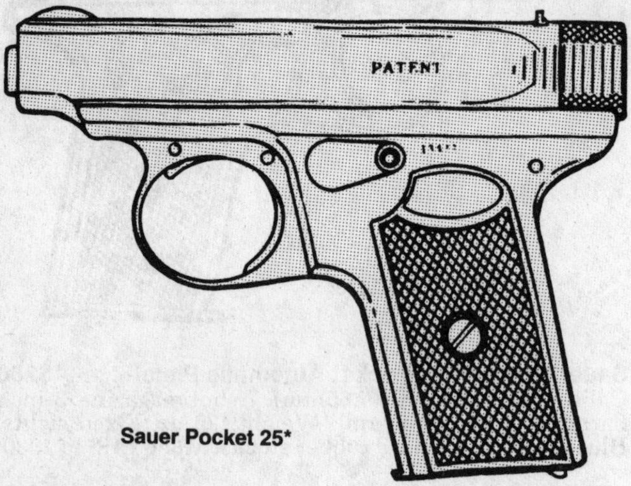

Sauer Pocket 25*

Sauer Pocket 25 Automatic Pistol $275
Smaller version of Model 1913, issued about same time as 32 caliber model. Caliber: 25 Automatic (6.35mm). 7-shot magazine. $2\frac{1}{2}$-inch barrel. $4\frac{1}{4}$ inches overall. Weight: $14\frac{1}{2}$ oz. Fixed sights. Blued finish. Black hard rubber stocks. Made from 1913 to 1930.

Sauer Single Action Revolvers
See listings under Hawes.

SIG-Sauer Model P220

SIG-Sauer Model P220 Double Action Automatic Pistol $450
Calibers: 22 Long Rifle, 7.65mm Luger, 9mm Luger, 38 Super, 45 Automatic. 10-shot magazine in 22, 7-shot in 45, 9-shot in other calibers. 4.4-inch barrel. 7.8 inches overall. Weight: 9mm, 26.5 oz. Fixed sights. Blued finish. Checkered plastic stocks. Made from 1976 to date. *Note:* Also sold in U.S. as Browning BDA.

SIG-Sauer Model P230

SIG-Sauer Model P230 Double Action Automatic Pistol $365
Calibers: 22 Long Rifle, 32 Automatic (7.65mm), 380 Automatic (9mm Short), 9mm Police. 10-shot magazine in 22, 8-shot in 32, 7-shot in 9mm. 3.6-inch barrel. 6.6 inches overall. Weight: 32 Auto, 18.2 oz. Fixed sights. Blued finish. Plastic stocks. Made from 1976 to date.

SAVAGE ARMS CO.
Utica, New York

Savage Model 101

Savage Model 101 Single Action Single Shot Pistol $130
Barrel integral with swing-out cylinder. Caliber: 22 Short, Long, Long Rifle. $5\frac{1}{2}$-inch barrel. Weight: 20 oz. Blade front sight, slotted rear sight adjustable for windage. Blued finish. Grips of compressed, impregnated wood. Made from 1960 to 1968.

Savage Model 1910

Savage Model 1910 Automatic Pistol $260
Calibers: 32 Auto, 380 Auto. 10-shot magazine (32 cal.), 9-shot (380 cal.). $3\frac{3}{4}$-inch barrel (32 cal.), $4\frac{1}{2}$-inch (380 cal.). $6\frac{1}{2}$ inches overall (32 cal.), 7 inch (380 cal.). Weight: about 23 oz. Fixed sights. Blued finish. Hard rubber stocks. *Note:* This model was made in hammerless type with grip safety as well as with exposed hammer spur. Made 1910-17.

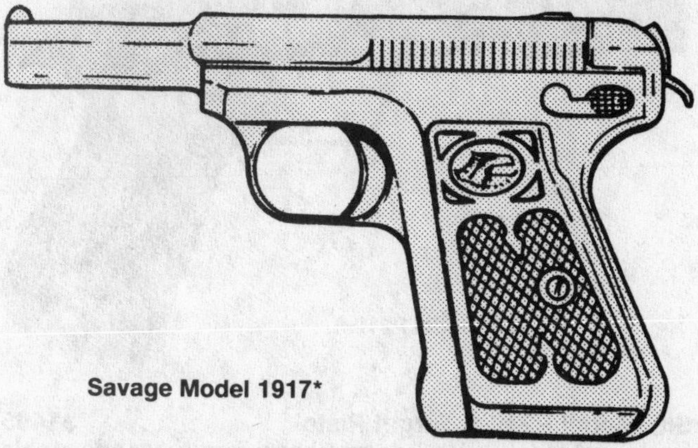

Savage Model 1917*

Savage Model 1917 Automatic Pistol $300
Same specifications as 1910 Model, except has spur-type hammer and redesigned heavier grip. Made from 1917 to 1928.

SEARS, ROEBUCK & COMPANY
Chicago, Illinois

Sears/J.C. Higgins Model 80 Auto Pistol $135
Caliber: 22 Long Rifle. 10-shot magazine. $4\frac{1}{2}$- or $6\frac{1}{2}$-inch interchangeable barrel. $10\frac{7}{8}$ inches overall w/$6\frac{1}{2}$-inch bbl. Weight: 41 oz. w/$6\frac{1}{2}$-inch bbl. Fixed Patridge sights. Blued finish. Checkered stocks with thumb rest.

Sears/J.C. Higgins Model 88 DA Revolver $75
Caliber: 22 Long Rifle. 9-shot cylinder. 4- or 6-inch barrel. $9\frac{1}{2}$ inches overall w/4-inch bbl. Weight: 23 oz. w/4-inch bbl. Fixed sights. Blued or nickel finish. Checkered plastic stocks.

Sears/J.C. Higgins Ranger DA Revolver $85
Caliber: 22 Long Rifle. 9-shot cylinder. $5\frac{1}{2}$-inch barrel. $10\frac{3}{4}$ inches overall. Weight: 28 oz. Fixed sights. Blued or chrome finish. Checkered plastic stocks.

SECURITY INDUSTRIES OF AMERICA
Little Ferry, New Jersey

Security Model PM357 Double Action Revolver . $185
Caliber: 357 Magnum. 5-shot cylinder. $2\frac{1}{2}$-inch barrel. $7\frac{1}{2}$ inches overall. Weight: 21 oz. Fixed sights. Stainless steel. Walnut stocks. Intro. 1975. Discontinued.

Security Model PPM357 Double Action Revolver $185
Caliber: 357 Magnum. 5-shot cylinder. 2-inch barrel. $6\frac{1}{8}$ inches overall. Weight: 18 oz. Fixed sights. Stainless steel.

Security Model PM357

Security Model PPM357

Security Model PPM357 (cont.)
Walnut stocks. Made from 1976 to date. *Note:* Spurless hammer (illustrated) was discontinued in 1977; this model now has the same conventional hammer as in other Security revolvers.

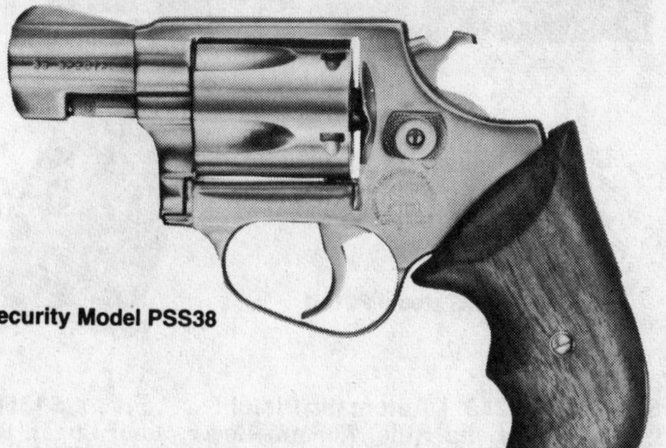

Security Model PSS38

Security Model PSS38 Double Action Revolver . $150
Caliber: 38 Special. 5-shot cylinder. 2-inch barrel. $6\frac{1}{2}$ inches overall. Weight: 18 oz. Fixed sights. Stainless steel. Walnut stocks. Intro. 1973. Discontinued.

R. F. SEDGLEY, INC.
Philadelphia, Pennsylvania

Sedgley Baby Hammerless Ejector Double Action Revolver $130
Solid frame. Folding trigger. Caliber: 22 Long. 6-shot cylinder. 4 inches overall. Weight: 6 oz. Fixed sights. Blued or nickel finish. Rubber stocks. Made c. 1930 to 1939.

SHERIDAN PRODUCTS, INC.
Racine, Wisconsin

Sheridan Knocabout

Sheridan Knocabout Single Shot Pistol $110
Tip-up type. Caliber: 22 Long Rifle, Long, Short. 5-inch barrel. 6¾ inches overall. Weight: 24 oz. Fixed sights. Checkered plastic stocks. Blue finish. Made 1953 to 1960.

SIG PISTOLS
Neuhausen am Rheinfall, Switzerland
Mfd. by SIG Schweizerische Industrie-Gesellschaft

SIG Model P210-1

SIG Model P210-1 Automatic Pistol $1350
Calibers: 22 Long Rifle, 7.65mm Luger, 9mm Luger. 8-shot magazine. 4¾-inch barrel. 8½ inches overall. Weight: 33 oz., 22 cal.; 35 oz., 7.65mm and 9mm. Fixed sights. Polished blued finish. Checkered wood stocks. Made from 1949 to date.

SIG Model P210-2 . . . . $1195
Same as Model P210-1, except has sandblasted finish, plastic stocks; not available in 22 Long Rifle.

SIG Model P210-5 Target Pistol $1425
Same as Model P210-2, except has 6-inch barrel, micrometer adjustable rear sight, target front sight, adjustable trigger stop. 9.7 inches overall. Weight: about 38.3 oz. Discontinued.

SIG Model P210-6

SIG Model P210-6 Target Pistol $1495
Same as Model P210-2, except has micrometer adjustable rear sight, target front sight, adjustable trigger stop. Weight: about 37 oz.

SIG P210 22 Conversion Unit $450
Converts P210 pistol to 22 Long Rifle. Consists of barrel with recoil spring, slide and magazine.

SIG-Hämmerli Model P240 Automatic Pistol $950
For data see listing under Hämmerli.

SIG-Sauer Model 220 Double Action Automatic . $395
Caliber: 38 Super, 9mm Parabellum, 45 ACP. 9-shot magazine (7-shot in 45 ACP). 4.4-inch barrel. 8 inches overall. Weight: 26½ oz.

SIG-Sauer Model 225 Double Action Automatic . $465
Caliber: 9mm Parabellum. 8-shot magazine. 3.85-inch barrel. 7 inches overall. Weight: 26½ oz. Blue finish.

SIG-Sauer Model 226 Double Action Automatic . $475
Caliber: 9mm Parabellum. 15-shot magazine. 4.4-inch barrel. 7¾ inches overall. Weight: 30 oz. Blue finish. Made from 1985 to date.

SIG-Sauer Model 230 Double Action Automatic . $340
Caliber: 380 ACP. 7-shot magazine. 3.6-inch barrel. 6.6 inches overall. Weight: 16¼ oz. Blue or stainless steel finish. Made from 1985 to date.

SIG-Sauer Model P220 Double Action Automatic $450
For data see listing under Sauer. *Note:* Also sold in U.S. as Browning BDA.

SIG-Sauer Model P230 Double Action Automatic $365
For data see listing under Sauer.

SMITH & WESSON, INC.
Springfield, Massachusetts

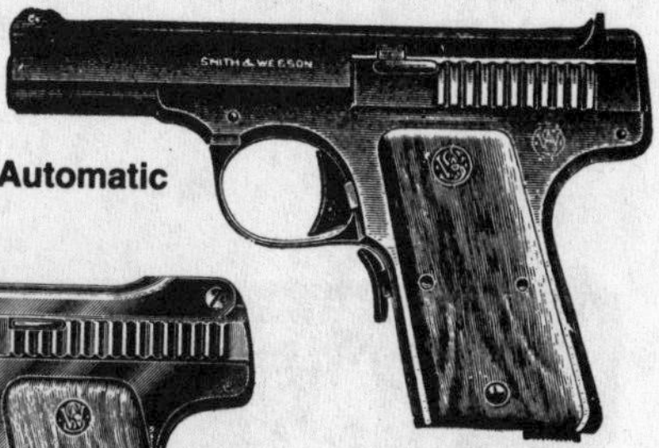

S&W 32 Automatic

S&W 35 Automatic

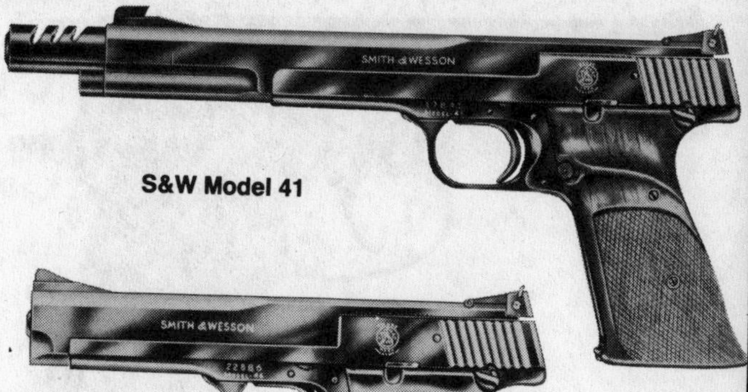

S&W Model 41

S&W Model 46

SMITH & WESSON PISTOLS

Smith & Wesson 32 Automatic Pistol $1295
Caliber: 32 Automatic. Same general specifications as 35 caliber model, but barrel is fastened to the receiver instead of hinged. Made from 1924 to 1937.

Smith & Wesson 35 Automatic Pistol $695
Caliber: 35 S&W Automatic. 7-shot magazine. $3\frac{1}{2}$-inch barrel (hinged to frame). $6\frac{1}{2}$ inches overall. Weight: 25 oz. Fixed sights. Blued or nickel finish. Plain walnut stocks. Made from 1913 to 1921.

S&W Model 39

Smith & Wesson Model 39 9mm Double Action Automatic Pistol
Caliber: 9mm Luger. 8-shot magazine. 4-inch barrel. Overall length: $7\frac{7}{16}$ inches. Weight: $26\frac{1}{2}$ oz. Click adjustable rear sight, ramp front sight. Blued or nickel finish. Checkered walnut stocks. Made from 1954 to date. *Note:* Between 1954 and 1966, 927 pistols of this model were made with steel, instead of alloy, frames.
With steel frame **$850**
With alloy frame **275**

Smith & Wesson Model 41 22 Automatic Pistol . $395
Caliber: 22 Long Rifle, 22 Short (not interchangeably). 10-shot magazine. Barrel lengths: 5-, $5\frac{1}{2}$-, $7\frac{3}{8}$-inch; latter has detachable muzzle brake. 12 inches overall ($7\frac{3}{8}$-inch bbl.). Weight: $43\frac{1}{2}$ oz. ($7\frac{3}{8}$-inch bbl.). Click adjustable rear sight, undercut Patridge front sight. Blued finish. Checkered walnut stocks with thumb rest. Made 1957 to date.

Smith & Wesson Model 46 22 Automatic Pistol . $475
Caliber: 22 Long Rifle. 10-shot magazine. Barrel lengths: 5-, $5\frac{1}{2}$-, 7-inch. $10\frac{9}{16}$ inches overall (7-inch bbl.). Weight: 42 oz. (7-inch bbl.). Click adjustable rear sight, under cut Patridge front sight. Blue finish. Molded nylon stocks with thumb rest. Only 4000 produced. Made from 1957 to 1966.

S&W Model 52

Smith & Wesson Model 52 38 Master Automatic $450
Caliber: 38 Special (mid-range wadcutter only). 5-shot magazine. 5-inch barrel. Overall length: $8\frac{5}{8}$ inches. Weight: 41 oz. Micrometer click rear sight, Patridge front sight on ramp base. Blued finish. Checkered walnut stocks. Made from 1961 to date.

Smith & Wesson Model 59 9mm Double Action Automatic Pistol $295
Similar to Model 39 with same general specifications, except has 14-shot magazine, checkered nylon stocks. Made from 1971 to date.

S&W Model 59

S&W Model 61

Smith & Wesson Model 61 Escort Pocket Automatic Pistol $250
Caliber: 22 Long Rifle. 5-shot magazine. 2$\frac{1}{8}$-inch barrel. 4$\frac{13}{16}$ inches overall. Weight: 14 oz. Fixed sights. Blued or nickel finish. Checkered plastic stocks. Made 1970-74.

S&W Model 439

Smith & Wesson Model 439 9mm Double Action Automatic Pistol $295
Caliber: 9mm Luger. Two 8-round magazines. 4-inch barrel. Overall length: 7$\frac{7}{16}$ inches. Weight: 30 oz. Serrated ramp square front sight, square notch rear. Checkered walnut grips. Blue or nickel finish.

S&W Model 459

Smith & Wesson Model 459 9mm Double Action Automatic Pistol $325
Caliber: 9mm Luger. Two 14-round magazines. 4-inch barrel. Overall length: 7$\frac{7}{16}$ inches. Weight: 28 oz. Blue or nickel finish.

S&W Model 469

Smith & Wesson Model 469 9mm Double Action Automatic Pistol $295
Caliber: 9mm Luger. Two 12-round magazines. 3$\frac{1}{2}$-inch barrel. Overall length: 6$\frac{7}{8}$ inches. Weight: 26 oz. Yellow ramp front sight, dovetail mounted square notch rear. Sandblasted blue finish. Optional ambidextrous safety.

S&W Model 639

S&W Model 645

Smith & Wesson Model 639 Automatic **$350**
Caliber: 9mm Luger Parabellum. Two 12-round magazines. $3\frac{1}{2}$-inch barrel. 6.9 inches overall. Weight: 26 oz. Non-glare blued finish.

Smith & Wesson Model 645 Double Action Automatic Pistol **$425**
Caliber: 45 ACP. 8-shot. 5-inch barrel. Overall length: $8\frac{1}{2}$ inches. Weight: Approx. 38 oz. Red ramp front, fixed rear sights. Stainless.

Smith & Wesson Model 659 9mm Double Action Automatic **$395**
Similar to S&W Model 459, except weight is $39\frac{1}{2}$ oz. and finish is satin stainless steel.

Smith & Wesson Model 669 Automatic **$375**
Caliber: 9mm. 12-shot magazine. Barrel: $3\frac{1}{2}$ inches. 6.9 inches overall. Weight: 26 oz. Serrated ramp front sight with red bar, fixed rear sight. Non-glare stainless steel finish.

S&W Model 659
Stainless

S&W Model 745
Automatic Pistol

Smith & Wesson Model 745 Automatic Pistol
Caliber: 45 ACP. 8-shot magazine. 5-inch barrel. $8\frac{5}{8}$ inches overall. Weight: $38\frac{3}{4}$ oz. Fixed sights. Blued slide and stainless frame. Checkered walnut grips. Similar to the model 645, but without double action capability. Made from 1987 to date.
With Standard Competition Features **$525**
IPSC Commemorative (first 5000) **570**

S&W Model 1891
Single Shot Pistol

Smith & Wesson Model 1891 Single Shot Target Pistol, First Model
Hinged frame. Calibers: 22 Long Rifle, 32 S&W, 38 S&W. Barrel lengths: 6-, 8- and 10-inch. Approximately $13\frac{1}{2}$ inches overall with 10-inch bbl. Weight: about 25 oz. Target sights, barrel catch rear sight adjustable for windage and elevation. Blued finish. Square butt, hard rubber

Smith & Wesson Model 1891, First Model (cont.)
stocks. Made from 1893 to 1905. *Note:* This model was available also as a combination arm with accessory 38 revolver barrel and cylinder to convert the single-shot target pistol to a pocket revolver. It has the frame of the 38 Single Action Revolver Model 1891 with side flanges, hand and cylinder stop slots.
Single-shot pistol, 22 Long Rifle . . . . **$ 340**
Single-shot pistol, 32 S&W or 38 S&W **1000**
Combination set, revolver and single-shot barrel **945**

Smith & Wesson Model 1891 Single Shot Target Pistol, Second Model $340
Basically the same as the First Model, except side flanges, hand and stop slots eliminated, cannot be converted to revolver, redesigned rear sight. Caliber: 22 Long Rifle only. 10-inch barrel only. Made from 1905 to 1909.

Smith & Wesson Perfected Single Shot Target Pistol
Also called Olympic Model (see note below). Similar to 1891 Single Shot Second Model except has double-action lockwork. Caliber: 22 Long Rifle only. 10-inch bbl. Checkered walnut stocks, extended square butt target type. Made from 1909 to 1923. *Note:* In 1920 and thereafter, pistols of this model were made with barrels having bore diameter of .223 instead of .226 and tight, short chambering. The first of these pistols were produced for the U.S. Olympic Team of 1920 and, therefore, the designation Olympic Model was adopted.
Pre-1920 Type **$400**
Olympic Model **550**

S&W Straight Line

Smith & Wesson Straight Line Single Shot Target Pistol $1150
Frame shaped like that of an automatic pistol, barrel swings to the left on pivot for extracting and loading, straight line trigger and hammer movement. Caliber: 22 Long Rifle. 10-inch bbl. 11¼ inches overall. Weight: 34 oz. Target sights. Blued finish. Smooth walnut stocks. Supplied in metal case with screwdriver and cleaning rod. Made from 1925 to 1936.

SMITH & WESSON REVOLVERS

Smith & Wesson Model I

Smith & Wesson Model I Hand Ejector Double Action Revolver $490
First Model. Forerunner of the current 32 Hand Ejector and Regulation Police models, this was the first S&W revolver of the solid-frame, swing-out cylinder type. Top strap of this model is longer than later models and it lacks the usual S&W cylinder latch. Caliber: 32 S&W Long. Barrel lengths: 3¼-, 4¼-, and 6-inch. Fixed sights. Blued or nickel finish. Round butt, hard rubber stocks. Made from 1896 to 1903.

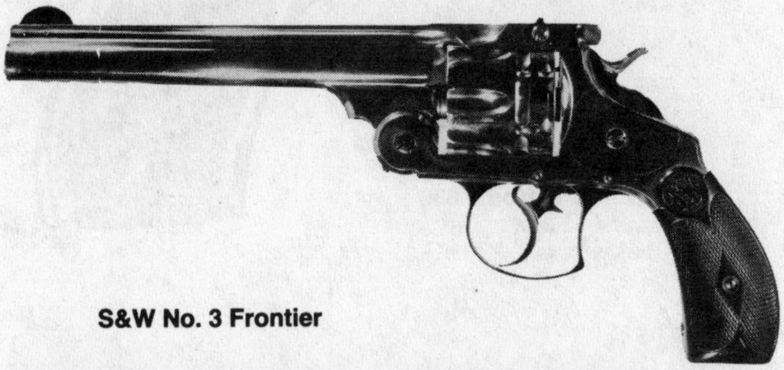
S&W No. 3 Frontier

Smith & Wesson No. 3 Single Action (Frontier) Revolver $1250
Caliber: 44-40 Winchester. Barrel lengths: 4-, 5- and 6½-inch. Fixed or target sights. Blued or nickel finish. Round buttstocks, hard rubber or checkered walnut. Made from 1885 to 1908.

Smith & Wesson No. 3 Single Action (New Model) Revolver $1095
Hinged frame. 6-shot cylinder. Caliber: 44 S&W Russian. Barrel lengths: 4-, 5-, 6-, 6½-, 7½- and 8-inch. Fixed or target sights. Blued or nickel finish. Round buttstocks, hard rubber or checkered walnut. Made from 1878 to 1908. *Note:* Value shown is for standard model. Specialist collectors recognize numerous variations with a wide range of higher values.

Smith & Wesson No. 3 Single Action Target Revolver $1295
Hinged frame. 6-shot cylinder. Calibers: 32/44 S&W, 38/44 S&W Gallery & Target. 6½-inch barrel only. Fixed or target sights. Blued or nickel finish. Round buttstocks, hard rubber or checkered walnut. Made from 1887 to 1910.

S&W Model 10 M & P Model of 1905

S&W Model 10 Round Butt

Smith & Wesson Model 10 38 Military & Police Double Action Revolver

Also called Hand Ejector Model of 1902, Hand Ejector Model of 1905, Model K. Manufactured substantially in its present form since 1902, this model has undergone numerous changes, most of them minor. Both round and square butt models available, the latter introduced in 1904. Caliber: 38 Special. 6-shot cylinder. Barrel lengths: 2- (introduced 1933), 4-, 5-, 6- and $6^{1}/_{2}$-inch (latter discontinued 1915), also 4-inch heavy barrel (introduced 1957). $11^{1}/_{8}$ inches overall in square butt model with 6-inch barrel. Round butt model is $^{1}/_{4}$-inch shorter, weighs about $^{1}/_{2}$ oz. less. Fixed sights. Blued or nickel finish. Checkered walnut stocks, hard rubber available in round butt style. Current Model 10 has short action. Made from 1902 to date. *Note:* S&W Victory Model, wartime version of the M & P 38, was produced for the U.S. Government from 1940 to the end of the war. A similar revolver, designated 38/200 British Service Revolver, was produced for the British Government during the same period. These arms have either brush-polish or sandblast blue finish, and most of them have plain, smooth walnut stocks, lanyard swivels.

Model of 1902 (1902-1905)	**$395**
Model of 1905 (1905-1940)	**290**
38/200 British Service (1940-1945)	**220**
Victory Model (1942-1945)	**220**
Model of 1944 (1945-1948)	**195**
Model 10 (1948-date)	**180**

S&W Model 10 Heavy Barrel

Smith & Wesson Model 10 38 Military & Police Heavy Barrel $175

Same as standard Model 10, except has heavy 4-inch barrel, weighs 34 oz. Made from 1957 to date.

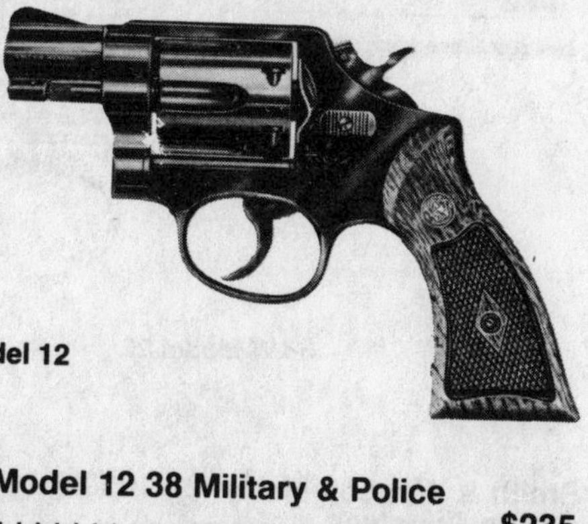

S&W Model 12

Smith & Wesson Model 12 38 Military & Police Airweight $235

Same as standard Military & Police, except has light alloy frame, furnished with 2- or 4-inch barrel only, weighs 18 oz. (with 2-inch barrel). Made from 1952 to 1986.

S&W Model 13

Smith & Wesson Model 13 357 Military & Police . . $195

Same as Model 10 38 Military & Police Heavy Barrel, except chambered for 357 Magnum. Made from 1974 to date.

Smith & Wesson Model 13 (Heavy Barrel) Double Action Revolver $195

Caliber: 357 Mag. 6-shot cylinder. Barrel lengths: 3 and 4 inches. $9^{1}/_{4}$ inches overall. Weight: 34 oz. Square notch rear sight, ramp front sight.

S&W Models 14, 16, 17 Masterpiece DA Revolver, Model 17 (shown)

Smith & Wesson Models 14 (K38), 16 (K32), 17 (K22) Masterpiece DA Revolvers

Calibers: 22 Long Rifle, 22 Magnum Rimfire, 32 S&W Long, 38 Special. 6-shot cylinder. Barrel lengths: 4- (22 MRF only), 6-, $8^{3}/_{8}$-inch (latter not available in K32). $11^{1}/_{8}$ inches overall (6-inch bbl.). Weight: $38^{1}/_{2}$ oz., K22 with 6-inch bbl. Click adjustable rear sight, Patridge front sight. Blued finish. Checkered walnut stocks. Made from 1947 to date. (Model 16 discontinued 1974; only 3630 were produced.)

Model 14 (K38)	**$250**
Model 16 (K32)	**395**
Model 17 (K22)	**250**

S&W Model 14 Single Action

Smith & Wesson Model 14 (K38) Masterpiece SA
Same as standard Model 14, except single action only, with target hammer and trigger.
With 6-inch barrel **$230**
With $8\frac{3}{8}$-inch barrel **250**

S&W Model 15

Smith & Wesson Models 15 (38) and 18 (22) Combat Masterpiece Double Action Revolvers
Same as K22 and K38 Masterpiece but with 2- (38) or 4-inch barrel and Baughman quick-draw front sight. $9\frac{1}{8}$ inches overall with 4-inch bbl. Weight: 34 oz., 38 cal. Introduced 1950; Model 18 discontinued 1985.
Model 15 .... **$195**
Model 18 .... **225**

S&W Model 19
Round Butt

S&W Model 19

Smith & Wesson Model 19 357 Combat Magnum Double Action Revolver **$245**
Caliber: 357 Magnum. 6-shot cylinder. Barrel lengths: $2\frac{1}{2}$-, 4-, 6-inch. $9\frac{1}{2}$ inches overall (4-inch bbl.). Weight: 35 oz. (4-inch bbl.). Click adjustable rear sight, ramp front sight. Blued or nickel finish. Target stocks of checkered Goncalo Alves. Model with $2\frac{1}{2}$-inch barrel has round butt. Made from 1956 to date.

S&W Model 20

Smith & Wesson Model 20 38/44 Heavy Duty Double Action Revolver
Caliber: 38 Special (especially designed for high speed ammunition). 6-shot cylinder. Barrel lengths: 4-, 5- and $6\frac{1}{2}$-inch. $10\frac{3}{8}$ inches overall with 5-inch bbl. Weight: 40 oz. with 5-inch bbl. Fixed sights. Blued or nickel finish. Checkered walnut stocks. Short action after 1948. Made from 1930 to 1967.
Pre-World War II **$400**
Postwar **300**

S&W Model 21

Smith & Wesson Model 21 1950 44 Military Double Action Revolver **$795**
Postwar version of the 1926 Model 44 Military. Same specifications as that model. Redesigned hammer. Made from 1950 to 1967.

S&W Model 22

Smith & Wesson Model 22 1950 Army Double Action Revolver **$495**
Postwar version of the 1917 Army. Same specifications as that model. Redesigned hammer. Made from 1950 to 1967.

S&W 22/32 Kit Gun

Smith & Wesson 22/32 Kit Gun **$255**
Same as 22/32 Target, except has 4-inch barrel and round buttstocks. 8 inches overall. Weight: 21 oz. Made from 1935 to 1953.

S&W 22/32 Target

Smith & Wesson 22/32 Target DA Revolver **$560**
Also known as the Bekeart Model. Design based upon "32 Hand Ejector." Caliber: 22 Long Rifle (recessed head cylinder for high speed cartridges introduced 1935). 6-shot cylinder. 6-inch barrel. 10½ inches overall. Weight: 23 oz. Adjustable target sights. Blued finish. Checkered walnut stocks. Made from 1911 to 1953. *Note:* In 1911, San Francisco gun dealer Phil Bekeart, who suggested this model, received 292 pieces. These are the true "Bekeart Model" revolvers worth about double the value shown for the standard 22/32 Target.

S&W Model 23

Smith & Wesson Model 23 38/44 Outdoorsman Double Action Revolver
Target version of the 38/44 Heavy Duty. 6½-inch barrel only. Weight: 41¾ oz. Target sights, micrometer click rear on postwar models. Blued finish only. 1950 model has ribbed barrel, redesigned hammer. Made from 1930 to 1967.
Prewar **$525**
Postwar **450**

S&W Model 24

Smith & Wesson Model 24 1950 44 Target DA Revolver **$525**
Postwar version of the 1926 Model 44 Target with same general specifications, except has redesigned hammer, ribbed barrel, micrometer click rear sight. Made from 1950 to 1967.

Smith & Wesson Model 25 1950 45 Target DA Revolver **$395**
Same as 1950 Model 44 Target but chambered for 45 Automatic cartridge. Made from 1950 to date.

S&W Model 27

Smith & Wesson Model 27 357 Magnum Double Action Revolver
Caliber: 357 S&W Magnum. 6-shot cylinder. Barrel lengths: 3½-, 5-, 6-, 6½- and 8⅜-inch. 11⅜ inches overall with 6-inch bbl. Weight: 44 oz. with 6-inch bbl. Adjustable target sights, Baughman quick-draw ramp front sight on 3½-inch barrel. Blued or nickel finish. Checkered walnut stocks. Made from 1935 to date. *Note:* Until 1938, the 357 Magnum was custom made in any barrel length from 3½-inch to 8¾-inch; each of these revolvers was accompanied by a registration certificate and has its registration number stamped on the inside of the yoke. Postwar Magnums have a redesigned hammer with shortened fall and the new S&W micrometer click rear sight.
Prewar registered model **$895**
Prewar model without registration number **550**
Current model with 8⅜-inch barrel **365**
Current model, other barrel lengths **350**

Smith & Wesson Model 28 Highway Patrolman Double Action Revolver **$235**
Caliber: 357 Magnum. 6-shot cylinder. Barrel lengths: 4- or 6-inch. Overall length: with 6-inch bbl., 11¼ inches. Weight: with 6-inch bbl., 44 oz. Adjustable rear sight, ramp

S&W Model 28

Smith & Wesson Model 28 (cont.)
front sight. Blued finish. Checkered walnut stocks, Magna or target type. Made from 1954 to 1986.

Smith & Wesson Model 29 44 Magnum Double Action Revolver
Caliber: 44 Magnum. 6-shot cylinder. Barrel lengths: 4-, 6½-, 8⅜-inch. 11⅞ inches overall (6½-inch bbl.). Weight: 47 oz., 6½-inch bbl. Click adjustable rear sight, ramp front sight. Blued or nickel finish. Target stocks of checkered Goncalo Alves. Made from 1956 to date.
With 8⅜-inch barrel **$375**
Other barrel lengths **360**

S&W Model 30

Smith & Wesson Model 30 32 Hand Ejector Double Action Revolver $215
Caliber: 32 S&W Long. 6-shot cylinder. Barrel lengths: 2- (introduced 1949), 3-, 4- and 6-inch. 8 inches overall with 4-inch bbl. Weight: 18 oz. with 4-inch bbl. Fixed sights. Blued or nickel finish. Checkered walnut or hard rubber stocks, round butt. Made from 1903 to 1976. Numerous changes, mostly minor, as in M & P model.

S&W Model 31 Regulation Police

Smith & Wesson Models 31 & 33 Regulation Police Double Action Revolver $225
Same basic type as 32 Hand Ejector, except has square buttstocks. Calibers: 32 S&W Long (Model 31), 38 S&W (Model 33). 6-shot cylinder in 32 caliber, 5-shot in 38 caliber. Barrel lengths: 2- (introduced 1949), 3-, 4- and 6-inch in 32 cal.; 4-inch only in 38 cal. 8½ inches overall with 4-inch bbl. Weight: 18 oz., 38 cal. with 4-inch barrel;

Smith & Wesson Models 31 & 33 (cont.)
32 cal., ¾-oz. heavier. Fixed sights. Blued or nickel finish. Checkered walnut stocks. Made from 1917 to date; Model 33 discontinued in 1974.

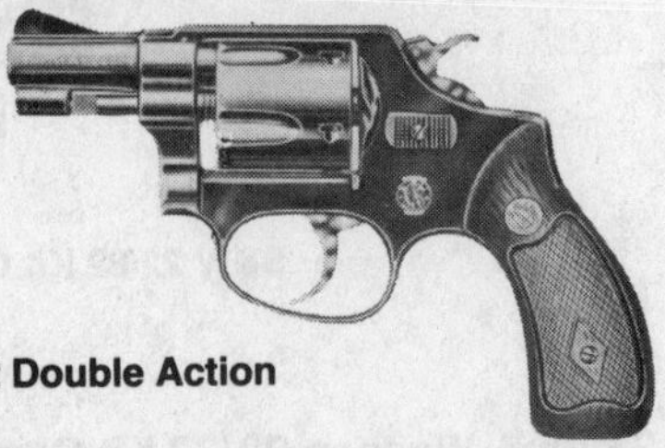

S&W Model 32 Double Action

Smith & Wesson 32 Double Action Revolver . . . $225
Hinged frame. Caliber: 32 S&W. 5-shot cylinder. Barrel lengths: 3-, 3½- and 6-inch. Fixed sights. Blued or nickel finish. Hard rubber stocks. Made from 1880 to 1919. *Note:* Value shown applies generally to the several varieties. Exception is the very rare first issue of 1880 (identified by squared side plate and serial number 1 to 30); value, $2000.

Smith & Wesson Model 32 Terrier Double Action Revolver $255
Caliber: 38 S&W. 5-shot cylinder. 2-inch barrel. 6¼ inches overall. Weight: 17 oz. Fixed sights. Blued or nickel finish. Checkered walnut or hard rubber stocks. Built on 32 Hand Ejector frame. Made from 1936 to 1974.

Smith & Wesson 32-20 Military & Police Double Action Revolver
Same as M & P 38, except chambered for 32-20 Winchester cartridge. First introduced in the 1899 model, M & P Revolvers were produced in this caliber until about 1940. Values same as for corresponding M & P 38 models.

S&W Model 34

Smith & Wesson Model 34 1953 22/32 Kit Gun . . $225
Same general specifications as previous 22/32 Kit Gun, except furnished in choice of 2-inch or 4-inch barrel and round or square buttstocks, blue or nickel finish. Made from 1953 to date.

S&W Model 35

Smith & Wesson Model 35 1953 22/32 Target . . $330
Same general specifications as previous model 22/32 Target, except has micrometer click rear sight, Magna-type target stocks, weighs 25 oz. Made from 1953 to 1974.

S&W Model 36 Chiefs Special

Smith & Wesson Model 36 Chiefs Special DA Revolver $195
Based on 32 Hand Ejector with frame lengthened to permit longer cylinder necessary for 38 Special cartridge. Caliber: 38 Special. 5-shot cylinder. Barrel lengths: 2- or 3-inch. Overall length: with 2-inch bbl., $6\frac{1}{2}$ inches. Weight: 19 oz. Fixed sights. Blued or nickel finish. Checkered walnut stocks, round or square butt. Made from 1952 to date.

Smith & Wesson Model 37 Airweight Chiefs Special $225
Same general specifications as standard Chiefs Special, except has light alloy frame, weighs $12\frac{1}{2}$ oz. with 2-inch bbl., blued finish only. Made from 1954 to date.

Smith & Wesson Model 38 Airweight Double Action Revolver $240
Caliber: 38 Special. 5-shot cylinder. Barrel length: 2 or 4 inches. $6\frac{7}{8}$ inches (2-inch barrel) overall. Weight: 18 oz. Square notch rear sight, ramp front sight.

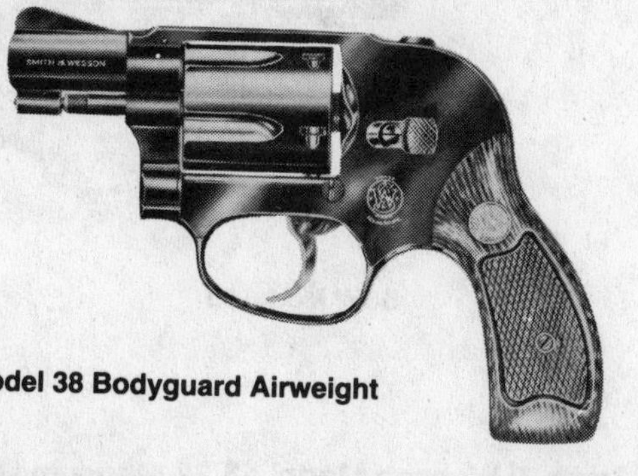

S&W Model 38 Bodyguard Airweight

Smith & Wesson Model 38 Bodyguard Airweight Double Action Revolver $225
"Shrouded" hammer. Light alloy frame. Caliber: 38 Special. 5-shot cylinder. 2-inch barrel. $6\frac{3}{8}$ inches overall. Weight: $14\frac{1}{2}$ oz. Fixed sights. Blued or nickel finish. Checkered walnut stocks. Made from 1955 to date.

Smith & Wesson 38 Double Action Revolver . . . $825
Hinged frame. Caliber: 38 S&W. 5-shot cylinder. Barrel lengths: 4-, $4\frac{1}{4}$-, 5-, 6-, 8- and 10-inch. Fixed sights. Blued or nickel finish. Hard rubber stocks. Made from 1880 to 1911. *Note:* Value shown applies generally to the several varieties. Exceptions are the first issue of 1880 (identified by squared side plate and serial number 1 to 4000) and the 8- and 10-inch barrel models of the third issue (1884-1895).

Smith & Wesson Model 38 Hand Ejector Double Action Revolver $650
Military & Police—First Model. Resembles Colt New Navy in general appearance, lacks barrel lug and locking bolt common to all later S&W hand ejector models. Caliber: 38 Long Colt. 6-shot cylinder. Barrel lengths: 4-, 5-, 6- and $6\frac{1}{2}$-inch. $11\frac{1}{2}$ inches overall with $6\frac{1}{2}$-inch bbl. Fixed sights. Blued or nickel finish. Checkered walnut or hard rubber stocks, round butt. Made from 1899 to 1902.

S&W 38 M&P Target

Smith & Wesson 38 Military & Police Target Double Action Revolver
Target version of the Military & Police with standard features of that model. Caliber: 38 Special. 6-inch barrel. Weight: $32\frac{1}{4}$ oz. Adjustable target sights. Blued finish. Checkered walnut stocks. Made from 1899 to 1940. For values, add $50 to those shown for corresponding M&P 38 models.

Smith & Wesson Model 38 Perfected Double Action Revolver $525
Hinged frame. Similar to earlier 38 Double Action Model, but heavier frame, side latch as in solid frame models, improved lockwork. Caliber: 38 S&W. 5-shot cylinder. Barrel lengths: $3\frac{1}{4}$-, 4-, 5- and 6-inch. Fixed sights. Blued or nickel finish. Hard rubber stocks. Made from 1909 to 1920.

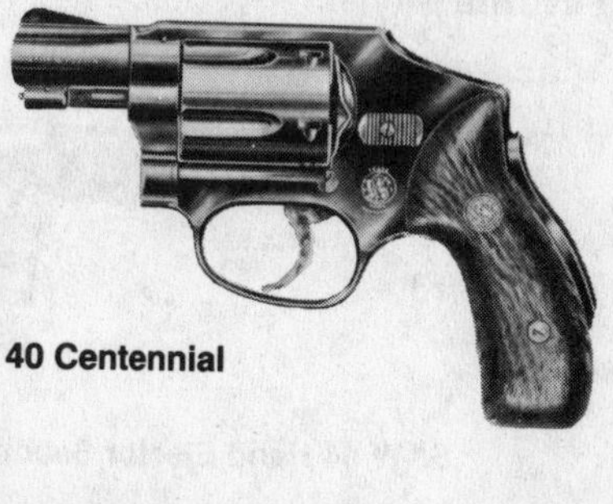

S&W Model 40 Centennial

Smith & Wesson Model 40 Centennial Double Action Hammerless Revolver $350
Similar to Chiefs Special, but has Safety Hammerless type mechanism with grip safety. 2-inch barrel. Weight: 19 oz. Made from 1953 to 1974.

Smith & Wesson Model 42 Centennial Airweight $425
Same as standard Centennial model except has light alloy frame, weighs 13 oz. Made from 1954 to 1974.

S&W Model 43

Smith & Wesson Model 43 1955 22/32 Kit Gun Airweight $355
Same as Model 34 Kit Gun, except has light alloy frame, furnished with 3½-inch barrel only, weighs 14¼ oz., square buttstock. Made from 1954 to 1974.

Smith & Wesson Model 44 1926 Military Double Action Revolver $600
Basically the same as the early New Century model, having the extractor rod casing but lacking the "Triple Lock" feature. Caliber: 44 S&W Special. 6-shot cylinder. Barrel lengths: 4-, 5- and 6½-inch. 11¾ inches overall with 6½-inch bbl. Weight: 39½ oz., 6½-inch bbl. Fixed sights. Blued or nickel finish. Checkered walnut stocks. Made from 1926 to 1941.

Smith & Wesson Model 44 1926 Target Double Action Revolver $525
Target version of the 1926 Model 44 Military. 6½-inch barrel only. Target sights. Blued finish only. Made from 1926 to 1941.

Smith & Wesson 44 Double Action Revolver
Also called Wesson Favorite (lightweight model), Frontier (caliber 44-40). Hinged frame. 6-shot cylinder. Calibers: 44 S&W Russian, 38-40, 44-40. Barrel lengths: 4-, 5-, 6- and 6½-inch. Weight: with 6½-inch bbl., 37½ oz. Fixed sights. Blued or nickel finish. Hard rubber stocks. Made from 1881 to 1913, except Frontier discont. 1910.

Standard Model, 44 Russian	**$ 800**
Standard Model, 38-40	**1200**
Frontier Model	**1200**
Favorite Model	**2000**

S&W 44 Hand Ejector Second Model

Smith & Wesson 44 Hand Ejector Second Model Double Action Revolver $750
Basically the same as New Century, except crane lock ("Triple Lock" feature) and extractor rod casing eliminated. Calibers: 44 S&W Special, 44-40 Winchester, 45 Colt. Barrel lengths: 4-, 5-, 6½- and 7½-inch. 11¾ inches overall with 6½-inch bbl. Weight: 38 oz. with 6½-inch bbl. Fixed sights. Blued or nickel finish. Checkered walnut stocks. Made from 1915 to 1937.

Smith & Wesson Model 48 (K-22) Masterpiece M.R.F. Double Action Revolver $300
Caliber: 22 Mag and 22 RF. 6-shot cylinder. Barrel lengths: 4 and 6 inches. 11⅛ inches overall. Weight: 39 oz. Adjustable rear sight, ramp front sight.

Smith & Wesson Model 49 Bodyguard $235
Same as Model 38 Bodyguard Airweight, except has steel frame, weighs 20½ oz. Made from 1959 to date.

S&W Model 51

Smith & Wesson Model 51 1960 22/32 Kit Gun M.R.F. $425
Same as Model 34 Kit Gun, except chambered for 22 Winchester Magnum Rimfire; has 3½-inch barrel, weighs 24 oz. Made from 1960 to 1974.

S&W Model 53

Smith & Wesson Model 53 22 Magnum Double Action Revolver $610
Caliber: 22 Remington Jet C.F. Magnum. 6-shot cylinder (inserts permit use of 22 Short, Long, or L.R. cartridges). Barrel lengths: 4-, 6-, 8⅜-inches. Overall length: (with 6-inch bbl.), 11¼ inches. Weight: with 6-inch barrel, 40 oz. Micrometer click rear sight, ramp front sight. Checkered walnut stocks. Made from 1960 to 1974.

Smith & Wesson Model 57 41 Magnum Double Action Revolver
Caliber: 41 Magnum. 6-shot cylinder. Barrel lengths: 4-, 6-, 8⅜-inches. Weight: with 6-inch barrel, 40 oz. Micrometer click rear sight, ramp front sight. Target stocks of checkered Goncalo Alves. Made from 1964 to date.

With 8⅜-inch barrel	**$325**
Other barrel lengths	**280**

S&W Model 58 41 M&P

Smith & Wesson Model 58 41 Military & Police Double Action Revolver $295
Caliber: 41 Magnum. 6-shot cylinder. 4-inch barrel. Overall length: 9¼ inches. Weight: 41 oz. Fixed sights. Checkered walnut stocks. Made from 1964 to date.

S&W Model 60

Smith & Wesson Model 60 Stainless Double Action Revolver $250
Caliber: 38 Special. 5-shot cylinder. Barrel length: 2 inches. 6½ inches overall. Weight: 19 oz. Square notch rear sight, ramp front sight. Satin finish stainless steel. Made 1965 to date.

Smith & Wesson Model 63 (1977) Kit Gun Double Action Revolver $235
Caliber: 22 LR. 6-shot cylinder. Barrel length: 4 inches. 6½ inches overall. Weight: 24½ oz. Adjustable rear sight, ramp front sight.

Smith & Wesson Model 64 38 Military & Police Stainless $210
Same as standard Model 10, except satin-finished stainless steel; available in square butt type with 4-inch heavy barrel, round butt-type with 2-inch barrel. Made 1970 to date.

S&W Model 65 357 M&P

Smith & Wesson Model 65 357 Military & Police Stainless $225
Same as Model 13, except satin-finished stainless steel. Made from 1974 to date.

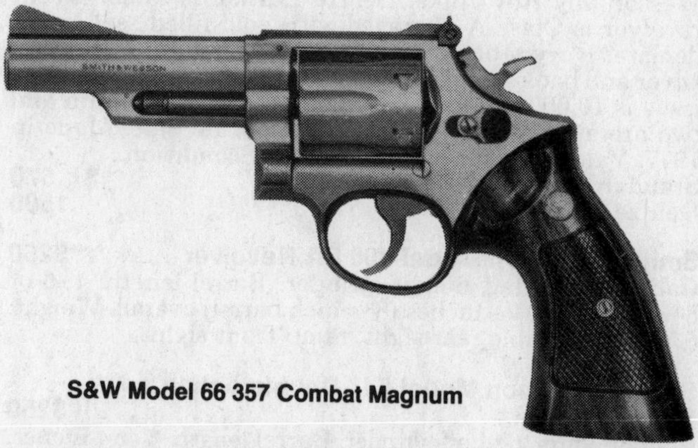

S&W Model 66 357 Combat Magnum

Smith & Wesson Model 66 357 Combat Magnum Stainless $265
Same as Model 19, except satin-finished stainless steel. Made from 1971 to date.

S&W Model 67 Combat Masterpiece

Smith & Wesson Model 67 38 Combat Masterpiece Stainless $235
Same as Model 15, except satin-finished stainless steel; available only with 4-inch barrel. Made from 1972 to date.

S&W 125th Anniversary Commemorative, Deluxe Edition

Smith & Wesson 125th Anniversary Commemorative
Issued to celebrate the 125th anniversary of the 1852 partnership of Horace Smith and Daniel Baird Wesson. Standard Edition is Model 25 revolver, caliber 45 Colt, with 6½-inch barrel, bright blued finish, gold-filled barrel

Smith & Wesson 125th Anniversary (cont.)
roll mark "Smith & Wesson 125th Anniversary," sideplate marked with gold-filled Anniversary seal, smooth Goncalo Alves stocks, in presentation case with nickel silver Anniversary medallion and book, "125 Years with Smith & Wesson" by Roy Jinks. Deluxe Edition is same, except revolver is Class A engraved with gold-filled seal on sideplate, ivory stocks; Anniversary medallion is sterling silver and book is leather bound; limited to 50 units. Total issue is 10,000 units, of which 50 are Deluxe Edition and two are a Custom Deluxe Edition not for sale. Made in 1977. Values are for revolvers in new condition.
Standard Edition . . . . **$ 570**
Deluxe Edition **1500**

Smith & Wesson Model 486 DA Revolver $260
Caliber: 357 Mag. 6-shot cylinder. Barrel length: 4, 6 or $8^3/_8$ inches. $13^{13}/_{16}$ inches ($8^3/_8$-inch barrel) overall. Weight: 53 oz. Adjustable rear sight, ramp front sight.

Smith & Wesson Model 547 Double Action Revolver $250
Caliber: 9mm. 6-shot cylinder. Barrel length: 3 or 4 inches. $7^5/_{16}$ inches overall. Weight: 32 oz. Square notch rear sight, ramp front sight. Discontinued 1986.

Smith & Wesson Model 581 Revolver $225
Caliber: 357 Magnum. Barrel: 4 inches. Weight: 34 oz. Serrated ramp front sight, square notch rear. Checkered walnut grips.

S&W Model 586
Distinguished Combat Magnum

Smith & Wesson Model 586 Distinguished Combat Magnum $255
Caliber: 357 Magnum. 6-shot. Barrel lengths: 4, 6 and $8^3/_8$ inches. Overall length: $9^3/_4$ inches w/4-inch bbl.; $13^{13}/_{16}$ inches w/$8^3/_8$-inch bbl. Weight: 42, 46, 53 oz., respectively. Red ramp front sight, micrometer click adjustable rear. Checkered grip. S&W blue or nickel finish.

Smith & Wesson Model 649 Stainless Double Action Revolver $240
Caliber: 38 Special. 5-shot cylinder. Barrel length: 2 inches. $6^1/_4$ inches overall. Weight: 20 oz. Square notch rear sight, ramp front sight.

Smith & Wesson Model 650 Revolver $245
Caliber: 22 LR. 6-shot cylinder. 3-inch barrel. 7 inches overall. Weight: $23^1/_2$ oz. Serrated ramp front sight, fixed square notch rear sight. Round butt, checkered walnut monogrammed stocks. Stainless steel finish.

Smith & Wesson Model 651 Stainless Double Action Revolver $250
Caliber: 22 Mag. RF. 6-shot cylinder. Barrel length: 3 and 4 inches. 7 and $8^5/_8$ inches, respectively, overall. Weight: $24^1/_2$ oz. Adjustable rear sight, ramp front sight.

Smith & Wesson Model 657 Revolver
Caliber: 41 Mag. 6-shot cylinder. Barrel: 4, 6 or 8.4 inches. 9.6, 11.4, and 13.9 inches overall. Weight: 44.2, 48 and 52.5 oz. Serrated black ramp front sight on ramp base; click rear sight adjustable for windage and elevation. Satin finish stainless steel.
With 4- or 6-inch barrel **$325**
With 8.4-inch barrel **340**

S&W Model 681 Nickel

Smith & Wesson Model 681 . . . . $235
Same as S&W Model 581, except in nickel finish.

Smith & Wesson Model 686 . . . . $270
Same as S&W Model 586 Distinguished Combat Magnum, except in stainless steel finish.

Smith & Wesson Model 1891 Single Action Revolver
Hinged frame. Caliber: 38 S&W. 5-shot cylinder. Barrel lengths: $3^1/_4$-, 4-, 5- and 6-inch. Fixed sights. Blued or nickel finish. Hard rubber stocks. Made 1891 to 1911. *Note:* Until 1906, an accessory single-shot target barrel (see Model 1891 Single Shot Target Pistol) was available for this revolver.
Revolver only . . . . **$ 505**
Set with 22 single-shot barrel **1015**

Smith & Wesson 1917 Army Double Action Revolver
Caliber: 45 Automatic, using 3-cartridge half-moon clip; 45 Auto Rim, without clip. 6-shot cylinder. $5^1/_2$-inch barrel. $10^3/_4$ inches overall. Weight: $36^1/_4$ oz. Fixed sights. Blued finish (blue-black finish on commercial model, brush polish on military). Checkered walnut stocks (commercial model, smooth on military). Made under U.S. Government contract from 1917 to 1919; produced commercially from 1919 to 1941. *Note:* About 175,000 of these revolvers were produced during World War I. The DCM sold these to NRA members during the 1930s at $16.15 each.
Commercial model **$450**
Military model **400**

Smith & Wesson K-22 Masterpiece Double Action Revolver $595
Improved version of K-22 Outdoorsman with same specifications but with micrometer click rear sight, short action and anti-backlash trigger. Manufactured 1940.

S&W K-22 Outdoorsman

Smith & Wesson K-22 Outdoorsman Double Action Revolver $390
Design based upon the 38 Military & Police Target. Caliber: 22 Long Rifle. 6-shot cylinder barrel. $11^{1}/_{8}$ inches overall. Weight: 35 oz. Adjustable target sights. Blued finish. Checkered walnut stock. Made from 1931 to 1940.

Smith & Wesson K32 and K38 Heavy Masterpiece Double Action Revolvers
Same as K32 and K38 Masterpiece, but with heavy weight barrel. Weight: $38^{1}/_{2}$ oz. Made from 1950 to 1953. *Note:* All K32 and K38 revolvers made after September 1953 have heavy barrels and the "Heavy Masterpiece" designation was discontinued. Values for Heavy Masterpiece models are the same as shown for Models 14 and 16. (*See* separate listing).

Smith & Wesson K-32 Target Double Action Revolver $895
Same as 38 Military & Police Target, except chambered for 32 S&W Long cartridge, slightly heavier barrel. Weight: 34 oz. Only 98 produced. Made from 1938 to 1940.

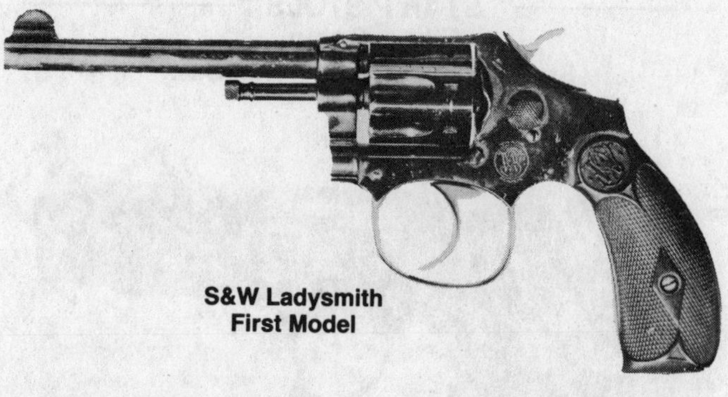

S&W Ladysmith
First Model

Smith & Wesson Ladysmith (Model M Hand Ejector) Double Action Revolver
Caliber: 22 Long Rifle. 7-shot cylinder. Barrel lengths: $2^{1}/_{4}$-, 3-, $3^{1}/_{2}$- and 6-inch (Third Model only). Approximately 7 inches overall with $3^{1}/_{2}$-inch barrel. Weight: about $9^{1}/_{2}$ oz. Fixed sights, adjustable target sights were available on Third Model. Blued or nickel finish. Round butt, hard rubber stocks on First and Second Model; checkered walnut or hard rubber square buttstocks on Third Model. First Model—1902 to 1906: cylinder locking bolt operated by button on left side of frame, no barrel lug and front locking bolt. Second Model—1906 to 1911: rear cylinder latch eliminated, has barrel lug, forward cylinder lock with draw-bolt fastening. Third Model—1911 to 1921: same as Second Model except has square buttstocks, target sights and 6-inch barrel available. *Note:* Legend has it

S&W Ladysmith
Second Model

S&W Ladysmith
Third Model

Smith & Wesson Ladysmith (cont.)
that a straight-laced D.B. Wesson ordered discontinuance of the Ladysmith when he learned of the little revolver's reputed popularity with ladies of the evening. The story, which undoubtedly has enhanced the appeal of this model to collectors, is not true: Wesson Ladysmith was discontinued because of difficulty of manufacture and high frequency of repairs.

First Model	**$ 895**
Second Model	**750**
Third Model, fixed sights, 3- or $3^{1}/_{2}$-inch barrel . .	**695**
Third Model, fixed sights, $2^{1}/_{4}$- or 6-inch barrel . .	**1095**
Third Model, adjustable sights, 6-inch barrel . . .	**1095**

Smith & Wesson New Century Model Hand Ejector Double Action Revolver $570
Also called "Triple Lock" because of its third cylinder lock at the crane. 6-shot cylinder. Calibers: 44 S&W Special, 450 Eley, 455 Mark II. Barrel lengths: 4-, 5-, $6^{1}/_{2}$- and $7^{1}/_{2}$-inch. Weight: with $6^{1}/_{2}$-inch bbl., 39 oz. Fixed sights. Blued or nickel finish. Checkered walnut stocks. Made from 1907 to 1915.

S&W Regulation Police Target

Smith & Wesson Regulation Police Target Double Action Revolver $235
Target version of the Regulation Police with standard features of that model. Caliber: 32 S&W Long. 6-inch barrel. $10^{1}/_{4}$ inches overall. Weight: 20 oz. Adjustable target sights. Blued finish. Checkered walnut stocks. Made from about 1917 to 1940.

Smith & Wesson Safety Hammerless Revolver . $370
Also called New Departure Double Action. Hinged frame. Calibers: 32 S&W, 38 S&W. 5-shot cylinder. Barrel lengths: 32 cal.—2-, 3- and $3^{1}/_{2}$-inch; 38 cal.—2-, $3^{1}/_{4}$-, 4-,

S&W Safety Hammerless

Smith & Wesson Safety Hammerless (cont.)
5- and 6-inch. Length overall: 32 cal. with 3-inch bbl., 6³/₄ inches; 38 cal. with 3¹/₄-inch bbl., 7¹/₂ inches. Weight: 32 cal. with 3-inch bbl., 14¹/₄ oz.; 38 cal. with 3¹/₄-inch bbl., 18¹/₄ oz. Fixed sights. Blued or nickel finish. Hard rubber stocks. 32 cal. made from 1888 to 1937, 38 cal. from 1887 to 1941. Various minor changes.

S&W Texas Ranger Commemorative

Smith & Wesson Texas Ranger Commemorative **$750**
Issued to honor the 150th anniversary of the Texas Rangers. Model 19 357 Combat Magnum with 4-inch barrel, sideplate stamped with Texas Ranger Commemorative Seal, smooth Goncalo Alves stocks. Special Bowie knife. In presentation case. 8000 sets were made in 1973. Value is for set in new condition.

SPRINGFIELD ARMORY
Geneseo, Illinois

Springfield Armory
Model 1911-A1 Auto Pistol

Springfield Armory 1911-A1 Automatic Pistol
Calibers: 9mm Parabellum, 45 ACP. 7- or 8-shot magazine. 5-inch barrel. 8¹/₂ inches overall. Weight: 36 oz. Fixed combat sights. Blued or parkerized finish. Checkered walnut stocks. *Note:* This is an exact duplicate of the M1911-A1 used by the U.S. Armed Forces for over 70 years.
Blued Finish **$290**
Parkerized Finish **275**

STAR PISTOLS
Eibar, Spain
Star, Bonifacio Echeverria, S.A.

Star Model 30M

Star Model 30M Double Action Auto Pistol **$360**
Caliber: 9mm Parabellum. 15-shot magazine. 4³/₈-inch barrel. 8 inches overall. Weight: 40 oz. Steel frame with combat features. Adjustable sights. Checkered composition stocks. Blued finish. Made from 1984 to date.

Star Model 30PK

Star Model 30PK Double Action Auto Pistol $355
Same basic specifications as Star Model 30M, except with 3.8-inch barrel, 30-oz. weight, and alloy frame. Made from 1984 to date.

Star Model AS

Star Model A Automatic Pistol $225
Modification of the Colt Government Model 45 Auto which it closely resembles; lacks grip safety. Caliber: 38 Super. 8-shot magazine. 5-inch barrel. 8-inches overall. Weight: 35 oz. Fixed sights. Blued finish. Checkered stocks. Made from 1934 to date.

Star Models AS, BS, PS $275
Same as Models A, B and P, except have magazine safety. Made from 1975 to date.

Star Model B $230
Same as Model A, except caliber 9mm Luger. Made from 1934 to 1975.

Star Model BKM $240
Similar to Model BKS, except has 4-inch barrel, checkered backstrap, checkered walnut stocks. Made 1976 to date.

Star Model BKS

Star Model BKS Starlight Automatic Pistol $220
Light alloy frame. Caliber: 9mm Luger. 8-shot magazine. $4\frac{1}{4}$-inch barrel. 7 inches overall. Weight: 25 oz. Fixed sights. Blued or chrome finish. Plastic stocks. Made from 1970 to date.

Star Model CO Pocket Automatic Pistol $160
Caliber: 25 Automatic (6.35mm). $2\frac{3}{4}$-inch barrel. $4\frac{1}{2}$ inches overall. Weight: 13 oz. Fixed sights. Blued finish. Plastic stocks. Made from 1941 to 1957.

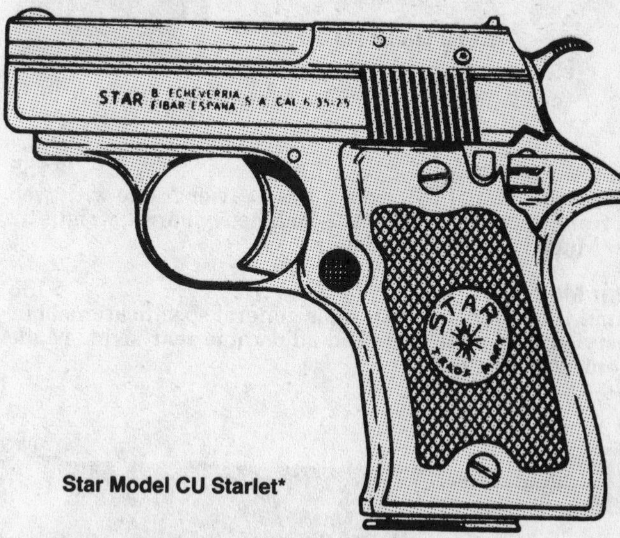

Star Model CU Starlet*

Star Model CU Starlet Pocket Automatic Pistol . $170
Light alloy frame. Caliber: 25 Automatic (6.35mm). 8-shot magazine. $2\frac{3}{8}$-inch barrel. $4\frac{3}{4}$ inches overall. Weight: $10\frac{1}{2}$ oz. Fixed sights. Blued or chrome-plated slide; frame anodized in black, blue, green, gray or gold. Plastic stocks. Made from 1957 to date. U.S. importation discont. 1968.

Star Model F Automatic Pistol $145
Caliber: 22 Long Rifle. 10-shot magazine. $4\frac{1}{2}$-inch barrel. $7\frac{1}{4}$ inches overall. Weight: 25 oz. Fixed sights. Blued finish. Plastic stocks. Made from 1942 to 1967.

Star Model F Olympic Rapid-Fire $220
Caliber: 22 Short. 9-shot magazine. 7-inch barrel. $11\frac{1}{16}$ inches overall. Weight: 52 oz. with weights. Adjustable target sight. Adjustable 3-piece barrel weight. Aluminum alloy slide. Muzzle brake. Plastic stocks. Made 1942-67.

Star Model F Automatic

Star Model FM

Star Model FM **$155**
Similar to Model FR, except has heavier frame with web in front of trigger guard, $4\frac{1}{4}$-inch heavy barrel; weighs 32 oz. Made from 1972 to date.

Star Model FR **$155**
Similar to Model F with same general specifications, but restyled, has slide stop and adjustable rear sight. Made from 1967 to 1972.

Star Model FRS

Star Model FRS **$155**
Same as Model FR, except has 6-inch barrel, weighs 28 oz.; also available in chrome finish. Made from 1967 to date.

Star Model FS

Star Model FS **$155**
Same as regular Model F, but with 6-inch barrel and adjustable sights. Weight: 27 oz. Made from 1942 to 1967.

Star Model H*

Star Model H **$145**
Same as Model HN except caliber 32 Automatic (7.65mm). 7-shot magazine. Weight: 20 oz. Made from 1934 to 1941.

Star Model HK Lancer*

Star Model HK Lancer Automatic Pistol **$185**
Similar to Starfire with same general specifications, except caliber 22 Long Rifle. Made from 1955 to 1968.

Star Model HN Automatic Pistol **$145**
Caliber: 380 Automatic (9mm Short). 6-shot magazine. $2\frac{3}{4}$-inch barrel. $5\frac{9}{16}$ inches overall. Weight: 20 oz. Fixed sights. Blued finish. Plastic stocks. Made 1934 to 1941.

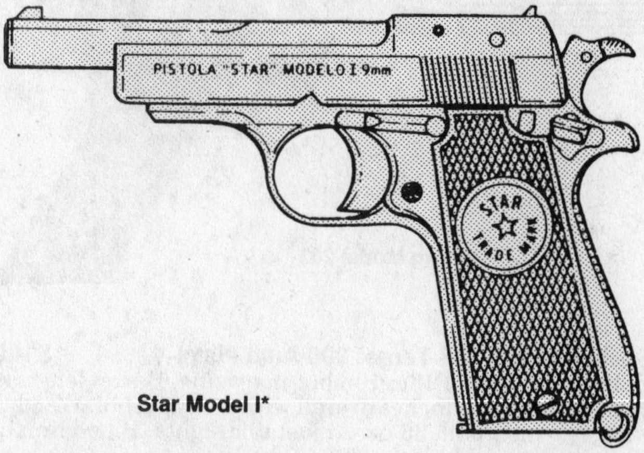

Star Model I*

Star Model I Automatic Pistol **$145**
Caliber: 32 Automatic (7.65mm). 9-shot magazine. $4\frac{13}{16}$-inch barrel. $7\frac{1}{2}$ inches overall. Weight: 24 oz. Fixed sights. Blued finish. Plastic stocks. Made from 1934 to 1936.

Star Model IN **$150**
Same as Model I, except caliber 380 Automatic (9mm Short), 8-shot magazine, weighs $24\frac{1}{2}$ oz. Made from 1934 to 1936.

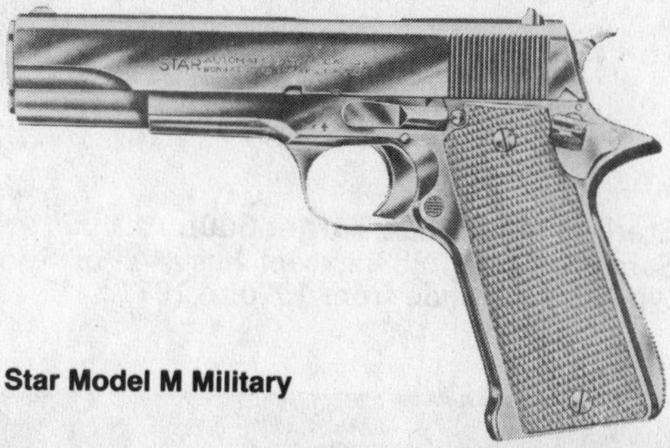

Star Model M Military

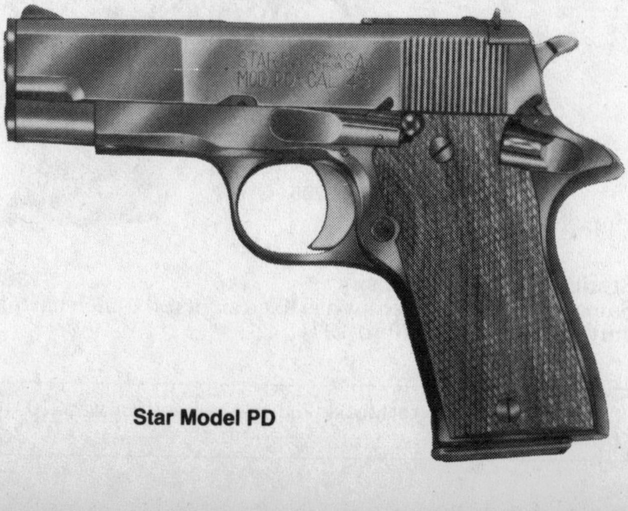

Star Model PD

Star Model M Military Automatic Pistol **$225**
Modification of the Colt Government Model 45 Auto, which it closely resembles; lacks grip safety. Calibers: 9mm Bergmann, 38 Super, 9mm Luger. 8-shot magazine, except 7-shot in 45 caliber. 5-inch barrel. $8\frac{1}{2}$ inches overall. Weight: 36 oz. Fixed sights. Blued finish. Checkered stocks. Made from 1934 to 1939.

Star Model P **$235**
Same as Model A, except caliber 45 Automatic; has 7-shot magazine. Made from 1934 to 1975.

Star Model PD Automatic Pistol **$250**
Caliber: 45 Automatic. 6-shot magazine. $3\frac{3}{4}$-inch barrel. 7 inches overall. Weight: 25 oz. Adjustable rear sight, ramp front sight. Blued finish. Checkered walnut stocks. Made from 1975 to date.

Star Model S

Star Model SI

Star Model S **$210**
Same as Model SI except caliber 380 Automatic (9mm), 7-shot magazine, weighs 19 oz. Made from 1941 to 1965.

Star Model SI Automatic Pistol **$200**
Reduced-size modification of the Colt Government Model 45 Auto; lacks grip safety. Caliber: 32 Automatic (7.65mm). 8-shot magazine. 4-inch barrel. $6\frac{1}{2}$ inches overall. Weight: 20 oz. Fixed sights. Blued finish. Plastic stocks. Made from 1941 to 1965.

Star Starfire Automatic Pistol **$185**
Light alloy frame. Caliber: 380 Automatic (9mm Short). 7-shot magazine. $3\frac{1}{8}$-inch barrel. $5\frac{1}{2}$ inches overall. Weight: $14\frac{1}{2}$ oz. Fixed sights. Blued or chrome-plated slide; frame anodized in black, blue, green, gray or gold. Plastic stocks. Made from 1957 to date. U.S. importation discont. 1968.

Star Models Super A, Super B, Super P **$250**
Same as Models A, B and P, except with improvements described under Super Star. Made from c. 1946 to date.

Star Models Super SI, Super S **$220**
Same general specifications as the regular Model SI and S, except with improvements described under Super Star. Made from c. 1946 to 1972.

Star Model Super SM

Star Model Super SM **$225**
Similar to Model Super S, except has adjustable rear sight, wood stocks. Made from 1973 to date.

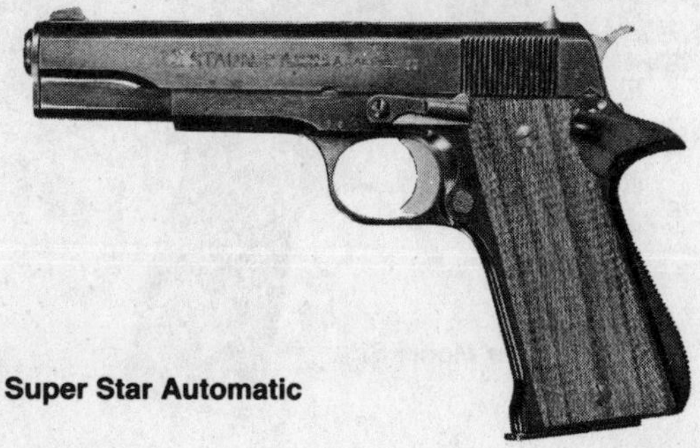

Super Star Automatic

Super Star Automatic Pistol **$245**
Improved version of the Model M with same general specifications; has disarming bolt permitting easier takedown, indicator of cartridge in chamber, magazine safety, takedown magazine, improved sights with luminous spots for aiming in darkness. Calibers: 38 Super, 9mm Luger. This is the standard service pistol of the Spanish Armed Forces, adopted 1946.

Super Star Target Model **$275**
Same as regular Super Star, except with adjustable target rear sight. Discontinued.

STENDA-WERKE PISTOL
Suhl, Germany

Stenda Pocket Automatic Pistol **$225**
Essentially the same as the Beholla; see listing of that pistol for specifications. Made c. 1920 to 1925. *Note:* This pistol may be marked "Beholla" along with the Stenda name and address.

STERLING ARMS CORPORATION
Gasport, New York

Sterling Model 283

Sterling Model 283 Target 300 Auto Pistol **$145**
Caliber: 22 Long Rifle. 10-shot magazine. Barrel lengths: $4\frac{1}{2}$-, 6-, 8-inch. 9 inches overall with $4\frac{1}{2}$-inch bbl. Weight: with $4\frac{1}{2}$-inch bbl., 36 oz. Adjustable sights. Blued finish. Plastic stocks. Made from 1970 to 1971.

Sterling Model 284

Sterling Model 284 Target 300L **$145**
Same as Model 283, except has $4\frac{1}{2}$- or 6-inch "Luger"-type barrel. Made from 1970 to 1971.

Sterling Model 285

Sterling Model 285 Husky **$130**
Same as Model 283, except has fixed sights, $4\frac{1}{2}$-inch barrel only. Made from 1970 to 1971.

Note: Total production of Models 283, 284, 285 and 286 was 2700 pieces.

Sterling Model 286

Sterling Model 286 Trapper **$130**
Same as Model 284, except has fixed sights. Made from 1970 to 1971.

Sterling Model 287 PPL-380 Automatic Pistol **$70**
Caliber: 380 Automatic. 6-shot magazine. 1-inch barrel. 5$^{3}/_{8}$ inches overall. Weight: 22$^{1}/_{2}$ oz. Fixed sights. Blued finish. Plastic stocks. Made from 1971 to 1972.

Sterling Model 300

Sterling Model 400

Sterling Model 300 Automatic Pistol **$85**
Caliber: 25 Automatic. 6-shot magazine. 2$^{1}/_{3}$-inch barrel. 4$^{1}/_{2}$ inches overall. Weight: 13 oz. Fixed sights. Blued or nickel finish. Plastic stocks. Made from 1972 to date.

Sterling Model 300S **$105**
Same as Model 300, except stainless steel. Made from 1976 to date.

Sterling Model 302 . . . . **$105**
Same as Model 300, except caliber 22 Long Rifle. Made from 1973 to date.

Sterling Model 302S **$125**
Same as Model 302, except stainless steel. Made from 1976 to date.

Sterling Model 400 Double Action Automatic Pistol **$185**
Caliber: 380 Automatic. 7-shot magazine. 3$^{1}/_{2}$-inch barrel. 6$^{1}/_{2}$ inches overall. Weight: 24 oz. Adjustable rear sight. Blued or nickel finish. Checkered walnut stocks. Made from 1975 to date.

Sterling Model 400S **$225**
Same as Model 400, except stainless steel. Introduced in 1977.

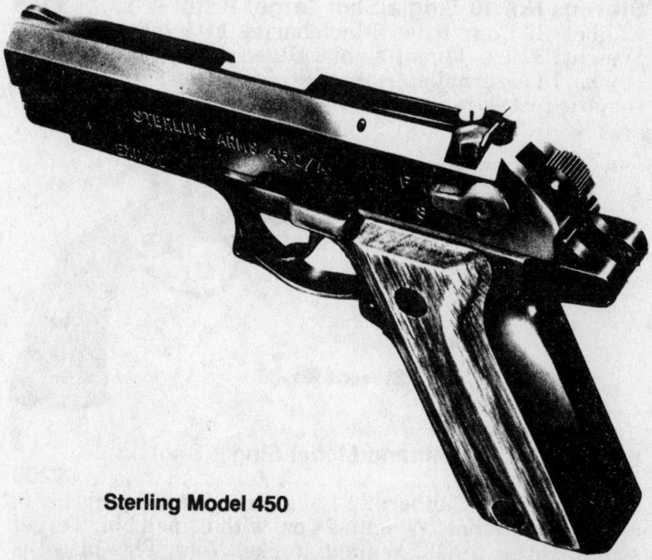

Sterling Model 450

Sterling Model PPL-22

Sterling Model 450 DA Auto Pistol **$300**
Caliber: 45 Automatic. 8-shot magazine. 4-inch barrel. 7$^{1}/_{2}$ inches overall. Weight: 36 oz. Adjustable rear sight. Blued finish. Smooth walnut stocks. Introduced in 1977.

Sterling Model PPL-22 Automatic Pistol $130
Caliber: 22 Long Rifle. 10-shot magazine. 1-inch barrel. 5½ inches overall. Weight: about 24 oz. Fixed sights. Blued finish. Wood stocks. Made from 1970 to 1971. *Note:* Only 382 were produced.

J. STEVENS ARMS CO.
Chicopee Falls, Mass.

Stevens No. 10

Stevens No. 10 Single Shot Target Pistol $195
Caliber: 22 Long Rifle. 8-inch barrel. 11½ inches overall. Weight: 37 oz. Target sights. Blued finish. Hard rubber stocks. In external appearance this arm resembles an automatic pistol; it has a tip-up action. Made 1919 to 1939.

Stevens No. 35

Stevens No. 35 Offhand Model Single Shot Target Pistol $200
Tip-up action. Caliber: 22 Long Rifle. Barrel lengths: 6, 8, 10, 12¼ inches. Weight: 24 oz. with 6-inch bbl. Target sights. Blued finish. Walnut stocks. *Note:* This pistol is similar to the earlier "Gould" model. No. 35 was also supplied chambered for .410 shotshell. Made 1907 to 1939.

STEYR PISTOLS
Steyr, Austria

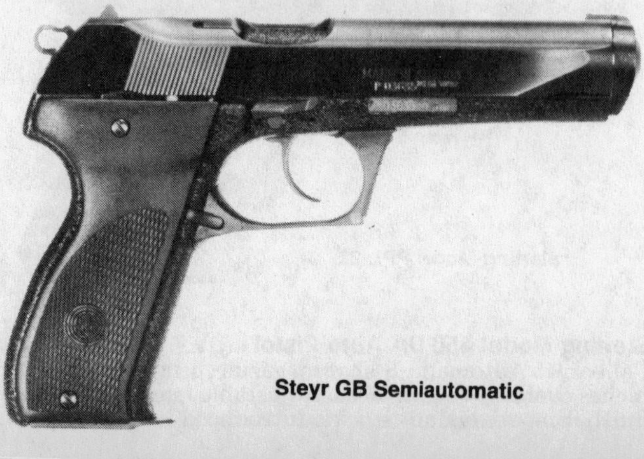
Steyr GB Semiautomatic

Steyr GB Semiautomatic Pistol $395
Caliber: 9mm Parabellum. 18-round magazine. 5.4-inch barrel. 8.9 inches overall. Weight: 2.9 lbs. Post front sight; fixed, notched rear sight. Double, gas-delayed, blow-back action. Currently in production.

Steyr-Hahn M12

Steyr-Hahn M12 Automatic Pistol $400
Caliber: 9mm Steyr. 8-shot fixed magazine, charger loaded. 5.1-inch barrel. 8.5 inches overall. Weight: 35 oz. Fixed sights. Blued finish. Checkered wood stocks. Made from 1911 to 1919. Adopted by the Austro-Hungarian Army in 1912. *Note:* Confiscated by the Germans in 1938, an estimated 250,000 of these pistols were converted to 9mm Luger and stamped with an identifying "08" on the left side of the slide. Mfd. by Osterreichische Waffenfabrik-Gesellschaft.

STOEGER LUGERS
Formerly mfd. by Stoeger Industries, So. Hackensack, N.J.; now by Classic Arms, Union City, N.J.

Stoeger Standard Luger

Stoeger Standard Luger 22 Automatic Pistol . . . $135
Caliber: 22 Long Rifle. 10-shot magazine. Barrels: 4½, 5½ inches. 8⅞ inches overall with 4½-inch bbl. Weight: with 4½-inch bbl., 29½ oz. Fixed sights. Black finish. Smooth wood stocks. Made from 1969 to date.

Stoeger Steel Frame Luger 22 Automatic Pistol . . $150
Caliber: 22 LR. 10-shot magazine. $4\frac{1}{2}$-inch barrel. $8\frac{7}{8}$ inches overall. Blued finish. Checkered wood stocks. Features one-piece solidly forged and machined steel frame. Made from 1980 to date.

Stoeger Target Luger 22 Automatic Pistol $185
Same as Standard Luger 22, except has target sights. $9\frac{3}{8}$ inches overall with $4\frac{1}{2}$-inch bbl. Checkered wood stocks. Made from 1975 to date.

TARGA PISTOLS ITALY

Manufactured by Armi Tanfoglio Guiseppe.

Targa Model GT26S Automatic Pistol $40
Caliber: 25 ACP. 6-shot magazine. $2\frac{1}{2}$-inch barrel. $4\frac{5}{8}$ inches overall. Weight: 15 oz. Fixed sights. Checkered composition stocks. Blued or chrome finish.

Targa Model GT32 Automatic Pistol
Caliber: 32 ACP. 6-shot magazine. $4\frac{7}{8}$-inch barrel. $7\frac{3}{8}$ inches overall. Weight: 26 oz. Fixed sights. Checkered composition or walnut stocks. Blued or chrome finish.
Blued finish **$100**
Chrome finish **110**

Targa Model GT380 Automatic Pistol
Same as the Targa GT32, except chambered for 380 ACP.
Blued finish **$120**
Chrome finish **125**

Targa Model GT380XE

Targa Model GT380XE Automatic Pistol $155
Caliber: 380 ACP. 11-shot magazine. $3\frac{3}{4}$-inch barrel. $7\frac{3}{8}$ inches overall. Weight: 28 oz. Fixed sights. Blued or satin nickel finish. Smooth wooden stocks. Made from 1980 to date.

FORJAS TAURUS S.A. Porto Alegre, Brazil

Taurus Model 65 Double Action Revolver $145
Caliber: 357 Magnum. 6-shot cylinder. 3- or 4-inch barrel. Weight: 32 oz. Front ramp sight, square notch rear. Checkered walnut target stock. Royal blue or satin nickel finish. Currently in production.

Taurus Model 66 Double Action Revolver $155
Calibers: 357 Magnum, 38 Special. 6-shot cylinder. Barrels: 3, 4 and 6 inches. Weight: 35 oz. Serrated ramp front sight; rear click adjustable sight. Checkered walnut grips. Royal blue or nickel finish. Currently in production.

Taurus Model 73 Double Action Revolver $135
Caliber: 32 Long. 6-shot cylinder. 3-inch heavy barrel. Weight: 20 oz.. Checkered grips. Blued or satin finish. Currently in production.

Taurus Model 74

Taurus Model 74 Target Grade Double Action Revolver $100
Caliber: 32 S&W Long. 6-shot cylinder. 3-inch barrel. $8\frac{1}{4}$ inches overall. Weight: 20 oz. Adjustable rear sight, ramp front sight. Blued or nickel finish. Checkered walnut stocks. Made from 1971 to date.

Taurus Model 80

Taurus Model 80 Double Action Revolver $135
Caliber: 38 Special. 6-shot cylinder. Barrel lengths: 3, 4 inches. $9\frac{1}{4}$ inches overall with 4-inch bbl. Weight: with 4-inch bbl., 30 oz. Fixed sights. Blued or nickel finish. Checkered walnut stocks. Made from 1971 to date.

Taurus Model 82

Taurus Model 82 Heavy Barrel $135
Same as Model 80, except has heavy barrel. Weight: with 4-inch bbl., 33 oz. Made from 1971 to date.

Taurus Model 83

Taurus Model 83 Heavy Barrel Target Grade . . . $140
Same as Model 84, except has heavy barrel, weighs $34\frac{1}{2}$ oz. Introduced in 1977.

Taurus Model 84

Taurus Model 84 Target Grade Revolver $125
Caliber: 38 Special. 6-shot cylinder. 4-inch barrel. $9\frac{1}{4}$ inches overall. Weight: 31 oz. Adjustable rear sight, ramp front sight. Blued or nickel finish. Checkered walnut stocks. Made from 1971 to date.

Taurus Model 85

Taurus Model 85 Double Action Revolver
Caliber: 38 Special. 5-shot cylinder. Barrel. 2- or 3-inch Weight: 21 oz. Fixed sights. Checkered walnut grips. Blued, satin nickel or stainless steel finish. Currently in production.

Blue or Satin	**$145**
Stainless Steel	**175**

Taurus Model 86

Taurus Model 86 Target Master Double Action Revolver $160
Caliber: 38 Special. 6-shot cylinder. 6-inch barrel. $11\frac{1}{4}$ inches overall. Weight: 34 oz. Adjustable rear sight, Patridge-type front sight. Blued finish. Checkered walnut stocks. Made from 1971 to date.

Taurus Model 94 Target Grade $125
Same as Model 74, except caliber 22 Long Rifle, 4-inch barrel, $9\frac{1}{4}$ inches overall, weighs 23 oz. Made from 1971 to date.

Taurus Model 96 Target Master $150
Same as Model 86, except caliber 22 Long Rifle. Made from 1971 to date.

Taurus Model PT 92AF

Taurus Model PT 92AF Semiautomatic Double Action Pistol $275
Caliber: 9mm Parabellum. 15-round magazine. Barrel: about 5 inches. 8½ inches overall. Weight: 34 oz. Blade front sight, notched bar rear sight. Smooth Brazilian walnut grips. Blued finish. Currently in production.

Taurus Model PT 99AF

Taurus Model PT 99AF Semiautomatic Pistol . . . $295
Same general specifications as Model PT 92AF, except rear sight is adjustable for elevation and windage, and finish is blued or satin nickel. Currently in production.

TEXAS LONGHORN ARMS
Richmond, Texas

Texas Longhorn Arms Single Action Revolver Cased Set
Set contains one each of the Texas Longhorn Single Actions. Each chambered in the same caliber and with the same serial number. Introduced in 1984. Ten sets were produced.
Standard Set **$4300**
Engraved Set **5700**

Texas Longhorn Arms Keith No. 5 Single Action Revolver $730
Caliber: 44 Magnum. 6-shot cylinder. 5½-inch barrel. 11 inches overall. Weight: 44 oz. Adjustable rear sight blade front. One-piece deluxe walnut stock. Blued finish. Introduced in 1987. 1200 produced.

Texas Longhorn Arms Sesquicentennial Single Action Revolver $1875
Same as South Texas Army Limited Edition, except engraved and nickel-plated with one-piece ivory stock. Introduced in 1986. 150 produced.

Texas Longhorn Arms South Texas Army Limited Edition Single Action Revolver $1125
Calibers: all popular centerfire pistol calibers. 6-shot cylinder. 4¾-inch barrel. 10¼ inches overall. Weight: 40 oz. Fixed sights. Color casehardened frame. One-piece deluxe walnut stocks. Blued barrel. Introduced in 1984. 1000 produced.

Texas Longhorn Arms Texas Border Special Single Action Revolver $1125
Same as South Texas Army Limited Edition, except with 3½-inch barrel and bird's-head grips. Introduced in 1984.

Texas Longhorn Arms West Texas Flat Top Target Single Action Revolver $1125
Same as South Texas Army Limited Edition, except with choice of barrel lengths from 7½ to 15 inches. Same special features with flat top style frame and adjustable rear sight. Introduced in 1984.

THOMPSON PISTOL
West Hurley, New York
Mfd. by Auto-Ordnance Corporation

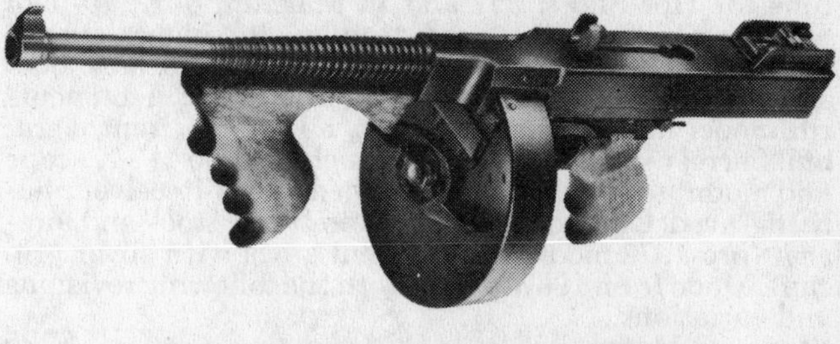

Thompson Model 27A-5 w/Drum Magazine

Thompson Model 27A-5 Semiautomatic Pistol
Similar to Thompson Model 1928A submachine gun, except has no provision for automatic firing, does not have detachable buttstock. Caliber: 45 Automatic. 20-shot detachable box magazine (5-, 15- and 30-shot box magazines, 39-shot drum also available). 13-inch finned barrel. Overall length: 26 inches. Weight: about 6¾ pounds. Adjustable rear sight, blade front sight. Blued finish. Walnut grips. Intro. 1977.
With box magazine **$400**
With drum magazine (as illustrated) **440**

THOMPSON/CENTER ARMS
Rochester, New Hampshire

Thompson/Center Contender Standard Model, 1967-Type

Thomspon/Center Contender Vent-Rib Model

Thompson/Center Contender Single Shot Pistol
Break frame, underlever action. Calibers: (rimfire) 22 LR, 22 WMR, 5mm RRM; (standard centerfire), 218 Bee, 22 Hornet, 22 Rem. Jet, 221 Fireball, 222 Rem., 25-35, 256 Win. Mag., 30 M1 Carbine, 30-30, 38 Auto, 38 Special, 357 Mag./Hot Shot, 9mm Luger, 45 Auto, 45 Colt, 44 Magnum/Hot Shot; (wildcat centerfire) 17 Ackley Bee, 17 Bumblebee, 17 Hornet, 17 K Hornet, 17 Mach IV, 17-222, 17-223, 22 K Hornet, 30 Herrett, 357 Herrett, 357-4 B&D. Interchangeable barrels: $8^3/_4$- or 10-inch standard octagon (357 Mag., 44 Mag. and 45 Colt available with detachable choke for use with Hot Shot cartridges); 10-inch with ventilated rib and detachable internal choke tube for Hot Shots, 357 and 44 Magnum only; 10-inch bull barrel, 30 or 357 Herrett only. $13^1/_2$ inches overall with 10-inch bbl. Weight: with standard 10-inch bbl., about 43 oz. Adjustable rear sight, ramp front sight; vent-rib model has folding rear sight, adjustable front sight; bull barrel available with or w/o sights; Lobo $1^1/_2$ X scope and mount (add $40 to value). Blued finish. Receiver photoengraved. Checkered walnut thumb-rest stock and forearm (pre-1972 model has different stock with silver grip cap). Made from 1967 to date, with the following revisions and variations.

Standard Model	**$225**
Ventilated-Rib Model	**240**
Bull Barrel Model, with sights	**220**
Bull Barrel Model, without sights	**215**
Extra standard barrel	**85**
Extra ventilated rib or bull barrel	**90**

Thompson/Center Contender Early Bull Barrel Model w/Scope

Thompson/Center Contender Bull Barrel—New Model

Thompson/Center Contender Bull Barrel Model **$250**
Responding to the popularity of the design, the caliber offerings of the bull barrel version expanded in 1973, with another bump in 1978, now making it the Contender with the widest range of caliber options: 22 LR, 22 Win. Mag., 22 Hornet, 223 Rem., 7mm T.C.U., 7×30 Waters, 30 M1 Carbine, 30-30 Win., 32 H&R Mag., 32-20 Win., 357 Rem. Max., 357 Mag., 10mm Auto, 44 Magnum, 445 Super Magnum. 10-inch heavy barrel. Patridge-style iron sights. Contoured Competitor™ grip. Blued finish.

Thompson/Center Contender Internal Choke Model
Originally made in 1968-69 with octagonal barrel, this Internal Choke version in 45 Colt/.410 caliber only was reintroduced in 1986 with 10-inch bull barrel. Vent rib also available. Iron sights: fixed rear, bead front. Detachable choke screws into muzzle. Blued finish. Contoured American black walnut Competitor™ Grip, also introduced in 1986, has non-slip rubber insert permanently bonded to back of grip.

With Bull Barrel	**$255**
With Vent Rib	**265**

Thompson/Center Contender Octagon Barrel

Thompson/Center Contender Octagon Barrel Model **$250**
The original Contender design, this octagonal barrel version began to see the discontinuance of caliber offerings in 1980, so that now it is available in 22 Long Rifle only. 10-inch octagonal barrel. Patridge-style iron sights. Contoured Competitor™ Grip. Blued finish.

Thompson/Center Contender Super 14

Thompson/Center Contender Super 14 . . . . **$245**
Calibers: 22 Long Rifle, 222 Rem., 223 Rem., 6mm T.C.U., 6.5mm T.C.U., 7mm T.C.U., 7 × 30 Waters, 30 Herrett, 30/30 Win., 357 Herrett, 357 Rem. Max., 35 Rem., 10mm Auto, 44 Mag., 445 Super Mag. 14-inch bull barrel. 18 inches overall. Weight: 56 oz. Patridge-style ramp front sight, adjustable target rear sight. Blued finish. Made from 1978 to date.

Thompson/Center Contender T/C Alloy II with Vent Rib

Thompson/Center Contender TC Alloy II
Calibers: 22 LR, 223 Rem., 357 Magnum, 357 Rem. Max., 44 Magnum, 7mm T.C.U., 30-30 Win.; 45 Colt/.410 with internal choke; 35 Rem. and 7×30 Waters (14-inch bbl.). 10- or 14-inch bull barrel or 10-inch vent-rib barrel (w/ internal choke). All metal parts permanently electroplated with T/C Alloy II, which is harder than stainless steel, ensuring smoother action, 30% longer barrel life. Other design specifications the same as late model Contenders. Made from 1986 to 1989.
T/C Alloy II 10-inch bull barrel **$300**
T/C Alloy II vent-rib bbl. w/choke **305**
T/C Alloy II Super 14 . . . . **310**

UNIQUE PISTOLS
Hendaye, France
Mfd. by Manufacture d'Armes des Pyrénées Francaises

Unique Model B/cf

Unique Model B/cf Automatic Pistol **$185**
Calibers: 32 Automatic (7.65mm), 380 Automatic (9mm Short). 9-shot magazine in 32, 8-shot in 380. 4-inch barrel. 6.6 inches overall. Weight: 24.3 oz. Blued finish. Plain or thumb-rest plastic stocks. Made from 1954 to date.

Unique Model D2 . . . . **$265**
Same as Model D6, except has 4¼-inch barrel, 7½ inches overall, weighs 24½ oz. Made from 1954 to date.

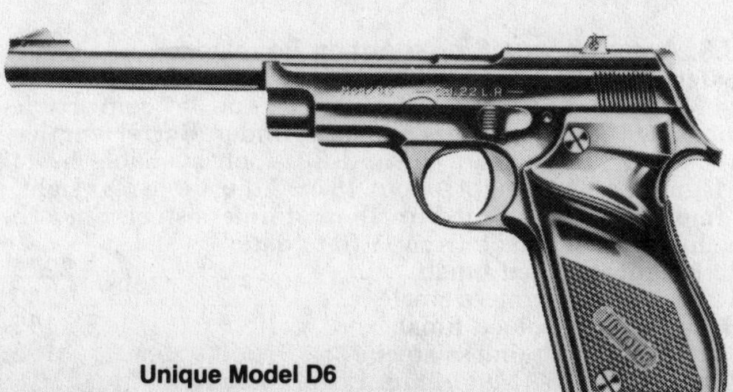
Unique Model D6

Unique Model D6 Automatic Pistol **$265**
Caliber: 22 Long Rifle. 10-shot magazine. 6-inch bbl. 9¼ inches overall. Weight: about 26 oz. Adjustable sights. Blued finish. Plain or thumb-rest plastic stocks. Made from 1954 to date.

Unique Model DES/69

Unique Model DES/69 Standard Match Automatic Pistol **$495**
Caliber: 22 Long Rifle. 5-shot magazine. 5.9-inch barrel. 10.6 inches overall. Weight: 35 oz. (barrel weight adds about 9 oz.). Click adjustable rear sight, ramp front sight. Blued finish. Checkered walnut thumb-rest stocks with adjustable hand-rest. Made from 1969 to date.

Unique Model DES/VO

Unique Model DES/VO Rapid Fire Match Automatic Pistol **$420**
Caliber: 22 Short. 5-shot magazine. 5.9-inch barrel. 10.4 inches overall. Weight: 43 oz. Click adjustable rear sight, blade front sight. Checkered walnut thumb-rest stocks with adjustable hand-rest. Trigger adjustable for length of pull. Made from 1974 to date.

Unique Kriegsmodell Automatic Pistol **$150**
Caliber: 32 Automatic (7.65mm). 9-shot magazine. 3.2-inch barrel. 5.8 inches overall. Weight: 26.5 oz. Fixed sights. Blued finish. Plastic stocks. Manufactured during German occupation of France 1940-1945. *Note:* Bears German military acceptance marks, may have stocks marked "7.65m/m 9 SCHUSS."

Unique Kriegsmodell

Unique Model L

Unique Model L Automatic Pistol **$245**
Calibers: 22 Long Rifle, 32 Automatic (7.65mm), 380 Automatic (9mm Short). 10-shot magazine in 22, 7 in 32, 6 in 380. 3.3-inch barrel. 5.8 inches overall. Weight: about 16½ oz. in 380 with light alloy frame; 23 oz. with steel frame. Fixed sights. Blued finish. Plastic stocks. Made from 1955 to date.

Unique Model Mikros

Unique Model Mikros Pocket Automatic Pistol . . **$195**
Calibers: 22 Short, 25 Automatic (6.35mm). 6-shot magazine. 2¼-inch barrel. 4 7/16 inches overall. Weight: 9½ oz. with light alloy frame; 12½ oz. with steel frame. Fixed sights. Blued finish. Plastic stocks. Made 1957 to date.

Unique Model Rr

Unique Model Rr Automatic Pistol **$180**
Postwar commercial version of WWII Kriegsmodell with same general specifications. Made from 1951 to date.

— UNITED STATES ARMS CORPORATION — Riverhead, New York

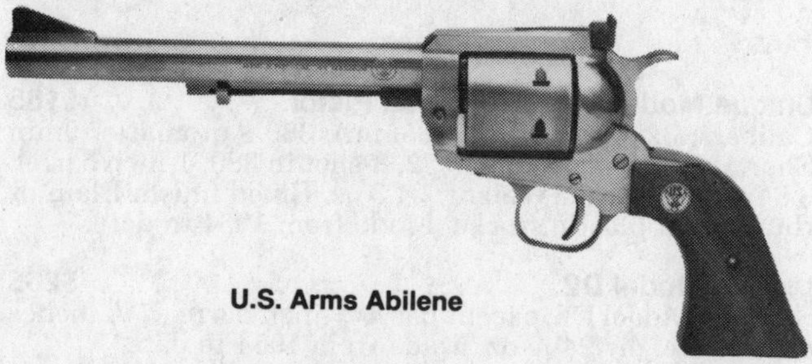

U.S. Arms Abilene

U.S. Arms Abilene Single Action Revolver
Safety Bar action. Calibers: 357 Magnum, 41 Magnum, 44 Magnum, 45 Colt; also 9mm Luger and 357 convertible model with two cylinders. 6-shot cylinder. Barrel lengths: 4⅝-, 5½-, 6½-inch. 7½- and 8½-inch available in 44 Magnum only. Weight: about 48 oz. Adjustable rear sight, ramp front sight. Blued finish or stainless steel. Smooth walnut stocks. Made from 1976 to date.

44 Magnum, blued finish **$225**
44 Magnum, stainless steel **240**
Other calibers, blued finish **185**
357 Magnum, stainless steel **195**
Convertible, 357 Mag./9mm Luger, blued finish **175**

UNIVERSAL FIREARMS CORPORATION
Hialeah, Florida

This company was purchased by Iver Johnson's Arms in the mid-1980's, when the Enforcer listed below was discontinued. An improved version was issued under the Iver Johnson name (*see* separate listing).

Universal Enforcer

Universal Enforcer Semiautomatic Pistol $200
M-1 Carbine-type action. Caliber: 30 Carbine. 5-, 15- or 30-shot clip magazine. 10$^{1}/_{4}$-inch barrel. 17$^{3}/_{4}$ inches overall. Weight: with 30-shot magazine, 4$^{1}/_{2}$ pounds. Adjustable rear sight, blade front sight. Blued finish. Walnut stock with pistol grip and handguard. Made from 1964 to 1985.

UZI PISTOLS
Mfd. by Israel Military Industries, Israel

Uzi 9mm Semiautomatic

Uzi Semiautomatic Pistol $460
Caliber: 9mm Parabellum. 20-round magazine. 4$^{1}/_{2}$-inch barrel. About 9$^{1}/_{2}$ inches overall. Weight: 3.8 pounds. Front post-type sight; rear open-type, both adjustable.

WALTHER PISTOLS
Manufactured by German, French and Swiss firms.

The following Walther pistols were made prior to and during World War II by Waffenfabrik Walther, Zella-Mehlis (Thür.), Germany.

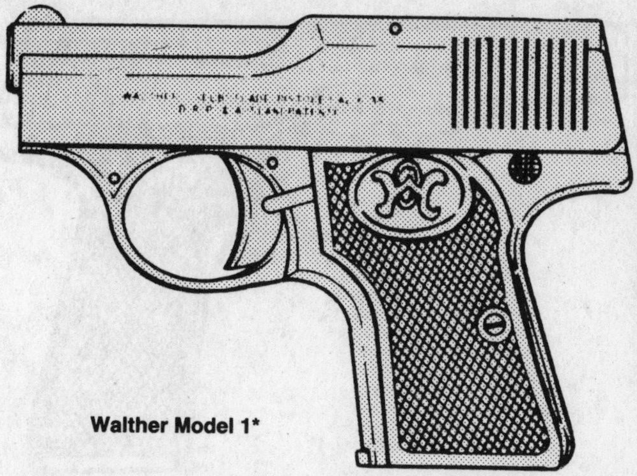

Walther Model 1*

Walther Model 1 Automatic Pistol $300
Caliber: 25 Automatic (6.35mm). 6-shot magazine. 2.1-inch barrel. 4.4 inches overall. Weight: 12.8 oz. Fixed sights. Blued finish. Checkered hard rubber stocks. Introduced in 1908.

Walther Model 2*

Walther Model 2 Automatic Pistol $350
Caliber: 25 Automatic (6.35mm). 6-shot magazine. 2.1-inch barrel. 4.2 inches overall. Weight: 9.8 oz. Fixed sights. Blued finish. Checkered hard rubber stocks. Introduced in 1909.

Walther Model 3 Automatic Pistol $450
Caliber: 32 Automatic (7.65mm). 6-shot magazine. 2.6-inch barrel. 5 inches overall. Weight: 16.6 oz. Fixed sights. Blued finish. Checkered hard rubber stocks. Introduced in 1910.

Walther Model 4 Automatic Pistol $425
Caliber: 32 Automatic (7.65mm). 8-shot magazine. 3.5-inch barrel. 5.9 inches overall. Weight: 18.6 oz. Fixed sights. Blued finish. Checkered hard rubber stocks. Made from 1910 to 1918.

Walther Model 4*

Walther Model 5 Automatic Pistol $325
Improved version of Model 2 with same general specifications. Distinguished chiefly by better workmanship and appearance. Introduced in 1913.

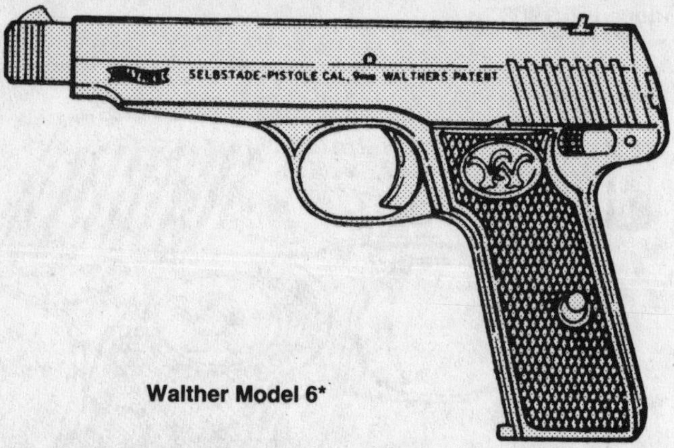

Walther Model 6*

Walther Model 6 Automatic Pistol $595
Caliber: 9mm Luger. 8-shot magazine. 4¾-inch barrel. 8¼ inches overall. Weight: 34 oz. Fixed sights. Blued finish. Checkered hard rubber stocks. Made from 1915 to 1917. *Note:* Since the powerful 9mm Luger cartridge is too much for the simple blowback system of this pistol, firing is not recommended.

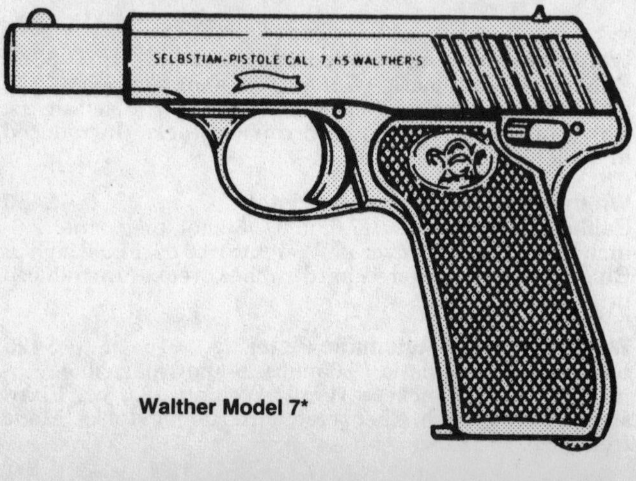

Walther Model 7*

Walther Model 7 Automatic Pistol $350
Caliber: 25 Automatic (6.35mm). 8-shot magazine. 3-inch barrel. 5.3 inches overall. Weight: 11.8 oz. Fixed sights. Blued finish. Checkered hard rubber stocks. Made from 1917 to 1918.

Walther Model 8*

Walther Model 8 Automatic Pistol $325
Caliber: 25 Automatic (6.35mm). 8-shot magazine. 2⅞-inch barrel. 5⅛ inches overall. Weight: 12⅜ oz. Fixed sights. Blued finish. Checkered plastic stocks. Made 1920 to 1945.

Walther Model 8 Lightweight Automatic Pistol . . $395
Same as standard Model 8 except about 25 percent lighter due to use of aluminum alloys.

Walther Model 9

Walther Model 9 Vest Pocket Automatic Pistol . . $325
Caliber: 25 Automatic (6.35mm). 6-shot magazine. 2-inch barrel. 3$^{15}/_{16}$ inches overall. Weight: 9 oz. Fixed sights. Blue finish. Checkered plastic stocks. Made 1921 to 1945.

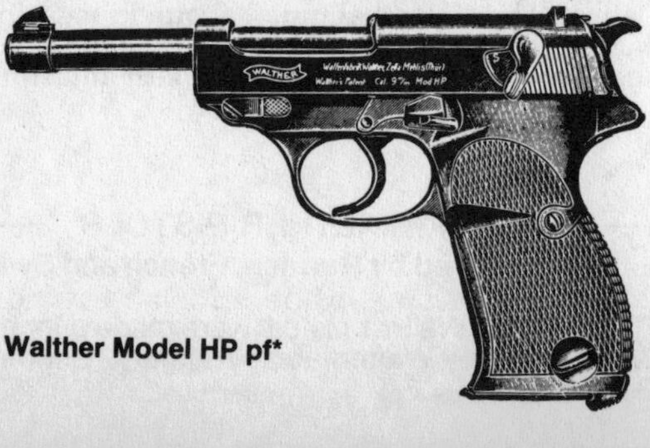

Walther Model HP pf*

Walther Model HP Double Action Automatic . . . $1100
Prewar commercial version of the P38. "HP" is abbreviation of "Heeres Pistole" (Army Pistol). Caliber: 9mm Luger. 8-shot magazine. 5-inch barrel. 8 3/8 inches overall. Weight: about 34 1/2 oz. Fixed sights. Blued finish. Checkered wood or plastic stocks. The Model HP is distinguished by its notably fine material and workmanship. Introduced in 1937.

Walther Olympia Funfkampf

Walther Olympia Funfkampf Model Automatic . $1300
Caliber: 22 Long Rifle. 10-shot magazine. 9.6-inch barrel. 13 inches overall. Weight: 33 oz., less weight. Set of 4 detachable weights. Adjustable target sights. Blued finish. Checkered stocks.

Walther Olympia Hunting Model Automatic Pistol $700
Same general specifications as Olympia Sport Model, but with 4-inch barrel. Weight: 28 1/2 oz.

Walther Olympia Rapid Fire Model Automatic Pistol $1100
Caliber: 22 Short. 6-shot magazine. 7.4-inch barrel. 10.7 inches overall. Weight: without 12 3/8 oz. detachable muzzle weight, 27 1/2 oz. Adjustable target sights. Blued finish. Checkered stocks. Introduced 1936.

Walther Olympia Sport Model Automatic Pistol . $700
Caliber: 22 Long Rifle. 10-shot magazine. 7.4-inch barrel. 10.7 inches overall. Weight: 30 1/2 oz., less weight. Adjustable target sights. Blued finish. Checkered stocks. Set of four detachable weights was supplied at extra cost. Introduced about 1936.

Walther Model P38 (WWII)

Walther P38 Military Double Action Automatic . . $450
Modification of the Model HP adopted as an official German Service arm in 1938 and produced throughout WWII by Walther (code "ac"), Mauser (code "byf") and a number of other manufacturers. General specifications are the same as Model HP, but there is a vast difference in quality, the P38 being a mass-produced military pistol; some of the late wartime models were very roughly finished and tolerances were quite loose.

Walther Model PP (Prewar)

Walther Model PP Double Action Automatic Pistol
Polizeipistole (Police Pistol). Calibers: 22 Long Rifle (5.6mm), 25 Auto (6.35mm), 32 Auto (7.65mm), 380 Auto (9mm). 8-shot magazine, 7-shot in 380. 3 7/8-inch barrel. 6 5/16 inches overall. Weight: 23 oz. Fixed sights. Blued finish. Checkered plastic stocks. *Note:* Wartime models are inferior in workmanship to prewar commercial pistols. Made from 1929 to 1945.

22 caliber, commercial model	**$550**
25 caliber, commercial model	**500**
32 and 380 caliber, commercial model	**550**
Wartime model	**325**

Walther Model PP Lightweight
Same as standard Model PP, except about 25 percent lighter due to use of aluminum alloys. Values 50 percent higher.

Walther Model PP 7.65mm Presentation $1350
Made of soft aluminum alloy in green-gold color, these pistols were not intended to be fired.

Walther Model PPK (WWII)

Walther Model PPK Double Action Automatic Pistol
Polizeipistole Kriminal (Detective Pistol). Calibers: 22 Long Rifle (5.6mm), 25 Auto (6.35mm), 32 Auto (7.65mm), 380 Auto (9mm). 7-shot magazine, 6-shot in 380. 3 1/4-inch barrel. 5 7/8 inches overall. Weight: 19 oz. Fixed sights. Blued finish. Checkered plastic stocks. *Note:* Wartime

Walther Model PPK (cont.)
models are inferior in workmanship to prewar commercial pistols. Made from 1931 to 1945.

22 and 25 caliber, commercial model	**$750**
32 and 380 caliber, commercial model	**675**
Wartime model	**450**

Walther Model PPK Lightweight
Same as standard Model PPK, except about 25 percent lighter due to use of aluminum alloys. Values 50 percent higher.

Walther Model PPK 7.65mm Presentation $1150
Made of soft aluminum alloy in green-gold color, these pistols were not intended to be fired.

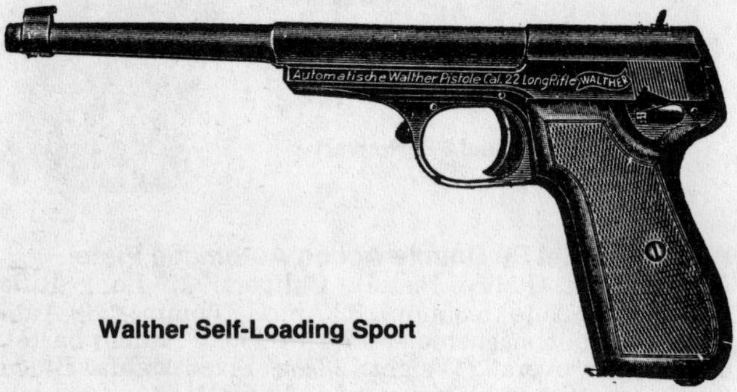

Walther Self-Loading Sport

Walther Self-Loading Sport Pistol $600
Caliber: 22 Long Rifle. 10-shot magazine. Barrel lengths: 6- and 9-inch. 9⅞ inches overall with 6-inch barrel. Target sights. Blued finish. One-piece, wood or plastic stocks, checkered. Introduced in 1932.

> *Note:* The following Walther pistols are currently manufactured by Carl Walther Waffenfabrik, Ulm/Donau, West Germany.

Walther Model GSP, 22 Long Rifle

Walther Model GSP
32 S&W Long Wadcutter

Walther Model GSP Target Automatic Pistol
Calibers: 22 Long Rifle, 32 S&W Long Wadcutter. 5-shot magazine. 4.5-inch barrel. 11.8 inches overall. Weights: 44.8 oz., 22 cal.; 49.4 oz., 32 cal. Adjustable target sights. Black finish. Walnut thumb-rest stocks with adjustable hand-rest. Made from 1969 to date.

22 Long Rifle	**$675**
32 S&W Long Wadcutter	**820**
Conversion unit, 22 Short or 22 Long Rifle, extra	**495**

Walther Model OSP

Walther Model OSP Rapid Fire Target Automatic Pistol $675
Caliber: 22 Short. 5-shot magazine. 4.5-inch barrel. 11.8 inches overall. Weight: 42.3 oz. Adjustable target sights. Black finish. Walnut thumb-rest stocks with adjustable hand-rest. 22 Long Rifle conversion unit available (add $275). Made from 1968 to date.

Walther Model P4

Walther Model P4 (P38-IV) Double Action Automatic Pistol $585
Similar to P38, except has an uncocking device instead of a manual safety. Caliber: 9mm Luger only. 4.3-inch barrel. 7.9 inches overall. Other general specifications same as for current model P38. Made from 1974 to date.

Walther Model P38 (P1) Double Action Automatic
Postwar commercial version of the P38, has light alloy frame. Calibers: 22 Long Rifle, 7.65mm Luger, 9mm Luger. 8-shot magazine. Barrel lengths: 5.1-inch in 22 caliber, 4.9-inch in 7.65mm and 9mm. 8.5 inches overall. Weight: 28.2 oz. Fixed sights. Non-reflective black finish. Checkered plastic stocks. Made from 1957 to date. *Note:* The "P1" is W. German Armed Forces official pistol.

Walther Model P38 (Current)

Walther Model P38 (P1) (cont.)
22 Long Rifle **$635**
Other calibers **560**

Walther Model P38 Deluxe Engraved Pistol
Elaborately engraved. Available in blued finish, chrome-, silver- or gold-plated.
Blued finish **$1175**
Chrome-plated **1300**
Silver-plated **1400**
Gold-plated **1500**

Walther Model P38K

Walther Model P38K **$590**
Short-barreled version of current P38—"K" is for *kurz* (short). Same general specifications as standard model, except 2.8-inch barrel, 6.3 inches overall, weighs 27.2 oz., front sight is slide mounted. Caliber: 9mm Luger only. Made from 1974 to date.

Walther Model PP (Current)

Walther Model PP Double Action Automatic Pistol
Calibers: 22 Long Rifle, 32 Auto (7.65mm), 380 Auto (9mm Short). 8-shot magazine in 22 and 32, 7-shot in 380. 3.9-inch barrel. 6.7 inches overall. Weight: 32 cal., 23.3 oz. Fixed sights. Blued finish. Checkered plastic stocks. Made from 1963 to date.
22 Long Rifle **$385**
Other calibers **375**

Walther Model PP Super

Walther Model PP Super Double Action Automatic Pistol **$630**
Caliber: 9x18mm. 7-shot magazine. 3.6-inch barrel. 6.9 inches overall. Weight: 30 oz. Fixed sights. Blued finish. Checkered plastic stocks. Made from 1974 to date.

Walther Model PPK (Current)

Walther Model PPK Double Action Automatic Pistol
Steel or dural frame. Calibers: 22 Long Rifle, 32 Auto (7.65mm), 380 Auto (9mm Short); latter caliber not available in model with dural frame. 3.3-inch barrel. 6.1 inches overall. Weight (32 caliber): with steel frame, 20.8 oz.; with dural frame, 16.6 oz. Fixed sights. Blued finish. Checkered plastic stocks. Made from 1963 to date. U.S. importation discontinued in 1968.
22 Long Rifle **$500**
Other calibers **400**

Walther Model PPK/S Double Action Automatic Pistol
Designed to meet the requirements of the U.S. Gun Control Act of 1968, this model has the frame of the PP and the shorter slide and barrel of the PPK. Overall length: 6.1 inches. Weight: 23 oz. Other specifications are the same

Walther Model PPK/S

Walther Model PPK/S (cont.)
as those of standard PPK, except steel frame only. Made from 1971 to date.
22 Long Rifle $350
Other calibers 325

Walther Models PP, PPK, PPK/S Deluxe Engraved Pistols
These elaborately engraved models are available in blued finish, chrome-, silver- or gold-plated.
Blued finish .... $ 995
Chrome-plated 1130
Silver-plated 1175
Gold-plated 1270
Add for 22 Long Rifle 25

Walther Model TPH

Walther Model TPH Double Action Pocket Automatic Pistol **$495**
Light alloy frame. Calibers: 22 Long Rifle, 25 Automatic (6.35mm). 6-shot magazine. 2.8-inch barrel. 5.3 inches overall. Weight: 11.5 oz. Fixed sights. Blued finish. Checkered plastic stocks. Made from 1969 to date. *Note:* Few of these have reached the U.S. due to import restrictions.

Note: The following Mark IIs have been made in France since 1950 by Manufacture de Machines du Haut-Rhin (MANURHIN) at Mulhouse-Bourtzwiller. The designation "Mark II" is used here to distinguish between these and the prewar models. Early (1950-1954) production bears MANURHIN trademark on slide and grips. Later models are marked "Walther Mark II." U.S. importation discont.

Walther Mark II Model PP Auto Pistol **$395**
Same general specifications as prewar Model PP.

Walther Mark II Model PPK Auto Pistol **$495**
Same general specifications as prewar Model PPK.

Walther Mark II Model PPK Lightweight **$490**
Same as standard PPK except has dural receiver. Calibers: 22 Long Rifle and 32 Auto.

Note: The Walther Olympia Model pistols were manufactured 1952-1963 by Hämmerli AG Jagd-und Sportwaffenfabrik, Lenzburg, Switzerland, and marketed as "Hämmerli-Walther." *See* Hämmerli listings for specific data.

Hämmerli-Walther Olympia Model 200 Auto Pistol, 1952 Type **$620**
Similar to 1936 Walther Olympia Funfkampf Model.

Hämmerli-Walther Olympia Model 200, 1958 Type **$700**

Hämmerli-Walther Olympia Model 201 .... **$620**

Hämmerli-Walther Olympia Model 202 .... **$700**

Hämmerli-Walther Olympia Model 203
1955 Type $700
1958 Type 775

Hämmerli-Walther Olympia American Model 204
1956 Type $735
1958 Type 810

Hämmerli-Walther Olympia American Model 205
1956 Type $810
1958 Type 890

WARNER PISTOL
Norwich, Connecticut
Warner Arms Corp. (or Davis-Warner Arms Co.)

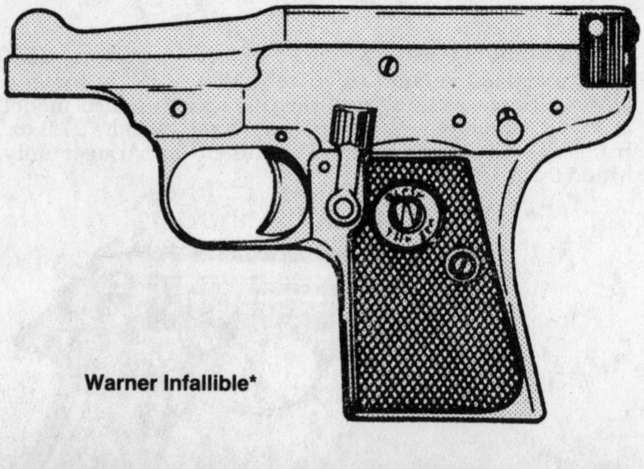

Warner Infallible*

Warner Infallible Pocket Automatic Pistol **$195**
Caliber: 32 Automatic. 7-shot magazine. 3-inch barrel. $6\frac{1}{2}$ inches overall. Weight: about 24 oz. Fixed sights. Blued finish. Hard rubber stocks. Made from 1917 to 1919.

WEBLEY & SCOTT LTD.
London and Birmingham, England

Webley 9mm M&P

Webley 9mm Military & Police Auto Pistol $250
Caliber: 9mm Browning Long. 8-shot magazine. 8 inches overall. Weight: 32 oz. Fixed sights. Blued finish. Checkered vulcanite stocks. Made from 1909 to 1930.

Webley 25 Hammer Model

Webley 25 Hammer Model Automatic Pistol $170
Caliber: 25 Automatic. 6-shot magazine. Overall length: 4³/₄ inches. Weight: 11³/₄ oz. No sights. Blued finish. Checkered vulcanite stocks. Made from 1906 to 1940.

Webley 25 Hammerless

Webley 25 Hammerless Model Auto Pistol $175
Caliber: 25 Automatic. 6-shot magazine. Overall length: 4¹/₄ inches. Weight: 9³/₄ oz. Fixed sights. Blued finish. Checkered vulcanite stocks. Made from 1909 to 1940.

Webley Mark I 455 Automatic*

Webley Mark I 455 Automatic Pistol $350
Caliber: 455 Webley Automatic. 7-shot magazine. 5-inch barrel. 8¹/₂ inches overall. Weight: about 39 oz. Fixed sights. Blued finish. Checkered vulcanite stocks. Made from 1912 to 1945. *Note:* **Mark I No. 2** is same pistol with adjustable rear sight and modified manual safety.

Webley Mark III

Webley Mark III 38 Military & Police Model Revolver $195
Hinged frame. Double action. Caliber: 38 S&W. 6-shot cylinder. Barrel lengths: 3- and 4-inch. Overall length: with 4-inch bbl., 9¹/₂ inches. Weight: with 4-inch bbl., 21 oz. Fixed sights. Blued finish. Checkered walnut or vulcanite stocks. Made from 1897 to 1945.

Webley Mark IV 22

Webley Mark IV 22 Caliber Target Revolver $225
Same frame and general appearance as Mark IV 38. Caliber: 22 Long Rifle. 6-shot cylinder. 6-inch barrel. 10¹/₈ inches overall. Weight: 34 oz. Target sights. Blued finish. Checkered stocks. Discont. 1945.

Webley Mark IV 38 M&P

Webley Mark IV 38 Military & Police Model Revolver **$185**
Hinged frame. Double action. Caliber: 38 S&W. 6-shot cylinder. Barrel lengths: 3-, 4- and 5-inch. $9\frac{1}{8}$ inches overall with 5-inch bbl. Weight: with 5-inch bbl., 27 oz. Fixed sights. Blued finish. Checkered stocks. Made from 1929 to c. 1957.

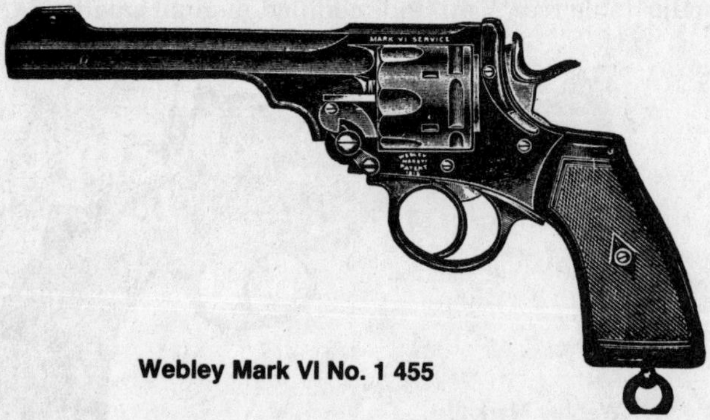

Webley Mark VI No. 1 455

Webley Mark VI No. 1 455 British Service Revolver **$180**
Double action. Hinged frame. Caliber: 455 Webley. 6-shot cylinder. Barrel lengths: 4-, 6- and $7\frac{1}{2}$-inch. Overall length: with 6-inch bbl., $11\frac{1}{4}$ inches. Weight: with 6-inch bbl., 38 oz. Fixed sights. Blued finish. Checkered walnut or vulcanite stocks. Made from 1915 to 1947.

Webley Mark VI 22

Webley Mark VI 22 Target Revolver **$170**
Same frame and general appearance as the Mark VI 455. Caliber: 22 Long Rifle. 6-shot cylinder. 6-inch barrel. $11\frac{1}{4}$ inches overall. Weight: 40 oz. Target sights. Blued finish. Checkered walnut or vulcanite stocks. Discontinued 1945.

Webley Metropolitan Police

Webley Metropolitan Police Automatic Pistol . . . **$150**
Calibers: 32 Automatic, 380 Automatic. 8-shot magazine (32 cal.), 7-shot (380 cal.). $3\frac{1}{2}$-inch barrel. $6\frac{1}{4}$ inches overall. Weight: 20 oz. Fixed sights. Blued finish. Checkered vulcanite stocks. Made from 1906 to 1940 (32), 1908 to 1920 (380).

Webley RIC Model

Webley RIC Model Revolver **$140**
Royal Irish Constabulary or Bulldog Model. Double action. Solid frame. Caliber: 455 Webley. 5-shot cylinder. $2\frac{1}{4}$-inch barrel. Weight: 21 oz. Fixed sights. Blued finish. Checkered walnut or vulcanite stocks. Discontinued.

Webley "Semiautomatic" Single Shot Pistol **$200**
Similar in appearance to the Webley Metropolitan Police Model Automatic, this pistol is "semiautomatic" in the sense that the fired case is extracted and ejected and the hammer cocked as in a blowback automatic pistol; it is loaded singly and the slide manually operated in loading. Caliber: 22 Long. Barrel lengths: $4\frac{1}{2}$- and 9-inch. Overall length: with 9-inch bbl., $10\frac{3}{4}$ inches. Weight: with 9-inch bbl., 24 oz. Adjustable sights. Blued finish. Checkered vulcanite stocks. Made from 1911 to 1927.

Webley Single Shot Target

Webley Single Shot Target Pistol **$225**
Hinged frame. Caliber: 22 Long Rifle. 10-inch barrel. 15 inches overall. Weight: 37 oz. Fixed sights on earlier models, current production has adjustable rear sight. Blued finish. Checkered walnut or vulcanite stocks. Made from 1909 to date.

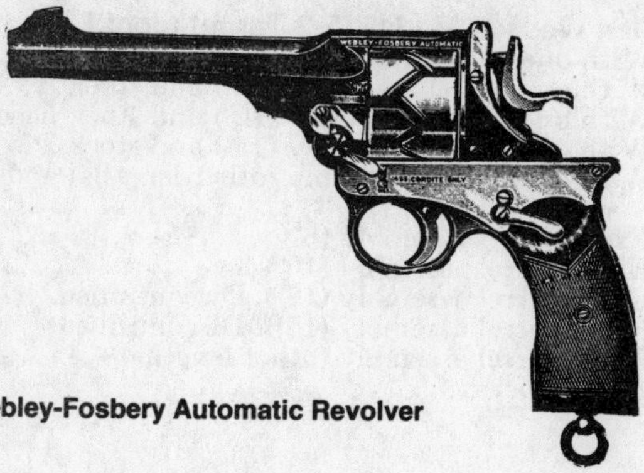

Webley-Fosbery Automatic Revolver

Dan Wesson Model 11

Webley-Fosbery Automatic Revolver **$395**
Hinged frame. Recoil action revolves cylinder and cocks hammer. Caliber: 455 Webley. 6-shot cylinder. 6-inch barrel. 12 inches overall. Weight: 42 oz. Fixed sights. Blued finish. Checkered walnut stocks. Made from 1901 to 1939. *Note:* A few were produced in caliber 38 Colt Auto with an 8-shot cylinder; this is a very rare collector's item.

DAN WESSON ARMS, INC.
Monson, Massachusetts

Dan Wesson Model 8 Service
Same general specifications as Model 14, except caliber 38 Special. Made from 1971 to 1975. Values same as for Model 14.

Dan Wesson Model 8-2 Service
Same general specifications as Model 14-2, except caliber 38 Special. Made from 1975 to date. Values same as for Model 14-2.

Dan Wesson Model 9 Target
Same as Model 15, except caliber 38 Special. Made from 1971 to 1975. Values same as for Model 15.

Dan Wesson Model 9-2 Target
Same as Model 15-2, except caliber 38 Special. Made from 1975 to date. Values same as for Model 15-2.

Dan Wesson Model 9-2H Heavy Barrel
Same as Model 15-2H, except caliber 38 Special. Made from 1975 to date. Values same as for Model 15-2H. Discontinued 1983.

Dan Wesson Model 9-2HV Vent-Rib Heavy Barrel
Same as Model 15-2HV, except caliber 38 Special. Made from 1975 to date. Values same as for Model 15-2HV.

Dan Wesson Model 9-2V Ventilated Rib
Same as Model 15-2V, except caliber 38 Special. Made from 1975 to date. Values same as for Model 15-2H.

Dan Wesson Model 11 Service Double Action Revolver
Caliber: 357 Magnum. 6-shot cylinder. Barrel lengths: $2^1/_2$-, 4-, 6-inch; interchangeable barrel assemblies. 9 inches overall with 4-inch bbl. Weight: with 4-inch bbl., 38 oz. Fixed sights. Blued finish. Interchangeable stocks. Made from 1970 to 1971. *Note:* The Model 11 has an external barrel nut.

Dan Wesson Model 11 (cont.)
With one barrel assembly and stock **$240**
Extra barrel assembly **50**
Extra stock **25**

Dan Wesson Model 12

Dan Wesson Model 12 Target
Same general specifications as Model 11, except has adjustable sights. Made from 1970 to 1971.
With one barrel assembly and stock **$255**
Extra barrel assembly **50**
Extra stock **25**

Dan Wesson Model 14

Dan Wesson Model 14 Service Double Action Revolver
Caliber: 357 Magnum. 6-shot cylinder. Barrel lengths: $2^1/_4$-, $3^3/_4$-, $5^3/_4$-inch; interchangeable barrel assemblies. 9 inches overall with $3^3/_4$-inch bbl. Weight: with $3^3/_4$-inch bbl., 36 oz. Fixed sights. Blued or nickel finish. Interchangeable stocks. Made from 1971 to 1975. *Note:* Model 14 has recessed barrel nut.
With one barrel assembly and stock **$200**
Extra barrel assembly **50**
Extra stock **25**

Dan Wesson Model 14-2

Dan Wesson Model 14-2 Service DA Revolver
Caliber: 357 Magnum. 6-shot cylinder. Barrel lengths: $2\frac{1}{2}$-, 4-, 6-, 8-inch; interchangeable barrel assemblies. $9\frac{1}{4}$ inches overall with 4-inch bbl. Weight: with 4-inch bbl., 34 oz. Fixed sights. Blued finish. Interchangeable stocks. Made from 1975 to date. *Note:* Model 14-2 has recessed barrel nut.
With one barrel assembly (8″) and stock **$225**
With one barrel assembly (other lengths) and stock **220**
Extra barrel assembly, 8″ **65**
Extra barrel assembly, other lengths **50**
Extra stock **25**

Dan Wesson Model 15

Dan Wesson Model 15 Target
Same general specifications as Model 14, except has adjustable sights. Made from 1971 to 1975.
With one barrel assembly and stock **$225**
Extra barrel assembly **50**
Extra stock **25**

Dan Wesson Model 15-2

Dan Wesson Model 15-2 Target
Same general specifications as Model 14-2, except has adjustable rear sight and interchangeable blade front sight; also available with 10-, 12- and 15-inch barrels. Made from 1975 to date.

Dan Wesson Model 15-2 Target (cont.)
With one barrel assembly (8″) and stock **$230**
With one barrel assembly (10″) and stock **235**
With one barrel assembly (12″) and stock Disc. **250**
With one barrel assembly (15″) and stock Disc. **265**
With one barrel assembly (other lengths) and stock **180**
Extra barrel assembly (8″) **75**
Extra barrel assembly (10″) **95**
Extra barrel assembly (12″). Discontinued. **100**
Extra barrel assembly (15″). Discontinued. **115**
Extra barrel assembly (other lengths) **50**
Extra stock **20**

Dan Wesson Model 15-2H
Interchangeable Heavy Barrel Assemblies

Dan Wesson Model 15-2H Heavy Barrel
Same as Model 15-2, except has heavy barrel assembly; weight, with 4-inch barrel, 38 oz. Made from 1975 to 1983.
With one barrel assembly (8″) and stock **$265**
With one barrel assembly (10″) and stock **260**
With one barrel assembly (12″) and stock **295**
With one barrel assembly (15″) and stock **315**
With one barrel assembly (other lengths) and stock **240**
Extra barrel assembly (8″) **80**
Extra barrel assembly (10″) **100**
Extra barrel assembly (12″) **110**
Extra barrel assembly (15″) **125**
Extra barrel assembly (other lengths) **60**
Extra stock **20**

Dan Wesson Model 15-2HV Vent-Rib Heavy Barrel
Same as Model 15-2, except has ventilated-rib heavy barrel assembly; weight, with 4-inch barrel, 37 oz. Made from 1975 to date.
With one barrel assembly (8″) and stock **$260**
With one barrel assembly (10″) and stock **270**
With one barrel assembly (12″) and stock **305**
With one barrel assembly (15″) and stock **330**
With one barrel assembly (other lengths) and stock **255**
Extra barrel assembly (8″) **90**
Extra barrel assembly (10″) **110**
Extra barrel assembly (12″) **125**
Extra barrel assembly (15″) **140**
Extra barrel assembly (other lengths) **70**
Extra stock **20**

Dan Wesson Model 15-2V
Interchangeable Vent-Rib Barrel Assemblies

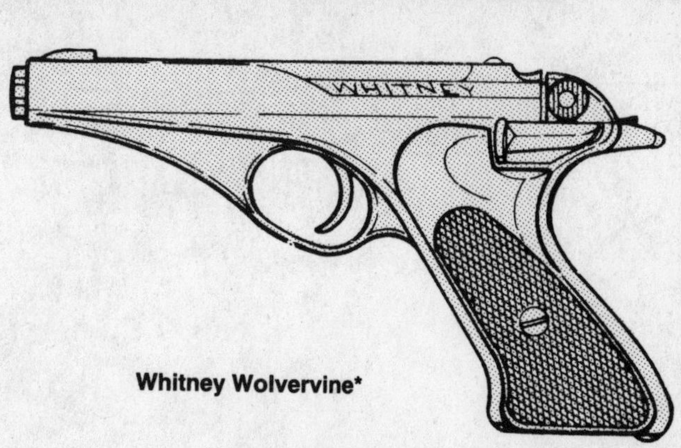

Whitney Wolvervine*

Dan Wesson Model 15-2V Ventilated Rib
Same as Model 15-2, except has ventilated-rib barrel assembly; weight, with 4-inch barrel, 35 oz. Made from 1975 to date. Values same as for 15-2H.

Dan Wesson Hunter Pacs
Dan Wesson Hunter Pacs are offered in all magnum calibers and include heavy vent 8-inch shroud barrel revolver, Burris scope mounts, barrel changing tool in a case.

HP22M-V	$560
HP22M-2	505
HP722M-V	620
HP722M-2	565
HP32-V	550
HP32-2	500
HP732-V	600
HP732-2	545
HP15-V	550
HP15-2	495
HP715-V	600
HP715-2	545
HP41-V	605
HP741-V	665
HP741-2	545
HP44-V	615
HP44-2	560
HP744-V	695
HP744-2	645
HP40-V	665
HP40-2	610
HP740-V	740
HP740-2	685
HP375-V	665
HP375-2	610

WHITNEY FIREARMS COMPANY
Hartford, Connecticut

Whitney Wolverine Automatic Pistol $295
Dural frame/shell contains all operating components. Caliber: 22 Long Rifle. 10-shot magazine. $4\frac{5}{8}$-inch barrel. 9 inches overall. Weight: 23 oz. Patridge-type sights. Blue or nickel finish. Plastic stocks. Made from 1955 to 1962.

WICHITA ARMS
Wichita, Kansas

Wichita Classic Pistol
Caliber: Chambered to order. Bolt-action, single shot. $11\frac{1}{4}$-inch octagonal barrel. 18 inches overall. Weight: 78 oz. Open micro sights. Custom-grade checkered walnut stock. Blued finish. Made from 1980 to date.

Standard	$2250
Presentation Grade (engraved)	3675

Wichita Hunter Pistol $365
Calibers: 22 Long Rifle, 22 WRF., 7mm Super Mag., 7-30 Waters, 30-30 Win., 32 H&R Mag., 357 Mag., 357 Super Mag. Bolt-action, single shot. $10\frac{1}{2}$-inch barrel. $16\frac{1}{2}$ inches overall. Weight: 60 oz. No sights (scope mount only). Stainless steel finish. Walnut stock. Made from 1983 to date.

Wichita International Pistol $365
Same as Wichita Hunter, except with adjustable target sights.

Wichita MK-40 Silhouette Pistol $600
Calibers: 22-250, 7mm IHMSA, 308 Win. Bolt-action, single shot. 13-inch barrel. $19\frac{1}{2}$ inches overall. Weight: 72 oz. Wichita Multi-Range sight system. Aluminum receiver with blued barrel. Gray fiberthane glass stock. Made from 1981 to date.

Wichita Silhouette Pistol $675
Caliber: 22-250, 7mm IHMSA, 308 Win. Bolt-action, single shot. $14\frac{15}{16}$-inch barrel. $21\frac{3}{8}$ inches overall. Weight: 72 oz. Wichita Multi-Range sight system. Blued finish. Walnut or gray fiberthane glass stock. Walnut center or rear grip. Made from 1979 to date.

WILKINSON ARMS
Parma, Idaho

Wilkinson "Linda" Semiautomatic Pistol $245
Caliber: 9mm Luger Parabellum. 31-shot magazine. $8\frac{1}{4}$-inch barrel. $12\frac{1}{4}$ inches overall. Weight: 77 oz., empty. Rear peep sight with blade front. Blued finish. Checkered composition stocks.

Wilkinson "Sherry" Semiautomatic Pistol $110
Caliber: 22 Long Rifle. 8-shot magazine. $2\frac{1}{8}$-inch barrel. $4\frac{3}{8}$ inches overall. Weight: $9\frac{1}{4}$ oz., empty. Crossbolt safety. Fixed sights. Blued or blue-gold finish. Checkered composition stocks. Made from 1985 to date.

Section II

RIFLES

Alpha Arms Alaskan

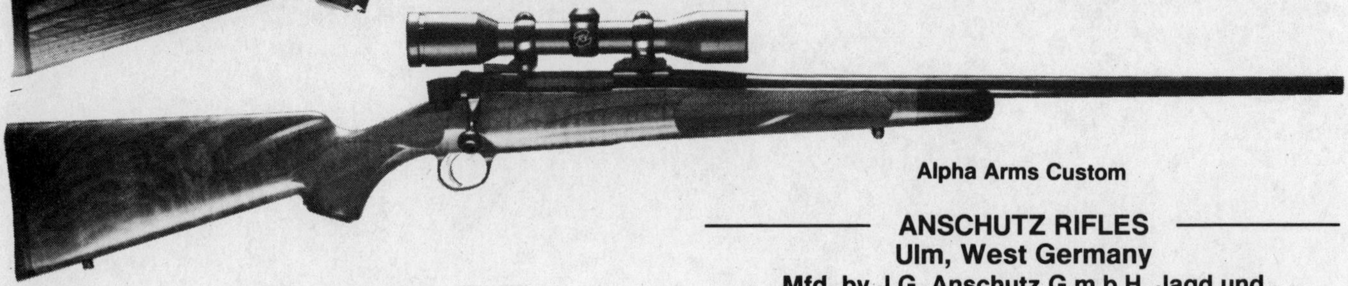

Alpha Arms Custom

ALPHA ARMS, INC.
Dallas, Texas

Alpha Alaskan Bolt Action Rifle $1680
Same as Custom model, except with stainless steel barrel and receiver and all other parts coated with Nitex; sling swivel stud attached to barrel. Left-hand model available. Made from 1984 to date.

Alpha Custom Bolt Action Rifle $1740
Calibers: 17 Rem. through 338 Win. Mag. Three action lengths with three-lug locking system and 60-degree bolt rotation. 20- to 24-inch barrel; round or octagonal. Weight: 6 to $7\frac{1}{4}$ pounds. No sights. Pistol-grip stock of presentation-grade California claro walnut; hand-rubbed oil finish. Custom inletted sling swivel stud attached to forend. Ebony forend tip. Left-hand models available. Made from 1984 to date.

Alpha Grand Slam Bolt Action Rifle $1475
Same as Custom model, except with Alphawood (fiberglass and wood) classic- style stock featuring Niedner-style grip cap. Weight: $6\frac{1}{2}$ pounds. Left-hand models available. Made from 1984 to date.

ANSCHUTZ RIFLES
Ulm, West Germany
Mfd. by J.G. Anschutz G.m.b.H. Jagd und Sportwaffenfabrik

Anschutz Models 1407 ISU, 1408-ED, 1411, 1413, 1418, 1432, 1433, 1518 and 1533 were marketed in the U.S. by Savage Arms. Further, Anschutz Models 1403, 1416, 1422D, 1441, 1516 and 1522D were sold as Savage/Anschutz with Savage model designations. (See also listings under Savage Arms.) Precision Sales Int'l., Inc. of Westfield, Mass., is now the U.S. distributor for all Anschutz rifles.

Anschutz Model 54.18MS 725
Bolt action, single shot. Caliber: 22 Long Rifle. 20-inch barrel. European hardwood stock with cheekpiece. Forend and Wundhammer swell pistol grip stipple checkered. Receiver grooved, drilled and tapped for scope blocks. Weight: $8\frac{3}{8}$ pounds. Made from 1982 to date.

Anschutz Model 64 MS Bolt Action Single Shot Rifle
Bolt action, single shot. Caliber: 22 Long Rifle. $21\frac{1}{4}$-inch barrel. European hardwood silhouette-style stock with cheekpiece. Forend base and Wundhammer swell pistol grip stipple checkered. Adjustable two-stage trigger. Receiver grooved, drilled and tapped for scope blocks. Weight: 8 pounds. Made from 1982 to date.
Standard or Featherweight **$565**
Left-hand Model **630**

Anschutz Model 54.18 MS

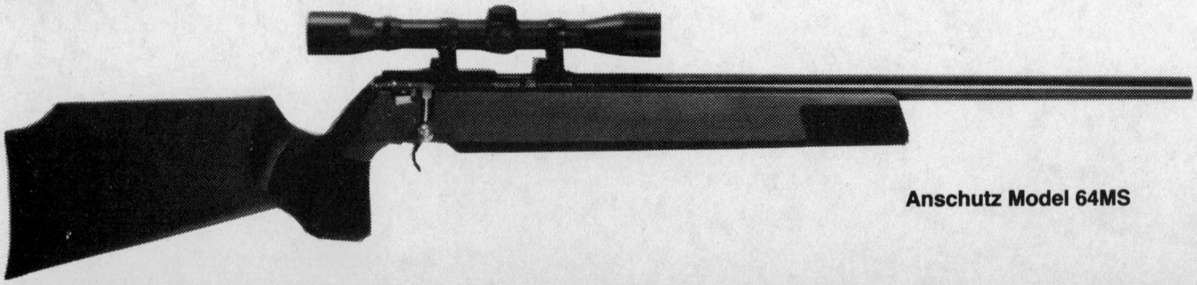

Anschutz Model 64MS

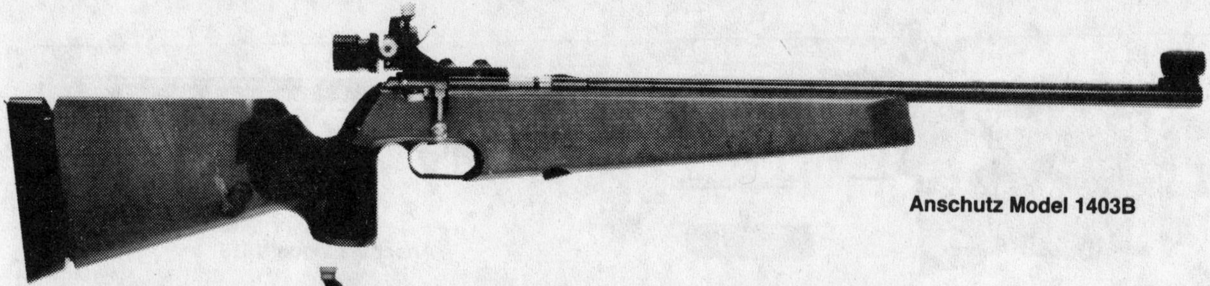

Anschutz Model 1403B

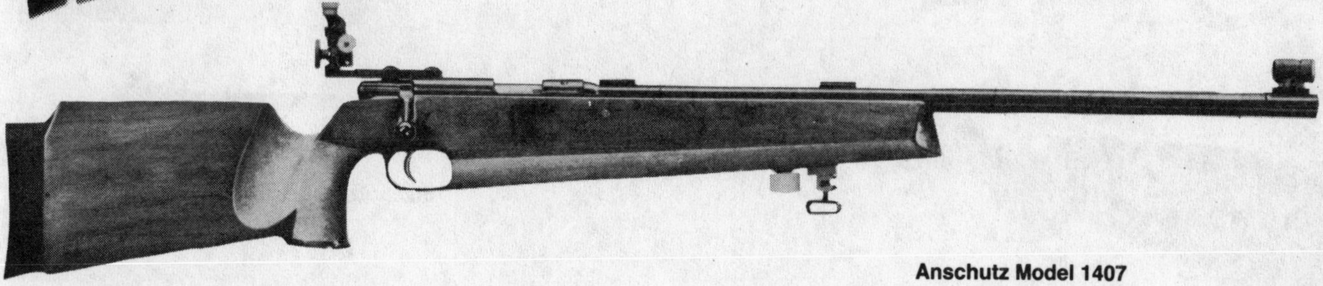

Anschutz Model 1407

Anschutz Model 520/61 Semiautomatic $235
Caliber: 22 Long Rifle. 10-shot magazine. 24-inch barrel. Folding leaf rear sight, hooded ramp front sight. Receiver grooved for scope mounting. Rotary-style safety. Monte Carlo stock and beavertail forend, checkered. Weight: 6½ pounds. Made from 1982 to date.

Anschutz Model 1403B $440
A lighter weight model designed for Biathlon competition. Caliber: 22 Long Rifle. 21½-inch barrel. Adjustable two-stage trigger. Adjustable grooved wood butt plate, stipple-checkered deep thumb rest flute and straight pistol grip. Weight: about 9 pounds with sights. Made 1982 to date.

Anschutz Model 1407 ISU Match 54 Rifle $695
Bolt action, single shot. Caliber: 22 Long Rifle. 26⅞-inch barrel. Scope bases. Receiver grooved for Anschutz sights. Single-stage adjustable trigger. Select walnut target stock with deep forearm for position shooting, adjustable butt plate, hand stop and swivel. Model 1407-L has left-hand stock. Weight: about 10 pounds. Made from 1970. Discontinued. Value is for rifle less sights; add $65 for Anschutz International sight set.

Anschutz Model 1408-ED Super Running Boar . . $640
Bolt action, single shot. Caliber: 22 Long Rifle. 23½-inch barrel with sliding weights. No metallic sights. Receiver drilled and tapped for scope bases. Single-stage adjustable trigger. Oversize bolt knob. Select walnut stock with thumb hole, adjustable comb and butt plate. Weight: about 9½ pounds. Introduced 1976; discontinued.

Anschutz Model 1411 Match 54 Rifle
Bolt action, single shot. Caliber: 22 Long Rifle. 27½-inch extra heavy barrel. Scope bases. Receiver grooved for Anschutz sights. Single-stage adjustable trigger. Select walnut target stock with cheekpiece (adjustable in 1973 and later production), full pistol grip, beavertail forearm, adjustable butt plate, hand stop and swivel. Model 1411-L has left-hand stock. Weight: about 11 pounds. Discont.
With nonadjustable cheekpiece **$550**
With adjustable cheekpiece **650**
Extra for Anschutz International sight set **100**

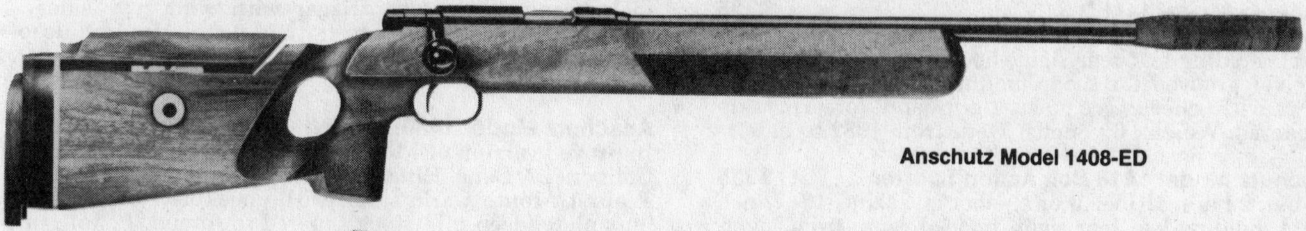

Anschutz Model 1408-ED

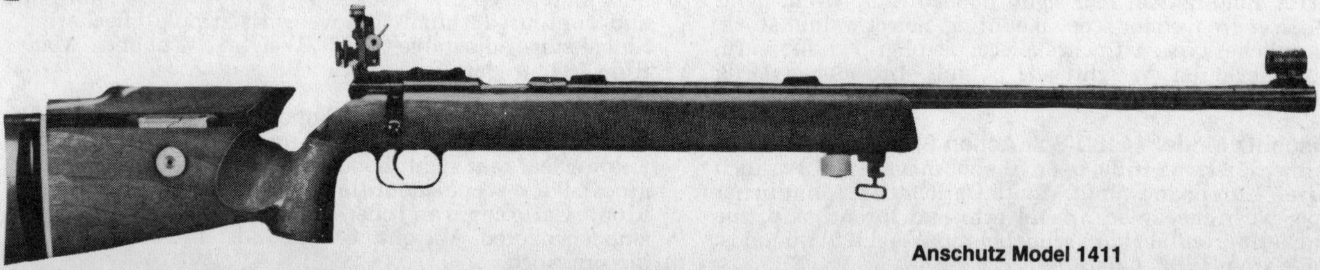

Anschutz Model 1411

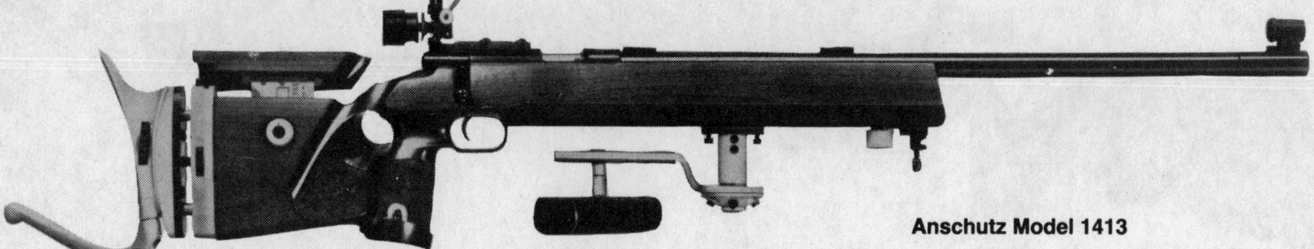

Anschutz Model 1413

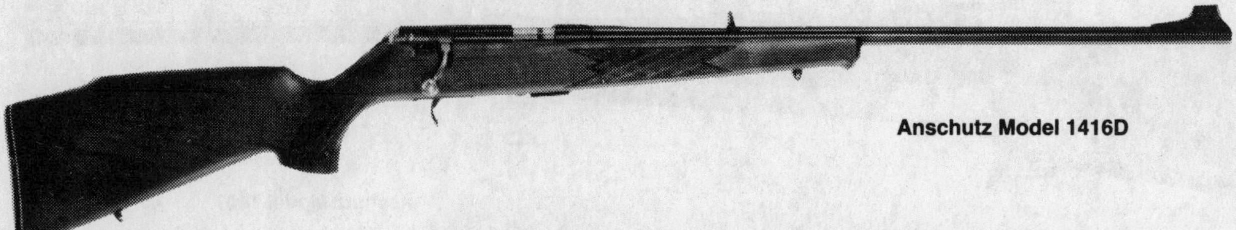

Anschutz Model 1416D

Anschutz Model 1418

Anschutz Model 1413 Super Match 54 Rifle
Freestyle international target rifle with specifications similar to those of Model 1411, except has special stock with thumb hole, adjustable pistol grip, adjustable cheekpiece in 1973 and later production, adjustable hook butt plate, adjustable palmrest. Model 1413-L has left-hand stock. Weight: about 15½ pounds. Discontinued.
With nonadjustable cheekpiece **$795**
With adjustable cheekpiece **850**
Extra for Anschutz International sight set **100**

Anschutz Model 1416D $325
Bolt-action sporter. Caliber: 22 Long Rifle. 22½-inch barrel. Folding leaf rear sight, hooded ramp front sight. Receiver grooved for scope mounting. Select European stock, with cheekpiece, pistol grip and forearm skip checkered. Weight: 6 pounds. Made from 1982 to date.

Anschutz Model 1418 Bolt Action Sporter $335
Caliber: 22 Long Rifle. 5- or 10-shot magazine. 19¾-inch barrel. Folding leaf rear sight, hooded ramp front sight. Receiver grooved for scope mounting. Select walnut stock, Mannlicher type, with cheekpiece, pistol grip and forearm skip checkered. Weight: 5½ pounds. Introduced 1976; discontinued.

Anschutz Model 1418D Bolt Action Sporter $435
Caliber: 22 Long Rifle. 5- or 10-shot magazine. 19¾-inch barrel. European walnut Monte Carlo stock, Mannlicher type, with cheekpiece, pistol grip and forend skip line checkering, buffalo horn schnabel tip. Weight: 5½ pounds. Made from 1982 to date.

Anschutz Model 1422D Classic $515
Bolt-action sporter. Caliber: 22 Long Rifle. 5-shot removable straight feed clip magazine. 24-inch barrel. Folding leaf rear sight, hooded ramp front sight. Select European walnut stock, classic type. Weight: 7¼ pounds. Made from 1982 to date.

Anschutz Model 1422D Custom $565
Same as Model 1422D Classic except has fancy grade Monte Carlo stock of European walnut with hand-carved roll-over cheekpiece. Weight: 6½ pounds. Made from 1982 to date.

Anschutz Model 1427B Biathlon Rifle $725
Bolt-action clip repeater. Caliber: 22 Long Rifle. 21½-inch barrel. Two-stage trigger with wing-type safety. Hardwood stock with deep fluting, pistol grip and deep forestock with adjustable hand stop rail. Weight: about 9 pounds with sights. Made from 1982 to date.

Anschutz Model 1430D Match $395
Improved version of Model 64S. Bolt-action, single shot. Caliber: 22 Long Rifle. 26-inch medium heavy barrel. Walnut Monte Carlo stock with cheekpiece, adjustable butt plate, deep mid stock tapered to forend. Pistol grip and contoured thumb groove with stipple checkering. Single-stage adjustable trigger. Weight: 8⅜ pounds. Made from 1982 to date.

Anschutz Model 1432 Bolt Action Sporter $580
Caliber: 22 Hornet. 5-shot box magazine. 24-inch barrel. Folding leaf rear sight, hooded ramp front sight. Receiver grooved for scope mounting. Select walnut stock with Monte Carlo comb and cheekpiece, pistol grip and forearm skip checkered. Weight: 6¾ pounds. Introduced 1974; discontinued.

Anschutz Model 1422D Classic

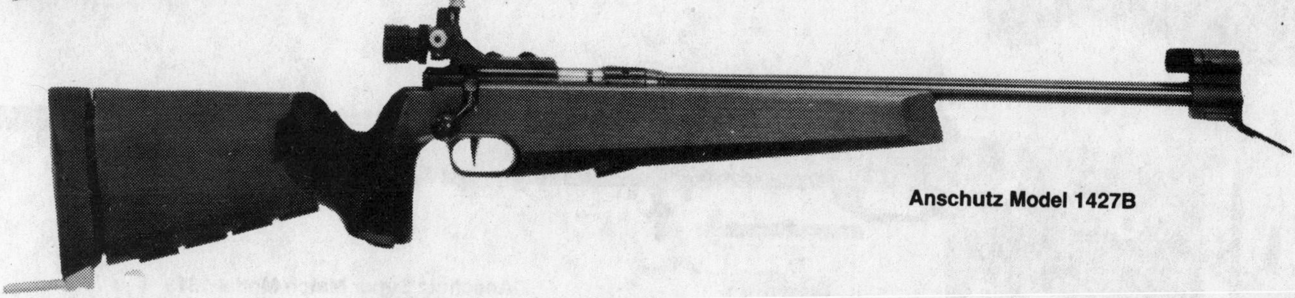

Anschutz Model 1427B

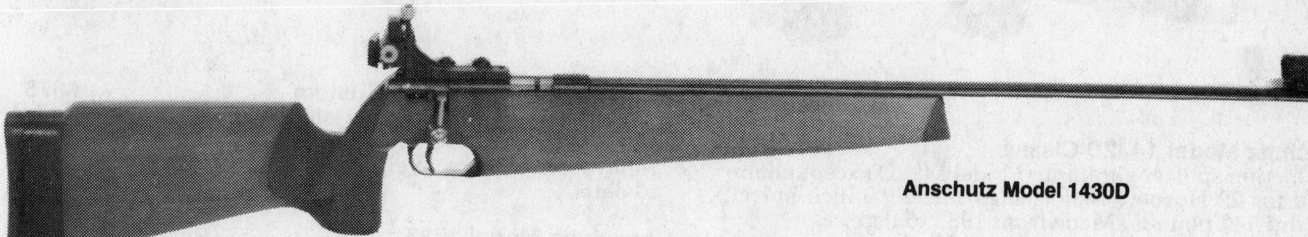

Anschutz Model 1430D

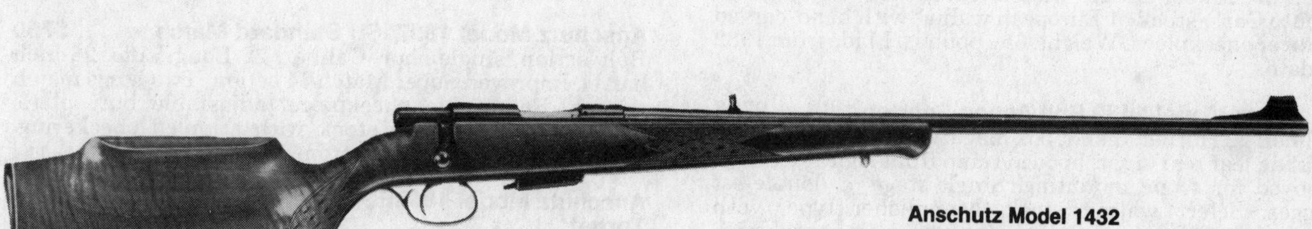

Anschutz Model 1432

Anschutz Model 1432D Classic

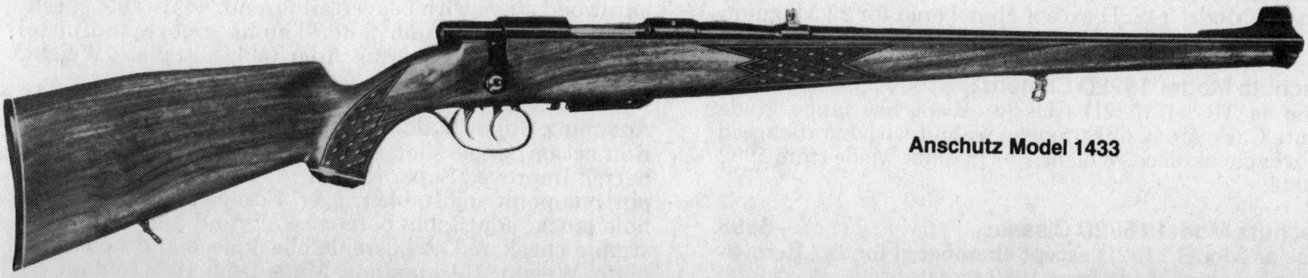

Anschutz Model 1433

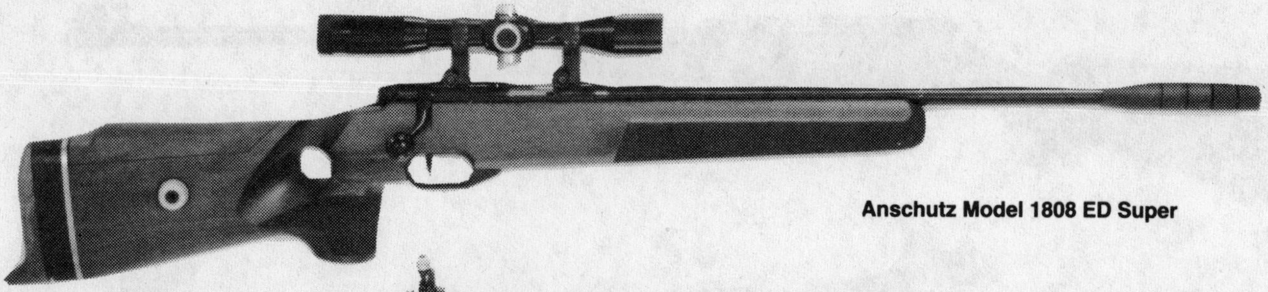

Anschutz Model 1808 ED Super

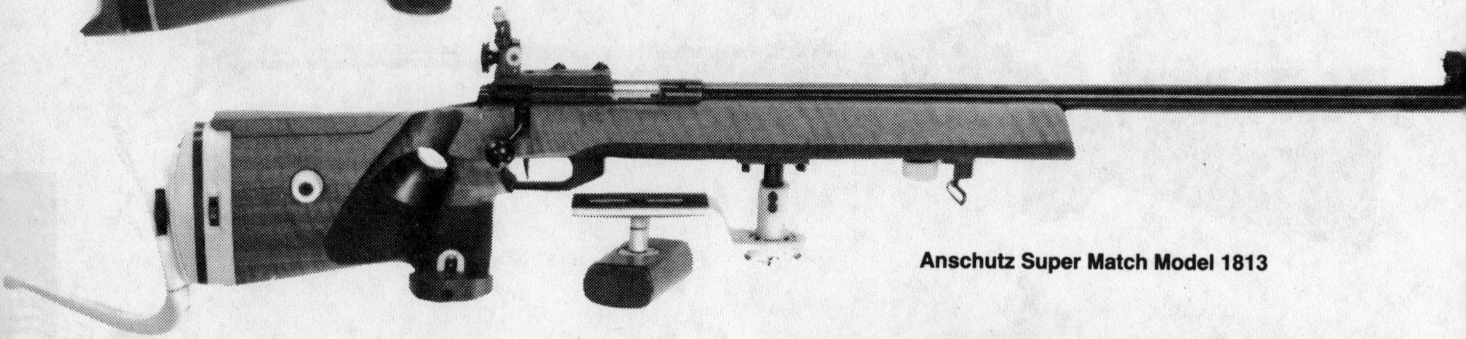

Anschutz Super Match Model 1813

Anschutz Model 1432D Classic **$650**
Bolt-action sporter similar to Model 1422D except chambered for 22 Hornet. 4-shot magazine. 23½-inch barrel. Weight: 7¾ pounds. Made from 1982 to date.

Anschutz Model 1432D Custom **$695**
Same as Model 1432D Classic except has fancy grade Monte Carlo stock of European walnut with hand-carved rollover cheekpiece. Weight: 6½ pounds. Made from 1982 to date.

Anschutz Model 1433 Bolt Action Sporter **$725**
Caliber: 22 Hornet. 5-shot box magazine. 19¾-inch barrel. Folding leaf rear sight, hooded ramp front sight. Receiver grooved for scope mounting. Single-stage or double-set trigger. Select walnut stock, Mannlicher type, with cheekpiece, pistol grip and forearm skip checkered. Weight: 6½ pounds. Introduced 1976; discontinued.

Anschutz Model 1516D Bolt Action Sporter **$395**
Same as Model 1416D except chambered for 22 Magnum RF. Made from 1982 to date.

Anschutz Model 1518 .... **$365**
Same as Model 1418 except chambered for 22 Magnum RF, 4-shot box magazine. Introduced 1976; discontinued.

Anschutz Model 1518D **$525**
Same as Model 1418D except chambered for 22 Magnum RF, 4-shot magazine. Made from 1982 to date.

Anschutz Model 1522D Classic **$485**
Same as Model 1422D except chambered for 22 Magnum RF, 4-shot magazine. Made from 1982 to date.

Anschutz Model 1522D Custom **$665**
Same as Model 1522D Classic except has fancy grade Monte Carlo stock of European walnut with hand-carved rollover cheekpiece. Weight: 6½ pounds. Made from 1982 to date.

Anschutz Model 1532D Classic **$595**
Same as Model 1432D except chambered for 222 Rem. 3-shot magazine. Made from 1982 to date.

Anschutz Model 1532D Custom **$675**
Same as Model 1532D Classic except has fancy grade Monte Carlo stock of European walnut with hand-carved rollover cheekpiece. Weight: 6½ pounds. Made from 1982 to date.

Anschutz Model 1533 .... **$695**
Same as Model 1433 except chambered for 222 Rem. 3-shot box magazine. Introduced 1976; discontinued.

Anschutz Model 1807 ISU Standard Match **$750**
Bolt action, single shot. Caliber: 22 Long Rifle. 26-inch barrel. Improved Super Match 54 action. Two-stage match trigger. Removable cheekpiece, adjustable butt plate, thumb piece and fore stock with stippled checkering. Weight: 10 pounds. Made from 1982 to date.

Anschutz Model 1808ED Super-Running Target **$885**
Bolt action, single shot. Caliber: 22 Long Rifle. 23½-inch barrel with sliding weights. Improved Super Match 54 action. Heavy beavertail forend, adjustable cheekpiece and butt plate. Adjustable single-stage trigger. Weight: 9¼ pounds. Made from 1982 to date.

Anschutz Model 1810 Super Match II **$1100**
A less detailed version of the Super Match 1813 Model. Tapered forend with deep receiver area. Select European hardwood stock. Weight: about 13½ pounds. Made from 1982 to date.

Anschutz Model 1811 Prone Match **$895**
Bolt action, single shot. Caliber: 22 Long Rifle. 27¼-inch barrel. Improved Super Match 54 action. Select European hardwood stock with beavertail forend, adjustable cheekpiece, and deep thumb flute. Thumb groove and pistol grip with stipple checkering. Adjustable butt plate. Weight: about 11½ pounds. Made from 1982 to date.

Anschutz Super Match Model 1813 .... **$1295**
Bolt action, single shot. Caliber: 22 Long Rifle. 27¼-inch barrel. Improved Super Match 54 action with light firing pin, one-point adjustable trigger. European walnut thumb hole stock, adjustable palm rest, forend and pistol grip stipple checkered. Adjustable cheekpiece and hook butt plate. Weight: 15¼ pounds. Made from 1982 to date.

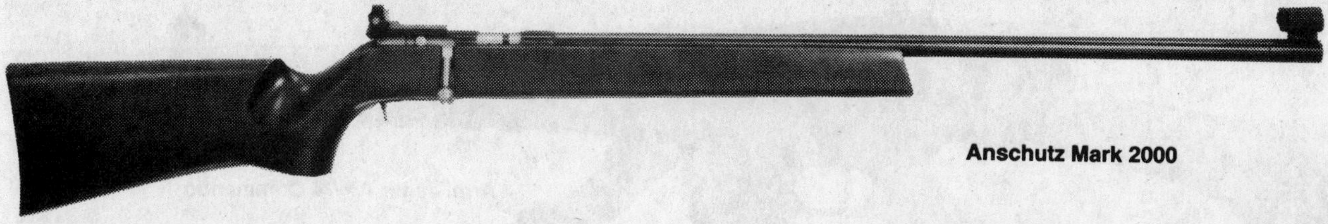

Anschutz Mark 2000

Anschutz Achiever Bolt Action Rifle **$300**
Caliber: 22 Long Rifle. 5-shot magazine. Mark 2000-type repeating action. 19½-inch barrel. 36¼ inches overall. Weight: 5 pounds. Adjustable open rear sight; hooded ramp front. Plain European hardwood target-style stock with vented forend and adjustable buttplate. Imported since 1987.

Anschutz Mark 2000 Match **$295**
Takedown. Bolt action, single shot. Caliber: 22 Long Rifle. 26-inch heavy barrel. Walnut stock with deep fluted thumb groove, Wundhammer swell pistol grip, beavertail-style forend. Adjustable butt plate, single-stage adjustable trigger. Weight: 8½ pounds. Made from 1982 to date.

Armalite AR-7 Explorer

Armalite Custom AR-7

Armalite AR-180

ARMALITE INC.
Costa Mesa, California

Armalite AR-7 Custom Rifle **$125**
Same as AR-7 Survival Rifle, except has deluxe walnut stock with cheekpiece and pistol grip. Weight: 3½ pounds. Made 1964 to 1970.

Armalite AR-7 Explorer Survival Rifle **$85**
Takedown. Semiautomatic. Caliber: 22 Long Rifle. 8-shot box magazine. 16-inch cast aluminum barrel with steel liner. Peep rear sight, blade front sight. Brown plastic stock, recessed to stow barrel, action, and magazine. Weight: 2¾ pounds. Will float, either stowed or assembled. Made from 1959 to 1973. *Note:* Now manufactured by Charter Arms Corp., Stratford, Conn.

Armalite AR-180 Semiautomatic Rifle **$595**
Commercial version of full automatic AR-18 Combat Rifle. Gas-operated semiautomatic. Caliber: 223 Rem. (5.56mm). 5-, 20-, 30-round magazines. 18¼-inch barrel with flash hider/muzzle brake. Flip-up "L" type rear sight, adjustable for windage; post front sight, adjustable for elevation. Accessory 3X scope and mount (add $60 to value). Folding buttstock of black nylon, rubber butt plate, pistol grip, heat-dissipating fiberglass forend (hand guard), swivels, sling. 38 inches overall, 28¾ inches folded. Weight: 6½ pounds. *Note:* Made by Armalite Inc. 1969 to 1972; manufactured for Armalite by Howa Machinery Ltd., Nagoya, Japan, 1972-73, by Sterling Armament Co. Ltd., Dagenham, Essex, England, 1976 to date.

Armi Jager AP-74 Commando

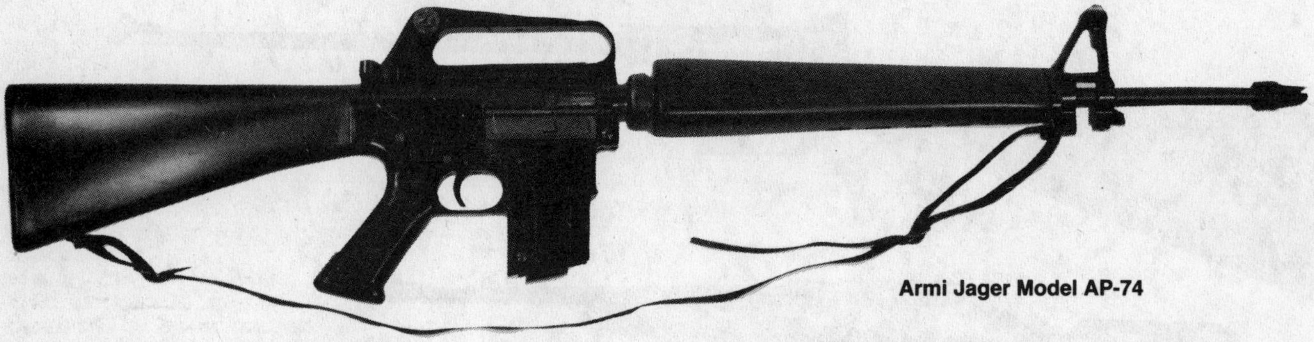

Armi Jager Model AP-74

ARMI JAGER
Turin, Italy

Armi Jager AP-74 Commando $195
Similar to standard AP-74, but styled to resemble original version of Uzi 9mm submachine gun with wood buttstock; lacks carrying handle and flash suppressor, has different type front sight mount and guards, wood stock, pistol grip and forearm. Made from 1976 to date.

Armi Jager AP-74 Semiautomatic Rifle
Styled after U.S. M16 military rifle. Calibers: 22 Long Rifle, 32 Auto (pistol cartridge). Detachable clip magazine; capacity: 14 rounds 22 LR, 9 rounds 32 ACP. 20-inch barrel with flash suppressor. Weight: about 6½ pounds. M16 type sights. Stock, pistol grip and forearm of black plastic, swivels and sling. Made from 1974 to date.
22 Long Rifle **$185**
32 Automatic **195**

Armi Jager AP-74 with Wood Stock
Same as standard AP-74, except has wood stock, pistol grip and forearm, weighs about 7 pounds.
22 Long Rifle **$225**
32 Automatic **235**

AUSTRIAN MILITARY RIFLES
Steyr, Austria
Manufactured at Steyr Armory

Austrian Model 90 Steyr-Mannlicher Carbine . . . $130
Same general specifications as Model 95 Rifle, except has 19½-inch barrel, weighs about 7 pounds.

Austrian Model 95 Rifle

Austrian Model 95 Steyr-Mannlicher Service Rifle $115
Straight-pull bolt action. Caliber: 8×50R Mannlicher (many of these rifles were altered during World War II to use the 7.9mm German service ammunition). 5-shot Mannlicher-type box magazine. 30-inch barrel. Weight: about 8½ pounds. Blade front sight, rear sight adjustable for elevation. Military-type full stock.

AUTO-ORDNANCE CORPORATION
West Hurley, New York

Auto-Ordnance Model 22-27A-3 Thompson $375
Smallbore version of Deluxe Model 27A-1. Same general specifications, except caliber 22 Long Rifle, has lightweight alloy receiver, weighs about 6½ pounds; magazines include 5-, 20-, 30- and 50-shot box types, 80-shot drum. Introduced in 1977.

Auto-Ordnance Deluxe Thompson Model 27A-1 . . . . $495
Same as Standard Model 27A-1, except has finned barrel with compensator, adjustable rear sight, pistol-grip forestock, weighs about 15 pounds. Made from 1976 to date.

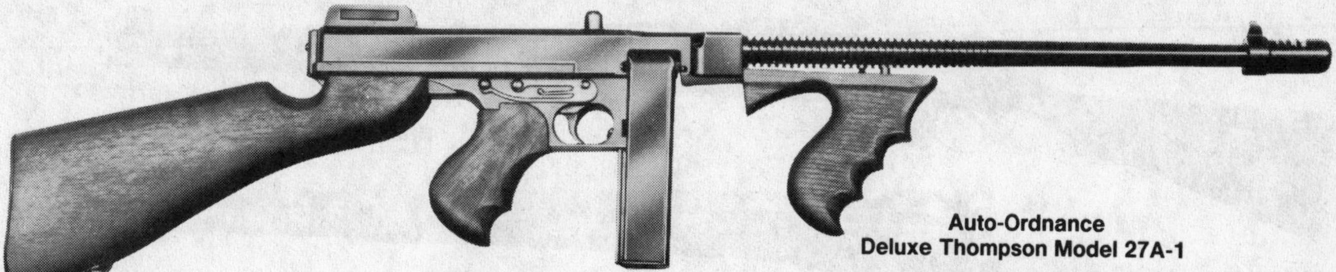

Auto-Ordnance
Deluxe Thompson Model 27A-1

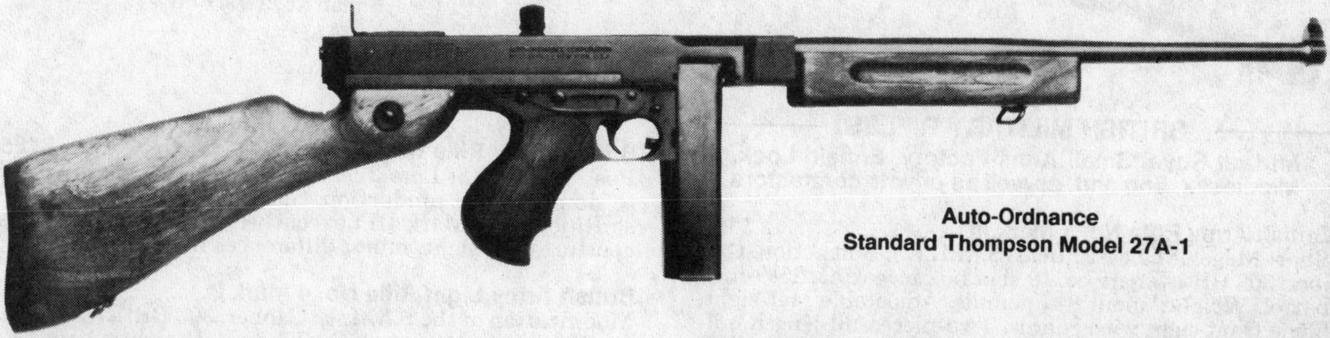

Auto-Ordnance
Standard Thompson Model 27A-1

Auto-Ordnance Standard Thompson Model 27A-1 Semiauto Carbine $350
Similar to Thompson submachine gun ("Tommy Gun"), except has no provision for automatic firing. Caliber: 45 Automatic. 20-shot detachable box magazine (5-, 15- and 30-shot box magazines, 39-shot drum also available). 16-inch plain barrel. Weight: about 14 pounds. Aperture rear sight, blade front sight. Walnut buttstock, pistol grip and grooved forearm, sling swivels. Made from 1976 to date.

BELGIAN MILITARY RIFLES

Mfd. by Fabrique Nationale D'Armes de Guerre, Herstal, Belgium; Fabrique D'Armes de L'Etat, Luttich, Belgium

Hopkins & Allen Arms Co. of Norwich, Conn., as well as contractors in Birmingham, England, also produced these arms during World War I.

Belgian Model 1889 Mauser Carbine $165
Same as Model 1889 Rifle except has $20\frac{3}{4}$-inch barrel, weighs about 8 pounds. The Model 1916 Carbine is virtually the same except for minor difference in the rear sight graduations, the lower band which is closer to the muzzle and the swivel plate located on the side of the buttstock.

Beretta AR-70 Sporter

Beretta AR-70 Semiautomatic Rifle $770
Caliber: 223 Rem. (5.56mm). 30-shot magazine. $17\frac{3}{4}$-inch barrel. Weight: $8\frac{1}{4}$ pounds. Rear peep sight adjustable for windage and elevation; blade front sight. High-impact synthetic buttstock. Made from 1984 to date.

Belgian Model 1889 Mauser Military Rifle $95
Caliber: 7.65mm Belgian Service (7.65mm Mauser). 5-shot projecting box magazine. $30\frac{3}{4}$-inch barrel with jacket. Weight: about $8\frac{1}{2}$ pounds. Adjustable rear sight, blade front sight. Straight-grip military stock. Made from 1889 to about 1935; this and the carbine model of the same type were the principal weapons of the Belgian Army at the start of WWII.

Belgian Model 1935 Mauser Military Rifle $170
Same general specifications as F.N. Model 1924; differences are minor. Caliber: 7.65mm Belgian Service. Mfd. by Fabrique Nationale D'Armes de Guerre.

Belgian Model 1936 Mauser Military Rifle $165
An adaptation of the Model 1889 with German M/98-type bolt, Belgian M/89 protruding box magazine. Caliber: 7.65mm Belgian Service. Mfd. by Fabrique Nationale D'Armes de Guerre.

BERETTA U.S.A. CORP.
Accokeek, Maryland

Manufactured by Fabbrica D'Armi Pietro Beretta S.p.A. in the Gardone Valtrompia (Brescia), Italy.

Beretta Small Bore Sporting Carbine $225
Semiautomatic with bolt handle raised, conventional bolt-action repeater with handle in lowered position. Caliber: 22 Long Rifle. 4-, 8-, or 20-shot magazines. $20\frac{1}{2}$-inch barrel. 3-leaf folding rear sight, patridge front sight. Stock with checkered pistol grip, sling swivels. Weight: $5\frac{1}{2}$ pounds.

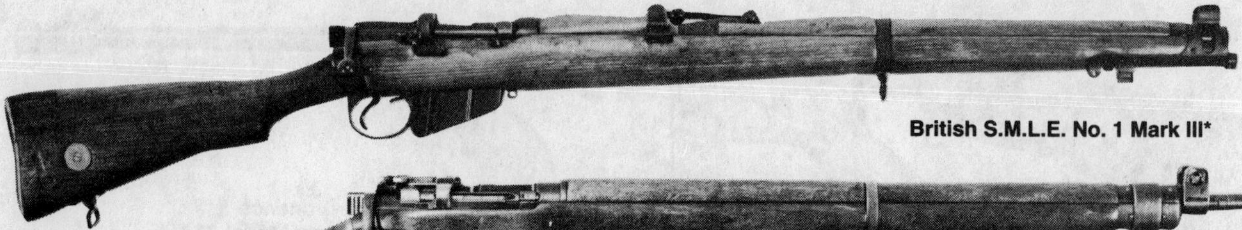

British S.M.L.E. No. 1 Mark III*

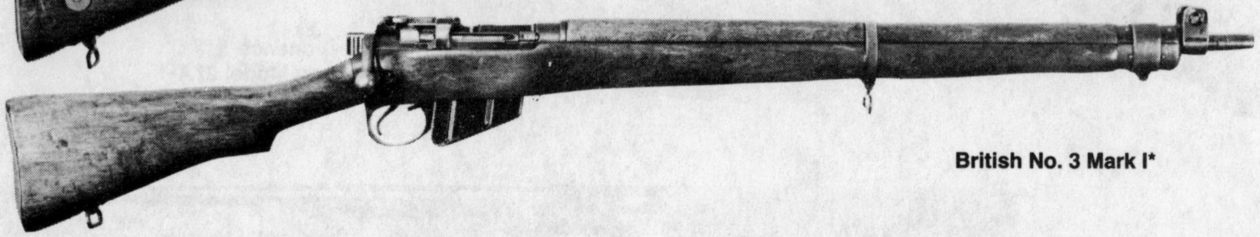

British No. 3 Mark I*

BRITISH MILITARY RIFLES

Mfd. at Royal Small Arms Factory, Enfield Lock, Middlesex, England, as well as private contractors

British Army Rifle No. 1 Mark III* $150
Short Magazine Lee-Enfield (S.M.L.E.). Bolt action. Caliber: 303 British Service. 10-shot box magazine. $25\frac{1}{4}$-inch barrel. Weight: about $8\frac{3}{4}$ pounds. Adjustable rear sight, blade front sight with guards. Two-piece, full-length military stock. *Note:* The earlier Mark III (approved 1907) is virtually the same as the Mark III* (adopted 1918) except for sights and different magazine cut-off which was eliminated on the latter.

British Army Rifle No. 3 Mark I* (Pattern '14) . . . $150
Modified Mauser-type bolt action. Except for caliber, 303 British Service, and long range sights, this rifle is the same as U.S. Model 1917 Enfield. See listing of the latter for general specifications.

British Army Rifle No. 4 Mark I* $125
Post-World War I modification of the S.M.L.E. intended to simplify mass production. General specifications same as Rifle No. 1 Mark III* except weighs $9\frac{1}{4}$ pounds, has aperture rear sight, minor differences in construction.

British Army Light Rifle No. 4 Mark I* $95
Modification of the S.M.L.E. Caliber: 303 British Service. 10-shot box magazine. 23-inch barrel. Weight: about $6\frac{3}{4}$ pounds. Micrometer click rear peep sight, blade front sight. One-piece military-type stock with recoil pad. Made during WWII.

British Army Rifle No. 5 Mark I* $140
Jungle Carbine. Modification of the S.M.L.E. similar to Light Rifle No. 4 Mark I* except has $20\frac{1}{2}$-inch barrel with flash hider, carbine-type stock. Made during WWII, originally designed for use in the Pacific Theater.

Brno Model II

Brno Model 21H

BRNO SPORTING RIFLES

Brno, Czechoslovakia
Manufactured by Ceska Zbrojovka

Brno Model I Bolt Action Sporting Rifle $435
Caliber: 22 Long Rifle. 5-shot detachable magazine. $22\frac{3}{4}$-inch barrel. Weight: about 6 pounds. Three-leaf open rear sight, hooded ramp front sight. Sporting stock with checkered pistol grip, swivels. Discontinued.

Brno Model II $485
Same as Model I except with deluxe grade stock. Discont.

Brno Model 21H Bolt Action Sporting Rifle $660
Mauser-type action. Calibers: 6.5×57mm, 7×57mm, 8×57mm. 5-shot box magazine. $20\frac{1}{2}$-inch barrel. Double set trigger. Weight: about $6\frac{3}{4}$ pounds. Two-leaf open rear sight, hooded ramp front sight. Half-length sporting stock with cheekpiece, checkered pistol grip and forearm, swivels. Discontinued.

Brno Model 22F

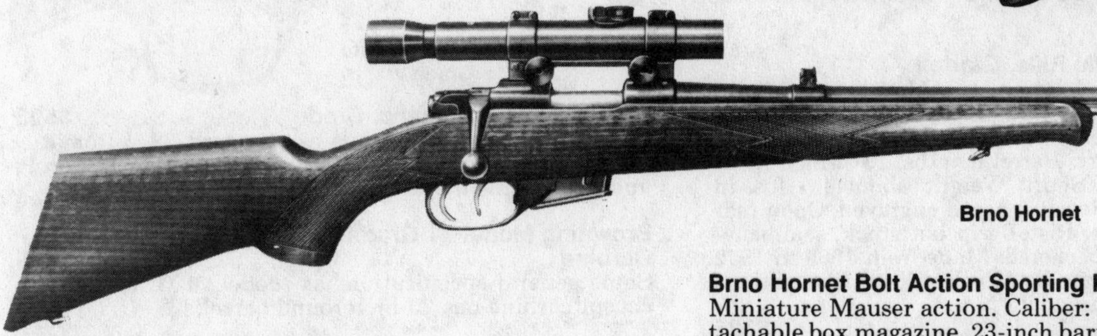

Brno Hornet

Brno Model 22F **$695**
Same as Model 21H except has full-length Mannlicher-type stock, weighs about 6 lbs. 14 oz. Discontinued.

Brno Hornet Bolt Action Sporting Rifle **$675**
Miniature Mauser action. Caliber: 22 Hornet. 5-shot detachable box magazine. 23-inch barrel. Double set trigger. Weight: about 6¼ pounds. Three-leaf open rear sight, hooded ramp front sight. Sporting stock with checkered pistol grip and forearm, swivels. Discontinued. *Note:* This rifle was also marketed in the U.S. as the "Z-B Mauser."

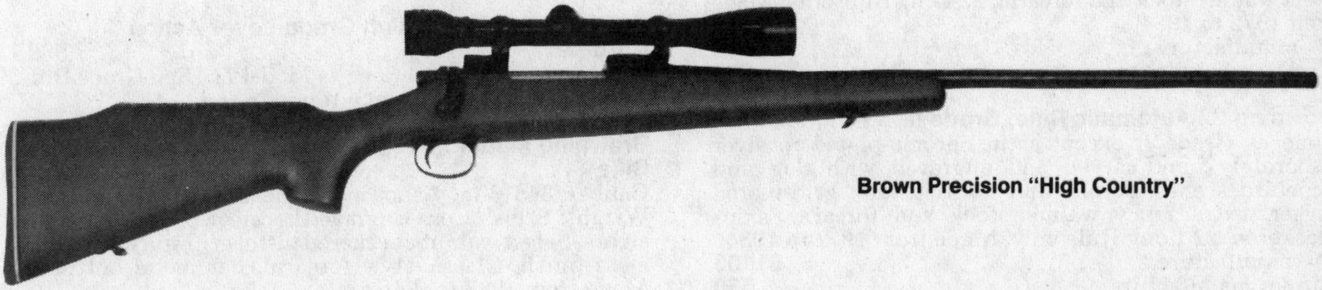

Brown Precision "High Country"

BROWN PRECISION COMPANY
Los Molinos, California

Brown Precision "High Country" Bolt Action Sporter **$595**
Calibers: 243 Win., 25-06, 270 Win., 7mm Rem. Mag., 308 Win., 30-06. 5-shot magazine (except 4-shot in 7mm Magnum). Remington Model 700 action. 22- or 24-inch barrel. No sights. Fiberglass stock with recoil pad and sling swivels. Weight: about 6½ pounds. Made from 1975 to date. Add $100 for stainless steel barrel.

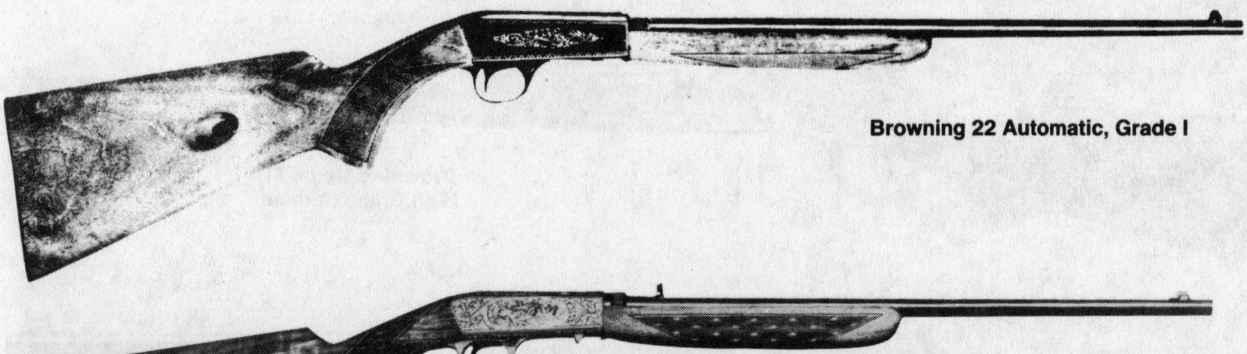

Browning 22 Automatic, Grade I

Browning 22 Automatic, Grade III

BROWNING RIFLES
Morgan, Utah

Mfd. for Browning by Fabrique Nationale d'Armes de Guerre (now Fabrique Nationale Herstal), Herstal, Belgium; Miroku Firearms Mfg. Co., Tokyo, Japan; Oy Sako Ab, Riihimaki, Finland

Browning 22 Automatic Rifle, Grade I
Similar to discontinued Remington Model 241A. Autoloading. Takedown. Calibers: 22 Long Rifle, 22 Short (not interchangeably). Tubular magazine in buttstock holds 11 Long Rifle, 16 Short. Barrel lengths: $19\frac{1}{4}$-inch in 22 L.R., $22\frac{1}{4}$-inch in 22 Short. Weight: about $4\frac{3}{4}$ lbs. in L.R.; 5 lbs. in Short. Receiver scroll engraved. Open rear sight, bead front sight. Pistol-grip buttstock, semibeavertail forearm, both checkered. Made from 1965 to 1972 by FN, from 1972 to date by Miroku. *Note:* Illustrations are of rifles manufactured by FN.
FN manufacture **$325**
Miroku manufacture **200**

Browning 22 Automatic Rifle, Grade II
Same as Grade I, except satin chrome-plated receiver engraved with small game animal scenes, gold-plated trigger, select walnut stock and forearm. 22 Long Rifle only. Made from 1972 to 1984.
FN manufacture **$495**
Miroku manufacture **295**

Browning 22 Automatic Rifle, Grade III
Same as Grade I, except satin chrome-plated receiver elaborately hand-carved and engraved with dog and gamebird scenes, scrolls and leaf clusters: gold-plated trigger, extra fancy walnut stock and forearm, skip-checkered. 22 Long Rifle only. Made from 1972 to 1984.
FN manufacture **$1100**
Miroku manufacture **650**

Browning 22 Auto
Grade VI

Browning 22 Automatic, Grade VI **$505**
Same general specifications as standard 22 Automatic, except for engraving, high-grade stock with checkering and glossy finish. Made from 1986 to date.

Browning Model 71 Grade I Lever Action Carbine **$425**
Same general specifications as Model 71 Grade I Rifle, except carbine has 20-inch round barrel.

Browning Model 71 Grade I Lever Action Rifle . . . **$435**
Caliber: 348 Win. 4-shot magazine. 24-inch round barrel. Weight: 8 lbs. 2 oz. Open buckhorn sights. Select walnut straight grip stock with satin finish. Classic-style forearm, flat metal buttplate. Made from 1987 to date.

Browning Model 71 High Grade Lever Action Carbine **$695**
Same general specifications as Model 71 High Grade Rifle, except carbine has 20-inch round barrel.

Browning Model 71 High Grade Lever Action Rifle **$735**
Caliber: 348 Win. 4-shot magazine. 24-inch round barrel. Weight: 8 lbs. 2 oz. Engraved receiver. Open buckhorn sights. Select walnut checkered pistol grip stock with high gloss finish. Classic-style forearm, flat metal buttplate. Made from 1987 to date.

Browning Model 71
Grade I Rifle

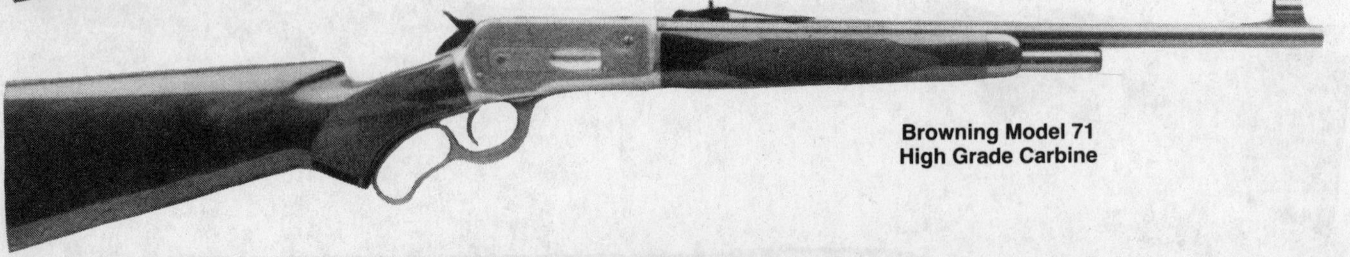
Browning Model 71
High Grade Carbine

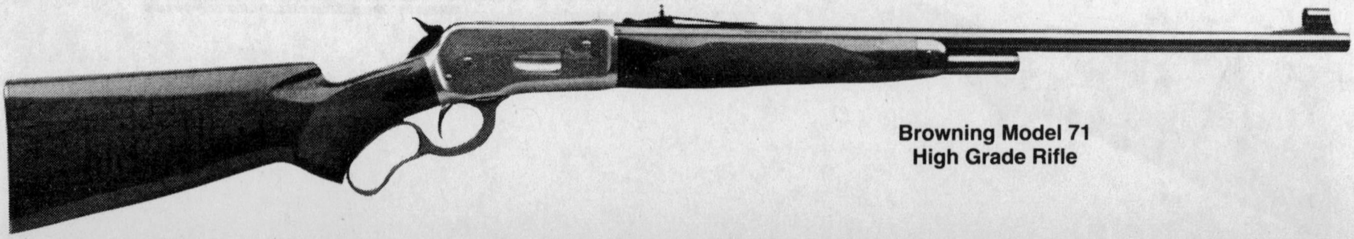
Browning Model 71
High Grade Rifle

Browning 78, 45-70

Browning 78 w/Monte Carlo Stock

Browning 78 Bicentennial

Browning 78 Bicentennial Set **$1800**
Special Model 78 45-70 with same specifications as standard type, except sides of receiver engraved with bison and eagle, scroll engraving on top of receiver, lever, both ends of barrel, and butt plate; high grade walnut stock and forearm. Accompanied by an engraved hunting knife and stainless steel commemorative medallion, all in an alder wood presentation case. Each item in set has matching serial number beginning with "1776" and ending with numbers 1 to 1000. Edition limited to 1000 sets. Made in 1976. Value is for set in new condition.

Browning 78 Single Shot Rifle **$415**
Falling-block lever action similar to Winchester 1885 High Wall S.S. Calibers: 22-250, 6mm Rem., 243 Win., 25-06, 7mm Rem. Mag., 30-06, 45-70 Govt. 26-inch octagon or heavy round barrel; 24-inch octagon bull barrel on 45-70 model. Weight: with octagon barrel, about 7¾ lbs.; with

Browning 78 Single Shot Rifle (cont.)
round barrel, 8½ lbs.; 45-70, 8¾ lbs. Furnished without sights, except 45-70 model has open rear sight, blade front sight. Fancy walnut stock and forearm, both checkered. 45-70 model has straight-grip stock with curved butt plate; others have stock with Monte Carlo comb and cheekpiece, pistol grip with cap, recoil pad. Made from 1973 to 1983 by Miroku.

Browning Model 1885 Single Shot Rifle **$435**
Calibers: 22-250, 270, 7mm Rem. Mag., 45-70 Govt. (223 and 30-06 scheduled for 1988). 28-inch octagonal barrel. 43½ inches overall. Weight: 8 lbs. 12 oz. Blued receiver. Gold-colored adjustable trigger. Drilled and tapped for scope mounts, open sights on 45-70 Govt. caliber only. Walnut straight-grip stock and schnabel forearm with cut checkering and high gloss finish. Made from 1985 to date.

Browning Model 1886 Grade I Lever Action Rifle . **$425**
Caliber: 45-70 Govt. 8-round magazine. 26-inch octagonal barrel. 45 inches overall. Weight: 9 lbs. 5 oz. Deep blued finish on receiver. Open buckhorn sights. Straight-grip walnut stock. Classic-style forearm. Metal buttplate. Satin finish. Made from 1986 in limited issue 1 of 7,000 by Miroku.

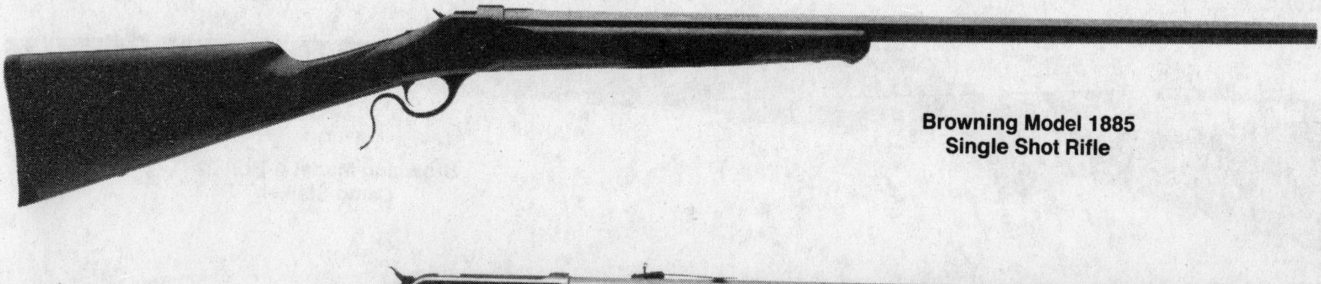

Browning Model 1885
Single Shot Rifle

Browning Model 1886
Grade I Rifle

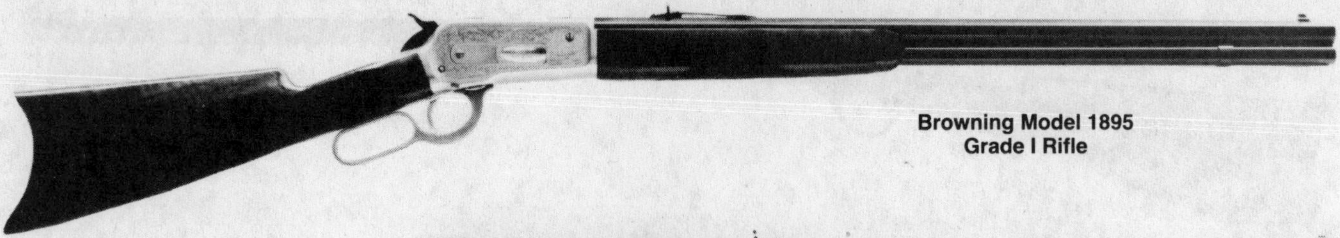

Browning Model 1895
Grade I Rifle

Browning Model 1895
High Grade Rifle

Browning Model 1886
High Grade Rifle

Browning Model 1886 High Grade Lever Action . . $655
Same general specifications as the Model 1886 Grade I, except receiver is grayed steel embellished with scroll; game scenes of elk and American bison engraving. Stock is high gloss. Made from 1986 in limited issue 1 of 3,000 by Miroku.

Browning Model 1886 Montana Centennial Rifle $850
Same general specifications as the Model 1886 High Grade Lever Action, except has specially engraved receiver designating Montana Centennial; also different stock design. Made from 1986 in limited issue 1 of 2,000 by Miroku.

Browning Model 1895 Grade I Lever Action Rifle $440
Caliber: 30-06, 30-40 Krag. 4-shot magazine. 24-inch round barrel. 42 inches overall. Weight: 8 pounds. French walnut stock and schnabel forend. Rear buckhorn sight; gold bead on elevated ramp front sight. Made from 1984 in limited issue 1 of 6,000. The 30-40 Krag caliber made from 1985 to date in limited issue 1 of 2,000. Mfd. by Miroku.

Browning Model 1895 High Grade Lever Action Rifle $595
Same general specifications as Model 1895 Grade I except engraved receiver and Grade III French walnut stock and forend with fine checkering. Made from 1984 in limited issue 1 of 1,000 by Miroku.

Browning Model A-Bolt 22 Camo Stalker Rifle $275
Same general specifications as Model A-Bolt 22 Rifle, except has laminated multi-colored stock with checkering. Made from 1987 to date.

Browning Model A-Bolt 22 . . . . $300
Caliber: 22 RF. 5- and 15-shot magazines. 22-inch round barrel. 40¼ inches overall. Weight: 5 lbs. 9 oz. Gold-colored adjustable trigger. Laminated walnut stock with checkering. Rosewood forend grip cap; pistol grip. Available with or without sights. Ramp front and adjustable folding leaf rear on open sight model. Made 1985 to date.

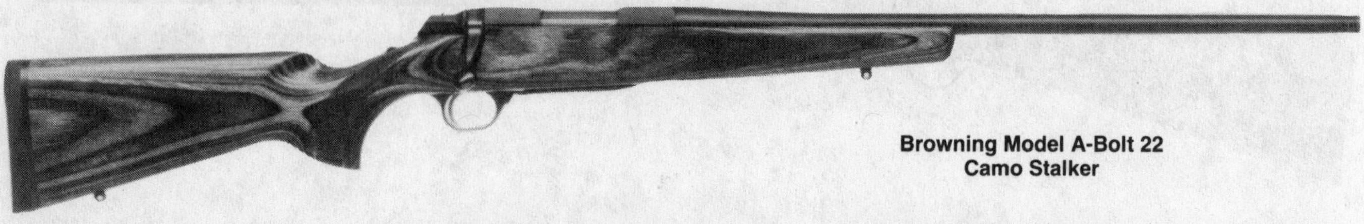

Browning Model A-Bolt 22
Camo Stalker

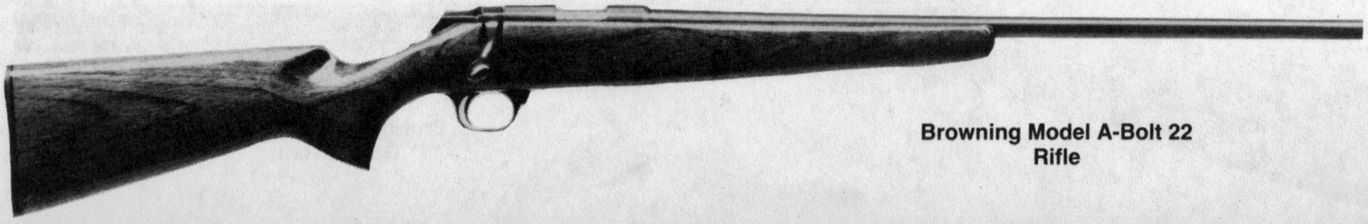

Browning Model A-Bolt 22
Rifle

Browning Model A-Bolt 22
Stainless Stalker

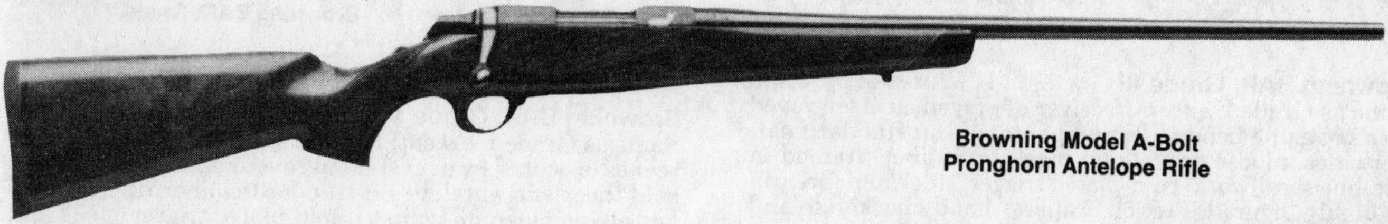

Browning Model A-Bolt
Pronghorn Antelope Rifle

Browning Model A-Bolt 22 Stainless Stalker Rifle $275
Same general specifications as Model A-Bolt 22 Camo Stalker, except has stainless steel bolt, barrel, etc. Made from 1987 to date.

Browning Model A-Bolt Big Horn Sheep Rifle . . . $1025
Same general specifications as the Model A-Bolt 22 Rifle, except has higher grade finish and special engraving. Chambered for 270 Win. Made in 1986 in Japan in limited issue (600).

Browning Model A-Bolt Pronghorn Antelope Rifle $900
Same general specifications as the Model A-Bolt 22 Rifle, except has higher grade finish and special engraving. Chambered for 243 Win. Made in 1987.

Browning Model B-92 Lever Action Rifle $250
Calibers: 357 Mag. and 44 Rem. Mag. 11-shot magazine. 20-inch round barrel. $37\frac{1}{2}$ inches overall. Weight: $5\frac{1}{2}$ lbs. to 6 lbs. 6 oz. Seasoned French walnut stock with high gloss finish. Cloverleaf rear sight; steel post front. Made from 1979 to date by Miroku.

Browning BAR Automatic Rifle, Grade I, Standard Calibers $450
Gas-operated semiautomatic. Calibers: 243 Win., 270 Win., 308 Win., 30-06. 4-round box magazine. 22-inch barrel. Weight: about $7\frac{1}{2}$ pounds. Folding leaf rear sight, hooded ramp front sight. French walnut stock and forearm, checkered, QD swivels. Made from 1967 to date by FN.

Browning BAR, Grade I, Magnum Calibers $495
Same as BAR in standard calibers, except chambered for 7mm Rem. Mag., 300 Win. Mag.; has 3-round box magazine, 24-inch barrel, recoil pad. Weight: about $8\frac{1}{2}$ pounds. Made from 1969 to date by FN.

Browning BAR, Grade II
Same as Grade I, except receiver engraved with big game heads (deer and antelope on standard-caliber rifles, ram and grizzly on magnum-caliber) and scrollwork, higher grade wood. Made 1967 to 1974 by FN.
Standard calibers **$650**
Magnum calibers **695**

RIFLES

Browning Model B-92
Lever Action Rifle

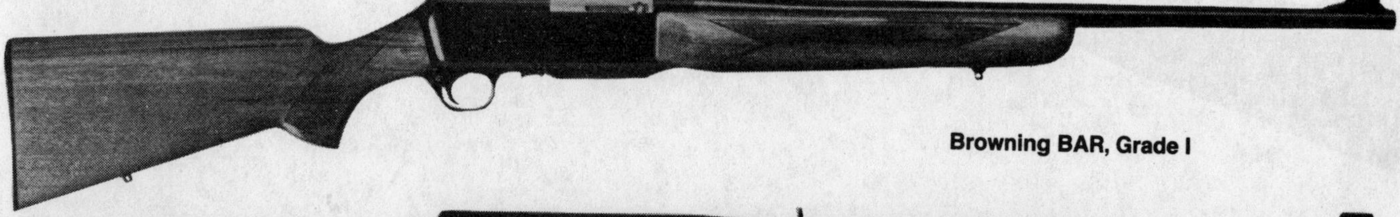

Browning BAR, Grade I

Browning BAR, Grade II

Browning BAR, Grade III

Browning BAR, Grade III $995
Same as Grade I, except receiver of grayed steel engraved with big game heads (deer and antelope on standard-caliber rifles, moose and elk on magnum-caliber) framed in fine-line scrollwork, gold-plated trigger, stock and forearm of highly figured French walnut, hand-checkered and carved. Made 1971-74 by FN.

Browning BAR, Grade IV

Browning BAR, Grade IV $1500
Same as Grade I, except: receiver of grayed steel engraved with full detailed rendition of running deer and antelope on standard-caliber rifles, moose and elk on magnum-caliber, gold-plated trigger, stock and forearm of highly figured French walnut, hand checkered and carved. Made from 1971 to 1986 by FN.

Browning BAR, Grade V

Browning BAR, Grade V $3000
Same as Grade I, except: receiver with complete big game scenes executed by a master engraver and inlaid with 18K gold (deer and antelope on standard-caliber rifles, moose and elk on magnum-caliber), gold-plated trigger, stock and forearm of finest French walnut, intricately hand-checkered and carved. Made 1971-74 by FN.

Browning BAR-22 Automatic Rifle $165
Semiautomatic. Caliber: 22 Long Rifle. Tubular magazine holds 15 rounds. 20¼-inch barrel. Weight: 6¼ pounds. Folding leaf rear sight, gold bead front sight on ramp. Receiver grooved for scope mounting. French walnut pistol-grip stock and forearm, checkered. Made 1977 to 1981.

Browning BAR-22, 1982 Version $185
Similar to BAR-22 Automatic Rifle except redesigned with new look and weight-forward balance. Weight: 6 pounds. Made 1982-84.

Browning BBR Lightning Bolt Action Rifle $325
Bolt-action rifle with short throw bolt of 60-degrees. Calibers: 25-06 Rem., 270 Win., 30-06, 7mm Rem. Mag., 300 Win. Mag. 24-inch barrel. Weight: 8 pounds. Made from 1979 to 1984.

Browning BAR-22

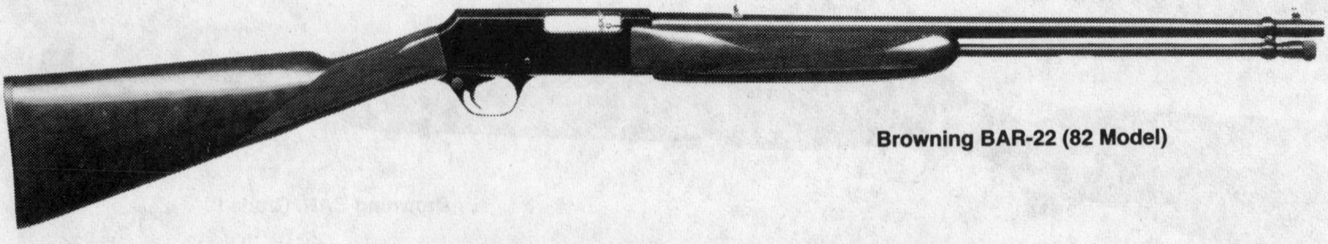

Browning BAR-22 (82 Model)

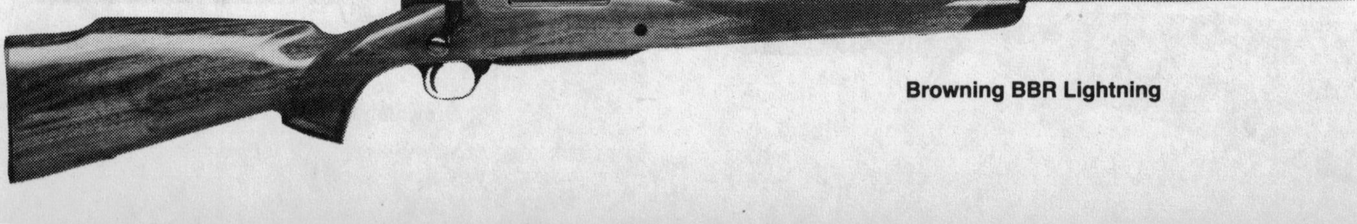

Browning BBR Lightning

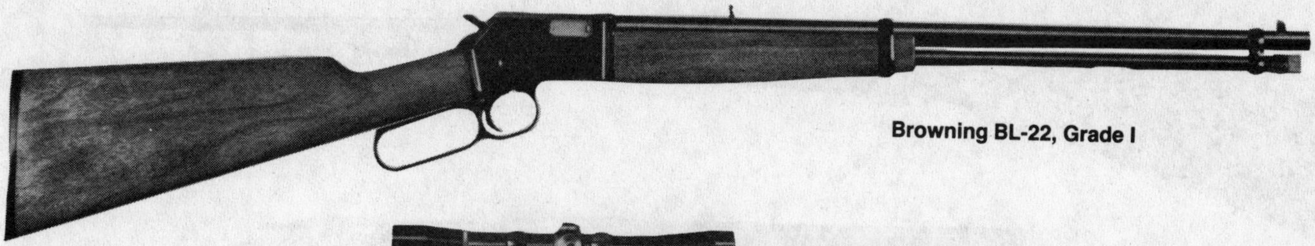

Browning BL-22, Grade I

Browning BL-22, Grade II

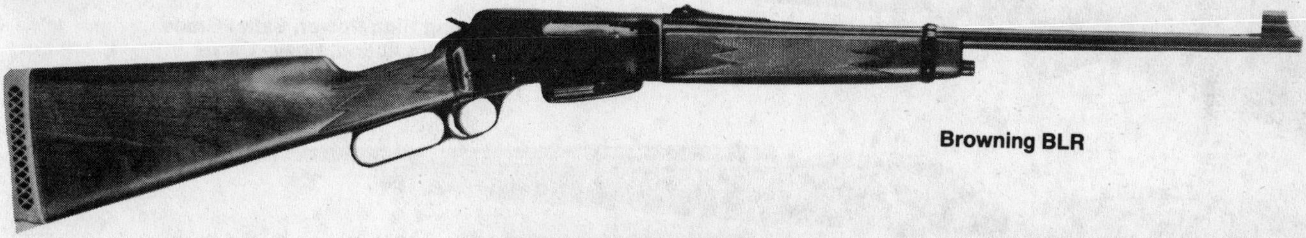

Browning BLR

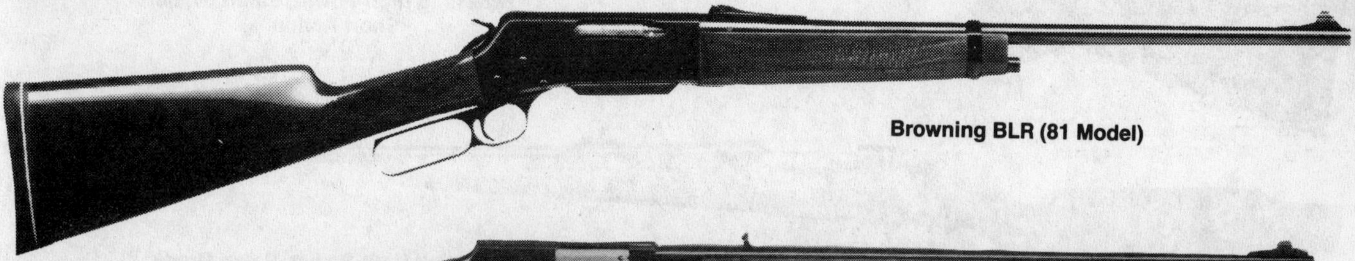

Browning BLR (81 Model)

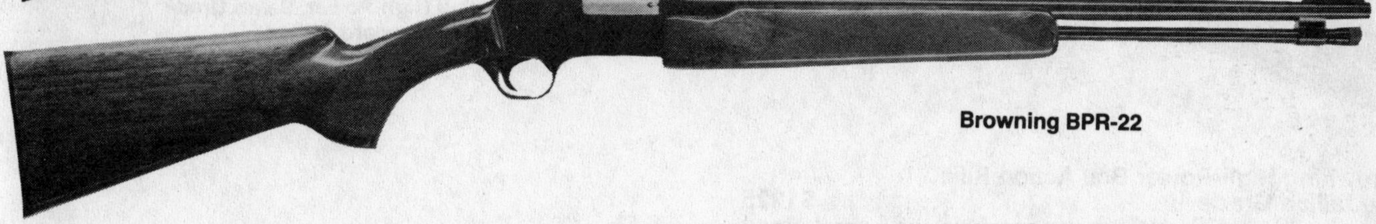

Browning BPR-22

Browning BL-22 Lever Action Repeating Rifle, Grade I $200
Short-throw lever action. Caliber: 22 Long Rifle, Long, Short. Tubular magazine holds 15 Long Rifle, 17 Long, 22 Short. 20-inch barrel. Weight: 5 pounds. Folding leaf rear sight, bead front sight. Receiver grooved for scope mounting. Walnut straight-grip stock and forearm, barrel band. Made from 1970 to date by Miroku.

Browning BL-22, Grade II $225
Same as Grade I, except scroll engraving on receiver, hand checkered grip and forearm. Made from 1970 to date by Miroku.

Browning BLR Lever Action Repeating Rifle $325
Calibers: 243 Win., 308 Win., 358 Win. 4-round detachable box magazine. 20-inch barrel. Weight: about 7 pounds. Windage and elevation adjustable open rear sight, hooded ramp front sight. Walnut straight-grip stock and forearm, checkered, barrel band, recoil pad. Made 1971 by FN, 1972 to date by Miroku.

Browning BLR Model '81 . . . . $350
Redesigned version of the Browning BLR. Calibers: 22-250 Rem., 243 Win., 308 Win., 358 Win. 4-round detachable box magazine. 20-inch barrel. Weight: about 7 pounds. Walnut straight-grip stock and forearm, cut checkering, recoil pad. Introduced 1982.

Browning BPR-22 Pump Rifle $185
Hammerless slide-action repeater. Specifications same as for BAR-22, except also available chambered for 22 Magnum RF; magazine capacity, 11 rounds. Introduced 1977 (Miroku); discontinued 1982.

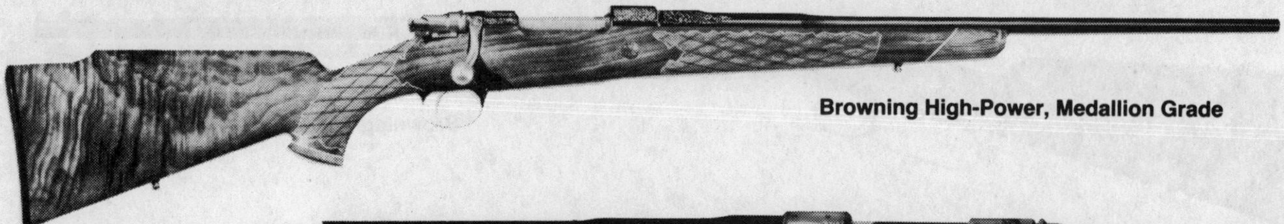

Browning High-Power, Medallion Grade

Browning High-Power, Olympian Grade

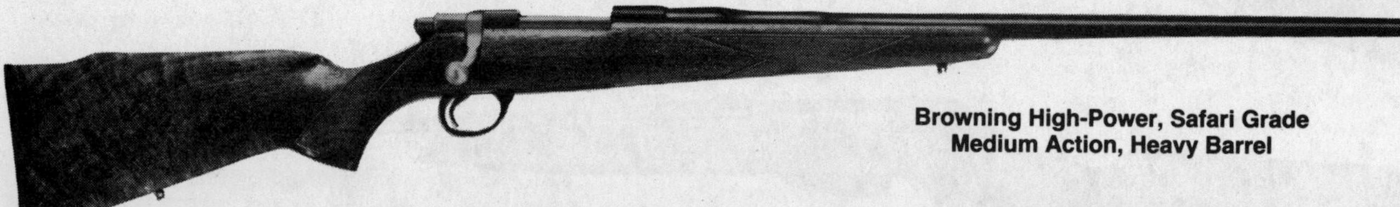

Browning High-Power, Safari Grade
Medium Action, Heavy Barrel

Browning High-Power, Safari Grade
Short Action

Browning High-Power, Safari Grade
Standard Action

Browning High-Power Bolt Action Rifle, Medallion Grade $1225
Same as Safari Grade, except: receiver and barrel scroll engraved, ram's head engraved on floorplate; select walnut stock with rosewood forearm tip and grip cap. Made 1961 to 1974.

Browning High-Power Bolt Action Rifle, Olympian Grade $1995
Same as Safari Grade, except: barrel engraved; receiver, trigger guard and floorplate satin chrome-plated and engraved with game scenes appropriate to caliber; finest figured walnut stock with rosewood forearm tip and grip cap, latter with 18K gold medallion. Made 1961 to 1974.

Browning High-Power Bolt Action Rifle, Safari Grade, Medium Action $725
Same as Standard, except medium action. Calibers: 22/250, 243 Win., 264 Win. Mag., 284 Win. Mag., 308 Win. Barrel: 22-inch lightweight barrel; 22/250 and 243 also available with 24-inch heavy barrel. Weight: 6 lbs. 12 oz. with lightweight barrel; 7 lbs. 13 oz. with heavy barrel. Made 1963 to 1974 by Sako.

Browning High-Power Bolt Action Rifle, Safari Grade, Short Action $695
Same as Standard, except short action. Calibers: 222 Rem., 222 Rem. Mag. 22-inch lightweight barrel or 24-inch heavy barrel. No sights. Weight: 6 lbs. 2 oz. with lightweight barrel; 7½ lbs. with heavy barrel. Made 1963 to 1974 by Sako.

Browning High-Power Bolt Action Rifle, Safari Grade, Standard Action $795
Mauser-type action. Calibers: 270 Win., 30-06, 7mm Rem. Mag., 300 H&H Mag., 300 Win. Mag., 308 Norma Mag., 338 Win. Mag., 375 H&H Mag., 458 Win. Mag. Cartridge capacity: 6 rounds in 270, 30-06; 4 in magnum calibers. Barrel length: 22 in., 270, 30-06; 24 in., magnum calibers. Weight: 7 lbs. 2 oz., 270, 30-06; 8¼ lbs., mag. calibers. Folding leaf rear sight, hooded ramp front sight. Checkered stock with pistol grip, Monte Carlo cheekpiece, QD swivels; recoil pad on magnum models. Made from 1959 to 1974 by FN.

Browning "T-Bolt" T-1

Browning "T-Bolt" T-2

Browning "T-Bolt" T-1 22 Repeating Rifle $335
Straight-pull bolt action. Caliber: 22 Long Rifle. 5-shot clip magazine. 24-inch barrel. Peep rear sight, blade/ramp front sight. Plain walnut stock with pistol grip. Weight: 6 lbs. Also available in left-hand model. Made 1965 to 1974 by FN.

Browning "T-Bolt" T-2 . . . . $420
Same as T-1, except fancy figured walnut stock, checkered. Discontinued 1974.

F.N. Browning Semiautomatic Rifle $2195
Same as F.N. FAL Semiautomatic Rifle. See listing of that rifle for specifications. Sold by Browning for a brief period c. 1960.

BSA GUNS LTD.
Birmingham, England

BSA No. 12 Martini Single Shot Target Rifle $240
Caliber: 22 Long Rifle. 29-inch barrel. Weight: about 8¾ pounds. Parker-Hale Model 7 rear sight and Model 2 front sight. Straight-grip stock, checkered forearm. *Note:* This model was also available with open sights or with BSA No. 30 and 20 sights. Made prior to WWII.

BSA Model 12/15 Martini Heavy $350
Same as Standard Model 12/15 except has extra heavy barrel, weighs about 11 pounds.

BSA Model 12/15 Martini Single Shot Target Rifle $315
Caliber: 22 Long Rifle. 29-inch barrel. Weight: about 9 pounds. Parker-Hale No. PH-7A rear sight and No. FS-22 front sight. Target stock with high comb and cheekpiece, beavertail forearm. *Note:* This is a post-WWII model; however, a similar rifle, the BSA-Parker Model 12/15, was produced c. 1938.

BSA No. 13 Martini Single Shot Target Rifle $235
Caliber: 22 Long Rifle. Lighter version of the No. 12 with same general specifications, except has 25-inch barrel, weighs 6½ pounds. Made prior to WWII.

BSA No. 13 Sporting Rifle
Same as No. 13 Target except fitted with Parker-Hale "Sportarget" rear sight and bead front sight. Also available in caliber 22 Hornet. Made prior to WWII.
22 Long Rifle **$240**
22 Hornet **330**

BSA Model 15 Martini Single Shot Target Rifle . . $400
Caliber: 22 Long Rifle. 29-inch barrel. Weight: about 9½ pounds. BSA No. 30 rear sight and No. 20 front sight. Target stock with cheekpiece and pistol grip, long semi-beavertail forearm. Made prior to WWII.

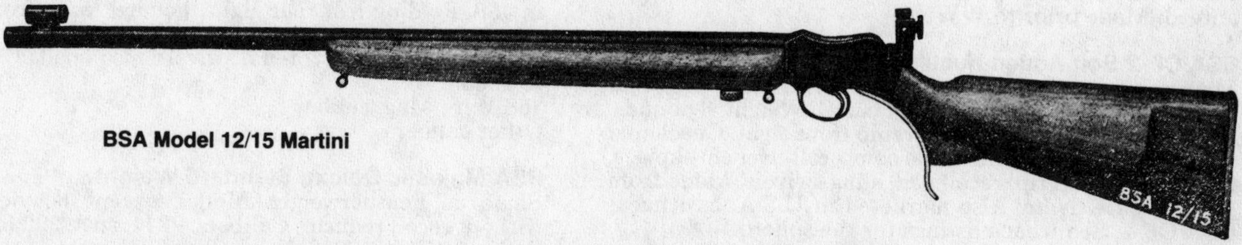

BSA Model 12/15 Martini

BSA No. 13 Martini

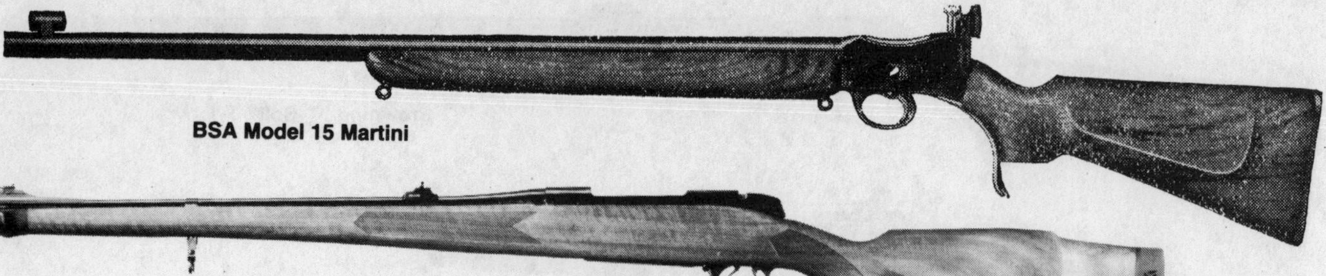

BSA Model 15 Martini

BSA CF-2 Stutzen Rifle

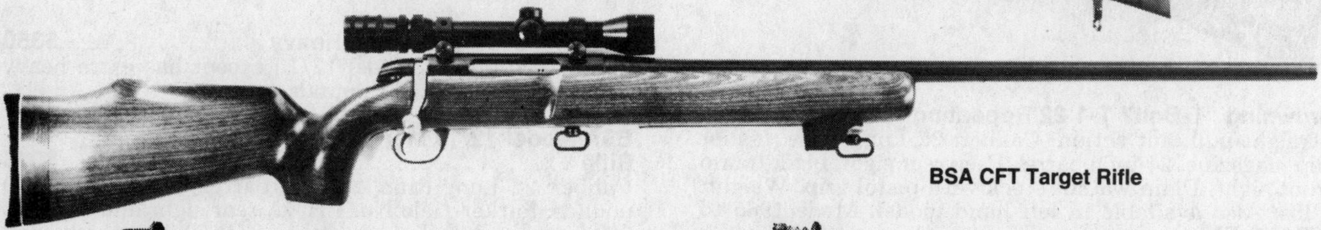

BSA CFT Target Rifle

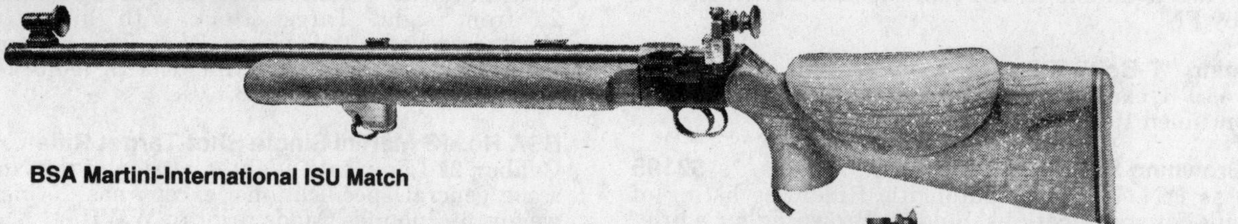

BSA Martini-International ISU Match

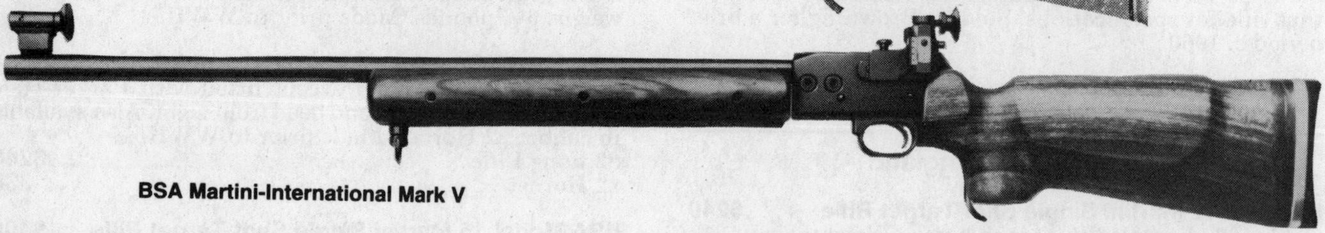

BSA Martini-International Mark V

BSA Centurion Model Match Rifle **$325**
Same general specifications as Model 15 except has "Centurion" match barrel, 1½-inch groups at 100 yards guaranteed. Made prior to WWII.

BSA CF-2 Bolt Action Hunting Rifle **$295**
Mauser-type action. Calibers: 7mm Rem. Mag., 300 Win. Mag. 3-shot magazine. 23.6-inch barrel. Weight: 8 pounds. Adjustable rear sight, hooded ramp front sight. Checkered walnut stock with Monte Carlo comb, roll-over cheekpiece, rosewood forend tip, recoil pad, sling swivels. Made from 1975 to date. *Note:* Also marketed in U.S.A. as Ithaca-BSA CF-2. See Ithaca listings for that photo.

BSA CF-2 Stutzen Rifle **$295**
Calibers: 222 Rem., 22/250, 243 Win., 270 Win., 308 Win., 30-06. 4-round capacity (5 in 222 Rem.). 20.6-inch barrel. 41½ inches (approx.) overall length. Weight: 7½ to 8 lbs. Williams front and rear sights. Hand-finished European walnut stock. Monte Carlo cheekpiece and Wundhammer palm swell. Double-set triggers.

BSA CFT Target Rifle **$550**
Single shot, bolt action. Caliber: 7.62mm. 26½-inch barrel. About 47½ inches overall. Weight: 11 pounds, incl. accessories. Barrel and action weight: 6 lbs. 12 oz.

BSA Majestic Deluxe Featherweight Bolt Action Hunting Rifle
Mauser-type action. Calibers: 243 Win., 270 Win., 308 Win., 30-06, 458 Win. Mag. 4-shot magazine. 22-inch barrel with BESA recoil reducer. Weight: 6¼ lbs.; 8¾ lbs. in 458. Folding leaf rear sight, hooded ramp front sight. European-style walnut stock, checkered, with cheekpiece, pistol grip, schnabel forend, swivels, recoil pad. Made 1959 to 1965.
458 Win. Mag. caliber **$355**
Other calibers **285**

BSA Majestic Deluxe Standard Weight **$325**
Same as Featherweight Model, except heavier barrel without recoil reducer. Calibers: 22 Hornet, 222 Rem., 243 Win., 7×57mm, 308 Win., 30-06. Weight: 7¼ to 7¾ pounds.

BSA Martini-International ISU Match Rifle **$550**
Similar to MK III, but modified to meet International Shooting Union "Standard Rifle" specifications. 28-inch standard weight barrel. Weight: 10¾ pounds. Redesigned stock and forearm; latter attached to barrel with "V" section alloy strut. Made from 1968 to date.

BSA Martini-International Mark V Match Rifle . . . **$575**
Same as ISU model, except has heavier barrel. Weight: 12¼ pounds. Made from 1976 to date.

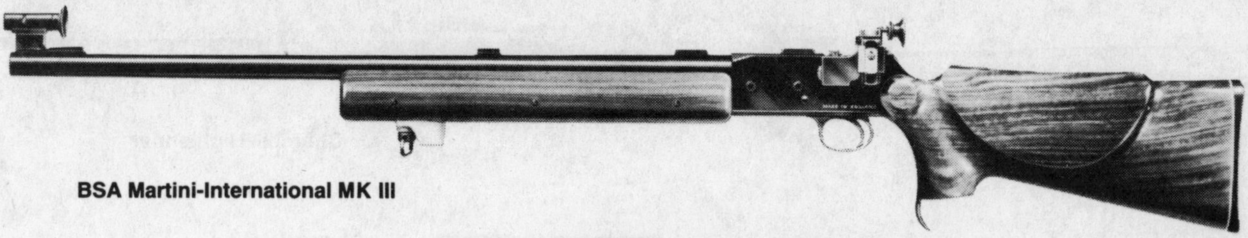

BSA Martini-International MK III

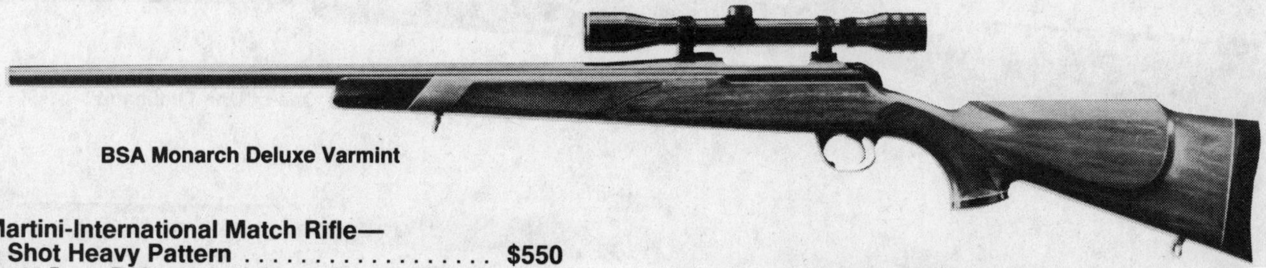

BSA Monarch Deluxe Varmint

BSA Martini-International Match Rifle— Single Shot Heavy Pattern $550
Caliber: 22 Long Rifle. 29-inch heavy barrel. Weight: about 14 pounds. Parker-Hale "International" front and rear sights. Target stock with full cheekpiece and pistol grip, broad beavertail forearm, handstop, swivels. Available in right-hand and left-hand models. Mfd. 1950-53.

BSA Martini-International Match Rifle— Light Pattern $425
Same general specifications as Heavy Pattern, except has 26-inch lighter weight barrel. Weight: about 11 pounds.

BSA Martini-International MK II Match Rifle $410
Same general specifications as original model. Heavy and Light Pattern. Improved trigger mechanism and ejection system. Redesigned stock and forearm. Made 1953 to 1959.

BSA Martini-International MK III Match Rifle $495
Same general specifications as MK II Heavy Pattern. Longer action frame with I-section alloy strut to which forearm is attached; barrel is fully floating. Redesigned stock and forearm. Made 1959 to 1967.

BSA Monarch Deluxe Bolt Action Hunting Rifle . $325
Same as Majestic Deluxe Standard Weight Model, except has redesigned stock of U.S. style with contrasting hardwood forend tip and grip cap. Calibers: 222 Rem., 243 Win., 270 Win., 7mm Rem. Mag., 308 Win., 30-06. 22-inch barrel. Weight: 7 to 7¼ pounds. Made 1965 to 1974.

BSA Monarch Deluxe Varmint Rifle $330
Same as Monarch Deluxe, except has 24-inch heavy barrel and weighs 9 pounds. Calibers: 222 Rem., 243 Win.

CANADIAN MILITARY RIFLES
Quebec, Canada
Manufactured by Ross Rifle Co.

Canadian Model 1907 Mark II Ross Military Rifle $185
Straight pull bolt action. Caliber: 303 British. 5-shot box magazine. 28-inch barrel. Weight: about 8½ pounds. Adjustable rear sight, blade front sight. Military-type full stock. *Note:* The Ross was originally issued as a Canadian service rifle in 1907. There were a number of variations; it was the official weapon at the beginning of WWI, but has been obsolete for many years. For Ross sporting rifle, see listing under Ross Rifle Co.

CHARTER ARMS CORPORATION
Stratford, Connecticut

Charter AR-7 Explorer (Disassembled and Stowed in Stock)

Charter AR-7 Explorer Survival Rifle $80
Same as Armalite AR-7, except has black, instead of brown, "wood grain" plastic stock. See listing of that rifle for specifications. Made from 1973 to date.

CHIPMUNK MANUFACTURING INC.
Medford, Oregon

Chipmunk Bolt Action Single Shot Rifle
Caliber: 22 RF or 22 RF Mag. Barrel: 16⅛ inches. Weight: about 2½ pounds. Peep rear sight, ramp front sight. Plain American walnut stock. Made from 1982 to date.

Standard Model	$95
Presentation Grade	400

CHURCHILL, GUNMAKERS, LTD.
London, England

Churchill Highlander Bolt Action Rifle $360
Calibers: 243 Win., 25-06 Rem., 270 Win., 308 Win., 30-06, 7mm Rem. Mag., 300 Win. Mag. 4-shot magazine (standard); 3-shot (magnum). Barrel length: 22-inch (standard); 24-inch (magnum). 42½ to 44½ inches overall.

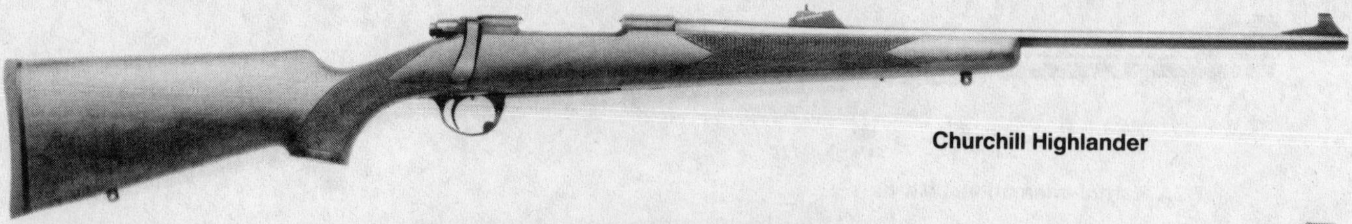

Churchill Highlander

Churchill "One of One Thousand"

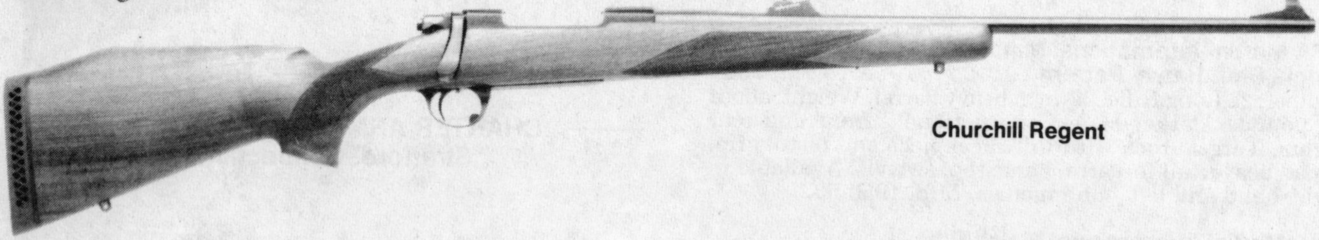

Churchill Regent

Churchill Highlander Bolt Action Rifle (cont.)
Weight: 7½ pounds. Adjustable rear sight, blade front. Checkered European walnut pistol-grip stock. Imported since 1986.

Churchill "One of One Thousand" Rifle $1400
Made for Interarms to commemorate that firm's 20th anniversary. Mauser-type action. Calibers: 270, 7mm Rem. Mag., 308, 30-06, 300 Win. Mag., 375 H&H Mag., 458 Win. Mag. 5-shot magazine (3-shot in magnum calibers). 24-inch barrel. Weight: about 8 pounds. Classic-style French walnut stock with cheekpiece, black forend tip,

Churchill "One of One Thousand" Rifle (cont.)
checkered pistol grip and forearm, swivel-mounted recoil pad with cartridge trap, pistol-grip cap with trap for extra front sight, barrel-mounted sling swivel. Issue limited to 1000 rifles. Made 1973.

Churchill Regent Bolt Action Rifle $410
Calibers: 243 Win., 25-06 Rem., 270 Win., 308 Win., 30-06, 7mm Rem. Mag., 300 Win. Mag. 4-shot magazine. 22-inch round barrel. 42.5 inches overall. Weight: 7.5 pounds. Ramp front sight w/gold bead; adjustable rear. Hand-checkered Monte Carlo-style stock of select European walnut; recoil pad. Made from 1986 to date.

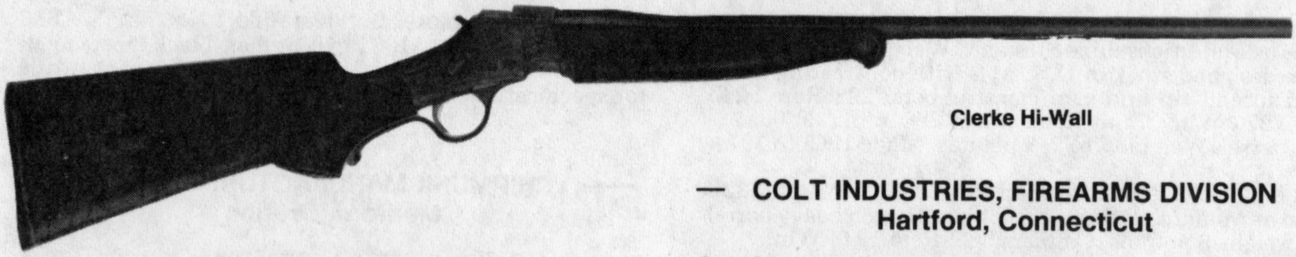

Clerke Hi-Wall

— CLERKE RECREATION PRODUCTS —
Santa Monica, California

Clerke Hi-Wall Single Shot Rifle $275
Falling-block lever action similar to Winchester 1885 High Wall S.S. Color casehardened investment-cast receiver. Calibers: 222 Rem., 22-250, 243 Rem., 6mm Rem., 25-06, 270 Win., 7mm Rem. Mag., 30-06, 45-70 Govt. 26-inch medium-weight barrel. Weight: about 8 pounds. Furnished without sights. Checkered walnut pistol-grip stock and schnabel forearm. Made 1972-74.

Clerke Deluxe Hi-Wall $350
Same as standard model, except has adjustable trigger, half-octagon barrel, select wood, stock with cheekpiece and recoil pad. Made 1972-74.

— COLT INDUSTRIES, FIREARMS DIVISION —
Hartford, Connecticut

Colt 22 Lightning Magazine Rifle $850
Slide action. Caliber: 22 Rimfire (Short or Long). Tubular magazine holding 15 long or 16 short. 24-inch barrel, round or octagon. Weight: 5¾ pounds (round barrel). Open rear sight, bead front sight. Walnut stock and forearm. Available in small, medium and large frames. Made from 1887 to 1904.

Colt AR-15 Adjustable Stock $695
Same as AR-15, except has collapsible buttstock and redesigned forearm.

Colt AR-15 Compact 9mm Carbine $650
Semiautomatic. Caliber: 9mm NATO. 20-round detachable magazine. Barrel: 16-inch round. Weight: 6.3 pounds. Adjustable rear and front sights. Collapsible buttstock. Ribbed round handguard. Made from 1985 to date.

Colt AR-15 Adjustable Stock

Colt AR-15 9mm Carbine

Colt AR-15 Sporter

Colt AR-15 A2 Sporter II

Colt Stagecoach

Colt AR-15 Sporter **$680**
Commercial semiautomatic version of U.S. M16 rifle. Gas-operated. Takedown. Caliber: 223 Rem. (5.56mm). 20-round magazine with spacer to reduce capacity to 5 rounds. 20-inch barrel with flash suppressor. Rear peep sight with windage adjustment in carrying handle. Front sight adjustable for windage, 3× scope and mount available as accessory equipment (adds $70 to value). Black molded buttstock of high-impact synthetic material, rubber butt plate. Barrel surrounded by handguards of black fiberglass with heat-reflecting inner shield. Swivels, black web sling strap. Weight: w/o accessories, 6.3 pounds. Made from 1964 to date.

Colt AR-15 A2 Sporter II **$695**
Same general specifications as standard AR-15 Sporter except heavier barrel, improved pistol grip, weight of 7½ pounds and optional 3× or 4× scope. Made 1985 to date.

Colt Lightning Carbine **$1450**
Same as Lightning Magazine Rifle, except has 12-shot magazine, 20-inch barrel, weighs 6¼ pounds.

Colt Lightning Baby Carbine **$3000**
Same as Lightning Carbine, except lighter weight (5½ pounds).

Colt Lightning Magazine Rifle **$925**
Slide action. Calibers: 32-20, 38-40, 44-40. 15-shot tubular magazine. 26-inch barrel, round or octagon. Weight: 6¾ pounds (round barrel). Open rear sight, bead or blade front sight. Walnut stock and forearm. Made 1884 to 1902.

Colt Stagecoach 22 Autoloader **$155**
Same as Colteer 22 Autoloader, except has engraved receiver, saddle ring, 16½-inch barrel. Weight: 4 lbs. 10 oz. Made 1965 to 1975.

Colteer 1-22 Single Shot Bolt Action Rifle **$95**
Caliber: 22 Long Rifle, Long, Short. 20- or 22-inch barrel. Open rear sight, ramp front sight. Pistol-grip stock with Monte Carlo comb. Weight: about 5 pounds. Made 1957 to 1967.

Colteer 22 Autoloader **$150**
Caliber: 22 Long Rifle. 15-round tubular magazine. 19⅜-inch barrel. Open rear sight, hooded ramp front sight. Straight-grip stock, Western carbine-style forearm with barrel band. Weight: about 4¾ pounds. Made 1964 to 1975.

Coltsman Custom Bolt Action Sporting Rifle **$425**
FN Mauser action, side safety, engraved floorplate. Calibers: 30-06, 300 H&H Mag. 5-shot box magazine. 24-inch barrel, ramp front sight. Fancy walnut stock, Monte Carlo comb, cheekpiece, pistol grip, checkered, QD swivels. Weight: about 7¼ pounds. Made from 1957 to 1961. Value shown is for rifle, as furnished by manufacturer, without rear sight.

Coltsman Deluxe Rifle **$395**
FN Mauser action. Same as Custom model except plain floorplate, plainer wood and checkering. Made from 1957 to 1961. Value shown is for rifle, as furnished by manufacturer, without rear sight.

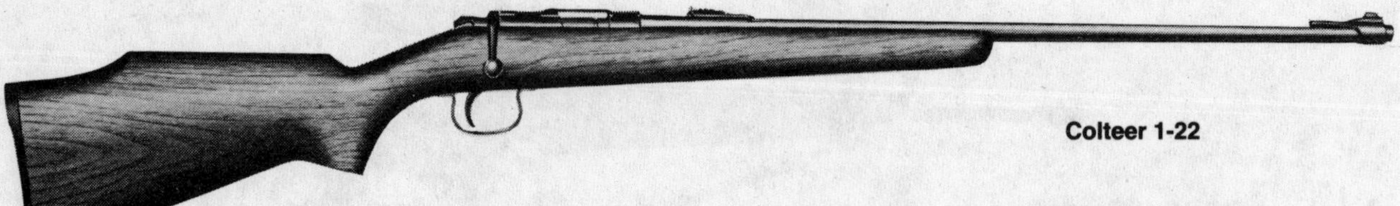

Colteer 1-22

Colteer 22 Autoloader

Coltsman Deluxe

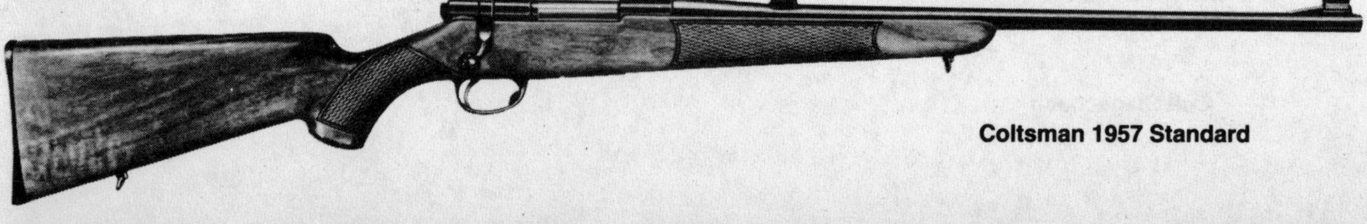

Coltsman 1957 Standard

Coltsman Models of 1957 Rifles
Sako Medium action. Calibers: 243, 308. Weight: about 6 3/4 pounds. Other specifications similar to those of models with FN actions. Made 1957 to 1961.

Custom **$425**
Deluxe **395**
Standard **340**

Coltsman Model of 1961, Custom Rifle $440
Sako action. Calibers: 222, 222 Mag., 223, 243, 264, 270, 308, 30-06, 300 H&H. 23-, 24-inch barrel. Folding leaf rear sight, hooded ramp front sight. Fancy French walnut stock with Monte Carlo comb, rosewood forend tip and grip cap, skip checkering, recoil pad, sling swivels. Weight: 6 1/2 to 7 1/2 pounds. Made from 1963 to 1965.

Coltsman Model of 1961, Standard Rifle $395
Same as Custom model, except plainer, American walnut stock. Made 1963-65.

Coltsman Standard Rifle $335
FN Mauser action. Same as Deluxe model except stock has no cheekpiece, barrel length is 22 inches. Made from 1957 to 1961. Value shown is for rifle, as furnished by manufacturer, without rear sight.

Note: The following Colt-Sauer rifles are manufactured for Colt by J. P. Sauer & Sohn, Eckernförde, West Germany.

Colt-Sauer Grand African $1050
Same specifications as standard model, except caliber 458 Win. Mag., weighs 9 1/2 pounds, adjustable leaf rear sight, hooded ramp front sight, magnum-style stock of Bubinga. Made from 1973 to date.

Colt-Sauer Grand Alaskan $995
Same specifications as standard model, except caliber 375 H&H, weighs 8 1/2 pounds, adjustable leaf rear sight, hooded ramp front sight, magnum-style stock of walnut.

Colt-Sauer Magnum $925
Same specifications as standard model, except calibers 7mm Rem. Mag., 300 Win. Mag., 300 Weatherby. Weight: 8 1/2 pounds. Made from 1973 to date.

Colt-Sauer Short Action $850
Same specifications as standard model, except calibers 22-250, 243 Win., 308 Win. Weight: 7 1/2 lbs.; 8 1/4 lbs. in 22-250. Made from 1973 to date.

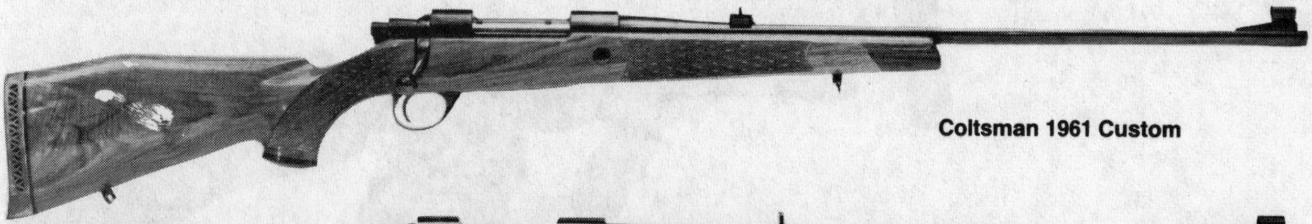

Coltsman 1961 Custom

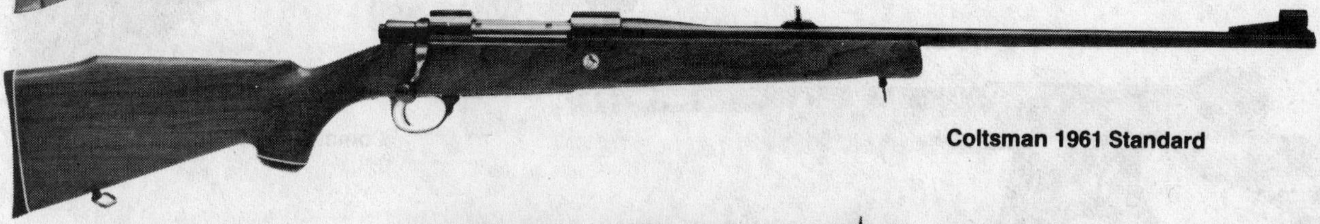

Coltsman 1961 Standard

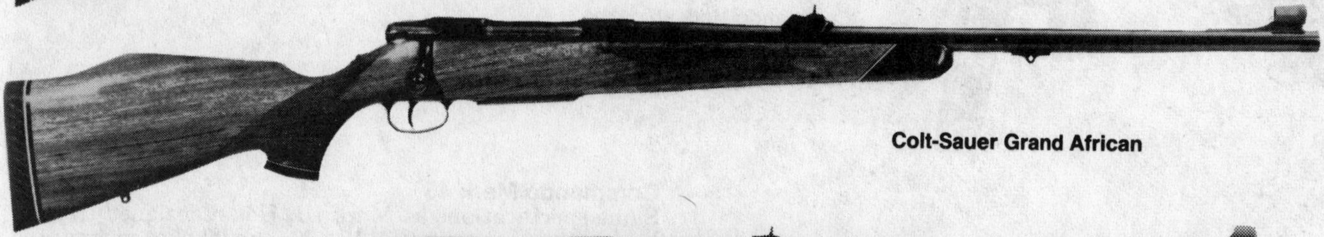

Colt-Sauer Grand African

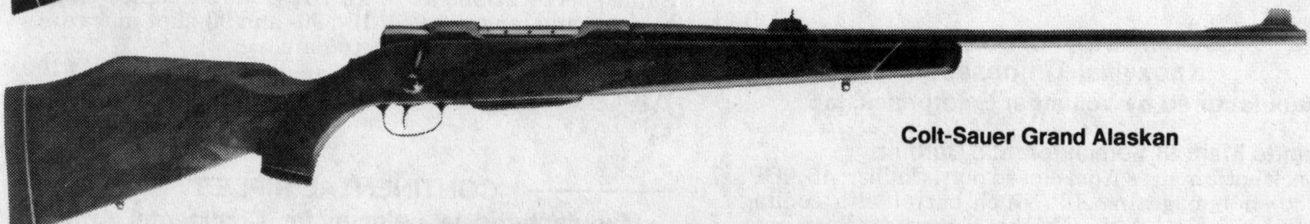

Colt-Sauer Grand Alaskan

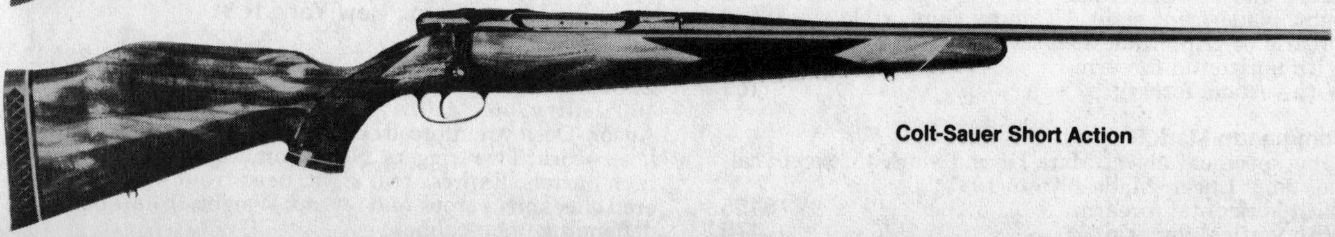

Colt-Sauer Short Action

Colt-Sauer Standard

Colt-Sauer Sporting Rifle, Standard Model $850
Sauer 80 nonrotating bolt-action. Calibers: 25-06, 270 Win., 30-06. 3-round detachable box magazine. 24-inch barrel. Weight: $7\frac{3}{4}$ lbs.; $8\frac{1}{2}$ lbs. in 25-06. Furnished with-

Colt-Sauer Sporting Rifle, Standard (cont.)
out sights. American walnut stock with Monte Carlo cheekpiece, checkered pistol grip and forearm, rosewood forend tip and pistol-grip cap, recoil pad. Made from 1973 to date.

Commando Mark III

Commando Mark 9

Commando Mark 45

COMMANDO CARBINES
Knoxville, Tennessee
Manufactured by Volunteer Enterprises, Inc.

Commando Mark III Semiautomatic Carbine
Blow-back action, fires from closed bolt. Caliber: 45 ACP. 15- or 30-shot magazine. $16\frac{1}{2}$-inch barrel with cooling sleeve and muzzle brake. Weight: 8 pounds. Peep rear sight, blade front sight. "Tommy Gun" style stock and forearm or grip. Made 1969 to 1976.
With horizontal forearm **$150**
With vertical foregrip **165**

Commando Mark 9
Same specifications as Mark III and Mark 45, except caliber 9mm Luger. Made 1976 to 1981.
With horizontal forearm **$155**
With vertical foregrip **175**

Commando Mark 45
Same specifications as Mark III. Has redesigned trigger housing and magazine. 5-, 15-, 30- and 90-shot magazines available. Made from 1976 to date.
With horizontal forearm **$180**
With vertical foregrip **195**

CONTINENTAL RIFLES
Manufactured in Belgium for Continental Arms Corp., New York, N.Y.

Continental Double Rifle $3995
Calibers: 270, 303 Sav., 30-40, 348 Win., 30-06, 375 H&H, 400 Jeffrey, 465, 470, 475 No. 2, 500, 600. Side-by-side. Anson-Deeley reinforced boxlock action with triple bolting lever-work. Two triggers. Nonautomatic safety. 24- or 26-inch barrels. Express rear sight, bead front sight. Checkered cheekpiece stock and forend. Weight: from 7 pounds, depending upon caliber.

— CZECHOSLOVAKIAN MILITARY RIFLES —
Brno, Czechoslovakia
Manufactured by Ceska Zbrojovka

Czech Model 1924 (VZ24) Mauser Military Rifle . . $175
Basically the same as the German Kar., 98k and F.N. (Belgian Model 1924.) Caliber: 7.9mm Mauser. 5-shot box magazine. 23¼-inch barrel. Weight: about 8½ pounds. Adjustable rear sight, blade front sight with guards. Military stock of Belgian-type, full handguard. Mfd. from 1924 through WWII. Many of these rifles were made for export. As produced during the German occupation, this model was known as Gewehr 24t.

Czech Model 1933 (VZ33) Mauser Military Carbine $195
Modification of the German M/98 action with smaller receiver ring. Caliber: 7.9mm Mauser. 19¼-inch barrel. Weight: about 7½ pounds. Adjustable rear sight, blade front sight with guards. Military-type full stock. Mfd. from 1933 through WWII; a similar model produced during the German occupation was designated Gew., 33/40.

DAISY RIFLES
Rogers, Arkansas

Daisy V/L rifles carry the first and only commercial caseless cartridge system. It is expected that these rifles will appreciate considerably in future years. The cartridge, no longer made, is also a collector's item.

Daisy V/L Collector's Kit $450
Presentation grade rifle with a gold plate inscribed with the owner's name and gun serial number mounted on the stock. Kit also includes a special gun case, pair of brass gun cradles for wall-hanging, 300 rounds of 22 V/L ammunition, and a certificate signed by Daisy president Cass S. Hough. Approx. 1000 mfd. 1968-69.

Daisy V/L Presentation Grade $295
Same specifications as standard model, except has walnut stock. Approximately 4000 manufactured 1968-69.

Daisy V/L Standard Rifle $225
Single shot, under-lever action. Caliber: 22 V/L (caseless cartridge; propellant ignited by jet of hot air). 18-inch barrel. Weight: 5 pounds. Adjustable open rear sight, ramp with blade front sight. Wood-grained Lustran stock (foam-filled). Approx. 19,000 mfd. 1968-69.

CHARLES DALY RIFLE
Made by Franz Jaeger & Co., Suhl, Germany, and distributed in the U.S. by Outdoor Sports Headquarters, Inc., Dayton, Ohio.

Charles Daly Hammerless Drilling
See listing under Charles Daly shotguns.

Charles Daly Hornet Rifle $950
Same as Herold Rifle. See listing of that rifle for specifications. Imported during the 1930s.

RIFLES

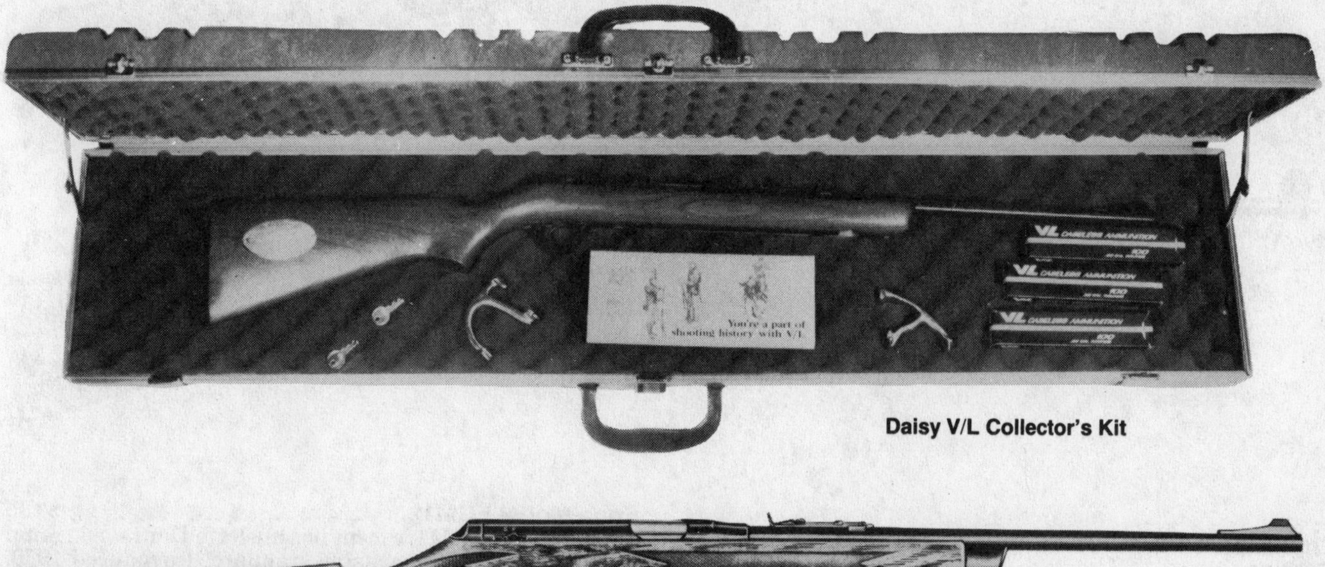

Daisy V/L Collector's Kit

Daisy V/L Standard

ERMA-WERKE
Dachau, West Germany

Erma EG72 Pump Action Repeater $110
Visible hammer. Caliber: 22 Long Rifle. 15-shot magazine. 18½-inch barrel. Weight: about 5¼ pounds. Open rear sight, hooded ramp front sight. Receiver grooved for scope mounting. Straight-grip stock, grooved slide handle. Made 1970-76.

Erma Model EG73 . . . . $160
Same as Model EG712, except chambered for 22 Winchester Magnum Rimfire, has 12-shot tubular magazine, 19.3-inch barrel. Made from 1973 to date.

Erma Model EG72

Erma Model EG712

Erma Model EGM1

Erma Model EM1 22

Erma Model EG712 Lever Action Repeating Carbine $150
Styled after Winchester Model 94. Caliber: 22 Long Rifle, Long, Short. Tubular magazine holds 15 LR, 17 Long, 21 Short. 18½-inch barrel. Weight: about 5½ pounds. Open rear sight, hooded ramp front sight. Receiver grooved for scope mounting. Western carbine-style stock and forearm with barrel band. Made from 1976 to date. *Note:* A similar carbine of Erma manufacture is marketed in the U.S. as Ithaca Model 72 Saddlegun.

Erma Model EGM1 . . . . $135
Same as Model EM1, except has unslotted buttstock, ramp front sight, 5-shot magazine standard. Introduced 1970; discontinued.

Erma Model EM1 22 Semiautomatic Carbine . . . $140
Styled after U.S. Carbine Cal. 30 M1. Caliber: 22 Long Rifle. 10- or 15-round magazine. 18-inch barrel. Weight: about 5½ pounds. Carbine-type sights. Receiver grooved for scope mounting. Military stock and handguard. Introduced 1966; discontinued.

FABRIQUE NATIONALE HERSTAL
Herstal, Belgium
Formerly Fabrique Nationale d'Armes de Guerre

F.N. Models 1924, 1934/30 and 1930 Mauser Military Rifles $225
Basically the same as the German Kar. 98k. Straight bolt handle. Calibers: 7mm, 7.65mm and 7.9mm Mauser. 5-shot box magazine. $23\frac{1}{2}$-inch barrel. Weight: about $8\frac{1}{2}$ pounds. Adjustable rear sight, blade front sight. Military stock of M/98 pattern with slight modification. Model differences are minor. Also produced in a short carbine model with $17\frac{1}{4}$-inch barrel. *Note:* These rifles were manufactured under contract for Abyssinia, Argentina, Belgium, Bolivia, Brazil, Chile, China, Colombia, Ecuador, Iran, Luxembourg, Mexico, Peru, Turkey, Uruguay and Yugoslavia. Such arms usually bear the coat of arms of the country for which they were made, together with the contractor's name and the date of manufacture. Also sold commercially and exported to all parts of the world.

F.N. Model 1949 Semiautomatic Military Rifle . . . $495
Gas-operated. Calibers: 7mm, 7.65mm, 7.92mm, 30M2 (30-06). 10-round box magazine, clip fed or loaded singly. 23.2-inch barrel. Weight: $9\frac{1}{2}$ pounds. Tangent rear sight, shielded post front sight. Pistol-grip stock, handguard. *Note:* Adopted in cal. 30 by Belgium in 1949 and also by Belgian Congo, Brazil, Colombia, Luxembourg, and Netherlands East Indies; Venezuela bought this rifle in 7mm, Egypt in 7.92mm. Approx. 160,000 were made.

F.N. Model 1950 Mauser Military Rifle $250
Same as previous F.N. models of Kar. 98k type, except chambered for 30-06.

F.N. Deluxe Mauser Bolt Action Sporting Rifle . . $585
American calibers: 220 Swift, 243 Win., 244 Rem., 250/3000, 257 Roberts, 270 Win., 7mm, 300 Sav., 308 Win., 30-06. European calibers: 7×57, 8×57JS, 8×60S, 9.3×62, 9.5×57, 10.75×68mm. 5-shot box magazine. 24-inch barrel. Weight: about $7\frac{1}{2}$ lbs.; in 270, $8\frac{1}{4}$ lbs. American model is standard with hooded ramp front sight and Tri-Range rear sight; Continental model has two-leaf rear sight. Checkered stock with cheekpiece, pistol grip, swivels. Made 1947 to 1963.

F.N. Deluxe Mauser—Presentation Grade $980
Same as regular model, except has select grade stock; engraving on receiver, trigger guard, floorplate and barrel breech. Discontinued 1963.

F.N. Supreme Mauser Bolt Action Sporting Rifle . . $600
Calibers: 243, 270, 7mm, 308, 30-06. 4-shot magazine in 243 and 308; 5-shot in other calibers. 22-inch barrel in 308; 24-inch in other calibers. Hooded ramp front sight, Tri-Range peep rear sight. Checkered stock with Monte Carlo cheekpiece, pistol grip, swivels. Weight: about $7\frac{3}{4}$ pounds. Made 1957 to 1975.

F.N. Supreme Magnum Mauser $685
Calibers: 264 Mag., 7mm Mag., 300 Win. Mag. Specifications same as for standard-caliber model except 3-shot magazine capacity.

F.N.-FAL Semiautomatic Rifle $795
Same as the standard FAL military rifle except without provision for automatic firing. Gas-operated. Caliber: 7.62mm NATO (.308 Win.). 10- or 20-round box magazine. $25\frac{1}{2}$-inch barrel (including flash hider). Weight: about 9

FN Model 1949 Semiautomatic Rifle

FN Model 1950 Mauser

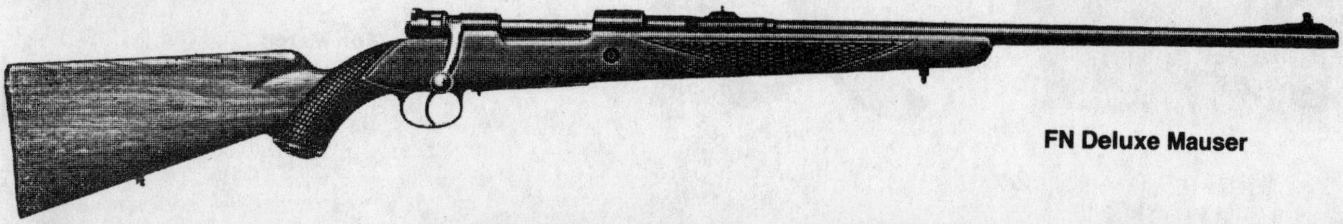

FN Deluxe Mauser

FN Supreme Mauser

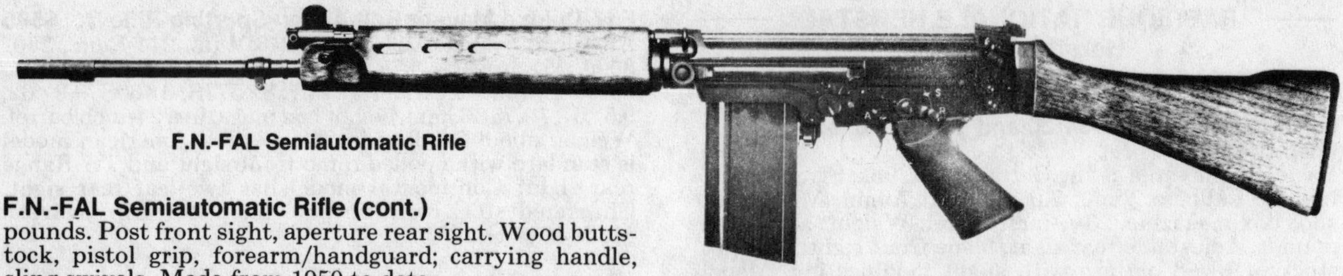

F.N.-FAL Semiautomatic Rifle

F.N.-FAL Semiautomatic Rifle (cont.)
pounds. Post front sight, aperture rear sight. Wood buttstock, pistol grip, forearm/handguard; carrying handle, sling swivels. Made from 1950 to date.

FINNISH LION RIFLES
Jyväskylä, Finland
Manufactured by Valmet Oy, Tourula Works

Finnish Lion Match Rifle **$450**
Bolt action, single shot. Caliber: 22 Long Rifle. 28$\frac{3}{4}$-inch heavy barrel. Weight: about 14$\frac{1}{2}$ pounds. Extension rear peep sight, aperture front sight. Walnut free-rifle stock with full pistol grip, thumb hole, beavertail forearm, hook butt plate, palm rest, hand stop, swivel. Made 1937 to 1972.

Finnish Lion Champion Free Rifle **$525**
Bolt action, single shot. Double-set trigger. Caliber: 22 Long Rifle. 28$\frac{3}{4}$-inch heavy barrel. Weight: about 16 pounds. Extension rear peep sight, aperture front sight.

Finnish Lion Champion Free Rifle (cont.)
Walnut free-rifle stock with full pistol grip, thumb hole, beavertail forearm, hook butt plate, palm rest, hand stop, swivel. Made 1965 to 1972.

Finnish Lion Standard ISU Target Rifle **$375**
Bolt action, single shot. Caliber: 22 Long Rifle. 27$\frac{1}{2}$-inch barrel. Weight: about 10$\frac{1}{2}$ pounds. Extension rear peep sight, aperture front sight. Walnut target stock with full pistol grip, checkered beavertail forearm, adjustable butt plate, sling swivel. Made 1966 to 1977.

Finnish Lion Standard Target Rifle
Bolt action. Single shot. Caliber: 22 LR. 27$\frac{1}{2}$-inch barrel. 44$\frac{1}{2}$ inches overall. Weight: 10$\frac{1}{2}$ pounds. No sights; micrometer rear and globe front International-style sights available. Select walnut stock in target configuration. Currently in production.
Standard Model **$500**
Thumbhole Stock Model **695**

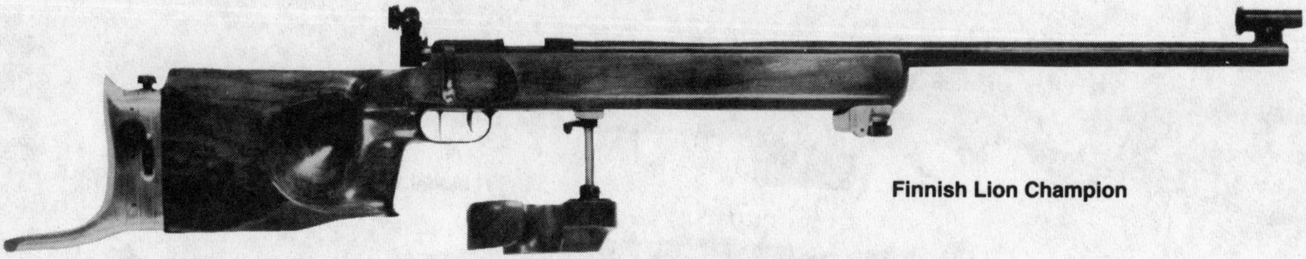

Finnish Lion Champion

Finnish Lion Match

Finnish Lion Standard

Franchi Deluxe Centennial

French Model 1936 MAS

LUIGI FRANCHI, S.P.A.
Brescia, Italy

Franchi Centennial Automatic Rifle
Commemorates Franchi's 100th anniversary (1868-1968). Centennial seal engraved on receiver. Semiautomatic. Takedown. Caliber: 22 Long Rifle. 11-shot magazine in buttstock. 21-inch barrel. Weight: 5 1/8 pounds. Open rear sight, goldbead front sight on ramp. Checkered walnut stock and forend. Deluxe model has fully engraved receiver, premium grade wood. Made 1968.
Standard Model **$300**
Deluxe Model **375**

FRENCH MILITARY RIFLE
Saint Etienne, France

French Model 1936 MAS Military Rifle $85
Bolt action. Caliber: 7.5mm MAS. 5-shot box magazine. 22 1/2-inch barrel. Weight: about 8 1/4 pounds. Adjustable rear sight, blade front sight. Two-piece military-type stock. Bayonet carried in forend tube. Made 1936 to 1940 by Manufacture Francaise d'Armes et de Cycles de St. Etienne (MAS).

Galil Model 223 AR Semiauto Rifle

GALIL RIFLES
Manufactured by Israel Military Industries, Israel

Galil AR Semiautomatic Rifle
Calibers: 308 Win. (7.62 NATO), 223 Rem. (5.56mm). 25-shot (308) or 35-shot (223) magazine. 16-inch (223) or 18 1/2-inch (308) barrel with flash suppressor. Weight: 9 1/2 pounds. Folding aperture rear sight, post front. Folding metal stock with carrying handle. Imported during the early 1980's.
Model 223 AR **$875**
Model 308 AR **950**

Garcia Bronco 22

GARCIA CORPORATION
Teaneck, New Jersey

Garcia Bronco 22 Single Shot Rifle $75
Swing-out action. Takedown. Caliber: 22 Long Rifle, Long, Short. 16 1/2-inch barrel. Weight: 3 pounds. Open rear sight, blade front sight. One-piece stock and receiver, crackle finish. Introduced 1967; discontinued.

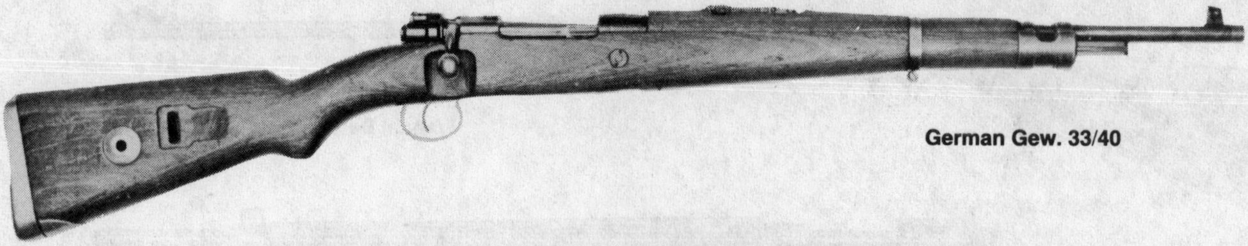

German Gew. 33/40

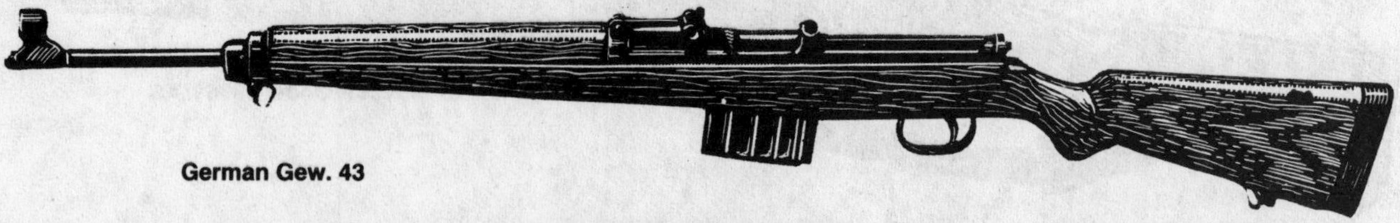

German Gew. 43

German Gew. 98

GERMAN MILITARY RIFLES

Mfd. by Ludwig Loewe & Co., Berlin, other contractors and by German arsenals and various plants under German Government control.

German Model 24T (Gew. 24T) Mauser Rifle . . . $145
Same general specifications as the Czech Model 24 (VZ24) Mauser Rifle with minor modifications, has laminated wood stock. Weight: about 9¼ pounds. Made in Czechoslovakia during German occupation; adopted 1940.

German Model 29/40 (Gew. 29/40) Mauser Rifle . . $175
Same general specifications as Kar. 98K, with minor differences. Made in Poland during German occupation; adopted 1940.

German Model 33/40 (Gew. 33/40) Mauser Rifle . . $245
Same general specifications as the Czech Model 33 (VZ33) Mauser Carbine with minor modifications, has laminated wood stock as found in war-time Model 98K carbines. Made in Czechoslovakia during German occupation; adopted 1940.

German Models 41 and 41-W (Gew. 41, Gew. 41-W) Semiautomatic Military Rifles $395
Gas-operated, muzzle cone system. Caliber: 7.9mm Mauser. 10-shot box magazine. 22½-inch barrel. Weight: about 10¾ pounds. Adjustable leaf rear sight, blade front sight. Military-type stock with semi-pistol grip, plastic handguard. *Note:* Model 41 lacks bolt release found on Model 41-W, otherwise the two models are the same. This is a Walther design and the early models were manufactured in that firm's Zella-Mehlis plant. Made about 1941-43.

German Model 43 (Gew. 43, Kar. 43) Semiauto Military Rifles $425
Gas-operated, barrel vented as in Russian Tokarev. Caliber: 7.9mm Mauser. 10-shot detachable box magazine. 22- or 24-inch barrel. Weight: about 9 pounds. Adjustable rear sight, hooded front sight. Military-type stock with semipistol grip, wooden handguard. *Note:* These rifles are alike except for minor details, have characteristic late WWII mfg. short cuts: cast receiver and bolt cover, stamped steel parts, etc. Gew. 43 may have either 22- or 24-inch barrel; the former length was standardized in late 1944 when weapon designation was changed to "Kar. 43." Made 1943-45.

German Model 1888 (Gew. 88) Mauser-Mannlicher Service Rifle $75
Bolt action, straight handle. Caliber: 7.9mm Mauser (8×57mm). 5-shot Mannlicher box magazine. 29-inch barrel with jacket. Weight: about 8½ pounds. Fixed front sight, adjustable rear. Military-type full stock. Mfd. by Ludwig Loewe & Co., Haenel, Schilling and other contractors.

German Kar. 88

German Model 1888 (Kar. 88) Mauser-Mannlicher Carbine $85
Same general specifications as Gew. 88, except has 18-inch barrel, without jacket, flat turned-down bolt handle, weighs about 6¾ pounds. Mfd. by Ludwig Loewe & Co., Haenel, Schilling and other contractors.

German Model 1898 (Gew. 98) Mauser Military Rifle $175
Bolt action, straight handle. Caliber: 7.9mm Mauser (8×57mm). 5-shot box magazine. 29-inch steeped barrel. Weight: 9 pounds. Blade front sight, adjustable rear sight. Military-type full stock with rounded bottom pistol grip. Adopted 1898.

German Kar. 98K

> *Note:* German Mauser Military Rifles (Gew. 98, Kar. 98) were made prior to and during WWI at the government arsenals at Amberg, Brunn, Danzig, Erfurt and Spandau; they were also manufactured by contractors such as Haenel, Loewe, Mauser, Schilling and Steyr. These rifles bear the Imperial Crown, maker's name and date of manufacture on the receiver ring. Post-WWI Kar. 98B bears maker's name and date. During WWII as well as the years immediately preceding (probably from c. 1935), a letter or number code was used to indicate maker. This code and date of manufacture will be found stamped on the receiver ring of rifles of this period. German Service Mausers also bear the model number (Gew. 98, Kar. 98K, G. 33/40, etc.) on the left side of the receiver. An exception is Model VK98, which usually bears no identifying marks. Gew. is abbreviation for *gewehr* (rifle), Kar. for *karabiner* (carbine).

German Model 1898A (Kar. 98A) Mauser Carbine **$210**
Same general specifications as Model 1898 (Gew. 98) Rifle, except has turned-down bolt handle, smaller receiver ring, light $23\frac{1}{2}$-inch straight taper barrel, front sight guards, sling is attached to left side of stock, weighs 8 pounds. *Note:* Some of these carbines are marked "Kar. 98"; the true Kar. 98 is the earlier original M/98 carbine with 17-inch barrel and is rarely encountered.

German Model 1898B (Kar. 98B) Mauser Carbine **$225**
Same general specifications as Model 1898 (Gew. 98) Rifle, except has turned-down bolt handle and sling attached to left side of stock. This is post-WWI model.

German Model 1898K (Kar. 98K) Mauser Carbine **$215**
Same general specifications as Model 1898 (Gew. 98) Rifle, except has turned-down bolt handle, $23\frac{1}{2}$-inch barrel, may have hooded front sight, sling is attached to left side of stock, weighs about $8\frac{1}{2}$ pounds. Adopted in 1935, this was the standard German Service rifle of WWII. *Note:* Late-war models had stamped sheet steel trigger guards and many of the Model 98K carbines made during WWII had laminated wood stocks; these weigh about $\frac{1}{2}$ to $\frac{3}{4}$ pound more than the previous Model 98K. Value shown is for earlier type.

German Model VK 98 People's Rifle ("Volksgewehr") **$100**
Kar. 98K-type action. Caliber: 7.9mm. Single shot or repeater (latter with rough hole-in-the-stock 5-shot "magazine" or fitted with 10-shot clip of German Model 43 semiauto rifle). 20.9-inch barrel. Weight: 7 pounds. Fixed V-notch rear sight dovetailed into front receiver ring; front blade welded to barrel. Crude, unfinished, half-length stock without butt plate. Last ditch weapon made in 1945 for issue to German civilians. *Note:* Of value only as a military arms collector's item, this hastily made rifle should be regarded as *unsafe* to shoot.

Gévarm E-1

Golden Eagle Model 7000

GÉVARM RIFLE
Saint Etienne, France
Manufactured by Gévelot

Gévarm E-1 Autoloading Rifle **$150**
Caliber: 22 Long Rifle. 8-shot clip magazine. $19\frac{1}{2}$-inch barrel. Open rear sight, post front sight. Pistol-grip stock and forearm of French walnut.

GOLDEN EAGLE RIFLES
Houston, Texas
Mfd. by Nikko Firearms Ltd., Tochigi, Japan

Golden Eagle Model 7000 Grade I African **$550**
Same as standard model, except calibers 375 H&H Mag. and 458 Win. Mag., 2-shot magazine in 458, weighs $8\frac{3}{4}$ lbs. in 375 and $10\frac{1}{2}$ lbs. in 458, furnished with sights. Introduced 1976; discontinued.

Golden Eagle Model 7000 Grade I Big Game . . . $475
Bolt action. Calibers: 22-250, 243 Win., 25-06, 270 Win., 270 Weatherby Mag., 7mm Rem. Mag., 30-06, 300 Weath. Mag., 300 Win. Mag., 338 Win. Mag. Magazine capacity: 4 rounds in 22-250, 3 rounds in other calibers. 24- or 26-inch barrel (26-inch only in 338). Weight: 7 lbs., 22-250; 8¾ lbs., other calibers. Furnished without sights. Fancy American walnut stock, skip checkered, contrasting wood forend tip and grip cap with gold eagle head, recoil pad. Introduced 1976; discontinued.

GREIFELT & CO.
Suhl, Germany

Greifelt Sport Model 22 Hornet Bolt Action Rifle . . $900
Caliber: 22 Hornet. 5-shot box magazine. 22-inch Krupp steel barrel. Weight: 6 pounds. Two-leaf rear sight, ramp front sight. Walnut stock, checkered pistol grip and forearm. Made prior to WWII.

Carl Gustaf Deluxe

Carl Gustaf Grand Prix

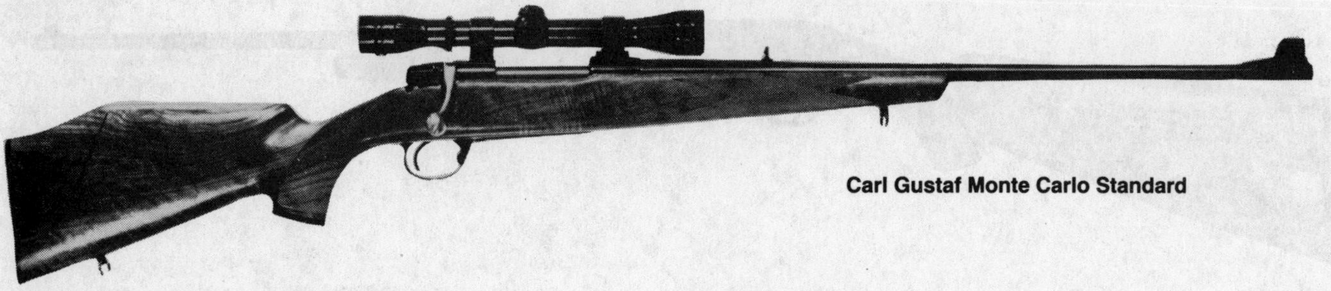

Carl Gustaf Monte Carlo Standard

CARL GUSTAF RIFLES
Eskilstuna, Sweden
Mfd. by Carl Gustafs Stads Gevärsfaktori

Carl Gustaf Deluxe $730
Same specifications as Monte Carlo Standard. Calibers: 6.5×55, 308 Win., 30-06, 9.3×62. 4-shot magazine in 9.3×62. Jewelled bolt. Engraved floorplate and trigger guard. Stock of deluxe French walnut with rosewood forend tip. Made 1970-77.

Carl Gustaf Grand Prix Single Shot Target Rifle . . $500
Special bolt action with "world's shortest lock time." Single-stage trigger adjusts down to 18 oz. Caliber: 22 Long Rifle. 26¾-inch heavy barrel with adjustable trim weight. Weight: about 9¾ pounds. Furnished without sights. Target-type Monte Carlo stock of French walnut, adjustable cork butt plate. Made 1970 to date.

Carl Gustaf Monte Carlo Standard Bolt Action Sporting Rifle $465
Carl Gustaf 1900 action. Calibers: 6.5×55, 7×64, 270 Win., 7mm Rem. Mag., 308 Win., 30-06, 9.3×62. 5-shot magazine, except 4-shot in 9.3×62 and 3-shot in 7mm Rem. Mag. 23½-inch barrel. Weight: about 7 pounds. Folding leaf rear sight, hooded ramp front sight. French walnut Monte Carlo stock with cheekpiece, checkered forearm and pistol grip, sling swivels. Also available in left-hand model. Made 1970-77.

Carl Gustaf Special $540
Also designated "Grade II" in U.S. and "Model 9000" in Canada. Same specifications as Monte Carlo Standard. Calibers: 22-250, 243 Win., 25-06, 270 Win., 7mm Rem. Mag., 308 Win., 30-06, 300 Win. Mag. 3-shot magazine in magnum calibers. Select wood stock with rosewood forend tip. Also available in left-hand model. Made 1970-77.

Carl Gustaf Special

Carl Gustaf Sporter

Carl Gustaf Trofé

Carl Gustaf Sporter **$490**
Also designated "Varmint-Target" in U.S. Fast bolt action with large bakelite bolt knob. Trigger pull adjusts down to 18 oz. Calibers: 222 Rem., 22-250, 243 Win., 6.5×55. 5-shot magazine, except 6-shot in 222 Rem. 26$\frac{3}{4}$-inch heavy barrel. Weight: about 9$\frac{1}{2}$ pounds. Furnished without sights. Target-type Monte Carlo stock of French walnut. Made 1970 to date.

Carl Gustaf Standard **$440**
Same specifications as Monte Carlo Standard. Calibers: 6.5×55, 7×64, 270 Win., 308 Win., 30-06, 9.3×62. Classic-style stock without Monte Carlo. Made 1970-77.

Carl Gustaf Trofé **$635**
Also designated "Grade III" in U.S. and "Model 8000" in Canada. Same specifications as Monte Carlo Standard. Calibers: 22-250, 25-06, 6.5×55, 270 Win., 7mm Rem. Mag., 308 Win., 30-06, 300 Win. Mag. 3-shot magazine in magnum calibers. Furnished without sights. Stock of fancy wood with rosewood forend tip, high-gloss lacquer finish. Made 1970-77.

C.G. HAENEL
Suhl, Germany

Haenel '88 Mauser Sporter **$495**
Same general specifications as Haenel Mauser-Mannlicher, except has Mauser 5-shot box magazine.

Haenel Mauser-Mannlicher Bolt Action Sporting Rifle **$495**
Mauser M/88-type action. Calibers: 7×57, 8×57, 9×57mm. Mannlicher clip-loading box magazine, 5-shot. 22- or 24-inch half or full octagon barrel with raised matted rib. Double-set trigger. Weight: about 7$\frac{1}{2}$ pounds. Leaf-type open rear sight, ramp front sight. Sporting stock with cheekpiece, checkered pistol grip, raised side-panels, schnabel tip, swivels.

HÄMMERLI AG JAGD-UND SPORTWAFFENFABRIK
Lenzburg, Switzerland

Hämmerli Model 45 Smallbore Bolt Action Single Shot Match Rifle **$660**
Calibers: 22 Long Rifle, 22 Extra Long. 27$\frac{1}{2}$-inch heavy barrel. Weight: about 15$\frac{1}{2}$ pounds. Micrometer peep rear sight, globe front sight. Free rifle stock with cheekpiece, full pistol grip, thumb hole, beavertail forearm, palm rest, Swiss-type butt plate, swivels. Made 1945 to 1957.

Hämmerli Model 45

Hämmerli Model 503

Hämmerli Model 506

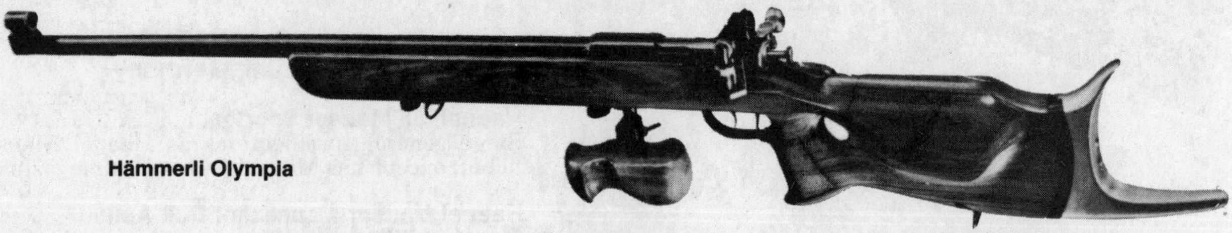

Hämmerli Olympia

Hämmerli-Tanner 300M

Hämmerli Model 54 Smallbore Match Rifle $625
Bolt action, single shot. Caliber: 22 Long Rifle. $27\frac{1}{2}$-inch heavy barrel. Weight: about 15 pounds. Micrometer peep rear sight, globe front sight. Free rifle stock with cheekpiece, thumb hole, adjustable hook butt plate, palm rest, swivel. Made 1954 to 1957.

Hämmerli Model 503 Free Rifle $600
Bolt action, single shot. Caliber: 22 Long Rifle. $27\frac{1}{2}$-inch heavy barrel. Weight: about $15\frac{1}{2}$ pounds. Micrometer peep rear sight, globe front sight. Free rifle stock with cheekpiece, thumb hole, adjustable hook butt plate, palm rest, swivel. Made 1957 to 1962.

Hämmerli Model 506 Smallbore Match Rifle $650
Bolt action, single shot. Caliber: 22 Long Rifle. $26\frac{3}{4}$-inch heavy barrel. Weight: about $16\frac{1}{2}$ pounds. Micrometer peep rear sight, globe front sight. Free rifle stock with cheekpiece, thumb hole, adjustable hook butt plate, palm rest, swivel. Made 1963-66.

Hämmerli Model Olympia 300 Meter Bolt Action Single Shot Free Rifle $800
Calibers: 30-06, 300 H&H Magnum for U.S.A.; ordinarily produced in 7.5mm, other calibers available on special order. $29\frac{1}{2}$-inch heavy barrel. Double-pull trigger or double-set trigger. Micrometer peep rear sight, globe front sight. Free rifle stock with cheekpiece, full pistol grip, thumb hole, beavertail forearm, palm rest, Swiss-type butt plate, swivels. Made 1945 to 1959.

Hämmerli-Tanner 300 Meter Free Rifle $860
Bolt action, single shot. Caliber: 7.5mm standard, available in most popular centerfire calibers. $29\frac{1}{2}$-inch heavy barrel. Weight: about $16\frac{3}{4}$ pounds. Micrometer peep rear sight, globe front sight. Free rifle stock with cheekpiece, thumb hole, adjustable hook butt plate, palm rest, swivel. Made 1962 to date.

HARRINGTON & RICHARDSON, INC.
Gardner, Massachusetts

Formerly Harrington & Richardson Arms Co. of Worcester, Mass. After a long and distinguished career in gunmaking this firm suspended operation in 1986.

Harrington & Richardson Model 60 Reising Semiautomatic Rifle $400
Caliber: 45 Automatic. 12- and 20-shot detachable box magazines. 18¼-inch barrel. Weight: about 7½ pounds. Open rear sight, blade front sight. Plain pistol-grip stock. Made 1944 to 1946.

Harrington & Richardson Model 65 Military Autoloading Rifle $295
Also called "General." Caliber: 22 Long Rifle. 10-shot detachable box magazine. 23-inch heavy barrel. Weight: about 9 pounds. Redfield 70 rear peep sight, blade front sight with protecting "ears." Plain pistol-grip stock, "Garand" dimensions. Made 1944-46. *Note:* This model was used as a training rifle by the U.S. Marine Corps.

Harrington & Richardson Model 150 Leatherneck Autoloader $135
Caliber: 22 Long Rifle only. 5-shot detachable box magazine. 22-inch barrel. Weight: about 7¼ pounds. Open rear sight, blade front sight on ramp. Plain pistol-grip stock. Made 1949 to 1953.

Harrington & Richardson Model 151 . . . . $145
Same as Model 150 except with Redfield 70 rear peep sight.

Harrington & Richardson Model 155 Single Shot Rifle $80
Model 158 action. Calibers: 44 Rem. Mag., 45-70 Govt. 24- or 28-inch barrel (latter in 44 only). Weight: 7 or 7½ pounds. Folding leaf rear sight, blade front sight. Straight-grip stock, forearm with barrel band, brass cleaning rod. Made 1972 to 1982.

Harrington & Richardson Model 157 Single Shot Rifle $95
Model 158 action. Calibers: 22 Win. Mag. RF, 22 Hornet, 30-30. 22-inch barrel. Weight: 6¼ pounds. Folding leaf rear sight, blade front sight. Pistol-grip stock, full-length forearm, swivels. Made from 1976 to 1986.

Harrington & Richardson Model 158 Topper Jet Single Shot Combination Rifle
Shotgun-type action with visible hammer, side lever, auto ejector. Caliber: 22 Rem. Jet. 22-inch barrel (interchanges with 30-30, 410 ga., 20 ga. barrels). Weight: 5 pounds. Lyman folding adjustable open rear sight, ramp front sight. Plain pistol-grip stock and forearm, recoil pad. Made from 1963 to 1967.

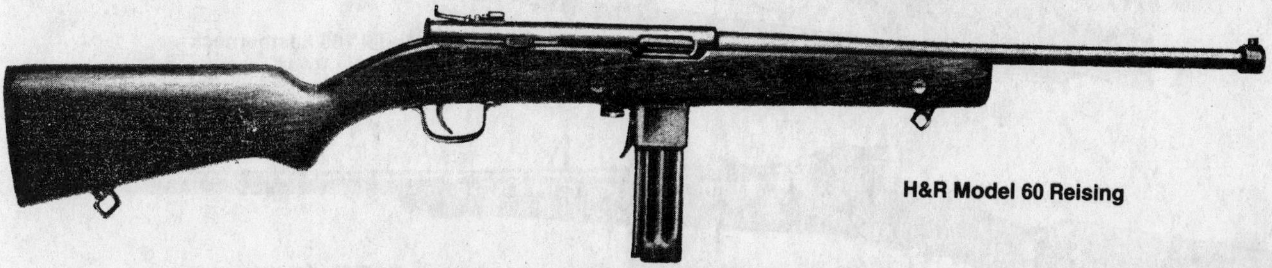

H&R Model 60 Reising

H&R Model 65

H&R Model 155

H&R Model 157

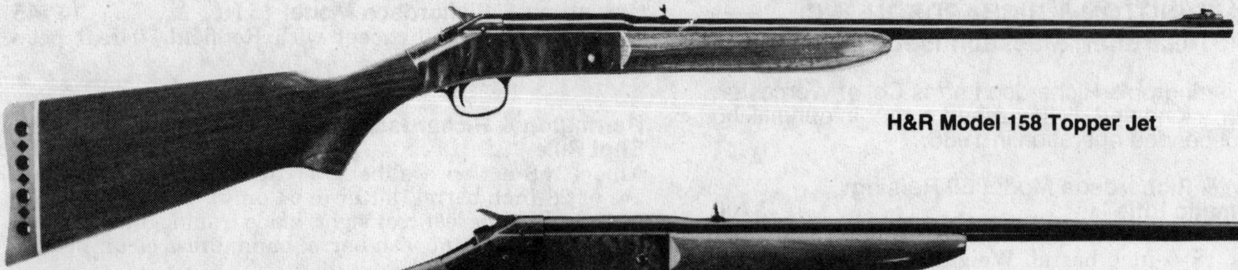

H&R Model 158 Topper Jet

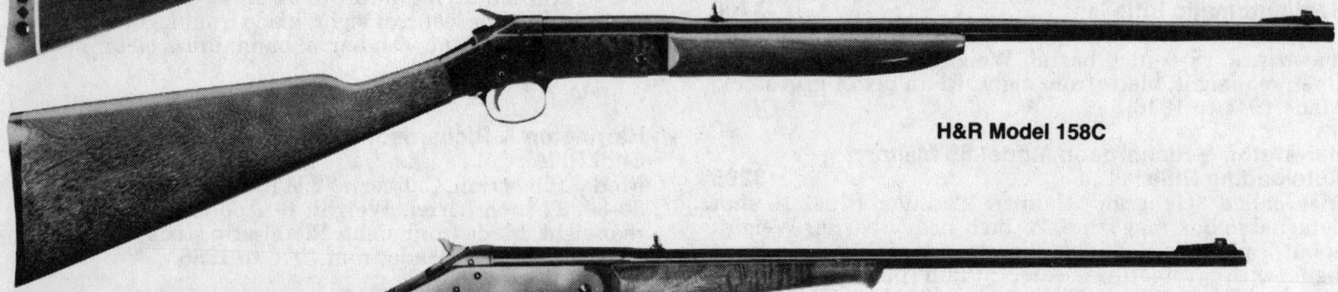

H&R Model 158C

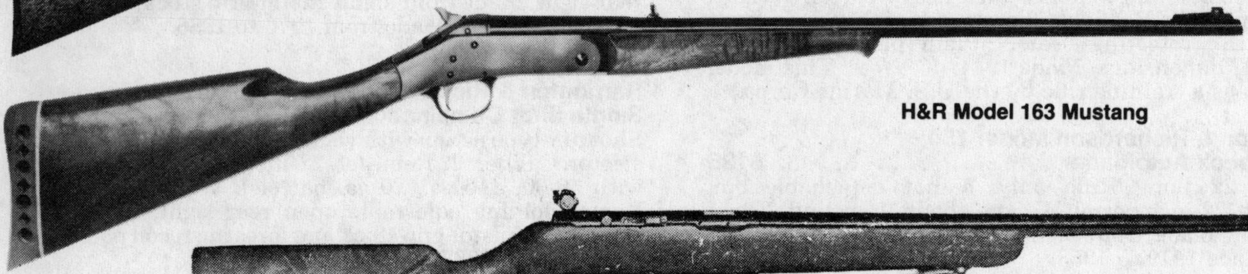

H&R Model 163 Mustang

H&R Model 165 Leatherneck

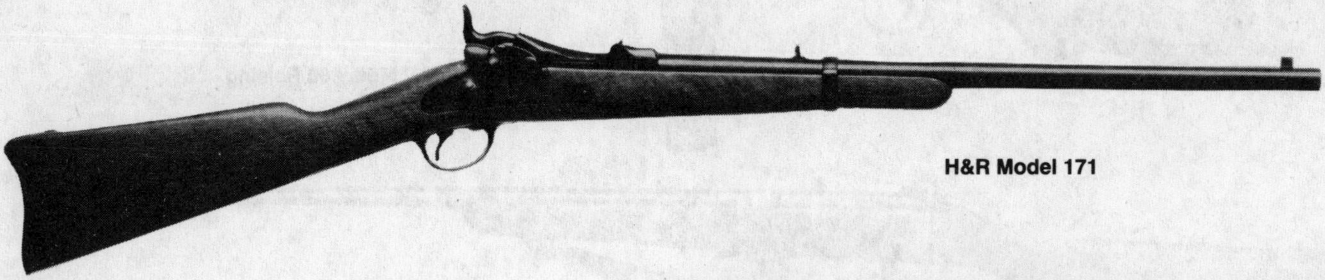

H&R Model 171

Harrington & Richardson Model 158 (cont.)
Rifle only **$110**
Interchangeable barrel—30-30, shotgun **30**

Harrington & Richardson Model 158C $110
Same as Model 158 Topper Jet, except calibers 22 Hornet, 30-30, 357 Mag., 357 Max., 44 Mag. Straight-grip stock. Made from 1963 to 1986.

Harrington & Richardson Model 163 Mustang Single Shot Rifle $110
Same as Model 158 Topper except has gold-plated hammer and trigger, straight-grip stock and contoured forearm. Made 1964-67.

Harrington & Richardson Model 165 Leatherneck Autoloader $135
Caliber: 22 Long Rifle. 10-shot detachable box magazine. 23-inch barrel. Weight: about 7½ pounds. Redfield 70 rear peep sight, blade front sight on ramp. Plain pistol-grip stock, swivels, web sling. Made 1945 to 1961.

Harrington & Richardson Model 171 .... $240
Model 1873 Springfield Cavalry Carbine replica. Caliber: 45-70. 22-inch barrel. Weight: 7 pounds. Leaf rear sight, blade front sight. Plain walnut stock. Made 1972 to 1981.

Harrington & Richardson Model 171 Deluxe $290
Same as Model 171, except engraved action and different sights. Made from 1972 to 1986.

Harrington & Richardson Model 172 .... $995
Same as Model 171 Deluxe, except silver-plated, has fancy walnut stock, checkered, with grip adapter; tang-mounted aperture sight. Made from 1972 to 1986.

Harrington & Richardson Model 173 .... $325
Model 1873 Springfield Officer's Model replica, same as 100th Anniversary Commemorative, except without plaque on stock. Made from 1972 to 1986.

Harrington & Richardson Model 174 .... $395
Little Big Horn Commemorative Carbine. Same as Model 171 Deluxe, except has tang-mounted aperture sight, grip adapter. Made from 1972 to 1984. Value is for carbine in new, unfired condition.

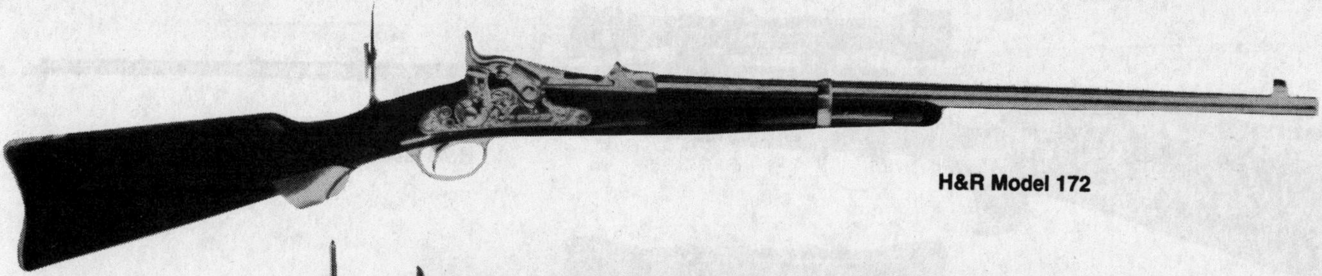

H&R Model 172

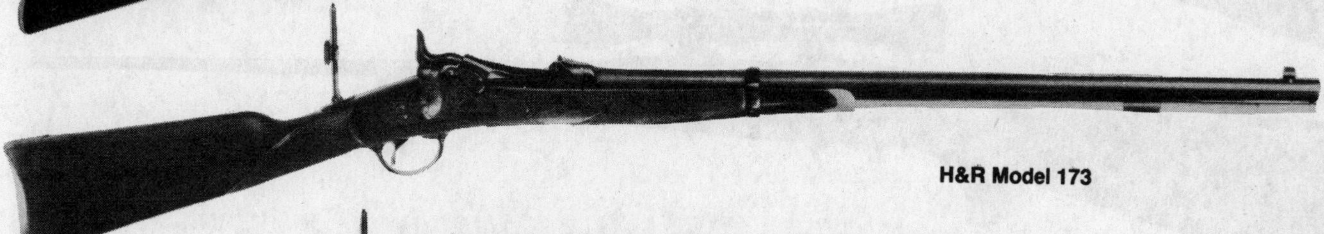

H&R Model 173

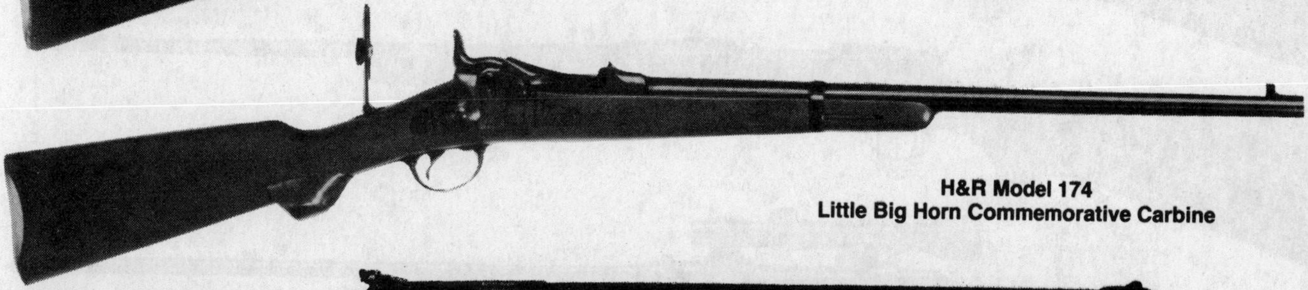

H&R Model 174
Little Big Horn Commemorative Carbine

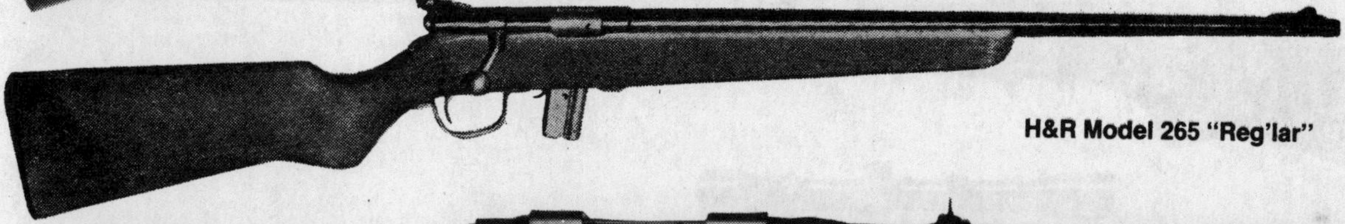

H&R Model 265 "Reg'lar"

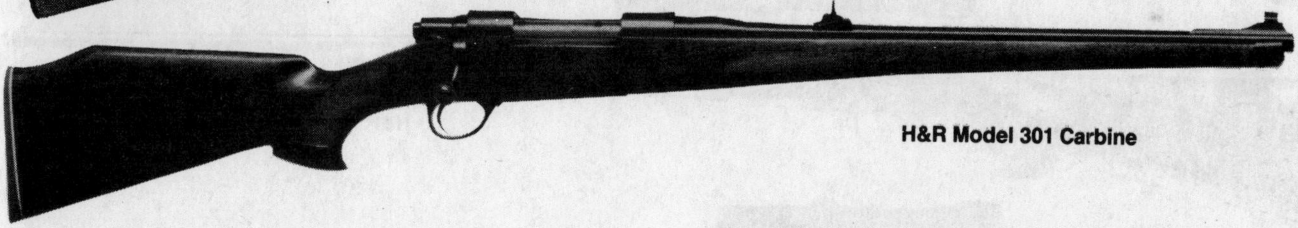

H&R Model 301 Carbine

Harrington & Richardson Model 178 . . . . $325
Model 1873 Springfield Infantry Rifle replica. Caliber: 45-70. 32-inch barrel. Weight: 8 lbs. 10 oz. Leaf rear sight, blade front sight. Full-length stock with barrel bands, swivels, ramrod. Made from 1973 to 1986.

Harrington & Richardson Model 250 Sportster Bolt Action Repeating Rifle $75
Caliber: 22 Long Rifle. 5-shot detachable box magazine. 23-inch barrel. Weight: about 6½ pounds. Open rear sight, blade front sight on ramp. Plain pistol-grip stock. Made 1948 to 1961.

Harrington & Richardson Model 251 . . . . $65
Same as Model 250 except has Lyman 55H rear sight.

Harrington & Richardson Model 265 "Reg'lar" Bolt Action Repeating Rifle $80
Caliber: 22 Long Rifle. 10-shot detachable box magazine. 22-inch barrel. Weight: about 6½ pounds. Lyman 55 rear peep sight, blade front sight on ramp. Plain pistol-grip stock. Made 1946-49.

Harrington & Richardson Model 300 Ultra Bolt Action Rifle $435
Mauser-type action. Calibers: 22-250, 243 Win., 270 Win., 30-06, 308 Win., 7mm Rem. Mag., 300 Win. Mag. 3-round magazine in 7mm and 300 Mag. calibers, 5-round in others. 22- or 24-inch barrel. Open rear sight, ramp front sight. Checkered stock with roll-over cheekpiece and full pistol grip, contrasting wood forearm tip and pistol grip, rubber butt plate, swivels. Weight: 7¼ pounds. Made from 1965 to 1982.

Harrington & Richardson Model 301 Carbine . . . $425
Same as Model 300, except has 18-inch barrel, Mannlicher-style stock, weighs 7¼ pounds; not available in caliber 22-250. Made 1967 to 1982.

Harrington & Richardson Model 317 Ultra Wildcat Bolt Action Rifle $525
Sako short action. Calibers: 17 Rem., 17/223 (handload), 222 Rem., 223 Rem. 6-round magazine. 20-inch barrel. No sights, receiver dovetailed for scope mounts. Checkered stock with cheekpiece and full pistol grip, contrasting wood forearm tip and pistol-grip cap, rubber butt plate. Weight: 5¼ pounds. Made 1968 to 1976.

H&R Model 317 Ultra Wildcat

H&R Model 317P

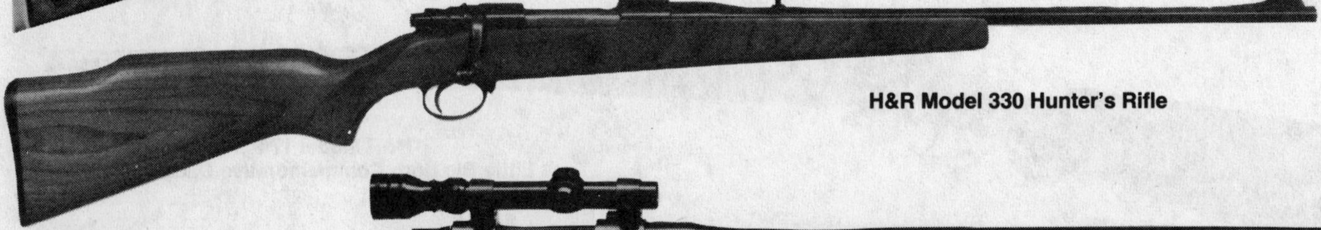

H&R Model 330 Hunter's Rifle

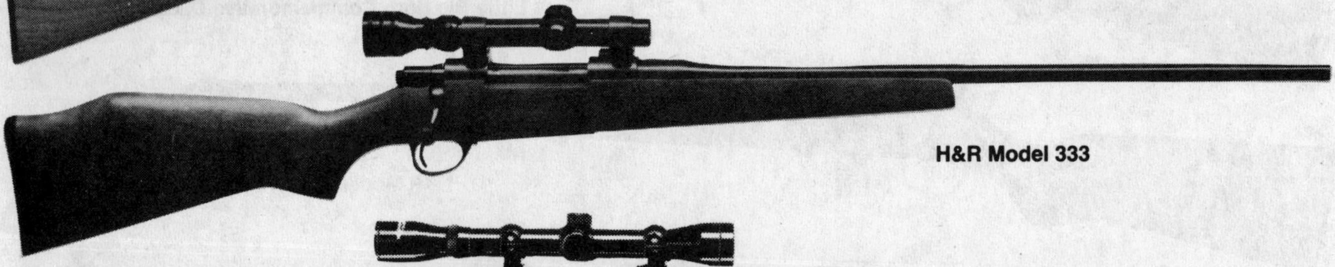

H&R Model 333

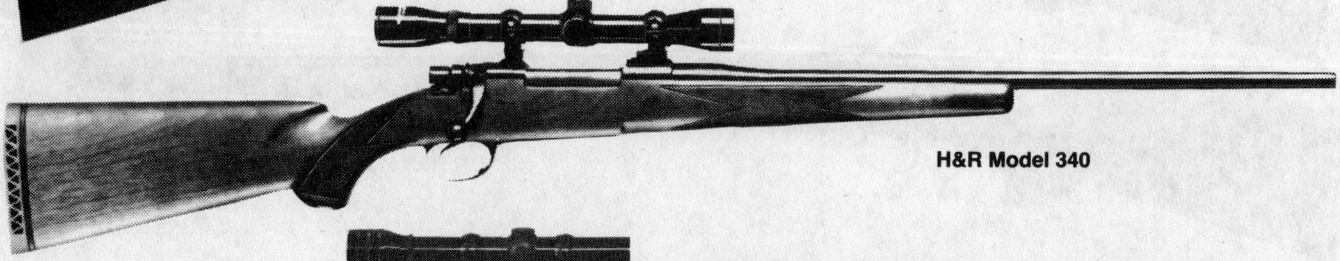

H&R Model 340

H&R Model 360 Ultra Automatic

Harrington & Richardson Model 317P Presentation Grade $595
Same as Model 317, except has select grade fancy walnut stock with basketweave carving on forearm and pistol grip. Made 1968 to 1976.

Harrington & Richardson Model 330 Hunter's Rifle $325
Similar to Model 300, but with plainer stock. Calibers: 243 Win., 270 Win., 30-06, 308 Win., 7mm Rem. Mag., 300 Win. Mag. Weight: about 7¹/₈ pounds. Made from 1967 to 1972.

Harrington & Richardson Model 333 . . . . $225
Plainer version of Model 300 with uncheckered walnut-finished hardwood stock. Calibers: 7mm Rem. Mag., 30-06. 22-inch barrel. Weight: 7¹/₄ pounds. No sights. Made 1974.

Harrington & Richardson Model 340 . . . . $325
Mauser-type action. Calibers: 243 Win., 308 Win., 270 Win., 30-06, 7×57mm. 22-inch barrel. Weight: 7¹/₄ pounds. Hand-checkered stock of American walnut. Made 1982-84.

Harrington & Richardson Model 360 Ultra Automatic Rifle $335
Gas-operated semiautomatic. Calibers: 243 Win., 308 Win. 3-round detachable box magazine. 22-inch barrel. Open rear sight, ramp front sight. Checkered stock with roll-

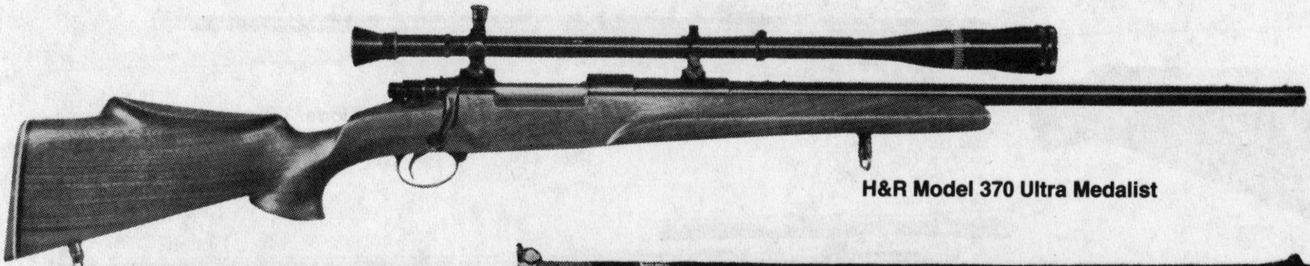

H&R Model 370 Ultra Medalist

H&R Model 465 Targeteer

Harrington & Richardson Model 360 (cont.)
over cheekpiece, full pistol grip, contrasting wood forearm tip and pistol-grip cap, rubber butt plate, sling swivels. Weight: 7½ pounds. Introduced 1965; discontinued. (*Note:* Originally designated Model 308, changed to 360 in 1967).

Harrington & Richardson Model 361 .... $340
Same as Model 360, except has full roll-over cheekpiece for right- or left-hand shooters. Made 1970-73.

Harrington & Richardson Model 365 Ace Bolt Action Single Shot Rifle $75
Caliber: 22 Long Rifle. 22-inch barrel. Weight: about 6½ pounds. Lyman 55 rear peep sight, blade front sight on ramp. Plain pistol-grip stock. Made 1946-47.

Harrington & Richardson Model 370 Ultra Medalist $450
Varmint and target rifle based on Model 300. Calibers: 22-250, 243 Win., 6mm Rem. 5-round magazine. 24-inch varmint weight barrel. No sights. Target-style stock with semibeavertail forearm. Weight: 9½ pounds. Made 1968 to 1973.

Harrington & Richardson Model 422 Slide Action Repeater $125
Caliber: 22 Long Rifle, Long, Short. Tubular magazine holds 21 Short, 17 Long, 15 Long Rifle. 24-inch barrel. Weight: about 6 pounds. Open rear sight, ramp front sight. Plain pistol-grip stock, grooved slide handle. Made from 1956 to 1958.

Harrington & Richardson Model 450 .... $135
Same as Model 451, except without front and rear sights.

Harrington & Richardson Model 451 Medalist Bolt Action Target Rifle $165
Caliber: 22 Long Rifle. 5-shot detachable box magazine. 26-inch barrel. Weight: about 10½ pounds. Lyman 524F extension rear sight, Lyman 77 front sight, scope bases. Target stock with full pistol grip and forearm, swivels and sling. Made 1948 to 1961.

Harrington & Richardson Model 465 Targeteer Special Bolt Action Repeater $120
Caliber: 22 Long Rifle. 10-shot detachable box magazine. 25-inch barrel. Weight: about 9 pounds. Lyman 57 rear peep sight, blade front sight on ramp. Plain pistol-grip stock, swivels, web sling strap. Made 1946-47.

Harrington & Richardson Model 700 Autoloading Rifle $160
Caliber: 22 Win. Mag. Rimfire. 5-shot magazine. 22-inch barrel. Weight: about 6½ pounds. Folding leaf rear sight, blade front sight on ramp. Monte Carlo-style stock of American walnut. Introduced 1977; discontinued.

Harrington & Richardson Model 700 Deluxe $195
Same as Model 700 Standard except has select custom polished and blued finish, select walnut stock, hand checkering, and no iron sights. Fitted with H&R Model 432 4× scope. Made from 1980 to 1986.

H&R Model 700

H&R Model 700 Deluxe

H&R Model 750

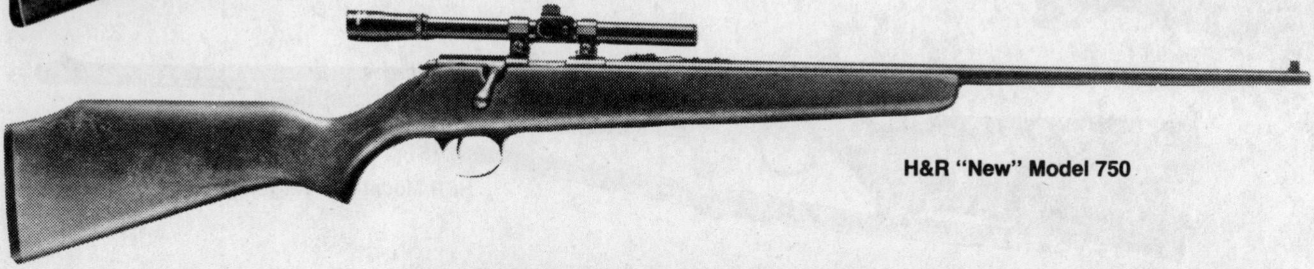

H&R "New" Model 750

H&R Model 755 Sahara

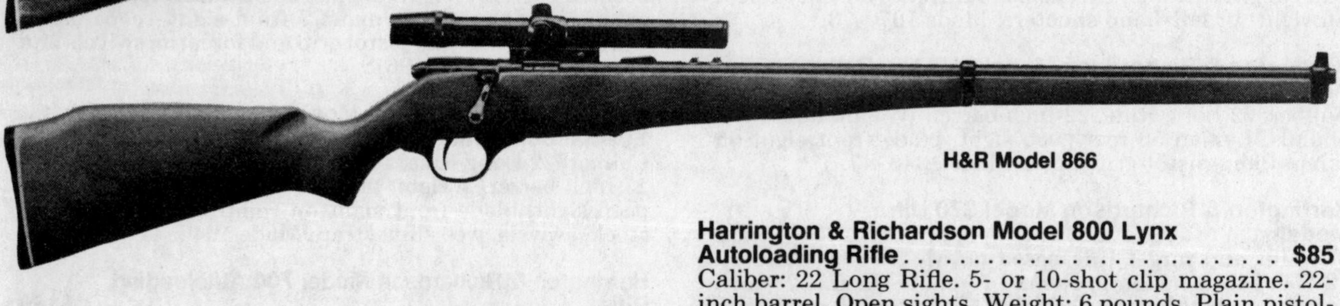

H&R Model 866

Harrington & Richardson Model 750 Pioneer Bolt Action Single Shot Rifle $65
Caliber: 22 Long Rifle, Long, Short. 22- or 24-inch barrel. Weight: about 5 pounds. Open rear sight, bead front sight. Plain pistol-grip stock. Made 1954 to 1981. Redesigned 1982.

Harrington & Richardson Model 751 Single Shot Rifle $65
Same as Model 750, except has Mannlicher-style stock. Made 1971.

Harrington & Richardson Model 755 Sahara Single Shot Rifle $70
Blow-back action, automatic ejection. Caliber: 22 Long Rifle, Long, Short. 18-inch barrel. Weight: 4 pounds. Open rear sight, military-type front sight. Mannlicher-style stock. Made 1963 to 1971.

Harrington & Richardson Model 760 Single Shot $70
Same as Model 755, except has conventional sporter stock. Made 1965 to 1970.

Harrington & Richardson Model 765 Pioneer Bolt Action Single Shot Rifle $50
Caliber: 22 Long Rifle, Long, Short. 24-inch barrel. Weight: about 5 pounds. Open rear sight, hooded bead front sight. Plain pistol-grip stock. Made 1948 to 1954.

Harrington & Richardson Model 800 Lynx Autoloading Rifle $85
Caliber: 22 Long Rifle. 5- or 10-shot clip magazine. 22-inch barrel. Open sights. Weight: 6 pounds. Plain pistol-grip stock. Made 1958 to 1960.

Harrington & Richardson Model 852 Fieldsman Bolt Action Repeater $80
Caliber: 22 Long Rifle, Long, Short. Tubular magazine holds 21 Short, 17 Long, 15 Long Rifle. 24-inch barrel. Weight: about 5½ pounds. Open rear sight, bead front sight. Plain pistol-grip stock. Made 1952-53.

Harrington & Richardson Model 865 Plainsman Bolt Action Repeater $75
Caliber: 22 Long Rifle, Long, Short. 5-shot detachable box magazine. 22- or 24-inch barrel. Weight: about 5¼ pounds. Open rear sight and bead front sight. Plain pistol-grip stock. Made from 1949 to 1986.

Harrington & Richardson Model 866 Bolt Action Repeater $85
Same as Model 865, except has Mannlicher-style stock. Made 1971.

Harrington & Richardson Model 1873 100th Anniversary (1871-1971) Commemorative Officer's Springfield Replica $425
Model 1873 "trap door" single-shot action. Engraved breech block, receiver, hammer, lock, band and butt plate. Caliber: 45-70. 26-inch barrel. Peep rear sight, blade front sight. Checkered walnut stock with anniversary plaque. Ramrod. Weight: about 8 pounds. 10,000 made 1971. Value is for rifle in new, unfired condition.

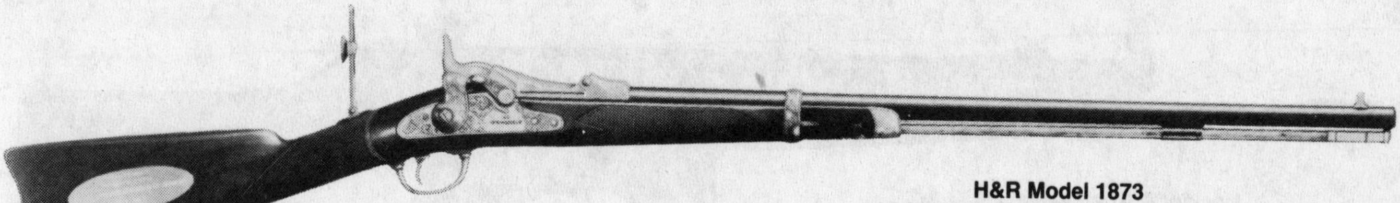

H&R Model 1873
100th Anniversary Springfield Replica

H&R Model 5200

Harrington & Richardson Model 5200 Sporter . . . $295
Turn-bolt repeater. Caliber: 22 Long Rifle. 24-inch barrel. Classic style American walnut stock. Adjustable trigger. Peep receiver sight, hooded ramp front sight. Weight: 6½ pounds.

Harrington & Richardson Model 5200 Match Rifle $275
Same action as 5200 Sporter. Caliber: 22 Long Rifle. 28-inch target weight barrel. Target stock of American walnut. Weight: 11 pounds. Made from 1982 to 1986.

Harrington & Richardson Custer Memorial Issue
Limited Edition Model 1873 Springfield Carbine replica, richly engraved and inlaid with gold, fancy walnut stock, in mahogany display case. Made 1973. Value is for carbine in new, unfired condition.
Officers' Model, limited to 25 pieces **$3500**
Enlisted Men's Model, limited to 243 pieces . . . **2250**

Harrington & Richardson Targeteer Jr. Bolt Action Rifle $100
Caliber: 22 Long Rifle. 5-shot detachable box magazine. 20-inch barrel. Weight: about 7 pounds. Redfield 70 rear peep sight. Lyman 17A front sight. Target stock, junior size with pistol grip, swivels and sling. Made 1948 to 1951.

Heckler & Koch Model HK91 A-2

Heckler & Koch Model HK91 A-3

HECKLER & KOCH, GMBH
Oberndorf/Neckar, West Germany

Heckler & Koch Model HK91 A-2 Semiautomatic $595
Delayed roller-locked blow-back action. Caliber: 7.62mm × 51 NATO (308 Win.). 5- or 20-round box magazine. 19-inch barrel. Weight: w/o magazine, 9.37 pounds. "V" and aperture rear sight, post front sight. Plastic buttstock and forearm. Currently manufactured.

Heckler & Koch Model HK91 A-3 . . . . $625
Same as Model HK91 A-2, except has retractable metal buttstock, weighs 10.56 pounds. Currently mfd.

Heckler & Koch Model HK93 A-2

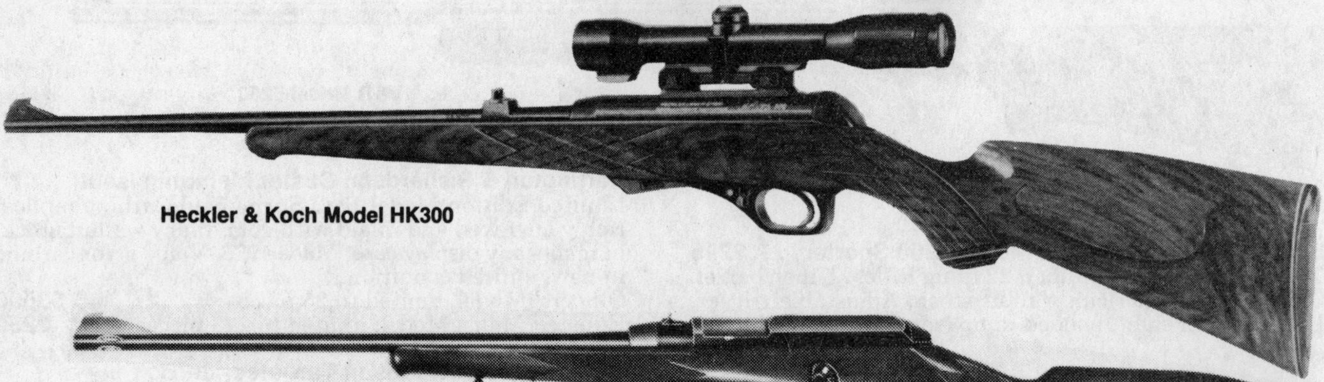

Heckler & Koch Model HK300

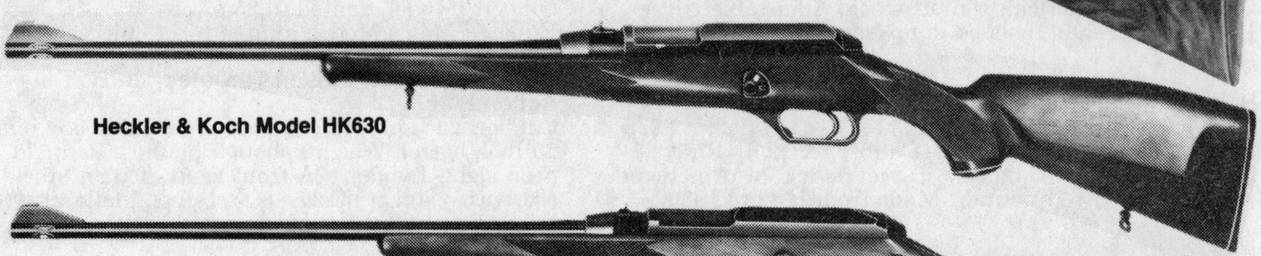

Heckler & Koch Model HK630

Heckler & Koch Model HK770

Heckler & Koch Model HK940

Heckler & Koch Model HK93 Semiautomatic $595
Delayed roller-locked blow-back action. Caliber: 5.56mm × 45 (223 Rem.). 5- or 20-round magazine. 16.13-inch barrel. Weight: w/o magazine, 7.6 pounds. "V" and aperture sight, post front sight. Plastic buttstock and forearm. Currently manufactured.
HK93, A-2 . . . . **$595**
HK93, A-3 with retractable stock **600**

Heckler & Koch Model HK94 Semiautomatic Carbine
Caliber: 9mm Para. 15-shot magazine. 16-inch barrel. Weight: 6¾ pounds. Aperture rear sight, front post. Plastic buttstock and forend or retractable metal stock. Made from 1983 to date.
HK94-A2 w/Standard Stock . . . . **$ 940**
HK94-A3 w/Retractable Stock **1100**

Heckler & Koch Model HK300 Semiautomatic . . . $395
Caliber: 22 Win. Mag. Rimfire. 5- or 15-round box magazine. 19.7-inch barrel. Weight: about 5¾ pounds. V-notch rear sight, ramp front sight. European walnut stock with cheekpiece, checkered forearm and pistol grip. Currently manufactured.

Heckler & Koch Model HK630 Semiautomatic . . . $495
Caliber: 223 Rem. 4- or 10-round magazine. Overall length: 42 inches. Weight: 7 pounds. Open rear sight, ramp front sight. European walnut stock with Monte Carlo cheekpiece. Made 1983 to date.

Heckler & Koch Model HK770 Semiautomatic . . . $535
Caliber: 308 Win. 3- or 10-round magazine. Overall length: 44.5 inches. Weight: 8 pounds. Open rear sight, ramp front sight. European walnut stock with Monte Carlo cheekpiece. Made 1983 to date.

Heckler & Koch Model HK940 Semiautomatic . . . $500
Caliber: 30-06 Springfield. 3- or 10-round magazine. Overall length: 47 inches. Weight: 8.8 pounds. Open rear sight, ramp front sight. European walnut stock with Monte Carlo cheekpiece. Made 1983 to date.

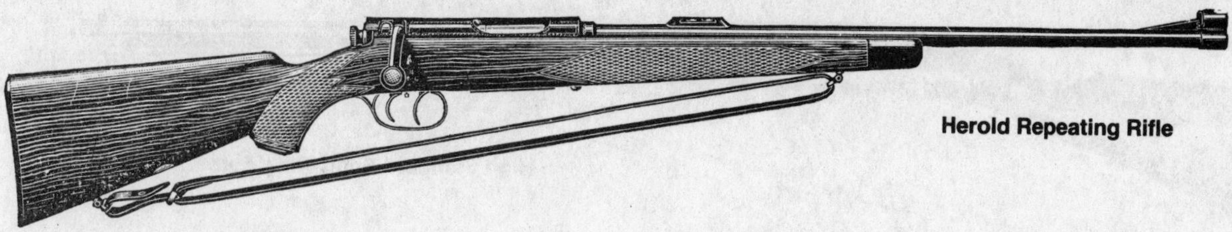

Herold Repeating Rifle

HERCULES RIFLES

See listings under "W" for Montgomery Ward.

HEROLD RIFLE
Suhl, Germany
Made by Franz Jaeger & Company

Herold Bolt Action Repeating Sporting Rifle $940
"Herold-Repetierbüchse." Miniature Mauser-type action with unique 5-shot box magazine on hinged floorplate.

Herold Repeating Rifle (cont.)
Double-set triggers. Caliber: 22 Hornet. 24-inch barrel. Leaf rear sight, ramp front sight. Weight: about 7³/₄ pounds. Fancy checkered stock. Made prior to WWII. *Note:* These rifles were imported by Charles Daly and A.F. Stoeger Inc. of New York City and sold under their own names.

J.C. HIGGINS RIFLES

See Sears, Roebuck & Company.

High Standard Flite-King Pump

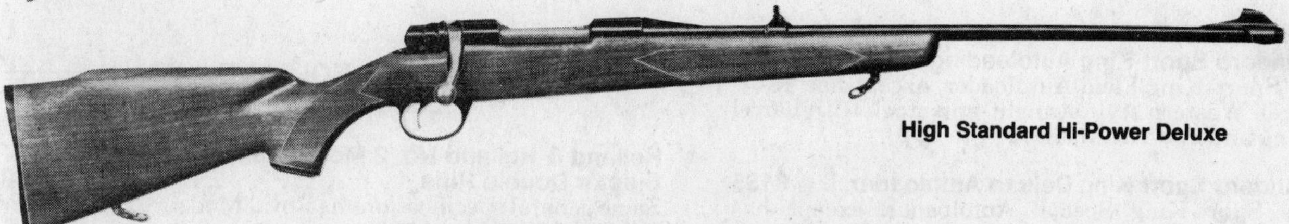

High Standard Hi-Power Deluxe

High Standard Hi-Power Field

THE HIGH STANDARD MFG. CORP.
Hamden, Connecticut

High Standard Flite-King Pump Rifle $120
Hammerless slide action. Caliber: 22 Long Rifle, 22 Long, 22 Short. Tubular magazine holds 17 Long Rifle, 19 Long, or 24 Short. 24-inch barrel. Weight: 5¹/₂ pounds. Patridge rear sight, bead front sight. Monte Carlo stock with pistol grip, serrated semibeavertail forearm. Made 1962 to 1975.

High Standard Hi-Power Deluxe Bolt Action Rifle $275
Mauser-type action, sliding safety. Calibers: 270, 30-06. 4-shot magazine. 22-inch barrel. Weight: 7 pounds. Folding open rear sight, ramp front sight. Walnut stock with checkered pistol grip and forearm, Monte Carlo comb, QD swivels. Made 1962-66.

High Standard Hi-Power Field Bolt Action Rifle . $230
Same as Hi-Power Deluxe, except has plain field style stock. Made 1962-66.

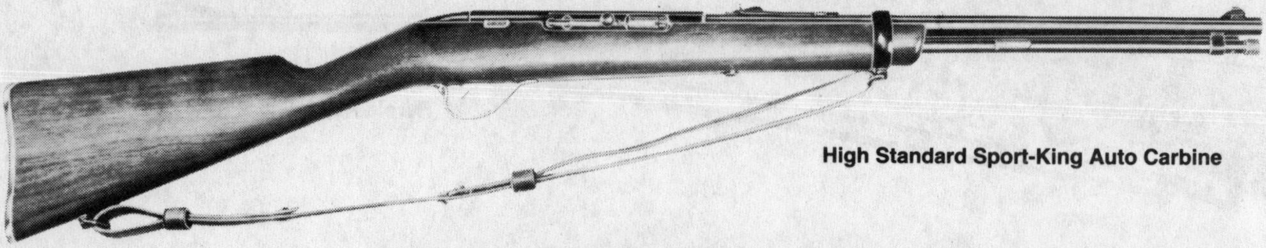

High Standard Sport-King Auto Carbine

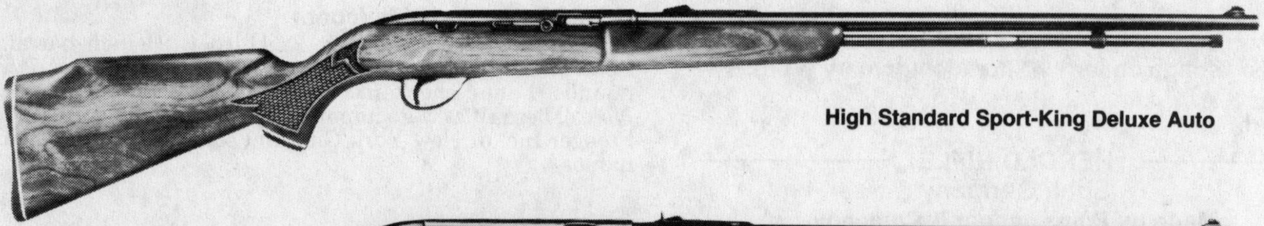

High Standard Sport-King Deluxe Auto

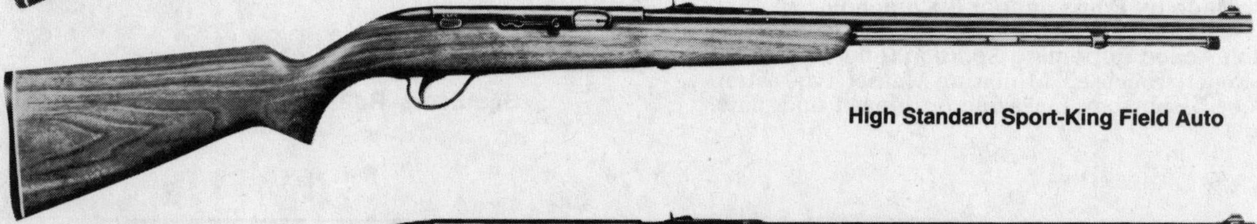

High Standard Sport-King Field Auto

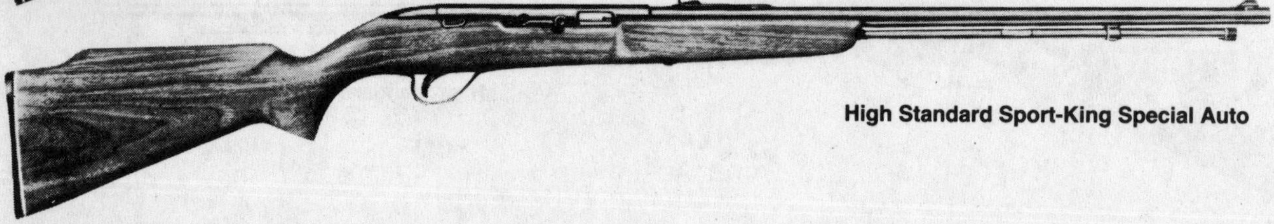

High Standard Sport-King Special Auto

High Standard Sport-King Autoloading Carbine . $125
Same as Sport-King Field Autoloader, except has 18¼-inch barrel, Western style straight-grip stock with barrel band, sling and swivels. Made 1964 to 1973.

High Standard Sport-King Deluxe Autoloader . . . $135
Same as Sport-King Special Autoloader, except has checkered stock. Made 1966 to 1975.

High Standard Sport-King Field Autoloader $95
Caliber: 22 Long Rifle, 22 Long, 22 Short (high speed). Tubular magazine holds 15 L.R., 17 Long, or 21 Short. 22¼-inch barrel. Weight: 5½ pounds. Open rear sight, beaded post front sight. Plain pistol-grip stock. Made 1960-66.

High Standard Sport-King Special Autoloader . . $110
Same as Sport-King Field, except stock has Monte Carlo comb and semibeavertail forearm. Made 1960-66.

HOLLAND & HOLLAND, LTD.
London, England

Holland & Holland No. 2 Model Hammerless Ejector Double Rifle $12,500
Same general specifications as Royal Model, except plainer finish. Discontinued 1960.

Holland & Holland Best Quality Magazine Rifle . . $4950
Mauser or Enfield action. Calibers: 240 Apex, 300 H&H Magnum, 375 H&H Magnum. 4-shot box magazine. 24-inch barrel. Weight: about 7¼ lbs., 240 Apex; 8¼ lbs., 300 Mag. and 375 Mag. Folding leaf rear sight, hooded ramp front sight. Detachable French walnut stock with cheekpiece, checkered pistol grip and forearm, swivels. Currently mfd. Specifications given are those of the present model; however, in general they apply also to prewar models.

H & H Best Quality Magazine Rifle

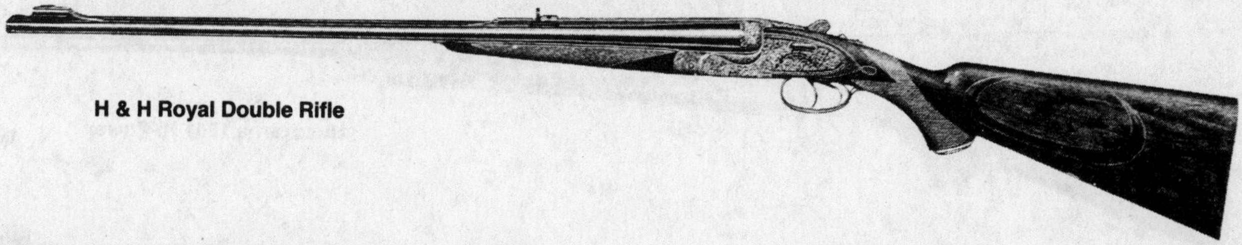

H & H Royal Double Rifle

Holland & Holland Deluxe Magazine Rifle $5400
Same specifications as Best Quality, except has exhibition grade stock and special engraving. Currently mfd.

Holland & Holland Royal Deluxe Double Rifle . . $24,500
Formerly designated "Modele Deluxe." Same specifications as Royal Model, except has exhibition grade stock and special engraving. Currently mfd.

Holland & Holland Royal Hammerless Ejector Double Rifle $9300
Side lock. Calibers: 240 Apex, 7mm H&H Mag., 300 H&H Mag., 300 Win. Mag., 30-06, 375 H&H Mag., 458 Win. Mag., 465 H&H Mag. 24- to 28-inch barrels. Weight: from 7½ pounds. Folding leaf rear sight, ramp front sight. Cheekpiece stock of select French walnut, checkered pistol grip and forearm. Currently mfd. Same general specifications apply to prewar model.

HUNGARIAN MILITARY RIFLES
Budapest, Hungary
Manufactured at Government Arsenal

Hungarian Model 1935M Mannlicher Military Rifle $195
Caliber: 8×52mm Hungarian. Bolt action, straight handle. 5-shot projecting box magazine. 24-inch barrel. Weight: about 9 pounds. Adjustable leaf rear sight, hooded front blade. Two-piece military-type stock. Made 1935 to c.1940.

Hungarian Model 1943M (German Gew. 98/40) Mannlicher Military Rifle $225
Modification, during German occupation, of the Model 1935M. Caliber: 7.9mm Mauser. Turned-down bolt handle and Mauser M/98-type box magazine; other differences are minor. Made from 1940 to end of war in Europe.

Husqvarna Model 456

Husqvarna 1100 Deluxe

HUSQVARNA VAPENFABRIK A.B.
Huskvarna, Sweden

Husqvarna Model 456 Lightweight Full-Stock Sporter $495
Same as Series 4000/4100 except has sporting-style full stock with slope-away cheek rest. Weight: 6½ pounds. Made 1959 to 1970.

Husqvarna Series 1000 Super Grade $475
Same as 1951 Model, except has European walnut sporter stock with Monte Carlo comb and cheekpiece. Made from 1952 to 1956.

Husqvarna Series 1100 Deluxe Model Hi-Power Bolt Action Sporting Rifles $450
Same as 1951 Model, except has "jeweled" bolt, European walnut stock. Made 1952-56.

Husqvarna 1950 Model Hi-Power Bolt Action Sporting Rifle $350
Mauser-type action. Calibers: 220 Swift, 270 Win., 30-06 (see note below), 5-shot box magazine. 23¾-inch barrel. Weight: about 7¾ pounds. Open rear sight, hooded ramp front sight. Sporting stock of Arctic beech, checkered pistol grip and forearm, swivels. *Note:* Husqvarna sporters were first introduced in the U.S. about 1948; earlier models were also available in calibers 6.5×55, 8×57 and 9.3×57. Made 1946 to 1951.

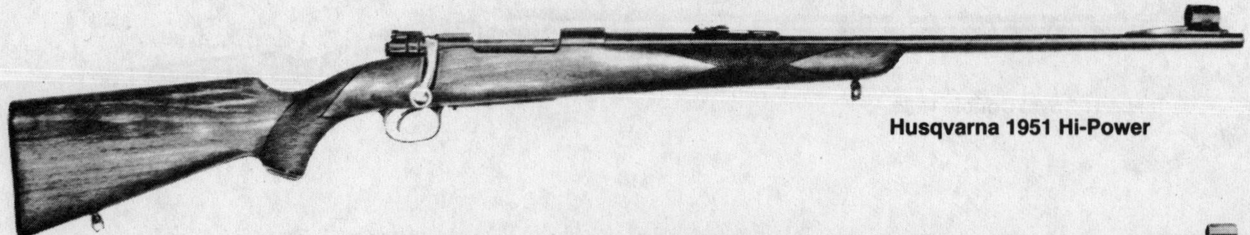

Husqvarna 1951 Hi-Power

Husqvarna 3000 Crown Grade

Husqvarna 4100 Lightweight

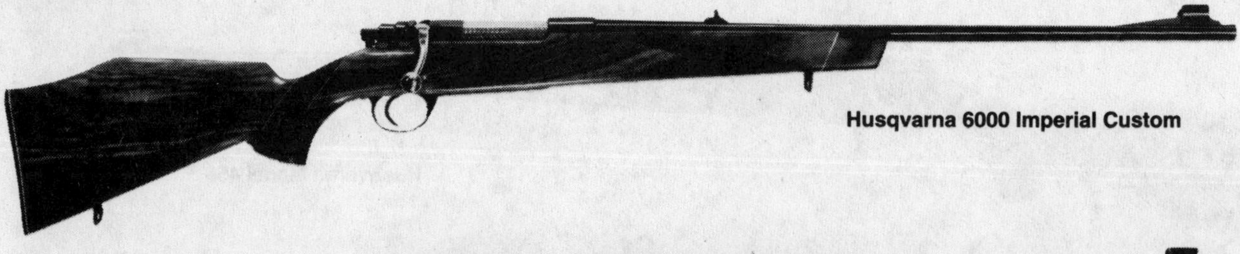

Husqvarna 6000 Imperial Custom

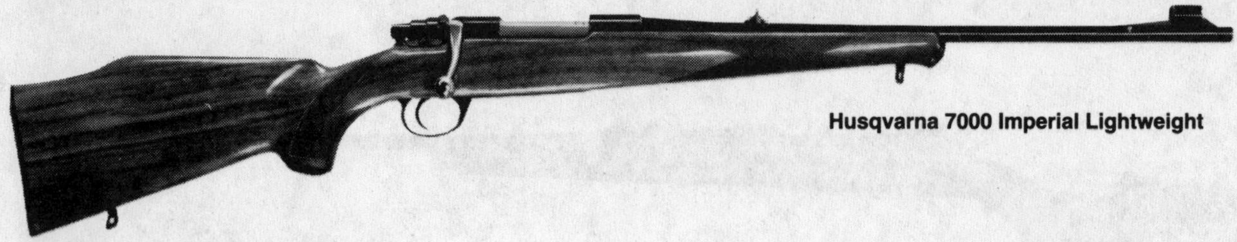

Husqvarna 7000 Imperial Lightweight

Husqvarna 1951 Model **$375**
Same as 1950 Model, except has high comb stock, low safety.

Husqvarna Series 3000 Crown Grade **$425**
Same as Series 3100, except has Monte Carlo comb stock.

Husqvarna Series 3100 Crown Grade **$425**
HVA improved Mauser action. Calibers: 243, 270, 7mm, 30-06, 308 Win. 5-shot box magazine. $23\frac{3}{4}$-inch barrel. Weight: $7\frac{1}{4}$ pounds. Open rear sight, hooded ramp front sight. European walnut stock, checkered, cheekpiece, pistol-grip cap, black foretip, swivels. Made 1954 to 1972.

Husqvarna Series 4000 Lightweight Rifle **$475**
Same as Series 4100, except has no rear sight and has Monte Carlo comb stock.

Husqvarna Series 4100 Lightweight Rifle **$450**
HVA improved Mauser action. Calibers: 243, 270, 7mm, 30-06, 308 Win. 5-shot box magazine. $20\frac{1}{2}$-inch barrel. Weight: about $6\frac{1}{4}$ pounds. Open rear sight, hooded ramp front sight. Lightweight walnut stock with cheekpiece, pistol grip, schnabel foretip, checkered, swivels. Made 1954 to 1972.

Husqvarna Series 6000 Imperial Custom Grade **$495**
Same as Series 3100, except fancy grade stock, 3-leaf folding rear sight, adjustable trigger. Calibers: 243, 270, 7mm Rem. Mag., 308, 30-06. Made 1968 to 1970.

Husqvarna Series 7000 Imperial Monte Carlo Lightweight **$525**
Same as Series 4000 Lightweight, except fancy grade stock, 3-leaf folding rear sight, adjustable trigger. Calibers: 243, 270, 308, 30-06. Made 1968 to 1970.

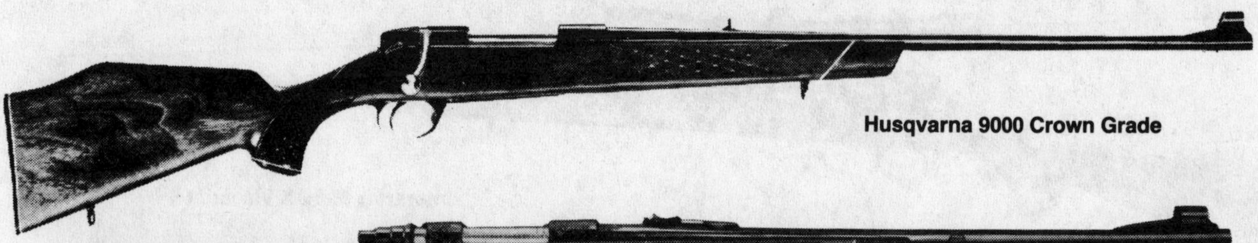

Husqvarna 9000 Crown Grade

Husqvarna P-3000 Presentation Grade

Husqvarna Model 8000 Imperial Grade Rifle $695
Same as Model 9000, except has jeweled bolt, engraved floorplate, deluxe French walnut stock, no sights. Made 1971-72.

Husqvarna Model 9000 Crown Grade Rifle $475
New design Husqvarna bolt action. Adjustable trigger. Calibers: 270, 7mm Rem. Mag., 30-06, 300 Win. Mag. 5-shot box magazine, hinged floorplate. 23$^{3}/_{4}$-inch barrel.

Husqvarna Model 9000 Crown Grade Rifle (cont.)
Folding leaf rear sight, hooded ramp front sight. Checkered walnut stock with Monte Carlo cheekpiece, rosewood forearm tip and pistol-grip cap. Weight: 7 lbs. 3 oz. Made 1971-72.

Husqvarna Series P-3000 Presentation Rifle . . . $725
Same as Crown Grade Series 3000, except specially selected stock, engraved action, adjustable trigger. Calibers: 243, 270, 7mm Rem. Mag., 30-06. Made 1968 to 1970.

RIFLES

Interarms Mark X

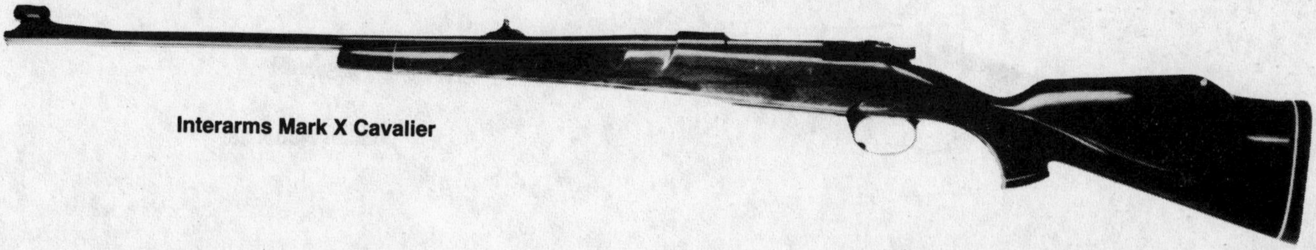

Interarms Mark X Cavalier

INTERARMS RIFLES
Alexandria, Virginia

The following Mark X rifles are manufactured by Zavodi Crvena Zastava, Belgrade, Yugoslavia.

Interarms Mark X Alaskan $395
Same specifications as Mark X Sporter, except calibers 375 H&H Mag. and 458 Win. Mag., 3-round magazine, weighs 8$^{1}/_{4}$ pounds, has stock with recoil-absorbing cross bolt and heavy duty recoil pad. Made from 1976 to date.

Interarms Mark X Bolt Action Sporting Rifle $235
Mauser-type action. Calibers: 22-250, 243, 25-06, 270, 7×57, 7mm Rem. Mag., 308, 30-06, 300 Win. Mag. 5-shot magazine (3-shot in magnum calibers). 24-inch barrel. Weight: 7$^{1}/_{2}$ pounds. Adjustable leaf rear sight, ramp front sight with hood. Classic-style stock of European walnut with Monte Carlo comb and cheekpiece, checkered pistol grip and forearm, black forend tip, QD swivels. Made from 1972 to date.

Interarms Mark X Cavalier $330
Same specifications as Mark X Sporter, except has contemporary style stock with roll-over cheekpiece, rosewood forend tip and grip cap, recoil pad. Made 1974 to date.

Interarms Mark X Viscount

Interarms Whitworth Express

Interarms Mark X Continental Mannlicher Style Carbine $340
Same specifications as Mark X Sporter, except straight European-style comb stock with sculptured cheekpiece. Precise double-set triggers and classic "butter-knife" bolt handle. French checkering. Weight: about 7¼ pounds.

Interarms Mark X Marquis Mannlicher Style Carbine $345
Same specifications as Mark X Sporter, except has 20-inch barrel, full-length Mannlicher-type stock with metal forend/muzzle cap. Calibers: 270, 7×57, 308, 30-06. Made from 1976 to date.

Interarms Mark X Viscount $195
Same specifications as Mark X Sporter, except has plainer field grade stock. Made from 1974 to date.

Interarms Whitworth Express Rifle, African Series $475
Mauser-type bolt action. Calibers: 375 H&H Mag., 458 Win. Mag. 3-shot magazine. 24-inch barrel. Weight: about 8 pounds. 3-leaf express open rear sight, ramp front sight with hood. English-style stock of European walnut, with cheekpiece, black forend tip, checkered pistol grip and forearm, recoil pad, QD swivels. Made from 1974 to date by Whitworth Rifle Co., England.

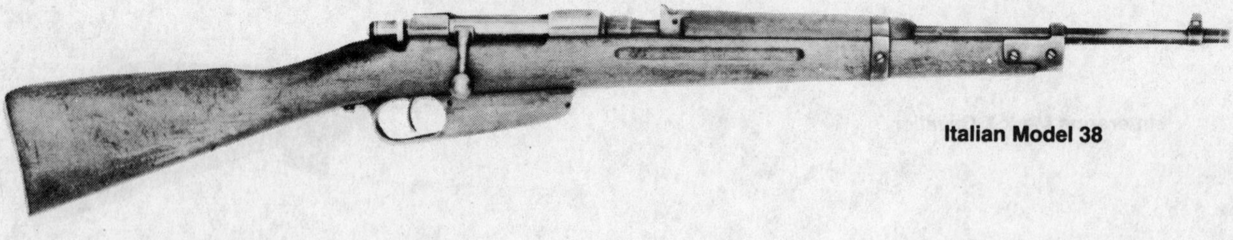

Italian Model 38

ITALIAN MILITARY RIFLES

Manufactured by Government plants at Brescia, Gardone, Terni and Turin, Italy

Italian Model 1891 Mannlicher-Carcano Military Rifle $85
Bolt action, straight handle. Caliber, 6.5mm. Italian Service. 6-shot modified Mannlicher-type box magazine. 30¾-inch barrel. Weight: about 9 pounds. Adjustable rear sight, blade front sight. Military-type straight-grip stock. Adopted 1891.

Italian Model 38 Military Rifle $95
Modification of Model 1891, has turned-down bolt handle, detachable folding bayonet. Caliber: 7.35mm Italian Service (many arms of this model were later converted to the old 6.5mm caliber). 6-shot box magazine. 21¼-inch barrel. Weight: about 7½ pounds. Adjustable rear sight, blade front sight. Military straight-grip stock. Adopted 1938.

Ithaca Model 49 Deluxe

Ithaca Model 49 Presentation

Ithaca Model 49

Ithaca Model 49R Repeater

Ithaca Model 72 Deluxe

ITHACA GUN COMPANY, INC.
Ithaca, New York

Ithaca Model 49 Deluxe Saddlegun $100
Same as standard Model 49, except has gold-plated hammer and trigger, figured walnut stock, sling swivels. Made 1962 to 1975.

Ithaca Model 49 Magnum Saddlegun $95
Same as standard Model 49, except chambered for 22 Win. Mag. R.F. cartridge. Made 1962 to 1978.

Ithaca Model 49 Presentation Saddlegun $225
Same as standard Model 49 Saddlegun, except has gold-plated hammer and trigger, engraved receiver, full fancy figured walnut stock with gold nameplate. Available in 22 Long Rifle or 22 WMR. Made 1962 to 1974.

Ithaca Model 49 Saddlegun Lever Action Single Shot Rifle $85
Martini-type action. Hand-operated rebounding hammer. Caliber: 22 Long Rifle, Long, Short. 18-inch barrel. Open sights. Western carbine-style stock. Weight: 5½ pounds. Made 1961 to 1978.

Ithaca Model 49 St. Louis Bicentennial Saddlegun $200
Same as Model 49 Deluxe, except has commemorative inscription. 200 made in 1964. Value is for rifle in new, unfired condition.

Ithaca Model 49 Youth Saddlegun $85
Same as standard Model 49, except shorter stock for young shooters. Made 1961 to 1978.

Ithaca Model 49R Saddlegun Repeating Rifle . . . $125
Similar in appearance to Model 49 Single Shot. Caliber: 22 Long Rifle, Long, Short. Tubular magazine holds 15 LR, 17 Long, 21 Short. 20-inch barrel. Weight: 5½ pounds. Open rear sight, bead front sight. Western-style stock, checkered grip. Made 1968 to 1971.

Ithaca Model 72 Deluxe $185
Same as standard Model 72, except has silver-finished and engraved receiver, octagon barrel, higher grade walnut stock and forearm. Made 1974-76.

Ithaca Model 72 Magnum $160
Same as standard Model 72, except chambered for 22 Winchester Magnum Rimfire, has 11-shot tubular magazine, 18½-inch barrel. Made 1975-78.

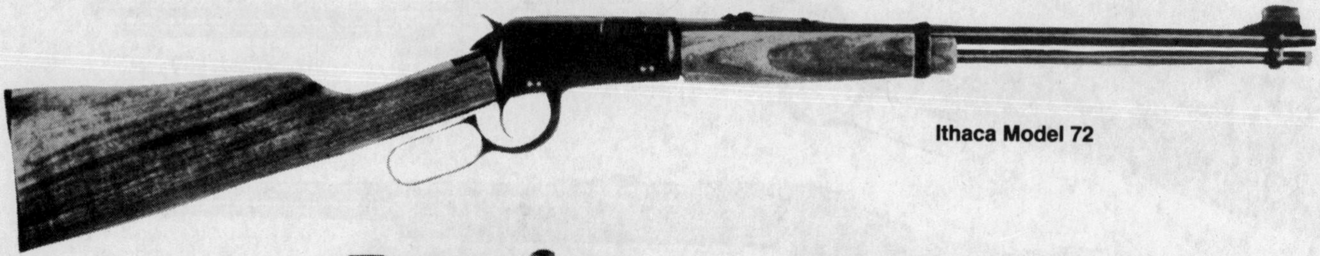

Ithaca Model 72

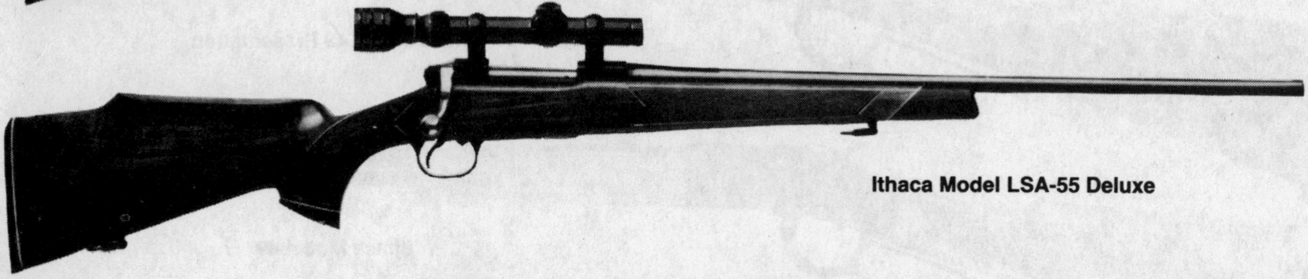

Ithaca Model LSA-55 Deluxe

Ithaca Model LSA-55 Standard

Ithaca Model LSA-65 Standard

Ithaca Model 72 Saddlegun Lever Action Repeating Carbine **$160**
Caliber: 22 Long Rifle, Long, Short. Tubular magazine holds 15 LR, 17 Long, 21 Short. 18½-inch barrel. Weight: about 5½ pounds. Open rear sight, hooded ramp front sight. Receiver grooved for scope mounting. Western carbine stock and forearm of American walnut. Made 1973-78. *Note:* Barrel and action are manufactured by Erma-Werke, Dachau, W. Germany; wood installed by Ithaca.

Ithaca Model LSA-55 Deluxe **$395**
Same as Model LSA-55 Standard Grade, except has roll-over cheekpiece, rosewood grip-cap and forend tip, skip checkering, high-luster blue, no iron sights, scope mount standard equipment. Made 1969 to 1977.

Ithaca Model LSA-55 Heavy Barrel **$410**
Same as Model LSA-55, except calibers 222 Rem. and 22-250 only; has 23-inch heavy barrel, no sights, special stock with beavertail forearm, weighs about 8½ pounds. Made 1974-77.

Ithaca Model LSA-55 Standard Grade Bolt Action Repeating Rifle **$340**
Mauser-type action. Calibers: 222 Rem., 22-250, 6mm Rem., 243 Win., 308 Win. 3-shot detachable clip magazine. 22-inch barrel. Weight: 6½ pounds. Folding leaf rear sight, hooded ramp front sight. Checkered walnut stock with Monte Carlo cheekpiece, detachable swivels. Made 1969 to 1977. Mfd. by Oy Tikkakoski AB, Tikkakoski, Finland.

Ithaca Model LSA-65 Deluxe **$380**
Same as Model LSA-65 Standard Grade, except has special features of Model LSA-55 Deluxe. Made 1969 to 1977.

Ithaca Model LSA-65 Standard Grade **$355**
Same as Model LSA-55 Standard Grade, except calibers 25-06, 270, 30-06; 4-shot magazine, 23-inch barrel, weighs 7 pounds. Made 1969 to 1977.

Ithaca Model X5-C Lightning Autoloader Clip Repeating Rifle **$135**
Takedown. Caliber: 22 Long Rifle. 7-shot clip magazine. 22-inch barrel. Weight: 6 pounds. Open rear sight. Raybar front sight. Pistol-grip stock, grooved forearm. Made 1958 to 1964.

Ithaca Model X5-T

Ithaca Model X-15

Ithaca-BSA CF-2

Ithaca Model X5-T Lightning Autoloader Tubular Repeating Rifle $135
Same as Model X5-C except has 16-shot tubular magazine, stock with plain forearm. Made 1959 to 1963.

Ithaca Model X-15 Lightning Autoloader $125
Same general specifications as Model X5-C, except forearm is not grooved. Made 1964-67.

Ithaca-BSA CF-2 Bolt Action Repeating Rifle . . . $315
Mauser-type action. Calibers: 7mm Rem. Mag., 300 Win. Mag. 3-shot magazine. 23.6-inch barrel. Weight: 8 pounds. Adjustable rear sight, hooded ramp front sight. Checkered walnut stock with Monte Carlo comb, roll-over cheekpiece, rosewood forend tip, recoil pad, sling swivels. Made 1976-77. Mfd. by BSA Guns Ltd., Birmingham, England.

JAPANESE MILITARY RIFLES
Tokyo, Japan
Manufactured by Government Plant

Japanese Model 38 Arisaka Carbine $125
Same general specifications as Model 38 Rifle, except has 19-inch barrel, heavy folding bayonet, weighs about 7¼ pounds.

Japanese Model 38 Arisaka Service Rifle $95
Mauser-type bolt action. Caliber: 6.5mm Japanese. 5-shot box magazine. Barrel lengths: 25⅜ and 31¼ inches. Weight: about 9¼ pounds with long barrel. Fixed front sight, adjustable rear sight. Military-type full stock. Adopted in 1905, the 38th year of the Meiji reign, hence designation "Model 38."

Japanese Model 44 Cavalry Carbine $135
Same general specifications as Model 38 Rifle except has 19-inch barrel, heavy folding bayonet, weighs about 8½ pounds. Adopted in 1911, the 44th year of the Meiji reign, hence the designation "Model 44."

Japanese Model 99 Service Rifle $140
Modified Model 38. Caliber: 7.7mm Japanese. 5-shot box magazine. 25¾-inch barrel. Weight: about 8¾ pounds. Fixed front sight, adjustable aperture rear sight, anti-aircraft sighting bars on some early models; fixed rear sight on some late WWII rifles. Military-type full stock, may have bipod. Takedown paratroop model was also made during WWII. Adopted in 1939, Japanese year 2599 from which the designation "Model 99" is taken. *Note:* The last Model 99 rifles made were of very poor quality; some have cast steel receivers. Value shown is for earlier type.

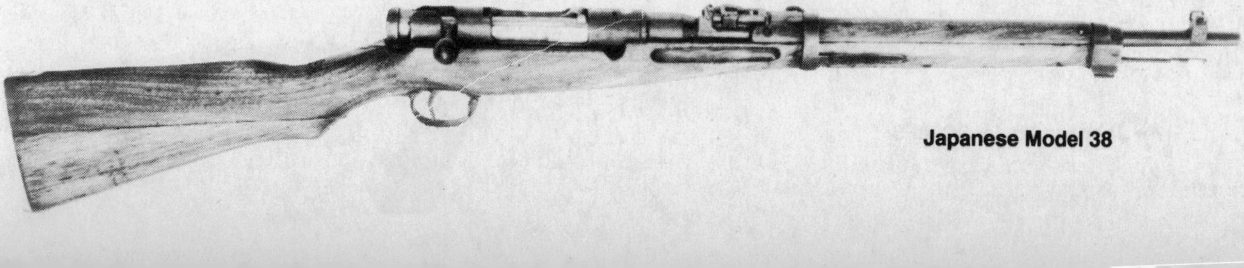

Japanese Model 38

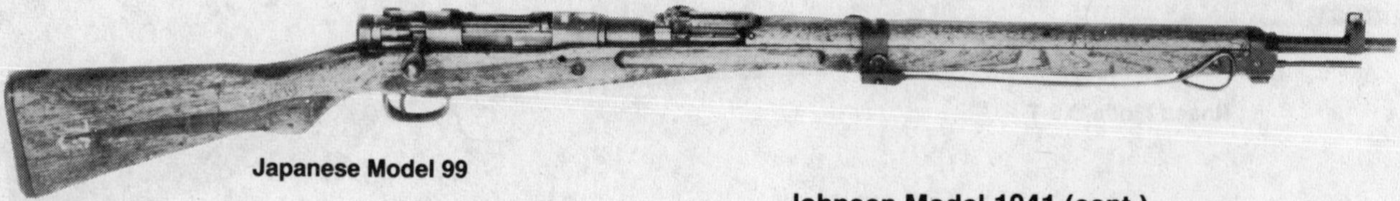

Japanese Model 99

JOHNSON AUTOMATICS, INC.
Providence, Rhode Island

Johnson Model 1941 Semiauto Military Rifle . . . $795
Short-recoil-operated. Removable, air-cooled, 22-inch barrel. Calibers: 30-06, 7mm Mauser. 10-shot rotary magazine. Two-piece, wood stock, pistol grip; perforated metal radiator sleeve over rear half of barrel. Receiver peep sight, protected post front sight. Weight: 9½ pounds. *Note:* The Johnson M/1941 was adopted by the Netherlands Government in 1940-41 and the major portion of the production of this rifle, 1941-43, was on Dutch orders. A quantity was also purchased by the U.S. Government for use by Marine Corps parachute troops (1943) and for Lend Lease. All of these rifles were caliber 30-06; the 7mm Johnson rifles were made for a South American government.

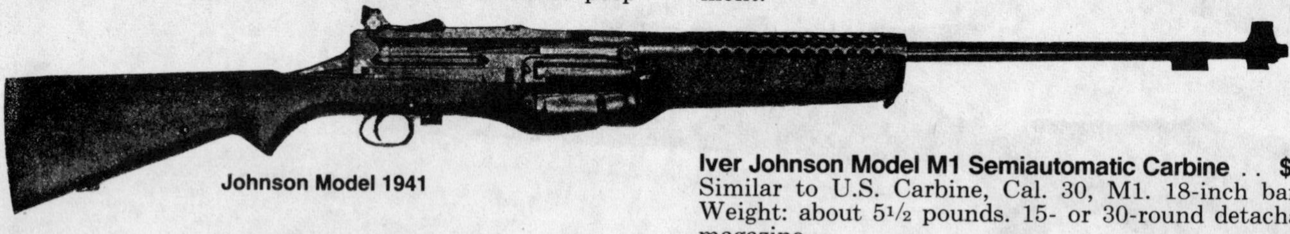

Johnson Model 1941

IVER JOHNSON'S ARMS, INC.
Jacksonville, Arkansas
Formerly of Fitchburg, Massachusetts, and Middlesex, New Jersey

Iver Johnson Li'l Champ Bolt Action Rifle $90
Caliber: 22 S, L, LR. Single shot. 16¼-inch barrel. 32½ inches overall. Weight: 3¼ pounds. Adjustable rear sight, blade front. Synthetic composition stock. Made from 1986 to date.

Iver Johnson Model M1 Semiautomatic Carbine . . $175
Similar to U.S. Carbine, Cal. 30, M1. 18-inch barrel. Weight: about 5½ pounds. 15- or 30-round detachable magazine.

Iver Johnson Model PM.30 Semiautomatic Carbine $180
Similar to U.S. Carbine, Cal. .30 M1. 18-inch barrel. Weight: about 5½ pounds. 15- or 30-round detachable magazine. Both hardwood and walnut stock.

Iver Johnson Model SC30FS Semiautomatic Carbine $225
Similar to Survival Carbine except has folding stock. Made from 1983 to date.

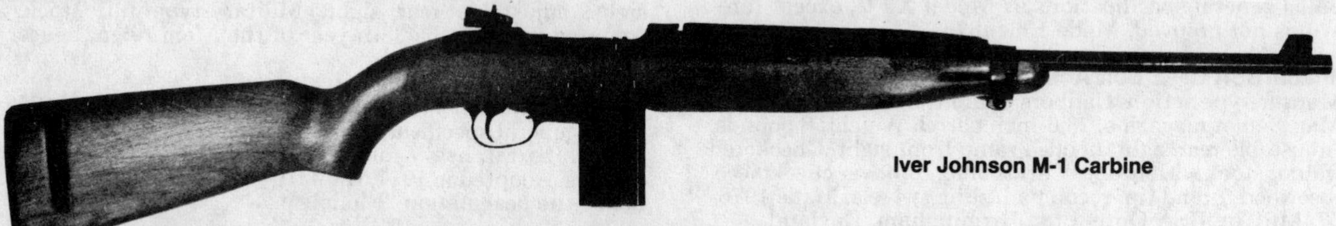

Iver Johnson M-1 Carbine

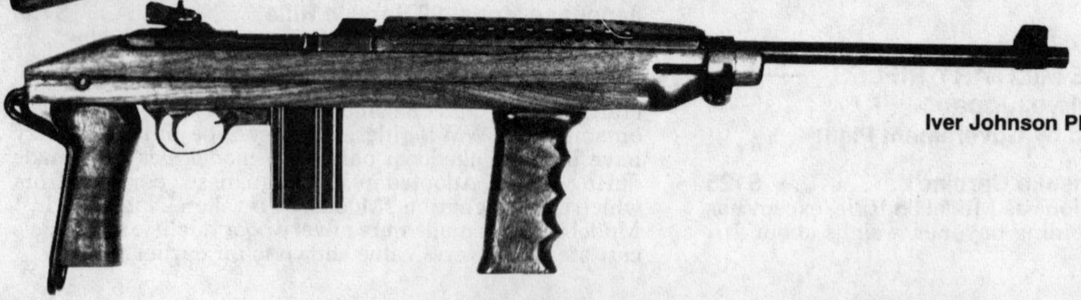

Iver Johnson PM30

Iver Johnson Model SC30FS

Iver Johnson Survival Carbine

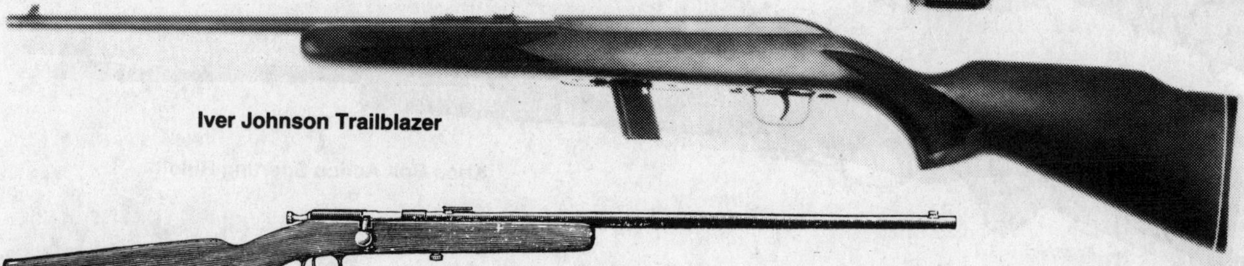

Iver Johnson Trailblazer

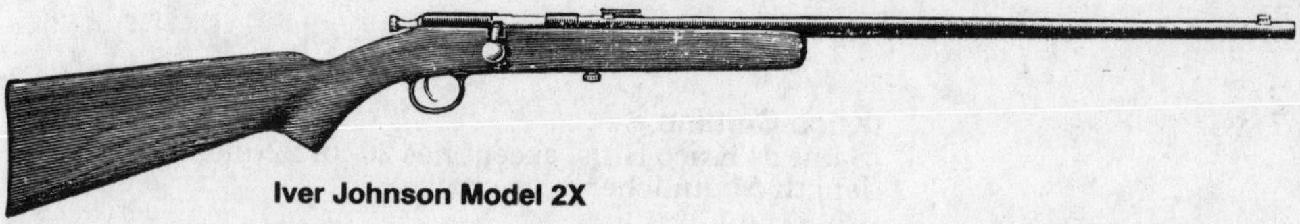

Iver Johnson Model 2X

Iver Johnson Survival Semiautomatic Carbine . . $220
Similar to Model PM.30 except in stainless steel with high-impact plastic, one-piece stock. Made from 1983 to date. With folding high-impact plastic stock add $35.

Iver Johnson Trailblazer Semiauto Rifle $95
Caliber: 22 Long Rifle. 18-inch barrel. Weight: 5½ pounds. Open rear sight, blade front sight. Hardwood stock. Made from 1983 to 1985.

Iver Johnson Model X Bolt Action Rifle $100
Takedown. Single shot. Caliber: 22 Short, Long and Long Rifle. 22-inch barrel. Weight: about 4 pounds. Open rear sight, blade front sight. Pistol-grip stock with knob forend tip. Made 1928 to 1932.

Iver Johnson Model XX (2X) Bolt Action $125
Improved version of the Model X, has heavier 24-inch barrel, larger stock (without knob tip), weighs about 4½ pounds. Made 1932 to 1955.

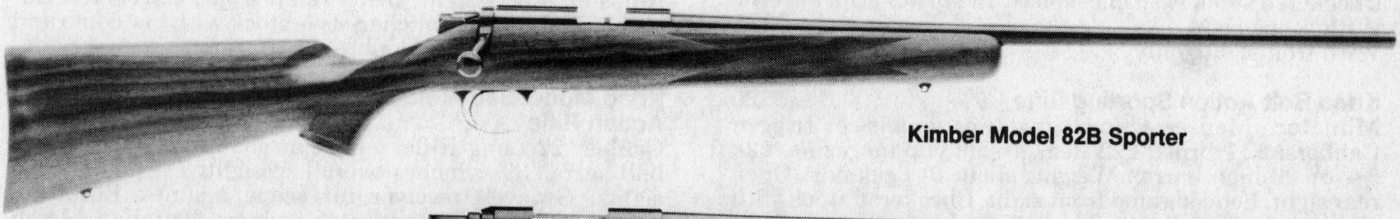

Kimber Model 82B Sporter

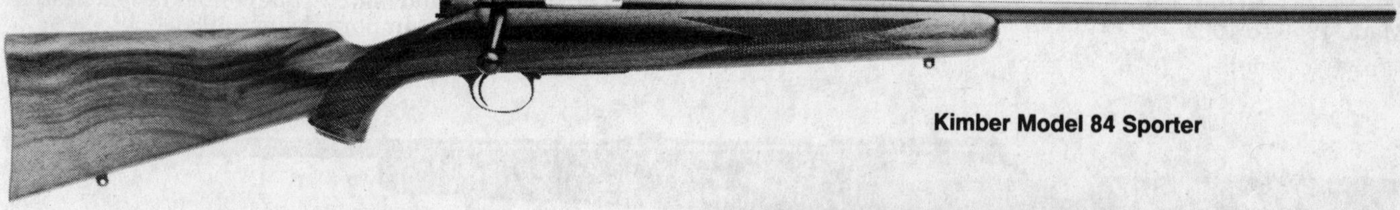

Kimber Model 84 Sporter

KIMBER OF OREGON, INC.
Colton, Oregon

Kimber Model 82B Rimfire Bolt Action Sporter
Caliber: 22 Long Rifle. 5- or 10-shot magazine. 22-inch barrel. 40½ inches overall. Weight: about 6½ pounds. No sights furnished. Round top receiver dovetailed for Kimber's machined steel scope mount rings. Special 4X scope or open iron sights optional. Checkered claro walnut stock with ebony forend tip. Neidner-style checkered steel buttplate, no cheekpiece (Deluxe Grade) or beaded cheekpiece (Super Grade). Inletted sling swivels.
Deluxe Grade **$825**
Super Grade **850**

Kimber Model 84 Centerfire Sporting Rifle
Calibers: 17 Rem., 221 Rem., 223 Rem. 22- or 24-inch barrel. Weight: 6½ to 7¾ pounds. Adjustable folding-leaf rear sight, hooded ramp front (optional). Checkered claro walnut stock with ebony forend tip and Niedner-style buttplate. Three-position safety available in 1987. *Deluxe and Super Grade* have 22-inch Sporterweight barrel; no cheekpiece or beaded cheekpiece; *Ultra Varmint* has 24-inch med. heavy stainless barrel, laminated birch stock, no cheekpiece; *Super Varmint* has 24-inch med. heavy barrel, AAA claro walnut stock, beaded cheekpiece. Made from 1984 to date.
Deluxe Grade **$895**
Super Grade **985**
Ultra Varmint **925**
Super Varmint **995**

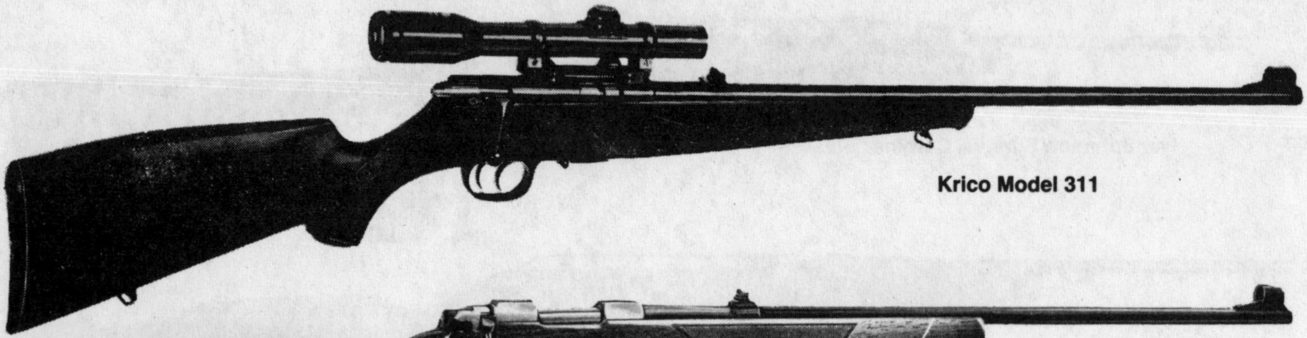

Krico Model 311

Krico Bolt Action Sporting Rifle

KRICO RIFLES
Stuttgart-Hedelfingen, W. Germany
Mfd. by Sportwaffenfabrik Kriegeskorte GmbH

Krico Model 311 Small Bore Rifle
Bolt action. Caliber: 22 Long Rifle. 5- or 10-shot clip magazine. 22-inch barrel. Weight: about 6 pounds. Single- or double-set trigger. Open rear sight, hooded ramp front sight; available with factory-fitted Kaps $2\frac{1}{2}\times$ scope. Checkered stock with cheekpiece and pistol grip, swivels.
With scope sight **$375**
With iron sights only **290**

Krico Bolt Action Sporting Rifle $520
Miniature Mauser action. Single- or double-set trigger. Calibers: 22 Hornet, 222 Rem. 4-shot clip magazine. 22-, 24- or 26-inch barrel. Weight: about $6\frac{1}{4}$ pounds. Open rear sight, hooded ramp front sight. Checkered stock with cheekpiece, pistol grip, black forend tip, sling swivels. Made 1956 to 1962.

Krico Carbine $575
Same as Krico Rifle, except has 20- or 22-inch barrel, full-length Mannlicher-type stock.

Krico Special Varmint Rifle $540
Same as Krico Rifle, except has heavy barrel, no sights, weighs about $7\frac{1}{4}$ pounds. Caliber: 222 Rem. only.

Note: The following Krico rifles are currently imported by Beeman Precision Arms, Inc., Santa Rosa, California

Krico Model 320 Bolt Action Sporter $695
Caliber: 22 Long Rifle. 5-shot detachable box magazine. $19\frac{1}{2}$-inch barrel. $38\frac{1}{2}$ inches overall. Weight: 6 pounds. Adjustable rear sight, blade ramp front. Checkered European walnut Mannlicher-style stock with low comb and cheekpiece. Single or double-set triggers.

Krico Model 340 Metallic Silhouette Bolt Action Rifle $740
Caliber: 22 Long Rifle. 5-shot magazine. 21-inch heavy, bull barrel. $39\frac{1}{2}$ inches overall. Weight: $7\frac{1}{2}$ pounds. No sights. Grooved receiver for scope mounts. European walnut stock in off-hand match-style configuration. Match or double-set triggers. Imported since 1983.

Krico Model 320 Sporter

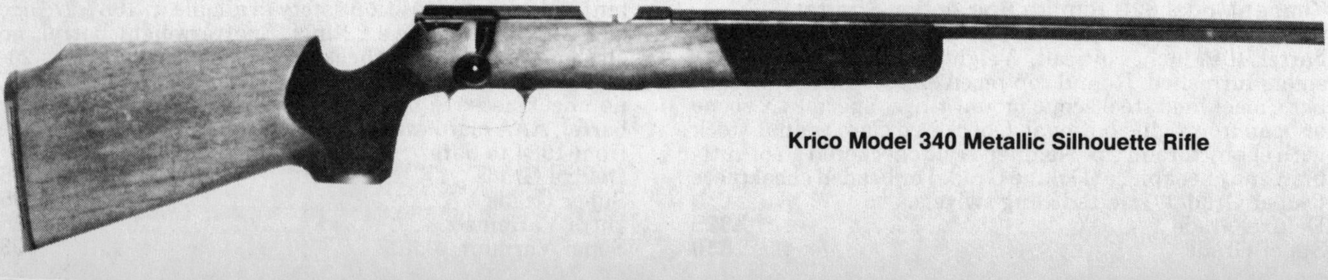

Krico Model 340 Metallic Silhouette Rifle

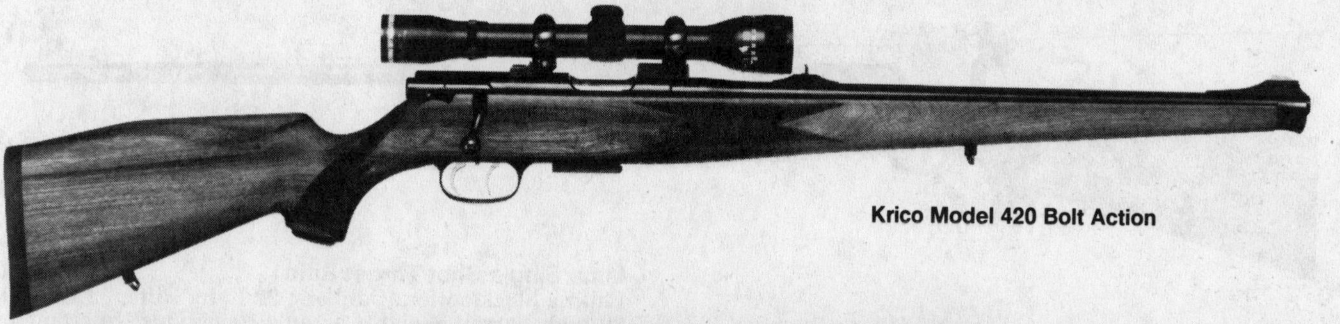

Krico Model 420 Bolt Action

Krico Model 640 Super Sniper

Krico Model 400 Bolt Action Rifle **$795**
Caliber: 22 Hornet. 5-shot detachable box magazine. 23½-inch barrel. Weight: 6¾ pounds. Adjustable open rear sight, ramp front. European walnut stock.

Krico Model 420 Bolt Action Rifle **$890**
Same as Model 400, except has full-length Mannlicher-style stock and double-set triggers. Scope optional, extra.

Krico Model 440 S Bolt Action Rifle **$895**
Caliber: 22 Hornet. Detachable box magazine. 20-inch barrel. 36½ inches overall. Weight: 7½ pounds. No sights. French walnut stock with ventilated forend.

Krico Model 620 Bolt Action Rifle **$1150**
Same as Model 700, except has short action chambered 308 Win. and full-length Mannlicher-style stock with schnabel forend tip. 20¾-inch barrel. Weight: 6½ pounds.

Krico Model 640 Super Sniper Bolt Action Repeating Rifle **$1595**
Calibers: 223 Rem., 308 Win. 3-shot magazine. 26-inch barrel. 44¾ inches overall. Weight: 9½ pounds. No sights, drilled and tapped for scope mounts. Single or double-set triggers. Select walnut stock with adjustable cheekpiece and recoil pad.

Krico Model 640 Varmint Rifle **$1150**
Caliber: 222 Rem. 4-shot magazine. 23¾-inch barrel. Weight: 9½ pounds. No sights. European walnut stock.

Krieghoff Teck Over/Under

Krieghoff Ulm Over/Under

KRIEGHOFF RIFLES
Ulm (Donau), West Germany
Mfd. by H. Krieghoff Jagd und Sportwaffenfabrik

See also combination guns under Krieghoff shotgun listings.

Krieghoff Teck Over/Under Rifle
Kersten action, double crossbolt, double underlugs. Box lock. Calibers: 7×57r5, 7×64, 7×65r5, 30-30, 308 Win., 30-06, 300 Win. Mag., 9.3×74r5, 375 H&H Mag., 458 Win. Mag. 25-inch barrels. Weight: 8 to 9½ pounds. Express rear sight, ramp front sight. Checkered walnut stock and forearm. Made from 1967 to date.
Standard calibers **$3500**
375 H&H Mag., 458 Win. Mag. **4700**

Krieghoff Ulm Over/Under Rifle **$4395**
Same general specifications as Teck model, except has side locks with leaf arabesque engraving. Made from 1963 to date.

Krieghoff ULM-Primus Over/Under Rifle **$5850**
Deluxe version of Ulm model, has detachable side locks, higher grade engraving and stock wood. Made from 1963 to date.

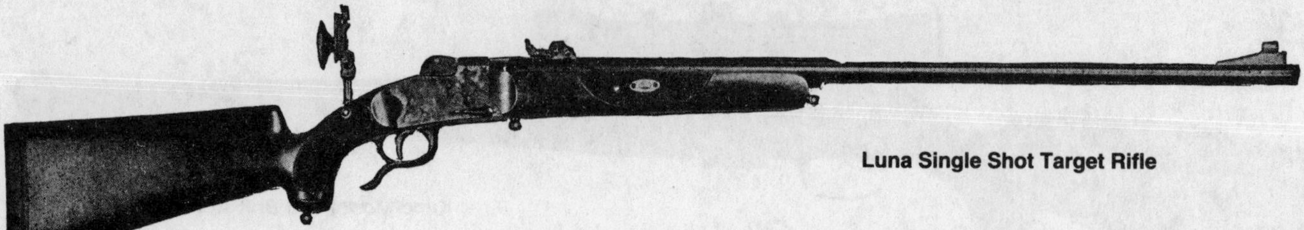

Luna Single Shot Target Rifle

LUNA RIFLE
Mehlis, Germany
Manufactured by Ernst Friedr. Büchel

Luna Single Shot Target Rifle **$750**
Falling block action. Calibers: 22 Long Rifle, 22 Hornet. 29-inch barrel. Weight: about 8¼ pounds. Micrometer peep rear tang sight, open rear sight, ramp front sight. Cheekpiece stock with full pistol grip, semibeavertail forearm, checkered, swivels. Made prior to WWII.

Mannlicher Model L Carbine

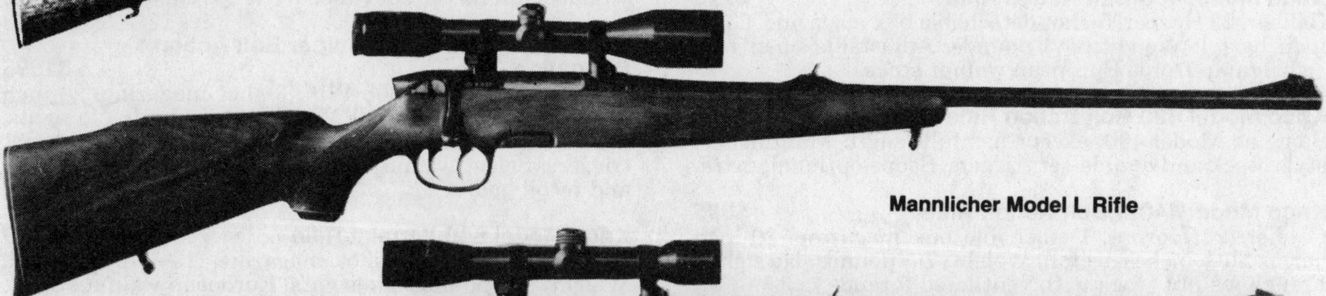

Mannlicher Model L Rifle

Mannlicher Model M Carbine

MANNLICHER SPORTING RIFLES
Steyr, Austria
Manufactured by Steyr-Daimler-Puch, A.-G.

In 1967, Steyr-Daimler-Puch introduced a series of sporting rifles with a bolt action that is a departure from the Mannlicher-Schoenauer system of earlier models. In the latter, the action is locked by lugs symmetrically arranged behind the bolt head as well as by placing the bolt handle ahead of the right flank of the receiver, the rear section of which is open on top for backward movement of the bolt handle. The current action, made in four lengths to accommodate different ranges of cartridges, has a closed-top receiver; the bolt locking lugs are located toward the rear of the bolt (behind the magazine), and the Mannlicher-Schoenauer rotary magazine has been redesigned as a detachable box type of Makrolon.

Mannlicher Model L Carbine **$745**
Same general specifications as Model SL Carbine, except has type "L" action, weighs about 6.2 pounds. Calibers same as for Model L Rifle. Made from 1968 to date.

Mannlicher Model L Rifle **$655**
Same general specifications as Model SL Rifle, except has type "L" action, weighs about 6.3 pounds. Calibers: 22-250, 5.6×57, 243 Win., 6mm Rem., 308 Win. Made from 1968 to date.

Mannlicher Model L Varmint Rifle **$625**
Same general specifications as Model SL Varmint Rifle, except has type "L" action. Calibers: 22-250, 243 Win., 308 Win. Made from 1969 to date.

Mannlicher Model Luxus Bolt Action Rifle
Same general specifications as Models L and M, except with 3-shot detachable box magazine and single-set trigger. Full or half-stock with low luster oil or high-gloss lacquer finish.
Full stock **$1450**
Half stock **1400**

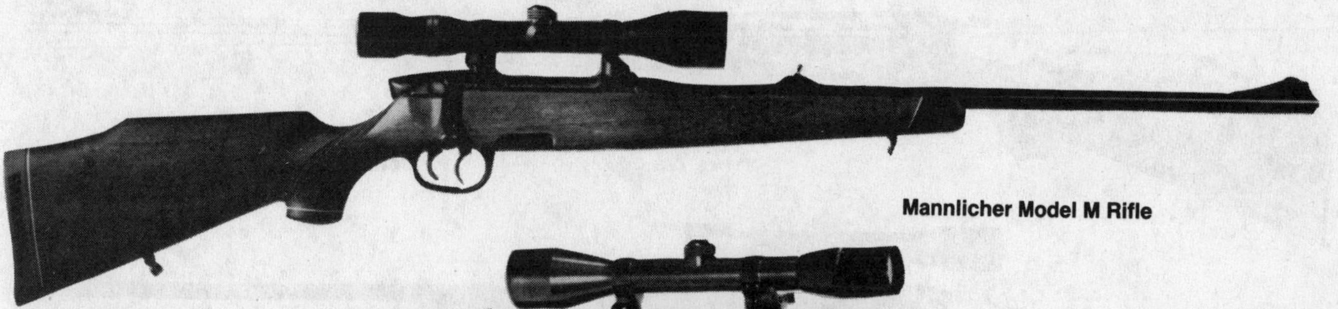

Mannlicher Model M Rifle

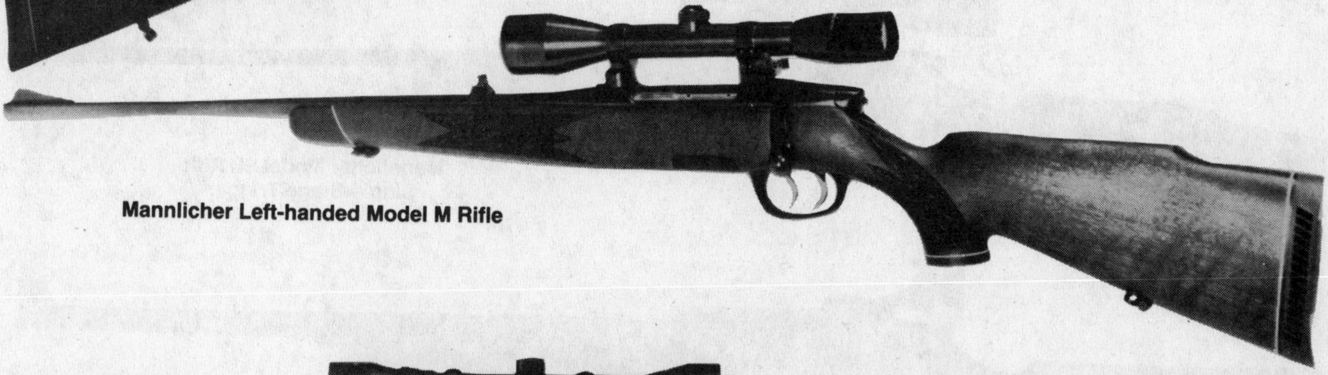

Mannlicher Left-handed Model M Rifle

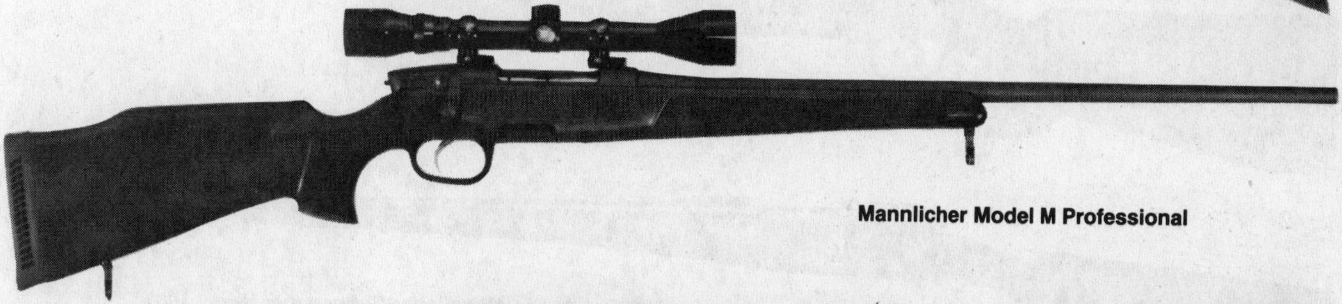

Mannlicher Model M Professional

Mannlicher Model SL Carbine

Mannlicher Model M Carbine
Same general specifications as Model SL Carbine, except has type "M" action, stock with recoil pad, weighs about 6.8 pounds. Made from 1969 to date. Left-hand version with additional 6.5 × 55 and 9.3 × 62 calibers introduced in 1977.
Right-hand Carbine **$755**
Left-hand Carbine **695**

Mannlicher Model M Professional Rifle $595
Same as standard Model M Rifle, except has synthetic (Cycolac) stock, weighs about 7½ pounds. Calibers: 6.5×55, 6.5×57, 270 Win., 7×57, 7×64, 7.5 Swiss, 30-06, 8×57JS, 9.3×62. Introduced 1977.

Mannlicher Model M Rifle
Same general specifications as Model SL Rifle, except has type "M" action, stock with forend tip and recoil pad, weighs about 6.9 pounds. Calibers: 6.5×57, 270 Win., 7×57, 7×64, 30-06, 8×57JS, 9.3×62. Made 1969 to date. Left-

Mannlicher Model M Rifle (cont.)
hand version with additional calibers 6.5 × 55 and 7.5 Swiss introduced in 1977.
Right-hand Rifle **$575**
Left-hand Rifle **645**

Mannlicher Model S Rifle $675
Same general specifications as Model SL Rifle, except has type "S" action, 4-round magazine, 25⅝-inch barrel, stock with forend tip and recoil pad, weighs about 8.4 pounds. Calibers: 6.5×68, 257 Weatherby Mag., 264 Win. Mag., 7mm Rem. Mag., 300 Win. Mag., 300 H&H Mag., 308 Norma Mag., 8×68S, 338 Win. Mag., 9.3×64, 37 H&H Mag. Made from 1970 to date.

Mannlicher Model SL Carbine $695
Same general specifications as Model SL Rifle, except has 20-inch barrel and full-length stock, weighs about 5.95 pounds. Made from 1968 to date.

Mannlicher Model SL Rifle Double-Set Trigger

Mannlicher Model SL Rifle Single-Stage Trigger

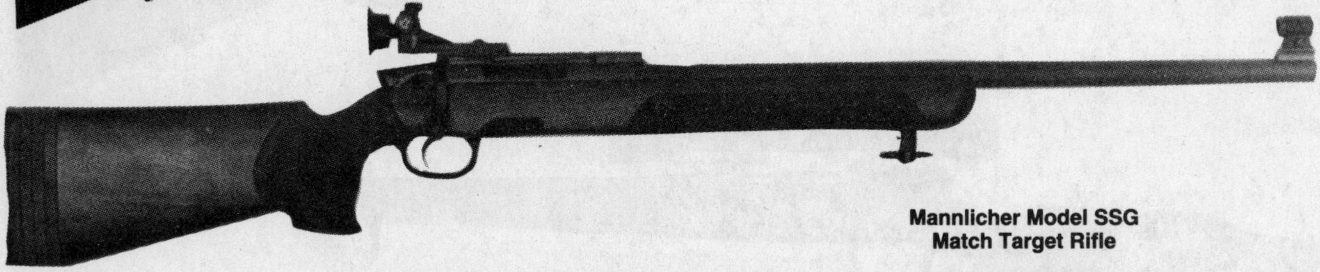

Mannlicher Model SSG Match Target Rifle

Mannlicher-Schoenauer Model 1903 Sporting Carbine

Mannlicher Model SL Rifle $725
Steyr-Mannlicher SL bolt action. Calibers: 222 Rem., 222 Rem. Mag., 223 Rem. 5-shot rotary magazine, detachable. $23\frac{5}{8}$-inch barrel. Weight: about 6.05 pounds. Single- or double-set trigger (mechanisms interchangeable). Open rear sight, hooded ramp front sight. Half stock of European walnut with Monte Carlo comb and cheekpiece, skip-checkered forearm and pistol grip, rubber butt pad, QD swivels. Made from 1967 to date.

Mannlicher Model SL Varmint Rifle $575
Same general specifications as Model SL Rifle, except caliber 222 Rem. only, has $25\frac{5}{8}$-inch heavy barrel, no sights, weighs about 7.92 pounds. Made from 1969 to date.

Mannlicher Model SSG Match Target Rifle
Type "L" action. Caliber: 308 Win. (7.62×51 NATO). 5- or 10-round magazine, single-shot plug. $25\frac{1}{2}$-inch heavy barrel. Weight: $10\frac{1}{4}$ pounds. Single trigger. Micrometer peep rear sight, globe front sight. Target stock, European walnut or synthetic, with full pistol grip, wide forearm with swivel rail, adjustable rubber butt plate. Made 1969 to date.
With walnut stock **$795**
With synthetic stock **725**

Mannlicher Model S/T Rifle $695
Same as Model S Rifle, except has heavy $25\frac{5}{8}$-inch barrel, weighs about 9 pounds. Calibers: 9.3×64, 375 H&H Mag., 458 Win. Mag. Option of $23\frac{5}{8}$-inch barrel in latter caliber. Made from 1975 to date.

Note: Certain Mannlicher-Schoenauer models were produced before WWII. Manufacture of sporting rifles and carbines was resumed at the Steyr-Daimler-Puch plant in Austria in 1950 during which time the Model 1950 rifles and carbines were introduced.

Mannlicher-Schoenauer Model 1903 Bolt Action Sporting Carbine $1000
Caliber: 6.5×53mm (referred to in some European gun catalogues as 6.7×53mm, following the Austrian practice of designating calibers by bullet diameter). 5-shot rotary magazine. 450mm (17.7-inch) barrel. Weight: about $6\frac{1}{2}$ pounds. Double-set trigger. Two-leaf rear sight, ramp front sight. Full-length sporting stock with cheekpiece, pistol grip, trap butt plate, swivels. Pre-WWII.

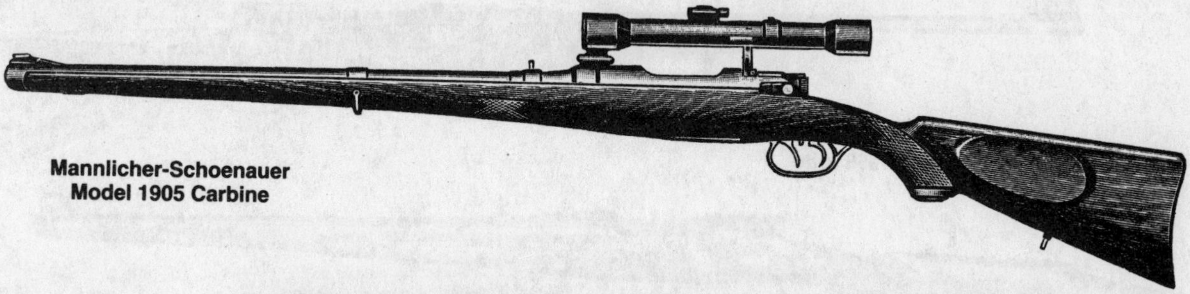

Mannlicher-Schoenauer Model 1905 Carbine

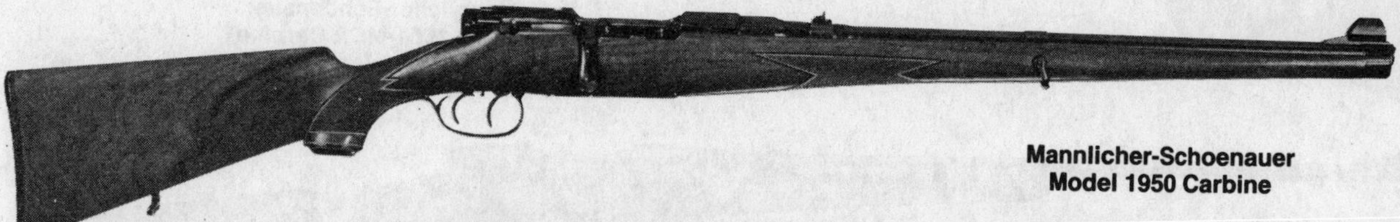

Mannlicher-Schoenauer Model 1950 Carbine

Mannlicher-Schoenauer Model 1950 Rifle

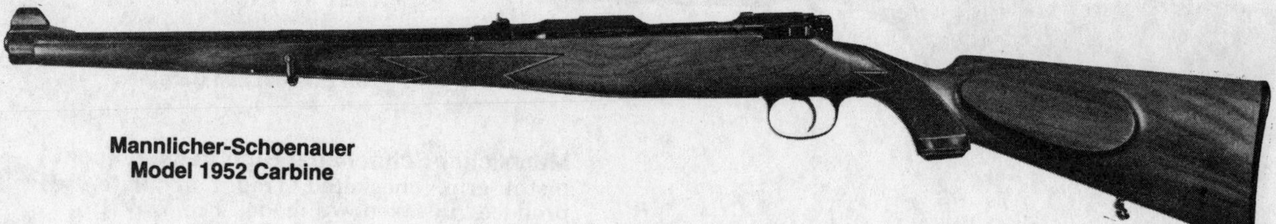

Mannlicher-Schoenauer Model 1952 Carbine

Mannlicher-Schoenauer Model 1905 Carbine . . . $910
Same as Model 1903, except caliber 9×56mm and has 19.7-inch barrel, weighs about 6¾ pounds. Pre-WWII.

Mannlicher-Schoenauer Model 1908 Carbine . . . $915
Same as Model 1905, except calibers 7×57mm and 8×56mm. Pre-WWII.

Mannlicher-Schoenauer Model 1910 Carbine . . . $925
Same as Model 1905, except caliber 9.5×57mm. Pre-WW II.

Mannlicher-Schoenauer Model 1924 Carbine . . $1200
Same as Model 1905, except caliber 30-06 (7.62×63mm). Pre-WWII.

Mannlicher-Schoenauer Model 1950 Bolt Action Sporting Rifle $995
Calibers: 257 Roberts, 270 Win., 30-06. 5-shot rotary magazine. 24-inch barrel. Weight: about 7¼ pounds. Single trigger or double-set trigger. Redesigned low bolt handle, shot-gun-type safety. Folding leaf open rear sight, hooded ramp front sight. Improved half-length stock with cheekpiece, pistol grip, checkered, ebony forend tip, swivels. Made 1950-52.

Mannlicher-Schoenauer Model 1950 Carbine . . . $825
Same general specifications as Model 1950 Rifle except has 20-inch barrel, full-length stock, weighs about 7 pounds. Made 1950-52.

Mannlicher-Schoenauer Model 1950 6.5 Carbine $875
Same as other Model 1950 Carbines except caliber 6.5×53mm, has 18¼-inch barrel, weighs 6¾ pounds. Made 1950-52.

Mannlicher-Schoenauer Model 1952 Improved Carbine $995
Same as Model 1950 Carbine except has swept-back bolt handle, redesigned stock. Calibers: 257, 270, 7mm, 30-06. Made 1952-56.

Mannlicher-Schoenauer Model 1952 Improved 6.5 Carbine $995
Same as Model 1952 Carbine except caliber 6.5×53mm, has 18¼-inch barrel. Made 1952-56.

Mannlicher-Schoenauer Model 1952 Improved Sporting Rifle $1095
Same as Model 1950 except has swept-back bolt handle, redesigned stock. Calibers: 257, 270, 30-06, 9.3×62mm. Made 1952-56.

Mannlicher-Schoenauer
Model 1956 Rifle

Mannlicher-Schoenauer
Model 1961-MCA Carbine

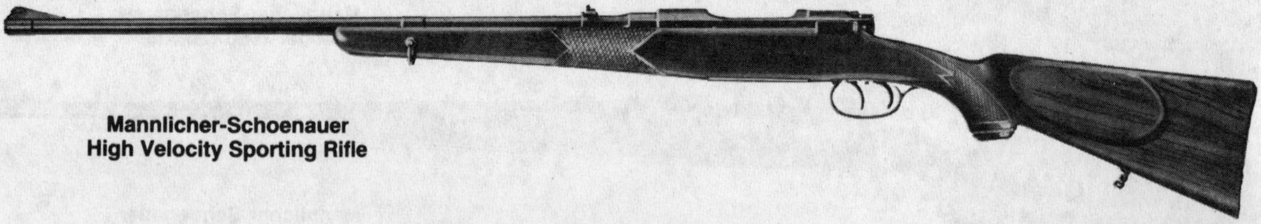

Mannlicher-Schoenauer
High Velocity Sporting Rifle

Mannlicher-Schoenauer
M72 Model L/M Carbine

Mannlicher-Schoenauer Model 1956 Custom Carbine $850
Same general specifications as Models 1950 and 1952 Carbines, except has redesigned stock with high comb. Calibers: 243, 6.5mm, 257, 270, 7mm, 30-06, 308. Made 1956 to 1960.

Mannlicher-Schoenauer Model 1956 Custom Sporting Rifle $795
Same general specifications as Models 1950 and 1952 except 22-inch barrel, redesigned stock with high comb. Calibers: 243 and 30-06. Made 1956 to 1960.

Mannlicher-Schoenauer Carbine, Model 1961-MCA $795
Same as Model 1956 Carbine, except has universal Monte Carlo design stock. Calibers: 243 Win., 6.5mm, 270, 308, 30-06. Made 1961 to 1971.

Mannlicher-Schoenauer Rifle, Model 1961-MCA . . $775
Same as Model 1956 Rifle, except has universal Monte Carlo design stock. Calibers: 243, 270, 30-06. Made 1961 to 1971.

Mannlicher-Schoenauer High Velocity Bolt Action Sporting Rifle $1000
Calibers: 7×64 Brenneke, 30-06 (7.62×63), 8×60 Magnum, 9.3×62, 10.75×68mm. 23.6-inch barrel. Weight: about 7½ pounds. British-style 3-leaf open rear sight, ramp front sight. Half-length sporting stock with cheek-piece,

Mannlicher-Schoenauer High Velocity (cont.)
pistol grip, checkered, trap butt plate, swivels. Also produced in takedown model. Pre-WWII.

Mannlicher-Schoenauer M72 Model L/M Carbine $560
Same general specifications as M72 Model L/M Rifle, except has 20-inch barrel and full-length stock, weighs about 7.2 pounds. Made from 1972 to date.

Mannlicher-Schoenauer M72 Model L/M Rifle . . $560
M72 bolt action, type L/M receiver, front-locking bolt, internal rotary magazine (5-round). Calibers: 22-250, 5.6×57, 6mm Rem., 243 Win., 6.5×57, 270 Win., 7×57, 7×64, 308 Win., 30-06. 23⅝-inch barrel. Weight: about 7.3 pounds. Single- or double-set trigger (mechanisms interchangeable). Open rear sight, hooded ramp front sight. Half stock of European walnut, checkered forearm and pistol grip, Monte Carlo cheekpiece, rosewood forend tip, recoil pad, QD swivels. Made from 1972 to date.

Mannlicher-Schoenauer M72 Model S Rifle $725
Same general specifications as M72 Model L/M Rifle, except has magnum action, 4-round magazine, 25⅝-inch barrel, weighs about 8.6 pounds. Calibers: 6.5×68, 7mm Rem. Mag., 8×68S, 9.3×64, 375 H&H Mag. Made from 1972 to date.

Mannlicher-Schoenauer M72 Model S/T Rifle . . . $775
Same as M72 Model S Rifle, except has heavy 25⅝-inch barrel, weighs about 9.3 pounds. Calibers: 300 Win. Mag., 9.3×64, 375 H&H Mag., 458 Win. Mag. Option of 23⅝-inch barrel in latter caliber. Made from 1975 to date.

MARLIN FIREARMS CO.
North Haven, Connecticut

Marlin Model 9 Carbine $185
Same general specifications as the Model 45, except comes in caliber 9mm with 12-shot clip. Made from 1985 to date.

Marlin Model 15Y $80
Bolt-action, single-shot "Little Buckaroo" rifle. Caliber: 22 Short, Long or Long Rifle. 16 1/4-inch barrel. Weight: 4 1/4 pounds. Thumb safety. Ramp front sight, adjustable open rear. One-piece walnut Monte Carlo stock with full pistol grip. Made from 1984 to date.

Marlin Model 18 Baby Slide Action Repeater . . . $285
Exposed hammer. Solid frame. Caliber: 22 Long Rifle, Long, Short. Tubular magazine holds 14 Short. 20-inch barrel, round or octagon. Weight: 3 3/4 pounds. Open rear sight, bead front sight. Plain straight-grip stock and slide handle. Made 1906 to 1909.

Marlin Model 20 Slide Action Repeating Rifle . . . $250
Exposed hammer. Takedown. Caliber: 22 Long Rifle, Long, Short. Tubular magazine: half-length holds 15 Short, 12 Long, 10 Long Rifle; full-length holds 25 Short, 20 Long, 18 Long Rifle. 24-inch octagon barrel. Weight: about 5 pounds. Open rear sight, bead front sight. Plain straight-grip stock, grooved slide handle. Made 1907 to 1922. *Note:* After 1920 was designated "Model 20-S."

Marlin Model 25 Bolt Action Rifle $80
Caliber: 22 Short, Long or Long Rifle. 7-shot clip. 22-inch barrel. Weight: 5 1/2 pounds. Ramp front sight, adjustable open rear. One-piece walnut Monte Carlo stock with full pistol grip. Mar-Shield finish. Made from 1984 to date.

Marlin Model 25 Slide Action Repeating Rifle . . . $295
Exposed hammer. Takedown. Caliber: 22 Short (also handles 22 CB Caps). Tubular magazine holds 15 Short. 23-inch barrel. Weight: about 4 pounds. Open rear sight, beaded front sight. Plain straight-grip stock and slide handle. Made 1909 to 1910.

Marlin Model 9
9mm Carbine

Marlin Model 15Y
"Little Buckaroo"

Marlin Model 20

Marlin Model 25
Bolt Action Rifle

Marlin Model 25M Bolt Action W/Scope $100
Caliber: 22 Win. Mag. RF. 7-shot clip. 22-inch barrel. Weight: 6 pounds. Ramp front sight with brass bead, adjustable open rear. Walnut-finished stock with Monte Carlo styling and full pistol grip. Sling swivels. Made from 1986 to date.

Marlin Model 25 MB
Midget Magnum

Marlin Model 25MB Midget Magnum $125
Bolt action. Caliber: 22 Win. Mag. RF. 7-shot capacity. $16^1/_4$-inch barrel. Weight: $4^3/_4$ pounds. Walnut-finished Monte Carlo-style stock with full pistol grip and abbreviated forend. Ramp front sight with brass bead, adjustable open rear sight. Thumb safety. Made from 1986 to date.

Marlin Model 27 Slide Action Repeating Rifle . . . $275
Exposed hammer. Takedown. Calibers: 25-20, 32-20. $^2/_3$ magazine (tubular) holds 7 shots. 24-inch octagon barrel. Weight: about $5^3/_4$ pounds. Open rear sight, bead front sight. Plain straight-grip stock, grooved slide handle. Made 1910-16.

Marlin Model 27S $250
Same as Model 27, except has round barrel, also chambered for 25 Stevens R.F. Made 1920 to 1932.

Marlin Model 29 Slide Action Repeating Rifle . . . $250
Similar to Model 20, has 23-inch round barrel, half magazine only, weighs about $5^3/_4$ pounds. **Model 37** is same type except has 24-inch barrel and full magazine. Made 1913-16.

Marlin Model 30AS Lever Action $225
Caliber: 30/30 Win. 6-shot tubular magazine. 20-inch barrel with Micro-Groove rifling. $38^1/_4$ inches overall. Weight: 7 pounds. Brass bead front sight, adjustable rear. Solid top receiver, offset hammer spur for scope use. Walnut-finished hardwood stock with pistol grip. Mar-Shield finish. Made from 1985 to date.

Marlin Model 32 Slide Action Repeating Rifle . . . $275
Hammerless. Takedown. Caliber: 22 Long Rifle, Long, Short. $^2/_3$ tubular magazine holds 15 Short, 12 Long, 10 L.R.; full magazine, 25 Short, 20 Long, 18 L.R. 24-inch octagon barrel. Weight: about $5^1/_2$ pounds. Open rear sight, bead front sight. Plain pistol-grip stock, grooved slide handle. Made 1914-15.

Marlin Model 25M w/Scope

Marlin Model 27

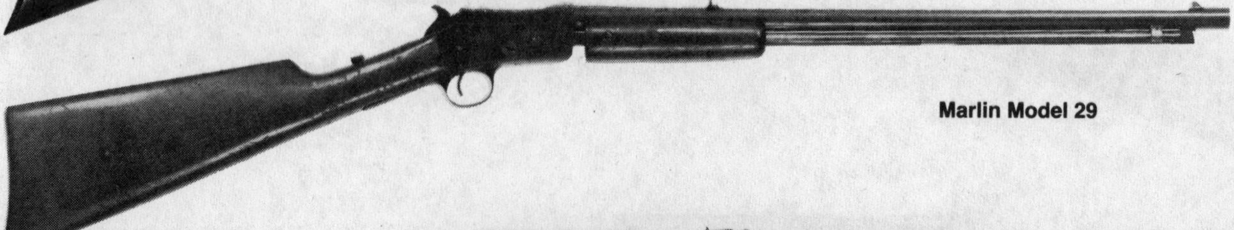
Marlin Model 29

Marlin Model 30AS
Lever Action Rifle

Marlin Model 36 Lever Action Repeating Carbine **$295**
Calibers: 30-30, 32 Special. 6-shot tubular magazine. 20-inch barrel. Weight: about 6½ pounds. Open rear sight, bead front sight. Pistol-grip stock, semibeavertail forearm with carbine barrel band. Made 1936 to 1948. *Note:* In 1936, this was designated "Model 1936."

Marlin Model 36 Sporting Carbine **$325**
Same as Model 36A rifle except has 20-inch barrel, weighs 6¼ pounds.

Marlin Model 36A Lever Action Repeating Rifle .. **$300**
Same as Model 36 Carbine, except has ⅔ magazine holding 5 cartridges, 24-inch barrel, weighs 6¾ pounds, has hooded front sight, semibeavertail forearm.

Marlin Model 36A-DL **$325**
Same as Model 36A, except has deluxe checkered stock and forearm, swivels and sling.

Marlin Model 38 Slide Action Repeating Rifle ... **$275**
Hammerless. Takedown. Caliber: 22 Long Rifle, Long, Short. ⅔ magazine (tubular) holds 15 Short, 12 Long, 10 Long Rifle. 24-inch octagon barrel. Weight: about 5½ pounds. Open rear sight, bead front sight. Plain pistol-grip stock, grooved slide handle. Made 1920 to 1930.

Marlin Model 39 Carbine **$180**
Same as Model 39M, except has lightweight barrel, ¾ magazine (capacity: 18 Short, 14 Long, 12 Long Rifle), slimmer forearm. Weight: 5¼ pounds. Made 1963-67.

Marlin Model 39 90th Anniversary Carbine **$500**
Carbine version of 90th Anniversary Model 39A. 500 made in 1960. Value is for carbine in new, unfired condition.

Marlin 39 Century Ltd. **$245**
Commemorative version of Model 39A. Receiver inlaid with brass medallion, Marlin Centennial 1870-1970. Square lever. 20-inch octagon barrel. Fancy walnut straight-grip stock and forearm; brass forend cap, butt plate, nameplate in buttstock. 35,388 made in 1970.

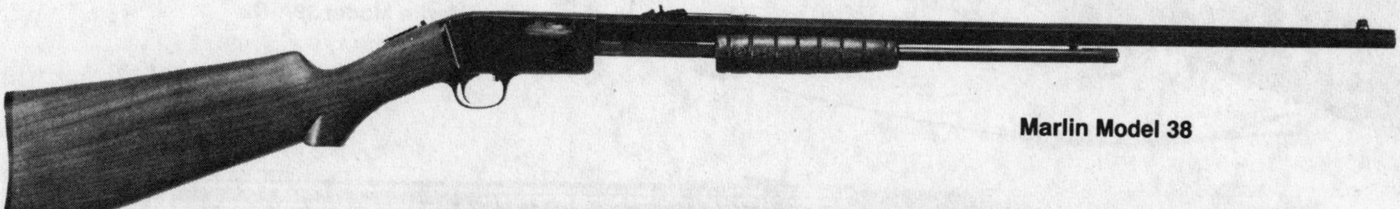

Marlin Model 38

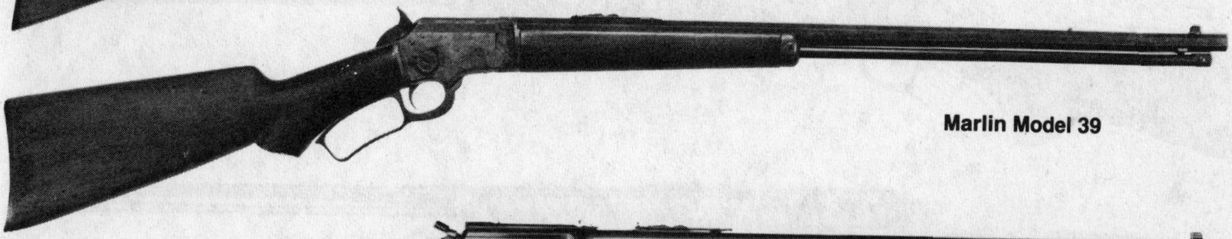

Marlin Model 39

Marlin Model 39 Carbine

Marlin Model 39
90th Anniversary Carbine

Marlin 39 Century Ltd.

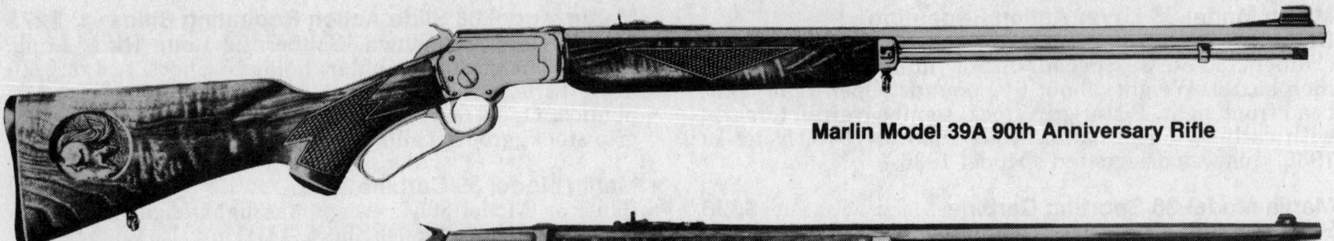

Marlin Model 39A 90th Anniversary Rifle

Marlin 39A Article II Rifle

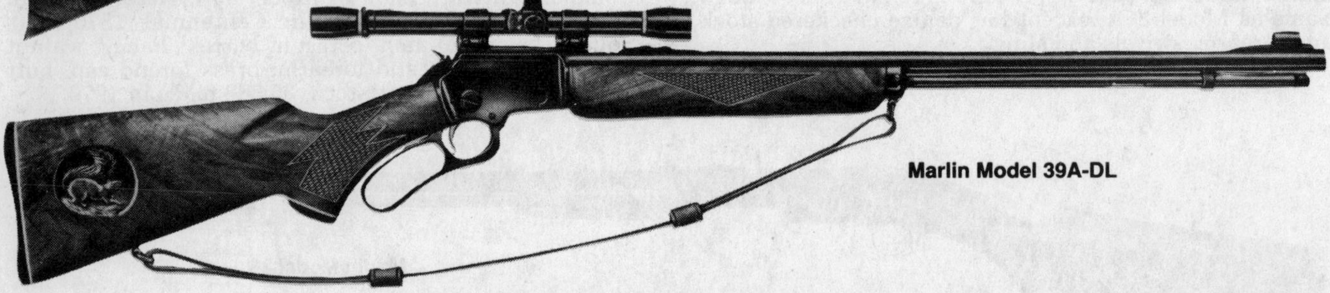

Marlin Model 39A-DL

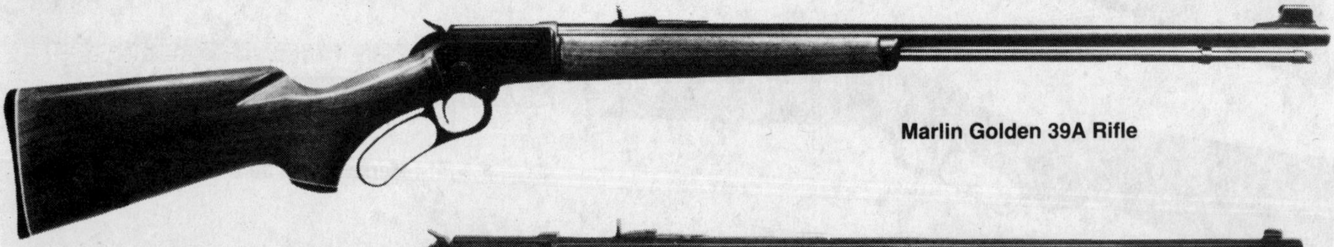

Marlin Golden 39A Rifle

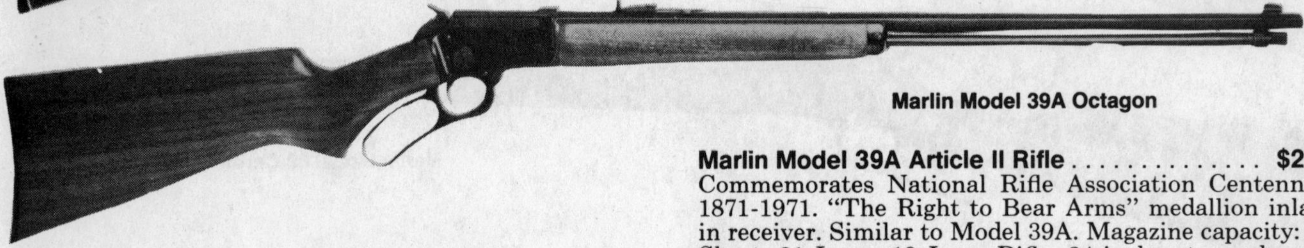

Marlin Model 39A Octagon

Marlin Model 39 Lever Action Repeating Rifle . . $395
Takedown. Casehardened receiver. Caliber: 22 Long Rifle, Long, Short. Tubular magazine holds 25 Short, 20 Long, 18 Long Rifle. 24-inch octagon barrel. Weight: about 5¾ pounds. Open rear sight, bead front sight. Plain pistol-grip stock and forearm. Made 1922 to 1947.

Marlin Model 39A $195
General specifications same as Model 39, except has blued receiver, round barrel, heavier stock with semibeavertail forearm, weighs about 6½ pounds. Made 1938 to 1960.

Marlin Model 39A 90th Anniversary Rifle $510
Commemorates Marlin's 90th anniversary. Same general specifications as Golden 39A, except has chrome-plated barrel and action, stock and forearm of select walnut, finely checkered, carved figure of a squirrel on right side of buttstock. 500 made in 1960. Value is for rifle in new, unfired condition.

Marlin Model 39A Article II Rifle $240
Commemorates National Rifle Association Centennial 1871-1971. "The Right to Bear Arms" medallion inlaid in receiver. Similar to Model 39A. Magazine capacity: 26 Short, 21 Long, 19 Long Rifle. 24-inch octagon barrel. Fancy walnut pistol-grip stock and forearm; brass forend cap, butt plate. 6,244 made in 1971.

Marlin Model 39A-DL $225
Same as 90th Anniversary Model 39A, except blued barrel and action. Made 1960-63.

Marlin Golden 39A Rifle $180
Same as Model 39A, except has gold-plated trigger, hooded ramp front sight, sling swivels. Made from 1960 to date.

Marlin Model 39A "Mountie" Lever Action Repeating Rifle $185
Same as Model 39A, except has lighter, straight-grip stock, slimmer forearm. Weight: 6¼ pounds. Made 1953 to 1960.

Marlin Model 39A Octagon $215
Same as Golden 39A, except has octagon barrel, plain bead front sight, slimmer stock and forearm, no pistol-grip cap or swivels. Made 1973.

Marlin Model 39D

Marlin 39M Article II Carbine

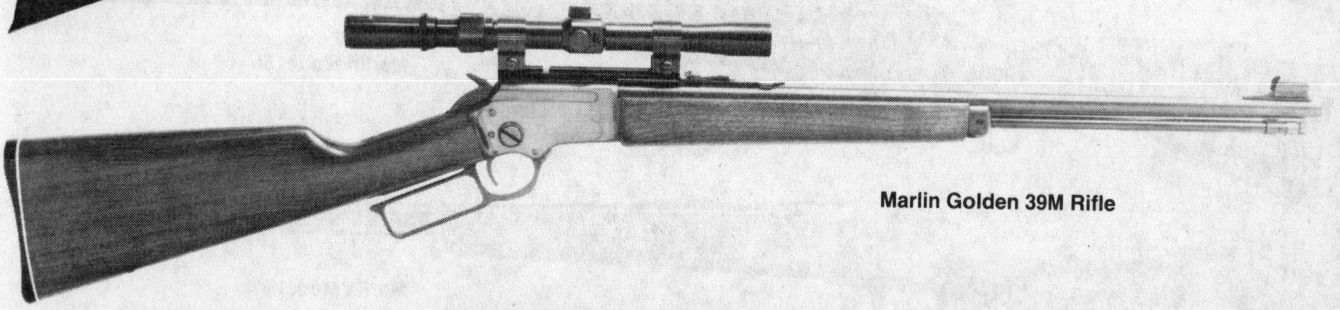

Marlin Golden 39M Rifle

Marlin Model 39M Octagon

Marlin Model 45

Marlin Model 39D **$160**
Same as Model 39M, except has pistol-grip stock, forearm with barrel band. Made 1970-74.

Marlin 39M Article II Carbine **$250**
Same as 39A Article II Rifle, except has straight-grip buttstock, square lever, 20-inch octagon barrel, reduced magazine capacity. 3,824 made in 1971.

Marlin Golden 39M **$180**
Calibers: 22 Short, Long and Long Rifle. Tubular magazine holds 21 Short, 16 Long or 15 Long Rifle cartridges. 20-inch barrel. 36 inches overall. Weight: about 6 pounds. Gold-plated trigger. Hooded ramp front sight, adjustable folding semi-buckhorn rear. Two-piece, straight-grip American black walnut stock. Sling swivels. Mar-Shield finish. Originally designated "Golden 39 Mountie." Made from 1960 to date.

Marlin Model 39M "Mountie" Carbine **$185**
Same as Model 39A "Mountie" Rifle, except has 20-inch barrel and reduced magazine capacity: 21 Short, 16 Long, 15 Long Rifle. Weight: 6 pounds. Made 1954 to 1960.

Marlin Model 39M Octagon **$195**
Same as Golden 39M, except has octagon barrel, plain bead front sight, no swivels. Made 1973.

Marlin Model 45 . . . . **$190**
Semiautomatic action. Caliber: 45 Auto. 7-shot clip. $16^1/_2$-inch barrel. $35^1/_2$ inches overall. Weight: $6^3/_4$ pounds. Manual bolt hold-open. Ramp front sight with brass bead, adjustable folding rear sight. Receiver drilled and tapped for scope mount. Walnut-finished hardwood stock with pistol grip. Made from 1985 to date.

Marlin Model 49DL

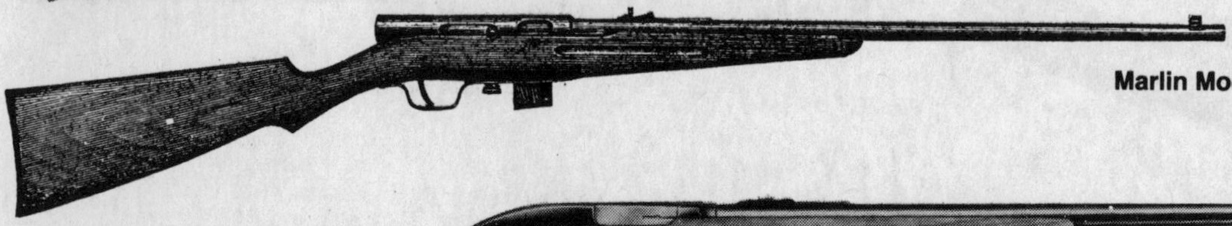

Marlin Model 50

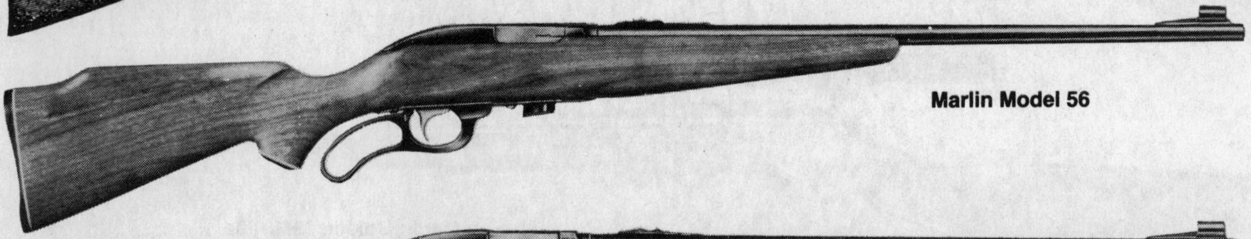

Marlin Model 56

Marlin Model 57

Marlin Model 62

Marlin Model 49 . . . . $90
Same as Model 99C, except has two-piece stock, checkered after 1970. Made 1968 to 1971.

Marlin Model 49DL $100
Same as Model 49, except has scrollwork on sides of receiver, checkered stock and forearm. Made 1971 to date.

Marlin Model 50 Autoloading Rifle $85
Takedown. Caliber: 22 Long Rifle. 6-shot detachable box magazine. 22-inch barrel. Weight: about 6 pounds. Open rear sight, bead front sight. Plain pistol-grip stock, forearm with finger grooves. Made 1931-34.

Marlin Model 50E $95
Same as Model 50, except has peep rear sight, hooded front sight.

Marlin Model 56 Levermatic Rifle $155
Same as Model 57 except clip-loading. Magazine holds eight rounds. Weight: about 5¾ pounds. Made 1955 to 1964.

Marlin Model 57 Levermatic Rifle $165
Lever action. Caliber: 22 Long Rifle, 22 Long, 22 Short. Tubular magazine holds 19 Long Rifle, 21 Long, 27 Short. 22-inch barrel. Weight: about 6¼ pounds. Open rear sight, hooded ramp front sight. Monte Carlo-style stock with pistol grip. Made 1959 to 1965.

Marlin Model 57M Levermatic $175
Same as Model 57, except chambered for 22 Winchester Magnum Rimfire cartridge, has 24-inch barrel, 15-shot magazine. Made 1960-69.

Marlin Model 62 Levermatic Rifle $225
Lever action. Calibers: 256 Magnum, 30 Carbine. 4-shot clip magazine. 23-inch barrel. Weight: 7 pounds. Open rear sight, hooded ramp front sight. Monte Carlo-style stock with pistol grip, swivels and sling. Made in 256 Magnum 1963 to 1966; in 30 Carbine 1966-69.

Marlin Model 65 Bolt Action Single Shot Rifle $65
Takedown. Caliber: 22 Long Rifle, Long, Short. 24-inch barrel. Weight: about 5 pounds. Open rear sight, bead front sight. Plain pistol-grip stock with grooved forearm. Made 1932-38. **Model 65E** is same as Model 65, except has rear peep sight and hooded front sight.

Marlin Model 70P "Papoose"

Marlin Model 75C Semiautomatic

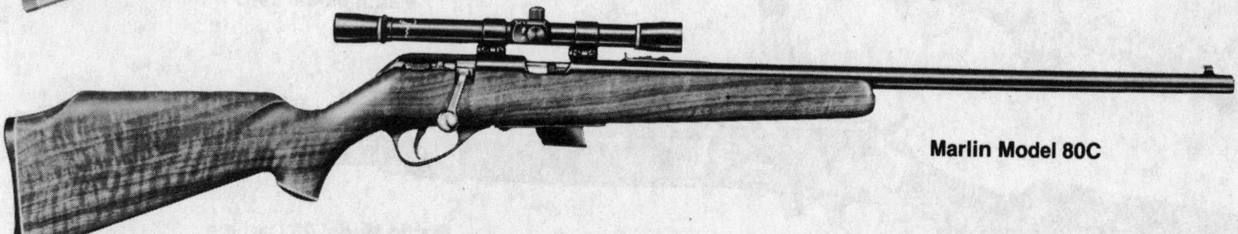

Marlin Model 80C

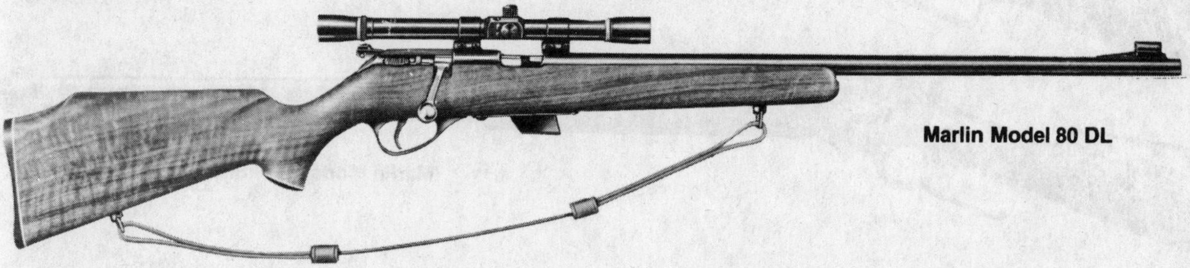

Marlin Model 80 DL

Marlin Model 70P Semiautomatic **$95**
"Papoose." Caliber: 22 Long Rifle. 7-shot clip. 16¼-inch barrel. 35¼ inches overall. Weight: 3¾ pounds. Ramp front sight, adjustable open rear sight. Side ejection, manual bolt hold-open. Cross-bolt safety. Walnut-finished hardwood stock with abbreviated forend, pistol grip. Made from 1984 to date.

Marlin Model 75C Semiautomatic **$80**
Caliber: 22 Long Rifle. 13-shot tubular magazine. 18-inch barrel. 36½ inches overall. Weight: 5 pounds. Side ejection. Cross-bolt safety. Ramp front sight, adjustable open rear sight. Monte Carlo-style walnut-finished hardwood stock with pistol grip. Made from 1985 to date.

Marlin Model 80 Bolt Action Repeating Rifle **$75**
Takedown. Caliber: 22 Long Rifle, Long, Short. 8-shot detachable box magazine. 24-inch barrel. Weight: about 6 pounds. Open rear sight, bead front sight. Plain pistol-grip stock. Made 1934-39.

Marlin Model 80C **$85**
Improved version of Model 80 with same general specifications, has stock with semibeavertail forearm. Made 1940 to 1970.

Marlin Model 80DL **$95**
Same as Model 80C except has peep rear sight, hooded front sight, swivels. Made 1940 to 1965.

Marlin Model 80E **$85**
Same as Model 80, except has peep rear sight, hooded front sight. Made 1934 to 1940.

Marlin Model 81 Bolt Action Repeating Rifle **$80**
Takedown. Caliber: 22 Long Rifle, Long, Short. Tubular magazine holds 24 Short, 20 Long, 18 Long Rifle. 24-inch barrel. Weight: about 6¼ pounds. Open rear sight, bead front sight. Plain pistol-grip stock. Made 1937 to 1940.

Marlin Model 81C **$90**
Improved version of Model 81 with same general specifications, has stock with semibeavertail forearm. Made 1940 to 1970.

Marlin Model 81 DL

Marlin Model 88-C

Marlin Model 89-C

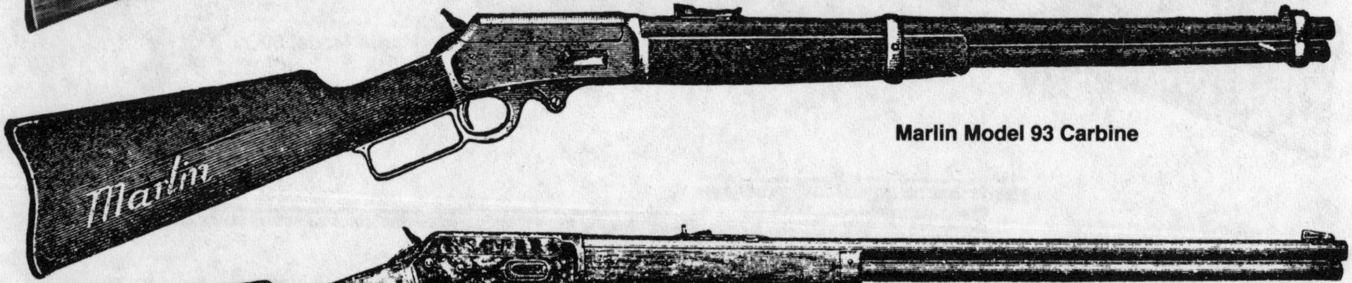

Marlin Model 93 Carbine

Marlin Model 93 Rifle

Marlin Model 81DL **$90**
Same as Model 81C, except has peep rear sight, hooded front sight, swivels. Discontinued 1965.

Marlin Model 81E **$85**
Same as Model 81, except has peep rear sight and hooded front sight.

Marlin Model 88-C Autoloading Rifle **$75**
Takedown. Caliber: 22 Long Rifle. Tubular magazine in buttstock holds 14 cartridges. 24-inch barrel. Weight: about 6³/₄ pounds. Open rear sight, hooded front sight. Plain pistol-grip stock. Made 1947 to 1956.

Marlin Model 88-DL **$90**
Same as Model 88-C except has receiver peep sight, checkered stock and sling swivels. Made 1953-56.

Marlin Model 89-C Autoloading Rifle **$75**
Clip magazine version of Model 88-C. 7-shot clip (12-shot in later models); other specifications same. Made 1950 to 1961.

Marlin Model 89-DL **$95**
Same as Model 89-C except has receiver peep sight and sling swivels.

Marlin Model 92 Lever Action Repeating Rifle . . **$425**
Calibers: 22 Short, Long, Long Rifle; 32 Short, Long (rimfire or centerfire by changing firing pin). Tubular magazines: holding 25 Short, 20 Long, 18 Long Rifle (22); 17 Short, 14 Long (32); 16-inch barrel model has shorter magazine holding 15 Short, 12 Long, 10 Long Rifle. Barrel lengths: 16 (22 cal. only), 24, 26, 28 inches. Weight: with 24-inch bbl., about 5¹/₂ pounds. Open rear sight, blade front sight. Plain straight-grip stock and forearm. Made 1892 to 1916. *Note:* Originally designated "Model 1892."

Marlin Model 93 Carbine **$595**
Same as Standard Model 93, except calibers 30-30 and 32 Special only; has 7-shot magazine, 20-inch round barrel, weighs about 6³/₄ pounds, carbine sights.

Marlin Model 93 Lever Action Repeating Rifle . . **$425**
Solid frame or takedown. Calibers: 25-36 Marlin, 30-30, 32 Special, 32-40, 38-55. Tubular magazine holds 10 cartridges. 26-inch round or octagon barrel standard; also

Marlin Model 98

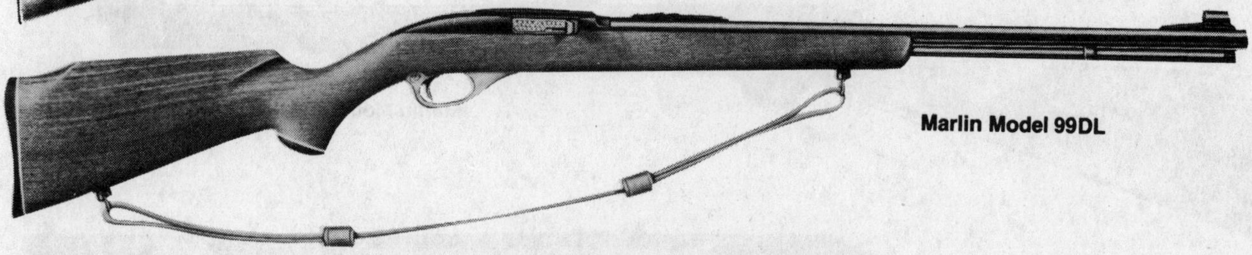

Marlin Model 99DL

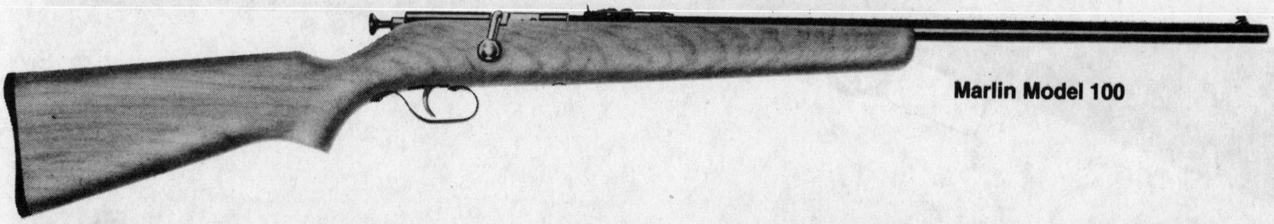

Marlin Model 100

Marlin Model 93 Lever Action Repeating Rifle (cont.)
made with 28-, 30- and 32-inch barrels. Weight: about $7\frac{1}{4}$ pounds. Open rear sight, bead front sight. Plain straight-grip stock and forearm. Made from 1893 to 1936. *Note:* Prior to 1915 designated "Model 1893."

Marlin Model 93 Musket **$895**
Same as Standard Model 93, except has 30-inch barrel, angular bayonet, ramrod under barrel, musket stock, full-length military-style forearm. Weight: 8 pounds. Made 1893 to 1915.

Marlin Model 93SC Sporting Carbine **$695**
Same as Model 93 Carbine, except has $\frac{2}{3}$ magazine holding 5 shots, weighs $6\frac{1}{2}$ pounds.

Marlin Model 94 Lever Action Repeating Rifle . . **$695**
Solid frame or takedown. Calibers: 25-20, 32-20, 38-40, 44-40. 10-shot tubular magazine. 24-inch round or octagon barrel. Weight: about 7 pounds. Open rear sight, bead front sight. Plain straight-grip stock and forearm (also available with pistol-grip stock). Made 1894 to 1934. *Note:* Prior to 1906 designated "Model 1894."

Marlin Model 97 Lever Action Repeating Rifle . . **$465**
Takedown. Caliber: 22 Long Rifle, Long, Short. Tubular magazine; full length holds 25 Short, 20 Long, 18 Long Rifle; half length holds 16 Short, 12 Long and 10 Long Rifle. Barrel lengths: 16, 24, 26, 28 inches. Weight: about 6 pounds. Open rear sight and bead front sight. Plain straight-grip stock and forearm (also available with pistol-grip stock). Made 1897 to 1922. *Note:* Prior to 1905 designated "Model 1897."

Marlin Model 98 Autoloading Rifle **$75**
Solid frame. Caliber: 22 Long Rifle. Tubular magazine holds 15 cartridges. 22-inch barrel. Weight: about $6\frac{3}{4}$ pounds. Open rear sight, hooded ramp front sight. Monte Carlo stock with cheekpiece. Made 1950 to 1961.

Marlin Model 99 Autoloading Rifle **$75**
Caliber: 22 Long Rifle. Tubular magazine holds 18 cartridges. 22-inch barrel. Weight: about $5\frac{1}{2}$ pounds. Open rear sight, hooded ramp front sight. Plain pistol-grip stock. Made 1959 to 1961.

Marlin Model 99C **$75**
Same as Model 99 except has gold-plated trigger, receiver grooved for tip-off scope mounts, Monte Carlo stock (checkered in current production). Made 1962 to date.

Marlin Model 99DL **$70**
Same as Model 99 except has gold-plated trigger, jeweled breech bolt, Monte Carlo stock with pistol grip, swivels and sling. Made 1960-65.

Marlin Model 99M1 Carbine **$90**
Same as Model 99C except styled after U.S. 30M1 Carbine; 9-shot tubular magazine, 18-inch barrel, open rear sight, military-style ramp front sight, carbine stock with handguard and barrel band, sling swivels. Weight: $4\frac{1}{2}$ pounds. Made 1966 to 1979.

Marlin Model 100 Bolt Action Single Shot Rifle . . . **$65**
Takedown. Caliber: 22 Long Rifle, Long, Short. 24-inch barrel. Weight: about $4\frac{1}{2}$ pounds. Open rear sight, bead front sight. Plain pistol-grip stock. Made 1936 to 1960.

Marlin Model 100SB **$150**
Same as Model 100 except smoothbore for use with 22 shot cartridges, shotgun sight. Made 1936 to 1941.

Marlin Model 100 Tom Mix Special **$275**
Same as Model 100 except has peep rear sight and hooded front sight, sling. Made 1936 to 1946.

Marlin Model 101 . . . . **$125**
Improved version of Model 100 with same general specifications except has stock with beavertail forearm, weighs about 5 pounds. Introduced 1951; discontinued.

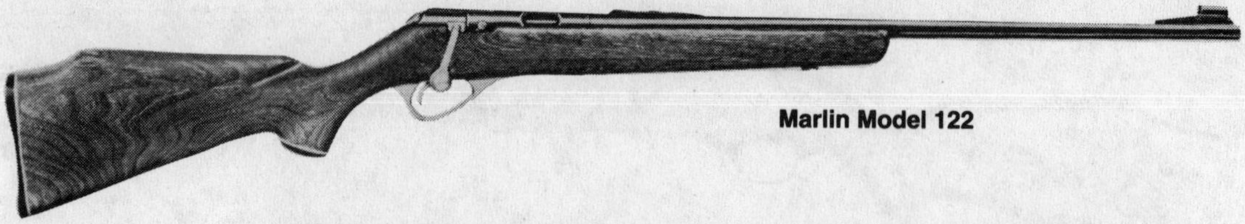

Marlin Model 122

Marlin Model 336 Marauder

Marlin Model 336 Octagon

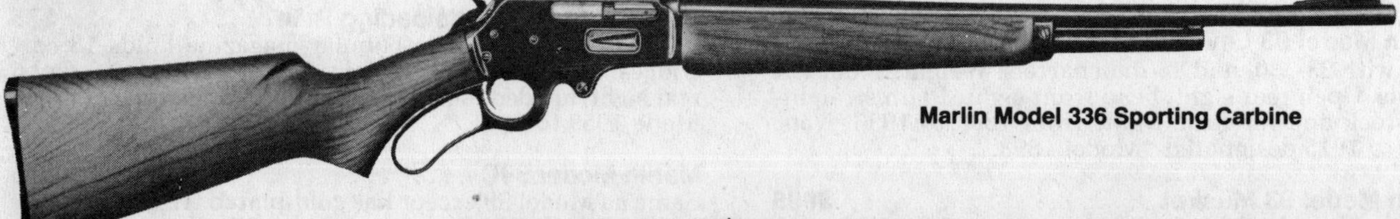

Marlin Model 336 Sporting Carbine

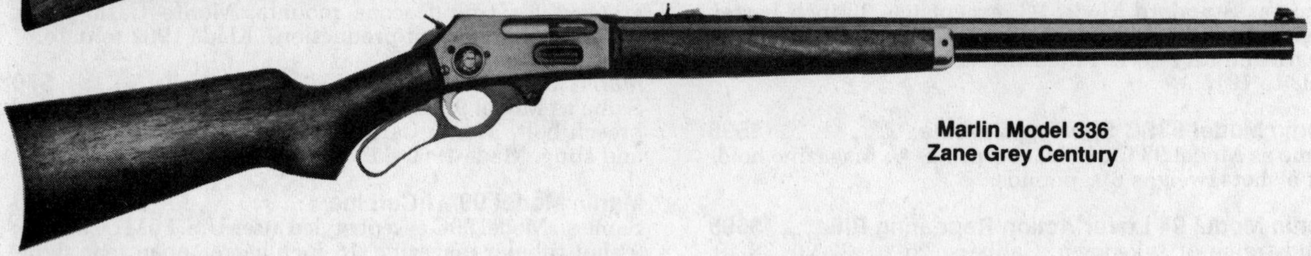

Marlin Model 336
Zane Grey Century

Marlin Model 101DL $130
Same as Model 101 except has peep rear sight, hooded front sight, swivels. Discontinued.

Marlin Model 122 Single Shot Junior Target Rifle $85
Bolt action. Caliber: 22 Long Rifle, 22 Long, 22 Short. 22-inch barrel. Weight: about 5 pounds. Open rear sight, hooded ramp front sight. Monte Carlo stock with pistol grip, swivels, sling. Made 1961-65.

Marlin Model 322 Bolt Action Varmint Rifle $375
Sako short Mauser action. Caliber: 222 Rem. 3-shot clip magazine. 24-inch medium weight barrel. Checkered stock. Two-position peep sight, hooded ramp front sight. Weight: about $7\frac{1}{2}$ pounds. Made 1954-57.

Marlin Model 336 Marauder $250
Same as Model 336 Texan Carbine except has $16\frac{1}{4}$-inch barrel, weighs about $6\frac{1}{4}$ pounds. Made from 1963-64.

Marlin Model 336 Micro Groove Zipper $495
General specifications same as Model 336 Sporting Carbine, except caliber 219 Zipper. Made 1955 to 1961.

Marlin Model 336 Octagon $225
Same as Model 336T, except chambered for 30-30 only, has 22-inch octagon barrel. Made 1973.

Marlin Model 336 Sporting Carbine $185
Same as Model 336A rifle, except has 20-inch barrel, weighs $6\frac{1}{4}$ pounds. Made 1948 to 1963.

Marlin Model 336 Zane Grey Century $325
Similar to Model 336A, except has 22-inch octagonal barrel, caliber 30-30; Zane Grey Centennial 1872-1972 medallion inlaid in receiver; selected walnut stock with classic pistol grip and forearm; brass butt plate, forend cap. Weight: 7 pounds. 10,000 produced (numbered ZG1 through ZG10,000). Made 1972.

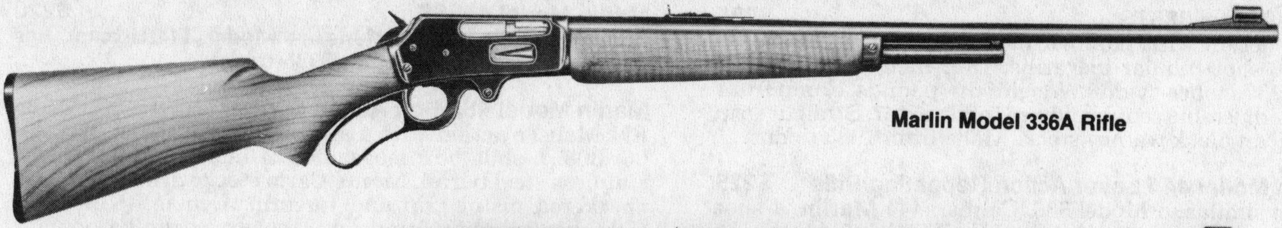

Marlin Model 336A Rifle

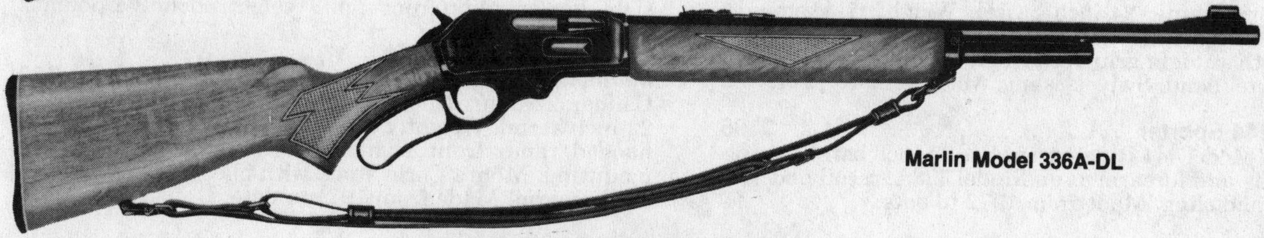

Marlin Model 336A-DL

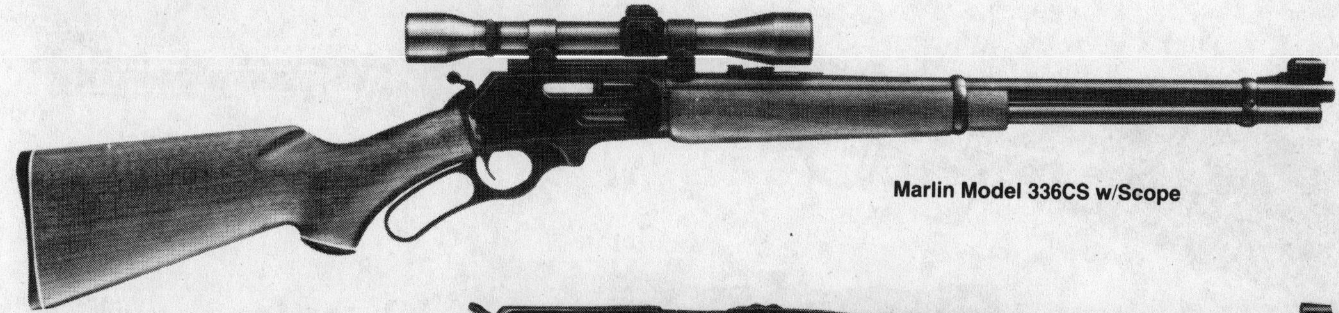

Marlin Model 336CS w/Scope

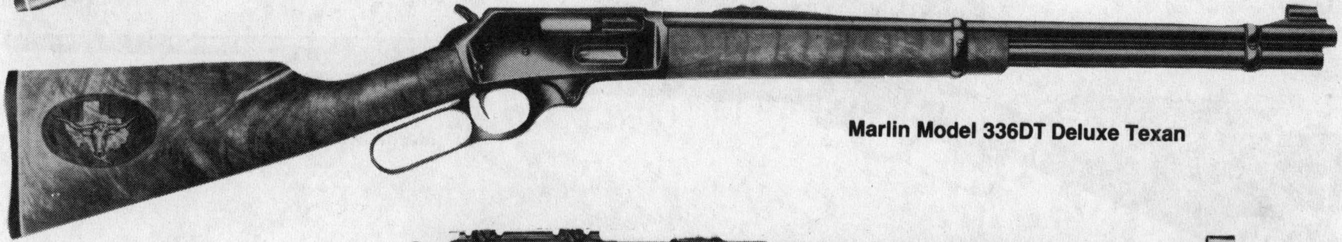

Marlin Model 336DT Deluxe Texan

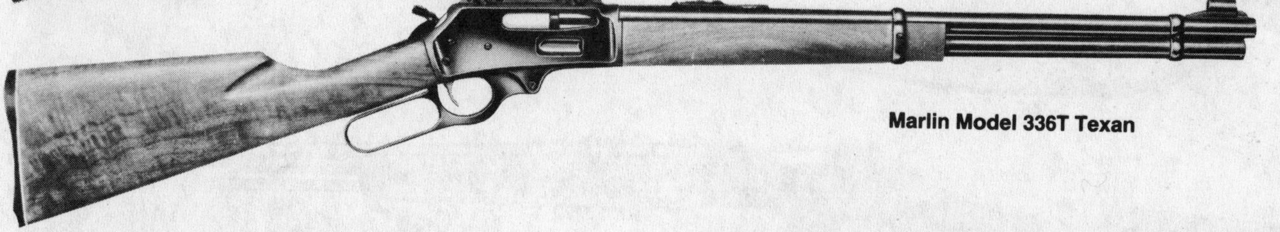

Marlin Model 336T Texan

Marlin Model 336A Lever Action Rifle $185
Improved version of Model 36A Rifle with same general specifications, has improved action with round breech bolt. Calibers: 30-30, 32 Special (discontinued 1963), 35 Rem. (introduced 1952). Made 1948 to 1963; reintroduced 1973, still in production. *Note:* Recent production has sling swivels and carrying strap.

Marlin Model 336A-DL $235
Same as Model 336A Rifle except has deluxe checkered stock and forearm, swivels and sling. Made 1948 to 1963.

Marlin Model 336C Lever Action Carbine $210
Improved version of Model 36 Carbine with same general specifications, has improved action with round breech bolt. Made 1948 to date. *Note:* Cal. 35 Rem. introduced 1953. Cal. 32 Win. Spl. discontinued 1963. Recent production has squared finger lever.

Marlin Model 336CS W/Scope $245
Lever action with hammer block safety. Caliber: 30/30 Win. or 35 Rem. 6-shot tubular magazine. 20-inch barrel with Micro-Groove rifling. 38½ inches overall. Weight: 7 pounds. Ramp front sight, adjustable semibuckhorn folding rear. Solid top receiver for scope mount or receiver sight; offset hammer spur for scope use. American black walnut stock with pistol grip, fluted comb. Mar-Shield finish. Made from 1985 to date.

Marlin Model 336DT Deluxe Texan $225
Same as Model 336T, except has select walnut stock and forearm, hand-carved longhorn steer and map of Texas on buttstock. Made 1962-64.

Marlin Model 336T Texan Lever Action Carbine . . $195
Same as Model 336 Carbine, except has straight-grip stock and is not available in caliber 32 Special. Made from 1953 to date. Caliber 44 Magnum made 1963-67.

Marlin Model 336TS **$225**
Lever action with hammer block safety. Caliber: 30/30 Win. 6-shot tubular magazine. 18½-inch Micro-Groove barrel. 37 inches overall. Weight: 6½ pounds. Ramp front sight, adjustable semibuckhorn folding rear. Straight-grip American black walnut stock. Made from 1985 to date.

Marlin Model 444 Lever Action Repeating Rifle . **$225**
Action similar to Model 336. Caliber: 444 Marlin. 4-shot tubular magazine. 24-inch barrel. Weight: 7½ pounds. Open rear sight, hooded ramp front sight. Monte Carlo stock with straight grip, recoil pad. Carbine-style forearm with barrel band. Swivels, sling. Made 1965 to 1971.

Marlin 444 Sporter **$195**
Same as Model 444 Rifle, except has 22-inch barrel, pistol-grip stock and forearm as on Model 336A, recoil pad, QD swivels and sling. Made from 1972 to date.

Marlin Model 444SS **$220**
Same general specifications as Model 444, except has hammer safety. Made from 1985 to date.

Marlin Model 455 Bolt Action Sporter **$395**
FN Mauser action with Sako trigger. Calibers: 270, 30-06, 308. 5-shot box magazine. 24-inch medium weight stainless steel barrel. Monte Carlo stock with cheekpiece, checkered pistol grip and forearm. Lyman 48 receiver sight, hooded ramp front sight. Weight: about 8½ pounds. Made 1957-59.

Marlin Model 780 Bolt Action Repeating Rifle **$90**
Caliber: 22 Long Rifle, Long, Short. 7-shot clip magazine. 22-inch barrel. Weight: about 5½ pounds. Open rear sight, hooded ramp front sight. Receiver grooved for scope mounting. Monte Carlo stock with checkered pistol grip and forearm. Made from 1971 to date.

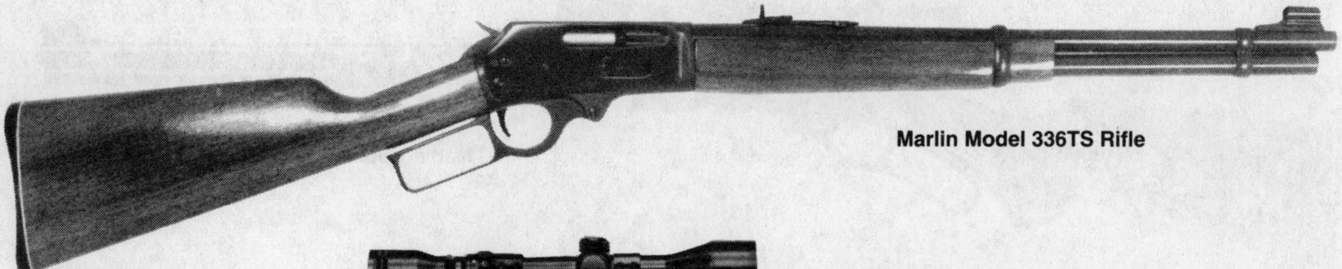

Marlin Model 336TS Rifle

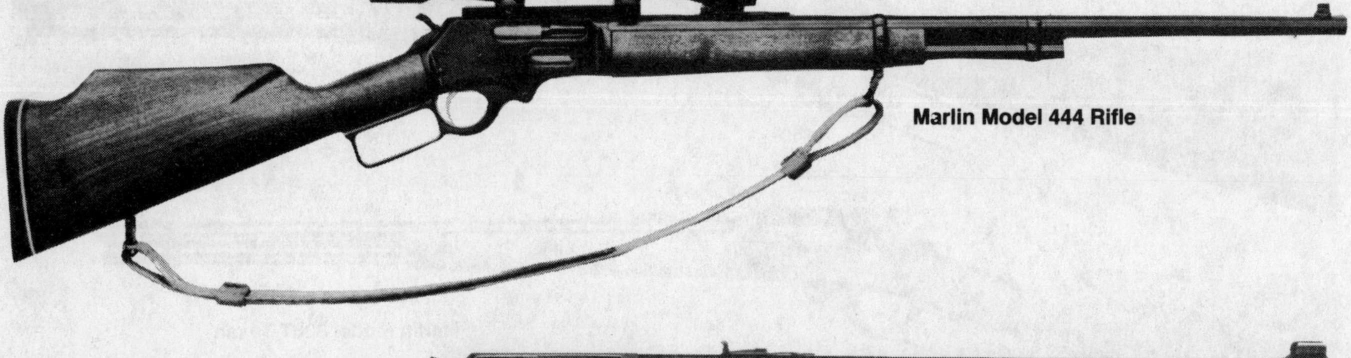

Marlin Model 444 Rifle

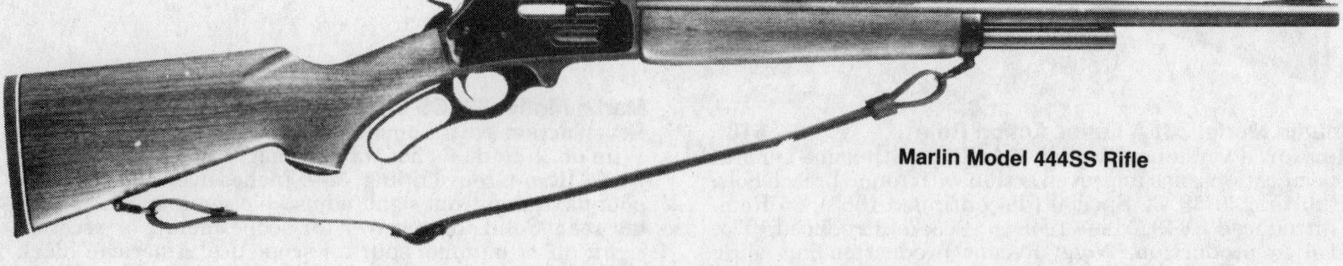

Marlin Model 444SS Rifle

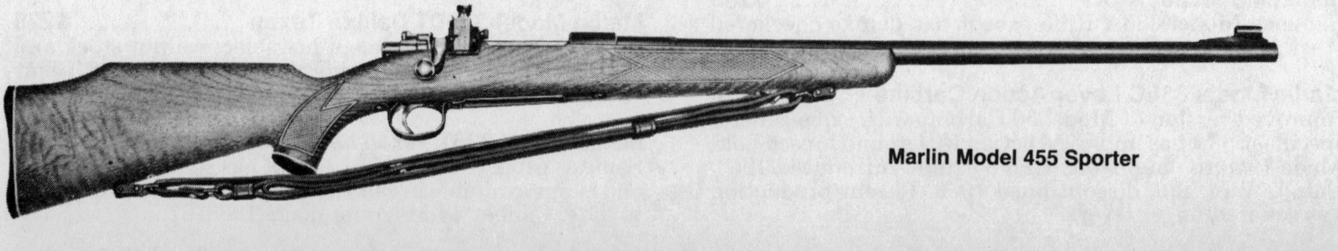

Marlin Model 455 Sporter

Marlin Model 780

Marlin Model 781

Marlin Model 783

Marlin Model 781 . . . . **$95**
Same general specifications as Model 780, except has tubular magazine (capacity: 17 LR, 19 Long, 25 Short), weighs about 6 pounds. Made from 1971 to date.

Marlin Model 782 . . . . **$100**
Same general specifications as Model 780, except chambered for 22 Win. Magnum R.F., weighs about 6 pounds, has swivels and sling. Made from 1971 to date.

Marlin Model 783 . . . . **$105**
Same as Model 782, except has 12-shot tubular magazine. Made from 1971 to date.

Marlin Model 980 22 Magnum **$95**
Bolt action. Caliber: 22 Win. Magnum R.F. 8-shot clip magazine. 24-inch barrel. Weight: about 6 pounds. Open rear sight, hooded ramp front sight. Monte Carlo stock, swivels, sling. Made 1962 to 1970.

Marlin Model 989 Autoloading Rifle **$95**
Caliber: 22 Long Rifle. 7-shot clip magazine. 22-inch barrel. Weight: about 5½ pounds. Open rear sight, hooded ramp front sight. Monte Carlo walnut stock with pistol grip. Made 1962-66.

Marlin Model 989M2 Carbine **$100**
Same as Model 99M1, except clip-loading, 7-shot magazine. Made 1966 to 1979.

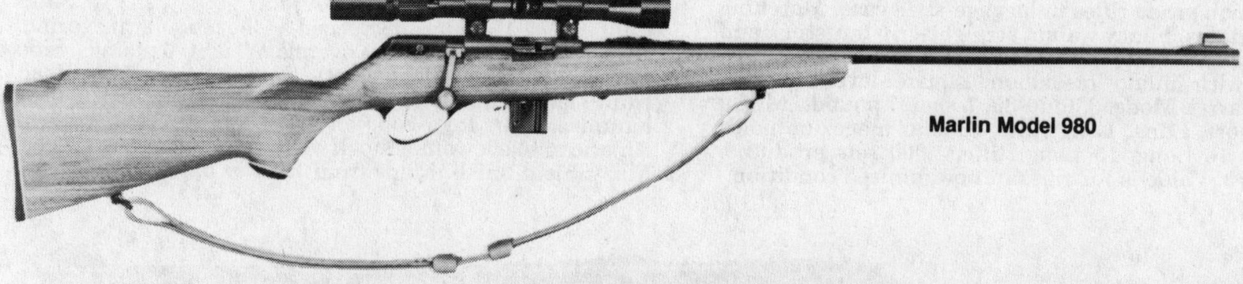

Marlin Model 980

Marlin Model 989

Marlin Model 989M2

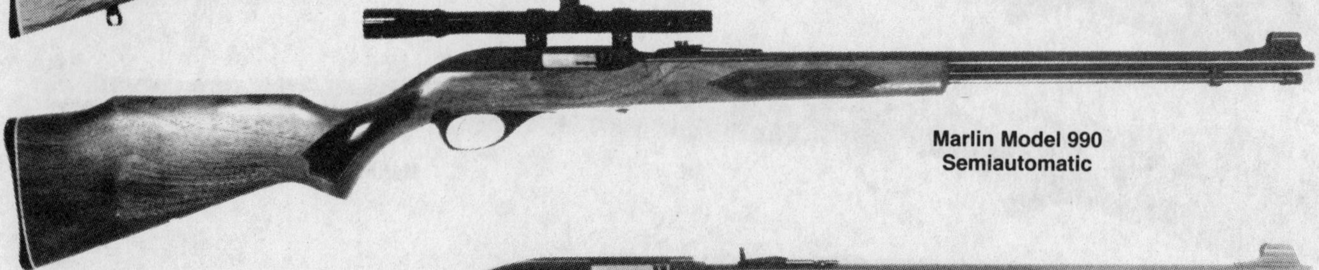

Marlin Model 990 Semiautomatic

Marlin Model 995 Semiautomatic

Marlin Model 990 Semiautomatic **$110**
Caliber: 22 Long Rifle. 17-shot tubular magazine. 22-inch barrel. 40¾ inches overall. Weight: 5½ pounds. Side ejection. Cross-bolt safety. Ramp front sight with brass bead, adjustable semibuckhorn folding rear. Receiver grooved for tip-off scope mount. Monte Carlo-style American black walnut stock with checkered pistol grip and forend. Made from 1985 to date.

Marlin Model 995 Semiautomatic **$105**
Caliber: 22 Long Rifle. 7-shot clip magazine. 18-inch barrel. 36¾ inches overall. Weight: about 5 pounds. Cross-bolt safety. Ramp front sight with brass bead, adjustable folding semibuckhorn rear sight. Monte Carlo-style American black walnut stock with checkered pistol grip and forend. Made from 1984 to date.

Marlin 1870-1970 Centennial Matched Pair, Models 336 and 39 . . . . **$1460**
Presentation grade rifles in luggage-style case. Matching serial numbers. Fancy walnut straight-grip buttstock and forearm, brass butt plate and forend cap. Engraved receiver with inlaid medallion; square lever. 20-inch octagon barrel. Model 336: 30-30, 7-shot, 7 pounds. Model 39: 22 Short, Long, Long Rifle; tubular magazine holds 21 Short, 16 Long, 15 Long Rifle. 1,000 sets produced. Made 1970. Value is for rifles in new, unfired condition.

Marlin Model 1892 Lever Action Rifle
See Marlin Model 92.

Marlin Model 1893 Lever Action Rifle
See Marlin Model 93.

Marlin Model 1894 Carbine **$215**
Replica of original Model 94. Caliber: 44 Rem. 10-shot magazine. 20-inch round barrel. Weight: 6 pounds. Open rear sight, ramp front sight. Straight-grip stock, forearm with barrel band. Made from 1969 to date.

Marlin Model 1894 Lever Action Rifle
See Marlin Model 94.

Marlin Model 1894 Octagon **$295**
Same general specifications as Model 1894 Carbine, except has octagon barrel, bead front sight. Made 1973.

Marlin Model 1894 Sporter **$215**
Same general specifications as Model 1894 Carbine, except has 22-inch barrel, 6-shot magazine. Made 1973.

Marlin Model 1894CS Lever Action **$205**
Caliber: 357 Magnum, 38 Special. 9-shot tubular magazine. 18½-inch barrel. 36 inches overall. Weight: 6 pounds. Side ejection. Hammer block safety. Square finger lever. Bead front sight, adjustable semibuckhorn folding rear. Offset hammer spur for scope use. Two-piece straight-grip American black walnut stock with white butt plate spacer. Mar-Shield finish. Made from 1985 to date.

Marlin Model 1894 Carbine

Marlin 1870-1970 Centennial Matched Pair

Marlin Model 1894 Octagon

Marlin Model 1894 Sporter

Marlin Model 1894CS

Marlin Model 1894M

Marlin Model 1894M Lever Action $225
Caliber: 22 Win. Mag. RF. 11-shot tubular magazine. 20-inch barrel. Weight: 6¼ pounds. Ramp front sight with brass bead and Wide-Scan hood; adjustable semibuckhorn folding rear sight. Offset hammer spur for scope use. Straight-grip American black walnut stock with white butt plate spacer. Squared finger lever. Made from 1986 to date.

Marlin Model 1894S Lever Action $200
Calibers: 44 Rem. Mag., 44 S&W Special, 41 Mag. 10-shot tubular magazine. 20-inch barrel. 37½ inches overall. Weight: 6 pounds. Sights and stock same as Model 1894M. Made from 1984 to date.

Marlin 1895 45/70 Repeater $225
Model 336-type action. Caliber: 45/70 Government. 4-shot magazine. 22-inch barrel. Weight: about 7 pounds. Open rear sight, bead front sight. Straight-grip stock, forearm with metal end cap, QD swivels, leather sling. Made from 1972 to date.

Marlin Model 1895 Lever Action Repeating Rifle . . $750
Solid frame or takedown. Calibers: 33 WCF, 38-56, 40-65, 40-70, 40-82, 45-70. 9-shot tubular magazine. 24-inch round or octagon barrel standard (other lengths available). Weight: about 8 pounds. Open rear sight, bead front sight. Plain stock and forearm (also available with pistol-grip stock). Made 1895 to 1915.

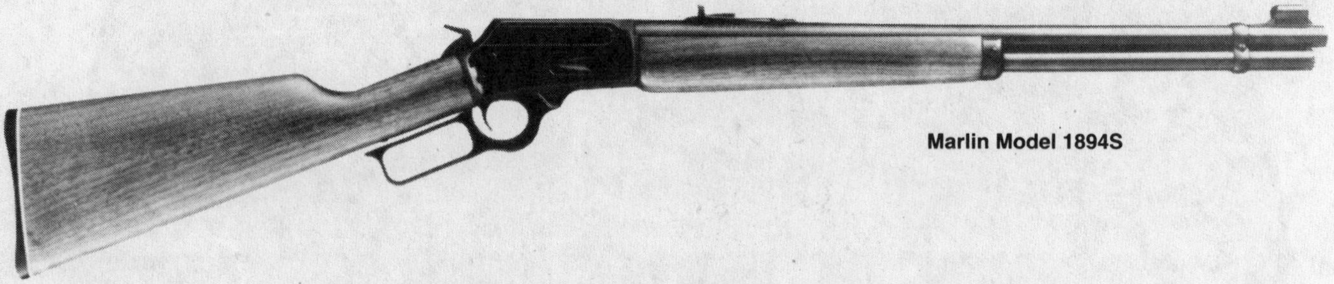
Marlin Model 1894S

Marlin Model 1895
45/70 Repeater

Marlin Model 1895

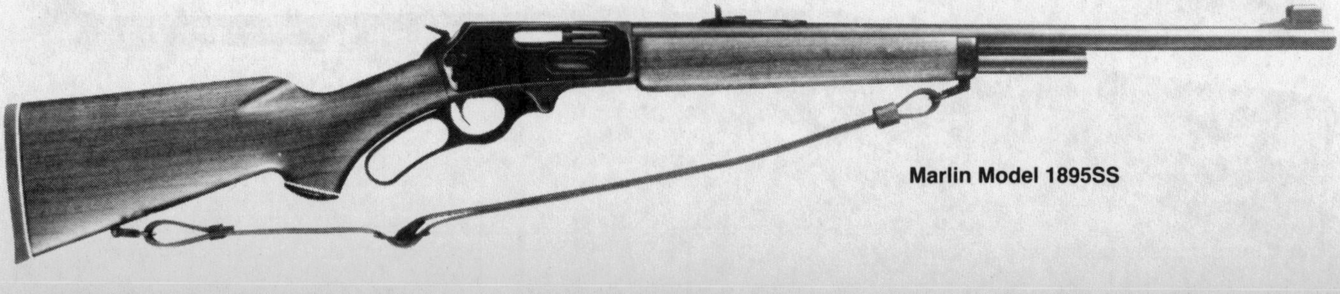
Marlin Model 1895SS

Marlin Model A-1 Autoloader

Marlin 1895SS Lever Action $255
Caliber: 45/70 Govt. 4-shot tubular magazine. 22-inch barrel with Micro-Groove rifling. 40½ inches overall. Weight: 7½ pounds. Ramp front sight with brass bead and Wide-Scan hood; adjustable semibuckhorn folding rear. Solid top receiver tapped for scope mount or receiver sight. Offset hammer spur for scope use. Two-piece American black walnut stock with fluted comb, pistol grip, sling swivels. Made from 1984 to date.

Marlin Model 1897 Lever Action Rifle
See Marlin Model 97.

Marlin Model 1936 Lever Action Carbine
See Marlin Model 36.

Marlin Model A-1 Autoloading Rifle $130
Takedown. Caliber: 22 Long Rifle. 6-shot detachable box magazine. 24-inch barrel. Weight: about 6 pounds. Open rear sight. Plain pistol-grip stock. Made 1935 to 1946.

Marlin Model A-1C Autoloading Rifle $145
Improved version of Model A-1 with same general specifications, has stock with semibeavertail forearm. Made 1940-46.

Marlin Model A-1DL $150
Same as Model A-1C, except has peep rear sight, hooded front sight, swivels.

Marlin Model A-1E $130
Same as Model A-1, except has peep rear sight, hooded front sight.

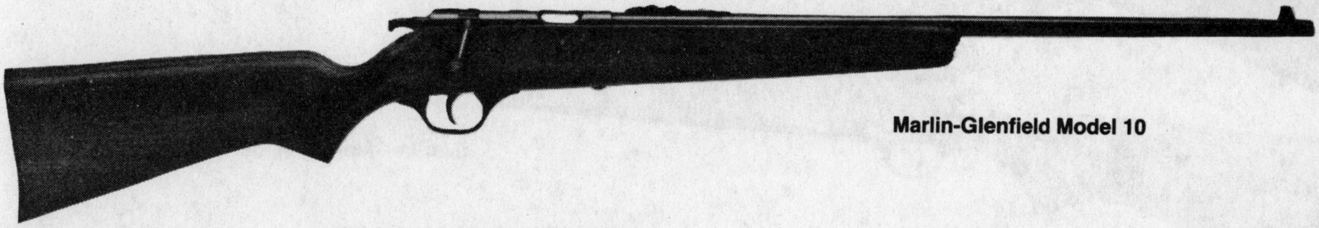

Marlin-Glenfield Model 10

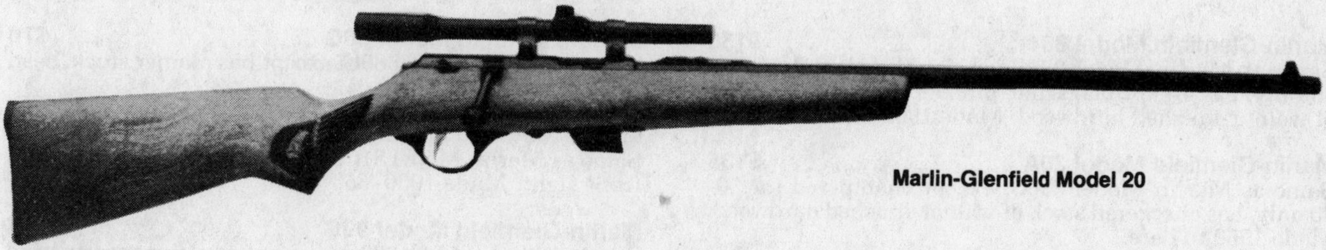

Marlin-Glenfield Model 20

Marlin-Glenfield Model 10 . . . . $65
Same as Marlin Model 101, except has walnut-finished hardwood stock. Made 1966 to 1979. *Note:* Later production has checkered pistol grip.

Marlin-Glenfield Model 20 . . . . $60
Same as Marlin Model 80/780, except has bead front sight, walnut-finished hardwood stock. Made from 1966 to date. *Note:* Recent production has checkered pistol grip.

Marlin-Glenfield Model 30A

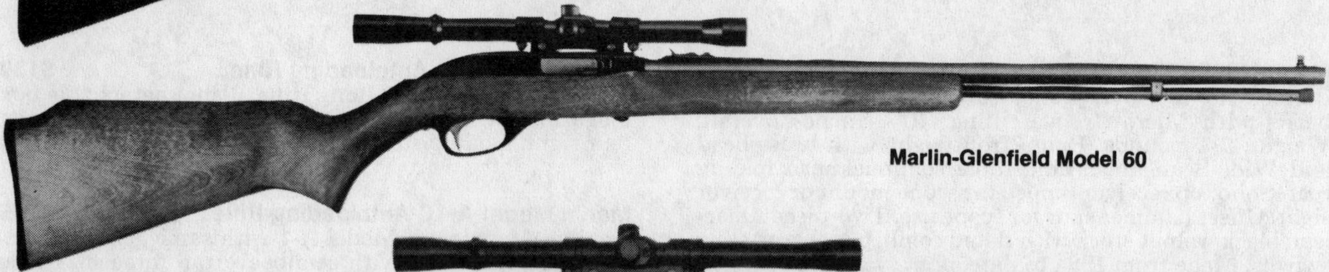

Marlin-Glenfield Model 60

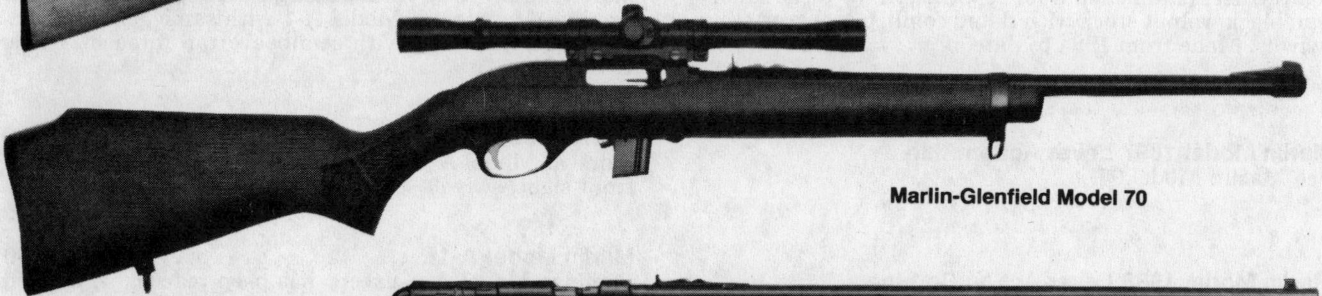

Marlin-Glenfield Model 70

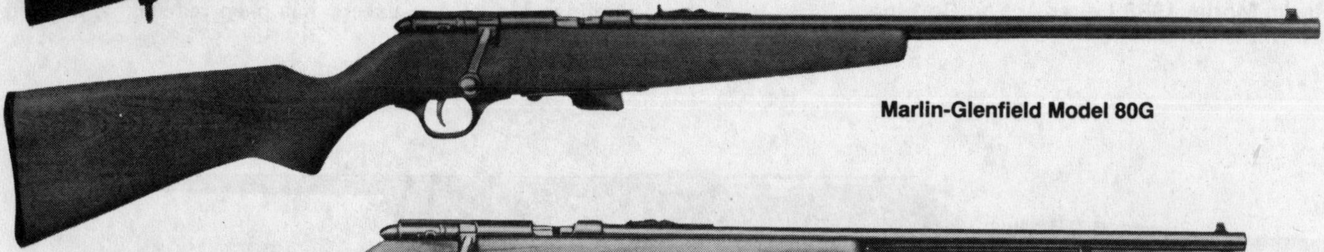

Marlin-Glenfield Model 80G

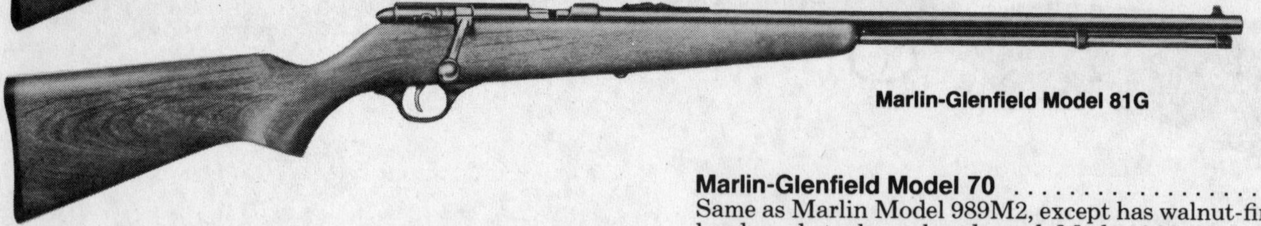

Marlin-Glenfield Model 81G

Marlin-Glenfield Model 30 . . . . **$150**
Same as Marlin Model 336C, except chambered for 30-30 only, has 4-shot magazine, plainer stock and forearm of walnut-finished hardwood. Made 1966-68.

Marlin-Glenfield Model 30A **$135**
Same as Marlin Model 336C, except chambered for 30-30 only, has checkered stock of walnut-finished hardwood. Made 1969 to date.

Marlin-Glenfield Model 36G **$220**
Same as Marlin Model 336C, except chambered for 30-30 only, has 5-shot magazine, plainer stock. Made 1960-65.

Marlin-Glenfield Model 60 . . . . **$70**
Same as Marlin Model 99C, except has walnut-finished hardwood stock. Made from 1966 to date. *Note:* Recent production has checkered pistol grip and forearm.

Marlin-Glenfield Model 70 . . . . **$70**
Same as Marlin Model 989M2, except has walnut-finished hardwood stock, no handguard. Made 1966-69.

Marlin-Glenfield Model 80G **$70**
Same as Marlin Model 80C, except has plainer stock, bead front sight. Made 1960-65.

Marlin-Glenfield Model 81G **$75**
Same as Marlin Model 81C, except has plainer stock, bead front sight. Made 1960-65.

Marlin-Glenfield Model 99G **$75**
Same as Marlin Model 99C, except has plainer stock, bead front sight. Made 1960-65.

Marlin-Glenfield Model 101G **$65**
Same as Marlin Model 101, except has plainer stock. Made 1960-65.

Marlin-Glenfield Model 989G Autoloading Rifle . . **$65**
Same as Marlin Model 989, except has plain stock, bead front sight. Made 1962-64.

MAUSER SPORTING RIFLES
Oberndorf am Neckar, Germany
Manufactured by Mauser-Werke GmbH

Prior to the end of WWI, the name of the Mauser firm was "Waffenfabrik Mauser A.-G." Shortly after WWI, it was changed to "Mauser-Werke A.-G." This may be used as a general clue to the age of genuine Original-Mauser sporting rifles made prior to WWII, since all bear either of these firm names as well as the "Mauser" banner trademark.

The first four rifles listed were manufactured prior to WWI. Those that follow were produced between World Wars I and II. The early Mauser models can generally be identified by the pistol grip, which is rounded instead of capped, and the M/98 military-type magazine floorplate and catch; the later models have hinged magazine floorplate with lever or button release.

PRE-WORLD WAR I MODELS

Mauser Bolt Action Sporting Carbine $750
Calibers: 6.5×54, 6.5×58, 7×57, 8×57, 957mm. 19¾-inch barrel. Weight: about 7 pounds. Full-stocked to muzzle. Other specifications same as for standard rifle.

Mauser Bolt Action Sporting Rifle $695
Calibers: 6.5×55, 6.5×58, 7×57, 8×57, 9×57, 9.3×62, 10.75×68. 5-shot box magazine, 23½-inch barrel. Weight: 7 to 7½ pounds. Double-set trigger. Tangent curve rear sight, ramp front sight. Pistol-grip stock, forearm with schnabel tip, swivels.

Mauser Bolt Action Sporting Rifle, Military Type $495
So-called because of "stepped" M/98-type barrel, military front sight and double-pull trigger. Calibers: 7×57, 8×57, 9×57mm. Other specifications same as for standard rifle.

Mauser Bolt Action Sporting Rifle, Short Model . $695
Calibers: 6.5×54, 8×51mm. 19¾-inch barrel. Weight: about 6¼ pounds. Other specifications same as for standard rifle.

PRE-WORLD WAR II MODELS

Mauser Model DSM34 Bolt Action Single Shot Sporting Rifle $395
Also called "Sport-model." Caliber: 22 Long Rifle. 26-inch barrel. Weight: about 7¾ pounds. Tangent curve open rear sight, barleycorn front sight. M/98 military-type stock, swivels. Introduced about 1935.

> *Note:* The "B" series of Mauser 22 rifles (Model MS350B, etc.) were improved versions of their corresponding models and were introduced about 1935.

Mauser Model EL320 Bolt Action Single Shot Sporting Rifle $250
Caliber: 22 Long Rifle. 23½-inch barrel. Weight: about 4¼ pounds. Adjustable open rear sight, bead front sight. Sporting stock with checkered pistol grip, swivels.

Mauser Model EN310 Bolt Action Single Shot Sporting Rifle $225
Caliber: 22 Long Rifle. ("22 Lang für Büchsen.") 19¾-inch barrel. Weight: about 4 pounds. Fixed open rear sight, blade front sight. Plain pistol-grip stock.

Mauser Model ES340 Bolt Action Single Shot Target Rifle $295
Caliber: 22 Long Rifle. 25½-inch barrel. Weight: about 6½ pounds. Tangent curve rear sight, ramp front sight. Sporting stock with checkered pistol grip and grooved forearm, swivels.

Mauser Model ES340B Bolt Action Single Shot Target Rifle $325
Caliber: 22 Long Rifle. 26¾-inch barrel. Weight: about 8 pounds. Tangent curve open rear sight, ramp front sight. Plain pistol-grip stock, swivels.

Mauser Model ES350 Bolt Action Single Shot Target Rifle $425
"Meistershaftsbüchse" (Championship Rifle). Caliber: 22 Long Rifle. 27½-inch barrel. Weight: about 7¾ pounds. Open micrometer rear sight, ramp front sight. Target stock with checkered pistol grip and forearm, grip cap, swivels.

Mauser Model ES350B Bolt Action Single Shot Target Rifle $370
Same general specifications as Model MS350B except single shot, weighs about 8¼ pounds.

Mauser Model KKW Bolt Action Single Shot Target Rifle $385
Caliber: 22 Long Rifle. 26-inch barrel. Weight: about 8¾ pounds. Tangent curve open rear sight, barleycorn front sight. M/98 military-type stock, swivels. *Note:* This rifle has an improved design Mauser 22 action with separate non-rotating bolt head. In addition to being produced for commercial sale, this model was used as a training rifle by the German armed forces; it was also made by Walther and Gustloff. Introduced just prior to WWII.

Mauser Model M410 Bolt Action Repeating Sporting Rifle $350
Caliber: 22 Long Rifle. 5-shot detachable box magazine. 23½-inch barrel. Weight: about 5 pounds. Tangent curve open rear sight, ramp front sight. Sporting stock with checkered pistol grip, swivels.

Mauser Model ES340B

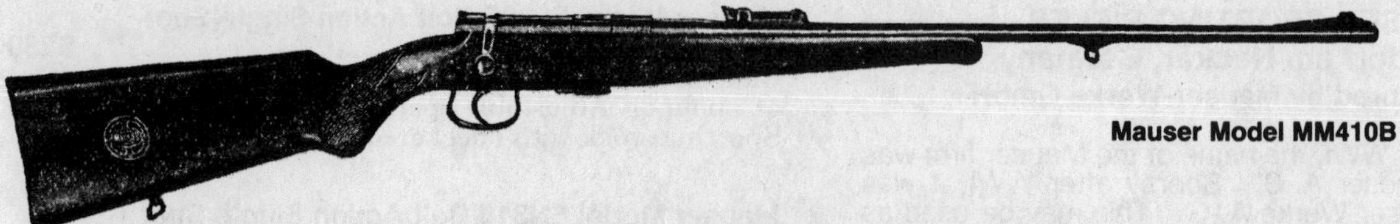

Mauser Model MM410B

Mauser Model MS350B

Mauser Model MS420B

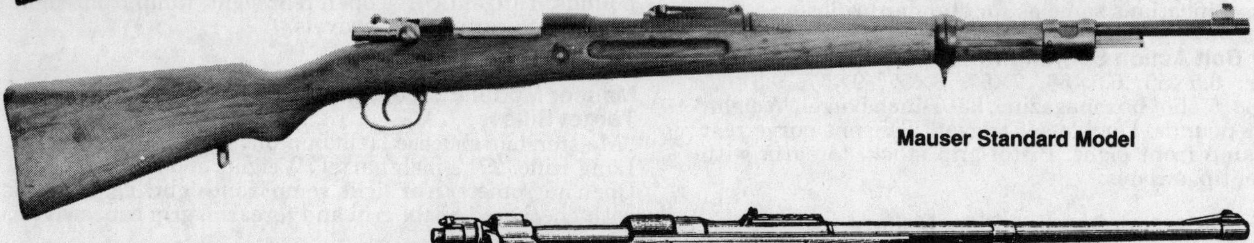

Mauser Standard Model

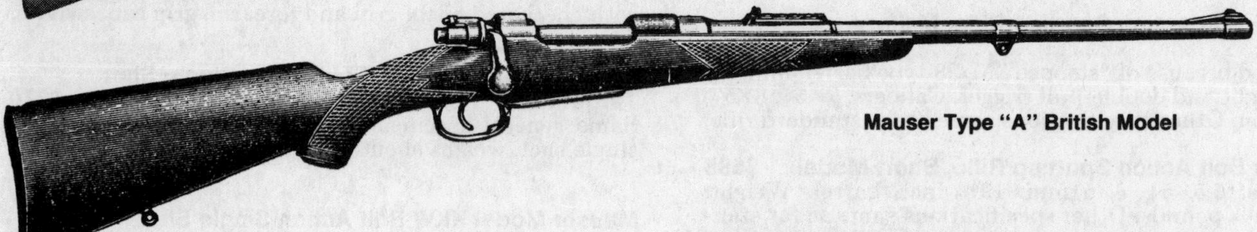

Mauser Type "A" British Model

Mauser Model MM410B Bolt Action Repeating Sporting Rifle $395
Caliber: 22 Long Rifle. 5-shot detachable box magazine. 23½-inch barrel. Weight: about 6¼ pounds. Tangent curve open rear sight, ramp front sight. Lightweight sporting stock with checkered pistol grip, swivels.

Mauser Model MS350B, Bolt Action Repeating Target Rifle $420
Caliber: 22 Long Rifle. 5-shot detachable box magazine. Receiver and barrel grooved for detachable rear sight or scope. 26¾-inch barrel. Weight: about 8½ pounds. Micrometer open rear sight, ramp front sight. Target stock with checkered pistol grip and forearm, grip cap, sling swivels.

Mauser Model MS420 Bolt Action Repeating Sporting Rifle $345
Caliber: 22 Long Rifle. 5-shot detachable box magazine. 25½-inch barrel. Weight: about 6½ pounds. Tangent curve open rear sight, ramp front sight. Sporting stock with checkered pistol grip, grooved forearm swivels.

Mauser Model MS420B Bolt Action Repeating Target Rifle $395
Caliber: 22 Long Rifle. 5-shot detachable box magazine. 26¾-inch barrel. Weight: about 8 pounds. Tangent curve open rear sight, ramp front sight. Target stock with checkered pistol grip, grooved forearm, swivels.

Mauser Standard Model Rifle $625
Refined version of the German Service Kar. 98k. Straight bolt handle. Calibers: 7mm Mauser (7×57mm), 7.9mm Mauser (8×57mm). 5-shot box magazine. 23½-inch barrel. Weight: about 8½ pounds. Blade front sight, adjustable rear sight. Walnut stock of M/98 military-type. *Note:* These rifles were made for commercial sale and are of the high quality found in the Oberndorf Mauser sporters. They bear the Mauser trademark on the receiver ring.

Mauser Type "A" Bolt Action Sporting Rifle $625
Special British Model. Calibers: 7×57, 30-06 (7.62×63), 8×60, 9×57, 9.3×62mm. 5-shot box magazine. 23½-inch round barrel. Weight: about 7¼ pounds. Military-type single trigger. Express rear sight, hooded ramp front sight. Circassian walnut sporting stock with checkered pistol grip and forearm, with or without cheekpiece, buffalo horn forend tip and grip cap, detachable swivels. Variations: octagon barrel, double-set trigger, shotgun-type safety, folding peep rear sight, tangent curve rear sight, three-leaf rear sight.

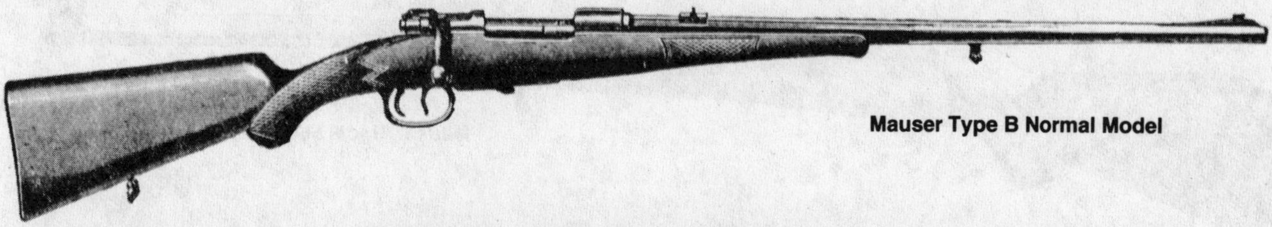

Mauser Type B Normal Model

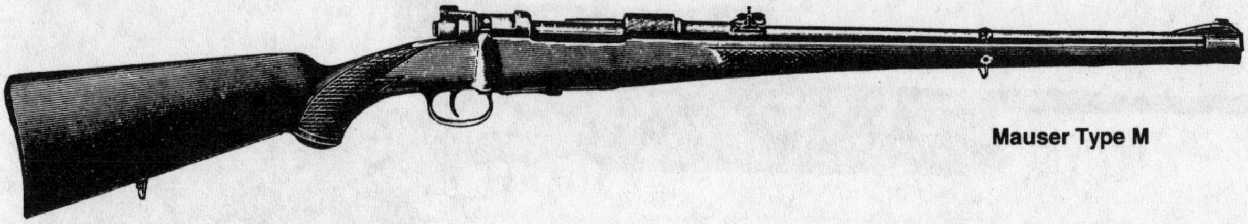

Mauser Type M

RIFLES

Mauser Type "A" Bolt Action Sporting Rifle, Magnum Model $725
Same general specifications as standard Type "A," except has Magnum action, weighs 7½ to 8½ pounds. Calibers: 280 Ross, 318 Westley Richards Express, 10.75×68mm, 404 Nitro Express.

Mauser Type "A" Bolt Action Sporting Rifle, Short Model $620
Same as standard Type "A," except has short action, 21½-inch round barrel, weighs about 6 pounds. Calibers: 250-3000, 6.5×54, 8×51mm.

Mauser Type "B" Bolt Action Sporting Rifle $695
Normal Model. Calibers: 7×57, 30-06 (7.62×63), 8×57, 8×60, 9×57, 9.3×62, 10.75×68mm. 5-shot box magazine. 23½-inch round barrel. Weight: about 7¼ pounds. Double-set trigger. Three-leaf rear sight, ramp front sight. Fine walnut stock with checkered pistol grip, schnabel forend tip, cheekpiece, grip cap, swivels. Variations: octagon or half-octagon barrel, military-type single trigger, shotgun-type trigger, shotgun-type safety, folding peep rear sight, tangent curve rear sight, telescopic sight.

Mauser Type "K" Bolt Action Sporting Rifle $595
Light Short Model. Same general specifications as Normal Type "B" model except has short action, 21½-inch round barrel, weighs about 6 pounds. Calibers: 250-3000, 6.5×54, 8×51mm.

Mauser Type "M" Bolt Action Sporting Carbine . . $625
Calibers: 6.5×54, 7×57, 30-06 (7.62×63), 8×51, 8×60, 9×57mm. 5-shot box magazine. 19¾-inch round barrel. Weight: 6 to 6¾ pounds. Double-set trigger, flat bolt handle. Three-leaf rear sight, ramp front sight. Stocked to muzzle, cheekpiece, checkered pistol grip and forearm, grip cap, steel forend cap, swivels. Variations: military-type single trigger, shotgun-type trigger, shotgun-type safety, tangent curve rear sight, telescopic sight.

Mauser Type "S" Bolt Action Sporting Carbine . $700
Calibers: 6.5×54, 7×57, 8×51, 8×60, 9×57mm. 5-shot box magazine. 19¾-inch round barrel. Weight: about 6 to 6¾ pounds. Double-set trigger. Three-leaf rear sight, ramp front sight. Stocked to muzzle, schnabel forend tip, cheekpiece, checkered pistol grip with cap, swivels. Variations: same as listed for Normal Model Type "B."

Mauser Model 66S Deluxe

Note: Production of original Mauser sporting rifles (66 Series) resumed at the Oberndorf plant in 1965 by Mauser-Jagdwaffen GmbH, now Mauser-Werke Oberndorf GmbH. The Series 2000-3000-4000 rifles, however, were made for Mauser by Friedrich Wilhelm Heym Gewehrfabrik, Muennerstadt, West Germany.

POST-WORLD WAR II MODELS

Mauser Model 66S Deluxe
On special order, Model 66S rifles and carbines are available with elaborate engraving, gold and silver inlays, and carved stocks of the finest select walnut. Added value is upwards of $1000.

Mauser Model 66S Standard

Mauser Model 66SP Super Match Target Rifle

Mauser Model 66ST Carbine

Mauser Model 66S Standard Bolt Action Sporting Rifle
Telescopic short action. Barrels interchangeable within caliber group. Single- or double-set trigger (interchangeable). Calibers: 243 Win., 6.5×57, 270 Win., 7×64, 308 Win., 30-06. 3-round magazine. 23.6-inch barrel (25.6-inch in 7×64). Weight: about 7.3 pounds (7.5 pounds in 7×64). Adjustable open rear sight, hooded ramp front sight. Select European walnut stock, Monte Carlo with cheekpiece, rosewood forend tip and pistol-grip cap, skip checkering, recoil pad, sling swivels. Made from 1965 to date; export to U.S. discontinued 1974. *Note:* U.S. designation, 1971-73, was "Model 660."
With one barrel **$995**
Extra barrel assembly **225**

Mauser Model 66S Ultra
Same general specifications as Model 66S Standard, except has 20.9-inch barrel, weighs about 6.8 pounds.
With one barrel **$1295**
Extra barrel assembly **225**

Mauser Model 66SG Big Game
Same general specifications as Model 66S Standard, except has 25.6-inch barrel, weighs about 9.3 pounds. Calibers: 375 H&H Mag., 458 Win. Mag. *Note:* U.S. designation, 1971-73, was "Model 660 Safari."
With one barrel **$1495**
Extra barrel assembly **325**

Mauser Model 66SH High Performance
Same general specifications as Model 66S Standard, except has 25.6-inch barrel, weighs about 7.5 pounds (9.3 pounds in 9.3×64). Calibers: 6.5×68, 7mm Rem. Mag., 7mm S.E.v. Hofe, 300 Win. Mag., 8×68S, 9.3×64.
With one barrel **$950**
Extra barrel assembly **250**

Mauser Model 66SP Super Match Bolt Action Target Rifle **$1095**
Telescopic short action. Adjustable single-stage trigger. Caliber: 308 Win. (chambering for other cartridges available on special order). 3-shot magazine. 27.6-inch heavy barrel with muzzle brake, dovetail rib for special scope mount. Weight: about 12 pounds. Target stock with wide and deep forearm, full pistol grip, thumb hole, adjustable cheekpiece, adjustable rubber butt plate.

Mauser Model 66ST Carbine
Same general specifications as Model 66S Standard, except has 20.9-inch barrel, full-length stock, weighs about 7 pounds.
With one barrel **$995**
Extra barrel assembly **210**

Mauser Model 83 Bolt Action Rifle **$1890**
Centerfire single-shot, bolt-action rifle for 300-meter competition. Caliber: 308 Win. 25½-inch fluted barrel. Weight: 10½ pounds. Adjustable micrometer rear sight, globe front. Fully adjustable competition stock.

Mauser Model 2000 Bolt Action Sporting Rifle .. **$295**
Modified Mauser-type action. Calibers: 270 Win., 308 Win., 30-06. 5-shot magazine. 24-inch barrel. Weight: about 7½ pounds. Folding leaf rear sight, hooded ramp front sight. Checkered walnut stock with Monte Carlo comb and cheekpiece, forend tip, sling swivels. Made 1969 to 1971. *Note:* Model 2000 is similar in appearance to Model 3000.

Mauser Model 3000

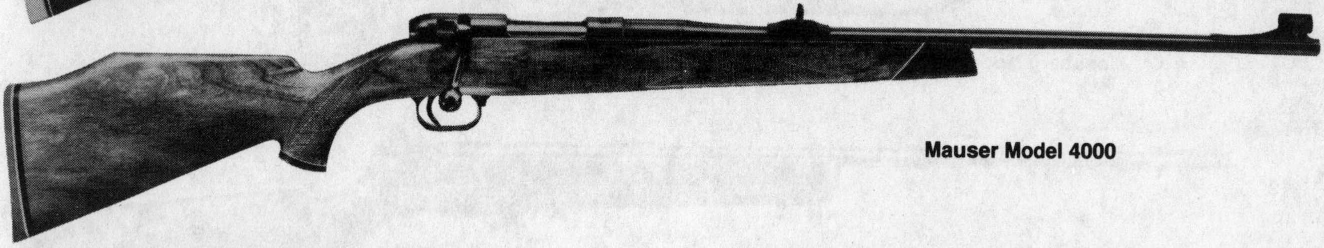

Mauser Model 4000

Mauser Model 3000 Bolt Action Sporting Rifle .. $475
Modified Mauser-type action. Calibers: 243 Win., 270 Win., 308 Win., 30-06. 5-shot magazine. 22-inch barrel. Weight: about 7 pounds. No sights. Select European walnut stock, Monte Carlo style with cheekpiece, rosewood forend tip and pistol-grip cap, skip checkering, recoil pad, sling swivels. Made 1971-74.

Mauser Model 3000 Magnum $550
Same general specifications as standard Model 3000, except has 3-shot magazine, 26-inch barrel, weighs about 8 pounds. Calibers: 7mm Rem. Mag., 300 Win. Mag., 375 H&H Mag.

Mauser Model 4000 Varmint Rifle $450
Same general specifications as standard Model 3000, except has smaller action, folding leaf rear sight and hooded ramp front sight, rubber butt plate instead of recoil pad, weighs about 6¾ pounds. Calibers: 222 Rem., 223 Rem.

GEBRÜDER MERKEL
Suhl, Germany

For Merkel combination guns and drillings, see listings under Merkel shotguns.

Merkel Over/Under Rifles ("Bock-Doppelbüchsen")
Calibers: 5.6×35 Vierling, 6.5×58r5, 7×57r5, 8×57JR, 8×60R Magnum, 9.3×53r5, 9.3×72r5, 9.3×74r5, 10.3×60R as well as most of the British calibers for African and Indian big game. Various barrel lengths, weights. In general, specifications correspond to those of Merkel over/under shotguns. Values of these over/under rifles (in calibers for which ammunition is obtainable) are about the same as those of comparable shotgun models. Currently manufactured. For more specific data, see Merkel shotgun models indicated below.

Merkel O/U Rifle Model 221

Merkel Over/Under Rifles (cont.)

Model 220 (see shotgun Model 200)	**$1095**
Model 220E (see shotgun Model 200E)	**1395**
Model 221 (see shotgun Model 201)	**1775**
Model 221E (see shotgun Model 201E)	**2050**
Model 320 (see shotgun Model 300)	**1995**
Model 320E (see shotgun Model 300E)	**2495**
Model 321 (see shotgun Model 301)	**2600**
Model 321E (see shotgun Model 301E)	**3200**
Model 322 (see shotgun Model 302)	**3400**
Model 323 (see shotgun Model 303E)	**6450**
Model 324 (see shotgun Model 304E)	**7500**

MEXICAN MILITARY RIFLE
Mfd. by Government Arsenal, Mexico, D.F.

Mexican Model 1936 Mauser Military Rifle $175
Same as the German Kar. 98k with minor variations, has U.S. M/1903 Springfield-type knurled cocking piece.

O.F. MOSSBERG & SONS, INC.
North Haven, Connecticut

Mossberg Model 10 Bolt Action Single Shot Rifle .. $85
Takedown. Caliber: 22 Long Rifle, Long, Short. 22-inch barrel. Weight: about 4 pounds. Open rear sight, bead front sight. Plain pistol-grip stock with swivels and sling. Made 1933-35.

Mossberg Model 14 Bolt Action Single Shot Rifle .. $65
Takedown. Caliber: 22 Long Rifle, Long, Short. 24-inch barrel. Weight: about 5¼ pounds. Peep rear sight, hooded ramp front sight. Plain pistol-grip stock with semibeavertail forearm, 1¼-inch swivels. Made 1934-35.

Mossberg Model 20 Bolt Action Single Shot Rifle .. $80
Takedown. Caliber: 22 Long Rifle, Long, Short. 24-inch barrel. Weight: about 4½ pounds. Open rear sight, bead front sight. Plain pistol-grip stock and forearm with finger grooves, sling and swivels. Made 1933-35.

Mossberg Model 25 Bolt Action Single Shot Rifle .. $60
Takedown. Caliber: 22 Long Rifle, Long, Short. 24-inch barrel. Weight: about 5 pounds. Peep rear sight, hooded ramp front sight. Plain pistol-grip stock with semibeavertail forearm. 1¼-inch swivels. Made 1935-36.

Mossberg Model 26B

Mossberg Model 35

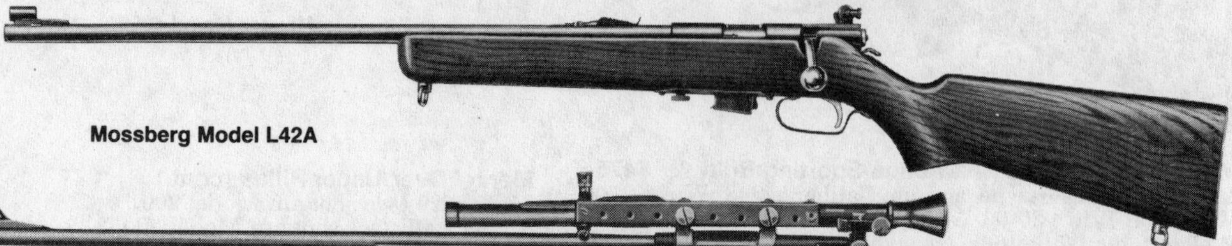

Mossberg Model L42A

Mossberg Model 42B

Mossberg Model 25A $60
Same as Model 25 with minor improvements. Made 1936 to 1938.

Mossberg Model 26B Bolt Action Single Shot Rifle $65
Takedown. Caliber: 22 Long Rifle, Long, Short. 26-inch barrel. Weight: about 5½ pounds. Micrometer click rear peep sight, open rear sight, hooded ramp front sight. Plain pistol-grip stock, swivels. Made 1938 to 1941.

Mossberg Model 26C $60
Same as Model 26B except without rear peep sight and swivels.

Mossberg Model 30 Bolt Action Single Shot Rifle .. $60
Takedown. Caliber: 22 Long Rifle, Long, Short. 24-inch barrel. Weight: about 4½ pounds. Peep rear sight, bead front sight on hooded ramp. Plain pistol-grip stock, forearm with finger grooves. Made 1933-35.

Mossberg Model 34 Bolt Action Single Shot Rifle .. $75
Takedown. Caliber: 22 Long Rifle, Long, Short. 24-inch barrel. Weight: 5½ pounds. Peep rear sight, hooded ramp front sight. Plain pistol-grip stock with semibeavertail forearm, 1¼-inch swivels. Made 1934-35.

Mossberg Model 35 Target Grade Bolt Action Single Shot Rifle $145
Caliber: 22 Long Rifle. 26-inch heavy barrel. Weight: about 8¼ pounds. Micrometer click rear peep sight, hooded ramp front sight. Large target stock with full pistol grip, cheekpiece, full beavertail forearm, 1¼-inch swivels. Made 1935-37.

Mossberg Model 35A Bolt Action Single Shot Rifle $120
Caliber: 22 Long Rifle. 26-inch heavy barrel. Weight: about 8¼ pounds. Micrometer click peep rear sight and hooded front sight. Target stock with cheekpiece, full pistol grip and forearm, 1¼-inch sling swivels. Made 1937-38.

Mossberg Model 35A-LS $135
Same as Model 35A but with Lyman 57 rear sight and 17A front sight.

Mossberg Model 35B $110
Same specifications as Model 44B, except single shot. Made 1938 to 1940.

Mossberg Model 40 Bolt Action Repeater $60
Same specifications as Model 30, except has a tubular magazine (holds 16 Long Rifle) and weighs about 5 pounds. Made 1933-35.

Mossberg Model 42 Bolt Action Repeater $60
Takedown. Caliber: 22 Long Rifle, Long, Short. 7-shot detachable box magazine. 24-inch barrel. Weight: about 5 pounds. Receiver peep sight, open rear sight, hooded ramp front sight. Pistol-grip stock. 1¼-inch swivels. Made 1935-37.

Mossberg Model 42A Bolt Action Repeater $70
Takedown. Caliber: 22 Long Rifle, Long, Short. 7-shot detachable box magazine. 24-inch barrel. Weight: about 5 pounds. Receiver peep sight, open rear sight, ramp front sight. Plain pistol-grip stock. Made 1937-38.

Mossberg Model L42A $90
Same as Model 42A but with left-hand action. Made 1937 to 1941.

Mossberg Model 42B Bolt Action Repeater $70
Takedown. Caliber: 22 Long Rifle, Long, Short. 5-shot detachable box magazine. 24-inch barrel. Weight: about 6 pounds. Micrometer click receiver peep sight, open rear sight, hooded ramp front sight. Plain pistol-grip stock, swivels. Made 1938 to 1941.

Mossberg Model 42C **$75**
Same as Model 42B except without rear peep sight.

Mossberg Model 42M Bolt Action Repeater **$95**
Caliber: 22 Long Rifle, Long, Short. 7-shot detachable box magazine. 23-inch barrel. Weight: about 6$^{3}/_{4}$ pouonds. Microclick receiver peep sight, open rear sight, hooded ramp front sight. Two-piece Mannlicher-type stock with cheekpiece and pistol grip, swivels. Made 1940 to 1950.

Mossberg Model 43 Bolt Action Repeater **$95**
Speedlock, adjustable trigger pull. Caliber: 22 Long Rifle. 7-shot detachable box magazine. 26-inch heavy barrel. Weight: about 8$^{1}/_{4}$ pounds. Lyman 57 rear sight, selective aperture front sight. Target stock with cheekpiece, full pistol grip, beavertail forearm, adjustable front swivel. Made 1937-38. **Model L43** is same as Model 43 except has left-hand action.

Mossberg Model 43B **$155**
Same as Model 44B, except with Lyman 57 receiver sight and 17A front sight. Made 1938-39.

Mossberg Model 44 Bolt Action Repeater **$65**
Takedown. Caliber: 22 Long Rifle, Long, Short. Tubular magazine holds 16 Long Rifle. 24-inch barrel. Weight: 6 pounds. Peep rear sight, hooded ramp front sight. Plain pistol-grip stock with semibeavertail forearm, 1$^{1}/_{4}$-inch swivels. Made 1934-35. *Note:* Do not confuse this rifle with the later Models 44B and 44US which are clip repeaters.

Mossberg Model 44B Bolt Action Target Rifle . . **$135**
Caliber: 22 Long Rifle. 7-shot detachable box magazine. 26-inch heavy barrel. Weight: about 8 pounds. Micrometer click receiver peep sight, hooded front sight. Target stock with full pistol grip, cheekpiece, beavertail forearm, adjustable swivel. Made 1938 to 1941.

Mossberg Model 44US Bolt Action Repeater . . . **$100**
Caliber: 22 Long Rifle. 7-shot detachable box magazine. 26-inch heavy barrel. Weight: about 8$^{1}/_{2}$ pounds. Micrometer click receiver peep sight, hooded front sight. Target stock, swivels. Made 1943-48. *Note:* This model was used as a training rifle by the U.S. Armed Forces during WWII.

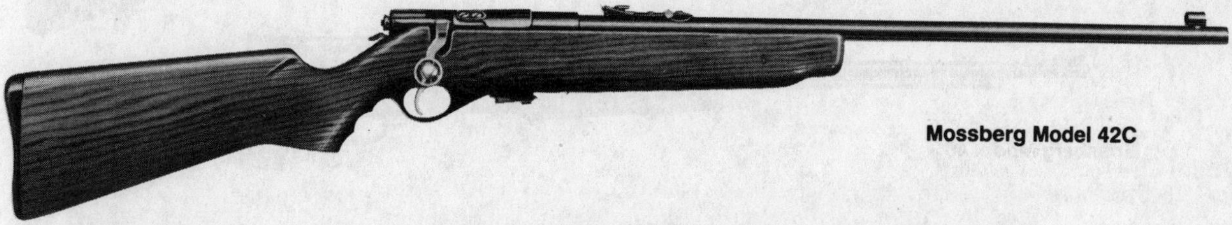
Mossberg Model 42C

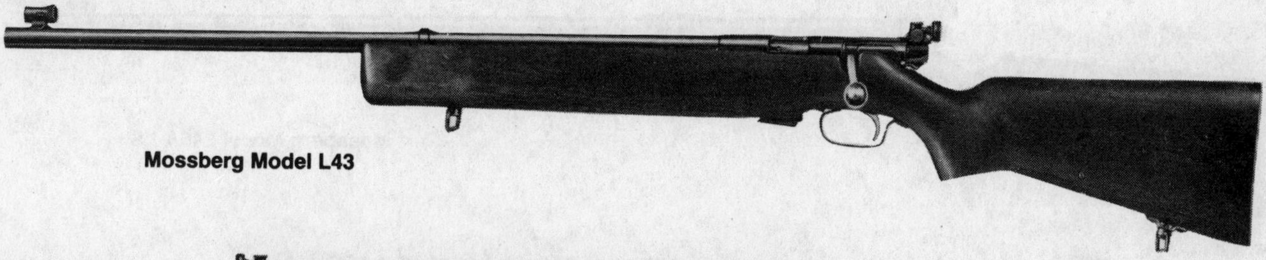
Mossberg Model L43

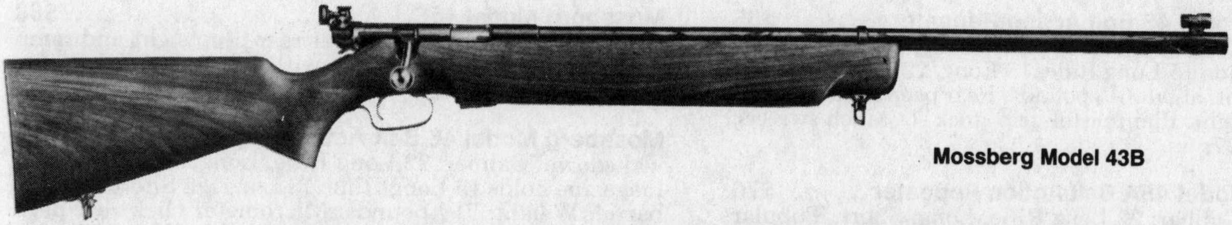
Mossberg Model 43B

Mossberg Model 44B

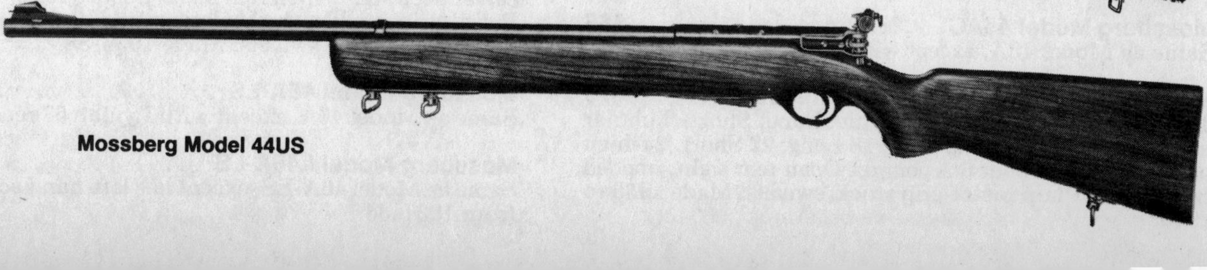
Mossberg Model 44US

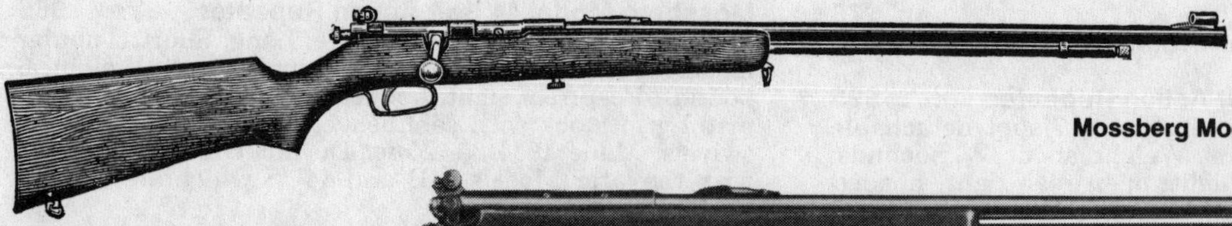

Mossberg Model 45

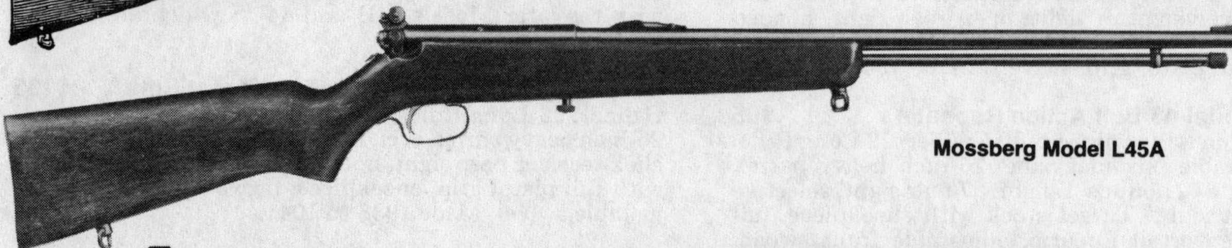

Mossberg Model L45A

Mossberg Model 45B

Mossberg Model 46

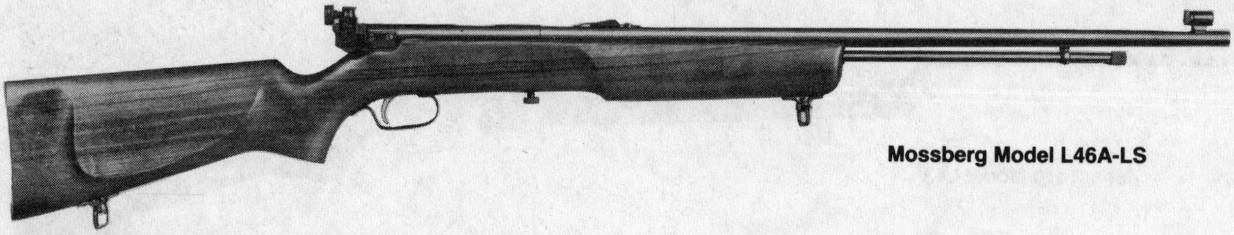

Mossberg Model L46A-LS

Mossberg Model 45 Bolt Action Repeater $65
Takedown. Caliber: 22 Long Rifle, Long, Short. Tubular magazine holds 15 Long Rifle, 18 Long, 22 Short. 24-inch barrel. Weight: about $6\frac{3}{4}$ pounds. Rear peep sight, hooded ramp front sight. Plain pistol-grip stock, $1\frac{1}{4}$-inch swivels. Made 1935-37.

Mossberg Model 45A Bolt Action Repeater $70
Takedown. Caliber: 22 Long Rifle, Long, Short. Tubular magazine holds 15 Long Rifle, 18 Long, 22 Short. 24-inch barrel. Weight: about $6\frac{3}{4}$ pounds. Receiver peep sight, open rear sight, hooded ramp front sight. Plain pistol-grip stock, $1\frac{1}{4}$-inch swivels. Made 1937-38.

Mossberg Model L45A $75
Same as Model 45A, except has left-hand action. Made 1937-38.

Mossberg Model 45AC $65
Same as Model 45A, except without receiver peep sight.

Mossberg Model 45B Bolt Action Repeater $75
Takedown. Caliber: 22 Long Rifle, Long, Short. Tubular magazine holds 15 Long Rifle, 18 Long, 22 Short. 24-inch barrel. Weight: about $6\frac{1}{4}$ pounds. Open rear sight, hooded front sight. Plain pistol-grip stock, swivels. Made 1938 to 1940.

Mossberg Model 45C $60
Same as Model 45 but without rear peep sight and ramp front sight; intended for use with telescopic sight only. Made 1935-37.

Mossberg Model 46 Bolt Action Repeater $65
Takedown. Caliber: 22 Long Rifle, Long, Short. Tubular magazine holds 15 Long Rifle, 18 Long, 22 Short. 26-inch barrel. Weight: $7\frac{1}{2}$ pounds. Micrometer click rear peep sight, hooded ramp front sight. Pistol-grip stock with cheekpiece, full beavertail forearm, $1\frac{1}{4}$-inch swivels. Made 1935-37.

Mossberg Model 46A Bolt Action Repeater $75
Takedown. Caliber: 22 Long Rifle, Long, Short. Tubular magazine holds 15 Long Rifle, 18 Long, 22 Short. 26-inch barrel. Weight: about $7\frac{1}{4}$ pounds. Micrometer click receiver peep sight, open rear sight, hooded ramp front sight. Pistol-grip stock with cheekpiece and beavertail forearm, quick-detachable swivels. Made 1937-38.

Mossberg Model 46A-LS $90
Same as Model 46A, except with Lyman 57 receiver sight.

Mossberg Model L46A-LS $90
Same as Model 46A-LS, except has left-hand action. Made from 1937-38.

Mossberg Model 46B

Mossberg Model 46M

Mossberg Model 50

Mossberg Model 51

Mossberg Model 51M

Mossberg Model 46B Bolt Action Repeater $70
Takedown. Caliber: 22 Long Rifle, Long, Short. Tubular magazine holds 15 Long Rifle, 18 Long, 22 Short. 26-inch barrel. Weight: about 7 pounds. Micrometer click receiver peep sight, open rear sight, hooded front sight. Plain pistol-grip stock with cheekpiece, swivels. *Note:* Postwar version of this model has full magazine holding 20 Long Rifle, 23 Long, 30 Short. Made 1938 to 1950.

Mossberg Model 46BT $90
Same as Model 46B, except has heavier barrel and stock, weighs 7¾ pounds. Made from 1938 to 1939.

Mossberg Model 46C $70
Same as Model 46 except has a heavier barrel and stock than that model, weighs 8½ pounds. Made 1936-37.

Mossberg Model 46M Bolt Action Repeater $90
Caliber: 22 Long Rifle, Long, Short. Tubular magazine holds 22 Short, 18 Long, 15 Long Rifle. 23-inch barrel. Weight: about 7 pounds. Microclick receiver peep sight, open rear sight, hooded ramp front sight. Two-piece Mannlicher-type stock with cheekpiece and pistol grip, swivels. Made 1940 to 1952.

Mossberg Model 50 Autoloading Rifle $95
Same as Model 51, except has plain stock without beavertail, cheekpiece, swivels or receiver peep sight. Made 1939 to 1942.

Mossberg Model 51 Autoloading Rifle $95
Takedown. Caliber: 22 Long Rifle. 15-shot tubular magazine in buttstock. 24-inch barrel. Weight: about 7¼ pounds. Micrometer click receiver peep sight, open rear sight, hooded ramp front sight. Cheekpiece stock with full pistol grip and beavertail forearm, swivels. Made in 1939 only.

Mossberg Model 51M Autoloading Rifle $115
Caliber: 22 Long Rifle. 15-shot tubular magazine. 20-inch barrel. Weight: about 7 pounds. Microclick receiver peep sight, open rear sight, hooded ramp front sight. Two-piece Mannlicher-type stock with pistol grip and cheekpiece, swivels. Made 1939 to 1946.

Mossberg Model 140B Sporter-Target Rifle $85
Same as Model 140K, except has peep rear sight, hooded ramp front sight. Made 1957-58.

Mossberg Model 140K Bolt Action Repeater $75
Caliber: 22 Long Rifle, 22 Long, 22 Short. 7-shot clip magazine. $24\frac{1}{2}$-inch barrel. Weight: $5\frac{3}{4}$ pounds. Open rear sight, bead front sight. Monte Carlo stock with cheekpiece and pistol grip, sling swivels. Made 1955-58.

Mossberg Model 142-A Bolt Action Repeating Carbine $75
Caliber: 22 Short, Long, Long Rifle. 7-shot detachable box magazine. 18-inch barrel. Weight: about 6 pounds. Peep rear sight, military-type front sight. Monte Carlo stock with pistol grip, hinged forearm pulls down to form hand grip, sling swivels mounted on left side of stock. Made 1949 to 1957.

Mossberg Model 142K $75
Same as Model 142, except has open rear sight. Made from 1953-57.

Mossberg Model 144 Bolt Action Target Rifle . . . $150
Caliber: 22 Long Rifle. 7-shot detachable box magazine. 26-inch heavy barrel. Weight: about 8 pounds. Microclick receiver peep sight, hooded front sight. Pistol-grip target stock with beavertail forearm, adjustable hand stop, swivels. Made from 1949 to 1954. *Note:* This model designation was resumed c.1973 for previous Model 144LS. See listing below.

Mossberg Model 144LS $160
Same as Model 144 except has Lyman 57MS or Mossberg S331 receiver sight and Lyman 17A front sight. Made from 1954 to date. *Note:* This model since c.1973 has been marketed as Model 144.

Mossberg Model 146B Bolt Action Repeater $85
Takedown. Caliber: 22 Long Rifle, Long, Short. Tubular magazine holds 30 Short, 23 Long, 20 Long Rifle. 26-inch barrel. Weight: about 7 pounds. Micrometer click rear peep sight, open rear sight, hooded front sight. Plain stock with pistol grip, Monte Carlo comb and cheekpiece, knob forend tip, swivels. Made 1949 to 1954.

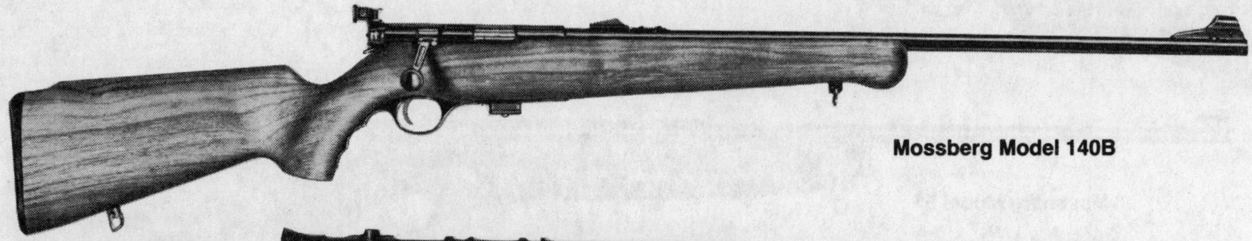

Mossberg Model 140B

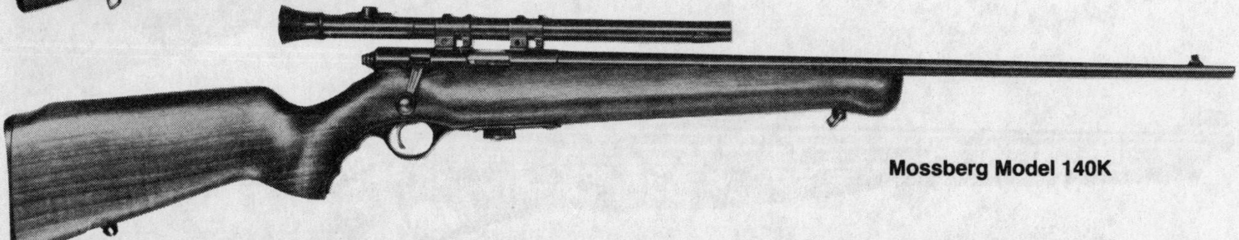

Mossberg Model 140K

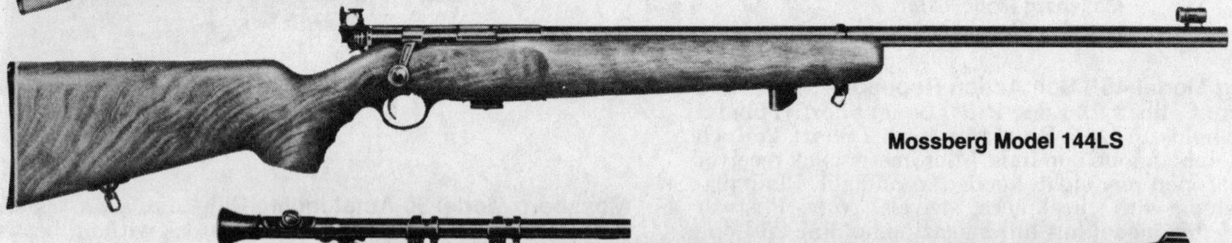

Mossberg Model 144LS

Mossberg Model 146B

Mossberg Model 151K

Mossberg Model 151M

Mossberg Model 152

Mossberg Model 151K **$125**
Same as Model 151M except has 24-inch barrel, weighs about 6 pounds, has no peep sight, plain stock with Monte Carlo comb and cheekpiece, pistol-grip knob, forend tip, without swivels. Made 1950-51.

Mossberg Model 151M Autoloading Rifle **$125**
Improved version of Model 51M with same general specifications, complete action is instantly removable without use of tools. Made 1946 to 1958.

Mossberg Model 152 Autoloading Carbine **$125**
Caliber: 22 Long Rifle. 7-shot detachable box magazine. 18-inch barrel. Weight: about 5 pounds. Peep rear sight, military-type front sight. Monte Carlo stock with pistol grip, hinged forearm pulls down to form hand grip, sling mounted on swivels on left side of stock. Made 1948 to 1957.

Mossberg Model 152K **$110**
Same as Model 152, except with open instead of peep rear sight. Made 1950-57.

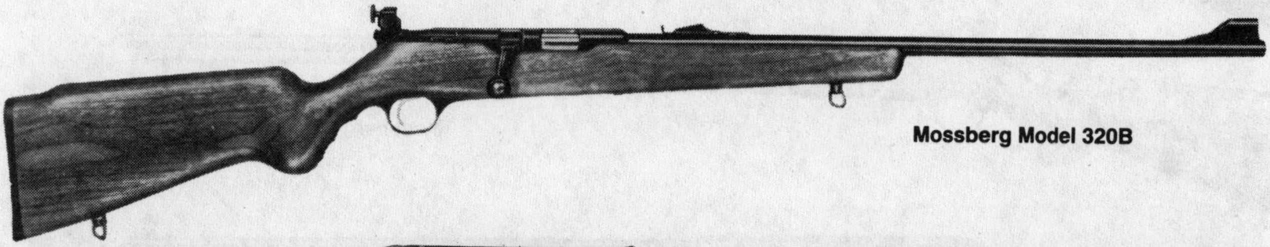

Mossberg Model 320B

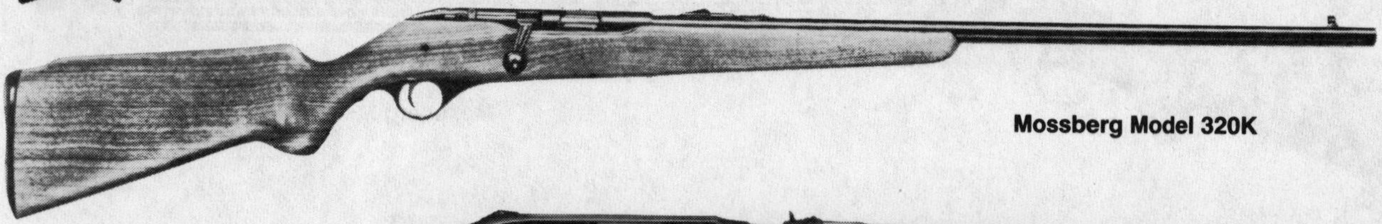

Mossberg Model 320K

Mossberg Model 333

Mossberg Model 320B Boy Scout Target Rifle . . . **$95**
Same as Model 340K, except single shot with automatic safety. Made 1960-1971.

Mossberg Model 320K Hammerless Bolt Action Single Shot **$80**
Same as Model 346K except single shot, has drop-in loading platform, automatic safety. Weight: about 5¾ pounds. Made 1958 to 1960.

Mossberg Model 321B **$80**
Same as Model 321K, except has receiver peep sight. Made 1972-75.

Mossberg Model 321K Bolt Action Single Shot . . . **$75**
Same as Model 341, except single shot. Made from 1972 to 1980.

Mossberg Model 333 Autoloading Carbine **$95**
Caliber: 22 Long Rifle. 15-shot tubular magazine. 20-inch barrel. Weight: about 6¼ pounds. Open rear sight, ramp front sight. Monte Carlo stock with checkered pistol grip and forearm, barrel band, swivels. Made 1972-73.

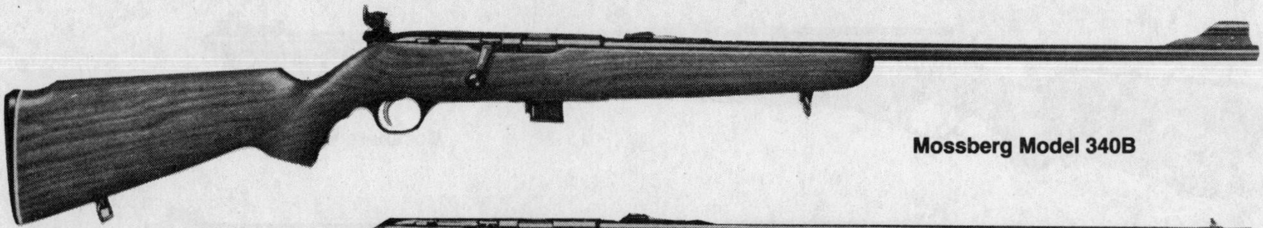

Mossberg Model 340B

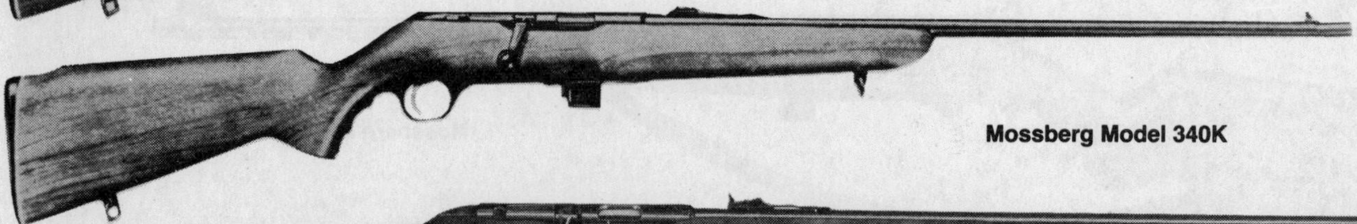

Mossberg Model 340K

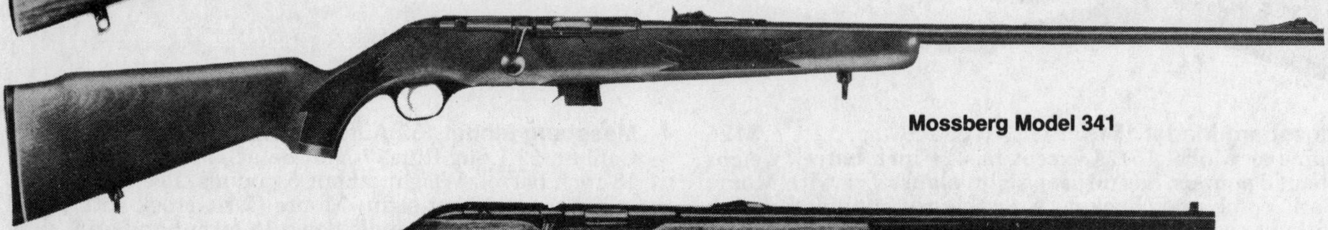

Mossberg Model 341

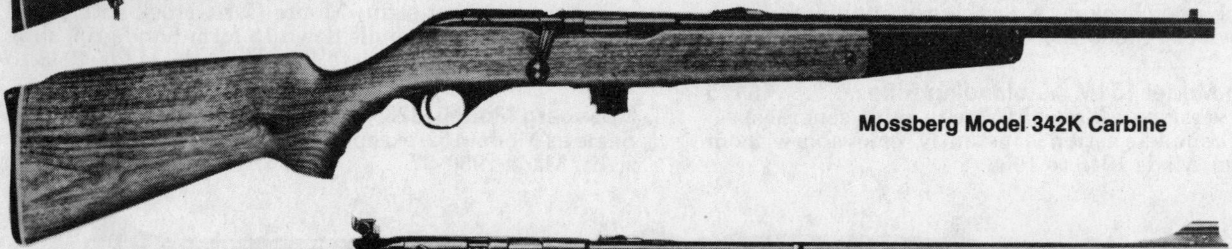

Mossberg Model 342K Carbine

Mossberg Model 346B

Mossberg Model 346K

Mossberg Model 340B Target Sporter.......... $65
Same as Model 340K, except has peep rear sight, hooded ramp front sight. Made 1958 to 1981.

Mossberg Model 340K Hammerless Bolt Action Repeater $60
Same as Model 346K, except clip type, 7-shot magazine. Made 1958 to 1971.

Mossberg Model 340M $80
Same as Model 340K, except has $18\frac{1}{2}$-inch barrel, Mannlicher-style stock with swivels and sling. Weight: $5\frac{1}{4}$ pounds. Made 1970-71.

Mossberg Model 341 Bolt Action Repeater...... $65
Caliber: 22 Short, Long, Long Rifle. 7-shot clip magazine. 24-inch barrel. Weight: $6\frac{1}{2}$ pounds. Open rear sight, ramp front sight. Monte Carlo stock with checkered pistol grip and forearm, sling swivels. Made from 1972 to date.

Mossberg Model 342K Hammerless Bolt Action Carbine $65
Same as Model 340K, except has 18-inch barrel, stock has no cheekpiece, extension forend is hinged, pulls down to form hand grip; sling swivels and web strap on left side of stock. Weight: about 5 pounds. Made 1958 to 1974.

Mossberg Model 346B $80
Same as Model 346K, except has peep rear sight, hooded ramp front sight. Made 1958 to 1967.

Mossberg Model 346K Hammerless Bolt Action Repeater $75
Caliber: 22 Short, Long, Long Rifle. Tubular magazine holds 25 Short, 20 Long, 18 Long Rifle. 24-inch barrel. Weight: about $6\frac{1}{2}$ pounds. Open rear sight, bead front sight. Walnut stock with Monte Carlo comb, cheekpiece, pistol grip, sling swivels. Made 1958 to 1971.

Mossberg Model 350K Clip

Mossberg Model 351K Sporter

Mossberg Model 352K Carbine

Mossberg Model 353 Carbine

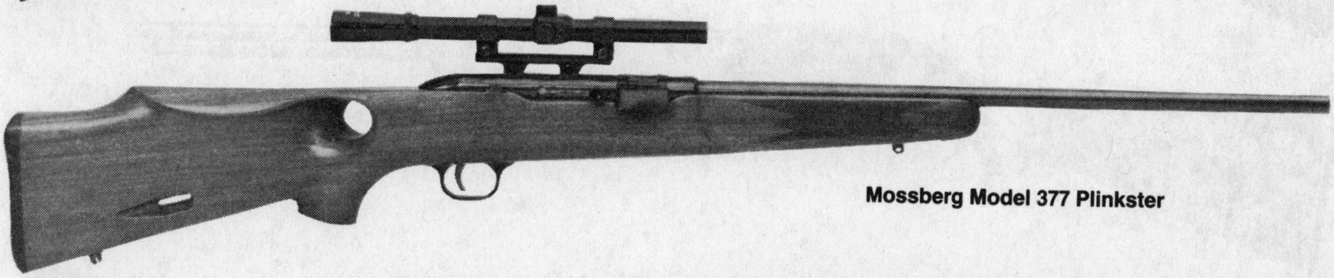

Mossberg Model 377 Plinkster

Mossberg Model 350K Autoloading Rifle— Clip Type $85
Caliber: 22 Short (high speed), Long, Long Rifle. 7-shot clip magazine. 23½-inch barrel. Weight: about 6 pounds. Open rear sight, bead front sight. Monte Carlo stock with pistol grip. Made 1958 to 1971.

Mossberg Model 351C Automatic Carbine $85
Same as Model 351K, except has 18½-inch barrel, Western carbine-style stock with barrel band and sling swivels. Weight: 5½ pounds. Made 1965 to 1971.

Mossberg Model 351K Automatic Sporter $80
Caliber: 22 Long Rifle. 15-shot tubular magazine in buttstock. 24-inch barrel. Weight: about 6 pounds. Open rear sight, bead front sight. Monte Carlo stock with pistol grip. Made 1960 to 1971.

Mossberg Model 352K Autoloading Carbine $80
Caliber: 22 Short, Long, Long Rifle. 7-shot clip magazine. 18-inch barrel. Weight: about 5 pounds. Open rear sight, bead front sight. Monte Carlo stock with pistol grip; extension forend of Tenite is hinged, pulls down to form hand grip; sling swivels, web strap. Made 1958 to 1971.

Mossberg Model 353 Autoloading Carbine $85
Caliber: 22 Long Rifle. 7-shot clip magazine. 18-inch barrel. Weight: about 5 pounds. Open rear sight, ramp front sight. Monte Carlo stock with checkered pistol grip and forearm; black Tenite extension forend pulls down to form hand grip. Made from 1972 to 1985.

Mossberg Model 377 Plinkster Autoloader $75
Caliber: 22 Long Rifle. 15-shot tubular magazine. 20-inch barrel. Weight: about 6¼ pounds. 4X scope sight. Thumbhole stock with roll-over cheekpiece, Monte Carlo comb, checkered forearm; molded of modified polystyrene foam in walnut finish; sling swivel studs. Introduced 1977.

Mossberg Model 380 Semiautomatic Rifle $80
Caliber: 22 Long Rifle. 15-shot buttstock magazine. 20-inch barrel. Weight: 5½ pounds. Open rear sight, bead front sight. Made from 1980 to 1985.

Mossberg Model 400 Palomino Lever Action Rifle $95
Hammerless. Caliber: 22 Short, Long, Long Rifle. Tubular magazine holds 20 Short, 17 Long, 15 Long Rifle. 24-inch barrel. Weight: about 5½ pounds. Open rear sight, bead front sight. Monte Carlo stock with checkered pistol grip; and beavertail forearm. Made 1959 to 1964.

Mossberg Model 402 Palomino Carbine $120
Same as Model 400, except has 18½-inch (1961-64) or 20-inch barrel (1964-71), forearm with barrel band, swivels; magazine holds two less rounds. Weight: about 4¾ pounds. Made 1961 to 1971.

Mossberg Model 430 Automatic Rifle $85
Caliber: 22 Long Rifle. 18-shot tubular magazine. 24-inch barrel. Weight: about 6¼ pounds. Open rear sight, bead front sight. Monte Carlo stock with checkered pistol grip; checkered forearm. Made 1970-71.

Mossberg Model 432 Western-Style Auto Carbine $80
Same as Model 430 except has plain straight-grip carbine-type stock and forearm, barrel band, sling swivels. Magazine capacity: 15 cartridges. Weight: about 6 pounds. Made 1970-71.

Mossberg Model 472 Brush Gun $175
Same as Model 472 Carbine with straight-grip stock, except has 18-inch barrel, weighs about 6½ pounds. Caliber: 30-30. Magazine capacity: 5 rounds. Made 1974-76.

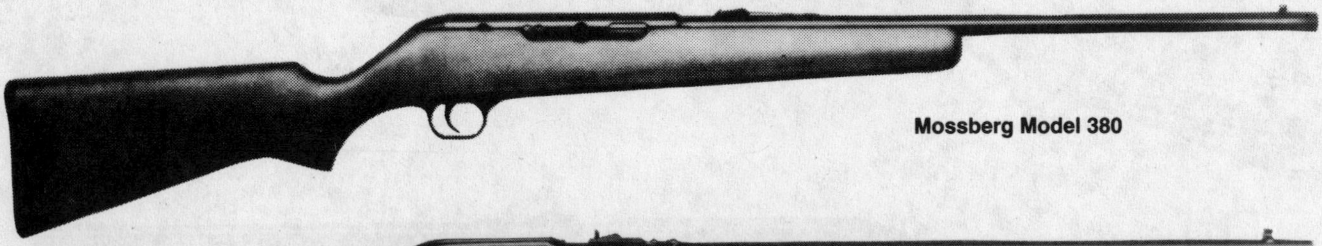
Mossberg Model 380

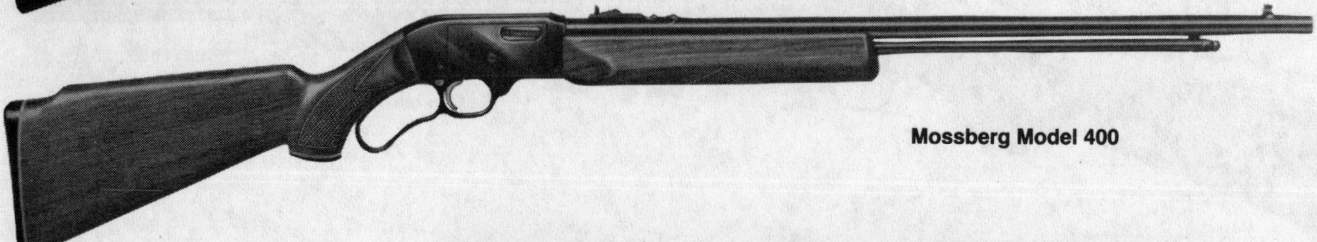
Mossberg Model 400

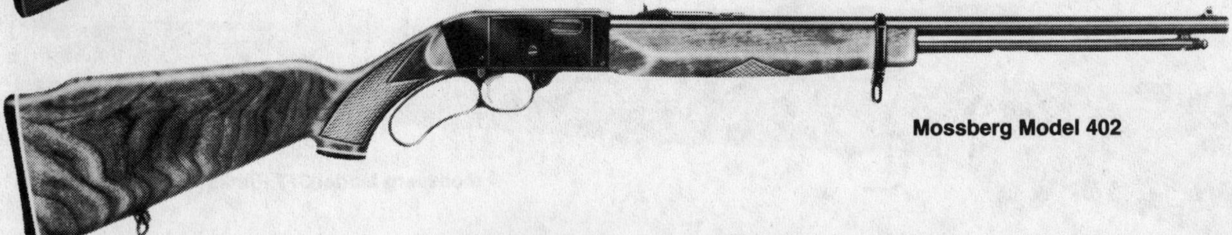
Mossberg Model 402

Mossberg Model 472 Brush Gun

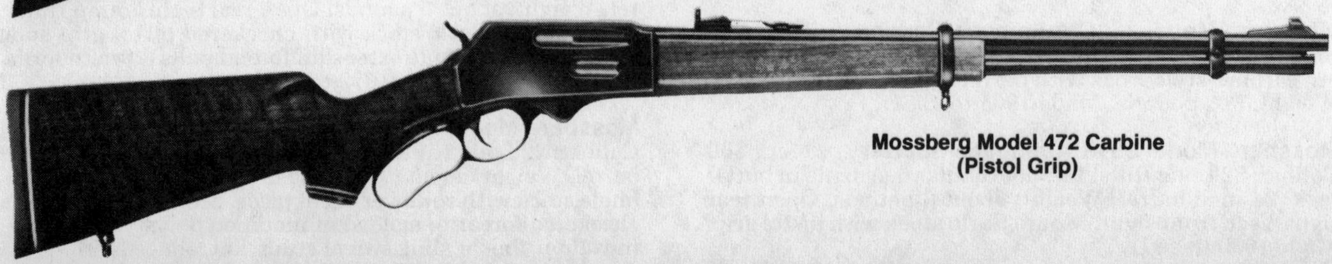
Mossberg Model 472 Carbine (Pistol Grip)

Mossberg Model 472 Carbine (Straight Grip)

Mossberg Model 472 "One in Five Thousand"

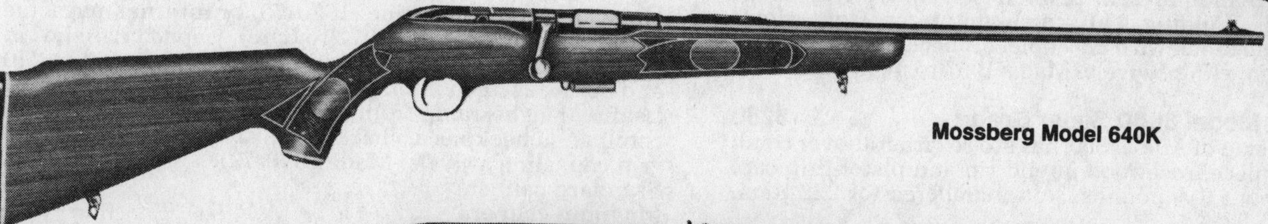

Mossberg Model 640K

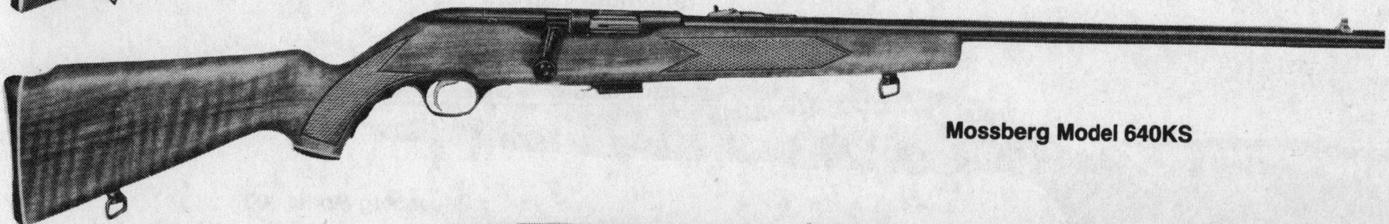

Mossberg Model 640KS

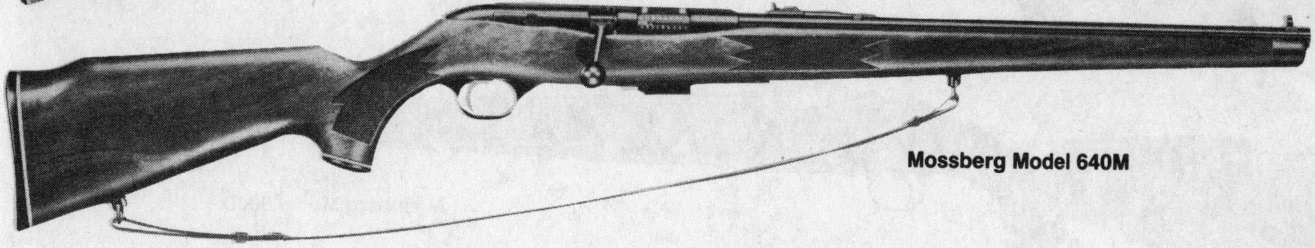

Mossberg Model 640M

Mossberg Model 472 Lever Action Carbine $155
Calibers: 30-30, 35 Rem. centerfire. 6-shot tubular magazine. 20-inch barrel. Weight: 6¾ to 7 pounds. Open rear sight, ramp front sight. Pistol-grip or straight-grip stock, forearm with barrel band; sling swivels on pistol-grip model, saddle ring on straight-grip model. Made 1972-79.

Mossberg Model 472 One in Five Thousand $300
Same as Model 472 Brush Gun, except has Indian scenes etched on receiver; brass butt plate, saddle ring and barrel bands, gold-plated trigger; bright blued finish; select walnut stock and forearm. Limited edition of 5000, serial numbered 1 to 5000. Made in 1974.

Mossberg Model 472 Rifle $160
Same as Model 472 Carbine with pistol-grip stock, except has 24-inch barrel, 5-shot magazine, weighs about 7 pounds. Made 1974-76.

Mossberg Model 620K $65
Same as Model 640K, except single shot. Made 1960-64.

Mossberg Model 640K Chuckster Hammerless Bolt Action Rifle $70
Caliber: 22 R.F. Magnum. 5-shot detachable clip magazine. 24-inch barrel. Weight: about 6 pounds. Open rear sight, bead front sight. Monte Carlo stock with cheekpiece, pistol grip, sling swivels. Made from 1959 to date.

Mossberg Model 640KS $90
Deluxe version of Model 640K, has select walnut stock, hand checkering; gold-plated front sight, rear sight elevator, and trigger. Made 1960-64.

Mossberg Model 640M $100
Similar to Model 640K, except chambered for 22 Win. Mag. R.F.; has 20-inch barrel, Mannlicher-style stock with Monte Carlo comb and cheekpiece, swivels. Made 1967 to 1973.

Mossberg Model 642K

Mossberg Model 642K **$80**
Same as Model 640K, except has 18½-inch barrel, forearm with black Tenite extension that pulls down to form hand grip. Made 1961-64.

Mossberg Model 800 Bolt Action Centerfire Rifle **$195**
Calibers: 222 Rem., 22-250, 243 Win., 308 Win. 4-shot magazine, 3-shot in 222. 22-inch barrel. Weight: about 7½ pounds. Folding leaf rear sight, ramp front sight. Monte Carlo stock with cheekpiece, checkered pistol grip and forearm, sling swivels. Made 1967 to 1979.

Mossberg Model 800D Super Grade **$260**
Deluxe version of Model 800; has stock with roll-over comb and cheekpiece, rosewood forend tip and pistol-grip cap. Weight: about 6¾ pounds. Not chambered for 222 Rem. Made 1970-73.

Mossberg Model 800M **$250**
Same as Model 800, except has flat bolt handle, 20-inch barrel, Mannlicher-style stock. Weight: 6½ pounds. Calibers: 22-250, 243 Win., 308 Win. Made 1969 to 1972.

Mossberg Model 800VT Varmint/Target **$245**
Similar to Model 800, except has 24-inch heavy barrel, no sights. Weight: about 9½ pounds. Calibers: 222 Rem., 22-250, 243 Win. Made 1968 to 1979.

Mossberg Model 810 Bolt Action Centerfire Rifle
Calibers: 270 Win., 30-06, 7mm Rem. Mag., 338 Win. Mag. Detachable box magazine (1970-75) or internal magazine with hinged floorplate (1972 to date). Capacity: 4-shot in 270 and 30-06, 3-shot in magnums. 22-inch barrel in 270 and 30-06, 24-inch in magnums. Weight: 7½ to 8 pounds. Leaf rear sight, ramp front sight. Stock with Monte Carlo comb and cheekpiece, checkered pistol grip and forearm, grip cap, sling swivels. Made 1970-79.
Standard calibers **$200**
Magnum calibers **225**

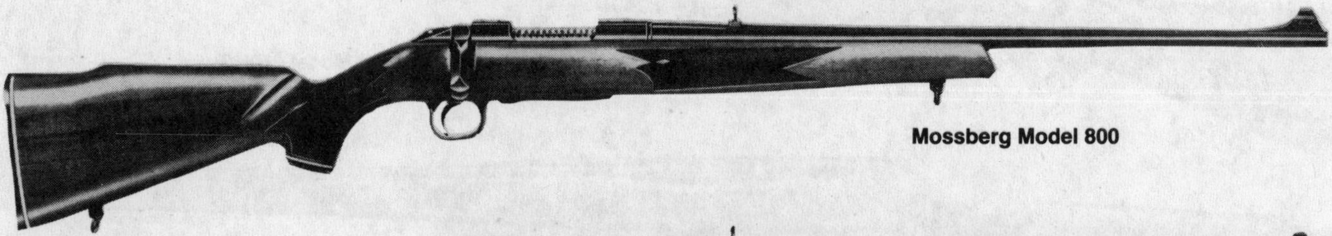

Mossberg Model 800

Mossberg Model 800D

Mossberg Model 800M

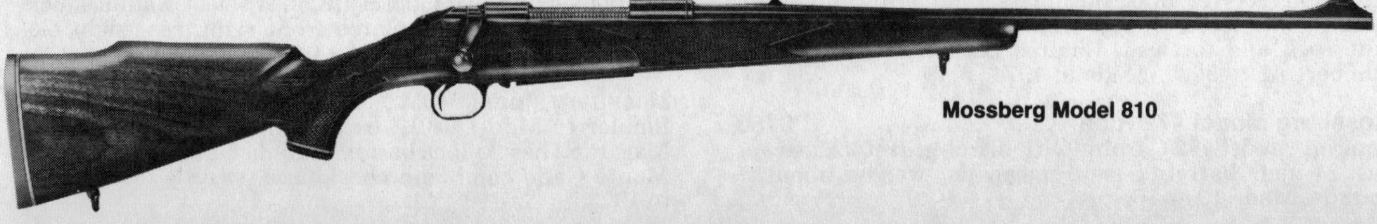

Mossberg Model 810

Mossberg Model K

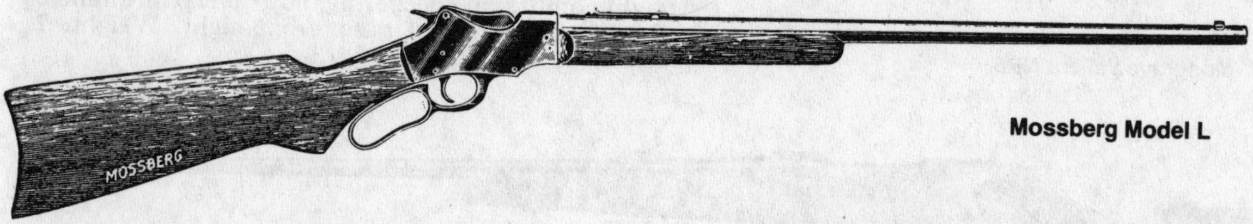

Mossberg Model L

Mossberg Model 1500 Mountaineer Grade I Centerfire Rifle $225
Calibers: 223, 243, 270, 30-06, 7mm Mag. 22-inch or 24-inch (7mm Mag.) barrel. Weight: 7 lbs. 10 oz. Hardwood walnut finished checkered stock. Hooded ramp front sight with gold bead, fully adjustable rear sight. Drilled and tapped for scope mounts. Sling swivel studs. Made from 1987 to date.

Mossberg Model B Bolt Action Rifle $125
Takedown. Caliber: 22 Long Rifle, Long, Short. Single shot. 22-inch barrel. Open rear sight, bead front sight. Plain pistol-grip stock. Made 1930-32.

Mossberg Model K Slide Action Repeater $175
Hammerless. Takedown. Caliber: 22 Long Rifle, Long, Short. Tubular magazine holds 20 Short, 16 Long, 14 Long Rifle. 22-inch barrel. Weight: about 5 pounds. Open rear sight, bead front sight. Plain straight-grip stock, grooved slide handle. Made 1922 to 1931.

Mossberg Models L42A, L43, L45A, L46A-LS
See Models 42A, 43, 45A and 46A-LS respectively; "L" refers to left-hand version of those rifles.

Mossberg Model L Single Shot Rifle $300
Martini-type falling-block lever action. Takedown. Caliber: 22 Long Rifle, Long, Short. 24-inch barrel. Weight: about 5 pounds. Open rear sight and bead front sight. Plain pistol-grip stock and forearm. Made 1929 to 1932.

Mossberg Model M Slide Action Repeater $185
Specifications same as for Model K except has 24-inch octagon barrel, pistol-grip stock, weighs about 5½ pounds. Made 1928 to 1931.

Mossberg Model R Bolt Action Repeater $75
Takedown. Caliber: 22 Long Rifle, Long, Short. Tubular magazine. 24-inch barrel. Open rear sight, bead front sight. Plain pistol-grip stock. Made 1930-32.

Musgrave Premier NR5

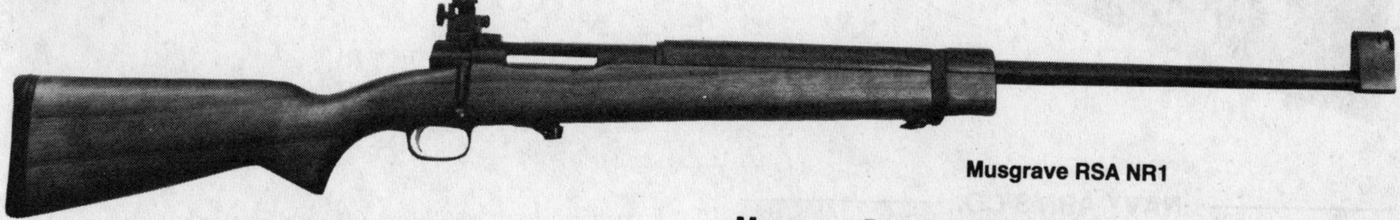

Musgrave RSA NR1

— MUSGRAVE MFRS. & DIST. (PTY) LTD. — Bloemfontein, South Africa

The following Musgrave bolt-action rifles were manufactured from 1971 to 1976.

Musgrave Premier NR5 Bolt Action Hunting Rifle $325
Calibers: 243 Win., 270 Win., 30-06, 308 Win., 7mm Rem. Mag. 5-shot magazine. 25½-inch barrel. Weight: 8¼

Musgrave Premier NR5 (cont.)
pounds. Furnished without sights. Select walnut Monte Carlo stock with cheekpiece, checkered pistol grip and forearm, contrasting pistol-grip cap and forend tip, recoil pad, swivel studs.

Musgrave RSA NR1 Bolt Action Single Shot Target Rifle $300
Caliber: 308 Win. (7.62mm NATO). 26.4-inch heavy barrel. Weight: about 10 pounds. Aperture receiver sight, tunnel front sight. Walnut target stock with beavertail forearm, handguard, barrel band, rubber butt plate, sling swivels.

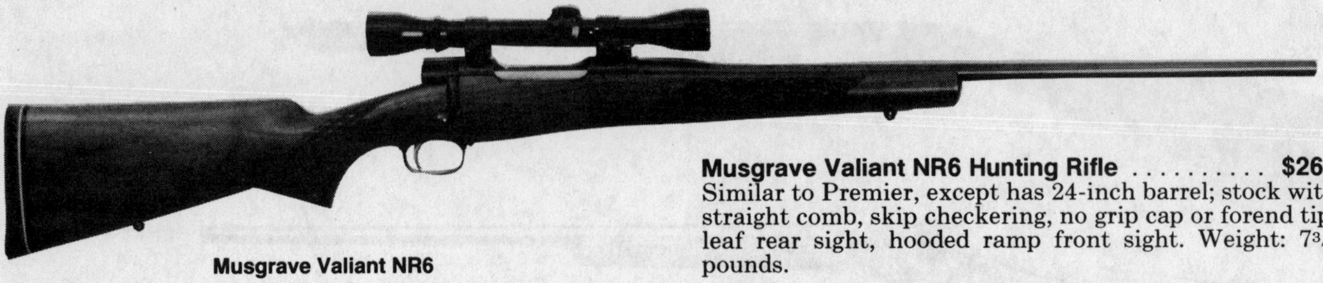

Musgrave Valiant NR6

Musgrave Valiant NR6 Hunting Rifle $260
Similar to Premier, except has 24-inch barrel; stock with straight comb, skip checkering, no grip cap or forend tip; leaf rear sight, hooded ramp front sight. Weight: 7 3/4 pounds.

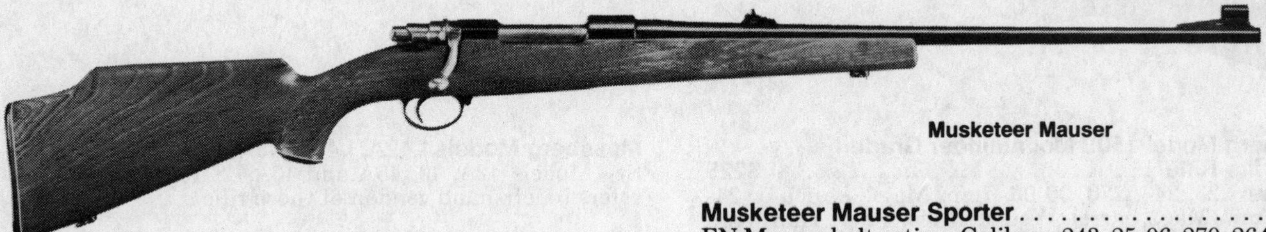

Musketeer Mauser

Musketeer Mauser Sporter $275
FN Mauser bolt action. Calibers: 243, 25-06, 270, 264 Mag., 308, 30-06, 7mm Mag., 300 Win. Mag. Magazine holds 5 standard, 3 magnum cartridges. 24-inch barrel. Weight: about 7 1/4 pounds. No sights. Monte Carlo stock with checkered pistol grip and forearm, swivels. Made from 1963 to 1972.

MUSKETEER RIFLES
Washington, D.C.
Mfd. by Firearms International Corp.

Navy Arms 45-70 Mauser Rifle

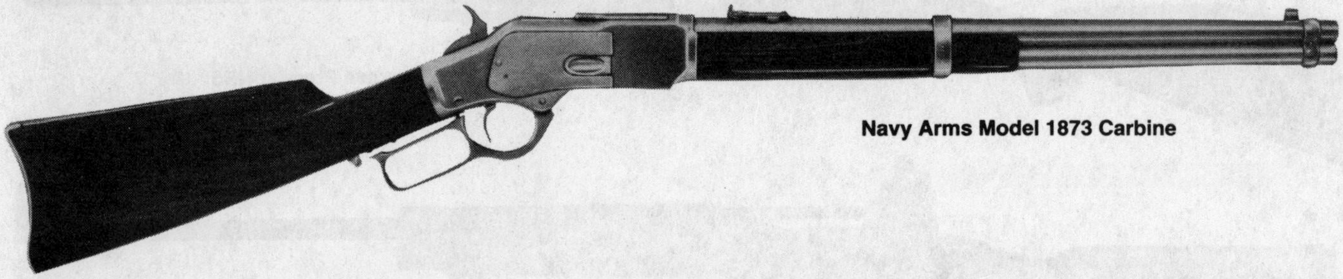

Navy Arms Model 1873 Carbine

NAVY ARMS CO.
Ridgefield, New Jersey

Navy Arms 45-70 Mauser Carbine $175
Same as 45-70 Mauser Rifle, except has 18-inch barrel, straight-grip stock with low comb, weighs about 7 1/2 pounds. Discontinued.

Navy Arms 45-70 Mauser Rifle $165
Siamese Mauser bolt action. Caliber: 45-70 Government. 3-round magazine. 24- or 26-inch barrel. Weight: about 8 1/2 pounds with 26-inch barrel. Open rear sight, ramp front sight. Checkered stock with Monte Carlo comb. Intro. 1973; discontinued.

Navy Arms 1873 Carbine $250
Similar to Model 1873 Rifle, except has blued receiver, 10-shot magazine, 19-inch round barrel, carbine-style forearm with barrel band, weighs about 6 3/4 pounds. Discontinued.

Navy Arms Model 1873 Lever Action Rifle $265
Replica of Winchester Model 1873. Casehardened receiver. Calibers: 22 Long Rifle, 357 Magnum, 44-40. 15-shot magazine. 24-inch octagon barrel. Weight: about 8 pounds. Open rear sight, blade front sight. Straight-grip stock, forearm with end cap. Discontinued.

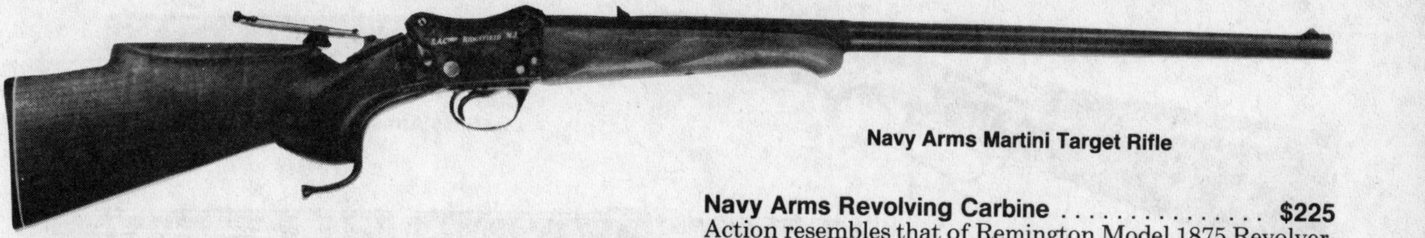

Navy Arms Martini Target Rifle

Navy Arms 1873 Trapper's Model **$250**
Same as Model 1873 Carbine, except has 16½-inch barrel, 8-shot magazine, weighs about 6¼ pounds. Discontinued.

Navy Arms Engraved Models
Yellowboy and Model 1873 rifles and carbines are available in deluxe models with select walnut stocks and forearms and engraving in three grades. Grade "A" has delicate scrollwork in limited areas. Grade "B" is more elaborate with about 40 percent coverage. Grade "C" has highest grade engraving. Add to value:
Grade "A" **$100**
Grade "B" **135**
Grade "C" **350**

Navy Arms Martini Target Rifle **$265**
Martini single-shot action. Calibers: 444 Marlin, 45-70. 26- or 30-inch half-octagon or full-octagon barrel. Weight: about 9 pounds with 26-inch barrel. Creedmore tang peep sight, open middle sight, blade front sight. Stock with cheekpiece and pistol grip, forearm with schnabel tip, both checkered. Introduced 1972; discontinued.

Navy Arms Revolving Carbine **$225**
Action resembles that of Remington Model 1875 Revolver. Casehardened frame. Calibers: 357 Magnum, 44-40, 45 Colt. 6-shot cylinder. 20-inch barrel. Weight: about 5 pounds. Open rear sight, blade front sight. Straight-grip stock, brass trigger guard and butt plate. Introduced 1968; discontinued.

Navy Arms Rolling Block Baby Carbine **$150**
Replica of small Remington Rolling Block single-shot action. Casehardened frame, brass trigger guard. Calibers: 22 Long Rifle, 22 Hornet, 357 Magnum, 44-40. 20-inch octagon or 22-inch round barrel. Weight: about 5 pounds. Open rear sight, blade front sight. Straight-grip stock, plain forearm, brass butt plate. Made 1968 to 1981.

Navy Arms Rolling Block Buffalo Carbine **$150**
Same as Buffalo Rifle, except has 18-inch barrel, weighs about 10 pounds.

Navy Arms Rolling Block Buffalo Rifle **$225**
Replica Remington Rolling Block single-shot action. Casehardened frame, brass trigger guard. Calibers: 444 Marlin, 45-70, 50-70. 26- or 30-inch heavy half-octagon or full-octagon barrel. Weight: 11 to 12 pounds. Open rear sight, blade front sight. Straight-grip stock with brass butt plate, forearm with brass barrel band. Made from 1971 to date.

Navy Arms Revolving Carbine

Navy Arms Rolling Block Baby Carbine

Navy Arms Rolling Block Buffalo Rifle

Navy Arms Yellowboy Carbine

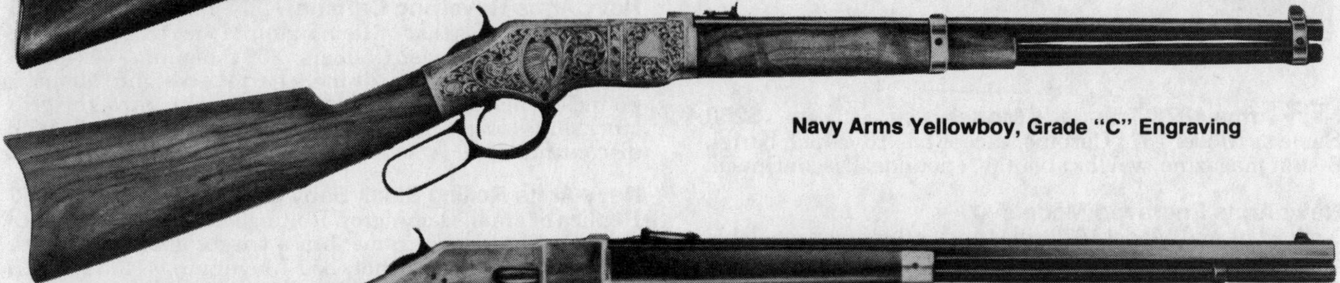

Navy Arms Yellowboy, Grade "C" Engraving

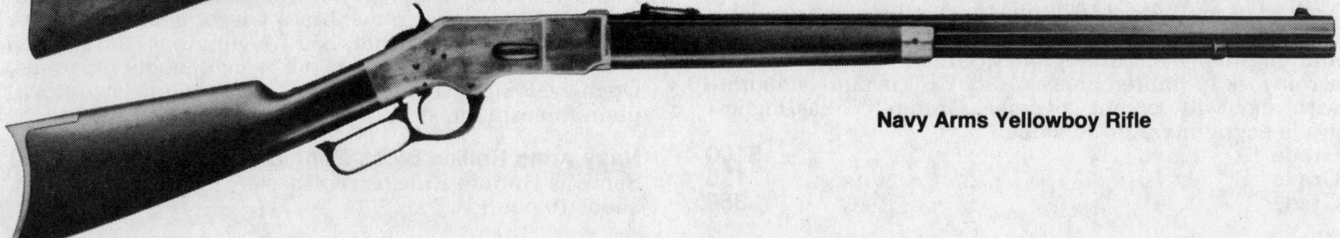

Navy Arms Yellowboy Rifle

Navy Arms Rolling Block Creedmoor Rifle $245
Same as Buffalo Rifle, except calibers 45-70 and 50-70 only, 28- or 30-inch heavy half-octagon or full-octagon barrel, Creedmoor tang peep sight.

Navy Arms Yellowboy Carbine $225
Similar to Yellowboy Rifle, except has 19-inch barrel, 10-shot magazine (14-shot in 22 Long Rifle), carbine-style forearm. Weight: about 6¾ pounds. Discontinued.

Navy Arms Yellowboy Lever Action Repeating Rifle $275
Replica of Winchester Model 1866. Calibers: 38 Special, 44-40. 15-shot magazine. 24-inch octagon barrel. Weight: about 8 pounds. Folding leaf rear sight, blade front sight. Straight-grip stock, forearm with end cap. Introduced 1966; discontinued.

Navy Arms Yellowboy Trapper's Model $225
Same as Yellowboy Carbine, except has 16½-inch barrel, magazine holds two fewer rounds, weighs about 6¼ pounds. Discontinued.

NEWTON SPORTING RIFLES
Buffalo, New York
Mfd. by Newton Arms Co., Charles Newton Rifle Corp. and Buffalo Newton Rifle Co.

Buffalo Newton Sporting Rifle $750
Same general specifications as Standard Model—Second Type. Made c. 1922-32 by Buffalo Newton Rifle Co.

Newton-Mauser Sporting Rifle $625
Mauser (Oberndorf) action. Caliber: 256 Newton. 5-shot box magazine, hinged floorplate. Double-set triggers. 24-inch barrel. Open rear sight, ramp front sight. Sporting stock with checkered pistol grip. Weight: about 7 pounds. Made c.1914 by Newton Arms Co.

Newton Standard Model Sporting Rifle—First Type $725
Newton bolt action, interrupted screw-type breech-locking mechanism, double-set triggers. Calibers: 22, 256, 280, 30, 33, 35 Newton; 30-06. 24-inch barrel. Open rear sight or cocking-piece peep sight, ramp front sight. Checkered pistol-grip stock. Weight: 7 to 8 pounds, depending upon caliber. Made c.1916-18 by Newton Arms Co.

Newton Standard Model Sporting Rifle—Second Type $750
Newton bolt action, improved design; distinguished by reversed-set trigger and 1917-Enfield-type bolt handle. Calibers: 256, 30, 35 Newton; 30-06. 5-shot box magazine. 24-inch barrel. Open rear sight, ramp front sight. Checkered pistol-grip stock. Weight: 7¾ to 8¼ pounds. Made c. 1921 by Charles Newton Rifle Corp.

NIKKO FIREARMS LTD.
Tochiga, Japan
See listings under Golden Eagle Rifles.

NOBLE MFG. CO.
Haydenville, Massachusetts

Noble Model 10 Bolt Action Single Shot Rifle $65
Caliber: 22 Long Rifle, Long, Short. 24-inch barrel. Plain pistol-grip stock. Open rear sight, bead front sight. Weight: about 4 pounds. Made 1955-58.

Noble Model 20 Bolt Action Single Shot Rifle $65
Manually cocked. Caliber: 22 Long Rifle, Long, Short. 22-inch barrel. Weight: about 5 pounds. Open rear sight, bead front sight. Walnut stock with pistol grip. Made from 1958 to 1963.

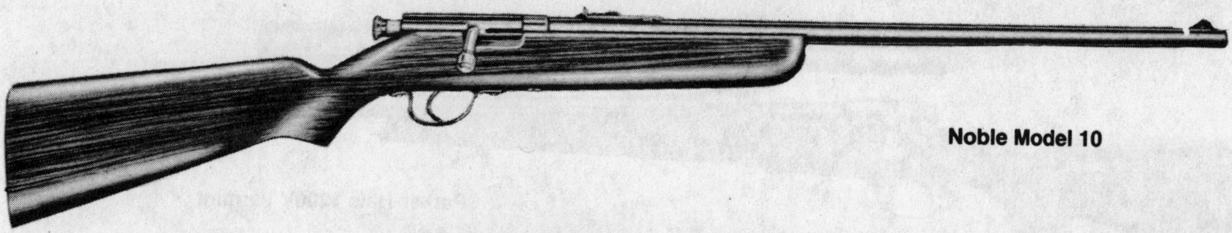

Noble Model 10

Noble Model 222

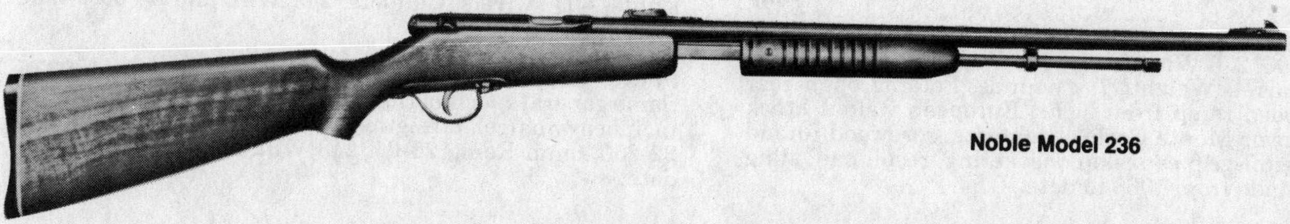

Noble Model 236

Noble Model 275

Noble Model 33 Slide Action Repeater $70
Hammerless. Caliber: 22 Long Rifle, Long, Short. Tubular magazine holds 21 Short, 17 Long, 15 Long Rifle. 24-inch barrel. Weight: 6 pounds. Open rear sight, bead front sight. Tenite stock and slide handle. Made 1949 to 1953.

Noble Model 33A $65
Same general specifications as Model 33 except has wood stock and slide handle. Made 1953-55.

Noble Model 222 Bolt Action Single Shot Rifle . . . $75
Manually cocked. Caliber: 22 Long Rifle, Long, Short. Barrel integral with receiver. Overall length: 38 inches. Weight: about 5 pounds. Interchangeable V-notch and

Noble Model 222 Bolt Action Single Shot Rifle (cont.)
peep rear sight, ramp front sight. Scope mounting base. Pistol-grip stock. Made 1958 to 1971.

Noble Model 236 Slide Action Repeating Rifle . . . $85
Hammerless. Caliber: 22 Short, Long, Long Rifle. Tubular magazine holds 21 Short, 17 Long, 15 Long Rifle. 24-inch barrel. Weight: about 5½ pounds. Open rear sight, ramp front sight. Pistol-grip stock, grooved slide handle. Made from 1951 to date.

Noble Model 275 Lever Action Rifle $95
Hammerless. Caliber: 22 Short, Long, Long Rifle. Tubular magazine holds 21 Short, 17 Long, 15 Long Rifle. 24-inch barrel. Weight: about 5½ pounds. Open rear sight, ramp front sight. Stock with semipistol grip. Made 1958 to 1971.

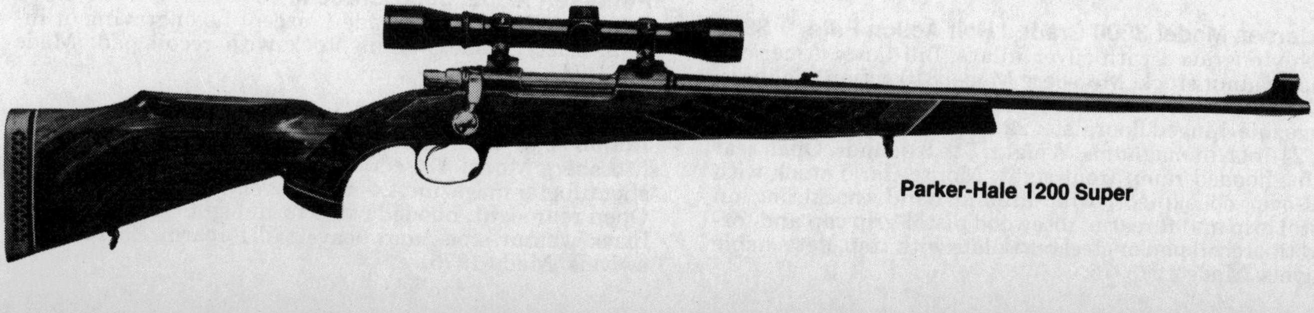

Parker-Hale 1200 Super

Parker-Hale 1200V Varmint

PARKER-HALE LIMITED
Birmingham, England

Parker-Hale 1200 Super Bolt Action Sporting Rifle $325
Mauser-type bolt action. Calibers: 22-250, 243 Win., 6mm Rem., 25-06, 270 Win., 30-06, 308 Win. 4-shot magazine. 24-inch barrel. Weight: 7¼ pounds. Folding open rear sight, hooded ramp front sight. European walnut stock with roll-over Monte Carlo cheekpiece, rosewood forend tip and pistol-grip cap, skip checkering, recoil pad, sling swivels. Made from 1968 to date.

Parker-Hale 1200 Super Magnum $395
Same general specifications as 1200 Super, except calibers 7mm Rem. Mag. and 300 Win. Mag., 3-shot magazine.

Parker-Hale 1200P Presentation $525
Same general specifications as 1200 Super, except has scroll-engraved action, trigger guard and floorplate, no sights. QD swivels. Calibers: 243 Win. and 30-06. Made 1969 to 1975.

Parker-Hale 1200V Varmint $375
Same general specifications as 1200 Super, except has 24-inch heavy barrel, no sights, weighs 9½ pounds. Calibers: 22-250, 6mm Rem., 25-06, 243 Win. Made from 1969 to date.

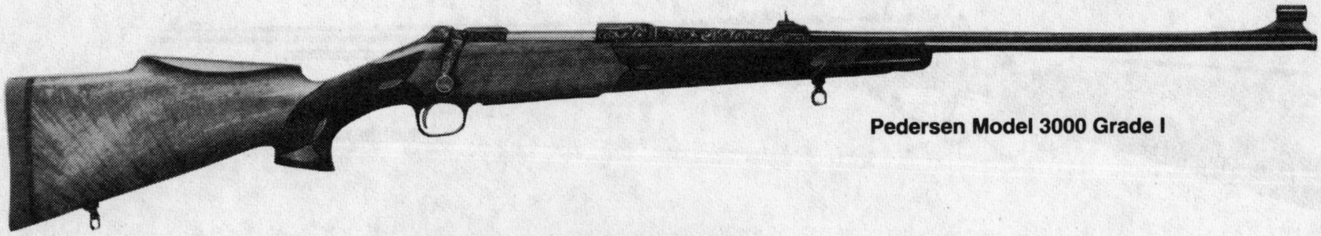

Pedersen Model 3000 Grade I

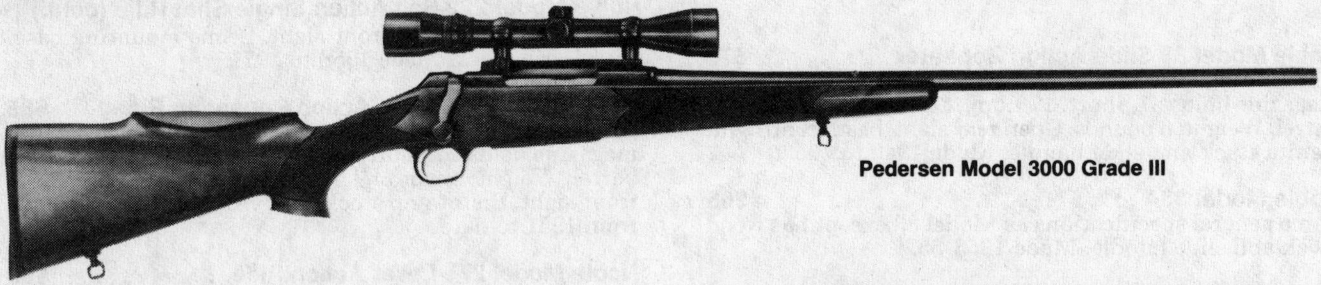

Pedersen Model 3000 Grade III

PEDERSEN CUSTOM GUNS
North Haven, Connecticut
Division of O.F. Mossberg & Sons, Inc.

Pedersen Model 3000 Grade I Bolt Action Rifle . $800
Richly engraved with silver inlays, full-fancy American black walnut stock. Mossberg Model 810 action. Calibers: 270 Win., 30-06, 7mm Rem. Mag., 338 Win. Mag. 3-shot magazine, hinged floorplate. 22-inch barrel in 270 and 30-06, 24-inch in magnums. Weight: 7 to 8 pounds. Open rear sight, hooded ramp front sight. Monte Carlo stock with roll-over cheekpiece, wrap-around hand checkering on pistol grip and forearm, rosewood pistol-grip cap and forend tip, recoil pad or steel butt plate with trap, detachable swivels. Made 1973-75.

Pedersen Model 3000 Grade II.............. $595
Same as Model 3000 Grade I, except less elaborate engraving, no inlays, fancy grade walnut stock with recoil pad. Made 1973-75.

Pedersen Model 3000 Grade III $500
Same as Model 3000 Grade I, except no engraving or inlays, select grade walnut stock with recoil pad. Made 1973-74.

Pedersen Model 4700 Custom Deluxe Lever Action Rifle $235
Mossberg Model 472 action. Calibers: 30-30, 35 Rem. 5-shot tubular magazine. 24-inch barrel. Weight: 7½ pounds. Open rear sight, hooded ramp front sight. Hand-finished black walnut stock and beavertail forearm, barrel band swivels. Made 1975.

J. C. PENNEY CO., INC.
New York, New York

Firearms sold under the J.C. Penney label have been manufactured by Marlin, High Standard, Stevens, Savage and Springfield.

J.C. Penney Model 2025 Bolt Action Repeating Rifle $50
Takedown. Caliber: 22 RF. 8-shot detachable box magazine. 24-inch barrel. Weight: about 6 pounds. Open rear sight, bead front sight. Plain pistol-grip stock. Mfd. by Marlin.

J.C. Penney Model 2035 Bolt Action Repeating Rifle $50
Takedown. Caliber: 22 RF. 8-shot detachable box magazine. 24-inch barrel. Weight: about 6 pounds. Open rear sight, bead front sight. Plain pistol-grip stock. Mfd. by Marlin.

J.C. Penney Model 2935 Lever Action Rifle $125
Same general specifications as Marlin Model 336.

J.C. Penney Model 6400 Bolt Action Centerfire Rifle $120
Same general specifications as Savage Model 340.

J.C. Penney Model 6660 Autoloading Rifle $65
Caliber: 22 RF. Tubular magazine. 22-inch barrel. Weight: about 5½ pounds. Open rear sight, hooded ramp front sight. Plain pistol-grip stock. Mfd. by Marlin.

PLAINFIELD MACHINE COMPANY
Dunellen, New Jersey

Plainfield M-1 Carbine $155
Same as U.S. Carbine, Cal. 30, M-1, except also available in caliber 5.7mm (22 with necked-down 30 Carbine cartridge case). Current production has ventilated metal handguard and barrel band without bayonet lug; earlier models have standard military-type fittings. Made 1960 to 1977.

Plainfield M-1 Carbine, Commando Model $165
Same as M-1 Carbine, except has paratrooper-type stock with telescoping wire shoulderpiece. Made 1960 to 1977.

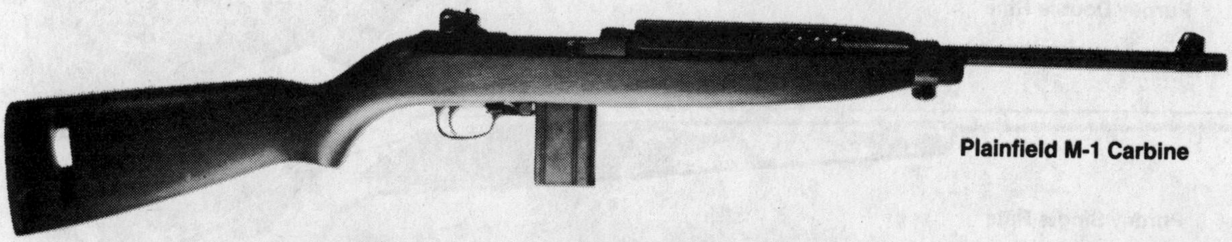

Plainfield M-1 Carbine

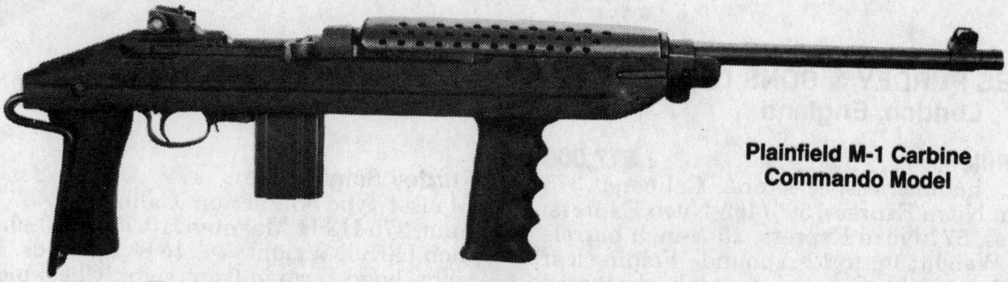

Plainfield M-1 Carbine Commando Model

Plainfield M-1 Carbine Military Sporter

Plainfielder M-1 Deluxe Sporter

Plainfield M-1 Carbine, Military Sporter $160
Same as M-1 Carbine, except has unslotted buttstock and wood handguard. Made 1960 to 1977.

Plainfielder M-1 Deluxe Sporter $185
Same as M-1 Carbine, except has Monte Carlo sporting stock. Made 1960 to 1973.

RIFLES

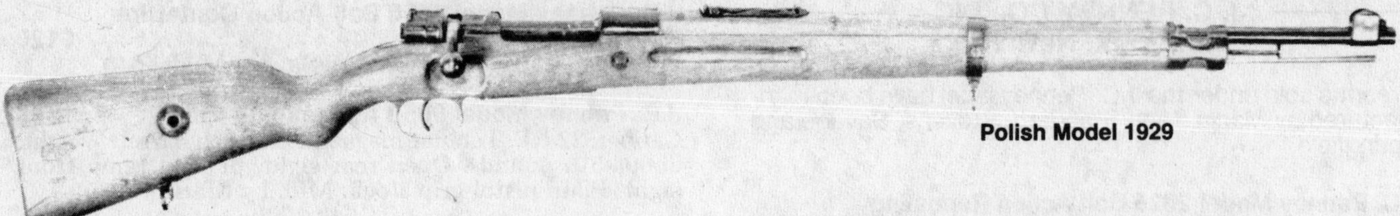

Polish Model 1929

POLISH MILITARY RIFLES

Manufactured by Government Arsenals at Radom and Warsaw, Poland

Polish Model 1898 (Karabin 98, WZ98A) Mauser Military Rifle **$95**
Same, except for minor details, as the German Gew. 98 used in WWI. Manufacture begun c. 1921.

Polish Model 1898 (Karabin 98, K98) Mauser Military Carbine **$130**
Same, except for minor details, as the German Kar. 98a. First manufactured during early 1920s.

Polish Model 1929 (Karabin 29, WZ29) Mauser Military Rifle **$150**
Same, except for minor details, as the Czech Model 24. Mfd. 1929 through WWII. A similar model produced during the German occupation was designated Gew. 29/40.

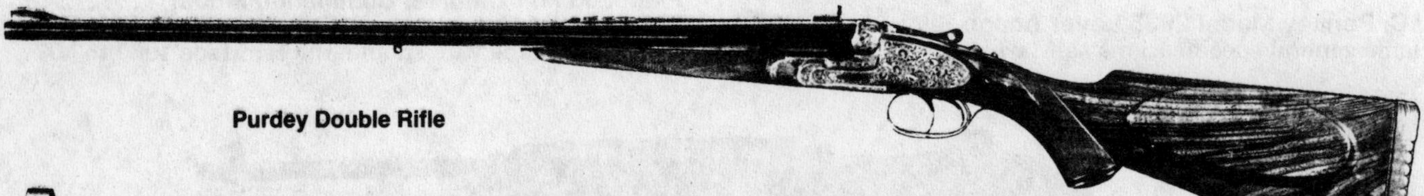

Purdey Double Rifle

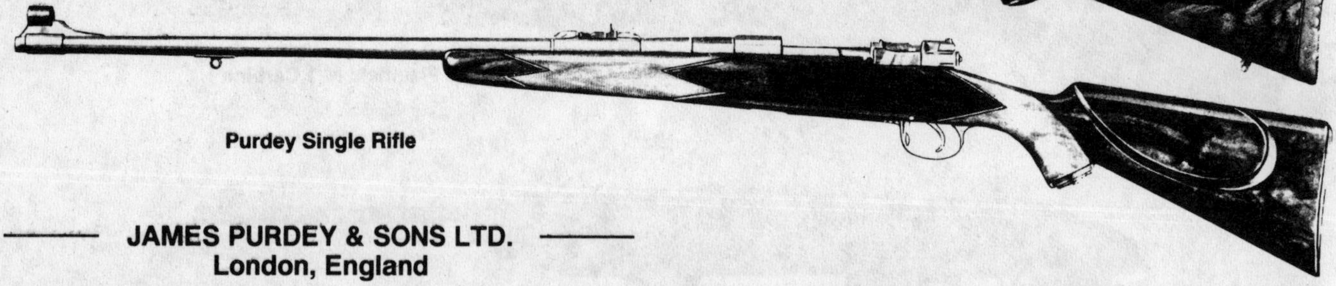

Purdey Single Rifle

JAMES PURDEY & SONS LTD.

London, England

Purdey Double Rifle **$17,000**
Sidelock action, hammerless, ejectors. Calibers: 375 Flanged Magnum Nitro Express, 500/465 Nitro Express, 470 Nitro Express, 577 Nitro Express. 25½-inch barrels (25-inch in 375). Weight: 9½ to 12¾ pounds. Folding leaf rear sight, ramp front sight. Cheekpiece stock, checkered forearm and pistol grip, recoil pad, swivels. Currently manufactured; same general specifications apply to pre-WWII model.

Purdey Single Rifle **$4500**
Mauser-type bolt action. Calibers: 7×57, 300 H&H Magnum, 375 H&H Magnum, 10.75×73. 3-shot magazine. 24-inch barrel. Weight: 7½ to 8¾ pounds. Folding leaf rear sight, hooded ramp front sight. Cheekpiece stock, checkered forearm and pistol grip, swivels. Currently manufactured; same general specifications apply to pre-WWII model.

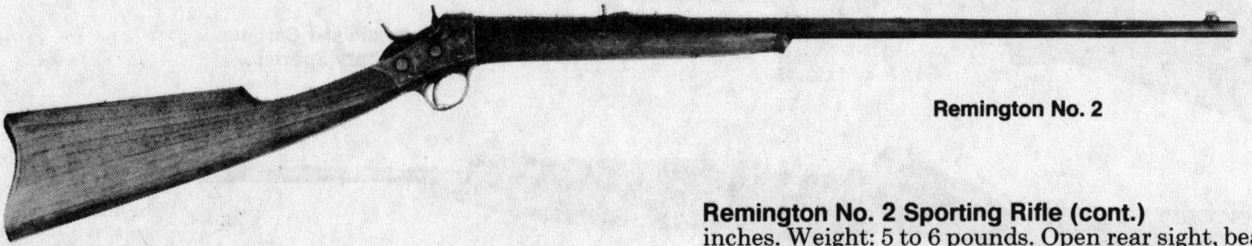

Remington No. 2

REMINGTON ARMS COMPANY

Ilion, New York

Remington No. 2 Sporting Rifle
Single-shot, rolling-block action. Calibers: 22, 25, 32, 38, 44 rimfire or centerfire. Barrel lengths: 24, 26, 28 or 30

Remington No. 2 Sporting Rifle (cont.)
inches. Weight: 5 to 6 pounds. Open rear sight, bead front sight. Straight-grip sporting stock and knobtip forearm of walnut. Made 1873 to 1910.
Calibers: 22, 25, 32 . . . . **$275**
Calibers: 38, 44 . . . . **425**

Remington Model 2C **$295**
Target Grade. Same as Model 12A, except has 24-inch octagon barrel, pistol-grip stock.

Remington No. 3 Creedmoor and Schuetzen Rifles . . . . **$5000+**
Produced in a variety of styles and calibers, these are collector's items and bring far higher prices than the sporting types. The Schuetzen Special, which has an under-lever action, is especially rare—perhaps less than 100 having been made.

Remington No. 3 High Power Rifle
Single shot. Hepburn falling-block action with side lever. Calibers: 30/30, 30/40, 32 Special, 32/40, 38/55, 38/72 (high-power cartridges). Barrel lengths: 26-, 28-, 30-inch. Weight: about 8 pounds. Open sporting sights. Checkered pistol-grip stock and forearm. Made 1893 to 1907.
Calibers: 30/30, 30/40, 32 Special, 32/40 . . . . **$1425**
Calibers: 38/55, 38/72 . . . . **1750**

Remington No. 3 Sporting Rifle **$725**
Single shot. Hepburn falling-block action with side lever. Calibers: 22 WCF, 22 Extra Long, 25/20 Stevens, 25/21 Stevens, 25/25 Stevens, 32 WCF, 32/40 Ballard & Marlin, 32/40 Rem., 38 WCF, 38/40 Rem., 38/50 Rem., 38/55 Ballard & Marlin, 40/60 Ballard & Marlin, 40/60 WCF, 40/65 Rem. Straight, 40/82 WCF, 45/70 Gov., 45/90 WCF; also was supplied on special order in bottle-necked 40/50, 40/70, 40/90, 44/77, 44/90, 44/105, 50/70 Gov., 50/90 Sharps Straight. Barrel lengths: 26-inch (22, 25, 32 cal. only), 28-inch, 30-inch; half-octagon or full-octagon. Weight: 8 to 10 pounds. Open rear sight, blade front sight. Checkered pistol-grip stock and forearm. Made 1880 to c. 1911.

Remington No. 3

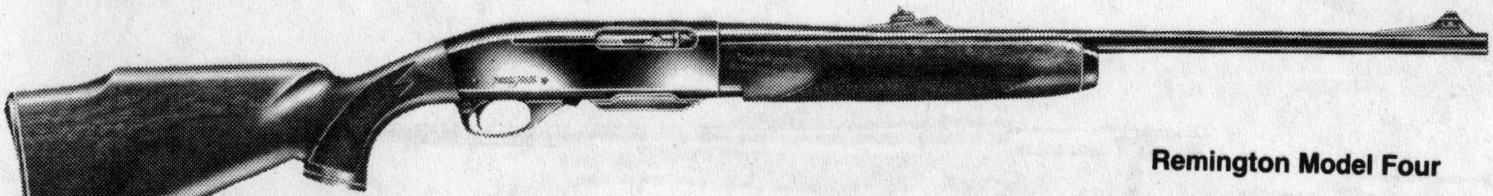

Remington Model Four

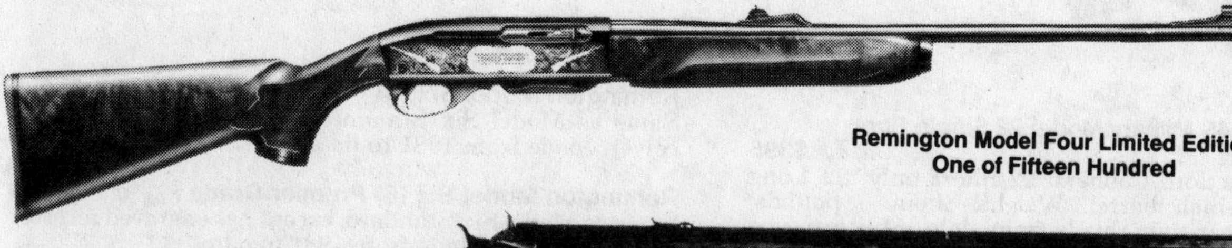

Remington Model Four Limited Edition
One of Fifteen Hundred

Remington No. 4

RIFLES

Remington Model Four (4) Autoloading Rifle . . . **$375**
Hammerless. Calibers: 6mm Rem., 243 Win., 270 Win., 7mm Express Rem., 30-06, 308 Win. 22-inch barrel. Weight: 7½ pounds. Open rear sight, bead front sight on ramp. Monte Carlo checkered stock and forearm. Made from 1981 to date.

Remington Model Four (4) Peerless Grade **$1235**
Same as Model Four Standard, except has engraved receiver. Made from 1981 to date.

Remington Model Four (4) Premier Grade **$3500**
Same as Model Four Standard, except has engraved receiver with gold inlay. Made from 1981 to date.

Remington No. 4 Single Shot Rifle **$215**
Rolling-block action. Solid frame or takedown. Calibers: 22 Short and Long, 22 Long Rifle, 25 Stevens R.F., 32 Short and Long R.F. 22½-inch octagon barrel, 24-inch available in 32 caliber only. Weight: about 4½ pounds. Open rear sight, blade front sight. Plain walnut stock and forearm. Made 1890 to 1933.

Remington No. 4S

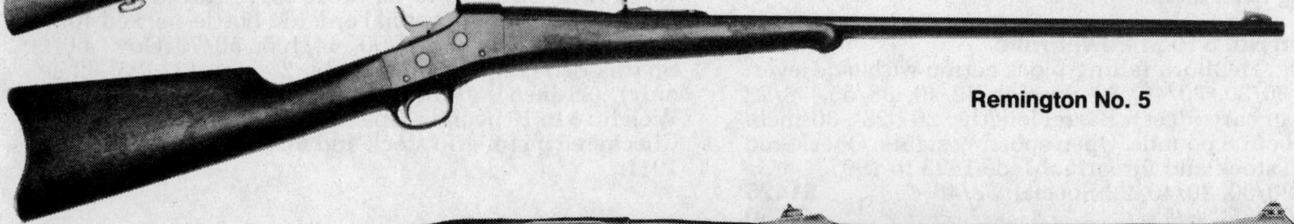

Remington No. 5

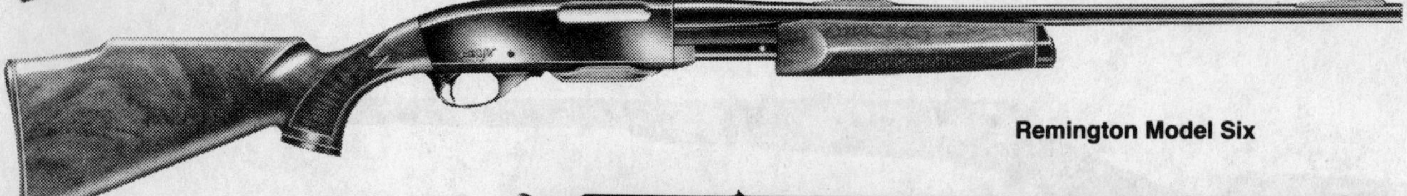

Remington Model Six

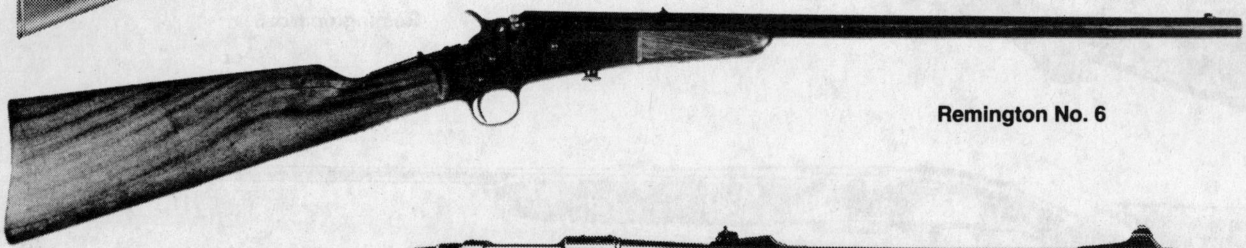

Remington No. 6

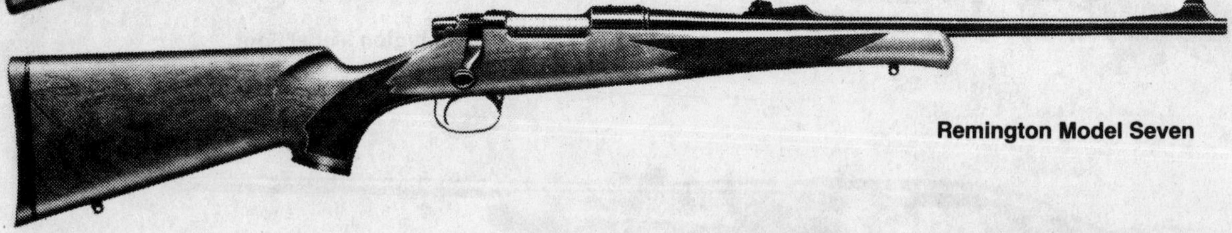

Remington Model Seven

Remington No. 4S Military Model 22 Single Shot Rifle **$395**
Rolling-block action. Calibers: 22 Short only, 22 Long Rifle only. 28-inch barrel. Weight: about 5 pounds. Military-type rear sight, blade front sight. Military-type stock with handguard, stacking swivel, sling. Has a bayonet stud on the barrel; bayonet and scabbard were regularly supplied. *Note:* At one time the "Military Model" was the official rifle of the Boy Scouts of America and was called the "Boy Scout Rifle." Made 1913 to 1933.

Remington No. 5 Special Rifle
Single shot. Rolling-block action. Calibers: 7mm Mauser, 30-30, 30-40 Krag, 303 British, 32-40, 32 Special, 38-55 (high-power cartridges). Barrel lengths: 24, 26 and 28 inches. Weight: about 7 pounds. Open sporting sights. Plain straight-grip stock and forearm. Made 1902 to 1918. *Note:* Models 1897 and 1902 Military Rifles, intended for the export market, are almost identical with the No. 5 except for 30-inch barrel, full military stock and weight (about $8^1/_2$ pounds); a carbine was also supplied. The military rifles were produced in caliber 8mm Lebel for France, 7.62mm Russian for Russia and 7mm Mauser for the Central and South American government trade. At one time, Remington also offered these military models to retail purchasers.
Sporting Model **$350**
Military Model **225**

Remington Model Six (6) Peerless Grade **$1235**
Same as Model Six Standard, except has engraved receiver. Made from 1981 to date.

Remington Model Six (6) Premier Grade **$3500**
Same as Model Six Standard, except has engraved receiver with gold inlay. Made from 1981 to date.

Remington Model Six (6) Slide Action Repeating Rifle **$345**
Hammerless. Calibers: 6mm Rem., 243 Win., 270 Win., 7mm Express Rem., 30-06, 308 Win. 22-inch barrel. Weight: $7^1/_2$ pounds. Checkered Monte Carlo stock and forearm. Made from 1981 to date.

Remington No. 6 Takedown Rifle **$165**
Single shot. Rolling-block action. Calibers: 22 Short, 22 Long, 22 Long Rifle, 32 Short and Long R.F. 20-inch barrel. Weight: about 4 pounds. Open front and rear sights, tang peep sight. Plain straight-grip stock and forearm. Made 1901 to 1933.

Remington Model Seven (7) Centerfire Bolt Action Rifle **$335**
Calibers: 222 Rem., 243 Win., 6mm Rem., 7mm-08 Rem., 308 Win. Magazine capacity: 5-shot in 222 Rem., 4-shot in other calibers. $18^1/_2$-inch barrel. Weight: $6^1/_4$ pounds. Walnut stock, checkering, and recoil pad. Made from 1983 to date. 223 Rem. added in 1984.

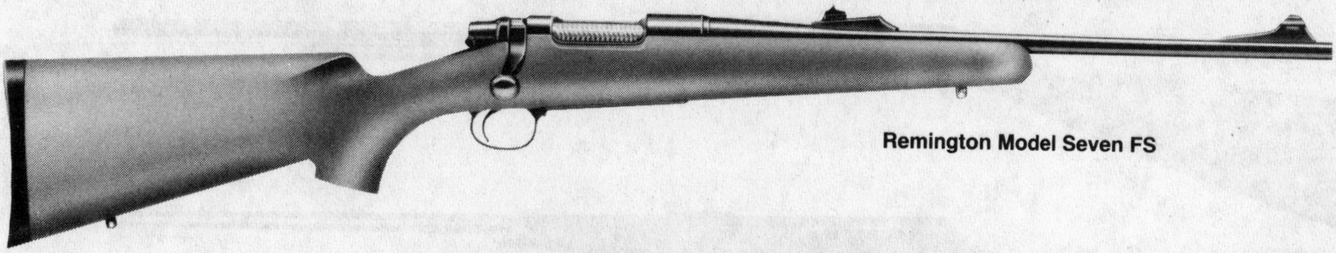

Remington Model Seven FS

Remington Model Seven KS Custom Rifle

Remington No. 7 Target

Remington Model 8A

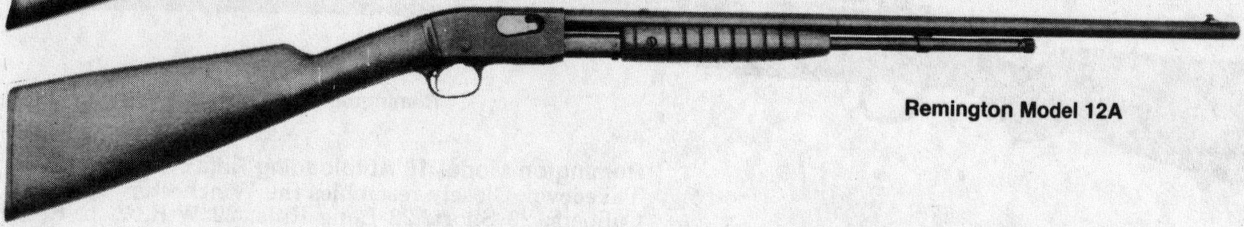

Remington Model 12A

Remington Model Seven (7) FS Centerfire Bolt Action Rifle $320
Calibers: 243, 7mm-08 Rem., 308 Win. 18½-inch barrel. 37½ inches overall. Weight: 5¼ pounds. Hand layup fiberglass stock, reinforced with DuPont Kevlar at points of bedding and stress. Made from 1987 to date.

Remington Model Seven (7) KS Custom Bolt Action Rifle $620
Calibers: 35 Rem and 350 Rem. Mag. 20-inch barrel. Custom made in Remington's Custom shop with Kevlar stock. Made from 1987 to date.

Remington No. 7 Target and Sporting Rifle $550
Single shot. Rolling-block Army Pistol frame. Calibers: 22 Short, 22 Long Rifle, 25 Stevens R.F. (other calibers as available in No. 2 Rifle were supplied on special order). Half-octagon barrels: 24-, 26-, 28-inch. Weight: about 6 pounds. Lyman combination rear sight, Beach combination front sight. Fancy walnut stock and forearm; Swiss butt plate available as an extra. Made 1903 to 1911.

Remington Model 8A Autoloading Rifle $350
Standard Grade. Takedown. Calibers: 25, 30, 32 and 35 Rem. Detachable box magazine holds five cartridges. 22-inch barrel. Weight: 7¾ pounds. Open rear sight, bead front sight. Plain straight-grip stock and forearm of walnut. Made 1906 to 1936.

Remington Model 12A Slide Action Repeating Rifle $250
Standard Grade. Hammerless. Takedown. Caliber: 22 Short, Long or Long Rifle. Tubular magazine holds 15 Short, 12 Long or 10 Long Rifle cartridges. 22-inch round barrel. Weight: 4½ pounds. Open rear sight, bead front sight. Plain, straight-grip stock, grooved slide handle. Made 1909 to 1936.

Remington Model 12B $220
Same as Model 12A, except chambered for 22 Short only.

Remington Model 12CS $225
Same as Model 12C, except chambered for 22 Remington Special (22 W.R.F.). Magazine holds 12 rounds.

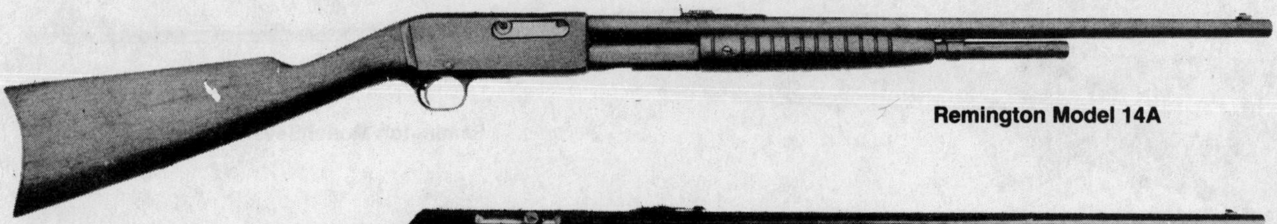

Remington Model 14A

Remington Model 16

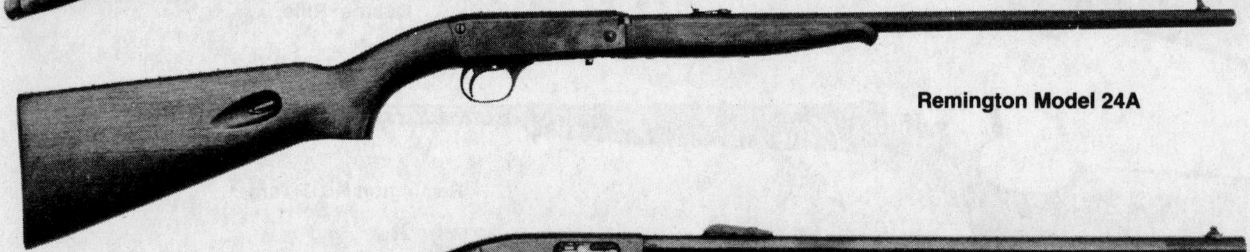

Remington Model 24A

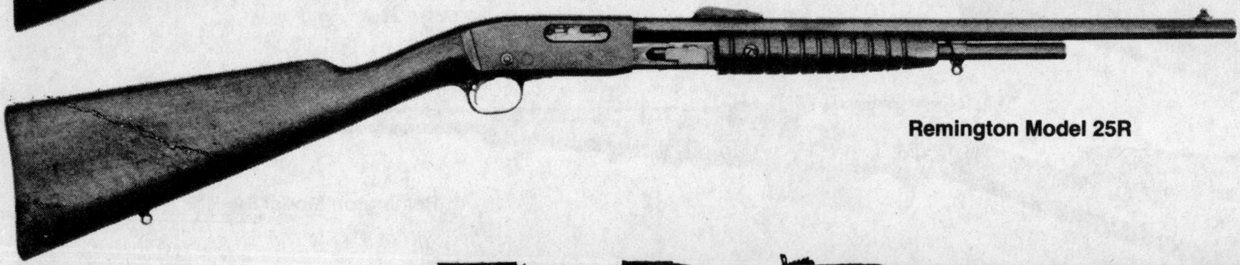

Remington Model 25R

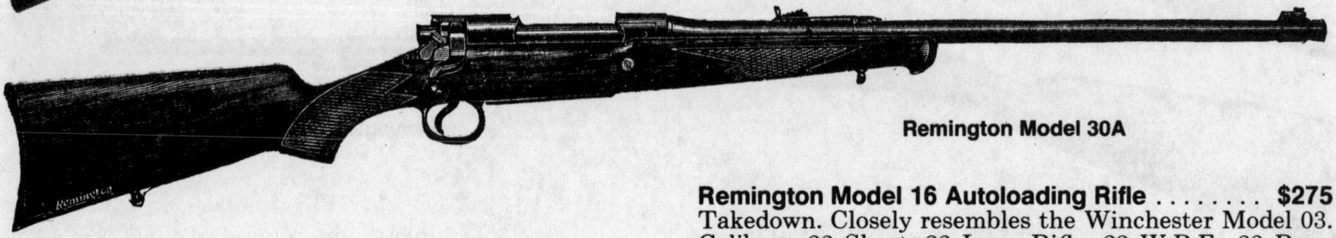

Remington Model 30A

Remington Model 14A High Power Slide Action Repeating Rifle $325
Standard Grade. Hammerless. Takedown. Calibers: 25, 30, 32 and 35 Rem. 5-shot tubular magazine. 22-inch barrel. Weight: about $6\frac{3}{4}$ pounds. Open rear sight, bead front sight. Plain, pistol-grip stock and grooved slide handle of walnut. Made 1912 to 1935.

Remington Model 14R Carbine $335
Same as Model 14A except has $18\frac{1}{2}$-inch barrel, straight-grip stock, weighs about 6 pounds.

Remington Model $14\frac{1}{2}$ Carbine $695
Same as Model $14\frac{1}{2}$ Rifle, except has 9-shot magazine, $18\frac{1}{2}$-inch barrel.

Remington Model $14\frac{1}{2}$ Rifle $595
Similar to Model 14A, except calibers 38/40 and 44/40, 11-shot full magazine, $22\frac{1}{2}$-inch barrel. Made 1912 to early 1920s.

Remington Model 16 Autoloading Rifle $275
Takedown. Closely resembles the Winchester Model 03. Calibers: 22 Short, 22 Long Rifle, 22 W.R.F., 22 Rem. Auto. 15-shot tubular magazine in buttstock. 22-inch barrel. Weight: $5\frac{3}{4}$ pounds. Open rear sight, bead front sight. Plain straight-grip stock and forearm. Made 1914 to 1928. *Note:* In 1918 this model was discontinued in all calibers except 22 Rem. Auto; specifications given are for that.

Remington Model 24A Autoloading Rifle $295
Standard Grade. Takedown. Calibers: 22 Short only, 22 Long Rifle only. Tubular magazine in buttstock, holds 15 Short or 10 Long Rifle. 21-inch barrel. Weight: about 5 pounds. Open rear sight, bead front sight. Plain walnut stock and forearm. Made 1922 to 1935.

Remington Model 25A Slide Action Repeating Rifle $360
Standard Grade. Hammerless. Takedown. Calibers: 25/20, 32/20. 10-shot tubular magazine. 24-inch barrel. Weight: about $5\frac{1}{2}$ pounds. Open rear sight, bead front sight. Plain, pistol-grip stock, grooved slide handle. Made 1923 to 1936.

Remington Model 25R Carbine $400
Same as Model 25A, except has 18-inch barrel. 6-shot magazine, straight-grip stock, weighs about $4\frac{1}{2}$ pounds.

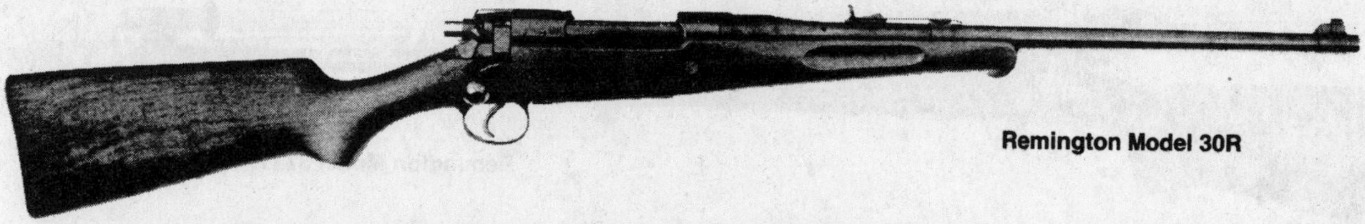

Remington Model 30R

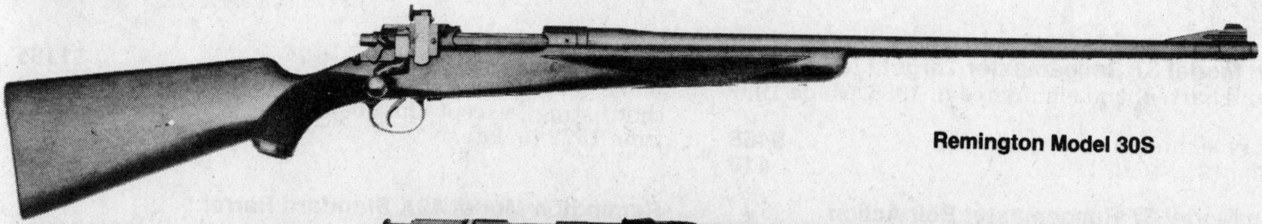

Remington Model 30S

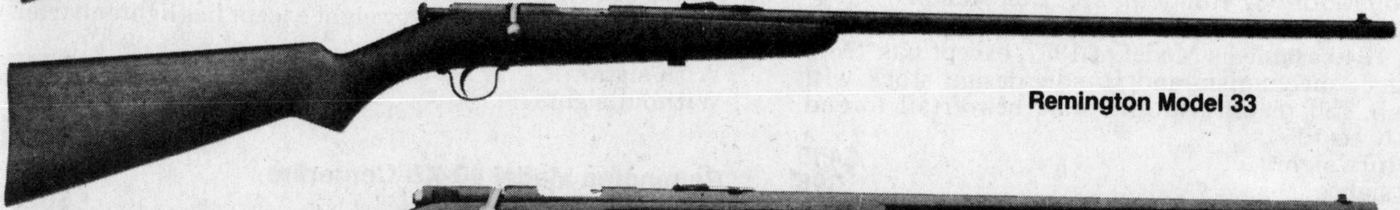

Remington Model 33

Remington Model 34

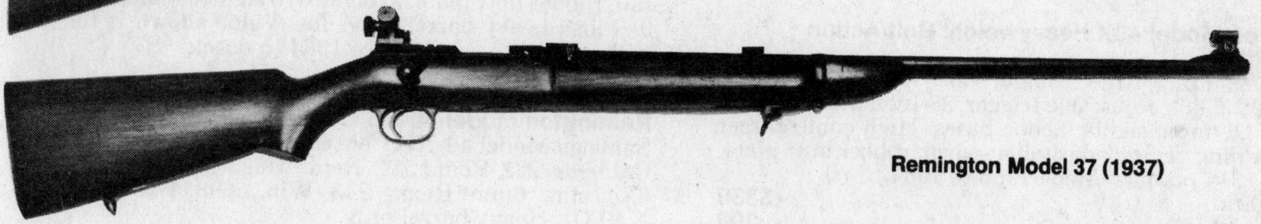

Remington Model 37 (1937)

Remington Model 30A Bolt Action Express Rifle $575
Standard Grade. Modified M/1917 Enfield Action. Calibers: 25, 30, 32 and 35 Rem., 7mm Mauser, 30-06. 5-shot box magazine. 22-inch barrel. Weight: about 7¼ pounds. Open rear sight, bead front sight. Walnut stock with checkered pistol grip and forearm. Made from 1921 to 1940. *Note:* Early Model 30s had a slender forend with schnabel tip, military-type double-pull trigger, 24-inch barrel.

Remington Model 30R Carbine $585
Same as Model 30A, except has 20-inch barrel, plain stock, weighs about 7 pounds.

Remington Model 30S Sporting Rifle $625
Special Grade. Same action as Model 30A. Calibers: 257 Roberts, 7mm Mauser, 30-06. 5-shot box magazine. 24-inch barrel. Weight: about 8 pounds. Lyman #48 Receiver sight, bead front sight. Special high comb stock with long, full forearm, checkered. Made 1930 to 1940.

Remington Model 33 Bolt Action Single Shot Rifle $125
Takedown. Caliber: 22 Short, Long, Long Rifle. 24-inch barrel. Weight: about 4½ pounds. Open rear sight, bead front sight. Plain, pistol-grip stock, forearm with grasping grooves. Made 1931-36.

Remington Model 33 NRA Junior Target Rifle . . . $145
Same as Model 33 Standard, except has Lyman peep rear sight, Patridge-type front sight, 7/8-inch sling and swivels, weighs about 5 pounds.

Remington Model 34 Bolt Action Repeating Rifle $150
Takedown. Caliber: 22 Short, Long, Long Rifle. Tubular magazine holds 22 Short, 17 Long or 15 Long Rifle. 24-inch barrel. Weight: about 5¼ pounds. Open rear sight, bead front sight. Plain, pistol-grip stock, forearm with grasping grooves. Made 1932-36.

Remington Model 34 NRA Target Rifle $175
Same as Model 34 Standard, except has Lyman peep rear sight, Patridge-type front sight, 7/8-inch sling and swivels, weighs about 5¾ pounds.

Remington Model 37 Rangemaster Bolt Action Target Rifle (I)
Model of 1937. Caliber: 22 Long Rifle. 5-shot box magazine, single shot adapter also supplied as standard equipment. 28-inch heavy barrel. Weight: about 12 pounds. Remington front and rear sights, scope bases. Target stock, swivels, sling. *Note:* Original 1937 model had a stock with outside barrel band similar in appearance to that of the old-style Winchester Model 52; forearm design was

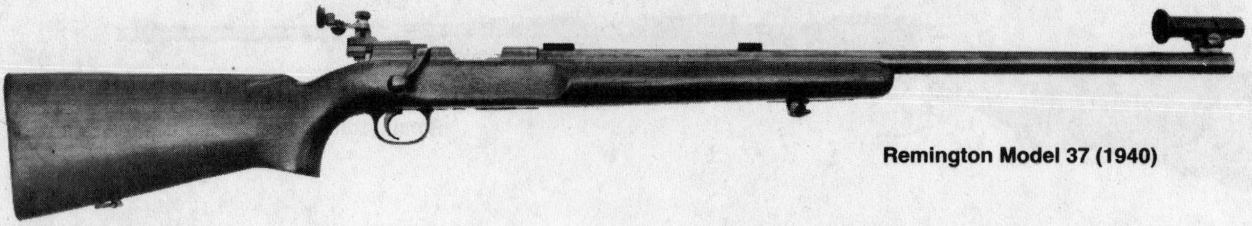

Remington Model 37 (1940)

Remington Model 37 Rangemaster Target I (cont.)
modified and barrel band eliminated in 1938. Made 1937 to 1940.
With factory sights **$465**
Without sights **410**

Remington Model 37 Rangemaster Bolt Action Target Rifle (II)
Model of 1940. Same as Model of 1937, except has "Miracle" trigger mechanism and Randle design stock with high comb, full pistol grip and wide beavertail forend. Made 1940 to 1954.
With factory sights **$450**
Without sights **395**

Remington Model 40X Centerfire Rifle $385
Specifications same as for Model 40X Rimfire (heavyweight). Calibers: 222 Rem., 222 Rem. Mag., 7.62mm NATO, 30-06 (others were available on special order). Made 1961-64. Value shown is for rifle without sights.

Remington Model 40X Heavyweight Bolt Action Target Rifle
Caliber: 22 Long Rifle. Single shot. Action similar to Model 722. Click adjustable trigger. 28-inch heavy barrel. Redfield Olympic sights. Scope bases. High comb target stock, bedding device, adjustable swivel, rubber butt plate. Weight: 12¾ pounds. Made 1955 to 1964.
With sights **$330**
Without sights **300**

Remington Model 40-X Sporter $1195
Same general specifications as Model 700C Custom (see that listing), except chambered for 22 Long Rifle. Made from 1972 to date.

Remington Model 40X Standard Barrel
Same as Model 40X Heavyweight except has lighter barrel. Weight: 10¾ pounds.
With sights **$315**
Without sights **275**

Remington Model 40-XB Centerfire Match Rifle $625
Bolt action, single shot. Calibers: 222 Rem., 222 Rem. Mag., 223 Rem., 22-250, 6×47mm, 6mm Rem., 243 Win., 25-06, 7mm Rem. Mag., 30-06, 308 Win. (7.62mm NATO), 30-338, 300 Win. Mag. 27¼-inch standard or heavy barrel. Target stock with adjustable front swivel block on guide rail, rubber butt plate. Weight w/o sights: standard barrel, 9¼ lbs.; heavy barrel, 11¼ lbs. Value shown is for rifle without sights. Made from 1964 to date.

Remington Model 40-XB Centerfire Repeater $565
Same as Model 40-XB Centerfire except 5-shot repeater. Calibers: 222 Rem., 222 Rem. Mag., 223 Rem., 22-250, 6×47mm, 6mm Rem., 243 Win., 308 Win. (7.62mm NATO). Heavy barrel only.

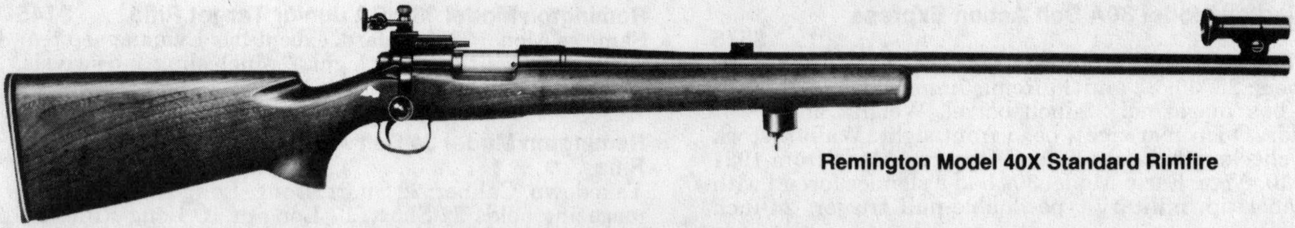

Remington Model 40X Standard Rimfire

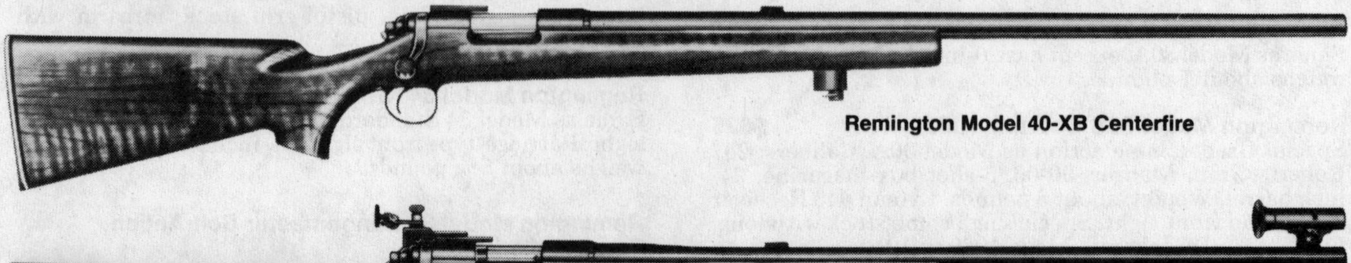

Remington Model 40-XB Centerfire

Remington Model 40-XB Rimfire

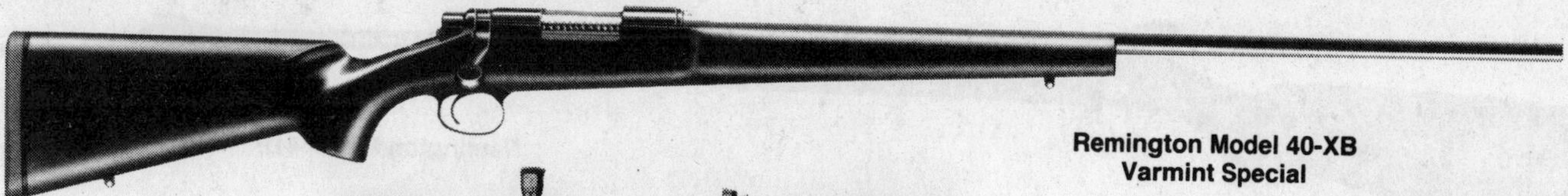

Remington Model 40-XB
Varmint Special

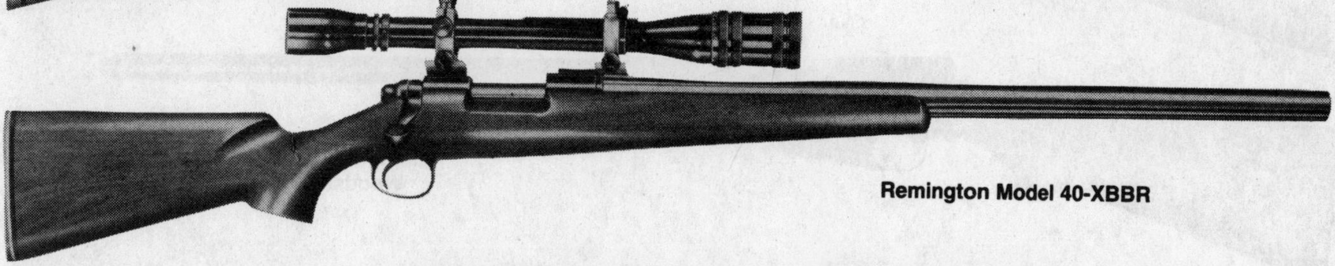

Remington Model 40-XBBR

Remington Model 40-XC

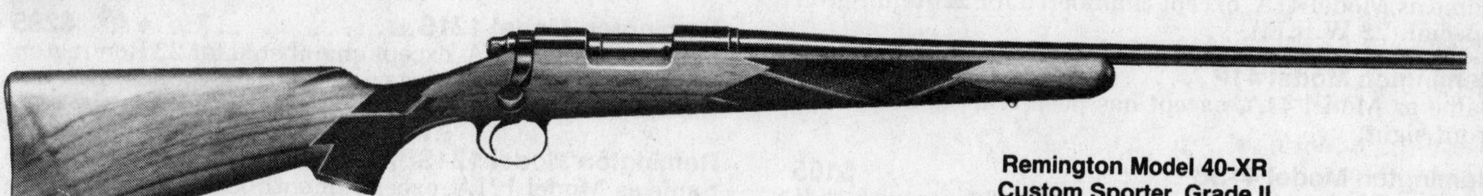

Remington Model 40-XR
Custom Sporter, Grade II

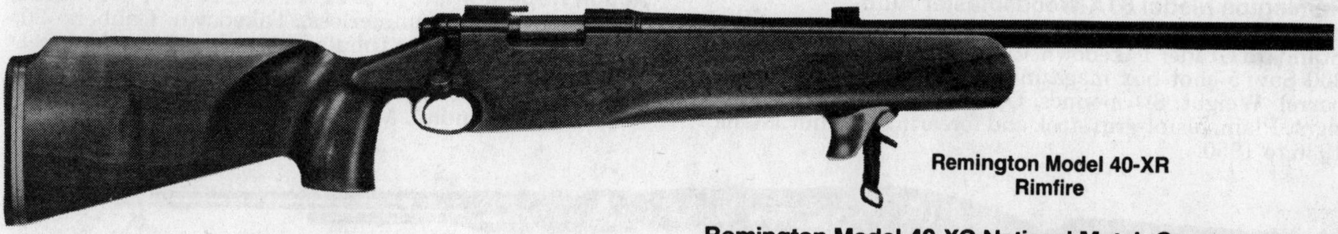

Remington Model 40-XR
Rimfire

Remington Model 40-XB Rangemaster Rimfire Match Rifle **$450**
Bolt action, single shot. Caliber: 22 Long Rifle. 28-inch standard or heavy barrel. Target stock with adjustable front swivel block on guide rail, rubber butt plate. Weight w/o sights: standard barrel, 10 lbs.; heavy barrel, 11¼ lbs. Value shown is for rifle without sights. Made 1964 to 1974.

Remington Model 40-XB Varmint Special Rifle . . $785
Same general specifications as Model 40-XB Repeater, except has synthetic stock of Kevlar. Made from 1987 to date.

Remington Model 40-XBBR Bench Rest Rifle . . . $695
Bolt action, single shot. Calibers: 222 Rem., 222 Rem. Mag., 223 Rem., 6×47mm, 308 Win. (7.62mm NATO). 20- or 26-inch unblued stainless steel barrel. Supplied without sights. Weight: with 20-inch bbl., 9¼ lbs.; with 26-inch bbl., 12 lbs. Varmint-style stock. Made from 1969 to date.

Remington Model 40-XC National Match Course Rifle **$695**
Bolt-action repeater. Caliber: 308 Win. (7.62mm NATO). 5-shot magazine; clip slot in receiver. 24-inch barrel. Supplied without sights. Weight: 11 pounds. Thumb groove stock with adjustable hand stop and sling swivel, adjustable butt plate. Made from 1974 to date.

Remington Model 40-XR Custom Sporter Rifle
Caliber: 22 RF. 24-inch contoured barrel. Supplied without sights. Made in four grades of checkering, engraving and other custom features. Made from 1987 to date.

Grade I	**$ 850**
Grade II	**1540**
Grade III	**2450**
Grade IV	**3800**

Remington Model 40-XR Rimfire Position Rifle **$425**
Bolt action, single shot. Caliber: 22 Long Rifle. 24-inch heavy barrel. Supplied without sights. Weight: about 10 pounds. Position style with thumb groove, adjustable hand stop and sling swivel on guide rail, adjustable butt plate. Made from 1974 to date.

Remington Model 41P

Remington Model 81A
Woodsmaster

Remington Model 41A Targetmaster Bolt Action Single Shot Rifle $125
Takedown. Caliber: 22 Short, Long, Long Rifle. 27-inch barrel. Weight: about $5\frac{1}{2}$ pounds. Open rear sight, bead front sight. Plain pistol-grip stock. Made 1936 to 1940.

Remington Model 41AS $125
Same as Model 41A, except chambered for 22 Remington Special (22 W.R.F.).

Remington Model 41P $135
Same as Model 41A, except has peep rear sight, hooded front sight.

Remington Model 41SB $165
Same as Model 41A, except smoothbore for use with shot cartridges.

Remington Model 81A Woodsmaster Autoloader $325
Standard Grade. Takedown. Calibers: 30, 32 and 35 Rem., 300 Sav. 5-shot box magazine (not detachable). 22-inch barrel. Weight: $8\frac{1}{4}$ pounds. Open rear sight, bead front sight. Plain, pistol-grip stock and forearm of walnut. Made 1936 to 1950.

Remington Model 121A Fieldmaster Slide Action Repeater $275
Standard Grade. Hammerless. Takedown. Caliber: 22 Short, Long, Long Rifle. Tubular magazine holds 20 Short, 15 Long or 14 Long Rifle cartridges. 24-inch round barrel. Weight: 6 pounds. Plain, pistol-grip stock and grooved semibeavertail slide handle. Made 1936 to 1954.

Remington Model 121S $295
Same as Model 121A, except chambered for 22 Remington Special (22 W.R.F.). Magazine holds 12 rounds. Discontinued.

Remington Model 121SB $350
Same as Model 121A, except smoothbore. Discontinued.

Remington Model 141A Gamemaster Slide Action Repeater $325
Standard Grade. Hammerless. Takedown. Calibers: 30, 32 and 35 Rem. 5-shot tubular magazine. 24-inch barrel. Weight: about $7\frac{3}{4}$ pounds. Open rear sight, bead front sight on ramp. Plain, pistol-grip stock, semibeavertail forend (slide-handle). Made 1936 to 1950.

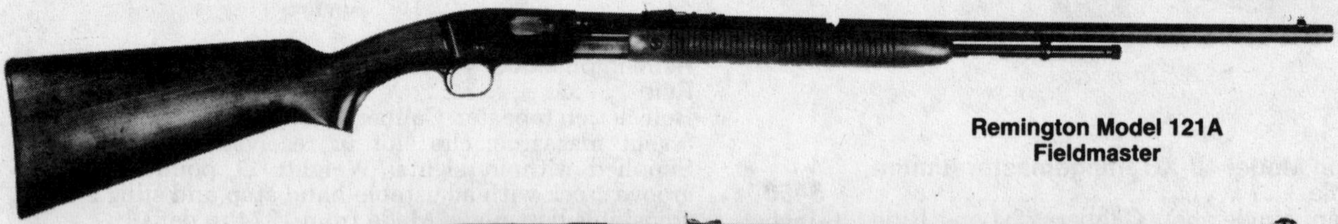

Remington Model 121A
Fieldmaster

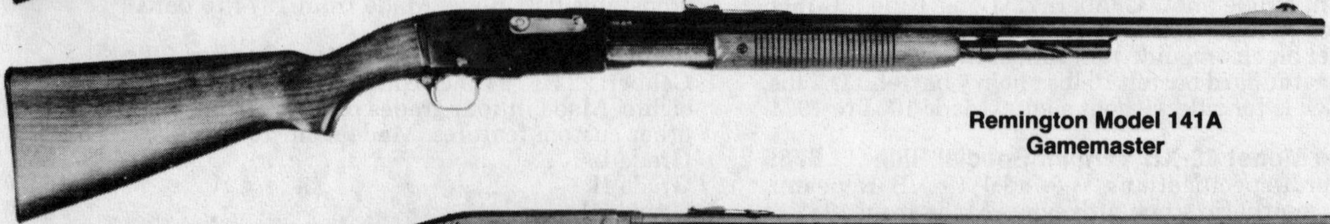

Remington Model 141A
Gamemaster

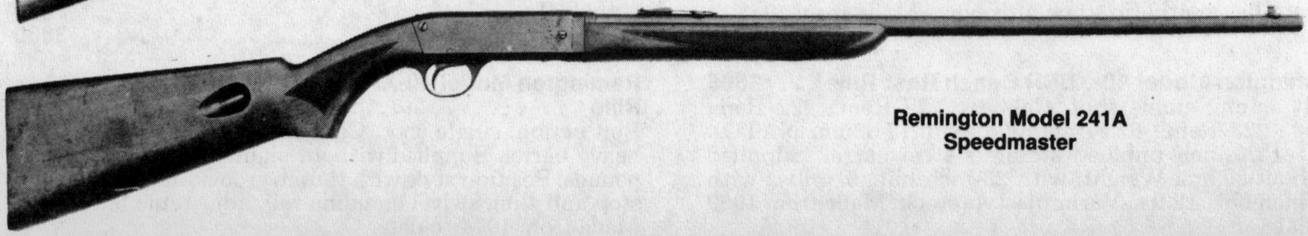

Remington Model 241A
Speedmaster

Remington Model 341A Sportsmaster

Remington Model 241A Speedmaster Autoloader **$275**
Standard Grade. Takedown. Calibers: 22 Short only, 22 Long Rifle only. Tubular magazine in buttstock, holds 15 Short or 10 Long Rifle. 24-inch barrel. Weight: about 6 pounds. Open rear sight, bead front sight. Plain walnut stock and forearm. Made 1935 to 1951.

Remington Model 341A Sportsmaster Bolt Action Repeater **$125**
Takedown. Caliber: 22 Short, Long, Long Rifle. Tubular magazine holds 22 Short, 17 Long, 15 Long Rifle. 27-inch barrel. Weight: about 6 pounds. Open rear sight, bead front sight. Plain pistol-grip stock. Made 1936 to 1940.

Remington Model 341P **$140**
Same as Model 341A, except has peep rear sight, hooded front sight.

Remington Model 341SB **$130**
Same as Model 341A, except smoothbore for use with shot cartridges.

Remington Model 510A Targetmaster Bolt Action Single Shot Rifle **$125**
Takedown. Caliber: 22 Short, Long, Long Rifle. 25-inch barrel. Weight: about 5½ pounds. Open rear sight, bead front sight. Plain pistol-grip stock. Made 1939 to 1962.

Remington Model 510P **$135**
Same as Model 510A, except has peep rear sight, Patridge front sight on ramp.

Remington Model 510SB **$165**
Same as Model 510A, except smoothbore for use with shot cartridges, shotgun bead front sight, no rear sight.

Remington Model 510X Bolt Action Single Shot Rifle **$140**
Same as Model 510A, except improved sights. Made 1964 to 1966.

Remington Model 511A Scoremaster Bolt Action Box Magazine Repeater **$115**
Takedown. Caliber: 22 Short, Long, Long Rifle. 6-shot detachable box magazine. 25-inch barrel. Weight: about 5½ pounds. Open rear sight, bead front sight. Plain pistol-grip stock. Made 1939 to 1962.

Remington Model 511P **$120**
Same as Model 511A, except has peep rear sight, Patridge-type blade front sight on ramp.

Remington Model 511X Bolt Action Repeater . . . **$130**
Clip type. Same as Model 511A, except improved sights. Made 1964-66.

Remington Model 510X

Remington Model 511A

Remington Model 511X

RIFLES

Remington Model 512A Sportsmaster Bolt Action Repeater $125
Takedown. Caliber: 22 Short, Long, Long Rifle. Tubular magazine holds 22 Short, 17 Long, 15 Long Rifle. 25-inch barrel. Weight: about 5¾ pounds. Open rear sight, bead front sight. Plain pistol-grip stock with semibeavertail forend. Made 1940 to 1962.

Remington Model 512P $135
Same as Model 512A, except has peep rear sight, blade front sight on ramp.

Remington Model 512X Bolt Action Repeater . . . $140
Tubular magazine type. Same as Model 512A, except has improved sights. Made 1964-66.

Remington Model 513S Bolt Action Sporting Rifle $225
Caliber: 22 Long Rifle. 6-shot detachable box magazine. 27-inch barrel. Weight: about 6¾ pounds. Marble open rear sight, Patridge-type front sight. Checkered sporter stock. Made 1941 to 1956.

Remington Model 513TR Matchmaster Bolt Action Target Rifle $250
Caliber: 22 Long Rifle. 6-shot detachable box magazine. 27-inch barrel. Weight: about 9 pounds. Redfield No. 75 rear sight and globe front sight. Target stock. Sling and swivels. Made 1941 to 1969.

Remington Model 514 Bolt Action Single Shot . . . $95
Takedown. Caliber: 22 Short, Long, Long Rifle. 24-inch barrel. Weight: 4¾ pounds. Open rear sight, bead front sight. Plain pistol-grip stock. Made 1948 to 1971.

Remington Model 514BC Boy's Carbine $125
Same as Model 514, except has 21-inch barrel, 1-inch shorter stock. Made 1961 to 1971.

Remington Model 514P $105
Same as Model 514, except has receiver peep sight.

Remington Model 512A Sportsmaster

Remington Model 513S

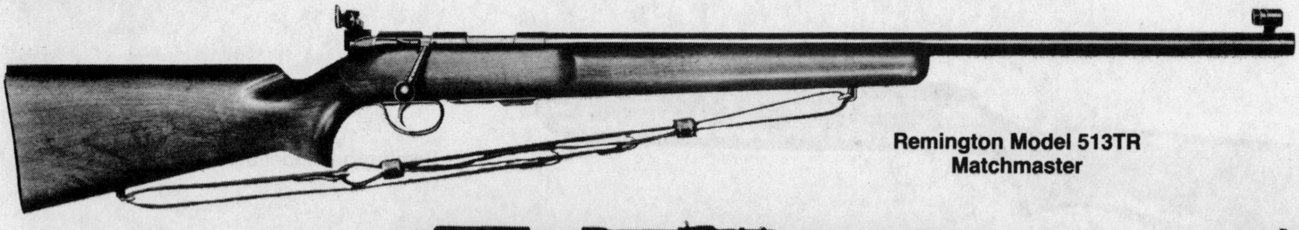
Remington Model 513TR Matchmaster

Remington Model 514BC

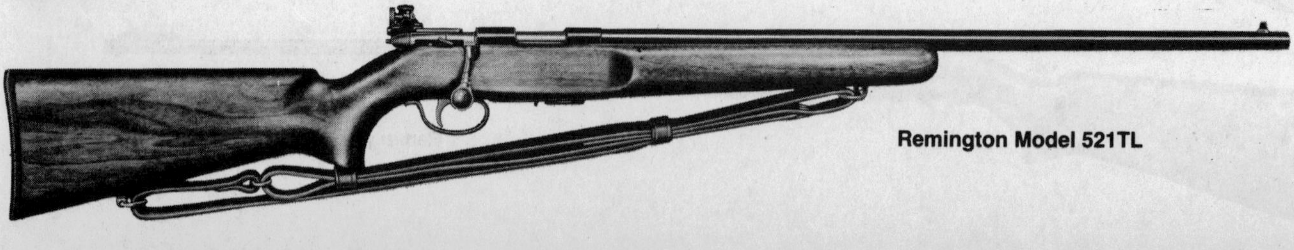
Remington Model 521TL

Remington Model 521TL Junior Target Bolt Action Repeater **$140**
Takedown. Caliber: 22 Long Rifle. 6-shot detachable box magazine. 25-inch barrel. Weight: about 7 pounds. Lyman No. 57RS rear sight, blade front sight. Target stock. Sling and swivels. Made 1947 to 1969.

Remington Model 540-X Rimfire Target Rifle . . . **$225**
Bolt action, single shot. Caliber: 22 Long Rifle. 26-inch heavy barrel. Supplied without sights. Weight: about 8 pounds. Target stock with Monte Carlo cheekpiece and thumb groove, guide rail for hand stop and swivel, adjustable butt plate. Made 1969 to 1974.

Remington Model 540-XR Rimfire Position Rifle **$250**
Bolt action, single shot. Caliber: 22 Long Rifle. 26-inch medium-weight barrel. Supplied without sights. Weight: 8 lbs. 13 oz. Position-style stock with thumb groove, guide rail for hand stop and swivel, adjustable butt plate. Made 1974 to 1984.

Remington Model 540-XRJR **$250**
Same as Model 540-XR, except $1\frac{3}{4}$-inch shorter stock. Made 1974 to 1984.

Remington Model 541-S Custom Sporter **$375**
Bolt-action repeater. Scroll engraving on receiver and trigger guard. Caliber: 22 Short, Long, Long Rifle. 5-shot clip magazine. 24-inch barrel. Weight: $5\frac{1}{2}$ pounds. Supplied without sights. Checkered walnut stock with rosewood-finished forend tip, pistol-grip cap and butt plate. Made 1972 to 1984.

Remington Model 541-T Bolt Action Rifle **$250**
Caliber: 22 RF. Clip-fed, 5-shot. 24-inch barrel. Weight: $5\frac{7}{8}$ pounds. Checkered walnut stock. Made 1986 to date.

Remington Model 550A Autoloader **$125**
Has "Power Piston" or floating chamber which permits interchangeable use of 22 Short, Long or Long Rifle cartridges. Tubular magazine holds 22 Short, 17 Long, 15 Long Rifle. 24-inch barrel. Weight: about $6\frac{1}{4}$ pounds. Open rear sight, bead front sight. Plain, one-piece pistol-grip stock. Made 1941 to 1971.

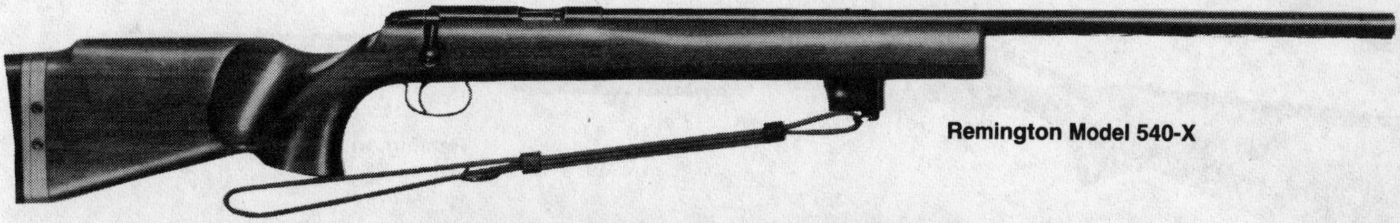

Remington Model 540-X

Remington Model 540-XR

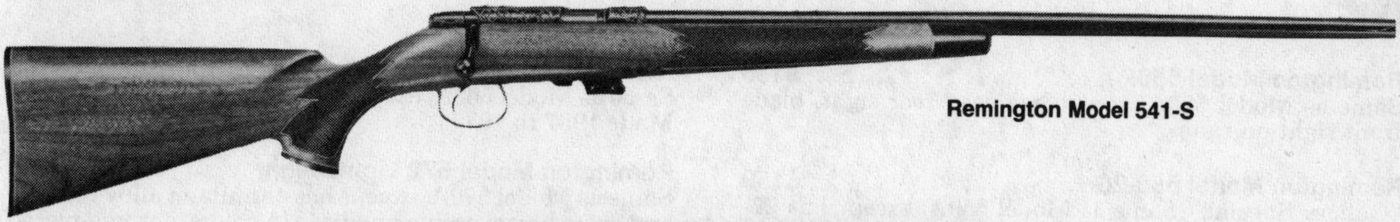

Remington Model 541-S

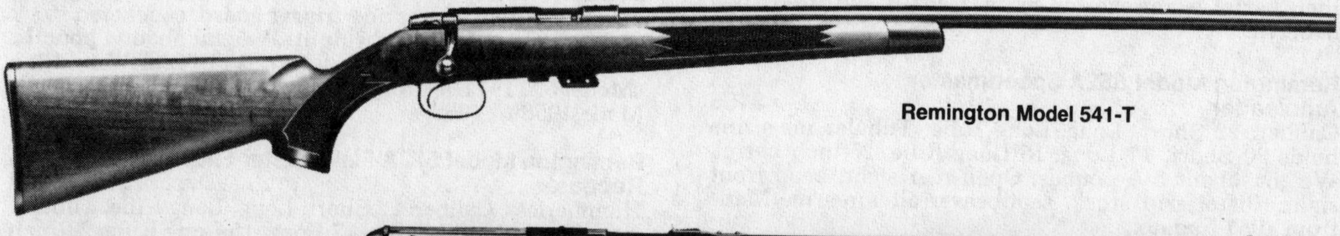

Remington Model 541-T

Remington Model 550A

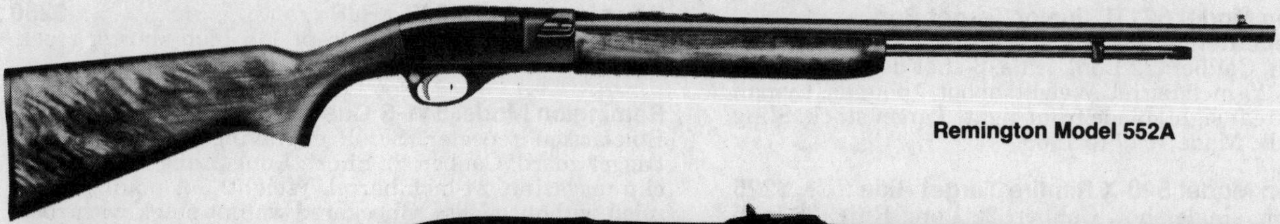

Remington Model 552A

Remington Model 552BDL

Remington Model 572 Lightweight

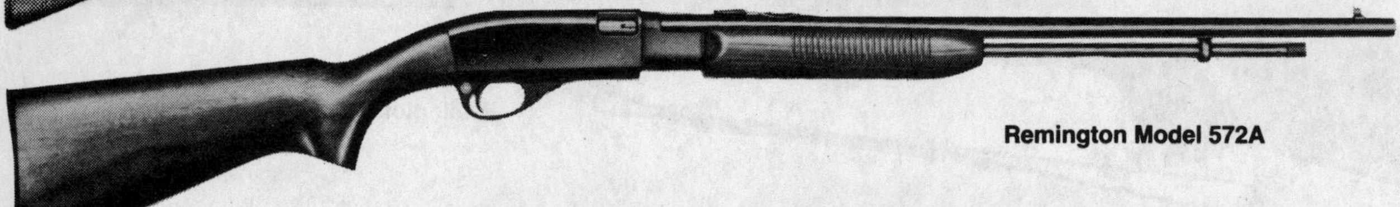

Remington Model 572A

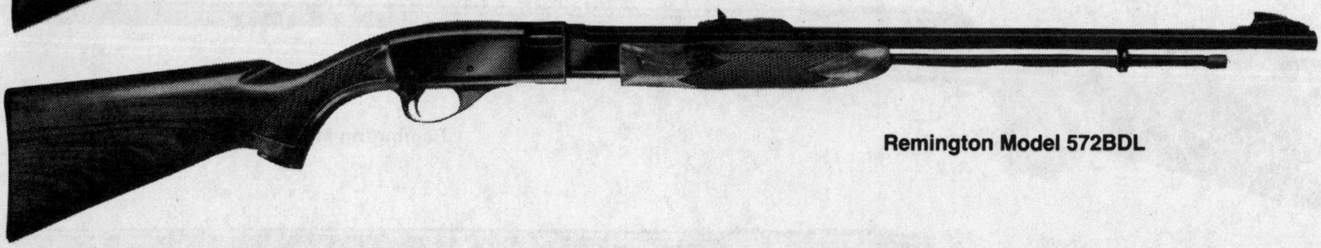

Remington Model 572BDL

Remington Model 550P $130
Same as Model 550A, except has peep rear sight, blade front sight on ramp.

Remington Model 550-2G $150
"Gallery Special." Same as Model 550A, except has 22-inch barrel, screweye for counter chain and fired shell deflector.

Remington Model 552A Speedmaster Autoloader $135
Caliber: 22 Short, Long, Long Rifle. Tubular magazine holds 20 Short, 17 Long, 15 Long Rifle. 25-inch barrel. Weight: about 5½ pounds. Open rear sight, bead front sight. Pistol-grip stock, semibeavertail forearm. Made from 1957 to date.

Remington Model 552BDL Deluxe $155
Same as Model 552A, except has checkered walnut stock and forearm. Made from 1966 to date.

Remington Model 552C Carbine $150
Same as Model 552A, except has 21-inch barrel. Made 1961 to 1977.

Remington Model 552GS Gallery Special $150
Same as Model 552A, except chambered for 22 Short only. Made 1957 to 1977.

Remington Model 572 Lightweight $140
Same as Model 572A, except has aluminum alloy receiver and outer barrel casing anodized in colors, chrome-plated magazine tube, trigger and trigger guard, checkered stock and forearm of light tan walnut. Weight: about 4 pounds. Colors: Buckskin Tan (Model 572BT), Teal Wing Blue (Model 572TWB), Crown Wing Black (Model 572CWB). Made 1958 to 1962.

Remington Model 572A Fieldmaster Slide Action Repeater $140
Hammerless. Caliber: 22 Short, Long, Long Rifle. Tubular magazine holds 20 Short, 17 Long, 15 Long Rifle. 23-inch barrel. Weight: about 5½ pounds. Open rear sight, ramp front sight. Pistol-grip stock, grooved forearm. Made from 1955 to date.

Remington Model 572BDL Deluxe $160
Same as Model 572A, except has blade ramp front sight, sliding ramp rear sight, checkered stock and forearm. Made from 1966 to date.

Remington Model 580

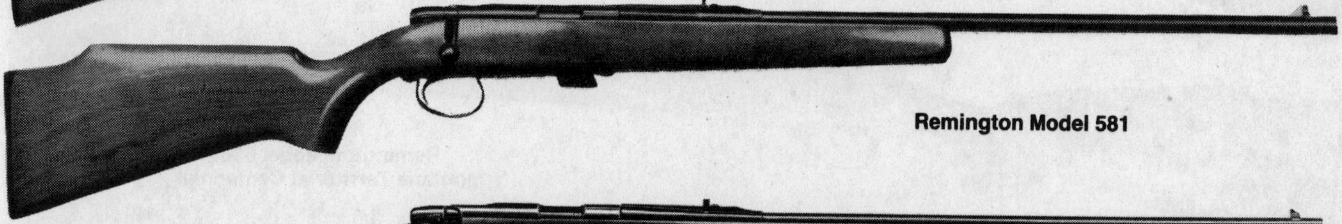

Remington Model 581

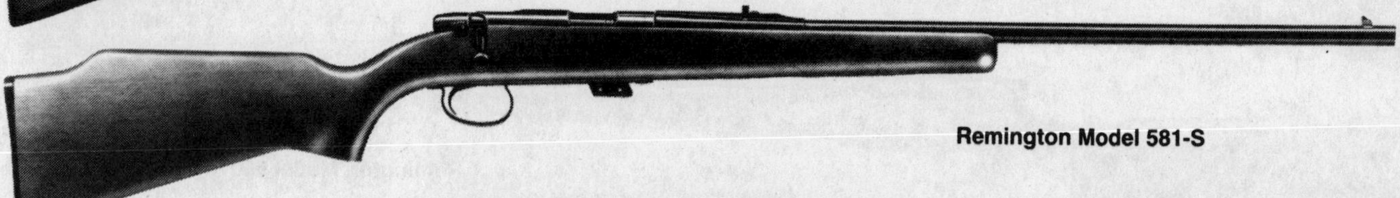

Remington Model 581-S

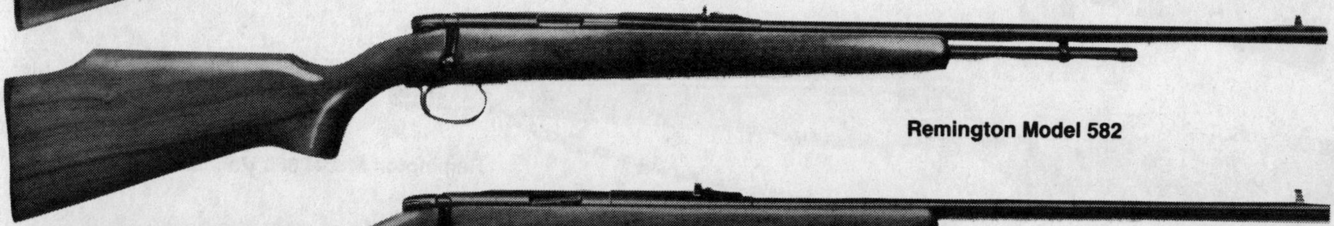

Remington Model 582

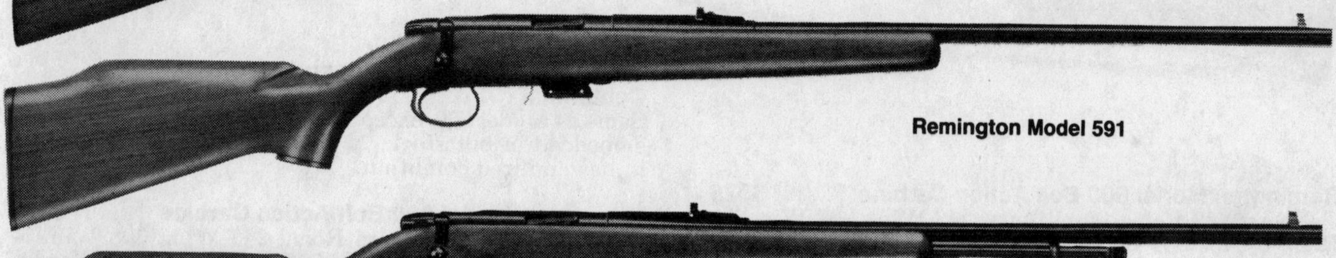

Remington Model 591

Remington Model 592

Remington Model 572SB Smooth Bore $165
Same as Model 572A, except smooth bore for 22 Long Rifle shot cartridges. Made from 1961 to date.

Remington Model 580 Bolt Action Single Shot . . . $85
Caliber: 22 Short, Long, Long Rifle. 24-inch barrel. Weight: 4¾ pounds. Bead front sight, U-notch rear sight. Monte Carlo stock. Made 1967 to 1978.

Remington Model 580BR Boy's Rifle $90
Same as Model 580, except has 1-inch shorter stock. Made 1971-78.

Remington Model 580SB Smooth Bore $100
Same as Model 580, except smooth bore for 22 Long Rifle shot cartridges. Made 1967 to 1978.

Remington Model 581 Clip Repeater $130
Same general specifications as Model 580, except has 5-shot clip magazine. Made 1967 to 1984.

Remington Model 581 Left Hand $145
Same as Model 581, except has left-hand bolt action. Made 1969 to 1984.

Remington Model 581-S Bolt Action Rifle $140
Caliber: 22 RF. Clip-fed, 5-shot. 24-inch barrel. Weight: about 4¾ pounds. Plain walnut-colored stock. Made from 1987 to date.

Remington Model 582 Tubular Repeater $125
Same general specifications as Model 580, except has tubular magazine holding 20 Short, 15 Long, 14 Long Rifle. Weight: about 5 pounds. Made 1967 to 1984.

Remington Model 591 Bolt Action Clip Repeater . . $195
Caliber: 5mm Rimfire Magnum. 4-shot clip magazine. 24-inch barrel. Weight: 5 pounds. Bead front sight, U-notch rear sight. Monte Carlo stock. Made 1970-73.

Remington Model 592 Tubular Repeater $190
Same as Model 591, except has tubular magazine holding 10 rounds, weighs 5½ pounds. Made 1970-73.

Remington Model 600

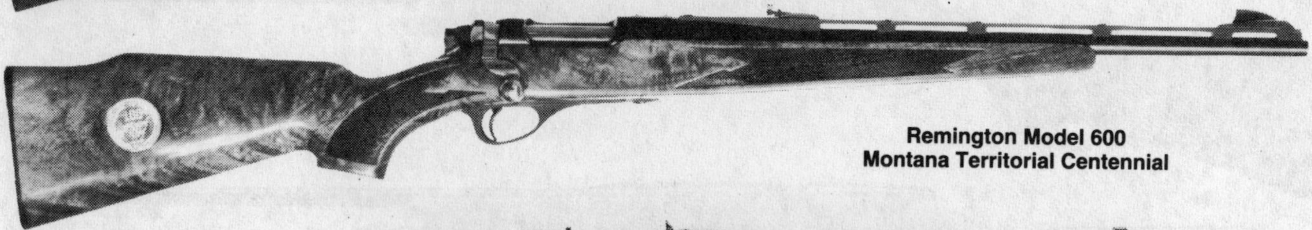

Remington Model 600
Montana Territorial Centennial

Remington Model 660

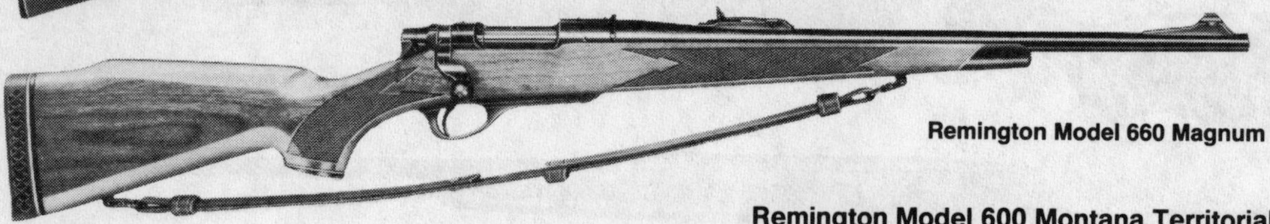

Remington Model 660 Magnum

Remington Model 600 Bolt Action Carbine **$325**
Calibers: 222 Rem., 6mm Rem., 243 Win., 308 Win., 35 Rem. 5-shot box magazine (6-shot in 222 Rem.). 18½-inch barrel with ventilated rib. Weight: 6 pounds. Open rear sight, blade ramp front sight. Monte Carlo stock with pistol grip. Made 1964-67.

Remington Model 600 Magnum **$540**
Same as Model 600, except calibers 6.5mm Rem. Mag. and 350 Rem. Mag., 4-shot magazine, special magnum type barrel with racket for scope back-up, laminated walnut-and-beech stock with recoil pad. QD swivels and sling; weight: about 6½ pounds. Made 1965-67.

Remington Model 600 Montana Territorial Centennial **$575**
Same as Model 600, except has commemorative medallion embedded in buttstock. Made in 1964. Value is for rifle in new, unfired condition.

Remington Model 660 Bolt Action Carbine **$425**
Calibers: 222 Rem., 6mm Rem., 243 Win., 308 Win. 5-shot box magazine (6-shot in 222). 20-inch barrel. Weight: 6½ pounds. Open rear sight, bead front sight on ramp. Monte Carlo stock, checkered, black pistol-grip cap and forend tip. Made 1968 to 1971.

Remington Model 660 Magnum **$525**
Same as Model 660, except calibers 6.5mm Rem. Mag. and 350 Rem. Mag., 4-shot magazine, laminated walnut-and-beech stock with recoil pad, QD swivels and sling. Made 1968 to 1971.

Remington Model 700 Classic

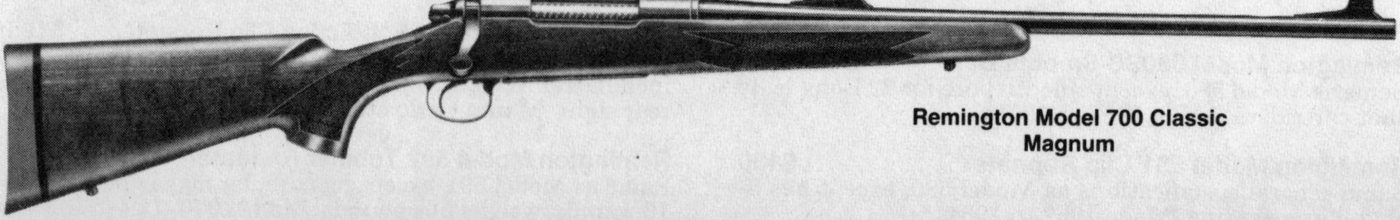

Remington Model 700 Classic
Magnum

Remington Model 700 Classic
Same general specifications as Model 700 BDL, except has "Classic" stock of high-quality walnut with full-pattern cut checkering, special satin-wood finish; schnabel forend. Brown rubber butt pad. Hinged floorplate. No sights. Weight: 7 pounds. Also chambered for "Classic" cartridges such as 257 Roberts and 250-3000. Introduced 1981.
Standard calibers **$300**
Magnum calibers **340**

Remington Model 700 Custom Bolt Action Rifle
Same general specifications as Model 700BDL except custom built, and available in four grades—each with different checkering patterns, engraving and similar custom features.
Grade I . . . . **$ 850**
Grade II **1540**
Grade III **2450**
Grade IV **3800**

Remington Model 700 FS Bolt Action Rifle $450
Calibers: 243, 270 Win., 30-06, 308 and 7mm Rem. Mag. 22-inch barrel. Weight: 6¼ pounds. Straight-line fiberglass stock with solid black English-style butt pad and sling swivels. Made from 1987 to date.

Remington Model 700 KS Custom Mountain Rifle $620
Calibers: 270 Win., 280 Rem., 30-06, 7mm Rem. Mag., 300 Win. Mag., 338 Win. Mag., 8mm Rem. Mag. and 375 H&H. 22-inch barrel. Weight: 6¾ pounds. Available in both right- and left-hand models. Synthetic stock with Kevlar aramid fiber. Made from 1987 to date.

Remington Model 700 RS Bolt Action Rifle $400
Calibers: 270 Win., 280 Rem. and 30-06. 22-inch barrel. Weight: 7¼ pounds. Stock made of Du Pont Rynite. Made from 1987 to date.

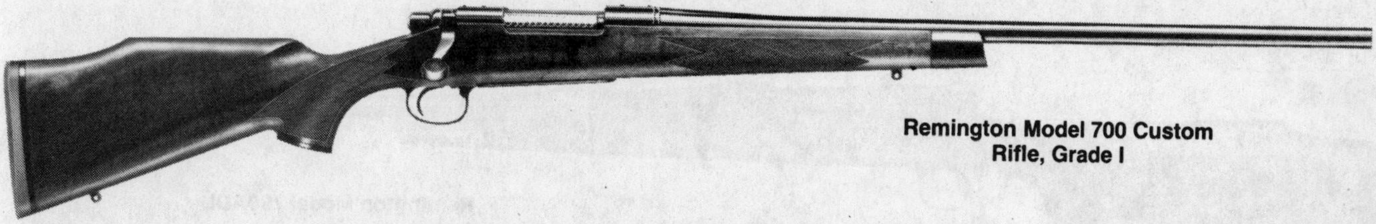
Remington Model 700 Custom Rifle, Grade I

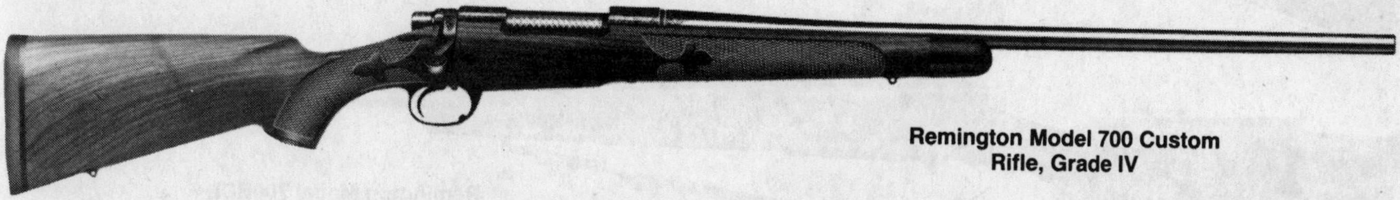
Remington Model 700 Custom Rifle, Grade IV

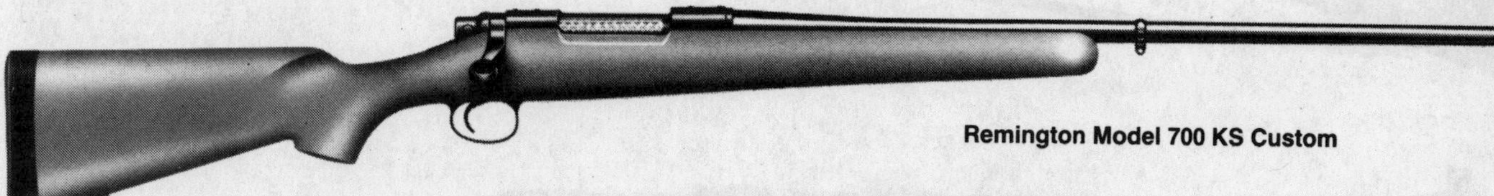
Remington Model 700 KS Custom

Remington Model 700 RS

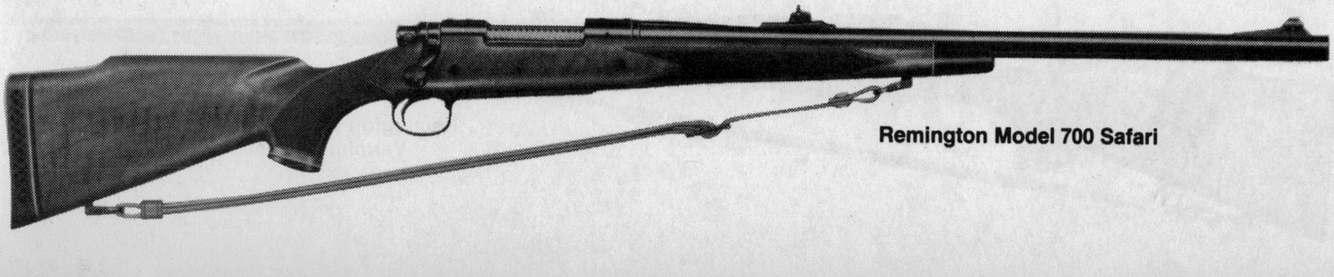
Remington Model 700 Safari

Remington Model 700 Safari Grade **$625**
Similar to magnum Model 700BDL, except calibers 375 H&H Mag. and 458 Win. Mag., has heavier barrel and stock, weighs 9 pounds. Made from 1962 to date.

Remington Model 700ADL Centerfire Bolt Action Rifle
Calibers: 22-250, 222 Rem., 25-06, 6mm Rem., 243 Win., 270 Win., 30-06, 308 Win., 7mm Rem. Mag. Magazine capacity: 6-shot in 222 Rem., 4-shot in 7mm Rem. Mag., 5-shot in other calibers. Barrel lengths: 24-inch in 22-250, 222 Rem., 25-06, 7mm Rem. Mag.; 22-inch in other calibers. Weight: 7 lbs. standard; 7½ lbs. in 7mm Rem. Mag. Ramp front sight, sliding ramp open rear sight. Monte Carlo stock with cheekpiece, skip checkering, recoil pad on magnum. Made from 1962 to date.
Standard calibers **$295**
7mm Rem. Mag. **315**

Remington Model 700BDL Custom Deluxe
Same as Model 700 ADL, except has hinged floorplate, hooded ramp front sight, stock with black forend tip and pistol-grip cap, cut checkering, QD swivels and sling. Additional calibers: 17 Rem., 264 Win. Mag., 300 Win. Mag., 8mm Rem. Mag. All have 24-inch barrels. Magnums have 4-shot magazine, recoil pad, weigh 7½ pounds; 17 Rem. has 6-shot magazine, weighs 7 pounds. Made from 1962 to date.
Standard calibers except 17 Rem. **$340**
Magnum calibers and 17 Rem. **355**

Remington Model 700BDL Left Hand
Same as Model 700BDL, except has left-hand bolt action, stock with cheekpiece on right side. Calibers: 270 Win., 30-06, 7mm Rem. Mag. Made from 1973 to date.
270 and 30-06 . . . . **$375**
7mm Rem. Mag. **395**

Remington Model 700BDL Varmint Special **$355**
Same as Model 700BDL, except has 24-inch heavy barrel, no sights, weighs 9 lbs. (8¾ lbs. in 308 Win.). Calibers: 22-250, 222 Rem., 223 Rem., 25-06, 6mm Rem., 243 Win., 308 Win. Made from 1967 to date.

Remington Model 700ADL

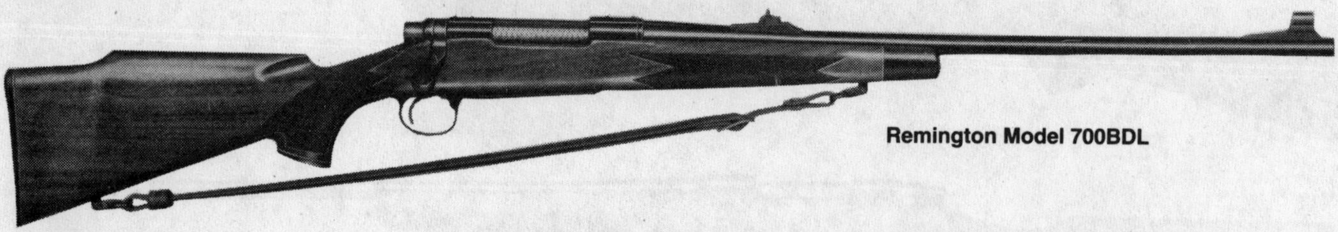

Remington Model 700BDL

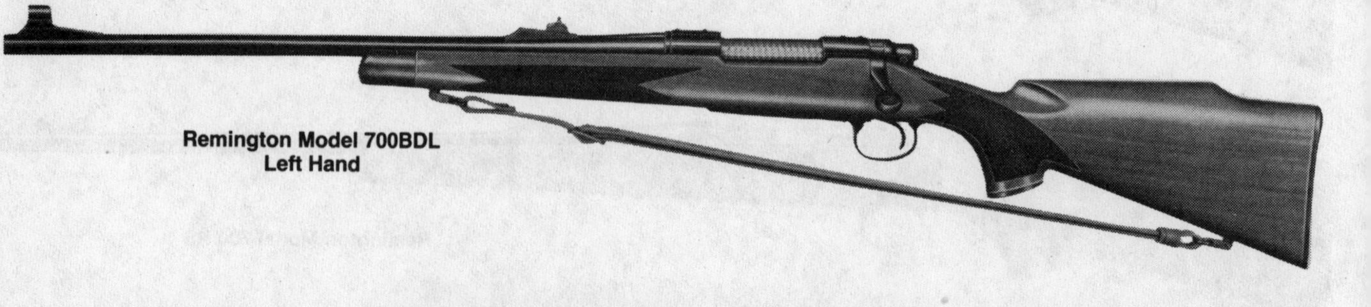

Remington Model 700BDL Left Hand

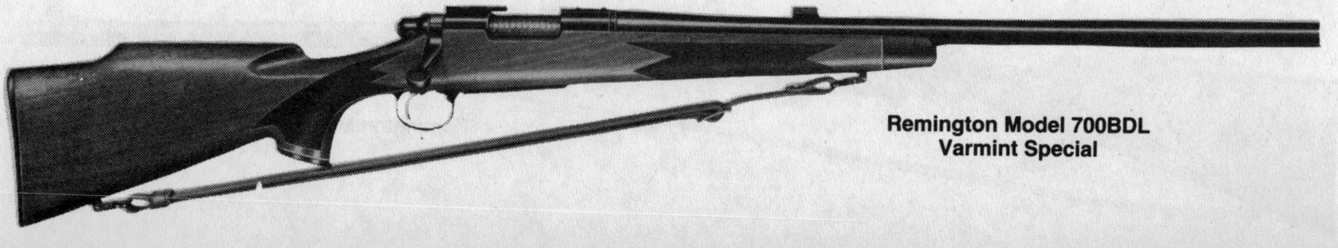

Remington Model 700BDL Varmint Special

Remington Model 700C Custom

Remington Model 700C Custom $895
Same general specifications as Model 700BDL, except special made-to-order grade with higher quality wood and high-gloss blued finish. Available in all Model 700BDL calibers except 17 Rem., 223 Rem., 8mm Rem. Mag., 264 Win. Mag., 375 H&H Mag., 458 Win. Mag. Made from 1965 to date.

Remington Model 700D Peerless Grade $1050
Same as Model 700C Custom, except scroll engraved, fancy wood. Made from 1965 to date.

Remington Model 700F Premier Grade $2060
Same as Model 700D Peerless Grade, except more elaborately engraved, finest grade wood. Made 1965 to date.

Remington Model 720A Bolt Action High Power Rifle $300
Modified M/1917 Enfield action. Calibers: 257 Roberts, 270 Win., 30-06. 5-shot box magazine. 22-inch barrel. Weight: about 8 pounds. Open rear sight, bead front sight on ramp. Pistol-grip stock, checkered. Made 1941.

Remington Model 720R $325
Same as Model 720A, except has 20-inch barrel.

Remington Model 720S. $325
Same as Model 720, except has 24-inch barrel.

Remington Model 721A Standard Grade Bolt Action High Power Rifle $265
Calibers: 264 Win., 270 Win., 30-06. 4-shot box magazine. 24-inch barrel. Weight: about 7¼ pounds. Open rear sight, bead front sight on ramp. Plain sporting stock. Made 1948 to 1962.

Remington Model 721A 300 Magnum Standard Grade $425
Caliber: 300 H&H Magnum. Same as standard model, except has 26-inch heavy barrel, 3-shot magazine, recoil pads, weighs 8¼ pounds.

Remington Model 721ADL 300 Magnum Deluxe . . $450
Same as Model 721A 300 Magnum, except has deluxe checkered stock.

Remington Model 721ADL Deluxe Grade $295
Same as Model 721A, except has deluxe checkered stock.

Remington Model 721BDL 300 Magnum Deluxe Special Grade $495
Same as Model 721ADL 300 Magnum, except selected wood.

Remington Model 721BDL Deluxe Special Grade $350
Same as Model 721ADL, except selected wood.

Remington Model 722A Standard Grade Bolt Action Sporting Rifle $265
Same as Model 721A, except shorter action, calibers 257 Roberts, 308 Win., 300 Savage, weighs 7 pounds. Made 1948 to 1962.

Remington Model 722A 222 Standard Grade . . . $265
Caliber: 222 Rem. Same as standard model, except has 26-inch barrel, 5-shot magazine, weighs about 8 pounds. Made 1950 to 1962.

Remington Model 722A 244 Standard Grade . . . $285
Caliber: 244 Rem. Specifications same as Model 722A 222, except magazine capacity is four rounds. Made 1955 to 1962.

Remington Model 722ADL Deluxe Grade $325
Same as Model 722A, except has deluxe checkered stock.

Remington Model 722ADL 222 Deluxe Grade . . . $325
Same as Model 722A 222, except has deluxe checkered stock.

Remington Model 722ADL 244 Deluxe Grade . . . $330
Same as Model 722A 244, except has deluxe checkered stock.

Remington Model 722BDL Deluxe Special Grade $350
Same as Model 722ADL, except selected wood.

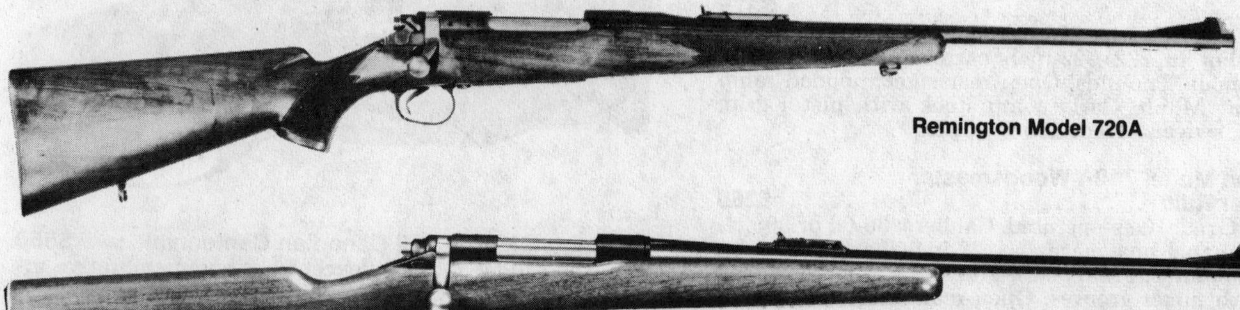

Remington Model 720A

Remington Model 721A

RIFLES

Remington Model 725 Kodiak

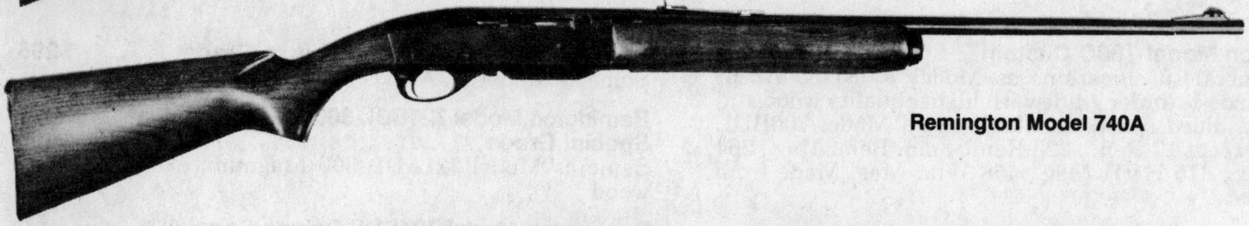

Remington Model 740A

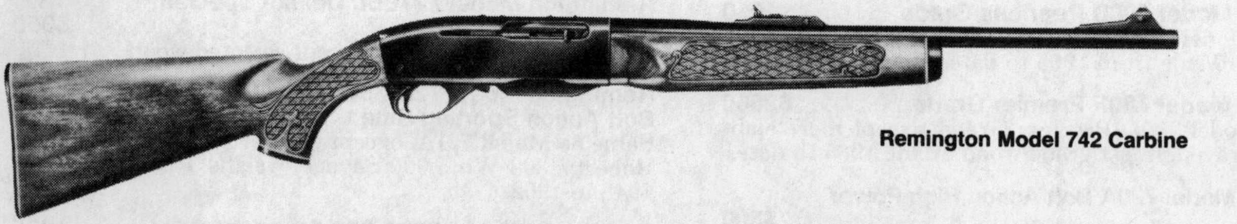

Remington Model 742 Carbine

Remington Model 742
Bicentennial Commemorative

Remington Model 722BDL 222 Deluxe Special Grade **$350**
Same as Model 722ADL 222, except selected wood.

Remington Model 722BDL 244 Deluxe Special Grade **$360**
Same as Model 722ADL, except selected wood.

Remington Model 725 Kodiak Magnum Rifle . . . **$650**
Similar to Model 725ADL. Calibers: 375 H&H Mag., 458 Win. Mag. 3-shot magazine. 26-inch barrel with recoil reducer built into muzzle. Weight: about 9 pounds. Deluxe, reinforced Monte Carlo stock with recoil pad, black forend tip, swivels, sling. Made 1961.

Remington Model 725ADL Bolt Action Repeating Rifle **$375**
Calibers: 222, 243, 244, 270, 280, 30-06. 4-shot box magazine (5-shot in 222). 22-inch barrel (24-inch in 222). Weight: about 7 pounds. Open rear sight, hooded ramp front sight. Monte Carlo comb stock with pistol grip, checkered, swivels. Made 1958 to 1961.

Remington Model 740A Woodsmaster Autoloader Rifle **$260**
Standard Grade. Gas-operated. Calibers: 30-06 or 308. 4-shot detachable box magazine. 22-inch barrel. Weight: about $7^{1}/_{2}$ pounds. Plain pistol-grip stock, semibeavertail forend with finger grooves. Open rear sight, ramp front sight. Made 1955 to 1960.

Remington Model 740ADL Deluxe Grade **$295**
Same as Model 740A, except has deluxe checkered stock, standard or high comb, grip cap, sling swivels. Made 1955 to 1960.

Remington Model 740BDL Deluxe Special Grade **$325**
Same as Model 740ADL, except selected wood. Made 1955 to 1960.

Remington Model 742 Bicentennial Commemorative **$500**
Same as Model 742 rifle, except has commemorative inscription on receiver. Made 1976.

Remington Model 742 Canadian Centennial **$550**
Same as Model 742 rifle, except has commemorative inscription on receiver. Made 1967. Value is for rifle in new, unfired condition.

Remington Model 742 Carbine **$345**
Same as Model 742 Rifle, except made in calibers 30-06 and 308 only, has $18^{1}/_{2}$-inch barrel, weighs $6^{3}/_{4}$ pounds. Made 1961 to 1980.

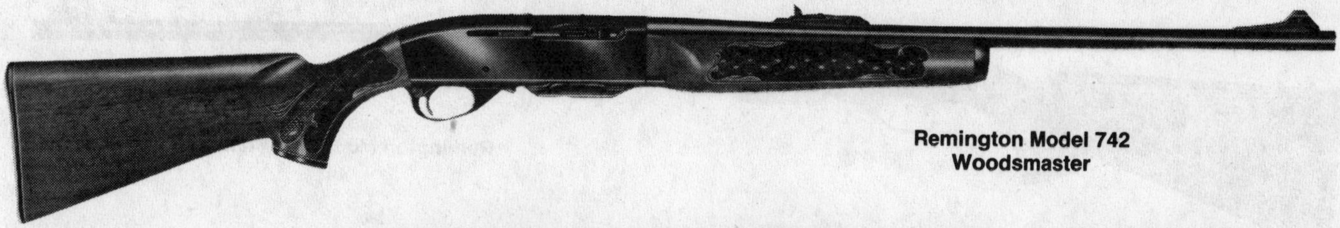

Remington Model 742 Woodsmaster

Remington Model 742BDL

Remington Model 742F

Remington Model 742 Woodsmaster Automatic Big Game Rifle $295
Gas-operated semiautomatic. Calibers: 6mm Rem., 243 Win., 280 Rem., 30-06, 308 Win. 4-shot clip magazine. 22-inch barrel. Weight: 7½ pounds. Open rear sight, bead front sight on ramp. Checkered pistol-grip stock and forearm. Made 1960 to 1980.

Remington Model 742BDL Custom Deluxe $330
Same as Model 742 Rifle, except made in calibers 30-06 and 308 only, has Monte Carlo cheekpiece stock, forearm with black tip, basket-weave checkering. Available in left-hand model. Made 1966 to 1980.

Remington Model 742D Peerless Grade $845
Same as Model 742 except scroll engraved, fancy wood. Made 1961 to 1980.

Remington Model 742F Premier Grade $2165
Same as Model 742 except extensively engraved with game scenes and scroll, finest grade wood. Also available with receiver inlaid with gold; adds 50 percent to value. Made 1961 to 1980.

Remington Model 760 Bicentennial Commemorative $495
Same as Model 760, except has commemorative inscription on receiver. Made 1976.

Remington Model 760 Carbine $295
Same as Model 760 Rifle, except made in calibers 270 Win., 280 Rem., 30-06 and 308 Win. only, has 18½-inch barrel, weighs 7¼ pounds. Made 1961 to 1980.

Remington Model 760 Gamemaster Standard Grade Slide Action Repeating Rifle $275
Hammerless. Calibers: 223 Rem., 6mm Rem., 243 Win., 257 Roberts, 270 Win., 280 Rem., 30-06, 300 Sav., 308

Remington Model 760 Bicentennial Commemorative

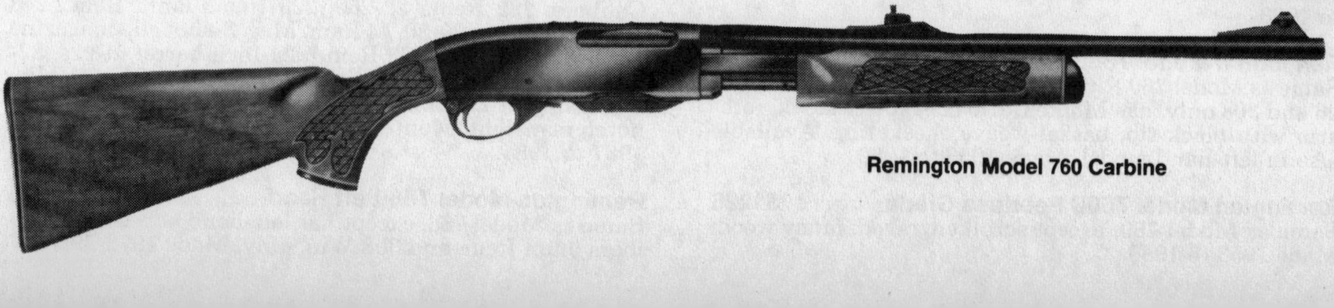

Remington Model 760 Carbine

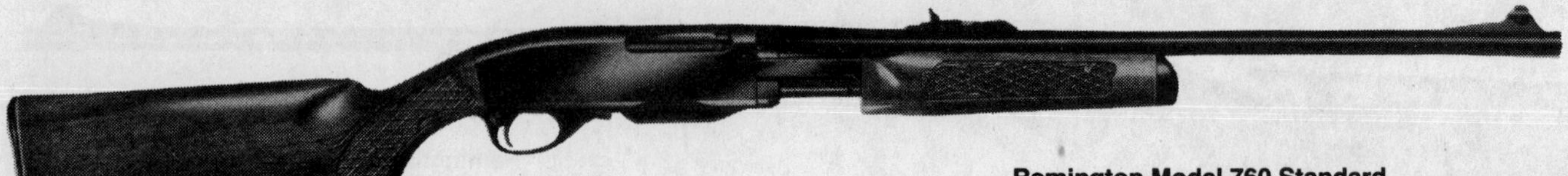

Remington Model 760 Standard

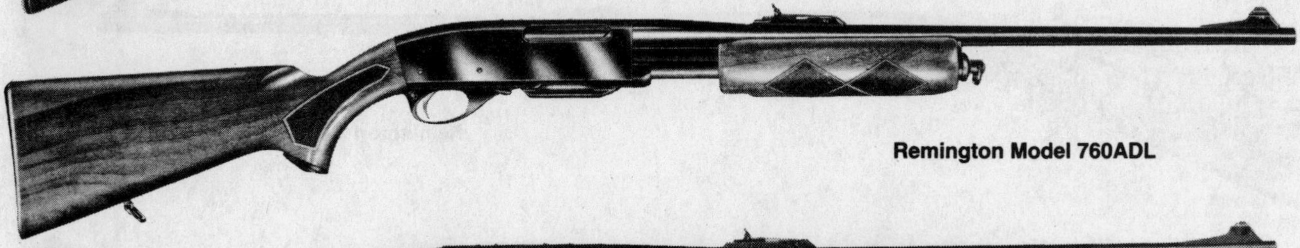

Remington Model 760ADL

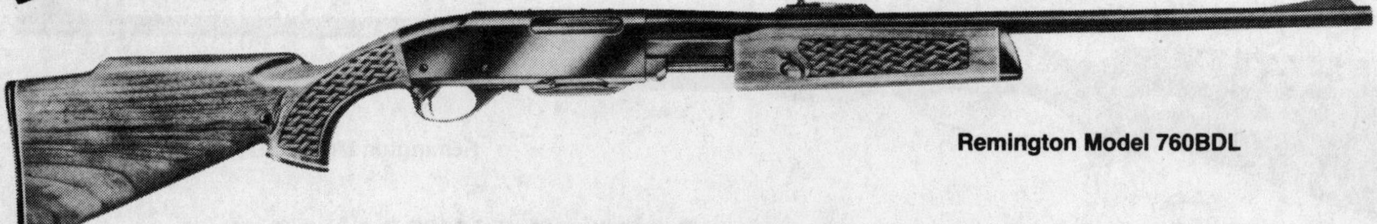

Remington Model 760BDL

Remington Model 788

Remington Model 788 Left Hand

Remington Model 760 Gamemaster (cont.)
Win., 35 Rem. 22-inch barrel. Weight: about 7½ pounds. Open rear sight, bead front sight on ramp. Plain pistol-grip stock, grooved slide handle on early models; current production has checkered stock and slide handle. Made 1952 to 1980.

Remington Model 760ADL Deluxe Grade $285
Same as Model 760, except has deluxe checkered stock, standard or high comb, grip cap, sling swivels. Made 1953 to 1963.

Remington Model 760BDL Custom Deluxe $295
Same as Model 760 Rifle, except made in calibers 270, 30-06 and 308 only, has Monte Carlo cheekpiece stock, forearm with black tip, basket-weave checkering. Available also in left-hand model. Made 1953 to 1980.

Remington Model 760D Peerless Grade $1225
Same as Model 760, except scroll engraved, fancy wood. Made 1953 to 1980.

Remington Model 760F Premier Grade $2370
Same as Model 760, except extensively engraved with game scenes and scroll, finest grade wood. Also available with receiver inlaid with gold; adds 50 percent to value. Made 1953 to 1980.

Remington Model 788 Centerfire Bolt Action . . . $195
Calibers: 222 Rem., 22-250, 223 Rem., 6mm Rem., 243 Win., 308 Win., 30-30, 44 Rem. Mag. 3-shot clip magazine (4-shot in 222 and 223 Rem.). 24-inch barrel in 22s, 22-inch in other calibers. Weight: 7½ lbs. with 24-inch bbl.; 7¼ lbs. with 22-inch bbl. Blade front sight on ramp, U-notch rear sight. Monte Carlo stock, no checkering. Made 1967 to 1984.

Remington Model 788 Left Hand $225
Same as Model 788, except has left-hand bolt action, calibers 6mm Rem. and 308 Win. only. Made 1972-79.

Remington Model 7400 Autoloader **$295**
Similar to Model Four, except has lower grade finishes. Made from 1981 to date.

Remington Model 7600 Carbine **$290**
Same general specifications as Model 7600 Rifle, except has 18½-inch barrel and weighs 7¼ pounds. Made from 1987 to date.

Remington Model 7600 Rifle **$280**
Similar to Model Six, except has lower grade finishes. Made from 1981 to date.

Remington International Free Rifle **$605**
Same as Model 40-XB rimfire and centerfire, except has "free rifle" -type stock with adjustable butt plate and hook, adjustable palm rest, movable front sling swivel, 2-oz. trigger. Weight: about 15 pounds. Made 1964 to 1974. Value shown is for rifle with professionally finished stock, no sights.

Remington International Match Free Rifle **$660**
Calibers: 22 Long Rifle, 222 Rem., 222 Rem. Mag., 7.62mm NATO, 30-06 (others were available on special order). Model 40X-type bolt action, single shot. 2-oz. adjustable trigger. 28-inch heavy barrel. Weight: about 15½ pounds. "Free rifle" -style stock with thumb hole (furnished semi-finished by mfr.); interchangeable and adjustable rubber butt plate and hook butt plate, adjustable palm rest, sling swivel. Made 1961-64. Value shown is for rifle with professionally finished stock, no sights.

Remington Light Baby Carbine **$325**
Single shot. Rolling-block action. Caliber: 44 Win. 20-inch barrel. Weight: 5¾ pounds. Open rear sight, blade front sight. Plain straight-grip carbine-stock and forearm, barrel band. Made 1883 to 1910.

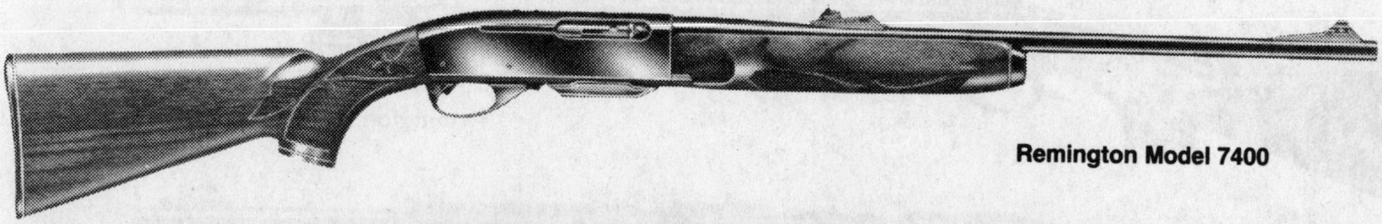
Remington Model 7400

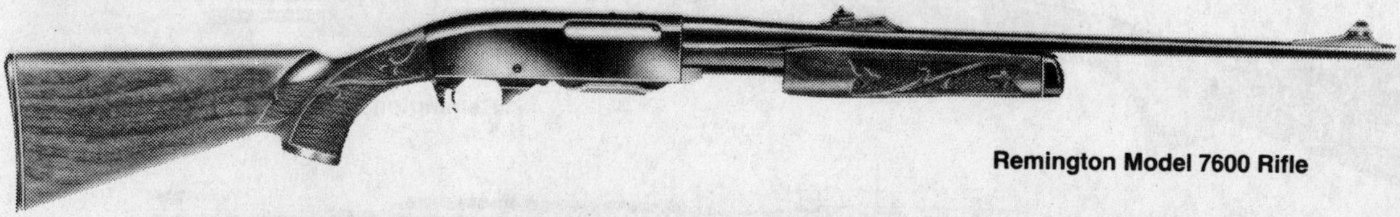
Remington Model 7600 Rifle

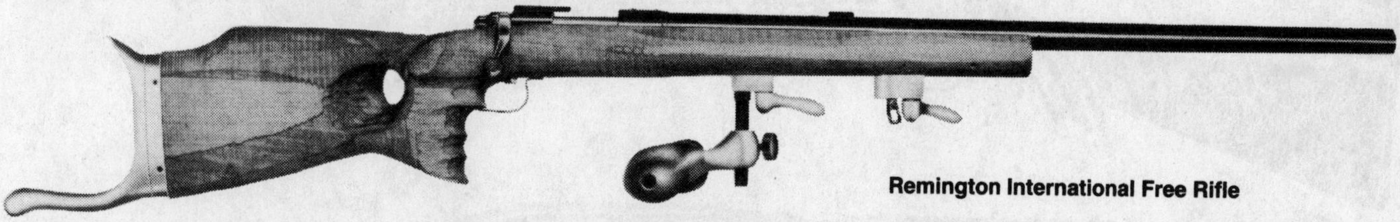
Remington International Free Rifle

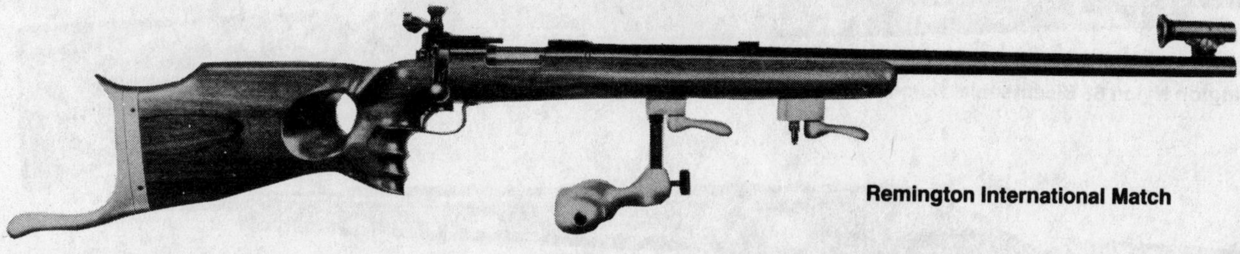
Remington International Match

Remington Light Baby Carbine

Remington Nylon 10 Bolt Action Single Shot Rifle $65
Same as Nylon 11 except single shot. Made from 1962 to 1966.

Remington Nylon 11 Bolt Action Repeater $75
Clip type. Caliber: 22 Short, Long, Long Rifle. 6- or 10-shot clip magazine. $19\frac{5}{8}$-inch barrel. Weight: about $4\frac{1}{2}$ pounds. Open rear sight, blade front sight. Nylon stock. Made 1962-66.

Remington Nylon 12 Bolt Action Repeater $70
Same as Nylon 11 except has tubular magazine holding 22 Short, 17 Long, 15 Long Rifle. Made 1962-66.

Remington Nylon 66 Apache Black $95
Same as Nylon 66 Mohawk Brown, except barrel and receiver cover chrome-plated, black stock. Made from 1962 to 1984.

Remington Nylon 66 Bicentennial Commemorative $110
Same as Nylon 66, except has commemorative inscription on receiver. Made 1976.

Remington Nylon 66 GS Gallery Special $95
Same as Nylon 66 Mohawk Brown except chambered for 22 Short only. Made 1959 to 1980.

Remington Nylon 66 Mohawk Brown Autoloader . $95
Caliber: 22 Long Rifle. Tubular magazine in buttstock holds 14 rounds. $19\frac{1}{2}$-inch barrel. Weight: about 4 pounds. Open rear sight, blade front sight. Brown nylon stock and forearm. Made from 1959 to date.

Remington Nylon 76 Lever Action Repeater $90
Short-throw lever action. Other specifications same as for Nylon 66. Made 1962-64.

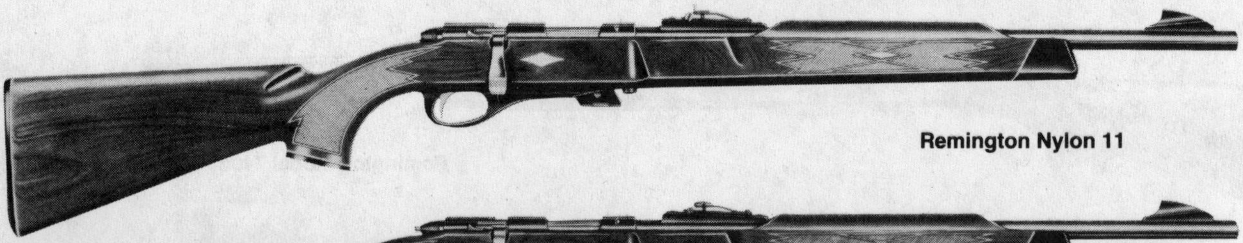

Remington Nylon 11

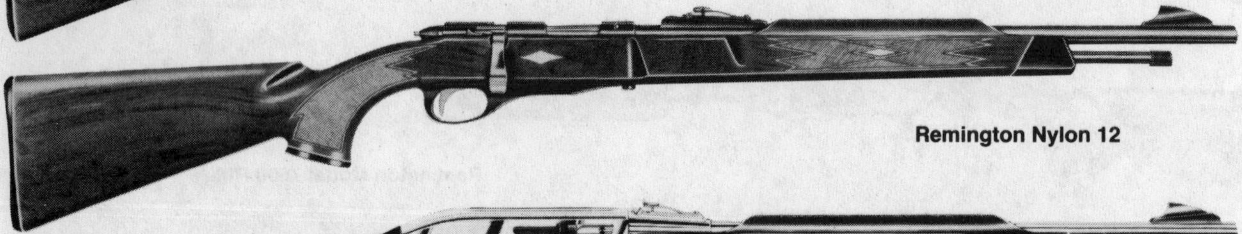

Remington Nylon 12

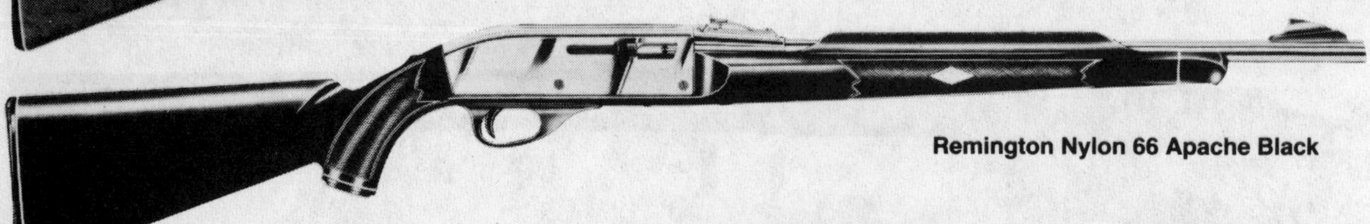

Remington Nylon 66 Apache Black

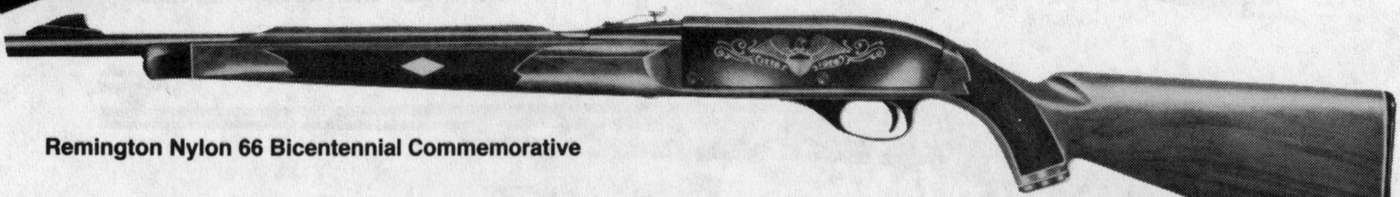

Remington Nylon 66 Bicentennial Commemorative

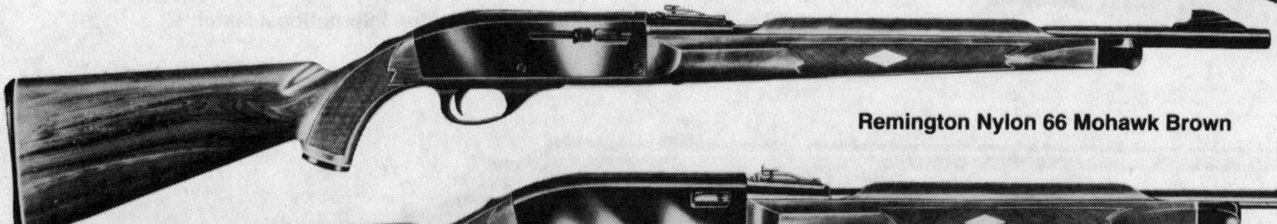

Remington Nylon 66 Mohawk Brown

Remington Nylon 76

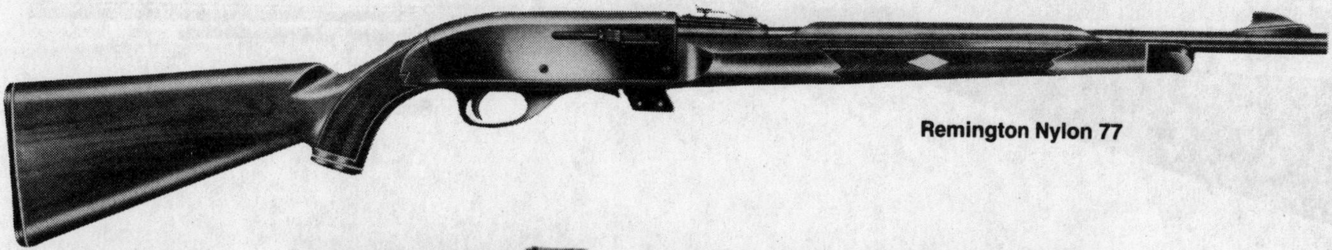

Remington Nylon 77

Remington-Lee Sporter

Remington Nylon 77 Clip Repeater **$90**
Same as Nylon 66, except has 5-shot clip magazine. Made 1970-71.

Remington-Lee Bolt Action Sporting Rifle
Calibers: 6mm U.S.N., 30-30, 30-40, 7mm Mauser, 7.65 Mauser, 32 Rem., 32-40, 35 Rem., 38-55, 38-72, 405 Win., 43 Spanish, 44/77 Sharps, 45/70, 45/90. Detachable box magazine holding 5 cartridges. 24- or 26-inch barrel. Weight: 7 pounds. Open rear sight, bead or blade front sight. Walnut stock with checkered pistol grip. Made 1886 to 1906. *Note:* A limited number were produced in "Special" Grade with deluxe walnut stock, half-octagon barrel, Lyman sights; these sold for approximately twice the price of the Standard Grade.
Standard Model **$500**
Deluxe Model **750**

JOHN RIGBY & CO.
London, England

Rigby 275 Lightweight Model Magazine Rifle **$3500**
Same as standard 275 rifle, except has 21-inch barrel and weighs only $6^3/_4$ pounds.

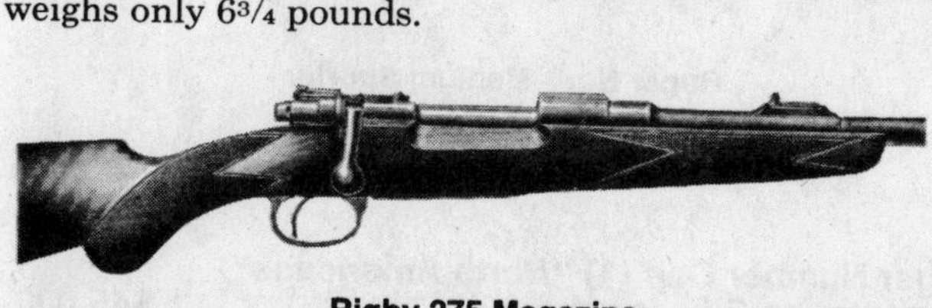

Rigby 275 Magazine

Rigby 275 Magazine Sporting Rifle **$3500**
Mauser action. Caliber: 275 High Velocity or 7×57mm. 5-shot box magazine. 25-inch barrel. Weight: about $7^1/_2$ pounds. Folding leaf rear sight, bead front sight. Sporting stock with half-pistol grip, checkered. Specifications given are those of current model; however, in general, they apply also to prewar model.

Rigby 350 Magnum Magazine Sporting Rifle .. **$5000**
Mauser action. Caliber: 350 Magnum. 5-shot box magazine. 24-inch barrel. Weight: about $7^3/_4$ pounds. Folding leaf rear sight, bead front sight. Sporting stock with full pistol grip, checkered. Currently mfd.

Rigby 416 Big Game Magazine Sporting Rifle . **$5000**
Mauser action. Caliber: 416 Big Game. 4-shot box magazine. 24-inch barrel. Weight: 9 to $9^1/_4$ pounds. Folding leaf rear sight, bead front sight. Sporting stock with full pistol grip, checkered. Currently manufactured.

Rigby Best Quality Hammerless Ejector Double Rifle **$20,000**
Side locks. Calibers: 275 Magnum, 350 Magnum, 470 Nitro Express. 24- to 28-inch barrels. Weight: $7^1/_2$ to $10^1/_2$ pounds. Folding leaf rear sight, bead front sight. Checkered pistol-grip stock and forearm.

Rigby 350 Magnum

Rigby Best Quality Double Rifle

Rigby Second Quality Double Rifle

Rigby Second Quality Hammerless Ejector Double Rifle **$16,000**
Same general specifications as Best Quality double rifle, except box lock.

Rigby Third Quality Hammerless Ejector Double Rifle **$12,000**
Same as Second Quality double rifle, except plainer finish and not of as high quality.

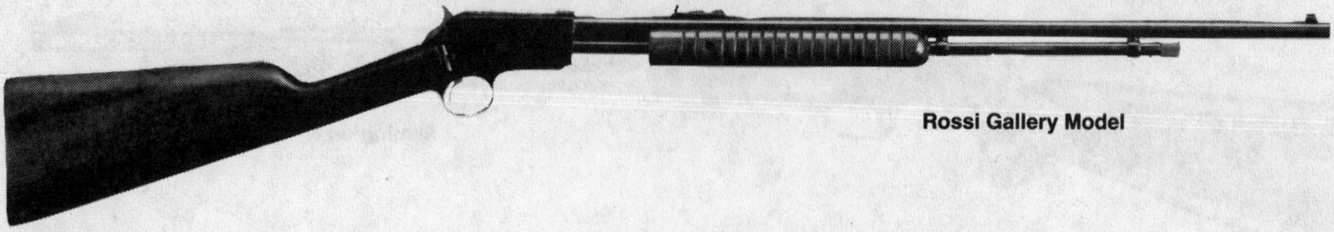

Rossi Gallery Model

ROSS RIFLE CO.
Quebec, Canada

Ross Model 1910 Bolt Action Sporting Rifle $295
Straight-pull bolt action with interrupted-screw-type lugs. Calibers: 280 Ross, 303 British. 4-shot or 5-shot magazine. Barrel lengths: 22, 24, 26 inches. Two-leaf open rear sight, bead front sight. Checkered sporting stock. Weight: about 7 pounds. Made from c. 1910 to end of World War I. *Note:* Most firearm authorities are of the opinion that this and other Ross models with interrupted-screw-type lugs are unsafe to fire.

ROSSI RIFLES
Sao Leopoldo, Brazil
Manufactured by Amadeo Rossi, S.A.

Rossi Gallery Model Carbine $125
Same as standard Gallery Model, except has $16^1/_4$-inch barrel, weighs $5^1/_2$ pounds. Made from 1975 to date.

Rossi Gallery Model Magnum $135
Same as standard Gallery Model, except chambered for 22 Win. Mag. R.F., 10-shot magazine. Made 1975.

Rossi Gallery Model Slide Action Repeater $125
Similar to Winchester Model 62. Caliber: 22 Long Rifle, Long, Short. Tubular magazine holds 13 LR, 16 Long, 20 Short. 23-inch barrel. Weight: $5^3/_4$ pounds. Open rear sight, bead front sight. Straight-grip stock, grooved slide handle. made from 1970 to date.

Rossi Lever Action Carbine $175
Similar to Winchester Model 92. Caliber: 357 Mag. Tubular magazine. 20-inch barrel. Weight: $5^3/_4$ pounds. Open rear sight, bead front sight. Straight-grip walnut stock. Made from 1978 to date.

Rossi Lever Action Carbine Engraved Model ... $200
Same as standard model, except has engraved action. Made from 1981 to date.

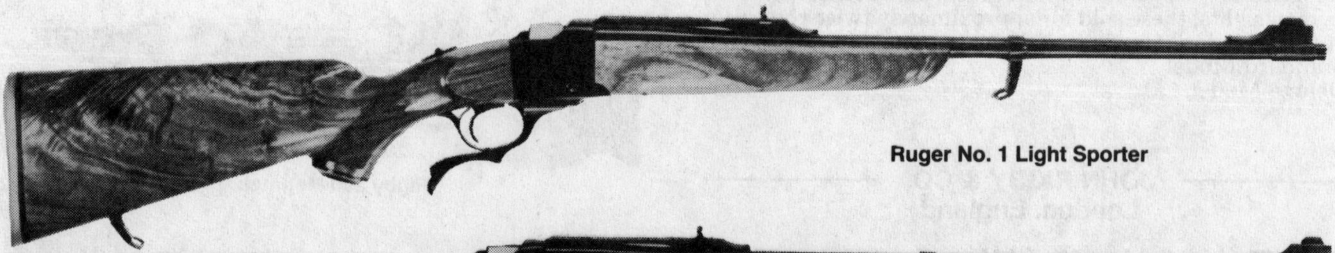

Ruger No. 1 Light Sporter

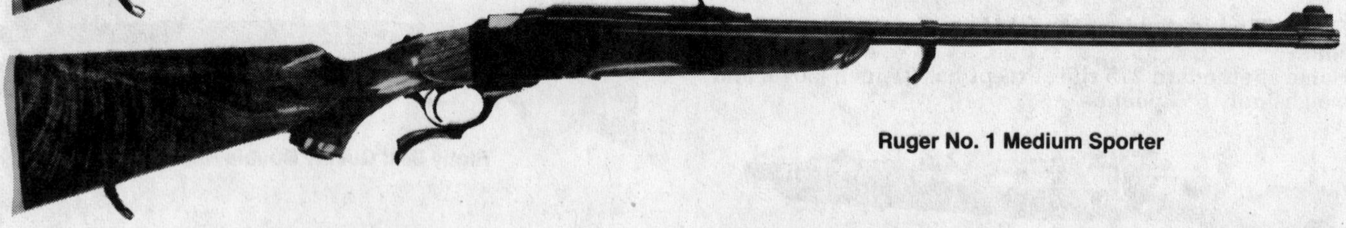

Ruger No. 1 Medium Sporter

RUGER RIFLES
Southport, Connecticut
Manufactured by Sturm, Ruger & Co.

Ruger Number One (1) Light Sporter $375
Same as No. 1 Standard, except has 22-inch barrel, folding leaf rear sight on quarter-rib and ramp front sight, Henry pattern forearm, front swivel on barrel band. Weight: $7^1/_4$ pounds. Calibers: 243 Win., 270 Win., 7×57mm, 30-06. Made 1966 to 1983.

Ruger Number One (1) Medium Sporter $385
Same as No. 1 Light Sporter, except has 26-inch barrel (22-inch in 45-70); weight is 8 pounds ($7^1/_4$ pounds in 45-70). Calibers: 7mm Rem. Mag., 300 Win. Mag., 45-70. Made from 1966 to date.

Ruger Number One (1) "North Americans" Presentation Rifle $45,000
Same general specifications as the Ruger No. 1 Standard, except highly customized with elaborate engravings, carvings, fine-line checkering and gold inlays. A series of 21 is planned, each rifle depicting a North American big-game animal, chambered in the caliber appropriate to the game. Stock is of Northern California English walnut. Comes in trunk-style Huey case with Leupold scope and other accessories.

Ruger Number One (1) Special Varminter $365
Same as No. 1 Standard, except has heavy 24-inch barrel with target scope bases, no quarter-rib. Weight: 9 pounds. Calibers: 22-250, 25-06, 7mm Rem. Mag., 300 Win. Mag. Made from 1966 to date.

Ruger No. 1 Special Varminter

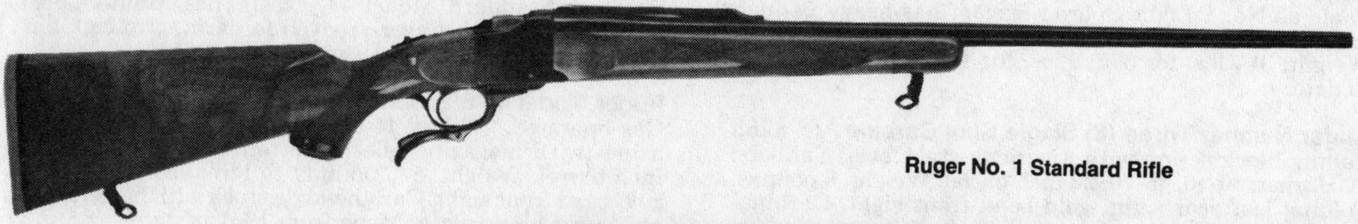

Ruger No. 1 Standard Rifle

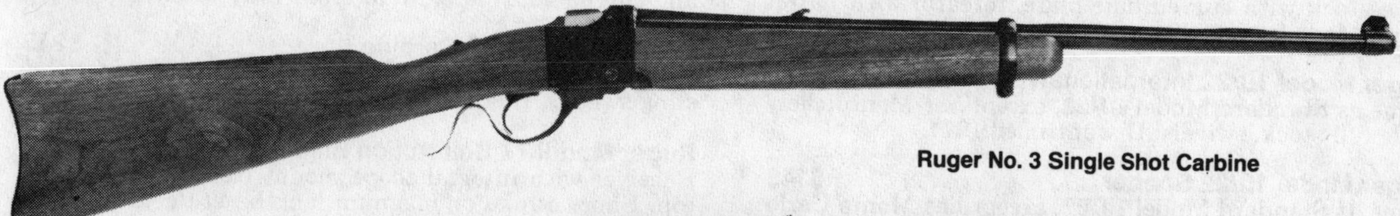

Ruger No. 3 Single Shot Carbine

Ruger 10/22 International

Ruger 10/22 Sporter

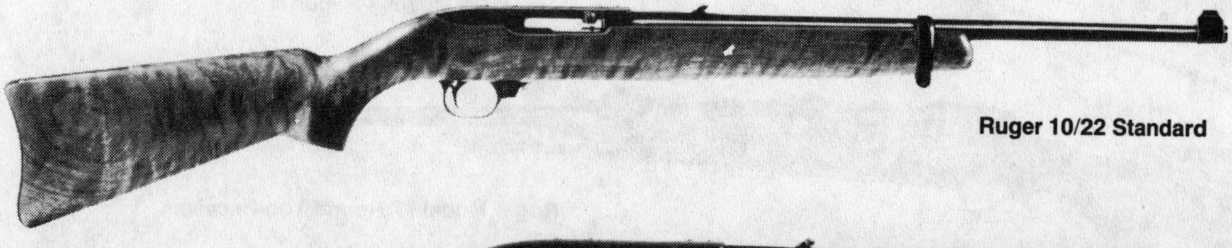

Ruger 10/22 Standard

Ruger Model 10/22SP Deluxe Sporter

Ruger Number One (1) Standard Rifle $385
Falling-block single-shot action with Farquharson-type lever. Calibers: 22-250, 243 Win., 6mm Rem., 25-06, 270 Win., 30-06, 7mm Rem. Mag., 300 Win. Mag. 26-inch barrel. Weight: 8 pounds. No sights, has quarter-rib for scope mounting. Checkered pistol-grip buttstock and semibeavertail forearm, QD swivels, rubber butt plate. Made from 1966 to date.

Ruger Number One (1) Tropical Rifle $425
Same as No. 1 Light Sporter, except has heavy 24-inch barrel; calibers are 375 H&H Mag. and 458 Win. Mag. Weight: $8\frac{1}{4}$ lbs. for 375; 9 lbs. for 458. Made from 1966 to date.

Ruger Number Three (3) Single Shot Carbine . . . $265
Falling-block action with American-style lever. Calibers: 22 Hornet, 30-40, 45-70. 22-inch barrel. Weight, 6 pounds. Folding leaf rear sight, gold bead front sight. Carbine-style stock with curved butt plate, forearm with barrel band. Made from 1972 to date.

Ruger Model 10/22 International $355
Same as Standard Model 10/22, except has Mannlicher-style full stock, swivels. Discontinued 1971.

Ruger Model 10/22 Sporter $145
Same as Standard Model 10/22, except has Monte Carlo sporter stock with finger-grooved forearm, grip cap, flat butt plate, sling swivels. Discontinued 1971.

Ruger Model 10/22 Standard Autoloading Carbine $125
Caliber: 22 Long Rifle. Detachable 10-shot rotary magazine. $18\frac{1}{2}$-inch barrel. Weight: 5 pounds. Folding leaf rear sight, bead front sight. Carbine-style stock with barrel band and curved butt plate. Made from 1964 to date. Walnut stock discontinued 1980.

Ruger Model 10/22SP Deluxe Sporter $160
Same as Standard Model 10/22, except has checkered stock with flat butt plate and sling swivels. Made from 1966 to date.

Ruger Model 44 International $495
Same as Standard Model 44, except has Mannlicher-style full stock, swivels. Discontinued 1971.

Ruger Model 44 Sporter $330
Same as Standard Model 44, except has Monte Carlo sporter stock with finger-grooved forearm, grip cap, flat butt plate, sling swivels. Discontinued 1971.

Ruger Model 44 Standard Autoloading Carbine . . $240
Gas-operated. Caliber: 44 Magnum. 4-shot tubular magazine (with magazine release button since 1967). $18\frac{1}{2}$-inch barrel. Weight: $5\frac{3}{4}$ pounds. Folding leaf rear sight, gold bead front sight. Carbine-style stock with barrel band and curved butt plate. Made from 1961 to date.

Ruger Model 44RS Carbine $245
Same as Standard Model 44, except has built-in peep sight, sling swivels. Discontinued 1978.

Ruger Model 77 Bolt Action Rifle
Receiver with integral scope mount base or with round top. Short stroke or magnum length action (depending upon caliber) in the former type receiver, magnum only in the latter. Calibers: 22-250, 220 Swift, 6mm Rem., 243 Win., 250-3000, 25-06, 257 Roberts, 270 Win., 7×57mm, 7mm Rem. Mag., 280 Rem., 308 Win., 30-06, 300 Win. Mag., 338 Win. Mag., 458 Win. Mag. 5-shot magazine standard, 4-shot in 220 Swift, 3-shot in magnum calibers. 22-, 24- or 26-inch barrel (depending upon caliber). Weight: about 7 lbs.; 458 Mag. model, $8\frac{3}{4}$ lbs. Round top model furnished with folding leaf rear sight and ramp front sight; integral base model furnished with scope rings and

Ruger 44 Standard

Ruger 44 Sporter

Ruger Model 77 Round Top Receiver

Ruger Model 77 Magnum Action

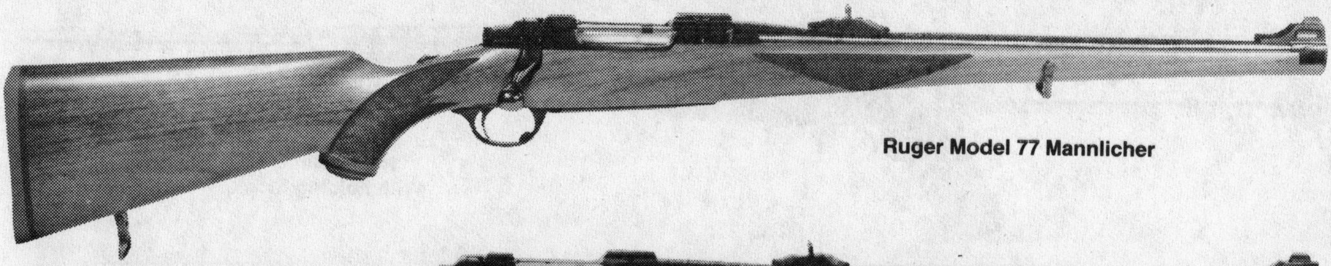

Ruger Model 77 Mannlicher

Ruger Model 77 Short Action

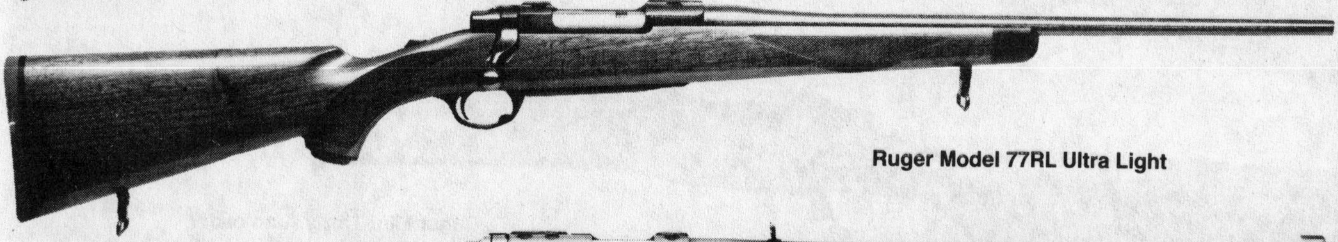

Ruger Model 77RL Ultra Light

Ruger Model 77/22R

Ruger Model 77 Bolt Action Rifle (cont.)
with or without open sights. Stock with checkered pistol grip and forearm, pistol-grip cap, rubber recoil pad, QD swivel studs. Made from 1968 to date.

Model 77r5, integral base, no sights	**$300**
Model 77, 338 Win. Mag.	**325**
Model 77RS, integral base, open sights	**335**
Model 77RS, 338 Win. Mag., 458 Win. Mag. with standard stock	**425**
Model 77RS, 458 Win. Mag. with fancy Circassian walnut stock	**495**
Model 77ST, round top, open sights	**300**
Model 77ST, 338 Win. Mag.	**325**

Ruger Model 77 (M-77) Ultra Light Carbine $330
Bolt action. Calibers: 270, 30-06, 243, 308. 18½-inch barrel. About 39 inches overall. Weight: 6 pounds. Handcheckered American walnut stock with pistol grip. Open sights and equipped with Ruger Integral Scope bases with one-inch Ruger rings. Sling swivels. Made 1986 to date.

Ruger Model 77RL Ultra Light Bolt Action Rifle . . . $345
Same general specifications as standard Model 77, except has no sights, 20- or 22-inch barrel and weighs 6 pounds.

Ruger Model 77V, Varmint Rifle $310
Same as standard Model 77 with integral base receiver, except has heavy 24-inch (26-inch in 220 Swift) barrel drilled and tapped for target scope bases. Weight: 9 pounds. Calibers: 22-250, 220 Swift, 243 Win., 6mm Rem., 25-06, 308. Made from 1968 to date.

Ruger Model 77/22R Bolt Action Rifle $260
Caliber: 22 RF. 10-shot rotary magazine. Barrel: 20 inches. Weight: 5¾ pounds. Integral scope bases. American hardwood stock. Made from 1985 to date.

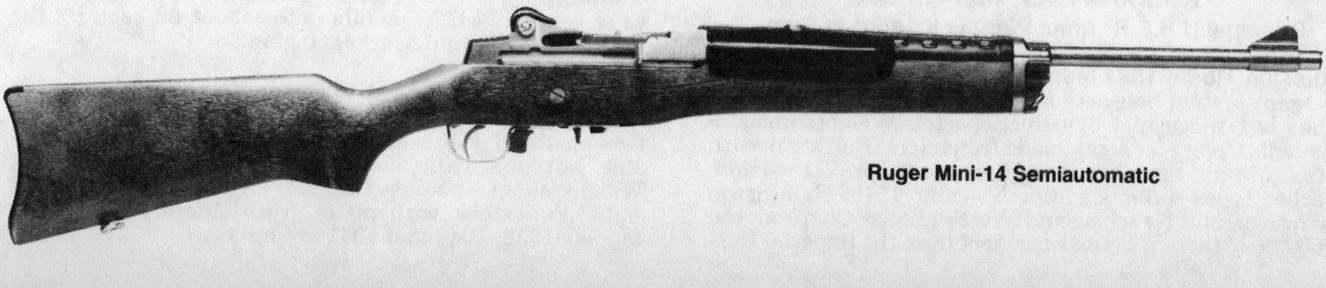

Ruger Mini-14 Semiautomatic

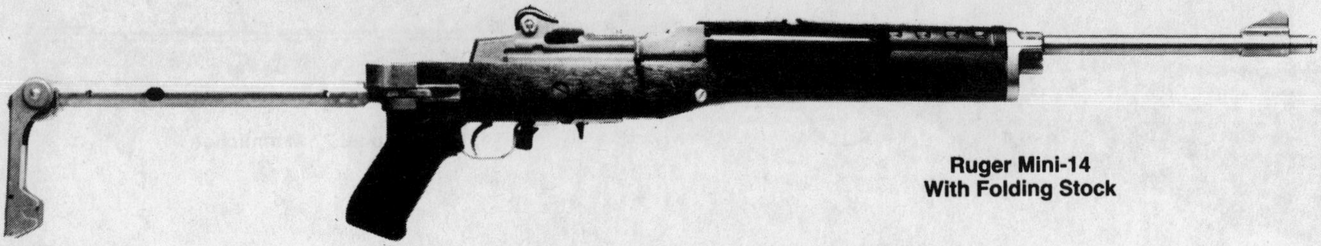

Ruger Mini-14
With Folding Stock

Ruger Mini-14/5

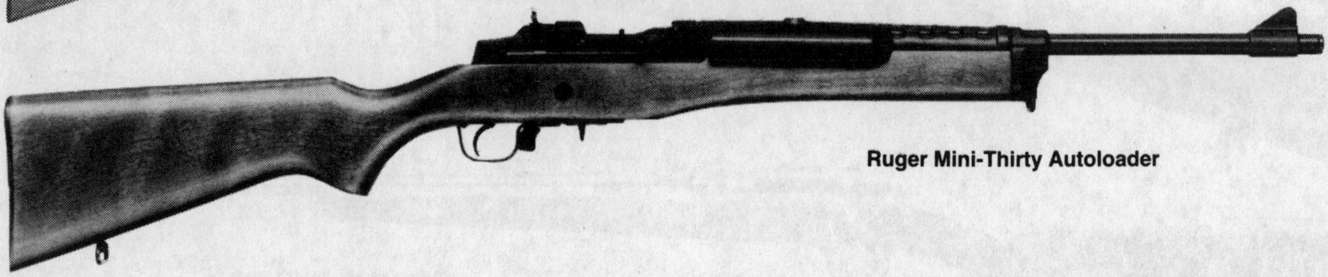

Ruger Mini-Thirty Autoloader

Ruger Mini-14 Semiautomatic Rifle
Gas-operated. Caliber: 223 Rem. (5.56mm). 5-, 10- or 20-shot box magazine. $18^1/_2$-inch barrel. Weight: about $6^1/_2$ pounds. Peep rear sight, blade front sight. Pistol-grip stock with curved butt plate, handguard. Made 1976 to date.
Mini-14/5 blued version **$275**
K-Mini-14/5 stainless steel version **295**
Mini-14/5F blued version **285**
K-Mini-14/5 stainless steel version, folding stock **345**

Ruger Mini-14 Semiautomatic Ranch Rifle $295
Same general specifications as standard Mini-14 except designed for telescopic sights and weighs approximately $6^1/_4$ pounds.

Ruger Mini-Thirty (30) Autoloader $350
Caliber: 7.62 × 39mm. 5-shot detachable magazine. $18^1/_2$-inch barrel. $37^1/_4$ inches overall. Weight: 7 lbs. 3 oz. Designed for use with telescopic sights. Walnut stained stock. Blued metal finish. Made from 1986 to date.

Russian Model 1891 Mosin

RUSSIAN MILITARY RIFLES

Principal U.S.S.R. Arms Plant is located at Tula

Russian Model 1891 Mosin Military Rifle $95
Nagant system bolt action. Caliber: 7.62mm Russian. 5-shot box magazine. $31^1/_2$-inch barrel. Weight: about 9 pounds. Open rear sight, blade front sight. Full stock with straight grip. Specifications given are for WWII version; earlier types differ slightly. *Note:* In 1916, Remington Arms Co. and New England Westinghouse Co. produced 250,000 of these rifles on a contract from the Imperial Rus-

Russian Model 1891 Mosin Military Rifle (cont.)
sian Government. Few were delivered to Russia and the balance were purchased by the U.S. Government for training purposes in 1918. Eventually, many of these rifles were sold to N.R.A. members for about $3 each by the Director of Civilian Marksmanship.

Russian Tokarev Model 40 Semiautomatic Military Rifle $325
Gas-operated. Caliber: 7.62mm Russian. 10-shot detachable box magazine. $24^1/_2$-inch barrel. Muzzle brake. Weight: about 9 pounds. Leaf rear sight, hooded post front sight. Full stock with pistol grip. Differences between Models 1938, 1940 and 1941 are minor.

SAKO RIFLES
Riihimaki, Finland
Manufactured by Oy Sako Ab

Sako Model 72 .... $495
Single model designation replacing Vixen Sporter, Vixen Carbine, Vixen Heavy Barrel, Forester Sporter, Forester Carbine, Forester Heavy Barrel, Finnbear Sporter, and Finnbear Carbine, with same specifications except all but heavy barrel models fitted with open rear sight. Values same as for corresponding earlier models. Made 1972-74.

Sako Model 73 Lever Action Rifle $500
Same as Finnwolf, except has 3-shot clip magazine, flush floorplate; stock has no cheekpiece. Made 1973-75.

Sako Model 74 Carbine $545
Long Mauser-type bolt action. Caliber: 30-06. 5-shot magazine. 20-inch barrel. Weight: about $7\frac{1}{2}$ pounds. No sights. Checkered Mannlicher-type full stock of European walnut, Monte Carlo cheekpiece. Made 1974-78.

Sako Model 74 Heavy Barrel Rifle, Long Action .. $575
Same specifications as with short action, except has 24-inch heavy barrel, weighs about $8\frac{3}{4}$ pounds; magnum has 4-shot magazine. Calibers: 25-06, 7mm Rem. Mag. Made 1974-78.

Sako Model 74 Heavy Barrel Rifle, Medium Action $595
Same specifications as with short action, except has 23-inch heavy barrel, weighs about $8\frac{1}{2}$ pounds. Calibers: 220 Swift, 22-250, 243 Win., 308 Win. Made 1974-78.

Sako Model 74 Heavy Barrel Rifle, Short Action $600
Mauser-type bolt action. Calibers: 222 Rem., 223 Rem. 5-shot magazine. $23\frac{1}{2}$-inch heavy barrel. Weight: about $8\frac{1}{4}$ pounds. No sights. Target-style checkered European walnut stock with beavertail forearm. Made 1974-78.

Sako Model 74 Super Sporter, Long Action $525
Same specifications as with short action, except has 24-inch barrel, weighs about 8 pounds; magnums have 4-shot magazine, recoil pad. Calibers: 25-06, 270 Win. 7mm Rem. Mag., 30-06, 300 Win. Mag., 338 Win. Mag., 375 H&H Mag. Made 1974-78.

Sako Model 74 Super Sporter, Medium Action .. $575
Same specifications as with short action, except weight is $7\frac{1}{4}$ pounds. Calibers: 220 Swift, 22-250, 243 Win. Made 1974-78.

Sako Model 74 Super Sporter, Short Action $595
Mauser-type bolt action. Calibers: 222 Rem., 223 Rem. 5-shot magazine. $23\frac{1}{2}$-inch barrel. Weight: about $6\frac{1}{2}$ pounds. No sights. Checkered European walnut stock with Monte Carlo cheekpiece, QD swivel studs. Made from 1974 to date.

Sako Model 78 Super Hornet Sporter $395
Same specifications as Model 78 Rimfire, except caliber 22 Hornet, 4-shot magazine. Introduced 1977; discont.

Sako Model 78 Super Rimfire Sporter $325
Bolt action. Caliber: 22 Long Rifle. 5-shot magazine. $22\frac{1}{2}$-inch barrel. Weight, about $6\frac{3}{4}$ pounds. No sights. Checkered European walnut stock, Monte Carlo cheekpiece. Introduced 1977; discontinued.

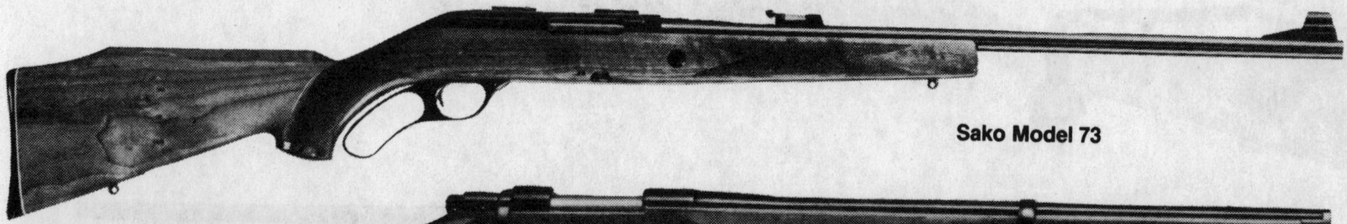

Sako Model 73

Sako Model 74 Carbine

Sako Model 74 Super Sporter

Sako Model 78 Super Rimfire

RIFLES

Sako Classic Bolt Action Rifle $625
Type AII action. Calibers: 243 Win., 270 Win., 30-06, 7mm Rem. Mag. American walnut stock.

Sako Deluxe Grade AI $640
Same specifications as Standard Grade, except with 22 lines to the inch French checkering, rosewood grip cap and forend tip, semibeavertail forend.

Sako Deluxe Grade AII $635
Same specifications as Standard Grade, except with 22 lines per inch French checkering, rosewood grip cap and forend tip, semibeavertail forend.

Sako Deluxe Grade AIII $695
Same specifications as with standard, except with French checkering, rosewood grip cap and forend tip, semibeavertail forend.

Sako Deluxe Lightweight Bolt Action Rifle $845
Same general specifications as Hunter Lightweight, except has beautifully grained French walnut stock, superb high-gloss finish, fine hand-cut checkering, rosewood forend tip and grip cap. Introduced 1985.

Sako Fiberglass Bolt Action Rifle $795
All-weather fiberglass stock version of Sako barreled long action. Calibers: 25-06, 270, 30-06, 7mm Rem. Mag., 300 Win. Mag., 338 Win. Mag., 375 H&H Mag. Barrel length: 22½ inches. Overall length: 44¼ inches. Weight: 7¼ pounds. Made 1984 to date.

Sako Finnbear Carbine $695
Same as Finnbear Sporter, except has 20-inch barrel, Mannlicher-type full stock. Made 1971.

Sako Finnbear Sporter $520
Long Mauser-type bolt action. Calibers: 25-06, 264 Mag., 270, 30-06, 300 Win. Mag., 338 Mag., 7mm Mag., 375 H&H Mag. Magazine holds 5 standard or 4 magnum cartridges. 24-inch barrel. Weight: about 7 pounds. Hooded ramp front sight. Sporter stock with Monte Carlo cheekpiece, checkered pistol grip and forearm, recoil pad, swivels. Made 1961 to 1971.

Sako Finnwolf Lever Action Rifle $795
Hammerless. Calibers: 243 Win., 308 Win. 4-shot clip magazine. 23-inch barrel. Weight: 6¾ pounds. Hooded ramp front sight. Sporter stock with Monte Carlo cheekpiece, checkered pistol grip and forearm, swivels (available with right- or left-hand stock). Made 1963 to 1972.

Sako Finsport 2700 . . . . $750
Bolt-action centerfire rifle. Calibers: 270, 30-06, 7mm Rem. Mag., 300 Win. Mag. Barrel length: 24 inches. Weight: 8 pounds. Discontinued.

Sako Forester Carbine $595
Same as Forester Sporter, except has 20-inch barrel, Mannlicher-type full stock. Made 1958 to 1971.

Sako Forester Heavy Barrel $585
Same as Forester Sporter, except has 24-inch heavy barrel, weighs 7½ pounds. Made 1958 to 1971.

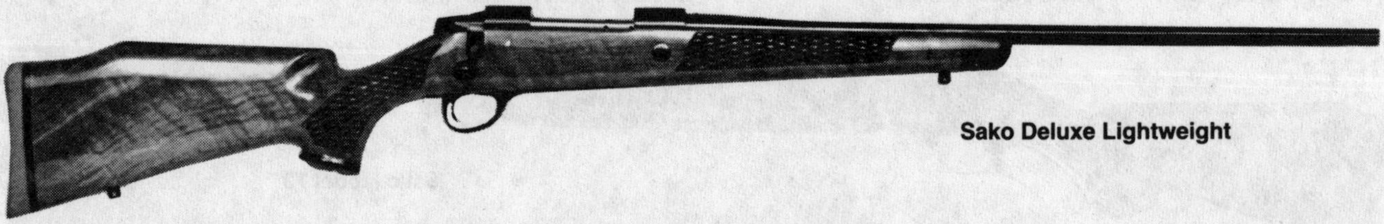

Sako Deluxe Lightweight

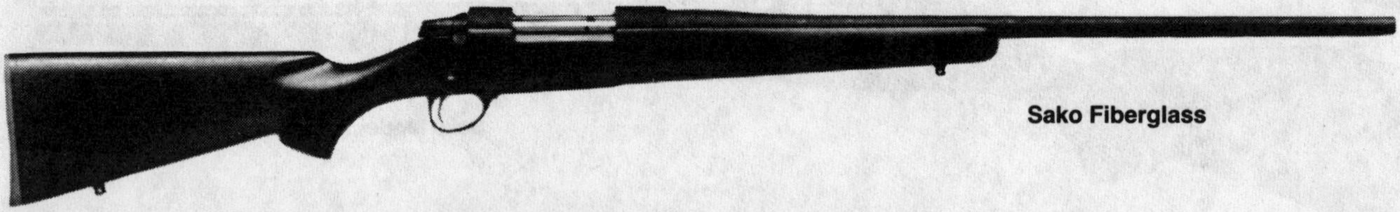

Sako Fiberglass

Sako Finnbear Sporter

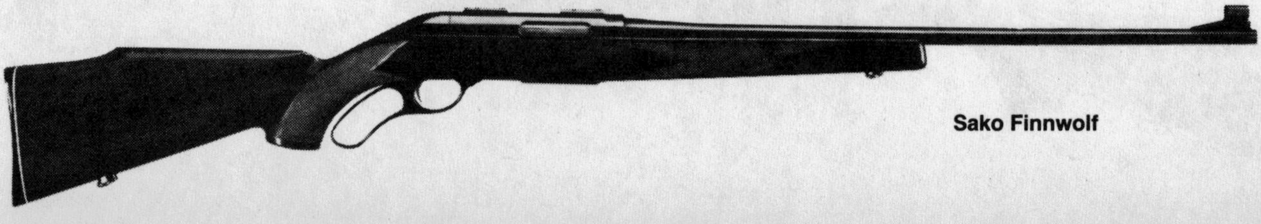

Sako Finnwolf

Sako Forester Sporter

Sako Golden Anniversary Model

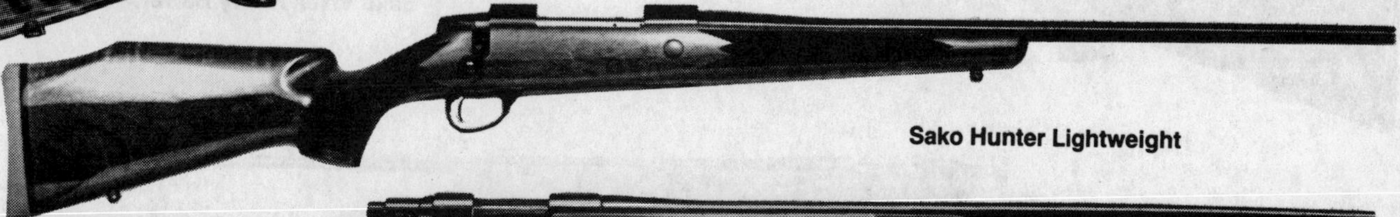

Sako Hunter Lightweight

Sako Sporter Deluxe

Sako Forester Sporter **$565**
Medium-length Mauser-type bolt action. Calibers: 22-250, 243 Win., 308 Win. 5-shot magazine. 23-inch barrel. Weight: 6½ pounds. Hooded ramp front sight. Sporter stock with Monte Carlo cheekpiece, checkered pistol grip and forearm, swivels. Made 1957 to 1971.

Sako Golden Anniversary Model **$1550**
Special presentation grade rifle issued in 1973 to commemorate Sako's 50th anniversary. 1000 (numbered 1 to 1000) made. Same specifications as Deluxe Sporter, long action, 7mm Rem. Mag. Receiver, trigger guard and floorplate decorated with gold oak leaf and acorn motif. Stock of select European walnut, checkering bordered with hand-carved oak leaf pattern.

Sako High-Power Mauser Sporting Rifle **$495**
FN Mauser action. Calibers: 270, 30-06. 5-shot magazine. 24-inch barrel. Open rear leaf sight, Patridge front sight, hooded ramp. Checkered stock with Monte Carlo comb and cheekpiece. Weight: about 7½ pounds. Made 1950-57.

Sako Hunter Lightweight Bolt Action Rifle
5- or 6-shot magazine. Barrel length: 21½ inches, AI; 22 inches, AII; 22½ inches, AIII. Overall length: 42¼-44½ inches. Weight: 5¾ lbs., AI; 6¾ lbs. AII; 7¼ lbs., AIII. Monte Carlo-style European walnut stock, oil finished. Hand-checkered pistol grip and forend. Introduced 1985. Left-hand version introduced 1987.

AI (Short Action) 17 Rem.	**$595**
222 Rem., 223 Rem.	**570**
AII (Medium Action)	
22-250 Rem., 243 Win., 308 Win.	**570**
AIII (Long Action)	
25-06 Rem., 270 Win., 30-06	**585**
338 Win. Mag.	**625**
375 H&H Mag.	**795**
Left-hand Model (Standard Cal.)	**985**
Magnum Calibers	**1020**

Sako Laminated Stock Bolt Action Rifles
Similar in style and specifications to the Hunter Grade, except with stock of resin-bonded, hardwood veneers. Available 18 calibers in AI (Short), AII (Medium) or AV action; left-handed version in 10 calibers, AV only. Introduced in 1987.

Short or Medium Action	**$690**
Long Action/Magnum	**715**

Sako Magnum Mauser **$595**
Same general specifications as Standard Model, except has recoil pad. Calibers: 300 H&H Magnum, 375 H&H Magnum.

Sako Safari Grade **$1500**
Classic bolt action. Calibers: 300 Win. Mag., 338 Win. Mag., 375 H&H. Oil-finished European walnut stock with hand-checkering. Barrel band swivel, express-type sight rib; satin or matte blue finish.

Sako Sporter Deluxe **$625**
Same as Vixen, Forester, Finnbear and Model 74, except has fancy French walnut stock with skip checkering, rosewood forend tip and pistol-grip cap, recoil pad, inlaid trigger guard and floorplate.

Sako Standard Grade AI **$495**
Short bolt action. Calibers: 17 Rem., 222 Rem., 223 Rem. 5-shot magazine. 23½-inch barrel. Weight: about 6½ pounds. No sights. Checkered European walnut stock with Monte Carlo cheekpiece, QD swivel studs. Made from 1978 to date.

Sako Standard Grade AII **$595**
Medium bolt action. Calibers: 22-250 Rem., 243 Win., 308 Win. 23½-inch barrel in 22-250; 23-inch barrel in other calibers. 5-shot magazine. Weight: about 7¼ pounds. Checkered European walnut stock with Monte Carlo cheekpiece, QD swivel studs. Made from 1978 to date.

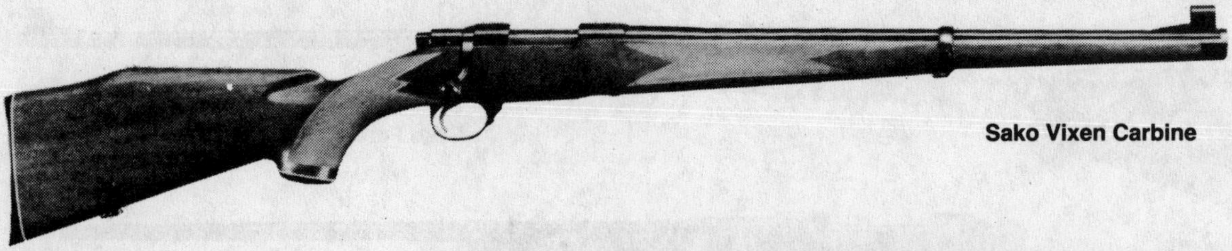

Sako Vixen Carbine

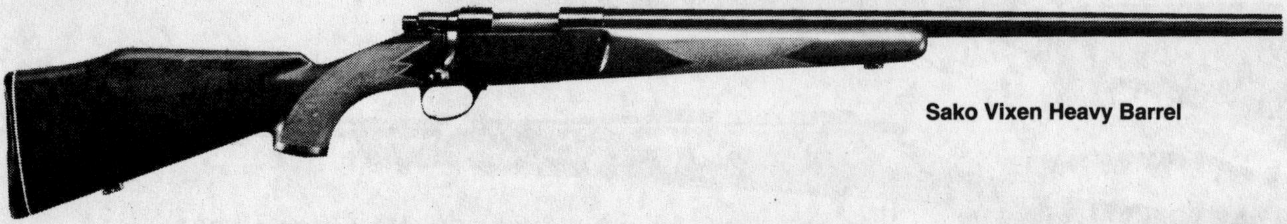

Sako Vixen Heavy Barrel

Sako Vixen Sporter

Sako Standard Grade AIII **$550**
Long bolt action. Calibers: 25-06 Rem., 270 Win., 30-06, 7mm Rem. Mag., 300 Win. Mag., 338 Win. Mag., 375 H&H. 24-inch barrel. 4-shot magazine. Weight: 8 pounds. Made from 1978 to date.

Sako Super Deluxe Rifle **$1500**
Available in AI, AII, AIII action calibers. Select European walnut stock, hand-checkered, deep oak leaf hand-engraved design.

Sako Vixen Carbine **$670**
Same as Vixen Sporter, except has 20-inch barrel, Mannlicher-type full stock. Made 1947 to 1971.

Sako Vixen Heavy Barrel **$525**
Same as Vixen Sporter, except calibers (222 Rem., 222 Rem. Mag., 223 Rem.), heavy barrel, target-style stock with beavertail forearm. Weight: 7½ pounds. Made 1947 to 1971.

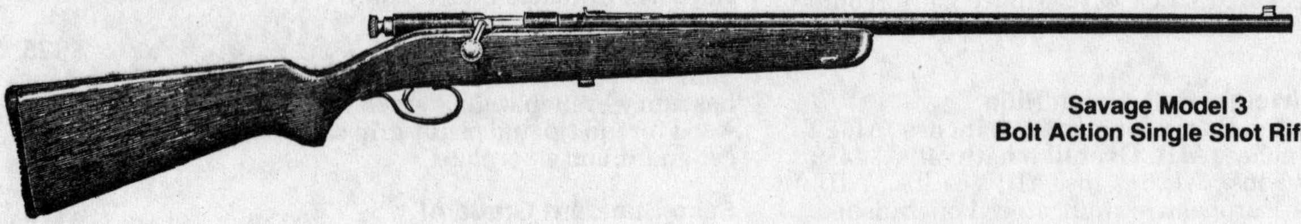

Savage Model 3
Bolt Action Single Shot Rifle

SAVAGE INDUSTRIES
Westfield, Massachusetts
Formerly of Utica, New York

Savage Model 3 Bolt Action Single Shot Rifle . . . **$100**
Takedown. Caliber: 22 Short, Long, Long Rifle. 26-inch barrel on prewar rifles, postwar production has 24-inch barrel. Weight: about 5 pounds. Open rear sight, bead front sight. Plain pistol-grip stock. Made 1933 to 1952.

Sako Vixen Sporter **$525**
Short Mauser-type bolt action. Calibers: 218 Bee, 22 Hornet, 222 Rem., 222 Rem. Mag., 223 Rem. 5-shot magazine. 23½-inch barrel. Weight: 6½ pounds. Hooded ramp front sight. Sporter stock with Monte Carlo cheekpiece, checkered pistol grip and forearm, swivels. Made 1946 to 1971.

J. P. SAUER & SOHN
Suhl, West Germany

Sauer Mauser Bolt Action Sporting Rifle **$895**
Calibers: 7×57 and 8×57mm most common, but these rifles were produced in a variety of calibers including most of the popular Continental numbers as well as our 30-06. 5-shot box magazine. 22- or 24-inch Krupp steel barrel, half-octagon with raised matted rib. Double-set trigger. Weight: about 7½ pounds. Three-leaf open rear sight, ramp front sight. Sporting stock with cheekpiece, checkered pistol grip, raised side-panels, schnabel tip, swivels. Also made with 20-inch barrel and full-length stock. Mfd prior to WWII.

Savage Model 3S **$130**
Same as Model 3, except has peep rear sight and hooded front sight. Made 1933 to 1942.

Savage Model 3ST **$100**
Same as Model 3S, except fitted with swivels and sling. Made 1933 to 1942.

Savage Model 4 Bolt Action Repeating Rifle $100
Takedown. Caliber: 22 Short, Long, Long Rifle. 5-shot detachable box magazine. 24-inch barrel. Weight: about $5^{1}/_{2}$ pounds. Open rear sight, bead front sight. Checkered pistol-grip stock on prewar models, early production had grooved forearm; postwar rifles have plain stocks. Made 1933 to 1965.

Savage Model 4M $85
Same as Model 4, except chambered for 22 Rimfire Magnum. Made 1961-65.

Savage Model 4S $110
Same as Model 4, except has peep rear sight and hooded front sight. Made 1933 to 1942.

Savage Model 5 Bolt Action Repeating Rifle $85
Same as Model 4, except has tubular magazine (holds 21 Short, 17 Long, 15 Long Rifle), weighs about 6 pounds. Made 1936 to 1961.

Savage Model 5S $90
Same as Model 5, except has peep rear sight and hooded front sight. Made 1936 to 1942.

Savage Model 6 Autoloading Rifle $110
Takedown. Caliber: 22 Short, Long, Long Rifle. Tubular magazine holds 21 Short, 17 Long, 15 Long Rifle. 24-inch barrel. Weight: about 6 pounds. Open rear sight, bead front sight. Checkered pistol-grip stock on prewar models, postwar rifles have plain stocks. Made 1938 to 1968.

Savage Model 6S $125
Same as Model 6, except has peep rear sight, bead front sight. Made 1938 to 1942.

Savage Model 7 Autoloading Rifle $100
Same general specifications as Model 6, except has 5-shot detachable box magazine. Made 1939 to 1951.

Savage Model 7S $100
Same as Model 7, except has peep rear sight and hooded front sight. Made 1938 to 1942.

Savage Model 19 Bolt Action Target Rifle $190
Model of 1933. Speed lock. Caliber: 22 Long Rifle. 5-shot detachable box magazine. 25-inch barrel. Weight: about 8 pounds. Adjustable rear peep sight and blade front sight on early models, later production equipped with extension rear sight and hooded front sight. Target stock with full pistol grip and beavertail forearm. Made 1933 to 1946.

Savage Model 4

Savage Model 4M

Savage Model 5

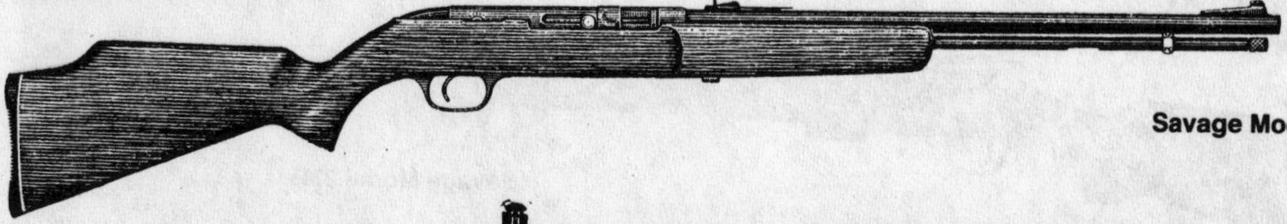

Savage Model 6

Savage Model 19 NRA (1933)

Savage Model 19 NRA Bolt Action Match Rifle . . $235
Model of 1919. Caliber: 22 Long Rifle. 5-shot detachable box magazine. 25-inch barrel. Weight: about 7 pounds. Adjustable rear peep sight, blade front sight. Full military stock with pistol grip. Made 1919 to 1933.

Savage Model 19H $325
Same as standard Model 19 (1933), except chambered for 22 Hornet, has Model 23D-type bolt mechanism, loading port and magazine. Made 1933 to 1942.

Savage Model 19L $195
Same as standard Model 19 (1933), except equipped with Lyman 48Y receiver sight and 17A front sight. Made 1933 to 1942.

Savage Model 19M $225
Same as standard Model 19 (1933), except has heavy 28-inch barrel with scope bases, weighs about 9¼ pounds. Made 1933 to 1942.

Savage Model 20-1926 Hi-Power Bolt Action Rifle $350
Same as Model 1920, except has 24-inch medium weight barrel, improved stock, Lyman 54 rear peep sight, weighs about 7 pounds. Made 1926-29.

Savage Model 23A Bolt Action Sporting Rifle . . . $160
Caliber: 22 Long Rifle. 5-shot detachable box magazine. 23-inch barrel. Weight: about 6 pounds. Open rear sight, blade or bead front sight. Plain pistol-grip stock with slender forearm and schnabel tip. Made 1923 to 1933.

Savage Model 23AA $185
Model of 1933. Improved version of the Model 23A with same general specifications, except has speed lock, improved stock, weighs about 6½ pounds. Made 1933 to 1942.

Savage Model 23B $240
Same as Model 23A, except caliber 25/20, has 25-inch barrel. Model of 1933 has improved stock with full forearm instead of the slender forearm with schnabel found on earlier production. Weight: about 6½ pounds. Made 1923 to 1942.

Savage Model 23C $250
Same as Model 23B, except caliber 32/20. Made 1923 to 1942.

Savage Model 23D $265
Same as Model 23B, except caliber 22 Hornet. Made 1933 to 1947.

Savage Model 25 Slide Action Repeating Rifle . . $225
Takedown. Hammerless. Caliber: 22 Short, Long, Long Rifle. Tubular magazine holds 20 Short, 17 Long, 15 Long Rifle. 24-inch octagon barrel. Weight: about 5¾ pounds. Open rear sight, blade front sight. Plain pistol-grip stock, grooved slide handle. Made 1925-29.

Savage Model 29 Slide Action Repeating Rifle . . $275
Takedown. Hammerless. Caliber: 22 Short, Long, Long Rifle. Tubular magazine holds 20 Short, 17 Long, 15 Long Rifle. 24-inch barrel, octagon on prewar, round on postwar production. Weight: about 5½ pounds. Open rear sight, bead front sight. Stock with checkered pistol grip and slide handle on prewar, plain stock and grooved forearm on postwar production. Made 1929 to 1967.

Savage Model 20 (1926)

Savage Model 23A

Savage Model 23AA

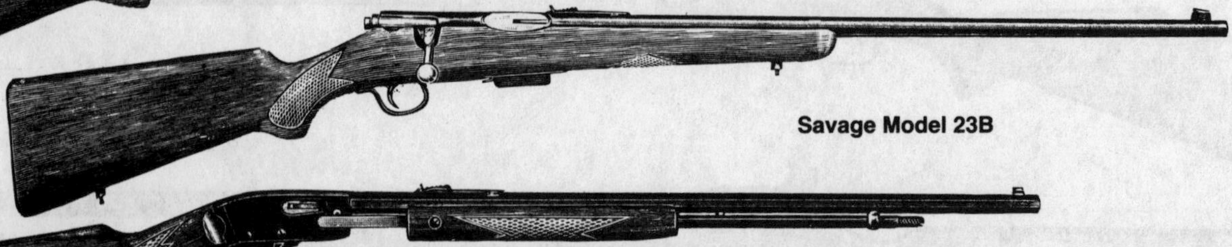
Savage Model 23B

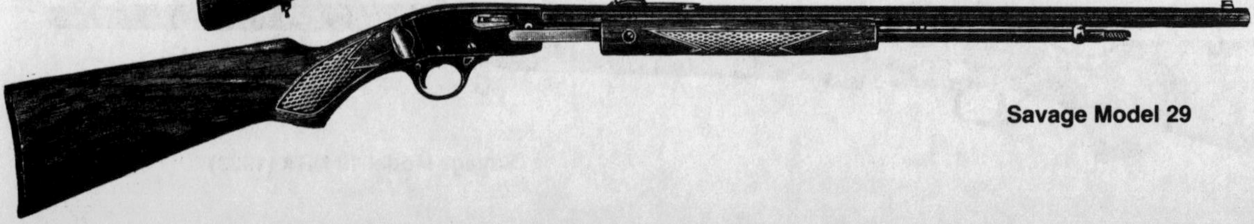
Savage Model 29

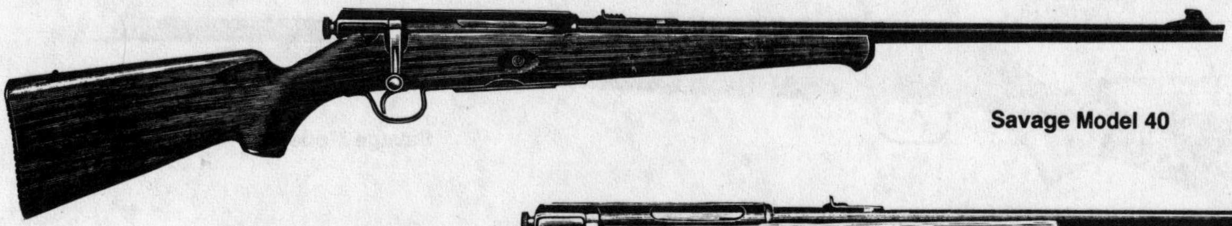

Savage Model 40

Savage Model 45

Savage Model 60

Savage Model 63K

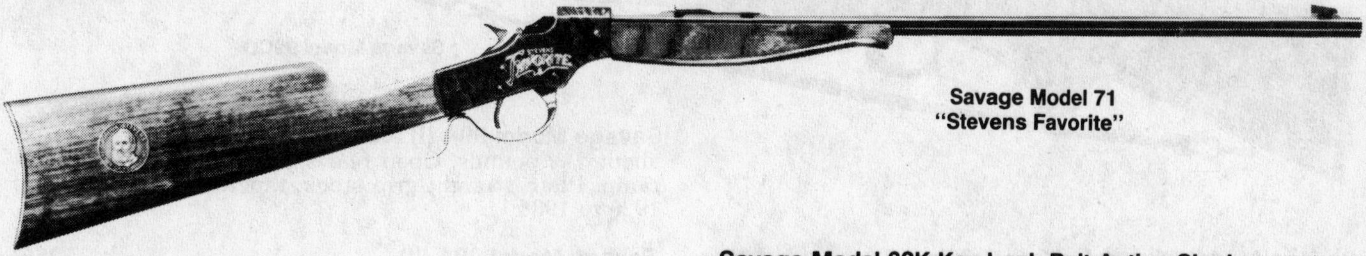

Savage Model 71
"Stevens Favorite"

Savage Model 40 Bolt Action Sporting Rifle $250
Standard Grade. Calibers: 250/3000, 300 Sav., 30/30, 30/06. 4-shot detachable box magazine. 22-inch barrel in calibers 250/3000 and 30/30; 24-inch in 300 Sav. and 30/06. Weight: about 7½ pounds. Open rear sight, bead front sight on ramp. Plain pistol-grip stock with tapered forearm and schnabel tip. Made 1928 to 1940.

Savage Model 45 Super Sporter $325
Special Grade. Same as Model 40, except has checkered pistol grip and forearm, Lyman No. 40 receiver sight. Made 1928 to 1940.

Savage Model 60 Autoloading Rifle $75
Caliber: 22 Long Rifle. 15-shot tubular magazine. 20-inch barrel. Weight: 6 pounds. Open rear sight, ramp front sight. Monte Carlo stock of walnut with checkered pistol grip and forearm. Made 1969 to 1972.

Savage Model 63K Key Lock Bolt Action Single Shot $60
Trigger locked with key. Caliber: 22 Short, Long, Long Rifle. 18-inch barrel. Weight: 4 pounds. Open rear sight, hooded ramp front sight. Full-length stock with pistol grip, swivels. Made 1970-72.

Savage Model 63KM $65
Same as Model 63K, except chambered for 22 Win. Mag. R.F. Made 1970-72.

Savage Model 71 "Stevens Favorite" Single Shot Lever Action Rifle $145
Replica of the original Stevens Favorite issued as a tribute to Joshua Stevens, "Father of 22 Hunting." Caliber: 22 Long Rifle. 22-inch full-octagon barrel. Brass-plated hammer and lever. Open rear sight, brass blade front sight. Weight: 4½ pounds. Plain straight-grip buttstock and schnabel forend; brass commemorative medallion inlaid in buttstock, brass crescent-shaped butt plate. 10,000 produced. Made in 1971 only. Value is for new, unfired specimen.

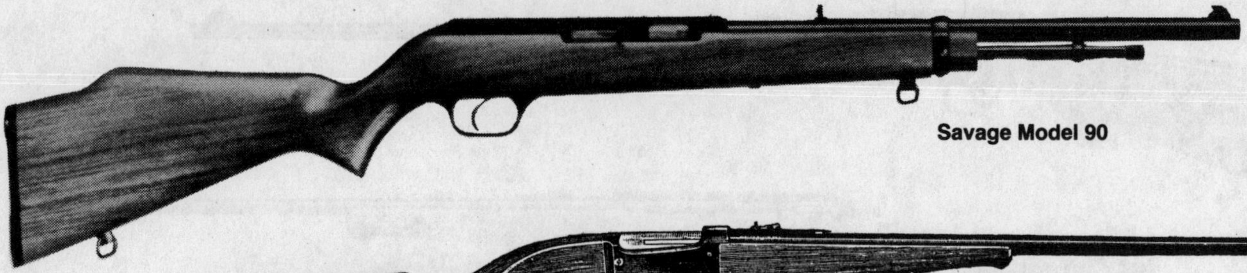

Savage Model 90

Savage Model 99A

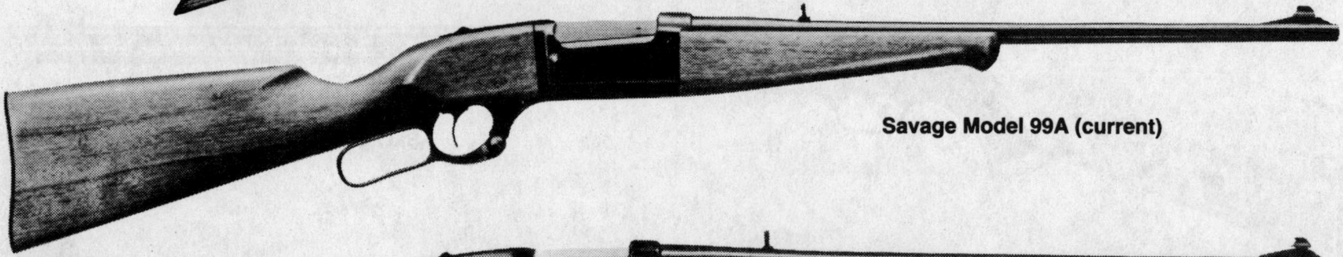

Savage Model 99A (current)

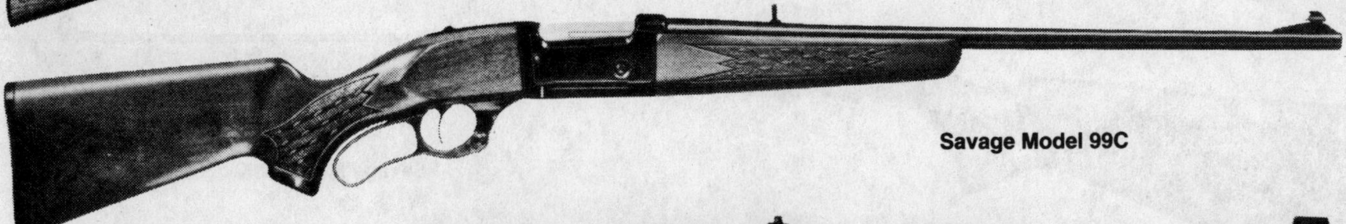

Savage Model 99C

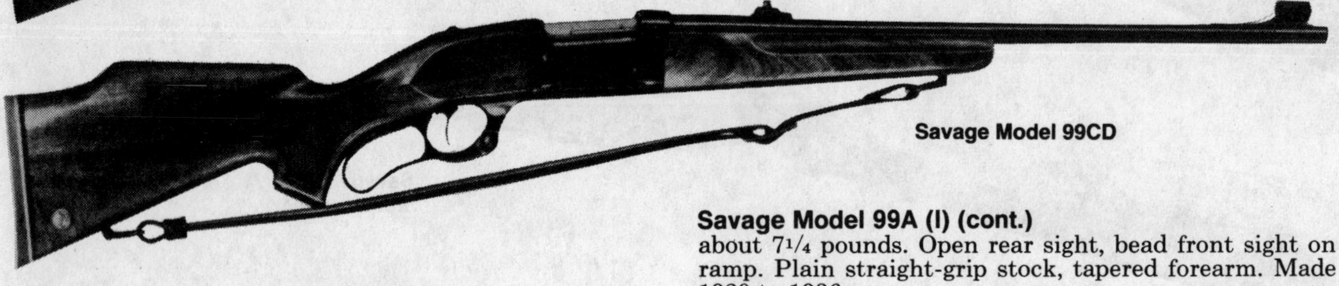

Savage Model 99CD

Savage Model 90 Autoloading Carbine **$80**
Similar to Model 60, except has 16½-inch barrel, 10-shot tubular magazine, folding leaf rear sight, bead front sight, carbine-style stock of uncheckered walnut with barrel band and sling swivels. Weight: 5¾ pounds. Made 1969 to 1972.

Savage Model 99 Lever Action Repeating Rifle
Introduced in 1899, this model has been produced in a variety of styles and calibers. Original designation "Model 1899" was changed to "Model 99" circa 1920. Earlier rifles and carbines—similar to Models 99A, 99B and 99H—were supplied in calibers 25-35, 30-30, 303 Sav., 32-40 and 38-55. Post-WWII Models 99A, 99C, 99CD, 99DE, 99DL, 99F and 99PE have top tang safety; other 99s have slide safety on right side of trigger guard. Current Models 99C and 99CD have detachable box magazine instead of traditional Model 99 rotary magazine.

Savage Model 99A (I) **$495**
Hammerless. Solid frame. Calibers: 30/30, 300 Sav., 303 Sav. Five-shot rotary magazine. 24-inch barrel. Weight: about 7¼ pounds. Open rear sight, bead front sight on ramp. Plain straight-grip stock, tapered forearm. Made 1920 to 1936.

Savage Model 99A (II) **$265**
Current model. Similar to original Model 99A, except has top tang safety, 22-inch barrel, folding leaf rear sight, no crescent butt plate. Calibers: 243 Win., 250 Sav., 300 Sav., 308 Win. Made 1971 to 1982.

Savage Model 99B **$495**
Takedown. Otherwise same as Model 99A, except weight about 7½ pounds. Made 1920 to 1936.

Savage Model 99C **$265**
Current model. Same as Model 99F, except has clip magazine instead of rotary. Calibers: 243 Win., 284 Win., 308 Win. (4-shot detachable magazine holds one round less in 284). Weight: about 6¾ pounds. Made 1965 to date.

Savage Model 99CD **$295**
Deluxe version of Model 99C. Calibers: 243 Win., 250 Sav., 308 Win. Hooded ramp front sight. Weight: 8¼ pounds. Stock with Monte Carlo comb and cheekpiece, checkered pistol grip, grooved forearm, swivels and sling. Made 1975 to 1981.

Savage Model 99DE Citation Grade $540
Same as Model 99PE, except has less elaborate engraving. Made 1968 to 1970.

Savage Model 99DL Deluxe $250
Postwar model. Calibers: 243 Win., 308 Win. Same as Model 99F, except has high comb Monte Carlo stock, sling swivels. Weight: about 6$\frac{3}{4}$ pounds. Made 1960 to 1973.

Savage Model 99E Carbine (I) $540
Pre-WWII type. Solid frame. Calibers: 22 Hi-Power, 250/3000, 30/30, 300 Sav., 303 Sav. with 22-inch barrel; 300 Sav. 24-inch. Weight: about 7 pounds. Other specifications same as Model 99A. Made 1920 to 1936.

Savage Model 99E Carbine (II) $235
Current model. Solid frame. Calibers: 250 Sav., 243 Win., 300 Sav., 308 Win. 20- or 22-inch barrel. Checkered pistol-grip stock and forearm. Made from 1960 to date.

Savage Model 99EG (I) $285
Pre-WWII type. Solid frame. Plain pistol-grip stock and forearm. Otherwise same as Model G. Made 1936 to 1941.

Savage Model 99EG (II) $345
Post-WWII type. Same as prewar model, except has checkered stock and forearm. Calibers: 250 Sav., 300 Sav., 308 Win. (introduced 1955), 243 Win., and 358 Win. Made 1946 to 1960.

Savage Model 99F Featherweight (I) $395
Pre-WWII type. Takedown. Specifications same as Model 99E, except weight about 6$\frac{1}{2}$ pounds. Made 1920 to 1942.

Savage Model 99F Featherweight (II) $240
Postwar model. Solid frame. Calibers: 243 Win., 300 Sav., 308 Win. 22-inch barrel. Checkered pistol-grip stock and forearm. Weight: about 6$\frac{1}{2}$ pounds. Made 1955 to 1973.

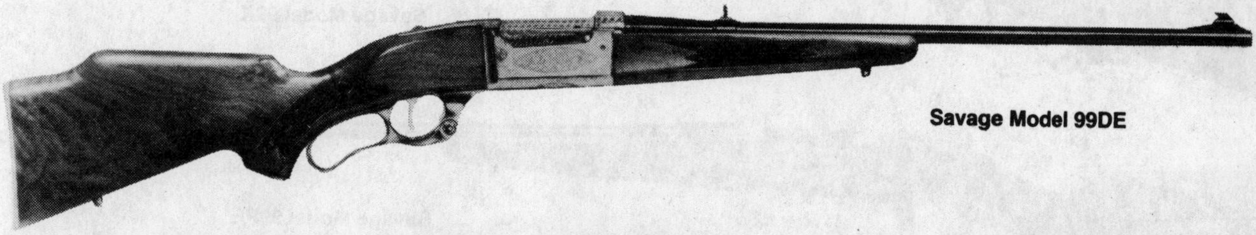

Savage Model 99DE

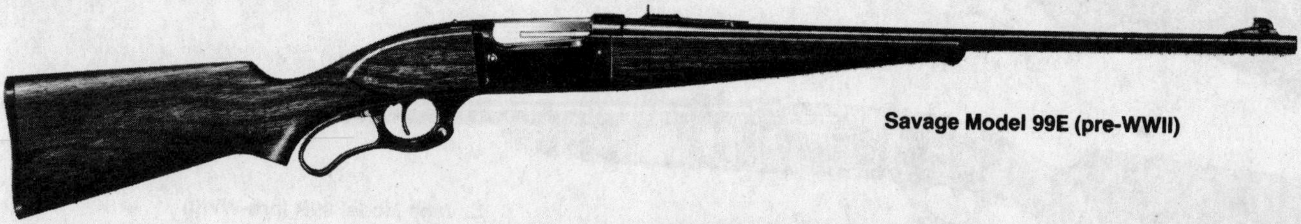

Savage Model 99E (pre-WWII)

Savage Model 99E (current)

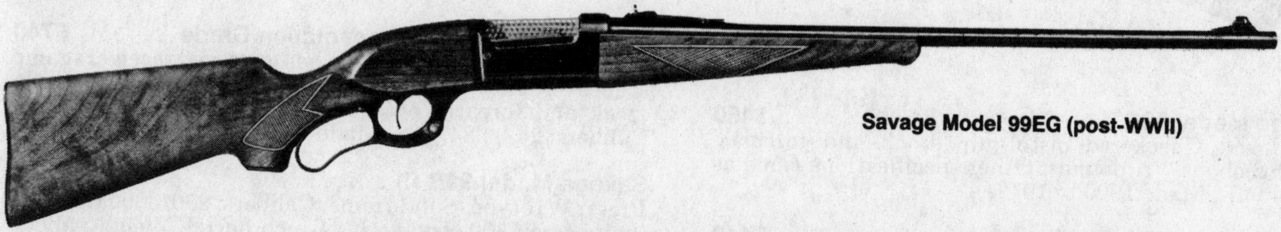

Savage Model 99EG (post-WWII)

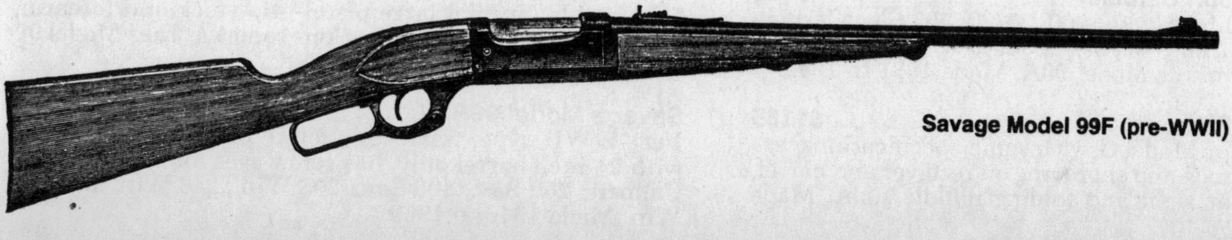

Savage Model 99F (pre-WWII)

Savage Model 99G

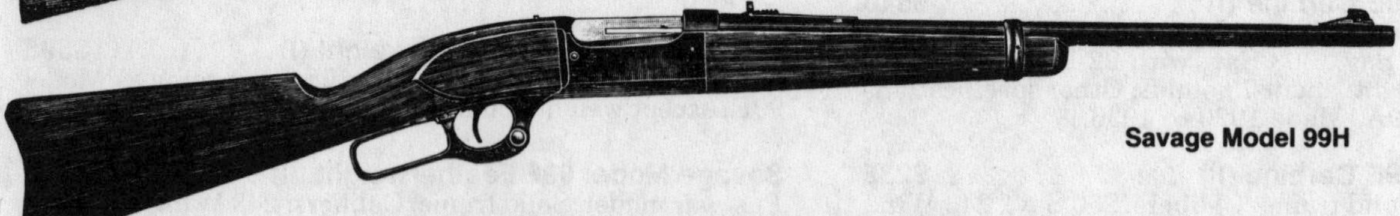

Savage Model 99H

Savage Model 99K

Savage Model 99PE

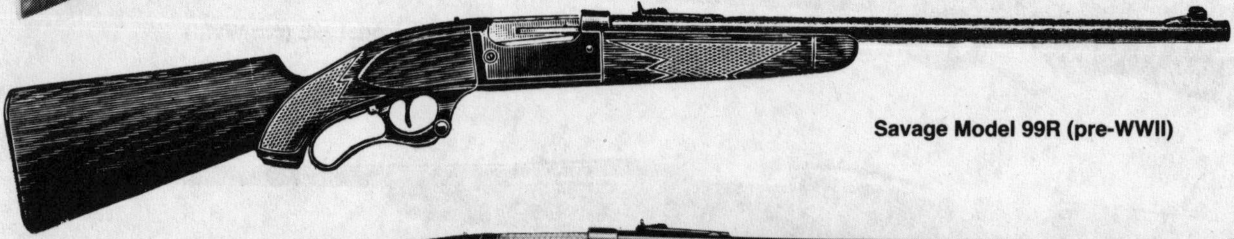

Savage Model 99R (pre-WWII)

Savage Model 99R (post-WWII)

Savage Model 99G **$450**
Takedown. Checkered pistol-grip stock and forearm. Weight: about 7¼ pounds. Other specifications same as Model 99E. Made 1920 to 1942.

Savage Model 99H Carbine **$440**
Solid frame. Calibers: 250/3000, 30/30, 303 Sav. Carbine stock and forearm. Weight: about 6½ pounds. Other specifications same as Model 99A. Made 1931 to 1942.

Savage Model 99K **$1165**
Deluxe version of Model G with same specifications, except has fancy stock and engraving on receiver and barrel, Lyman peep rear sight and folding middle sight. Made 1931 to 1942.

Savage Model 99PE Presentation Grade **$740**
Same as Model 99DL, except has engraved receiver (game scenes on sides), tang and lever; fancy walnut Monte Carlo stock and forearm with hand checkering, QD swivels. Calibers: 243, 284, 308. Made 1968 to 1970.

Savage Model 99R (I) **$445**
Pre-WWII type. Solid frame. Calibers: 250/3000 with 22-inch barrel; 300 Sav. with 24-inch barrel. Weight: about 7½ pounds. Special large pistol-grip stock and forearm, checkered. General specifications same as other Model 99 rifles. Made 1936 to 1942.

Savage Model 99R (II) **$295**
Post-WWII type. Same as prewar model, except made with 24-inch barrel only, has screw eyes for sling swivels. Calibers: 250 Sav., 300 Sav., 308 Win., 243 Win. and 358 Win. Made 1946 to 1960.

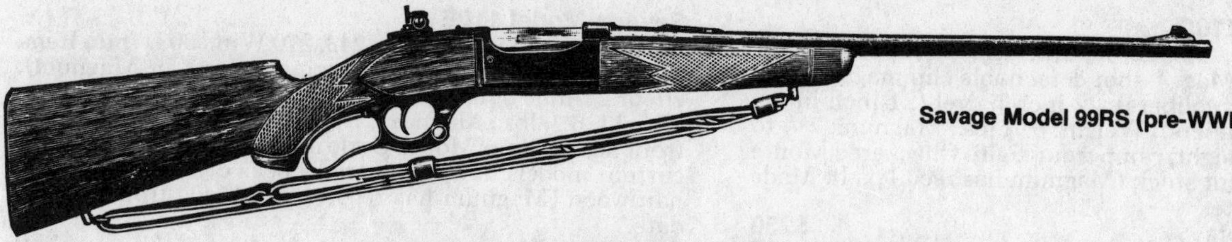

Savage Model 99RS (pre-WWII)

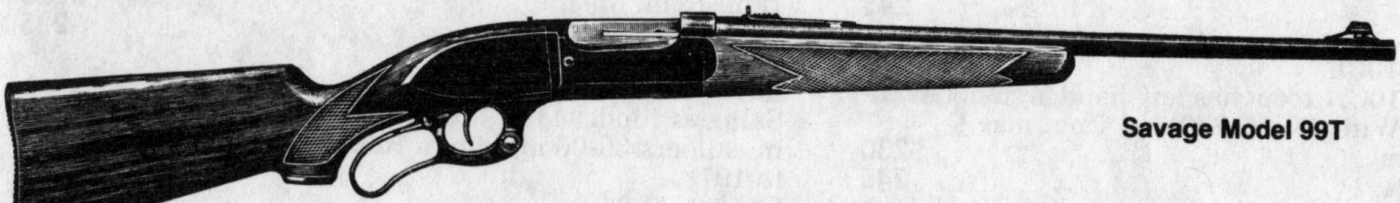

Savage Model 99T

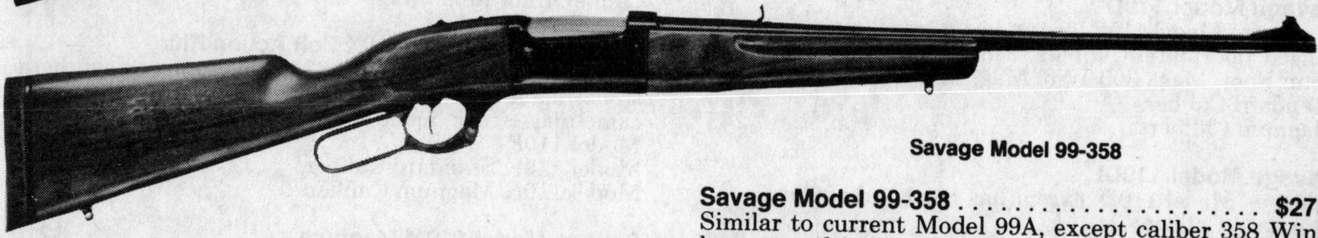

Savage Model 99-358

Savage Model 99RS (I) **$450**
Pre-WWII type. Same as prewar Model 99r5, except equipped with Lyman rear peep sight and folding middle sight, quick detachable swivels and sling. Made 1936 to 1942.

Savage Model 99RS (II) **$325**
Post-WWII type. Same as postwar Model 99r5, except equipped with Redfield 70LH receiver sight, blank in middle sight slot. Made 1946 to 1958.

Savage Model 99T **$345**
Featherweight. Solid frame. Calibers: 22 Hi-Power, 30/30, 303 Sav. with 20-inch barrel; 300 Sav. with 22-inch barrel. Checkered pistol-grip stock and beavertail forearm. Weight: about 7 pounds. General specifications same as other Model 99 rifles. Made 1936 to 1942.

Savage Model 99-358 . . . . **$275**
Similar to current Model 99A, except caliber 358 Win., has grooved forearm, recoil pad, swivel studs. Made 1977 to 1980.

Savage Model 110 Sporter Bolt Action Repeating Rifle **$160**
Calibers: 243, 270, 308, 30-06. 4-shot box magazine. 22-inch barrel. Weight: about 6¾ pounds. Open rear sight, ramp front sight. Standard sporter stock with pistol grip, checkered. Made 1958 to 1963.

Savage Model 110B Bolt Action Rifle
Same as Model 110E, except with checkered select walnut Monte Carlo-style stock (early models) or brown laminated stock (late models). Calibers: 243 Win., 270 Win., 30-06, 7mm Rem. Mag., 338 Win. Mag. Made from 1976 to date.

Early Model **$240**
Laminated Stock Model **370**

Savage Model 110BL **$250**
Same as Model 110B, except has left-hand action.

Savage Model 110

Savage Model 110B

Savage Model 110C
Calibers: 22-250, 243, 25-06, 270, 308, 30-06, 7mm Rem. Mag., 300 Win. Mag. 4-shot detachable clip magazine (3-shot in Magnum calibers). 22-inch barrel (24-inch in 22-250 Magnum calibers). Weight: 6 3/4 lbs.; Magnum, 7 3/4 to 8 lbs. Open rear sight, ramp front sight. Checkered Monte Carlo-style walnut stock (Magnum has recoil pad). Made from 1966 to date.
Standard Calibers **$230**
Magnum Calibers **245**

Savage Model 110CL
Same as Model 110C, except has left-hand action. (Available only in 243 Win., 30-06, 270 and 7mm mag.)
Standard Calibers **$230**
Magnum Calibers **245**

Savage Model 110D
Similar to Model 110C, except has internal magazine with hinged floorplate. Calibers: 243 Win., 270 Win., 30-06, 7mm Rem. Mag., 300 Win. Mag. Made 1972 to date.
Standard Calibers **$220**
Magnum Calibers **245**

Savage Model 110DL
Same as Model 110D, except has left-hand action.
Standard Calibers **$235**
Magnum Calibers **245**

Savage Model 110E
Calibers: 22-250, 223 Rem., 243, 270 Win., 308, 7mm Rem. Mag., 30-06. 4-shot box magazine (3-shot in Magnum). 20- or 22-inch barrel (24-inch stainless steel in Magnum). Weight: 6 3/4 lbs.; Magnum, 7 3/4 lbs. Open rear sight, ramp front sight. Plain Monte Carlo stock on early production; current models have checkered stocks of walnut-finished hardwood (Magnum has recoil pad). Made from 1963 to date.
7mm Rem. Mag. **$250**
Other Calibers **225**

Savage Model 110EL
Same as Model 110E, except has left-hand action, made in calibers 30-06 and 7mm Rem. Mag. only. Made 1969 to 1973.
Caliber 30-06 . . . . **$200**
Caliber 7mm Rem. Mag. **215**

Savage Model 110F/110K Bolt Action Rifle
Same as Model 110E, except Model 110F with synthetic stock; made 1988 to date. Model 110K with laminated camouflage stock; made 1986 to date.
Model 110F **$370**
Model 110K Standard Calibers **340**
Model 110K Magnum Calibers **400**

Savage Model 110M Magnum $210
Same as Model 110MC, except calibers: 7mm Rem. Mag., 264, 300 and 338 Win. 24-inch barrel. Stock with recoil pad. Weight: 7 3/4 to 8 pounds. Made 1963-69.

Savage Model 110BL

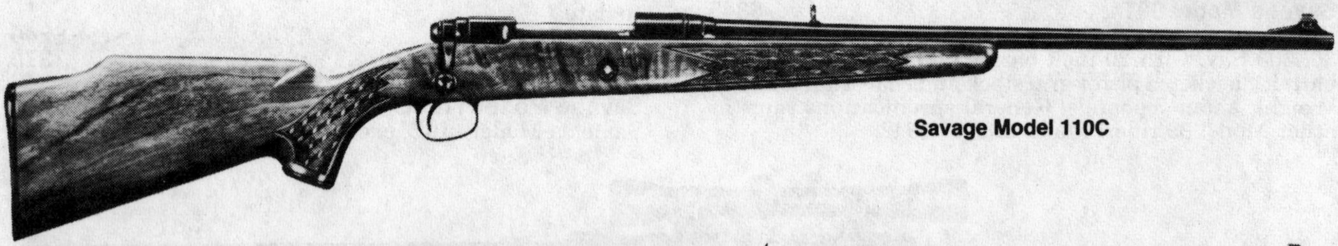
Savage Model 110C

Savage Model 110DL

Savage Model 110E

Savage Model 110MC
Same as Model 110, except has Monte Carlo-style stock. Calibers: 22-250, 243, 270, 308, 30-06. 24-inch barrel in 22-250. Made 1959 to 1969.
Model 110MC **$175**
Model 100MCL w/Left-hand Action **200**

Savage Model 110ML Magnum **$215**
Same as Model 110M Magnum, except has left-hand action.

Savage Model 110P Premier Grade
Calibers: 243 Win., 7mm Rem. Mag., 30-06. 4-shot magazine (3-shot in Magnum). 22-inch barrel (24-inch stainless steel in Magnum). Weight: 7 lbs.; Magnum, $7\frac{3}{4}$ lbs. Open rear folding leaf sight, ramp front sight. French walnut stock with Monte Carlo comb and cheekpiece, rosewood forend tip and pistol-grip cap, skip checkering, sling swivels (Magnum has recoil pad). Made 1964 to 1970.
Calibers 243 Win. and 30-06 .... **$400**
Caliber 7mm Rem. Mag. **420**

Savage Model 110PE Presentation Grade
Same as Model 110P, except has engraved receiver, floorplate and trigger guard, stock of choice grade French walnut. Made 1968 to 1970.
Calibers 243 and 30-06 .... **$655**
Caliber 7mm Rem. Mag. **700**

Savage Model 110PEL Presentation Grade
Same as Model 110PE, except has left-hand action.
Calibers 243 and 30-06 .... **$670**
Caliber 7mm Rem. Mag. **695**

Savage Model 110PL Premier Grade
Same as Model 110P, except has left-hand action.
Calibers 243 Win. and 30-06 .... **$400**
Caliber 7mm Rem. Mag. **425**

Savage Model 111 Chieftain Bolt Action Rifle
Calibers: 243 Win., 270 Win., 7×57mm, 7mm Rem. Mag., 30-06. 4-shot clip magazine (3-shot in Magnum). 22-inch barrel (24-inch in Magnum). Weight: $7\frac{1}{2}$ lbs.; $8\frac{1}{4}$ lbs., Magnum. Leaf rear sight, hooded ramp front sight. Select walnut stock with Monte Carlo comb and cheekpiece, checkered, pistol-grip cap, QD swivels and sling. Made 1974-79.
Standard calibers **$265**
Caliber 7mm Rem. Mag. **275**

Savage Model 112V Varmint Rifle **$250**
Bolt action, single shot. Caliber: 220 Swift, 222 Rem., 223 Rem., 22-250, 243 Win., 25-06. 26-inch heavy barrel with scope bases. Supplied without sights. Weight: $9\frac{1}{4}$ pounds. Select walnut stock in varmint style with checkered pistol grip, high comb, QD sling swivels. Made 1975-79.

Savage Model 110MCL

Savage Model 110P

Savage Model 110PE

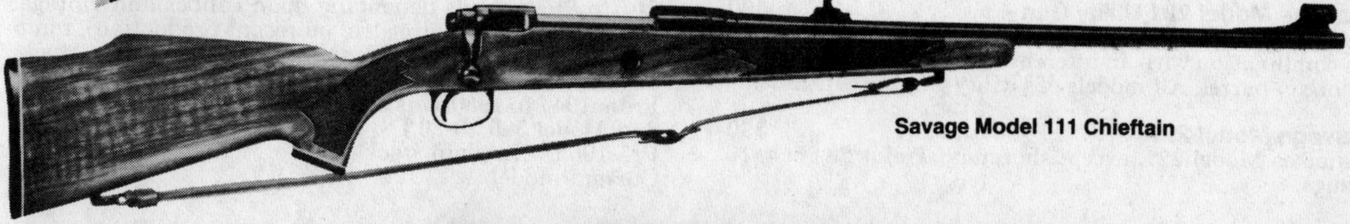
Savage Model 111 Chieftain

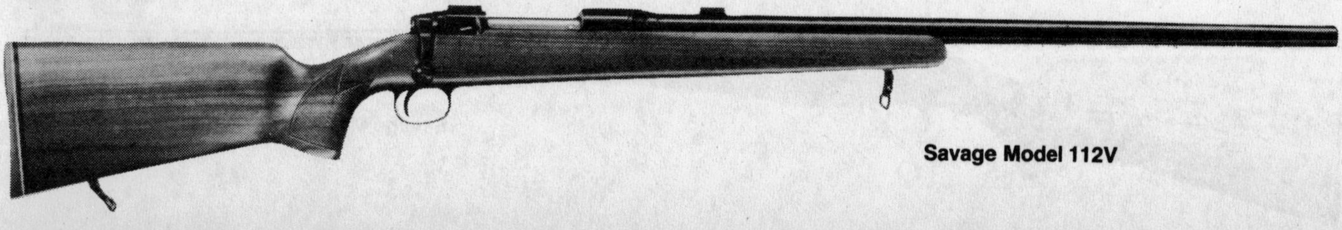
Savage Model 112V

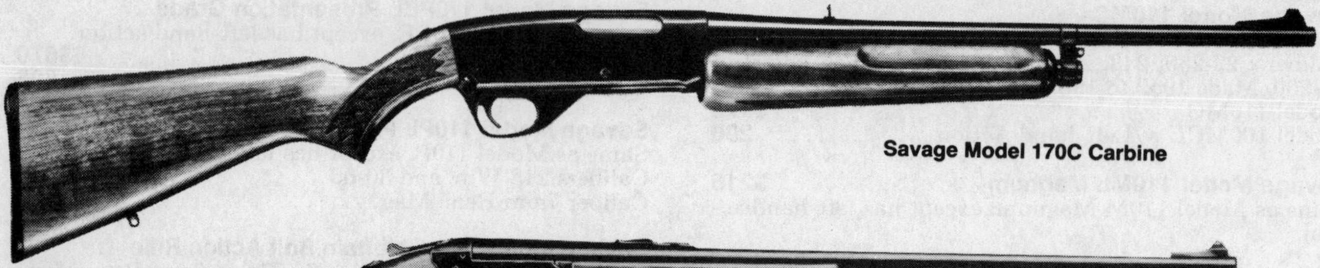

Savage Model 170C Carbine

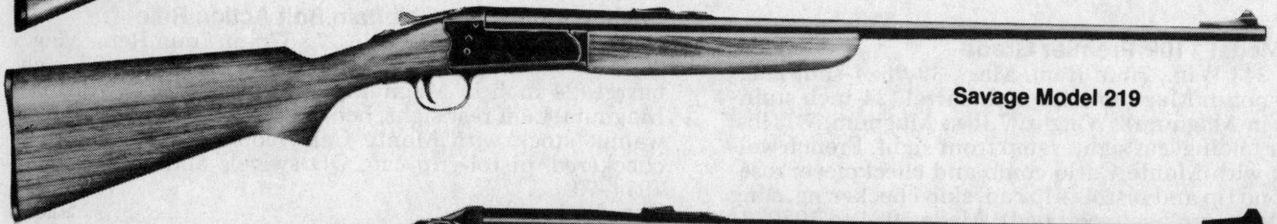

Savage Model 219

Savage Model 219L

Savage Model 170 Pump Action Centerfire Rifle . . $150
Calibers: 30-30, 35 Rem. 3-shot tubular magazine. 22-inch barrel. Weight: 6¾ pounds. Folding leaf rear sight, ramp front sight. Select walnut stock with checkered pistol grip, Monte Carlo comb, grooved slide handle. Made 1970 to 1981.

Savage Model 170C Carbine $150
Same as Model 170 Rifle, except has 18½-inch barrel, straight comb stock, weighs 6 pounds; caliber 30-30 only. Made 1974 to 1981.

Savage Model 219 Single Shot Rifle $85
Hammerless. Takedown. Shotgun-type action with top lever. Calibers: 22 Hornet, 25/20, 32/20, 30/30. 26-inch barrel. Weight: about 6 pounds. Open rear sight, bead front sight. Plain pistol-grip stock and forearm. Made 1938 to 1965.

Savage Model 219L $80
Same as Model 219, except has side lever. Made 1965-67.

Savage Model 221 Utility Gun $90
Same as Model 219, except caliber 30/30 only, supplied in combination with an interchangeable 30-inch 12 gauge shotgun barrel. All models of Utility Gun discontinued.

Savage Model 222 . . . . $90
Same as Model 221, except shotgun barrel is 28-inch, 16 gauge.

Savage Model 223 . . . . $90
Same as Model 221, except shotgun barrel is 28-inch, 20 gauge.

Savage Model 227 . . . . $90
Same as Model 221, except caliber 22 Hornet and 30-inch, 12 gauge barrel.

Savage Model 228 . . . . $90
Same as Model 227, except shotgun barrel is 28-inch, 16 gauge.

Savage Model 229 . . . . $90
Same as Model 227, except shotgun barrel is 28-inch, 20 gauge.

Savage Model 340 Bolt Action Repeater
Calibers: 22 Hornet, 222 Rem., 223 Rem., 225 Win., 30-30. Clip magazine; 4-shot capacity (3-shot in 30-30). Barrel lengths: originally 20-inch in 30-30, 22-inch in 22 Hornet; later 22-inch in 30-30, 24-inch in other calibers. Weight: 6½ to 7½ pounds depending upon caliber and vintage. Open rear sight (folding leaf on recent production), ramp front sight. Early models had plain pistol-grip stock; checkered since 1965. Made from 1950 to 1985. (*Note:* From 1947 to 1950, this was Stevens Model 322 22 Hornet and Model 325 30-30.)
Pre-1965 with plain stock **$155**
Current model **185**

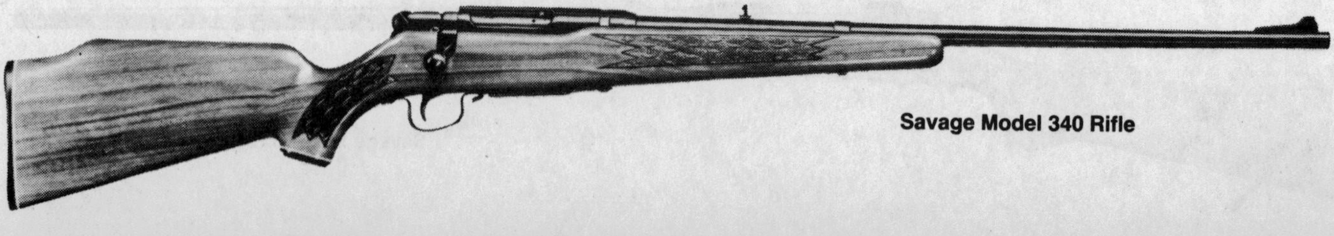

Savage Model 340 Rifle

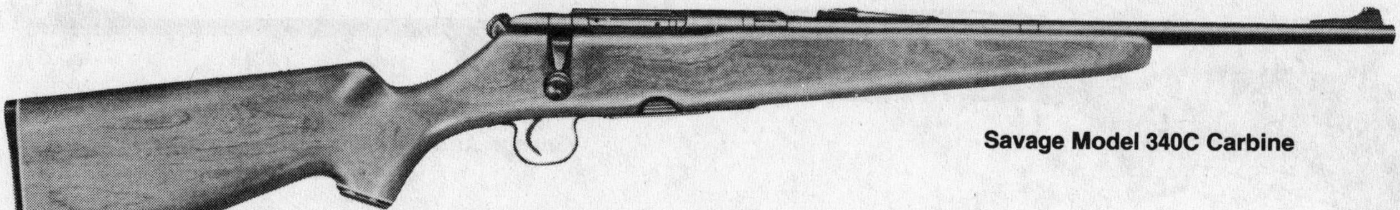

Savage Model 340C Carbine

Savage Anniversary Model 1895

Savage Model 340C Carbine $155
Same as Model 340, except caliber 30-30, 18½-inch barrel. Weight: about 6 pounds. Made 1962-64.

Savage Model 340S Deluxe $180
Same as Model 340, except has checkered stock, screw eyes for sling, peep rear sight and hooded front sight. Made 1955 to 1960.

Savage Model 342 .... $150
Designation, 1950 to 1955, of Model 340 22 Hornet.

Savage Model 342S Deluxe $170
Designation, 1950 to 1955, of Model 340S 22 Hornet.

Savage Anniversary Model 1895 Lever Action Rifle $290
Replica of Savage Model 1895 Hammerless Lever Action Rifle issued to commemorate the 75th anniversary (1895-1970) of Savage Arms. Caliber: 308 Win. 5-shot rotary magazine. 24-inch full-octagon barrel. Engraved receiver. Brass-plated lever. Open rear sight, brass blade front sight. Plain straight-grip buttstock, schnabel-type forend; brass medallion inlaid in buttstock, brass crescent-shaped butt plate. 9,999 produced. Made in 1970 only. Value is for new, unfired specimen.

Savage Model 1903 Slide Action Repeater $195
Hammerless. Takedown. Caliber: 22 Short, Long, Long Rifle. Detachable box magazine. 24-inch octagon barrel. Weight: about 5 pounds. Open rear sight, bead front sight. Pistol-grip stock, grooved slide handle. Made 1903 to 1921.

Savage Model 1904 Bolt Action Single Shot Rifle .. $110
Takedown. Caliber: 22 Short, Long, Long Rifle. 18-inch barrel. Weight: about 3 pounds. Open rear sight, bead front sight. Plain, straight-grip, one-piece stock. Made 1904 to 1917.

Savage Model 1905 Bolt Action Single Shot Rifle .. $110
Takedown. Caliber: 22 Short, Long, Long Rifle. 22-inch barrel. Weight: about 5 pounds. Open rear sight, bead front sight. Plain, straight-grip one-piece stock. Made 1905 to 1919.

Savage Model 1909 Slide Action Repeater $185
Hammerless. Takedown. Similar to Model 1903, except has 20-inch round barrel, plain stock and forearm, weighs about 4¾ pounds. Made 1909 to 1915.

Savage Model 1912 Autoloading Rifle $325
Takedown. Caliber: 22 Long Rifle only. 7-shot detachable box magazine. 20-inch barrel. Weight: about 4½ pounds. Open rear sight, bead front sight. Plain straight-grip stock and forearm. Made 1912-16.

Savage Model 1914 Slide Action Repeater $225
Hammerless. Takedown. Caliber: 22 Short, Long, Long Rifle. Tubular magazine holds 20 Short, 17 Long, 15 Long Rifle. 24-inch octagon barrel. Weight: about 5¾ pounds. Open rear sight, bead front sight. Plain pistol-grip stock, grooved slide handle. Made 1914 to 1924.

Savage Model 1920 Hi-Power Bolt Action Rifle . $400
Short Mauser-type action. Calibers: 250/3000, 300 Sav. 5-shot box magazine. 22-inch barrel in 250 cal.; 24-inch in 300 cal. Weight: about 6 pounds. Open rear sight, bead front sight. Checkered pistol-grip stock with slender forearm and schnabel tip. Made 1920-26.

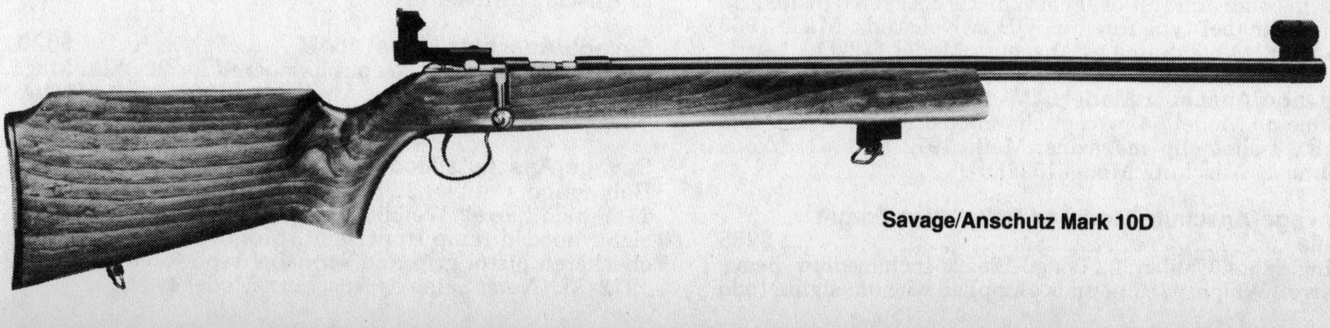

Savage/Anschutz Mark 10D

Savage/Anschutz Model 54 Sporter

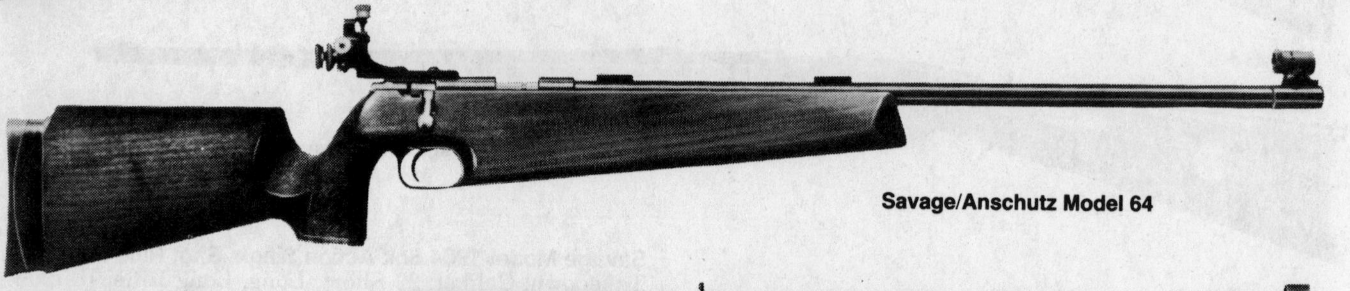

Savage/Anschutz Model 64

Savage/Anschutz Model 164

Note: In 1965, Savage began the importation of rifles manufactured by J. G. Anschutz GmbH, Ulm, West Germany. Models designated "Savage/Anschutz" are listed in this section; those marketed in the U.S. under the "Anschutz" name are included in that firm's listings. Anschutz rifles are now distributed in the U.S. by Precision Sales Int'l., Westfield, Mass.

Savage/Anschutz Mark 10 Bolt Action Target Rifle $255
Single shot. Caliber: 22 Long Rifle. 26-inch barrel. Weight: 8½ pounds. Anschutz micrometer rear sight, globe front sight. Target stock with full pistol grip and cheekpiece, adjustable hand stop and swivel. Made 1967 to 1972.

Savage/Anschutz Mark 10D $255
Same as Mark 10, except has redesigned stock with Monte Carlo comb, different rear sight. Weight: 7¾ pounds. Made 1972.

Savage/Anschutz Model 54 Custom Sporter . . . $320
Bolt action. Caliber: 22 Long Rifle. 5-shot clip magazine. 24-inch barrel. Weight: 6¾ pounds. Folding leaf rear sight, hooded ramp front sight. Select walnut stock with Monte Carlo comb and roll-over cheekpiece, checkered pistol grip and schnabel-type forearm, QD swivel studs. Made 1969 to 1981. (*Note:* Same as Anschutz Model 1422D.)

Savage/Anschutz Model 54M $495
Same as Model 54, except chambered for 22 Win. Mag. R.F., 4-shot clip magazine. Made 1972 to 1981. (*Note:* Same as Anschutz Model 1522D.)

Savage/Anschutz Model 64 Bolt Action Target Rifle $285
Single shot. Caliber: 22 Long Rifle. 26-inch medium-heavy barrel. Weight: 7¾ pounds. Supplied without sights (add

Savage/Anschutz Model 64 (cont.)
$40 for Anschutz match sight set). Target stock with thumb groove, checkered pistol grip, high comb and cheekpiece, adjustable butt plate, swivel rail. Model 64L has left-hand stock. Made 1965 to 1981. (*Note:* Same as Anschutz Model 1403.)

Savage/Anschutz Model 153 Bolt Action Sporter $495
Caliber: 222 Rem. 3-shot clip magazine. 24-inch barrel. Folding leaf open rear sight, hooded ramp front sight. Weight: 6¾ pounds. French walnut stock with cheekpiece, skip checkering, rosewood forend tip and grip cap, swivels. Made 1964-67.

Savage/Anschutz Model 153S $425
Same as Model 153, except has double-set trigger. Made 1965-67.

Savage/Anschutz Model 164 Custom Sporter . . $325
Bolt action. Caliber: 22 Long Rifle. 5-shot clip magazine. 23-inch barrel. Weight: 6 pounds. Folding leaf rear sight, hooded ramp front sight. Select walnut stock with Monte Carlo comb and cheekpiece, checkered pistol grip and schnabel-type forearm. Made 1969 to 1981 (*Note:* Same as Anschutz Model 1416.)

Savage/Anschutz Model 164M $320
Same as Model 164, except chambered for 22 Win. Mag. R.F., 4-shot clip magazine. Made from 1969 to date. (*Note:* Same as Anschutz Model 1516.)

Savage/Anschutz Model 184 Sporter $240
Bolt action. Caliber: 22 Long Rifle. 5-shot clip magazine. 21½-inch barrel. Weight: 4½ pounds. Folding leaf rear sight, hooded ramp front sight. Monte Carlo stock with checkered pistol grip and schnabel-type forearm. Made 1972-75. (*Note:* Same as Anschutz Model 1441.)

> *Note:* Since J. Stevens Arms (see also separate listing) is a division of Savage Industries, certain Savage models carry the "Stevens" name.

Savage-Stevens Model 34 Bolt Action Repeater . $65
Caliber: 22 Short, Long, Long Rifle. 5-shot clip magazine. 20-inch barrel. Weight: $5\frac{1}{2}$ pounds. Open rear sight, bead front sight. Checkered stock with Monte Carlo comb. Made 1969 to 1981.

Savage-Stevens Model 34M $70
Same as Model 34, except chambered for 22 Win. Mag. R.F. Made 1969 to 1973.

Savage-Stevens Model 35 . . . . $65
Bolt-action repeater. Caliber: 22 Long Rifle. 6-shot clip magazine. 22-inch barrel. Weight: about 5 pounds. Open rear sight, ramp front sight. Monte Carlo stock with checkered pistol grip and forearm. Made 1982 to date.

Savage-Stevens Model 35M $75
Same as Model 35, except chambered for 22 Win. Mag. R.F. Made from 1982 to date.

Savage-Stevens Model 46 Bolt Action Tubular Repeater $65
Caliber: 22 Short, Long, Long Rifle. Tubular magazine holds 22 Short, 17 Long, 15 Long Rifle. 20-inch barrel. Weight: 5 pounds. Plain pistol-grip stock on early production; later models have Monte Carlo stock with checkering. Made 1969 to 1973.

Savage-Stevens Model 65 Bolt Action Repeater . $70
Caliber: 22 Short, Long, Long Rifle. 5-shot clip magazine. 20-inch barrel. Weight: 5 pounds. Open rear sight, ramp front sight. Monte Carlo stock with checkered pistol grip and forearm. Made 1969 to 1973.

Savage-Stevens Model 65M $75
Same as Model 65, except chambered for 22 Win. Mag. R.F., has 22-inch barrel, weighs $5\frac{3}{4}$ pounds. Made 1969 to 1981.

Savage-Stevens Model 72 Crackshot Single Shot Lever Action Rifle $85
Falling-block action. Casehardened frame. Caliber: 22 Short, Long, Long Rifle. 22-inch octagon barrel. Weight: $4\frac{1}{2}$ pounds. Open rear sight, bead front sight. Plain

RIFLES

Savage-Stevens Model 34

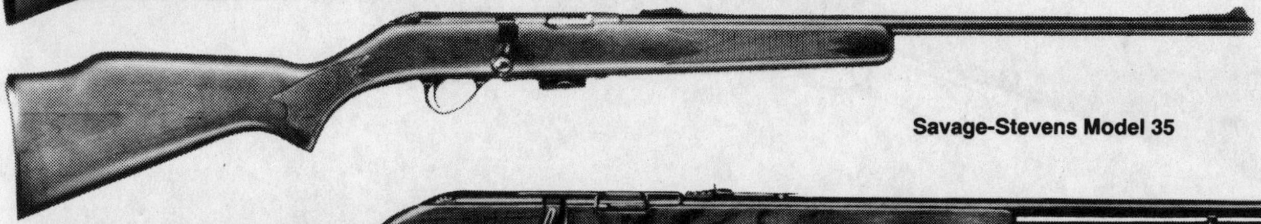

Savage-Stevens Model 35

Savage-Stevens Model 46

Savage-Stevens Model 65

Savage-Stevens Model 72 Crackshot

Savage-Stevens Model 72 Crackshot (cont.)
straight-grip stock and forearm of walnut. Made from 1972 to date. (*Note:* Model 72 is a "Favorite" type single shot, unlike the smaller original "Crackshot" made by Stevens 1913-39.)

Savage-Stevens Model 73 Bolt Action Single Shot **$60**
Caliber: 22 Short, Long, Long Rifle. 20-inch barrel. Weight: $4^{3}/_{4}$ pounds. Open rear sight, bead front sight. Plain pistol-grip stock. Made 1965 to 1980.

Savage-Stevens 73Y Youth Model **$60**
Same as Model 73, except has 18-inch barrel, $1^{1}/_{2}$-inch shorter buttstock, weighs $4^{1}/_{2}$ pounds. Made 1965 to 1980.

Savage-Stevens Model 74 Little Favorite **$85**
Same as Model 72 Crackshot, except has black-finished frame, 22-inch round barrel, walnut-finished hardwood stock. Weight: $4^{3}/_{4}$ pounds. Made 1972-74.

Savage-Stevens Model 73

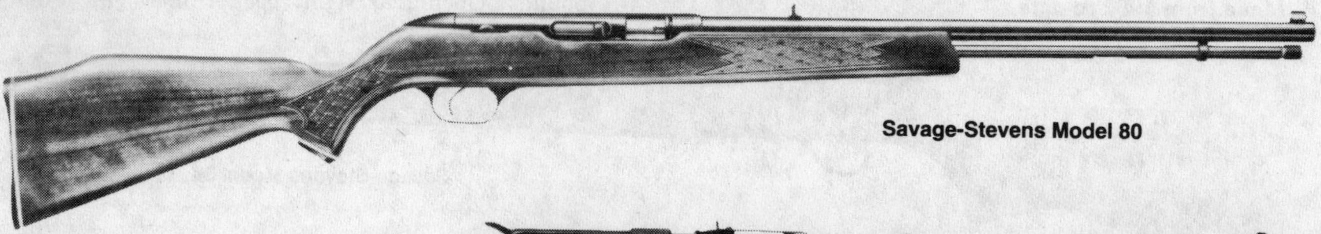

Savage-Stevens Model 80

Savage-Stevens Model 89

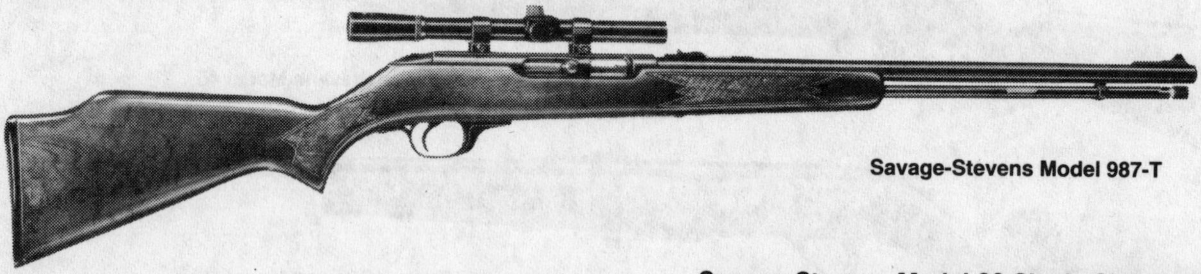

Savage-Stevens Model 987-T

Savage-Stevens Model 80 Autoloading Rifle **$65**
Caliber: 22 Long Rifle. 15-shot tubular magazine. 20-inch barrel. Weight: 6 pounds. Open rear sight, bead front sight. Monte Carlo stock of walnut with checkered pistol grip and forearm. Made from 1976 to date. (*Note:* This rifle is essentially the same as Model 60 of 1969-72, except that it has a different style of checkering, side instead of top safety, and plain bead instead of ramp front sight.)

Savage-Stevens Model 88 Autoloading Rifle **$60**
Similar to Model 60, except has walnut-finished hardwood stock, plain bead front sight; weight, $5^{3}/_{4}$ pounds. Made 1969 to 1972.

Savage-Stevens Model 89 Single Shot Lever Action Carbine **$55**
Martini-type action. Caliber: 22 Short, Long, Long Rifle. $18^{1}/_{2}$-inch barrel. Weight: 5 pounds. Open rear sight, bead front sight. Western-style carbine stock with straight grip, forearm with barrel band. Made from 1976 to date.

Savage-Stevens Model 987-T Autoloading Rifle. . . . **$70**
Caliber: 22 Long Rifle. 15-shot tubular magazine. 20-inch barrel. Weight: 6 pounds. Open rear sight, ramp front sight. Monte Carlo stock with checkered pistol grip and forearm. Made from 1981 to date.

Savage "Stevens Favorite"
See Savage Model 71.

V. C. SCHILLING
Suhl, Germany

Schilling Mauser-Mannlicher Bolt Action Sporting Rifle $525
Same general specifications as given for the Haenel Mauser-Mannlicher Sporter. See separate listing.

Schilling '88 Mauser Sporter $525
Same general specifications as Haenel '88 Mauser Sporter. See separate listing.

SCHULTZ & LARSEN GEVAERFABRIK
Otterup, Denmark

Schultz & Larsen Match Rifle No. 47 . . . . $575
Caliber: 22 Long Rifle. Bolt action, single shot, set trigger. 28½-inch heavy barrel. Weight: about 14 pounds. Micrometer receiver sight, globe front sight. Free-rifle stock with cheekpiece, thumb hole, adjustable Schuetzen-type butt plate, swivels, palm rest.

Schultz & Larsen Free Rifle Model 54 . . . . $750
Calibers: 6.5×55mm or any standard American centerfire caliber. Schultz & Larsen M54 bolt action, single shot, set trigger. 27½-inch heavy barrel. Weight: about 15½ pounds. Micrometer receiver sight, globe front sight. Free-rifle stock with cheekpiece, thumb hole, adjustable Schuetzen-type butt plate, swivels, palm rest.

Schultz & Larsen Model 54J Sporting Rifle $500
Calibers: 270 Win., 30-06, 7×61 Sharpe & Hart. Schultz & Larsen bolt action. 3-shot magazine. 24-inch barrel in 270 and 30-06, 26-inch in 7×61 S&H. Checkered stock with Monte Carlo comb and cheekpiece. Value shown is for rifle less sights.

SEARS, ROEBUCK & COMPANY
Chicago, Illinois

The most encountered brands or model designations used by Sears are J. C. Higgins and Ted Williams. Firearms sold under these designations have been manufactured by various firms including Winchester, Marlin, Savage, Mossberg, etc.

Sears Model 2C Bolt Action Rifle $80
Caliber: 22RF. 7-shot clip magazine. 21-inch barrel. Weight: 5 pounds. Open rear sight, ramp front sight. Plain Monte Carlo stock. Mfd. by Winchester.

Sears Model 42 Bolt Action Repeating Rifle $75
Takedown. Caliber: 22RF. 8-shot detachable box magazine. 24-inch barrel. Weight: 6 pounds. Open rear sight, bead front sight. Plain pistol-grip stock. Mfd. by Marlin.

Sears Model 42DL Bolt Action Repeating Rifle . . . $80
Same general specifications as Model 42 except fancier grade with peep sight, hooded front sight and swivels.

Sears Model 44DL Lever Action Rifle $125
Caliber: 22RF. Tubular magazine holds 19 Long Rifle cartridges. 22-inch barrel. Weight: 6¼ pounds. Open rear sight, hooded ramp front sight. Monte Carlo-style stock with pistol grip. Mfd. by Marlin.

Sears Model 53 Bolt Action Rifle $175
Calibers: 243, 270, 308, 30-06. 4-shot magazine. 22-inch barrel. Weight: 6¾ pounds. Open rear sight, ramp front sight. Standard sporter stock with pistol grip, checkered. Mfd. by Savage.

Sears Model 54 Lever Action Rifle $125
Similar general specifications as Winchester Model 94 carbine. Made in 30-30 caliber only. Mfd. by Winchester.

Sears Model 103 Series Bolt Action Repeating Rifle $80
Same general specifications as Model 103.2 with minor changes. Mfd. by Marlin.

Sears Model 103.2 Bolt Action Repeating Rifle . . $80
Takedown. Caliber: 22RF. 8-shot detachable box magazine. 24-inch barrel. Weight: 6 pounds. Open rear sight, bead front sight. Plain pistol-grip stock. Mfd. by Marlin.

R. F. SEDGLEY, INC.
Philadelphia, Pennsylvania

Sedgley Springfield Sporter $495
Springfield '03 bolt action. Calibers: 220 Swift, 218 Bee, 22-3000, R2, 22-4000, 22 Hornet, 25-35, 250-3000, 257 Roberts, 270 Win., 7mm, 30-06. 24-inch barrel. Weight: 7½ pounds. Lyman No. 48 receiver sight, bead front sight on matted ramp. Checkered walnut stock, grip cap, sling swivels. Discontinued 1941.

Sedgley Springfield Left-Hand Sporter $610
Bolt action reversed for left-handed shooter; otherwise the same as standard Sedgley Springfield Sporter.

RIFLES

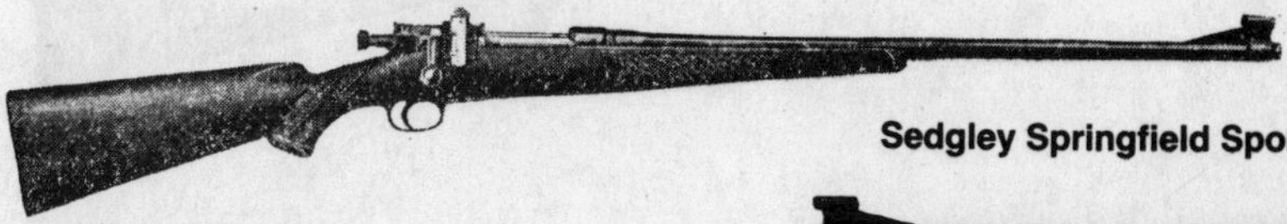

Sedgley Springfield Sporter

Sedgley Springfield Left Hand

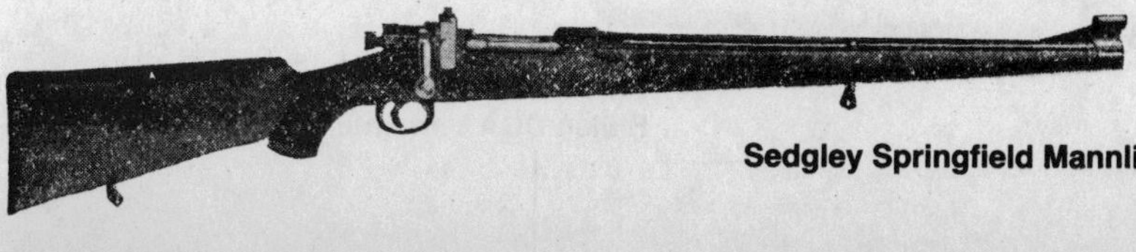

Sedgley Springfield Mannlicher

Sedgley Springfield Mannlicher-Type Sporter . . $625
Same as the standard Sedgley Springfield Sporter, except has 20-inch barrel, Mannlicher-type full stock with cheekpiece, weighs 7¾ pounds.

SHILEN RIFLES, INC.
Ennis, Texas

Shilen DGA Benchrest Rifle $575
DGA single-shot bolt action. Calibers as listed for Sporter. 26-inch medium-heavy or heavy barrel. Weight: from 10½ pounds. No sights. Fiberglass or walnut stock, classic or thumb-hole pattern. Currently manufactured.

Shilen DGA Sporter $525
DGA bolt action. Calibers: 17 Rem., 222 Rem., 223 Rem., 22-250, 220 Swift, 6mm Rem., 243 Win., 250 Sav., 257 Roberts, 284 Win., 308 Win., 358 Win. 3-shot blind magazine. 24-inch barrel. Average weight: 7½ pounds. No sights. Selected Claro walnut stock with cheekpiece, pistol grip, sling swivel studs. Currently manufactured.

Shilen DGA Varminter $510
Same as Sporter, except has 25-inch medium-heavy barrel. Weight: about 9 pounds.

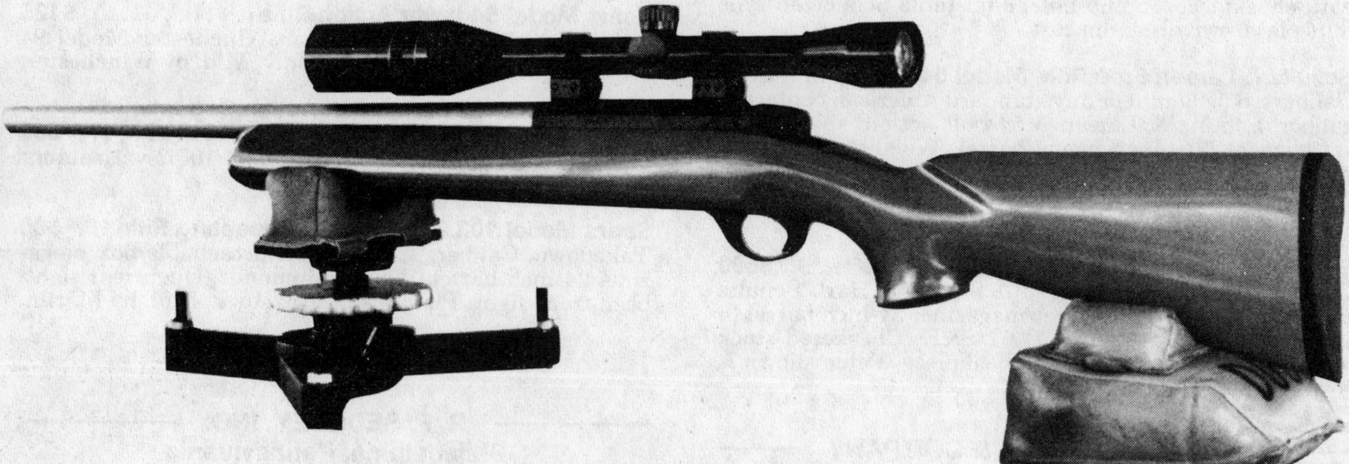

Shilen DGA Benchrest Rifle

Shilen DGA Sporter

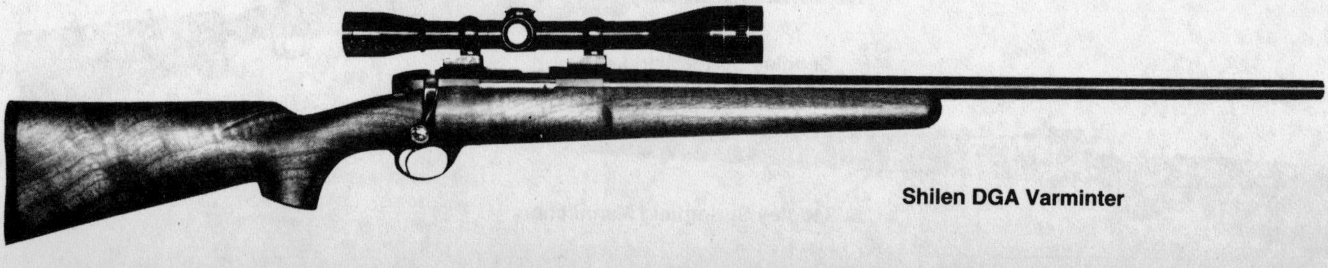

Shilen DGA Varminter

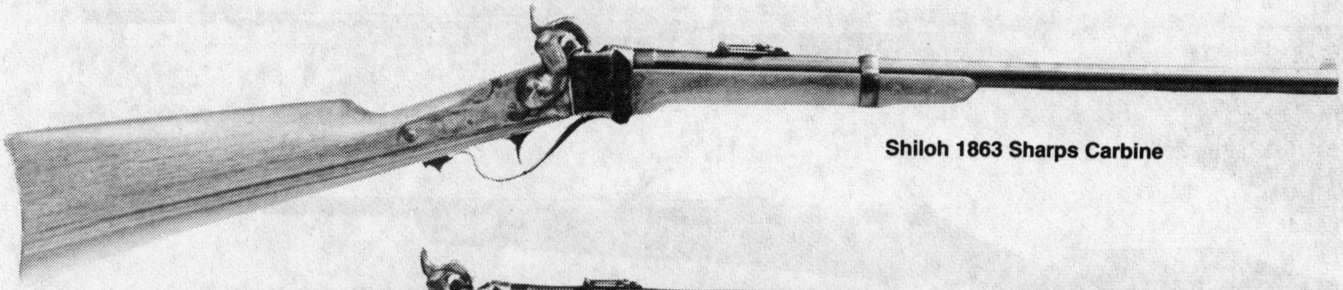

Shiloh 1863 Sharps Carbine

Shiloh 1863 Sharps Rifle

SHILOH ARMS COMPANY
Farmingdale, New York

Shiloh New Model 1863 Sharps Carbine $395
Same as 1863 Sharps Rifle, except has 22-inch barrel and available in 50 caliber only.

Shiloh New Model 1863 Sharps Rifle $475
Replica of 1863 Sharps rifle. Breechloading single shot rifle. Calibers: 50 and 54. 30-inch barrel. Walnut buttstock and forearm. Color casehardened patchbox, receiver, lockplate, hammer and butt plate. Barrel finish is blue-black. Weight: 8¾ pounds.

SIG AMT Sporting Rifle

SIG SWISS INDUSTRIAL COMPANY
Neuhausen-Rhine Falls, Switzerland

SIG-AMT Semiautomatic Rifle $1995
Caliber: 308 Win.(7.62 NATO). 5, 10, or 20-shot magazine. 18½-inch barrel with flash suppressor. Weight: 9½ pounds. Adjustable aperture rear sight, post front. Walnut buttstock and forend with synthetic pistol grip. Imported during the 1980's.

SIG-AMT Sporting Rifle $995
Semiautomatic version of SG510-4 automatic assault rifle based on Swiss Army StGW57. Roller-delayed blowback action. Caliber: 7.62×51mm NATO (308 Win.). 5-, 10- and 20-round magazines. 19-inch barrel. Weight: about 10 pounds. Aperture rear sight, post front sight. Wood buttstock and forearm, folding bipod. Made 1960 to 1974.

SIG-PE57 Semiautomatic Rifle $1995
Caliber: 7.65 Swiss. 24-shot magazine. 23¾-inch barrel. Weight: 12½ pounds. Adjustable aperture rear sight, post front. High-impact synthetic stock. Imported from Switzerland during the 1980's.

SMITH & WESSON
Springfield, Massachusetts
Mfd. by Husqvarna Vapenfabrik A.B., Huskvarna, Sweden

Smith & Wesson Model 1500 . . . . $235
Bolt action. Calibers: 243 Win., 270 Win., 30-06, 7mm Rem. Mag. 22-inch barrel (24-inch in 7mm Rem. Mag.). Weight: about 7½ pounds. American walnut stock with Monte Carlo comb and cheekpiece, cut checkering. Open rear sight, hooded ramp gold bead front. Introduced in 1979, this model is now produced by Mossberg (see separate listings).

Smith and Wesson Model 1500 DL

Smith & Wesson Model A

Smith & Wesson Model B

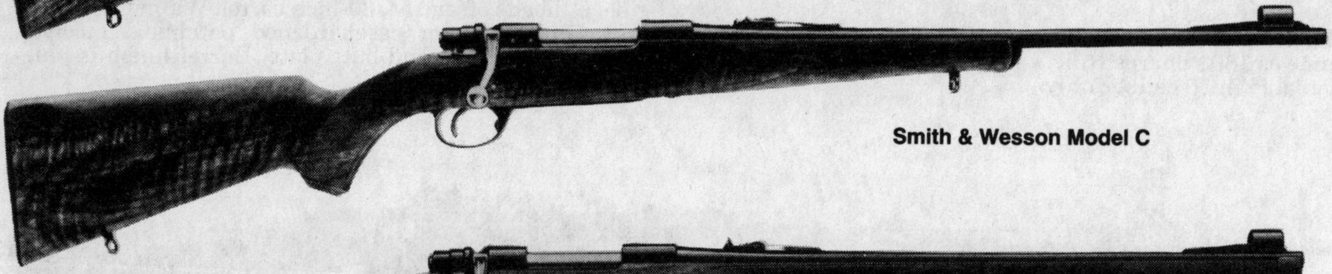

Smith & Wesson Model C

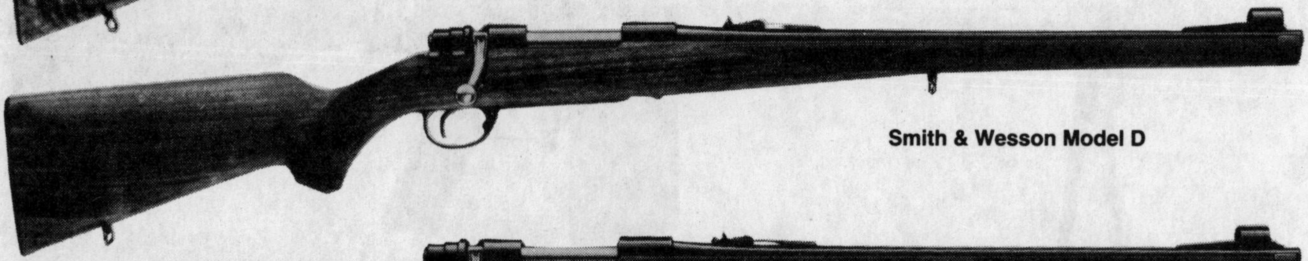

Smith & Wesson Model D

Smith & Wesson Model E

Smith & Wesson Model 1500 Deluxe **$240**
Same as standard model, except without sights; has engine-turned bolt, decorative scroll on floorplate, French checkering.

Smith & Wesson Model A Bolt-Action Sporting Rifle **$350**
Similar to Husqvarna Model 9000 Crown Grade. Mauser-type bolt action. Calibers: 22-250, 243 Win., 270 Win., 308 Win., 30-06, 7mm Rem. Mag., 300 Win. Mag. 5-shot magazine, except 3-round capacity in latter two calibers. 23¾-inch barrel. Weight: about 7 pounds. Folding leaf rear sight, hooded ramp front sight. Checkered walnut stock with Monte Carlo cheekpiece, rosewood forend tip and pistol-grip cap, swivels. Made 1969 to 1972.

Smith & Wesson Model B **$315**
Same as Model A, except has 20¾-inch extra-light barrel, Monte Carlo cheekpiece with schnabel-style forearm, weighs about 6 lbs. 10 oz. Calibers: 243 Win., 30-06.

Smith & Wesson Model C **$315**
Same as Model B, except has cheekpiece stock with straight comb.

Smith & Wesson Model D **$360**
Same as Model C, except has full-length Mannlicher-style forearm.

Smith & Wesson Model E **$360**
Same as Model B, except has full-length Mannlicher-style forearm.

Springfield Armory M1A

SPRINGFIELD ARMORY
Geneseo, Illinois

This is a private firm, not to be confused with the former U.S. Government facility of the same name in Springfield, Mass.

Springfield Armory BM-59 Semiautomatic Rifle
Gas-operated. Caliber: 308 Win. (7.62mm NATO). 20-shot detachable box magazine. 19.3-inch barrel with flash suppressor. About 43 inches overall. Weight: 9¼ pounds. Adjustable military aperture rear sight, square post front; direct and indirect grenade launcher sights. European walnut stock with handguard or folding buttstock (Alpine Paratrooper). Made from 1981 to date.
Standard Model **$1200**
Paratrooper Model **1595**

Springfield Armory M-1 Garand Semiautomatic Rifle
Gas-operated. Calibers: 308 Win. (7.62 NATO), 30-06. 8-shot stripper clip. 24-inch barrel. 43½ inches overall. Weight: 9½ pounds. Adjustable aperture rear sight, military sqaure blade front. Standard "Issue-grade" walnut stock or folding buttstock. Made from 1979 to date.
Standard Model **$750**
National Match **835**

Springfield Armory M-1 Garand Semiauto (cont.)
Ultra Match **$950**
Sniper Model **975**
Paratrooper with folding stock **775**

Springfield Armory Match M1A
Same as Standard M1A, except has National Match grade barrel with modified flash suppressor, National Match sights, turned trigger pull, gas system assembly in one unit, modified mainspring guide, glass-bedded walnut stock. Super Match M1A has premium-grade heavy barrel (weighs 10 pounds).
Match M1A **$795**
Super Match M1A **895**

Springfield Armory Standard M1A Semiautomatic
Gas-operated. Similar to U.S. M14 service rifle, except has no provision for automatic firing. Caliber: 7.65mm NATO (308 Win.). 5-, 10- or 20-round detachable box magazine. 25 1/16-inch barrel with flash suppressor. Weight: about 9 pounds. Adjustable aperture rear sight, blade front sight. Fiberglass, birch or walnut stock, fiberglass hand guard, sling swivels. Made from 1974 to date.
With fiberglass or birch stock **$550**
With walnut stock **650**

RIFLES

Squires Bingham Model M16

Squires Bingham Model M20D

SQUIRES BINGHAM CO., INC.
Makati, Rizal, Philippines

Squires Bingham Model 14D Deluxe Bolt Action Repeating Rifle **$80**
Caliber: 22 Long Rifle. 5-shot box magazine. 24-inch barrel. V-notch rear sight, hooded ramp front sight. Receiver grooved for scope mounting. Pulong Dalaga stock with contrasting forend tip and grip cap, checkered forearm and pistol grip. Weight: about 6 pounds. Currently mfd.

Squires Bingham Model 15 .... **$85**
Same as Model 14D, except chambered for 22 Magnum R.F. Currently manufactured.

Squires Bingham Model M16 Semiautomatic Rifle $95
Styled after U.S. M16 military rifle. Caliber: 22 Long Rifle. 15-shot box magazine. 19½-inch barrel with muzzle brake/flash hider. Rear sight in carrying handle, post front on high ramp. Black-painted mahogany buttstock and forearm. Weight: about 6½ pounds. Currently manufactured.

Squires Bingham Model M20D Deluxe Semiautomatic Rifle $100
Caliber: 22 Long Rifle. 15-shot box magazine. 19½-inch barrel with muzzle brake/flash hider. V-notch rear sight, blade front sight. Receiver grooved for scope mounting. Pulong Dalaga stock with contrasting forend tip and grip cap, checkered forearm and pistol grip. Weight: about 6 pounds. Currently manufactured.

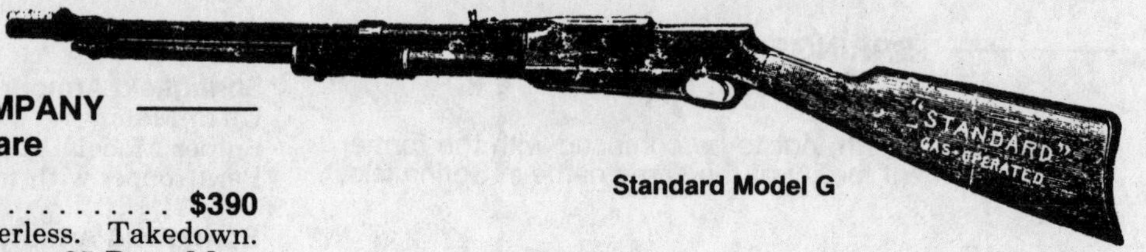

Standard Model G

STANDARD ARMS COMPANY
Wilmington, Delaware

Standard Model G Automatic Rifle $390
Gas-operated. Autoloading. Hammerless. Takedown. Calibers: 25-35, 30-30, 25 Rem., 30 Rem., 35 Rem. Magazine capacity: 4 rounds in 35 Rem., 5 rounds in other calibers. 22⅜-inch barrel. Weight: about 7¾ pounds. Open sporting rear sight, ivory bead front sight. Shotgun-type stock. Made c. 1910. *Note:* This was the first gas-operated rifle manufactured in the U.S. While essentially an autoloader, the gas port can be closed and the rifle operated as a slide-action repeater.

Standard Model M Hand-Operated Rifle $265
Slide-action repeater with same general specifications as Model G, except lacks autoloading feature. Weight: about 7 pounds.

Star Rolling Block

STAR
Eibar, Spain
Mfd. by Bonifacio Echeverria, S.A.

Star Rolling Block Carbine $185
Single-shot action similar to Remington Rolling Block. Calibers: 30-30, 357 Mag., 44 Mag. 20-inch barrel. Weight: about 6 pounds. Folding leaf rear sight, ramp front sight. Walnut straight-grip stock with crescent butt plate, forearm with barrel band. Made 1973-75.

STERLING
Imported by Lanchester U.S.A., Inc., Dallas, Texas

Sterling Mark 6 Semi-Automatic Carbine $495
Caliber: 9mm Parabellum. 34-shot magazine. Barrel: 16.1 inches. Weight: about 7½ pounds. Flip-type rear peep sight, ramp front. Folding metal skeleton stock. Made from 1983 to date.

Stevens Youth's Model 15Y

J. STEVENS ARMS CO.
Chicopee Falls, Massachusetts
Now a Div. of Savage Industries, Westfield, Mass.

Since J. Stevens Arms is a division of Savage Industries, the "Stevens" brand name is used for some rifles by Savage; see separate Savage-Stevens listings under Savage.

Stevens No. 12 Marksman Single Shot Rifle $125
Lever action, tip-up. Takedown. Calibers: 22 Long Rifle, 25 R.F., 32 R.F. 22-inch barrel. Plain straight-grip stock, small tapered forearm.

Stevens No. 14½ Little Scout Single Shot Rifle $125
Rolling block. Takedown. Caliber: 22 Long Rifle. 18- or 20-inch barrel. Weight: about 2¾ pounds. Open rear sight, blade front sight. Plain straight-grip stock, small tapered forearm.

Stevens No. 12 Marksman

Stevens No. 14½ Little Scout

Stevens No. 44 Ideal

Stevens Ideal Schuetzen

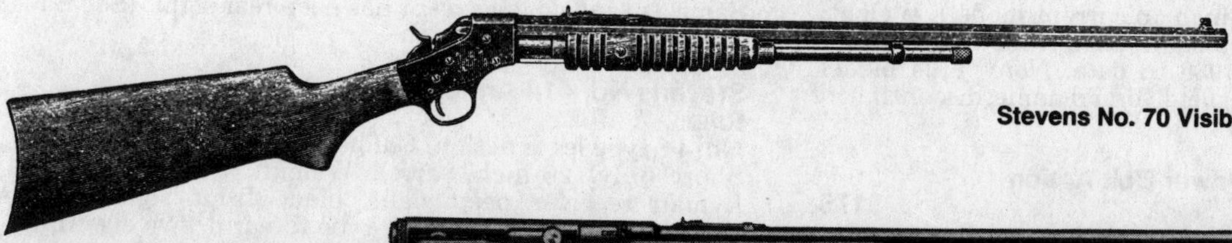

Stevens No. 70 Visible Loading

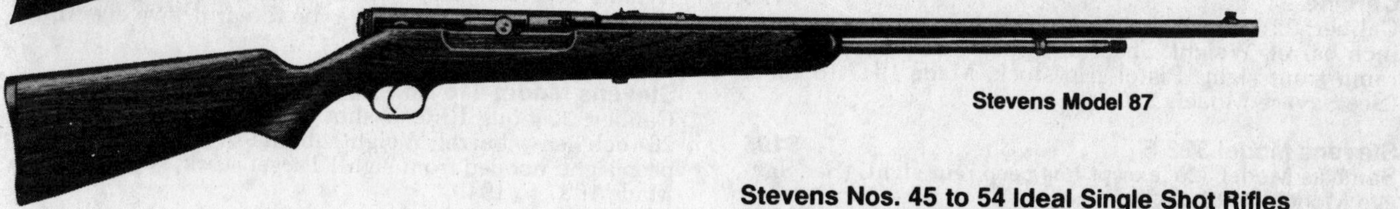

Stevens Model 87

Stevens Model 15 . . . . $110
Same as Stevens-Springfield Model 15, except has 24-inch barrel, weighs about 5 pounds, has redesigned stock. Made 1948 to 1965.

Stevens Model 15Y Youth's Rifle $95
Same as Model 15, except has 21-inch barrel, short butt-stock, weighs about 4¾ pounds. Made 1958 to 1965.

Stevens No. 44 Ideal Single Shot Rifle $395
Rolling block. Lever action. Takedown. Calibers: 22 Long Rifle, 25 R.F., 32 R.F., 25-20 S.S., 32-20, 32-40, 38-40, 38-55, 44-40. Barrel lengths: 24-inch, 26-inch (round, half-octagon, full-octagon). Weight: about 7 pounds with 26-inch round bbl. Open rear sight, Rocky Mountain front sight. Plain straight-grip stock and forearm. Made 1894 to 1932.

Stevens No. 44½ Ideal Single Shot Rifle $465
Falling-block lever action. Aside from the new design action introduced in 1903, the specifications of this model are the same as those of Model 44. Model 44½ discontinued about 1916.

Stevens Nos. 45 to 54 Ideal Single Shot Rifles
These are the higher grade models, differing from the standard No. 44 and No. 44½ chiefly in finish, engraving, set triggers, levers, barrels, stocks, etc. The Schuetzen types (including the "Stevens-Pope" models) are in this series. Model Nos. 45 to 54 were introduced about 1896 and originally had the No. 44-type rolling-block action which was superseded in 1903 by the No. 44½-type falling-block action. These models were all discontinued about 1916. Generally speaking the 45-54 series rifles, particularly the "Stevens-Pope" and higher grade Schuetzen models, are collector's items, bringing much higher prices than the ordinary No. 44 and 44½.

Stevens No. 66 Bolt Action Repeating Rifle $75
Takedown. Caliber: 22 Short, Long, Long Rifle. Tubular magazine holds 13 Long Rifle, 15 Long, 19 Short. 24-inch barrel. Weight: about 5 pounds. Open rear sight, bead front sight. Plain pistol-grip stock with grooved forearm. Made 1931-35.

Stevens No. 70 Visible Loading Slide Action Repeating Rifle $195
Exposed hammer. Caliber: 22 Long Rifle, Long, Short. Tubular magazine holds 11 Long Rifle, 13 Long, 15 Short. 22-inch barrel. Weight: about 4½ pounds. Open rear sight, bead front sight. Plain straight-grip stock, grooved slide handle. Made 1907 to 1934. *Note:* Nos. 70½, 71, 71½, 72, 72½ are essentially the same as No. 70, differing chiefly in barrel length or sight equipment.

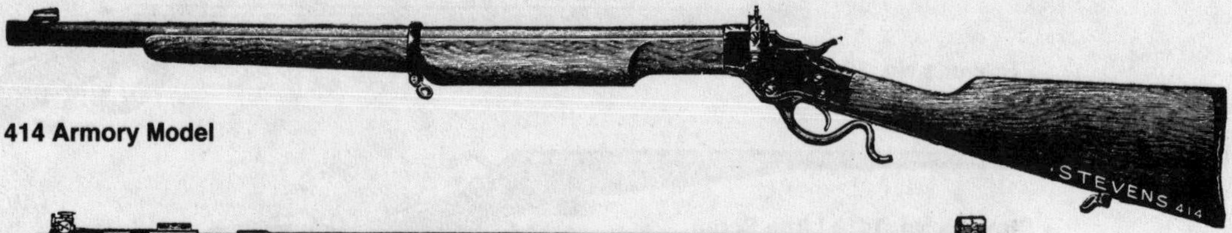

Stevens No. 414 Armory Model

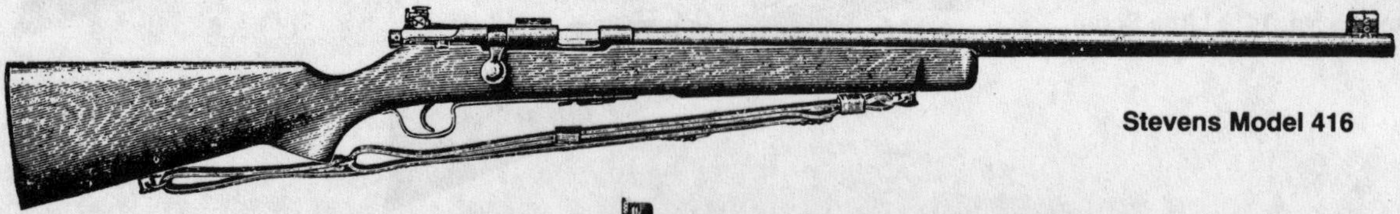

Stevens Model 416

Stevens No. 419

Stevens Model 87 Autoloading Rifle $125
Takedown. Caliber: 22 Long Rifle. 15-shot tubular magazine. 24-inch barrel (20-inch on current model). Weight: about 6 pounds. Open rear sight, bead front sight. Pistol-grip stock. Made from 1938 to date. *Note:* This model originally bore the "Springfield" brand name, discontinued in 1948.

Stevens Model 322 Hi-Power Bolt Action Carbine $175
Caliber: 22 Hornet. 4-shot detachable box magazine. 21-inch barrel. Weight: about 6¾ pounds. Open rear sight, ramp front sight. Pistol-grip stock. Made 1947 to 1950. (See Savage Models 340, 342.)

Stevens Model 322-S $195
Same as Model 325, except has peep rear sight. (See Savage Models 340S, 342S.)

Stevens Model 325 Hi-Power Bolt Action Carbine $125
Caliber: 30-30. 3-shot detachable box magazine. 21-inch barrel. Weight: about 6¾ pounds. Open rear sight, bead front sight. Plain pistol-grip stock. Made 1947 to 1950. (See Savage Model 340.)

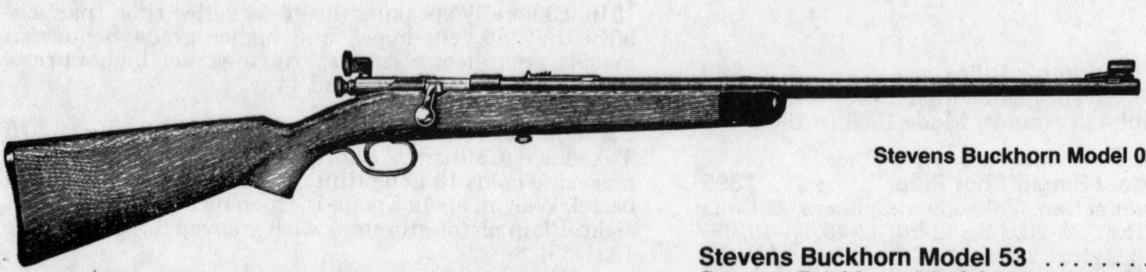

Stevens Buckhorn Model 053

Stevens Buckhorn Model 053 Bolt Action Single Shot Rifle $95
Takedown. Calibers: 22 Short, Long, Long Rifle, 22 W.R.F., 25 Stevens R.F. 24-inch barrel. Weight: about 5½ pounds. Receiver peep sight, open middle sight, hooded front sight. Sporting stock with pistol grip and black forend tip. Made 1935 to 1948.

Stevens Model 325-S $130
Same as Model 325, except has peep rear sight. (See Savage Model 340S.)

Stevens No. 414 Armory Model Single Shot Rifle $360
No. 44-type lever action. Calibers: 22 Long Rifle only, 22 Short only. 26-inch barrel. Weight: about 8 pounds. Lyman receiver peep sight, blade front sight. Plain straight-grip stock, military-type forearm, swivels. Made 1912 to 1932.

Stevens Model 416 Bolt Action Target Rifle $175
Caliber: 22 Long Rifle. 5-shot detachable box magazine. 26-inch heavy barrel. Weight: about 9½ pounds. Receiver peep sight, hooded front sight. Target stock, swivels, sling. Made 1937 to 1949.

Stevens No. 419 Junior Target Model Bolt Action Single Shot Rifle $85
Takedown. Caliber: 22 Long Rifle. 26-inch barrel. Weight: about 5½ pounds, Lyman No. 55 rear peep sight, blade front sight. Plain junior target stock with pistol grip and grooved forearm, swivels, sling. Made 1932-36.

Stevens Buckhorn Model 53 . . . . $95
Same as Buckhorn Model 053, except has open rear sight and plain bead front sight.

Stevens Buckhorn Model 056 Bolt Action Repeating Rifle $95
Takedown. Caliber: 22 Long Rifle, Long, Short. 5-shot detachable box magazine. 24-inch barrel. Weight: about 6 pounds. Receiver peep sight, open middle sight, hooded front sight. Sporting stock with pistol grip and black forend tip. Made 1935 to 1948.

Stevens Buckhorn Model 56 . . . . $90
Same as Buckhorn Model 056, except has open rear sight and plain bead front sight.

Stevens Buckhorn No. 057 . . . . $100
Same as Buckhorn Model 076, except has 5-shot detachable box magazine. Made 1939 to 1948.

Stevens Buckhorn No. 57 . . . . $100
Same as Buckhorn Model 76, except has 5-shot detachable box magazine. Made 1939 to 1948.

Stevens Buckhorn Model 066 Bolt Action Repeating Rifle $115
Takedown. Caliber: 22 Long Rifle, Long, Short. Tubular magazine holds 21 Short, 17 Long, 15 Long Rifle. 24-inch barrel. Weight: about 6 pounds. Receiver peep sight, open middle sight, hooded front sight. Sporting stock with pistol grip and black forend tip. Made 1935 to 1948.

Stevens Buckhorn Model 66 . . . . $100
Same as Buckhorn Model 066, except has open rear sight, plain bead front sight.

Stevens Buckhorn No. 076 Autoloading Rifle . . . $135
Takedown. Caliber: 22 Long Rifle. 15-shot tubular magazine. 24-inch barrel. Weight: about 6 pounds. Receiver peep sight, open middle sight, hooded front sight. Sporting stock with pistol grip, black forend tip. Made 1938 to 1948.

Stevens Buckhorn No. 76 . . . . $100
Same as Buckhorn No. 076, except has open rear sight, plain bead front sight.

Stevens Crack Shot No. 26 Single Shot Rifle . . . $135
Lever action. Takedown. Calibers: 22 Long Rifle, 32 R.F. 18-inch or 22-inch barrel. Weight: about 3 1/4 pounds. Open rear sight, blade front sight. Plain straight-grip stock, small tapered forearm. Made 1913 to 1939.

Stevens Crack Shot No. 26 1/2 . . . . $130
Same as Crack Shot No. 26, except has smoothbore barrel for shot cartridges.

Stevens Favorite No. 17 Single Shot Rifle $135
Lever action. Takedown. Calibers: 22 Long Rifle, 25 R.F., 32 R.F. 24-inch round barrel, other lengths were available. Weight: about 4 1/2 pounds. Open rear sight, Rocky Mountain front sight. Plain straight-grip stock, small tapered forearm. Made 1894 to 1935.

Stevens Favorite No. 18 . . . . $180
Same as Favorite No. 17 except has Vernier peep rear sight, leaf middle sight, Beach combination front sight.

Stevens Favorite No. 19 . . . . $195
Same as Favorite No. 17 except has Lyman combination rear sight, leaf sight, Lyman front sight.

Stevens Favorite No. 20 . . . . $145
Same as Favorite No. 17, except has smoothbore barrel for 22 R.F. and 32 R.F. shot cartridges.

Stevens Favorite No. 27 . . . . $175
Same as Favorite No. 17, except has octagon barrel.

Stevens Favorite No. 28 . . . . $205
Same as Favorite No. 18, except has octagon barrel.

Stevens Buckhorn Model 066

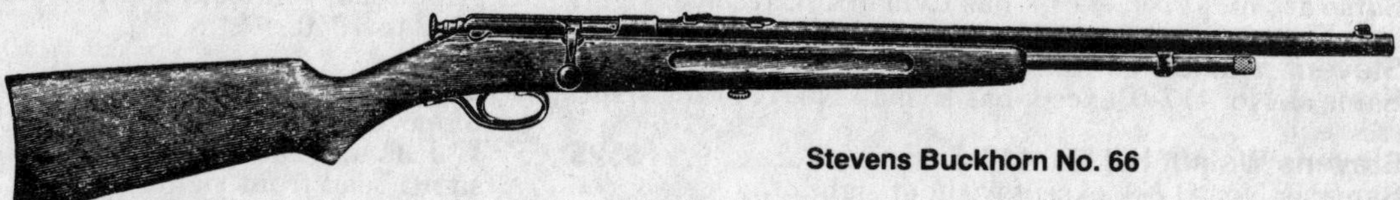
Stevens Buckhorn No. 66

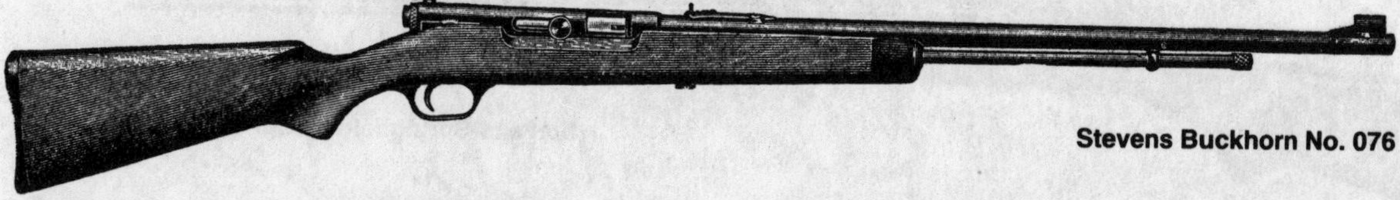
Stevens Buckhorn No. 076

Stevens Crack Shot No. 26

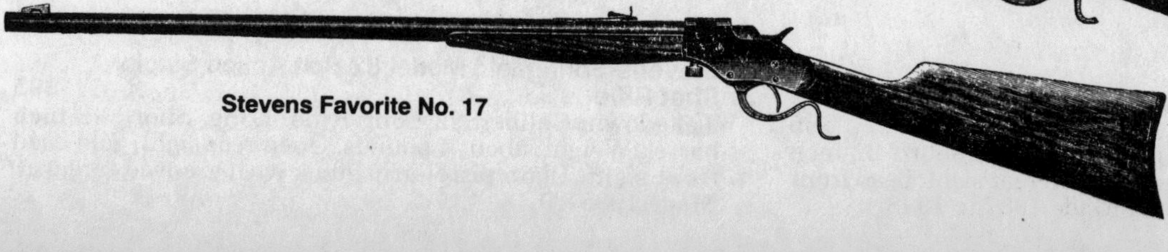
Stevens Favorite No. 17

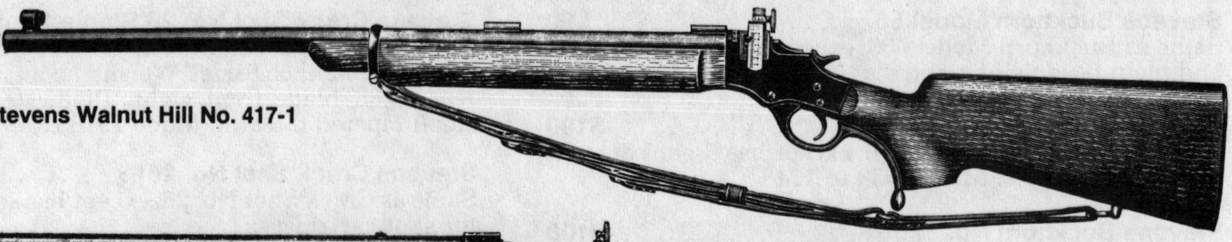

Stevens Walnut Hill No. 417-1

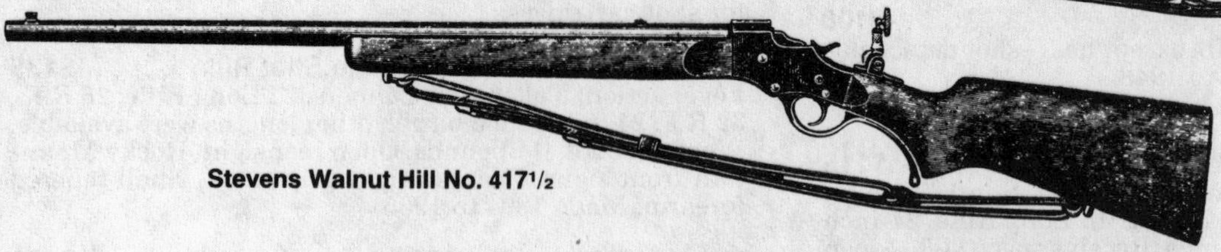

Stevens Walnut Hill No. 417½

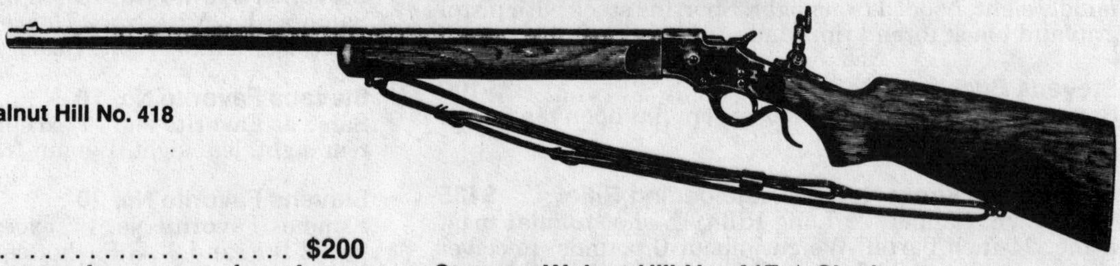

Stevens Walnut Hill No. 418

Stevens Favorite No. 29 . . . . $200
Same as Favorite No. 19, except has octagon barrel.

Stevens Walnut Hill No. 417-0 Single Shot Target Rifle $500
Lever action. Calibers: 22 Long Rifle only, 22 Short only, 22 Hornet. 28-inch heavy barrel (extra heavy 29-inch barrel also available). Weight: about 10½ pounds. Lyman 52L extension rear sight, 17A front sight, scope bases. Target stock with full pistol grip, beavertail forearm, barrel band, swivels, sling. Made 1932 to 1947.

Stevens Walnut Hill No. 417-1 . . . . $595
Same as No. 417-0, except has Lyman 48L receiver sight.

Stevens Walnut Hill No. 417-2 . . . . $725
Same as No. 417-0, except has Lyman No. 144 tang sight.

Stevens Walnut Hill No. 417-3 . . . . $525
Same as No. 417-0, except without sights.

Stevens Walnut Hill No. 417½ Single Shot Rifle $595
Lever action. Calibers: 22 Long Rifle, 22 W.R.F., 25 R.F., 22 Hornet. 28-inch barrel. Weight: about 8½ pounds. Lyman No. 144 tang peep sight, folding middle sight, bead front sight. Sporting stock with pistol grip, semibeavertail forearm, swivels, sling. Made 1932 to 1940.

Stevens Walnut Hill No. 418 Single Shot Rifle . . . $395
Lever action. Takedown. Calibers: 22 Long Rifle only, 22 Short only. 26-inch barrel. Weight: about 6½ pounds. Lyman No. 144 tang peep sight, blade front sight. Pistol-grip stock, semibeavertail forearm, swivels, sling. Made 1932 to 1940.

Stevens Walnut Hill No. 418½ $435
Same as No. 418, except also available in calibers 22 W.R.F. and 25 Stevens R.F., has Lyman No. 2A tang peep sight, bead front sight.

Stevens-Springfield Model 15

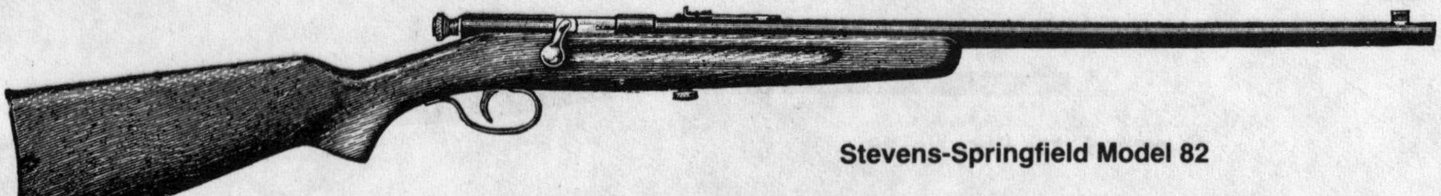

Stevens-Springfield Model 82

Stevens-Springfield Model 15 Single Shot Bolt Action Rifle $95
Takedown. Caliber: 22 Long Rifle, Long, Short. 22-inch barrel. Weight: about 4 pounds. Open rear sight, bead front sight. Plain pistol-grip stock. Made 1937 to 1948.

Stevens-Springfield Model 82 Bolt Action Single Shot Rifle $95
Takedown. Caliber: 22 Long Rifle, Long, Short. 22-inch barrel. Weight: about 4 pounds. Open rear sight, gold bead front sight. Plain pistol-grip stock with grooved forearm. Made 1935-39.

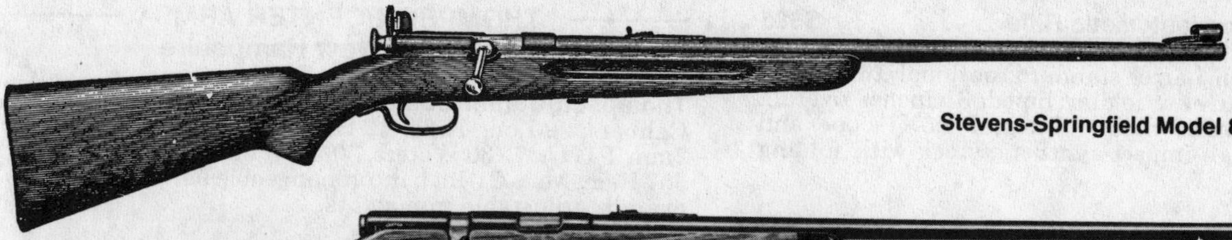

Stevens-Springfield Model 83

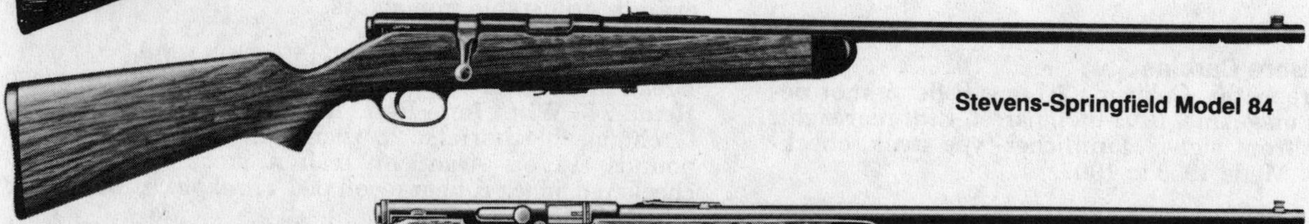

Stevens-Springfield Model 84

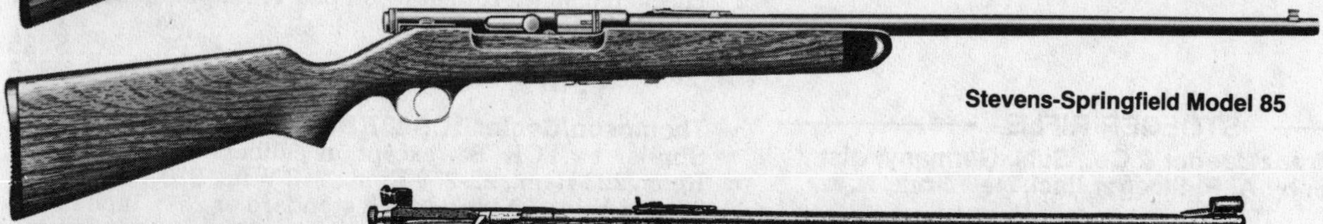

Stevens-Springfield Model 85

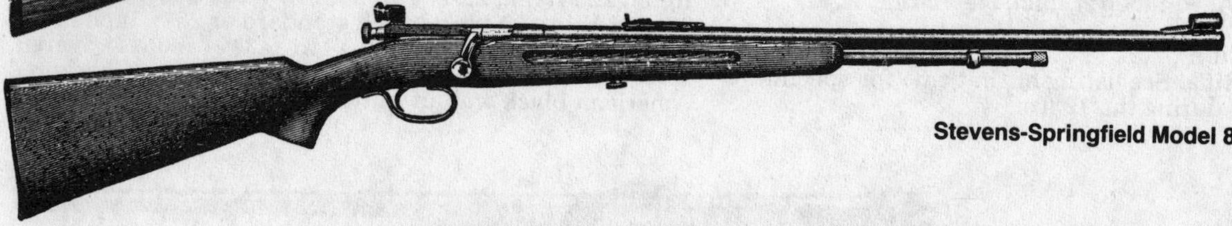

Stevens-Springfield Model 86-S

Stevens-Springfield Model 83 Bolt Action Single Shot Rifle $95
Takedown. Calibers: 22 Long Rifle, Long, Short; 22 W.R.F., 25 Stevens R.F. 24-inch barrel. Weight: about 4½ pounds. Peep rear sight, open middle sight, hooded front sight. Plain pistol-grip stock with grooved forearm. Made 1935-39.

Stevens-Springfield Model 84 . . . . $100
Same as Model 86, except has 5-shot detachable box magazine. Pre-1948 rifles of this model were designated Springfield Model 84, later known as Stevens Model 84. Made 1940 to 1965.

Stevens-Springfield Model 84-S (084) $100
Same as Model 84, except has peep rear sight and hooded front sight. Pre-1948 rifles of this model were designated Springfield Model 084, later known as Stevens Model 84-S. Discontinued.

Stevens-Springfield Model 85 . . . . $130
Same as Stevens Model 87, except has 5-shot detachable box magazine. Made from 1939 to date. Pre-1948 rifles of this model were designated Springfield Model 85, currently known as Stevens Model 85.

Stevens-Springfield Model 85-S (085) $130
Same as Model 85, except has peep rear sight and hooded front sight. Pre-1948 rifles of this model were designated Springfield Model 085, currently known as Stevens Model 85-S.

Stevens-Springfield Model 86 Bolt Action Repeating Rifle $100
Takedown. Caliber: 22 Long Rifle, Long, Short. Tubular magazine holds 15 Long Rifle, 17 Long, 21 Short. 24-inch barrel. Weight: about 6 pounds. Open rear sight, gold bead front sight. Pistol-grip stock, black forend tip on later production. Made 1935 to 1965. *Note:* The "Springfield" brand name was discontinued in 1948.

Stevens-Springfield Model 86-S (086) $110
Same as Model 86, except has peep rear sight and hooded front sight. Pre-1948 rifles of this model were designated as Springfield Model 086, later known as Stevens Model 86-S. Discontinued.

Stevens-Springfield Model 87-S (087) $130
Same as Stevens Model 87, except has peep rear sight and hooded front sight. Pre-1948 rifles of this model were designated as Springfield Model 087, later known as Stevens Model 87-S. Discontinued.

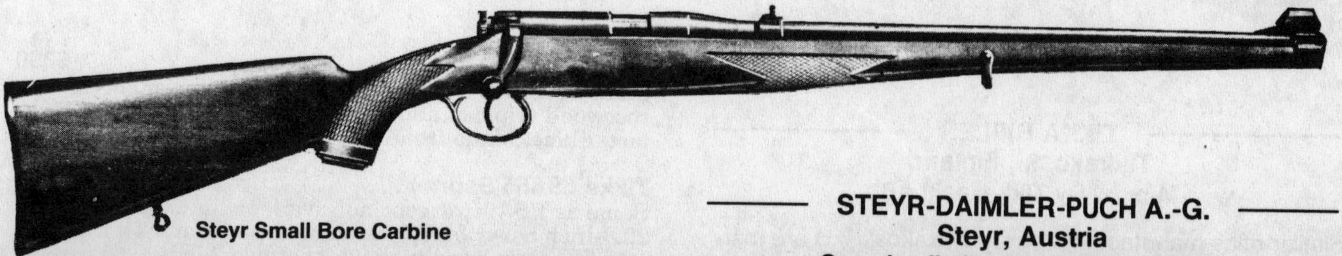

Steyr Small Bore Carbine

STEYR-DAIMLER-PUCH A.-G.
Steyr, Austria
See also listings under Mannlicher.

Steyr AUG-SA Semiautomatic Rifle **$995**
Gas-operated. Caliber: 223 Rem. (5.56mm). 30- or 40-shot magazine. 20-inch barrel standard; optional 16-inch or 24-inch heavy barrel w/folding bipod. 31 inches overall. Weight: $8\frac{1}{2}$ pounds. Sights: Integral 1.5X scope and mount. Green high-impact synthetic stock with folding vertical grip.

Steyr Small Bore Carbine **$400**
Bolt-action repeater. Caliber: 22 Long Rifle. 5-shot detachable box magazine. $19\frac{1}{2}$-inch barrel. Leaf rear sight, hooded bead front sight. Mannlicher-type stock, checkered, swivels. Made 1953 to 1967.

STOEGER RIFLE

Mfd. by Franz Jaeger & Co., Suhl, Germany; dist. in the U.S. by A. F. Stoeger, Inc., New York, N.Y.

Stoeger Hornet Rifle **$1200**
Same as Herold Rifle. See listing of that rifle for specifications. Imported during the 1930s.

THOMPSON/CENTER ARMS
Rochester, New Hampshire

Thompson/Center Contender Carbine **$250**
Calibers: 22 Long Rifle, 22 Hornet, 222 Rem., 223 Rem., 7mm T.C.U., 7×30 Waters, 30/30 Win., 35 Rem., 44 Mag., 357 Rem. Max. 21-inch interchangeable barrels. 35 inches overall. Adjustable iron sights.

Thompson/Center TCR '83 Single Shot Rifle
Break frame, overlever action. Calibers: 223 Rem., 22/250 Rem., 243 Win., 7mm Rem. Mag., 30-06 Springfield. Interchangeable barrels: 23 inches in length. Weight: 6 pounds, 14 oz. American walnut stock and forearm, checkered, black rubber recoil pad, cheekpiece. Made 1983 to date.
TCR '83 Standard Model **$295**
TCR '83 Aristocrat **335**

Thompson/Center TCR '87 Hunter Rifle **$300**
Similar to TCR '83, except in calibers 22 Hornet, 222 Rem., 223 Rem., 22-250 Rem., 243 Win., 270 Win., 7mm-08, 308 Win., 30-06. 23-inch standard or $25\frac{7}{8}$-inch heavy barrel∞terchangeable. $39\frac{1}{2}$ to $43\frac{3}{8}$ inches overall. Weight: 6 lbs. 14 oz. to $7\frac{1}{2}$ lbs. Iron sights. Checkered American black walnut buttstock with fluted forend.

Thompson/Center Contender Carbine

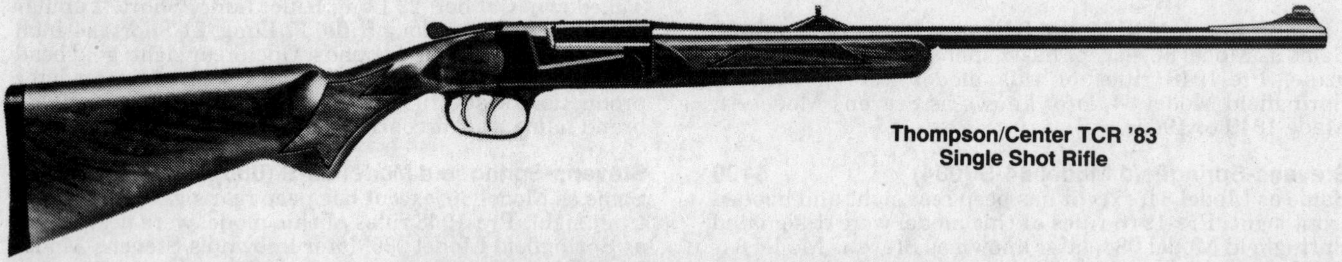

Thompson/Center TCR '83 Single Shot Rifle

Thompson/Center TCR'87 Hunter

TIKKA RIFLES
Tikkakoski, Finland
Mfd. by Oy Tikkakoski AB

Similar rifles manufactured by Oy Tikkakoski AB are marketed in the U.S. as Ithaca-LSA. See separate listings.

Tikka LSA55 Deluxe **$350**
Same as LSA55 Standard, except has roll-over cheekpiece, rosewood grip cap and forend tip, skip checkering, high-luster blue. Made from 1965 to date.

Tikka LSA55 Sporter **$375**
Same as LSA55, except not available in 6mm Rem., has 22.8-inch heavy barrel, no sights, special stock with beavertail forearm, weighs about 9 pounds. Made 1965 to date.

Tikka LSA55 Deluxe

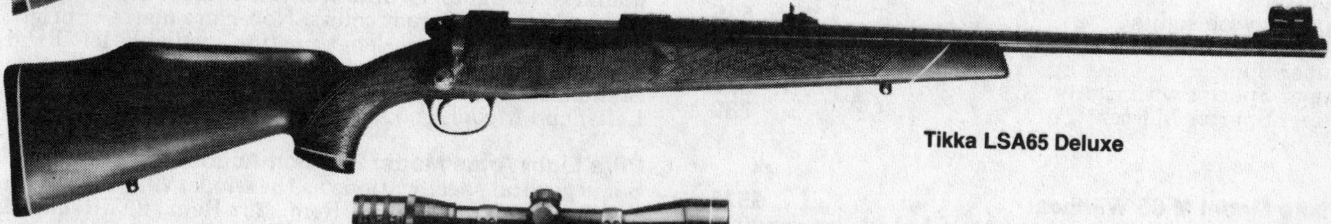

Tikka LSA65 Deluxe

Tikka Model M 55 Deluxe

Tikka Model M 55 Standard

Tikka Model M 65 Sporter

Tikka LSA55 Standard Bolt Action Repeating Rifle **$325**
Mauser-type action. Calibers: 222 Rem., 22-250, 6mm Rem. Mag., 243 Win., 308 Win. 3-shot clip magazine. 22.8-inch barrel. Weight: 6.8 pounds. Folding leaf rear sight, hooded ramp front sight. Checkered walnut stock with Monte Carlo cheekpiece, swivels. Made from 1965 to date.

Tikka LSA65 Deluxe **$375**
Same as LSA65 Standard, except has special features of LSA55 Deluxe. Made from 1970 to date.

Tikka LSA65 Standard **$320**
Same as LSA55 Standard, except calibers: 25-06, 6.5×55, 270 Win., 30-06. 5-shot magazine, 22-inch barrel, weighs 7½ pounds. Made from 1970 to date.

Tikka Model M 55
Bolt action. Calibers: 222 Rem., 22-250 Rem., 223 Rem., 243 Win., 308 Win. (6mm Rem. and 17 Rem. available in Standard and Deluxe models only). 23.2-inch barrel (24.8-inch in Sporter and Heavy Barrel models). 42.8 inches overall (44 inches in Sporter and Heavy Barrel models). Weight: 7¼ to 9 pounds. Monte Carlo-style stock with pistol grip. Sling swivels.

Continental	**$470**
Deluxe Model	**470**
Sporter	**445**
Sporter with sights	**460**
Standard	**430**
Super Sporter	**530**
Super Sporter with sights	**545**
Trapper	**450**

Tikka Model M 65
Bolt action. Calibers: 25-06, 270 Win., 308 Win., 30-06, 7mm Rem. Mag., 300 Win. Mag. (Sporter and Heavy Barrel models in 270 Win., 308 Win. and 30-06 only). 22.4-inch barrel (24.8-inch in Sporter and Heavy Barrel mod-

Tikka Model M 65 (cont.)
els). 43.2 inches overall (44 inches in Sporter, 44.8 inches in Heavy Barrel). Weight: 7½ to 9.9 pounds. Monte Carlo-style stock with pistol grip.

Continental	**$495**
Deluxe Magnum	**530**
Deluxe Model	**495**
Magnum	**490**
Sporter	**490**
Sporter with sights	**525**
Standard	**460**
Super Sporter	**575**
Super Sporter with sights	**595**
Super Sporter Master	**730**

Tikka Model M 65 Wildboar $525
Same general specifications as Model M 65, except 20.8-inch barrel, overall length of 41.6 inches and weight of 7½ pounds.

ULTRA-HI PRODUCTS COMPANY
Hawthorne, New Jersey

Ultra-Hi Model 2200 Single Shot Bolt Action Rifle . . $75
Caliber: 22 Long Rifle, Long, Short. 23-inch barrel. Weight: about 5 pounds. Open rear sight, blade front sight. Monte Carlo stock with pistol grip. Made in Japan. Introduced 1977. Discontinued.

ULTRA LIGHT ARMS COMPANY
Granville, West Virginia

Ultra Light Arms Model 20 Bolt Action Rifle
Calibers: 22-250 Rem., 243 Win., 6mm Rem., 250-3000 Savage, 257 Roberts, 257 Ack., 7mm Mauser, 7mm Ack., 7mm-08 Rem., 284 Win., 300 Savage, 308 Win., 358 Win. Box magazine. 22-inch ultra light barrel. Weight: 4¾ pounds. No sights. Synthetic stock of Kevlar or graphite finished seven different colors. Non-glare matte or bright metal finish. Medium-length action available left-hand models.

Standard Model	**$1300**
Left-hand Model	**1400**

Ultra Light Arms Model 20S Bolt Action Rifle
Same general specifications as the Model 20, except with short action in calibers 17 Rem., 222 Rem., 223 Rem., 22 Hornet only.

Standard Model	**$1300**
Left-hand Model	**1400**

Ultra Light Arms Model 24 Bolt Action Rifle
Same general specifications as the Model 20, except with long action in calibers 25-06, 270 Win., 30-06 and 7mm Express only.

Standard Model	**$1375**
Left-hand Model	**1475**

Ultra Light Arms Model 28 Bolt Action Rifle . . . $2150
Same general specifications as the Model 20, except with long magnum action in calibers 264 Win. Mag., 7mm Rem. Mag., 300 Win. Mag., 338 Win. Mag. only. Offered with recoil arrestor. Left-hand model available.

Ultra-Hi Model 2200

Ultra Light Arms Model 20 Series

Unique T66 Match

UNIQUE RIFLE
Hendaye, France
Mfd. by Manufacture d'Armes des Pyrénées Francaises

Unique T66 Match Rifle $610
Single-shot bolt action. Caliber: 22 Long Rifle. 25½-inch barrel. Weight: about 10½ pounds. Micrometer aperture rear sight, globe front sight. French walnut target stock with Monte Carlo comb, bull pistol grip, wide and deep forearm, stippled grip surfaces, adjustable swivel on accessory track, adjustable rubber butt plate. Made from 1966 to date.

U.S. MILITARY RIFLES

Mfd. by Springfield Armory, Remington Arms Co., Winchester Repeating Arms Co., Inland Mfg. Div. of G.M.C., and other contractors. See notes.

Unless otherwise indicated, the following U.S. Military rifles were manufactured at Springfield Armory, Springfield, Mass.

U.S. Model 1898 Krag-Jorgensen Carbine $395
Same general specifications as Model 1898 Rifle, except has 22-inch barrel, weighs about 8 pounds, carbine-type stock. *Note:* The foregoing specifications apply, in general, to Carbine Models 1896 and 1899 which differed from Model 1898 only in minor details.

U.S. Model 1898 Krag-Jorgensen Military Rifle . . $255
Bolt action. Caliber: 30-40 Krag. 5-shot hinged box magazine. 30-inch barrel. Weight: about 9 pounds. Adjustable rear sight, blade front sight. Military-type stock, straight grip. *Note:* The foregoing specifications apply, in general, to Rifle Models 1892 and 1896 which differed from Model 1898 only in minor details. Made 1894 to 1904.

U.S. Model 1903 Mark I Springfield $295
Same as Standard Model 1903, except altered to permit use of the Pedersen Device. This device, officially designated "U.S. Automatic Pistol Model 1918," converted the M/1903 to a semiautomatic weapon firing a 30 caliber cartridge similar to the 32 automatic pistol ammunition. Mark I rifles have a slot milled in the left side of the receiver to serve as an ejection port when the Pedersen Device was in use; these rifles were also fitted with a special sear and cut-off. Some 65,000 of these devices were manufactured and presumably a like number of M/1903 rifles converted to handle them. During the early 1930s all Pedersen Devices were ordered destroyed and the Mark I rifles were reconverted by replacement of the special sear and cut-off with standard components. Some 20-odd specimens are known to have escaped destruction and are in government museums and private collections. Probably more are extant. Rarely is a Pedersen Device offered for sale and so a current value cannot be assigned. However, many of the altered rifles were purchased by members of the National Rifle Association through the Director of Civilian Marksmanship. Value shown is for the Mark I rifle without the Pedersen Device.

U.S. Model 1903 National Match Springfield $800
Same general specifications as the Standard Model 1903, except specially selected with star-gauged barrel, Type C pistol-grip stock, polished bolt assembly; early types have headless firing pin assembly and reversed safety lock. Produced especially for target shooting.

U.S. Model 1903 Springfield Military Rifle
Modified Mauser-type bolt action. Caliber: 30-06. 5-shot box magazine. 23.79-inch barrel. Weight: about 8¾ pounds. Adjustable rear sight, blade front sight. Military-type stock, straight grip. *Note:* M/1903 rifles of Springfield manufacture with serial numbers under 800,000 (1903-1918) have casehardened receivers; those between 800,000 and 1,275,767 (1918-1927) were double-heat-treated; rifles numbered over 1,275,767 have nickel-steel bolts and receivers. Rock Island production from No. 1 to 285,507 have casehardened receivers. Improved heat treatment was adopted in May 1918 with No. 285,207; about three months later with No. 319,921 the use of nickel steel was begun, but the production of some double-heat-treated carbon-steel receivers and bolts continued. Made from 1903 to 1930 at Springfield Armory; during WWI, M/1903 rifles were also made at Rock Island Arsenal, Rock Island, Ill.
With casehardened receiver **$185**
With double-heat-treated receiver **200**
With nickel steel receiver **250**

U.S. Model 1903 Springfield Sporter $795
Same general specifications as the National Match, except has sporting design stock, Lyman No. 48 receiver sight.

U.S. Model 1903 Style T Springfield Match Rifle $900
Same general specifications as the Springfield Sporter, except has heavy barrel (26-, 28- or 30-inch), scope bases, globe front sight, weighs about 12½ pounds with 26-inch barrel.

U.S. Model 1903 Type A Springfield Free Rifle . . $1000
Same as Style T, except made with 28-inch barrel only, has Swiss butt plate, weighs about 13¼ pounds.

U.S. Model 1903 Type B Springfield Free Rifle . . $1185
Same as Type A, except has cheekpiece stock, palm rest, Woodie double-set triggers, Garand fast firing pin, weighs about 14¾ pounds.

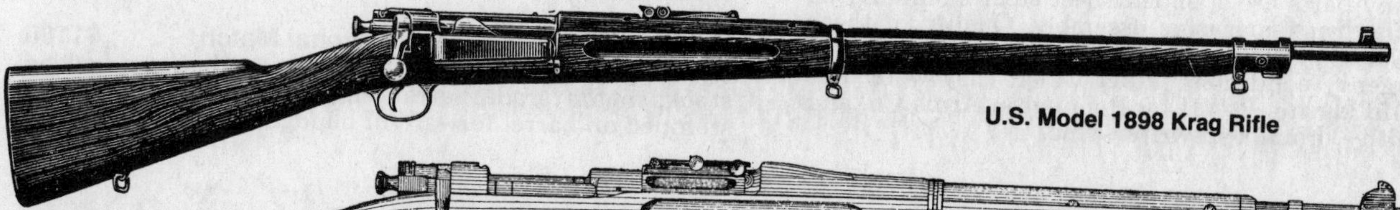

U.S. Model 1898 Krag Rifle

U.S. Model 1903 Springfield

U.S. Model 1903 Springfield Sporter

RIFLES

U.S. Model 1903-A1 Springfield

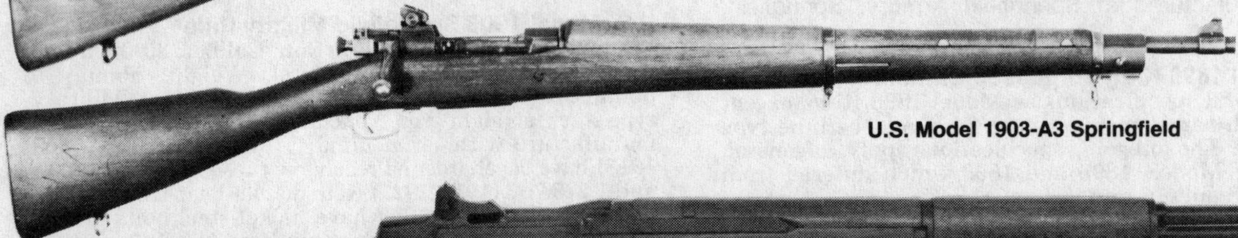

U.S. Model 1903-A3 Springfield

U.S. Rifle Cal. 30 M1 (Garand)

U.S. Model 1903-A1 Springfield
Same general specifications as Model 1903, except may have Type C pistol-grip stock adopted in 1930. The last Springfields produced at the Springfield Armory were of this type, final serial number was 1,532,878 made in 1939. *Note:* Late in 1941, the Remington Arms Co., Ilion, N.Y., began production under government contract of Springfield rifles of this type with a few minor modifications. These rifles are numbered from 3,000,001 to 3,348,085 and were manufactured prior to the adoption of Model 1903-A3.
Springfield manufacture **$250**
Remington manufacture **215**

U.S. Model 1903-A3 Springfield $195
Same general specifications as Model 1903-A1, except modified to permit increased production and lower cost; may have either straight-grip or pistol-grip stock, bolt is not interchangeable with earlier types, has receiver peep sight, many parts are stamped sheet steel including the trigger guard and magazine assembly. Quality of these rifles, lower than that of other 1903 Springfields, reflects the emergency conditions under which they were produced. Mfd. during WWII by Remington Arms Co. and L. C. Smith Corona Typewriters, Inc.

U.S. Model 1922-M1 22 Springfield Target Rifle $375
Modified Model 1903. Caliber: 22 Long Rifle. 5-shot detachable box magazine. 24½-inch barrel. Weight: about 9 pounds. Lyman No. 48C receiver sight, blade front sight. Sporting-type stock similar to that of the Model 1903 Springfield Sporter. Issued 1927. *Note:* The earlier Model 1922, which is seldom encountered, differs from the foregoing chiefly in the bolt mechanism and magazine.

U.S. M2 22 Springfield Target Rifle $550
Same general specifications as Model 1922-MI, except has speedlock, improved bolt assembly adjustable for headspace. *Note:* These improvements were later incorporated in many rifles of the preceding models (M1922, M1922MI) and arms so converted were marked "M1922M2" or "M1922MII."

U.S. Rifle, Caliber 30, M1 (Garand) Military Rifle $695
Clip-fed, gas-operated, air-cooled semiautomatic. Uses a clip containing 8 rounds. 24-inch barrel. Weight: without bayonet, 9½ pounds. Adjustable peep rear sight, blade front sight with guards. Pistol-grip stock, handguards. Made 1937 to 1957. *Note:* Garand rifles have also been produced by Winchester Repeating Arms Co., Harrington & Richardson Arms Co., and International Harvester Co.

U.S. Rifle, Caliber 30, M1, National Match $1100
Accurized target version of the Garand. Glass-bedded stock; match grade barrel, sights, gas cylinder. "NM" stamped on barrel forward of handguard.

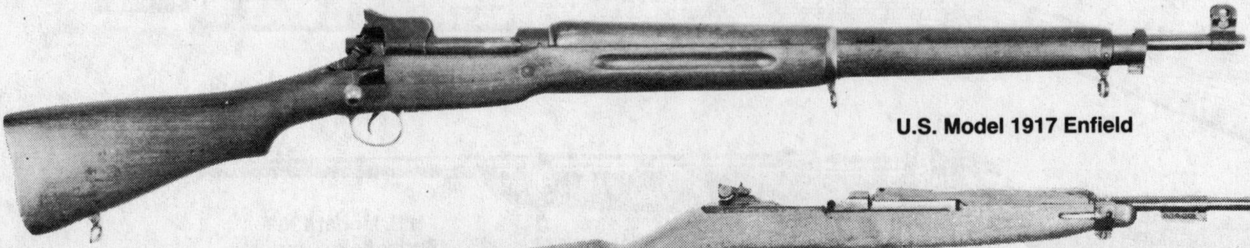

U.S. Model 1917 Enfield

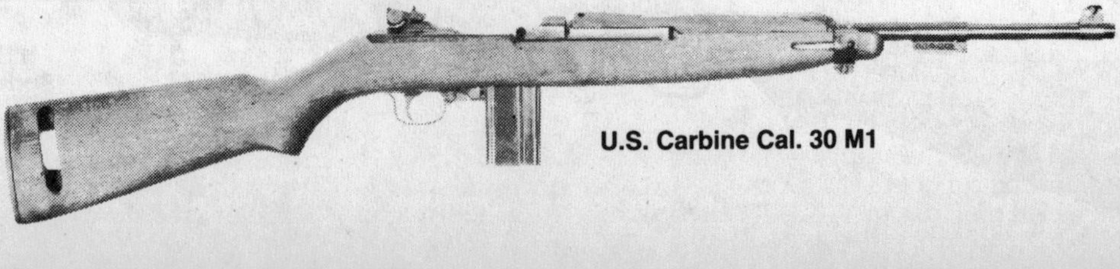

U.S. Carbine Cal. 30 M1

> *Note:* The U.S. Model 1917 Enfield was mfd. 1917-18 by Remington Arms Co. of Delaware (later Midvale Steel & Ordnance Co.), Eddystone, Penn.; Remington Arms Co., Ilion, N.Y.; Winchester Repeating Arms Co., New Haven, Conn.

U.S. Model 1917 Enfield Military Rifle **$175**
Modified Mauser-type bolt action. Caliber: 30-06. 5-shot box magazine. 26-inch barrel. Weight: about 9¼ pounds. Adjustable rear sight, blade front sight with guards. Military-type stock with semi-pistol grip. This design originated in Great Britain as their "Pattern '14" and was manufactured in caliber 303 for the British Government in three U.S. plants. In 1917, the U.S. Government contracted with these firms to produce the same rifle in caliber 30-06; over two million of these Model 1917 Enfields were mfd. While no more were produced after WWI, the U.S. supplied over a million of them to Great Britain during WWII.

U.S. Carbine, Caliber 30, M1 .... **$265**
Gas-operated (short-stroke piston), semiautomatic. 15- or 30-round detachable box magazine. 18-inch barrel.

U.S. Carbine, Caliber 30, M1 (cont.)
Weight: about 5½ pounds. Adjustable rear sight, blade front sight with guards. Pistol-grip stock with handguard, side-mounted web sling. Made 1942-45. *Note:* In 1963, 150,000 surplus M1 Carbines were sold at $20 each to members of the National Rifle Assn. by the Dept. of the Army.

> *Note:* The WWII-vintage 30-caliber U.S. Carbine was mfd. by Inland Mfg. Div. of G.M.C., Dayton, Ohio; Winchester Repeating Arms Co., New Haven, Conn.; and other contractors: International Business Machines Corp., Poughkeepsie, N.Y.; National Postal Meter Co., Rochester, N.Y.; Quality Hardware & Machine Co., Chicago, Ill.; Rock-Ola Co., Chicago, Ill.; Saginaw Steering Gear Div. of G.M.C., Saginaw, Mich.; Standard Products Co., Port Clinton, Ohio; Underwood-Elliott-Fisher Co., Hartford, Conn.

U.S. REPEATING ARMS CO.
See Winchester Rifle listings.

Universal Deluxe 30 Carbine

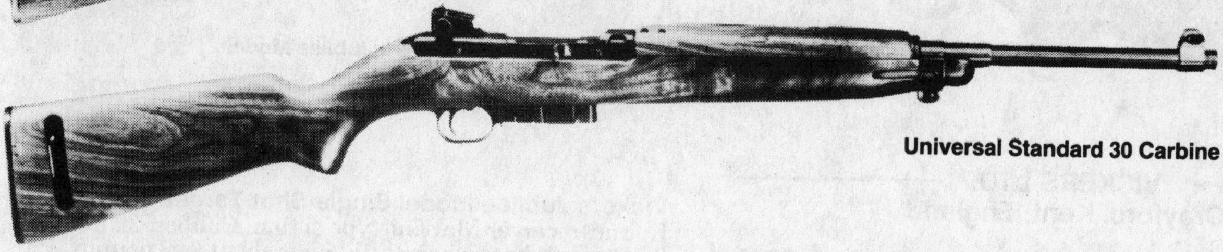
Universal Standard 30 Carbine

UNIVERSAL SPORTING GOODS, INC.
Miami, Florida

Universal Deluxe Carbine **$185**
Same as standard model, except also available in caliber 256, has deluxe walnut Monte Carlo stock and handguard. Made from 1965 to date.

Universal Standard M-1 Carbine **$175**
Same as U.S. Carbine, Cal. 30, M1, except may have either wood or metal handguard, barrel band with or without bayonet lug; 5-shot magazine standard. Made from 1964 to date.

Valmet M-62S

VALMET OY RIFLES
Punanotkonkatu, Finland

Valmet M-62S Semiautomatic Rifle **$695**
Semiautomatic version of Finnish M-62 automatic assault rifle based on Russian AK-47. Gas-operated rotating-bolt

Valmet M-62S Semiautomatic Rifle (cont.)
action. Caliber: 7.62mm × 39 Russian. 15- and 30-round magazines. 16⅝-inch barrel. Weight: about 8 pounds with metal stock. Tangent aperture rear sight, hooded blade front sight with luminous flip-up post for low-light use. Tubular steel or wood stock. Made from 1962 to date.

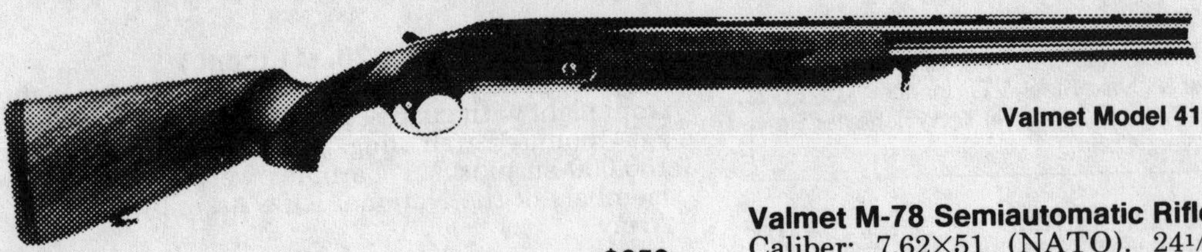
Valmet Model 412 S

Valmet M-71S **$650**
Same specifications as M-62S, except caliber 5.56mm×45 (223 Rem.), has open rear sight, reinforced resin or wood stock, weighs 7¾ pounds with former. Made from 1971

Valmet M-76 Semiautomatic Rifle
Semiautomatic assault rifle. Gas-operated, rotating bolt action. Caliber: 223 Rem. 15- and 30-shot magazines. Made from 1984 to date.
Wooden stock **$595**
Folding stock **625**

Valmet M-78 Semiautomatic Rifle **$635**
Caliber: 7.62×51 (NATO). 24⅛-inch barrel. Overall length: 43⅛ inches. Weight: 10½ pounds.

Valmet M-82 Semiautomatic Carbine **$525**
Caliber: 223 Rem. 15- or 30-shot magazine. 17-inch barrel. 27 inches overall. Weight: 7¾ pounds.

Valmet Model 412 S Shotgun/Rifle **$695**
Boxlock. Manual or automatic extraction. Calibers: 243, 308, 30-06, 375 Win., 9.3×74R. Barrels: 24-inch over/under. Weight: 8⅝ pounds. American walnut checkered stock and forend.

Vickers Empire Model

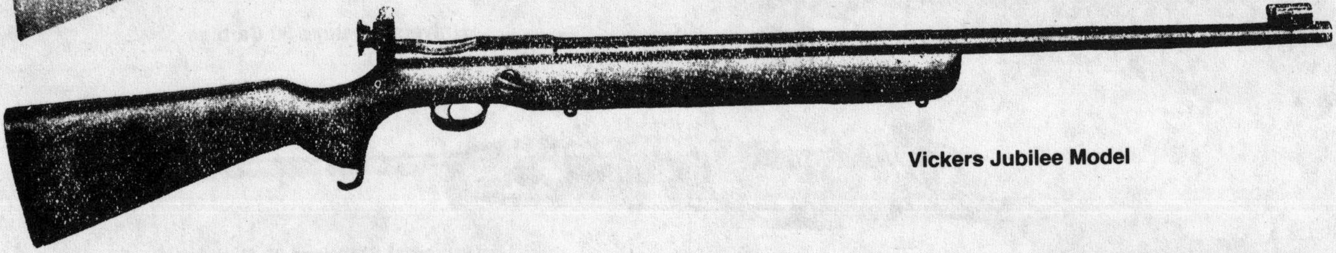
Vickers Jubilee Model

VICKERS LTD.
Crayford, Kent, England

Vickers Empire Model **$300**
Similar to Jubilee Model, except has 27- or 30-inch barrel, straight-grip stock, weighs about 9¼ pounds with 30-inch barrel. Made prior to WWII.

Vickers Jubilee Model Single Shot Target Rifle . **$375**
Round-receiver Martini-type action. Caliber: 22 Long Rifle. 28-inch heavy barrel. Weight: about 9½ pounds. Parker-Hale No. 2 front sight, Perfection rear peep sight. One-piece target stock with full forearm and pistol grip. Made prior to WWII.

Walther Model 2

WALTHER RIFLES
Mfd. by the German firms of Waffenfabrik Walther and Carl Walther Sportwaffenfabrik

The following Walther rifles were mfd. prior to WWII by Waffenfabrik Walther, Zella-Mehlis (Thür.), Germany.

Walther Model 1 Autoloading Rifle, Light Model **$410**
Similar to Standard Model 2, but with 20-inch barrel, lighter stock, weighs about 4½ pounds.

Walther Model 2 Autoloading Rifle **$40**
Bolt action, may be used as autoloader, manually operated repeater or single shot. Caliber: 22 Long Rifle. 5- or 9 shot detachable box magazine. 24½-inch barrel. Weight about 7 pounds. Tangent-curve rear sight, ramp front sight. Sporting stock with checkered pistol grip, grooved forearm, swivels.

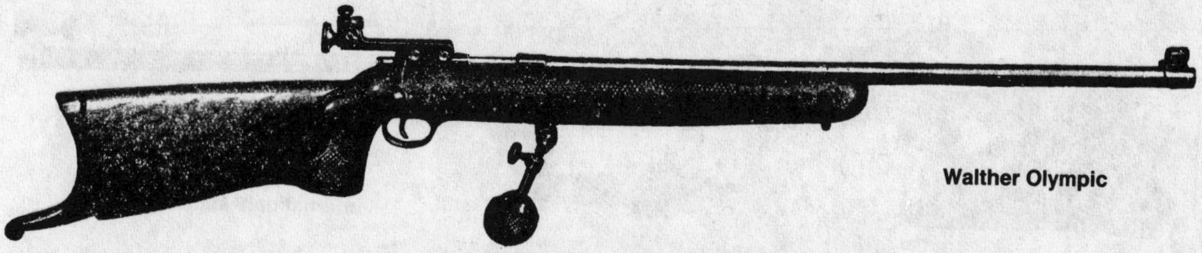

Walther Olympic

Walther Model V Meisterbuchse

Walther Olympic Bolt Action Single Shot Match Rifle $900
Caliber: 22 Long Rifle. 26-inch heavy barrel. Weight: about 13 pounds. Micrometer extension rear sight, interchangeable front sights. Target stock with checkered pistol grip, thumb hole, full beavertail forearm covered with corrugated rubber, palm rest, adjustable Swiss-type butt plate, swivels.

Walther Model V Bolt Action Single Shot Rifle . . $340
Caliber: 22 Long Rifle. 26-inch barrel. Weight: about 7 pounds. Open rear sight, ramp front sight. Plain pistol-grip stock with grooved forearm.

Walther Model V "Meisterbuchse" (Champion Rifle) $400
Same as standard Model V, except has micrometer open rear sight and checkered pistol grip.

Note: The Walther rifles listed below have been mfd. since WWII by Carl Walther Sportwaffenfabrik, Ulm/Donau, W. Germany.

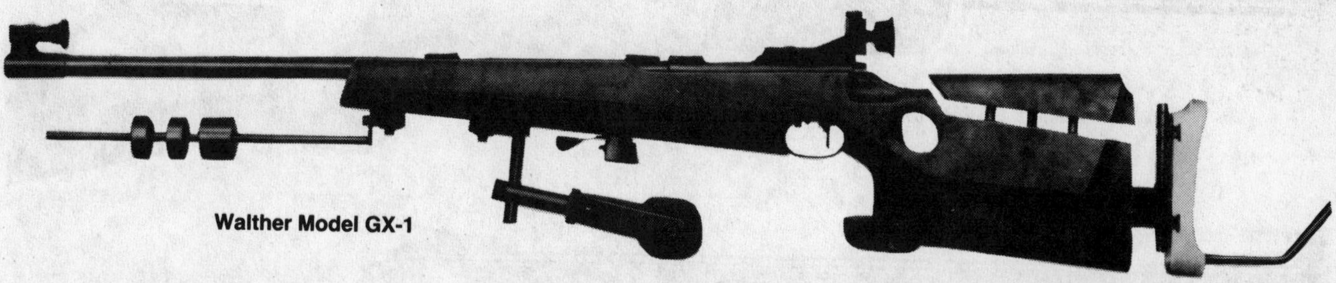

Walther Model GX-1

Walther Model KKJ

Walther Model GX-1 Free Rifle $790
Bolt action, single shot. Caliber: 22 Long Rifle. 25½-inch heavy barrel. Weight: 15.9 pounds. Micrometer aperture rear sight, globe front sight. Thumb-hole stock with adjustable cheekpiece and butt plate with removable hook, accessory rail. Left-hand stock available. Accessories furnished include hand stop and sling swivel, palm rest, counterweight assembly.

Walther Model KKJ Sporter $495
Bolt action. Caliber: 22 Long Rifle. 5-shot box magazine. 22½-inch barrel. Weight: 5½ pounds. Open rear sight. hooded ramp front sight. Stock with cheekpiece, checkered pistol grip and forearm, sling swivels.

Walther Model KKJ-Ho $525
Same as Model KKJ, except chambered for 22 Hornet.

Walther Model KKJ-Ma $425
Same as Model KKJ, except chambered for 22 Win. Mag. R.F.

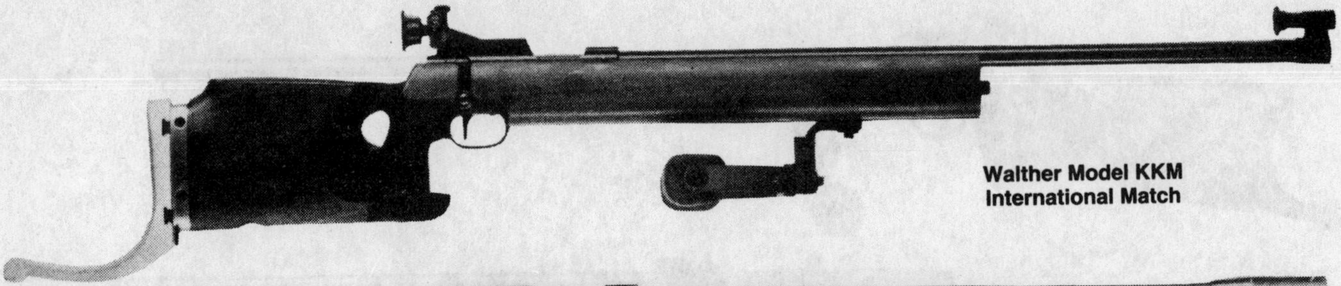

Walther Model KKM International Match

Walther Moving Target Match

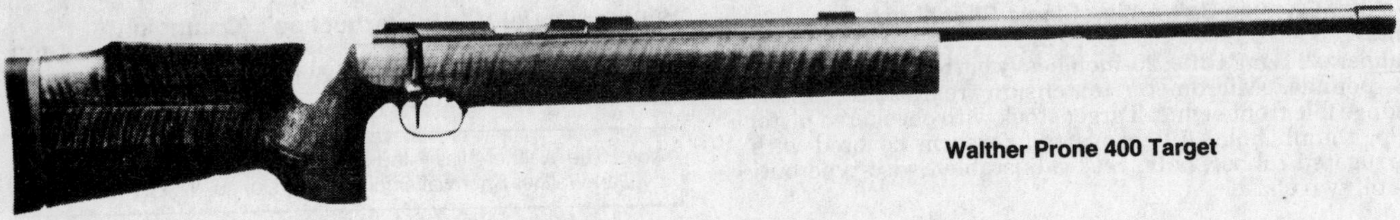

Walther Prone 400 Target

Walther Model SSV Varmint

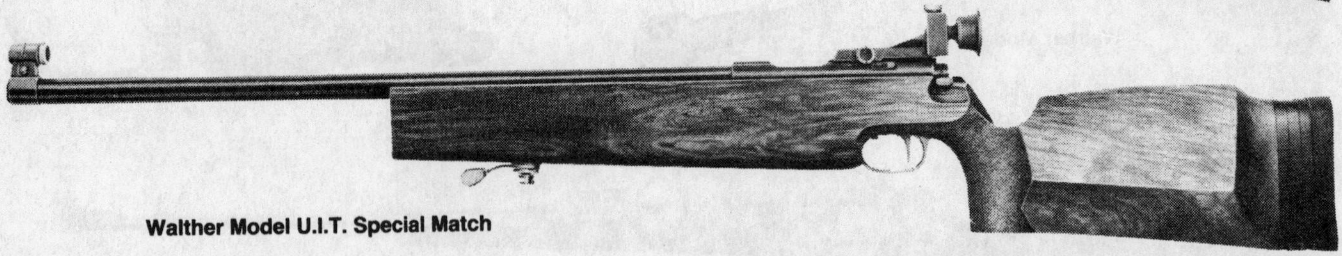

Walther Model U.I.T. Special Match

Walther Model KKM International Match Rifle . . . $740
Bolt action, single shot. Caliber: 22 Long Rifle. 28-inch heavy barrel. Weight: 15½ pounds. Micrometer aperture rear sight, globe front sight. Thumb-hole stock with high comb, adjustable hook butt plate, accessory rail. Left-hand stock available.

Walther Model KKM-S $750
Same specifications as Model KKM, except has adjustable cheekpiece.

Walther Moving Target Match Rifle $525
Bolt action, single shot. Caliber: 22 Long Rifle. 23.6-inch barrel with weight. Weight: 8.6 pounds. Supplied without sights. Thumb-hole stock with adjustable cheekpiece and butt plate. Left-hand stock available.

Walther Prone 400 Target Rifle $525
Bolt action, single shot. Caliber: 22 Long Rifle. 25½-inch heavy barrel. Weight: 10¼ pounds. Supplied without sights. Prone stock with adjustable cheekpiece and butt plate, accessory rail. Left-hand stock available.

Walther Model SSV Varmint Rifle $490
Bolt action, single shot. Calibers: 22 Long Rifle, 22 Hornet. 25½-inch barrel. Weight: 6¾ pounds. Supplied without sights. Monte Carlo stock with high cheekpiece, full pistol grip and forearm.

Walther Model U.I.T. Special Match Rifle $600
Bolt action, single shot. Caliber: 22 Long Rifle. 25½-inch barrel. Weight: 10.2 pounds. Micrometer aperture rear sight, globe front sight. Target stock with high comb, adjustable butt plate, accessory rail. Left-hand stock avail.

Walther Model U.I.T. Super Match

Walther Model U.I.T. Super Match Rifle $625
Bolt action, single shot. Caliber: 22 Long Rifle. 25½-inch heavy barrel. Weight: 10.2 pounds. Micrometer aperture rear sight, globe front sight. Target stock with support for off-hand shooting, high comb, adjustable butt plate and swivel. Left-hand stock available.

MONTGOMERY WARD
Chicago, Illinois
Western Field and Hercules Models

Firearms under the "private label" names of Western Field and Hercules are manufactured by such firms as Mossberg, Stevens, Marlin, and Savage for distribution and sale by Montgomery Ward.

Montgomery Ward Model 14M-497B Western Field Bolt Action Rifle $65
Caliber: 22 RF. 7-shot detachable box magazine. 24-inch barrel. Weight: about 5 pounds. Receiver peep sight, open rear sight, hooded ramp front sight. Pistol-grip stock. Mfd. by Mossberg.

Montgomery Ward Model M771 Western Field Lever Action Rifle $150
Calibers: 30-30, 35 Rem. 6-shot tubular magazine. 20-inch barrel. Weight: 6¾ pounds. Open rear sight, ramp front sight. Pistol-grip or straight stock, forearm with barrel band. Mfd. by Mossberg.

Montgomery Ward Model M772 Western Field Lever Action Rifle $160
Calibers: 30-30, 35 Rem. 6-shot tubular magazine. 20-inch barrel. Weight: 6¾ pounds. Open rear sight, ramp front sight. Pistol-grip or straight stock, forearm with barrel band. Mfd. by Mossberg.

Montgomery Ward Model M775 Bolt Action Rifle $190
Calibers: 222 Rem., 22-250, 243 Win., 308 Win. 4-shot magazine. Weight: about 7½ pounds. Folding leaf rear sight, ramp front sight. Monte Carlo stock with cheekpiece, pistol grip. Mfd by Mossberg.

Montgomery Ward Model M776 Bolt Action Rifle $195
Calibers: 222 Rem., 22-250, 243 Win., 308 Win. 4-shot magazine. Weight: about 7½ pounds. Folding leaf rear sight, ramp front sight. Monte Carlo stock with cheekpiece, pistol grip. Mfd. by Mossberg.

Montgomery Ward Model M778 Lever Action Rifle $150
Calibers: 30-30, 35 Rem. 6-shot tubular magazine. 20-inch barrel. Weight: 6¾ pounds. Open rear sight, ramp front

Montgomery Ward Model M778 (cont.)
sight. Pistol-grip or straight stock, forearm with barrel band. Mfd. by Mossberg.

Montgomery Ward Model M780 Bolt Action Rifle $195
Calibers: 222 Rem., 22-250, 243 Win., 308 Win. 4-shot magazine. Weight: about 7½ pounds. Folding leaf rear sight, ramp front sight. Monte Carlo stock with cheekpiece, pistol grip. Mfd. by Mossberg.

Montgomery Ward Model M782 Bolt Action Rifle $195
Same general specifications as Model M780.

Montgomery Ward Model M808 . . . . $75
Takedown. Caliber: 22RF. 15-shot tubular magazine. Barrels: 20- and 24-inch. Weight: about 6 pounds. Open rear sight, bead front sight. Pistol-grip stock. Mfd. by Stevens.

Montgomery Ward Model M832 Bolt Action Rifle $75
Caliber: 22 RF. 7-shot clip magazine. 24-inch barrel. Weight: 6½ pounds. Open rear sight, ramp front sight. Mfd. by Mossberg.

Montgomery Ward Model M836 . . . . $75
Takedown. Caliber: 22RF. 15-shot tubular magazine. Barrels: 20- and 24-inch. Weight: about 6 pounds. Open rear sight, bead front sight. Pistol-grip stock. Mfd. by Stevens.

Montgomery Ward Model M865 Lever Action Carbine $90
Hammerless. Caliber: 22RF. Tubular magazine. Made with both 18½-inch and 20-inch barrel, forearm with barrel band, swivels. Weight: about 5 pounds. Mfd. by Mossberg.

Montgomery Ward Model M894 Autoloading Carbine $90
Caliber: 22 RF. 15-shot tubular magazine. 20-inch barrel. Weight: about 6 pounds. Open rear sight, ramp front sight. Monte Carlo stock with pistol grip. Mfd. by Mossberg.

Montgomery Ward Model M-SD57 . . . . $75
Takedown. Caliber: 22RF. 15-shot tubular magazine. Barrels: 20- and 24-inch. Weight: about 6 pounds. Open rear sight, bead front sight. Pistol-grip stock. Mfd. by Stevens.

WEATHERBY, INC.
South Gate, California

Weatherby Deluxe 378 Magnum Rifle $1100
Same general specifications as Deluxe Magnum in other calibers, except caliber 378 W. M. Schultz & Larsen action; 26-inch barrel. Discontinued 1958.

Weatherby Deluxe Magnum

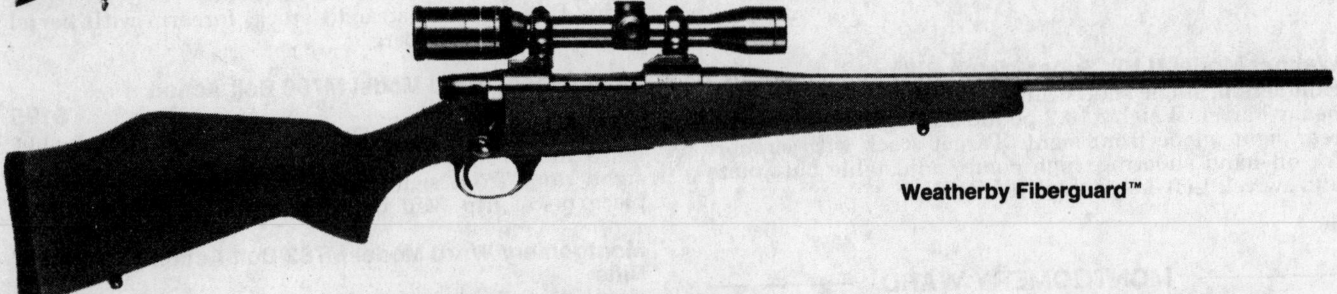

Weatherby Fiberguard™

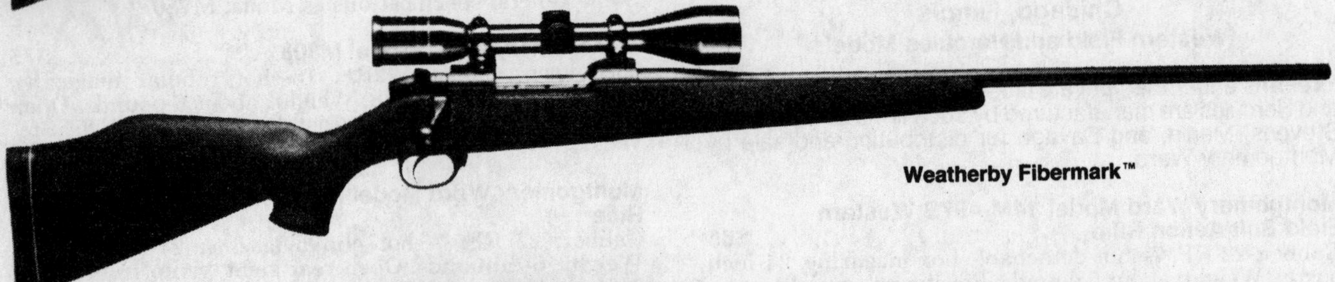

Weatherby Fibermark™

Weatherby Mark V

Weatherby Mark V Euromark

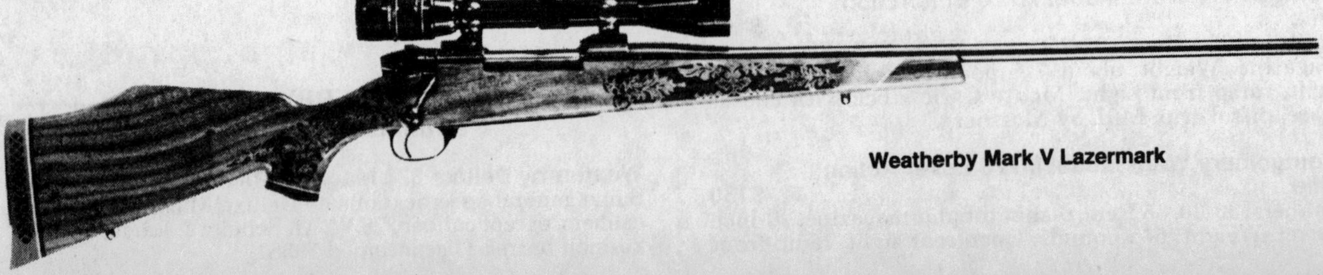

Weatherby Mark V Lazermark

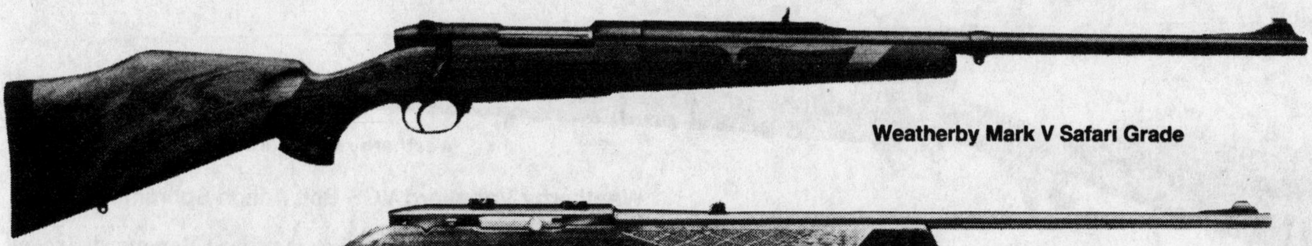

Weatherby Mark V Safari Grade

Weatherby Mark XXII Clip-fed

Weatherby Deluxe Magnum Rifle $900
Calibers: 220 Rocket, 257 Weatherby Mag., 270 W.M., 7mm W.M., 300 W.M., 375 W.M. Specially processed FN Mauser action. 24-inch barrel (26-inch in 375 cal.). Monte Carlo-style stock with cheekpiece, black forend tip, grip cap, checkered pistol grip and forearm, quick-detachable sling swivels. Value shown is for rifle without sights. Discontinued 1958.

Weatherby Deluxe Rifle $825
Same general specifications as Deluxe Magnum, except chambered for standard calibers such as 270, 30-06, etc. Discontinued 1958.

Weatherby Fiberguard Rifle $395
Same general specifications as Vanguard except for fiberglass stock and matte metal finish.

Weatherby Fibermark Rifle $650
Same general specifications as Mark V except with molded fiberglass stock, finished in a non-glare black wrinkle finish. The metal is finished in a non-glare matte finish.

Weatherby Mark V Deluxe Bolt Action Sporting Rifle
Mark V action, right or left hand. Calibers: 22/250, 30-06; 224 Weatherby Varmintmaster; 240, 257, 270, 7mm, 300, 340, 378, 460 Weatherby Magnums. Box magazine holds 2 to 5 cartridges depending upon caliber. 24- or 26-inch barrel. Weight: 6½ to 10½ pounds. Monte Carlo-style stock with cheekpiece, skip checkering, forend tip, pistol-grip cap, recoil pad, QD swivels. Values shown are for rifles without sights. Made in Germany (1958-69), Japan (1970 to date).

Calibers 22/250, 224	**$600**
Caliber 378 Weatherby Magnum	**695**
Caliber 460 Weatherby Magnum	**795**
Other calibers	**625**
Add for left-hand action	**50**
Deduct 30% if Japanese-made	

Weatherby Mark V Euromark Bolt Action Rifle $750
Same general specifications as other Mark V rifles, except has hand-rubbed, satin oil finish Claro walnut stock and non-glare special process blue matte barreled action. Left-hand models available. Made from 1986 to date.

Weatherby Mark V Lazermark Rifle $695
Same general specifications as Mark V except with lazer-carved stock.

Weatherby Mark V Safari Grade Rifle $1695
Same general specifications as Mark V except extra capacity magazine, barrel sling swivel, and express rear sight, typical "Safari" style.

Weatherby Mark XXII Deluxe 22 Automatic Sporter Clip-fed Model $275
Semiautomatic with single shot selector. Caliber: 22 Long Rifle. 5- and 10-shot clip magazines. 24-inch barrel. Weight: 6 pounds. Folding leaf open rear sight, ramp front sight. Monte Carlo-type stock with cheekpiece, pistol grip, forend tip, grip cap, skip checkering, QD swivels. Introduced 1964. Made in Italy 1964-69; in Japan, 1970 to 1981; in the U.S., 1982 to date.

Weatherby Mark XXII, Tubular Magazine Model $280
Same as Mark XXII, Clip-fed Model, except has 15-shot tubular magazine. Made in Japan 1973 to 1981; in the U.S., 1982 to date.

Weatherby Vanguard Bolt Action Sporting Rifle (I) $340
Mauser-type action. Calibers: 243 Win., 25-06, 270 Win., 7mm Rem. Mag., 30-06, 300 Win. Mag. 5-shot magazine (3-shot in magnum calibers). 24-inch barrel. Weight: 7 lbs. 14 oz. No sights. Monte Carlo-type stock with cheekpiece, rosewood forend tip and pistol-grip cap, checkering, rubber butt pad, QD swivels. Made in Japan 1970 to 1984.

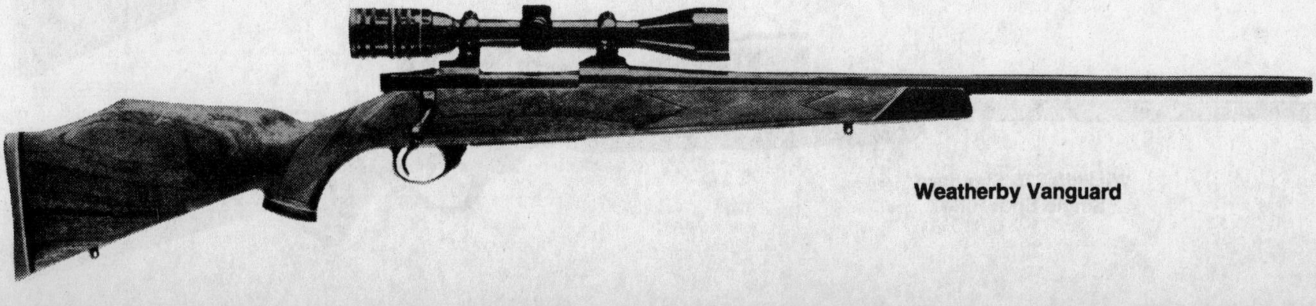

Weatherby Vanguard

Weatherby Vanguard VGX

Weatherby Vanguard VGL Bolt Action Sporting Rifle $300
Same general specifications as standard Vanguard, except has shorter action and lighter weight ($6\frac{1}{2}$ pounds). Made from 1985 to date.

Weatherby Vanguard VGS Bolt Action Sporting Rifle $300
Same general specifications as standard Vanguard, except has hand-bedded, hammer-forged barrel. Made from 1985 to date.

Weatherby Vanguard VGX Rifle $370
Same general specifications as early Vanguard except for higher grade finish.

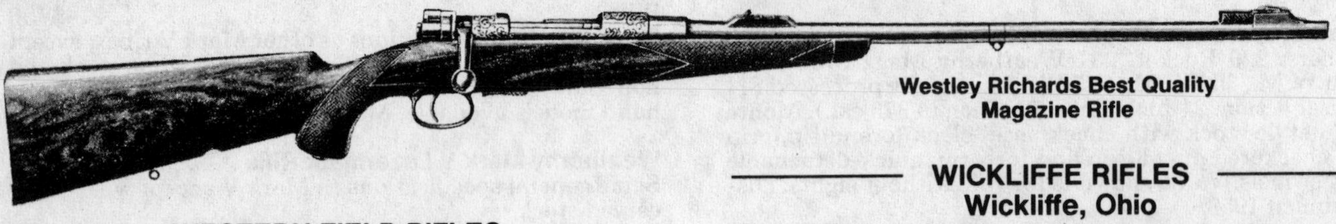

Westley Richards Best Quality
Magazine Rifle

WESTERN FIELD RIFLES

See listings under "W" for Montgomery Ward.

WESTLEY RICHARDS & CO., LTD.
London, England

Westley Richards Best Quality Double Rifle . . $17,500
Box lock, hammerless, ejector. Hand-detachable locks. Calibers: 30-06, 318 Accelerated Express, 375 Mag., 425 Mag. Express, 465 Nitro Express, 470 Nitro Express. 25-inch barrels. Weight: $8\frac{1}{2}$ to 11 pounds. Leaf rear sight, hooded front sight. French walnut stock with cheekpiece, checkered pistol grip and forend.

Westley Richards Best Quality Magazine Rifle $4,500
Mauser or Magnum Mauser action. Calibers: 7mm High Velocity, 30-06, 318 Accelerated Express, 375 Mag., 404 Nitro Express, 425 Mag. Barrel lengths: 24-inch; 7mm, 22-inch; 425 caliber, 25-inch. Weight: $7\frac{1}{4}$ to $9\frac{1}{4}$ pounds. Leaf rear sight, hooded front sight. French walnut sporting stock with cheekpiece, checkered pistol grip and forearm, horn forend tip, swivels.

WICKLIFFE RIFLES
Wickliffe, Ohio
Mfd. by Triple S Development Co., Inc.

Wickliffe '76 Commemorative Model $695
Limited edition of 100. Same as Deluxe Model, except has filled etching on receiver sidewalls, U.S. silver dollar inlaid in stock, 26-inch barrel only, comes in presentation case.

Wickliffe '76 Deluxe Model $375
Same as Standard Model, except 22-inch barrel in 30-06 only, has high-luster blued finish, fancy grade figured American walnut stock with nickel silver grip cap.

Wickliffe '76 Standard Model Single Shot Rifle . . $300
Falling block action. Calibers: 22 Hornet, 223 Rem., 22-250, 243 Win., 25-06, 308 Win., 30-06, 45-70. 22-inch lightweight barrel (243 and 308 only) or 26-inch heavy sporter barrel. Weight: $6\frac{3}{4}$ or $8\frac{1}{2}$ pounds, depending upon barrel. No sights. Select American walnut Monte Carlo stock with right or left cheekpiece and pistol grip, semi-beavertail forearm. Made from 1976 to date.

TED WILLIAMS RIFLES

See Sears, Roebuck and Company.

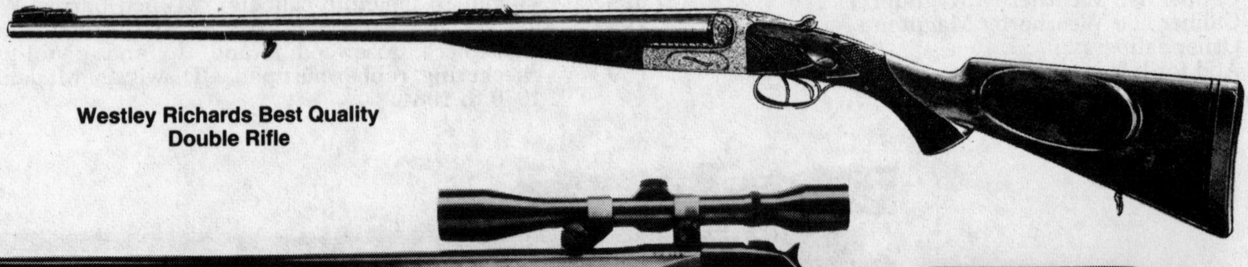

Westley Richards Best Quality
Double Rifle

Wickliffe '76 Standard
Single Shot Rifle

WINCHESTER RIFLES
New Haven, Connecticut

Formerly Winchester Repeating Arms Co. Now mfd. by Winchester Western Div., Olin Corp., and by U.S. Repeating Arms Co. both of New Haven, Conn.

Winchester Model 02 Bolt Action Single Shot Rifle $215
Takedown. Basically the same as Model 1900 with minor improvements. Calibers: 22 Short and Long, 22 Extra Long, 22 Long Rifle. Weight: 3 pounds. Made 1902 to 1931.

Winchester [Model 02] Thumb Trigger Bolt Action Single Shot Rifle $345
Takedown. Same as Model 02 except fired by pressing a button behind the cocking piece. Made from 1904 to 1923.

Winchester Model 03 Self-Loading Rifle $275
Takedown. Caliber: 22 Win. Auto Rimfire. 10-shot tubular magazine in buttstock. 20-inch barrel. Weight: 5¾ pounds. Open rear sight, bead front sight. Plain straight-grip stock and forearm (stock illustrated was extra-cost option). Made 1903 to 1936.

Winchester Model 04 Bolt Action Single Shot Rifle $215
Similar to Model 02. Takedown. Caliber: 22 Short, Long, Extra Long, Long Rifle. 21-inch barrel. Weight: 4 pounds. Made 1904 to 1931.

Winchester Model 05 Self-Loading Rifle $225
Takedown. Calibers: 32 Win. S.L., 35 Win. S.L. 5- or 10-shot detachable box magazine. 22-inch barrel. Weight: 7½ pounds. Open rear sight, bead front sight. Plain pistol-grip stock and forearm. Made 1905 to 1920.

Winchester Model 06 Slide Action Repeater $410
Takedown. Visible hammer. Caliber: 22 Short, Long, Long Rifle. Tubular magazine holds 20 Short, 16 Long or 14 Long Rifle. 20-inch barrel. Weight: 5 pounds. Open rear sight, bead front sight. Straight-grip stock and grooved forearm. Made 1906 to 1932.

Winchester Model 07 Self-Loading Rifle $330
Takedown. Caliber: 351 Win. S.L. 5- or 10-shot detachable box magazine. 20-inch barrel. Weight: 7¾ pounds. Open rear sight, bead front sight. Plain pistol-grip stock and forearm. Made 1907 to 1957.

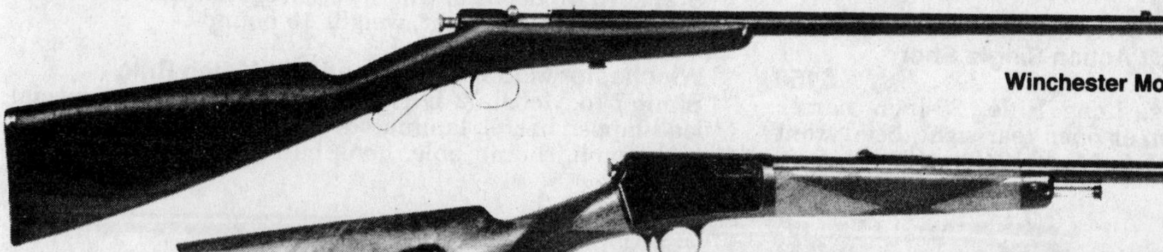
Winchester Model 02

Winchester Model 03

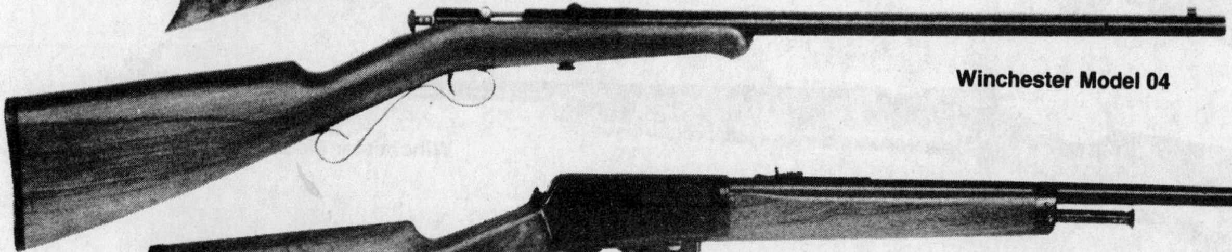
Winchester Model 04

Winchester Model 05

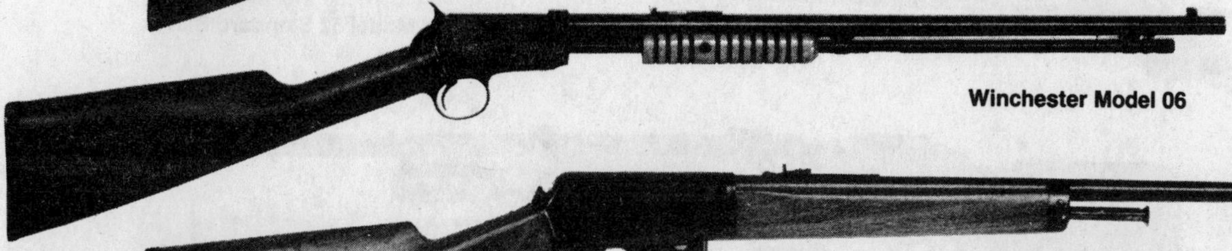
Winchester Model 06

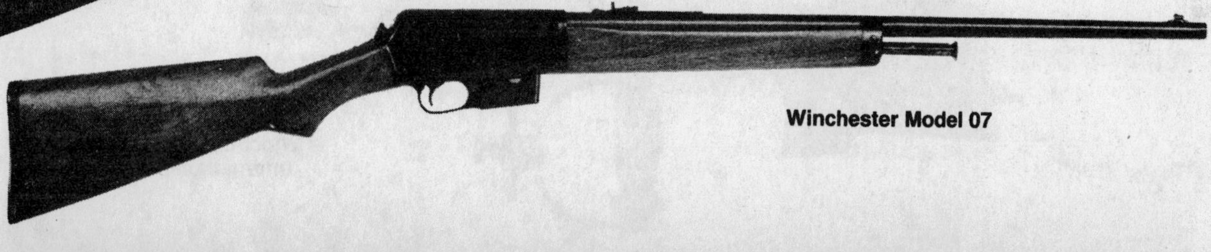
Winchester Model 07

Winchester Model 10

Winchester Model 10 Self-Loading Rifle $390
Takedown. Caliber: 401 Win. S.L. 4-shot detachable box magazine. 20-inch barrel. Weight: 8½ pounds. Open rear sight, bead front sight. Plain pistol-grip stock and forearm. Made 1910 to 1936.

Winchester Model 43 Bolt Action Sporting Rifle . . $470
Standard Grade. Calibers: 218 Bee, 22 Hornet, 25-20, 32-20 (latter two discontinued 1950). 3-shot detachable box magazine. 24-inch barrel. Weight: 6 pounds. Open rear sight, bead front sight on hooded ramp. Plain pistol-grip stock with swivels. Made 1949 to 1957.

Winchester Model 43 Special Grade $650
Same as Standard Model 43, except has checkered pistol grip and forearm, grip cap.

Winchester Model 47 Bolt Action Single Shot Rifle $150
Caliber: 22 Short, Long, Long Rifle. 25-inch barrel. Weight: 5½ pounds. Peep or open rear sight, bead front sight. Plain pistol-grip stock. Made 1949 to 1954.

Winchester Model 52 Bolt Action Target Rifle
Standard Barrel. First type. Caliber: 22 Long Rifle. 5-shot box magazine. 28-inch barrel. Weight: 8¾ pounds. Folding leaf peep rear sight, blade front sight, standard sights, various other combinations available. Scope bases. Semi-military type target stock with pistol grip; original model has grasping grooves in forearm; higher comb and semi-beavertail forearm on later models. Numerous changes were made in this model, the most important being the adoption of the speed lock in 1929; Model 52 rifles produced prior to this change are generally referred to as "slow lock" models. Last arms of this type bore serial numbers followed by the letter "A." Made 1919 to 1937.
Slow Lock Model **$425**
Speed Lock Model **575**

Winchester Model 52 Heavy Barrel $595
First type. Speed lock. Same general specifications as Standard Model 52 of this type, except has heavier barrel, Lyman 17G front sight, weighs 10 pounds.

Winchester Model 52 International Match Rifle
Similar to Model 52-D Heavy Barrel, except has special lead-lapped barrel, laminated "free rifle" style stock with high comb, thumb hole, hook butt plate, accessory rail,

Winchester Model 43 Special Grade

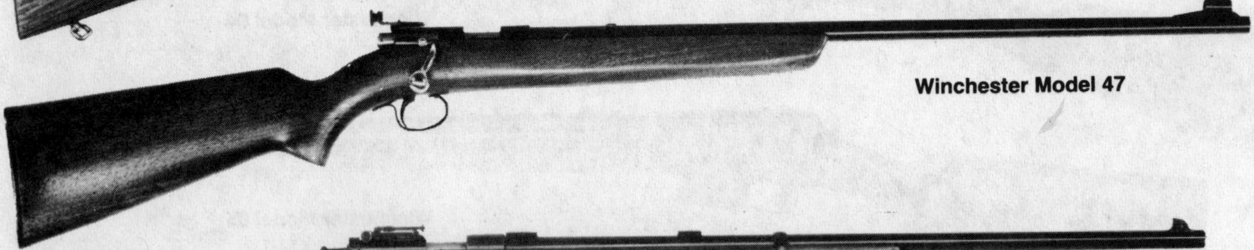

Winchester Model 47

Winchester Model 52 Standard Barrel

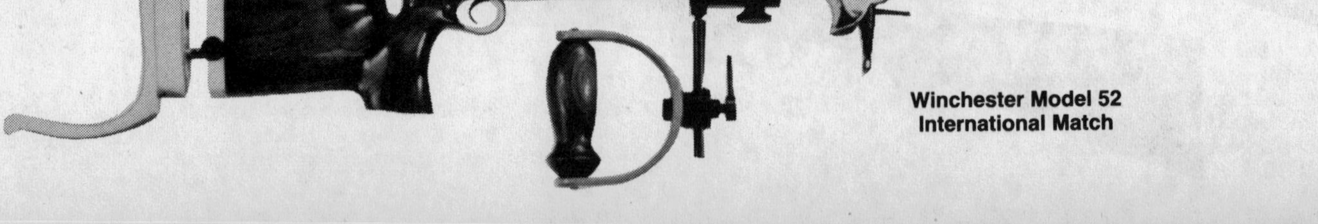

Winchester Model 52
International Match

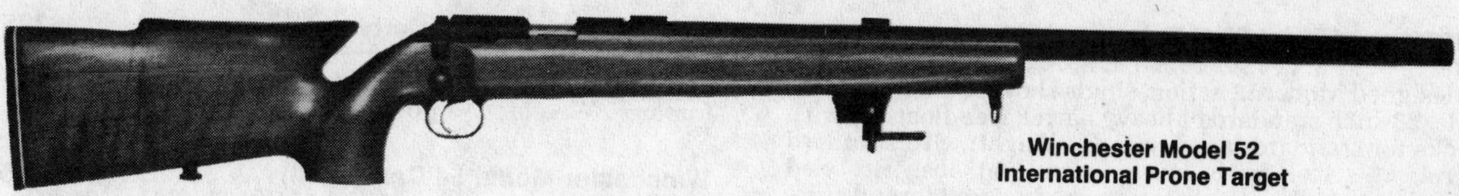

Winchester Model 52 International Prone Target

Winchester Model 52B Standard Barrel

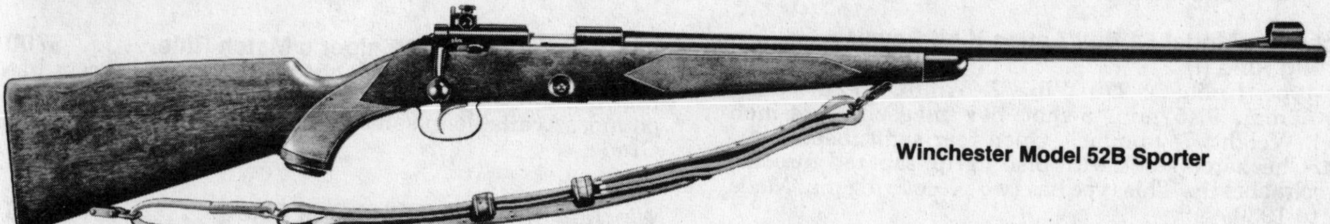

Winchester Model 52B Sporter

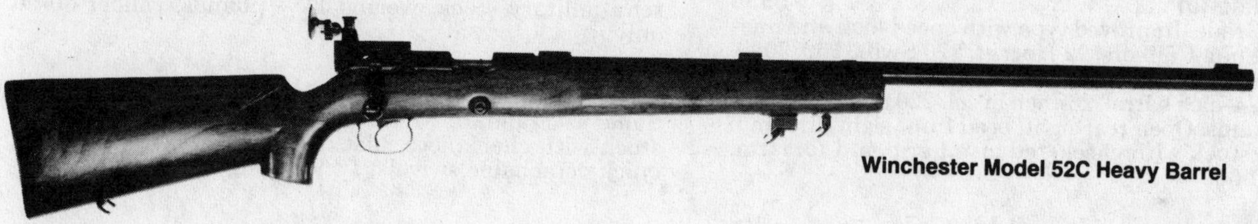

Winchester Model 52C Heavy Barrel

Winchester Model 52 International Match Rifle (cont.)
handstop/swivel assembly, palm rest. Weight: 13½ pounds. Made 1969 to 1978.
With standard trigger **$650**
With Kenyon or I.S.U. trigger **750**

Winchester Model 52 International Prone Target Rifle **$695**
Similar to Model 52-D Heavy Barrel, except has special lead-lapped barrel, prone stock with fuller pistol grip, roll-over cheekpiece removable for bore-cleaning. Weight: 11½ pounds. Made from 1975 to date.

Winchester Model 52 Sporting Rifle **$1580**
First type. Same as Standard Model 52 of this type, except has lightweight 24-inch barrel, Lyman No. 48 receiver sight and gold bead front sight on hooded ramp, deluxe checkered sporting stock with cheekpiece, black forend tip, etc. Weight: 7¾ pounds.

Winchester Model 52-B Bolt Action Target Rifle **$425**
Standard Barrel. Extensively redesigned action. Supplied with choice of "Target" stock, an improved version of the previous Model 52 stock, or "Marksman" stock with high comb, full pistol grip and beavertail forearm. Weight: 9 pounds. Offered with a wide choice of target sight combinations (Lyman, Marble-Goss, Redfield, Vaver, Winchester); value shown is for rifle less sight equipment. Other specifications as shown for first type. Made 1935 to 1947.

Winchester Model 52-B Bull Gun **$625**
Same general specifications as Standard Model 52-B, except has extra heavy barrel, Marksman stock only, weighs 12 pounds.

Winchester Model 52-B Heavy Barrel **$610**
Same general specifications as Standard Model 52-B, except has heavier barrel, weighs 11 pounds.

Winchester Model 52-B Sporting Rifle **$675**
Model 52-B action, otherwise same as Model 52 Sporting Rifle.

Winchester Model 52-C Bolt Action Target Rifle **$540**
Heavy Barrel. Improved action with "Micro-Motion" trigger mechanism and new type "Marksman" stock. General specifications same as shown for previous models. Made 1947 to 1961. Value shown is for rifle less sights.

Winchester Model 52-C Bull Gun **$650**
Same general specifications as Heavy Barrel Model, except has extra heavy "bull" barrel, weighs 12 pounds. Made 1952 to 1961.

Winchester Model 52-C Standard Barrel **$565**
Same general specifications as Heavy Barrel Model, except has standard weight barrel, weighs 9¾ pounds. Made 1947 to 1961.

Winchester Model 52-D Bolt Action Target Rifle $545
Redesigned Model 52 action, single shot. Caliber: 22 Long Rifle. 28-inch standard or heavy barrel, free-floating, with blocks for standard target scopes. Weight: with standard barrel, $9\frac{3}{4}$ lbs.; with heavy barrel, 11 lbs. Restyled Marksman stock with accessory channel and forend stop, rubber butt plate. Made 1961 to 1978. Value shown is for rifle without sights.

Winchester Model 53 Lever Action Repeater . . . $925
Modification of Model 92. Solid frame or takedown. Calibers: 25/20, 32/20, 44/40. 6-shot tubular half-magazine in solid frame model. 7-shot in takedown. 22-inch nickel steel barrel. Weight: $5\frac{1}{2}$ to $6\frac{1}{2}$ pounds. Open rear sight, bead front sight. Redesigned straight-grip stock and forearm. Made 1924 to 1932.

Winchester Model 54 Bolt Action High Power Sporting Rifle (I) $495
First type. Calibers: 270 Win., 7×57mm, 30-30, 30-06, 7.65×53mm, 9×57mm. 5-shot box magazine. 24-inch barrel. Weight: $7\frac{3}{4}$ pounds. Open rear sight, bead front sight. Checkered stock with pistol grip, tapered forearm with schnabel tip. This type has two-piece firing pin. Made 1925 to 1930.

Winchester Model 54 Bolt Action High Power Sporting Rifle (II) $550
Standard Grade. Improved type with speed lock and one-piece firing pin. Calibers: 22 Hornet, 220 Swift, 250/3000, 257 Roberts, 270 Win., 7×57mm, 30-06. 5-shot box magazine. 24-inch barrel, 26-inch in cal. 220 Swift. Weight: about 8 pounds. Open rear sight, bead front sight on ramp. NRA-type stock with checkered pistol grip and forearm. Made 1930-36.

Winchester Model 54 Carbine (I) $325
First type. Same as Model 54 rifle, except has 20-inch barrel, plain lightweight stock with grasping grooves in forearm. Weight: $7\frac{1}{4}$ pounds.

Winchester Model 54 Carbine (II) $595
Improved type. Same as Model 54 Standard Grade Sporting Rifle of this type, except has 20-inch barrel. Weight: about $7\frac{1}{2}$ pounds. This model may have either NRA-type stock or the lightweight stock found on the first-type Model 54 Carbine.

Winchester Model 54 National Match Rifle $710
Same as Standard Model 54, except has Lyman sights, scope bases, Marksman-type target stock, weighs $9\frac{1}{2}$ pounds. Same calibers as Standard Model.

Winchester Model 54 Sniper's Match Rifle $700
Similar to the earlier Model 54 Sniper's Rifle, except has Marksman-type target stock, scope bases, weighs $12\frac{1}{2}$ pounds. Available in same calibers as Model 54 Standard Grade.

Winchester Model 54 Sniper's Rifle $600
Same as Standard Model 54, except has heavy 26-inch barrel, Lyman #48 rear peep sight and blade front sight, semi-military stock, weighs $11\frac{3}{4}$ pounds, caliber 30-06 only.

Winchester Model 54 Super Grade $1095
Same as Standard Model 54 Sporter, except has deluxe stock with cheekpiece, black forend tip, pistol-grip cap, quick detachable swivels, 1-inch sling strap.

Winchester Model 52D Heavy Barrel

Winchester Model 53

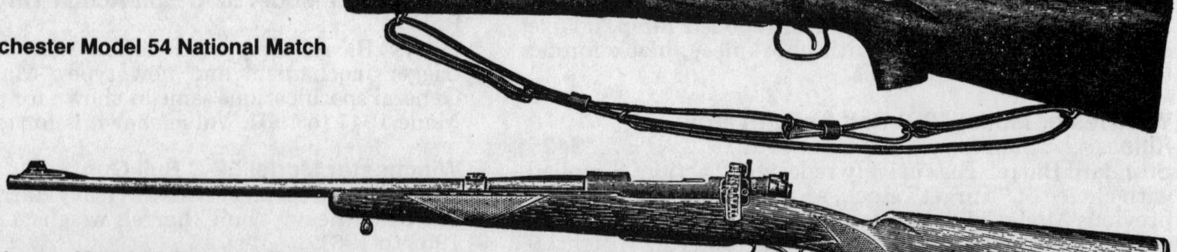

Winchester Model 54 National Match

Winchester Model 54 Standard Grade Improved Type

Winchester Model 54 Target Rifle **$750**
Same as Standard Model 54, except has 24-inch medium-weight barrel (26-inch in cal. 220 Swift), Lyman sights, scope bases, Marksman-type target stock, weighs 10½ pounds, same calibers as Standard Model.

Winchester Model 55 "Automatic" Single Shot Rifle **$100**
Caliber: 22 Short, Long, Long Rifle. 22-inch barrel. Open rear sight, bead front sight. One-piece walnut stock. Weight: about 5½ pounds. Made 1958 to 1960.

Winchester Model 55 Lever Action Repeater
Modification of Model 94. Solid frame or takedown. Calibers: 25/35, 30/30, 32 Win. Special. 3-shot tubular half magazine. 24-inch nickel steel barrel. Weight: about 7 pounds. Open rear sight, bead front sight. Made 1924 to 1932.

Straight Grip	**$ 680**
Pistol Grip	**1295**

Winchester Model 56 Bolt Action Sporting Rifle . . **$325**
Solid frame. Caliber: 22 Long Rifle, 22 Short. 5- or 10-shot detachable box magazine. 22-inch barrel. Weight: 4¾ pounds. Open rear sight, bead front sight. Plain pistol-grip stock with schnabel forend. Made 1926-29.

Winchester Model 57 Bolt Action Target Rifle . . **$495**
Solid frame. Same as Model 56, except available (until 1929) in 22 Short as well as Long Rifle, has semi-military style target stock, swivels and web sling, Lyman peep rear sight, blade front sight, weighs 5 lbs. Mfd. 1926 to 1936.

Winchester Model 54 Super Grade

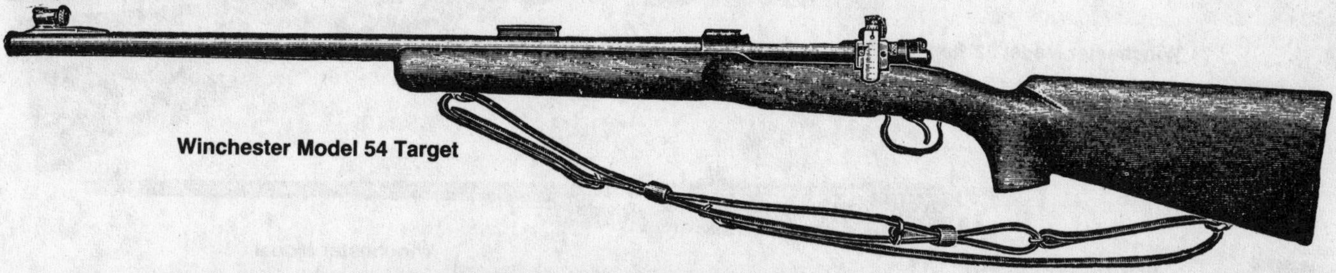

Winchester Model 54 Target

Winchester Model 55 "Automatic" Single Shot

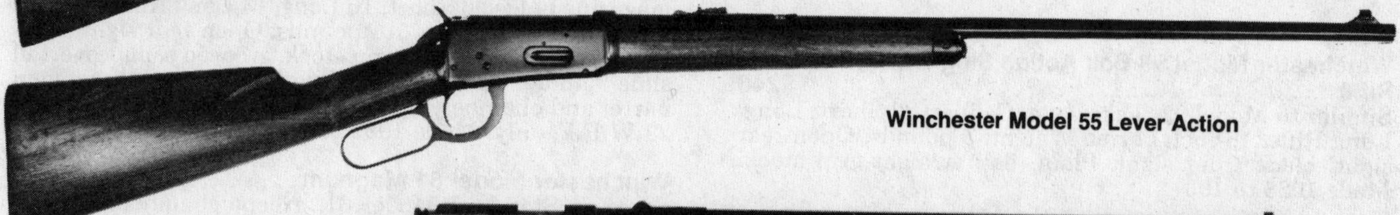

Winchester Model 55 Lever Action

Winchester Model 56

Winchester Model 57 Target

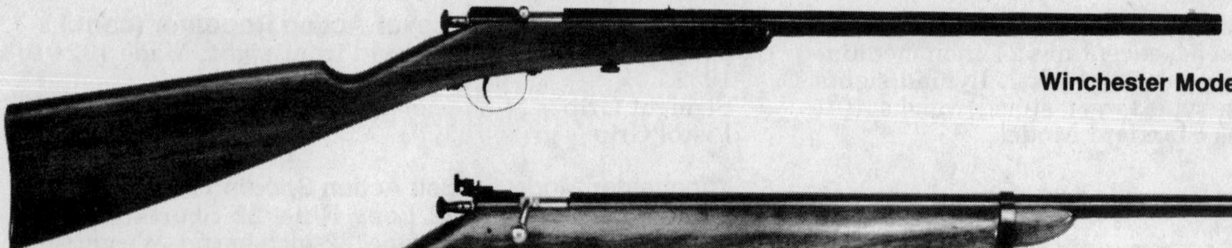

Winchester Model 58

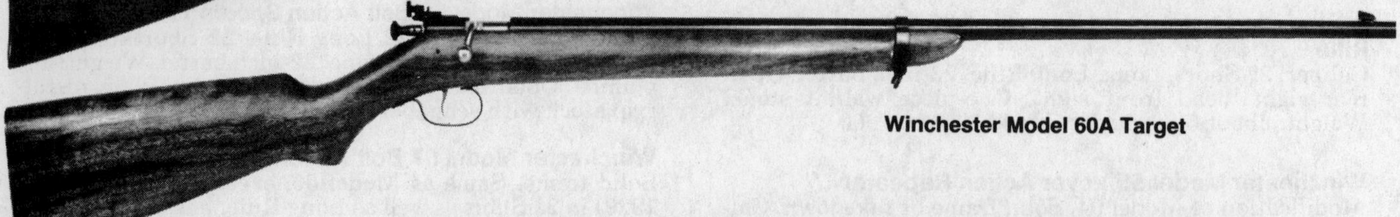

Winchester Model 60A Target

Winchester Model 61 Repeater

Winchester Model 62 Repeater

Winchester Model 63

Winchester Model 58 Bolt Action Single Shot Rifle $240
Similar to Model 02. Takedown. Caliber: 22 Short, Long, Long Rifle. 18-inch barrel. Weight: 3 pounds. Open rear sight, blade front sight. Plain, flat, straight-grip stock. Made 1928 to 1931.

Winchester Model 59 Bolt Action Single Shot Rifle $410
Improved version of Model 58, has 23-inch barrel, redesigned stock with pistol grip, weighs 4½ pounds. Made in 1930.

Winchester Model 60 Bolt Action Single Shot Rifle $125
Redesign of Model 59. Caliber: 22 Short, Long, Long Rifle. 23-inch barrel (27-inch after 1933). Weight: 4¼ pounds. Open rear sight, blade front sight. Plain stock with pistol grip. Made 1930-34.

Winchester Model 60A Target Rifle $495
Essentially the same as Model 60, except has Lyman peep rear sight and square top front sight, semi-military target stock and web sling, weighs 5½ pounds. Made 1932-39.

Winchester Model 61 Hammerless Slide Action Repeater $465
Takedown. Caliber: 22 Short, Long, Long Rifle. Tubular magazine holds 20 Short, 16 Long, 14 Long Rifle. 24-inch round barrel. Weight: 5½ pounds. Open rear sight, bead front sight. Plain pistol-grip stock, grooved semibeavertail slide handle. Also available with 24-inch full-octagon barrel and chambered for 22 L.R. only, 22 Short only or 22 W.R.F. only. Made 1932 to 1963.

Winchester Model 61 Magnum $550
Same as Standard Model 61, except chambered for 22 R.F. Magnum cartridge; magazine holds 12 rounds. Made 1960-63.

Winchester Model 62 Visible Hammer Slide Action Repeater $395
Modernized version of Model 1890. Caliber: 22 Short, Long, Long Rifle. 23-inch barrel. Weight: 5½ pounds. Plain straight-grip stock, grooved semibeavertail slide handle. Also available in Gallery Model chambered for 22 Short only. Made 1932 to 1959.

Winchester Model 63 Self-Loading Rifle $525
Takedown. Caliber: 22 Long Rifle High Speed only. 10-shot tubular magazine in buttstock. 23-inch barrel. Weight: 5½ pounds. Open rear sight, bead front sight. Plain pistol-grip stock and forearm. Originally available with 20-inch barrel as well as 23-inch. Made 1933 to 1959.

Winchester Model 64 Deer Rifle

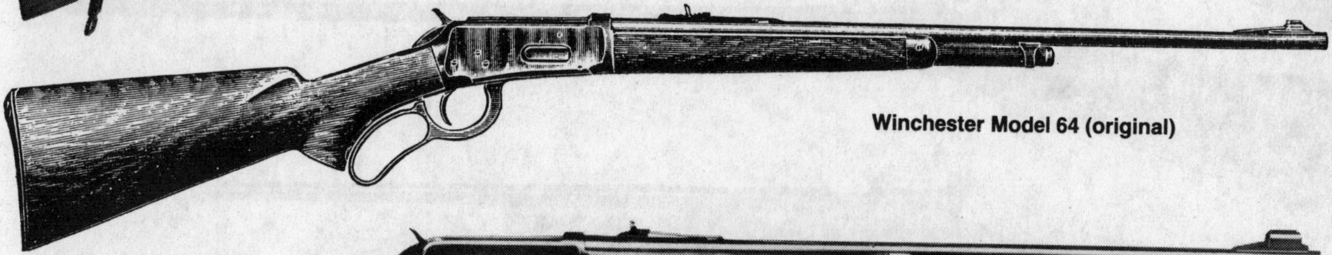

Winchester Model 64 (original)

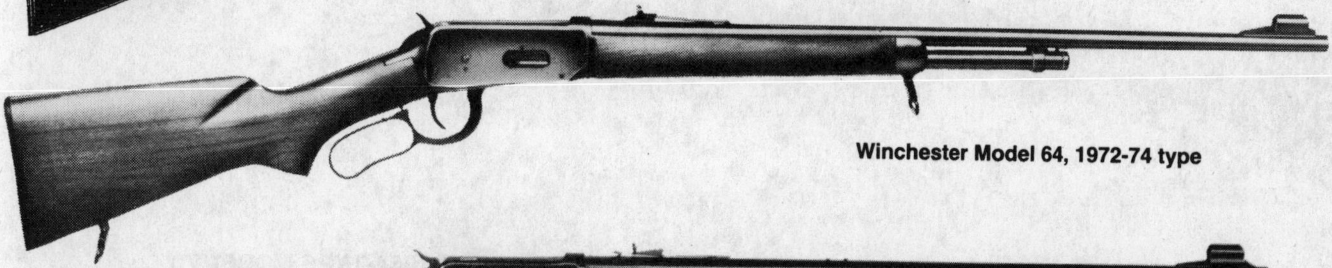

Winchester Model 64, 1972-74 type

Winchester Model 65

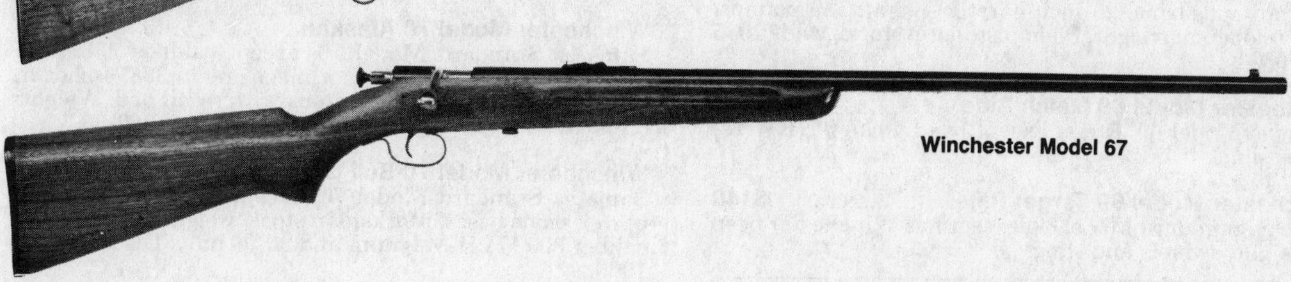

Winchester Model 67

Winchester Model 64 Deer Rifle $805
Same as Standard Model 64, calibers 30-30 and 32 Win. Special, except has checkered pistol grip and semibeavertail forearm, swivels and sling, weighs 7¾ pounds. Made 1933 to 1956.

Winchester Model 64 Lever Action Repeater
Standard Grade. Improved version of Models 94 and 55. Solid frame. Calibers: 25/35, 30-30, 32 Win. Special. 5-shot tubular ⅔ magazine. 20- or 24-inch barrel. Weight: about 7 pounds. Open rear sight, bead front sight on ramp with sight cover. Plain pistol-grip stock and forearm. Made from 1933 to 1956. Production resumed in 1972 (caliber 30-30, 24-inch barrel); discontinued 1974.
Original model **$505**
1972-74 model **285**

Winchester Model 64—219 Zipper $1395
Same as Standard Grade Model 64, except has 26-inch barrel, peep rear sight. Made 1937 to 1947.

Winchester Model 65 Lever Action Repeater . . $1195
Improved version of Model 53. Solid frame. Calibers: 25-20 and 32-20. Six-shot tubular half-magazine. 22-inch barrel. Weight: 6½ pounds. Open rear sight, bead front sight on ramp base. Plain pistol-grip stock and forearm. Made 1933 to 1947.

Winchester Model 65—218 Bee $1500
Same as Standard Model 65, except has 24-inch barrel, peep rear sight. Made 1938 to 1947.

Winchester Model 67 Bolt Action Single Shot Rifle $95
Takedown. Calibers: 22 Short, Long, Long Rifle, 22 L.R. shot (smoothbore), 22 W.R.F. 27-inch barrel. Weight: 5 pounds. Open rear sight, bead front sight. Plain pistol-grip stock (original model had grasping grooves in forearm). Made 1934 to 1963.

Winchester Model 67 Boy's Rifle $160
Same as Standard Model 67, except has shorter stock, 20-inch barrel, weighs 4¼ pounds.

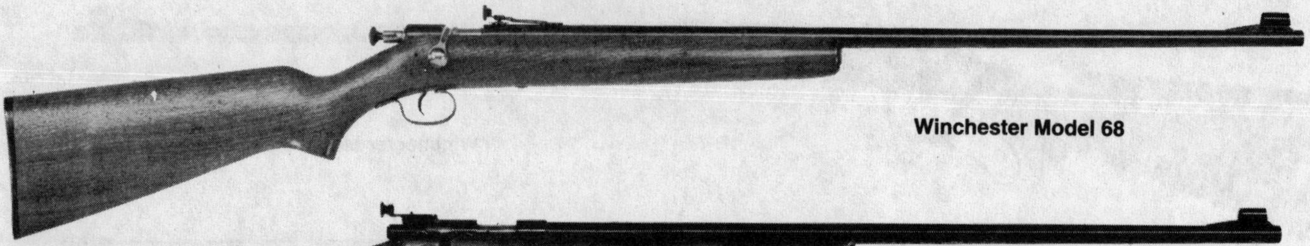

Winchester Model 68

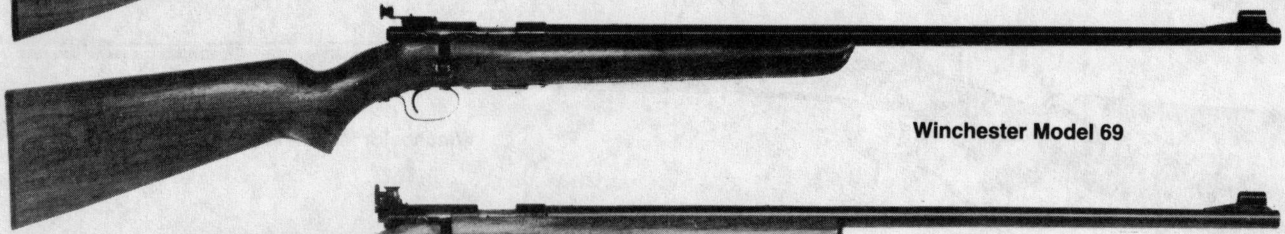

Winchester Model 69

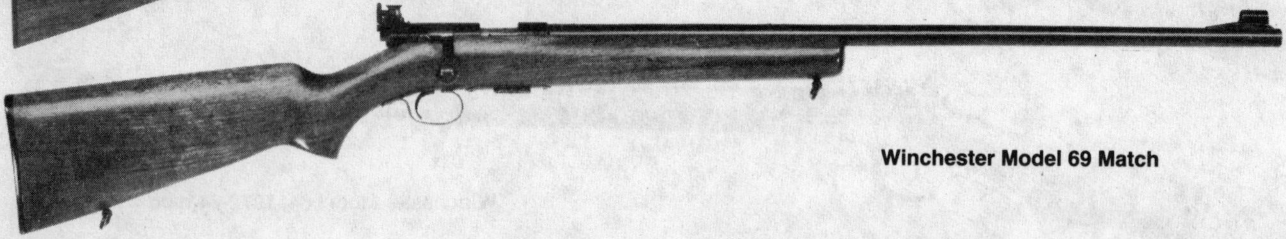

Winchester Model 69 Match

Winchester Model 68 Bolt Action Single Shot Rifle $140
Same as Model 67, except has rear peep sight. Made 1934 to 1946.

Winchester Model 69 Bolt Action Repeater $165
Takedown. Caliber: 22 Short, Long, Long Rifle. 5- or 10-shot box magazine. 25-inch barrel. Weight: 5½ pounds. Peep or open rear sight. Plain pistol-grip stock. Made 1935 to 1963.

Winchester Model 69 Match Rifle $305
Same as Model 69 Target except has Lyman #57EW receiver sight.

Winchester Model 69 Target Rifle $140
Same as Standard Model 69, except has Winchester peep rear sight, swivels and sling.

> *Note:* Introduced in 1937, the Model 70 Bolt Action Repeater was offered in a number of styles and calibers. Only minor design changes were made over a period of 27 years, and more than one-half million of these rifles were sold. In 1964, the original Model 70 was superseded by a revised version with redesigned action, improved bolt, swaged barrel, restyled stock (barrel free-floating). This model again underwent major changes in 1972—most visible: new stock with contrasting forend tip and grip cap, cut checkering (instead of impressed as in predecessor), knurled bolt handle. Action (machined from a solid block of steel) and barrel are chrome molybdenum steel.

PRE-1964-TYPE MODEL 70

Winchester Model 70 African Rifle $2395
Same general specifications as Super Grade Model 70, except has 25-inch barrel, 3-shot magazine, Monte Carlo stock with recoil pad. Weight: about 9½ pounds. Caliber: 458 Winchester Magnum. Made 1956 to 1963.

Winchester Model 70 Alaskan $1240
Same as Standard Model 70, except calibers 338 Win. Mag., 375 H&H Mag.; 3-shot magazine in 338, 4-shot in 375 caliber; 25-inch barrel; stock with recoil pad. Weight: 8 lbs. in 338; 8¾ lbs. in 375 caliber. Made 1960-63.

Winchester Model 70 Bull Gun $625
Same as Standard Model 70, except has heavy 28-inch barrel, scope bases, Marksman stock, weighs 13¼ pounds, caliber 300 H&H Magnum and 30-06 only. Discontinued 1963.

Winchester Model 70 Featherweight Sporter . . . $675
Same as Standard Model 70, except has redesigned stock and 22-inch barrel, aluminum trigger guard, floorplate and butt plate. Calibers: 243 Win., 264 Win. Mag., 270 Win., 308 Win., 30-06, 358 Win. Weight: about 6½ pounds. Made 1952 to 1963.

Winchester Model 70 National Match Rifle $895
Same as Standard Model 70, except has scope bases, Marksman-type target stock, weighs 9½ pounds, caliber 30-06 only. Discontinued 1960.

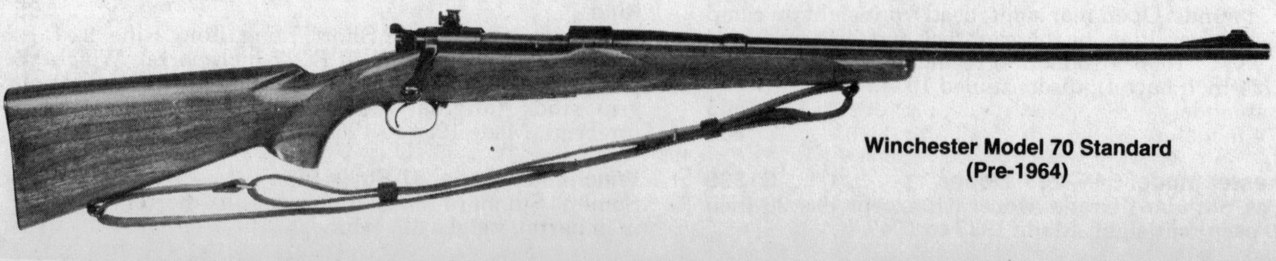

Winchester Model 70 Standard (Pre-1964)

Winchester Model 70 Standard Grade **$660**
Calibers: 22 Hornet, 220 Swift, 243 Win., 250-3000, 257 Roberts, 270 Win., 7×57mm, 30-06, 308 Win., 300 H&H Mag., 375 H&H Mag. 5-shot box magazine (4-shot in Magnum calibers). 24-inch barrel standard; 26-inch in 220 Swift and 300 Mag.; 25-inch in 375 Mag.; at one time a 20-inch barrel was available. Open rear sight, hooded ramp front sight. Checkered walnut stock; Monte Carlo comb standard on later production. Weight: from 7¾ pounds depending upon caliber and barrel length. Made 1937 to 1963.

Winchester Model 70 Super Grade **$1495**
Same as Standard Grade Model 70, except has deluxe stock with cheekpiece, black forend tip, pistol-grip cap, quick detachable swivels, sling. Discontinued 1960.

Winchester Model 70 Super Grade Featherweight **$1480**
Same as Standard Grade Featherweight except has deluxe stock with cheekpiece, black forend tip, pistol-grip cap, quick detachable swivels, sling. Discontinued 1960.

Winchester Model 70 Target Rifle **$875**
Same as Standard Model 70, except has 24-inch medium-weight barrel, scope bases, Marksman stock, weight about 10½ pounds. Originally offered in all of the Model 70 calibers, this rifle later was available in calibers 243 Win. and 30-06. Discontinued 1963.

Winchester Model 70 Varmint Rifle **$795**
Same general specifications as Standard Model 70, except has 26-inch heavy barrel, scope bases, special varminter stock. Calibers: 220 Swift, 243 Win. Made 1956 to 1963.

Winchester Model 70 Westerner **$895**
Same as Standard Model 70, except calibers 264 Win. Mag., 300 Win. Mag.; 3-shot magazine; 26-inch barrel in former caliber, 24-inch in latter. Weight: about 8¼ pounds. Made 1960-63.

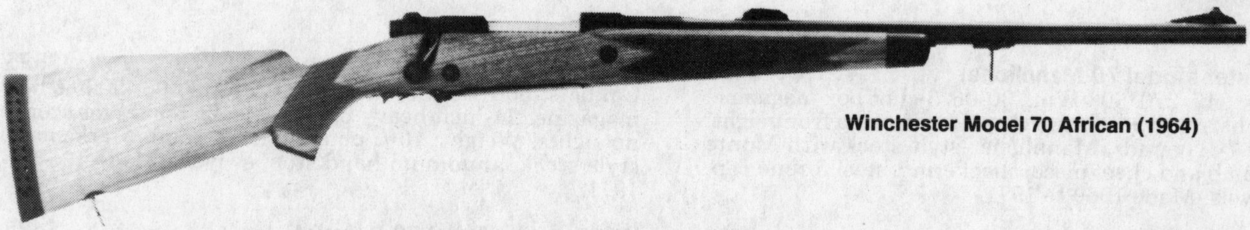

Winchester Model 70 African (1964)

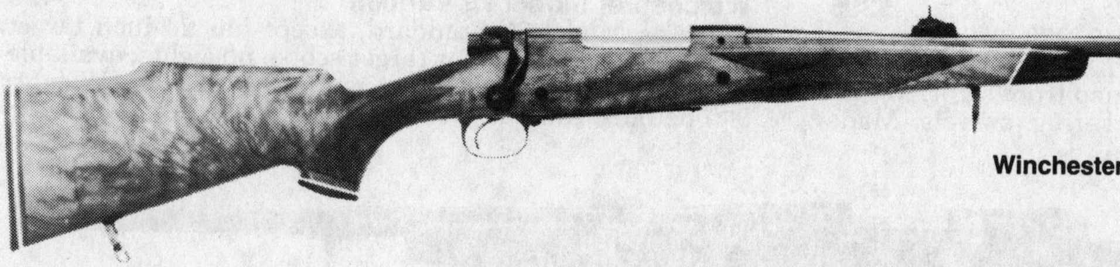

Winchester Model 70 Deluxe (1964)

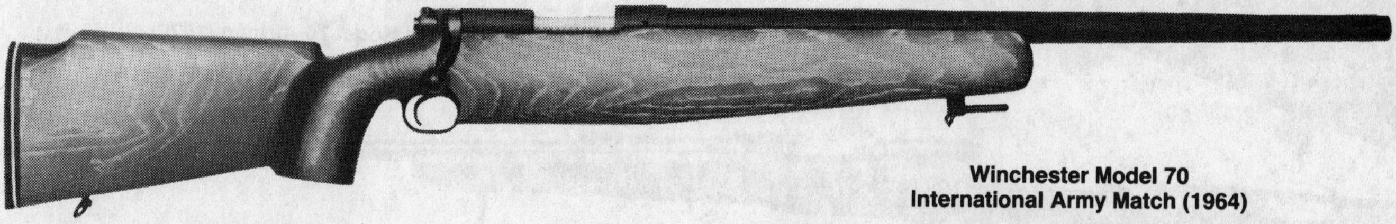

Winchester Model 70 International Army Match (1964)

1964-TYPE MODEL 70

Winchester Model 70 African **$595**
Caliber: 458 Win. Mag. 3-shot magazine. 22-inch barrel. Weight: 8½ pounds. Special "African" sights. Monte Carlo stock with ebony forend tip, hand-checkering, twin stock-reinforcing bolts, recoil pad, QD swivels. Made 1964 to 1971.

Winchester Model 70 Deluxe **$400**
Calibers: 243, 270 Win., 30-06, 300 Win. Mag. 5-shot box magazine (3-shot in Magnum). 22-inch barrel (24-inch in Magnum). Weight: 7½ pounds. Open rear sight, hooded ramp front sight, Monte Carlo stock with ebony forend tip, hand-checkering, QD swivels, recoil pad on Magnum. Made 1964 to 1971.

Winchester Model 70 International Army Match Rifle **$625**
Caliber: 308 Win. (7.62 NATO). 5-shot box magazine. 24-inch heavy barrel. Externally adjustable trigger. Weight: 11 pounds. ISU stock with military oil finish, forearm rail for standard accessories, vertically adjustable butt plate. Made in 1971. Value shown is for rifle without sights.

Winchester Model 70 Magnum
Calibers: 7mm Rem. Mag.; 264, 300, 338 Win. Mag.; 375 H&H Mag. 3-shot magazine. 24-inch barrel. Weight: 7¾ to 8½ pounds. Open rear sight, hooded ramp front sight. Monte Carlo stock with cheekpiece, checkering, twin stock-reinforcing bolts, recoil pad, swivels. Made 1964 to 1971.
Caliber 375 H&H Mag. **$400**
Other calibers **280**

Winchester Model 70 Mannlicher (1964)

Winchester Model 70 Standard (1964)

Winchester Model 70 Target (1964)

Winchester Model 70 Mannlicher $480
Calibers: 243, 270, 308 Win., 30-06. 5-shot box magazine. 19-inch barrel. Open rear sight, hooded ramp front sight. Weight: 7½ pounds. Mannlicher-style stock with Monte Carlo comb and cheekpiece, checkering, steel forend cap, QD swivels. Made 1969 to 1971.

Winchester Model 70 Standard $395
Calibers: 22-250, 222 Rem., 225, 243, 270, 308 Win., 30-06. 5-shot box magazine. 22-inch barrel. Weight: 7½ pounds. Open rear sight, hooded ramp front sight. Monte Carlo stock with cheekpiece, checkering, swivels. Made 1964 to 1971.

Winchester Model 70 Target $525
Calibers: 308 Win. (7.62 NATO) and 30-06. 5-shot box magazine. 24-inch heavy barrel. Blocks for target scope, no sights. Weight: 10¼ pounds. High comb Marksman-style stock, aluminum hand stop, swivels. Made 1964 to 1971.

Winchester Model 70 Varmint $425
Same as Model 70 Standard, except has 24-inch target weight barrel, blocks for target scope, no sights, available in calibers 22-250, 222 Rem., and 243 Win. only. Weight: 9¾ pounds. Made 1964 to 1971.

Winchester Model 70 African (1972)

Winchester Model 70 Golden 50th Anniversary Rifle

1972-TYPE MODEL 70

Winchester Model 70 African $580
Similar to Model 70 Magnum, except caliber 458 Win. Mag.; has 22-inch barrel, special African open rear sight, reinforced stock with ebony forend tip, detachable swivels and sling. Weight: about 8½ pounds. Made from 1972 to date.

Winchester Model 70 Golden 50th Anniversary Edition Bolt Action Rifle $895
Caliber: 300 Win. 3-shot magazine. 24-inch barrel. 44½ inches overall. Weight: 7¾ pounds. Checkered American walnut stock. Hand-engraved American scroll pattern on barrel, receiver, magazine cover, trigger guard and pistol grip cap. Adjustable rear sight, hooded front ramp sight. Inscription on barrel reads "The Rifleman's Rifle 1937-1987." Only 500 made from 1986 to 1987.

Winchester Model 70 International Army Match $600
Caliber: 308 Win. (7.62mm NATO). 5-shot magazine, clip slot in receiver bridge. 24-inch heavy barrel. Weight: 11 pounds. No sights. ISU target stock. Made from 1973 to date.

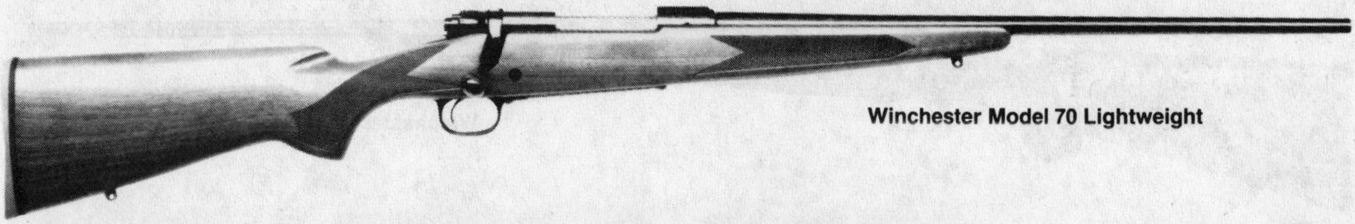

Winchester Model 70 Lightweight

Winchester Model 70 Magnum (1972)

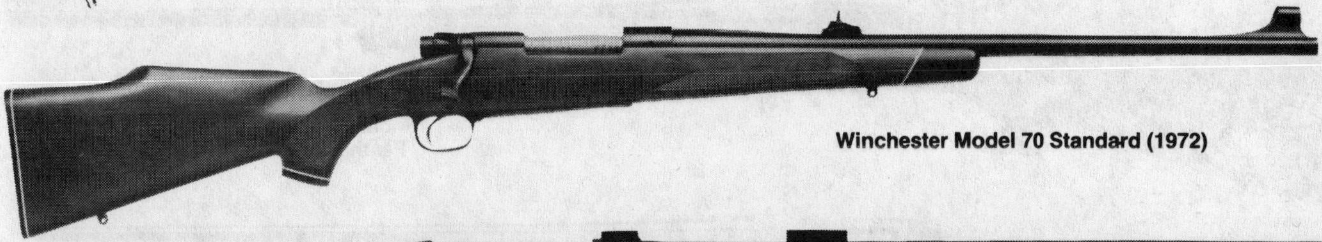

Winchester Model 70 Standard (1972)

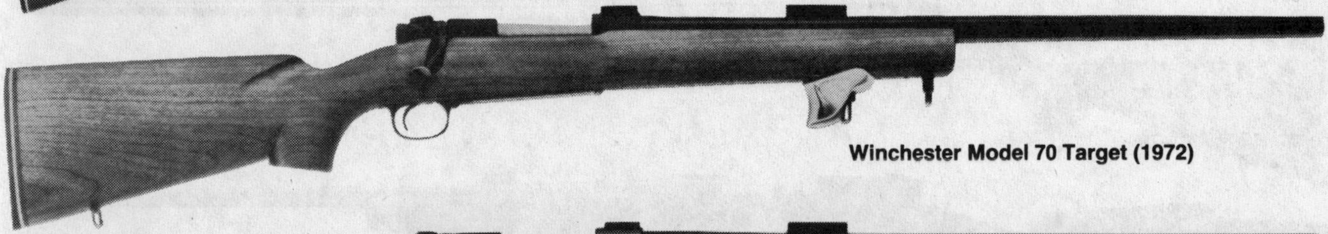

Winchester Model 70 Target (1972)

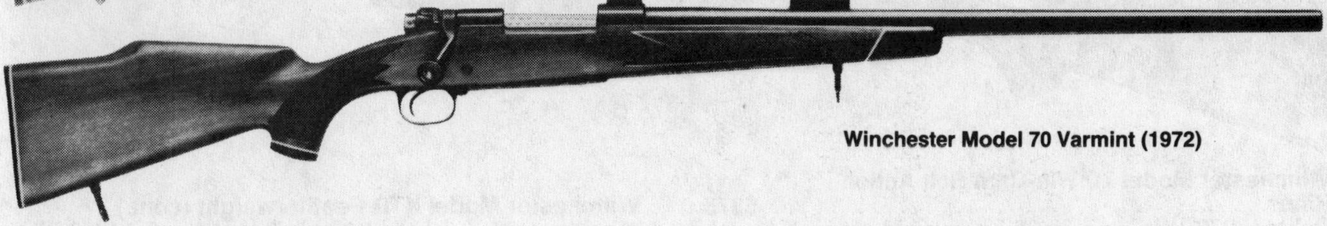

Winchester Model 70 Varmint (1972)

Winchester Model 70 Lightweight Bolt Action Rifle **$325**
Calibers: 22-250 and 223 Rem.; 243, 270 and 308 Win.; 30-06 Springfield. 5-shot magazine capacity (6-shot 223 Rem.). 22-inch barrel. 42 to 42½ inches overall. Weight: 6 to 6¼ pounds. Checkered classic straight stock. Sling swivel studs. Made from 1986 to date.

Winchester Model 70 Magnum
Same as Model 70, except has 3-shot magazine, 24-inch barrel, reinforced stock with recoil pad. Weight: about 7¾ pounds (except 8½ pounds in 375 H&H Mag.). Calibers: 264 Win. Mag., 7mm Rem. Mag., 300 Win. Mag., 338 Win. Mag., 375 H&H Mag. Made from 1972 to date.
375 H&H Magnum **$395**
Other magnum calibers **280**

Winchester Model 70 Standard **$325**
Same as Model 70A, except has 5-shot magazine, Monte Carlo stock with cheekpiece, black forend tip and pistol-

Winchester Model 70 Standard (cont.)
grip cap with white spacers, checkered pistol grip and forearm, detachable sling swivels. Same calibers plus 225 Win. Made from 1972 to date.

Winchester Model 70 Target **$525**
Calibers: 30-06 and 308 Win. (7.62mm NATO). 5-shot magazine. 26-inch heavy barrel. Weight: 10½ pounds. No sights. High-comb Marksman-style target stock, aluminum hand stop, swivels. Made from 1972 to date.

Winchester Model 70 Ultra Match **$500**
Similar to Model 70 Target, but custom grade; has 26-inch heavy barrel with deep counterbore, glass bedding, externally adjustable trigger. Made from 1972 to date.

Winchester Model 70 Varmint **$450**
Same as Model 70 Standard, except has medium-heavy 24-inch barrel, no sights, stock with less drop. Weight: about 9¾ pounds. Calibers: 222 Rem., 22-250, 243 Win. Made from 1972 to date.

Winchester Model 70 Win-Cam

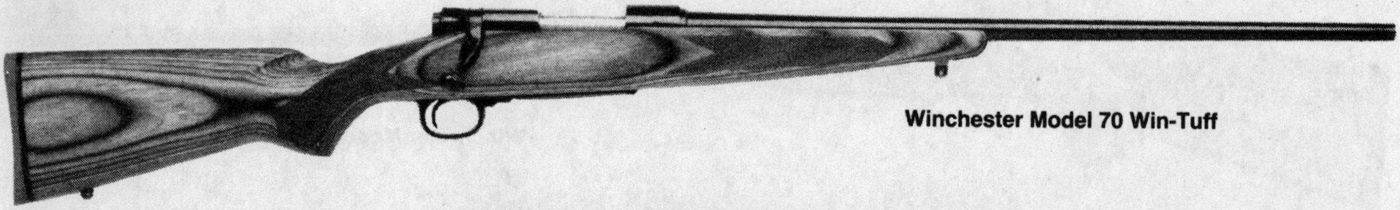

Winchester Model 70 Win-Tuff

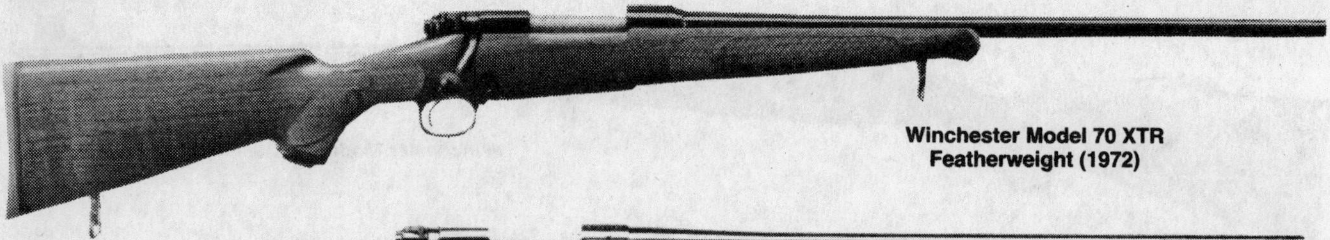

Winchester Model 70 XTR Featherweight (1972)

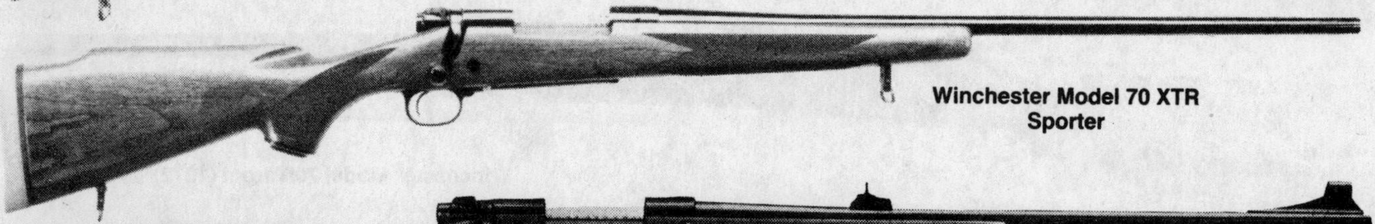

Winchester Model 70 XTR Sporter

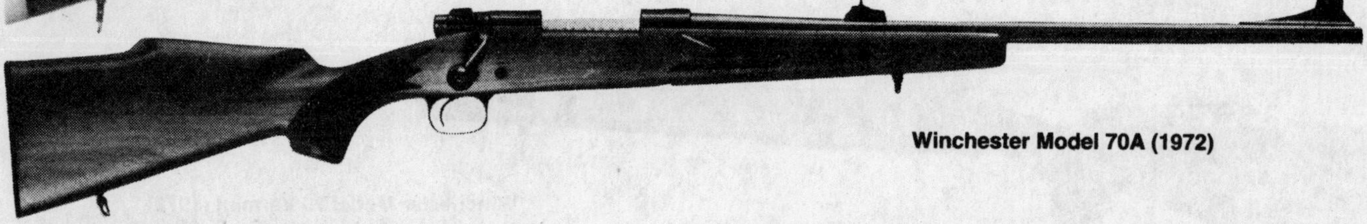

Winchester Model 70A (1972)

Winchester Model 70 Win-Cam Bolt Action Rifle **$375**
Caliber: 270 Win. and 30-06 Springfield. 24-inch barrel. Camouflage one-piece laminated stock. Recoil pad. Drilled and tapped for scope. Made from 1986 to date.

Winchester Model 70 Winlite Bolt Action Rifle **$460**
Calibers: 270 Win., 280 Rem., 30-06 Springfield, 7mm Rem., 300 Win. Mag., and 338 Win. Mag. 5-shot magazine; 3-shot for magnum calibers. 22-inch barrel; 24-inch for Magnum calibers. 42½ inches overall; 44½, magnum calibers. Weight: 6¼ to 7 pounds. Fiberglass stock with rubber recoil pad, sling swivel studs. Made from 1986 to date.

Winchester Model 70 Win-Tuff Bolt Action Rifle
Calibers: 270 Win. and 30-06 Springfield. 22-inch barrel. Weight: 6¼ pounds. Laminated dye-shaded brown wood stock with recoil pad. Barrel drilled and tapped for scope. Swivel studs. Made from 1986 to date.
Featherweight Model **$464**
Lightweight Model **400**

Winchester Model 70 XTR Featherweight **$315**
Similar to Standard Win. Model 70, except lightweight American walnut stock with classic schnabel forend, checkered. 22-inch barrel, hooded blade front sight, folding leaf rear sight. Stainless steel magazine follower. Weight: 6¾ pounds. Made from 1984 to date.

Winchester Model 70 XTR Sporter Rifle **$350**
Calibers: 264 Win. Mag., 7mm Rem. Mag., 300 Win. Mag., 200 Weatherby Mag., and 338 Win. Mag. 3-shot magazine. 24-inch barrel. 44½ inches overall. Weight: 7¾ pounds. Walnut Monte Carlo stock. Rubber butt pad. Receiver tapped and drilled for scope mounting. Made from 1986 to date.

Winchester Model 70A **$225**
Calibers: 222 Rem., 22-250, 243 Win., 25-06, 270 Win., 30-06, 308 Win. 4-shot magazine. 22-inch barrel (except 24- or 26-inch in 25-06). Weight: about 7½ pounds. Open rear sight, hooded ramp front sight. Monte Carlo stock with checkered pistol grip and forearm, sling swivels. Made from 1972 to date.

Winchester Model 70A Magnum **$250**
Same as Model 70A, except has 3-shot magazine, 24-inch barrel, recoil pad. Weight: about 7¾ pounds. Calibers: 264 Win. Mag., 7mm Rem. Mag., 300 Win. Mag. Made from 1972 to date.

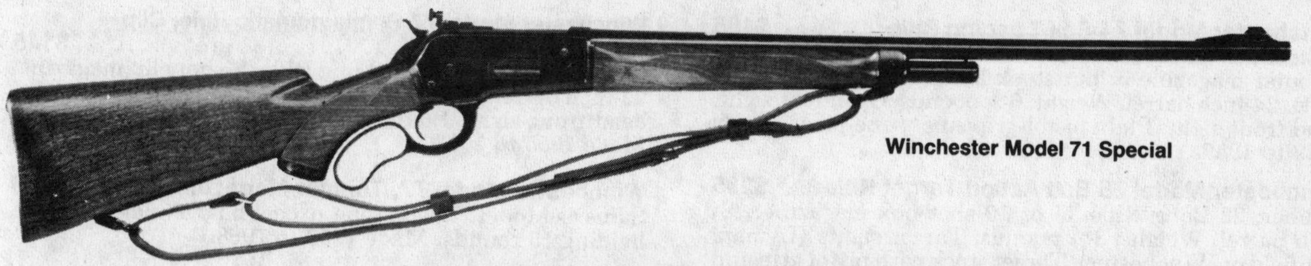
Winchester Model 71 Special

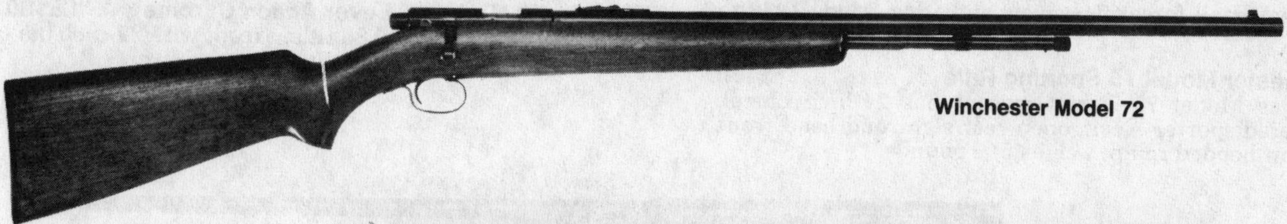
Winchester Model 72

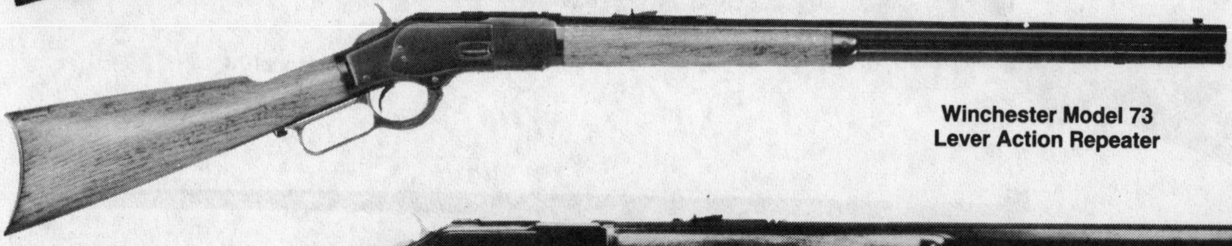
Winchester Model 73
Lever Action Repeater

Winchester Model 73
One of One Thousand

Closeup of Barrel Engraving
Winchester Model 73 One of One Thousand

Winchester Model 71 Special Lever Action Repeater $1010
Solid frame. Caliber: 348 Win. 4-shot tubular magazine. 20- or 24-inch barrel. Weight: 8 pounds. Open rear sight, bead front sight on ramp with hood. Walnut stock, checkered pistol grip and forearm, grip cap, quick-detachable swivels and sling. Made 1935 to 1957.

Winchester Model 71 Standard Grade $705
Plain Model. Same as Model 71 Special, except lacks checkering, grip car, sling and swivels.

Winchester Model 72 Bolt Action Repeater $170
Tubular magazine. Takedown. Caliber: 22 Short, Long, Long Rifle. Magazine holds 20 Short, 16 Long or 15 Long Rifle. 25-inch barrel. Weight: $5^{3}/_{4}$ pounds. Peep or open rear sight, bead front sight. Plain pistol-grip stock. Made 1938 to 1959.

Winchester Model 73 Lever Action Carbine . . . $3495
Same as Standard Model 73 Rifle, except has 20-inch barrel, 12-shot magazine, weighs $7^{1}/_{4}$ pounds.

Winchester Model 73 Lever Action Repeater . . $2795
Calibers: 32-20, 38-40, 44-40; a few were chambered for 22 rimfire. 15-shot magazine, also made with 6-shot half magazine. 24-inch barrel (round, half-octagon, octagon). Weight: about $8^{1}/_{2}$ pounds. Open rear sight, bead or blade front sight. Plain straight-grip stock and forearm. Made 1873 to 1924. 720,610 rifles of this model were mfd.

Winchester Model 73 Rifle—One of One Thousand . . . . $40,000+
During the late 1870s Winchester offered Model 73 rifles of superior accuracy and extra finish, designated "One of One Thousand" grade, at a price of $100. These rifles are marked "1 of 1000" or "One of One Thousand." Only 136 of this model are known to have been manufactured. This is one of the rarest of shoulder arms and, because so very few have been sold in recent years, it is extremely difficult to assign a value; however, in the author's opinion, an "excellent" specimen would probably bring a price upward of $25,000.

Winchester Model 73 Special Sporting Rifle . . . $2700
Same as Standard Model 73 Rifle, except this type has receiver casehardened in colors, pistol-grip stock of selected walnut, octagon barrel only.

Winchester Model 74 Self-Loading Rifle $165
Takedown. Calibers: 22 Short only, 22 Long Rifle only. Tubular magazine in buttstock holds 20 Short, 14 Long Rifle. 24-inch barrel. Weight: 6¼ pounds. Open rear sight, bead front sight. Plain pistol-grip stock, one-piece. Made 1939 to 1955.

Winchester Model 75 Bolt Action Target Rifle . . $295
Caliber: 22 Long Rifle. 5- or 10-shot box magazine. 28-inch barrel. Weight: 8¾ pounds. Target sights (Lyman, Redfield or Winchester). Target stock with pistol grip and semibeavertail forearm, swivels and sling. Made 1938 to 1959.

Winchester Model 75 Sporting Rifle $450
Same as Model 75 Target, except has 24-inch barrel, checkered sporter stock, open rear sight and bead front sight on hooded ramp, weighs 5½ pounds.

Winchester Model 77 Semiautomatic Rifle, Clip Type $145
Solid frame. Caliber: 22 Long Rifle. 8-shot clip magazine. 22-inch barrel. Weight: about 5½ pounds. Open rear sight, bead front sight. Plain, one-piece stock with pistol grip. Made 1955 to 1963.

Winchester Model 77, Tubular Magazine Type . . $145
Same as Model 77. Clip type, except has tubular magazine holding 15 rounds. Made 1955 to 1963.

Winchester Model 86 Lever Action Carbine . . . $5100
Same as standard Model 86 rifle, except with 22-inch barrel and weighs about 7¾ pounds.

Winchester Model 74

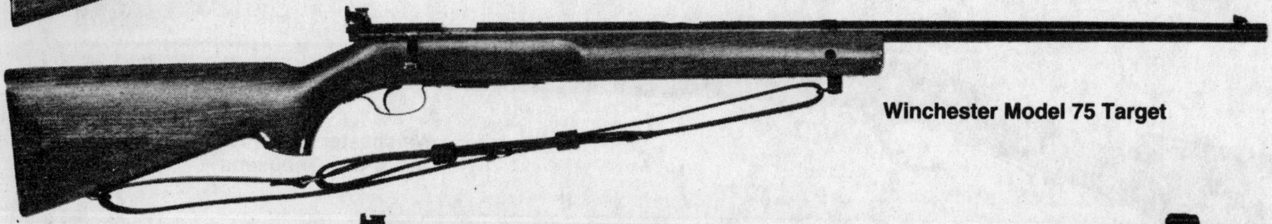

Winchester Model 75 Target

Winchester Model 75 Sporter

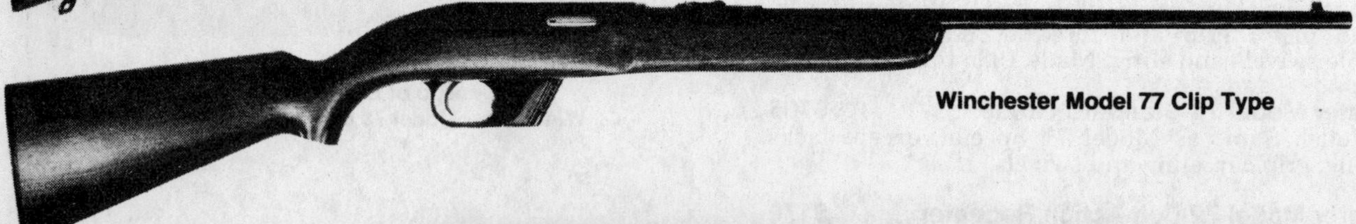

Winchester Model 77 Clip Type

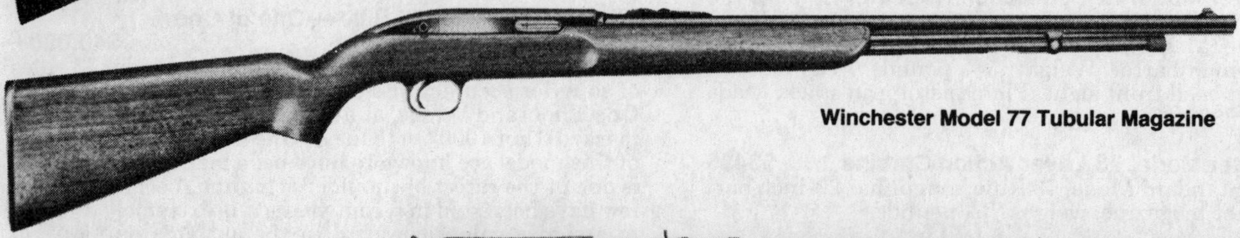

Winchester Model 77 Tubular Magazine

Winchester Model 86
Lever Action Repeater

Winchester Model 86 Lever Action Repeater . . $1250
Solid frame or takedown style. Calibers: 45/70, 38/56, 45/90/300, 40/82/260, 40/65/260, 38/56/255, 38/70/255, 40/70/330, 50/110/300, 50/100/450, 33 Win. All but the first cartridge listed are now obsolete. 33 Win. and 45/70 were the last calibers in which this model was supplied. 8-shot tubular magazine, also 4-shot half-magazine. 22- or 26-inch barrel (round, half-octagon, octagon). Weight: from $7\frac{1}{2}$ pounds up. Open rear sight, bead or blade front sight. Plain straight-grip stock and forearm. Made 1886 to 1935.

Winchester Model 88 Carbine $465
Same as Model 88 Rifle, except has 19-inch barrel, plain carbine-style stock and forearm with barrel band. Weight: 7 pounds. Made 1968 to 1973.

Winchester Model 88 Lever Action Rifle $415
Hammerless. Calibers: 243 Win., 284 Win., 308 Win., 358 Win. 4-shot box magazine. 3-shot in pre-1963 models and in current 284. 22-inch barrel. Weight: about $7\frac{1}{4}$ pounds. One-piece walnut stock with pistol grip, swivels (1965 and later models have basket-weave ornamentation instead of checkering). Made 1955 to 1973. *Note:* 243 and 358 introduced 1956, latter discontinued 1964; 284 introduced 1963.

Winchester Model 90 Slide Action Repeater $490
Visible hammer. Calibers: 22 Short, Long, Long Rifle; 22 W.R.F. (not interchangeable). Tubular magazine holds 15 Short, 12 Long, 11 Long Rifle; 12 W.R.F. 24-inch octagon barrel. Weight: $5\frac{3}{4}$ pounds. Open rear sight, bead front sight. Plain straight-grip stock, grooved slide handle. Originally solid frame, after No. 15,499 all rifles of this model were takedown type. Fancy checkered pistol-grip stock, stainless steel barrel supplied at extra cost. Made 1890 to 1932.

Winchester Model 92 Lever Action Carbine . . . $1075
Same as Model 92RR rifle, except has 20-inch barrel, 5-shot or 11-shot magazine, weighs about $5\frac{3}{4}$ pounds.

Winchester Model 92 Lever Action Repeater . . . $875
Solid frame or takedown. Calibers: 25/20, 32/20, 38/40, 44/40. 13-shot tubular magazine, also 7-shot half-magazine. 24-inch barrel (round, octagon, half-octagon). Weight: from $6\frac{3}{4}$ pounds up. Open rear sight, bead front sight. Plain straight-grip stock and forearm (stock illustrated was extra cost option). Made 1892 to 1941.

Winchester Model 88 Carbine

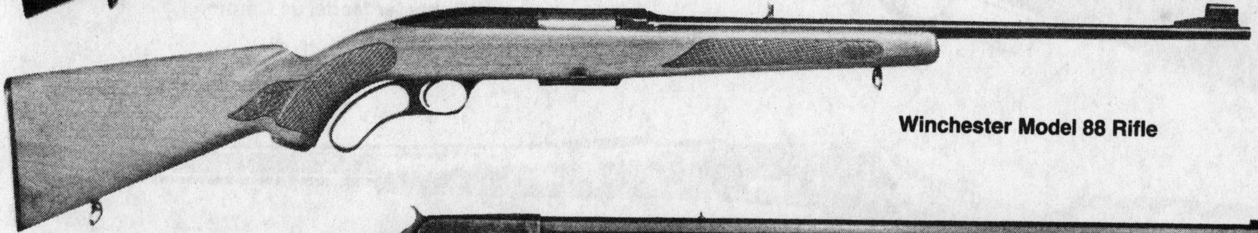
Winchester Model 88 Rifle

Winchester Model 90

Winchester Model 92 Repeater

Winchester Model 94 Antique Carbine

Winchester Model 94 Antique Carbine **$155**
Same as standard Model 94 Carbine, except has receiver with decorative scrollwork and casehardened in colors, brass-plated loading gate, saddle ring; caliber 30-30 only. Made 1964 to 1984.

Winchester Model 94 Carbine
Same as Model 94 Rifle, except 20-inch round barrel, 6-shot full-length magazine. Weight: about $6^1/_2$ pounds. Currently mfd. in calibers 30-30 and 32 Special, solid frame only.
Pre-World War II (under No. 1,300,000) **$360**
Postwar, pre-1964 . . . . **290**
Current model **140**

Winchester Model 94 Classic Carbine **$250**
Same as Model 67 Carbine, except without commemorative details; has scroll-engraved receiver, gold-plated loading gate. Made 1968 to 1970.

Winchester Model 94 Classic Rifle **$250**
Same as Model 67 Rifle, except without commemorative details; has scroll-engraved receiver, gold-plated loading gate. Made 1968 to 1970.

Winchester Model 94 Deluxe Carbine **$320**
Caliber: 30-30. 6-shot magazine. 20-inch barrel. $37^3/_4$ inches overall. Weight: $6^1/_2$ pounds. Semi-fancy American walnut stock with rubber butt pad, long forearm and specially cut checkering. Engraved with "Deluxe" script. Made from 1987 to date.

Winchester Model 94 Lever Action Rifle **$425**
Solid frame or takedown. Calibers: 25/35, 30/30, 32/40, 32 Special, 38/55. 7-shot tubular magazine or 4-shot half-magazine. 26-inch barrel (octagon, half-octagon, round). Weight: about $7^3/_4$ pounds. Open rear sight, bead front sight. Plain straight-grip stock and forearm. Made 1894 to 1937.

Winchester Model 94 Long Barrel Rifle **$205**
Caliber: 30-30. 7-round magazine. 24-inch barrel. $41^3/_4$ inches overall. Weight: 7 pounds. American walnut stock. Blade front sight. Made from 1987 to date.

Winchester Model 94 Trapper **$175**
Same as Winchester Model 94 Carbine, except 16-inch barrel and weighs 6 lbs. 2 oz. Made from 1980 to date.

Winchester Model 94 Carbine

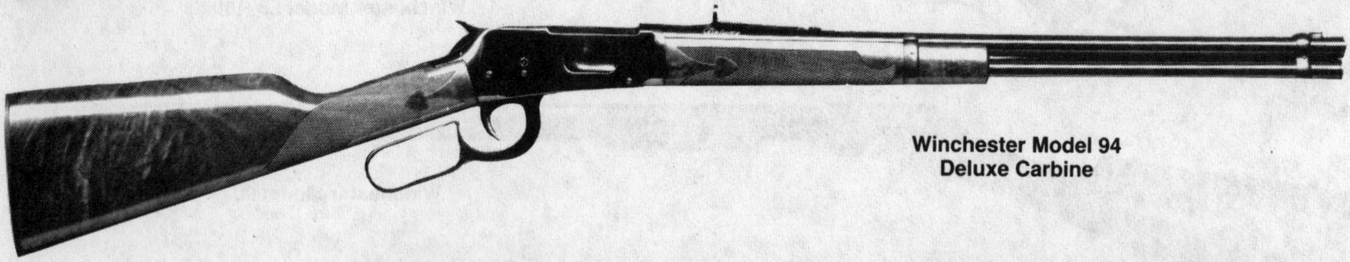

Winchester Model 94
Deluxe Carbine

Winchester Model 94
Lever Action Rifle

Winchester Model 94
Long Barrel Rifle

Winchester Model 94 Win-Tuff Lever Action Rifle **$205**
Caliber: 30-30. 6-round magazine. 20-inch barrel. 37¾ inches overall. Weight: 6½ pounds. Brown laminated wood stock. Made from 1987 to date.

Winchester Model 94 Wrangler II Angle Eject Carbine **$180**
Same as standard Model 94 Carbine, except has 16-inch barrel, engraved receiver and chambered for 38-55 Win. Introduced by U.S. Repeating Arms.

Winchester Model 94 XTR Big Bore
Modified Model 94 action for added strength. Caliber: 375 Win. 20-inch barrel. Rubber butt pad. Checkered stock and forearm. Weight: 6½ pounds. Made from 1978 to date.
Standard **$185**
Angle Eject **275**

Winchester Model 94 XTR in 7-30 Waters Lever Action Rifle **$220**
Same general specifications as standard Angle Eject M94 except chambered for 7-30 Waters cartridge and has 24-inch barrel. Weight: 7 pounds. Made from 1985 to date by U.S. Repeating Arms.

Winchester Model 94 Win-Tuff

Winchester Model 94
Wrangler II Angle Eject

Winchester Model 94 XTR Big Bore

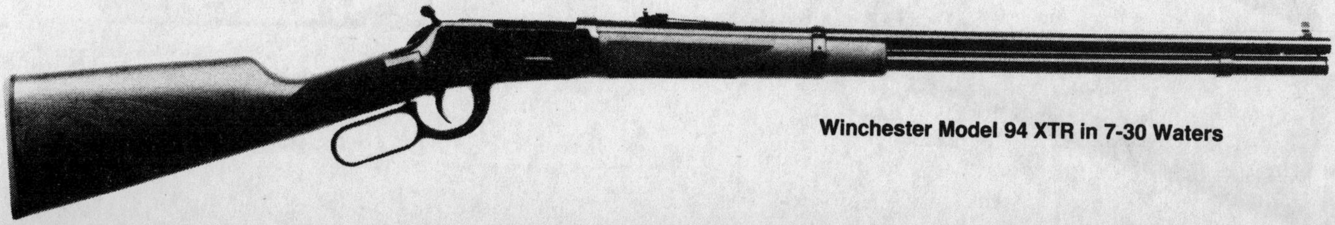
Winchester Model 94 XTR in 7-30 Waters

MODEL 94 COMMEMORATIVES

Values indicated are for commemorative Winchesters in new condition. Data on these models supplied by Mr. Robert E. P. Cherry, Cherry's Sporting Goods, Greensboro, N.C.

Winchester Model 94 Alaskan Purchase Centennial Commemorative Carbine $1785
Same as Wyoming issue, except different medallion and inscription. 1,501 made in 1967.

Winchester Model 94 Antlered Game Commemorative $400
Standard Model 94 action. Gold-colored medallion inlaid in stock. Antique gold-plated receiver, lever tang and barrel bands. Medallion and receiver engraved with elk, moose, deer and caribou. 20½-inch barrel. Curved steel butt plate. In 30-30 caliber. 19,999 made in 1978.

Winchester Model 94 Bicentennial '76 Carbine . $550
Same as Standard Model 94 Carbine, except caliber 30-30 only; antique silver-finished, engraved receiver; stock and forearm of fancy walnut, checkered, Bicentennial medallion embedded in buttstock, curved butt plate. 20,000 made in 1976.

Winchester Model 94 Buffalo Bill Commemorative Carbine $350
Same as Buffalo Bill Rifle, except has 20-inch barrel, magazine holds 6 rounds, weight is 7 pounds, forearm is shorter. Made in 1968.

Winchester Model 94 Buffalo Bill Commemorative Rifle $350
Same as Centennial '66 Rifle, except receiver is black-chromed, scroll-engraved and bears name "Buffalo Bill"; hammer, trigger, loading gate, saddle ring, forearm cap, and butt plate are nickel-plated; Buffalo Bill Memorial Assn. commemorative medallion embedded in buttstock; "Buffalo Bill Commemorative" inscribed on barrel, facsimile signature "W.F. Cody, Chief of Scouts" on tang. Made in 1968.

Winchester Model 94 Buffalo Bill Matched Set $795
Rifle and carbine were offered in sets with consecutive serial numbers. 120,751 Buffalo Bill 94s were made.

Winchester Canadian Centennial Commemorative Carbine (Model 67) $350
Same as Model 67 Rifle, except has 20-inch barrel, magazine holds 6 rounds, weight is 7 pounds, forearm is shorter. Made in 1967.

Winchester Canadian Centennial Commemorative Rifle (Model 67) $350
Same as Centennial '66 Rifle, except receiver—engraved with maple leaves—and forearm cap are black-chromed, butt plate is blued, commemorative inscription in gold on barrel and top tang: "Canadian Centennial 1867-1967." Made in 1967.

Winchester Canadian Centennial Matched Set (Model 67) $750
Rifle and carbine were offered in sets with consecutive serial numbers. *Note:* 90,398 Model 67s were made.

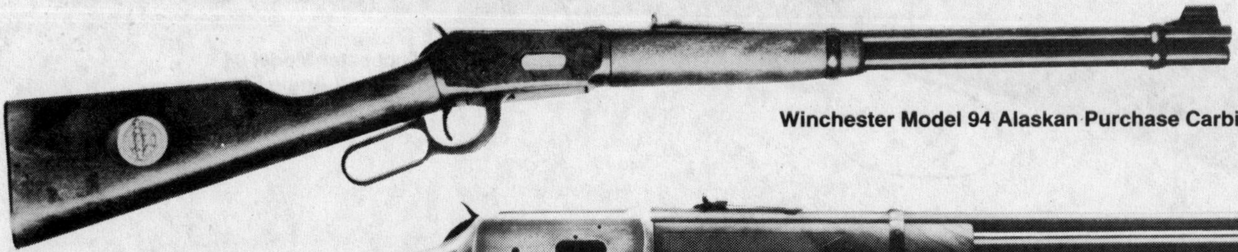

Winchester Model 94 Alaskan Purchase Carbine

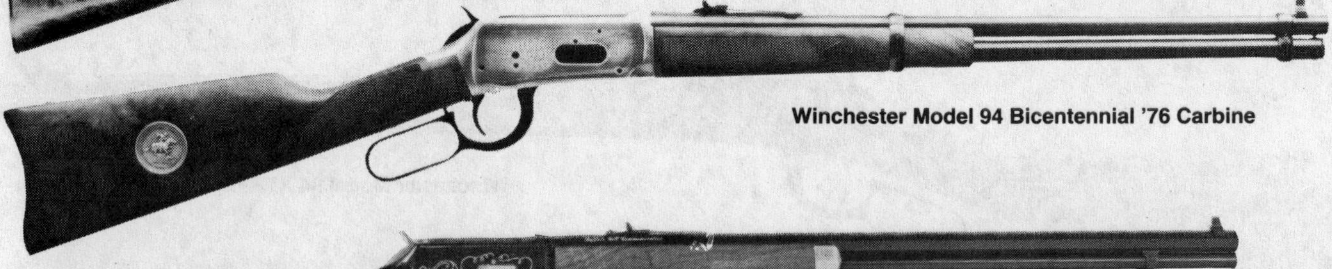

Winchester Model 94 Bicentennial '76 Carbine

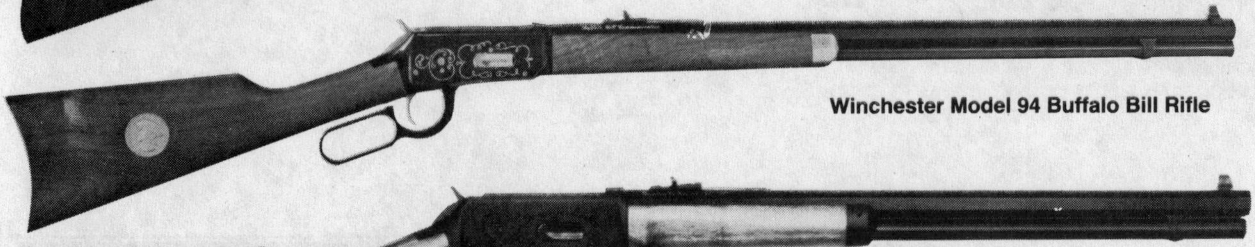

Winchester Model 94 Buffalo Bill Rifle

Winchester Canadian Centennial

Winchester Centennial '66 Rifle

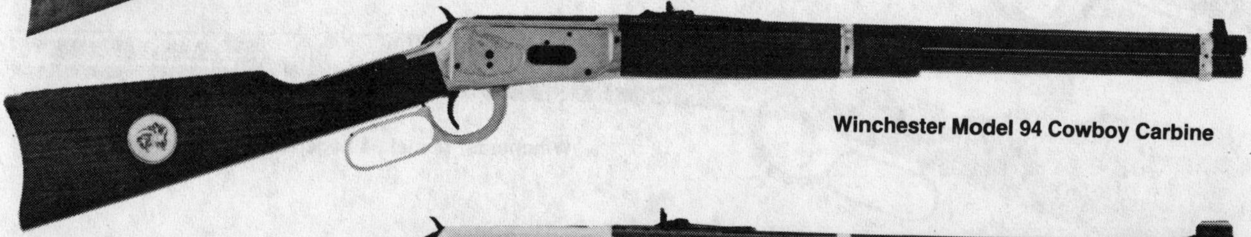

Winchester Model 94 Cowboy Carbine

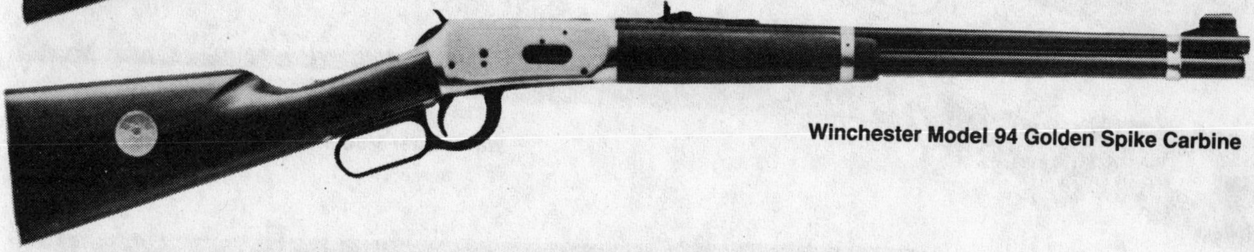

Winchester Model 94 Golden Spike Carbine

Winchester Colt Commemorative Set

Winchester Centennial '66 Carbine $350
Same as Centennial '66 Rifle, except has 20-inch barrel, magazine holds 6 rounds, weight is 7 pounds, forearm is shorter. Made in 1966.

Winchester Centennial '66 Commemorative Rifle $350
Commemorates Winchester's 100th anniversary. Standard Model 94 action. Caliber: 30-30. Full-length magazine holds 8 rounds. 26-inch octagon barrel. Weight: 8 pounds. Gold-plated receiver and forearm cap. Open rear sight, post front sight. Saddle ring. Walnut buttstock and forearm with high-gloss finish, solid brass butt plate. Commemorative inscription on barrel and top tang of receiver. Made in 1966.

Winchester Centennial '66 Matched Set $790
Rifle and carbine were offered in sets with consecutive serial numbers. *Note:* 100,478 Centennial '66s were made.

Winchester Model 94 Cheyenne Commemorative $450
Available in Canada only. Same as Standard Model 94 Carbine, except chambered for 44/40. 11,225 made in 1977.

Winchester Model 94 Colt Commemorative Carbine Set $2900
Standard Model 94 action. Caliber: 44-40 Win. 20-inch barrel. Weight: 6¼ pounds. Features a horse-and-rider trademark and distinctive WC monogram in gold etching on left side of receiver. Sold in set with Colt Single Action Revolver chambered for same caliber.

Winchester Model 94 Cowboy Commemorative Carbine $350
Same as Standard Model 94 Carbine, except caliber 30-30 only; nickel-plated receiver, tangs, lever, barrel bands; engraved receiver, "Cowboy Commemorative" on barrel, commemorative medallion embedded in buttstock; curved butt plate. 20,915 made in 1970.

Winchester Model 94 Golden Spike Commemorative Carbine $350
Same as Standard Model 94 Carbine, except caliber 30-30 only; gold-plated receiver, tangs and barrel bands; engraved receiver, commemorative medallion embedded in stock. 64,758 made in 1969.

Winchester Model 94 Illinois Sesquicentennial Commemorative Carbine $350
Same as Standard Model 94 Carbine, except caliber 30-30 only; gold-plated butt plate, trigger, loading gate, and saddle ring; receiver engraved with profile of Lincoln, commemorative inscriptions on receiver, barrel; souvenir medallion embedded in stock. 31,124 made in 1968.

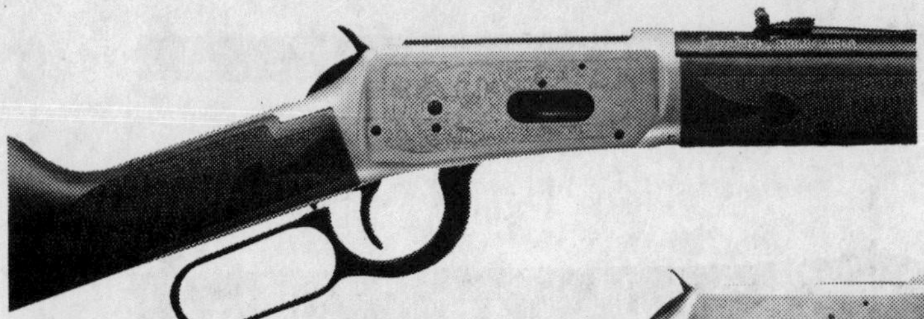

Winchester Model 94 Legendary Frontiersmen

Winchester Model 94 Legendary Lawmen Carbine

Winchester Model 94 Lone Star Rifle

Winchester Model 94 NRA Centennial Musket

Winchester Model 94 Nebraska Centennial Carbine

Winchester Model 94 Legendary Frontiersmen Commemorative $350
Standard Model 94 action. Caliber: 38-55. 24-inch round barrel. Nickel-silver medallion inlaid in stock. Antique silver-plated receiver engraved with scenes of the old frontier. Checkered walnut stock and forearm. 19,999 made in 1979.

Winchester Model 94 Legendary Lawmen Commemorative $380
Same as Standard Model 94 Carbine, except 30-30 only; antique silver-plated receiver engraved with action law-enforcement scenes. 16-inch Trapper barrel, antique silver-plated barrel bands. 19,999 made in 1978.

Winchester Model 94 Lone Star Commemorative Rifle $375
Same as Theodore Roosevelt Rifle, except yellow-gold plating; "Lone Star" engraving on receiver and barrel, commemorative medallion embedded in buttstock. Made in 1970.

Winchester Model 94 Lone Star Matched Set . . . $845
Rifle and carbine were offered in sets with consecutive serial numbers. 30,669 Lone Star 94s were made.

Winchester Model 94 NRA Centennial Musket $350
Commemorates 100th anniversary of National Rifle Association of America. Standard Model 94 action. Caliber: 30-30. 7-shot magazine. 26-inch barrel. Military folding rear sight and blade front sight. Black chrome-finished receiver engraved "NRA 1871-1971" plus scrollwork. Barrel inscribed "NRA Centennial Musket." Musket-style buttstock and full-length forearm; commemorative medallion embedded in buttstock. Weight: 7 1/8 pounds. Made in 1971.

Winchester Model 94 NRA Centennial Rifle $395
Same as Model 94 Rifle, except has commemorative details as in NRA Centennial Musket (barrel inscribed "NRA Centennial Rifle"); caliber 30-30, 24-inch barrel, QD sling swivels. Made in 1971.

Winchester NRA Centennial Matched Set $845
Rifle and carbine were offered in sets with consecutive serial numbers. *Note:* Production figures not available. These rifles were again offered in Winchester's 1972 catalog.

Winchester Model 94 Nebraska Centennial Commemorative Carbine $900
Same as Standard Model 94 Carbine, except caliber 30-30 only; gold-plated hammer, loading gate, barrel band, and butt plate; souvenir medallion embedded in stock, commemorative inscription on barrel. 2,500 made in 1966.

Winchester Model 94 Theodore Roosevelt Commemorative Carbine $365
Same as Theodore Roosevelt Rifle, except has 20-inch barrel, 6-shot full-length magazine, shorter forearm, weighs 7 pounds. Made in 1969.

Winchester Model 94 Theodore Roosevelt Commemorative Rifle $350
Standard Model 94 action. Caliber: 30-30. Half-magazine holds 6 rounds. 26-inch octagon barrel. Weight: 7½ pounds. White gold-plated receiver, upper tang, and forend cap; receiver engraved with American Eagle, "26th President 1901-1909," and Roosevelt's signature. Commemorative medallion embedded in buttstock. Saddle ring. Half pistol grip, contoured lever. Made in 1969.

Winchester Model 94 Theodore Roosevelt Matched Set $745
Rifle and carbine were offered in sets with consecutive serial numbers. 49,505 T. Roosevelt 94s were made.

Winchester Model 94 Texas Ranger Association Carbine $1950
Same as Texas Ranger Commemorative Model 94, except special edition of 150 carbines, numbered 1 through 150, with hand-checkered full-fancy walnut stock and forearm. Sold only through Texas Ranger Association. Made in 1973.

Winchester Model 94 Texas Ranger Commemorative Carbine $650
Same as Standard Model 94 Carbine, except caliber 30-30 only, stock and forearm of semi-fancy walnut, replica of Texas Ranger star embedded in buttstock, curved butt plate. 5,000 made in 1973.

Winchester Model 94 John Wayne Commemorative $695
Standard Model 94 action. Caliber: 32-40. 18½-inch barrel. Receiver is pewter-plated with engraving of Indian attack and cattle drive scenes. Oversized bow on lever. Nickel-silver medallion in buttstock bears a bas-relief portrait of Wayne. Selected American walnut stock with deep-cut checkering. Introduced by U.S. Repeating Arms.

Winchester Model 94 Wells Fargo & Co. Commemorative Carbine $375
Same as Standard Model 94 Carbine, except 30-30 only; antique silver-finished, engraved receiver; stock and forearm of fancy walnut, checkered, curved butt plate. Nickel-silver stagecoach medallion (inscribed "Wells Fargo & Co.—1852-1977—125 Years") embedded in buttstock. 20,000 made in 1977.

Winchester Model 94 Oliver F. Winchester Commemorative $525
Standard Model 94 action. Caliber: 38-55. 24-inch octago-

Winchester Model 94
Theodore Roosevelt Rifle

Winchester Model 94
Texas Ranger Carbine

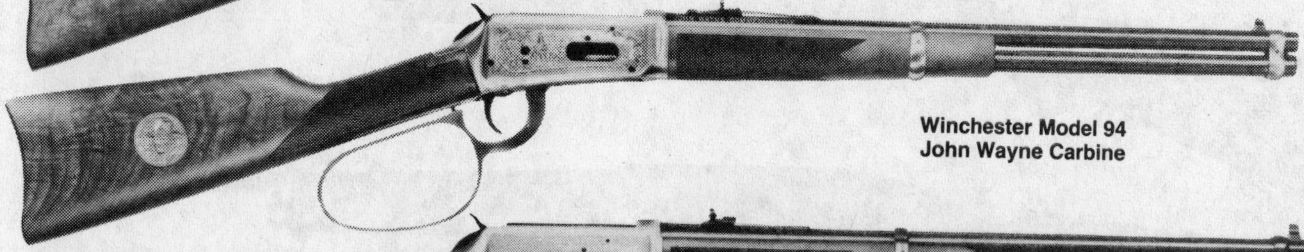

Winchester Model 94
John Wayne Carbine

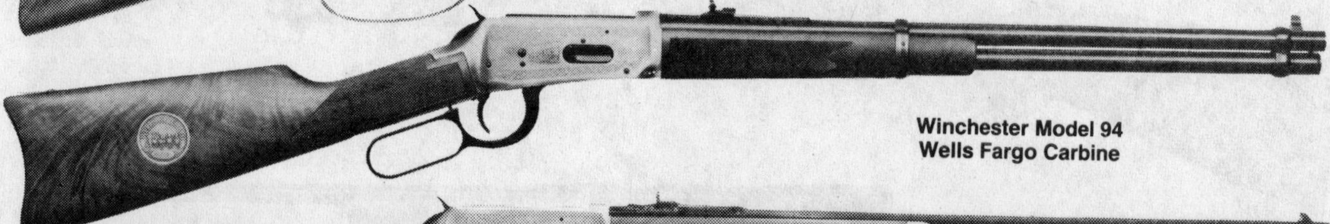

Winchester Model 94
Wells Fargo Carbine

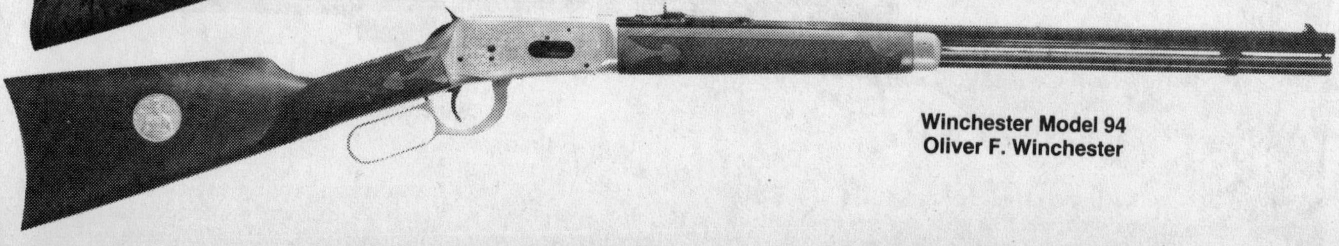

Winchester Model 94
Oliver F. Winchester

Winchester Model 94 Oliver F. Winchester (cont.)
nal barrel. Receiver is satin gold-plated with distinctive engravings. Stock and forearm semi-fancy American walnut with high grade checkering. 19,999 made in 1980.

Winchester Model 94 Wyoming Diamond Jubilee Commemorative Carbine $1750
Same as Standard Model 94 Carbine, except caliber 30-30 only, receiver engraved and casehardened in colors, brass saddle ring and loading gate, souvenir medallion embedded in buttstock, commemorative inscription on barrel. 1,500 made in 1964.

Winchester Model 95 Lever Action Carbine ... $1100
Same as Model 95 Standard Rifle, except has 22-inch barrel, carbine-style stock, weighs about 8 pounds, calibers 30-40, 30-30, 30-06 and 303, solid frame only.

Winchester Model 95 Lever Action Repeater .. $1035
Calibers: 30-40 Krag, 30-30, 30-06, 303 British, 35 Win., 405 Win.; original model supplied in the now obsolete 38/72 and 40/72 calibers. 4-shot box magazine, except 30-40 and 303 which have 5-shot magazine. Barrel lengths: 24-, 26-, 28-inches (round, half-octagon, octagon). Weight: about 8½ pounds. Open rear sight, bead or blade front sight. Plain straight-grip stock and forearm (standard). Both solid frame and takedown models were available. Made 1895 to 1931.

Winchester Model 100 Autoloading Rifle $395
Gas-operated semiautomatic. Calibers: 243, 284, 308 Win. 4-shot clip magazine (3-shot in 284). 22-inch barrel. Weight: 7¼ pounds. Open rear sight, hooded ramp front sight. One-piece stock with pistol grip, basket-weave checkering, grip cap, sling swivels. Made 1961 to 1973.

Winchester Model 100 Carbine $465
Same as Model 100 Rifle, except has 19-inch barrel, plain carbine-style stock and forearm with barrel band. Weight: 7 pounds. Made 1967 to 1973.

Winchester Model 121 Deluxe $95
Same as Model 121 Standard, except has ramp front sight, stock with fluted comb and sling swivels. Made 1967 to 1973.

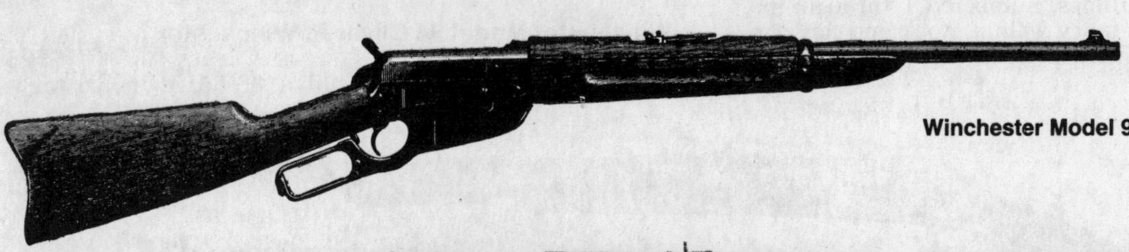

Winchester Model 95 Carbine

Winchester Model 95 Rifle

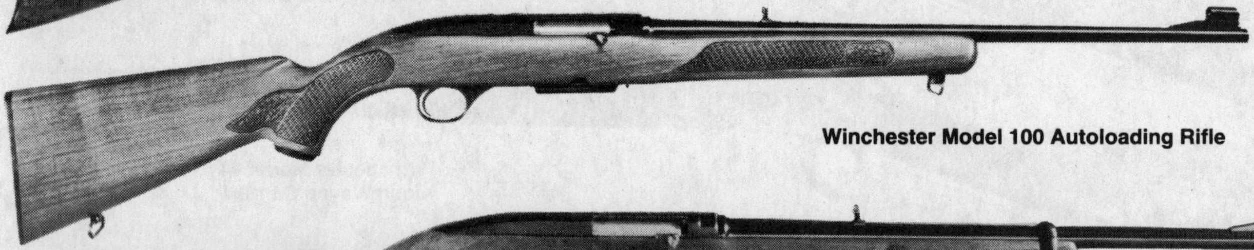

Winchester Model 100 Autoloading Rifle

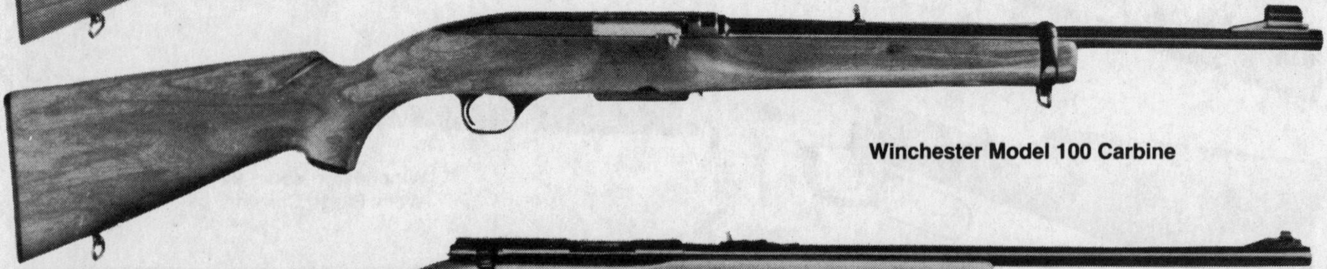

Winchester Model 100 Carbine

Winchester Model 121 Deluxe

Winchester Model 131

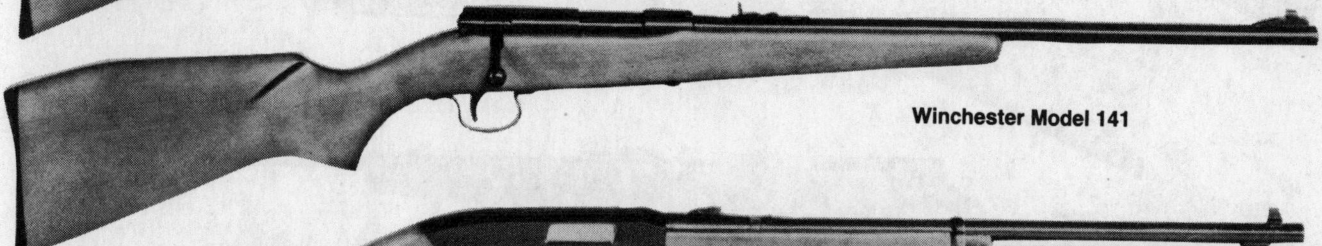

Winchester Model 141

Winchester Model 150 Carbine

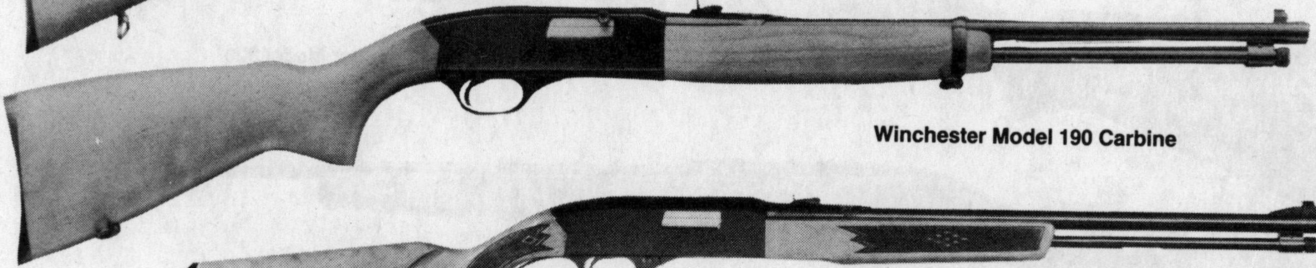

Winchester Model 190 Carbine

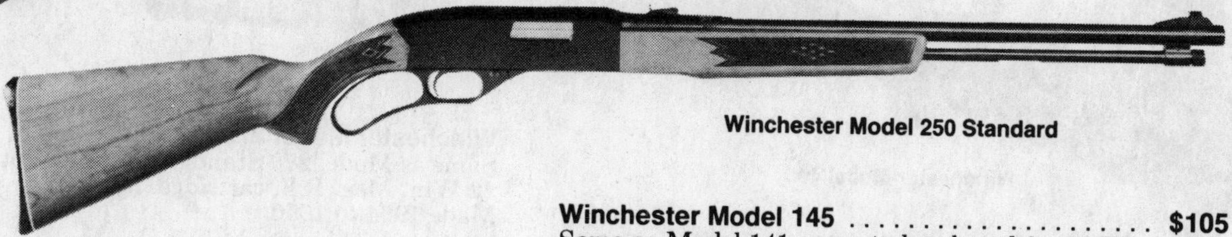

Winchester Model 250 Standard

Winchester Model 121 Standard Bolt Action Single Shot **$85**
Caliber: 22 Short, Long, Long Rifle. 20¾-inch barrel. Weight: 5 pounds. Open rear sight, bead front sight. Monte Carlo-style stock. Made 1967 to 1973.

Winchester Model 121 Youth **$90**
Same as Model 121 Standard, except has 1¼-inch shorter stock. Made 1967 to 1973.

Winchester Model 131 Bolt Action Repeater **$95**
Caliber: 22 Short, Long or Long Rifle. 7-shot clip magazine. 20¾-inch barrel. Weight: 5 pounds. Open rear sight, ramp front sight. Plain Monte Carlo stock. Made 1967 to 1973.

Winchester Model 135 .... **$100**
Same as Model 131, except chambered for 22 Win. Mag. R.F. cartridge. Magazine holds 5 rounds. Made in 1967.

Winchester Model 141 Bolt Action Tubular Repeater **$95**
Same as Model 131, except has tubular magazine in buttstock; holds 19 Short, 15 Long, 13 Long Rifle. Made 1967 to 1973.

Winchester Model 145 .... **$105**
Same as Model 141, except chambered for 22 Win. Mag. R.F.; magazine holds 9 rounds. Made in 1967.

Winchester Model 150 Lever Action Carbine **$85**
Same as Model 250, except has straight loop lever, plain carbine-style straight-grip stock and forearm with barrel band. Made 1967 to 1973.

Winchester Model 190 Carbine **$95**
Same as Model 190 rifle, except has carbine-style forearm with barrel band. Made 1967 to 1973.

Winchester Model 190 Semiautomatic Rifle **$85**
Same as current Model 290, except has plain stock and forearm. Made 1966 to 1978.

Winchester Model 250 Deluxe Rifle **$130**
Same as Model 250 Standard Rifle, except has fancy walnut Monte Carlo stock and forearm, sling swivels. Made 1965 to 1971.

Winchester Model 250 Standard Lever Action Rifle **$100**
Hammerless. Caliber: 22 Short, Long or Long Rifle. Tubular magazine holds 21 Short, 17 Long, 15 L.R. 20½-inch barrel. Open rear sight, ramp front sight. Weight: about 5 pounds. Plain stock and forearm on early production; later model has checkering. Made 1963 to 1973.

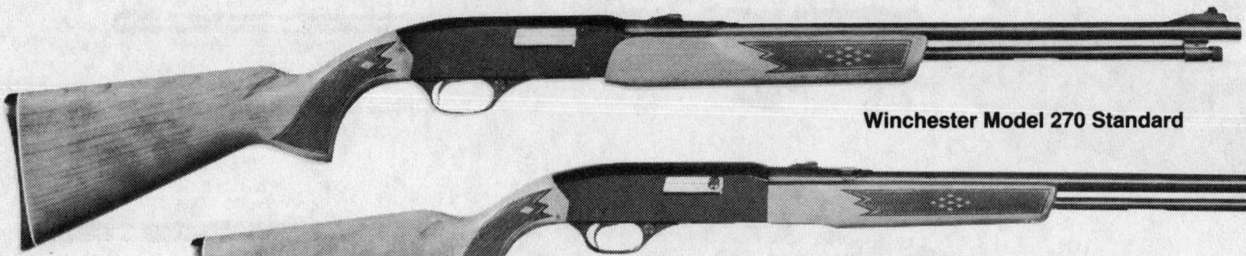

Winchester Model 270 Standard

Winchester Model 290 Standard

Winchester Model 310

Winchester Model 320

Winchester Model 490

Winchester Model 255 Deluxe Rifle $150
Same as Model 250 Deluxe Rifle, except chambered for 22 Win. Mag. R.F. cartridge. Magazine holds 11 rounds. Made 1965 to 1973.

Winchester Model 255 Standard Rifle $125
Same as Model 250 Standard Rifle, except chambered for 22 Win. Mag. R.F. cartridge. Magazine holds 11 rounds. Made 1964 to 1970.

Winchester Model 270 Deluxe Rifle $135
Same as Model 270 Standard Rifle, except has fancy walnut Monte Carlo stock and forearm. Made 1965 to 1973.

Winchester Model 270 Standard Slide Action Rifle $110
Hammerless. Caliber: 22 Short, Long or Long Rifle. Tubular magazine holds 21 Short, 17 Long, 15 L.R. 20½-inch barrel. Open rear sight, ramp front sight. Weight: about 5 pounds. Early production had plain walnut stock and forearm (slide handle); latter also furnished in plastic (Cycolac); last model has checkering. Made 1963 to 1973.

Winchester Model 275 Deluxe Rifle $145
Same as Model 270 Deluxe Rifle, except chambered for 22 Win. Mag. R.F. cartridge. Magazine holds 11 rounds. Made 1965 to 1970.

Winchester Model 275 Standard Rifle $115
Same as Model 270 Standard Rifle, except chambered for 22 Win. Mag. R.F. cartridge. Magazine holds 11 rounds. Made 1964 to 1970.

Winchester Model 290 Deluxe Rifle $120
Same as Model 290 Standard Rifle, except has fancy walnut Monte Carlo stock and forearm. Made 1965 to 1973.

Winchester Model 290 Standard Semiautomatic Rifle
Caliber: 22 Long or Long Rifle. Tubular magazine holds 17 Long, 15 L.R. 20½-inch barrel. Open rear sight, ramp front sight. Weight: about 5 pounds. Plain stock and forearm on early production; current model has checkering. Made 1963 to 1977.
With plain stock/forearm $125
With checkered stock/forearm 130

Winchester Model 310 Bolt Action Single Shot . . $125
Caliber: 22 Short, Long, Long Rifle. 22-inch barrel. Weight: 5⅝ pounds. Open rear sight, ramp front sight. Monte Carlo stock with checkered pistol grip and forearm, sling swivels. Made 1972-75.

Winchester Model 320 Bolt Action Repeater . . . $175
Same as Model 310, except has 5-shot clip magazine. Made 1972-74.

Winchester Model 490 Semiautomatic Rifle $190
Caliber: 22 Long Rifle. 5-shot clip magazine. 22-inch barrel. Weight: 6 pounds. Folding leaf rear sight, hooded ramp front sight. One-piece walnut stock with checkered pistol grip and forearm. Made 1975-77.

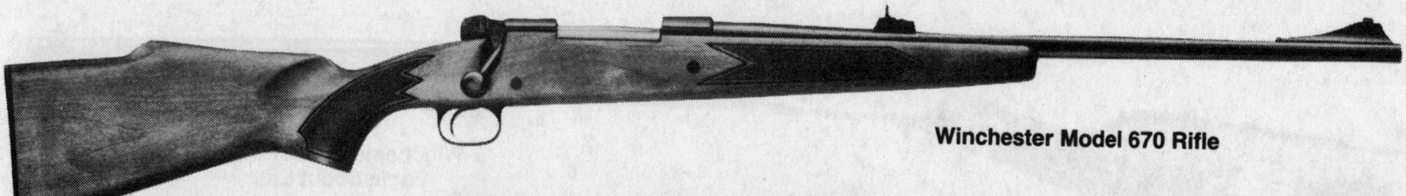

Winchester Model 670 Rifle

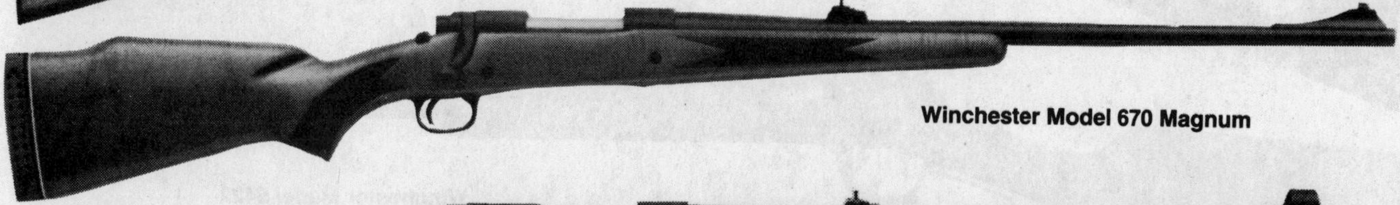

Winchester Model 670 Magnum

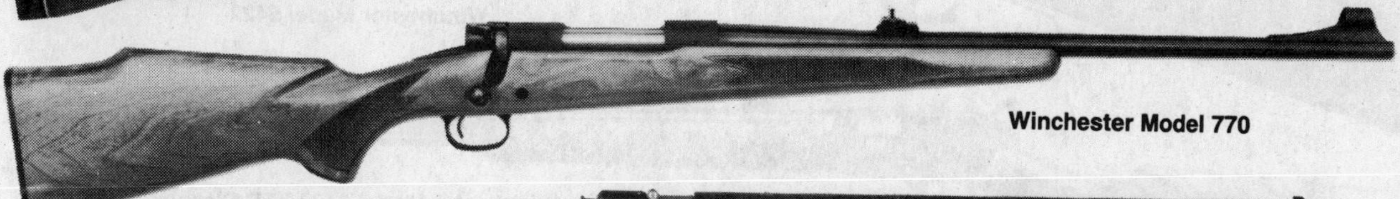

Winchester Model 770

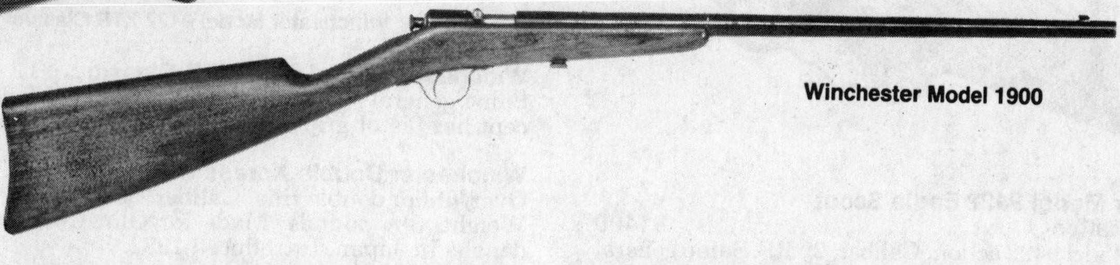

Winchester Model 1900

Winchester Model 670 Bolt Action Sporting Rifle $200
Calibers: 225 Win., 243 Win., 270 Win., 30-06, 308 Win. 4-shot magazine. 22-inch barrel. Weight: 7 pounds. Open rear sight, ramp front sight. Monte Carlo stock with checkered pistol grip and forearm. Made 1967 to 1973.

Winchester Model 670 Carbine $210
Same as Model 670 Rifle, except has 19-inch barrel. Weight: 6¾ pounds. Calibers: 243 Win., 270 Win., 30-06. Made 1967 to 1970.

Winchester Model 670 Magnum $225
Same as Model 670 Rifle, except has 24-inch barrel, reinforced stock with recoil pad. Weight: 7¼ pounds. Calibers: 264 Win. Mag., 7mm Rem. Mag., 300 Win. Mag. Made 1967 to 1970.

Winchester Model 770 Bolt Action Sporting Rifle $260
Model 70-type action. Calibers: 22-250, 222 Rem., 243, 270 Win., 30-06. 4-shot box magazine. 22-inch barrel. Open rear sight, hooded ramp front sight. Weight: 7⅛ pounds. Monte Carlo stock, checkered, swivels. Made 1969 to 1971.

Winchester Model 770 Magnum $275
Same as Standard Model 770, except 24-inch barrel, weight 7¼ pounds, recoil pad. Calibers: 7mm Rem. Mag., 264 and 300 Win. Mag. Made 1969 to 1971.

Winchester Model 1900 Bolt Action Single Shot Rifle $135
Takedown. Caliber: 22 Short and Long. 18-inch barrel. Weight: 2¾ pounds. Open rear sight, blade front sight. One-piece, straight-grip stock. Made 1899 to 1902.

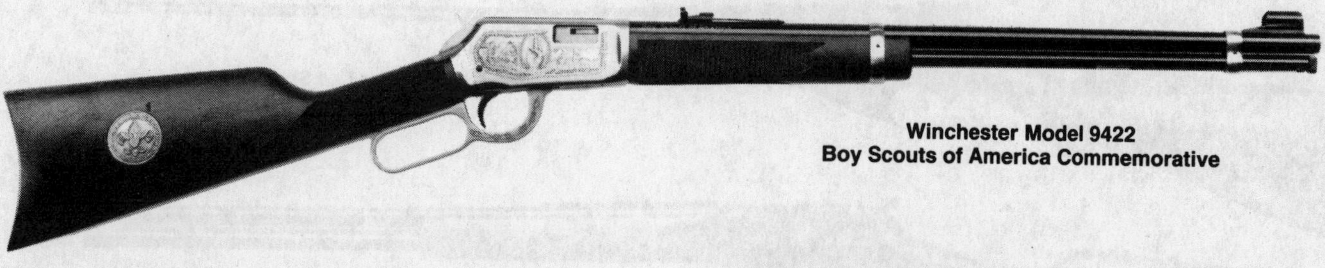

Winchester Model 9422
Boy Scouts of America Commemorative

Winchester Model 9422 Boy Scouts of America Commemorative $400
Standard Model 9422 action. Caliber: 22RF. 20½-inch round barrel. Receiver roll-engraved and plated in antique pewter, illustrating the Boy Scout oath and law. Frame

Winchester Model 9422 Boy Scouts of America (cont.)
carries inscription, "1910-1985." "Boy Scouts of America" inscribed on right side of barrel. Checkered stock and forearm of American walnut with satin finish. A maximum of 15,000 were produced by U.S. Repeating Arms beginning with serial number BSA1.

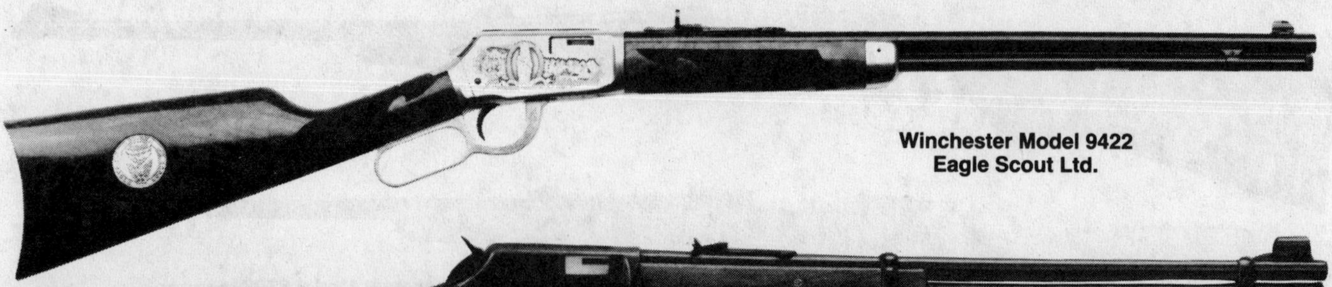

Winchester Model 9422
Eagle Scout Ltd.

Winchester Model 9422

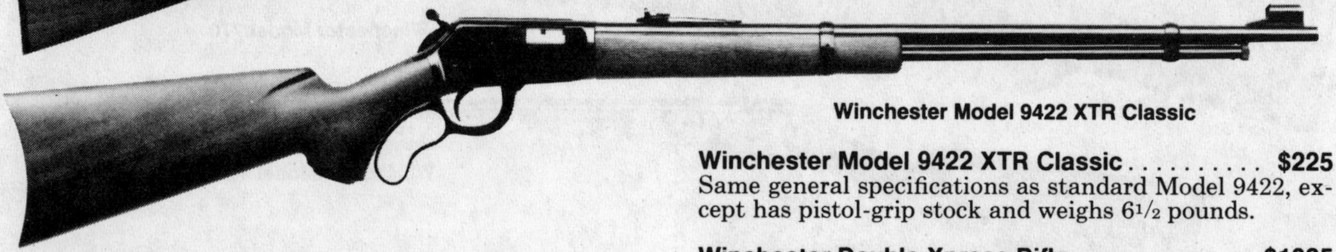

Winchester Model 9422 XTR Classic

Winchester Model 9422 Eagle Scout Commemorative **$1490**
Standard Model 9422 action. Caliber: 22 RF. Same general specifications as Boy Scout model except different engraving, jeweled bolt, antique gold-plated forearm cap and brass magazine tube. Only 1,000 were made by U.S. Repeating Arms bearing serial number Eagle 1 through Eagle 1000.

Winchester Model 9422 Lever Action Carbine . . **$215**
Styled after Model 94. Caliber: 22 Short, Long, Long Rifle. Tubular magazine holds 21 Short, 17 Long, 15 Long Rifle. $20^1/_2$-inch barrel. Weight: $6^1/_4$ pounds. Open rear sight, hooded ramp front sight. Carbine-style stock and forearm, barrel band. Made from 1972 to date.

Winchester Model 9422M **$245**
Same as Model 9422, except chambered for 22 Win. Mag. R.F.; magazine holds 11 rounds. Made from 1972 to date.

Winchester Model 9422 Win-Cam **$240**
Caliber: 22 RF. 11-shot magazine. $20^1/_2$-inch barrel. $37^1/_8$ inches overall. Weight: $6^1/_4$ pounds. Laminated non-glare green-shaded stock and forend. Made from 1987 to date.

Winchester Model 9422 XTR Classic **$225**
Same general specifications as standard Model 9422, except has pistol-grip stock and weighs $6^1/_2$ pounds.

Winchester Double Xpress Rifle **$1825**
Over/under double rifle. Caliber: 30-06. $23^1/_2$-inch barrel. Weight: $8^1/_2$ pounds. Made for Olin Corp. by Olin-Kodensha in Japan. Introduced 1982.

Winchester Lee Straight-Pull Bolt Action Repeating Rifle—Musket Model **$550**
Commercial version of U.S. Navy Model 1895 Rifle, caliber 6mm (1895-1897). Caliber: 236 U.S.N. 5-shot box magazine, clip-loaded. 28-inch barrel. Weight: $8^1/_2$ pounds. Folding leaf rear sight, post front sight. Military-type full stock with semi-pistol grip. Made 1897 to 1902.

Winchester Lee Straight-Pull Sporting Rifle **$700**
Same as Musket Model except has 24-inch barrel, sporter-style stock, open sporting rear sight, bead front sight. Weight: about $7^1/_2$ pounds. Made 1897 to 1902.

Winchester Ranger Angle Eject Lever Action Carbine **$195**
Caliber: 30-30. 5-shot tubular magazine. Barrel: 20-inch round. Weight: $6^1/_2$ pounds. American hardwood stock. Economy version of Model 94. Made from 1985 to date by U.S. Repeating Arms.

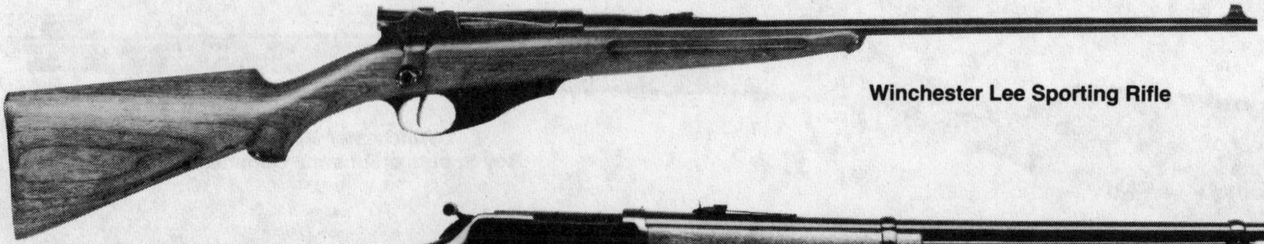

Winchester Lee Sporting Rifle

Winchester Ranger Angle Eject
Lever Action Carbine

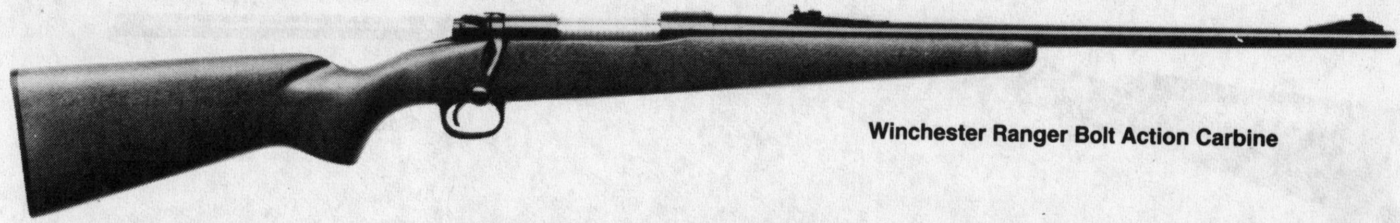

Winchester Ranger Bolt Action Carbine

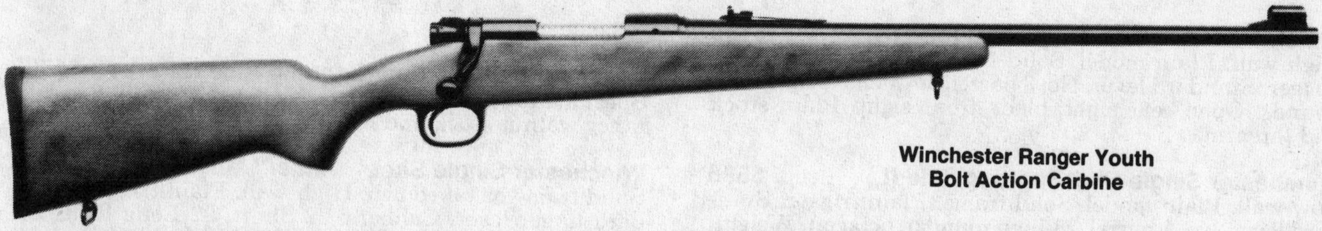

Winchester Ranger Youth Bolt Action Carbine

Winchester Ranger Bolt Action Carbine $245
Calibers: 270, 30-06, 7mm Rem. Mag. 3- and 4-shot magazine. Barrel: 24-inch in 7mm; 22-inch in 270 and 30-06. Open sights. American hardwood stock. Made from 1985 to date by U.S. Repeating Arms.

Winchester Ranger Youth Bolt Action Carbine $250
Calibers: 223 and 243. 4- and 5-shot magazine. Barrel: 20-inch. Weight: 5¾ pounds. American hardwood stock. Open rear sight. Made from 1985 to date by U.S. Repeating Arms.

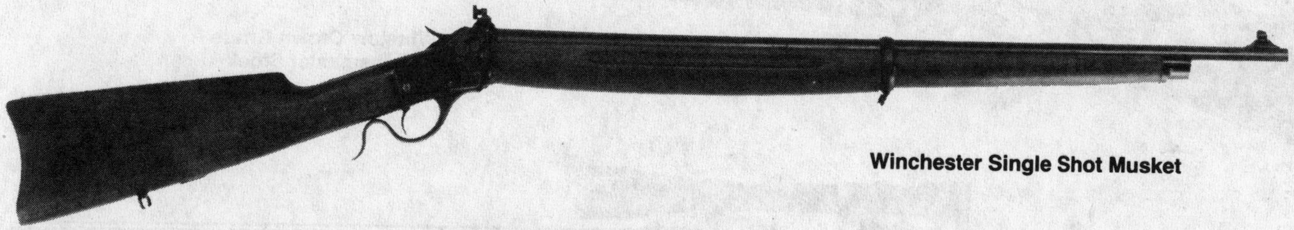

Winchester Single Shot Musket

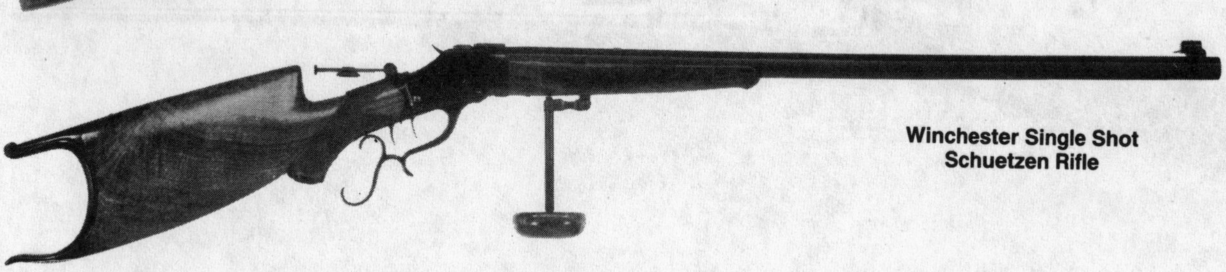

Winchester Single Shot Schuetzen Rifle

Note: Winchester Single Shot Rifle. Designed by John M. Browning, this falling-block lever action arm was manufactured from 1885 to 1920 in a variety of models and chambered for most of the popular cartridges of the period, rimfire and centerfire, from 22 to 50 caliber. There are two basic styles of frame, low-wall and high-wall. The former style was used only for low-powered calibers; the latter was supplied in all calibers and was made in three types: the standard model for #3 and heavier barrels is the type commonly encountered, the thin-walled version was supplied with #1 and #2 light barrels and the thick-walled action in the heavier calibers. Made in solid frame and takedown models. The latter are generally considered less desirable. Barrels were available in five weights, ranging from the lightweight #1 to the extra heavy #5 in round, half-octagon and full-octagon styles. Plain, single-set, double-set and double-Schuetzen triggers were offered. A complete listing of Winchester Single Shots is beyond the proper scope of this volume; included herein are the three standard types: Musket, Schuetzen Rifle and Sporting Rifle.

Winchester Single Shot Musket $495
Solid frame. Low-wall. Plain trigger. Standard finger lever. Calibers: 22 Short, 22 Long Rifle. 28-inch round barrel. Weight: 8½ pounds. Lyman rear peep sight, blade front sight. Military-type stock and forearm. *Note:* The U.S. Government purchased a large quantity of these Single Shot Muskets during WWI for training purposes. Many of these rifles were later sold through the Director of Civilian Marksmanship to National Rifle Association members for $1.50.

Winchester Single Shot Schuetzen Rifle $2300
Solid frame or takedown. High-wall action. Schuetzen double-set trigger. Spur finger level. No. 3 30-inch octagon barrel. Weight: 12 pounds. Vernier rear peep sight, wind-gauge front sight. Fancy walnut Schuetzen stock with checkered pistol grip and forearm. Schuetzen butt plate. Adjustable palm rest.

Winchester Single Shot
Sporting Rifle

Winchester Single Shot Sporting Rifle (H) $795
High-wall. Plain model. Solid frame or takedown. Plain trigger. Standard lever. No. 3 barrel, 30-inch. Weight: 9½ pounds. Open rear sight, blade front sight. Plain stock and forearm.

Winchester Single Shot Sporting Rifle (L) $595
Low-wall. Plain model. Solid frame. Plain trigger. Standard lever. No. 1 barrel, 28-inch round or octagon. Weight: 7 pounds. Open rear sight, blade front sight. Plain stock and forearm.

Winchester Single Shot Sporting Rifle (SP) $1850
Special Grade. Same as Plain Model High-wall, but with fancy walnut stock and forearm, checkered.

Winchester Single Shot "Winder" Musket $550
Solid frame or takedown. High-wall. Plain trigger. Standard finger lever. Calibers: 22 Short, 22 Long Rifle. 28-inch round barrel. Weight: 8½ pounds. Musket rear sight, blade front sight. Military-type stock and forearm.

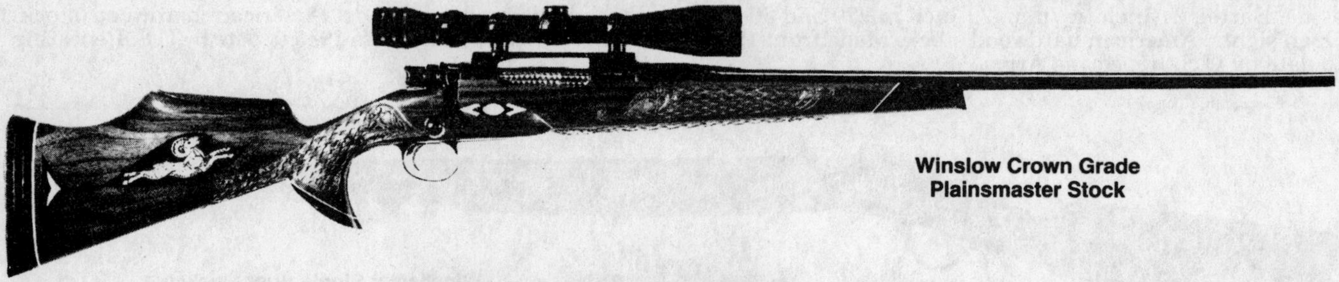

Winslow Crown Grade
Plainsmaster Stock

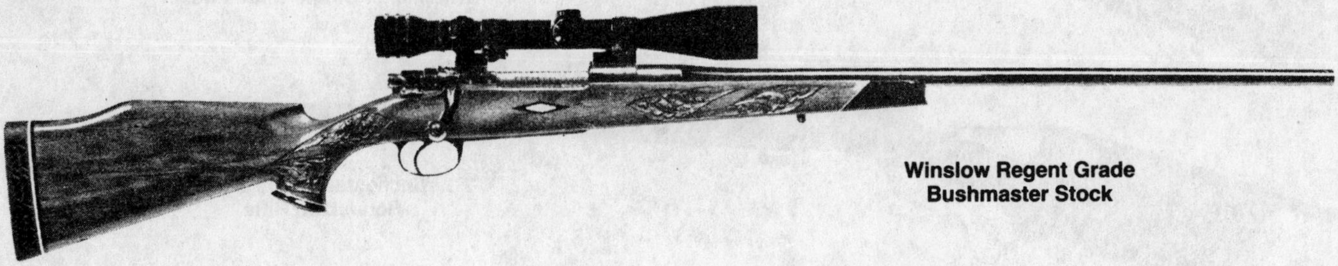

Winslow Regent Grade
Bushmaster Stock

WINSLOW ARMS COMPANY
Camden, South Carolina

Winslow Bolt Action Sporting Rifle
Action: FN Supreme Mauser, Mark X Mauser, Remington 700 and 788, Sako, Winchester 70. Standard calibers: 17/222, 17/223, 222 Rem., 22-250, 243 Win., 6mm Rem., 25-06, 257 Roberts, 270 Win., 7×57, 280 Rem., 284 Win., 308 Win., 30-06, 358 Win. Magnum calibers: 17/222 Mag., 257 Weatherby, 264 Win., 270 Weath., 7mm Rem., 7mm Weath., 300 H&H, 300 Weath., 300 Win., 308 Norma, 8mm Rem., 338 Win., 358 Norma, 375 H&H, 375 Weath., 458 Win. 3-shot magazine in standard calibers, 2-shot in magnum. 24-inch barrel in standard calibers, 26-inch in magnum. Weight: with 24-inch barrel, 7 to 7½ lbs.; with 26-inch barrel, 8 to 9 lbs. No sights. Stocks: "Bushmaster" with slender pistol grip and beavertail forearm, "Plainsmaster" with full curl pistol grip and flat forearm; both styles have Monte Carlo cheekpiece; rosewood forend tip

Winslow Bolt Action Sporting Rifle (cont.)
and pistol-grip cap, recoil pad, QD swivels; woods used include walnut, maple, myrtle. There are eight grades—Commander, Regal, Regent, Regimental, Royal, Imperial, Emperor—in ascending order of quality of wood, carving, inlays, engraving. Values shown are for basic rifle in each grade; extras such as special fancy wood, more elaborate carving, inlays and engraving can increase these figures considerably. Made 1962 to date.

Commander Grade	**$ 495**
Regal Grade	**575**
Regent Grade	**695**
Regimental Grade	**850**
Crown Grade	**1200**
Royal Grade	**1400**
Imperial Grade	**3000**
Emperor Grade	**5500**

Section III

SHOTGUNS

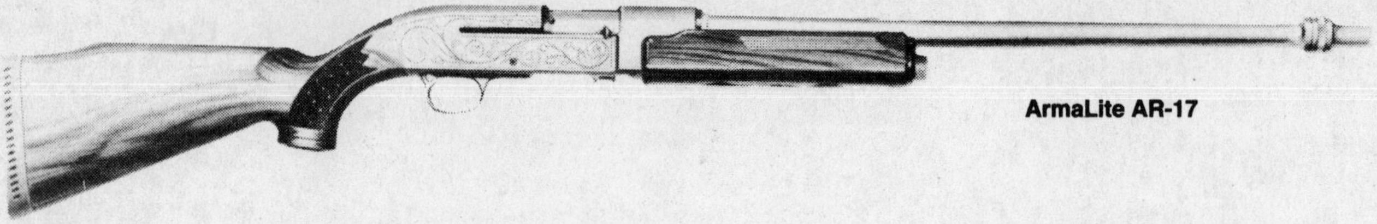

ArmaLite AR-17

ALDENS SHOTGUN
Chicago, Illinois

Aldens Model 670 Chieftain Slide Action $125
Hammerless. Gauges: 12, 20, and others. 3-shot tubular magazine. Barrel: 26- to 30-inch; various chokes. Weight: $6^1/_4$ to $7^1/_2$ pounds depending upon barrel length and gauge. Walnut finished hardwood stock.

ARMALITE, INC.
Costa Mesa, California

Armalite AR-17 Golden Gun $450
Recoil-operated semiautomatic. High-test aluminum barrel and receiver housing. 12 gauge only. 2-shot. 24-inch barrel with interchangeable choke tubes: improved cylinder, modified, and full. Weight: 5.6 pounds. Polycarbonate stock and forearm, recoil pad. Gold anodized finish standard; also made with black finish. Made from 1964 to 1965. Less than 2,000 produced.

ARMSPORT, INC.
Miami, Florida

Armsport Models 1050, 1053, 1054 Hammerless Doubles
Side-by-side with engraved receiver, double triggers and extractors. Gauges: 12, 20, .410; 3-inch chambers. *Model 1050:* 12 ga., 28-inch bbl., mod./full choke. *Model 1053:* 20 ga., 26-inch bbl., imp./mod. choke. *Model 1054:* .410 ga., 26-inch bbl., imp./mod. Weight: 6 pounds (12 ga.). European walnut buttstock and forend. Made in Italy from 1986 to date.
Model 1050 .... **$370**
Model 1053 .... **370**
Model 1054 .... **410**

Armsport Model 2700 Goose Gun $550
Similar to the 2700 Standard Model, except 10 gauge with $3^1/_2$-inch chambers. Double triggers with 28-inch barrel choked imp. cyl./mod. or 32-inch barrel, full/full. 12mm wide vent rib. Weight: $9^1/_2$ pounds. Canada geese engraved on receiver. Antiqued silver finished action. Checkered European walnut stock with rubber recoil pad. Made in Italy from 1986 to date.

Armsport Model 2700 Over/Under Shotgun
Hammerless, takedown shotgun with engraved receiver. Selective single or double triggers. Gauges: 12, 20 and .410. Barrel: 26- or 28-inch with fixed chokes or choke tubes. Weight: 8 pounds. Checkered European walnut buttstock and forend. Made in Italy.
12 or 20 ga. w/Extractors **$430**
12 or 20 ga. w/Ejectors **505**
With Ejectors, S/S trigger, C-tubes **560**
.410 w/Double Triggers **370**
.410 w/Single Trigger **410**

Armsport Model 2751 Autoloading Shotgun
Gas-operated, takedown, hammerless shotgun with tubular magazine. Gauge: 12; 3-inch chamber. Barrels: 28-inch (modified), 30-inch (full) or 28-inch with choke tubes; vent rib. Weight: 7 pounds. European walnut stock. Made in Italy from 1986 to date.
With Fixed Choke **$430**
With Choke Tubes **490**
Deluxe Model w/Silver Receiver **505**

Armsport Model 2755 Slide Action Shotgun
Pump action, hammerless shotgun. 12 gauge w/3-inch chamber. Tubular magazine. Barrels: 28- or 30-inch with fixed choke or choke tubes. Weight: 7 pounds; vent rib. European walnut stock. Made in Italy from 1986 to date.
Standard Model, Fixed Choke **$295**
Standard Model, Choke Tubes **350**
Police Model, 20-inch Barrel **280**

Armsport Models 1050, 1053, 1054
Side/Side Shotguns

Armsport Model 2700
10 Gauge O/U Goose Gun

ASTRA SHOTGUNS
Guernica, Spain
Manufactured by Unceta y Compania

Astra Model 650 Over/Under Shotgun
Hammerless, takedown with double triggers. 12 gauge w/ 2¾-inch chambers. Barrels: 28-inch (mod./full or Skeet/ Skeet); 30-inch (mod./full). Weight: 6¾ pounds. Checkered European walnut buttstock and forend.
With Extractors **$420**
With Ejectors **505**

Astra Model 750 Over/Under Shotgun
Similar to the Model 650, except with selective single trigger and ejectors. Made in Field, Skeet and Trap configurations since 1980.
Field Model w/Extractors **$490**
Field Model w/Ejectors **570**
Trap or Skeet **675**

AYA (AGUIRRE Y ARANZABAL)
Eibar, Spain

AyA Model 2 Hammerless Double
Sidelock action with selective single or double triggers, automatic ejectors and safety. Gauges: 12, 20, 28, (2¾-inch chambers); .410 (3-inch chambers). Barrels: 26- or 28-inch with various fixed choke combinations. Weight: 7 pounds (12 ga.). English-style straight walnut buttstock and splinter forend. Made from 1987 to date.
12 or 20 ga. w/Double Triggers **$1240**
12 or 20 ga. w/Single Trigger **1350**
28 or .410 ga. w/Double Triggers **1345**
28 or .410 ga. w/Single Trigger **1460**
Two Barrel Set **600**

AyA Model 37 Super Over/Under Shotgun $2100
Side lock. Automatic ejectors. Selective single trigger. Made in all gauges, barrel lengths and chokes. Vent-rib barrels. Elaborately engraved. Checkered stock (with straight or pistol grip) and forend. Discontinued 1985.

AyA Model 53E $1100
Same general specifications as Model 117, except more elaborate engraving and select figured wood. Discontinued 1986.

AyA Model 76 Hammerless Double $450
Anson & Deeley box lock. Auto ejectors. Selective single trigger. Gauges: 12, 20 (3-inch). Barrels: 26-, 28-, 30-inch (latter in 12 gauge only); any standard choke combination. Checkered pistol-grip stock and beavertail forend. Discontinued.

AyA Model 76—410 Gauge $410
Same general specifications as 12 and 20 gauge Model 76, except chambered for 3-inch shells in .410, has extractors, double triggers, 26-inch barrels only, English-style stock with straight grip and small forend. Discontinued.

AyA Model 117 Hammerless Double $700
Holland & Holland-type side locks, hand-detachable. Engraved action. Automatic ejectors. Selective single trigger. Gauges: 12, 20 (3-inch). Barrels: 26-, 27-, 28-, 30-inch; 27- and 30-inch in 12 gauge only; any standard choke combination. Checkered pistol-grip stock and beavertail forend of select walnut. Manufactured 1985.

AyA Bolero $345
Same general specifications as Matador except non-selective single trigger and extractors. Gauges: 12, 16, 20, 20 magnum (3-inch), .410 (3-inch). *Note:* This model, prior to 1956, was designated F. I. Model 400 by the importer. Made from 1955 to 1963.

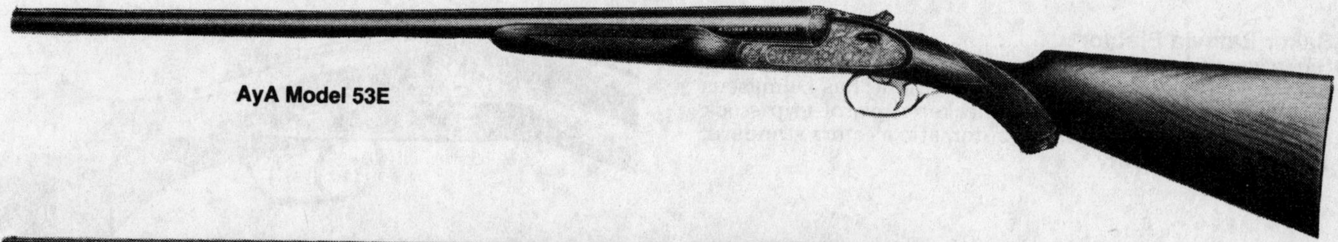
AyA Model 53E

AyA Model 76

AyA Model 117

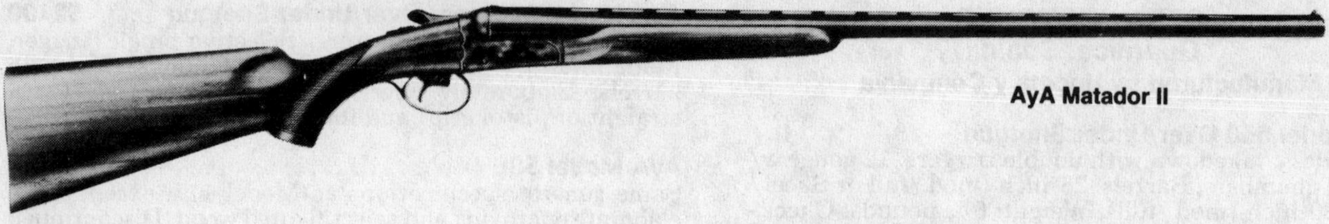

AyA Matador II

AyA Matador Hammerless Double $425
Anson & Deeley box lock. Selective automatic ejectors. Selective single trigger. Gauges: 12, 16, 20, 20 magnum (3-inch). Barrels: 26-, 28-, 30-inch; any standard choke combination. Weight: $6^{1}/_{2}$ to $7^{1}/_{2}$ pounds depending upon gauge and barrel length. Checkered pistol-grip stock and beavertail forend. *Note:* This model, prior to 1956, was designated F. I. Model 400E by the U.S. importer, Firearms International Corp., Washington, D.C. Made from 1955 to 1963.

AyA Matador II $475
Improved version of Matador with same general specifications, except has vent-rib barrels. Made 1964-69.

AyA Matador III $700
Same general specifications as AyA Matador II. Made from 1970 to 1985.

BAKER SHOTGUNS
Batavia, New York
Made from 1903 to 1933 by Baker Gun Company

Baker Batavia Ejector $695
Same general specifications as the Batavia Leader, except higher quality and finer finish throughout; has Damascus or homotensile steel barrels, checkered pistol-grip stock and forearm of select walnut; automatic ejectors standard; 12 and 16 gauge only.

Baker Batavia Leader

Baker Batavia Leader Hammerless Double
Side lock. Plain extractors or automatic ejectors. Double triggers. Gauges: 12, 16, 20. Barrels: 26- to 32-inch; any standard boring. Weight: about $7^{3}/_{4}$ pounds (12 gauge with 30-inch barrels). Checkered pistol-grip stock and forearm.
With plain extractors **$350**
With automatic ejectors **425**

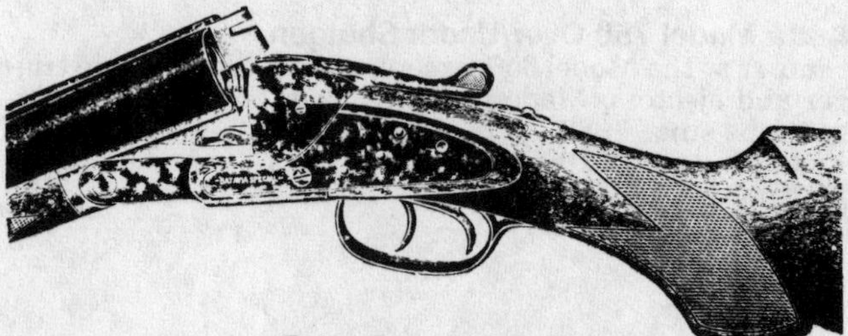

Baker Batavia Special

Baker Batavia Special $300
Same general specifications as the Batavia Leader, except plainer finish; 12 and 16 gauge only; has plain extractors, homotensile steel barrels.

Baker Black Beauty Special
Same general specifications as the Batavia Leader, except higher quality and finer finish throughout; has line engraving, special steel barrels, select walnut stock with straight, full or half-pistol grip.
With plain extractors **$610**
With automatic ejectors **710**

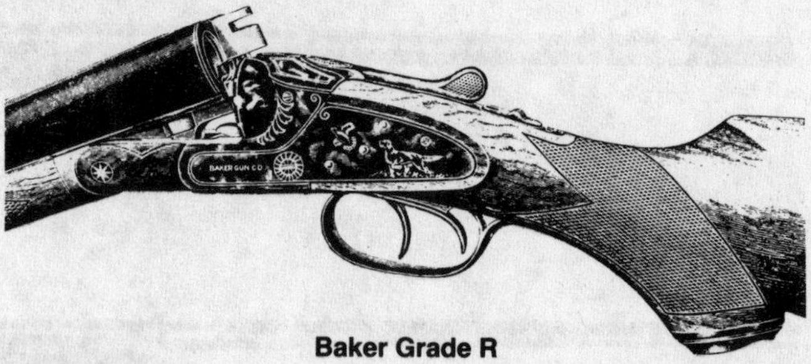

Baker Grade R

Baker Grade R
High-grade gun with same general specifications as the Batavia Leader, except has fine Damascus or Krupp fluid steel barrels, engraving in line, scroll and game scene designs, checkered stock and forearm of fancy European walnut; 12 and 16 gauges only.
Non-ejector **$1000**
With automatic ejectors **1200**

Baker Grade S
Same general specifications as the Batavia Leader, except higher quality and finer finish throughout; has Flui-tempered steel barrels, line and scroll engraving, checkered stock with half-pistol grip and forearm of semifancy imported walnut; 10, 12 and 16 gauges.
Non-ejector **$750**
With automatic ejectors **875**

Baker Paragon Grade

Baker Paragon, Expert and Deluxe Grades
Made to order only, these are the higher grades of Baker hammerless sidelock double-barrel shotguns. After 1909, the Paragon Grade, as well as the Expert and Deluxe introduced that year, had a cross bolt in addition to the regular Baker system taper wedge fastening. There are early Paragon guns with Damascus barrels and some are non-ejector, but this grade was also produced with automatic ejectors and with the finest fluid steel barrels, in lengths to 34 inches, standard on Expert and Deluxe guns. Differences among the three models are in overall quality, finish, elaborateness of engraving and grade of fancy figured walnut in the stock and forearm; Expert and Deluxe wood may be carved as well as checkered. Choice of straight, half- or full pistol grip was offered. A single trigger was available in the two higher grades. The Paragon was available in 10 gauge (Damascus barrels only); this and the other two models were regularly produced in 12, 16 and 20 gauges.

Paragon Grade, non-ejector **$1500**
Paragon Grade, automatic ejectors **1600**
Expert Grade **3000**
Deluxe Grade **5000**
Extra for single trigger **200**

BELKNAP SHOTGUNS
Louisville, Kentucky

Belknap Model B-63 Single Shot Shotgun $65
Takedown. Visible hammer. Automatic ejector. Gauges: 12, 20 and .410. Barrels: 26- to 36-inch; full choke. Weight: average 6 pounds. Plain pistol-grip stock and forearm.

Belknap Model B-63E Single Shot Shotgun $65
Same general specifications as Model B-68, except has side lever opening instead of top lever.

Belknap Model B-64 Slide Action Shotgun $125
Hammerless. Gauges: 12, 16, 20 and .410. 3-shot tubular magazine. Various barrel lengths and chokes from 26-inch to 30-inch. Weight: 6¼ to 7½ pounds. Walnut finished hardwood stock.

Belknap Model B-65C Autoloading Shotgun $250
Browning-type lightweight alloy receiver. 12 gauge only. 4-shot tubular magazine. Barrel: plain, 28-inch. Weight: about 8¼ pounds. Discontinued 1949.

Belknap Model B-68 Single Shot Shotgun $65
Takedown. Visible hammer. Automatic ejector. Gauges: 12, 16, 20 and .410. Barrels: 26-inch to 36-inch; full choke. Weight: 6 pounds. Plain pistol-grip stock and forearm.

BENELLI SHOTGUNS
Urbino, Italy

Benelli Model 121 M1 Military/Police Autoloading Shotgun $310
Gauge: 12. 7-shot magazine. 19¾-inch barrel. 39¾ inches overall. Cylinder choke, 2¾-inch chamber. Weight: 7.4 pounds. Matte black finish and European hardwood stock. Post front sight, fixed buckhorn rear sight. Made in 1985.

Benelli SL 121V Semiautomatic Shotgun $310
Gauge: 12. 5-shot capacity. Barrels: 26-, 28- and 30-inch. 26-inch choked mod., imp. mod., imp. cyl.; 28-inch, full, mod., imp. mod.; 30-inch, full choke (Mag.) Straight walnut stock with hand-checkered pistol grip and forend. Ventilated rib. Made in 1985.

Benelli Model SL 121V Slug Shotgun $325
Same general specifications as Benelli SL121V, except designed for rifled slugs and equipped with rifle sights. Made in 1985.

Benelli SL 123V Semiautomatic Shotgun $345
Gauge: 12. 26- and 28-inch barrels. 26-inch choked imp. mod., mod., imp. cyl.; 28-inch choked full, imp. mod., mod. Made in 1985.

SHOTGUNS

Benelli Model 121 M1 Military/Police Shotgun

Benelli SL 123V Semiautomatic

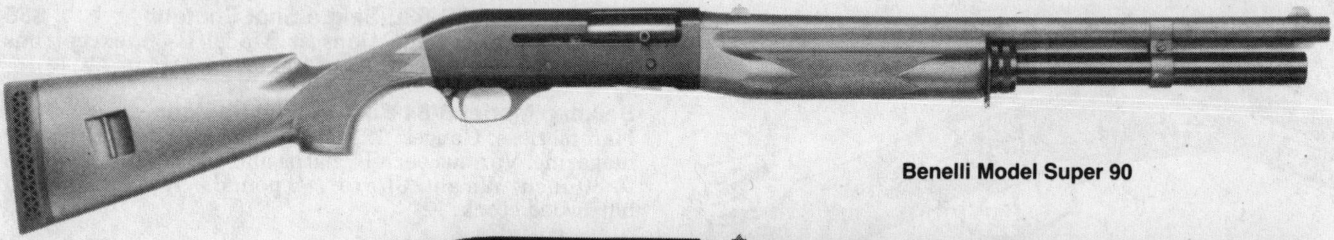

Benelli Model Super 90

Benelli Model Super 90
Buttstock w/ Pistol Grip

Benelli Model SL 201 Semiautomatic Shotgun . . $300
Gauge: 20. 26-inch barrel. Mod. choke. Weight: 5 lbs., 10 oz. Ventilated rib. Made in 1985.

Benelli Model Super 90 Autoloading Shotgun
Gauge: 12. 7-shot magazine. Cylinder choke. 19¾-inch barrel. 39¾ inches overall. Weight: 7 lbs. 4 oz. to 7 lbs. 10 oz. Matte black finish. Stock and forend made of fiberglass reinforced polymer. Post front sight, fixed buckhorn rear drift adjustable sight. Made from 1985 to date.
Standard **$495**
Buttstock w/Pistol Grip **520**

BERETTA USA CORP.
Accokeek, Maryland

Manufactured by Fabbrica D'Armi Pietro Beretta S.p.A. in the Gardone Valtrompia (Brescia), Italy.

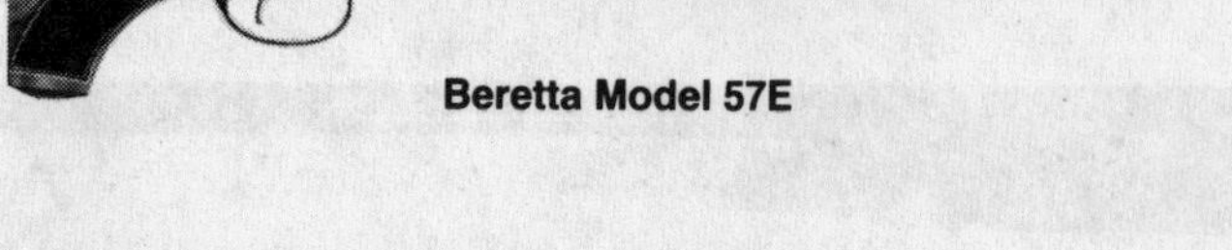

Beretta Model 57E

Beretta Model 57E Over-and-Under
Same general specifications as Golden Snipe, but higher quality throughout. Made from 1955 to 1967.
With non-selective single trigger **$795**
With selective single trigger **840**

Beretta Model 409 PB

Beretta Model 409PB Hammerless Double $725
Box lock. Double triggers. Plain extractors. Gauges: 12, 16, 20, 28. Barrels: 27½-, 28½- and 30-inch; improved cylinder and modified choke or modified and full choke. Weight: from 5½ to 7¾ pounds depending upon gauge and barrel length. Straight or pistol-grip stock and beavertail forearm, checkered. Made from 1934 to 1964.

Beretta Model 410 E

Beretta Model 410E $755
Same general specifications as Model 409PB, except has automatic ejectors and is of higher quality throughout. Made from 1934 to 1964.

Beretta Model 410, 10 Gauge Magnum $925
Same as Model 410E, except heavier construction. Plain extractors. Double triggers. 10 gauge magnum, 3½-inch chambers. 32-inch barrels, both full choke. Weight: about 10 pounds. Checkered pistol-grip stock and forearm, recoil pad. Made from 1934 to date.

Beretta Model 411E $1195
Same general specifications as Model 409PB except has side plates, automatic ejectors and is of higher quality throughout. Made from 1934 to 1964.

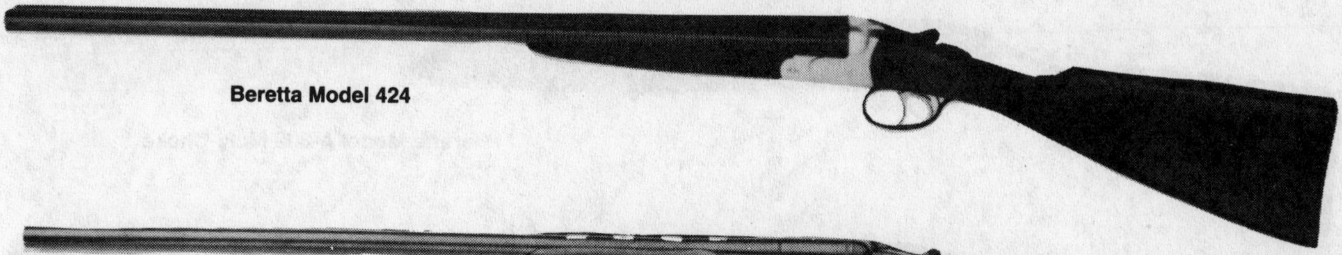

Beretta Model 424

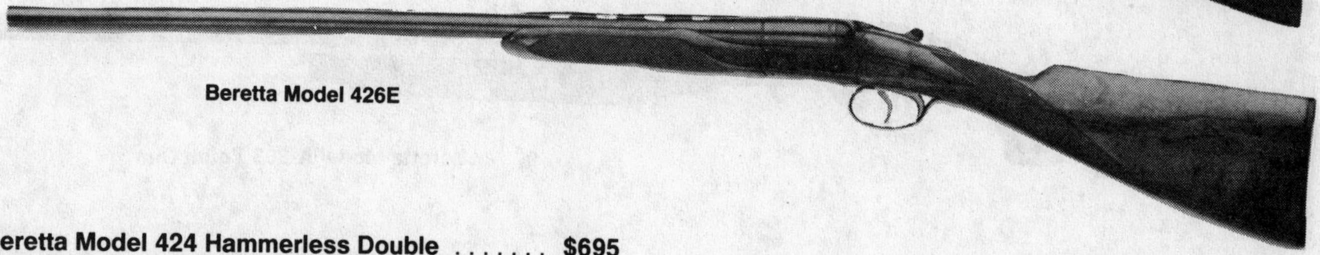

Beretta Model 426E

Beretta Model 424 Hammerless Double $695
Box lock. Light border engraving. Plain extractors. Gauges: 12, 20; chambers 2¾-inch in former, 3-inch in latter. Barrels: 28-inch modified and full choke; 26-inch improved cylinder and modified choke. Weight: 5 lbs. 14 oz. to 6 lbs. 10 oz. depending upon gauge and barrel length. English-style straight-grip stock and forearm, checkered. Introduced in 1977.

Beretta Model 426E $895
Same as Model 424, except action body is finely engraved, silver pigeon inlaid in top lever; has selective automatic ejectors and selective single trigger, stock and forearm of select European walnut. Introduced in 1977.

Beretta Model 626 S/S Hammerless Double $770
Field Grade side-by-side. Boxlock action with single selective trigger, extractors and automatic safety. Gauges: 12 (2¾-inch chambers); 20 (3-inch chambers). Barrels: 26- or 28-inch with various fixed choke combinations. Weight: 6¾ pounds (12 ga.). Bright chrome finish. Checkered European walnut buttstock and forend in straight English style. Made from 1985 to date.

Beretta Model 682 O/U Sporting Shotgun $1460
Hammerless takedown with selective single trigger. 12 gauge w/2¾-inch chambers. 28-inch barrels w/four screw-in choke tubes—full, modified, improved cylinder, skeet. Weight: 7¾ pounds. Checkered European walnut buttstock and forend.

Beretta Model A-301 Autoloading Shotgun $325
Field Gun. Gas-operated. Scroll-decorated receiver. Gauges: 12, 20; 2¾-inch chamber in former, 3-inch in latter. 3-shot magazine. Barrels: ventilated rib; 28-inch full or modified choke, 26-inch improved cylinder. Weight: 6 lbs. 5 oz. to 6 lbs. 14 oz. depending upon gauge and barrel length. Checkered pistol-grip stock and forearm. Made from 1977 to about 1982.

Beretta Model A-301 Magnum $375
Same as Model A-301 Field Gun, except chambered for 12 gauge 3-inch magnum shells; 30-inch full choke barrel only, stock with recoil pad. Weight: 7¼ pounds.

Beretta Model A-301 Skeet Gun $350
Same as Model A-301 Field Gun, except 26-inch barrel in skeet choke only, has skeet-style stock, gold-plated trigger.

Beretta Model A-301 Slug Gun............... $325
Same as Model A-301 Field Gun, except has plain 22-inch barrel, slug choke, with rifle sights. Weight: 6 lbs. 14 oz.

Beretta Model A-301 Trap Gun $350
Same as Model A-301 Field Gun, except has 30-inch barrel in full choke only, Monte Carlo stock with recoil pad, gold-plated trigger. Weight: 7 lbs. 10 oz.

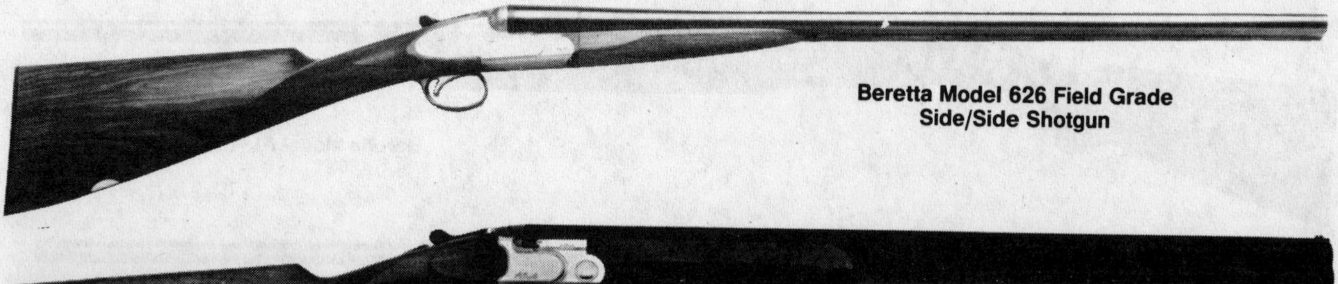

Beretta Model 626 Field Grade
Side/Side Shotgun

Beretta Model 682 Sporting

Beretta Model A-302 Multi-Choke

Beretta Model A-303 Youth Gun

Beretta Model A-302 Semiautoloading Shotgun
Similar to gas-operated Model 301. Hammerless, take-down shotgun with tubular magazine and Mag-Action that handles both 2¾- and 3-inch magnum shells. Gauges: 12, 20; 2¾- or 3-inch Mag. chambers. Barrels: ventilated or plain; 22-inch/Slug (12 ga.); 26-inch/improved cylinder (12 or 20); 28-inch/modified (20 ga.); 28-inch/Multi-choke (12 or 20 ga.); 30-inch/full (12 ga.). Weight: 6½ pounds (20 ga.); 7¼ pounds (12 ga.) Blue/black finish. Checkered European walnut, pistol-grip stock and forend. Made from 1983 to about 1987.
Standard Model with Fixed Choke **$360**
Standard Model with Multi-choke **460**

Beretta Model A-302 Super Lusso **$1875**
A custom A-302 in presentation grade with hand-engraved receiver and custom select walnut stock.

Beretta Model A-303 Semiautoloader **$520**
Similar to Model 302, except with target specifications in Trap, Skeet and Youth configurations, and weighs 6 to 7 pounds. Made from about 1987 to date.

Beretta Model AL-1 Field Gun **$295**
Same as Model AL-2 Field Gun, except has barrel without rib, no engraving on receiver. Made from 1971 to 1973.

Beretta Model AL-2 Autoloading Shotgun
Field Gun. Gas-operated. Engraved receiver (1968 version, 12 gauge only, had no engraving). Gauges: 12, 20. 2¾-inch chamber. 3-shot magazine. Barrels: ventilated rib; 30-inch full choke, 28-inch full or modified choke, 26-inch improved cylinder. Weight: 6½ to 7¼ pounds depending upon gauge and barrel length. Checkered pistol-grip stock and forearm. Made from 1968 to 1975.
With plain receiver **$300**
With engraved receiver **330**

Beretta Model AL-2 Magnum **$350**
Same as Model AL-2 Field Gun, except chambered for 12 gauge 3-inch magnum shells; 30-inch full, 28-inch modified choke barrels only. Weight: about 8 pounds. Made from 1973 to 1975.

Beretta Model AL-2 Skeet Gun **$375**
Same as Model AL-2 Field Gun, except has wide rib, 26-inch barrel in skeet choke only, beavertail forearm. Made from 1969 to 1975.

Beretta Model AL-2 Trap Gun **$350**
Same as Model AL-2 Field Gun, except has wide rib, 30-inch barrel in full choke only, beavertail forearm. Monte Carlo stock with recoil pad. Weight: about 7¾ pounds. Made from 1969 to 1975.

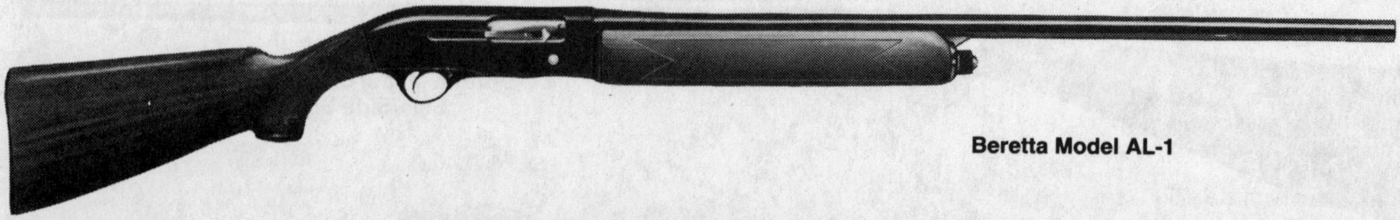

Beretta Model AL-1

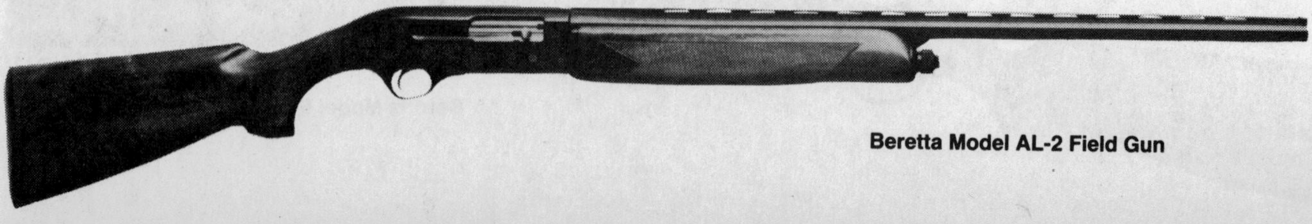

Beretta Model AL-2 Field Gun

Beretta Model AL-3
Similar to corresponding AL-2 models in design and general specifications. Made from 1975 to 1976.
Field model **$360**
Magnum model **390**
Skeet model **390**
Trap model **410**

Beretta Model AL-3 Deluxe Trap Gun $700
Same as standard Model AL-3 Trap Gun, except has fully engraved receiver, gold-plated trigger and safety, stock and forearm of premium grade European walnut, gold monogram escutcheon inlaid in buttstock. Made from 1975 to 1976.

Beretta Model Asel

Beretta Model Asel Over-and-Under Shotgun . . $1000
Box lock. Single non-selective trigger. Selective automatic ejectors. Gauges: 12, 20. Barrels: 26-, 28-, 30-inch; improved cylinder and modified choke or modified and full choke. Weight: 20 gauge, about 5¾ pounds; 12 gauge, about 7 pounds. Checkered pistol-grip stock and forearm. Made from 1947 to 1964.

Beretta Model BL-1

Beretta Model BL-2/S

Beretta Model BL-3

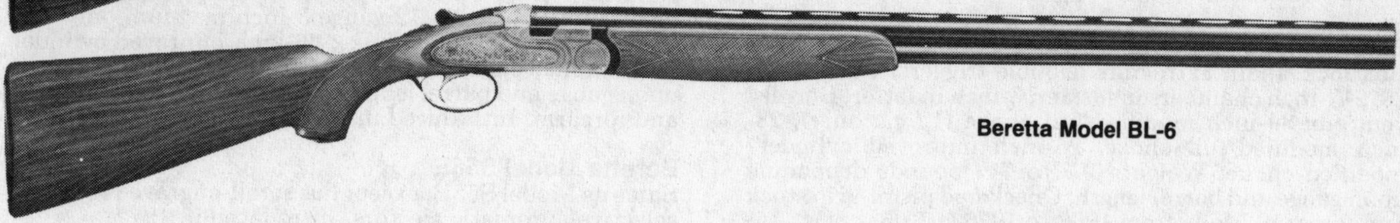
Beretta Model BL-6

Beretta Model BL-1 Over-and-Under Shotgun . . $350
Box lock. Plain extractors. Double triggers. 12 gauge, 2¾-inch chambers only. Barrels: 30- and 28-inch modified/full choke; 26-inch improved cylinder/modified choke. Weight: 6¾ to 7 pounds depending upon barrel length. Checkered pistol-grip stock and forearm. Made from 1968 to 1973.

Beretta Model BL-2 . . . . $395
Same as Model BL-1, except has more engraving, selective single trigger. Made from 1968 to 1973.

Beretta Model BL-2/S $395
Similar to Model BL-1, except has selective "Speed-Trigger," ventilated-rib barrels, 2¾- or 3-inch chambers. Weight: 7 to 7½ pounds. Made from 1974 to 1976.

Beretta Model BL-3 . . . . $575
Same as Model BL-1, except deluxe engraved receiver, selective single trigger, ventilated-rib barrels; 12 or 20 gauge, 2¾-inch or 3-inch chambers in former, 3-inch in latter. Weight: 6 to 7½ pounds depending upon gauge and barrel length. Made from 1968 to 1976.

Beretta Models BL-4, BL-5 and BL-6
Higher grade versions of Model BL-3 with more elaborate engraving and fancier wood; Model BL-6 has side plates. Selective automatic ejectors standard. Made from 1968 to 1976 (Model BL-6 introduced in 1973).
Model BL-4 . . . . **$ 725**
Model BL-5 . . . . **725**
Model BL-6 . . . . **895**

Beretta FS-1

Beretta Series "BL" Skeet Guns
Models BL-3, BL-4, BL-5 and BL-6 with standard features of their respective grades plus wider rib and skeet-style stock; 26-inch barrels skeet choked. Weight: 6 to 7¼ pounds depending upon gauge.

Model BL-3 Skeet Gun	$ 600
Model BL-4 Skeet Gun	750
Model BL-5 Skeet Gun	995
Model BL-6 Skeet Gun	1295

Beretta Series "BL" Trap Guns
Models BL-3, BL-4, BL-5 and BL-6 with standard features of their respective grades plus wider rib and Monte Carlo stock with recoil pad; 30-inch barrels, improved modified/full or both full choke. Weight: about 7½ pounds.

Model BL-3 Trap Gun	$ 600
Model BL-4 Trap Gun	795
Model BL-5 Trap Gun	995
Model BL-6 Trap Gun	1250

Beretta Model FS-1 Folding Single $125
Formerly "Companion." Folds to length of barrel. Hammerless. Underlever. Gauges: 12, 16, 20, 28, .410. Barrels: 30-inch in 12 ga.; 28-inch in 16 and 20 ga.; 26-inch in 28 and .410 ga.; all full choke. Checkered semipistol-grip stock and forearm. Weight: 4½ to 5½ pounds depending upon gauge. Discontinued 1971.

Beretta Golden Snipe Over-and-Under
Same as Silver Snipe, except has automatic ejectors, ventilated rib is standard feature. Made from 1959 to 1967.

With non-selective single trigger	$625
Extra for selective single trigger	75

Beretta Model GR-2 Hammerless Double $575
Box lock. Plain extractors. Double triggers. Gauges: 12, 20; 2¾-inch chambers in former, 3-inch in latter. Barrels: vent rib; 30-inch modified/full choke (12 ga. only), 28-inch modified/full choke, 26-inch improved cylinder/modified choke. Weight: 6½ to 7¼ pounds depending upon gauge and barrel length. Checkered pistol-grip stock and forearm. Made from 1968 to 1976.

Beretta Model GR-3 . . . . $700
Same as Model GR-2, except has selective single trigger; chambered for 12 gauge 3-inch as well as 2¾-inch shell. Magnum model has 30-inch modified and full choke barrel, recoil pad. Weight: about 8 pounds. Made 1968 to 1976.

Beretta Model GR-4 . . . . $795
Same as Model GR-2, except has automatic ejectors and selective single trigger, higher grade engraving and wood. 12 gauge, 2¾-inch chambers only. Made from 1968 to 1976.

Beretta Grade 100 Over-and-Under Shotgun . . $1695
Side lock. Double triggers. Automatic ejectors. 12 gauge only. Barrels: 26-, 28-, 30-inch; any standard boring. Weight: about 7½ pounds. Checkered stock and forend, straight grip or pistol grip. Discontinued.

Beretta Grade 200 . . . . $2100
Same general specifications as Grade 100 except higher quality, bores and action parts hard chrome-plated. Discontinued.

Beretta Mark II Single Barrel Trap Gun $575
Boxlock action similar to that of Series "BL" Over-and-Unders. Engraved receiver. Automatic ejector. 12 gauge only. 32- or 34-inch barrel with wide ventilated rib. Weight: about 8½ pounds. Monte Carlo stock with pistol grip and recoil pad, beavertail forearm. Made 1972—-76.

Beretta Model S55B Over-and-Under Shotgun . . $475
Box lock. Plain extractors. Selective single trigger. Gauges: 12, 20; 2¾- or 3-inch chambers in former, 3-inch in latter. Barrels: ventilated rib; 30-inch modified and full choke or both full choke in 12 gauge 3-inch magnum only; 28-inch modified and full choke; 26-inch improved cylinder and modified choke. Weight: 6½ to 7½ pounds, depending upon gauge and barrel length. Checkered pistol-grip stock and forearm. Introduced in 1977.

Beretta Model S56E $595
Same as Model S55B, except has scroll-engraved receiver, selective automatic ejectors. Introduced in 1977.

Beretta Model GR-2

Beretta Mark II Trap

Beretta S-58 Trap

Beretta Silver Hawk

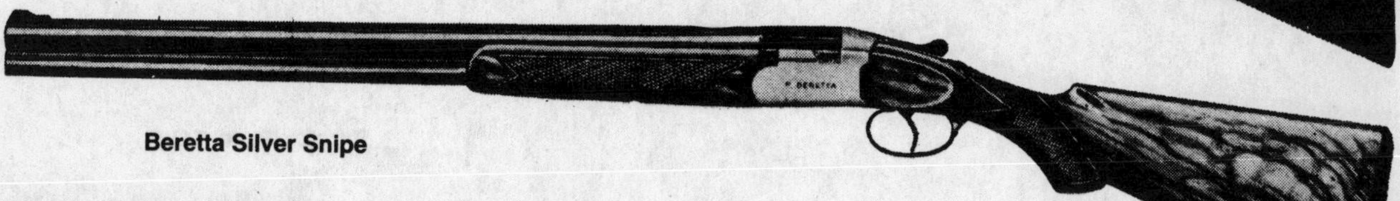

Beretta Silver Snipe

Beretta Model S58 Skeet Gun **$725**
Same as Model S56E, except has 26-inch barrels of Boehler Antinit Anticorro steel, skeet choked, with wide ventilated rib; skeet-style stock and forearm. Weight: 7½ pounds. Introduced in 1977.

Beretta Model S58 Trap Gun **$695**
Same as Model S58 Skeet Gun, except has 30-inch barrels bored improved modified and full trap, Monte Carlo stock with recoil pad. Weight: 7 lbs. 10 oz. Introduced in 1977.

Beretta Silver Hawk Featherweight Hammerless Double Barrel Shotgun
Box lock. Double triggers or non-selective single trigger. Plain extractor. Gauges: 12, 16, 20, 28, 12 mag. Barrels: 26- to 32-inch with high matted rib; all standard choke combinations. Weight: 12 ga. with 26-inch barrels, 7 pounds. Checkered walnut stock with beavertail forearm. Discontinued 1967.
With double triggers **$395**
Extra for non-selective single trigger **50**

Beretta Silver Snipe Over-and-Under Shotgun
Box lock. Non-selective or selective single trigger. Plain extractor. Gauges: 12, 20, 12 mag., 20 mag. Barrels: 26-, 28-, 30-inch; plain or ventilated rib; improved cylinder and modified choke, modified and full choke, skeet chokes #1 and #2, full and full. Weight: from about 6 pounds in

Beretta Silver Snipe Over-and-Under (cont.)
20 ga. to 8½ pounds in 12 ga. (trap gun). Checkered walnut pistol-grip stock and forearm. Made from 1955 to 1967.
With plain barrel, non-selective trigger **$375**
With ventilated-rib barrel, non-selective single trigger **425**
Extra for selective single trigger **50**

Beretta Model SL-2 Pump Gun **$255**
Hammerless. Takedown. 12 gauge only. 3-shot magazine. Barrels: ventilated rib; 30-inch full choke, 28-inch modified, 26-inch improved cylinder. Weight: about 7 to 7¼ pounds depending upon barrel length. Checkered pistol-grip stock and forearm. Made from 1968 to 1971.

Beretta Series "SO" Over-and-Under Shotguns
Side lock. Selective automatic ejectors. Selective single trigger or double triggers. 12 gauge only, 2¾- or 3-inch chambers. Barrels: ventilated rib (wide type on skeet and trap guns); 26-, 27-, 29-, 30-inch; any combination of standard chokes. Weight: from about 7 to 7¾ pounds depending upon barrel length, style of stock and density of

Beretta Model SL-2

Beretta Model SO-2
Over-and-Under

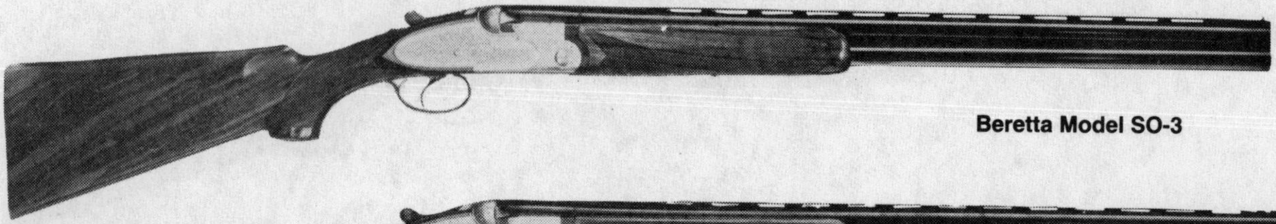
Beretta Model SO-3

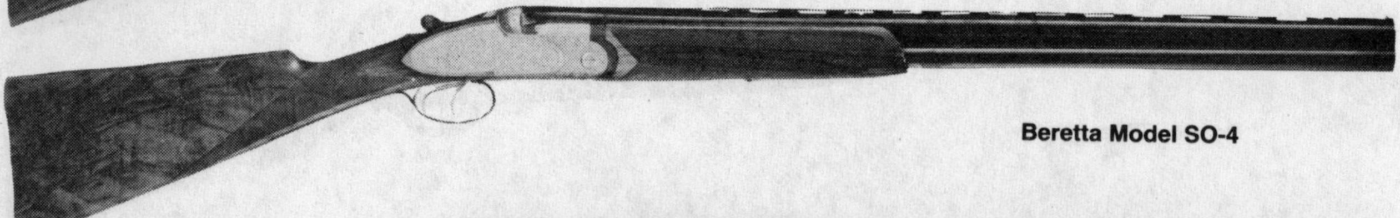
Beretta Model SO-4

Beretta Model SO-5

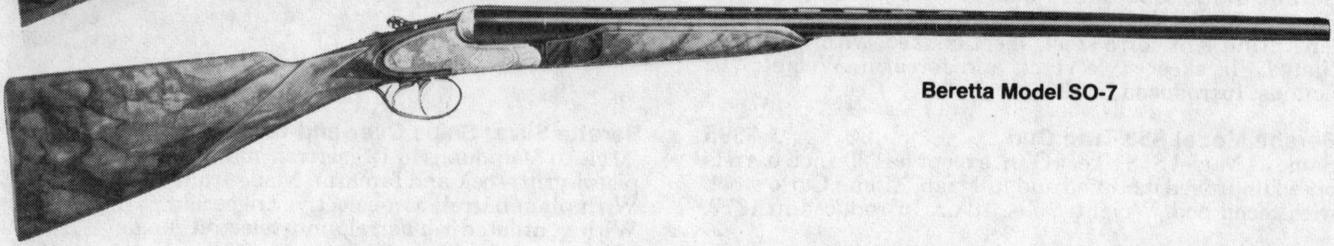
Beretta Model SO-7

Beretta Series "SO" Over-and-Unders (cont.)
wood. Stock and forearm of select walnut, finely checkered; straight or pistol grip; field, skeet and trap guns have appropriate styles of stock and forearm. The various models differ chiefly in quality of wood and grade of engraving. Models SO-3EL, SO-3EELL, SO-4 and SO-5 have hand-detachable locks. "SO-4" is used to designate current skeet and trap models derived from Model SO-3EL but with less elaborate engraving. Present Models SO-3EL and SO-3EELL are similar to the earlier SO-4 and SO-5, respectively. Made from 1948 to 1986.
Model SO-2 .... **$3100**
Model SO-3 .... **5100**
Model SO-4 Skeet or Trap Gun (current) **6500**
Model SO-4 (pre-1977) or SO-3EL **7100**
Model SO-5 or SO-3EELL **8100**

Beretta Models SO-6 and SO-7 Hammerless Doubles
Side-by-side guns with same general specifications as Series "SO" over-and-unders. Higher grade Model SO-7 has more elaborate engraving, fancier wood. Made from 1948 to date.
Model SO-6 .... **$8100**
Model SO-7 .... **9250**

Beretta Model TR-1 Single Barrel Trap Gun $220
Hammerless. Underlever action. Engraved frame. 12 gauge only. 32-inch barrel with ventilated rib. Weight: about 8¼ pounds. Monte Carlo stock with pistol grip and recoil pad, beavertail forearm. Made from 1968 to 1971.

Beretta Model TR-2 .... $250
Same as Model TR-1, except has extended ventilated rib. Made from 1969 to 1973.

Beretta Model TR-1

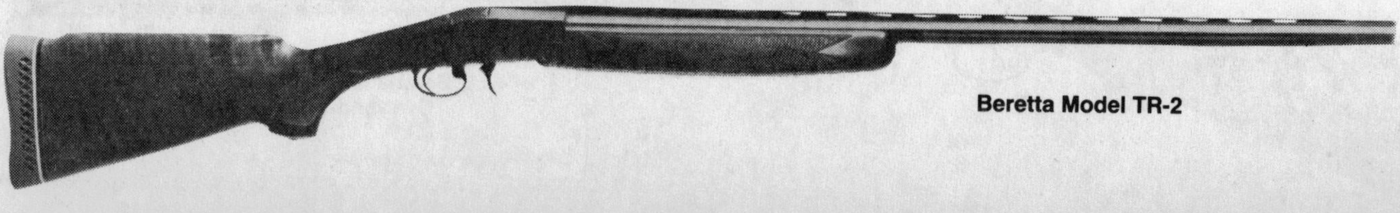
Beretta Model TR-2

VINCENZO BERNARDELLI
Gardone V.T. (Brescia), Italy

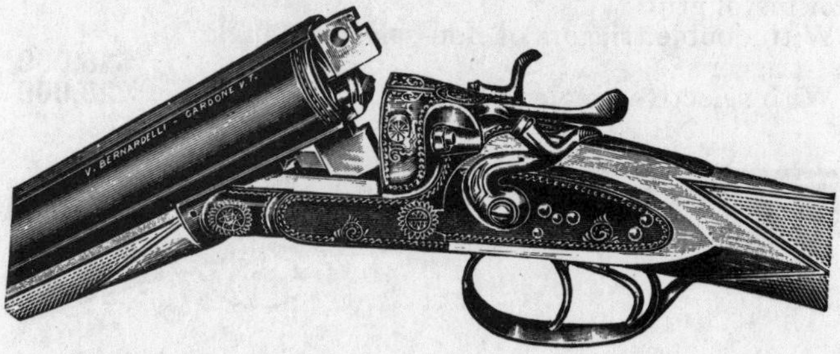

Bernardelli Brescia

Bernardelli Brescia Hammer Double $695
Back-action side lock. Plain extractors. Double triggers. Gauges: 12, 20. Barrels: $27\frac{1}{2}$ or $29\frac{1}{2}$-inch modified and full choke in 12 gauge, $25\frac{1}{2}$-inch improved cylinder and modified choke in 20 gauge. Weight: from $5\frac{3}{4}$ to 7 pounds depending upon gauge and barrel length. English-style stock and forearm, checkered. Currently manufactured.

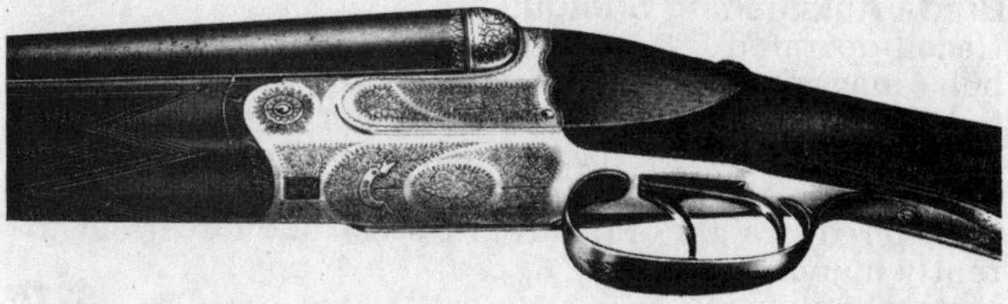

Bernardelli Elio

Bernardelli Elio $995
Lightweight game gun, 12 gauge only, with same general specifications as Standard Gamecock (S. Uberto 1), except weighs about 6 to $6\frac{1}{4}$ pounds, has automatic ejectors, fine English pattern scroll engraving. Currently manufactured.

Bernardelli Standard Gamecock

Bernardelli Gamecock, Standard (S. Uberto 1) Hammerless Double Barrel Shotgun $695
Box lock. Plain extractors. Double triggers. Gauges: 12, 16, 20; $2\frac{3}{4}$-inch chambers in 12 and 16, 3-inch in 20 gauge. Barrels: $25\frac{1}{2}$-inch improved cylinder/modified choke; $27\frac{1}{2}$-inch modified/full choke. Weight: $5\frac{3}{4}$ to $6\frac{1}{2}$ pounds depending upon gauge and barrel length. English-style straight-grip stock and forearm, checkered. Currently manufactured.

Bernardelli Premier Gamecock

Bernardelli Gamecock, Premier (Roma 3) $995
Same general specifications as Standard Gamecock (S. Uberto 1), except has side plates, auto ejectors, single trigger. Currently manufactured.

Bernardelli Italia

Bernardelli Italia $995
Same general specifications as Brescia, except higher grade engraving and wood. Discontinued 1986.

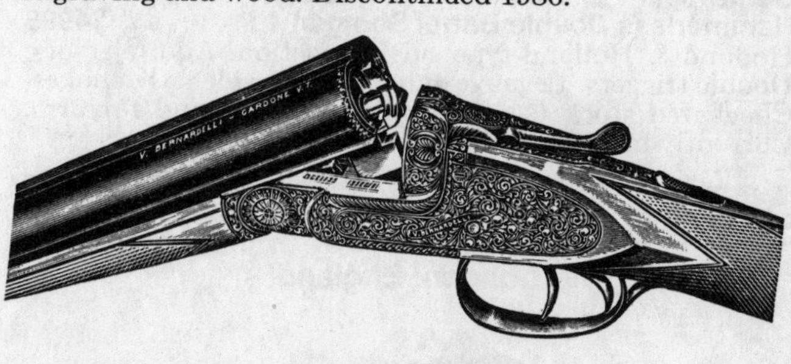

Bernardelli Roma 6

Bernardelli Roma 4 and Roma 6
Same as Premier Gamecock (Roma 3), except higher grade engraving and wood, double triggers. Currently manufactured.
Roma 4 . . . . $ 950
Roma 6 1295

Bernardelli S. Uberto 2

Bernadelli S. Uberto 2 . . . . $995
Same as Standard Gamecock (S. Uberto 1), except higher grade engraving and wood. Currently manufactured.

Bernardelli S. Uberto F.S.

Bernardelli S. Uberto F.S. **$1095**
Same as Standard Gamecock, except with higher grade engraving, wood and has auto ejectors. Currently manufactured.

Bernardelli V.B. Holland Liscio

Bernardelli V.B. Holland Liscio Deluxe Hammerless Double Barrel Shotgun **$4995**
Holland & Holland-type sidelock action. Auto ejectors. Double triggers. 12 gauge only. Any barrel length, chokes. Checkered stock (straight or pistol grip) and forearm. Currently manufactured.

BOSS & CO.
London, England

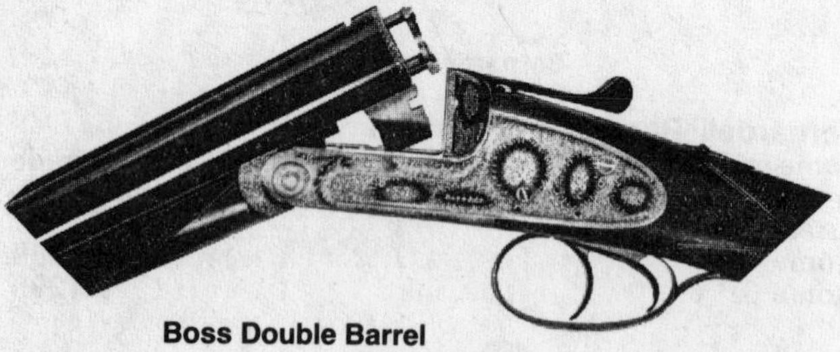

Boss Double Barrel

Boss Hammerless Double Barrel Shotgun
Side lock. Automatic ejectors. Double triggers, non-selective or selective single trigger. Made in all gauges, barrel lengths and chokes. Checkered stock and forend, straight or pistol grip.
With double triggers or non-selective single trigger **$16,000**
With selective single trigger **20,000**

Boss Over-and-Under

Boss Hammerless Over/Under Shotgun **$21,000**
Side lock. Automatic ejectors. Selective single trigger. Made in all gauges, barrel lengths and chokes. Checkered stock and forend, straight or pistol grip. Discontinued.

ERNESTO BREDA
Milan, Italy

Breda Autoloading Shotgun
Recoil-operated. 12 gauge, $2\frac{3}{4}$-inch chamber. 4-shell tubular magazine. Barrels: $25\frac{1}{2}$- and $27\frac{1}{2}$-inch; plain, matted rib or vent rib; improved cylinder, modified or full choke; current model has 26-inch vent-rib barrel with interchangeable choke tubes. Weight: about $7\frac{1}{4}$ pounds. Checkered straight or pistol-grip stock and forearm. Currently manufactured.
With plain barrel **$275**
With raised matted rib **295**
With ventilated rib **315**
With vent rib, interchangeable choke tube **350**

Breda Magnum
Same general specifications as standard model, except chambered for 12 gauge 3-inch magnum, 3-shot magazine; latest model has 29-inch vent-rib barrel. Currently manufactured.
With plain barrel **$395**
With ventilated rib **425**

BRNO SHOTGUNS
Rocky River, Ohio
Manufactured in Czechoslovakia.

Brno 500 Over/Under Shotgun **$675**
Hammerless boxlock with double triggers and ejectors. 12-gauge w/$2\frac{3}{4}$-inch chambers. $27\frac{1}{2}$-inch barrels choked modified and full. Weight: 7 pounds. Checkered walnut stock with classic-style cheekpiece.

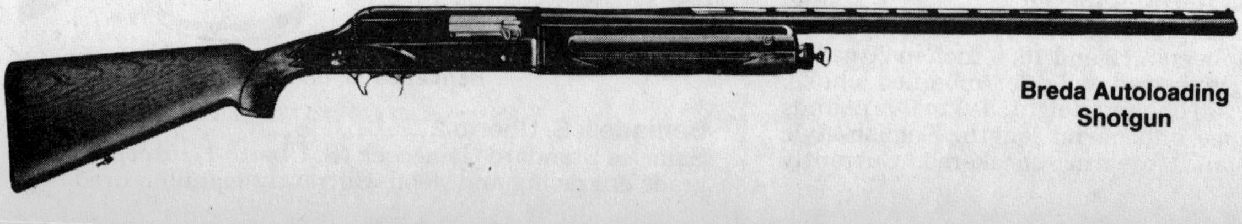

Breda Autoloading Shotgun

Brno CZ 581 Over/Under Shotgun **$490**
Hammerless boxlock with double triggers, ejectors and automatic safety. 12 gauge w/2¾- or 3-inch chambers. 28-inch barrels choked modified and full. Weight: 7½ pounds. Checkered walnut stock.

Brno Super Over/Under Shotgun **$675**
Hammerless sidelock with selective single or double triggers and ejectors. 12 gauge w/2¾- or 3-inch chambers. 27½-inch barrels choked modified and full. Weight: 7¼ pounds. Checkered European walnut stock with classic-style cheekpiece.

Brno ZH 301 Over/Under Shotgun **$450**
Hammerless boxlock with double triggers. 12 gauge w/ 2¾- or 3-inch chambers. 27½-inch barrels choked modified and full. Weight: 7 pounds. Skip-line checkered walnut stock with classic-style cheekpiece.

Brno ZP 149 Hammerless Double
Sidelock action with double triggers, automatic ejectors and automatic safety. 12 gauge w/2¾- or 3-inch chambers. 28½-inch barrels choked modified and full. Weight: 7¼ pounds. Checkered walnut buttstock with cheekpiece.
Standard Model **$440**
Engraved Model **465**

BROWNING SHOTGUNS
Morgan (formerly Ogden), Utah

Designated "American" Browning because they were produced in Ilion, New York, the following Remington-made Brownings are almost identical to the Remington Model 11A and Sportsman, and the Browning Auto-5. They are the only Browning shotguns manufactured in the U.S. during the 20th century, and were made for Browning Arms when production was suspended in Belgium because of WWII (*see Note* below).

AMERICAN BROWNING SHOTGUNS

American Browning Grade I Autoloading Shotgun **$495**
Recoil-operated. Gauges: 12, 16, 20. 2- or 4-shell tubular magazine. Plain barrel, 26- to 32-inch, any standard boring. Weight: about 6⅞ (20 ga.) to 8 pounds (12 ga.). Checkered pistol-grip stock and forearm. Made 1940 to 1949.

American Browning Special
Same general specifications as Grade I, except supplied with raised matted rib or vent rib. Discont. 1949.
With raised matted rib **$595**
With ventilated rib **625**

American Browning Special Skeet Model **$475**
Same general specifications as Grade I, except has 26-inch barrel with ventilated rib and Cutts Compensator. Discontinued in 1949.

American Browning Utility Field Gun **$400**
Same general specifications as Grade I, except has 28-inch plain barrel with Poly Choke. Discontinued in 1949.

Note: Fabrique Nationale Herstal (formerly Fabrique Nationale d'Armes de Guerre) of Herstal, Belgium, is the long-time manufacturer of Browning shotguns, dating back to 1900. Miroku Firearms Mfg. Co. of Tokyo, Japan, bought into the Browning company and has, since the early 1970s, undertaken some of the production. The following shotguns were manufactured for Browning by these two firms.

Browning 2000 Buck Special **$395**
Same as Field Model, except has 24-inch plain barrel specially bored for rifled slug and buck shot, fitted with rifle sights (open rear, ramp front). 12 gauge, 2¾-inch or 3-inch chamber; 20 gauge, 2¾-inch chamber. Weight: 12 ga., 7 lbs. 8 oz.; 20 ga., 6 lbs. 10 oz. Made 1974 to 1981 by FN.

Browning 2000 Gas Automatic Shotgun, Field Model
Gas-operated. Gauges: 12, 20. 2¾-inch chamber. 4-shot magazine. Barrels: 26-, 28-, 30-inch; any standard choke; plain matted barrel (12 gauge only) or vent rib. Weight: 6 lbs. 11 oz. to 7 lbs. 12 oz. depending upon gauge and barrel. Checkered pistol-grip stock and forearm. Made from 1974 to 1981 by FN.
With plain matted barrel **$350**
With ventilated rib **395**

Browning 2000 Magnum Model **$400**
Same as Field Model, except chambered for 3-inch shells, 3-shot magazine. Barrels: 26- (20 gauge only), 28-, 30- or 32-inch (latter two 12 gauge only); any standard choke; vent rib. Weight: 6 lbs. 11 oz. to 7 lbs. 13 oz. depending upon gauge and barrel length. Made from 1974 to 1981 by FN.

Browning 2000 Skeet Model **$425**
Same as Field Model, except has skeet-style stock with recoil pad, 26-inch vent-rib barrel, skeet choke. 12 or 20 gauge, 2¾-inch chamber. Weight: 12 ga., 8 lbs. 1 oz.; 20 ga., 6 lbs. 12 oz. Made from 1974 to 1981 by FN.

Browning 2000 Trap Model **$425**
Same as Field Model, except has Monte Carlo stock with recoil pad, 30- or 32-inch barrel with high-post ventilated rib and receiver extension; modified, improved or full choke. 12 gauge, 2¾-inch chamber. Weight: about 8 lbs. 5 oz. Made from 1974 to 1981 by FN.

Browning 2000 Field Model

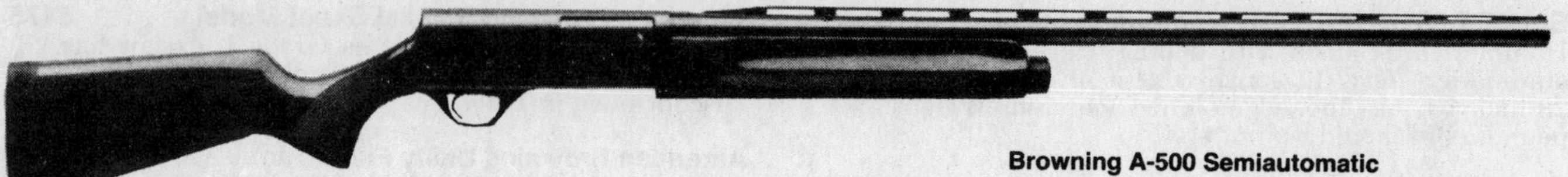

Browning A-500 Semiautomatic

Browning Automatic-5

Browning Automatic-5 Gold Classic

Browning A-500 Semiautomatic $415
Gauge: 12. 26- to 30-inch vent-rib barrels. Invector choke tube system. 2¾- or 3-inch magnum cartridges. Weight: 7 lbs. 3 oz. to 7 lbs. 7 oz. Cross-bolt safety. Gold-plated trigger. Scroll-engraved receiver. Gloss-finished walnut stock and forend. Made by F.N. from 1986 to date.

Browning Autoloading Shotguns, Grade III and IV
These higher grade models differ from the Standard or Grade I in general quality, grade of wood, checkering, engraving, etc., otherwise specifications are the same. Grade IV guns, sometimes called Midas Grade, are inlaid with yellow and green gold. Discontinued in 1940.
Grade III, plain barrel . . . . **$ 1695**
Grade IV, plain barrel **3000**
Extra for raised matted rib **200**
Extra for ventilated rib **400**

Browning Automatic-5, Buck Special Models
Same as Light 12, Magnum 12, Light 20, Magnum 20, in respective gauges, except 24-inch plain barrel specially bored for rifled slug and buckshot, fitted with rifle sights (open rear, ramp front). Weight: 6⅛ to 8¼ pounds depending upon gauge. Made from 1964 to 1976 by FN, since then by Miroku.
FN manufacture, with plain barrel **$600**
Miroku manufacture **475**

Browning Automatic-5 Classic $890
Gauge: 12. 5-shot capacity. 28-inch vent-rib barrels. Modified choke. 2¾-inch chambers. Engraved silver grey receiver. Gold-plated trigger. Cross-bolt safety. High-grade, hand-checkered select American walnut stock with rounded pistol grip. 5,000 issued; made in Japan in 1984, engraved in Belgium.

Browning Automatic-5 Gold Classic $4875
Same general specifications as Automatic-5 Classic, except engraved receiver inlaid with gold. Pearl border on stock and forend plus fine-line hand-checkering. Each gun numbered "1 of Five Hundred," etc. 500 issued in 1984; made in Belgium.

Browning Automatic-5, Light 12
12 gauge only. Same general specifications as Standard Model, except lightweight (about 7¼ pounds), has gold-plated trigger and guns without rib have striped matting on top of barrel. Fixed chokes or Invector tubes. Made 1948 to 1976 by FN, since then by Miroku.
FN manufacture, with plain barrel **$625**
FN manufacture, with raised matted rib **645**
FN manufacture, with ventilated rib **675**
Miroku manufacture, vent rib, fixed choke **455**
Miroku manufacture, vent rib, Invectors **475**

Browning Automatic-5, Light 20
Same general specifications as Standard Model, except lightweight and 20 gauge. Barrels: 26- or 28-inch; plain or vent rib. Weight: about 6¼ to 6½ pounds depending upon barrel. Made from 1958 to 1976 by FN, since then by Miroku.
FN manufacture, with plain barrel **$625**
FN manufacture, with ventilated rib barrel **650**
Miroku manufacture, vent rib, fixed choke **475**
Miroku manufacture, vent rib, Invectors **475**

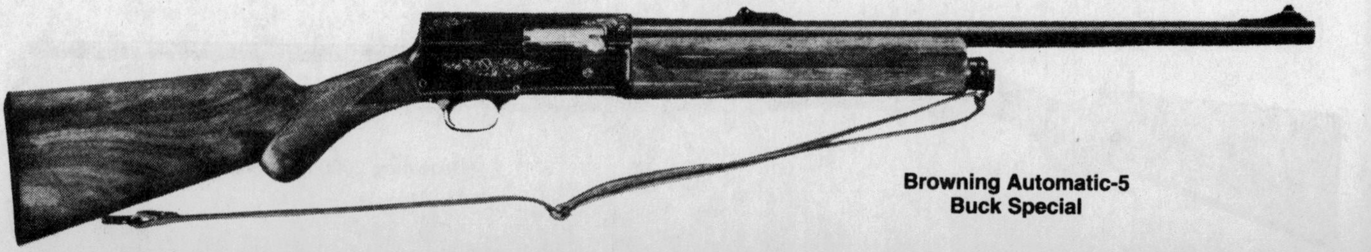

Browning Automatic-5
Buck Special

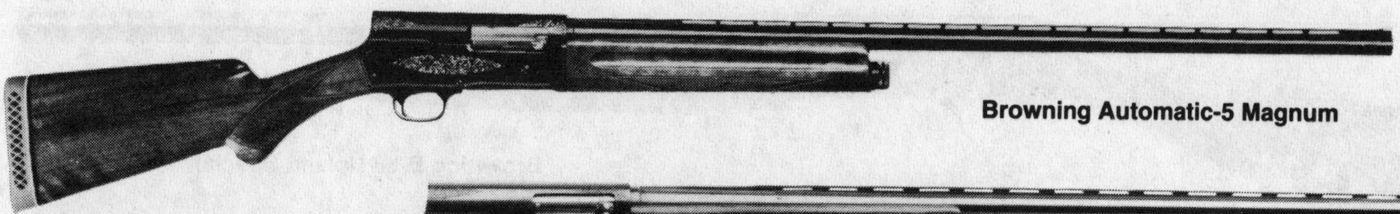

Browning Automatic-5 Magnum

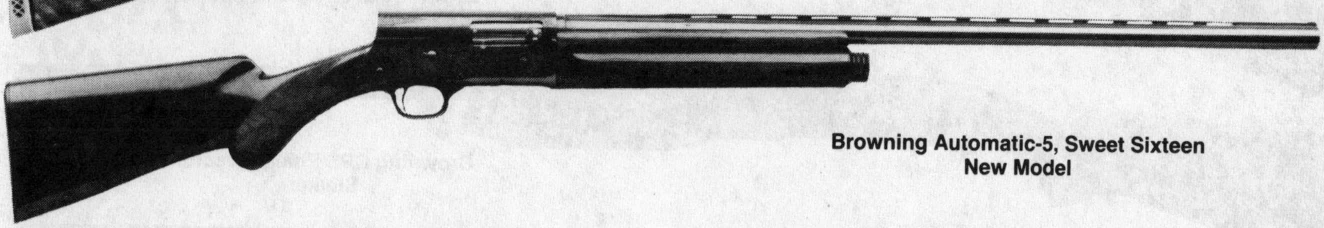

Browning Automatic-5, Sweet Sixteen New Model

Browning Automatic-5, Magnum 12 Gauge
Same general specifications as Standard Model. Chambered for 3-inch magnum 12 gauge shells. Barrels: 28-inch modified/full, 30- or 32-inch full/full; plain or vent rib. Weight: 8½ to 9 pounds depending upon barrel. Buttstock has recoil pad. Made from 1958 to 1976 by FN, since then by Miroku. Fixed chokes or Invector tubes.
FN manufacture, with plain barrel **$625**
FN manufacture, with ventilated rib **700**
Miroku manufacture, vent rib, fixed chokes **470**
Miroku manufacture, vent rib, Invectors **475**

Browning Automatic-5, Magnum 20 Gauge
Same general specifications as Standard Model, except chambered for 3-inch magnum 20 gauge shell. Barrels: 26- or 28-inch, plain or vent rib. Weight: 7 lbs. 5 oz. to 7 lbs. 7 oz. depending upon barrel. Made from 1967 to 1976 by FN, since then by Miroku.
FN manufacture, with plain barrel **$685**
FN manufacture, with ventilated rib **715**
Miroku manufacture, vent rib, Invectors **485**

Browning Automatic-5, Skeet Model
12 gauge only. Same general specifications as Light 12. Barrels: 26- or 28-inch, plain or vent rib, skeet choke. Weight: 7 lbs. 5 oz. to 7 lbs. 10 oz. depending upon barrel. Made by FN prior to 1976, since then by Miroku.
FN manufacture, with plain barrel **$650**
FN manufacture, with ventilated rib barrel **700**
Miroku manufacture, with ventilated rib barrel **450**

Browning Automatic-5, Standard (Grade I)
Recoil-operated. Gauges: 12 and 16 (16 gauge guns made prior to World War II were chambered for 2$^{9}/_{16}$-inch shells; standard 16 discontinued 1964). 4-shell magazine in five-shot model, prewar guns were also available in three-shot model. Barrels: 26- to 32-inch; plain, raised matted or vent rib; choice of standard chokes. Weight: about 8 pounds, 12 ga.; 7¼ pounds, 16 ga. Checkered pistol-grip stock and forearm. (*Note:* Browning Special, discontinued about 1940, is Grade I gun with either vent or raised matted rib.) Made from 1900 to 1973 by FN.
Grade I, plain barrel **$550**
Grade I or Browning Special, raised matted rib **575**
Grade I or Browning Special, ventilated rib **595**

Browning Automatic-5, Sweet 16
16 gauge only. Same general specifications as Standard Model, except lightweight (about 6¾ pounds), has gold-plated trigger and guns without rib have striped matting on top of barrel. Made from 1937 to 1976 by FN.
With plain barrel **$625**
With raised matted rib **650**
With ventilated rib **800**

Browning Automatic-5, Sweet Sixteen New Model **$475**
Reissue of popular 16 gauge Hunting Model with 5-shot capacity, 2¾-inch chambers, scroll-engraved blued receiver, high-gloss French walnut stock with rounded pistol grip. 26- or 28-inch vent-rib barrel. Full choke tube. Weight: 7 lbs. 5 oz. Reintroduced in 1987.

Browning Automatic-5, Trap Model **$625**
12 gauge only. Same general specifications as Standard Model, except has trap-style stock, 30-inch ventilated-rib barrel, full choke. Weight: 8½ pounds. Discontinued 1971.

Browning Model B-80 Gas-Operated Automatic .. **$415**
Gauges: 12, 20; 2¾-inch chamber. 4-shot magazine. Barrels: 26-, 28-, 30-inch; any standard choke; vent-rib barrel with fixed chokes or Invector tubes. Weight: 6 lbs. 12 oz. to 8 lbs. 1 oz. depending upon gauge and barrel. Checkered pistol-grip stock and forearm. Made from 1981 to date.

Browning Model B-80 Magnum **$425**
Same as Standard Model, except has 3-inch magnum chambers.

Browning Model B-80 Superlight **$410**
Same as Standard Model, except weighs 1 pound less.

SHOTGUNS

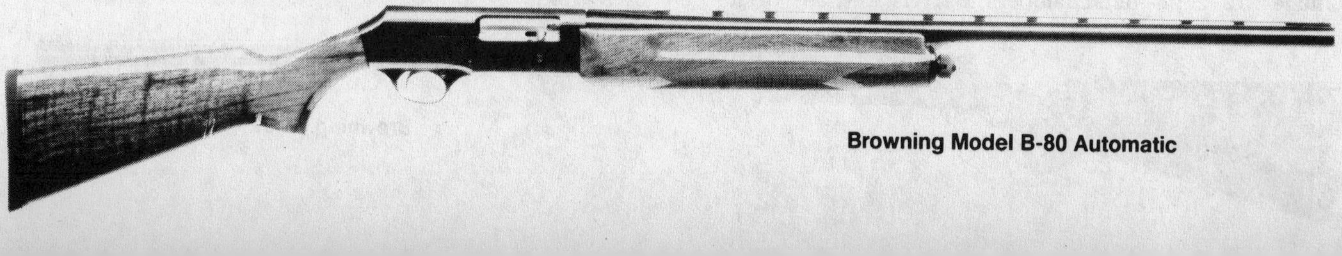

Browning Model B-80 Automatic

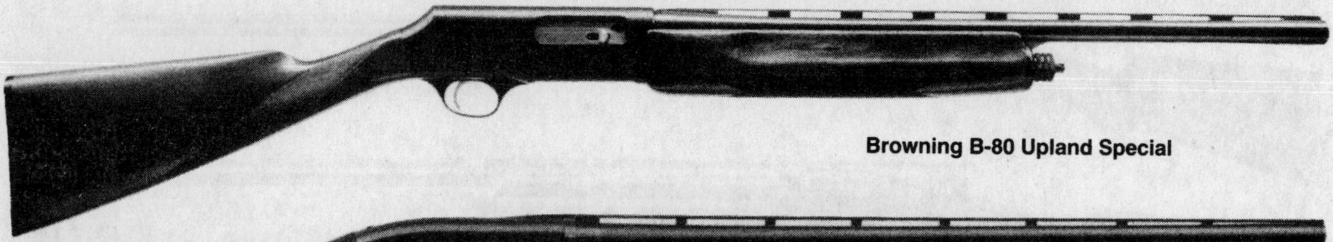

Browning B-80 Upland Special

Browning BPS Pump Invector Stalker

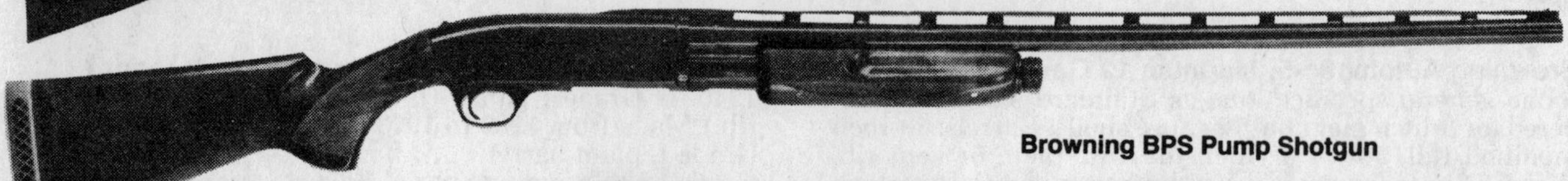

Browning BPS Pump Shotgun

Browning B-SS 20-Gauge Sporter

Browning B-80 Upland Special $420
Gauges: 12 and 20. 22-inch vent-rib barrel. Invector choke tube system. $2^{3}/_{4}$-inch chambers. 42 inches overall. Weight: 5 lbs. 7 oz. (20 ga.); 6 lbs. 10 oz. (12 ga.). German nickel-silver sight bead. Cross-bolt safety. Checkered walnut straight-grip stock and forend.

Browning BPS Pump Invector Stalker $300
Same general specifications as BPS Pump Shotgun, except in 12 gauge only with invector choke system and matte black finish.

Browning BPS Pump Shotgun $305
Takedown. 12 gauge. 3-inch chamber. Holds five $2^{3}/_{4}$-inch or four 3-inch shells. Barrels: 26-, 28-, 30-inch; improved cylinder, modified or full choke; vent rib; fixed choke or Invector tubes. Weight (with 28-inch barrel): about $7^{3}/_{4}$ pounds. Checkered pistol-grip stock and semibeavertail forearm (slide handle), recoil pad. Introduced in 1977. Made by Miroku.

Browning BPS Youth and Ladies' Model $310
Lightweight (6 lbs. 11 oz.) version of BPS Pump Shotgun in 20 gauge with 22-inch barrel and floating ventilated rib, full choke (invector) tube.

Browning B-SS Side-by-Side $575
Box lock. Automatic ejectors. Non-selective single trigger. Gauges: 12, 20; 3-inch chambers. Barrels: 26-, 28-, or 30-inch (latter in 12 gauge only); improved cylinder/modified, modified/full, both barrels full choke; matted solid rib. Weight (with 28-inch barrels): 12 ga., 7 lbs. 5 oz.; 20 ga., 7 lbs. Checkered straight-grip stock and beavertail forearm. Made from 1972 to date by Miroku.

Browning B-SS Side-by-Side (cont.)

Browning B-SS Side-by-Side Sidelock $1500
Same general specifications as B-SS boxlock models, except sidelock version available in 26- or 28-inch barrel lengths. 26-inch choked imp. cyl./mod. 28-inch choked mod./full. Double triggers. Satin greyed receiver engraved with rosettes and scrolls. German nickel-silver sight bead. Weight: $6^{1}/_{4}$ lbs. to 6 lbs. 11 oz. 12 ga. made in 1983; 20 ga. made in 1984.

Browning B-SS S/S 20 Gauge Sporter $595
Same as standard B-SS 20 gauge, except has selective single trigger, straight-grip stock. Introduced 1977.

Browning BT-99 Grade I Competition $595
Same as BT-99, except has super-high wide rib and Monte Carlo stock. Made from 1976 to date.

Browning BT-99 Grade I Single Barrel Trap $600
Box lock. Automatic ejector. 12 gauge only. 32- or 34-inch vent-rib barrel; modified, improved modified or full choke. Weight: about 8 pounds. Checkered pistol-grip stock and beavertail forearm, recoil pad. Made from 1971 to 1976 by Miroku.

Browning BT-99

Browning Citori O/U
Hunting Model

Browning Double Automatic
Standard Grade

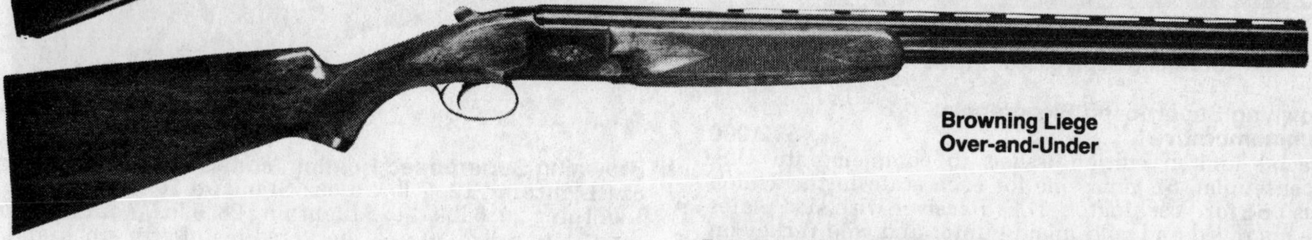

Browning Liege
Over-and-Under

Browning Citori Over/Under Hunting Models . . . $795
Boxlock. Gauges: 12, 16, 20, 28 and .410. Barrel lengths: 24-, 26-, 28-, or 30-inch with vent rib. Chokes: mod./full or invector (30-inch bbl.); invector, mod./full or imp. cyl./mod. (other bbl. lengths). Overall length ranges from 41 to 47 inches. $2\frac{1}{2}$-, 3- or 3-inch Mag. loads, depending on gauge. Weight: $5\frac{3}{4}$ lbs. to 7 lbs. 13 oz. Single selective, gold-plated trigger. Medium raised German nickel-silver sight bead. Checkered, rounded pistol-grip walnut stock with beavertail forend. Prices vary with the different grades. Made from 1973 to date by Miroku.

Browning Citori Skeet Gun
Same as Hunting Model, except has skeet-style stock and forearm, 26- or 28-inch barrels, both bored skeet choke. Available with either standard vent rib or special target-type, high-post, wide ventilated rib. Weight (with 26-inch barrels): 12 ga., 8 pounds; 20 ga., 7 pounds. Made from 1974 to date by Miroku.

With standard ventilated rib	**$895**
With target ventilated rib	**925**

Browning Citori Superlight O/U Shotguns
Similar to the Citori Hunting Model, except with straight-grip stock and schnabel forend tip. Made by Miroku from 1982 to date.

Grade I, Fixed Choke	**$ 670**
Grade I, Invector	**700**
Grade III, 12 and 20 ga.	**920**
Grade III, 28 and .410 ga.	**1010**
Grade VI, 12 and 20 ga.	**1345**
Grade VI, 28 and .410 ga.	**1420**

Browning Citori Trap Gun
Same as Hunting Model, except 12 gauge only, has Monte Carlo stock and beavertail forearm, trap-style recoil pad; 30- or 32-inch barrels; modified/full, improved modified/full, or full/full. Available with either standard vent rib or special target-type, high-post, wide vent rib. Weight: 8 pounds. Made from 1974 to date by Miroku.

With standard ventilated rib	**$895**
With target ventilated rib	**910**

Browning Double Automatic, Standard Grade (Steel Receiver)
Short recoil system. Takedown. 12 gauge only. Two shots. Barrels: 26-, 28-, 30-inch; any standard choke. Checkered pistol-grip stock and forearm. Weight: about $7\frac{3}{4}$ pounds. Made from 1955 to 1961.

With plain barrel	**$400**
With recessed-rib barrel	**510**

Browning Liege Over-and-Under Shotgun $695
Box lock. Automatic ejectors. Non-selective single trigger. 12 gauge only. Barrels: $26\frac{1}{2}$-, 28-, or 30-inch; $2\frac{3}{4}$-inch chambers in $26\frac{1}{2}$- and 28-inch, 3-inch in 30-inch; improved cylinder/modified, modified/full, both barrels full choke; vent rib. Weight: 7 lbs. 4 oz. to 7 lbs. 14 oz. depending upon barrels. Checkered pistol-grip stock and forearm. Made from 1973 to 1975 by FN.

Browning Over/Under Classic $1595
Gauge: 20. 26-inch blued barrels. Choked imp. cyl./mod. $2\frac{3}{4}$-inch chambers. Gold-plated, single selective trigger. Manual, top-tang-mounted safety. Engraved receiver. High-grade, select American walnut straight-grip stock with schnabel forend. Fine-line checkering with pearl borders. High-gloss finish. 5,000 issued in 1986; made in Japan, engraved in Belgium.

Browning Over/Under
Gold Classic

Browning Over/Under Gold Classic $4500
Same general specifications as Over/Under Classic, except more elaborate engravings, enhanced in gold, including profile of John M. Browning. Fine oil finish. 500 issued; made in 1986 in Belgium.

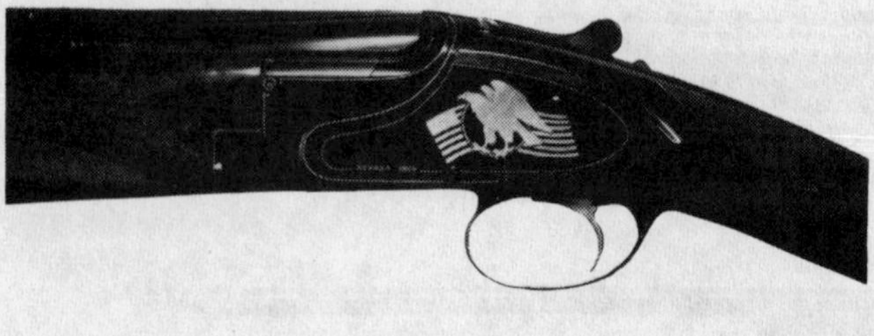

Browning Superposed Bicentennial (Left Side)

Browning Superposed Bicentennial (Right Side)

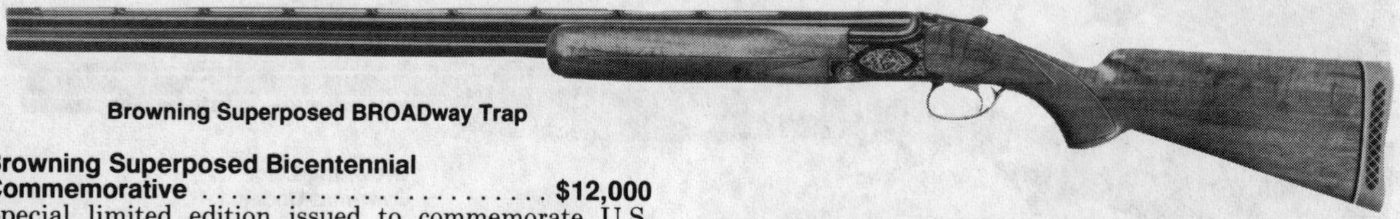

Browning Superposed BROADway Trap

Browning Superposed Bicentennial Commemorative $12,000
Special limited edition issued to commemorate U.S. Bicentennial. 51 guns, one for each state in the Union plus one for Washington, D.C. Receiver with side plates has engraved and gold-inlaid hunter and wild turkey on right side, U.S. flag and bald eagle on left side, together with state markings inlaid in gold, on blued background. Checkered straight-grip stock and schnabel-style forearm of highly figured American walnut. Velvet-lined wooden presentation case. Made in 1976 by FN. Value shown is for gun in new, unfired condition.

Browning Superposed BROADway 12 Trap . . . $1500
Same as standard Trap Gun, except has 30- or 32-inch barrels with wider BROADway rib. Discontinued 1976.

Browning Superposed Shotguns, Hunting Models
Over-and-under. Box lock. Selective automatic ejectors. Selective single trigger; earlier models (worth 25% less) supplied with double triggers, twin selective triggers or non-selective single trigger. Gauges: 12, 20 (introduced 1949, 3-inch chambers in later production), 28, .410 (latter two gauges introduced 1960). Barrels: 26½-, 28-, 30-, 32-inch; raised matted or vent rib; prewar Lightning Model made without ribbed barrel, postwar version supplied only with vent rib; any combination of standard chokes. Weight (with 26½-inch vent-rib barrels): Standard 12, 7 lbs. 11

Browning Superposed Hunting Models (cont.)
oz.; Lightning 12, 7 lbs. 6 oz.; Standard 20, 6 lbs. 8 oz.; Lightning 20, 6 lbs. 4 oz.; Lightning 28, 6 lbs. 7 oz.; Lightning .410, 6 lbs. 10 oz. Checkered pistol-grip stock and forearm. Higher grades—Pigeon, Pointer, Diana, Midas, Grade VI—differ from standard Grade I models in overall quality, engraving, wood and checkering; otherwise, specifications are the same. Midas Grade and Grade VI guns are richly gold-inlaid. Made by FN from 1928 to 1976. Prewar models may be considered as discontinued in 1940 when Belgium was occupied by Germany. Grade VI offered 1955—-1960. Pointer Grade discontinued in 1966, Grade I Standard in 1973, Pigeon Grade in 1974. Lightning Grade I, Diana and Midas Grades were not offered after 1976.

Grade I Standard **$1300**
Grade I Lightning **1495**
Grade I Lightning, prewar, matted barrel, no rib . **1795**
Grade II—Pigeon **1995**
Grade III—Pointer **2750**
Grade IV—Diana **$2995**
Grade V—Midas **4500**
Grade VI **5500**
Add for 28 or .410 gauge **300**
Values shown are for models with ventilated rib,
if gun has raised matted rib, *deduct* **150**

Browning Superposed Grade I Standard (Prewar)

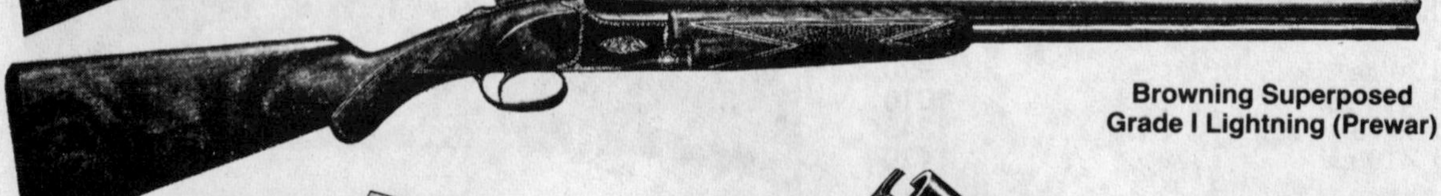

Browning Superposed Grade I Lightning (Prewar)

Pigeon Grade (Prewar)

Diana Grade (Prewar)

Midas Grade (Prewar)

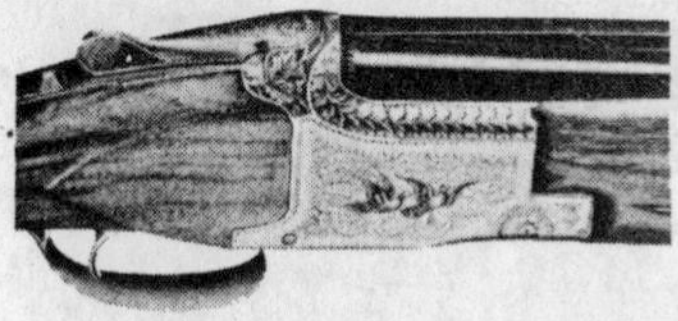

Grade II Pigeon (Postwar)

Grade III Pointer (Postwar)

Grade IV Diana (Postwar)

Grade V Midas (Postwar)

Browning Superposed Lightning and Superlight Models (Reissue)
Reissue of popular 12 and 20 gauge superposed shotguns. Lightning models available in 26½- and 28-inch barrel lengths with 2¾- or 3-inch chambering, full pistol grip. Superlight models available in 26½-inch barrel lengths with 2¾-inch chambering only, and straight-grip stock with schnabel forend. Both have hand-engraved receivers, fine-line checkering, gold-plated single selective trigger, automatic selective ejectors, manual safety. Weight: 6 to 7½ pounds. Reintroduced 1985-86.

Grade II, Pigeon	**$2890**
Grade III, Pointer	**3560**
Grade IV, Diana	**4240**
Grade V, Midas	**5250**

Browning Superposed Magnum $1450
Same as Grade I, except chambered for 12 gauge 3-inch shells, 30-inch vent-rib barrels, stock with recoil pad. Weight: about 8¼ pounds. Discontinued 1976.

Browning Superposed Ltd. Black Duck Issue . . $6000
Gauge: 12. Superposed Lightning action. 28-inch vent-rib barrels. Choked mod./full. 2¾-inch chambers. Weight: 7 lbs. 6 oz. Gold inlaid receiver and trigger guard engraved with Black Duck scenes. Gold-plated, single selective trigger. Top-tang mounted manual safety. Automatic, selective ejectors. Front and center ivory sights. High-grade, hand-checkered, hand-oiled select walnut stock and forend. 500 issued in 1983.

Browning Superposed Ltd. Pintail Duck Issue . $5775
Same general specifications as Ltd. Black Duck Issue, except Pintail Duck scenes engraved on receiver and trigger guard; stock is of dark French walnut with rounded pistol grip. 500 issued in 1983.

Browning Superposed, Presentation Grades
Custom versions of Super-Light, Lightning Hunting, Trap and Skeet Models, with same general specifications as those of standard guns, but of higher overall quality. The four Presentation Grades differ in receiver finish (greyed or blued), engraving, gold inlays, wood and checkering; Presentation 4 has side plates. Made by FN, these models were introduced in 1977.

Presentation 1	**$3200**
Presentation 1, gold-inlaid	**3600**
Presentation 2	**3800**
Presentation 2, gold-inlaid	**5500**
Presentation 3, gold-inlaid	**5700**
Presentation 4	**6500**
Presentation 4, gold-inlaid	**7500**

Browning Superposed Skeet Guns, Grade I
Same as standard Lightning 12, 20, 28 and .410 Hunting Models, except has skeet-style stock and forearm, 26½- or 28-inch vent-rib barrels bored skeet choke. Available also in All Gauge Skeet Set: Lightning 12 with one removable forearm and three extra sets of barrels in 20, 28 and .410 gauge in fitted luggage case. Discontinued 1976.

12 or 20 gauge	**$1495**
28 or .410 gauge	**1750**
All Gauge Skeet Set	**4250**

Browning Choke Marks. The following markings are used to indicate chokes on Browning shotguns:

Full *	Improved Cylinder **—
Improved Modified *—	Skeet **S
Modified **	Cylinder ***

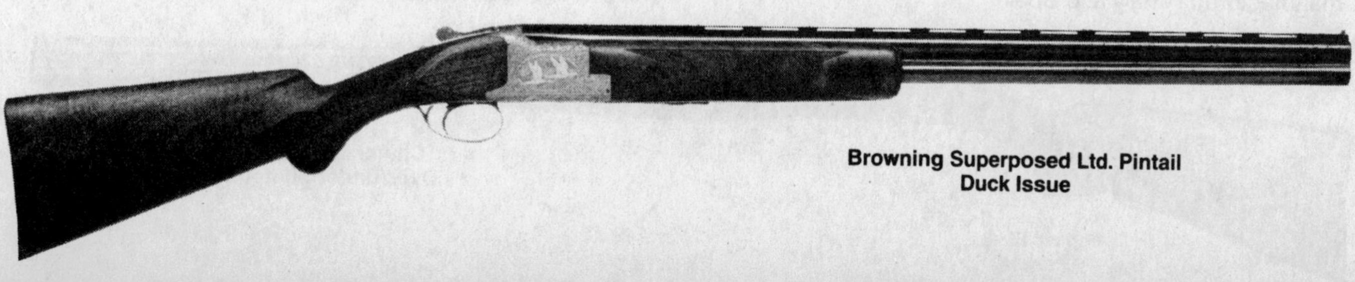

Browning Superposed Ltd. Pintail Duck Issue

Browning Superposed Trap

Browning Twelvette Double Automatic

Browning Twentyweight Double Automatic

Browning Superposed Super-Light Model $1425
Ultralight field gun version of Standard Lightning Model has classic straight-grip stock and slimmer forearm. Available only in 12 and 20 gauges (2 3/4-inch chambers), with 26 1/2-inch vent-rib barrels. Weight: 6 1/2 pounds, 12 ga.; 6 pounds, 20 ga. Made from 1967 to 1976.

Browning Superposed Trap Gun $1475
Same as Grade I, except has trap-style stock, beavertail forearm, 30-inch vent-rib barrels, 12 gauge only. Discont. 1976.

Browning Twelvette Double Automatic
Lightweight version of Double Automatic with same general specifications except aluminum receiver. Barrel with plain matted top or vent rib. Weight: 6 3/4 to 7 pounds depending upon barrel. Receiver is finished in black with gold engraving; from 1956 to 1961, receivers were also anodized in grey, brown, and green with silver engraving. Made from 1955 to 1971.
With plain barrel **$425**
With ventilated-rib barrel **475**

Browning Twentyweight Double Automatic
Same as Twelvette, but 3/4 pound lighter. 26 1/2-inch barrel only. Made from 1956 to 1971.
With plain barrel **$425**
With ventilated-rib barrel **475**

E.J. CHURCHILL, LTD. London, England

Originally made in London, Churchill shotguns are now manufactured in Italy and Spain.

Churchill Field Model Hammerless Double
Sidelock hammerless ejector gun with same general specifications as Premiere Model but of lower quality. Discontinued.
With double triggers **$8000**
Selective single trigger, extra **400**

Churchill Monarch Over/Under Shotgun
Hammerless, takedown with engraved receiver. Selective single or double triggers. Gauges: 12, 20, 28, .410; 3-inch chambers. Barrels: 25- or 26-inch (improved cylinder/modified); 28-inch (modified/full). Weight: 6 1/2 to 7 1/2 pounds. Checkered European walnut buttstock and forend. Made in Italy from 1986 to date.
With Double Triggers **$290**
With Single Trigger **370**

Churchill Premiere

Churchill Premiere Quality Hammerless Double
Side lock. Automatic ejectors. Double triggers or selective single trigger. Gauges: 12, 16, 20, 28. Barrels: 25-, 28-, 30-, 32-inch; any degree of boring. Weight: 5 to 8 pounds depending upon gauge and barrel length. Checkered stock and forend, straight or pistol grip. Discontinued.
With double triggers **$11,000**
Selective single trigger, extra **400**

Churchill Monarch Over/Under Shotgun

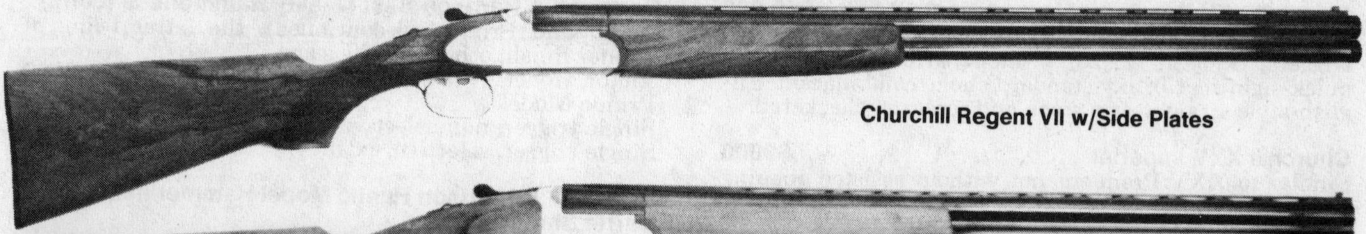

Churchill Regent VII w/Side Plates

Churchill Regent Trap

Churchill Windsor III Over/Under

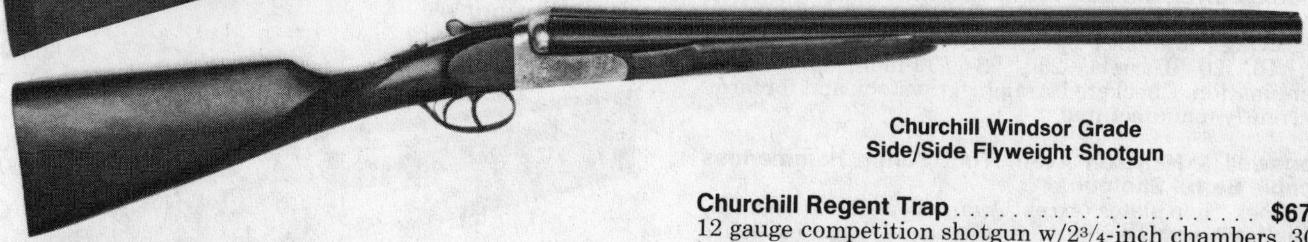

Churchill Windsor Grade
Side/Side Flyweight Shotgun

Churchill Premiere Quality Under-and-Over Shotgun
Side lock. Automatic ejectors. Double triggers or selective single trigger. Gauges: 12, 16, 20, 28. Barrels: 25-, 28-, 30-, 32-inch; any degree of boring. Weight: from 5 to 8 pounds depending upon gauge and barrel length. Checkered stock and forend, straight or pistol grip. Discontinued.
With double triggers **$12,500**
Selective single trigger, extra **400**
Raised ventilated rib, extra **400**

Churchill Regent Over/Under Shotguns
Gauges: 12 or 20; 2¾-inch chambers. 27-inch barrels w/ interchangeable choke tubes and wide vent rib. Single selective trigger, selective automatic ejectors. Checkered pistol-grip stock in fancy walnut. Imported from Italy from 1984 to date.
Regent V **$595**
Regent VII, w/Side Plates **770**

Churchill Regent Side-by-Side Shotguns
12 gauge s/s. 25-, 27- or 28-inch barrels w/fixed choke or interchangeable choke tubes. Double triggers. Automatic top tang safety. Double safety side lock, engraved antique silver receiver. Automatic selective ejectors. Oil-finished English-style stock of extra select European walnut. Imported from Spain from 1984 to date.
Regent Standard **$445**
Regent VI, Side Lock **655**

Churchill Regent Skeet **$640**
12 or 20 gauge with 2¾-inch chambers. Selective automatic ejectors, single-selective trigger. 26-inch over/under barrels w/vent rib. Weight: 7 pounds. Made in Italy from 1984 to date.

Churchill Regent Trap **$670**
12 gauge competition shotgun w/2¾-inch chambers. 30-inch over/under barrels choked imp. mod./full., ventilated side ribs. Weight: 8 pounds. Selective automatic ejectors, single-selective trigger. Checkered Monte Carlo stock with Supercushion recoil pad. Made in Italy from 1984 to date.

Churchill Utility Model Hammerless Double Barrel
Anson & Deeley boxlock action. Double triggers or single trigger. Gauges: 12, 16, 20, 28, .410. Barrels: 25-, 28-, 30-, 32-inch; any degree of boring. Weight: from 4½ to 8 pounds depending upon gauge and barrel length. Checkered stock and forend, straight or pistol grip. Discontinued.
With double triggers **$3500**
Selective single trigger, extra **400**

Churchill Windsor Over/Under Shotguns
Hammerless, boxlock with engraved receiver, selective single trigger. Extractors or ejectors. Gauges: 12, 20, 28 or .410; 3-inch chambers. Barrels: 24 to 30 inches with fixed chokes or choke tubes. Weight: 6 lbs. 3 oz. (Flyweight) to 7 lbs. 10 oz. (12 ga.). Checkered straight (Flyweight) or pistol-grip stock and forend of European walnut. Imported from Italy from 1984 to date.
Windsor III, w/Fixed Chokes **$450**
Windsor III, w/Choke Tubes **520**
Windsor IV, w/Fixed Chokes **490**
Windsor IV, w/Choke Tubes **600**

Churchill Windsor Side-by-Side Shotguns
Boxlock action with double triggers, ejectors or extractors and automatic safety. Gauges: 10, (3½-inch chambers); 12, 20, 28, .410 (3-inch chambers); 16 (2¾-inch chambers). Barrels: 23 to 32 inches with various fixed choke or choke tube combinations. Weight: from 5 lbs. 12 oz. (Flyweight) to 11½ lbs. (10 ga.). European walnut buttstock and forend. Imported from Spain from 1984 to date.
Windsor I, 10 ga. **$440**
Windsor I, 12 thru .410 ga. **355**
Windsor II, 12 or 20 ga. **465**

Churchill XXV Premiere Hammerless Double . . $10,000
Side lock. Assisted opening. Automatic ejectors. Double triggers. Gauges: 12, 20. 25-inch barrels with narrow, quick-sighting rib; any standard choke combination. English-style straight-grip stock and forearm, checkered.

Churchill XXV Imperial $9000
Similar to XXV Premiere, but without assisted opening feature.

Churchill XXV Hercules $6000
Box lock, otherwise specs same as for XXV Premiere.

Churchill XXV Regal $4200
Similar to XXV Hercules, but without assisted opening feature. Gauges: 12, 20, 28, .410.

COGSWELL & HARRISON, LTD.
London, England

Cogswell & Harrison Ambassador Hammerless Double Barrel Shotgun $3800
Box lock. Side plates with game scene or rose scroll engraving. Automatic ejectors. Double triggers. Gauges: 12, 16, 20. Barrels: 26-, 28-, 30-inch; any choke combination. Checkered straight-grip stock and forearm. Currently manufactured.

Cogswell & Harrison Avant Tout Series Hammerless Double Barrel Shotguns
Box lock. Side plates (except Avant Tout III Grade). Automatic ejectors. Double triggers or single trigger (selective or non-selective). Gauges: 12, 16, 20. Barrels: 25-, 27½-, 30-inch; any choke combination. Checkered stock and forend, straight grip standard. Made in three models—Avant Tout I or Konor, Avant Tout II or Sandhurst, Avant Tout III or Rex—which differ chiefly in overall quality, engraving, grade of wood, checkering, etc.; general specifications are the same. Discontinued.

Avant Tout I **$3000**
Avant Tout II **2700**
Avant Tout III **2000**
Single trigger, non-selective, extra **225**
Single trigger, selective, extra **300**

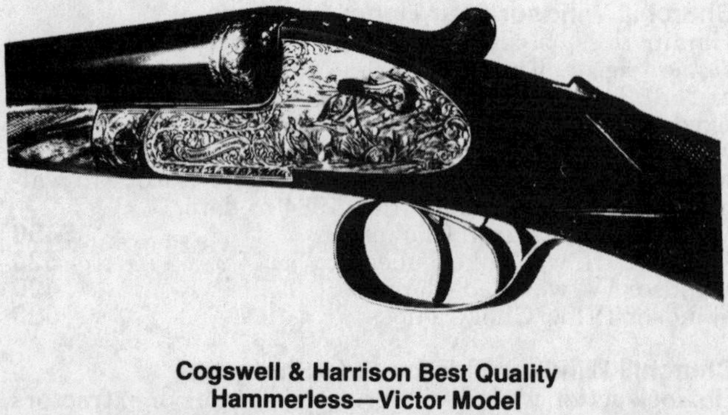

Cogswell & Harrison Best Quality Hammerless—Victor Model

Cogswell & Harrison Best Quality Hammerless Sidelock Double Barrel Shotgun
Hand-detachable locks. Automatic ejectors. Double triggers or single trigger (selective or non-selective). Gauges: 12, 16, 20. Barrels: 25-, 26-, 28-, 30-inch; any choke combination. Checkered stock and forend, straight grip standard. Made in two models: Victor (currently manufactured) and Primic (discontinued), the latter being of plainer finish, otherwise the same.

Victor Model **$6000**
Primic Model **4000**
Single trigger, non-selective, extra **225**
Single trigger, selective, extra **300**

Cogswell & Harrison Huntic Model Hammerless Double Barrel Shotgun
Side lock. Automatic ejectors. Double triggers or single trigger (selective or non-selective). Gauges: 12, 16, 20. Barrels: 25-, 27½-, 30-inch; any choke combination. Checkered stock and forend, straight grip standard. Discontinued.

With double triggers **$3400**
Single trigger, non-selective, extra **225**
Single trigger, selective, extra **300**

Cogswell & Harrison Markor Hammerless Double
Box lock. Non-ejector or ejector. Double triggers. Gauges: 12, 16, 20. Barrels: 27½- or 30-inch; any choke combination. Checkered stock and forend, straight grip standard. Discontinued.

Non-ejector Model **$1650**
Ejector Model **2000**

Cogswell & Harrison Regency

Cogswell & Harrison Regency Hammerless Double $3000
Anson & Deeley boxlock action. Automatic ejectors. Double triggers. Gauges: 12, 16, 20. Barrels: 26-, 28-, 30-inch; any choke combination. Checkered straight-grip stock and forearm. Introduced in 1970 to commemorate the firm's bicentenary, this model has deep scroll engraving and the name "Regency" inlaid in gold on the rib. Currently manufactured.

COLT INDUSTRIES
Hartford, Connecticut

Colt Auto Shotguns were made by Luigi Franchi S.p.A. and are similar to corresponding models of that manufacturer.

Colt Auto Shotgun—Magnum
Same as Standard Auto, except steel receiver, handles 3-inch magnum shells, 30- and 32-inch barrels in 12 gauge, 28-inch in 20 gauge. Weight: 12 ga., about 8¼ pounds. Made from 1964 to 1966.

With plain barrel **$245**
With solid-rib barrel **250**
With ventilated-rib barrel **265**

Colt Auto Shotgun—Magnum Custom
Same as Magnum, except has engraved receiver, select walnut stock and forearm. Made from 1964 to 1966.

With solid-rib barrel **$450**
With ventilated-rib barrel **495**

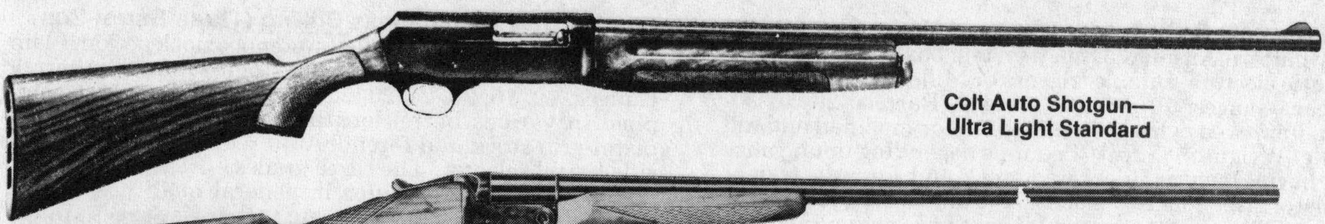

Colt Auto Shotgun—Ultra Light Standard

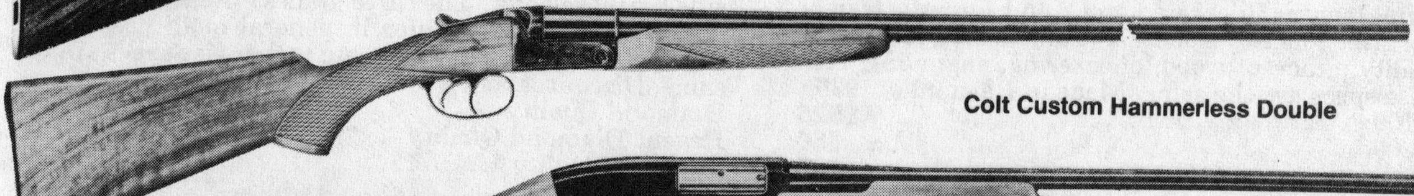

Colt Custom Hammerless Double

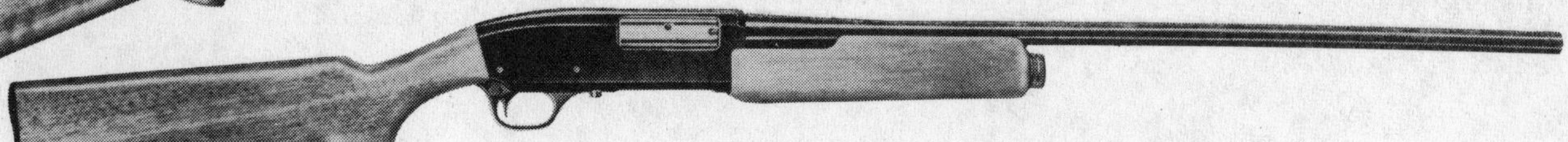

Coltsman Standard Pump

Colt-Sauer Drilling

Colt Auto Shotgun—Ultra Light Custom
Same as Standard Auto, except has engraved receiver, select walnut stock and forearm. Made from 1964 to 1966.
With solid-rib barrel **$295**
With ventilated-rib barrel **310**

Colt Auto Shotgun—Ultra Light Standard
Recoil-operated. Takedown. Alloy receiver. Gauges: 12, 20. Magazine holds 4 shells. Barrels: plain, solid or vent rib; chrome-lined; 26-inch improved cylinder or modified choke, 28-inch modified or full choke, 30-inch full choke, 32-inch full choke. Weight: 12 ga., about $6\frac{1}{4}$ pounds. Checkered pistol-grip stock and forearm. Made 1964-66.
With plain barrel **$225**
With solid-rib barrel **240**
With ventilated-rib barrel **250**

Colt Custom Hammerless Double **$375**
Box lock. Double triggers. Auto ejectors. Gauges: 12 Mag., 16. Barrels: 26-inch improved cylinder/modified; 28-inch modified/full; 30-inch full/full. Weight: 12 ga., about $7\frac{1}{2}$ pounds. Checkered pistol-grip stock and beavertail forearm. Made in 1961.

Coltsman Custom Pump **$250**
Same as Standard Pump except has checkered stock, ventilated-rib barrel. Weight: about $6\frac{1}{2}$ pounds. Made from 1961 to 1963.

Coltsman Standard Pump Shotgun **$195**
Takedown. Gauges: 12, 16, 20. Magazine holds 4 shells. Barrels: 26-inch improved cylinder; 28-inch modified or

Coltsman Standard Pump Shotgun (cont.)
full choke; 30-inch full choke. Weight: about 6 pounds. Plain pistol-grip stock and forearm. Made from 1961 to 1965 by Manufrance.

Colt-Sauer Drilling **$2695**
Three-barrel combination gun. Box lock. Set rifle trigger. Tang barrel selector, automatic rear sight positioner. 12 gauge over 30-06 or 243 rifle barrel. 25-inch barrels, full and modified choke. Weight: about 8 pounds. Folding leaf rear sight, blade front sight with brass bead. Checkered pistol-grip stock and beavertail forearm, recoil pad. Made from 1974 to date by J. P. Sauer & Sohn, Eckernförde, West Germany.

CHARLES DALY, INC.
New York, New York

The pre-WWII Charles Daly shotguns, with the exception of the Commander, were manufactured by various firms in Suhl, Germany. The postwar guns, except for the Novamatic series and the current models distributed by Outdoor Sports Headquarters, were produced by Miroku Firearms Mfg. Co., Tokyo.

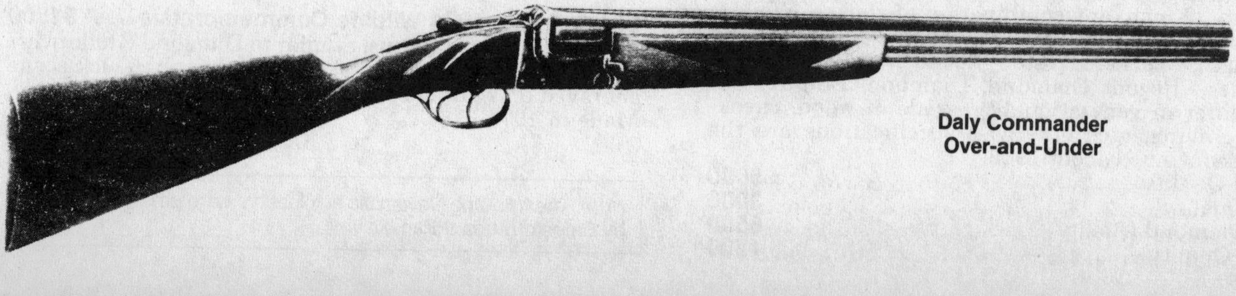

Daly Commander Over-and-Under

Charles Daly Commander Over-and-Under Shotgun

Daly pattern Anson & Deeley system boxlock action. Automatic ejectors. Double triggers or Miller selective single trigger. Gauges: 12, 16, 20, 28, .410. Barrels: 26- to 30-inch, improved cylinder and modified or modified and full choke. Weight: 5¼ to 7¼ pounds depending upon gauge and barrel length. Checkered stock and forend, straight or pistol grip. The two models, 100 and 200, differ in general quality, grade of wood, checkering, engraving, etc.; otherwise specs are the same. Made in Belgium c. 1939.

Model 100 .... **$525**
Model 200 .... **750**
Miller single trigger, extra **100**

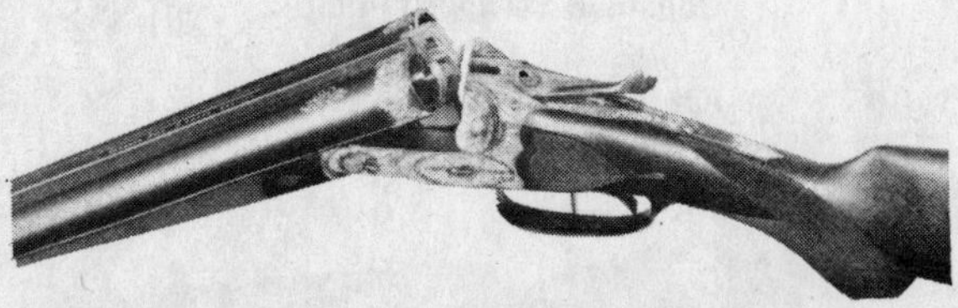

Daly Diamond Hammerless Double

Daly Regent Diamond Hammerless Double

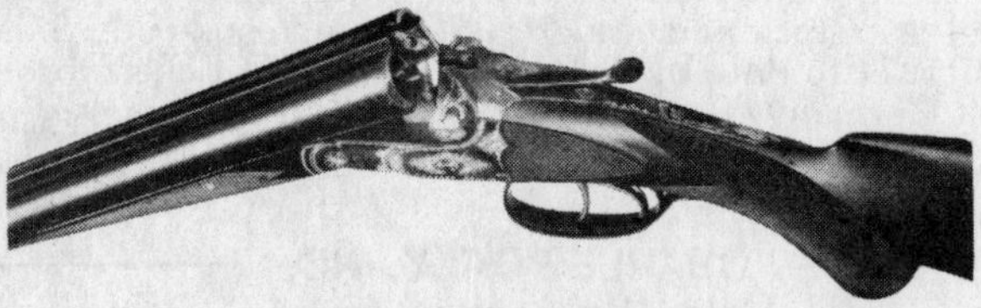

Daly Superior Hammerless Double

Charles Daly Hammerless Double Barrel Shotgun

Daly pattern Anson & Deeley system boxlock action. Automatic ejectors — except "Superior Quality" is non-ejector. Double triggers. Gauges: 10, 12, 16, 20, 28, .410. Barrels: 26- to 32-inch, any combination of chokes. Weight: from 4 pounds to 8½ pounds depending upon gauge and barrel length. Checkered pistol-grip stock and forend. The four grades—Regent Diamond, Diamond, Empire, Superior—differ in general quality, grade of wood, checkering, engraving, etc.; otherwise specifications are the same. Discontinued about 1933.

Diamond Quality **$5000**
Empire Quality **3000**
Regent Diamond Quality **6500**
Superior Quality **1500**

Charles Daly Hammerless Drilling (Three Barrel Gun)

Daly pattern Anson & Deeley system boxlock action. Plain extractors. Double triggers, front single set for rifle barrel. Gauges: 12, 16, 20, 25-20, 25-35, 30-30 rifle barrel. Supplied in various barrel lengths and weights. Checkered pistol-grip stock and forend. Auto rear sight operated by rifle barrel selector. The three grades—Regent Diamond, Diamond, Superior—differ in general quality, grade of wood, checkering, engraving, etc.; otherwise specs are the same. Discont. about 1933.

Diamond Quality **$5500**
Regent Diamond Quality **7500**
Superior Quality **4500**

Daly Empire Double Barrel

Charles Daly Empire Grade Hammerless Double $595

Box lock. Plain extractors. Non-selective single trigger. Gauges: 12, 16, 20; 3-inch chambers in 12 and 20, 2¾-inch in 16 gauge. Barrels: vent rib; 26-, 28-, 30-inch (latter in 12 gauge only); improved cylinder/modified, modified/full, full/full. Weight: 6 to 7¾ pounds depending upon gauge and barrels. Checkered pistol-grip stock and beavertail forearm. Made from 1968 to 1971.

Daly 1974 Wildlife Commemorative

Charles Daly 1974 Wildlife Commemorative . . . $1500

Limited issue of 500 guns. Similar to Diamond Grade over/under. 12-gauge trap and skeet models only. Duck scene engraved on right side of receiver, fine scroll on left side. Made in 1974.

> *Note:* The following Novamatic autoloaders were produced in 1968 by Ernesto Breda, Milan, Italy.

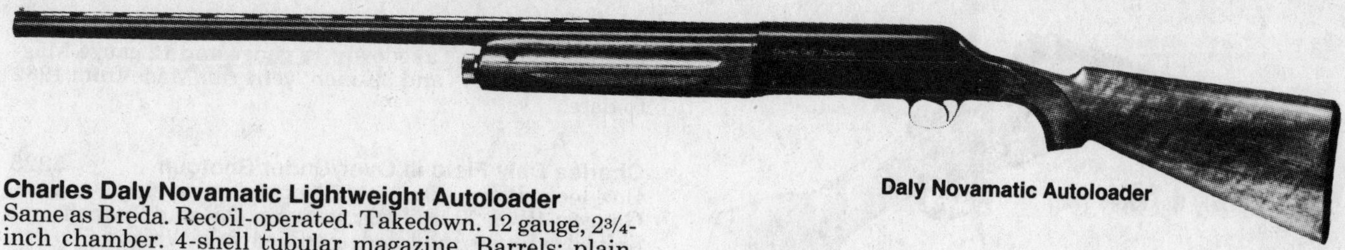

Daly Novamatic Autoloader

Charles Daly Novamatic Lightweight Autoloader
Same as Breda. Recoil-operated. Takedown. 12 gauge, $2\frac{3}{4}$-inch chamber. 4-shell tubular magazine. Barrels: plain, vent rib; 26-inch imp. cyl. or Quick-Choke with three interchangeable tubes, 28-inch modified or full choke. Weight (with 26-inch vent-rib barrel): 7 lbs. 6 oz. Checkered pistol-grip stock and forearm.

With plain barrel **$300**
With ventilated rib **325**
Extra for Quick-Choke **10**

Charles Daly Novamatic Super Lightweight
Lighter version of Novamatic Lightweight. Gauges: 12, 20. Weight (with 26-inch vent-rib barrel): 12 ga., 6 lbs. 10 oz.; 20 ga., 6 pounds. Skeet choke available in 26-inch vent-rib barrel. 28-inch barrels in 12 gauge only. Quick-Choke in 20 gauge with plain barrel.

12 gauge, plain barrel **$300**
12 gauge, ventilated rib **325**
20 gauge, plain barrel **290**
20 gauge, plain barrel with Quick-Choke **300**
20 gauge, ventilated rib **325**

Charles Daly Novamatic Super Lightweight 20 Gauge Magnum **$300**
Same as Novamatic Super Lightweight 20, except 3-inch chamber, has 3-shell magazine, 28-inch vent-rib barrel, full choke.

Charles Daly Novamatic 12 Gauge Magnum **$300**
Same as Novamatic Lightweight, except chambered for 12 gauge magnum 3-inch shell, has 3-shell magazine, 30-inch vent-rib barrel, full choke, and stock with recoil pad. Weight: $7\frac{3}{4}$ pounds.

Charles Daly Novamatic Trap Gun **$325**
Same as Novamatic Lightweight, except has 30-inch vent-rib barrel, full choke and Monte Carlo stock with recoil pad. Weight: $7\frac{3}{4}$ pounds.

Daly Over-and-Under Field Grade (Postwar)

Daly Over-and-Under Venture (Postwar)

Charles Daly Over-and-Under Shotguns (Prewar)
Daly pattern Anson & Deeley system boxlock action. Side plates. Auto ejectors. Double triggers. Gauges: 12, 16, 20. Supplied in various barrel lengths and weights. Checkered pistol-grip stock and forend. The two grades—Diamond and Empire—differ in general quality, grade of wood, checkering, engraving, etc.; otherwise specifications are the same. Discont. about 1933.

Diamond Quality **$6000**
Empire Quality **5000**

Charles Daly Over-and-Under Shotguns (Postwar)
Box lock. Auto ejectors or selective auto/manual ejection. Selective single trigger. Gauges: 12, 12 magnum (3-inch chambers), 20 (3-inch chambers), 28, .410. Barrels: vent rib; 26-, 28-, 30-inch; standard choke combinations. Weight: 6 to 8 pounds depending upon gauge and barrels. Select walnut stock with pistol grip, fluted forearm, checkered; Monte Carlo comb on trap guns; recoil pad on

Charles Daly Over-and-Unders (Postwar) (cont.)
12 ga. mag. and trap models. The various grades differ in quality of engraving and wood. Made 1963 to 1976.

Diamond Grade **$825**
Field Grade **530**
Superior Grade **550**
Venture Grade **520**

Charles Daly Sextuple Model Single Barrel Trap Gun
Daly pattern Anson & Deeley system boxlock action. Six locking bolts. Auto ejector. 12 gauge only. Barrels: 30-, 32-, 34-inch, vent rib. Weight: $7\frac{1}{2}$ to $8\frac{1}{4}$ pounds. Checkered pistol-grip stock and forend. This model was made in two grades, Empire and Regent Diamond, the guns differing in general quality, grade of wood, checkering, engraving, etc.; otherwise specs are the same. Discont. about 1933.

Regent Diamond Quality **$7500**
Empire Quality **5800**

Daly Sextuple Trap

Daly Single Barrel Trap

Charles Daly Single Barrel Trap Gun $5000
Daly pattern Anson & Deeley system boxlock action. Auto ejector. 12 gauge only. Barrels: 30-, 32-, 34-inch, vent rib. Weight: $7\frac{1}{2}$ to $8\frac{1}{4}$ pounds. Checkered pistol-grip stock and forend. This model was made in Empire Quality only. Discontinued about 1933.

Charles Daly Superior Grade Single Barrel Trap $550
Box lock. Automatic ejector. 12 gauge only. 32- or 34-inch ventilated-rib barrel, full choke. Weight: about 8 pounds. Monte Carlo stock with pistol grip and recoil pad, beavertail forearm, checkered. Made 1968 to 1976.

Note: The following Charles Daly shotguns are distributed in the U.S. by Outdoor Sports Headquarters, Dayton, Ohio. The Daly semiauto guns are currently manufactured in Japan while the over/under models are produced in Italy.

Charles Daly Field Semi-Auto Shotgun $250
Recoil-operated. Takedown. 12 gauge and 12 gauge Magnum. Barrels: 27- and 30-inch; vent rib. Made from 1982 to date.

Charles Daly Field III Over/Under Shotgun $325
Box lock. Plain extractors. Non-selective single trigger. Gauges: 12 or 20. Barrels: vent rib; 26- and 28-inch; improved cylinder/modified, modified/full. Weight: 6 to $7\frac{3}{4}$ pounds depending upon gauge and barrels. Chrome-molybdenum steel barrels. Checkered pistol-grip stock and forearm. Made from 1982 to date.

Charles Daly Multi-XII Self-loading Shotgun $375
Similar to the gas-operated field semiauto, except with new Multi-Action gas system designed to shoot all loads without adjustment. 12 gauge w/3-inch chamber. 27-inch barrel with Invector choke tubes, vent rib. Made in Japan from 1987 to date.

Charles Daly Over/Under Presentation Grade . . $760
Purdey double cross-bolt locks. Single selective trigger. Gauges: 12 or 20. Barrels: chrome-molybdenum steel, rectified, honed and internally chromed; 27-inch vent rib. Hand-checkered deluxe European walnut stock. Made from 1982 to 1986.

Charles Daly Over/Under Superior II Shotgun . . . $450
Box lock. Plain extractors. Non-selective single trigger. Gauges: 12 or 20. Barrels: chrome-molybdenum vent rib; 26-, 28-, 30-inch; latter in Magnum only; assorted chokes. Silver engraved receiver. Checkered pistol-grip stock and forearm. Made from 1982 to date.

Daly Field Semi-Auto

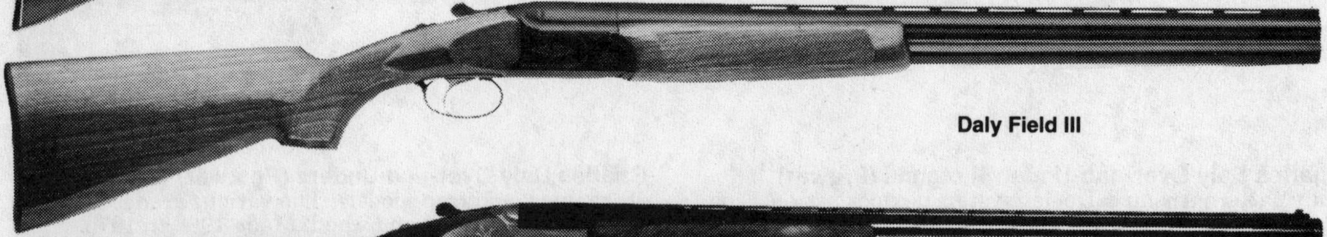

Daly Field III

Daly Presentation Grade

Daly Superior II

DARNE S.A.
Saint-Etienne, France

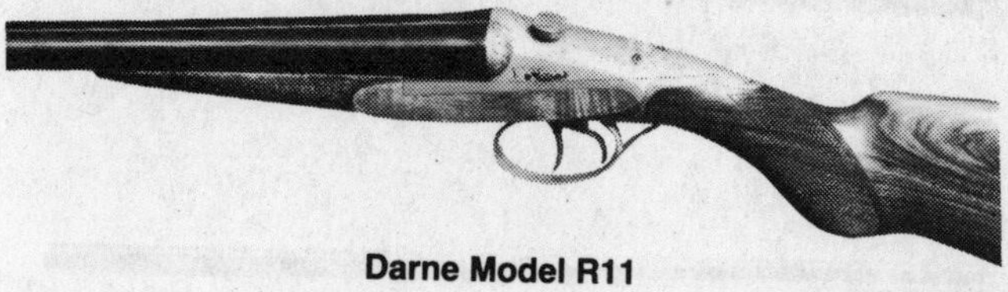

Darne Model R11

Darne Model V22

Darne Model V
Hors Série No. 1

Darne Hammerless Double Barrel Shotguns
Sliding-breech action with fixed barrels. Auto ejectors. Double triggers. Gauges: 12, 16, 20, 28; also 12 and 20 magnum with 3-inch chambers. Barrels: 27½-inch standard, 25½- to 31½-inch lengths available; any standard choke combination. Weight: 5½ to 7 pounds depending upon gauge and barrel length. Checkered straight-grip or pistol-grip stock and forearm. The various models differ in grade of engraving and wood. Currently manufactured.

Model R11 (Bird Hunter) .... **$ 800**
Model R15 (Pheasant Hunter) **1495**
Model R16 (Magnum) **1925**
Model V19 (Quail Hunter) **2450**
Model V22 .... **$3600**
Model V Hors Série No. 1 .... **4500**

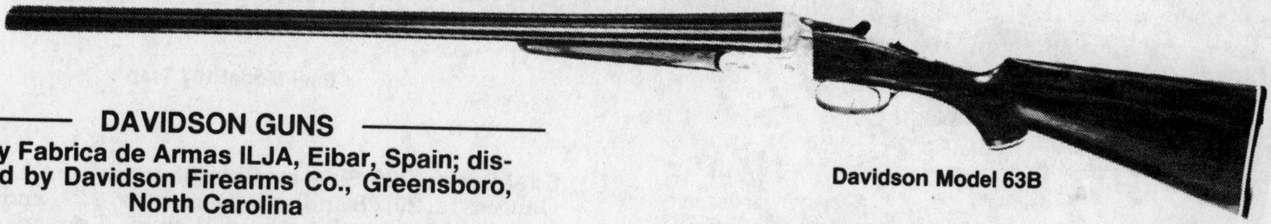

Davidson Model 63B

DAVIDSON GUNS
Mfd. by Fabrica de Armas ILJA, Eibar, Spain; distributed by Davidson Firearms Co., Greensboro, North Carolina

Davidson Model 63B Double Barrel Shotgun ... $255
Anson & Deeley boxlock action. Frame-engraved and nickel plated. Plain extractors. Auto safety. Double triggers. Gauges: 12, 16, 20, 28, .410. Barrel lengths: 25 (.410 only), 26, 28, 30 inches (latter 12 ga. only). Chokes: imp. cyl./mod., mod./full, full/full. Weight: 5 lb. 11 oz. (.410) to 7 pounds (12 ga.). Pistol-grip stock and forearm of European walnut, checkered. Made 1963 to date.

Davidson Model 63B Magnum
Similar to standard Model 63B, except chambered for 10 ga. 3½-inch, 12 and 20 ga. 3-inch magnum shells; 10 gauge has 32-inch barrels, choked full and full. Weight: 10 lb. 10 oz. Made from 1963 to date.

12 and 20 gauge Magnum **$325**
10 gauge Magnum **350**

Davidson Model 69SL Double Barrel Shotgun .. $400
Sidelock action with detachable side plates, engraved and nickel-plated. Plain extractors. Auto safety. Double triggers. 12 and 20 gauge. Barrels: 26-inch imp. cyl./mod., 28-inch mod./full. Weight: 12 ga., 7 pounds; 20 ga., 6½ pounds. Pistol-grip stock and forearm of European walnut, checkered. Made from 1963 to 1976.

Davidson Model 73 Stagecoach Hammer Double $250
Sidelock action with detachable side plates and exposed hammers. Plain extractors. Double triggers. Gauges: 12, 20; 3-inch chambers. 20-inch barrels, modified and full choke. Weight: 7 lbs., 12 ga.; 6½ lbs., 20 ga. Checkered pistol-grip stock and forearm. Made from 1976 to date.

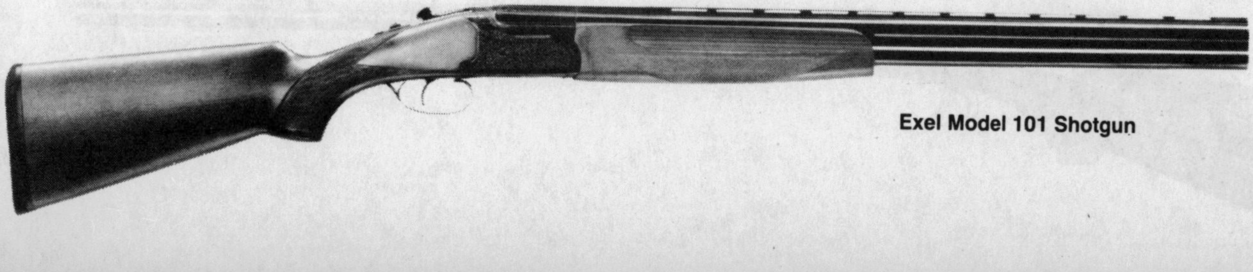

Exel Model 101 Shotgun

Exel Model 103 Shotgun

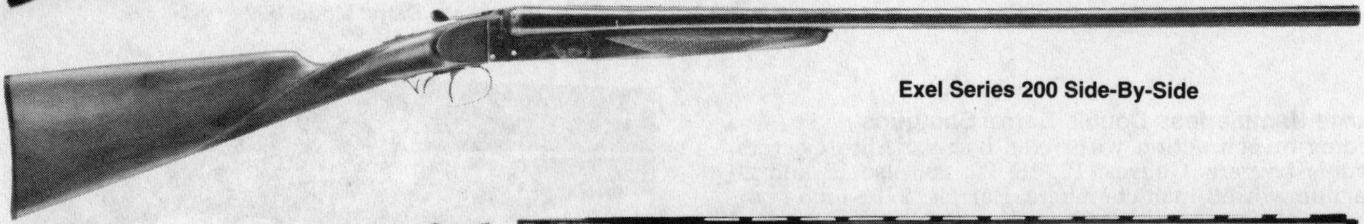

Exel Series 200 Side-By-Side

Exel Series 300 Over/Under

Exel Model 107 Trap

EXEL ARMS OF AMERICA
Gardner, Massachusetts

Exel Series 100 Over/Under Shotguns
Gauge: 12. Single selective trigger. Selective auto ejectors. Hand-checkered European walnut stock with full pistol grip, tulip forend. Black metal finish. Chambered for 2¾-inch shells (Model 103 for 3-inch). Weight: 6⅞ to 7⅞ pounds.

Model 101, 26-inch bbl., IC/M	$340
Model 102, 28-inch bbl., IC/IM	340
Model 103, 30-inch bbl., M/F	350
Model 104, 28-inch bbl., IC/IM	410
Model 105, 28-inch bbl., 5 choke tubes	485
Model 106, 28-inch bbl., 5 choke tubes	635
Model 107 Trap, 30-inch bbl., Full +5 tubes	635

Exel Series 200 Side-by-Side Shotgun $340
Gauges: 12, 20, 28 and .410. Barrels: 26-, 27- and 28-inch; various choke combinations. Weight: 7 pounds average. American or European-style stock and forend. Made from 1985 to date.

Exel Series 300 Over/Under Shotgun $450
Gauge: 12. Barrels: 26-, 28- and 29-inch. Non-glare black-chrome matte finish. Weight: 7 pounds average. Selective auto ejectors, engraved receiver. Hand-checkered European walnut stock and forend. Made from 1985 to 1986.

FOX SHOTGUNS

Made by A. H. Fox Gun Co., Philadelphia, Penn., from 1903 to 1930 and since then by Savage Arms, originally of Utica, N.Y., now of Westfield, Mass.

Values shown are for 12 and 16 gauge doubles made by A. H. Fox. Twenty gauge guns often are valued up to 75% higher. Savage-made Fox models generally bring prices 25% lower. With the exception of Model B, production of Fox shotguns was discontinued about 1942.

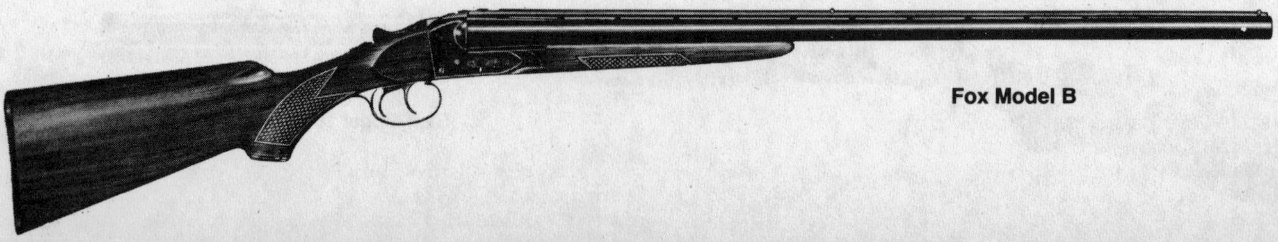

Fox Model B

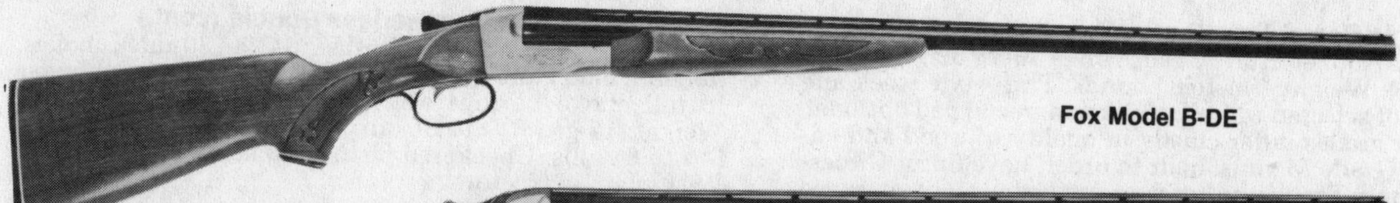

Fox Model B-DE

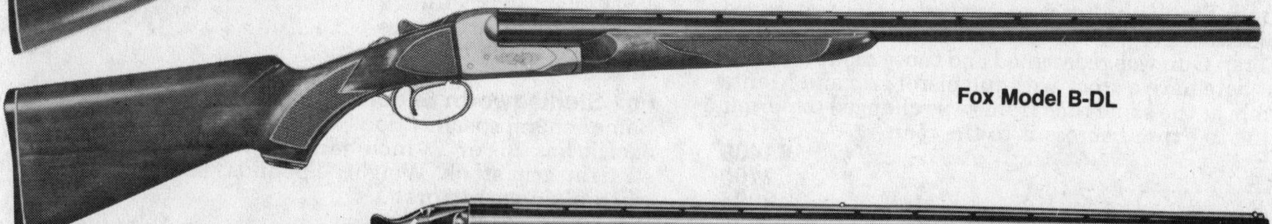

Fox Model B-DL

Fox Model B-ST

Fox Model B Hammerless Double **$225**
Box lock. Double triggers. Plain extractor. Gauges: 12, 16, 20, .410. 24- to 30-inch barrels; vent rib on current production; chokes: modified/full, cylinder/modified, both full (.410 only). Weight: about 7½ pounds, 12 ga. Checkered pistol-grip stock and forearm. Made about 1940 to date.

Fox Model B-DE **$270**
Same as Model B-ST except frame finished in satin chrome, select walnut buttstock with checkered pistol grip and beavertail forearm. Made from 1965 to 1966.

Fox Model B-DL **$300**
Same as Model B-ST except frame finished in satin chrome, select walnut buttstock with checkered pistol grip, side panels, beavertail forearm. Made 1962 to 1966.

Fox Model B-SE **$265**
Same as Model B except has selective ejectors and single trigger. Made from 1966 to date.

Fox Model B-ST **$230**
Same as Model B except has non-selective single trigger. Made from 1955 to 1966.

Fox Grade A

Fox Hammerless Double Barrel Shotguns
The higher grades have the same general specifications as the standard Sterlingworth model with differences chiefly in workmanship and materials. Higher grade models are stocked in fine selected walnut; quantity and quality of engraving increases with price. Except for Grade A, all have auto ejectors.

Grade A . . . . $ 925
Grade AE 1495

Fox Grade AE

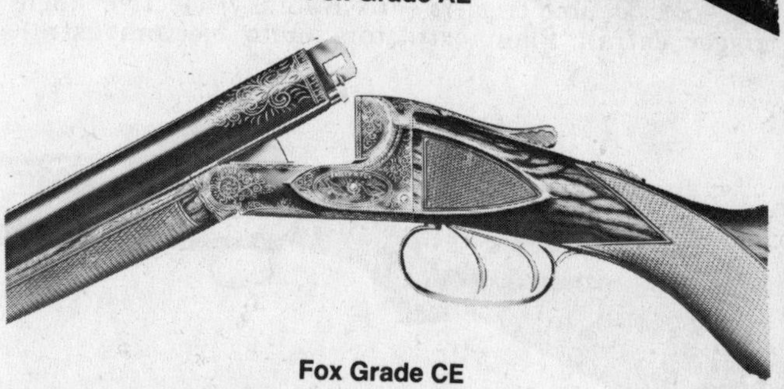

Fox Grade CE

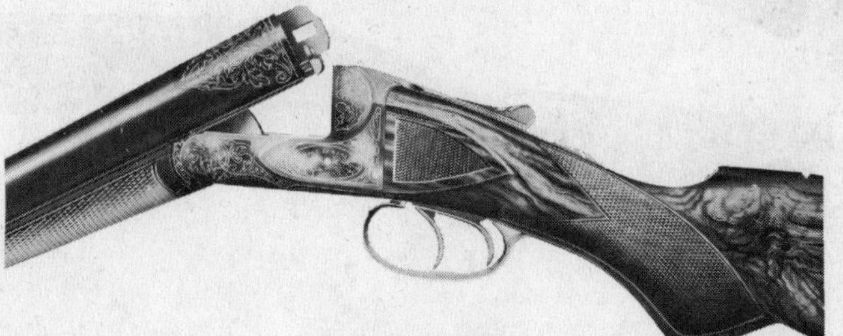

Fox Grade XE

Fox Hammerless Double Barrel Shotguns (cont.)

Grade BE . . . . $ 2050
Grade CE 2100
Grade DE 6000
Grade FE 14,000
Grade XE 3850
Fox-Kautzky selective single trigger, extra 200
Ventilated rib, extra 300
Beavertail forearm, extra 200

Fox Single Barrel Trap Guns
Box lock. Auto ejector. 12 gauge only. 30- or 32-inch vent-rib barrel. Weight: $7\frac{1}{2}$ to 8 pounds. Trap-style stock and forearm of selected walnut, checkered, recoil pad optional. The four grades differ chiefly in quality of wood and engraving; Grade M guns, built to order, have finest Circassian walnut. Stock and receiver are elaborately engraved and inlaid with gold. Discontinued 1942. *Note:* In 1932 the Fox Trap Gun was redesigned and those manufactured after that date have a stock with full pistol grip and Monte Carlo comb; at the same time frame was changed to permit the rib line to extend across it to the rear.
Grade JE **$1400**
Grade KE **2100**
Grade LE **2895**
Grade ME **7500**

Fox Sterlingworth Deluxe
Same general specifications as Sterlingworth, except 32-inch barrel was also available, has recoil pad, ivory bead sights.
With plain extractors **$775**
With automatic ejectors **810**

Fox Sterlingworth

Fox Sterlingworth Hammerless Double
Box lock. Double triggers (Fox-Kautzky selective single trigger extra). Plain extractors (auto ejectors extra).

Fox Sterlingworth Hammerless Double (cont.)
Gauges: 12, 16, 20. Barrel lengths: 26-, 28-, 30-inch; chokes, full/full, mod./full, cyl./mod. (any combination of cylinder to full choke borings was available at no extra cost). Weight: 12 ga., $6\frac{7}{8}$ to $8\frac{1}{4}$ lbs.; 16 ga., 6 to 7 lbs.; 20 ga., $5\frac{3}{4}$ to $6\frac{3}{4}$ lbs. Checkered pistol-grip stock and forearm.
With plain extractors **$825**
With automatic ejectors **950**
Selective single trigger, extra **200**

Fox Sterlingworth Skeet and Upland Game Gun
Same general specifications as the standard Sterlingworth, except has 26- or 28-inch barrels with skeet boring only, straight-grip stock. Weight: 7 pounds, 12 ga.
With plain extractors **$795**
With automatic ejectors **850**

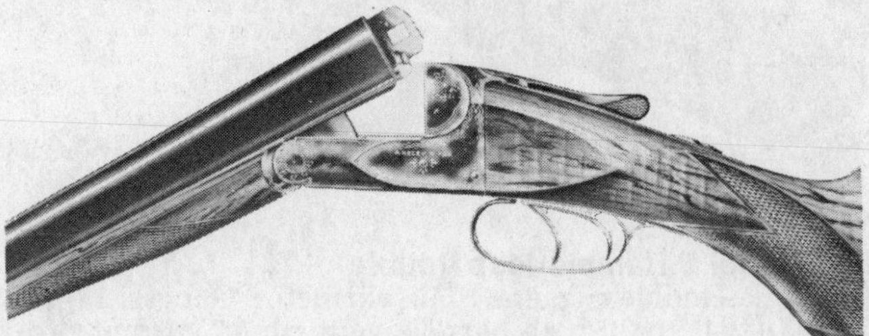

Super Fox HE

Super Fox HE Grade **$1595**
Long-range gun made in 12 gauge only (chambered for 3-inch shells on order), 30- or 32-inch full choke barrels, auto ejectors standard. Weight: $8\frac{3}{4}$ to $9\frac{3}{4}$ pounds. General specifications same as standard Sterlingworth.

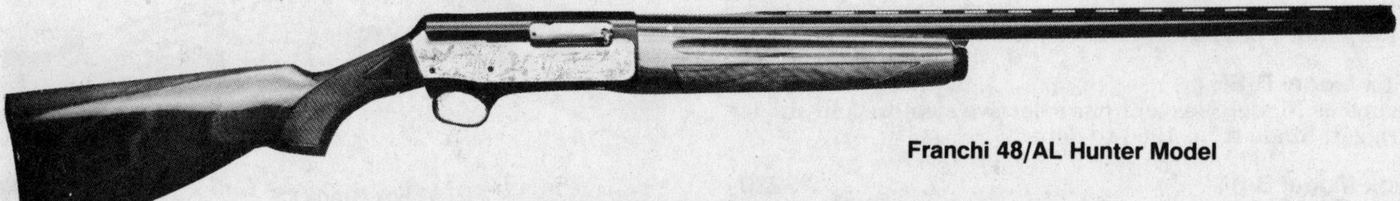

Franchi 48/AL Hunter Model

Franchi Model 500
Standard Autoloader

LUIGI FRANCHI S.P.A.
Brescia, Italy

Franchi 48/AL Ultra Light Shotgun
Recoil-operated, takedown, hammerless shotgun with tubular magazine. Gauges: 12 or 20 ($2\frac{3}{4}$-inch); 12 ga. Magnum (3-inch chamber). Barrels: 24- to 32-inch w/various choke combinations. Weight: 5 lbs. 2 oz. (20 ga.) to $6\frac{1}{4}$ lbs. (12 ga.). Checkered pistol-grip walnut stock and forend with high gloss finish.
Standard Model **$370**
Hunter or Magnum Models **410**

Franchi Model 500 Standard Autoloader **$310**
Gas-operated. 12 gauge. 4-shot magazine. Barrels: 26-, 28-inch; vent rib; improved cylinder, modified, improved modified, full choke. Weight: about 7 pounds. Checkered pistol-grip stock and forearm. Made 1976 to 1980.

Franchi Model 520 Deluxe

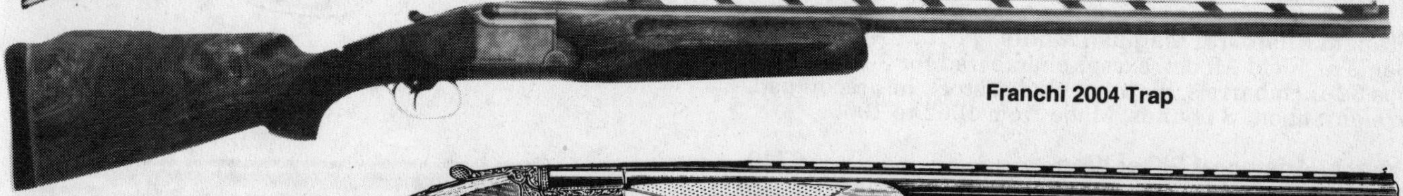

Franchi 2004 Trap

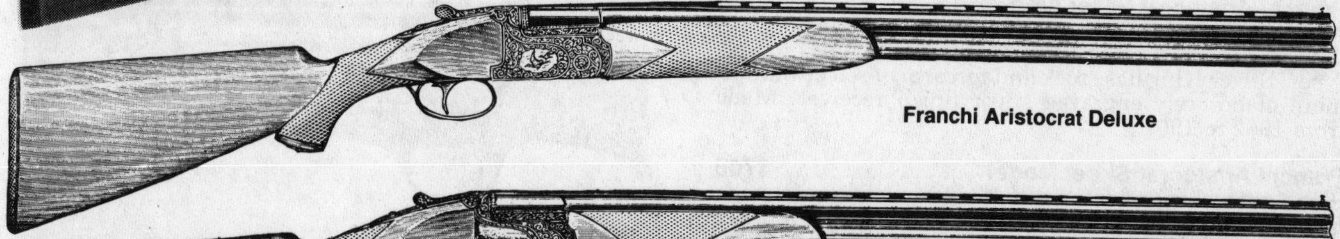

Franchi Aristocrat Deluxe

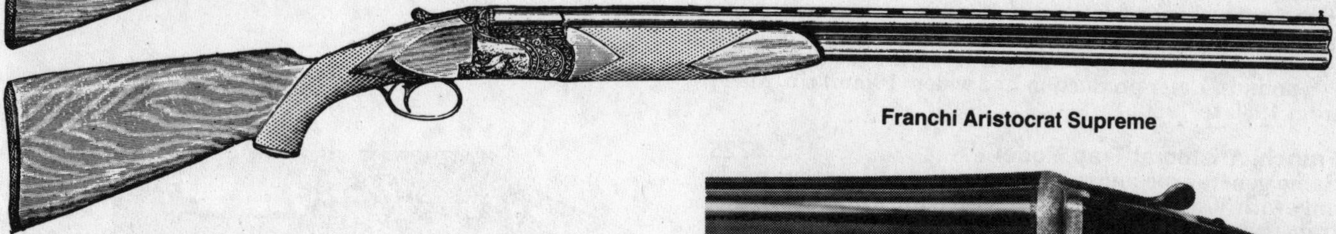

Franchi Aristocrat Supreme

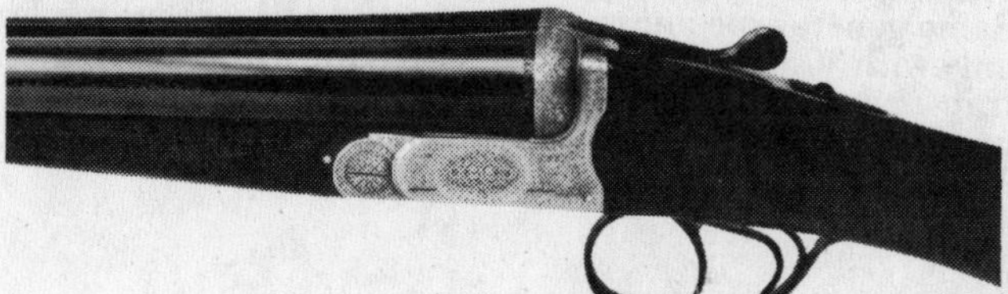

Franchi Airone

Franchi Model 520 Deluxe **$350**
Same as Model 500, except higher grade with engraved receiver. Made from 1975 to 1979.

Franchi Model 520 Eldorado Gold **$950**
Same as Model 520, except custom grade with engraved and gold-inlaid receiver, finer quality wood. Intro. 1977.

Franchi Model 2003 Trap Over-and-Under **$1100**
Box lock. Auto ejectors. Selective single trigger. 12 gauge. Barrels: 30-, 32-inch; improved modified/full, full/full; high vent rib. Weight (with 30-inch barrel): $8\frac{1}{4}$ pounds. Checkered walnut beavertail forearm and stock with straight or Monte Carlo comb, recoil pad. Luggage-type carrying case. Made from 1976 to date.

Franchi Model 2004 Trap Single Barrel **$1100**
Same as Model 2003, except single barrel, 32- or 34-inch, full choke. Weight (with 32-inch barrel): $8\frac{1}{4}$ pounds. Made from 1976 to date.

Franchi Model 2005 Combination Trap **$1320**
Model 2004/2005 type gun with two sets of barrels, single and over-and-under. Made from 1976 to date.

Franchi Model 2005/3 Combination Trap **$2200**
Model 2004/2005 type gun with three sets of barrels, any combination of single and over-and-under. Made from 1976 to date.

Franchi Model 3000/2 Combination Trap **$2500**
Box lock. Automatic ejectors. Selective single trigger. 12 gauge. Barrels: 32-inch over/under full and improved modified; 34-inch underbarrel modified choke; high vent rib. Weight (with 32-inch barrels): 8 lbs. 6 oz. Choice of six different castoff buttstocks. Made from 1979 to date.

Franchi Airone Hammerless Double **$1200**
Box lock. Anson & Deeley system action. Auto ejectors. Double triggers. 12 gauge. Various barrel lengths, chokes, weights. Checkered straight-grip stock and forearm. Made from 1940 to 1950.

Franchi Alcione Over/Under Shotgun **$600**
Hammerless, takedown shotgun with engraved receiver. Selective single trigger and ejectors. 12 gauge w/3-inch chambers. Barrels: 26-inch (imp. cyl./ mod.; 28-inch (mod./full). Weight: $6\frac{3}{4}$ pounds. Checkered French walnut buttstock and forend. Imported from Italy since 1982.

Franchi Aristocrat Field Model Over/Under **$525**
Box lock. Selective auto ejectors. Selective single trigger. 12 gauge. Barrels: 26-inch improved cylinder/modified; 28- and 30-inch modified/full choke; vent rib. Weight (with 26-inch barrels): 7 pounds. Checkered pistol-grip stock and forearm. Made from 1960 to 1969.

Franchi Aristocrat Deluxe and Supreme Grades
Available in Field, Skeet and Trap Models with the same general specifications as standard guns of these types. Deluxe and Supreme Grades are of higher quality with stock and forearm of select walnut, elaborate relief engraving on receiver, trigger guard, tang and top lever. Supreme Model has figures of game birds inlaid in gold. Made from 1960 to 1966.
Deluxe Grade .... **$ 995**
Supreme Grade **1400**

Franchi Aristocrat Imperial and Monte Carlo Grades
Custom guns made in Field, Skeet and Trap Models with the same general specifications as standard for these types. Imperial and Monte Carlo Grades are of highest quality with stock and forearm of select walnut, fine engraving—elaborate on the latter grade. Made from 1967 to 1969.
Imperial Grade **$2400**
Monte Carlo Grade **3100**

Franchi Aristocrat Magnum Model $545
Same as Field Model, except chambered for 3-inch shell, has 32-inch barrels, both full choke; stock has recoil pad. Weight: about 8 pounds. Made from 1962 to 1965.

Franchi Aristocrat Silver King $710
Available in Field, Magnum, Skeet and Trap Models with the same general specifications as standard guns of these types. Silver King has stock and forearm of select walnut, more elaborately engraved silver finish receiver. Made from 1962 to 1969.

Franchi Aristocrat Skeet Model $700
Same general specifications as Field Model, except made only with 26-inch ventilated-rib barrels bored skeet chokes #1 and #2; skeet-style stock and forearm. Weight: about 7½ pounds. Later production had wider (10mm) rib. Made from 1960 to 1969.

Franchi Aristocrat Trap Model $725
Same general specifications as Field Model, except made only with 30-inch vent-rib barrels, modified and full choke; trap-style stock with recoil pad, beavertail forearm. Later production had Monte Carlo comb, wider (10mm) rib. Made from 1960 to 1969.

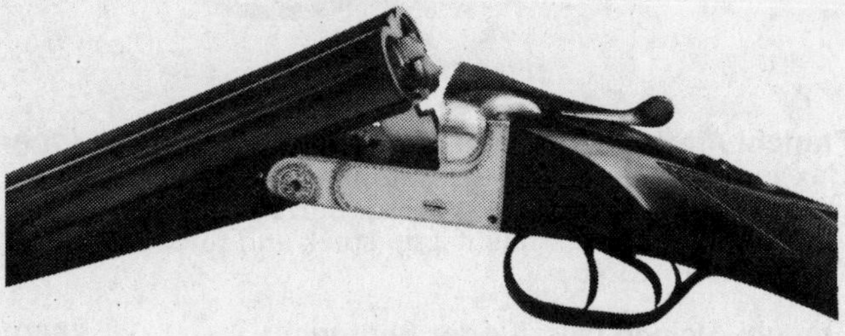

Franchi Astore

Franchi Astore Hammerless Double $995
Box lock. Anson & Deeley system action. Plain extractors. Double triggers. 12 gauge. Various barrel lengths, chokes, weights. Checkered straight-grip stock and forearm. Made from 1937 to 1960.

Franchi Astore II $1200
Similar to Astore S, but not as high grade. Furnished with either plain extractors or auto ejectors, double triggers, pistol-grip stock. Barrels: 27-inch imp. cyl./imp. mod.; 28-inch mod./full choke. Currently manufactured for Franchi in Spain.

Franchi Astore S $2100
Same as Astore, except has higher grade wood, fine engraving. Automatic ejectors, single trigger, 28-inch barrel (modified/full or improved modified/full choke) are standard on current production.

Franchi Astore S

Franchi Crown Grade

Franchi Diamond Grade

Franchi Crown, Diamond and Imperial Grade Autoloaders
Same general specifications as Standard Model, except these are custom guns of the highest quality. Crown Grade has hunting scene engraving; Diamond Grade has silver-inlaid scroll engraving; Imperial Grade has elaborately engraved hunting scenes with figures inlaid in gold. Stock and forearm of fancy walnut. Made 1954 to 1975.
Crown Grade **$1600**
Diamond Grade **1900**
Imperial Grade **2400**

Franchi Dynamic-12
Same general specifications and appearance as Standard Model, except 12 gauge only, has heavier steel receiver. Weight: about 7¼ pounds. Made from 1965 to 1972.
With plain barrel **$310**
With ventilated rib **340**

Franchi Dynamic-12 Slug Gun $320
Same as standard Slug Gun, except 12 gauge only, has heavier steel receiver. Made from 1965 to 1972.

Franchi Dynamic-12 Skeet Gun $375
Same general specifications and appearance as Standard Model, except has heavier steel receiver; made only in 12 gauge with 26-inch vent-rib barrel, skeet choke; stock and forearm of extra fancy walnut. Made from 1965 to 1972.

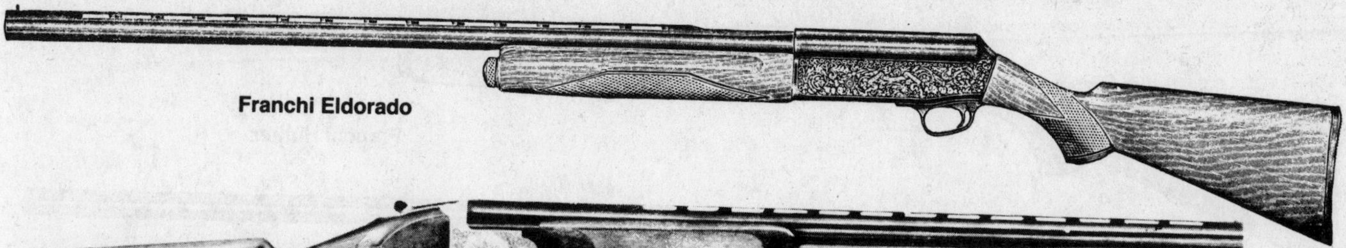

Franchi Eldorado

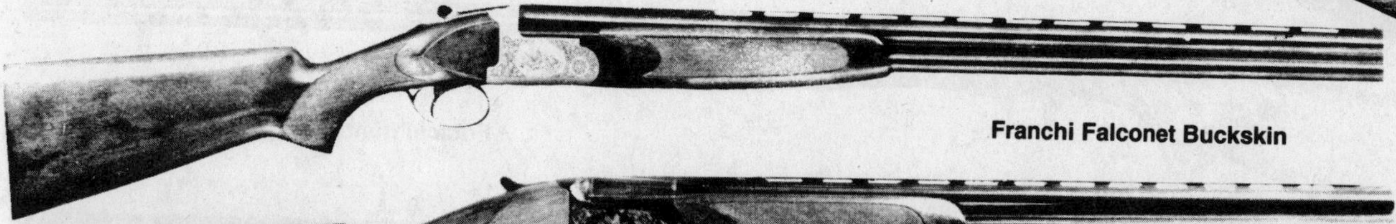

Franchi Falconet Buckskin

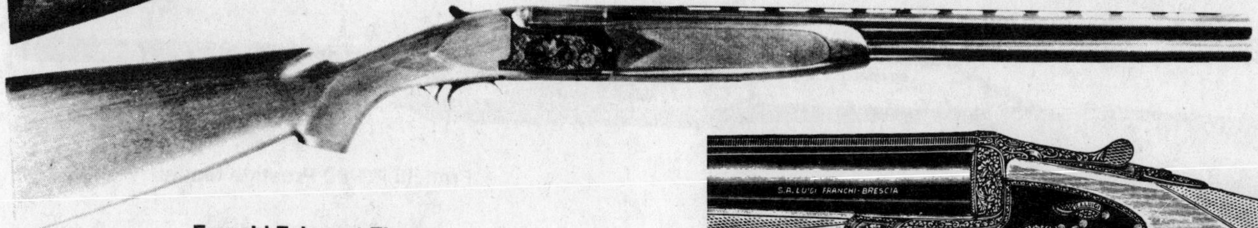

Franchi Falconet Ebony

Franchi Eldorado Model $450
Same general specifications as Standard Model except highest grade with gold-filled engraving, stock and forearm of selected walnut; furnished with vent-rib barrel only. Made from 1954 to date.

Franchi Falconet International Skeet Model $995
Similar to Standard Skeet Model, but higher grade. Made from 1970 to 1974.

Franchi Falconet International Trap Model $950
Similar to Standard Trap Model, but higher grade; with either straight or Monte Carlo comb stock. Made from 1970 to 1974.

Franchi Falconet Over-and-Under Field Models
Box lock. Auto ejectors. Selective single trigger. Gauges: 12, 16, 20, 28, .410. Barrels: 24-, 26-, 28-, 30-inch; vent rib. Chokes: cylinder/improved cylinder, improved cylinder/modified, modified/full. Weight: from about 6 pounds. Engraved lightweight alloy receiver; light-colored in Buckskin Model, blued in Ebony Model, pickled silver in Silver Model. Checkered walnut stock and forearm. Made from 1968 to 1975.
Buckskin or Ebony Model **$550**
Silver Model **600**

Franchi Falconet Standard Skeet Model $895
Same general specifications as Field Models, except made only with 26-inch barrels bored skeet chokes #1 and #2, wide vent rib, color-casehardened receiver, skeet-style stock and forearm. Weight: 12 ga., about 7¾ pounds. Made 1970 to 1974.

Franchi Falconet Standard Trap Model $925
Same general specifications as Field Models, except made only in 12 gauge with 30-inch barrels, modified and full choke; wide vent rib, color-casehardened receiver, Monte Carlo trap-style stock and forearm, recoil pad. Weight: about 8 pounds. Made from 1970 to 1974.

Franchi Hammerless Side Lock Doubles
Hand-detachable locks. Self-opening action. Auto ejectors. Double triggers or single trigger. Gauges: 12, 16, 20. Barrel

Franchi Condor

Franchi Imperiale Montecarlo Extra

Franchi Imperiale "S"

Franchi Hammerless Side Lock Doubles (cont.)
lengths, chokes, weights according to customer's specifications. Checkered stock and forend, straight or pistol grip. Made in six grades—Condor, Imperiale, Imperiale S, Imperiale Montecarlo No. 5, Imperiale Montecarlo No. 11, Imperiale Montecarlo Extra—which differ chiefly in overall quality, engraving, grade of wood, checkering, etc.; general specifications are the same. Only the Imperiale Montecarlo Extra Grade is currently manufactured.
Condor Grade . . . . **$ 7500**
Imperiale, Imperiale S Grades **9000**
Imperiale Montecarlo Grades No. 5, 11 . . . . **14,500**
Imperiale Montecarlo Extra Grade **16,500**

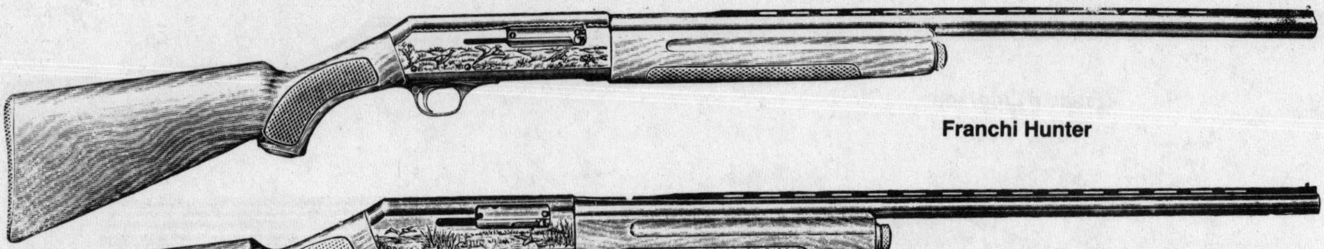

Franchi Hunter

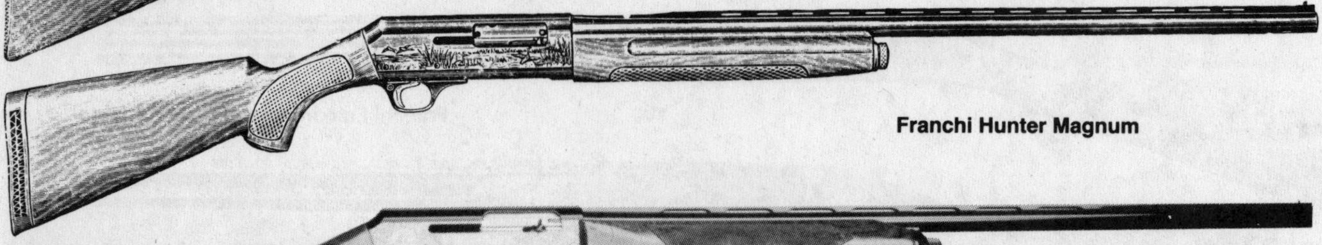

Franchi Hunter Magnum

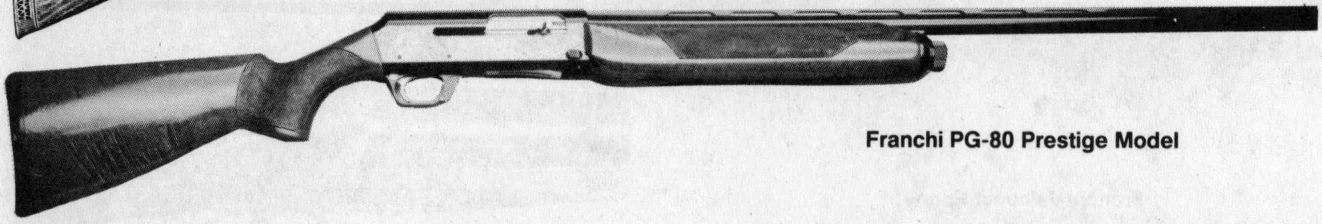

Franchi PG-80 Prestige Model

Franchi Hunter Model
Same general specifications as Standard Model except higher grade with engraved receiver; furnished with ribbed barrel only. Made from 1950 to date.
With solid rib **$325**
With ventilated rib **340**

Franchi Hunter Model Magnum $395
Same as Standard Model Magnum, except higher grade with engraved receiver, ventilated-rib barrel only. Formerly designated "Wildfowler Model." Made 1954 to 1973.

Franchi Peregrine Model 400 . . . . $580
Same general specifications as Model 451, except has steel receiver. Weight (with 26½-inch barrel): 6 lbs. 15 oz. Made from 1975 to 1978.

Franchi Peregrine Model 451 Over-and-Under . . $525
Box lock. Lightweight alloy receiver. Automatic ejectors. Selective single trigger. 12 gauge. Barrels: 26½-, 28-inch; cylinder and improved cylinder, improved cylinder and modified, modified and full choke; ventilated rib. Weight (with 26½-inch barrels): 6 lbs. 1 oz. Checkered pistol-grip stock and forearm. Made from 1975 to 1978.

Franchi PG-80 Gas-Operated Semiautomatic Shotgun
Gas-operated, takedown, hammerless shotgun with tubular magazine. 12 gauge w/2¾-inch chamber. 5-shot

Franchi PG-80 Gas-Operated Semiautomatic (cont.)
magazine. Barrels: 24 to 30 inches w/vent rib. Weight: 7½ pounds. Gold-plated trigger. Checkered pistol-grip stock and forend of European walnut. Imported from Italy since 1985.
Prestige Model **$410**
Elite Model **450**

Franchi Skeet Gun $395
Same general specifications and appearance as Standard Model, except made only with 26-inch vent-rib barrel, skeet choke. Stock and forearm of extra fancy walnut. Made from 1972 to 1974.

Franchi Slug Gun $345
Same as Standard Model, except has 22-inch plain barrel, cylinder bore, folding leaf open rear sight, gold bead front sight. Made from 1960 to date.

Franchi Standard Model Autoloader
Recoil operated. Light alloy receiver. Gauges: 12, 20. 4-shot magazine. Barrels: 26-, 28-, 30-inch; plain, solid or vent rib; improved cylinder, modified, full choke. Weight: 12 ga., about 6¼ lbs.; 20 ga., 5⅛ lbs. Checkered pistol-grip stock and forearm. Made 1950 to date.
With plain barrel **$300**
With solid rib **325**
With ventilated rib **340**

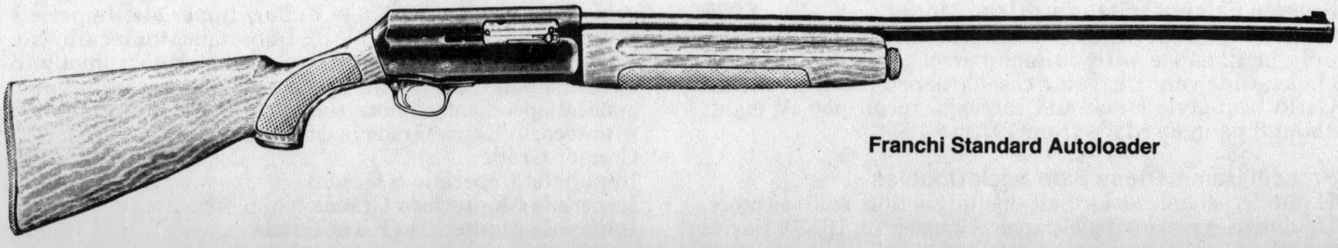

Franchi Standard Autoloader

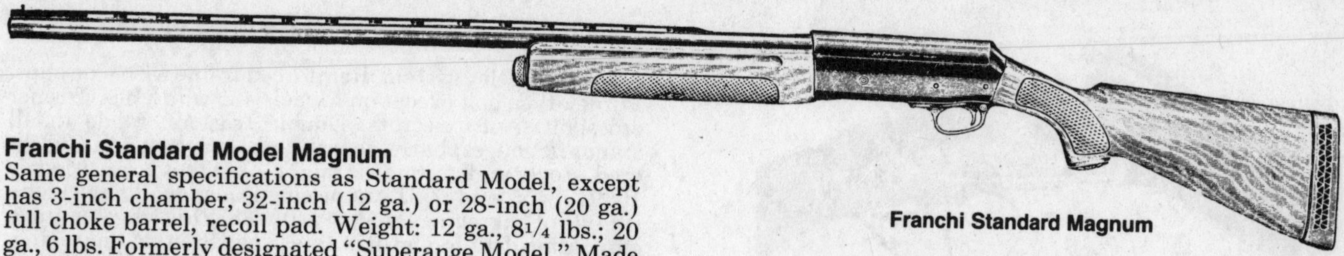

Franchi Standard Magnum

Franchi Standard Model Magnum
Same general specifications as Standard Model, except has 3-inch chamber, 32-inch (12 ga.) or 28-inch (20 ga.) full choke barrel, recoil pad. Weight: 12 ga., 8¼ lbs.; 20 ga., 6 lbs. Formerly designated "Superange Model." Made from 1954 to date.
With plain barrel **$345**
With ventilated rib **365**

Franchi Turkey Gun **$400**
Same as Standard Model Magnum, except higher grade with turkey scene engraved receiver, 12 gauge only, 36-inch matted-rib barrel, extra full choke. Made 1963-1965.

AUGUSTE FRANCOTTE & CIE., S.A.
Liege, Belgium

Francotte shotguns for many years were distributed in the U.S. by Abercrombie & Fitch of New York City. This firm has used a series of model designations for Francotte guns which do not correspond to those of the manufacturer. Because so many Francotte owners refer to their guns by the A & F model names and numbers, the A & F series is included in a listing separate from that of the standard Francotte numbers.

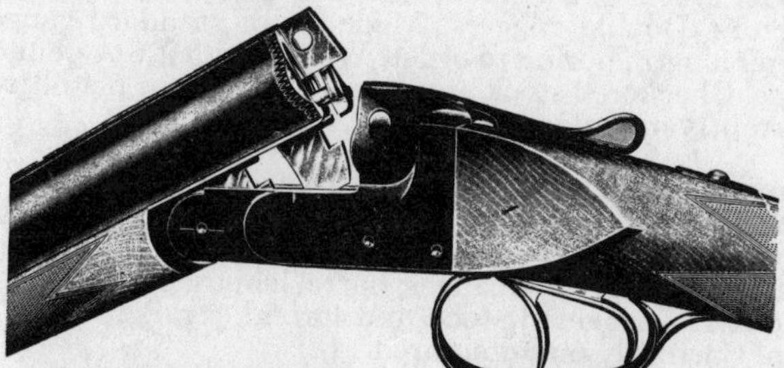

Francotte Model 6886

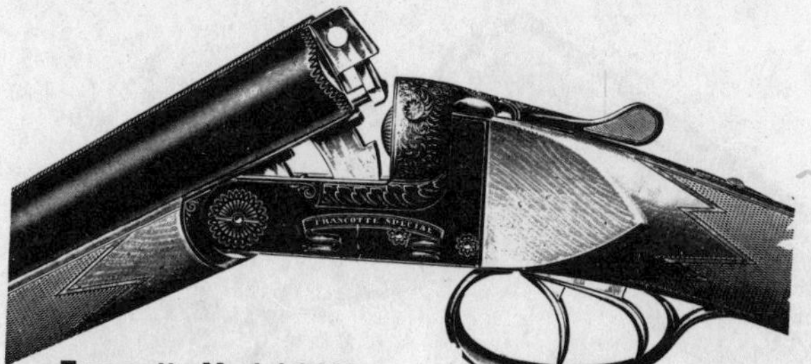

Francotte Model 8446

Francotte Model 9261

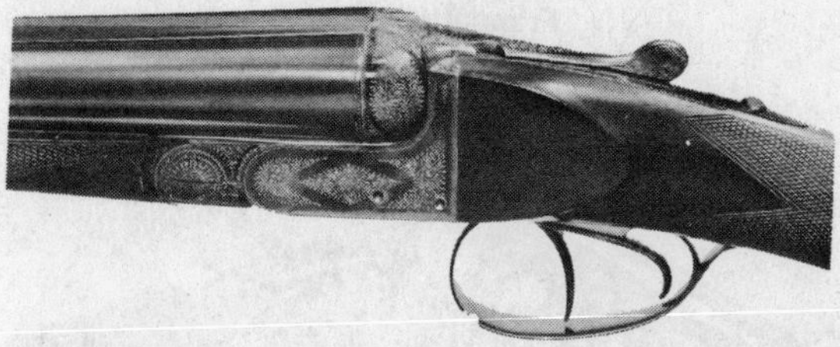

Francotte Model 10/18E/628

Francotte Box Lock Hammerless Doubles
Anson & Deeley system. Side clips. Greener crossbolt on Models 6886, 8446, 4996 and 9261; square crossbolt on Model 6930; Greener-Scott crossbolt on Model 8457; Purdey bolt on Models 11/18E and 10/18E/628. Auto ejectors. Double triggers. Made in all standard gauges, barrel lengths, chokes, weights. Checkered stock and forend, straight or pistol grip. The eight models listed vary chiefly in fastening as described above, finish and engraving, etc.; general specifications are the same. All except Model 10/18E/628 are discontinued.
Model 6886 . . . . **$2100**
Model 8446 ("Francotte Special"), 6930, 4996 . . . . **2500**
Model 8457, 9261 ("Francotte Original"), 11/18E . . . **2900**
Model 10/18E/628 . . . . **4100**

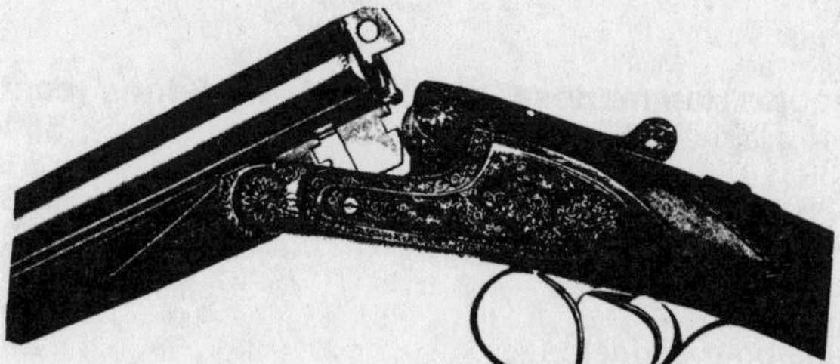

Francotte Box Lock Hammerless
A & F Series—No. 20

Francotte Box Lock Hammerless Doubles—A & F Series
Box lock, Anson & Deeley type. Crossbolt. Side plate on all except Knockabout Model. Side clips. Auto ejectors. Double triggers. Gauges: 12, 16, 20, 28, .410. Barrels: 26- to 32-inch in 12 gauge, 26- and 28-inch in other gauges; any boring. Weight: 4¾ to 8 pounds depending upon gauge and barrel length. Checkered stock and forend; straight, half or full pistol grip. The seven grades—No. 45 Eagle Grade, No. 30, No. 25, No. 20, No. 14, Jubilee Model, Knockabout Model—differ chiefly in overall quality, engraving, grade of wood, checkering, etc.; general specifications are the same. Discontinued.

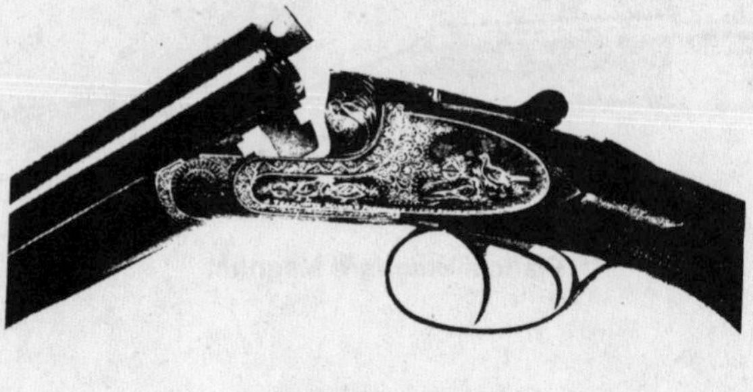

Francotte No. 30

Francotte No. 45 Eagle

Francotte Knockabout

Francotte Hammerless Doubles—A & F Series (cont.)

No. 45 Eagle Grade	**$6450**
No. 30	**5100**
No. 25	**4800**
No. 20	**4200**
No. 14	**3800**
Jubilee Model	**3800**
Knockabout Model	**2950**

Francotte Box Lock Hammerless
Model 6982

Francotte Box Lock Hammerless Doubles With Sideplates

Anson & Deeley system. Reinforced frame with side clips. Purdey-type bolt except on Model 8455 which has Greener crossbolt. Auto ejectors. Double triggers. Made in all standard gauges, barrel lengths, chokes, weights. Checkered stock and forend, straight or pistol grip. Models 10594, 8455 and 6982 are of equal quality, differ chiefly in style of engraving; Model 9/40E/38321 is a higher grade gun in all details and has fine English-style engraving. Currently manufactured.

Models 10594, 8455, 6982	**$3200**
Model 9/40E/38321	**4100**

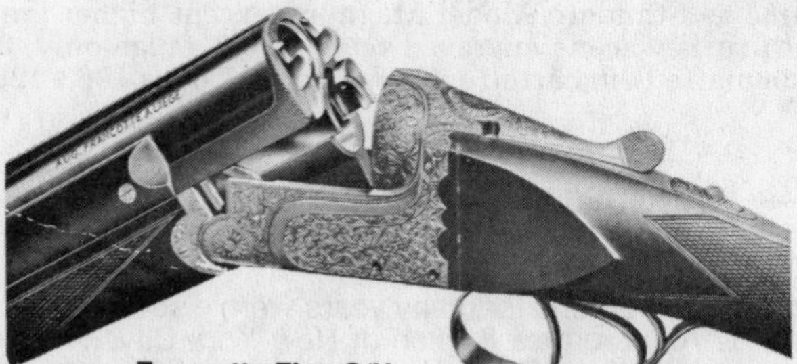

Francotte Fine O/U
Model 9/40.SE

Francotte Fine Over-and-Under Shotgun $8750

Model 9/40.SE. Box lock, Anson & Deeley system. Auto ejectors. Double triggers. Made in all standard gauges; barrel length, boring to order. Weight: about 6¾ pounds, 12 ga. Checkered stock and forend, straight or pistol grip. Currently manufactured.

Francotte Fine Side Lock Hammerless Double $8200

Model 120.HE/328. Automatic ejectors. Double triggers. Made in all standard gauges; barrel length, boring, weight to order. Checkered stock and forend, straight or pistol grip. Currently manufactured.

Francotte Half-Fine O/U
Model SOB.E/11082

Francotte Half-Fine Over-and-Under Shotgun . . $6500

Model SOB.E/11082. Box lock, Anson & Deeley system. Auto ejectors. Double triggers. Made in all standard gauges; barrel length, boring to order. Checkered stock and forend, straight or pistol grip. *Note:* This model is quite similar to No. 9/40.SE except general quality is not as high and frame is not fully engraved or scalloped. Discontinued.

GALEF SHOTGUNS

Manufactured for J. L. Galef & Son, Inc., New York, New York, by M.A.V.I., Gardone V.T., Italy, by Zabala Hermanos, Elquetta, Spain, and by Antonio Zoli, Gardone V.T., Italy

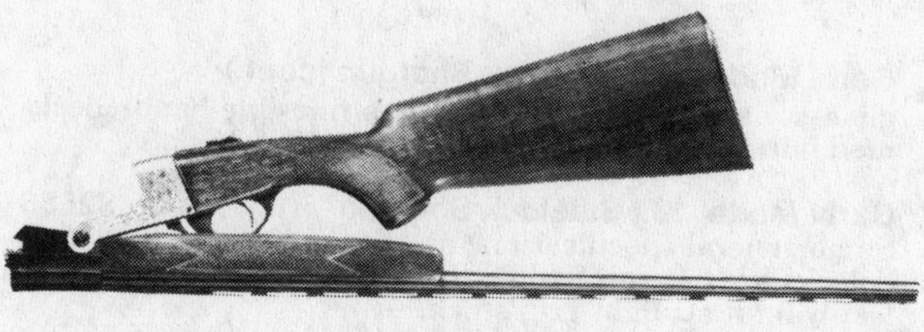

Galef Companion

Galef Companion Folding Single Barrel Shotgun
Hammerless. Underlever. Gauges: 12 mag., 16, 20 mag., 28, .410. Barrels: 26-inch (.410 only), 28-inch (12, 16, 20, 28), 30-inch (12 gauge only); full choke; plain or vent rib. Weight: 4½ lbs. for .410 to 5 lbs. 9 oz. for 12 gauge. Checkered pistol-grip stock and forearm. Made by M.A.V.I. from 1968 to date.
With plain barrel **$90**
With ventilated rib **105**

Galef Golden Snipe $425
Same as Silver Snipe, except has selective automatic ejectors. Made by Antonio Zoli from 1968 to date.

Galef Monte Carlo Trap Single Barrel Shotgun .. $195
Hammerless. Underlever. Plain extractor. 12 gauge. 32-inch barrel, full choke, vent rib. Weight: about 8¼ pounds. Checkered pistol-grip stock with Monte Carlo comb and recoil pad, beavertail forearm. Made by M.A.V.I. from 1968 to date.

Galef Silver Hawk Hammerless Double $410
Box lock. Plain extractors. Double triggers. Gauges: 12, 20; 3-inch chambers. Barrels: 26-, 28-, 30-inch (latter in 12 gauge only); improved cylinder/modified, modified/full choke. Weight: 12 ga. with 26-inch barrels, 6 lbs. 6 oz. Checkered walnut pistol-grip stock and beavertail forearm. Made by Antonio Zoli 1968 to 1972.

Galef Silver Snipe Over-and-Under Shotgun $395
Box lock. Plain extractors. Single trigger. Gauges: 12, 20; 3-inch chambers. Barrels: 26-, 28-, 30-inch (latter in 12 gauge only); improved cylinder/modified, modified/full choke; vent rib. Weight: 12 gauge with 28-inch barrels, 6½ pounds. Checkered walnut pistol-grip stock and forearm. Made by Antonio Zoli from 1968 to date.

Galef Zabala Hammerless Double Barrel Shotgun
Box lock. Plain extractors. Double triggers. Gauges: 10 mag., 12 mag., 16, 20 mag., 28, .410. Barrels: 22-, 26-, 28-, 30-, 32-inch; both improved cylinder, improved cylinder and modified, modified and full, both full choke. Weight: 12 gauge with 28-inch barrels, 7¾ pounds. Checkered walnut pistol-grip stock and beavertail forearm, recoil pad. Made by Zabala from 1972 to date.
10 gauge **$275**
Other gauges **225**

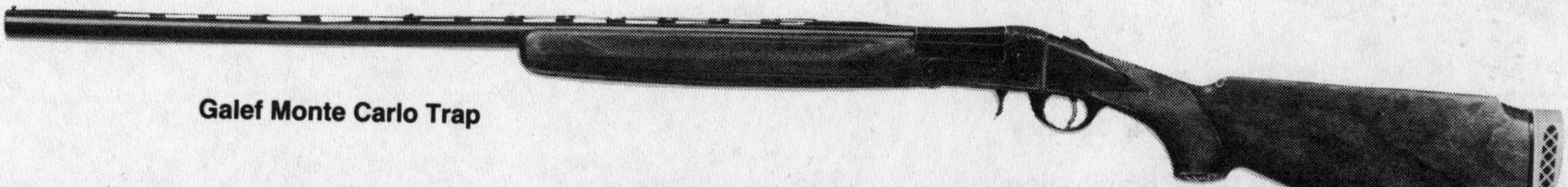

Galef Monte Carlo Trap

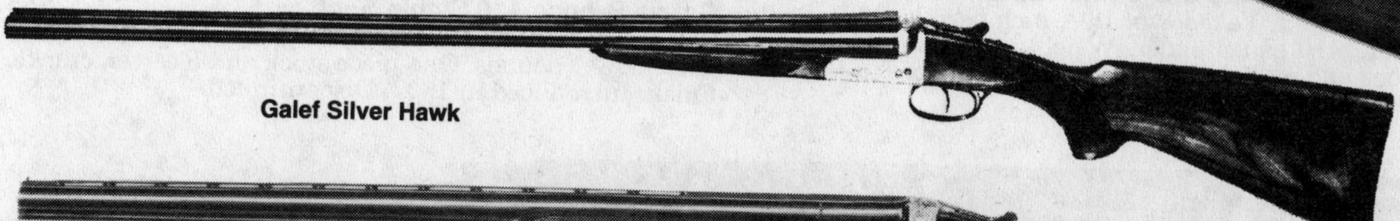

Galef Silver Hawk

Galef Silver Snipe

Galef Zabala

Garbi Model 100 Sidelock

GARBI SHOTGUNS
Eibar, Spain

Garbi Model 100 Sidelock Shotgun $2100
Gauges: 12, 16, 20 and 28. Barrels: 25-, 28-, 30-inch. Action: Holland & Holland pattern sidelock; automatic ejectors and double trigger. Weight: 5 lbs. 6 oz. to 7 lbs. 7 oz. English-style straight grip stock with fine-line hand-checkered butt; classic forend. Made from 1985 to date.

Garbi Model 101 Sidelock Shotgun $2630
Same general specifications as Model 100, except the sidelocks are handcrafted with hand-engraved receiver; select walnut straight grip stock.

Garcia Bronco 22/410

Garcia Bronco 410

GARCIA CORPORATION
Teaneck, New Jersey

Garcia Bronco 22/410 O/U Combination $95
Swing-out action. Takedown. 18½-inch barrels; 22 Long Rifle over, .410 gauge under. Weight: 4½ pounds. One-piece stock and receiver, crackle finish. Introduced in 1976. Discontinued.

Garcia Bronco 410 Single Shot $65
Swing-out action. Takedown. .410 gauge. 18½-inch barrel. Weight: 3½ pounds. One-piece stock and receiver, crackle finish. Introduced in 1967. Discontinued.

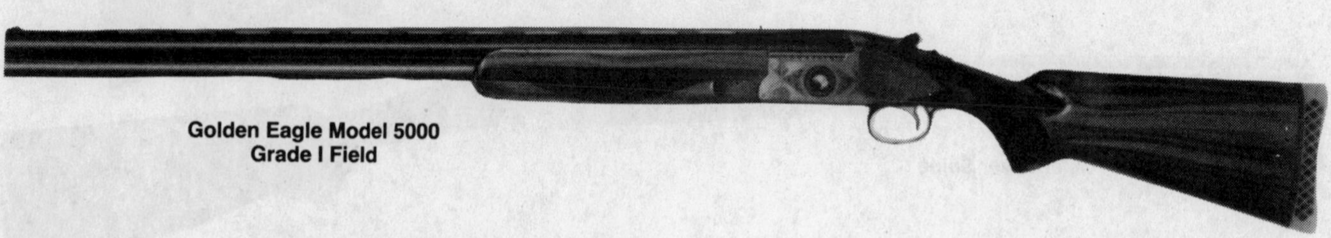

Golden Eagle Model 5000
Grade I Field

GOLDEN EAGLE FIREARMS INC.
Houston, Texas
Mfd. by Nikko Firearms Ltd., Tochigi, Japan

Golden Eagle Model 5000 Grade I Field O/U ... $795
Receiver engraved and inlaid with gold eagle head. Box lock. Auto ejectors. Selective single trigger. Gauges: 12, 20; 2¾- or 3-inch chambers, 12 ga., 3-inch, 20 ga. Barrels: 26-, 28-, 30-inch (latter only in 12 gauge 3-inch magnum); improved cylinder/modified, modified/full choke; vent rib. Weight: 6¼ lbs., 20 ga.; 7¼ lbs., 12 ga.; 8 lbs., 12 ga. Magnum. Checkered pistol-grip stock and semibeavertail forearm. Made from 1975 to date. *Note:* Guns marketed 1975-76 under the Nikko brand name have white receivers; those made since 1976 are blued.

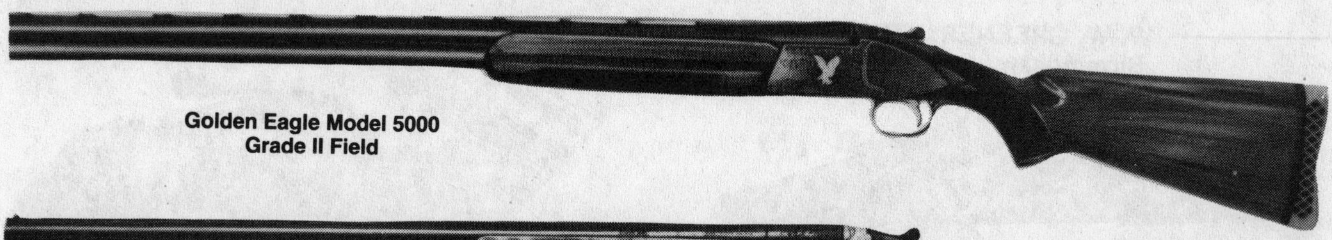

Golden Eagle Model 5000
Grade II Field

Golden Eagle Model 5000
Grade III Grandee

Golden Eagle Model 5000 Grade I Skeet $825
Same as Field Model, except has 26- or 28-inch barrels with wide (11mm) vent rib, skeet choked. Made 1975 to date.

Golden Eagle Model 5000 Grade I Trap $895
Same as Field Model, except has 30- or 32-inch barrels with wide (11mm) vent rib (modified/full, improved modified/full, both full choke), trap-style stock with recoil pad. Made from 1975 to date.

Golden Eagle Model 5000 Grade II Field $895
Same as Grade I Field Model, except higher grade with fancier wood, more elaborate engraving and "screaming eagle" inlaid in gold. Made from 1975 to date.

Golden Eagle Model 5000 Grade II Skeet $950
Same as Grade I Skeet Model, except higher grade with fancier wood, more elaborate engraving and "screaming eagle" inlaid in gold; inertia trigger, vent side ribs. Made 1975 to date.

Golden Eagle Model 5000 Grade II Trap $995
Same as Grade I Trap Model, except higher grade with fancier wood, more elaborate engraving and "screaming eagle" inlaid in gold; inertia trigger, ventilated side ribs. Made from 1975 to date.

Golden Eagle Model 5000 Grade III Grandee . . $2595
Best grade, available in Field, Skeet and Trap Models with same general specifications as lower grades. Has side plates with game scene engraving, scroll on frame and barrels, fancy wood (Monte Carlo comb, full pistol grip and recoil pad on Trap Model). Made from 1976 to date.

GOROSABEL SHOTGUNS
Spain

Gorosabel Model 503 Shotgun $720
Gauges: 12, 16, 20 and .410. Action: Anson & Deeley-style boxlock. Barrels: 26-, 27- and 28-inch. Select European walnut, English or pistol grip, sliver or beavertail forend, hand-checkering. Scalloped frame and scroll engraving. Made from 1985 to date.

Gorosabel Model 504 Shotgun $750
Gauge: 12 or 20. Action: Holland & Holland-style sidelock. Barrel: 26-, 27- or 28-inch. Select European walnut, English or pistol grip, sliver or beavertail forend, hand-checkering. Holland-style large scroll engraving. Made from 1985 to date.

Gorosabel Model 505 Shotgun $1000
Gauge: 12 or 20. Action: Holland & Holland-style sidelock. Barrels: 26-, 27- or 28-inch. Select European walnut, English or pistol grip, sliver or beavertail forend, hand-checkering. Purdey-style fine scroll and rose engraving. Made from 1985 to date.

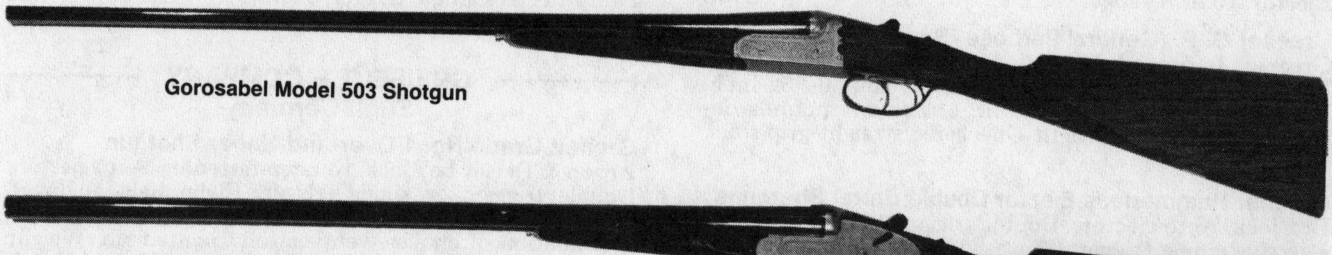

Gorosabel Model 503 Shotgun

Gorosabel Model 504 Shotgun

W. W. GREENER, LTD.
Birmingham, England

Greener Empire

Greener Empire Model Hammerless Doubles

Box lock. Non-ejector or with automatic ejectors. Double triggers. 12 gauge only (2¾-inch or 3-inch chamber). Barrels: 28- to 32-inch; any choke combination. Weight: from 7¼ to 7¾ pounds depending upon barrel length. Checkered stock and forend, straight- or half-pistol grip. Also furnished in "Empire Deluxe Grade," this model has same general specs, but deluxe finish.

Empire Model, non-ejector **$1500**
Empire Model, ejector **1700**
Empire Deluxe Model, non-ejector **1800**
Empire Deluxe Model, ejector **1900**

Greener Far-Killer

Greener Far-Killer Model Grade FH35 Hammerless Double Barrel Shotgun

Box lock. Non-ejector or with automatic ejectors. Double triggers. Gauges: 12 (2¾-inch or 3-inch), 10, 8. Barrels: 28-, 30- or 32-inch. Weight: from 7½ to 9 pounds in 12 gauge. Checkered stock, forend; straight- or half-pistol grip.

Non-ejector, 12 gauge **$2200**
Ejector, 12 gauge **2900**
Non-ejector, 10 or 8 gauge **2400**
Ejector, 10 or 8 gauge **3140**

Greener G. P. (General Purpose) Single Barrel . . $325

Greener Improved Martini Lever Action. Takedown. Ejector. 12 gauge only. Barrel lengths: 26-, 30-, 32-inch. Modified or full choke. Weight: 6¼ to 6¾ pounds depending upon barrel length. Checkered straight-grip stock and forearm.

Greener Hammerless Ejector Double Barrel Shotguns

Box lock. Auto ejectors. Double triggers, non-selective or selective single trigger. Gauges: 12, 16, 20, 28, .410 (two latter gauges not supplied in Grades DH40 and DH35). Barrels: 26-, 28-, 30-inch; any choke combination. Weight: from 4¾ to 8 pounds depending upon gauge and barrel length. Checkered stock and forend, straight- or half-pistol grip. The Royal, Crown, Sovereign and Jubilee Models differ in quality, engraving, grade of wood, checkering, etc. General specifications are the same.

Greener Royal

Greener Sovereign

Greener Jubilee

Greener Hammerless Ejector Double Barrel (cont.)

Royal Model Grade DH75 .... **$3900**
Crown Model Grade DH55 .... **2900**
Sovereign Model Grade DH40 .... **2500**
Jubilee Model Grade DH35 .... **2100**
Selective single trigger, extra **330**
Non-selective single trigger, extra **250**

GREIFELT & COMPANY
Suhl, Germany

Greifelt Grade No. 1 Over-and-Under Shotgun

Anson & Deeley box lock, Kersten fastening. Auto ejectors. Double triggers or single trigger. Elaborately engraved. Gauges: 12, 16, 20, 28, .410. Barrels: 26- to 32-inch, any combination of chokes, vent or solid matted rib. Weight: 4¼ to 8¼ pounds depending upon gauge and barrel length. Straight- or pistol-grip stock, Purdey-type forend, both checkered. Manufactured prior to World War II.

With solid matted-rib barrel, except .410 .... **$3800**
With solid matted-rib barrel, .410 gauge **4250**
Extra for ventilated rib **380**
Extra for single trigger **425**

Greifelt Grade No. 1 Over/Under

Greifelt Grade No. 3 Over-and-Under Shotgun
Same general specifications as Grade No. 1 except not as fancy engraving. Manufactured prior to World War II.
With solid matted-rib barrel, except .410 .... **$3100**
With solid matted-rib barrel, .410 gauge **3250**
Extra for ventilated rib **380**
Extra for single trigger **425**

Greifelt Model 22 Hammerless Double $1995
Anson & Deeley box lock. Plain extractors. Double triggers. Gauges: 12 and 16. Barrels: 28- or 30-inch, modified and full choke. Checkered stock and forend, pistol grip and cheekpiece standard, English-style stock also supplied. Manufactured since World War II.

Greifelt Model 22E Hammerless Double $2400
Same as Model 22, except has automatic ejectors.

Greifelt Model 103 Hammerless Double $1700
Anson & Deeley box lock. Plain extractors. Double triggers. Gauges: 12 and 16. Barrels: 28- or 30-inch, modified and full choke. Checkered stock and forend, pistol grip and cheekpiece standard, English-style stock also supplied. Manufactured since World War II.

Greifelt Model 103E Hammerless Double $1900
Same as Model 103, except has automatic ejectors.

Greifelt Model 143E Over-and-Under Shotgun
General specifications same as prewar Grade No. 1 Over-and-Under except this model is not supplied in 28 and .410 gauge or with 32-inch barrels. Model 143E is not as high quality as the Grade No. 1 gun. Mfd. since World War II.
With raised matted rib, double triggers **$2100**
With ventilated rib, selective single trigger **3400**

Greifelt Hammerless Drilling (Three Barrel Combination Gun) $4100
Box lock. Plain extractors. Double triggers, front single set for rifle barrel. Gauges: 12, 16, 20; rifle barrel in any caliber adapted to this type of gun. 26-inch barrels. Weight: about 7½ pounds. Auto rear sight operated by rifle barrel selector. Checkered stock and forearm, pistol grip and cheekpiece standard. Manufactured prior to WWII. *Note:* Value shown is for guns chambered for cartridges readily obtainable; if rifle barrel is an odd foreign caliber, value will be considerably less.

Greifelt Over-and-Under Combination Gun
Similar in design to this maker's over-and-under shotguns. Gauges: 12, 16, 20, 28, .410; rifle barrel in any caliber adapted to this type of gun. Barrels: 24- or 26-inch, solid matted rib. Weight: from 4¾ to 7¼ pounds. Folding rear sight. Manufactured prior to World War II. *Note:* Values shown are for gauges other than .410, with rifle barrel chambered for a cartridge readily obtainable; if in an odd foreign caliber, value will be considerably less. .410 gauge increases in value by about 50%.
With nonautomatic ejector **$4800**
With automatic ejector **5200**

— HARRINGTON & RICHARDSON ARMS CO. — Worcester, Massachusetts

H&R No. 3 Hammerless

Harrington & Richardson No. 3 Hammerless Single Barrel Shotgun $90
Takedown. Automatic ejector. Gauges: 12, 16, 20, .410. Barrels: plain, 26- to 32-inch, full choke. Weight: 6½ to 7¼ pounds depending upon gauge and barrel length. Plain pistol-grip stock and forend. Discontinued 1942.

H&R No. 5 Standard Lightweight

Harrington & Richardson No. 5 Standard Light Weight Hammer Single $100
Takedown. Auto ejector. Gauges: 24, 28, .410, 14mm. Barrels: 26- or 28-inch, full choke. Weight: about 4 to 4¾ pounds. Plain pistol-grip stock and forend. Discontinued 1942.

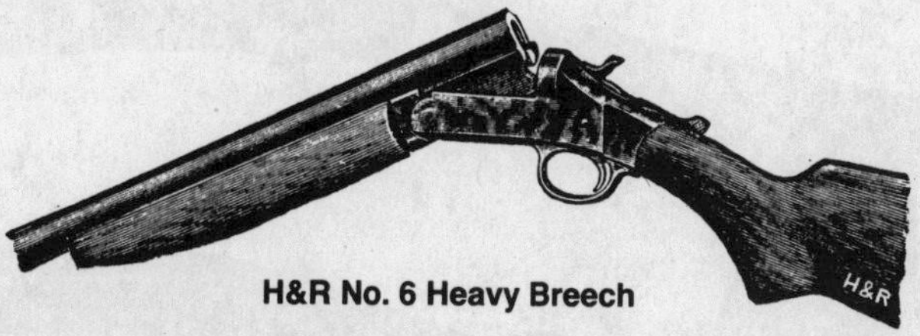

H&R No. 6 Heavy Breech

Harrington & Richardson No. 6 Heavy Breech Single Barrel Hammer Shotgun $100
Takedown. Automatic ejector. Gauges: 10, 12, 16, 20. Barrels: plain, 28- to 36-inch, full choke. Weight: about 7 to 7¼ pounds. Plain stock and forend. Discontinued 1942.

SHOTGUNS

H&R No. 7 Bay State

Harrington & Richardson No. 7 or 9 Bay State Single Barrel Hammer Shotgun $90
Takedown. Automatic ejector. Gauges: 12, 16, 20, .410. Barrels: plain, 26- to 32-inch, full choke. Weight: 5½ to 6½ pounds depending upon gauge and barrel length. Plain pistol-grip stock and forend. Discontinued 1942.

H&R No. 8 Single Barrel

Harrington & Richardson No. 8 Standard Single Barrel Hammer Shotgun $90
Takedown. Automatic ejector. Gauges: 12, 16, 20, 24, 28, .410. Barrels: plain, 26- to 32-inch, full choke. Weight: 5½ to 6½ pounds depending upon gauge and barrel length. Plain pistol-grip stock and forend. Made from 1908 to 1942.

Harrington & Richardson Model 348 Gamester Bolt Action Shotgun $95
Takedown. 12 and 16 gauge. 2-shot tubular magazine, 28-inch barrel, full choke. Plain pistol-grip stock. Weight: about 7½ pounds. Made from 1949 to 1954.

Harrington & Richardson Model 349 Gamester Deluxe $110
Same as Model 348, except has 26-inch barrel with adjustable choke device, recoil pad. Made from 1953 to 1955.

Harrington & Richardson Model 351 Huntsman Bolt Action Shotgun $125
Takedown. 12 and 16 gauge. 2-shot tubular magazine. Pushbutton safety. 26-inch barrel with H&R variable choke. Weight: about 6¾ pounds. Monte Carlo stock with recoil pad. Made from 1956 to 1958.

Harrington & Richardson Model 400 Pump $175
Hammerless. Gauges: 12, 16, 20. Tubular magazine holds 4 shells. 28-inch barrel, full choke. Weight: about 7¼ pounds. Plain pistol-grip stock (recoil pad in 12 and 16 ga.), grooved slide handle. Made from 1955 to 1967.

Harrington & Richardson Model 401 .... $175
Same as Model 400, except has H&R variable choke. Made from 1956 to 1963.

Harrington & Richardson Model 402 .... $185
Similar to Model 400, except .410 gauge, weighs about 5½ pounds. Made from 1959 to 1967.

Harrington & Richardson Model 403 Autoloader $200
Takedown. .410 gauge. Tubular magazine holds four shells. 26-inch barrel, full choke. Weight: about 5¾ pounds. Plain pistol-grip stock and forearm. Made in 1964.

Harrington & Richardson Model 404 Double $180
Box lock. Plain extractors. Double triggers. Gauges: 12, 20, .410. Barrels: 28-inch modified and full choke in 12 ga., 26-inch in 20 ga. (improved cylinder and modified) and .410 (full and full). Weight: 5½ to 7¼ pounds. Plain walnut-finished hardwood stock and forend. Made in Brazil by Amadeo Rossi from 1969 to 1972.

Harrington & Richardson Model 404C $195
Same as Model 404, except has checkered stock and forend. Made from 1969 to 1972.

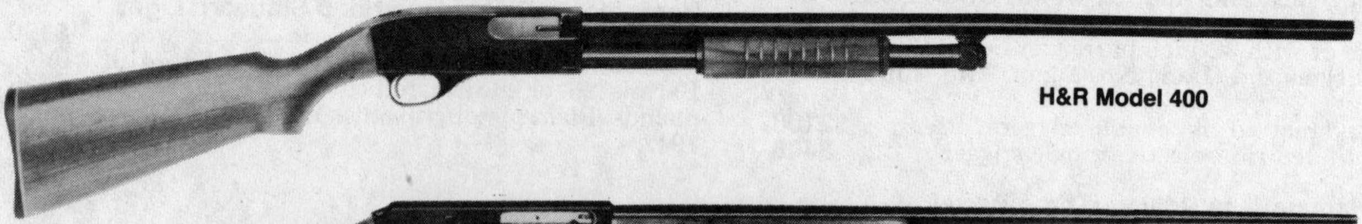

H&R Model 400

H&R Model 403

H&R Model 404C

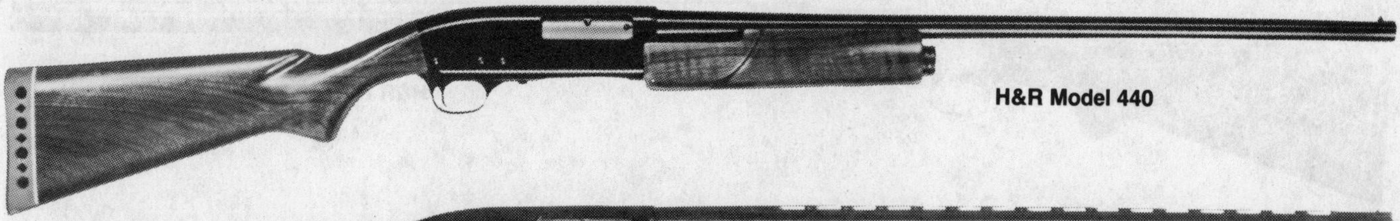

H&R Model 440

H&R Model 442

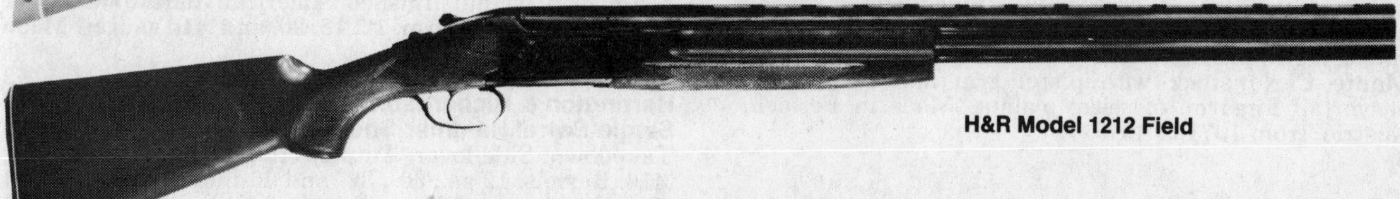

H&R Model 1212 Field

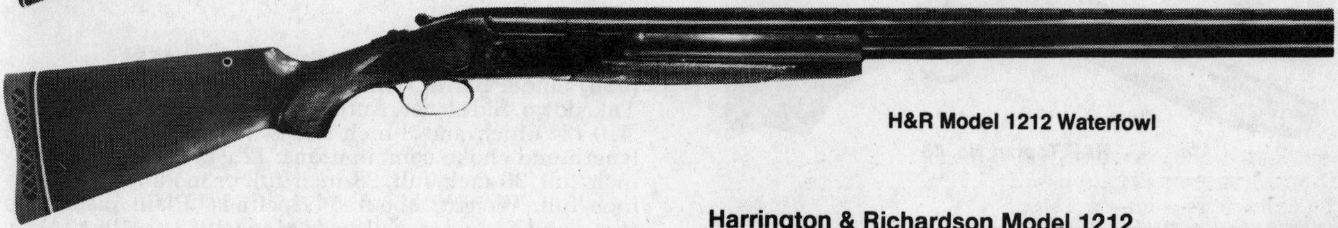

H&R Model 1212 Waterfowl

Harrington & Richardson Model 440 Pump $145
Hammerless. Gauges: 12, 16, 20. 2¾-inch chamber in 16 gauge, 3-inch in 12 and 20 gauges. 3-shot magazine. Barrels: 26-, 28-, 30-inch; improved cylinder, modified, full choke. Weight: 6¼ pounds. Plain pistol-grip stock and slide handle, recoil pad. Made from 1968 to 1973.

Harrington & Richardson Model 442 . . . . $185
Same as Model 440, except has ventilated-rib barrel, checkered stock and forearm, weighs 6¾ pounds. Made from 1969 to 1973.

Harrington & Richardson Model 1212 Over/Under Field Gun $325
Box lock. Plain extractors. Selective single trigger. 12 gauge, 2¾-inch chambers. 28-inch barrels, improved cylinder and improved modified, ventilated rib. Weight: 7 pounds. Checkered walnut pistol-grip stock and fluted forearm. Made from 1976 to 1980 by Lanber Arms S.A., Zaldibar (Vizcaya), Spain.

Harrington & Richardson Model 1212 Waterfowl Gun $395
Same as Field Gun, except chambered for 12 gauge 3-inch magnum shells, has 30-inch barrels, modified and full choke, stock and recoil pad, weighs 7½ pounds. Made from 1976 to 1980.

Harrington & Richardson Folding Gun $135
Single barrel hammer shotgun hinged at the front of the frame, the barrel folds down against the stock. *Light Frame Model:* gauges—28, 14mm, .410; 22-inch barrel; weighs about 4½ pounds. *Heavy Frame Model:* gauges—12, 16, 20, 28, .410; 26-inch barrel; weighs from 5¾ to 6½ pounds. Plain pistol-grip stock and forend. Discontinued 1942.

Harrington & Richardson Golden Squire Model 159 Single Barrel Hammer Shotgun $100
Hammerless. Side lever. Automatic ejection. Gauges: 12, 20. Barrels: 30-inch in 12 ga., 28-inch in 20 ga., both full choke. Weight: about 6½ pounds. Straight-grip stock with recoil pad, forearm with schnabel. Made from 1964 to 1966.

Harrington & Richardson Golden Squire Jr. Model 459 . . . . $100
Same as Model 159, except gauges 20 and .410, 26-inch barrel, youth-size stock. Made in 1964.

H&R Golden Squire Model 159

SHOTGUNS

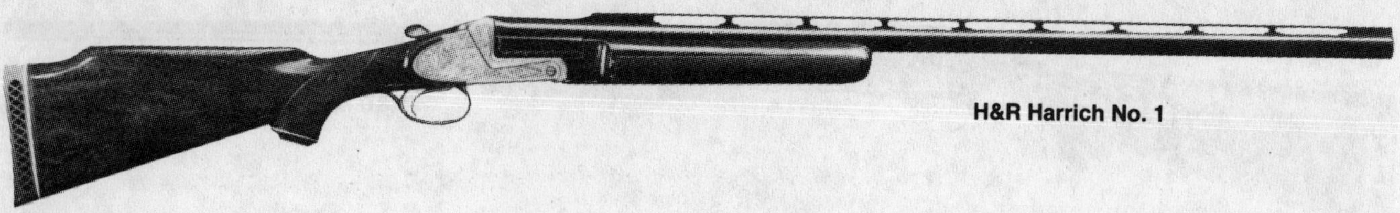

H&R Harrich No. 1

Harrington & Richardson Harrich No. 1 Single Barrel Trap Gun $2025

Anson & Deeley-type locking system with Kersten top locks and double underlocking lugs. Side plates engraved with hunting scenes. 12 gauge. Barrels: 32-, 34-inch; full choke; high ventilated rib. Weight: 8½ pounds. Checkered Monte Carlo stock with pistol grip and recoil pad, beavertail forearm, of select walnut. Made in Ferlach, Austria, from 1971 to 1975.

H&R Topper No. 48

Harrington & Richardson Topper No. 48 Single Barrel Hammer Shotgun $85

Similar to old Model 8 Standard. Takedown. Top lever. Auto ejector. Gauges: 12, 16, 20, .410. Barrels: plain; 26- to 30-inch; modified or full choke. Weight: 5½ to 6½ pounds depending upon gauge and barrel length. Plain pistol-grip stock and forend. Made from 1946 to 1957.

Harrington & Richardson Topper Model 099 Deluxe $85

Same as Model 158, except has matte nickel finish, semi-pistol grip walnut-finished American hardwood stock; semibeavertail forearm; 12, 16, 20, and .410 gauges. Made from 1982 to 1986.

Harrington & Richardson Topper Model 148 Single Barrel Hammer Shotgun $85

Takedown. Side lever. Auto ejection. Gauges: 12, 16, 20, .410. Barrels: 12 ga., 30-, 32- and 36-inch; 16 ga., 28- and 30-inch; 20 and .410 ga., 28-inch; full choke. Weight: 5 to 6½ pounds. Plain pistol-grip stock and forend, recoil pad. Made 1958 to 1961.

Harrington & Richardson Topper Model 158 (058) Single Barrel Hammer Shotgun $85

Takedown. Side lever. Automatic ejection. Gauges: 12, 20, .410 (2¾-inch and 3-inch shells); 16 (2¾-inch). Barrel length and choke combinations: 12 ga., 36-inch/full, 32-inch/full, 30-inch/full, 28-inch/full or modified; .410, 28-inch/full. Weight: about 5½ pounds. Plain pistol-grip stock and forend, recoil pad. Made 1962 to 1981. *Note:* Designation changed to 058 in 1974.

Harrington & Richardson Topper Model 162 Slug Gun $100

Same as Topper Model 158, except has 24-inch barrel, cylinder bore, with rifle sights. Made from 1968 to 1986.

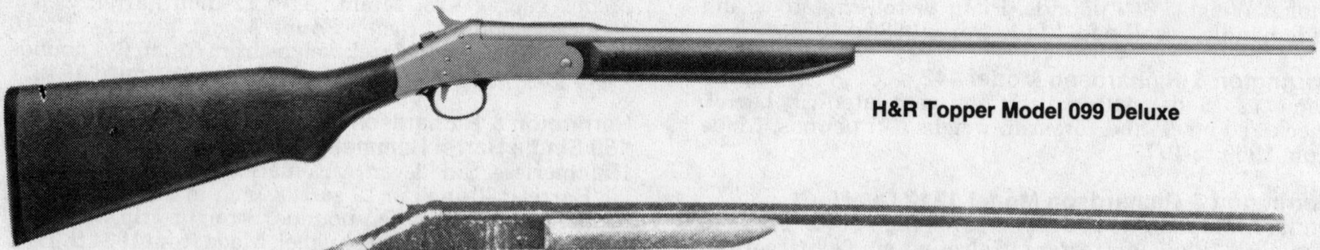

H&R Topper Model 099 Deluxe

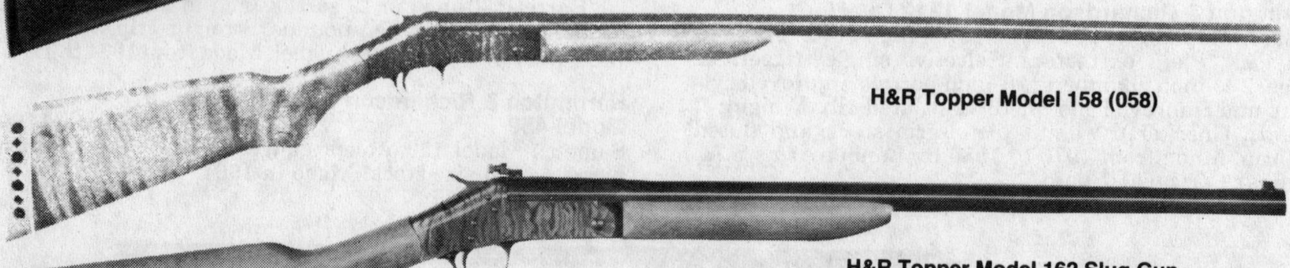

H&R Topper Model 158 (058)

H&R Topper Model 162 Slug Gun

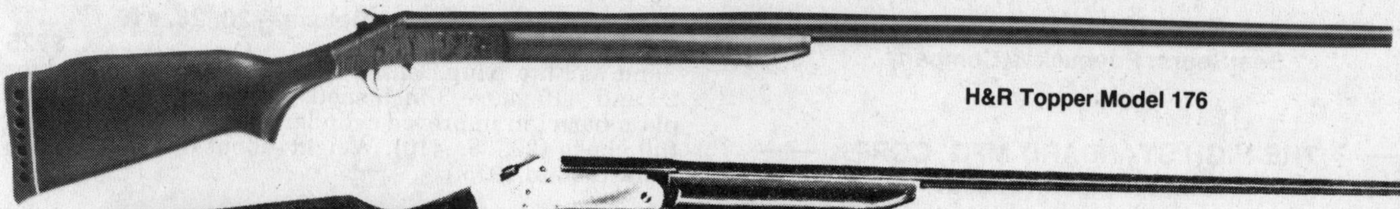

H&R Topper Model 176

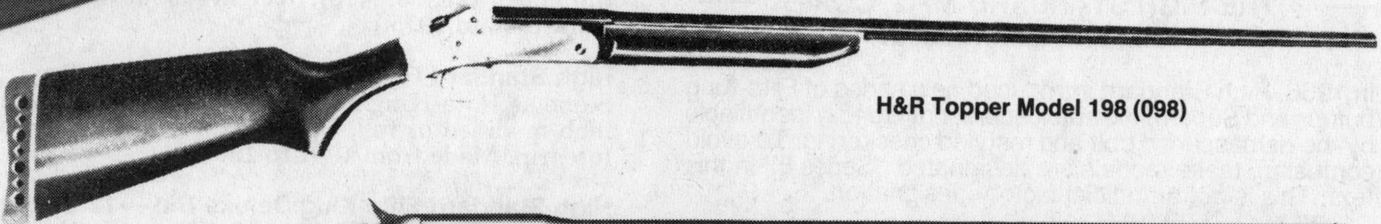

H&R Topper Model 198 (098)

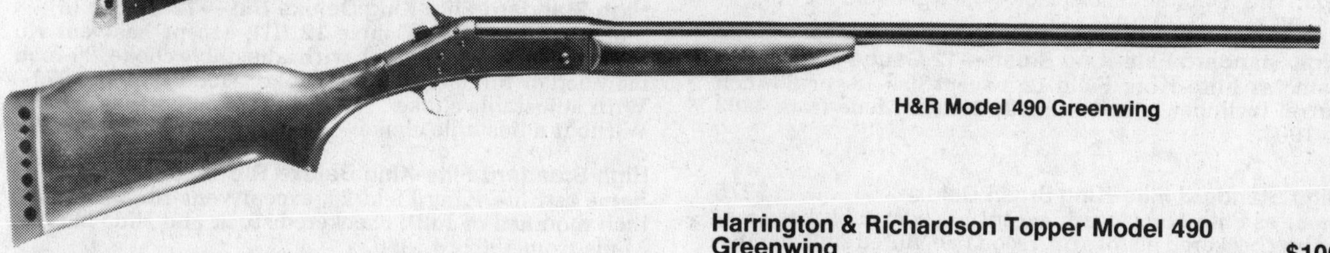

H&R Model 490 Greenwing

Harrington & Richardson Topper Model 176 10 Gauge Magnum $95
Similar to Model 158, but has 36-inch heavy barrel chambered for 3½-inch 10 gauge magnum shells, weighs 10 pounds; stock with Monte Carlo comb and recoil pad, longer and fuller forearm. Made 1977 to 1986.

Harrington & Richardson Topper Model 188 Deluxe $100
Same as standard Topper Model 148, except has chromed frame, stock and forend in black, red, yellow, blue, green, pink, or purple colored finish. .410 gauge only. Made from 1958 to 1961.

Harrington & Richardson Topper Model 198 (098) Deluxe $95
Same as Model 158, except has chrome-plated frame, black finished stock and forend; 12, 20 and .410 gauges. Made from 1962 to 1981. *Note:* Designation changed to 098 in 1974.

Harrington & Richardson Topper Jr. Model 480 . . $85
Similar to No. 48 Topper, except has youth-size stock, 26-inch barrel, .410 gauge only. Made from 1958 to 1961.

Harrington & Richardson Topper No. 488 Deluxe $95
Same as standard No. 48 Topper, except chrome-plated frame, black lacquered stock and forend, recoil pad. Discontinued 1957.

Harrington & Richardson Topper Model 490 . . . . . $95
Same as Model 158, except has youth-size stock (3 inches shorter), 26-inch barrel; 20 and 28 gauge (modified choke), .410 (full). Made from 1962 to 1986.

Harrington & Richardson Topper Model 490 Greenwing $100
Same as the Model 490, except has a special high-polished finish. Made from 1981 to 1986.

Harrington & Richardson Topper Jr. Model 580 . . $80
Same as Model 480, except has colored stocks as on Model 188. Made from 1958 to 1961.

Harrington & Richardson Topper Model 590 . . . . . $95
Same as Model 490, except has chrome-plated frame, black finished stock and forend. Made from 1962 to 1963.

HERCULES SHOTGUNS

See listings under "W" for Montgomery Ward.

HEYM SHOTGUNS
Münnerstadt, W. Germany

Heym Model 22S "Safety" Shotgun/Rifle Combination $1895
Gauges: 16 and 20. Calibers: 22 Mag., 22 Hornet, 222 Rem., 222 Rem. Mag., 5.6 × 50 R Mag., 6.5 × 57 R, 7 × 57 R, 243 Win. 24-inch barrels. 40 inches overall. Weight: about 5½ pounds. Single-set trigger. Left-side barrel selector. Integral dovetail base for scope mounting. Arabesque engraving. Walnut stock.

Heym Model 55 BF Shotgun/Rifle Combination $3895
Gauges: 12, 16 and 20. Calibers: 5.6 × 50 R Mag., 6.5 × 57 R, 7 × 57 R, 7 × 65 R, 243 Win., 308 Win., 30-06. 25-inch barrels. 42 inches overall. Weight: about 6¾ pounds. Black satin-finished, corrosion-resistant barrels of Krupps special steel. Hand-checkered walnut stock with long pistol grip. Hand-engraved leaf scroll. German cheekpiece.

Heym Model 55 BF Shotgun/Rifle

SHOTGUNS

J. C. HIGGINS SHOTGUNS

See Sears, Roebuck & Company.

THE HIGH STANDARD MFG. CORP.
Hamden, Connecticut

In 1966, High Standard introduced new series of Flite-King pumps and Supermatic autoloaders, both readily identifiable by the damascened bolt and restyled checkering. To avoid confusion, these models are designated "Series II" in this text. This is *not* an official factory designation.

High Standard Flite-King Brush—12 Gauge $225
Same as Flite-King Field 12, except has 18- or 20-inch barrel (cylinder bore) with rifle sights. Made from 1962 to 1964.

High Standard Flite-King Brush Deluxe $275
Same as Flite-King Brush, except has adjustable peep rear sight, checkered pistol grip, recoil pad, fluted slide handle, swivels and sling. Not available with 18-inch barrel. Made from 1964 to 1966.

High Standard Flite-King Brush (Series II) $255
Same as Flite-King Deluxe 12 (II), except has 20-inch barrel, cylinder bore, with rifle sights. Weight: 7 pounds. Made from 1966 to 1975.

High Standard Flite-King Brush Deluxe (II) $275
Same as Flite-King Brush (II), except has adjustable peep rear sight, swivels and sling. Made from 1966 to 1975.

High Standard Flite-King Deluxe—12 Ga. (Series II)
Hammerless. 5-shot magazine. Barrels: plain; 27-inch with adjustable choke. 26-inch improved cylinder, 28-inch modified or full, 30-inch full choke. Weight: about 7¼ pounds. Checkered pistol-grip stock and forearm, recoil pad. Made 1966 to 1975.
With adjustable choke **$295**
Without adjustable choke **275**

High Standard Flite-King Deluxe—20, 28, 410 Gauge (Series II) $225
Same as Flite-King Deluxe 12 (II), except chambered for 20 and .410 gauge 3-inch shell, 28 gauge 2¾-inch shell; plain barrel in improved cylinder (20), modified (20, 28), full choke (20, 28, .410). Weight: about 6 pounds. Made from 1966 to 1975.

High Standard Flite-King Deluxe Rib—12 Ga. . . $295
Same as Flite-King Field 12, except vent-rib barrel (28-inch modified or full, 30-inch full), checkered stock and forearm. Made from 1961 to 1966.

High Standard Flite-King Deluxe Rib—12 Gauge (II)
Same as Flite-King Deluxe 12 (II), except has vent-rib barrel; available in 27-inch with adjustable choke, 28-inch modified or full, 30-inch full choke. Made 1966 to 1975.
With adjustable choke **$300**
Without adjustable choke **295**

High Standard Flite-King Deluxe Rib—20 Ga. . . $275
Same as Flite-King Field 20, except vent-rib barrel (28-inch modified or full), checkered stock and slide handle. Made from 1962 to 1966.

High Standard Flite-King Deluxe Rib—20, 28, 410 Gauge (Series II)
Same as Flite-King Deluxe 20, 28, .410 (II), except 20 gauge available with 27-inch adjustable choke, 28-inch modified or full choke. Weight: about 6¼ pounds. Made from 1966 to 1975.
With adjustable choke **$300**
Without adjustable choke **295**

High Standard Flite-King Deluxe Skeet Gun—12 Gauge (Series II) $275
Same as Flite-King Deluxe Rib 12 (II), except available only with 26-inch ventilated-rib barrel, skeet choke; recoil pad optional. Made from 1966 to 1975.

High Standard Flite-King Deluxe Skeet Gun—20, 28, 410 Gauge (Series II) $305
Same as Flite-King Deluxe Rib 20, 28, .410 (II) except available only with 26-inch vent-rib barrel, skeet choke. Made from 1966 to 1975.

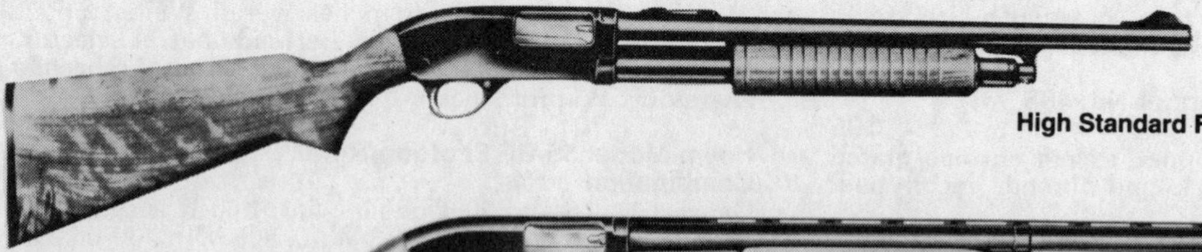
High Standard Flite-King Brush

High Standard Flite-King Deluxe Rib-12 Gauge

High Standard Flite-King Deluxe Rib—20 (II), Adjustable Choke

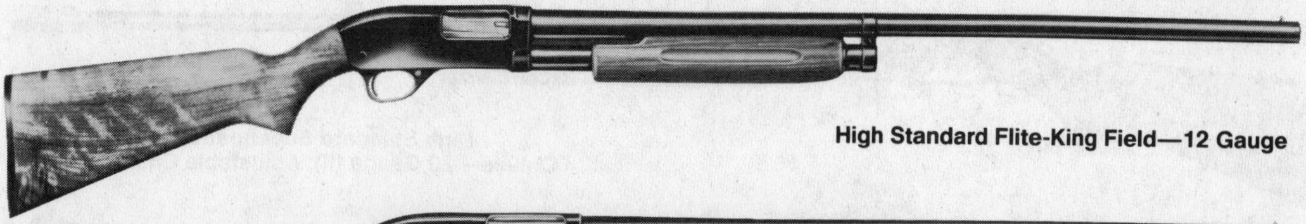

High Standard Flite-King Field—12 Gauge

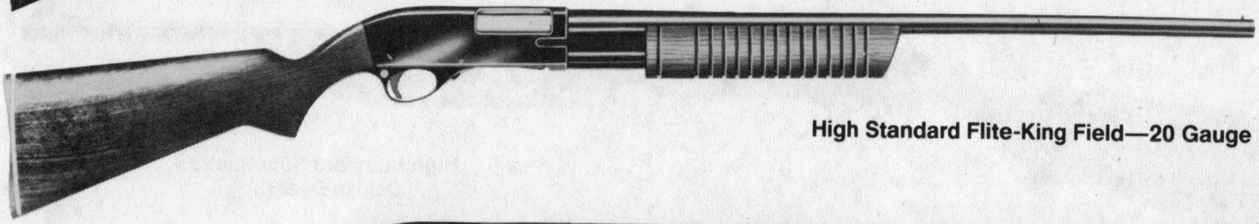

High Standard Flite-King Field—20 Gauge

High Standard Flite-King Trophy—20 Gauge

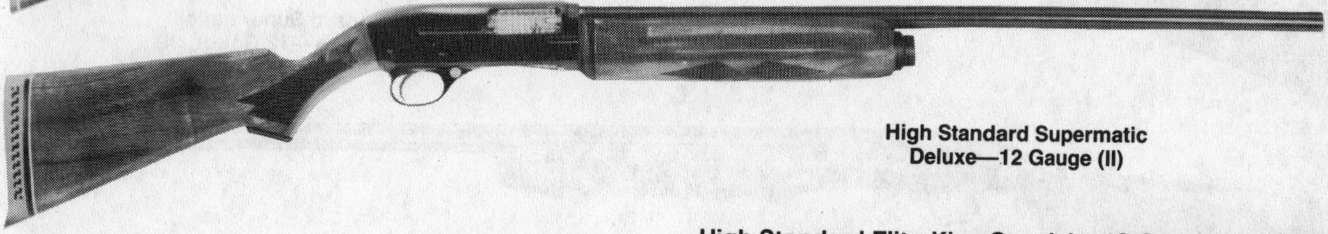

High Standard Supermatic Deluxe—12 Gauge (II)

High Standard Flite-King Deluxe Trap Gun (II) . . $300
Same as Flite-King Deluxe Rib 12 (II), except available only with 30-inch vent-rib barrel, full choke; trap-style stock. Made from 1966 to 1975.

High Standard Flite-King Field Pump—12 Ga. . . $275
Hammerless. Magazine holds 5 shells. Barrels: 26-inch improved cylinder, 28-inch modified or full, 30-inch full choke. Weight: 7¼ pounds. Plain pistol-grip stock and slide handle. Made from 1960 to 1966.

High Standard Flite-King Field Pump—20 Ga. . . $275
Hammerless. Chambered for 3-inch magnum shells, also handles 2¾-inch. Magazine holds four shells. Barrels: 26-inch improved cylinder, 28-inch modified or full choke. Weight: about 6 pounds. Plain pistol-grip stock and slide handle. Made from 1961 to 1966.

High Standard Flite-King Pump Shotguns—16 Gauge
Same general specifications as Flite-King 12, except not available in Brush, Skeet and Trap Models, or 30-inch barrel. Values same as for 12 gauge guns. Made 1961-65.

High Standard Flite-King Pump Shotguns—410 Gauge
Same general specifications as Flite-King 20, except not available in Special and Trophy Models, or with other than 26-inch full choke barrel. Values same as for 20-gauge guns. Made from 1962 to 1966.

High Standard Flite-King Skeet—12 Gauge $310
Same as Flite-King Deluxe Rib, except 26-inch vent-rib barrel, bored skeet choke. Made from 1962 to 1966.

High Standard Flite-King Special—12 Gauge . . . $225
Same as Flite-King Field 12, except has 27-inch barrel with adjustable choke. Made from 1960 to 1966.

High Standard Flite-King Special—20 Gauge . . . $230
Same as Flite-King Field 20, except has 27-inch barrel with adjustable choke. Made from 1961 to 1966.

High Standard Flite-King Trap—12 Gauge $325
Same as Flite-King Deluxe Rib 12, except 30-inch vent-rib barrel, full choke; special trap stock with recoil pad. Made from 1962 to 1966.

High Standard Flite-King Trophy—12 Gauge . . . $310
Same as Flite-King Deluxe Rib 12, except has 27-inch vent-rib barrel with adjustable choke. Made 1960 to 1966.

High Standard Flite-King Trophy—20 Gauge . . . $325
Same as Flite-King Deluxe Rib 20, except has 27-inch ventilated-rib barrel with adjustable choke. Made 1962-66.

High Standard Supermatic Deer Gun $300
Same as Supermatic Field 12, except has 22-inch barrel (cylinder bore) with rifle sights, checkered stock and forearm, recoil pad. Weight: 7¾ pounds. Made in 1965.

High Standard Supermatic Deluxe—12 Ga. (Series II)
Gas-operated autoloader. 4-shot magazine. Barrels: plain; 27-inch with adjustable choke (discontinued about 1970); 26-inch improved cylinder, 28-inch modified or full, 30-inch full choke. Weight: about 7½ pounds. Checkered pistol-grip stock and forearm, recoil pad. Made from 1966 to 1975.

With adjustable choke $295
Without adjustable choke 275

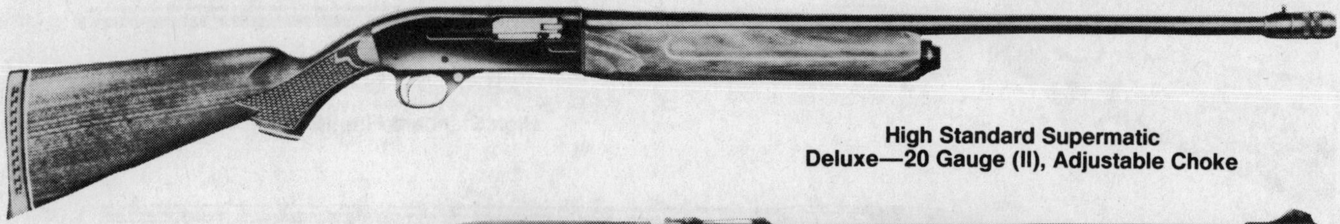

High Standard Supermatic Deluxe—20 Gauge (II), Adjustable Choke

High Standard Supermatic Deluxe Deer (II)

High Standard Supermatic Deluxe Duck Rib—12 Gauge (II)

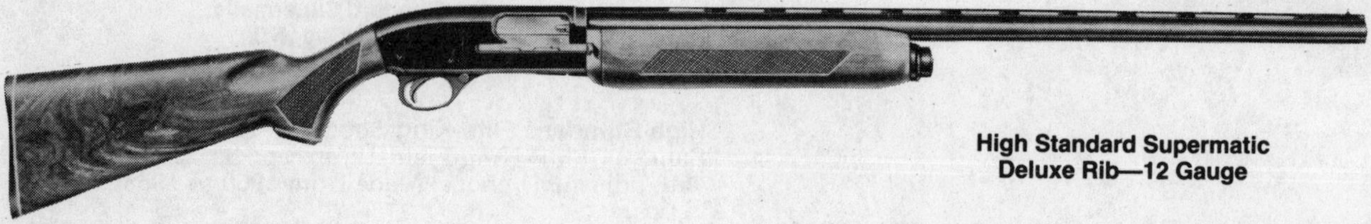

High Standard Supermatic Deluxe Rib—12 Gauge

High Standard Supermatic Deluxe—20 Ga. (Series II)
Same as Supermatic Deluxe 12 (II), except chambered for 20 gauge 3-inch shell; barrels available in 27-inch with adjustable choke (discontinued about 1970), 26-inch improved cylinder, 28-inch modified or full choke. Weight: about 7 pounds. Made from 1966 to 1975.
With adjustable choke **$295**
Without adjustable choke **275**

High Standard Supermatic Deluxe Deer Gun (II) .. $310
Same as Supermatic Deluxe 12 (II), except has 22-inch barrel, cylinder bore, with rifle sights. Weight: 7¾ pounds. Made from 1966 to 1974.

High Standard Supermatic Deluxe Duck—12 Gauge Magnum (Series II) $210
Same as Supermatic Deluxe 12 (II), except chambered for 3-inch magnum shell, 3-shot magazine; 30-inch plain barrel, full choke. Weight: 8 pounds. Made from 1966 to 1974.

High Standard Supermatic Deluxe Duck Rib—12 Gauge Magnum (Series II) $245
Same as Supermatic Deluxe Rib 12 (II), except chambered for 3-inch magnum shell, 3-shot magazine; 30-inch vent-rib barrel, full choke. Weight: 8 pounds. Made from 1966 to 1975.

High Standard Supermatic Deluxe Rib—12 Ga. .. $215
Same as Supermatic Field 12, except vent-rib barrel (28-inch modified or full, 30-inch full), checkered stock and forearm. Made from 1961 to 1966.

High Standard Supermatic Deluxe Rib—12 Gauge (II)
Same as Supermatic Deluxe 12 (II), except has vent-rib barrel; available in 27-inch with adjustable choke, 28-inch modified or full, 30-inch full choke. Made 1966 to 1975.
With adjustable choke **$275**
Without adjustable choke **250**

High Standard Supermatic Deluxe Rib—20 Ga. .. $275
Same as Supermatic Field 20, except vent-rib barrel (28-inch modified or full), checkered stock and forearm. Made from 1963 to 1966.

High Standard Supermatic Deluxe Rib—20 Ga. (II)
Same as Supermatic Deluxe 20 (II), except has vent-rib barrel. Made from 1966 to 1975.
With adjustable choke **$275**
Without adjustable choke **245**

High Standard Supermatic Deluxe Skeet Gun—12 Gauge (Series II) $240
Same as Supermatic Deluxe Rib 12 (II), except available only with 26-inch vent-rib barrel, skeet choke. Made from 1966 to 1975.

High Standard Supermatic Deluxe Skeet Gun—20 Gauge (Series II) $245
Same as Supermatic Deluxe Rib 20 (II), except available only with 26-inch vent-rib barrel, skeet choke. Made from 1966 to 1975.

High Standard Supermatic Deluxe Trap Gun (Series II) $260
Same as Supermatic Deluxe Rib 12 (II), except available only with 30-inch vent-rib barrel, full choke; trap-style stock. Made from 1966 to 1975.

High Standard Supermatic Duck—12 Ga. Mag. . $225
Same as Supermatic Field 12, except chambered for 3-inch magnum shell, 30-inch full choke barrel, recoil pad. Made from 1961 to 1966.

High Standard Supermatic Duck Rib—12 Gauge Magnum $245
Same as Supermatic Duck 12 Magnum, except has vent-rib barrel, checkered stock and forearm. Made 1961 to 1966.

High Standard Supermatic Field Autoloading Shotgun—12 Gauge $225
Gas-operated. Magazine holds four shells. Barrels: 26-inch improved cylinder, 28-inch modified or full choke, 30-inch full choke. Weight: about 7½ pounds. Plain pistol-grip stock and forearm. Made from 1960 to 1966.

High Standard Supermatic Field Autoloading Shotgun—20 Gauge $250
Gas-operated. Chambered for 3-inch magnum shells, also handles 2¾-inch. Magazine holds three shells. Barrels: 26-inch improved cylinder, 28-inch modified or full choke. Weight: about 7 pounds. Plain pistol-grip stock and forearm. Made 1963 to 1966.

High Standard Supermatic Shadow Automatic . . $310
Gas-operated. Gauge: 12, 20, 2¾- or 3-inch chamber in 12 gauges, 3-inch in 20 gauge. Magazine holds four 2¾-inch shells, three 3-inch. Barrels: full-size airflow rib; 26-inch (improved cylinder or skeet choke); 28-inch (modified, improved modified or full); 30-inch (trap or full choke); 12-gauge 3-inch magnum available only in 30-inch full choke; 20 gauge not available in 30-inch. Weight: 12 ga., 7 pounds. Checkered walnut stock and forearm. Made 1974 to 1975 by Caspoll Int'l., Inc., Tokyo.

High Standard Supermatic Shadow Indy O/U . . . $725
Box lock. Fully engraved receiver. Selective auto ejectors. Selective single trigger. 12 gauge. 2¾-inch chambers. Barrels: full-size airflow rib; 27½-inch both skeet choke, 29¾-inch improved modified/full or both full. Weight: with 29¾-inch barrels, 8 lbs. 2 oz. Pistol-grip stock with recoil pad, ventilated forearm, skip checkering. Made 1974 to 1975 by Caspoll Int'l., Inc., Tokyo.

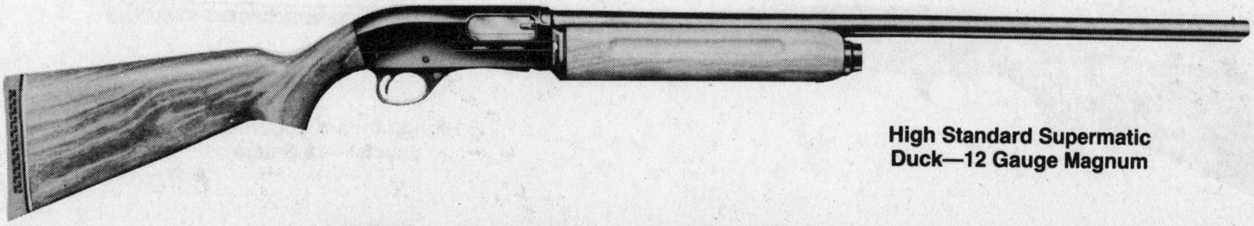

High Standard Supermatic Duck—12 Gauge Magnum

High Standard Supermatic Duck Rib—12 Gauge

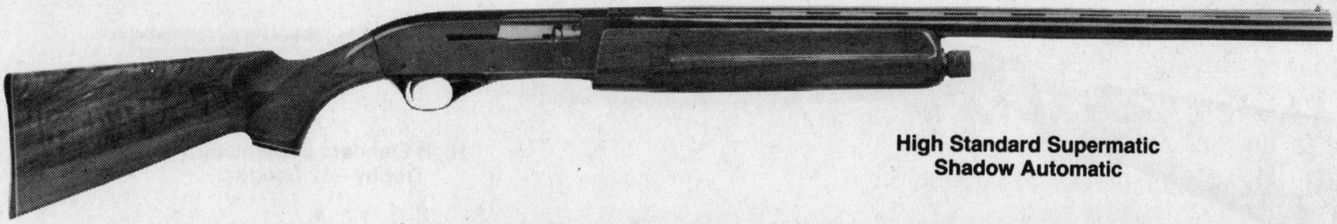

High Standard Supermatic Shadow Automatic

High Standard Supermatic Shadow Indy

SHOTGUNS

High Standard Supermatic Shadow Seven $600
Same general specifications as Shadow Indy, except has conventional vent rib, less elaborate engraving, standard checkering; forearm is not vented, no recoil pad. 27½-inch barrels also available in improved cylinder/modified, modified/full choke. Made 1974 to 1975.

High Standard Supermatic Skeet—12 Gauge . . . $225
Same as Supermatic Deluxe Rib 12, except 26-inch vent-rib barrel bored skeet choke. Made from 1962 to 1966.

High Standard Supermatic Skeet—20 Gauge . . . $275
Same as Supermatic Deluxe Rib 20, except 26-inch ventilated-rib barrel bored skeet choke. Made from 1964 to 1966.

High Standard Supermatic Special—12 Gauge . $200
Same as Supermatic Field 12, except has 27-inch barrel with adjustable choke. Made from 1960 to 1966.

High Standard Supermatic Special—20 Gauge . $210
Same as Supermatic Field 20, except has 27-inch barrel with adjustable choke. Made from 1963 to 1966.

High Standard Supermatic Trap—12 Gauge . . . $245
Same as Supermatic Deluxe Rib 12, except 30-inch vent-rib barrel, full choke, special trap stock with recoil pad. Made from 1962 to 1966.

High Standard Supermatic Trophy—12 Gauge . . $225
Same as Supermatic Deluxe Rib 12, except has 27-inch vent-rib barrel with adjustable choke. Made 1961 to 1966.

High Standard Supermatic Trophy—20 Gauge . . $230
Same as Supermatic Deluxe Rib 20, except has 27-inch vent-rib barrel with adjustable choke. Made 1963 to 1966.

High Standard Supermatic Shadow Seven

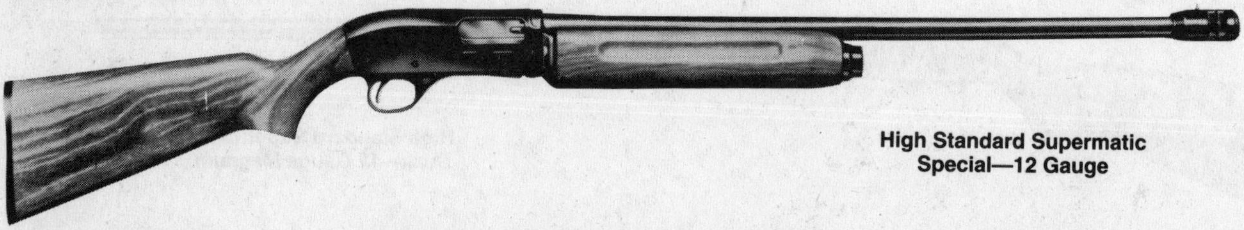
High Standard Supermatic Special—12 Gauge

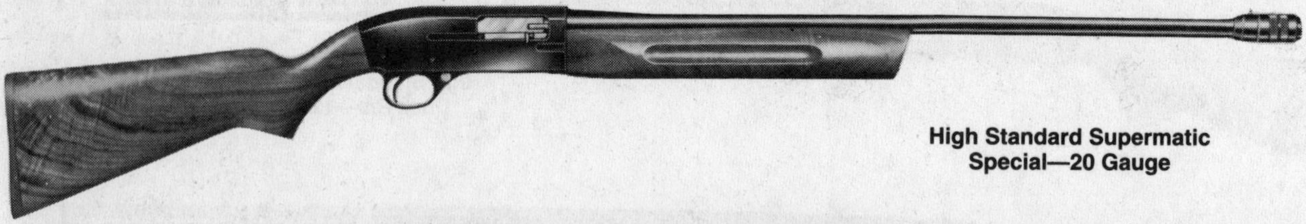
High Standard Supermatic Special—20 Gauge

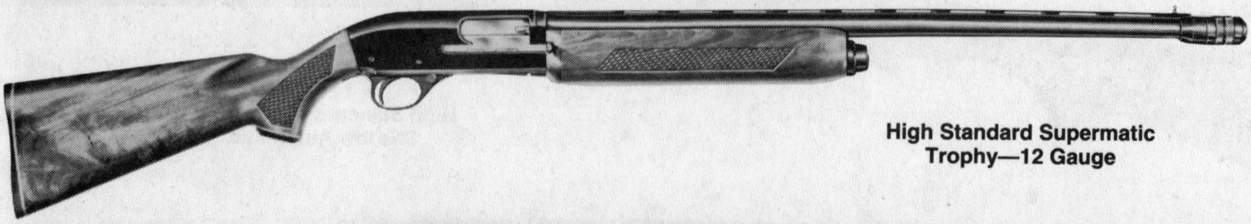
High Standard Supermatic Trophy—12 Gauge

High Standard Supermatic Trophy—20 Gauge

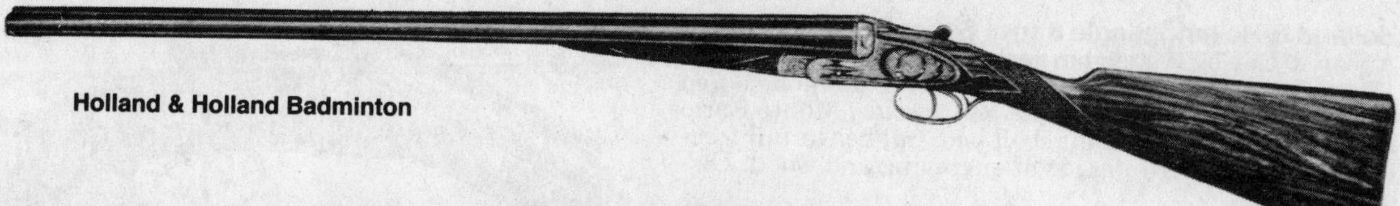

Holland & Holland Badminton

Holland & Holland Dominion

Holland & Holland Northwood

HOLLAND & HOLLAND, LTD. London, England

Holland & Holland Badminton Model Hammerless Double Barrel Shotgun. Originally No. 2 Grade
General specifications same as Royal Model except without self-opening action. Made as a Game Gun or Pigeon and Wildfowl Gun. Made from 1902 to date.
With double triggers **$8000**
With single trigger **8500**

Holland & Holland Centenary Model Hammerless Double Barrel Shotgun
Lightweight (5½ lbs.). 12 gauge game gun designed for 2-inch shell. Made in four grades—Model Deluxe, Royal, Badminton, Dominion—values same as shown for standard guns in those grades. Discontinued 1962.

Holland & Holland Dominion Model Hammerless Double Barrel Shotgun $4500
Game Gun. Side lock. Auto ejectors. Double triggers. Gauges: 12, 16, 20. Barrels: 25- to 30-inch, any standard boring. Checkered stock and forend, straight grip standard. Discontinued 1967.

Holland & Holland Model Deluxe Hammerless Double
Same as Royal Model, except has special engraving and exhibition grade stock and forearm. Currently mfd.
With double triggers **$15,000**
With single trigger **16,000**

Holland & Holland Northwood Model Hammerless Double Barrel Shotgun $3200
Anson & Deeley system box lock. Auto ejectors. Double triggers. Gauges: 12, 16, 20, 28 in Game Model; 28 gauge not offered in Pigeon Model; Wildfowl Model in 12 gauge only (3-inch chambers available). Barrels: 28-inch standard in Game and Pigeon Models, 30-inch in Wildfowl Model; other lengths, any standard choke combination available. Weight: from 5 to 7¾ pounds depending upon gauge and barrels. Checkered straight-grip or pistol-grip stock and forearm. Discontinued.

Holland & Holland Riviera Model Pigeon Gun . . $10,000
Same as Badminton Model but supplied with two sets of barrels, double triggers. Discontinued 1967.

Holland & Holland Royal Model Hammerless Double
Self-opening. Side locks, hand-detachable. Auto ejectors. Double triggers or single trigger. Gauges: 12, 16, 20, 28, .410. Built to customer's specifications as to barrel length, chokes, etc. Made as a Game Gun or Pigeon and Wildfowl Gun, the latter having treble-grip action and side clips. Checkered stock and forend, straight grip standard. Made from 1885 to date.
With double triggers **$12,500**
With single trigger **13,000**

Holland & Holland Royal Model Under-and-Over
Side locks, hand-detachable. Auto ejectors. Double triggers or single trigger. 12 gauge. Built to customer's specifications as to barrel length, chokes, etc. Made as a Game Gun or Pigeon and Wildfowl Gun. Checkered stock and forend, straight grip standard. *Note:* In 1951 Holland & Holland introduced their New Model Under/Over with an improved, narrower action body. Discont. 1960.
New Model with double triggers **$16,000**
New Model with single trigger **17,500**
Old Model with double triggers **12,500**
Old Model with single trigger **13,500**

Holland & Holland Royal Double Barrel

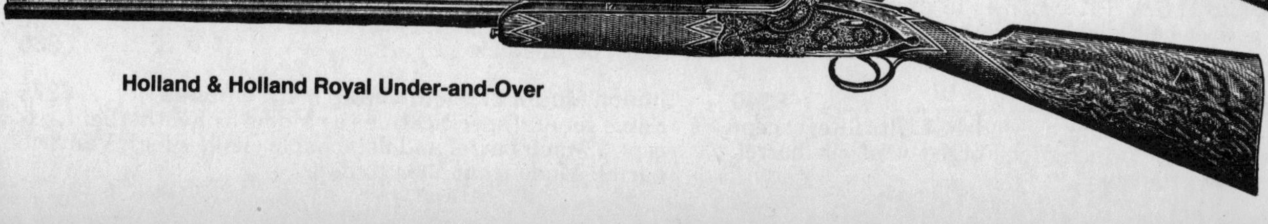

Holland & Holland Royal Under-and-Over

Holland & Holland Single Barrel Super Trap Gun
Anson & Deeley system box lock. Auto ejector. No safety. 12 gauge. Barrels: wide vent rib, 30- or 32-inch, bored extra full choke. Weight: about $8^{3}/_{4}$ pounds. Monte Carlo stock with pistol grip and recoil pad, full beavertail forearm. Models differ in grade of engraving and wood. Discontinued.
Standard Grade . . . . $ 9,000
Deluxe Grade 10,000
Exhibition Grade 12,000

HUNTER ARMS COMPANY
Fulton, New York

Hunter Fulton Hammerless Double Barrel Shotgun
Box lock. Plain extractors. Double triggers or non-selective single trigger. Gauges: 12, 16, 20. Barrels: 26- to 32-inch, various choke combinations. Weight: about 7 pounds. Checkered pistol-grip stock and forearm. Discont. 1948.
With double triggers $325
With single trigger 550

Hunter Special Hammerless Double Barrel Shotgun
Box lock. Plain extractors. Double triggers or non-selective single trigger. Gauges: 12, 16, 20. Barrels: 26- to 30-inch, various choke combinations. Weight: $6^{1}/_{2}$ to $7^{1}/_{4}$ pounds

Hunter Fulton

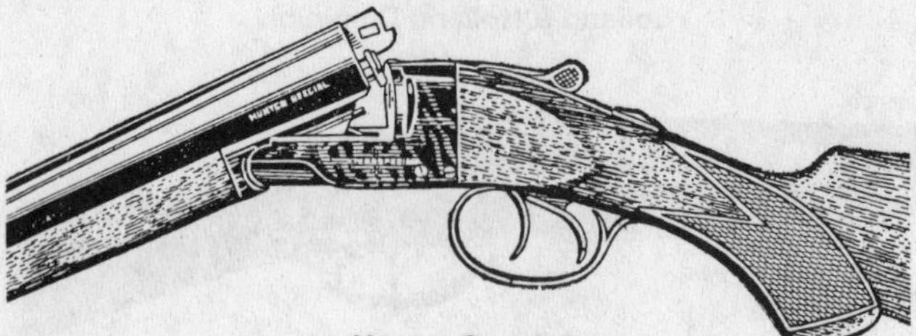
Hunter Special

Hunter Special Hammerless (cont.)
depending upon barrel length and gauge. Checkered full pistol-grip stock and forearm. Discont. 1948.
With double triggers $525
With single trigger 610

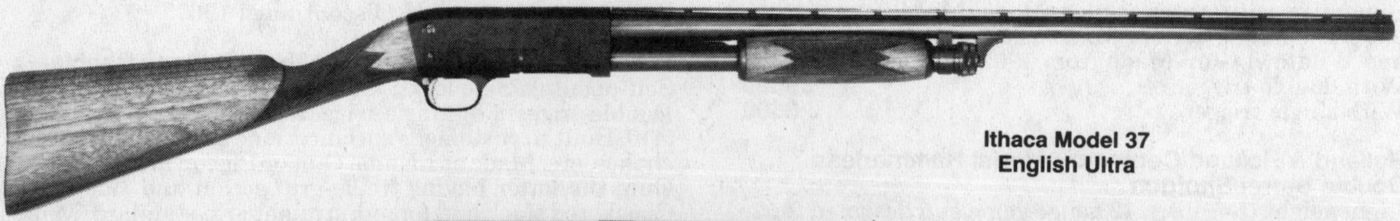
Ithaca Model 37
English Ultra

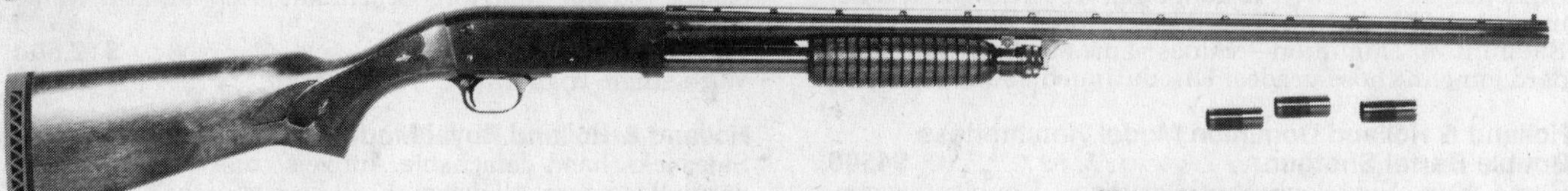
Ithaca Model 37
Field Grade Mag. w/Tubes

IGA SHOTGUNS
See Stoeger Shotguns.

ITHACA GUN COMPANY
Ithaca, New York

Ithaca Model 37 Bicentennial Commemorative . . $600
Limited to issue of 1976. Similar to Model 37 Supreme, except has special Bicentennial design etched on receiver, full-fancy walnut stock and slide handle. Serial numbers U.S.A. 0001 to U.S.A. 1976. Comes in presentation case with cast pewter belt buckle. Made in 1976. Value is for gun in new, unfired condition.

Ithaca Model 37 English Ultra $340
Same general specifications as Model 37 Ultralite, except straight buttstock, 25-inch Rot-Forged vent-rib barrel. Made from 1984 to date.

Ithaca Model 37 Featherlight Standard Grade Slide Action Repeating Shotgun
Adaptation of the earlier Remington Model 17, a Browning design patented in 1915. Hammerless. Takedown. Gauges: 12, 16 (discontinued 1973), 20. 4-shell magazine. Barrel lengths: 26-, 28-, 30-inch (the latter in 12 gauge only); standard chokes. Weight: from $5^{3}/_{4}$ to $7^{1}/_{2}$ pounds depending upon gauge and barrel length. Checkered pistol-grip stock and slide handle. Some guns made in the 1950s and 1960s have grooved slide handle; plain or checkered pistol grip. Made from 1937 to 1984.
With checkered pistol grip $250
With plain stock 230

Ithaca Model 37 Field Grade Mag. w/tubes $275
Same general specifications as Model 37 Featherlight, except 32-inch barrel and detachable choke tubes. Vent-rib barrel. Made from 1984 to date.

Ithaca Model 37 $5,000 Grade

Ithaca Model 37 Super Deluxe Deerslayer

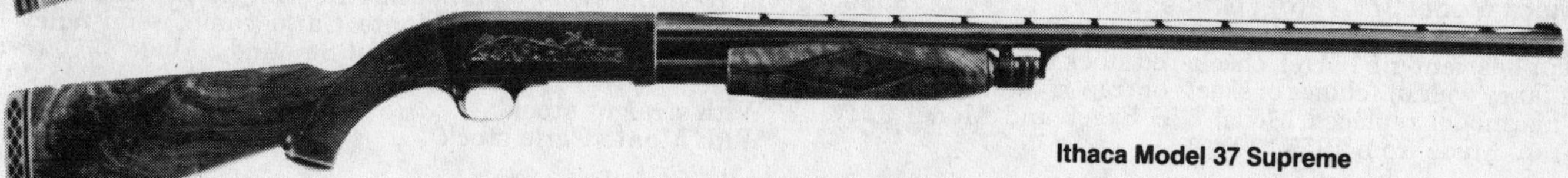

Ithaca Model 37 Supreme

Ithaca Model 37DV Deluxe Ventilated Rib

Ithaca Model 37 $5000 Grade **$6000**
Custom built, elaborately engraved and inlaid with gold, hand-finished working parts, stock and forend of selected figured walnut. General specifications same as standard Model 37. *Note:* The same gun was designated the $1000 Grade prior to World War II. Made from 1937 to 1967.

Ithaca Model 37 Standard Deerslayer **$285**
Same as Model 37 Standard, except has 20- or 26-inch barrel bored for rifled slugs, rifle-type open rear sight and ramp front sight. Weight: 5¾ to 6½ pounds depending upon gauge and barrel length. Made 1959 to date.

Ithaca Model 37 Super Deluxe Deerslayer **$295**
Formerly "Deluxe Deerslayer." Same as Model 37 Standard Deerslayer, except has stock and slide handle of fancy walnut. Made from 1962 to date.

Ithaca Model 37 Supreme Grade **$495**
Available in Skeet or Trap Gun, similar to Model 37T. Made from 1967 to date.

Ithaca Model 37 Ultralite
Same general specifications as Model 37 Featherlight, except streamlined forend, gold trigger, Sid Bell grip cap and vent rib. Weight: 5 to 5¾ pounds. Made from 1984 to date.
Standard **$315**
With Choke Tubes **340**

Ithaca Model 37D Deluxe **$280**
Same as Model 37 Standard, except checkered stock and beavertail forearm, recoil pad. Made 1954 to 1977.

Ithaca Model 37DV Deluxe Ventilated Rib **$300**
Same as Model 37D Deluxe, except has ventilated rib. Made from 1962 to 1984.

Ithaca Model 37R Deluxe Solid Rib **$350**
Same general specifications as Model 37R, except has fancy walnut stock and slide handle, checkered. Made from 1955 to 1961.

Ithaca Model 37R Solid Rib Grade
Same general specifications as the Model 37 Featherlight, except has a raised solid rib, adding about ¼ pound of weight. Made from 1937 to 1967.
With checkered grip and slide handle **$300**
With plain stock **295**

Ithaca Model 37R Deluxe Solid Rib

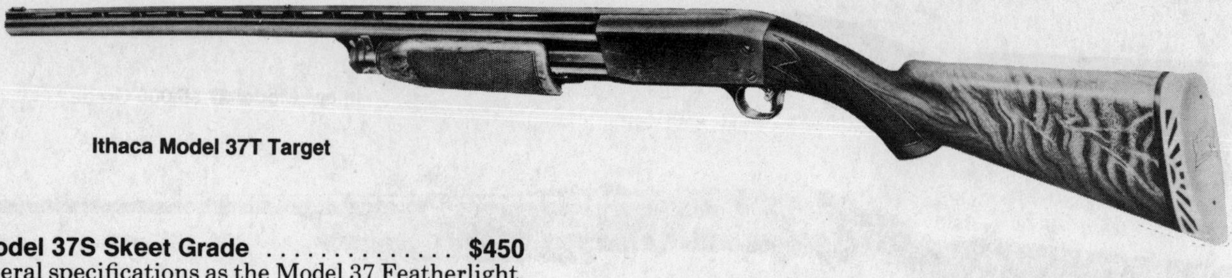

Ithaca Model 37T Target

Ithaca Model 37S Skeet Grade **$450**
Same general specifications as the Model 37 Featherlight, except has vent rib and large extension-type forend; weighs about 1/2 pound more. Made from 1937 to 1955.

Ithaca Model 37T Target Grade **$550**
Same general specifications as Model 37 Featherlight, except has vent-rib barrel, checkered stock and slide handle of fancy walnut (choice of skeet- or trap-style stock). *Note:* This model replaced Model 37S Skeet and Model 37T Trap. Made from 1955 to 1961.

Ithaca Model 37T Trap Grade **$550**
Same general specifications as Model 37S, except has straighter trap-style stock of selected walnut, recoil pad; weighs about 1/2 pound more. Made 1937 to 1955.

Ithaca Model 37V Standard Ventilated Rib **$275**
Same as Model 37 Standard, except has vent rib, adding about 1/4 pound of weight. Made 1962 to 1984.

Ithaca Model 51 Deerslayer **$260**
Same as Model 51 Standard, except has 24-inch plain barrel with slug boring, rifle sights, recoil pad. Weight: about 7 1/4 pounds. Made from 1972 to 1984.

Ithaca Model 51 Deluxe Skeet Grade **$300**
Same as Model 51 Standard, except 26-inch ventilated-rib barrel only, skeet choke, skeet-style stock, semi-fancy wood. Weight: about 8 pounds. Made from 1970 to date.

Ithaca Model 51 Deluxe Trap Grade
Same as Model 51 Standard, except 12 gauge only, 30-inch barrel with broad floating rib, full choke, trap-style stock with straight or Monte Carlo comb, semi-fancy wood, recoil pad. Weight: about 8 pounds. Made 1970 to date.
With straight stock **$255**
With Monte Carlo stock **265**

Ithaca Model 51 Standard Automatic Shotgun
Gas-operated. Gauges: 12, 20. 3-shot. Barrels: plain or vent rib; 30-inch full choke (12 gauge only), 28-inch full or modified, 26-inch imp. cyl. Weight: 7 1/4 to 7 3/4 pounds depending upon gauge and barrel. Checkered pistol-grip stock, forearm. Made 1970 to 1980. Still available in 12 and 20 ga., 28-inch mod. choke only.
With plain barrel **$250**
With ventilated rib **270**

Ithaca Model 51 Standard Magnum
Same as Model 51 Standard, except has 3-inch chamber, handles magnum shells only; 30-inch barrel in 12 gauge, 28-inch in 20 gauge, full or modified choke, stock with recoil pad. Weight: 7 3/4 or 8 pounds depending upon gauge. Made 1972 to date.
With plain barrel (discontinued 1976) **$250**
With ventilated rib **290**

Ithaca Model 51 Deerslayer

Ithaca Model 51 Deluxe Trap

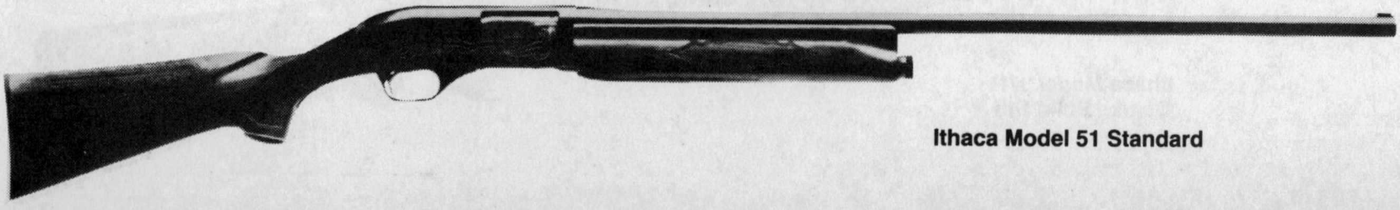

Ithaca Model 51 Standard

Ithaca Model 51A Turkey Gun

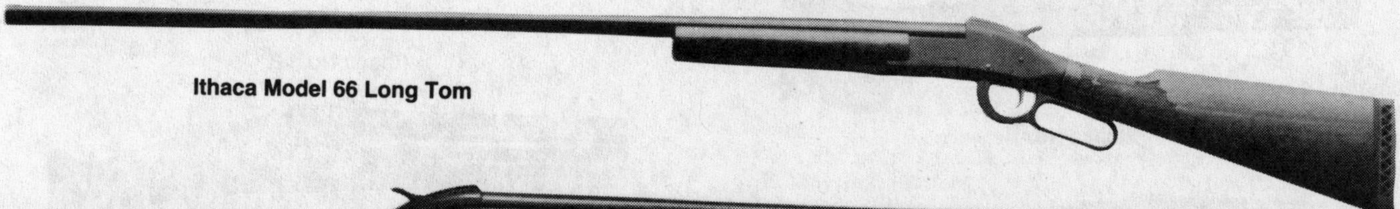

Ithaca Model 66 Long Tom

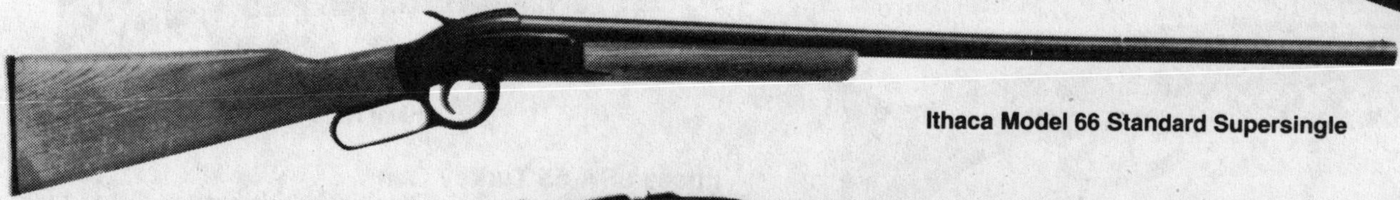

Ithaca Model 66 Standard Supersingle

Ithaca Model 66RS Buckbuster

Ithaca Model 51A Turkey Gun **$395**
Same general specifications as standard Model 51 Magnum, except 26-inch barrel and matte finish. Discontinued 1986.

Ithaca Model 66 Long Tom **$100**
Same as Model 66 Standard, except has 36-inch full choke barrel, 12 gauge only, checkered stock and recoil pad standard. Made from 1969 to 1974.

Ithaca Model 66 Standard Supersingle Lever **$95**
Single shot. Hand-cocked hammer. Gauges: 12 (discont. 1974), 20, .410; 3-inch chambers. Barrels: 12 ga., 30-inch full choke, 28-inch full or modified; 20 ga., 28-inch full or modified; .410, 26-inch full. Weight: about 7 pounds. Plain or checkered straight-grip stock, plain forend. Made from 1963 to 1978.

Ithaca Model 66 Ventilated Rib **$125**
Same as Model 66 Standard and Youth Model, except has vent-rib barrel, made in 20 ga. only, checkered stock and recoil pad standard. Made 1969 to 1974.

Ithaca Model 66 Youth **$95**
Same as Model 66 Standard, except 26-inch barrel, shorter stock and recoil pad; 20 and .410 gauges only. Made from 1965 to 1978.

Ithaca Model 66RS Buckbuster **$130**
Same as Model 66 Standard, except has 22-inch barrel, cylinder bore with rifle sights; later version has recoil pad. Originally offered in 12 and 20 gauges; the former was discont. in 1970. Made from 1967 to 1978.

Ithaca Hammerless Double Barrel Shotguns
Box lock. Plain extractors, auto ejectors standard on the "E" grades. Double triggers, non-selective or selective single trigger extra. Gauges: Magnum 10, 12; 12, 16, 20, 28, .410. Barrels: 26- to 32-inch, any standard boring. Weight: 5¾ (.410) to 10½ pounds (Magnum 10). Checkered pistol-grip stock and forearm standard. The higher grades differ from the Field Grade chiefly in quality of workmanship, grade of wood, checkering, engraving, etc.; general specifications are the same. Ithaca doubles made before 1925 had underbolts and a bolt through the rib extension. In 1925 (serial number 425,000) the rotary bolt and a stronger frame were adopted. Values shown are for this latter type; earlier models bring prices about 50 percent under those of the more recent types. Smaller gauge guns often bring prices up to 75 percent higher. Ithaca double barrel guns discontinued 1948.

Field Grade .... $ 610
No. 1 Grade 795
No. 2 Grade 1795
No. 3 Grade 2100
No. 4-E Grade (ejector) 3100
No. 5-E Grade (ejector) 4100
No. 7-E Grade (ejector) 7500
$2000 (prewar $1000) Grade (ejector and selective single trigger standard) 12,000

Extras:
Magnum 10 or 12 gauge (in other than the four highest grades), add 200
Automatic ejectors (Grades No. 1, 2, 3, with ejectors are designated No. 1E, 2E, 3E), add 200
Selective single trigger, add 150

Ithaca Field Grade

Ithaca No. 1

Ithaca No. 2

Ithaca No. 3

Ithaca Hammerless Doubles (cont.)

Non-selective single trigger, add	$100
Beavertail forend (Field No. 1 or 2), add	150
Beavertail forend (No. 3 or 4), add	175
Beavertail forend (No. 5, 7 or $2000 Grade), add	250
Ventilated rib (No. 4, 5, 7 or $2000 Grade), add	250
Ventilated rib (lower grades), add	175

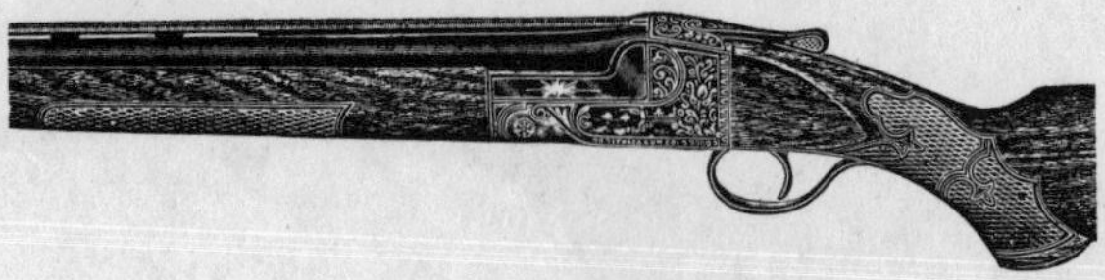

Ithaca No. 4E

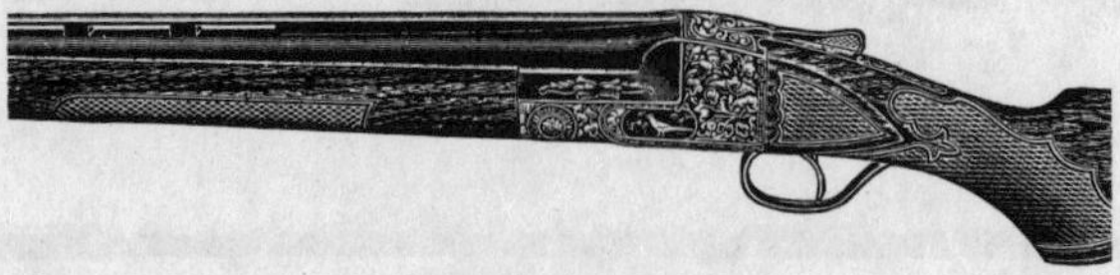

Ithaca No. 5E

Ithaca No. 7E

Ithaca LSA-55 Turkey Gun **$500**
Over-and-under shotgun/rifle combination. Box lock. Exposed hammer. Plain extractor. Single trigger. 12 gauge/222 Rem. 24½-inch ribbed barrels (rifle barrel has muzzle brake). Weight: about 7 pounds. Folding leaf rear sight, bead front sight. Checkered Monte Carlo stock and forearm. Made from 1970 to 1977 by Oy Tikkakoski AB, Tikkakoski, Finland.

Ithaca Mag-10 Automatic Shotgun
Gas-operated. 10 gauge. 3½-inch magnum. 3-shot. 32-inch plain (Standard Grade only) or vent-rib barrel. Full choke. Weight: 11 lbs., plain barrel; 11½ lbs., vent rib. Standard Grade has plain stock and forearm. Deluxe and Supreme Grades have checkering, semi-fancy and fancy wood respectively, and stud swivel. All have recoil pad. Deluxe and Supreme Grades made from 1974 to 1982. Standard Grade introduced in 1977. All grades discontinued 1986.

Camo Model	$625
Deluxe Grade	695
Roadblocker	555
Standard Grade, plain barrel	540
Standard Grade, ventilated rib	585
Standard Grade, with tubes	625
Supreme Grade	840

Ithaca LSA-55 Turkey Gun

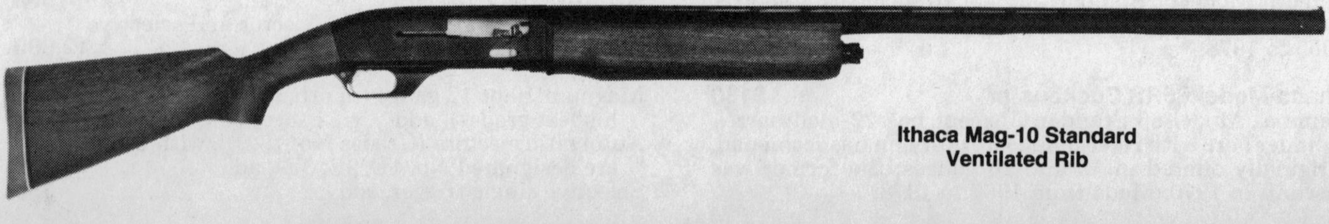

Ithaca Mag-10 Standard Ventilated Rib

Ithaca Single Barrel Trap
Model 5E

Ithaca Single Barrel Trap
"Dollar Grade"

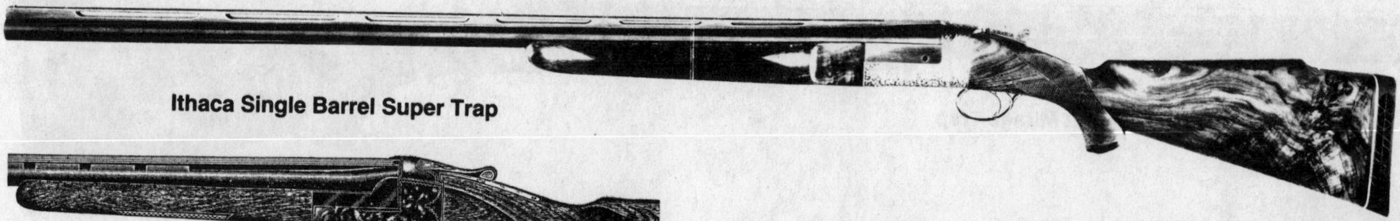

Ithaca Single Barrel Super Trap

Ithaca Single Barrel Trap
Victory Grade

Ithaca Single Barrel Trap, Flues and Knick Models
Box lock. Hammerless. Ejector. 12 gauge only. Barrel lengths: 30-, 32-, 34-inch (32-inch only in Victory Grade). Vent rib. Weight: about 8 pounds. Checkered pistol-grip stock and forend. Grades differ only in quality of workmanship, engraving, checkering, wood, etc. Flues Model, serial number under 400,000, made from 1908 to 1921. Triple-bolted Knick Model, serial number above 400,000, made since 1921. Victory Model discontinued in 1938, No. 7-E in 1964, No. 4-E in 1976, No. 5-E in 1986. $5000 Grade currently manufactured. Values shown are for Knick Model; Flues Model guns bring prices about 50 percent lower.

Ithaca Single Barrel Shotguns (cont.)

Victory Grade	**$1200**
No. 4-E	**2700**
No. 5-E	**3500**
No. 7-E	**5200**
$5000 Grade (prewar $1000 Grade)	**7000**

Ithaca-Perazzi Competition I Skeet

Ithaca-Perazzi Competition I Trap

Note: The following Ithaca-Perazzi shotguns were manufactured by Manifattura Armi Perazzi, Brescia, Italy. See also separate Perazzi listing.

Ithaca-Perazzi Competition I Skeet $1525
Same as Competition I Trap, except has 26³/₄-inch barrels with integral muzzle brakes, skeet choke, skeet-style stock and forearm. Weight: 7³/₄ pounds. Made 1969 to 1974.

Ithaca-Perazzi Competition I Trap O/U $1525
Box lock. Auto ejectors. Single trigger. 12 gauge. 30- or 32-inch vent-rib barrels, imp. mod./full choke. Weight: about 8¹/₂ pounds. Checkered pistol-grip stock, forearm; recoil pad. Made from 1969 to 1974.

Ithaca-Perazzi Competition I Trap Single Barrel $1695
Box lock. Auto ejection. 12 gauge. 32- or 34-inch barrel, vent rib, full choke. Weight: 8¹/₂ pounds. Checkered Monte Carlo stock and beavertail forearm, recoil pad. Made from 1973 to 1978.

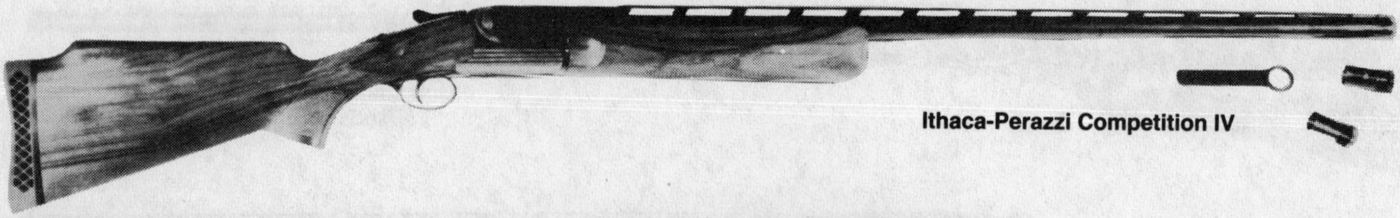

Ithaca-Perazzi Competition IV

Ithaca-Perazzi Light Game Model

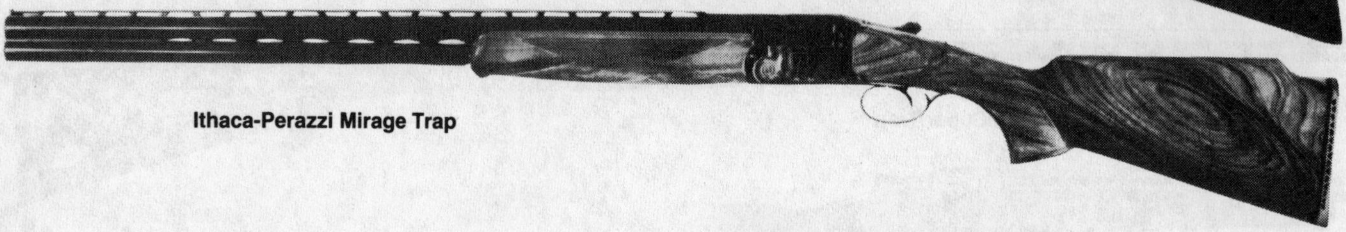

Ithaca-Perazzi Mirage Trap

Ithaca-Perazzi Competition IV Trap Gun $1895
Box lock. Auto ejection. 12 gauge. 32- or 34-inch barrel with high, wide vent rib, four interchangeable choke tubes (extra full, full, imp. mod., mod.). Weight: about 8¾ pounds. Checkered Monte Carlo stock and beavertail forearm, recoil pad. Fitted case. Made 1977 to 1978.

Ithaca-Perazzi Light Game O/U Field $1800
Box lock. Auto ejectors. Single trigger. 12 gauge. 27½-inch vent-rib barrels, modified/full or imp. cyl./mod. choke. Weight: 6¾ pounds. Checkered field-style stock and forearm. Made 1972 to 1974.

Ithaca-Perazzi Mirage Live Bird $1750
Same as Mirage Trap, except has 28-inch barrels, modified and extra full choke, special stock and forearm for live bird shooting. Weight: about 8 pounds. Made 1973 to 1978.

Ithaca-Perazzi Mirage Skeet $1695
Same as Mirage Trap, except has 28-inch barrels with integral muzzle brakes, skeet choke, skeet-style stock and forearm. Weight: about 8 pounds. Made 1973 to 1978.

Ithaca-Perazzi Mirage Trap $1750
Same general specifications as MX-8 Trap, except has tapered rib. Made from 1973 to 1978.

Ithaca-Perazzi MT-6 Skeet $1800
Same as MT-6 Trap, except has 28-inch barrels with two skeet choke tubes instead of extra full and full, skeet-style stock and forearm. Weight: about 8 pounds. Made from 1976 to 1978.

Ithaca-Perazzi MT-6 Trap Combo $3695
MT-6 with extra single under barrel with high-rise aluminum vent rib, 32- or 34-inch; seven interchangeable choke tubes (improved cylinder through extra full). Fitted case. Made from 1977 to 1978.

Ithaca-Perazzi MT-6 Trap Over-and-Under $1795
Box lock. Auto selective ejectors. Non-selective single trigger. 12 gauge. Barrels separated, wide vent rib, 30- or 32-inch, five interchangeable choke tubes (extra full, full, imp. mod., mod., imp. cyl.). Weight: about 8½ pounds. Checkered pistol-grip stock and forearm, recoil pad. Fitted case. Made 1976 to 1978.

Ithaca-Perazzi MT-6

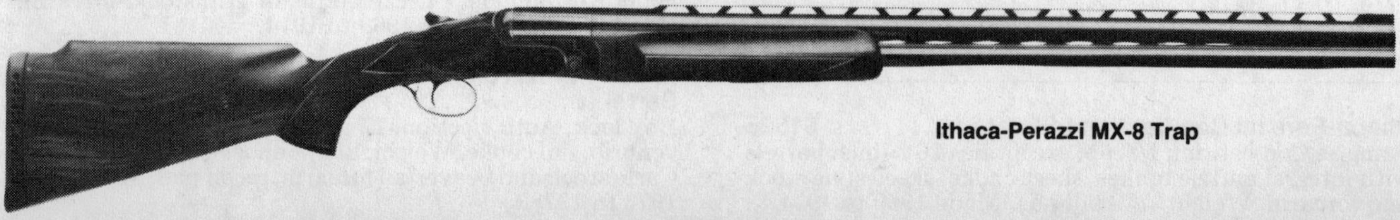

Ithaca-Perazzi MX-8 Trap

Ithaca-Perazzi Single Barrel Trap

Ithaca-Perazzi MX-8 Trap Combo **$3295**
MX-8 with extra single barrel, vent rib, 32- or 34-inch, full choke, forearm; two trigger groups included. Made 1973 to 1978.

Ithaca-Perazzi MX-8 Trap Over-and-Under **$2200**
Box lock. Auto selective ejectors. Non-selective single trigger. 12 gauge. Barrels: high vent rib; 30- or 32-inch, improved modified/full choke. Weight: 8¼ to 8½ pounds. Checkered Monte Carlo stock and forearm, recoil pad. Made 1969 to 1978.

Ithaca-Perazzi Single Barrel Trap Gun **$1525**
Box lock. Auto ejection. 12 gauge. 34-inch vent-rib barrel, full choke. Weight: about 8½ pounds. Checkered pistol-grip stock, forearm; recoil pad. Made 1971 to 1972.

Note: The following Ithaca-SKB shotguns, manufactured by SKB Arms Company, Tokyo, Japan, were distributed in the U.S. by Ithaca Gun Company from 1966 to 1976. See also listings under SKB.

Ithaca-SKB Model 100 Side-by-Side **$350**
Box lock. Plain extractors. Selective single trigger. Auto safety. Gauges: 12 and 20; 2¾-inch and 3-inch chambers respectively. Barrels: 30-inch, full/full (12 ga. only); 28-inch, full/modified; 26-inch, improved cylinder/modified (12 ga. only); 25-inch, improved cylinder/modified (20 ga. only). Weight: 12 ga., about 7 lbs.; 20 ga., about 6 lbs. Checkered stock and forend. Made 1966 to 1976.

Ithaca-SKB Model 150 Field Grade **$385**
Same as Model 100, except has fancier scroll engraving, beavertail forearm. Made from 1972 to 1974.

Ithaca-SKB Model 200E Field Grade S/S **$550**
Same as Model 100, except auto selective ejectors, engraved and silver-plated frame, gold-plated nameplate and trigger, beavertail forearm. Made 1966 to 1976.

Ithaca-SKB Model 200E Skeet Gun **$595**
Same as Model 200E Field Grade, except 26-inch (12 ga.) and 25-inch (20 ga./2¾-inch chambers) barrels, skeet choke; nonautomatic safety and recoil pad. Made 1966 to 1976.

Ithaca-SKB Model 280 English **$595**
Same as Model 200E, except has scrolled game scene engraving on frame, English-style straight-grip stock; 30-inch barrels not available; special quail gun in 20 gauge has 25-inch barrels, both bored improved cylinder. Made from 1971 to 1976.

Ithaca-SKB Model 300 Standard Automatic Shotgun
Recoil-operated. Gauges: 12, 20 (3-inch). 5-shot. Barrels: plain or vent rib; 30-inch full choke (12 gauge only), 28-inch full or modified, 26-inch improved cylinder. Weight: about 7 pounds. Checkered pistol-grip stock and forearm. Made 1968 to 1972.

With plain barrel **$230**
With ventilated rib **250**

SHOTGUNS

Ithaca-SKB Model 100

Ithaca-SKB Model 200E Field

Ithaca-SKB Model 280 English

Ithaca-SKB Model 500 Field Grade O/U $540
Box lock. Auto selective ejectors. Selective single trigger. Nonautomatic safety. Gauges: 12 and 20; 2¾-inch and 3-inch chambers respectively. Vent-rib barrels: 30-inch modified/full (12 ga. only); 28-inch modified/full; 26-inch improved cylinder/modified. Weight: 12 ga., about 7½ lbs.; 20 ga., about 6½ lbs. Checkered stock and forearm. Made 1966 to 1976.

Ithaca-SKB Model 500 Magnum $550
Same as Model 500 Field Grade, except chambered for 3-inch 12 gauge shells, has 30-inch barrels, improved modified/full choke. Weight: about 8 pounds. Made 1973-76.

Ithaca-SKB Model 600 Doubles Gun $700
Same as Model 600 Trap Grade, except specially choked for 21-yard first target, 30-yard second. Made 1973 to 1975.

Ithaca-SKB Model 600 Field Grade $650
Same as Model 500, except has silver-plated frame, higher grade wood. Made from 1969 to 1976.

Ithaca-SKB Model 600 Magnum $675
Same as Model 600 Field Grade, except chambered for 3-inch 12 gauge shells; has 30-inch barrels, improved modified/full choke. Weight: 8½ pounds. Made 1969-72.

Ithaca-SKB Model 600 Skeet Grade
Same as Model 500, except also available in 28 and .410 gauge, has silver-plated frame, higher grade wood, recoil pad, 26- or 28-inch barrels (28-inch only in 28 and .410), skeet choke. Weight: 7 to 7¾ pounds depending upon gauge and barrel length. Made 1966 to 1976.
12 or 20 gauge **$700**
28 or .410 gauge **725**

Ithaca-SKB Model 600 Skeet Combo Set $1895
Model 600 Skeet Grade with matched set of 20, 28 and .410 gauge barrels, 28-inch, fitted case. Made 1970 to 1976.

Ithaca-SKB Model 600 Trap Grade O/U $700
Same as Model 500, except 12 gauge only, has silver-plated frame, 30- or 32-inch barrels choked full/full or full/imp. mod., choice of Monte Carlo or straight stock of higher grade wood, recoil pad. Weight: about 8 pounds. Made 1966 to 1976.

Ithaca-SKB Model 680 English $690
Same as Model 600 Field Grade, except has intricate scroll engraving, English-style straight-grip stock and forearm of extra-fine walnut; 30-inch barrels not available. Made from 1973 to 1976.

Ithaca-SKB Model 300

Ithaca-SKB Model 500 Field

Ithaca-SKB Model 600 Field

Ithaca-SKB Model 600 Trap

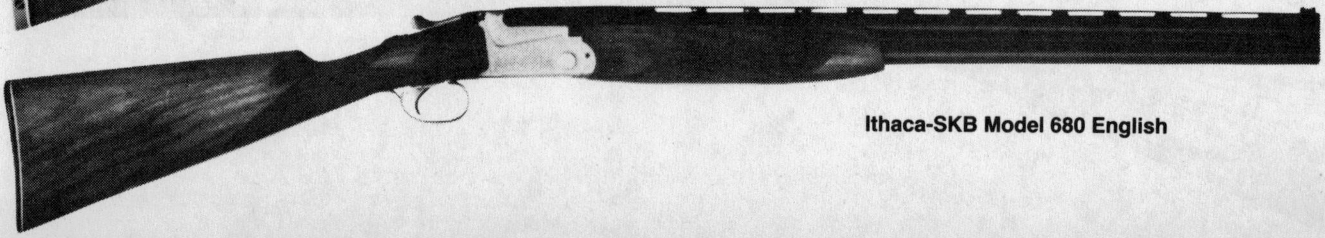

Ithaca-SKB Model 680 English

Ithaca-SKB Model 700 Skeet Grade

Ithaca-SKB Model 900 Deluxe

Ithaca-SKB Century Trap

Ithaca-SKB Century II Trap

Ithaca-SKB Model XL300

Ithaca-SKB Model 700 Doubles Gun $775
Same as Model 700 Trap Grade, except specially choked for 21-yard first target, 30-yard second target. Made from 1973 to 1975.

Ithaca-SKB Model 700 Skeet Combo Set $1980
Model 700 Skeet Grade with matched set of 20, 28 and .410 gauge barrels, 28-inch, fitted case. Made 1970 to 1971.

Ithaca-SKB Model 700 Skeet Grade $790
Same as Model 600 Skeet Grade, except not available in 28 and .410 gauge, has more elaborate scroll engraving, extra-wide rib, higher grade wood. Made 1969 to 1975.

Ithaca-SKB Model 700 Trap Grade $725
Same as Model 600 Trap Grade, except has more elaborate scroll engraving, extra-wide rib, higher grade wood. Made from 1969 to 1975.

Ithaca-SKB Model 900 Deluxe Automatic $275
Same as Model 300, except has game scene etched and gold-filled on receiver, vent rib standard. Made 1968 to 1972.

Ithaca-SKB Model 900 Slug Gun $255
Same as Model 900 Deluxe, except has 24-inch plain barrel with slug boring, rifle sights. Weight: about 6½ pounds. Made from 1970 to 1972.

Ithaca-SKB Century Single Barrel Trap Gun $495
Box lock. Auto ejector. 12 gauge. Barrels: 32- or 34-inch, vent rib, full choke. Weight: about 8 pounds. Checkered walnut stock with pistol grip, straight or Monte Carlo comb, recoil pad, beavertail forearm. Made 1973 to 1974. *Note:* Current SKB Century is same as Ithaca-SKB Century II.

Ithaca-SKB Century II $595
Improved version of Century. Same general specifications, except has higher stock, reverse-taper beavertail forearm with redesigned locking iron. Made 1975 to 1976.

Ithaca-SKB Model XL300 Standard Automatic
Gas-operated. Gauges: 12, 20 (3-inch). 5-shot. Barrels: plain or vent rib; 30-inch full choke (12 gauge only), 28-inch full or modified, 26-inch improved cylinder. Weight: 6 to 7½ pounds depending upon gauge and barrel. Checkered pistol-grip stock, forearm. Made 1972 to 1976.
With plain barrel **$235**
With ventilated rib **255**

Ithaca-SKB Model XL900 Deluxe Automatic $275
Same as Model XL300, except has game scene finished in silver on receiver, vent rib standard. Made 1972 to 1976.

Ithaca-SKB Model XL900 Skeet Grade $285
Same as Model XL900 Deluxe, except has scrolled receiver finished in black chrome, 26-inch barrel only, skeet choke, skeet-style stock. Weight: 7 or 7½ pounds depending upon gauge. Made 1972 to 1976.

Ithaca-SKB Model XL900 Deluxe

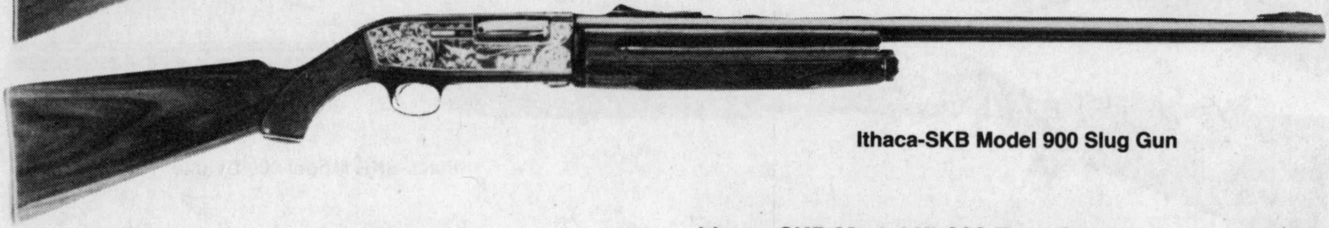

Ithaca-SKB Model 900 Slug Gun

Ithaca-SKB Model XL900 Slug Gun $265
Same as Model XL900 Deluxe, except has 24-inch plain barrel with slug boring, rifle sights. Weight: 6½ or 7 pounds depending upon gauge. Made 1972 to 1976.

Ithaca-SKB Model XL900 Trap Grade $300
Same as Model XL900 Deluxe, except 12 gauge only, has scrolled receiver finished in black chrome, 30-inch barrel only, improved modified or full choke, trap style with straight or Monte Carlo comb, recoil pad. Weight: about 7¾ pounds. Made from 1972 to 1976.

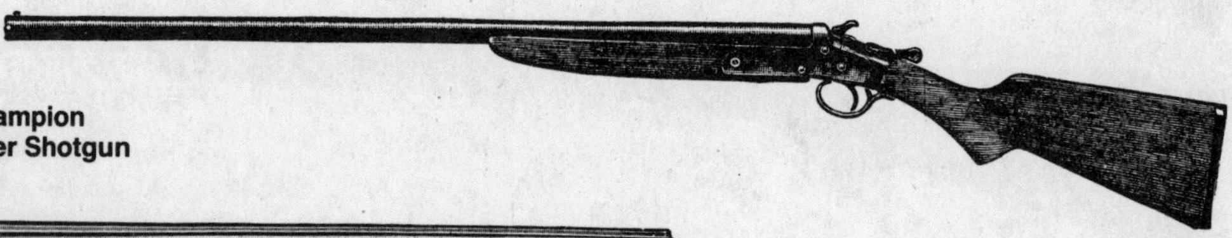

Iver Johnson Champion Single Barrel Hammer Shotgun

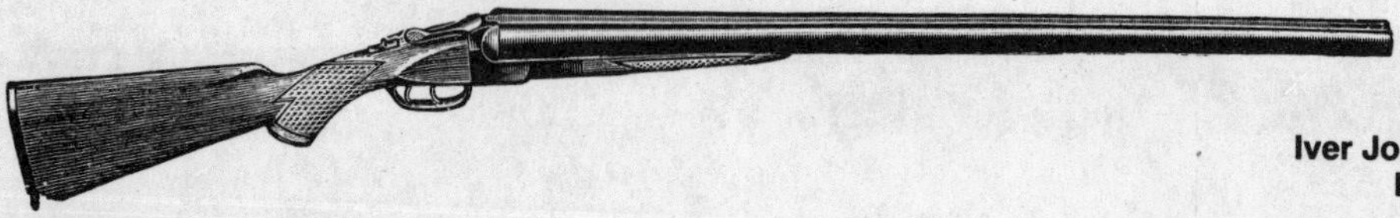

Iver Johnson Hercules Hammerless Double Barrel Shotgun

IVER JOHNSON'S ARMS
Jacksonville, Arkansas

Formerly Iver Johnson's Arms & Cycle Works of Fitchburg, Mass., and Middlesex, N.J. Now a division of the American Military Arms Corporation.

Iver Johnson Champion Grade Single Barrel Hammer Shotgun $140
Auto ejector. Gauges: 12, 16, 20, 28 and .410. Barrels: 26- to 36-inch, full choke. Weight: 5¾ to 6½ pounds depending upon gauge and barrel length. Plain pistol-grip stock and forend. Extras include checkered stock and forend, pistol-grip cap and knob forend. Known as Model 36. Also made in a Semi-Octagon Breech, Top Matted and Jacketed Breech (extra heavy) model. Made in Champion Lightweight as Model 39 in gauges 24, 28, 32 and .410; 44 and 45 caliber; 12 and 14mm with same extras—$200; add $100 in the smaller and obsolete gauges. Made from 1909 to 1973.

Iver Johnson Hercules Grade Hammerless Double Barrel Shotgun
Box lock. (Some made with false side plates.) Plain extractors and auto ejectors. Double or Miller Single triggers (both selective or non-selective). Gauges: 12, 16, 20 and .410. Barrel lengths: 26- to 32-inch, all chokes. Weight: 5¾ to 7¾ pounds depending upon gauge and barrel length. Checkered stock and forend. Straight grip in .410 gauge with both 2½ and 3-inch chambers. Extras include in

Iver Johnson Matted Rib

Iver Johnson Hercules Hammerless Double (cont.)
addition to Miller Single Trigger, Jostam Anti-Flinch Recoil Pad and Lyman Ivory Sights at extra cost. Discont. 1946.

With double triggers, extractors	**$545**
With double triggers, automatic ejectors	**650**
Extra for non-selective single trigger	**100**
Extra for selective single trigger	**135**
Extra for .410 gauge	**75**

Iver Johnson Matted Rib Single Barrel Hammer Shotgun in smaller gauges $200
Same general specifications as Champion Grade except has solid matted top rib, checkered stock and forend. Weight: 6 to 6¾ pounds. Discont. 1948.

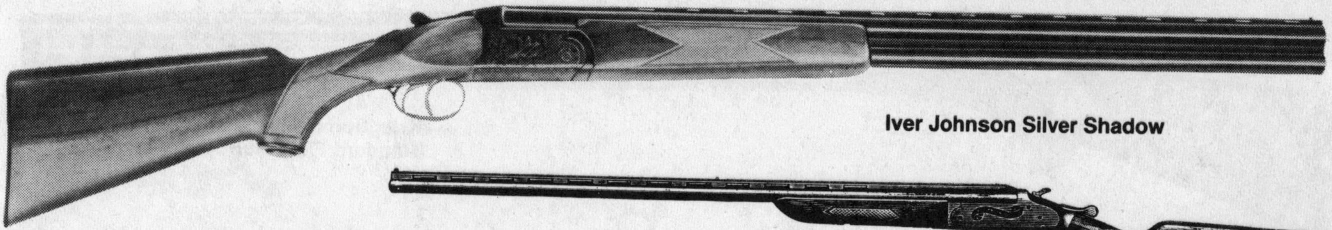

Iver Johnson Silver Shadow

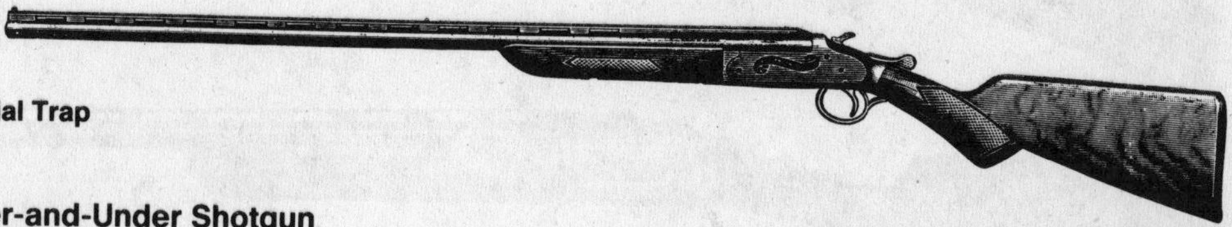

Iver Johnson Special Trap

Iver Johnson Silver Shadow Over-and-Under Shotgun

Box lock. Plain extractors. Double triggers or non-selective single trigger. 12 gauge, 3-inch chambers. Barrels: 26-inch improved cylinder/modified; 28-inch improved cylinder/modified; 28-inch modified/full; 30-inch both full choke; vent rib. Weight: with 28-inch barrels, $7\frac{1}{2}$ pounds. Checkered pistol-grip stock and forearm. Made by F. Marocchi, Brescia, Italy, 1973 to 1978.

Model 412 with double triggers **$450**
Model 422 with single trigger **510**

Iver Johnson Skeeter Model Hammerless Double Barrel Shotgun

Box lock. Plain extractors or selective auto ejectors. Double triggers or Miller Single Trigger (selective or non-selective). Gauges: 12, 16, 20, 28 and .410. 26- or 28-inch barrels, skeet boring standard. Weight: about $7\frac{1}{2}$ pounds; less in smaller gauges. Pistol- or straight-grip stock and beavertail forend, both checkered, of selected fancy figured black walnut. Extras include Miller Single Trigger, selective or non-selective, Jostam Anti-Flinch Recoil Pad and Lyman Ivory Rear Sight at additional cost. Discont. 1942.

With double triggers, plain extractors **$815**
With double triggers, automatic ejectors **995**
Extra for non-selective single trigger **100**
Extra for selective single trigger **135**
Extra for .410 gauge **200**
Extra for 28 gauge **300**

Iver Johnson Special Trap Single Barrel Hammer Shotgun $250

Auto ejector. 12 gauge only. 32-inch barrel with vent rib, full choke. Checkered pistol-grip stock and forend. Weight: about $7\frac{1}{2}$ pounds. Discontinued 1942.

Iver Johnson Super Trap

Iver Johnson Super Trap Hammerless Double Barrel Shotgun

Box lock. Plain extractors. Double triggers or Miller Single Trigger (selective or non-selective), 12 gauge only, 32-inch full choke barrels, vent rib. Weight: about $8\frac{1}{2}$ pounds. Checkered pistol-grip stock and beavertail forend, recoil pad. Discont. 1942.

With double triggers **$895**
Extra for non-selective single trigger **100**
Extra for selective single trigger **135**

KESSLER ARMS CORP.
Silver Creek, New York

Kessler Lever-Matic Repeating Shotgun $140

Lever action. Takedown. Gauges: 12, 16, 20; three-shot magazine. Barrels: 26-, 28-, 30-inch; full choke. Plain pistol-grip stock, recoil pad. Weight: 7 to $7\frac{3}{4}$ pounds. Discont. 1953.

Kessler Three Shot Bolt Action Repeater $75

Takedown. Gauges: 12, 16, 20. Two-shell detachable box magazine. Barrels: 28-inch in 12 and 16 gauge; 26-inch in 20 gauge; full choke. Weight: $6\frac{1}{4}$ to $7\frac{1}{4}$ pounds depending upon gauge and barrel length. Plain one-piece pistol-grip stock, recoil pad. Made 1951 to 1953.

H. KRIEGHOFF JAGD UND SPORTWAFFENFABRIK
Ulm (Donau), West Germany

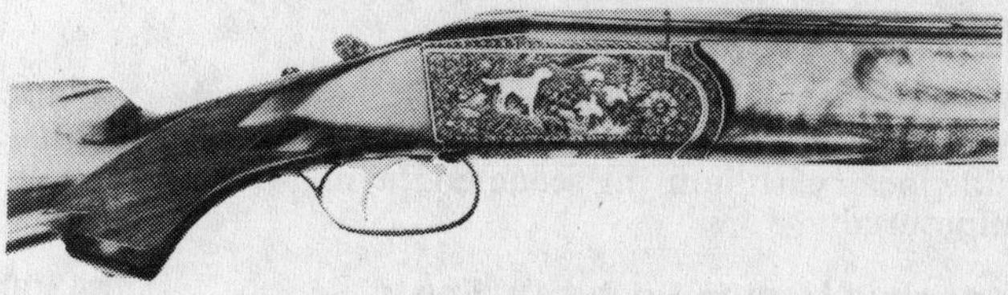

Krieghoff Model 32 Monte Carlo

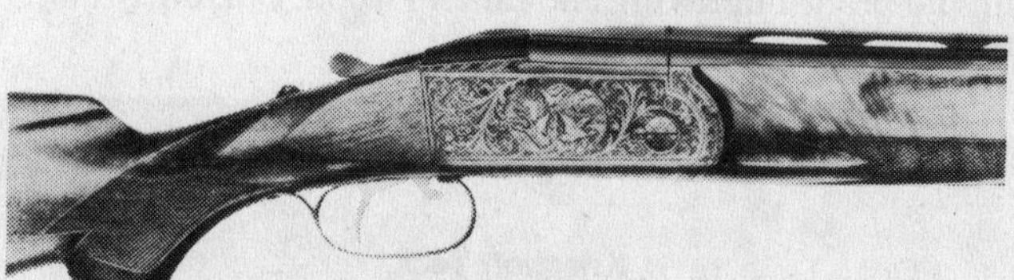

Krieghoff Model 32 San Remo

Krieghoff Model 32 Four-barrel Skeet Set

Over-and-under gun with four sets of matched barrels in 12, 20, 28 and .410 gauge, in fitted case. Available in six grades that differ in quality of engraving and wood. Currently manufactured.

Standard Grade .... **$ 4,940**
München Grade **6,370**
San Remo Grade **7,280**
Monte Carlo Grade **13,650**
Crown Grade **14,560**
Super Crown Grade **16,500**
Exhibition Grade **27,300**

Krieghoff Model 32
Standard Field Gun

Krieghoff Standard
Single Barrel Trap

Krieghoff Model 32 Standard Grade Over/Under
Similar to prewar Remington Model 23. Box lock. Auto ejector. Single trigger. Gauges: 12, 20, 28, .410. Barrels: vent rib, 26½- to 32-inch, any chokes. Weight: 12 gauge field gun with 28-inch barrels, about 7½ pounds. Checkered pistol-grip stock and forearm of select walnut; available in field, skeet and trap styles. Made from 1958 to 1981.

With one set of barrels **$1995**
Low-rib Two-barrel Trap Combo **3300**
Vandalia (high-rib) Two-barrel Trap Combo **4160**

Krieghoff Model 32 Standard Grade Single Barrel Trap Gun $1495
Same action as over-and-under. 12 gauge. 32- or 34-inch barrel with high vent rib; modified, improved modified, or full choke. Monte Carlo stock with recoil pad, beavertail forearm.

Krieghoff Neptun Drilling $3800
Same general specifications as Trumpf model, except has side locks with hunting scene engraving. Currently manufactured.

Krieghoff Neptun-Primus Drilling $4300
Deluxe version of Neptun model; has detachable side locks, higher grade engraving and fancier wood. Currently manufactured.

Krieghoff Teck Over/Under Rifle-Shotgun $2100
Box lock. Kersten double crossbolt system. Steel or dural receiver. Split extractor or ejector for shotgun barrel. Single or double triggers. Gauges: 12, 16, 20; latter with either 2¾- or 3-inch chamber. Calibers: 22 Hornet, 222 Rem., 222 Rem. Mag., 7×57r5, 7×64, 7×65r5, 30-30, 300 Win. Mag., 30-06, 308, 9.3×74R. 25-inch barrels with solid rib, folding leaf rear sight, post or bead front sight; over barrel is shotgun, under barrel rifle (later fixed or interchangeable; extra rifle barrel, $175). Weight: 7.9 to 9.5 pounds depending upon type of receiver and caliber. Checkered pistol-grip stock with cheekpiece and semibeavertail forearm of figured walnut, sling swivels. Made 1967 to date. *Note:* This combination gun is similar in appearance to the same model shotgun.

Krieghoff Teck Over-and-Under Shotgun $1950
Box lock. Kersten double crossbolt system. Auto ejector. Single or double triggers. Gauges: 12, 16, 20; latter with either 2¾- or 3-inch chambers. 28-inch vent-rib barrel, modified/full choke. Weight: about 7 pounds. Checkered walnut pistol-grip stock and forearm. Made 1967 to date.

Krieghoff Trumpf Drilling $2700
Box lock. Steel or dural receiver. Split extractor or ejector for shotgun barrels. Double triggers. Gauges: 12, 16, 20; latter with either 2¾- or 3-inch chambers. Calibers: 243, 6.5×57r5, 7×57r5, 7×65r5, 30-06; other calibers available. 25-inch barrels with solid rib, folding leaf rear sight, post or bead front sight; rifle barrel soldered or free floating. Weight: 6.6 to 7.5 pounds depending upon type of receiver, gauge and caliber. Checkered pistol-grip stock with cheekpiece and forearm of figured walnut, sling swivels. Made 1953 to date.

Krieghoff Teck
Over-and-Under

Krieghoff Trumpf Drilling

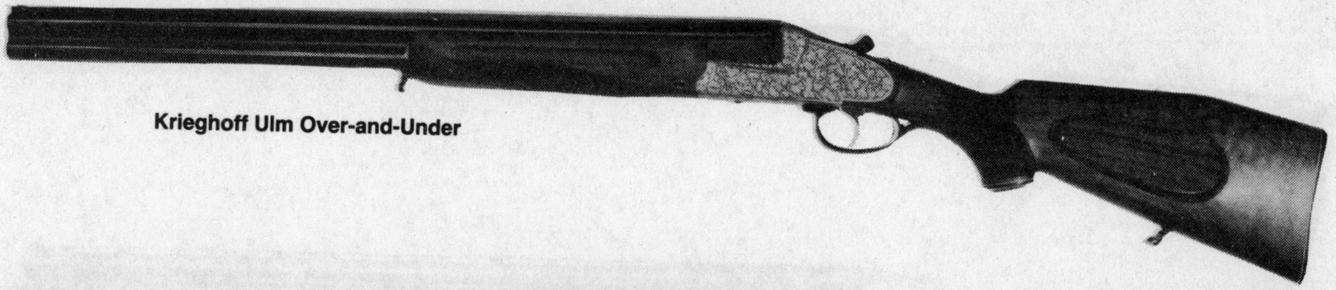

Krieghoff Ulm Over-and-Under

Krieghoff Model ULM-P
Live Pigeon Gun

Krieghoff Ulm Over/Under Rifle-Shotgun $2860
Same general specifications as Teck model, except has side locks with leaf arabesque engraving. Made from 1963 to date. *Note:* This combination gun is similar in appearance to the same model shotgun.

Krieghoff Ulm Over-and-Under Shotgun $3100
Same general specifications as Teck model, except has side locks with leaf arabesque engraving. Made 1958 to date.

Krieghoff Model ULM-P Live Pigeon Gun
Sidelock. Gauge: 12. 28- and 30-inch barrels. Chokes: full/imp. mod. Weight: 8 pounds. Oil-finished, fancy English walnut stock with semibeavertail forearm. Light scroll-work engraving. Tapered, ventilated rib. Made from 1983 to date
Bavaria $6740
Standard 5545

Krieghoff Ulm-Primus Over-and-Under $3770
Deluxe version of Ulm model; detachable side locks, higher grade engraving and fancier wood. Made 1958 to date.

Krieghoff Ulm-Primus O/U Rifle-Shotgun $3500
Deluxe version of Ulm model; has detachable side locks, higher grade engraving and fancier wood. Made 1963 to date. *Note:* This combination gun is similar in appearance to the same model shotgun.

Krieghoff Model ULM-S Skeet Gun
Sidelock. Gauge: 12. Barrel: 28-inch. Chokes: skeet/skeet. Other specifications similar to the Model ULM-P. Made from 1983 to 1986.
Bavaria 6740
Standard $5545

Krieghoff Model ULM-T O/U Live Trap Gun
Over/under sidelock. Gauge: 12. 30-inch barrel. Tapered ventilated rib. Chokes: imp. mod./full.; optional screw-in choke. Custom grade versions command a higher price. Discontinued 1986.
Bavaria $6740
Standard 5545

LANBER SHOTGUNS
Spain

Lanber Model 844 MST Magnum O/U $350
Field grade. Gauge: 12. 3-inch Mag. chambers. 30-inch flat vent-rib barrels. Chokes: mod./full. Weight: 7 lbs. 7 oz. Single selective trigger. Blued barrels and engraved receiver. European walnut stock with hand-checkered pistol grip and forend. Made from 1984 to date.

Lanber Model 844 MST
Magnum Over/Under

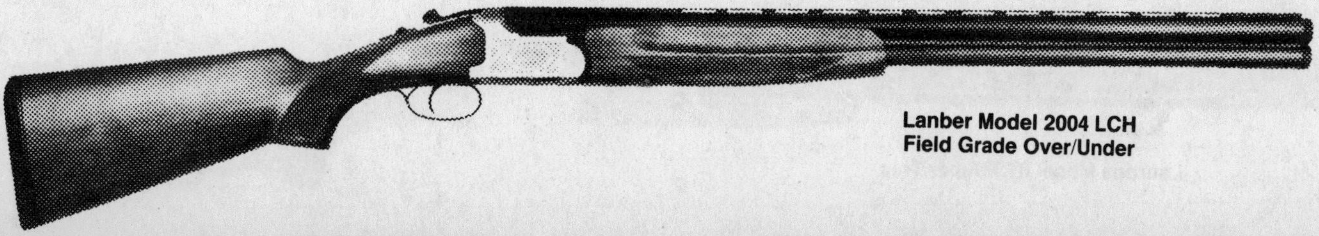

Lanber Model 2004 LCH
Field Grade Over/Under

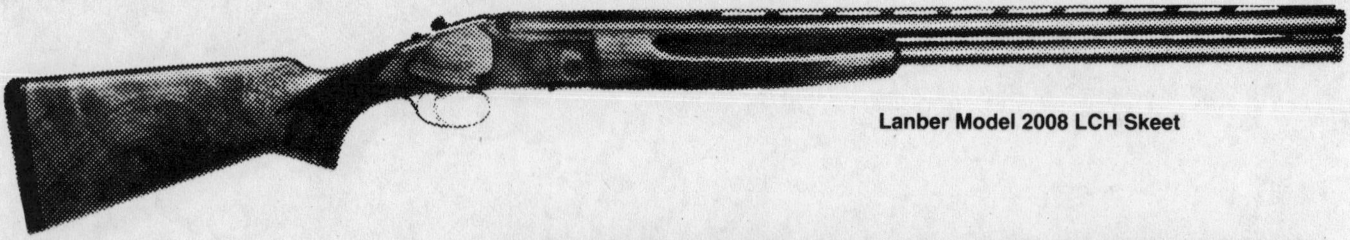

Lanber Model 2008 LCH Skeet

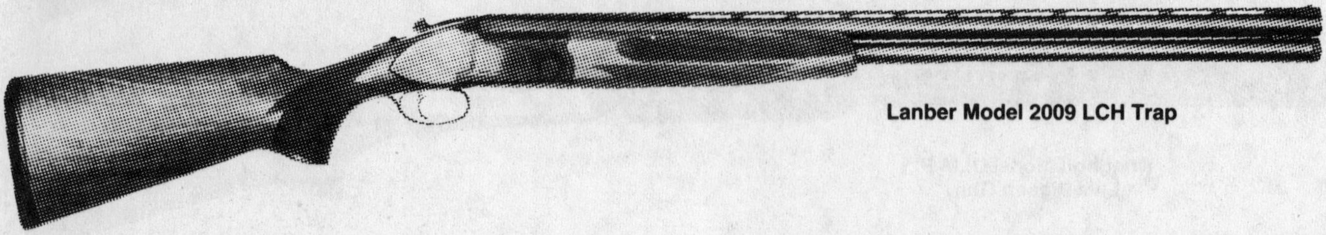

Lanber Model 2009 LCH Trap

Lanber Model 2004 LCH O/U $610
Field grade. Gauge: 12. 2¾-inch chambers. 28-inch flat vent-rib barrels. 5 interchangeable choke tubes: cyl., imp. cyl., mod., imp. mod., full. Weight: about 7 pounds. Single selective trigger. Engraved silver receiver with fine-line scroll. Walnut stock with checkered pistol grip and forend. Rubber recoil pad. Made from 1984 to date.

Lanber Model 2008 LCH O/U Skeet $630
Gauge: 12. 28-inch vent-rib barrels. 5 interchangeable choke tubes: same as Model 2004 LCH. Single selective trigger. Auto safety. Blued barrels and engraved receiver. Hand-checkered European walnut stock with pistol grip. Made from 1984 to date.

Lanber Model 2009 LCH O/U Trap $675
Gauge: 12. 30-inch vent-rib barrels. 3 interchangeable choke tubes: mod., imp. mod., full. Manual safety. Other specifications same as Model 2008 LCH Skeet. Made from 1984 to date.

LAURONA SHOTGUNS
Spain

Laurona Model 82 Super Game Over/Under Shotgun $430
Gauge: 12. 28-inch barrels. Chokes: mod. full or imp. cyl./imp. mod. Weight: 7 pounds. Checkered tulip forend and pistol grip stock of walnut. Plastic recoil pad. Anti-rust black chrome finish. Ventilated rib. Made 1985 to date.

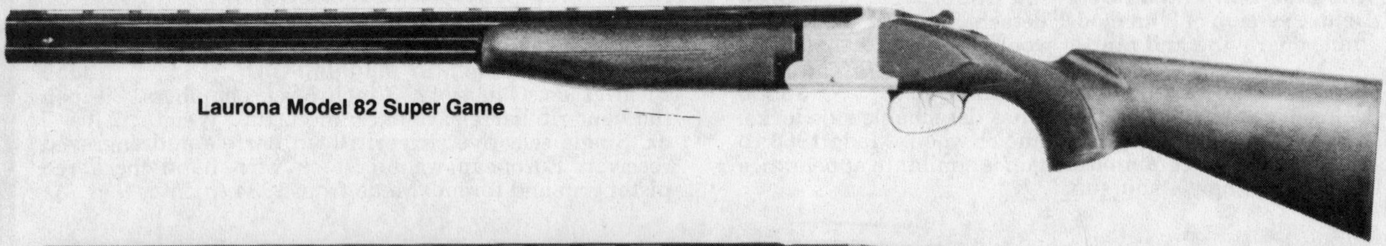

Laurona Model 82 Super Game

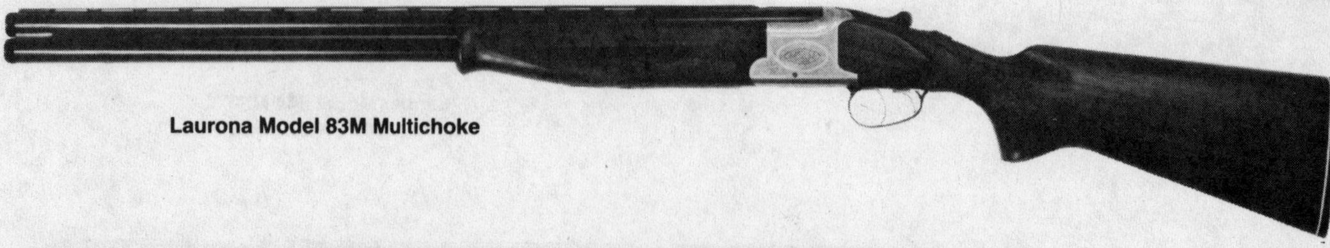

Laurona Model 83M Multichoke

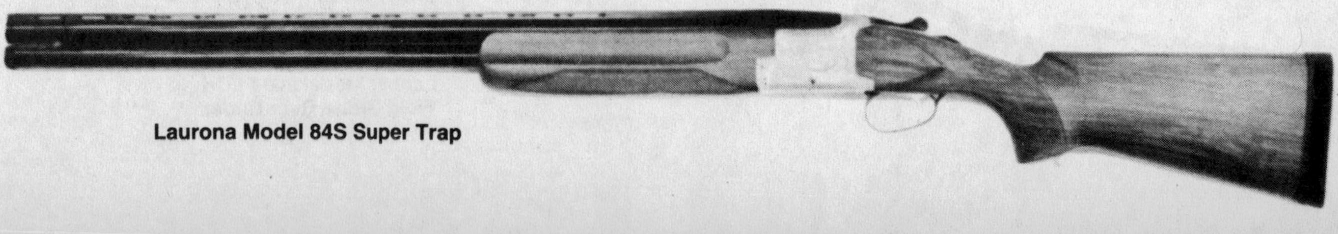

Laurona Model 84S Super Trap

Laurona Model 83M Over/Under Shotgun **$400**
Gauge: 12 or 20. 28- or 26-inch barrels. Weight: about 7 pounds. Chokes: full, imp. mod., mod., imp. cyl. Checkered pistol-grip walnut stock with tulip forend. Made from 1985 to date.

Laurona Model 84S Super Trap Over/Under Shotgun **$500**
Gauge: 12. 29-inch chrome-lined barrels with wide ventilated rib. Chokes: imp. mod./full or mod./full. Weight: 7 lbs. 12 oz. Checkered walnut stock with full pistol grip and beavertail forend. Made from 1985 to date.

LEBEAU-COURALLY SHOTGUNS
Belgium

Lebeau-Courally Boxlock Side-by-Side Shotguns **$7500**
Gauges: 12, 16, 20 and 28. barrels. 26- to 30-inch. Weight: 6½ pounds average. Checkered, hand-rubbed, oil-finished, straight-grip stock of French walnut. Classic forend. Made from 1986 to date.

LEFEVER ARMS COMPANY
Syracuse and Ithaca, N.Y.

Lefever sidelock hammerless double-barrel shotguns were made by Lefever Arms Company of Syracuse, New York, from about 1885 to 1915 (serial numbers 1 to 70,000) when the firm was sold to Ithaca Gun Company of Ithaca, New York. Production of these models was continued at the Ithaca plant until 1919 (serial numbers 70,001 to 72,000). Grades listed are those that appear in the last catalog of the Lefever Gun Company, Syracuse. In 1921, Ithaca introduced the boxlock Lefever Nitro Special double, followed in 1934 by the Lefever Grade A; there also were two single barrel Lefevers made from 1927 to 1942. Manufacture of Lefever brand shotguns was discontinued in 1948. *Note:* "New Lefever" boxlock shotguns made circa 1904-1906 by D. M. Lefever Company, Bowling Green, Ohio, are included in a separate listing.

Lefever A Grade

Lefever A Grade Hammerless Double Barrel Shotgun
Box lock. Plain extractors or auto ejector. Single or double triggers. Gauges: 12, 16, 20, .410. Barrels: 26- to 32-inch, standard chokes. Weight: about 7 pounds in 12 gauge. Checkered pistol-grip stock and forearm. Made 1934 to 1942.
With plain extractors, double triggers **$725**
Extra for automatic ejector **100**
Extra for single trigger **100**
Extra for beavertail forearm **75**

Lefever A Grade Skeet

Lefever A Grade Skeet Model **$1100**
Same as A Grade, except standard features include auto ejector, single trigger, beavertail forearm; 26-inch barrels, skeet boring. Discontinued 1942.

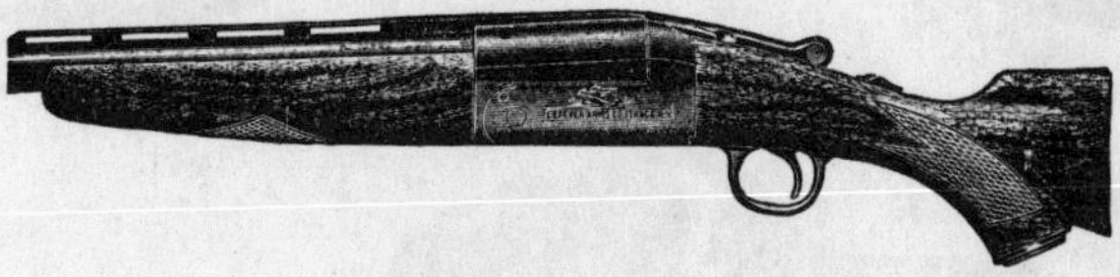

Lefever Single Barrel Trap

Lefever Hammerless Single Barrel Trap Gun . . . **$500**
Box lock. Ejector. 12 gauge only. Barrel lengths: 30- or 32-inch. Vent rib. Weight: about 8 pounds. Checkered pistol-grip stock and forend, recoil pad. Made 1927 to 1942.

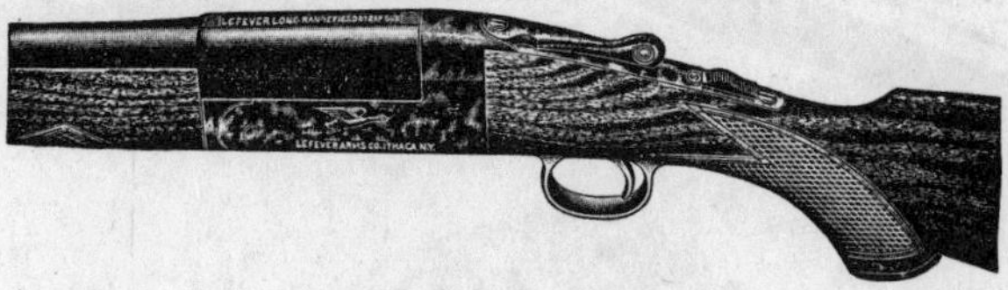

Lefever Long Range

Lefever Long Range Hammerless Single Barrel Field Gun **$250**
Box lock. Plain extractor. Gauges: 12, 16, 20, .410. Barrel lengths: 26- to 32-inch. Weight: 5½ to 7 pounds depending upon gauge and barrel length. Checkered pistol-grip stock and forend. Made from 1927 to 1942.

Lefever Nitro Special

Lefever Nitro Special Hammerless Double
Box lock. Plain extractors. Single or double triggers. Gauges: 12, 16, 20, .410. Barrels: 26- to 32-inch, standard chokes. Weight: about 7 pounds in 12 gauge. Checkered pistol-grip stock and forend. Made 1921 to 1948.
With double triggers **$525**
With single trigger **695**

SHOTGUNS

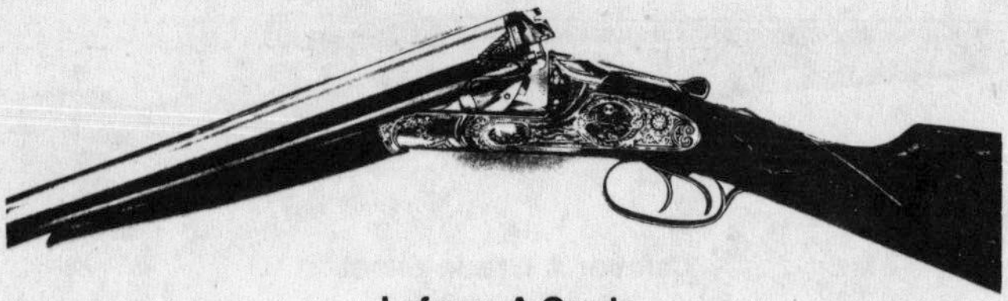

Lefever A Grade

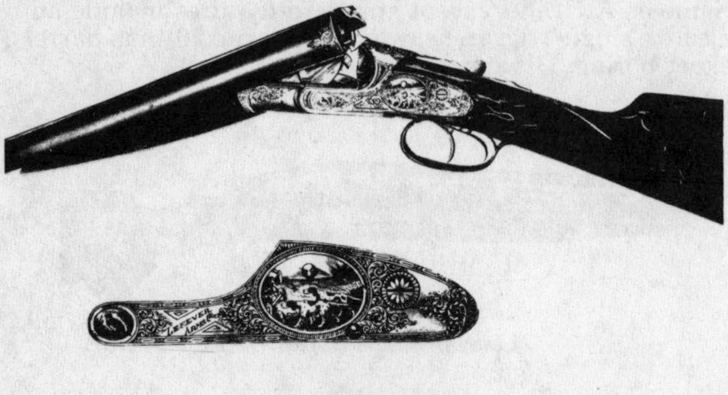

Lefever BE Grade

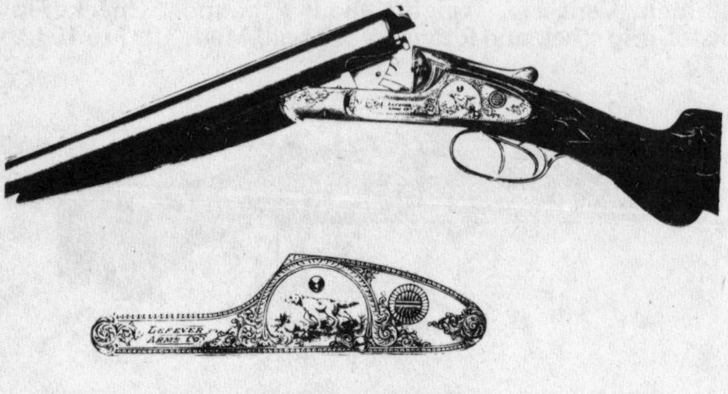

Lefever CE Grade

Lefever DE Grade

Lefever Side Lock Hammerless Doubles

Plain extractors or auto ejectors. Double triggers or selective single trigger. Gauges: 10, 12, 16, 20. Barrels: 26- to 32-inch, standard choke combinations. Weight: 5¾ to 10½ pounds depending upon gauge and barrel length. Checkered walnut straight-grip or pistol-grip stock and forearm. Grades differ chiefly in quality of workmanship, engraving, wood, checkering, etc.; general specifications are the same. DS and DSE Grade guns lack the cocking indicators found on all other models. Suffix "E" means model has auto ejector; also standard on A, AA, Optimus, and Thousand Dollar Grade guns.

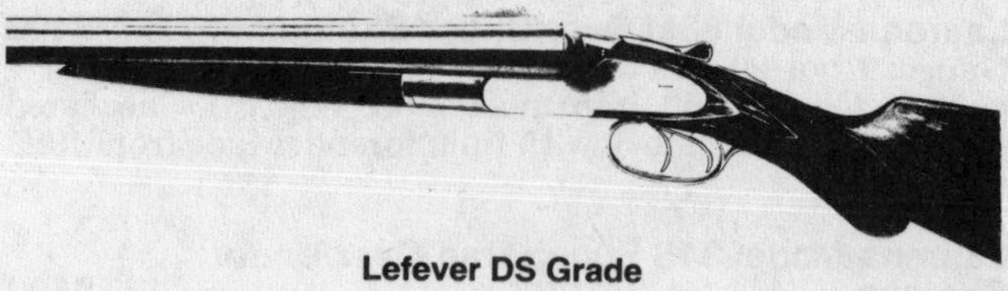

Lefever DS Grade

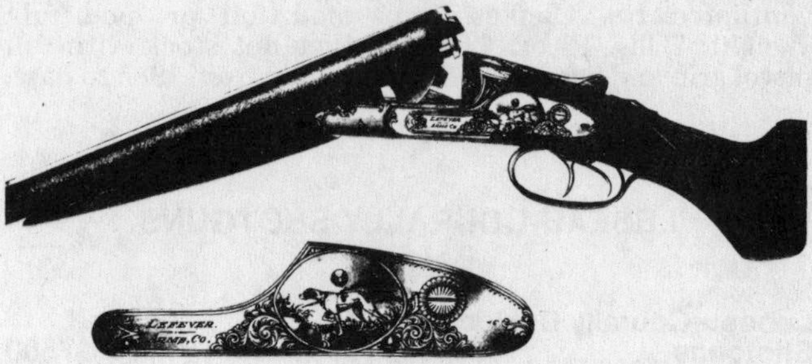

Lefever EE Grade

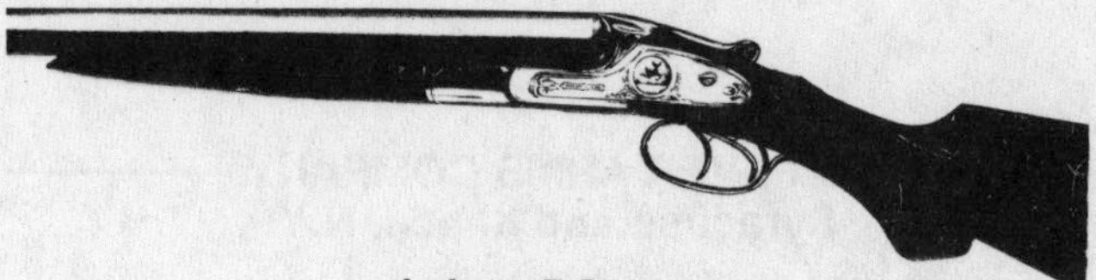

Lefever F Grade

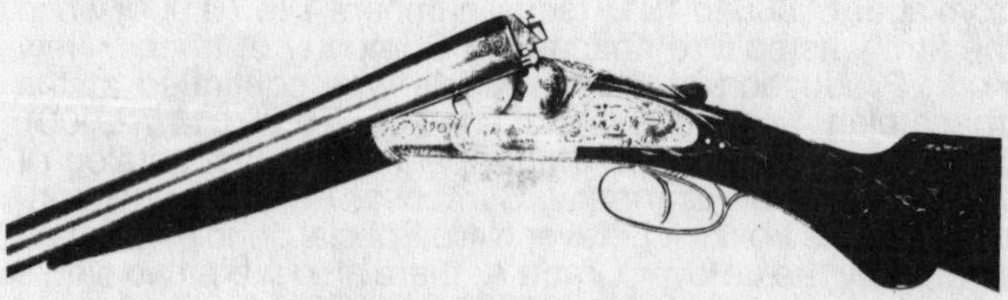

Lefever Optimus Grade

Lefever Side Lock Hammerless Doubles (cont.)

H Grade	$ 1095
HE Grade	1495
G Grade	1550
GE Grade	1795
F Grade	1495
FE Grade	2000
E Grade	1695
EE Grade	2100
D Grade	1895
DE Grade	2500
DS Grade	995
DSE Grade	1195
C Grade	3100
CE Grade	5000
B Grade	4850
BE Grade	7500
A Grade	10,000
AA Grade	15,000
Optimus Grade	20,000
Thousand Dollar Grade	25,000
Extra for single trigger	400

D. M. Lefever Single Trap

D. M. LEFEVER COMPANY
Bowling Green, Ohio

In 1901, D. M. "Uncle Dan" Lefever, founder of the Lefever Arms Company, withdrew from that firm to organize D. M. Lefever, Sons & Company (later D. M. Lefever Company) to manufacture the "New Lefever" boxlock double and single barrel shotguns. These were produced at Bowling Green, Ohio, from about 1904 to 1906, when Dan Lefever died and the factory closed permanently. Grades listed are those that appear in the last catalog of D. M. Lefever Company.

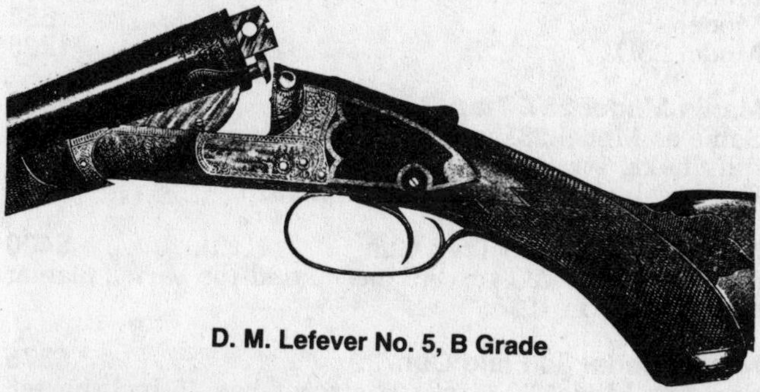

D. M. Lefever No. 5, B Grade

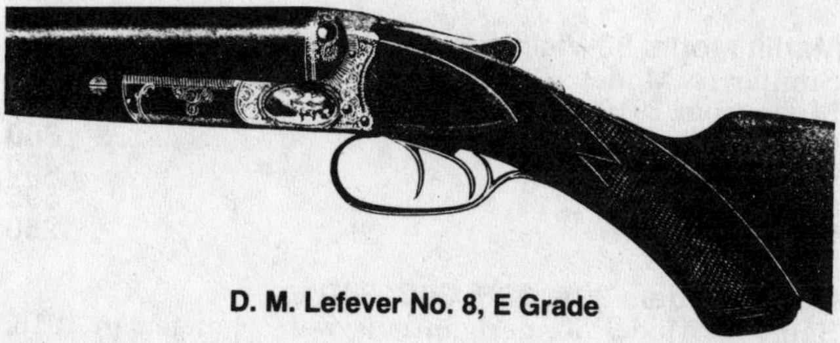

D. M. Lefever No. 8, E Grade

D. M. Lefever Hammerless Double Barrel Shotguns
"New Lefever." Box lock. Auto ejector standard on all grades except O Excelsior, which was regularly supplied with plain extractors (auto ejector offered as an extra). Double triggers or selective single trigger (latter standard on Uncle Dan Grade, extra on all others). Gauges: 12, 16, 20. Barrels: any length and choke combination. Weight:

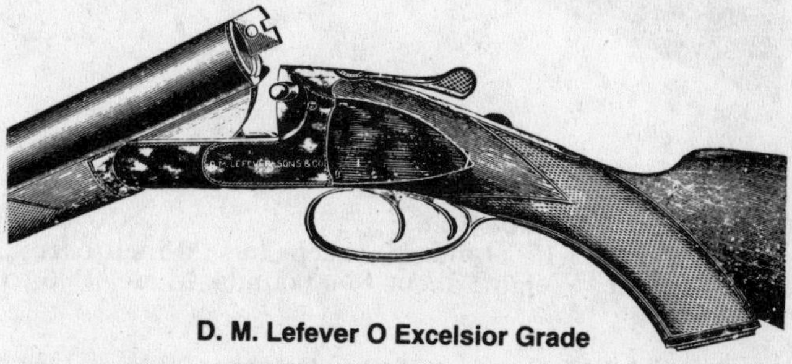

D. M. Lefever O Excelsior Grade

D. M. Lefever Hammerless Doubles (cont.)
5½ to 8 pounds depending upon gauge and barrel length. Checkered walnut straight-grip or pistol-grip stock and forearm. Grades differ chiefly in quality of workmanship, engraving, wood, checkering, etc.; general specifications are the same.

O Excelsior Grade with plain extractors .... **$ 1495**
O Excelsior Grade with automatic ejectors **1595**
No. 9, F Grade **2000**
No. 8, E Grade **3000**
No. 6, C Grade **4000**
No. 5, B Grade **4500**
No. 4, AA Grade **7500**
Uncle Dan Grade **12,000**
Extra for single trigger **400**

D. M. Lefever Single Barrel Trap Gun $1200
Box lock. Auto ejector. 12 gauge only. Barrels: 26- to 32-inches, full choke. Weight: 6½ to 8 pounds, depending upon barrel length. Checkered walnut pistol-grip stock and forearm.

MARLIN FIREARMS CO.
North Haven (formerly New Haven), Conn.

Marlin Model 16 Visible Hammer Slide Action Repeater
Takedown. 16 gauge. 5-shell tubular magazine. Barrels: 26- or 28-inch, standard chokes. Weight: about 6¼ pounds. Pistol-grip stock, grooved slide handle; checkering on higher grades. Difference among grades is in quality of wood, engraving on Grades C and D. Made 1904 to 1910.

Grade A .... **$ 360**
Grade B **475**
Grade C **600**
Grade D **1250**

Marlin Model 17 Brush Gun $430
Same as Model 17 Standard, except has 26-inch barrel, cylinder bore. Weight: about 7 pounds. Made 1906 to 1908.

Marlin Model 17 Standard

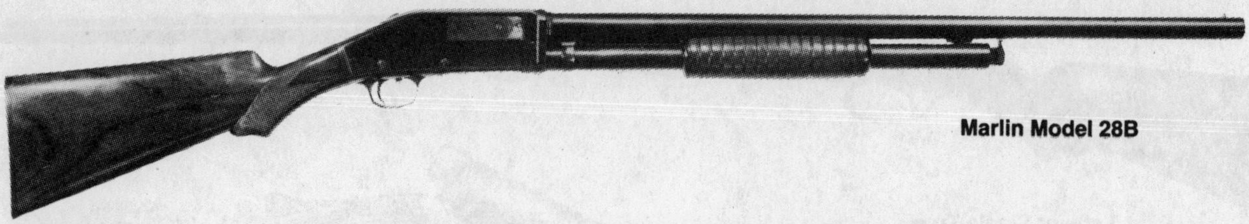

Marlin Model 28B

Marlin Model 17 Riot Gun $380
Same as Model 17 Standard, except has 20-inch barrel, cylinder bore. Weight: about 6 7/8 pounds. Made 1906 to 1908.

Marlin Model 17 Standard Visible Hammer Slide Action Repeater $425
Solid frame. 12 gauge. 5-shot tubular magazine. Barrels: 30- or 32-inch, full choke. Weight: about 7 1/2 pounds. Straight-grip stock, grooved slide handle. Made 1906 to 1908.

Marlin Model 19 Visible Hammer Slide Action Repeater
Similar to Model 1898, but improved, lighter weight, with two extractors, matted sighting groove on receiver top. Weight: about 7 pounds. Made 1906 to 1907.

Grade A	**$ 350**
Grade B	**460**
Grade C	**580**
Grade D	**1250**

Marlin Model 21 Trap Visible Hammer Slide Action Repeater
Similar to Model 19 with same general specifications, except has straight-grip stock. Made 1907 to 1909.

Grade A	**$ 360**
Grade B	**475**
Grade C	**600**
Grade D	**1260**

Marlin Model 24 Visible Hammer Slide Action Repeater
Similar to Model 19, but has improved takedown system and auto recoil safety lock, solid matted rib on frame. Weight: about 7 1/2 pounds. Made 1908 to 1915.

Grade A	**$ 350**
Grade B	**480**
Grade C	**610**
Grade D	**1330**

Marlin Model 26 Brush Gun $315
Same as Model 26 Standard, except has 26-inch barrel, cylinder bore. Weight: about 7 pounds. Made 1909 to 1915.

Marlin Model 26 Riot Gun $350
Same as Model 26 Standard, except has 20-inch barrel, cylinder bore. Weight: about 6 7/8 pounds. Made 1909 to 1915.

Marlin Model 26 Standard Visible Hammer Slide Action Repeater $295
Similar to Model 24 Grade A, except solid frame and straight-grip stock. 30- or 32-inch full choke barrel. Weight: about 7 1/8 pounds. Made from 1909 to 1915.

Marlin Model 28 Hammerless Slide Action Repeater
Takedown. 12 gauge. 5-shot tubular magazine. Barrels: 26-, 28-, 30-, 32-inch, standard chokes; matted-top barrel except on Model 28D which has solid matted rib. Weight: about 8 pounds. Pistol-grip stock, grooved slide handle; checkering on higher grades. Grades differ in quality of wood, engraving on Models 28C and 28D. Made from 1913 to 1922; all but Model 28A discont. in 1915.

Model 28A	**$ 360**
Model 28B	**470**
Model 28C	**650**
Model 28D	**1225**

Marlin Model 28T Trap Gun $575
Same as Model 28, except has 30-inch matted-rib barrel, full choke, straight-grip stock with high fluted comb of fancy walnut, checkered. Made in 1915.

Marlin Model 28TS Trap Gun $400
Same as Model 28T, except has matted-top barrel, plainer stock. Made in 1915.

Marlin Model 30 Field Gun $375
Same as Model 30 Grade B, except has 25-inch barrel, modified choke, straight-grip stock. Made 1913 to 1914.

Marlin Model 30 Visible Hammer Slide Action Repeater
Similar to Model 16, but with Model 24 improvements. Made from 1910 to 1914.

Grade A	**$ 360**
Grade B	**480**
Grade C	**595**
Grade D	**1250**

Marlin Models 30A, 30B, 30C, 30D
Same as Model 30; designations were changed in 1915. Also available in 20 gauge with 25- or 28-inch barrel; matted-top barrel on all grades. Suffixes "A," "B," "C" and "D" correspond to former grades. Made in 1915.

Model 30A	**$ 300**
Model 30B	**390**
Model 30C	**580**
Model 30D	**1050**

Marlin Model 30 Grade D

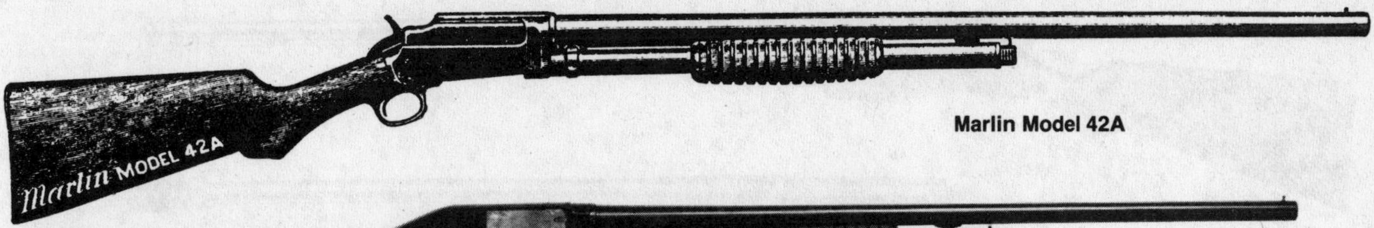

Marlin Model 42A

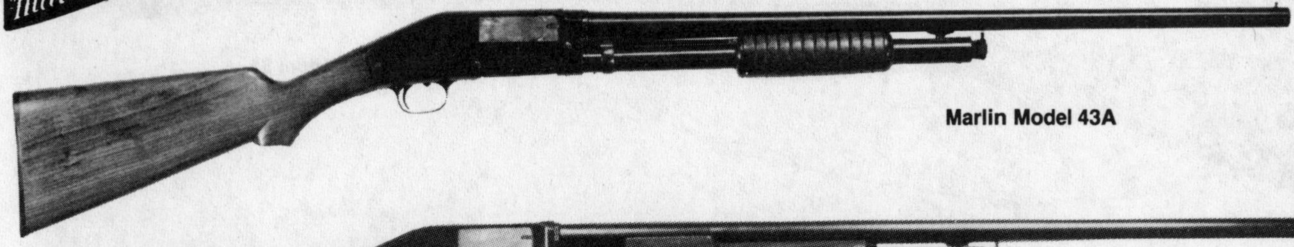

Marlin Model 43A

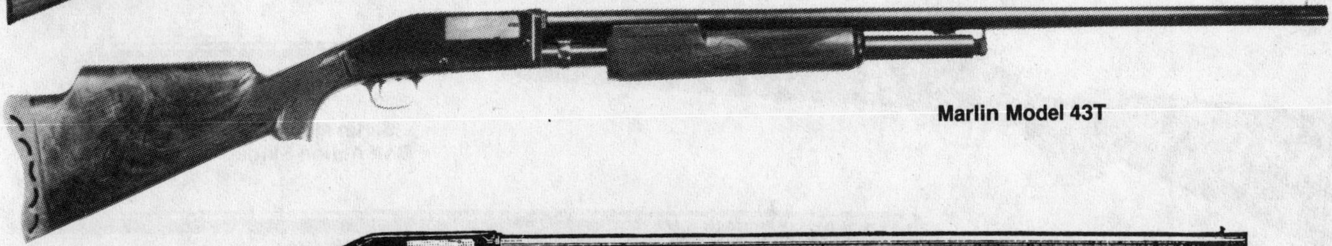

Marlin Model 43T

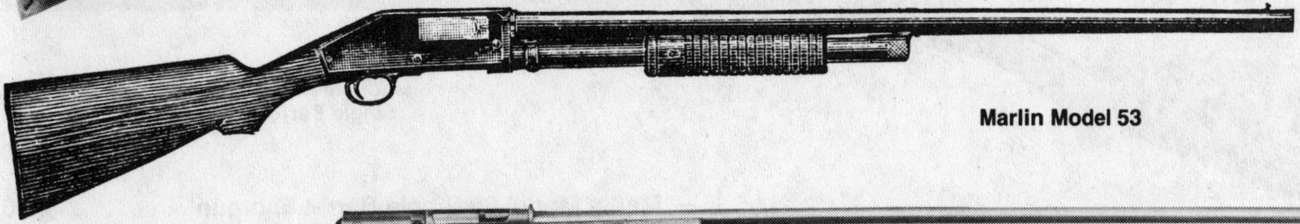

Marlin Model 53

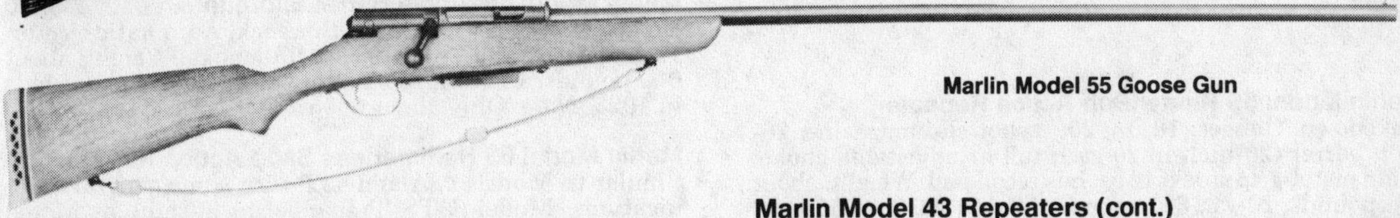

Marlin Model 55 Goose Gun

Marlin Model 31 Hammerless Slide Action Repeater
Similar to Model 28, except scaled down for 16 and 20 gauges. Barrels: 25-inch (20 gauge only), 26-inch (16 gauge only), 28-inch; all with matted top; standard chokes. Weight: 16 ga., about 6¾ pounds; 20 ga., about 6 pounds. Pistol-grip stock, grooved slide handle; checkering on higher grades; straight-grip stock optional on Model 31D. Made from 1915 to 1917; Model 31A until 1922.

Model 31A . . . . $ 360
Model 31B 475
Model 31C 600
Model 31D 1240

Marlin Model 31F Field Gun $475
Same as Model 31B, except has 25-inch barrel, modified choke, straight- or pistol-grip stock. Made 1915 to 1917.

Marlin Model 42A Visible Hammer Slide Action Repeater $230
Similar to pre-World War I Model 24 Grade A with same general specifications, but not of as high quality. Made from 1922 to 1934.

Marlin Model 43 Hammerless Slide Action Repeater
Similar to pre-World War I Models 28A, 28T and 28TS, with same general specifications, but not of as high quality. Made 1923 to 1930.

Marlin Model 43 Repeaters (cont.)
Model 43A $245
Model 43T 500
Model 43TS 510

Marlin Model 44 Hammerless Slide Action Repeater
Similar to pre-World War I Model 31A, with same general specifications, but not of as high quality. 20 gauge only. Model 44A is a standard grade field gun. Model 44S Special Grade has checkered stock and slide handle of fancy walnut. Made 1923 to 1935.

Model 44A $345
Model 44S 430

Marlin Model 49 Visible Hammer Slide Action Repeating Shotgun $410
Economy version of Model 42A, offered as a bonus on the purchase of four shares of Marlin stock. About 3000 were produced. Made 1925 to 1928.

Marlin Model 53 Hammerless Slide Action Repeater $345
Similar to Model 43A, with same general specifications. Made 1929 to 1930.

Marlin Model 55 Goose Gun $120
Same as Model 55 Hunter, except chambered for 12 gauge 3-inch magnum shell, has 36-inch barrel, full choke, swivels and sling. Weight: about 8 pounds. Made 1962 to date.

Marlin Model 55 Hunter

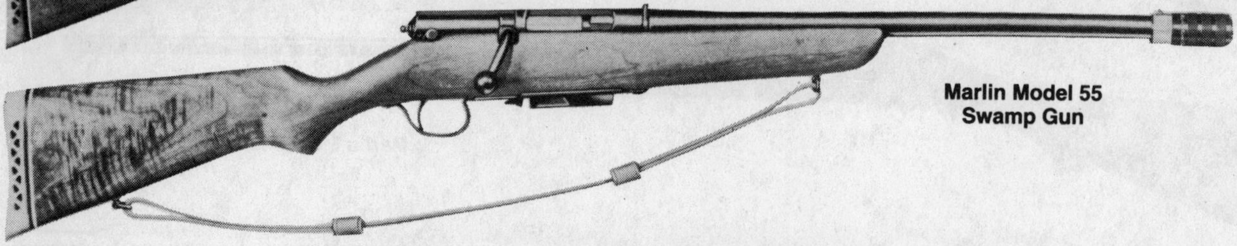

Marlin Model 55
Swamp Gun

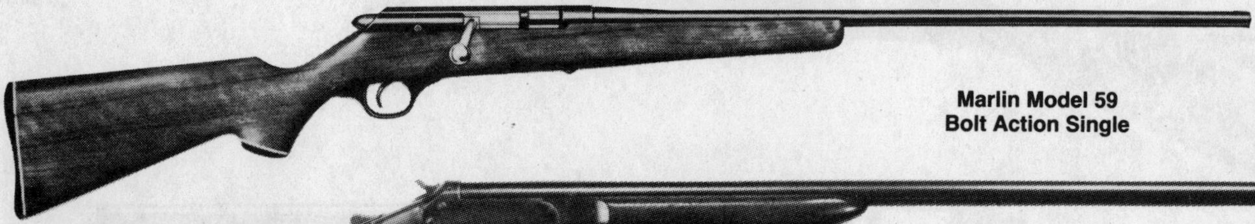

Marlin Model 59
Bolt Action Single

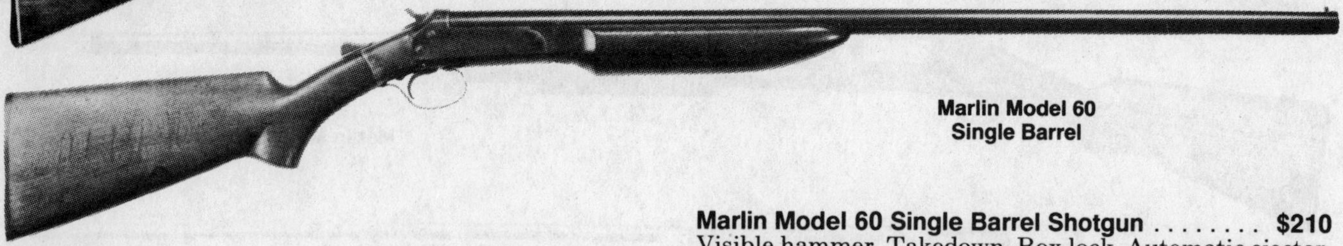

Marlin Model 60
Single Barrel

Marlin Model 55 Hunter Bolt Action Repeater
Takedown. Gauges: 12, 16, 20. 2-shot clip magazine. 28-inch barrel (26-inch in 20 ga.), full or adjustable choke. Plain pistol-grip stock; 12 ga. has recoil pad. Weight: about 7¼ pounds; 20 ga., 6½ pounds. Made 1950 to 1965.
With plain barrel . . . . **$ 85**
With adjustable choke **100**

Marlin Model 55 Swamp Gun **$100**
Same as Model 55 Hunter except chambered for 12 gauge 3-inch magnum shell, has 20½-inch barrel with adjustable choke, sling swivels. Weight: about 6½ pounds. Made 1963 to 1965.

Marlin Model 55S Slug Gun **$135**
Same as Model 55 Goose Gun, except has 24-inch barrel, cylinder bore, rifle sights. Weight: about 7½ pounds. Made 1974 to date.

Marlin Model 59 Auto-Safe Bolt Action Single . . . **$70**
Takedown. Auto thumb safety. 410 gauge. 24-inch barrel, full choke. Weight: about 5 pounds. Plain pistol-grip stock. Made from 1959 to 1961.

Marlin Model 60 Single Barrel Shotgun **$210**
Visible hammer. Takedown. Box lock. Automatic ejector. 12 gauge. 30- or 32-inch barrel, full choke. Weight: about 6½ pounds. Pistol-grip stock, beavertail forearm. Made in 1923. *Note:* Only about 600 were produced.

Marlin Model 63 Hammerless Slide Action Repeater
Similar to Models 43A and 43T with same general specifications. Model 63TS Trap Special is same as Model 63T Trap Gun except stock style and dimensions to order. Made 1931 to 1935.
Model 63A **$230**
Model 63T or 63TS **375**

Marlin Model 90 Standard Over-and-Under Shotgun
Hammerless. Box lock. Double triggers; non-selective single trigger was available as an extra on prewar guns except .410. Gauges: 12, 16, 20, .410. Barrels: plain; 26-, 28- or 30-inch; chokes improved cylinder/modified or modified/full; barrel design changed in 1949, eliminating full-length rib between barrels. Weight: 12 ga., about 7½ lbs.; 16 and 20 ga., about 6¼ lbs. Checkered pistol-grip stock and forearm, recoil pad standard on prewar guns. Postwar production: Model 90-DT (double trigger), Model 90-ST (single trigger). Made 1937 to 1958.
With double triggers **$450**
With single trigger **560**

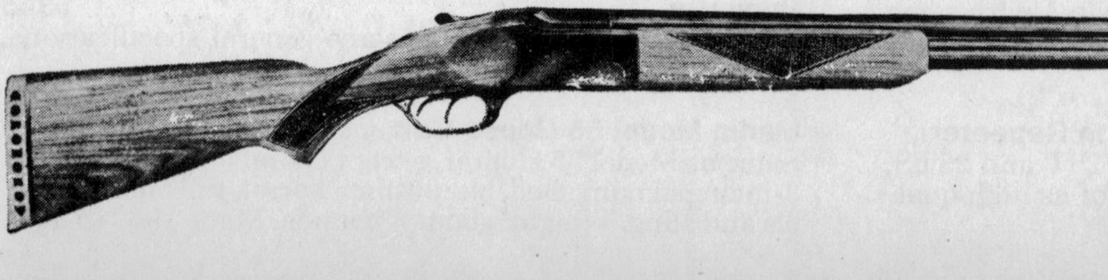

Marlin Model 90
Standard Over-and-Under

Marlin Model 120 Magnum

Marlin Model 410

Marlin Model 5510
Super Goose 10

Marlin Model 120 Magnum Slide Action Repeater $250
Hammerless. Takedown. 12 gauge (3-inch). 4-shot tubular magazine. Barrels: 26-inch vent rib, improved cylinder; 28-inch vent rib, modified choke; 30-inch vent rib, full choke; 38-inch plain, full choke; 40-inch plain, full choke; 26-inch slug barrel with rifle sights, improved cylinder. Weight: about $7\frac{3}{4}$ pounds. Checkered pistol-grip stock and forearm, recoil pad. Made 1971 to 1985.

Marlin Model 410 Lever Action Repeater $495
Action similar to that of Marlin Model 93 rifle. Visible hammer. Solid frame. .410 gauge ($2\frac{1}{2}$-inch shell). 5-shot tubular magazine. 22- or 26-inch barrel, full choke. Weight: about 6 pounds. Plain pistol-grip stock and grooved beavertail forearm. Made 1929 to 1932.

Marlin Model 1898 Visible Hammer Slide Action Repeater
Takedown. 12 gauge. 5-shell tubular magazine. Barrels: 26-, 28-, 30-, 32-inch; standard chokes. Weight: about $7\frac{1}{4}$

Marlin Model 1898 Repeater (cont.)
pounds. Pistol-grip stock, grooved slide handle; checkering on higher grades. Difference among grades is in quality of wood, engraving on Grades C and D. Made 1898 to 1905. *Note:* This was the first Marlin shotgun.

Grade A (Field)	$ 525
Grade B	685
Grade C	900
Grade D	1800

Marlin Model 5510 Super Goose 10 . . . . $190
Similar to Model 55 Goose Gun, except chambered for 10 gauge $3\frac{1}{2}$-inch magnum shell, has 34-inch heavy barrel, full choke. Weight: about $10\frac{1}{2}$ pounds. Made 1976 to 1985.

Marlin Premier Mark I Slide Action Repeater . . . $150
Hammerless. Takedown. 12 gauge. Magazine holds 3 shells. Barrels: 30-inch full choke, 28-inch modified, 26-inch improved cylinder or skeet choke. Weight: about 6 pounds. Plain pistol-grip stock and forearm. Made in France 1960 to 1963.

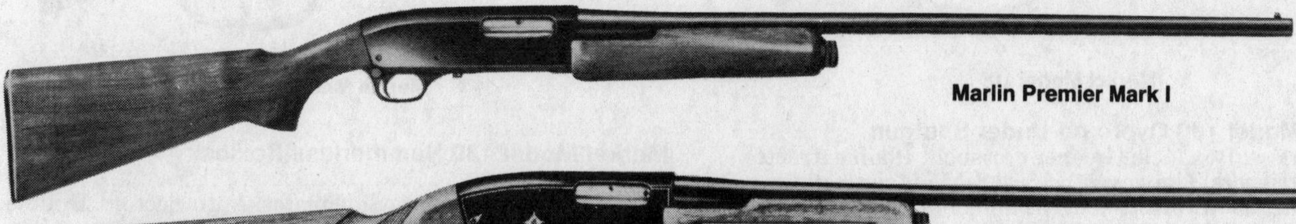
Marlin Premier Mark I

Marlin Premier Mark II

Marlin Premier Mark IV

Marlin-Glenfield Model 50

Marlin Premier Mark II **$200**
Same as Premier Mark I, except engraved receiver, checkered stock and forearm. Made 1960 to 1963.

Marlin Premier Mark IV
Same as Premier Mark II, except more elaborate engraving, fancier wood. Made 1960 to 1963.
With plain barrel **$295**
With ventilated-rib barrel **325**

Marlin-Glenfield Model 50 Bolt Action Repeater . . **$65**
Similar to Model 55 Hunter, except chambered for 12 or 20 gauge 3-inch magnum shell; has 28-inch barrel in 12 gauge, 26-inch in 20 gauge, full choke. Made 1966 to 1974.

Marlin-Glenfield 778 Slide Action Repeater
Hammerless. 12 gauge 2$^3/_4$-inch or 3-inch. 4-shot tubular magazine. Barrels: 26-inch improved cylinder, 28-inch modified, 30-inch full, 38-inch MXR, 20-inch slug barrel. Weight: 7$^3/_4$ pounds. Checkered pistol grip. Made from 1979 to date.
With plain barrel **$140**
With ventilated-rib barrel **175**

GEBRÜDER MERKEL
Suhl, Germany

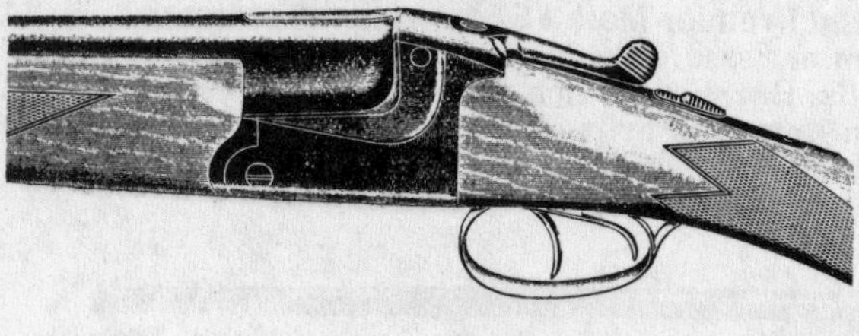

Merkel Model 100

Merkel Model 100 Over-and-Under Shotgun
Hammerless. Box lock. Greener crossbolt. Plain extractor. Double triggers. Gauges: 12, 16, 20. Made with plain or ribbed barrels in various lengths and chokes. Plain finish, no engraving. Checkered forend and stock with pistol grip and cheekpiece or English style. Made prior to WWII.
With plain barrel . . . . **$ 995**
With ribbed barrel **1050**

Merkel Model 101

Merkel Models 101 and 101E Over/Unders
Same as Model 100, except ribbed barrel standard, has separate extractors (ejectors on Model 101E), English engraving. Made prior to World War II.
Model 101 . . . . **$1295**
Model 101E **1350**

Merkel Model 127

Merkel Model 127 Hammerless Sidelock Double **$15,000**
Holland & Holland system, hand-detachable locks. Auto ejectors. Double triggers. Made in all standard gauges, barrel lengths and chokes. Checkered forend and stock with pistol grip and cheekpiece or English style. This is a highest quality deluxe gun, elaborately engraved in arabesque or hunting scene pattern. Manufactured prior to World War II.

Merkel Model 130

Merkel Model 130 Hammerless Boxlock Double **$7500**
Anson & Deeley system. Side plates. Auto ejectors. Double triggers. Elaborate hunting scene or arabesque engraving. Made in all standard gauges, various barrel lengths and chokes. Checkered forend and stock with pistol grip and cheekpiece or English style. Manufactured prior to World War II.

Merkel Model 147E Hammerless Boxlock Double Barrel Shotgun **$1250**
Anson & Deeley system. Auto ejectors. Double triggers. Gauges: 12, 16, 20 (3-inch chambers available in 12 and 20 gauge). Barrels: 26-inch standard, other lengths available; any standard choke combination. Weight: about 6$^1/_2$ pounds. Checkered straight-grip stock and forearm. Currently manufactured.

Merkel Model 147E

Merkel Model 147S

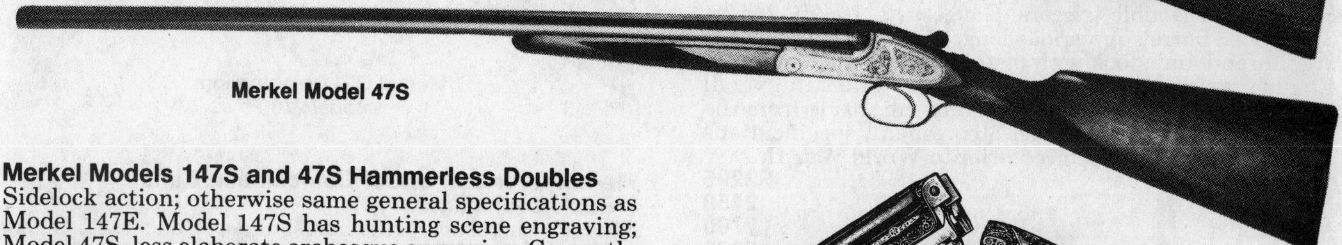

Merkel Model 47S

Merkel Models 147S and 47S Hammerless Doubles
Sidelock action; otherwise same general specifications as Model 147E. Model 147S has hunting scene engraving; Model 47S, less elaborate arabesque engraving. Currently manufactured.

Model 147S **$3200**
Model 47S **1800**

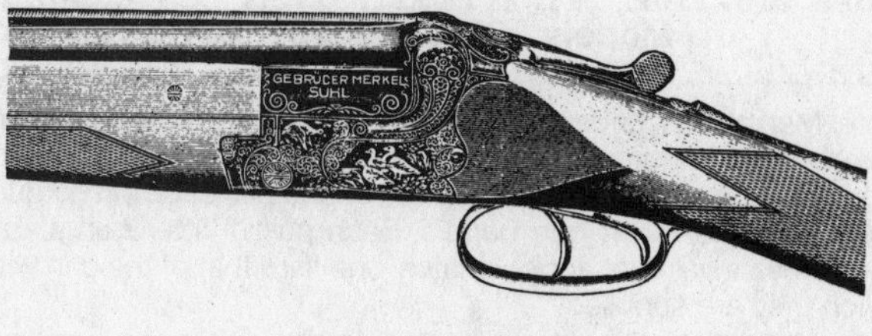

Merkel Model 201

Merkel Models 200, 200E, 201, 201E, 202 and 202E Over-and-Under Shotguns
Hammerless. Box lock. Kersten double crossbolt. Scalloped frame. Sideplates on Models 202 and 202E. Arabesque engraving, hunting engraving supplied on all except Models 200 and 200E. "E" models have ejectors, others have separate extractors. Signal pins. Double triggers. Gauges: 12, 16, 20, 24, 28, 32 (last three not available in postwar guns). Ribbed barrels in various lengths and chokes. Weight: $5\frac{3}{4}$ to $7\frac{1}{2}$ pounds depending upon barrel length and gauge. Checkered forend and stock with pistol grip and cheekpiece or English style. The 200, 201, and 202 differ in overall quality, engraving, wood, checkering, etc.; aside from the dummy sideplates on Models 202 and 202E, general specifications are the same. Models 200, 201, 202, and 202E, which were made before World War II, are discontinued.

Model 200 . . . . **$1100**
Model 200E **1350**
Model 201 . . . . **1400**
Model 201E **2650**
Model 202 . . . . **2850**
Model 202E **3100**

Merkel Model 203E

Merkel Model 203E Over-and-Under Shotgun . . $3850
Hammerless. Hand-detachable side locks, Kersten fastening, auto ejectors, double triggers. Arabesque engraving standard, hunting engraving also supplied. Gauges: 12, 16, 20. Ribbed barrels in various lengths and chokes. Checkered forend and stock with pistol grip and cheekpiece or English style. Currently manufactured.

Merkel Model 204E Over-and-Under Shotgun . . $4500
Similar to Model 203E; has Merkel sidelocks, fine English engraving. Made prior to World War II.

Merkel Model 300E

Merkel Models 300, 300E, 301, 301E and 302 O/U
Merkel-Anson system box lock. Kersten double crossbolt, two underlugs, scalloped frame, sideplates on Model 302. Arabesque or hunting engraving. "E" models and Model

Merkel Model 302

Merkel Models 300, 301, 302 (cont.)
302 have auto ejectors, others have separate extractors. Signal pins. Double triggers. Gauges: 12, 16, 20, 24, 28, 32. Ribbed barrels in various lengths and chokes. Checkered forend and stock with pistol grip and cheekpiece or English style. Grades 300, 301 and 302 differ in overall quality, engraving, wood, checkering, etc.; aside from the dummy sideplates on Model 302, general specifications are the same. Manufactured prior to World War II.
Model 300 . . . . **$2295**
Model 300E **2450**
Model 301 . . . . **2700**
Model 301E **5300**
Model 302 . . . . **5500**

Merkel Model 303E Over-and-Under Shotgun $10,500
Similar to Model 203E. Has Kersten crossbolt, double underlugs, Holland & Holland-type hand-detachable side locks, auto ejectors. This is a finer gun than Model 203E. Currently manufactured.

Merkel Model 304E

Merkel Model 304E Over/Under Shotgun $15,000
Special version of the Model 303E-type, but higher quality throughout. This is the top grade Merkel over/under. Currently manufactured.

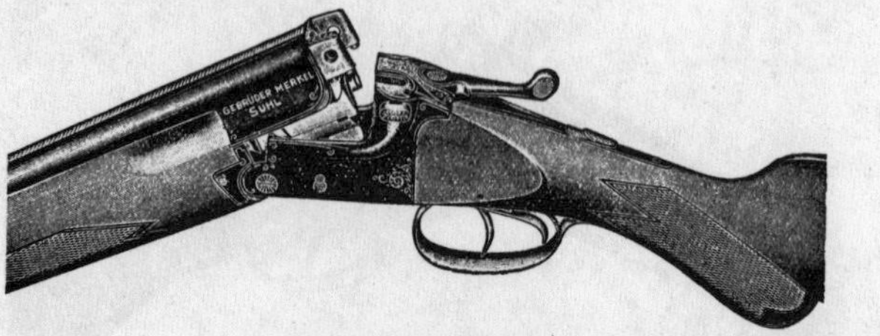

Merkel Model 400

Merkel Models 400, 400E, 401, 401E Over/Unders
Similar to Model 101 except have Kersten double crossbolt, arabesque engraving on Models 400 and 400E, hunting engraving on Models 401 and 401E, finer general quality. "E" models have Merkel ejectors, others have separate extractors. Made prior to World War II.

Merkel Models 400, 401 (cont.)
Model 400 . . . . **$1195**
Model 400E **1250**
Model 401 . . . . **1350**
Model 401E **1695**

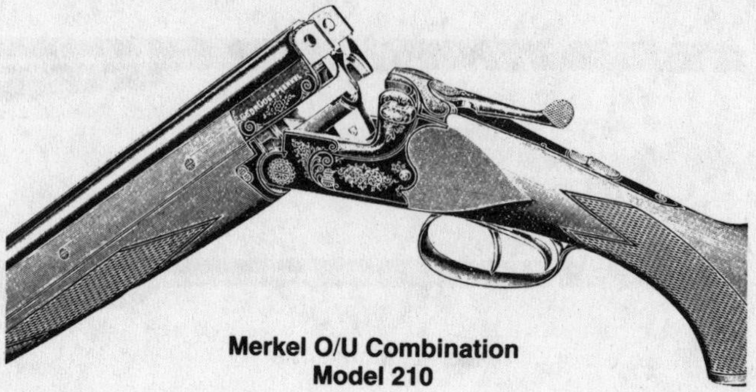

Merkel O/U Combination
Model 210

Merkel Over-and-Under Combination Guns ("Bock-Büchsflinten")
Shotgun barrel over, rifle barrel under. Gauges: 12, 16, 20; calibers: 5.6×35 Vierling, 7×57r5, 8×57JR, 8×60R Magnum, 9.3×53r5, 9.3×72r5, 9.3×74R and others. Various barrel lengths, chokes and weights. Other specifications and values correspond to those of Merkel over/under shotguns listed below. Currently manufactured.
Models 410, 410E, 411E . . . . **see shotgun Models 400, 400E, 401, 401E respectively**
Models 210, 210E, 211, 211E, 212, 212E . . **see shotgun Models 200, 200E, 201, 201E, 202, 202E**

Note: Merkel over/under guns were often supplied with accessory barrels, interchangeable to convert the gun into an arm of another type; for example, a set might consist of one pair each of shotgun, rifle and combination gun barrels. Each pair of interchangeable barrels has a value of approximately one-third that of the gun with which they are supplied.

Merkel Anson Drilling
Model 144

Merkel Anson Drillings
Three-barrel combination guns; usually made with double shotgun barrels, over rifle barrel, although "Doppelbüchsdrillingen" were made with two rifle barrels over and shotgun barrel under. Hammerless. Box lock. Anson & Deeley system. Side clips. Plain extractors. Double triggers. Gauges: 12, 16, 20; rifle calibers: 7×57r5, 8×57JR and 9.3×74R are most common, but these guns were produced in other calibers from 5.6mm to 10.75mm. Barrels: standard drilling, 25.6 inches; short drilling, 21.6 inches.

Merkel Anson Drillings (cont.)
Checkered pistol-grip stock and forend. The three models listed differ chiefly in overall quality, grade of wood, etc.; general specifications are the same. Manufactured prior to World War II.
Model 144 . . . . **$7000**
Model 142 . . . . **5500**
Model 145 . . . . **5500**

MIIDA SHOTGUNS

Manufactured for Marubeni America Corp., New York, N.Y., by Olin-Kodensha Co., Tochigi, Japan

Miida Model 612 Field Grade Over-and-Under . . $725
Box lock. Auto ejectors. Selective single trigger. 12 gauge. Barrels: vent rib; 26-inch, improved cylinder/modified; 28-inch, modified/full choke. Weight: with 26-inch barrel, 6 lbs. 11 oz. Checkered pistol-grip stock and forearm. Made 1972 to 1974.

Miida Model 2100 Skeet Gun $895
Similar to Model 612, except has more elaborate engraving on frame (50 percent coverage), skeet-style stock and forearm of select grade wood; 27-inch vent-rib barrels, skeet choke. Weight: 7 lbs. 11 oz. Made from 1972 to 1974.

Miida Model 2200T Trap Gun, Model 2200S Skeet Gun $945
Similar to Model 612, except more elaborate engraving on frame (60 percent coverage), trap- or skeet-style stock and semibeavertail forearm of fancy walnut, recoil pad on trap stock. Barrels: wide vent rib; 29¾-inch, improved modified/full choke on Trap Gun; 27-inch, skeet choke on Skeet Gun. Weight: Trap, 7 lbs. 14 oz.; Skeet, 7 lbs. 11 oz. Made 1972 to 1974.

Miida Model 2300T Trap Gun, Model 2300S Skeet Gun $1000
Same as Models 2200T and 2200S, except more elaborate engraving on frame (70 percent coverage). Made from 1972 to 1974.

Miida Grandee Model GRT Trap Gun, Model GRS Skeet Gun $2100
Box lock with side plates. Frame, breech ends of barrels, trigger guard and locking lever fully engraved and gold inlaid. Auto ejectors. Selective single trigger. 12 gauge. Barrels: wide vent rib; 29-inch, full choke on Trap Gun; 27-inch, skeet choke on Skeet Gun. Weight: Trap, 7 lbs. 14 oz.; Skeet, 7 lbs. 11 oz. Trap- or skeet-style stock and semibeavertail forearm of extra fancy wood, recoil pad on trap stock. Made 1972 to 1974.

Miida Model 612

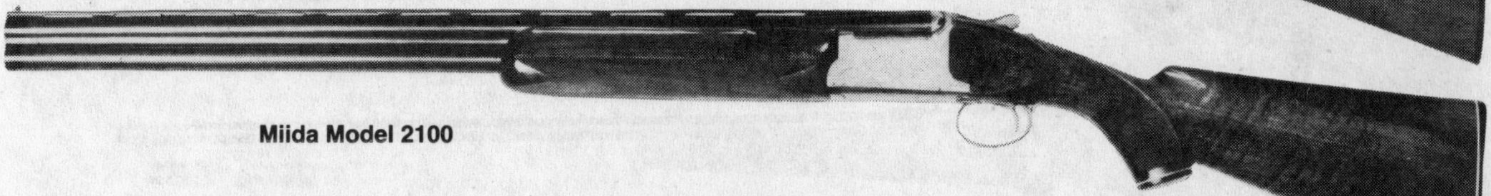
Miida Model 2100

Miida Model 2200T

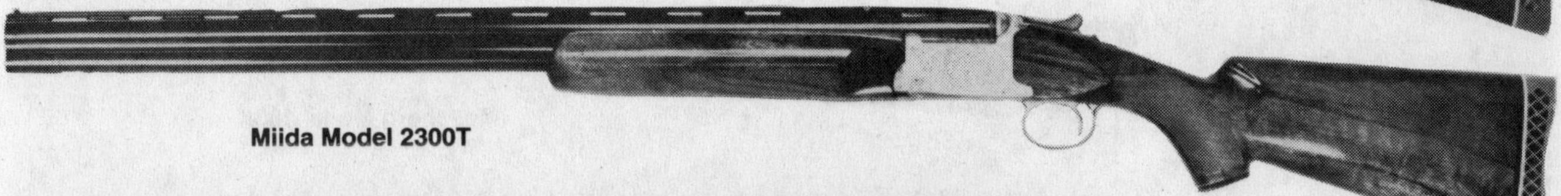
Miida Model 2300T

Miida Grandee Model GRT

MONTGOMERY WARD

See shotgun listings under "W."

MORRONE SHOTGUN

Manufactured by Rhode Island Arms Company, Hope Valley, R.I.

Morrone Standard Model 46 Over-and-Under . . . $725
Box lock. Plain extractors. Non-selective single trigger. Gauges: 12, 20. Barrels: plain, vent rib; 26-inch, improved cylinder/modified, 28-inch, modified/full choke. Weight: about 7 lbs., 12 ga.; 6 lbs., 20 ga. Checkered straight- or pistol-grip stock and forearm. Made from 1949 to 1953. *Note:* Less than 500 of these guns were produced, about 50 in 20 gauge; a few had vent-rib barrels. Value shown is for 12 gauge with plain barrels; the very rare 20 gauge and vent-rib types should bring considerably more.

O. F. MOSSBERG & SONS, INC.

North Haven, Connecticut
Formerly of New Haven, Conn.

Mossberg Model 83D or 183D $90
3-shot. Takedown. 410-gauge only. 2-shell fixed, top-loading magazine. 23-inch barrel with two interchangeable choke tubes (modified, full). Later production had 24-inch barrel. Plain, one-piece, pistol-grip stock. Weight: about 5½ pounds. Originally designated Model 83D, changed in 1947 to Model 183D. Made 1940 to 1971.

Mossberg Model 85D or 185D Bolt Action Repeating Shotgun $85
Takedown. 3-shot. 20 gauge only. 2-shell detachable box magazine. 25-inch barrel, three interchangeable choke tubes (full, modified, improved cylinder). Later production had 26-inch barrel with full and improved cylinder choke tubes. Weight: about 6¼ pounds. Plain, one-piece, pistol-grip stock. Originally designated Model 85D, changed in 1947 to Model 185D. Made 1940 to 1971.

Mossberg Model 183K $90
Same as Model 183D, except has 25-inch barrel with variable C-Lect-Choke instead of interchangeable choke tubes. Made 1953 to 1986.

Mossberg Model 185K $95
Same as Model 185D, except has variable C-Lect-Choke instead of interchangeable choke tubes. Made 1950 to 1963.

Mossberg Model 190D $95
Same as Model 185D, except in 16 gauge. Weight: about 6 pounds. Made 1955 to 1971.

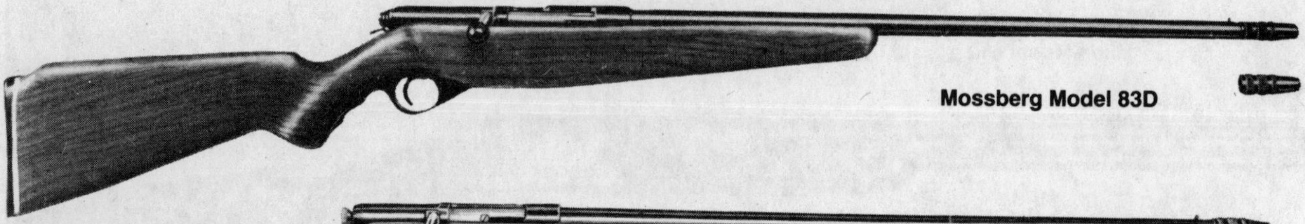

Mossberg Model 83D

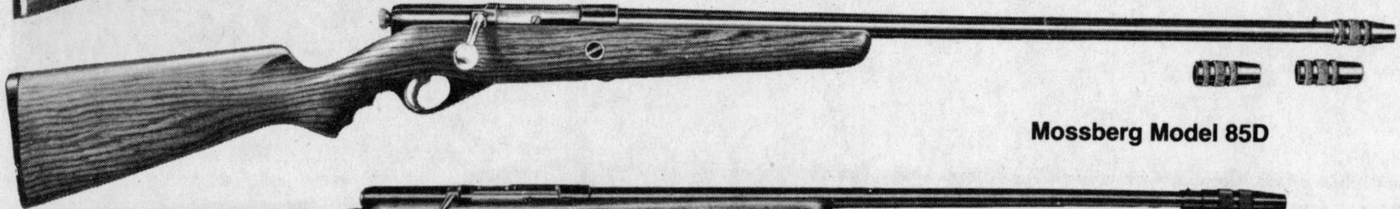

Mossberg Model 85D

Mossberg Model 183K

Mossberg Model 185K

Mossberg Model 190D

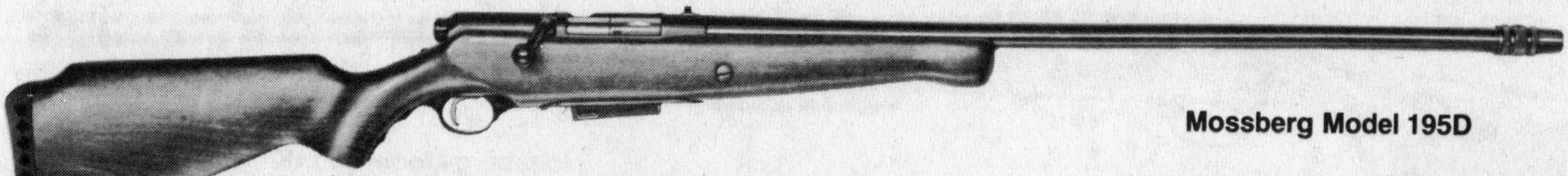

Mossberg Model 195D

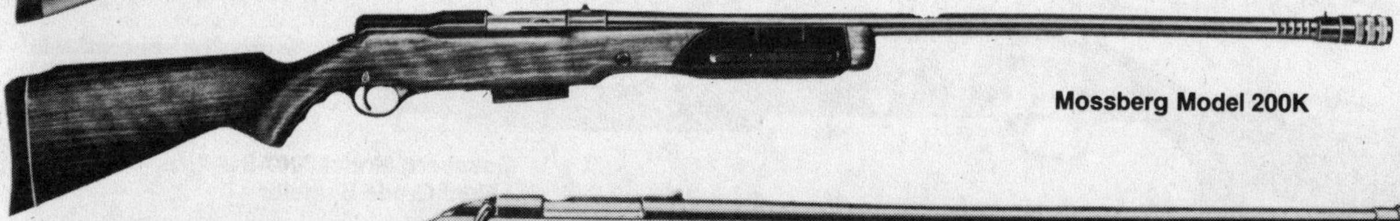

Mossberg Model 200K

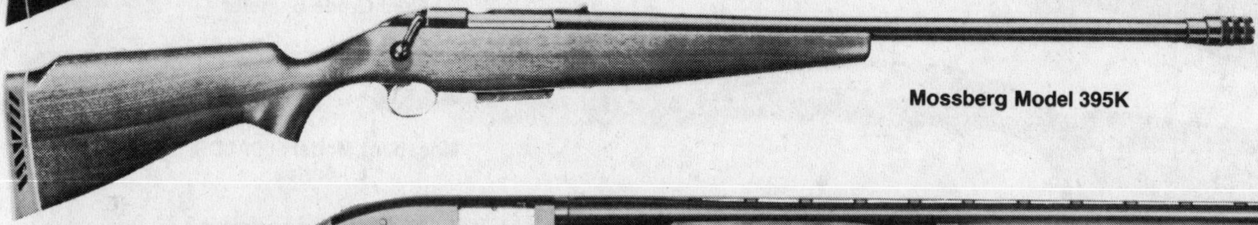

Mossberg Model 395K

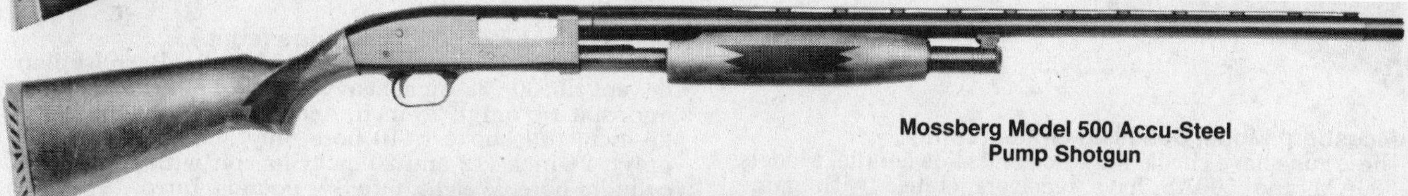

Mossberg Model 500 Accu-Steel Pump Shotgun

Mossberg Model 500A Field

Mossberg Model 190K **$100**
Same as Model 185K, except in 16 gauge. Weight: about 6¾ pounds. Made 1956 to 1963.

Mossberg Model 195D **$100**
Same as Model 185D, except in 12 gauge. Weight: about 6¾ pounds. Made 1955 to 1971.

Mossberg Model 195K **$100**
Same as Model 185K, except in 12 gauge. Weight: about 7½ pounds. Made 1956 to 1963.

Mossberg Model 200D **$125**
Same as Model 200K, except with two interchangeable choke tubes instead of C-Lect-Choke. Made 1955 to 1959.

Mossberg Model 200K Slide Action Repeater . . . **$175**
12 gauge. 3-shot detachable box magazine. 28-inch barrel. C-Lect-Choke. Plain pistol-grip stock. Black nylon slide handle. Weight: about 7½ pounds. Made 1955 to 1959.

Mossberg Model 385K **$95**
Same as Model 395K, except 20 gauge (3-inch), 26-inch barrel with C-Lect-Choke. Weight: about 6¼ pounds. Made 1963 to 1983.

Mossberg Model 390K **$90**
Same as Model 395K, except 16 gauge (2¾-inch). Made 1963 to 1974.

Mossberg Model 395K Bolt Action Repeater . . . **$100**
Takedown. 3-shot (detachable-clip magazine holds two shells). 12 gauge (3-inch chamber). 28-inch barrel with C-Lect-Choke. Weight: about 7½ pounds. Monte Carlo stock with recoil pad. Made 1963 to 1983.

Mossberg Model 395S Slugster **$110**
Same as Model 395K, except has 24-inch barrel, cylinder bore, rifle sights, swivels and web sling. Weight: about 7 pounds. Made 1968 to 1981.

Mossberg Model 500 Accu-Steel Shotgun **$250**
Pump. Gauge: 12. 24- or 28-inch barrel. Weight: 7¼ pounds. Checkered walnut-finished woodstock with ventilated recoil pad. Available with synthetic field or Speedfeed stocks. Drilled and tapped receivers, swivels and camo sling on camo models. Made from 1987 to date.

Mossberg Model 500 Bullpup Shotgun **$325**
Pump. Gauge: 12. 6- or 8-shot capacity. Barrel: 18½ to 20 inches. 26½ and 28½ inches overall. Weight: about 9½ pounds. Multiple independent safety systems. Dual pistol grips, rubber recoil pad. Fully enclosed rifle-type sights. Synthetic stock. Ventilated barrel heat shield. Made from 1987 to date.

Mossberg Model 500 Field Grade Hammerless Slide Action Repeater
Pre-1977 type. Takedown. Gauges: 12, 16, 20, .410. 3-inch chamber (2¾-inch in 16 gauge). Tubular magazine holds five 2¾-inch shells or four three-inch. Barrels: plain; 30-inch regular or heavy magnum, full choke (12 ga. only); 28-inch, modified or full; 26-inch, improved cylinder or adjustable C-Lect-Choke; 24-inch Slugster, cylinder bore, with rifle sights. Weight: 5¾ to 8 pounds. Plain pistol-grip stock with recoil pad, grooved slide handle. After 1973,

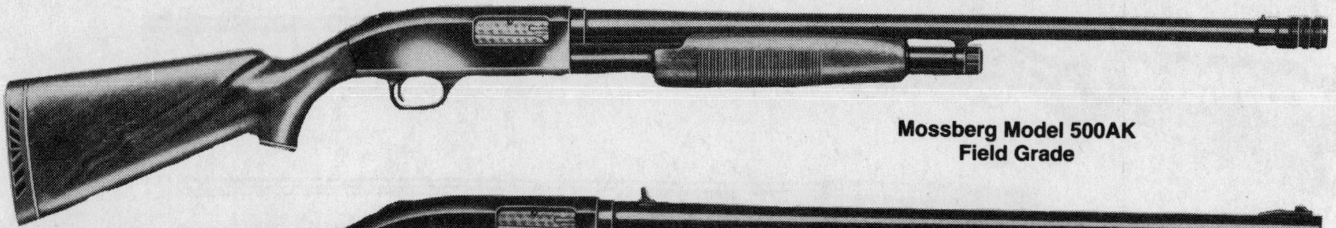

Mossberg Model 500AK
Field Grade

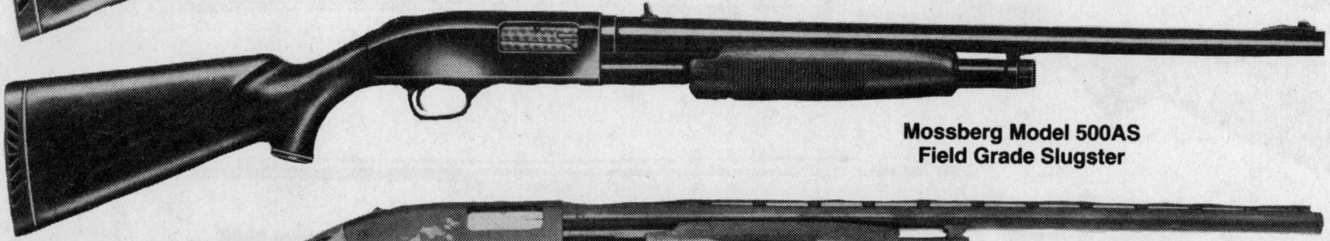

Mossberg Model 500AS
Field Grade Slugster

Mossberg Model 500ALDR
"L" Series

Mossberg Model 500 Field Grade (cont.)
these guns have checkered stock and slide handle, Models 500AM and 500AS have receivers etched with game scenes. The latter has swivels and sling. Made 1962 to 1976.

Model 500A, 12 gauge	**$200**
Model 500AM, 12 gauge, heavy magnum barrel	**200**
Model 500AK, 12 gauge, C-Lect-Choke	**225**
Model 500AS, 12 gauge, Slugster	**220**
Model 500B, 16 gauge	**200**
Model 500BK, 16 gauge, C-Lect-Choke	**250**
Model 500BS, 16 gauge, Slugster	**225**
Model 500C, 20 gauge	**200**
Model 500CK, 20 gauge, C-Lect-Choke	**250**
Model 500CS, 20 gauge, Slugster	**225**
Model 500E, .410 gauge	**240**
Model 500EK, .410 gauge, C-Lect-Choke	**275**

Mossberg Model 500 "L" Series
"L" in model designation. Same as pre-1977 Model 500 Field Grade, except not available in 16 gauge, has receiver etched with different game scenes; Accu-Choke with three interchangeable tubes (improved cylinder, modified, full) standard, restyled stock and slide handle. Barrels: plain or vent rib; 30-, 32-inch, heavy, full choke (12 ga. magnum and vent rib only), 28-inch, Accu-Choke (12 and 20 ga.), 26-inch, full choke (.410 bore only), 18½-inch (12 ga. only), 24-inch (12 and 20 ga.) Slugster with rifle sights, cylinder bore. Weight: 6 to 8½ pounds. Intro. 1977.

Model 500ALD, 12 gauge, plain barrel (Disc. 1980)	**$200**
Model 500ALDR, 12 gauge, ventilated rib	**250**
Model 500ALMR, 12 ga., Heavy Duck Gun (Disc. 1980)	**250**
Model 500ALS, 12 gauge, Slugster (Disc. 1981)	**200**
Model 500CLD, 20 gauge, plain barrel (Disc. 1980)	**200**
Model 500CLDR, 20 gauge, ventilated rib	**250**
Model 500CLS, 20 gauge, Slugster (Disc. 1980)	**250**
Model 500EL, .410 gauge, plain barrel (Disc. 1980)	**200**
Model 500ELR, .410 gauge, ventilated rib	**250**

Mossberg Model 500 Mariner Shotgun $265
Slide action. Gauge: 12. 18½ or 20-inch barrel. 6-shot and 8-shot respectively. Weight: 7¼ pounds. High-strength synthetic buttstock and forend. Available in extra round-carrying speedfeed synthetic buttstock. All metal treated for protection against saltwater corrosion. Intro. 1987.

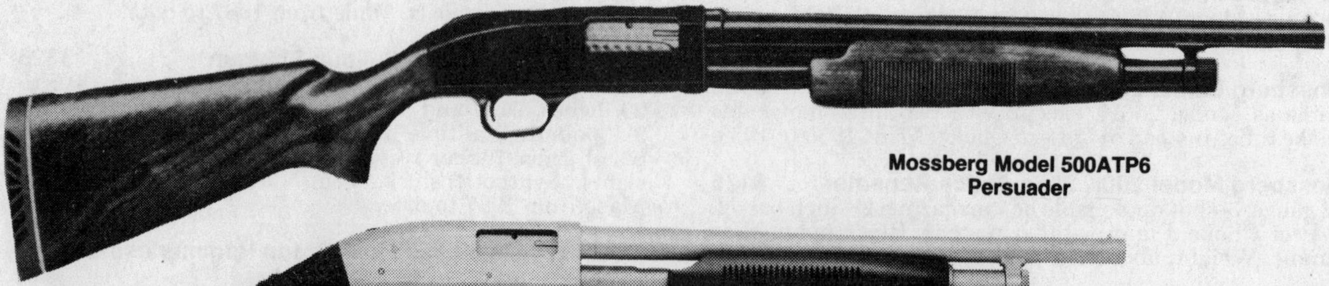

Mossberg Model 500ATP6
Persuader

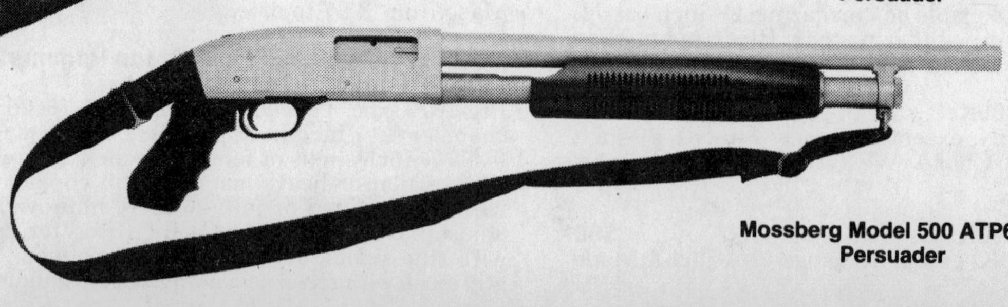

Mossberg Model 500 ATP6CN
Persuader

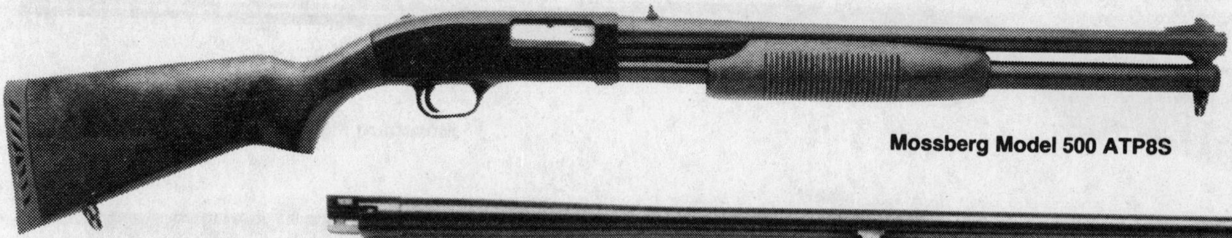

Mossberg Model 500 ATP8S

Mossberg Model 500
Security Combo 6-S

Mossberg Model 500 Persuader Law Enforcement Shotgun

Similar to pre-1977 Model 500 Field Grade, except 12 gauge only, 6- or 8-shot, has 18½- or 20-inch plain barrel, cylinder bore, either shotgun or rifle sights, plain pistol-grip stock and grooved slide handle, sling swivels. Special Model 500ATP8-SP has bayonet lug, Parkerized finish. Currently manufactured.

Model 500ATP6, 6-shot, 18½-inch barrel, shotgun sights **$145**
Model 500ATP6CN, 6-shot, nickel finish, "Cruiser" pistol grip **150**
Model 500ATP6N, 6-shot, nickel finish, 2¾- or 3-inch mag. shells **150**
Model 500ATP6S, 6-shot, 18½" barrel, rifle sights **160**
Model 500ATP8, 8-shot, 20-inch bbl., shotgun sights **180**
Model 500ATP8S, 8-shot, 20-inch barrel, rifle sights **180**
Model 500ATP8-SP Special Enforcement Shotgun **250**
Model 500 Bullpup **250**
Model 500 Security Combo Pack **150**
Model 500 Cruiser with pistol grip **150**

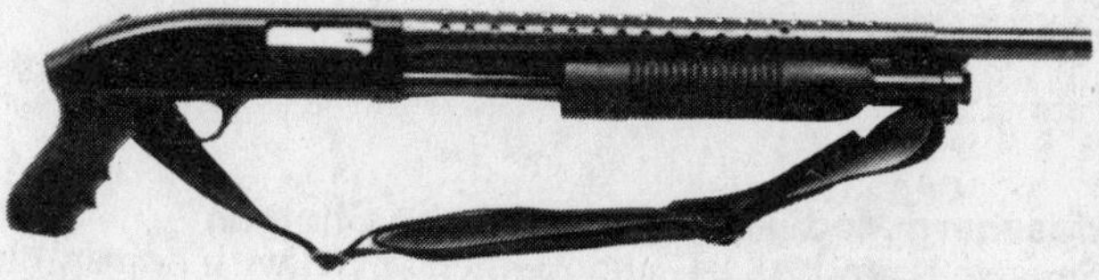

Mossberg Model 500 Cruiser

Mossberg Model 500 Pigeon Grade

Same as Model 500 Super Grade, except higher quality with fancy wood, floating vent rib; field gun hunting dog etching, trap and skeet guns have scroll etching. Barrels: 30-inch, full choke (12 gauge only); 28-inch, modified choke; 26-inch, skeet choke or C-Lect-Choke. Made 1971 to 1975.

Model 500APR, 12 gauge, Field, Trap or Skeet . . . **$325**
Model 500APKR, 12 gauge, Field Gun, C-Lect-Choke **330**
Model 500 APTR, 12 gauge, Trap Gun, Monte Carlo stock **395**
Model 500CPR, 20 gauge, Field or Skeet Gun **345**
Model 500EPR, .410 gauge, Field or Skeet Gun . . . **345**

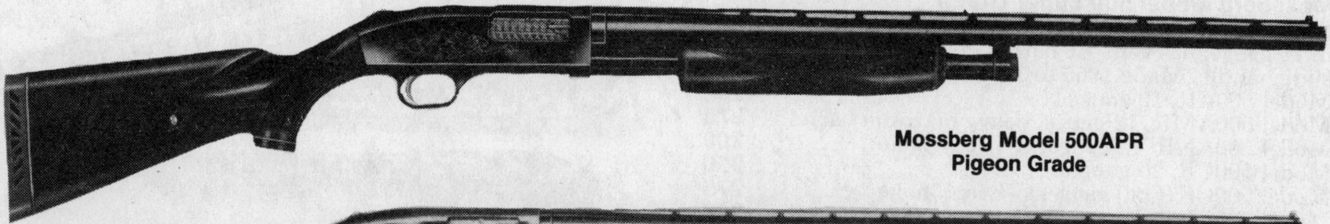

Mossberg Model 500APR
Pigeon Grade

Mossberg Model 500APTR
Pigeon Grade Trap

Mossberg Model 500 Regal

Mossberg Model 500-AKR
Super Grade

Mossberg Model 500 Turkey/Deer
Combination

Mossberg Model 500 Pump Combo Shotgun . . . $280
Gauges: 12 and 20. 24- and 28-inch barrel with adjustable rifle sights. Weight: 7 to 7¹/₄ pounds. Available with blued or camo finish. Drilled and tapped receiver with sling swivels and a camo web sling. Made from 1987 to date.

Mossberg Model 500 Pump Slugster Shotgun . . $240
Gauge: 12. 24-inch barrel with adjustable rifle sights. Weight: 7 pounds. Camo finish. Drilled and tapped receiver with camo sling and swivels. Made from 1987 to date.

Mossberg Model 500 Regal Slide Action Repeater
Similar to regular Model 500 except higher quality workmanship throughout. Gauges: 12 and 20. Barrels: 26- and 28-inch with various chokes, or Accu-Choke. Weight: 6³/₄ to 7¹/₂ pounds. Checkered walnut stock and forearm. Made 1985 to date.
Model 500 with Accu-Choke **$200**
Model 500 with fixed choke **190**

Mossberg Model 500 Super Grade
Same as pre-1977 Model 500 Field Grade, except not made in 16 gauge, has vent-rib barrel, checkered pistol grip and slide handle. Made 1965 to 1976.
Model 500AR, 12 gauge **$250**
Model 500AMR, 12 gauge, heavy magnum barrel . . **275**
Model 500AKR, 12 gauge, C-Lect-Choke **300**
Model 500CR, 20 gauge **250**
Model 500CKR, 20 gauge, C-Lect-Choke **275**
Model 500ER, .410 gauge **200**
Model 500EKR, .410 gauge, C-Lect-Choke **275**

Mossberg Model 500 Turkey/Deer Combo Shotgun $325
Pump. Gauge: 12. 20- and 24-inch barrels. Weight: 7¹/₄ pounds. Drilled and tapped receiver, camo sling and swivels. Adjustable rifle sights and camo finish. Vent rib. Made from 1987 to date.

Mossberg Model 500 Waterfowl/Deer Combo Shotgun $395
Same general specifications as the Turkey/Deer Combo, except with either 28- or 30-inch barrel along with the 24-inch barrel. Made from 1987 to date.

Mossberg Model 500ATR Super Grade Trap . . . $290
Same as pre-1977 Model 500 Field Grade, except 12 gauge only with vent-rib barrel; 30-inch full choke, checkered Monte Carlo stock with recoil pad, beavertail forearm (slide handle). Made 1968 to 1971.

Mossberg Model 500DSPR Duck Stamp Commemorative $600
Limited edition of 1000 to commemorate the Migratory Bird Hunting Stamp Program. Same as Model 500DSPR Pigeon Grade 12 Gauge Magnum Heavy Duck Gun with heavy 30-inch vent-rib barrel, full choke; receiver has special Wood Duck etching. Gun accompanied by a special wall plaque. Made in 1975. *Note:* Value is for gun in new, unfired condition.

Mossberg Model 500/410
Camper

Mossberg Model 500/410 Camper $175
Similar to regular Model 500 action, except in .410 only. Barrel: 18¹/₂-inch; imp. cyl. choke. Synthetic pistol-grip stock, ribbed forearm. Made from 1985 to date.

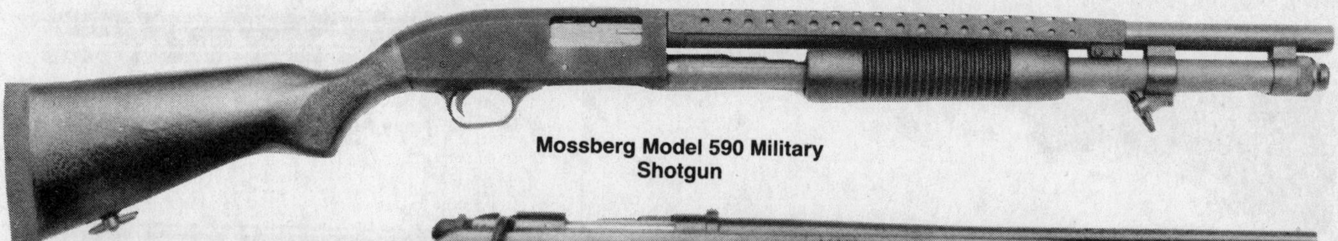

Mossberg Model 590 Military Shotgun

Mossberg Model 595 Bolt Action

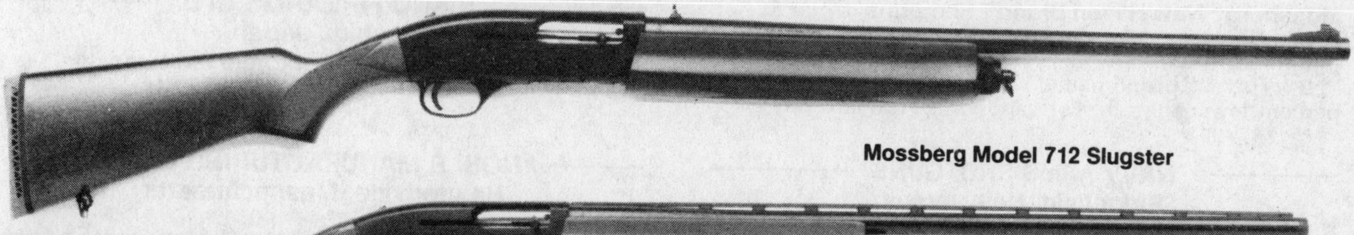

Mossberg Model 712 Slugster

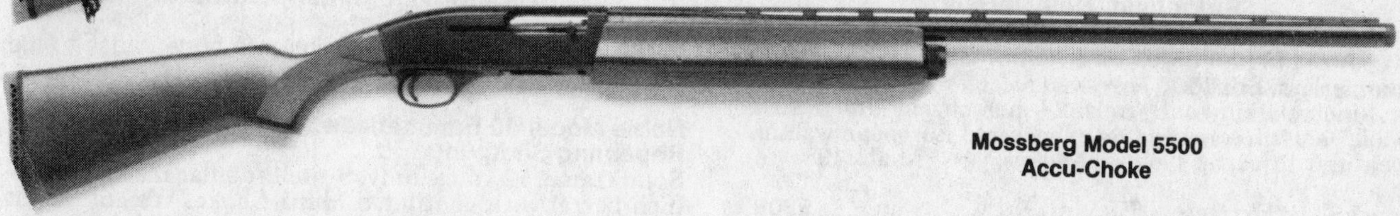

Mossberg Model 5500 Accu-Choke

Mossberg Model 590 Military Security Shotgun . $275
Same general specifications as the Model 590 Military, except there is no heat shield and gun has short pistol-grip style instead of buttstock. Weight: about 6¾ lbs. Made from 1987 to date.

Mossberg Model 590 Military Shotgun $275
Slide-action. Gauge: 12. 9-shot capacity. 20-inch barrel. Weight: about 7 pounds. Synthetic wood or hardwood buttstock and forend. Ventilated barrel heat shields. Equipped with bayonet lug. Blue or Parkerized finish. Made from 1987 to date.

Mossberg Model 595 Bolt Action Repeater $125
12 gauge only. 4-shot detachable magazine. 18½-inch barrel. Weight: about 7 pounds. Walnut finished stock with recoil pad and sling swivels. Made from 1985 to 1986.

Mossberg Model 712 Autoloading Shotgun $410
Gas-operated, takedown, hammerless shotgun with 5-shot (4-shot w/3-inch chamber) tubular magazine. 12 gauge. Barrels: 28-inch vent rib or 24-inch plain barrel Slugster with rifle sights; ACCU-CHOKE tube system. Weight: 7½ pounds. Plain alloy receiver, top-mounted ambidextrous safety. Checkered walnut stained hardwood stock with recoil pad. Imported from Japan since 1988.

Mossberg Model 1000 Autoloading Shotgun
Gas-operated, takedown, hammerless shotgun with tubular magazine. Gauges: 12, 20; 2¾- or 3-inch chamber. Barrels: 22- to 30-inch vent rib with fixed choke or ACCU-

Mossberg Model 1000 Autoloading (cont.)
CHOKE tubes; or 22-inch plain barrel Slugster with rifle sights. Weight: 6½ to 7½ pounds. Scroll-engraved alloy receiver, crossbolt-type safety. Checkered American walnut buttstock and forend. Imported from Japan.

Junior Model, 20 ga., 22-inch bbl.	$340
Standard Model with Fixed Choke	345
Standard Model with Choke Tubes	375

Mossberg Model 1000 Super Autoloading Shotgun
Similar to Model 1000, but in 12 gauge only with 3-inch chamber and new gas metering system. Barrels: 26-, 28- or 30-inch ventilated rib with ACCU-CHOKE tubes.

Standard Model w/Choke Tubes	$425
Waterfowler Model (Parkerized)	455

Mossberg Model 1000S Super Skeet $495
Similar to Model 1000 in 12 or 20 gauge, except with all-steel receiver and vented jug-type choke for reduced muzzle jump. Bright-point front sight and brass mid-bead. 1 and 2 oz. forend cap weights.

Mossberg Model 5500 Autoloading Shotgun
Gas-operated. Takedown. 12-gauge only. 4-shot magazine (3-shot with 3-inch shells). Barrels: 18½- to 30-inch; various chokes. Checkered walnut finished hardwood. Made 1985 to 1986.

Model 5500 w/Accu-choke	$200
Model 5500 Modified Junior	200
Model 5500 Slugster	200
Model 5500 12 gauge	200
Model 5500 Guardian	190

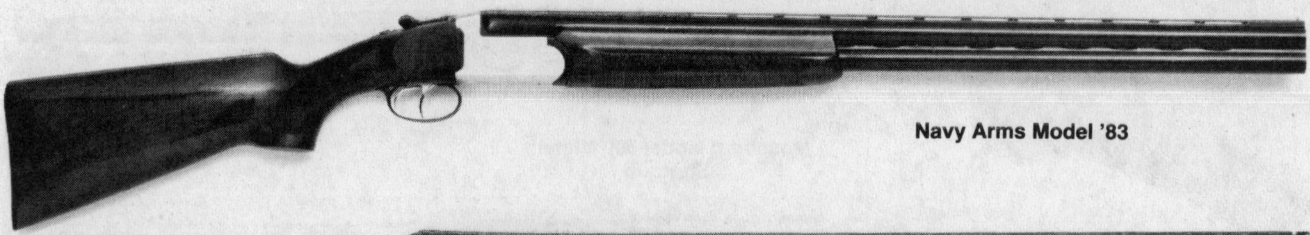

Navy Arms Model '83

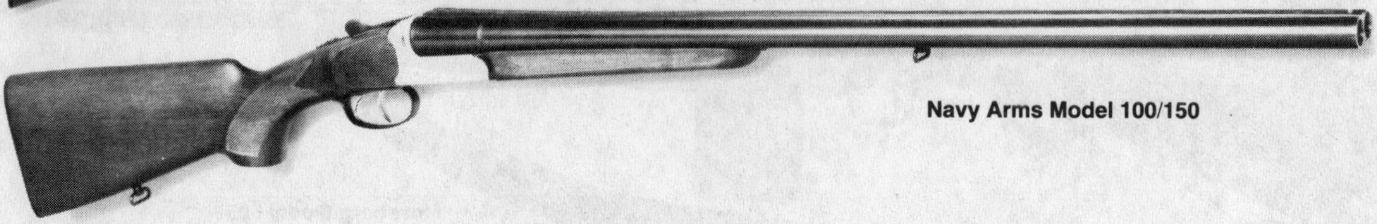

Navy Arms Model 100/150

Mossberg "New Haven Brand" Shotguns
Promotional models, similar to their standard guns but plainer in finish, are marketed by Mossberg under the "New Haven" brand name. Values generally are about 20 percent lower than for corresponding standard models.

NAVY ARMS SHOTGUNS
Ridgefield, New Jersey

Navy Arms Model 83/93 Bird Hunter Over/Under
Hammerless. Box lock, engraved receiver. Gauges: 12 and 20; 3-inch chambers. Barrels: 28-inch chrome lined with double vent-rib construction. Checkered European walnut stock and forearm. Gold plated triggers. Made 1984 to date.
Model 83 w/Extractors **$300**
Model 93 w/Ejectors **355**

Navy Arms Model 95/96 Over/Under Shotgun
Same as the Model 83/93, except with five interchangeable choke tubes. Imported from Italy.
Model 95 w/Extractors **$375**
Model 96 w/Ejectors **475**

Navy Arms Model 100/150 Field Hunter Double Barrel Shotgun
Box lock. Gauges: 12 and 20. Barrels: 28-inch chrome lined. Checkered European walnut stock and forearm. Made 1984 to date.
Model 100 .... **$295**
Model 150 (auto ejectors) **350**

Navy Arms Model 410 Over/Under Shotgun $225
Hammerless, takedown shotgun with engraved chrome receiver. Single trigger. .410 gauge w/3-inch chambers. Barrels: 26-inch (full/full or skeet/skeet); vent rib. Weight: 6¼ pounds. Checkered European walnut buttstock and forend. Imported from Italy since 1986.

NIKKO FIREARMS LTD.
Tochigi, Japan
See listings under Golden Eagle Firearms, Inc.

NOBLE MANUFACTURING CO.
Haydenville, Massachusetts

Noble Series 602 and 70 are similar in appearance to the corresponding Model 66 guns.

Noble Model 40 Hammerless Slide Action Repeating Shotgun $100
Solid frame. 12 gauge only. 5-shell tubular magazine. 28-inch barrel with ventilated Multi-Choke. Weight: about 7½ pounds. Plain pistol-grip stock, grooved slide handle. Made 1950 to 1955.

Noble Model 50 .... $95
Same as Model 40, except without Multi-Choke. Modified or full choke barrel. Made 1953 to 1955.

Noble Model 60 Hammerless Slide Action Repeating Shotgun $150
Solid frame. 12 and 16 gauge. 5-shot tubular magazine. 28-inch barrel with adjustable choke. Plain pistol-grip stock with recoil pad, grooved slide handle. Weight: about 7½ pounds. Made 1955 to 1966.

Noble Model 65 .... $130
Same as Model 60, except without adjustable choke and recoil pad. Modified or full choke barrel. Made 1955 to 1966.

Noble Model 66CLP $140
Same as Model 66RCLP, except has plain barrel. Introduced in 1967. Discontinued.

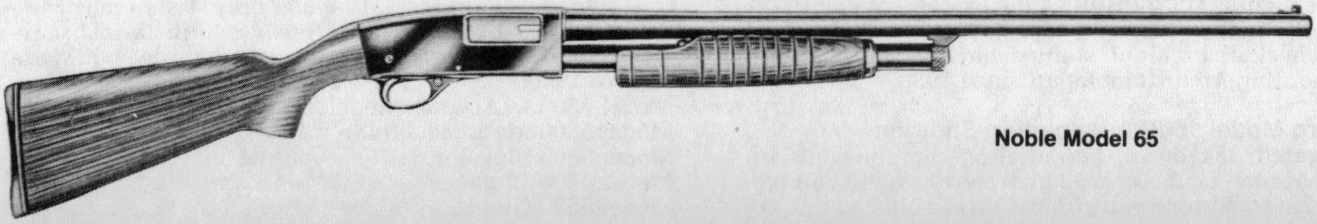

Noble Model 65

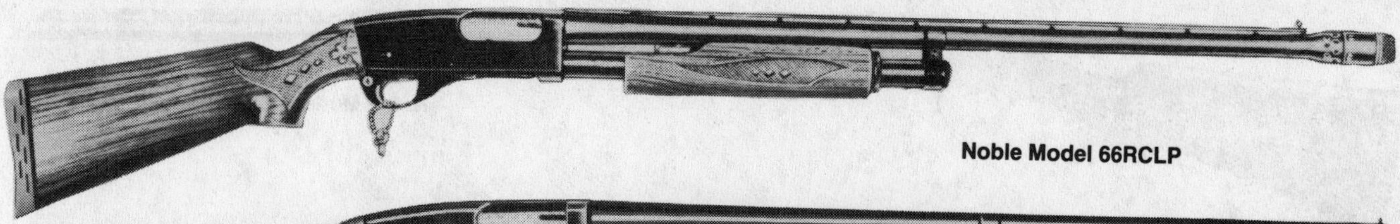

Noble Model 66RCLP

Noble Model 66XL

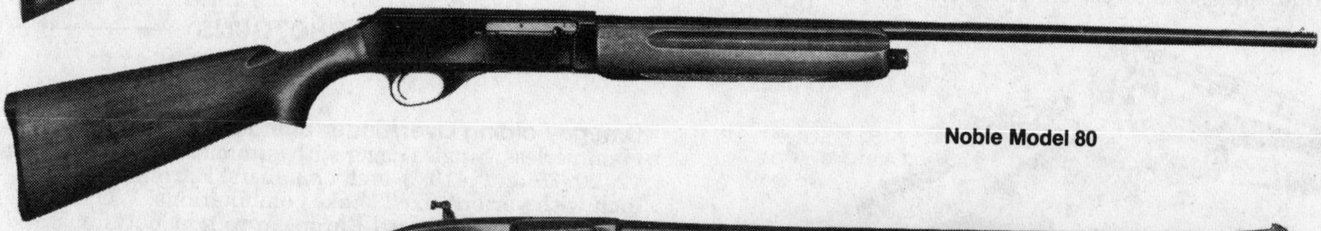

Noble Model 80

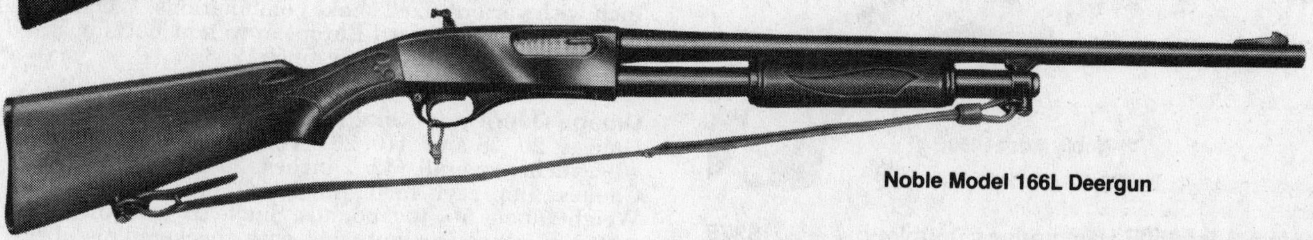

Noble Model 166L Deergun

Noble Model 66RCLP Hammerless Slide Action Repeating Shotgun **$175**
Solid frame. Key lock fire control mechanism. Gauges: 12, 16. 3-inch chamber in 12 gauge. 5-shot tubular magazine. 28-inch barrel, vent rib, adjustable choke. Weight: about $7\frac{1}{2}$ pounds. Checkered pistol-grip stock and slide handle, recoil pad. Made 1967 to 1970.

Noble Model 66RLP **$150**
Same as Model 66RCLP, except with full or modified choke. Made 1967 to 1970.

Noble Model 66XL **$125**
Same as Model 66RCLP, except has plain barrel, full or modified choke, slide handle only checkered, no recoil pad. Made 1967 to 1970.

Noble Model 70CLP Hammerless Slide Action Repeating Shotgun **$150**
Solid frame. .410 gauge. Magazine holds 5 shells. 26-inch barrel with adjustable choke. Weight: about 6 pounds. Checkered buttstock and forearm, recoil pad. Made 1958 to 1970.

Noble Model 70RCLP **$175**
Same as Model 70CLP, except has ventilated rib. Made 1967 to 1970.

Noble Model 70RLP **$160**
Same as Model 70CLP, except has vent rib and no adjustable choke. Made 1967 to 1970.

Noble Model 70XL **$110**
Same as Model 70CLP, except without adjustable choke and checkering on buttstock. Made 1958 to 1970.

Noble Model 80 Autoloading Shotgun **$225**
Recoil-operated. .410 gauge. Magazine holds three 3-inch shells, four $2\frac{1}{2}$-inch shells. 26-inch barrel, full choke. Weight: about 6 pounds. Plain pistol-grip stock and fluted forearm. Made 1964 to 1966.

Noble Key Lock Fire Control Mechanism

Noble Model 166L Deergun **$230**
Solid frame. Key lock fire control mechanism. 12 gauge. $2\frac{3}{4}$-inch chamber. 5-shot tubular magazine. 24-inch plain barrel, specially bored for rifled slug. Lyman peep rear sight, post ramp front sight. Receiver dovetailed for scope mounting. Weight: about $7\frac{1}{4}$ pounds. Checkered pistol-grip stock and slide handle, swivels and carrying strap. Made 1967 to 1970.

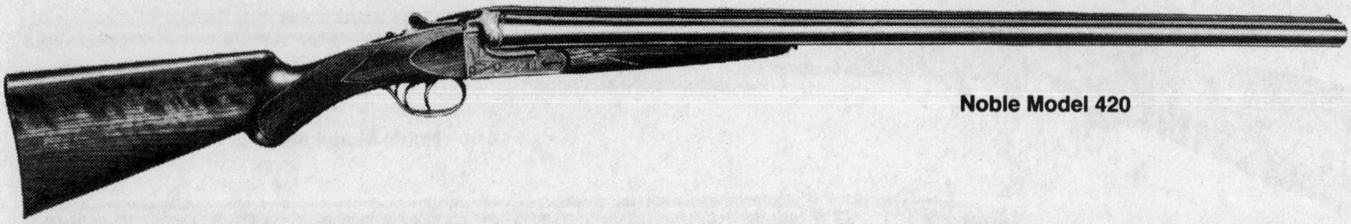
Noble Model 420

Noble Model 420 Hammerless Double **$275**
Box lock. Plain extractors. Double triggers. Gauges: 12 ga. 3-inch mag.; 16 ga.; 20 ga. 3-inch mag.; .410 ga. Barrels: 28-inch, except .410 in 26-inch, modified/full choke. Weight: about 6¾ pounds. Engraved frame. Checkered walnut stock and forearm. Made 1958 to 1970.

Noble Model 450E

Noble Model 450E Hammerless Double **$375**
Box lock. Engraved frame. Selective auto ejectors. Double triggers. Gauges: 12, 16, 20. 3-inch chambers in 12 and 20 gauge. 28-inch barrels, modified/full choke. Weight: about 6 lbs. 14 oz., 12 ga. Checkered pistol-grip stock and beavertail forearm, recoil pad. Made 1967 to 1970.

Noble Model 602CLP **$155**
Same as Model 602RCLP, except has plain barrel. Made 1958 to 1970.

Noble Model 602RCLP Hammerless Slide Action Repeating Shotgun **$195**
Solid frame. Key lock fire control mechanism. 20 gauge. 3-inch chamber. 5-shot tubular magazine. 28-inch barrel, vent rib, adjustable choke. Weight: about 6½ pounds. Checkered pistol-grip stock and slide handle, recoil pad. Made 1967 to 1970.

Noble Model 602RLP **$175**
Same as Model 602RCLP, except without adjustable choke, bored full or modified choke. Made 1967 to 1970.

Noble Model 602XL **$125**
Same as Model 602RCLP, except has plain barrel, full or modified choke, slide handle only checkered, no recoil pad. Made 1958 to 1970.

Noble Model 662 . . . . **$175**
Same as Model 602CLP, except has aluminum receiver and barrel. Weight: about 4½ pounds. Made 1966 to 1970.

OMEGA SHOTGUNS
Brescia, Italy, and Korea

Omega Folding Over/Under Shotgun **$270**
Hammerless. Single trigger with automatic safety. Gauges: 12, 20, 28 and .410; 3-inch chambers. Barrels: 26- or 28-inch with various fixed choke combinations. Weight: 5½ to 6 pounds. Checkered European walnut buttstock and forend. Imported from Italy since 1986.

Omega Over/Under Shotgun, Deluxe **$290**
Gauges: 20, 28 and .410. 26- or 28-inch vent-rib barrels. 40½ inches overall (42½ inches, 20 ga., 28-inch bbl.). Chokes: imp. cyl./mod., mod./full or full/full (.410). Weight: about 5½ to 6 pounds. Single trigger. Automatic safety. European walnut stock with checkered pistol grip and tulip forend. Made in Italy from 1984 to date.

Omega Side-by-Side Shotgun, Deluxe **$230**
Same general specifications as the Standard Side-by-Side, except has checkered European walnut stock and low barrel rib. Made in Italy from 1984 to date.

Omega Side-by-Side Shotgun, Standard **$220**
Gauge: .410. 26-inch barrel. 40½ inches overall. Choked full/full. Weight: 5½ pounds. Double trigger. Manual safety. Checkered beechwood stock and semi-pistol grip. Made in Italy from 1984 to date.

Omega Single Barrel Shotgun, Deluxe **$180**
Same general specifications as the Standard Single Barrel, except has checkered walnut stock, top lever break, fully blued receiver, vent rib. Made in Korea from 1984 to date.

Omega Single Barrel Shotgun, Standard **$140**
Gauges: 12, 16, 20, 28 and .410. Barrel lengths: 26-, 28- or 30-inch. Weight: 5 lbs. 4 oz. to 5 lbs. 11 oz. Indonesian walnut stock. Matte-chromed receiver and top lever break. Made in Korea from 1984 to date.

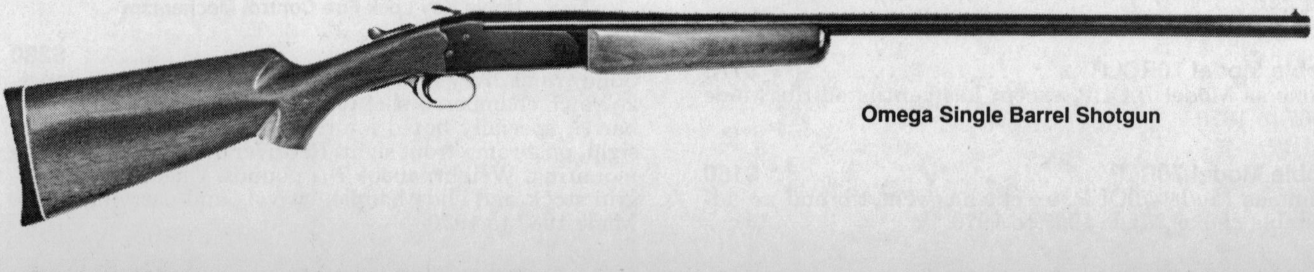
Omega Single Barrel Shotgun

PARKER BROTHERS
Meriden, Connecticut

This firm was taken over by Remington Arms Company in 1934 and its production facilities removed to Remington's Ilion, New York, plant.

Parker G.H.E.

Parker D.H.E.

Parker C.H.E.

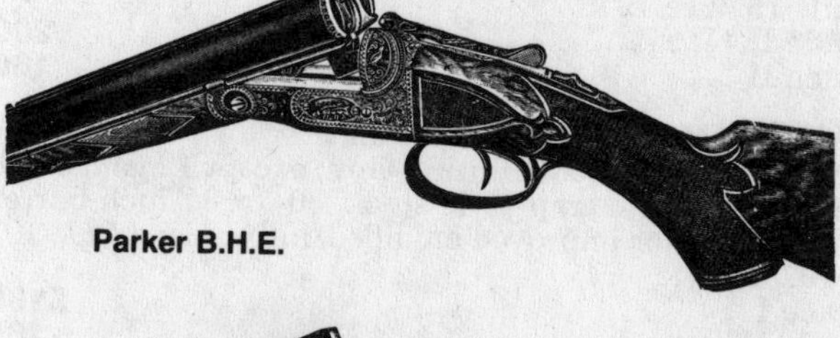

Parker B.H.E.

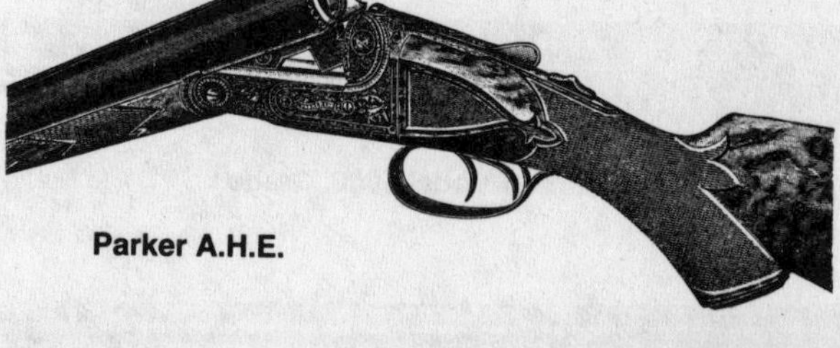

Parker A.H.E.

Parker Hammerless Double Barrel Shotguns

Grades V.H.E. through A-1 Special. Box lock. Auto ejectors. Double triggers or selective single trigger. Gauges: 10, 12, 16, 20, 28, .410. Barrels: 26- to 32-inch, any standard boring. Weight: $6^{7}/_{8}$ to $8^{1}/_{2}$ pounds, 12 ga. Stock and forearm of select walnut, checkered; straight, half or full pistol grip. Grades differ only in quality of workmanship, grade of wood, engraving, checkering, etc.; general specifications are the same for all. Discontinued about 1940.

V.H.E. Grade, 12 or 16 gauge	$ 2,060
V.H.E. Grade, 20 gauge	3,500
V.H.E. Grade, 28 gauge	4,480
V.H.E. Grade, .410 gauge	8,500
G.H.E. Grade, 12 or 16 gauge	2,495
G.H.E. Grade, 20 gauge	4,500
G.H.E. Grade, 28 gauge	6,000
G.H.E. Grade, .410 gauge	10,000
D.H.E. Grade, 12 or 16 gauge	3,500
D.H.E. Grade, 20 gauge	4,995
D.H.E. Grade, 28 gauge	12,500
D.H.E. Grade, .410 gauge	15,000
C.H.E. Grade, 12 or 16 gauge	7,000
C.H.E. Grade, 20 gauge	6,400
C.H.E. Grade, 28 gauge	18,200
C.H.E. Grade, .410 gauge	28,000
B.H.E. Grade, 12 or 16 gauge	7,500
B.H.E. Grade, 20 gauge	8,000
B.H.E. Grade, 28 gauge	10,000
B.H.E. Grade, .410 gauge	30,000
A.H.E. Grade, 12 or 16 gauge	6,000
A.H.E. Grade, 20 gauge	12,500
A.H.E. Grade, 28 gauge	15,000
A.A.H.E. Grade, 12 or 16 gauge	10,500
A.A.H.E. Grade, 20 gauge	35,000
A.A.H.E. Grade, 28 gauge	40,000
A-1 Special Grade, 12 or 16 gauge	20,000
A-1 Special Grade, 20 gauge	25,000
A-1 Special Grade, 28 gauge	130,000

Non-ejector guns, deduct 30 percent from values shown.
Vent-rib barrels, add 20 percent to values shown.

Parker Single Barrel Trap Guns

Hammerless. Box lock. Ejector. 12 gauge only. Barrel lengths: 30-, 32-, 34-inch; any boring. Ventilated rib. Weight: $7^{1}/_{2}$ to $8^{1}/_{2}$ pounds. Stock and forearm of select walnut, checkered; straight, half or full pistol grip. The five grades differ only in quality of workmanship, grade of wood, checkering, engraving, etc.; general specifications same for all. Discontinued about 1940.

S.C. Grade	$ 2,000
S.B. Grade	3,000
S.A. Grade	4,200
S.A.A. Grade	6,200
S.A.1 Special	10,000

Parker Skeet Gun

Same as other Parker doubles from Grade V.H.E. up, except selective single trigger and beavertail forearm are standard on this model, as are 26-inch barrels, skeet choke. Discontinued about 1940. Values are 20 percent higher.

Parker Single Barrel Trap

SHOTGUNS

Parker Trojan

Parker Trojan Hammerless Double Barrel Shotgun

Box lock. Plain extractors. Double trigger or single trigger. Gauges: 12, 16, 20. Barrels: 30-inch both full choke (12 ga. only), 26- or 28-inch modified and full choke. Weight: 6¼ to 7¾ pounds. Checkered pistol-grip stock and forearm. Discont. 1939.

12 or 16 gauge . . . . . **$ 1400**
20 gauge **2100**

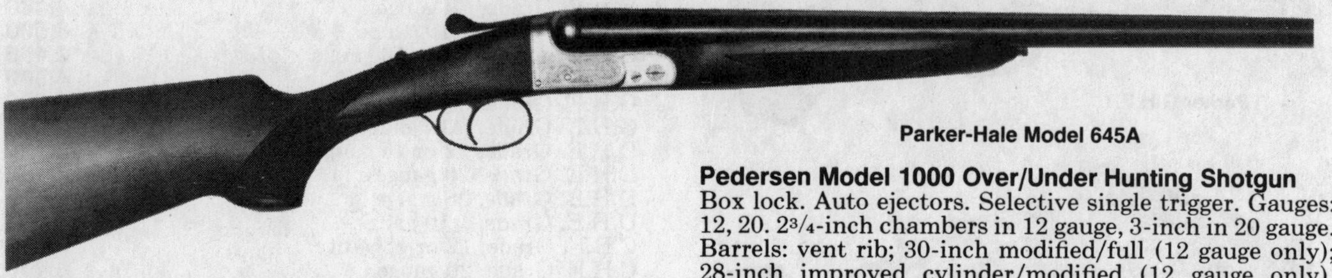
Parker-Hale Model 645A

PARKER-HALE SHOTGUNS

Mfd. by Ignacio Ugartechea, Spain

Parker-Hale Model 645A (American) Side-by-Side Shotgun $525

Gauges: 12, 16 and 20. Boxlock action. 26- and 28-inch barrels. Chokes: imp. cyl./mod., mod./full. Weight: 6 pounds average. Single non-selective trigger. Automatic safety. Hand-checkered pistol grip walnut stock with beavertail forend. Raised matted rib. English scroll-design engraved receiver.

Parker-Hale Model 645E (English) Side-by-Side Shotgun

Same general specifications as the Model 645A, except double triggers, straight grip, splinter forend, checkered butt and concave rib.

Model 645E
12, 16, 20 ga. with 26- or 28-inch bbl. **$430**
28, .410 ga. with 27-inch bbl. **500**

Model 645E-XXV
12, 16, 20 ga. with 25-inch bbl. **475**
28, .410 ga. with 25-inch bbl. **525**

PEDERSEN CUSTOM GUNS

North Haven, Connecticut
Division of O. F. Mossberg & Sons, Inc.

Pedersen Model 1000 Over/Under Hunting Shotgun

Box lock. Auto ejectors. Selective single trigger. Gauges: 12, 20. 2¾-inch chambers in 12 gauge, 3-inch in 20 gauge. Barrels: vent rib; 30-inch modified/full (12 gauge only); 28-inch improved cylinder/modified (12 gauge only), modified/full; 26-inch improved cylinder/modified. Checkered pistol-grip stock and forearm. Grade I is the higher quality gun with custom stock dimensions, fancier wood, more elaborate engraving, silver inlays. Made 1973 to 1975.

Grade I **$2000**
Grade II **1675**

Pedersen Model 1000 Magnum

Same as Model 1000 Hunting Gun, except chambered for 12 gauge magnum 3-inch shells, 30-inch barrels, improved modified/full choke. Made 1973 to 1975.

Grade I **$1800**
Grade II **1600**

Pedersen Model 1000 Skeet Gun

Same as Model 1000 Hunting Gun, except has skeet-style stock; 26- and 28-inch barrels (12 gauge only), skeet choke. Made 1973 to 1975.

Grade I **$2000**
Grade II **1600**

Pedersen Model 1000 Trap Gun

Same as Model 1000 Hunting Gun, except 12 gauge only, has Monte Carlo trap-style stock, 30- or 32-inch barrels, modified/full or improved modified/full choke. Made 1973 to 1975.

Grade I **$1800**
Grade II **1650**

Pedersen Model 1000, Grade I

Pedersen Model 1000, Grade II

Pedersen Model 1500 Trap

Pedersen Model 2500

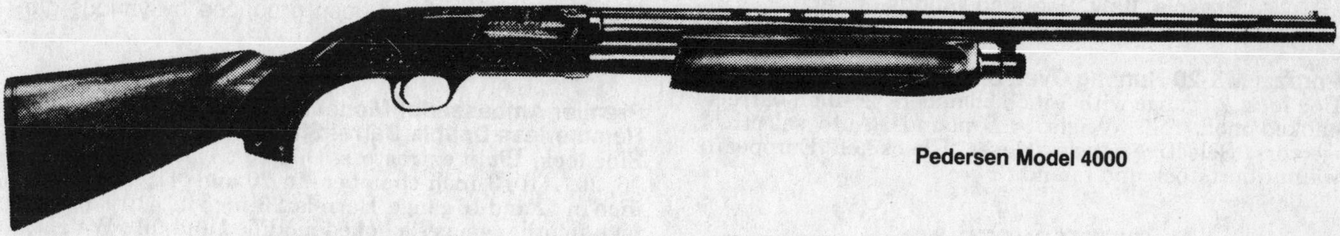

Pedersen Model 4000

Pedersen Model 1500 O/U Hunting Shotgun $395
Box lock. Auto ejectors. Selective single trigger. 12 gauge. 2¾- or 3-inch chambers. Barrels: vent rib; 26-inch improved cylinder/modified; 28- and 30-inch modified/full; Magnum has 30-inch, improved modified/full choke. Weight: 7 to 7½ pounds depending upon barrel length. Checkered pistol-grip stock and forearm. Made 1973 to 1975.

Pedersen Model 1500 Skeet Gun $480
Same as Model 1500 Hunting Gun, except has skeet-style stock, 27-inch barrels, skeet choke. Made 1973 to 1975.

Pedersen Model 1500 Trap Gun $490
Same as Model 1500 Hunting Gun, except has Monte Carlo trap-style stock, 30- or 32-inch barrels, modified/full or improved modified/full chokes. Made 1973 to 1975.

Pedersen Model 2000 Hammerless Double
Box lock. Auto ejectors. Selective single trigger. Gauges: 12, 20. 2¾-inch chambers in 12 gauge, 3-inch in 20 gauge. Barrels: vent rib; 30-inch modified/full (12 gauge only); 28-inch modified/full; 26-inch improved cylinder/modified choke. Checkered pistol-grip stock and forearm. Grade I is the higher quality gun with custom dimensions, fancier wood, more elaborate engraving, silver inlays. Made 1973 to 1974.
Grade I $1700
Grade II 1400

Pedersen Model 2500 Hammerless Double $425
Box lock. Auto ejectors. Selective single trigger. Gauges: 12, 20. 2¾-inch chambers in 12 gauge, 3-inch in 20 gauge. Barrels: vent rib; 28-inch modified/full; 26-inch improved cylinder/modified choke. Checkered pistol-grip stock and forearm. Made 1973 to 1974.

Pedersen Model 4000 Hammerless Slide Action Repeating Shotgun $420
Custom version of Mossberg Model 500. Full-coverage floral engraving on receiver. Gauges: 12, 20, .410. 3-inch chamber. Barrels: vent rib; 26-inch improved cylinder or skeet choke; 28-inch full or modified; 30-inch full. Weight: 6 to 8 pounds depending upon gauge and barrel. Checkered stock and slide handle of select wood. Made in 1975.

Pedersen Model 4000 Trap Gun $450
Same as standard Model 4000, except 12 gauge only, has 30-inch full choke barrel, Monte Carlo trap-style stock with recoil pad. Made in 1975.

Pedersen Model 4500 . . . . $390
Same as Model 4000, except has simpler scroll engraving. Made in 1975.

Pedersen Model 4500 Trap Gun $405
Same as Model 4000 Trap Gun, except has simpler scroll engraving. Made in 1975.

J. C. PENNEY CO., INC.
New York, New York

J. C. Penney Model 4011 Autoloading Shotgun . $160
Hammerless. 5-shot magazine. Barrels: 26-inch improved cylinder; 28-inch modified or full; 30-inch full choke. Weight: 7¼ lbs. Plain pistol-grip stock and slide handle.

J. C. Penney Model 6610 Single Shot Shotgun . . . $75
Hammerless. Takedown. Auto ejector. Gauges: 12, 16, 20 and .410. Barrel length: 28 to 36 inches. Weight: about 6 pounds. Plain pistol-grip stock and forearm.

J. C. Penney Model 6630 Bolt Action Shotgun . . $110
Takedown. Gauges: 12, 16, 20. 2-shot clip magazine. 26- and 28-inch barrel lengths; with or without adjustable choke. Plain pistol-grip stock. Weight: about 7¼ pounds.

J. C. Penney Model 6670 Slide Action Shotgun . $110
Hammerless. Gauges: 12, 16, 20, and .410. 3-shot tubular magazine. Barrels: 26- to 30-inch; various chokes. Weight: 6¼ to 7½ pounds. Walnut finished hardwood stock.

J. C. Penney Model 6870 Slide Action Shotgun . $195
Hammerless. Gauges: 12, 16, 20, .410. 4-shot magazine. Barrels: vent rib; 26- to 30-inch, various chokes. Weight: average 6½ pounds. Plain pistol-grip stock.

PERAZZI SHOTGUNS
Rome, New York
Manufactured by Manifattura Armi Perazzi, Brescia, Italy. See also listings under Ithaca-Perazzi.

Perazzi MX-20 Hunting Over/Under $3900
Box lock. 20 gauge with 3-inch chambers. 26-inch barrels choked mod./full. Weight: 6½ pounds. Auto selective ejectors. Selective single trigger. Checkered European walnut buttstock and forend.

PIOTTI SHOTGUNS
Italy

Piotti King No. 1 Sidelock $9000
Gauges: 10, 12, 16, 20, 28 and .410. 25- to 30-inch barrels (12 ga.); 25- to 28-inch (other gauges). Weight: about 5 lbs. (.410) to 8 lbs. (12 ga.) Holland & Holland pattern sidelock. Double triggers standard. Coin finish or color case-hardened. Level file-cut rib. Full-coverage scroll engraving, gold inlays. Hand-rubbed, oil-finished, straight-grip stock with checkered butt, splinter forend.

Piotti King Extra Side-by-Side Shotgun $11,000
Same general specifications as the Piotti King No. 1, except has choice of engraving, gold inlays plus stock is of exhibition grade wood.

Piotti Lunik Sidelock Shotgun $9050
Same general specifications as the Monte Carlo model, except has level, file-cut rib. Renaissance-style, large scroll engraving in relief, gold crown in top lever, gold name, and gold crest in forearm, finely figured wood.

Piotti Monte Carlo Sidelock Shotgun $7100
Gauges: 10, 12, 16, 20, 28 or .410. Barrels: 25- to 30-inch. Holland & Holland pattern sidelock. Weight: 5 to 8 pounds. Automatic ejectors. Double triggers. Hand-rubbed oil-finished straight-grip stock with checkered butt. Choice of Purdey-style scroll and rosette or Holland & Holland-style large scroll engraving.

Piotti Piuma Boxlock Side-by-Side Shotgun . . . $3400
Same general specifications as the Monte Carlo model, except has Anson & Deeley boxlock action with demi-bloc barrels, scalloped frame. Standard scroll and rosette engraving. Hand-rubbed, oil-finished straight-grip stock.

PREMIER SHOTGUNS
Brooklyn, New York

Premier shotguns have been produced by various gunmakers in Italy and Spain.

Premier Ambassador Model Field Grade Hammerless Double Barrel Shotgun $400
Side lock. Plain extractors. Double triggers. Gauges: 12, 16, 20, .410. 3-inch chambers in 20 and .410 gauge, 2¾-inch in 12 and 16 gauge. Barrels: 26-inch in .410 gauge, 28-inch in other gauges; choked modified and full. Weight: 6 lbs. 3 oz. to 7 lbs. 3 oz. depending upon gauge. Checkered pistol-grip stock and beavertail forearm. Made 1957 to date.

Premier Brush King $275
Same as standard Regent Model, except chambered for 12 (2¾-inch) and 20 gauge (3-inch) only; has 22-inch barrels, improved cylinder and modified choke, straight-grip stock. Weight: 6 lbs. 3 oz. in 12 gauge; 5 lbs. 12 oz. in 20 gauge. Made 1959 to date.

Premier Continental Model Field Grade Hammer Double Barrel Shotgun $330
Side lock. Exposed hammers. Plain extractors. Double triggers. Gauges: 12, 16, 20, .410. 3-inch chambers in 20 and .410 gauge, 2¾-inch in 12 and 16 gauge. Barrels: 26-inch in .410 gauge; 28-inch in other gauges; choked modified and full. Weight: 6 lbs. 3 oz. to 7 lbs. 3 oz. depending upon gauge. Checkered pistol-grip stock and English-style forearm. Made 1957 to date.

Premier Ambassador

Premier Continental

Premier Monarch

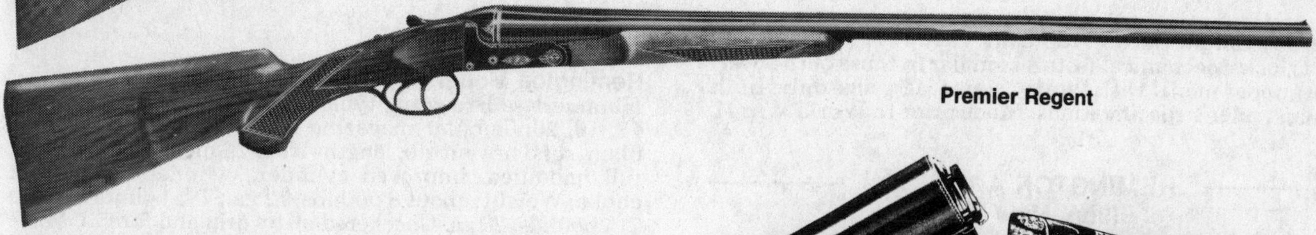

Premier Regent

Premier Monarch Supreme Grade Hammerless Double Barrel Shotgun **$450**
Box lock. Auto ejectors. Double triggers. Gauges: 12, 20. 2¾-inch chambers in 12 gauge, 3-inch in 20 gauge. Barrels: 28-inch modified/full; 26-inch improved cylinder/modified choke. Weight: 6 lbs. 6 oz. to 7 lbs. 2 oz. depending upon gauge and barrel. Checkered pistol-grip stock and beavertail forearm of fancy walnut. Made 1959 to date.

Premier Presentation Custom Grade **$1000**
Similar to Monarch model, but made to order; of higher quality with hunting scene engraving gold and silver inlaid, fancier wood. Made 1959 to date.

Premier Regent 10 Gauge Magnum Express . . . **$325**
Same as standard Regent Model, except chambered for 10 gauge magnum 3½-inch shells, has heavier construction, 32-inch barrels choked full and full, stock with recoil pad. Weight: 11¼ pounds. Made 1957 to date.

Premier Regent 12 Gauge Magnum Express . . . **$300**
Same as standard Regent Model, except chambered for 12 gauge magnum 3-inch shells, has 30-inch barrels choked full and full, stock with recoil pad. Weight: 7¼ pounds. Made 1957 to date.

Premier Regent Model Field Grade Hammerless Double Barrel Shotgun **$260**
Box lock. Plain extractors. Double triggers. Gauges: 12, 16, 20, 28, .410. 3-inch chambers in 20 and .410 gauge, 2¾-inch in other gauges. Barrels: 26-inch improved cylinder/modified, modified/full (28 and .410 gauge only); 28-inch modified/full; 30-inch modified/full (12 ga. only). Weight: 6 lbs. 2 oz. to 7 lbs. 4 oz. depending upon gauge and barrel. Checkered pistol-grip stock and beavertail forearm. Made 1955 to date.

JAMES PURDEY & SONS, LTD.
London, England

Purdey Hammerless Double Barrel

Purdey Hammerless Double Barrel Shotgun
Side lock. Auto ejectors. Single or double triggers. Gauges: 12, 16, 20. Barrels: 26-, 27-, 28-, 30-inch (latter in 12 gauge only); any boring, any shape or style of rib. Weight: 5¼ to 6½ pounds depending upon model, gauge and barrel length. Checkered stock and forearm, straight grip standard, pistol-grip also available. Purdey guns of this type have been made from about 1880 to date. Models include: Game Gun, Featherweight Game Gun, Two-Inch Gun (chambered for 12 gauge 2-inch shells), Pigeon Gun (with 3rd fastening and side clips); values of all models are the same.
With double triggers **$24,000**
With single trigger **29,000**

Purdey Over-and-Under Gun
Side lock. Auto ejectors. Single or double triggers. Gauges: 12, 16, 20. Barrels: 26-, 27-, 28-, 30-inch (latter in 12 gauge only); any boring, any style rib. Weight: 6 to 7½ pounds depending upon gauge and barrel length. Checkered stock and forend, straight or pistol grip. Prior to World War II, the Purdey Over-and-Under Gun was made with a Purdey action; since the war James Purdey & Sons have acquired the business of James Woodward & Sons and all Purdey over/under guns are now built on the Woodward principle. General specifications of both types are the same.
With Purdey action, double triggers **$25,000**
With Woodward action, double triggers **28,000**
Single trigger, extra **1,000**

Purdey Over-and-Under

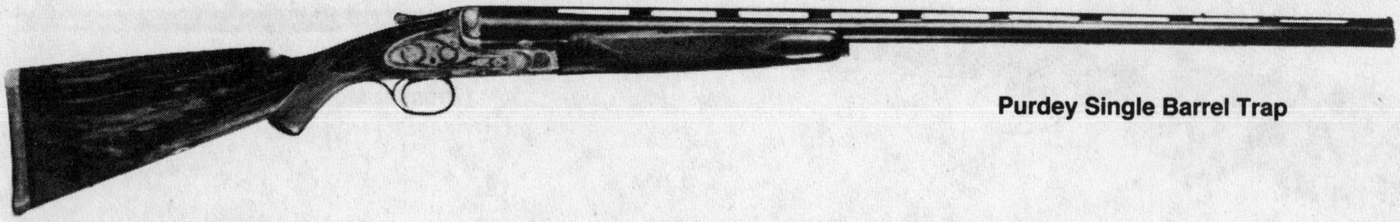

Purdey Single Barrel Trap

Purdey Single Barrel Trap Gun **$15,000**
Side lock. Mechanical features similar to those of the over-and-under model with Purdey action. 12 gauge only. Built to customer's specifications. Made prior to World War II.

REMINGTON ARMS CO.
Ilion, New York

Eliphalet Remington Jr. began making long arms with his father in 1816. In 1828 they moved their facility to Ilion, N.Y., where it remained a family-run business for decades. As the family died, other people bought controlling interests and today, still a successful gunmaking company, it is a subsidiary of the du Pont Corporation.

Remington Model 10A Standard Grade Slide Action Repeating Shotgun **$290**
Hammerless. Takedown. 6-shot. 12 gauge only. 5-shell tubular magazine. Barrels: plain; 26- to 32-inch; choked full, modified or cylinder. Weight: about 7½ pounds. Plain pistol-grip stock, grooved slide handle. Made 1907 to 1929.

Remington Model 11 Special, Tournament, Expert and Premier Grade Guns
These higher grade models differ from the Model 11A in general quality, grade of wood, checkering, engraving, etc. General specifications are the same.

Model 11B Special Grade	**$ 400**
Model 11D Tournament Grade	**795**
Model 11E Expert Grade	**1200**
Model 11F Premier Grade	**2000**

Remington Model 11A Standard Grade Autoloader
Hammerless Browning type. 5-shot. Takedown. Gauges: 12, 16, 20. Tubular magazine holds four shells. Barrels: plain, solid or vent rib; lengths from 26 inches to 32 inches; full, modified, improved cylinder, cylinder bore, skeet choke. Weight: about 8 pounds, 12 ga.; 7½ pounds, 16 ga.; 7¼ pounds, 20 ga. Checkered pistol grip and forend. Made 1905 to 1949.

With plain barrel	**$240**
With solid-rib barrel	**320**
With ventilated-rib barrel	**350**

Remington Model 11R Riot Gun **$210**
Same as Model 11A Standard Grade, except has 20-inch plain barrel, 12 gauge only.

Remington Model 11-48.
See Remington Sportsman-48 Series.

Remington Model 11-87 Premier Autoloader
Gas-operated. Hammerless. Gauge: 12; 3-inch chamber. Barrel: 26-, 28- or 30-inch with REM choke. Weight: 8⅛ to 8⅜ pounds, depending upon barrel length. Checkered walnut stock and forend in satin finish. Made from 1987 to date.

Left-Hand	**$410**
Skeet	**410**
SP Deer Gun	**375**
SP Magnum	**375**
Standard Autoloader	**380**
Trap	**420**

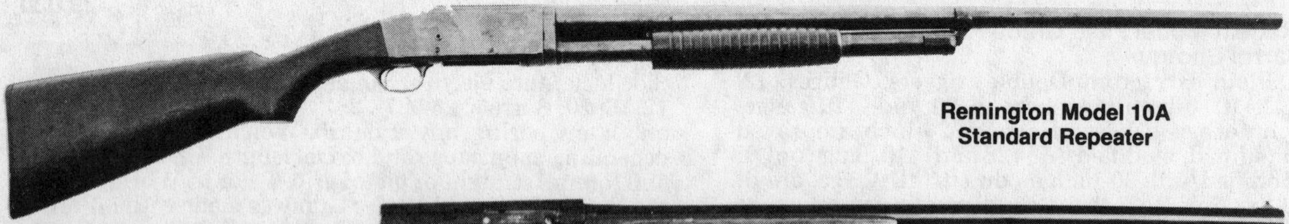

Remington Model 10A
Standard Repeater

Remington Model 11A
Autoloader

Remington Model 11-87 Premier
12 Gauge Autoloader

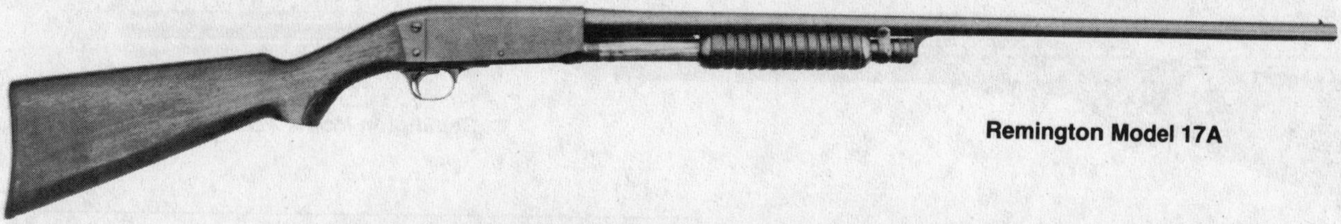

Remington Model 17A

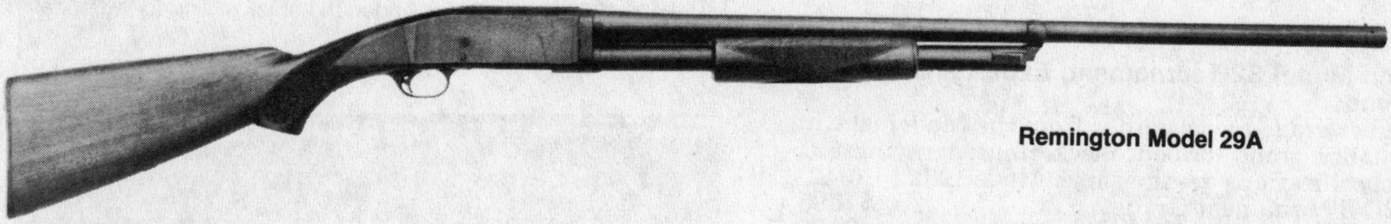

Remington Model 29A

Remington Model 17A Standard Grade Slide Action Repeating Shotgun **$250**
Hammerless. Takedown. 5-shot. 20 gauge only. 4-shell tubular magazine. Barrels: plain; 26- to 32-inch; choked full, modified or cylinder. Weight: about 5¾ pounds. Plain pistol-grip stock, grooved slide handle. Made 1921 to 1933. *Note:* The present Ithaca Model 37 is an adaptation of this Browning design.

Remington Model 29A Standard Grade Slide Action Repeating Shotgun **$300**
Hammerless. Takedown. 6-shot. 12 gauge only. 5-shell tubular magazine. Barrels: plain; 26- to 32-inch; choked full, modified or cylinder. Weight: about 7½ pounds. Checkered pistol-grip stock and slide handle. Made 1929 to 1933.

Remington Model 29T Target Grade **$340**
Same general specifications as Model 29A, except has trap-style stock with straight grip, extension slide handle, vent-rib barrel. Discontinued 1933.

Remington Model 31 Skeet Grade
Same general specifications as Model 31A, except has 26-inch barrel with raised solid or ventilated rib, skeet boring, checkered pistol-grip stock and beavertail forend. Weight: about 8 pounds, 12 ga.
With raised solid rib **$480**
With ventilated rib **800**

Remington Model 31 Special, Tournament, Expert and Premier Grade Guns
These higher grade models differ from the Model 31A in general quality, grade of wood, checkering, engraving, etc. General specifications are the same.
Model 31B Special Grade . . . . **$ 390**
Model 31D Tournament Grade **790**
Model 31E Expert Grade **1140**
Model 31F Premier Grade **1700**

Remington Model 31A Standard Grade Slide Action Repeater
Hammerless. Takedown. 3- or 5-shot. Gauges: 12, 16, 20. Tubular magazine holds two or four shells. Barrels: plain, solid or vent rib; lengths from 26 inches to 32 inches; full, modified, improved cylinder, cylinder or skeet choke. Weight: about 7½ pounds, 12 ga.; 6¾ pounds, 16 ga.; 6½ pounds, 20 ga. Earlier models have checkered pistol-grip stock and slide handle; later models have plain stock and grooved slide handle. Made 1931 to 1949.
With plain barrel **$265**
With solid-rib barrel **340**
With ventilated-rib barrel **360**

Remington Model 31H Hunters' Special **$400**
Same as Model 31S, except has sporting-style stock (shorter and with more drop).

Remington Model 31R Riot Gun **$215**
Same as Model 31A, except has 20-inch plain barrel, 12 gauge only.

Remington Model 31S Trap Special **$425**
Same general specifications as Model 31TC, except has solid-rib barrel, half-pistol-grip stock and forend of standard walnut.

Remington Model 31TC Trap Grade **$645**
Same general specifications as Model 31A, except 12 gauge only, has 30- or 32-inch vent-rib barrel, full choke, trap stock with full pistol grip and recoil pad, extension beavertail forend, both checkered. Weight: about 8 pounds.

Remington Model 32 Skeet Grade
Same general specifications as Model 32A, except 26- or 28-inch barrel, skeet boring, beavertail forend, selective single trigger only. Weight: about 7½ pounds. Made 1932 to 1942.
With plain barrels **$1250**
With raised solid rib **1395**
With ventilated rib **1550**

SHOTGUNS

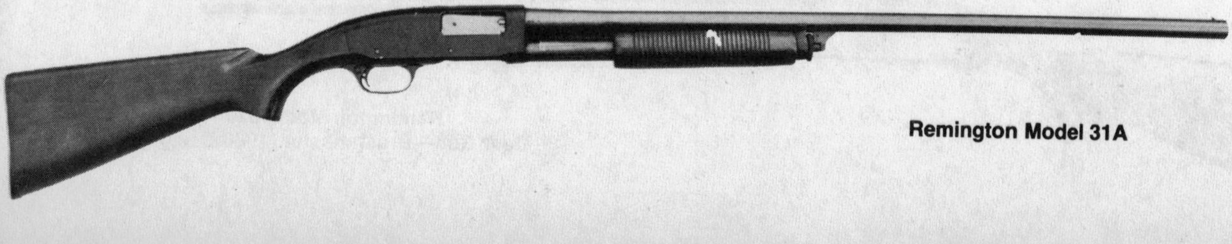

Remington Model 31A

Remington Model 32A

Remington Model 32 Tournament, Expert and Premier Grade Guns

These higher grade models differ from the Model 32A in general quality, grade of wood, checkering, engraving, etc. General specifications are the same. Made 1932 to 1942.

Model 32D Tournament Grade **$1895**
Model 32E Expert Grade **2600**
Model 32F Premier Grade **4200**

Remington Model 32A Standard Grade Over/Under

Hammerless. Takedown. Auto ejectors. Early model had double triggers, later built with selective single trigger only. 12 gauge only. Barrels: plain, raised matted solid or vent rib; 26-, 28-, 30-, 32-inch; full and modified choke standard, option of any combination of full, modified, improved cylinder, cylinder, skeet boring. Weight: about 7¾ pounds. Checkered pistol-grip stock and forend. Made 1932 to 1942.

With double triggers .... **$ 950**
With selective single trigger **1025**
Extra for raised solid rib **125**
Extra for ventilated rib **210**

Remington Model 32TC Target (Trap) Grade

Same general specifications as Model 32A, except 30- or 32-inch vent-rib barrel, full choke, trap-style stock with checkered pistol-grip and beavertail forend. Weight: about 8 pounds. Made 1932 to 1942.

With double triggers **$1395**
With selective single trigger **1495**

Remington Model 89 .... $950

Hammers. Circular action. Gauges: 10, 12, 16. 28- to 32-inch barrels; steel or damascus twist. Weight 7 to 10 pounds. Made from 1889 to 1908.

Note: In 1980 Remington changed the stock styling for all Model 870 shotguns.

Remington Model 870 "All American" Trap

Remington Model 870 "All American" Trap Gun $1250

Same as Model 870TB, except custom grade with engraved receiver, trigger guard and barrel; Monte Carlo or straight-comb stock and forend of fancy walnut; available only with 30-inch full choke barrel. Made 1972 to 1977.

Remington Model 870 Competition Trap $450

Based on standard Model 870 receiver, except is single-shot with gas-assisted recoil-reducing system, new choke design, a high step-up vent rib and redesigned stock and forend with cut checkering and a satin finish. Weight: 8½ pounds. Made 1981 to date.

Remington Model 870 Deer Gun Brushmaster Deluxe $310

Same as Model 870 Standard Deer Gun, except available in 20 gauge as well as 12 gauge, has checkered stock and forend, recoil pad.

Remington Model 870 Deer Gun Standard $310

Same as Model 870 Riot Gun, except has rifle-type sights.

Remington Model 870 Competition Trap

Remington Model 870 Deer Gun—Brushmaster

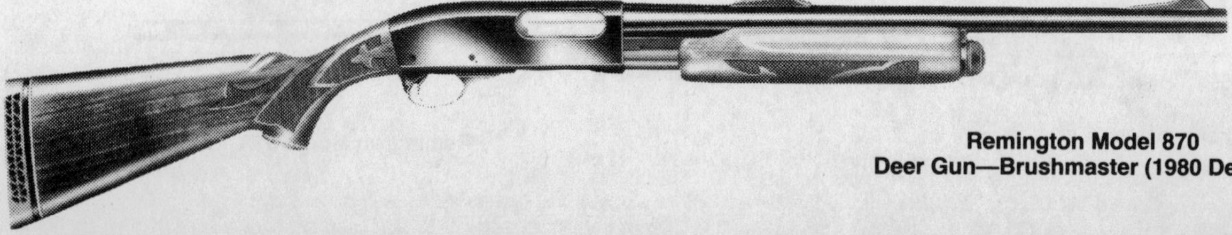
Remington Model 870 Deer Gun—Brushmaster (1980 Design)

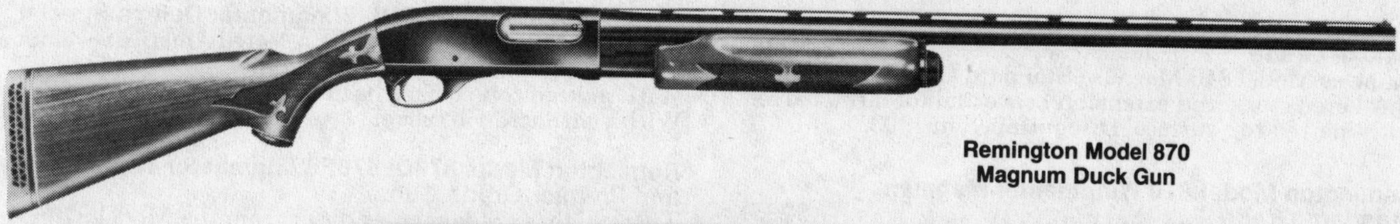

Remington Model 870
Magnum Duck Gun

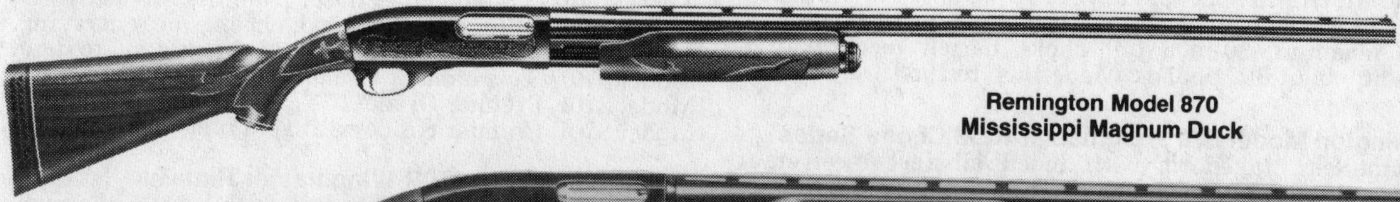

Remington Model 870
Mississippi Magnum Duck

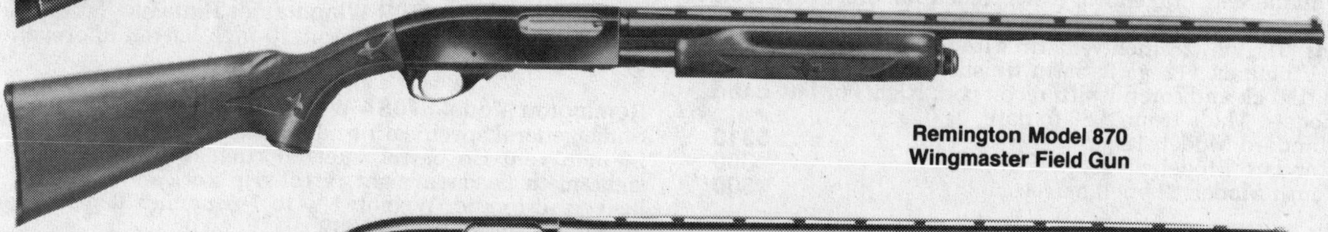

Remington Model 870
Wingmaster Field Gun

Remington Model 870
Wingmaster Field Gun (1980 Design)

Remington Model 870 Lightweight
Same as standard Model 870, but with scaled-down receiver and lightweight mahogany stock; 20 gauge only. $2\frac{3}{4}$-inch chamber. Barrels: plain or vent rib; 26-inch, improved cylinder; 28-inch, modified or full choke. Weight: $5\frac{3}{4}$ pounds with 26-inch plain barrel. Made 1972 to date.
With plain barrel **$230**
With ventilated-rib barrel **250**

Remington Model 870 Lightweight Magnum
Same as Model 870 Lightweight, but chambered for 20 gauge magnum 3-inch shell; 28-inch barrel, plain or vent rib, full choke. Weight: 6 pounds with plain barrel. Made 1972 to date.
With plain barrel **$230**
With ventilated-rib barrel **275**

Remington Model 870 Magnum Duck Gun
Same as Model 870 Field Gun, except has 3-inch chamber, 12 and 20 gauge magnum only. 28- or 30-inch barrel, plain or vent rib, modified or full choke; recoil pad. Weight: about $7\frac{1}{2}$ or $6\frac{3}{4}$ pounds. Made 1964 to date.
With plain barrel **$230**
With ventilated-rib barrel **275**

Remington Model 870 Mississippi Magnum Duck Gun **$350**
Same as Remington Model 870 Magnum Duck Gun except has 32-inch barrel. Engraved receiver, "Ducks Unlimited." Made 1983 to date.

Remington Model 870 SA Skeet Gun, Small Bore **$275**
Similar to Wingmaster Model 870SA, except chambered for 28 and .410 gauge ($2\frac{1}{2}$-inch chamber for latter); 25-inch vent-rib barrel, skeet choke. Weight: 6 lbs., 28 ga.; $6\frac{1}{2}$ lbs., .410. Made 1969 to 1982.

Remington Model 870 Special Field Shotgun . . . **$325**
Pump action. Hammerless. Gauge: 12 or 20. 21-inch vent-rib barrel with REM choke. $41\frac{1}{2}$ inches overall. Weight: 6 to 7 pounds. Straight-grip checkered walnut stock and forend. Made from 1987 to date.

Remington Model 870 Special Purpose Deer Gun **$265**
Similar to Special Purpose Magnum, except with 20-inch, improved cylinder choke, rifle sights on barrel. Matte black oxide and parkerized finish. Oil-finished, checkered buttstock and forend with recoil pad. Made 1986 to date.

Remington Model 870 Special Purpose Magnum **$300**
Similar to the 870 Magnum Duck Gun, except with 26- or 30-inch vent-rib REM Choke barrel. 12 gauge only; 3-inch chamber. Matte black finish. Field-grade stock with recoil pad. Made 1985 to date.

Remington Model 870 Wingmaster Field Gun
Same general specifications as Model 870AP, except checkered stock and forend. Later models have REM choke systems in 12 ga. Made 1964 to date.
With plain barrel **$250**
With ventilated-rib barrel **300**

Remington Model 870 Wingmaster Field Gun, Small Bore
Same as standard Model 870, but scaled down. Gauges: 28, .410. 25-inch barrel, plain or vent rib; improved cylinder, modified or full choke. Weight: $5\frac{1}{2}$ to $6\frac{1}{4}$ pounds depending upon gauge and barrel. Made 1969 to date.
With plain barrel **$250**
With ventilated-rib barrel **310**
With REM choke **310**

Remington Model 870 Wingmaster Magnum Deluxe Grade **$295**
Same as Model 870 Magnum Standard Grade, except has checkered stock and extension beavertail forearm, barrel with matted top surface. Discontinued in 1963.

Remington Model 870 Wingmaster Magnum Standard Grade **$295**
Same as Model 870AP, except chambered for 12 gauge 3-inch magnum, 30-inch full choke barrel, recoil pad. Weight: about 8¼ pounds. Made 1955 to 1963.

Remington Model 870 Wingmaster REM Choke Series
Hammerless, takedown with blued all-steel receiver. Gauges: 12, 20; 3-inch chamber. Tubular magazine. Barrels: 21-, 26-, 28-inch vent-rib with REM Choke. Weight: 7½ pounds (12 ga.). Satin-finished, checkered walnut buttstock and forend with recoil pad. Right- or left-hand models. Made from 1986 to date.
Standard Model, 12 ga. **$310**
Standard Model, 20 ga. **300**
Youth Model, 21-inch barrel **300**

Remington Model 870ADL Wingmaster Deluxe Grade
Same general specifications as Wingmaster Model 870AP, except has pistol-grip stock and extension beavertail forend, both finely checkered; matted top surface or vent-rib barrel. Made 1950 to 1963.
With matted top-surface barrel **$210**
With ventilated-rib barrel **230**

Remington Model 870AP Wingmaster Standard Grade 5-Shot Slide Action Repeater
Hammerless. Takedown. Gauges: 12, 16, 20. Tubular magazine holds four shells. Barrels: plain, matted top surface or vent rib; 26-inch improved cylinder, 28-inch modified or full choke, 30-inch full choke (12 ga. only). Weight: about 7 pounds, 12 ga.; 6¾ pounds, 16 ga.; 6½ pounds, 20 ga. Plain pistol-grip stock, grooved forend. Made 1950 to 1963.
With plain barrel **$200**
With matted top-surface barrel **210**
With ventilated-rib barrel **230**
Left-hand model **240**

Remington Model 870BDL Wingmaster Deluxe Special
Same as Model 870ADL, except selected American walnut stock and forend. Made 1950 to 1963.
With matted top-surface barrel **$230**
With ventilated-rib barrel **250**

Remington Model 870D, 870F Wingmaster Tournament and Premier Grade Guns
These higher grade models differ from the Model 870AP in general quality, grade of wood, checkering, engraving, etc. Gen. specifications are the same. Made 1950 to date.
Model 870D Tournament Grade **$1350**
Model 870F Premier Grade **2900**
Model 870F Premier Grade with gold inlay **4300**

Remington Model 870R Wingmaster Riot Gun . . **$200**
Same as Model 870AP, except 20-inch barrel, improved cylinder, 12 gauge only.

Remington Model 870SA Wingmaster Skeet Gun
Same general specifications as Model 870AP, except has 26-inch vent-rib barrel, skeet boring, ivory bead front sight, metal bead rear sight, pistol-grip stock and extension beavertail forend. Weight: 6¾ to 7½ pounds depending on gauge. Made 1950 to 1982.
Model 870SA Skeet Grade (Disc. 1982) . . . . **$ 260**
Model 870SC Skeet Target Grade (Disc 1980) **430**
Model 870SD Skeet Tournament Grade **1200**
Model 870SF Skeet Premier Grade **2400**

Remington Model 870TB Wingmaster Trap Special **$325**
Same general specifications as Model 870AP Wingmaster, except has 28- or 30-inch vent-rib barrel, full choke, metal bead front sight, no rear sight. "Special" grade trap-style stock and forend, both checkered, recoil pad. Weight: about 8 pounds. Made 1950 to 1981.

Remington Model 870TC Wingmaster Trap Grade
Same as Model 870TB, except higher grade walnut in stock and forend, has both front and rear sights. Made 1950 to 1979. Model 870 TC reissued in 1987. See separate listing.
Model 870TC Trap Grade . . . . **$ 400**
Model 870TD Trap Tournament Grade **1250**
Model 870TF Trap Premier Grade **2500**

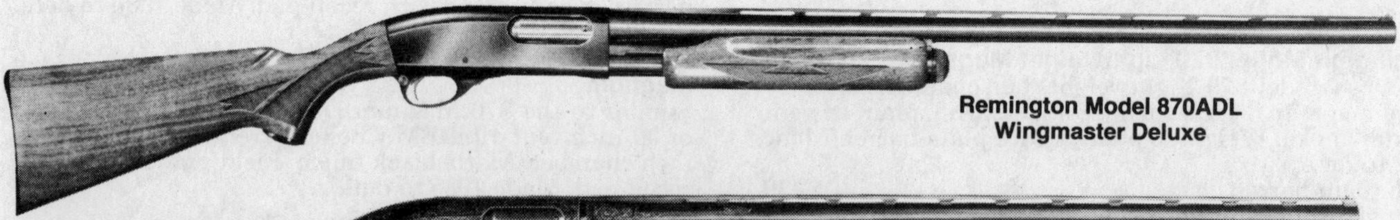

Remington Model 870ADL Wingmaster Deluxe

Remington Model 870F Wingmaster Premier Grade

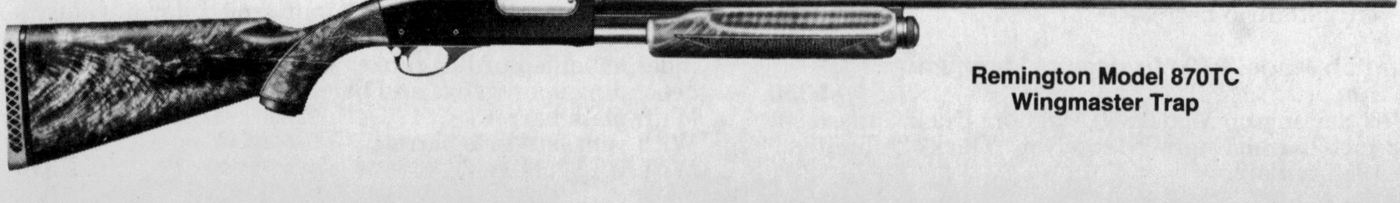

Remington Model 870TC Wingmaster Trap

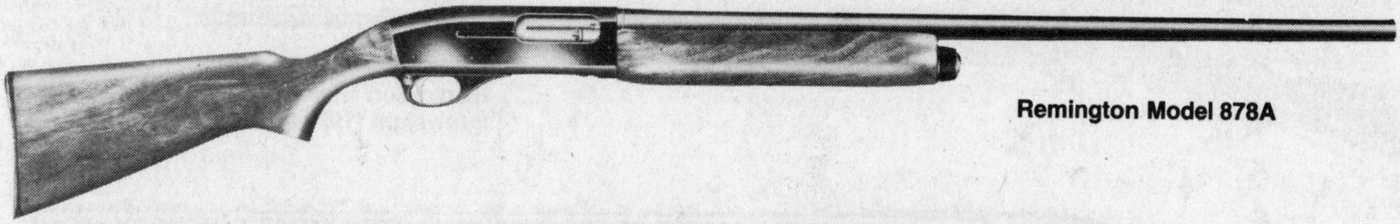

Remington Model 878A

Remington Model 1100
Left-hand Action

Remington Model 878A Automaster Autoloader **$250**

Gas-operated. 12 gauge, 3-shot magazine. Barrels: 26-inch improved cylinder, 28-inch modified choke, 30-inch full choke. Weight: about 7 pounds. Plain pistol-grip stock and forearm. Made 1959 to 1962.

> *Note:* New stock checkering patterns and receiver scroll markings were incorporated on all standard Model 1100 field, magnum, skeet and trap models in 1979.

Remington Model 1100 Automatic Field Gun

Gas-operated. Hammerless. Takedown. Gauges: 12, 16, 20. Barrels: plain or vent. rib; 30-inch/full, 28-inch/modified or full, 26-inch/improved cylinder; or REM choke tubes. Weight: average 7¼ to 7½ pounds depending upon gauge and barrel length. Checkered walnut pistol-grip stock and forearm in high-gloss finish. Made 1963 to date. 16 ga. discontinued.

With plain barrel **$300**
With ventilated-rib barrel **340**
REM choke model **370**
REM chokes, Left-hand action **400**

Remington Model 1100 Deer Gun **$395**

Same as Model 1100 Field Gun, except has 22-inch barrel, improved cylinder, with rifle-type sights; 12 and 20 gauge only; recoil pad. Weight: about 7¼ pounds. Made 1963 to date.

Remington Model 1100 Ducks Unlimited Atlantic Commemorative **$450**

Limited production for one year. Similar specifications to Model 1100 Field, except with 32-inch full choke, vent-rib barrel. 12-gauge magnum only. Made in 1982.

Remington Model 1100 Ducks Unlimited "The Chesapeake" Commemorative **$440**

Limited edition 1 to 2400. Same general specifications as Model 1100 Field, except sequentially serial numbered with markings "The Chesapeake." 12-gauge Magnum with 30-inch full choke, vent-rib barrel. Made in 1981.

Remington Model 1100 Field

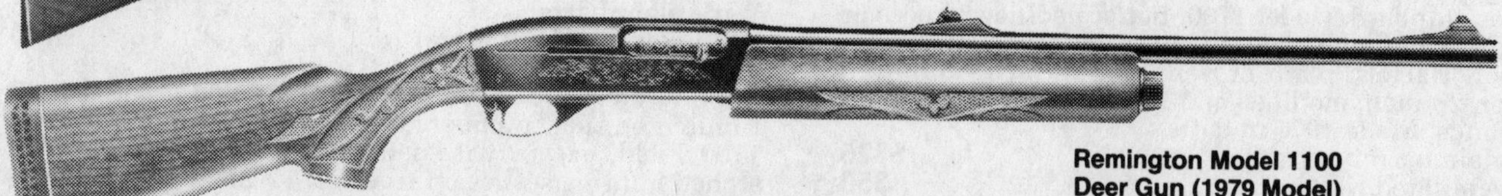

Remington Model 1100
Deer Gun (1979 Model)

Remington Model 1100 Ducks
Unlimited Atlantic Commemorative

Remington Model 1100 Ducks Unlimited
"The Chesapeake" Commemorative

Remington Model 1100 Lightweight (1979 Model)

Remington Model 1100 LT-20 Ducks Unlimited Special

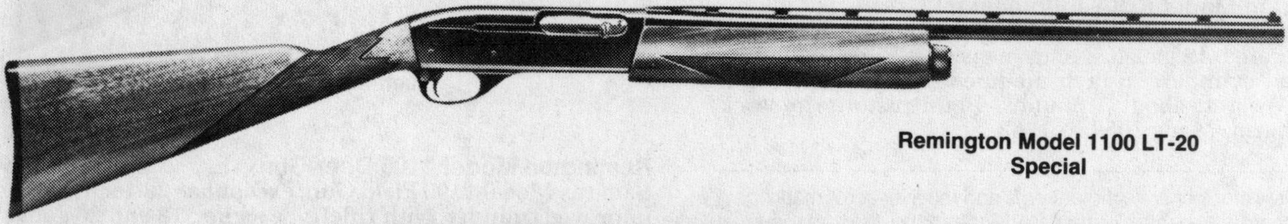

Remington Model 1100 LT-20 Special

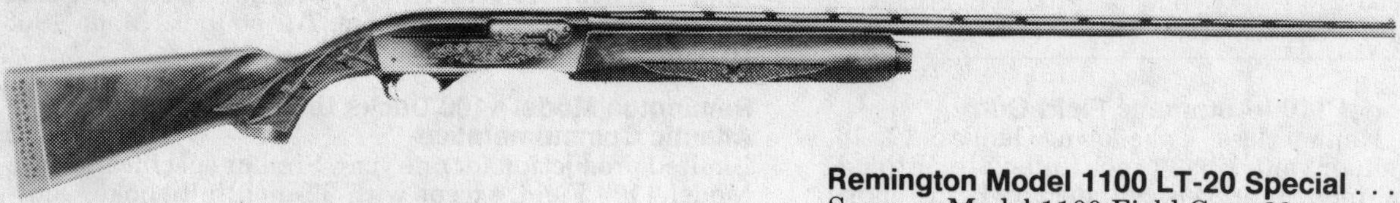

Remington Model 1100 Magnum Duck Gun

Remington Model 1100 Field Grade, Small Bore
Same as standard Model 1100, but scaled down. Gauges: 28, .410. 25-inch barrel, plain or vent rib; improved cylinder, modified or full choke. Weight: 6¼ to 7 pounds depending upon gauge and barrel. Made 1969 to date.
With plain barrel **$360**
With ventilated rib **375**

Remington Model 1100 Lightweight
Same as standard Model 1100, but scaled-down receiver and lightweight mahogany stock; 20 gauge only, 2¾-inch chamber. Barrels: plain or vent rib; 26-inch, improved cylinder, 28-inch, modified and full choke. Weight: about 6¼ pounds. Made 1971 to date.
With plain barrel **$325**
With ventilated rib **350**

Remington Model 1100 Lightweight Magnum
Same as Model 1100 Lightweight, but chambered for 20 gauge magnum 3-inch shell; 28-inch barrel, plain or vent rib, full choke. Weight: about 6½ pounds. Made 1971 to date.
With plain barrel **$330**
With ventilated rib **350**
With chokes tubes **375**

Remington Model 1100 LT-20 Ducks Unlimited Special Commemorative **$450**
Limited edition 1 to 2400. Same general specifications as Model 1100 Field, except sequentially serial numbered with markings "The Chesapeake." 20-gauge only. 26-inch improved cylinder, vent-rib barrel. Made in 1981.

Remington Model 1100 LT-20 Special **$375**
Same as Model 1100 Field Gun, 20 gauge, except has 23-inch vent-rib barrel. Stock is 1-inch shorter than standard, and has straight grip. REM choke series has 21-inch vent-rib barrel, choke tubes. Weight: 6¼ pounds. Checkered grip and forearm. Made 1983 to date.

Remington Model 1100 Magnum **$395**
Limited production. Similar to the Model 1100 Field, except with 26-inch full choke, vent-rib barrel and 3-inch chamber. Made in 1981.

Remington Model 1100 Magnum Duck Gun
Same as Model 1100 Field Gun, except has 3-inch chamber, 12 and 20 gauge magnum only. 30-inch plain or vent-rib barrel in 12 gauge, 28-inch in 20 gauge; modified or full choke. Recoil pad. Weight: about 7¾ pounds. Made 1963 to date.
With plain barrel **$375**
With ventilated-rib barrel **410**

Remington Model 1100 One of 3000 Field **$1000**
Limited edition, numbered 1 to 3000. Similar to Model 1100 Field, except with fancy wood and gold-trimmed etched hunting scenes on receiver. 12 gauge with 28-inch modified, vent-rib barrel. Made in 1980.

Remington Model 1100 Special Field Shotgun . . **$410**
Gas-operated. 5-shot. Hammerless. Gauges: 12 and 20. 21-inch vent-rib barrel with REM choke. Weight: 6½ to 7¼ pounds. Straight-grip checkered walnut stock and forend. Made from 1987 to date.

Remington Model 1100 SP Magnum
Same as Model 1100 Field, except 12 gauge only with 3-inch chambers. Barrels: 26-, 30-inch w/full choke; or 26-inch with REM Choke tubes; ventilated rib. Non-reflective, matte black, parkerized barrel and receiver. Satin-finished stock and forend. Made from 1981 to date.
With Fixed Choke **$395**
With REM Choke **410**

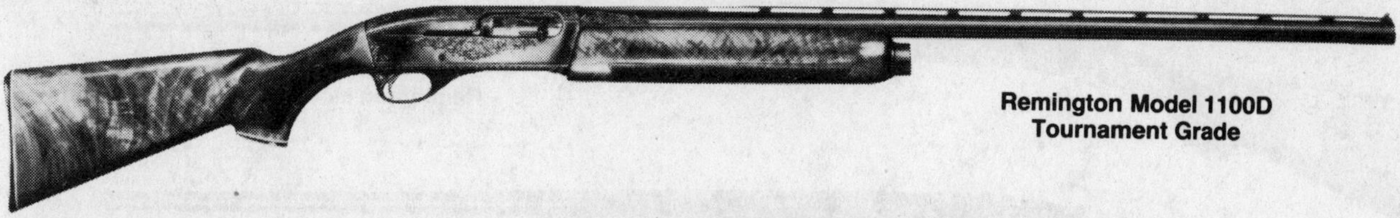

Remington Model 1100D Tournament Grade

Remington Model 1100SA Skeet Gun Left-hand Action

Remington Model 1100TB Trap

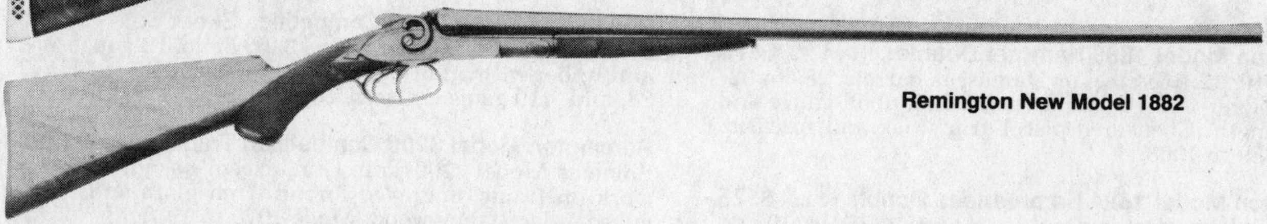

Remington New Model 1882

Remington Model 1100 Tournament and Premier
These higher grade guns differ from standard models in overall quality, grade of wood, checkering, engraving, gold inlays, etc. General specifications are the same. Made 1963 to date.
Model 1100D Tournament **$1395**
Model 1100F Premier **2895**
Model 1100F Premier with gold inlay **4295**

Remington Model 1100 Tournament Skeet $425
Similar to Model 1100 Field, except with 26-inch barrel, skeet bore. Gauges: 12, LT-20, 28, and .410. Features select walnut stocks and new cut-checkering patterns. Made 1979 to date.

Remington Model 1100 Tournament Trap
Similar to Model 1100 Field Gun, except with 30-inch full or modified trap barrels. 12-gauge. Features select walnut stocks with cut-checkering patterns. Made 1979 to date.
D Grade **$1495**
F Grade **2700**
F Grade w/Gold Inlay **4150**

Remington Model 1100SA Skeet Gun
Same as Model 1100 Field Gun, 12 and 20 gauge, except has 26-inch vent-rib barrel, skeet choke or with Cutts Compensator. Weight: 7¼ to 7½ pounds. Made 1963 to date.
With skeet-choked barrel **$375**
With Cutts Comp **395**
Left-hand action **410**

Remington Model 1100SA Lightweight Skeet ... $360
Same as Model 1100 Lightweight, except has skeet-style stock and forearm, 26-inch vent-rib barrel, skeet choke. Made 1971 to date.

Remington Model 1100SA Skeet Gun, Small Bore $375
Similar to standard Model 1100SA, except chambered for 28 and .410 gauge (2½-inch chamber for latter); 25-inch vent-rib barrel, skeet choke. Weight: 6¾ pounds, 28 ga.; 7¼ pounds, .410. Made 1969 to date.

Remington Model 1100SB Lightweight Skeet ... $375
Same as Model 1100SA Lightweight, except has selected wood. Introduced in 1977.

Remington Model 1100SB Skeet Gun $375
Same as Model 1100SA, except has selected wood. Made 1963 to date.

Remington Model 1100TA Trap Gun $360
Similar to Model 1100TB Trap Gun, except with regular-grade stocks. Available in both left- and right-hand versions. Made 1979 to date.

Remington Model 1100TB Trap Gun
Same as Model 1100 Field Gun, except has special trap stock, straight or Monte Carlo comb, recoil pad; 30-inch vent-rib barrel, full or modified trap choke; 12 gauge only. Weight: 8¼ pounds. Made 1963 to 1979.
With straight stock **$395**
With Monte Carlo stock **415**

Remington New Model 1882 Hammer Double ... $895
Gauges: 10, 12, 16. Plain or Damascus barrels, 28- to 32-inch. Weight: 6¾ to 10¼ pounds. Checkered pistol-grip stock and forearm. Made 1882 to 1910. *Note:* Value shown is for standard grade; this model was made in six higher grades, varying in quality of workmanship, engraving, grade of wood, etc.

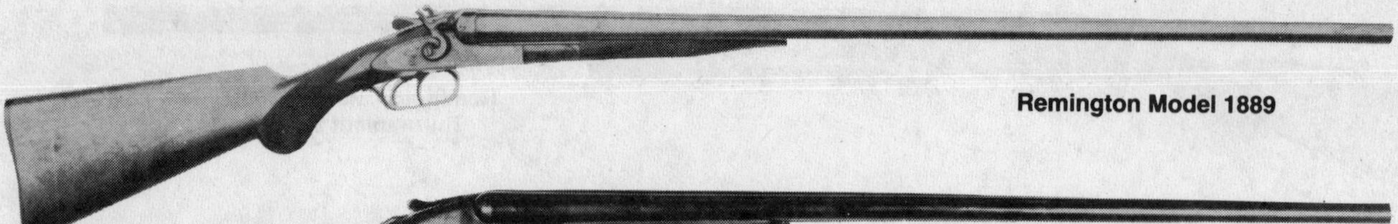

Remington Model 1889

Remington Model 1894

Remington Model 1900

Remington Model 1889 Hammer Double $875
Gauges: 10, 12, 16. Steel or Damascus barrels, 28- to 32-inch. Weight: 7 to 10 pounds depending upon gauge and barrel length. Checkered pistol-grip stock and forearm. Made 1889 to 1908.

Remington Model 1894 Hammerless Double . . . $525
Box lock. Auto ejector. Double triggers. Gauges: 10, 12, 16. Ordnance steel barrels, 28- to 32-inch. Weight: 7 to 10 pounds. Checkered stock and forearm. Made 1894 to 1910. *Note:* This model was made in seven higher grades, including a trap gun, which have a higher value than the standard grade value listed here. Guns with Damascus barrels have about 50 percent lower value.

Remington Model 1900 Hammerless Double . . . $595
Improved version of Model 1894 with same general specifications. Made 1900 to 1910. Value shown is for standard grade with ordnance steel barrels; see note under Model 1894.

Remington Model 3200 Competition Skeet Gun . $1210
Same as Model 3200 Skeet Gun, except has gilded scrollwork on frame, engraved forend latch plate and trigger guard, select fancy wood. Made 1973 to 1984.

Remington Model 3200 Competition Skeet Set . . $3800
Similar specifications to Model 3200 Field. 12-gauge over-and-under with additional, interchangeable barrels in 20, 28, and .410 gauges. Cased. Made 1980 to 1984.

Remington Model 3200 Competition Trap Gun . . $1200
Same as Model 3200 Trap Gun, except has gilded scrollwork on frame, engraved forend latch plate and trigger guard, select fancy wood. Made 1973 to 1984.

Remington Model 3200 Field Grade Magnum . . . $950
Same as Model 3200 Field Grade, except chambered for 12 gauge magnum 3-inch shell; 30-inch barrels, modified and full or both full choke. Made 1975 to 1984.

Remington Model 3200 Field Grade O/U $850
Box lock. Auto ejectors. Selective single trigger. 12 gauge. 2¾-inch chambers. Barrels: vent rib; 26- and 28-inch modified and full, 30-inch improved cylinder and modified. Weight: about 7¾ pounds with 26-inch barrels. Checkered pistol-grip stock and forearm. Made 1973 to 1978.

Remington Model 3200 "One of 1000" Skeet . . $1895
Same as Model 3200 "One of 1000" Trap Gun, except has 26- or 28-inch barrels bored skeet choke, skeet-style stock and forearm. Made in 1974.

Remington Model 3200 Field

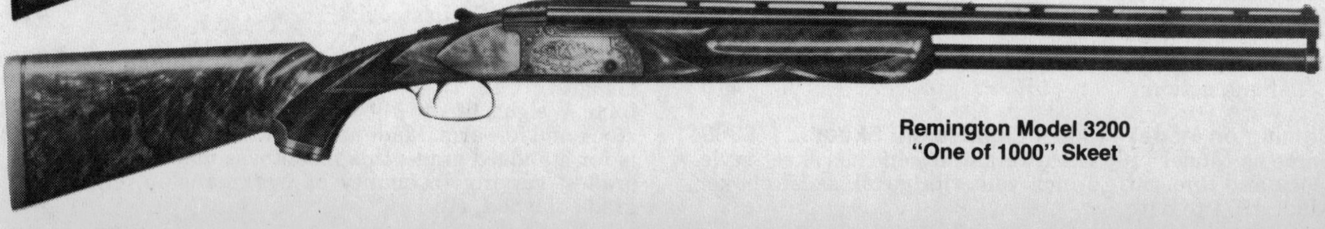

Remington Model 3200
"One of 1000" Skeet

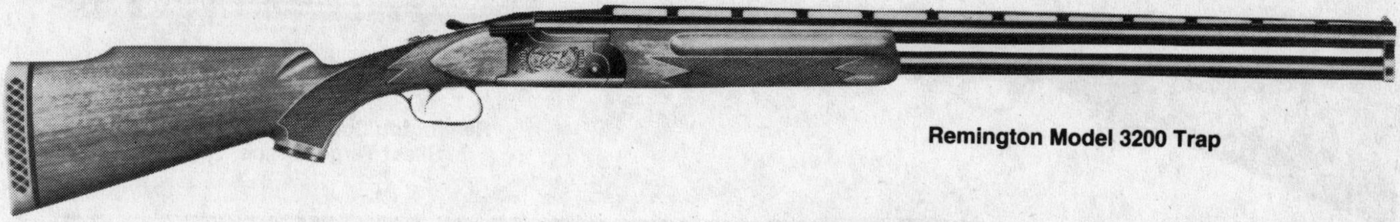

Remington Model 3200 Trap

Remington Model 3200 "One of 1000" Trap Gun $2195
Limited edition numbered 1 to 1000. Same general specifications as Model 3200 Trap Gun, but has frame, trigger guard and forend latch elaborately engraved (designation "One of 1,000" on frame side), stock and forearm of high grade walnut. Supplied in carrying case. Made in 1973.

Remington Model 3200 Skeet Gun $1000
Same as Model 3200 Field Grade, except skeet-style stock and full beavertail forearm; 26- or 28-inch barrels, skeet choke. Made 1973 to 1980.

Remington Model 3200 Special Trap Gun $1100
Same as Model 3200 Trap Gun, except has select wood. Made 1973 to 1984.

Remington Model 3200 Trap Gun $1000
Same as Model 3200 Field Grade, except trap-style stock with Monte Carlo or straight comb, beavertail forearm; 30- or 32-inch barrels, improved modified/full or both full choke. Made 1973 to 1977.

Remington Rider No. 3 Single Barrel Shotgun .. $210
Semi-hammerless. Gauges: 10, 12, 16, 20, 24, 28. Plain barrel, 30- to 32-inch. Weight: about 6 pounds. Plain pistol-grip stock and forearm. Made 1893 to 1903.

Remington Rider No. 9 Single Barrel Shotgun .. $225
Improved version of No. 3 Single; same general specifications, except has auto ejector. Made 1902 to 1910.

Remington Sportsman A Standard Grade Autoloader
Same general specifications as Model 11A, except magazine holds two shells. Also available in "B" Special Grade, "D" Tournament Grade, "E" Expert Grade, "F" Premier Grade. Made 1931 to 1948. Same values as for Model 11A, etc.

Remington Sportsman Skeet Gun
Same general specifications as the Sportsman A, except has 26-inch barrel (plain, solid or vent rib), skeet boring, beavertail forend. Discont. 1949.

With plain barrel	$340
With solid-rib barrel	410
With ventilated-rib barrel	450

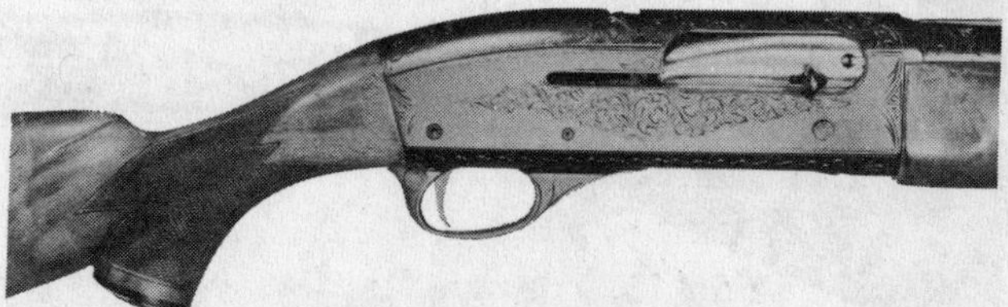

Remington Sportsman 48D Tournament Grade

Remington Sportsman-48 Special, Tournament and Premier Grade Guns
These higher grade models differ from the Sportsman-48A in general quality, grade of wood, checkering, engraving, etc. General specifications are the same. Made 1949 to 1959.

Sportsman-48B Special Grade	$ 340
Sportsman-48D Tournament Grade	725
Sportsman-48F Premier Grade	1500

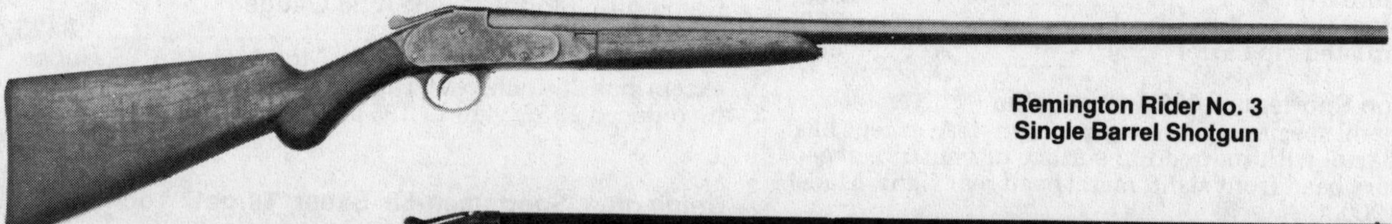

Remington Rider No. 3 Single Barrel Shotgun

Remington Rider No. 9

Remington Sportsman

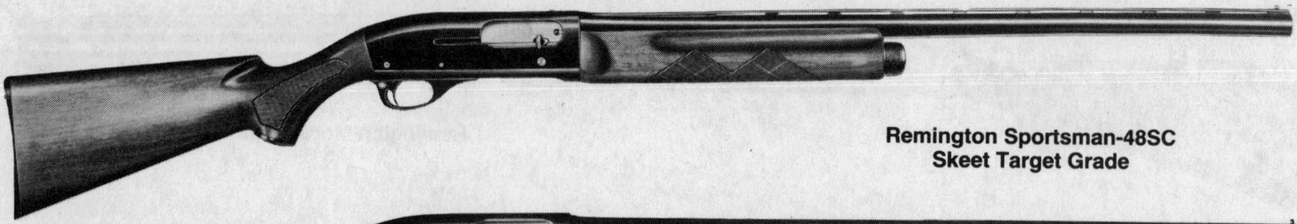

Remington Sportsman-48SC Skeet Target Grade

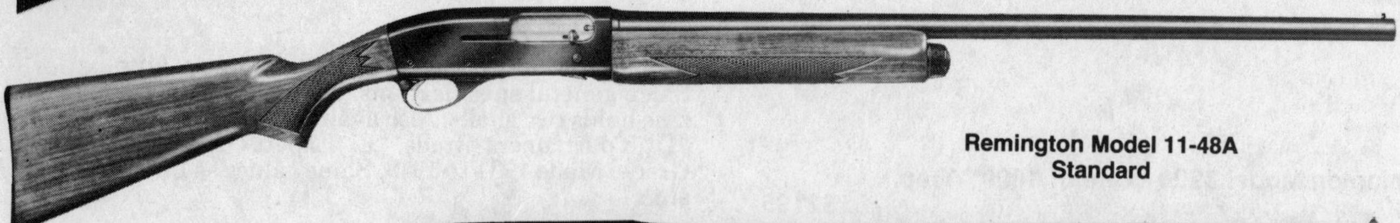

Remington Model 11-48A Standard

Remington Model 11-48A, 410 & 28

Remington Sportsman-58ADL

Remington Sportsman-48A Standard Grade 3-Shot Autoloader
Streamlined receiver. Hammerless. Takedown. Gauges: 12, 16, 20. Tubular magazine holds two shells. Barrels: plain, matted top surface or vent rib; 26-inch improved cylinder, 28-inch modified or full choke, 30-inch full choke (12 ga. only). Weight: about 7½ pounds, 12 ga.; 6¾ pounds, 16 ga.; 6½ pounds, 20 ga. Pistol-grip stock, grooved forend, both checkered. Made 1949 to 1959.
With plain barrel $230
With matted top-surface barrel 250
With ventilated-rib barrel 280

Remington Sportsman-48SA Skeet Gun
Same general specifications as Sportsman-48A, except has 26-inch barrel with matted top surface or vent rib, skeet choke, ivory bead front sight, metal bead rear sight. Made 1949 to 1960.
With matted top-surface barrel .... $ 245
With ventilated-rib barrel 290
Sportsman-48SC Skeet Target Grade 385
Sportsman-48SD Skeet Tournament Grade 785
Sportsman-48SF Skeet Premier Grade 1400

Remington Model 11-48A Riot Gun $250
Same as Model 11-48A, except 20-inch plain barrel and 12 gauge only. Discontinued in 1969.

Remington Model 11-48A Standard Grade 4-Shot Autoloader, 410 & 28 Gauge
Same general specifications as Sportsman-48A, except gauge, 3-shell magazine, 25-inch barrel. Weight: about 6¼ pounds. 28 gauge introduced 1952, .410 in 1954. Discontinued in 1969. Prices same as shown for Sportsman-48A.

Remington Model 11-48A Standard Grade 5-Shot Autoloader
Same general specifications as Sportsman-48A, except magazine holds four shells, forend not grooved. Also available in Special Grade (11-48B), Tournament Grade (11-48D) and Premier Grade (11-48F). Made 1949 to 1969. Prices same as shown for Sportsman-48A.

Remington Model 11-48SA 28 Gauge Skeet Gun $425
Same general specifications as Model 11-48A 28 Gauge, except has 25-inch vent-rib barrel, skeet choke. 28 gauge introduced 1952, .410 in 1954.

Remington Sportsman-58 Skeet Target, Tournament and Premier Grades
These higher grade models differ from the Sportsman-58SA in general quality, grade of wood, checkering, engraving, etc. General specifications are the same.
Sportsman-58C Skeet Target Grade .... $ 425
Sportsman-58D Skeet Tournament Grade 650
Sportsman-58SF Skeet Premier Grade 1270

Remington Sportsman-58 Tournament and Premier
These higher grade models differ from the Sportsman-58ADL with vent-rib barrel in general quality, grade of wood, checkering, engraving, etc. General specifications are the same.
Sportsman-58D Tournament Grade .... $ 690
Sportsman-58F Premier Grade 1300

Remington Sportsman-58ADL Autoloader
Deluxe Grade. Gas-operated. 12 gauge. 3-shot magazine. Barrels: plain or vent rib; 26-, 28- or 30-inch; improved cylinder, modified or full choke, or Remington Special Skeet boring. Weight: about 7 pounds. Checkered pistol-grip stock and forearm. Made 1956 to 1964.
With plain barrel **$250**
With ventilated-rib barrel **280**

Remington Sportsman-58BDL Deluxe Special Grade
Same as Model 58ADL, except select grade wood.
With plain barrel **$290**
With ventilated-rib barrel **330**

Remington Sportsman-58SA Skeet Grade $310
Same general specifications as Model 58ADL with vent-rib barrel, except special skeet stock and forearm.

REVELATION SHOTGUNS

See Western Auto listings.

RICHLAND ARMS COMPANY
Blissfield, Michigan
Manufactured in Italy and Spain

Richland Model 200 Field Grade Double $250
Hammerless, box lock, Anson & Deeley-type. Plain extractors. Double triggers. Gauges: 12, 16, 20, 28, .410 (3-inch chambers in 20 and .410; others have $2\frac{3}{4}$-inch). Barrels: 28-inch modified/full choke; 26-inch improved cylinder/modified; .410 with 26-inch modified/full only; 22-inch improved cylinder/modified in 20 ga. only. Weight: 6 lbs. 2 oz. to 7 lbs. 4 oz. Checkered walnut stock with cheekpiece, pistol grip, recoil pad; beavertail forend. Made in Spain 1963 to date.

Richland Model 202 All-Purpose Field Gun $295
Same as Model 200, except has two sets of barrels same gauge. 12 gauge: 30-inch barrels full/full, 3-inch chambers; 26-inch barrels improved cylinder/modified, $2\frac{3}{4}$-inch chambers. 20 gauge: 28-inch barrels modified/full; 22-inch barrels improved cylinder/modified, 3-inch chambers. Made 1963 to date.

Richland Model 707 Deluxe Field Gun $300
Hammerless, box lock, triple bolting system. Plain extractors. Double triggers. Gauges: 12, $2\frac{3}{4}$-inch chambers; 20, 3-inch chambers. Barrels: 12 gauge, 28-inch modified/full, 26-inch improved cylinder/modified; 20 gauge, 30-inch full/full, 28-inch modified/full, 26-inch improved cylinder/modified. Weight: 6 lbs. 4 oz. to 6 lbs. 15 oz. Checkered walnut stock and forend, recoil pad. Made 1963 to 1972.

Richland Model 711 Long Range Waterfowl Magnum Double Barrel Shotgun
Hammerless, box lock, Anson & Deeley-type, Purdey triple lock. Plain extractors. Double triggers. Auto safety. Gauges: 10, $3\frac{1}{2}$-inch chambers; 12, 3-inch chambers. Barrels: 10 ga., 32-inch; 12 ga., 30-inch; full and full. Weight: 10 ga., 11 pounds; 12 ga., $7\frac{3}{4}$ pounds. Checkered walnut stock and beavertail forend; recoil pad. Made in Spain 1963 to date.
10 Gauge Magnum **$350**
12 Gauge Magnum **230**

Richland Model 200 Field Grade Double

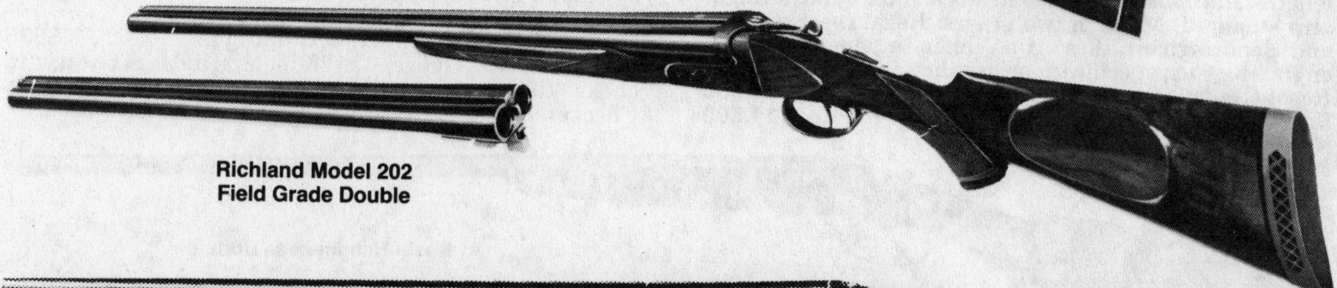
Richland Model 202 Field Grade Double

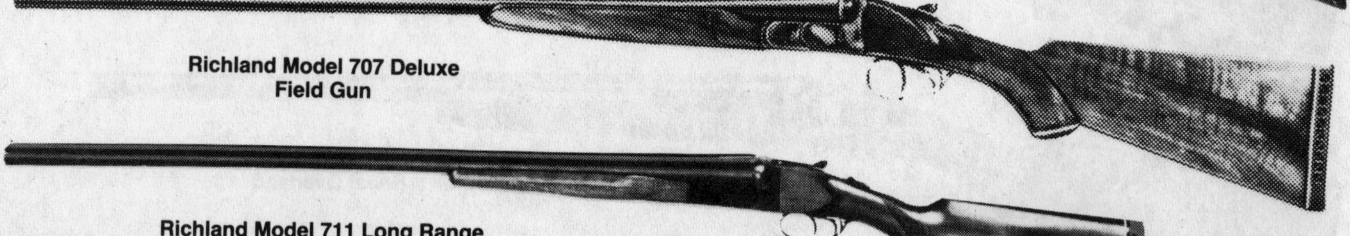
Richland Model 707 Deluxe Field Gun

Richland Model 711 Long Range Waterfowl Magnum

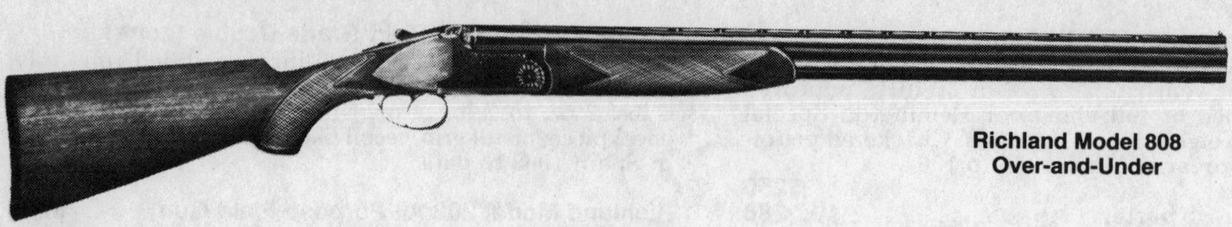

Richland Model 808
Over-and-Under

Richland Model 808 Over-and-Under Gun **$360**
Box lock. Plain extractors. Non-selective single trigger. 12 gauge only. Barrels (Vickers steel): 30-inch full/full; 28-inch modified/full; 26-inch improved cylinder/modified. Weight: 6 lbs. 12 oz. to 7 lbs. 3 oz. Checkered walnut stock and forend. Made in Italy 1963 to 1968.

JOHN RIGBY & CO.
London, England

Rigby Hammerless Box Lock Double Barrel Shotguns
Auto ejectors. Double triggers. Made in all gauges, barrel lengths and chokes. Checkered stock and forend, straight grip standard. Made in two grades: Sackville and Chatsworth. These guns differ in general quality, engraving, etc.; specifications are the same.
Sackville Grade **$5700**
Chatsworth Grade **4300**

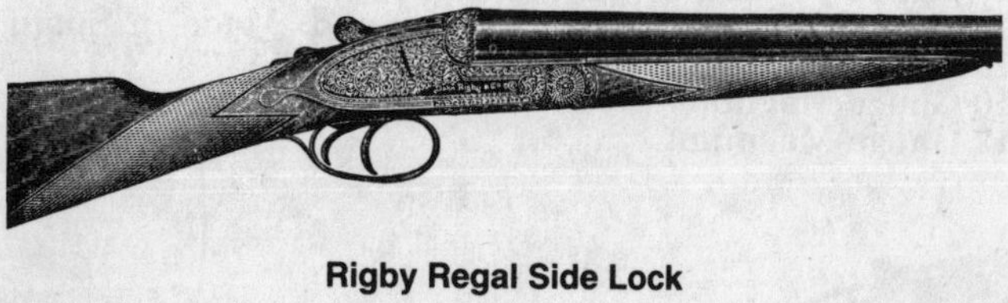

Rigby Regal Side Lock

Rigby Hammerless Side Lock Double Barrel Shotguns
Auto ejectors. Double triggers. Made in all gauges, barrel lengths and chokes. Checkered stock and forend, straight grip standard. Made in two grades: Regal (best quality) and Sandringham; these guns differ in general quality, engraving, etc.; specifications are the same.
Regal Grade **$19,000**
Sandringham Grade **14,500**

AMADEO ROSSI, S.A.
Sao Leopoldo, Brazil

Rossi Hammerless Double Barrel Shotgun **$225**
Box lock. Plain extractors. Double triggers. 12 gauge. 3-inch chambers. Barrels: 26-inch improved cylinder/modified; 28-inch modified/full choke. Weight: 7 to 7½ pounds. Pistol-grip stock and beavertail forearm, uncheckered. Made 1974 to date. *Note:* H&R Model 404 (1969-72) is same gun.

Rossi Overland Hammer Double **$195**
Side lock. Plain extractors. Double triggers. Gauges: 12, .410; 3-inch chambers. Barrels: 20-inch, improved cylinder/modified in 12 gauge; 26-inch, both full choke in .410. Weight: 7 lbs., 12 ga.; 6 lbs., .410. Pistol-grip stock and beavertail forearm, uncheckered. *Note:* Because of its resemblance to the short-barreled doubles carried by guards riding shotgun on 19th-century stagecoaches, the 12 gauge version originally was called the "Coach Gun." Made 1968 to date.

ROTTWEIL SHOTGUNS
West Germany

Rottweil Model 72 Over/Under Shotgun **$1725**
Hammerless, takedown with engraved receiver. 12 gauge; 2¾-inch chambers. 26¾-inch barrels with skeet/skeet chokes. Weight: 7½ pounds. Interchangeable trigger groups and buttstocks. Checkered French walnut buttstock and forend. Imported from West Germany.

Rottweil Model 650 Field O/U Shotgun **$635**
Breech action. Gauge: 12. 28-inch barrels. Six screw-in choke tubes. Automatic ejectors. Engraved receiver. Checkered pistol grip stock. Made from 1984 to 1986.

Rossi Hammerless Double

Rossi Overland

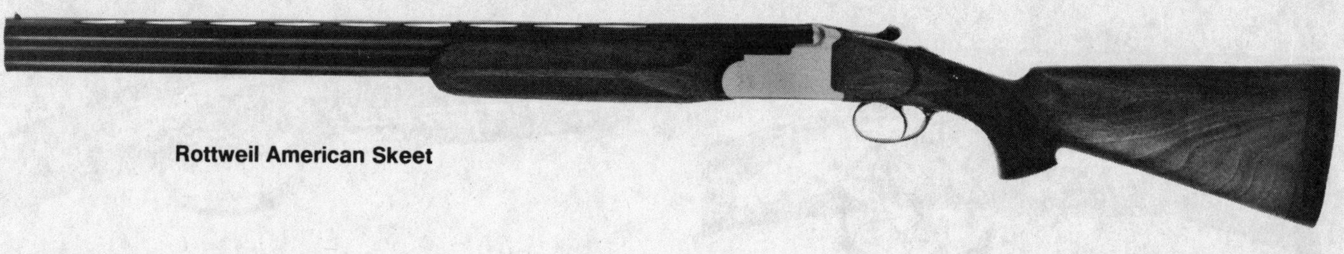

Rottweil American Skeet

Rottweil American Skeet **$1795**
Boxlock action. Gauge: 12. 27-inch vent-rib barrels. 44½ inches overall. Skeet chokes. Weight: 7½ pounds. Designed for tube sets. Hand-checkered European walnut stock with modified forend. Made from 1984 to date.

Rottweil International Trap Shotgun **$1720**
Boxlock action. Gauge: 12. 30-inch barrels. 48½ inches overall. Weight: 8 pounds. Choked imp. mod./full. Selective single trigger. Metal bead front sight. Checkered European walnut stock with pistol grip. Engraved action. Made from 1984 to date.

RUGER SHOTGUN
Southport, Connecticut
Manufactured by Sturm, Ruger & Company

Ruger Plain Grade Red Label Over/Under **$650**
Box lock. Auto ejectors. Selective single trigger. 20 gauge. 3-inch chambers. 26-inch vent-rib barrel, improved cylinder and modified or skeet choke. Weight: about 7 pounds. Checkered pistol-grip stock and forearm. Introduced in 1977; 12 gauge version, 1982. Chambers: 2¾- and 3-inch. Barrels: 26-, 28- and 30-inch. Weight: about 7½ pounds.

Ruger Red Label Over/Under Stainless **$725**
Gauges: 12 and 20. Barrels: 26- or 28-inch. Various chokes. Weight: 7 to 7½ pounds. Single selective trigger. Automatic top safety. Standard gold bead front sight. American walnut stock with hand-cut checkering. Made from 1985 to date.

VICTOR SARASQUETA, S. A.
Eibar, Spain

Sarasqueta Model 3

Sarasqueta Model 3 Hammerless Box Lock Double Barrel Shotgun
Plain extractors or auto ejectors. Double triggers. Gauges: 12, 16, 20. Made in various barrel lengths, chokes and weights. Checkered stock and forend, straight grip standard. Currently manufactured.
Model 3, plain extractors **$500**
Model 3E, automatic ejectors **550**

Sarasqueta Hammerless Side Lock Doubles
Automatic ejectors (except on Models 4 and 203 which have plain extractors). Double triggers. Gauges: 12, 16, 20. Barrel lengths, chokes and weights made to order. Checkered stock and forend, straight grip standard. Mod-

SHOTGUNS

Ruger Red Label O/U Stainless

Ruger Red Label—12 Gauge (1982)

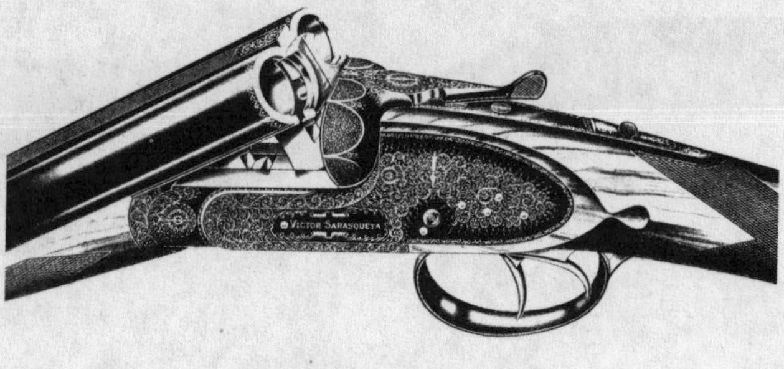

Sarasqueta Model 6E

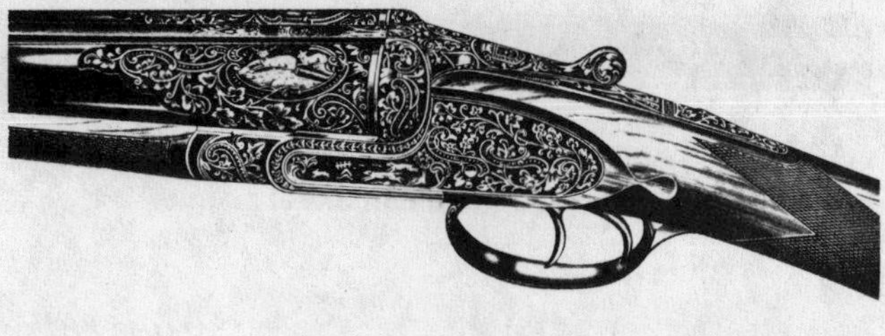

Sarasqueta Model 12E

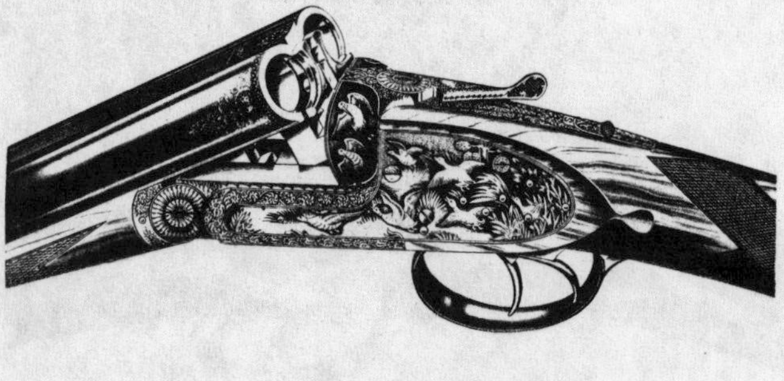

Sarasqueta Model 11E

Sarasqueta Hammerless Side Lock Doubles (cont.)
els differ chiefly in overall quality, engraving, grade of wood, checkering, etc.; general specifications are the same. Currently manufactured.

Model 4	$ 600
Model 4E	750
Model 203	800
Model 203E	825
Model 6E	900
Model 7E	910
Model 10E	2500
Model 11E	2800
Model 12E	3000

Sauer Model 66 Field, Grade I

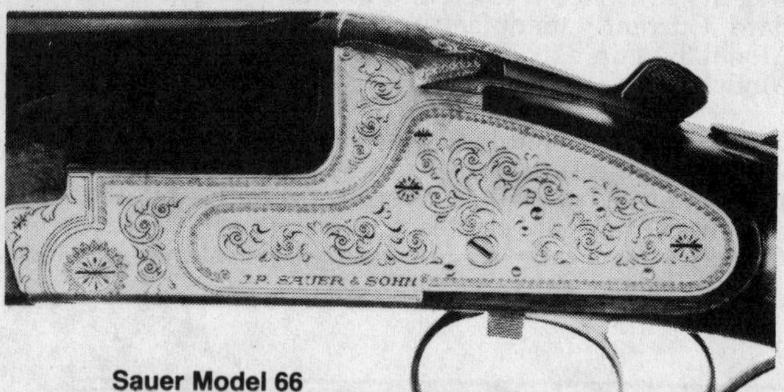

Sauer Model 66 Field, Grade II

Sauer Model 66 Field, Grade III

J. P. SAUER & SOHN
Eckernförde, West Germany
Formerly located in Suhl, W. Germany

Sauer Model 66 Over-and-Under Field Gun
Purdey-system action with Holland & Holland-type side locks. Selective single trigger. Selective auto ejectors. Automatic safety. Available in three grades of engraving. 12 gauge only. Krupp-Special steel barrels with vent rib, 28-inch, modified/full choke. Weight: about 7¼ pounds. Checkered walnut stock and forend; recoil pad. Made 1966 to 1975.

Grade I	$1600
Grade II	2100
Grade III	2900

Sauer Model 66 Over-and-Under Skeet Gun
Same as Model 66 Field Gun, except 26-inch barrels with wide vent rib, skeet choked; skeet-style stock and ventilated beavertail forearm; nonautomatic safety. Made 1966 to 1975.

Grade I	$1500
Grade II	2000
Grade III	3000

Sauer Model 66 Trap, Grade II

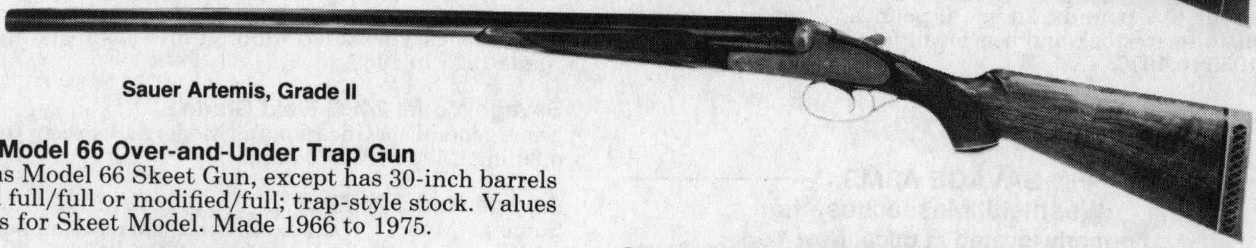

Sauer Artemis, Grade II

Sauer Model 66 Over-and-Under Trap Gun
Same as Model 66 Skeet Gun, except has 30-inch barrels choked full/full or modified/full; trap-style stock. Values same as for Skeet Model. Made 1966 to 1975.

Sauer Model 3000E Drilling, Standard

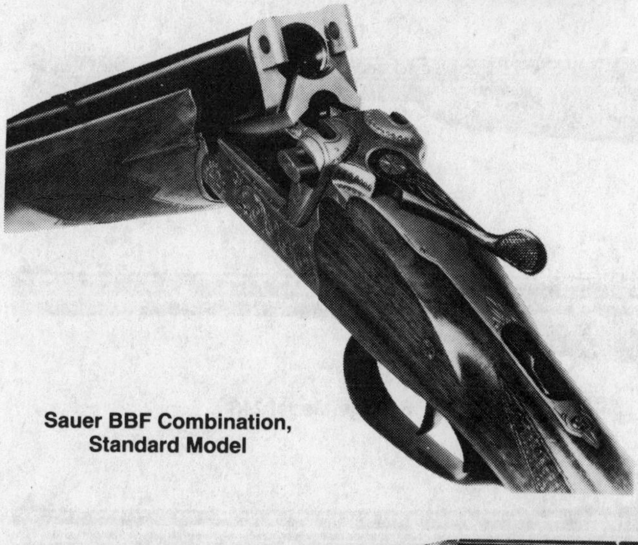

Sauer BBF Combination, Standard Model

Sauer Model 3000E Drilling
Combination rifle and double barrel shotgun. Blitz action with Greener crossbolt, double underlugs, separate rifle cartridge extractor, front set trigger, firing pin indicators, Greener side safety, sear slide selector locks right shotgun barrel for firing rifle barrel. Gauge/calibers: 12 gauge ($2\frac{3}{4}$-inch chambers); 222, 243, 30-06, 7X65R. 25-inch Krupp-Special steel barrels; modified and full choke, automatic folding leaf rear rifle sight. Weight: $6\frac{1}{2}$ to $7\frac{1}{4}$ pounds depending on rifle caliber. Checkered walnut stock and forend; pistol grip, modified Monte Carlo comb and cheekpiece, sling swivels. Standard Model with arabesque engraving; Deluxe Model with hunting scenes engraved on action. Currently manufactured. *Note:* Also see listing under Colt.

Standard Model **$1750**
Deluxe Model **3200**

Sauer Artemis Double Barrel Shotgun
Holland & Holland-type side lock with Greener crossbolt, double underlugs, double sear safeties, selective single trigger, selective auto ejectors. Grade I with fine line engraving; Grade II with full English arabesque engraving. 12 gauge ($2\frac{3}{4}$-inch chambers). Krupp-Special steel barrels, 28-inch, modified and full choke. Weight: about $6\frac{1}{2}$ pounds. Checkered walnut pistol-grip stock and beavertail forend; recoil pad. Made 1966 to 1977.

Grade I **$4300**
Grade II **5200**

Sauer BBF Over/Under Combination Rifle/Shotgun
Blitz action with Kersten lock, front set trigger fires rifle barrel, slide-operated sear safety. Gauge/calibers: 16 gauge; 30-30, 30-06, 7X65R. 25-inch Krupp-Special steel barrels; shotgun barrel full choke, folding leaf rear sight. Weight: about 6 pounds. Checkered walnut stock and forend; pistol grip, modified Monte Carlo comb and cheekpiece, sling swivels. Standard Model with arabesque engraving; Deluxe Model with hunting scenes engraved on action. Currently manufactured.

Standard Model **$1700**
Deluxe Model **2715**

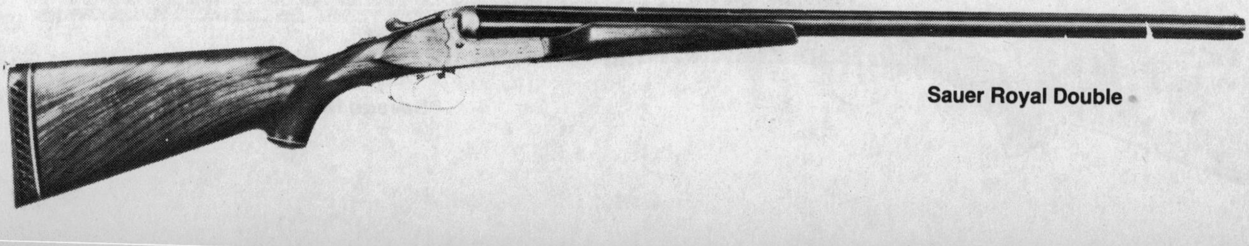

Sauer Royal Double

Sauer Royal Double Barrel Shotgun **$1450**
Anson & Deeley action (box lock) with Greener crossbolt, double underlugs, signal pins, selective single trigger, selective auto ejectors, auto safety. Scalloped frame with arabesque engraving. Krupp-Special steel barrels. Gauges: 12, 2³/₄-inch chambers; 20, 3-inch chambers. Barrels: 30-inch (12 ga. only) and 28-inch, modified/full; 26-inch (20 ga. only), improved cylinder/modified. Weight: 12 ga., about 6¹/₂ pounds; 20 ga., 6 pounds. Checkered walnut pistol-grip stock and beavertail forend; recoil pad. Made 1955 to 1977.

SAVAGE ARMS
Westfield, Massachusetts
Formerly located in Utica, New York

Savage Model 24C Camper's Companion **$125**
Same as Model 24FG, except made in 22 magnum/20 gauge only; has 20-inch barrels, shotgun tube cylinder bore. Weight: 5³/₄ pounds. Trap in butt provides ammunition storage; comes with carrying case. Made 1972 to date.

Savage Model 24 22-410 O/U Combination **$120**
Same as Stevens No. 22-.410, has walnut stock and forearm. Made 1950 to 1965.

Savage Model 24D **$140**
Same as Models 24DL and 24MDL, except frame has black or casehardened finish. Game scene decoration of frame eliminated in 1974; forearm uncheckered after 1976. Made 1970 to date.

Savage Model 24DL **$120**
Same general specifications as Model 24S, except top lever opening; satin-chrome-finished frame decorated with game scenes, checkered Monte Carlo stock and forearm. Made 1965 to 1969.

Savage Model 24FG Field Grade **$120**
Same general specifications as Model 24S, except top lever opening. Made 1972 to date.

Savage Model 24MDL **$140**
Same as Model 24DL, except rifle barrel chambered for 22 Win. magnum rimfire. Made 1965 to 1969.

Savage Model 24MS **$130**
Same as Model 24S, except rifle barrel chambered for 22 Win. magnum rimfire. Made 1965 to 1971.

Savage Model 24S Over/Under Combination ... **$130**
Box lock. Visible hammer. Side lever opening. Plain extractors. Single trigger. 20 ga. or .410 bore shotgun barrel under 22 long rifle bore barrel; 24-inch; open rear sight, ramp front sight, dovetail for scope mounting. Weight: about 6³/₄ pounds. Plain pistol-grip stock and forearm. Made 1965 to 1971.

Savage Model 24C

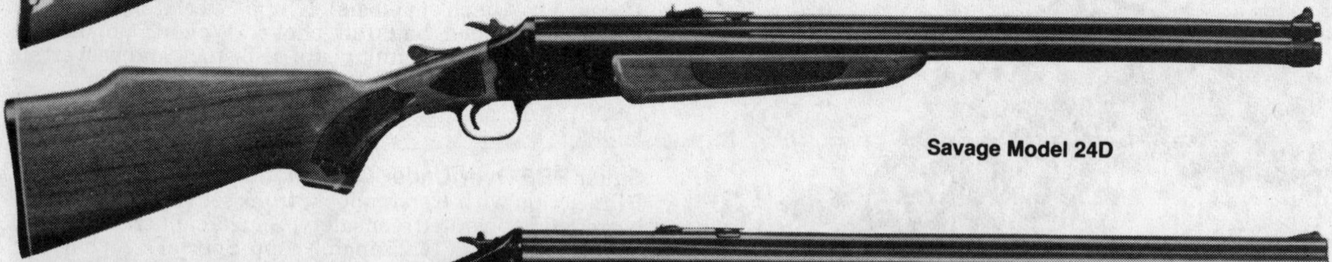

Savage Model 24D

Savage Model 24S

Savage Model 24V

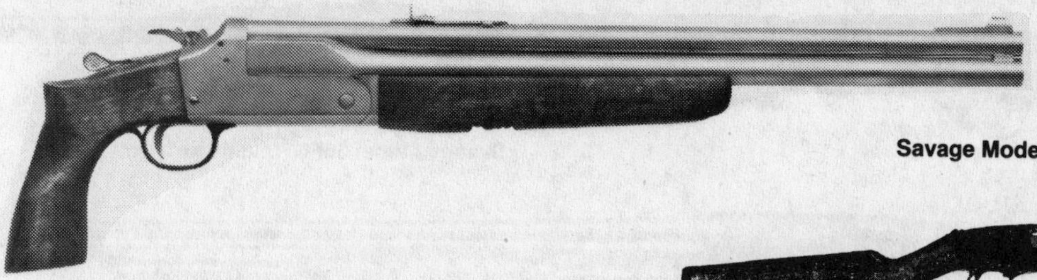

Savage Model 24-VS Camper/Survival

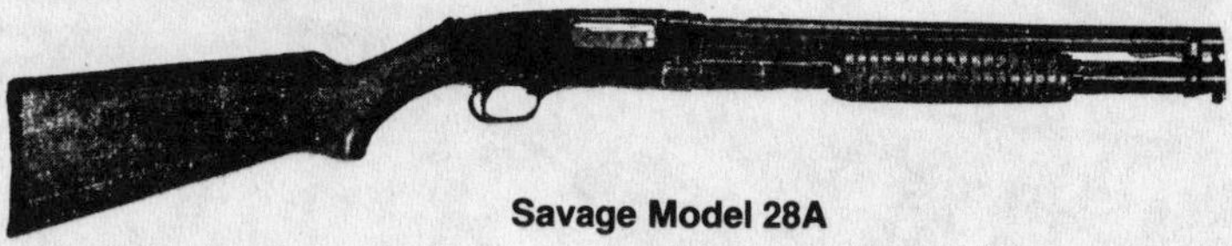

Savage Model 28A

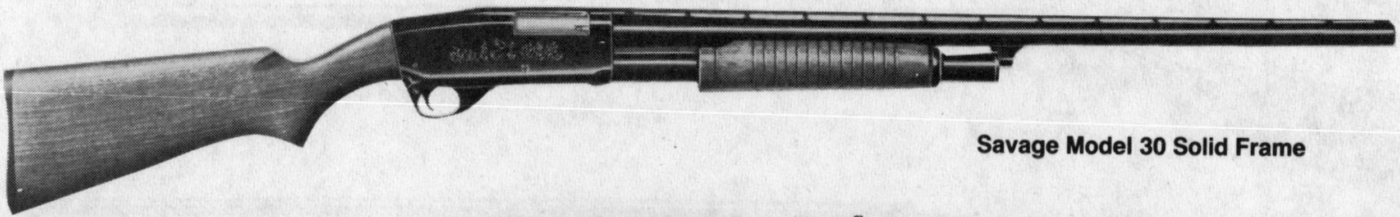

Savage Model 30 Solid Frame

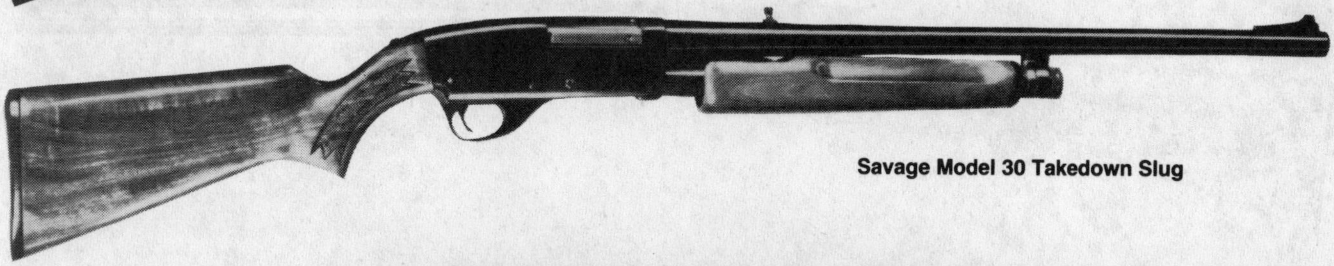

Savage Model 30 Takedown Slug

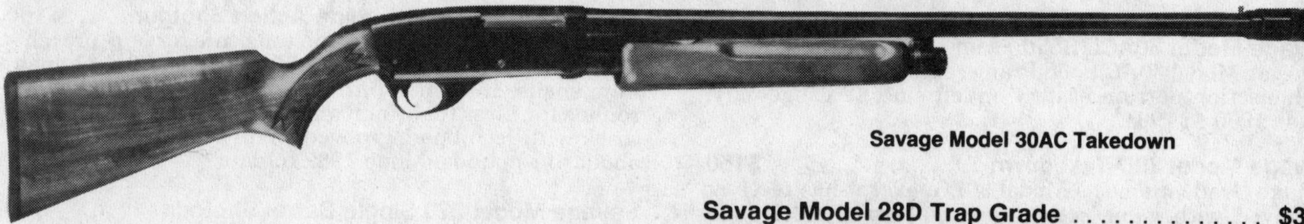

Savage Model 30AC Takedown

Savage Model 24V $165
Similar to Model 24D, except 20 gauge under 222 Rem., 22 Rem., 357 Mag., 22 Hornet or 30-30 rifle barrel. Made 1971 to date.

Savage Model 24-VS Camper/Survival/ Centerfire Rifle/Shotgun $120
Similar to Model 24V except 357 Rem. Mag. over 20 gauge. Nickel finish, full length stock and accessory pistol-grip stock. Overall length: 36 inches with full stock; 26 inches with pistol grip. Weight: about 6½ pounds. Made 1983 to date.

Savage Model 28A Standard Grade Slide Action Repeating Shotgun $225
Hammerless. Takedown. 12 gauge. 5-shell tubular magazine. Plain barrel; lengths: 26-, 28-, 30-, 32-inches; choked cylinder, modified, full. Weight: about 7½ pounds with 30-inch barrel. Plain pistol-grip stock, grooved slide handle. Made 1928 to 1931.

Savage Model 28B $250
Raised matted rib; otherwise the same as Model 28A.

Savage Model 28D Trap Grade $310
Same general specifications as Model 28A, except has 30-inch full choke barrel with matted rib, trap-style stock with checkered pistol grip, checkered slide handle of selected walnut.

Savage Model 30 Solid Frame Hammerless Slide Action Shotgun $165
Gauges: 12, 16, 20, .410. 2¾-inch chamber in 16 gauge, 3-inch in other gauges. Magazine holds four 2¾-inch shells or three 3-inch shells. Barrels: vent rib; 26-, 28-, 30-inch; improved cylinder, modified, full choke. Weight: average 6¼ to 6¾ pounds depending upon gauge. Plain pistol-grip stock (checkered on later production), grooved slide handle. Made 1958 to 1970.

Savage Model 30 Takedown Slug Gun $140
Same as Model 30FG, except 21-inch cylinder bore barrel with rifle sights. Made 1971 to 1979.

Savage Model 30AC Solid Frame $190
Same as Model 30 Solid Frame, except has 26-inch barrel with adjustable choke; 12 gauge only. Made 1959 to 1970.

Savage Model 30AC Takedown $175
Same as Model 30FG, except has 26-inch barrel with adjustable choke; 12 and 20 gauge only. Made 1971 to 1972.

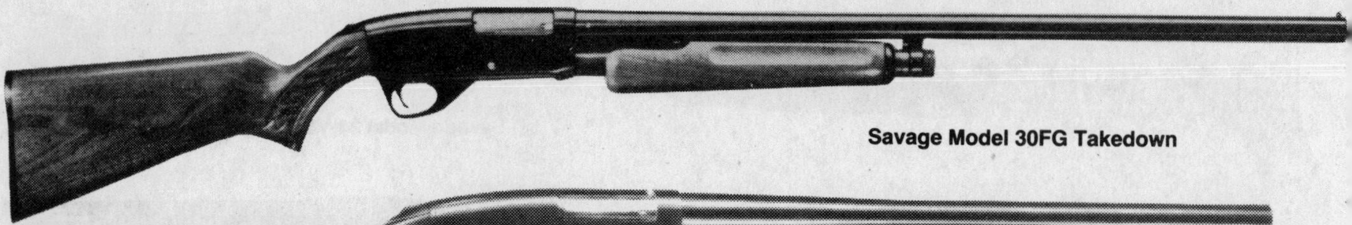

Savage Model 30FG Takedown

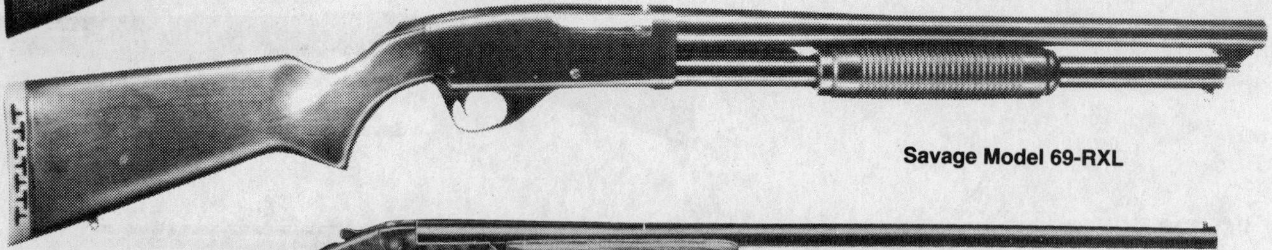

Savage Model 69-RXL

Savage Model 220

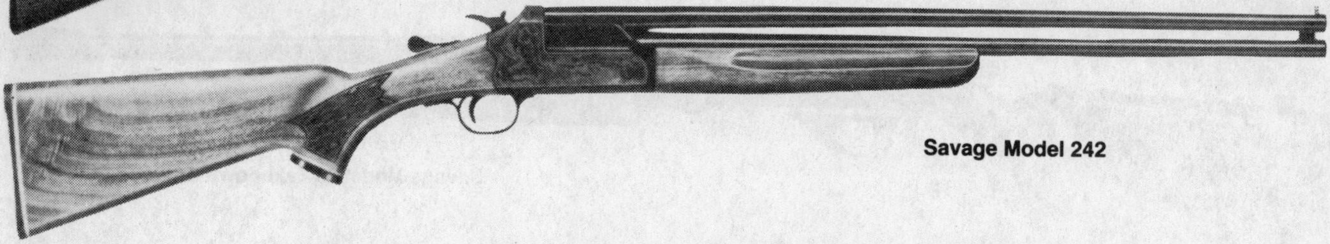

Savage Model 242

Savage Model 30ACL Solid Frame $190
Same as Model 30AC Solid Frame, except left-hand model with ejection port and safety on left side; 12 gauge only. Made 1960 to 1964.

Savage Model 30D Takedown $150
Deluxe Grade. Same as Model 30FG, except has receiver engraved with game scene, vent-rib barrel, recoil pad. Made 1971 to date.

Savage Model 30FG Takedown Hammerless Slide Action Shotgun $130
Field Grade. Gauges: 12, 20, .410. 3-inch chamber. Magazine holds four 2¾-inch shells or three 3-inch shells. Barrels: plain; 26-inch full choke (.410 ga. only); 28-inch modified, full choke; 30-inch full choke (12 ga. only). Weight: average 7 to 7¾ pounds depending upon gauge. Checkered pistol-grip stock, fluted slide handle. Made 1970 to 1979.

Savage Model 30L Solid Frame $175
Same as Model 30 Solid Frame, except left-handed model with ejection port and safety on left side; 12 gauge only. Made 1959 to 1970.

Savage Model 30T Solid Frame Trap and Duck . $195
Same as Model 30 Solid Frame, except only in 12 gauge with 30-inch full choke barrel; has Monte Carlo stock with recoil pad; weight, about 8 pounds. Made 1963 to 1970.

Savage Model 30T Takedown Trap Gun $175
Same as Model 30D, except only in 12 gauge with 30-inch full choke barrel. Monte Carlo stock with recoil pad. Made 1970 to 1973.

Savage Model 69-RXL Slide Action Shotgun . . . $160
Hammerless, side ejection, top tang safe for left- or right-hand use. 12 gauge, chambered for 2¾- and 3-inch magnum shells. 18¼-inch barrel. Tubular magazine holds 6 rounds (one less for 3-inch mag). Walnut finish hardwood stock with recoil pad, grooved operating handle. Weight: about 6½ pounds. Made 1982 to date.

Savage Model 220 Single Barrel Shotgun $90
Hammerless. Takedown. Auto ejector. Gauges: 12, 16, 20, .410. Single shot. Barrel lengths: 12 ga., 28- to 36-inch; 16 ga., 28- to 32-inch; 20 ga., 26- to 32-inch; .410 bore, 26- and 28-inch. Full choke. Weight: about 6 pounds. Plain pistol-grip stock and wide forearm. Made 1938 to 1965.

Savage Model 220AC $100
Same as Model 220, except has Savage adjustable choke.

Savage Model 220L $90
Same general specifications as Model 220, except has side lever opening instead of top lever. Made 1965 to 1972.

Savage Model 220P $100
Same as Model 220, except has Poly Choke built integrally with barrel; made in 12 gauge with 30-inch barrel, 16 and 20 gauge with 28-inch barrel, not made in .410 bore; has recoil pad.

Savage Model 242 Over-and-Under Shotgun . . . $160
Similar to Model 24D, except both barrels .410 bore, full choke. Weight: about 7 pounds. Made 1977 to 1980.

Note: Savage Models 330, 333T, 333, and 2400 were manufactured by Valmet Oy, Helsinki, Finland.

Savage Model 330

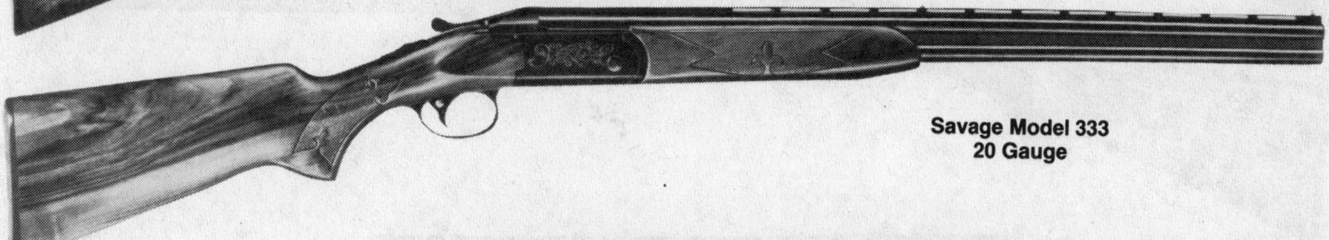

Savage Model 333
20 Gauge

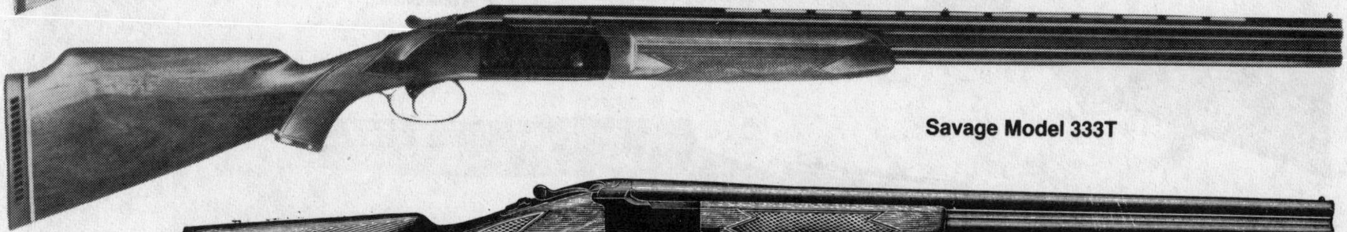

Savage Model 333T

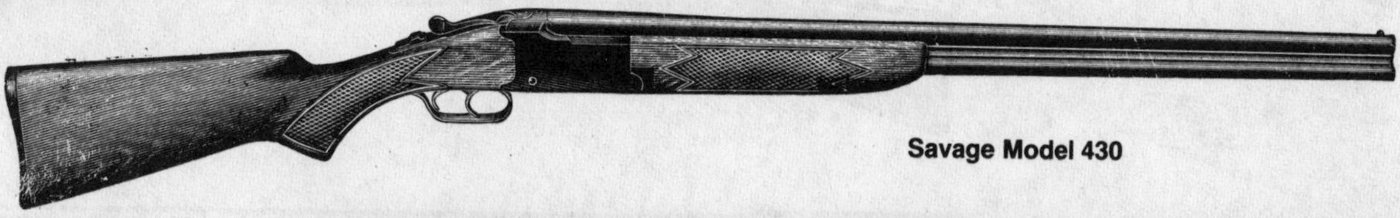

Savage Model 430

Savage Model 440

Savage Model 330 Over-and-Under Shotgun . . . $425
Box lock. Plain extractors. Selective single trigger. Gauges: 12, 20. 2³/₄-inch chambers in 12 gauge, 3-inch in 20 gauge. Barrels: 26-inch improved cylinder/modified; 28-inch modified/full; 30-inch modified/full choke (12 ga. only). Weight: 6¹/₄ to 7¹/₄ pounds, depending upon gauge. Checkered pistol-grip stock and forearm. Made 1969 to 1978.

Savage Model 333 Over-and-Under Shotgun . . . $525
Box lock. Auto ejectors. Selective single trigger. Gauges: 12, 20. 2³/₄-inch chambers in 12 gauge, 3-inch in 20 gauge. Barrels: vent rib; 26-inch skeet choke, improved cylinder/modified; 28-inch modified/full; 30-inch modified/full choke (12 ga. only). Weight: average 6¹/₄ to 7¹/₄ pounds. Checkered pistol-grip stock and forearm. Made 1973 to 1979.

Savage Model 333T Trap Gun $495
Similar to Model 330, except only in 12 gauge with 30-inch vent-rib barrels, improved modified/full choke; Monte Carlo stock with recoil pad. Weight: 7³/₄ pounds. Made 1972 to 1979.

Savage Model 420 Over-and-Under Shotgun
Box lock. Hammerless. Takedown. Automatic safety. Double triggers or non-selective single trigger. Gauges: 12, 16, 20. Barrels: plain; 26- to 30-inch (the latter in 12 gauge only); choked modified and full, cylinder and improved cylinder. Weight with 28-inch barrels: 12 ga., 7³/₄ lbs.; 16 ga., 7¹/₂ lbs.; 20 ga., 6³/₄ lbs. Plain pistol-grip stock and forearm. Made 1938 to 1942.
With double triggers **$450**
With single trigger **550**

Savage Model 430
Same as Model 420, except has matted top barrel, checkered stock of selected walnut with recoil pad, checkered forearm. Made 1938 to 1942.
With double triggers **$550**
With single trigger **600**

Savage Model 440 Over-and-Under Shotgun . . . $495
Box lock. Plain extractors. Selective single trigger. Gauges: 12, 20. 2³/₄-inch chambers in 12 gauge, 3-inch in 20 gauge. Barrels: vent rib; 26-inch skeet choke, improved cylinder and modified; 28-inch modified and full; 30-inch modified and full choke (12 ga. only). Weight: average 6 to 6¹/₂ pounds depending upon gauge. Made 1968 to 1972.

Savage Model 440T

Savage Model 550

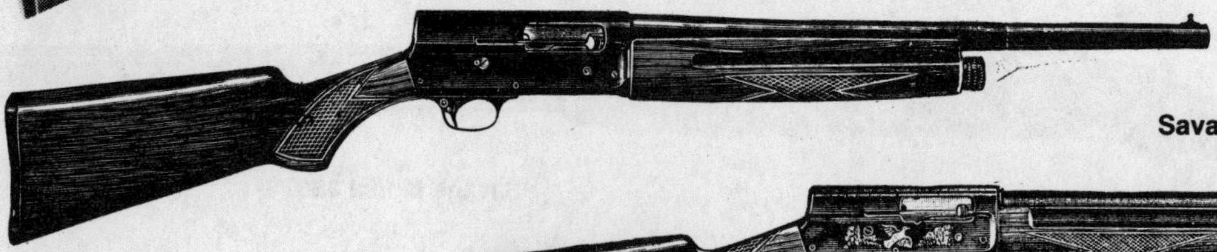

Savage Model 720

Savage Model 726

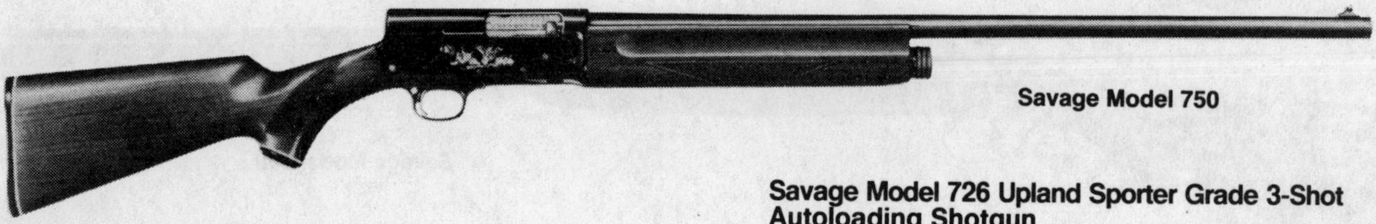

Savage Model 750

Savage Model 440T Trap Gun $500
Similar to Model 440, except only in 12 gauge with 30-inch barrels, extra-wide vent rib, improved modified and full choke. Trap-style Monte Carlo stock and semibeavertail forearm of select walnut, recoil pad. Weight: $7\frac{1}{2}$ pounds. Made 1969 to 1972.

Savage Model 444 Deluxe Over/Under Shotgun .. $510
Similar to Model 440, except has auto ejectors, select walnut stock and semibeavertail forearm. Made 1969 to 1972.

Savage Model 550 Hammerless Double $245
Box lock. Auto ejectors. Non-selective single trigger. Gauges: 12, 20. $2\frac{3}{4}$-inch chamber in 12 gauge, 3-inch in 20 gauge. Barrels: vent rib; 26-inch improved cylinder/modified; 28-inch modified/full; 30-inch modified/full choke (12 ga. only). Weight: 7 to 8 pounds. Checkered pistol-grip stock and semibeavertail forearm. Made 1971 to 1973.

Savage Model 720 Standard Grade 5-Shot Autoloading Shotgun $250
Browning type. Takedown. 12 and 16 gauge. 4-shell tubular magazine. Barrel: plain; 26- to 32-inch (the latter in 12 gauge only); choked cylinder, modified, full. Weight: about $8\frac{1}{4}$ pounds, 12 ga. with 30-inch barrel; 16 ga., about $\frac{1}{2}$ pound lighter. Checkered pistol-grip stock and forearm. Made 1930 to 1949.

Savage Model 726 Upland Sporter Grade 3-Shot Autoloading Shotgun $240
Same as Model 720, except has 2-shell magazine capacity. Made 1931 to 1949.

Savage Model 740C Skeet Gun $295
Same as Model 726, except has special skeet stock and full-beavertail forearm, equipped with Cutts Compensator, barrel length overall with spreader tube is about $24\frac{1}{2}$ inches. Made 1936 to 1949.

Savage Model 745 Lightweight Autoloader $210
Three- or five-shot model. Same general specifications as Model 720, except has lightweight alloy receiver, 12 gauge only, 28-inch plain barrel. Weight: about $6\frac{3}{4}$ pounds. Made 1940 to 1949.

Savage Model 750 Automatic Shotgun $210
Browning-type autoloader. Takedown. 12 gauge. 4-shot tubular magazine. Barrels: 28-inch full or modified choke; 26-inch improved cylinder. Weight: about $7\frac{1}{4}$ pounds. Checkered walnut pistol-grip stock and grooved forearm. Made 1960 to 1967.

Savage Model 750-AC $275
Same as Model 750, except has 26-inch barrel with adjustable choke. Made 1964 to 1967.

Savage Model 750-SC $250
Same as Model 750, except has 26-inch barrel with Savage Super Choke. Made 1962 to 1963.

Savage Model 775

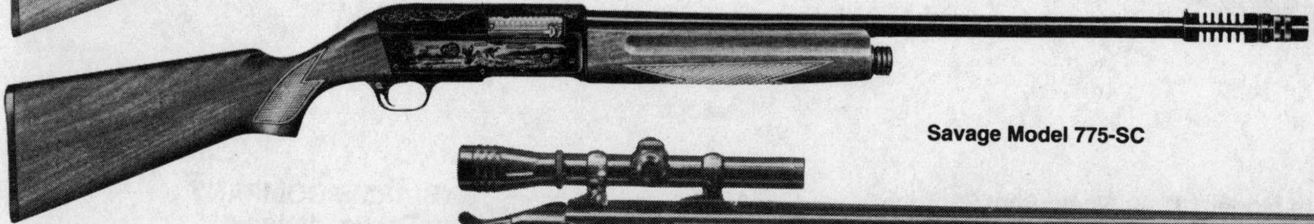

Savage Model 775-SC

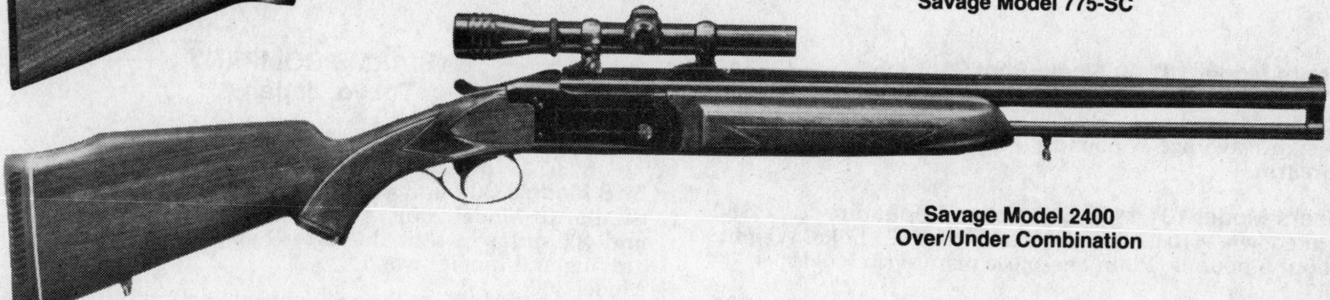

Savage Model 2400
Over/Under Combination

Savage Model 755 Standard Grade Autoloader $210
Streamlined receiver. Takedown. 12 and 16 gauge. 4-shell tubular magazine (a three-shot model with magazine capacity of two shells was also produced until 1951). Barrel: plain; 30-inch full choke (12 ga. only), 28-inch full or modified, 26-inch improved cylinder. Weight: about 8¼ pounds, 12 ga. Checkered pistol-grip stock and forearm. Made 1949 to 1958.

Savage Model 755-SC $200
Same as Model 755, except has 26-inch barrel with recoil-reducing, adjustable Savage Super Choke.

Savage Model 775 Lightweight $210
Same general specifications as Model 755, except has lightweight alloy receiver and weighs about 6¾ pounds. Made 1950 to 1965.

Savage Model 775-SC $210
Same as Model 775, except has 26-inch barrel with Savage Super Choke.

Savage Model 2400 Over/Under Combination . . $595
Box lock action similar to that of Model 330. Plain extractors. Selective single trigger. 12 gauge (2¾-inch chamber) shotgun barrel, full choke, over 308 Win. or 222 Rem. rifle barrel; 23½-inch; solid matted rib with blade front sight and folding leaf rear sight, dovetail for scope mounting. Weight: about 7½ pounds. Monte Carlo stock with pistol grip and recoil pad, semibeavertail forearm, checkered. Made 1975 to 1979.

SEARS, ROEBUCK & COMPANY
Chicago, Illinois
J. C. Higgins and Ted Williams Models

Although they do not correspond to specific models below, the names Ted Williams and J. C. Higgins have been used to designate various Sears shotguns at various times.

Sears Model 18 Bolt Action Repeater $80
Takedown. 3-shot top-loading magazine. Gauge: .410 only. Barrel: 25-inch with variable choke. Weight: about 5¾ pounds.

Sears Model 20 Slide Action Repeater $160
Hammerless. 5-shot magazine. Barrels: 26- to 30-inch with various chokes. Weight: 7¼ pounds. Plain pistol-grip stock and slide handle.

Sears Model 21 Slide Action Repeater $185
Same general specifications as the Model 20 except vent rib and adjustable choke.

Sears Model 30 Slide Action Repeater $185
Hammerless. Gauges: 12, 16, 20 and .410. 4-shot magazine. Barrels: 26- to 30-inch, various chokes. Weight: 6½ pounds. Plain pistol-grip stock, grooved slide handle.

Sears Model 97 Single Shot Shotgun $65
Takedown. Visible hammer. Automatic ejector. Gauges: 12, 16, 20 and .410. Barrels: 26- to 36-inch, full choke. Weight: average 6 pounds. Plain pistol-grip stock and forearm.

Sears Model 97-AC Single Shot Shotgun $80
Same general specifications as Model 97 except fancier stock and forearm.

Sears Model 101.7 Double Barrel Shotgun $160
Box lock. Double triggers. Gauges: 12, 16, 20, .410. Barrels: 26- to 32-inch, choked modified and full. Weight: from 6 to 7½ pounds. Plain stock and forend.

Sears Model 101.7C Double Barrel Shotgun $175
Same general specifications as Model 101.7 except checkered stock and forearm.

Sears Model 101.25 Bolt Action Shotgun $80
Takedown. .410 gauge. 5-shell tubular magazine. 24-inch barrel, full choke. Weight: about 6 pounds. Plain, one-piece pistol-grip stock.

SKB Model 880

Sears Model 101.40 Single Shot Shotgun **$65**
Takedown. Visible hammer. Automatic ejector. Gauges: 12, 16, 20 and .410. Barrels: 26- to 36-inch, full choke. Weight: average 6 pounds. Plain pistol-grip stock and forearm.

Sears Model 101.1120 Bolt Action Repeater **$80**
Takedown. .410 gauge. 24-inch barrel, full choke. Weight: about 5 pounds. Plain one-piece pistol-grip stock.

Sears Model 101.1380 Bolt Action Repeater **$90**
Takedown. Gauges: 12, 16, 20. 2-shell detachable box magazine. 26-inch barrel, full choke. Weight: about 7 pounds. Plain one-piece pistol-grip stock.

Sears Model 101.1610 Double Barrel Shotgun . . **$225**
Box lock. Double triggers. Plain extractors. Gauges: 12, 16, 20 and .410. Barrels: 24- to 30-inch. Various chokes, but mostly modified and full. Weight: about 7½ pounds, 12 ga. Checkered pistol-grip stock and forearm.

Sears Model 101.1701 Double Barrel Shotgun . . **$230**
Same general specifications as Model 101.1610 except satin chrome frame and select walnut buttstock and forearm.

Sears Model 101.5350-D Bolt Action Repeater . . . **$80**
Takedown. Gauges: 12, 16, 20. 2-shell detachable box magazine. 26-inch barrel, full choke. Weight: about 7¼ pounds. Plain one-piece pistol-grip stock.

Sears Model 101.5410 Bolt Action Repeater **$80**
Same general specifications as Model 101.5350-D.

Sears Model 103.720 Bolt Action Repeater **$75**
Takedown. Automatic thumb safety. .410 gauge. 24-inch barrel, full choke. Weight: about 5 pounds. Plain pistol-grip stock.

Sears Model 103.740 Bolt Action Repeater **$75**
Same general specifications as Model 103.720.

Sears Model 200 Slide Action Repeater **$165**
Front-locking rotary bolt. Takedown. 4-shot magazine. Gauges: 12, 16 and 20. Barrel: plain or vent rib. Weight: 6½ to 7¼ pounds. Checkered pistol grip and forearm.

Sears Model 300 Autoloading Shotgun **$195**
Gas-operated. Front-locking rotary bolt. Takedown. 2-shot magazine. Gauges: 12, 16, 20. Barrel: plain or vent rib. Various chokes. Weight: 6½ to 7½ pounds. Checkered pistol-grip stock and forearm, recoil pad.

Sears Model 5100 Double Barrel Shotgun **$160**
Box lock. Double triggers. Gauges: 12, 16, 20, .410. Barrels: 26- to 32-inch, various chokes. Weight: 6 to 7½ pounds.

SKB ARMS COMPANY
Tokyo, Japan

SKB Models 300 and 400 Side-by-Side Doubles
Similar to Model 200E, except higher grade. Models 300 and 400 differ in that the latter has more elaborate engraving and fancier wood.
Model 300 . . . . **$675**
Model 400 . . . . **900**

SKB Model 400 Skeet **$895**
Similar to Model 200E Skeet, except higher grade with more elaborate engraving and full fancy wood.

SKB Model 480 English **$895**
Similar to Model 280 English, except higher grade with more elaborate engraving and full fancy wood.

SKB Model 500 Small Gauge O/U Shotgun **$545**
Similar to Model 500, except gauges 28 and .410; has 28-inch vent-rib barrels, modified and full choke. Weight: about 6½ pounds.

SKB Model 600 Small Gauge **$600**
Same as Model 500 Small Gauge, except higher grade with more elaborate engraving and fancier wood.

SKB Model 800 Skeet Over/Under Shotgun **$925**
Similar to Model 700 Skeet, except higher grade with more elaborate engraving and fancier wood.

SKB Model 800 Trap **$950**
Similar to Model 700 Trap, except higher grade with more elaborate engraving and fancier wood.

SKB Model 880 Skeet **$1500**
Similar to Model 800 Skeet, except has side plates.

SKB Model 880 Trap **$1500**
Similar to Model 800 Trap, except has side plates.

Note: The following SKB shotguns were distributed by Ithaca Gun Co. from 1966 to 1976. For specific data, please see corresponding listings under Ithaca.

SKB Century Single Barrel Trap Gun
The SKB catalog does not differentiate between Century and Century II; however, specifications of current Century are those of Ithaca-SKB Century II.
Century **$495**
Century II **595**

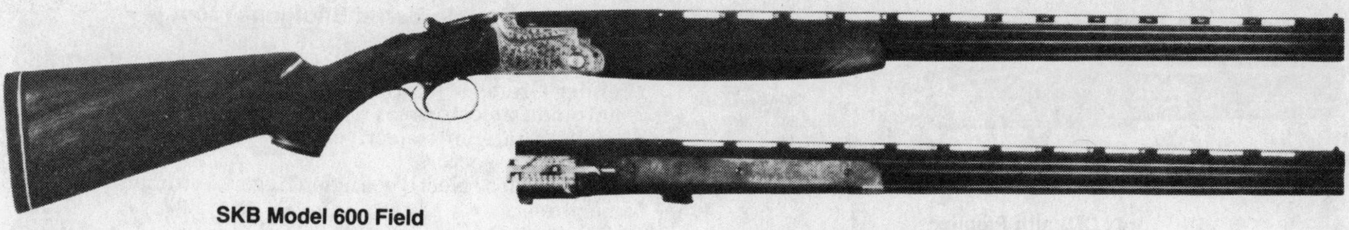

SKB Model 600 Field

SKB Gas-operated Automatic Shotguns

Model XL300—with plain barrel	$290
Model XL300—with ventilated rib	325
Model XL900	350
Model XL900 Trap	370
Model XL900 Skeet	350
Model XL900 Slug	290

SKB Over-and-Under Shotguns

Model 500 Field	$ 525
Model 500 Magnum	540
Model 600 Field	630
Model 600 Magnum	640
Model 600 Trap	650
Model 600 Doubles	650
Model 600 Skeet—12 or 20 gauge	635
Model 600 Skeet—28 or .410	650
Model 600 Skeet Combo	1900
Model 600 English	650
Model 700 Trap	810
Model 700 Doubles	810
Model 700 Skeet	810
Model 700 Skeet Combo	2100

SKB Recoil-operated Automatic Shotguns

Model 300—with plain barrel	$250
Model 300—with ventilated rib	260
Model 900	330
Model 900 Slug	280

SKB Side-by-Side Double Barrel Shotguns

Model 100	$385
Model 150	390
Model 200E	545
Model 200E Skeet	540
Model 280 English	550

L. C. SMITH SHOTGUNS

Made from 1890 to 1945 by Hunter Arms Company, Fulton, N.Y.; from 1946 to 1951 and from 1968 to 1973 by Marlin Firearms Company, New Haven, Conn.

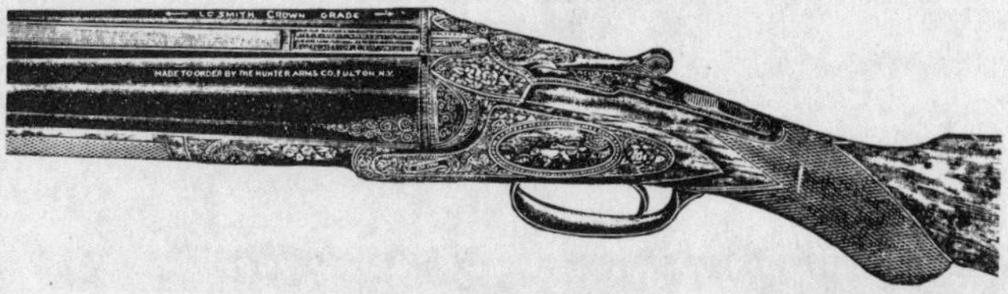

L. C. Smith Crown

L. C. Smith Double Barrel Shotguns

Values shown are for L. C. Smith doubles made by Hunter. Those of 1946—-1951 Marlin manufacture generally bring prices about 1/3 lower. Smaller gauge models, especially

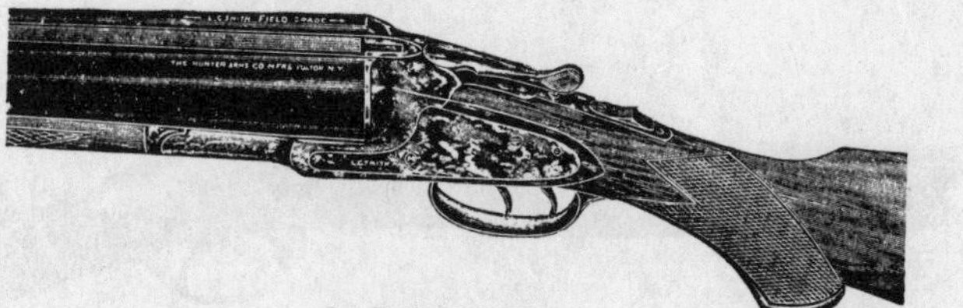

L. C. Smith Field

L. C. Smith Ideal

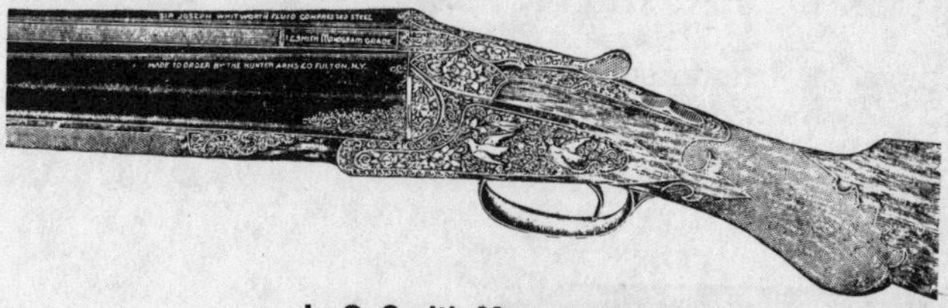

L. C. Smith Monogram

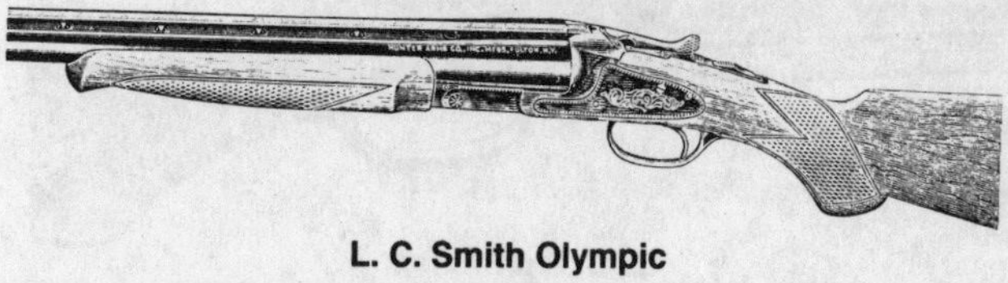

L. C. Smith Olympic

L. C. Smith Double Barrel Shotguns (cont.)

in the higher grades, command premium prices: up to 50 percent more for 20 gauge, up to 200 percent for .410 gauge.

Crown Grade, double triggers, automatic ejectors	$ 4,200
Crown Grade, selective single trigger, automatic ejectors	4,500
Deluxe Grade, selective single trigger, automatic ejectors	12,500
Field Grade, double triggers, plain extractors	995
Field Grade, double triggers, automatic ejectors	1,050
Field Grade, non-selective single trigger, plain extractors	995
Field Grade, selective single trigger, automatic ejectors	1,100
Ideal Grade, double triggers, plain extractors	1,200
Ideal Grade, double triggers, automatic ejectors	1,400
Ideal Grade, selective single trigger, automatic ejectors	1,795
Monogram Grade, selective single trigger, automatic ejectors	7,200

L. C. Smith Double Barrel Shotguns (cont.)

Olympic Grade, selective single trigger, automatic ejectors	$ 1,650
Premier Grade, selective single trigger, automatic ejectors	11,000
Skeet Special, non-selective single trigger, automatic ejectors	1,495
Skeet Special, selective single trigger, automatic ejectors	1,500
.410 Gauge	10,995
Specialty Grade, double triggers, auto ejectors	2,500
Specialty Grade, selective single trigger, automatic ejectors	2,600
Trap Grade, selective single trigger, automatic ejectors	1,200

L. C. Smith Field Grade Hammerless Double 1968 Model $400
"Re-creation" of the original L. C. Smith double. Side lock. Plain extractors. Double triggers. 12 gauge. 28-inch vent-rib barrels, modified/full choke. Weight: about $6\frac{3}{4}$ pounds. Checkered pistol-grip stock and forearm. Made 1968 to 1973.

L. C. Smith Deluxe Model $525
Same as 1968 Field Grade, except has Simmons floating vent rib, beavertail forearm. Made 1971 to 1973.

L. C. Smith Hammerless Double Barrel Shotguns
Side lock. Auto ejectors standard on higher grades, extra on Field and Ideal Grades. Double triggers or Hunter single trigger (non-selective or selective). Gauges: 12, 16, 20, .410. Barrels: 26- to 32-inch, any standard boring. Weight: $6\frac{1}{2}$ to $8\frac{1}{4}$ pounds, 12 ga. Checkered stock and forend; choice of straight, half or full pistol grip, beavertail or standard-type forend. Grades differ only in quality of workmanship, wood, checkering, engraving, etc. Same general specifications apply to all. Manufacture of these L. C. Smith guns was discontinued in 1951. Production of Field Grade 12 gauge was resumed 1968—-1973. *Note:* L. C. Smith Shotguns manufactured by the Hunter Arms Co. from 1890 to 1913 were designated by numerals to indicate grade, with the exception of Pigeon and Monogram.

00 Grade	$ 1050
0 Grade	1300
1 Grade	1500
2 Grade	1600
3 Grade	1500
Pigeon	4000

L. C. Smith Premier

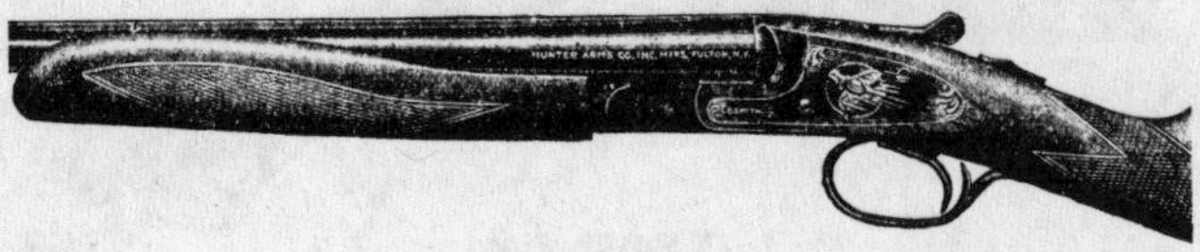
L. C. Smith Skeet

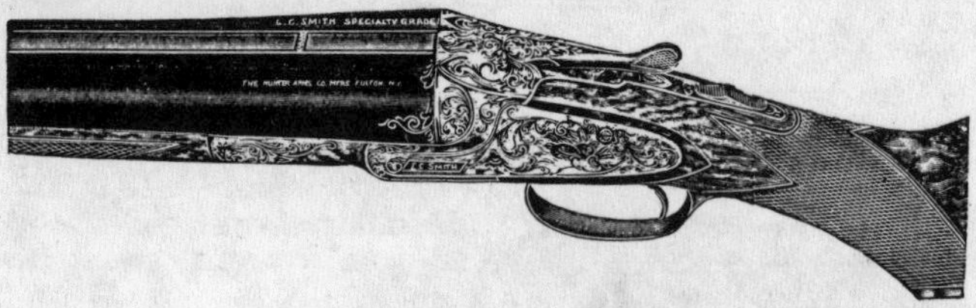
L. C. Smith Specialty

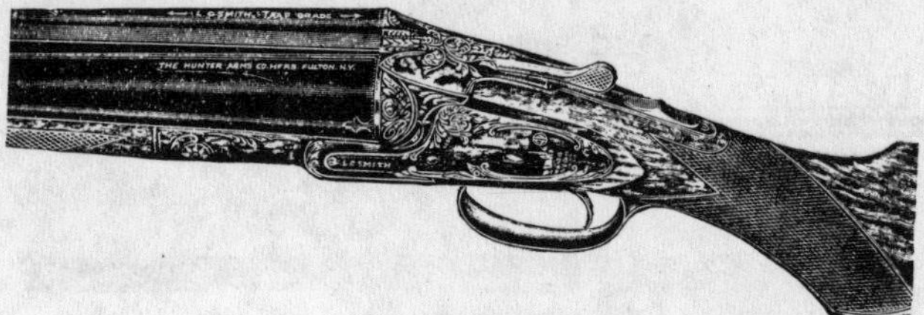
L. C. Smith Trap

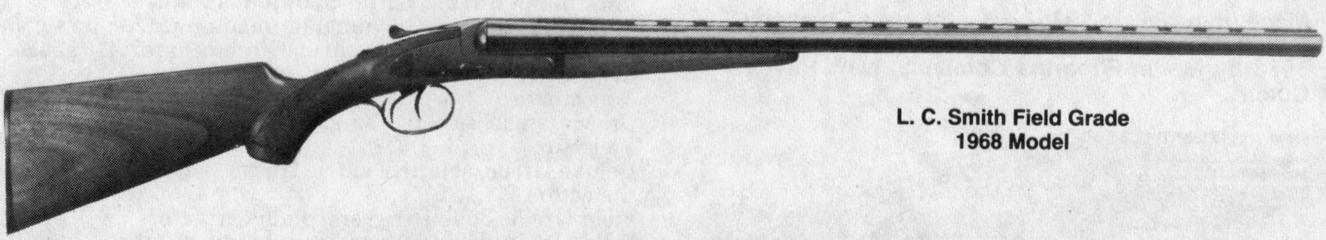
L. C. Smith Field Grade 1968 Model

L. C. Smith Deluxe Model

L. C. Smith Hammerless Doubles (cont.)

4 Grade . . . . $ 5000
5 Grade 5500
Monogram 9000
A1 5760
A2 8400
A3 . . . . +15,000

L. C. Smith Single Barrel Trap
Olympic Grade

L. C. Smith Single Barrel Trap Guns

Box lock. Hammerless. Auto ejector. 12 gauge only. Barrel lengths: 32- or 34-inch. Vent rib. Weight: 8 to 8$^1/_4$ pounds. Checkered pistol-grip stock and forend, recoil pad. Grades vary in quality of workmanship, wood, engraving, etc.; general specifications are the same. Discont. 1951. *Note:* Values shown are for L. C. Smith single barrel trap guns made by Hunter. Those of Marlin manufacture generally bring prices about one-third lower.

Olympic Grade $1000
Specialty Grade 2000
Crown Grade 3200
Monogram Grade 4000
Premier Grade 6400
Deluxe Grade 9000

SMITH & WESSON SHOTGUNS
Springfield, Massachusetts
Mfd. by Howa Machinery, Ltd., Nagoya, Japan

In 1985 Smith and Wesson sold its shotgun operation to O. F. Mossberg & Sons, Inc.

Smith & Wesson Model 916 Slide Action Repeater

Hammerless. Solid frame. Gauges: 12, 16, 20. 3-inch chamber in 12 and 20 gauge. 5-shot tubular magazine. Barrels: plain or vent rib; 20-inch cylinder (12 ga., plain only); 26-inch improved cylinder; 28-inch modified or full; 30-inch full choke (12 ga. only). Weight: with 28-inch plain barrel, 7$^1/_4$ pounds. Plain pistol-grip stock, fluted slide handle. Made 1972 to 1981.

With plain barrel $140
With ventilated-rib barrel 165

Smith & Wesson Model 916T

Same as Model 916, except takedown, 12 gauge only. Not available with 20-inch barrel. Made 1976 to 1981.

With plain barrel $160
With ventilated-rib barrel 175

Smith & Wesson Model 1000 Autoloader $330

Gas-operated. Takedown. Gauges: 12, 20. 2$^3/_4$-inch chamber in 12 ga., 3-inch in 20 ga. 4-shot magazine. Barrels: vent rib; 26-inch skeet choke, improved cylinder; 28-inch modified or full; 30-inch full choke (12 ga. only). Weight: with 28-inch barrel, 6$^1/_2$ lbs. in 20 ga., 7$^1/_2$ lbs. in 12 ga. Checkered pistol-grip stock and forearm. Made 1972 to date.

Smith & Wesson Model 1000 Magnum $395

Same as standard Model 1000, except chambered for 12 gauge magnum 3-inch shell; 30-inch barrel only, modified or full choke; stock with recoil pad. Weight: about 8 pounds. Introduced in 1977.

Smith & Wesson Model 3000 Slide Action $210

Hammerless. 20-gauge. Barrels: 26-inch improved cylinder; 28-inch modified or full. Chambered for 3-inch magnum and 2$^3/_4$-inch loads. American walnut stock and forearm. Checkered pistol grip and forearm. Intro. 1982.

SHOTGUNS

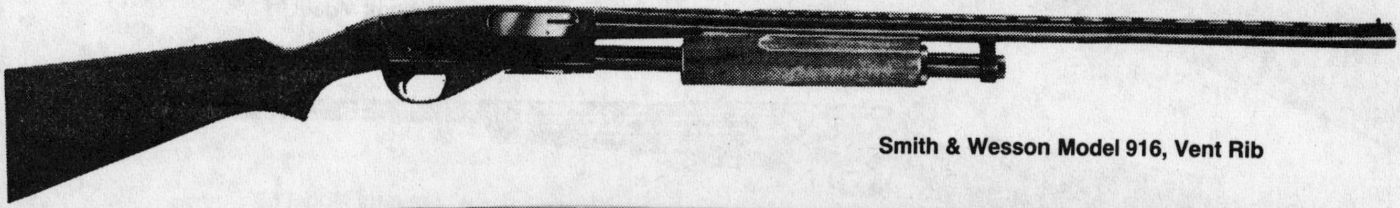

Smith & Wesson Model 916, Vent Rib

Smith & Wesson Model 1000 Magnum

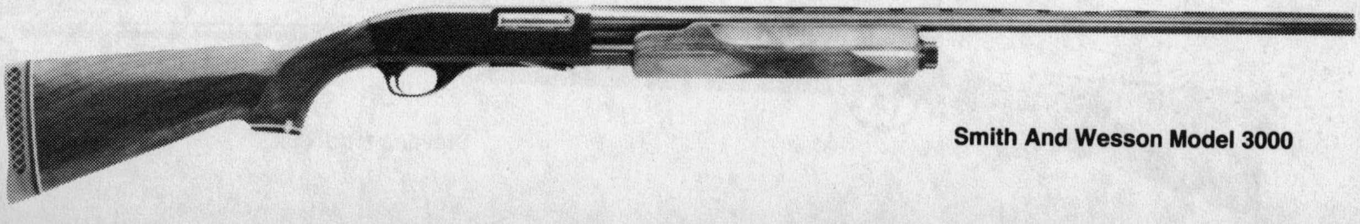

Smith And Wesson Model 3000

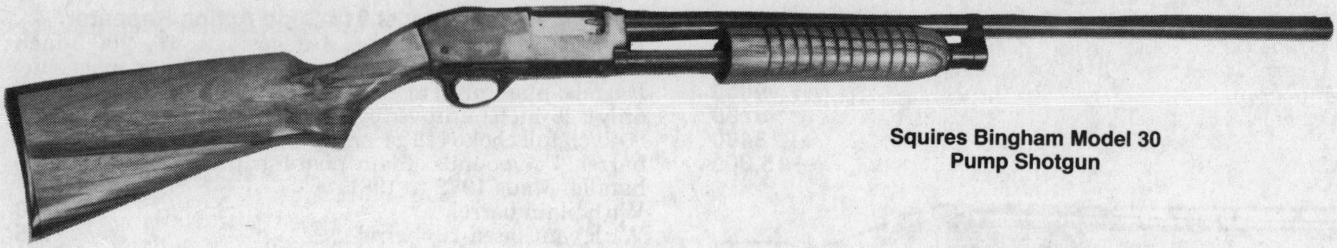

Squires Bingham Model 30
Pump Shotgun

SQUIRES BINGHAM CO., INC.
Makati, Rizal, Philippines

Squires Bingham Model 30 Pump Shotgun $150
Hammerless. 12 gauge. 5-shot magazine. Barrels: 20-inch cylinder; 28-inch modified; 30-inch full choke. Weight: about 7 pounds. Pulong Dalaga stock and slide handle. Currently manufactured.

J. STEVENS ARMS COMPANY
Chicopee Falls, Massachusetts
Division of Savage Arms Corporation

Stevens No. 22-410 Over-and-Under Combination Gun
22 caliber rifle barrel over .410 bore shotgun barrel. Visible hammer. Takedown. Single trigger. 24-inch barrels, shotgun barrel full choke. Weight: about 6 pounds. Open rear sight and ramp front sight of sporting rifle type. Plain pistol-grip stock and forearm; originally supplied with walnut stock and forearm. "Tenite" (plastic) was used in later production. Made 1938 to 1950. *Note:* This gun is now manufactured as the Savage Model 24.
With wood stock and forearm $125
With Tenite stock and forearm 105

Stevens Model 51 Bolt Action Shotgun $65
Single shot. Takedown. .410 gauge. 24-inch barrel, full choke. Weight: about 4¾ pounds. Plain one-piece pistol-grip stock, checkered on later models. Made 1962 to 1971.

Stevens Model 58 Bolt Action Repeater $75
Takedown. Gauges: 12, 16, 20. 2-shell detachable box magazine. 26-inch barrel, full choke. Weight: about 7¼ pounds. Plain one-piece pistol-grip stock. Made 1933 to 1981. *Note:* Later production models have 3-inch chamber in 20 gauge, checkered stock with recoil pad.

Stevens Model 58- 410 Bolt Action Repeater $75
Takedown. .410 gauge. 3-shell detachable box magazine. 24-inch barrel, full choke. Weight: about 5½ pounds. Plain one-piece pistol-grip stock, checkered on later production. Made 1937 to 1981.

Stevens Model 59 Bolt Action Repeater $100
Takedown. .410 gauge. 5-shell tubular magazine. 24-inch barrel, full choke. Weight: about 6 pounds. Plain, one-piece pistol-grip stock, checkered on later production. Made 1934 to 1973.

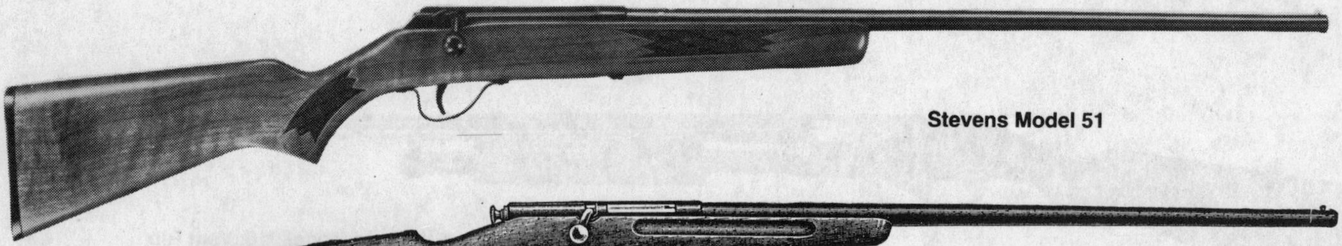

Stevens Model 51

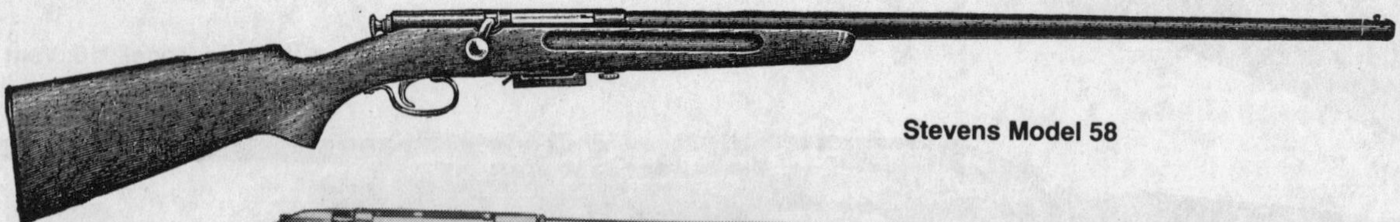

Stevens Model 58

Stevens Model 58-410

Stevens Model 59

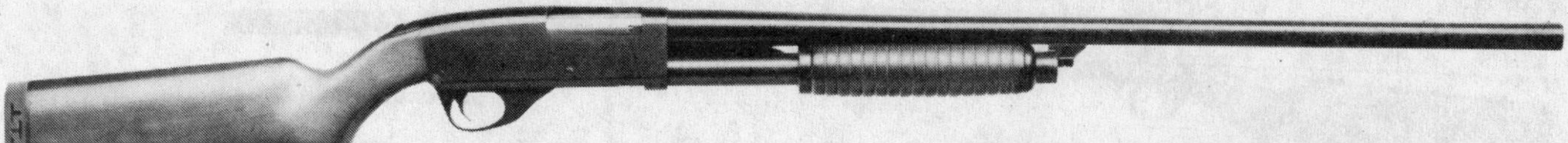

Stevens Model 67 Pump Shotgun

Stevens Model 67 Waterfowl Gun

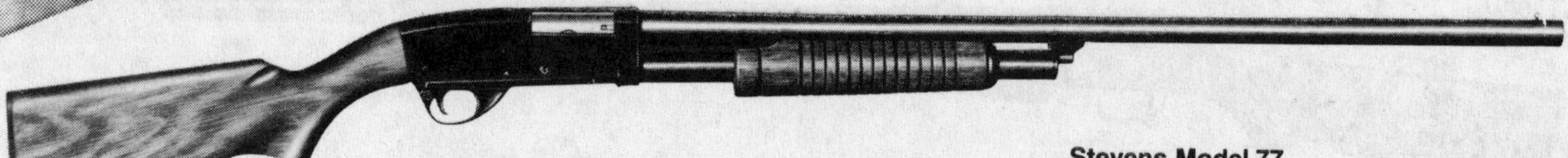

Stevens Model 77

Stevens Model 94C

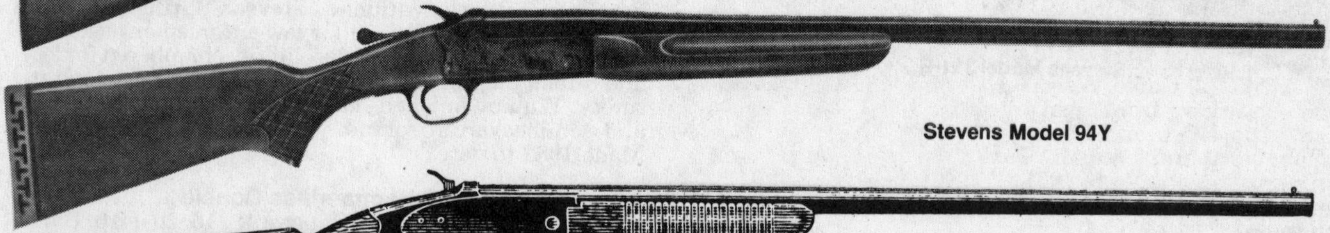

Stevens Model 94Y

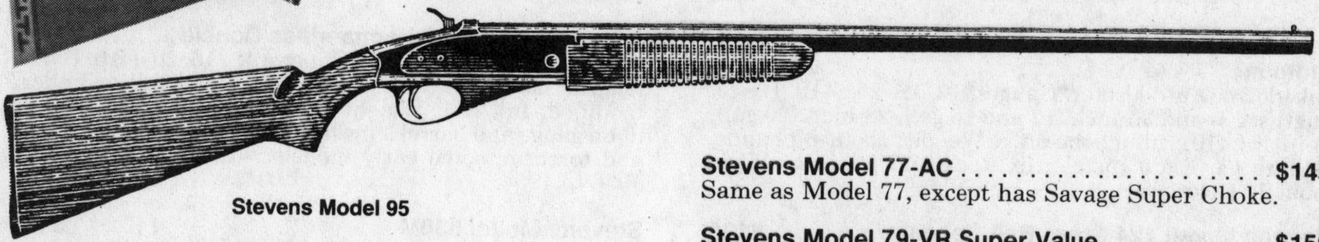

Stevens Model 95

Stevens Model 67 Pump Shotgun
Hammerless, side-ejection solid steel receiver. Gauges: 12, 20 and .410; 2¾- or 3-inch shells. Barrels: 21-, 26-, 28-, 30-inch with fixed chokes or interchangeable choke tubes; plain or vent rib. Weight: 6¼ to 7½ pounds. Optional rifle sights. Walnut-finished hardwood stock with corn cob-style forend.

Standard Model, Plain Barrel	**$155**
Standard Model, Vent Rib	**180**
Standard Model, w/Choke Tubes	**195**
Slug Model, w/Rifle Sights	**155**
Lobo Model, Matte Finish	**150**
Youth Model, 20 ga.	**120**
Camo Model, w/Choke Tubes	**220**

Stevens Model 67 Waterfowl Shotgun $140
Hammerless. Gauge: 12. 3-shot tubular magazine. Walnut finished hardwood stock. Weight: about 7½ pounds. Made 1972 to date.

Stevens Model 77 Slide Action Repeater $150
Solid frame. Gauges: 12, 16, 20. 5-shot tubular magazine. Barrels: 26-inch improved cylinder; 28-inch modified or full choke. Weight: about 7½ pounds. Plain pistol-grip stock with recoil pad, grooved slide handle. Made 1954 to 1971.

Stevens Model 77-AC $145
Same as Model 77, except has Savage Super Choke.

Stevens Model 79-VR Super Value $150
Hammerless, side ejection. Barrel: chambered for 2¾-inch and 3-inch mag. shells. 12, 20, and .410 gauge. Ventilated rib. Walnut finished hardwood stock with checkering on grip. Weight: 6¾-7 pounds. Made 1979 to date.

Stevens Model 94 Single Barrel Shotgun $75
Takedown. Visible hammer. Auto ejector. Gauges: 12, 16, 20, 28, .410. Barrels: 26-, 28-, 30-, 32-, 36-inch; full choke. Weight: about 6 pounds depending upon gauge and barrel. Plain pistol-grip stock and forearm. Made 1939 to 1961.

Stevens Model 94C $80
Same as Model 94, except has checkered stock, fluted forearm on late production. Made 1965 to date.

Stevens Model 94Y Youth Gun $75
Same as Model 94, except made in 20 and .410 gauge only; has 26-inch full choke barrel, 12½-inch buttstock with recoil pad; checkered pistol grip and fluted forearm on late production. Made 1959 to date.

Stevens Model 95 Single Barrel Shotgun $85
Solid frame. Visible hammer. Plain extractor. 12 gauge. 3-inch chamber. Barrels: 28-inch modified; 30-inch full choke. Weight: about 7¼ pounds. Plain pistol-grip stock, grooved forearm. Made 1965 to 1969.

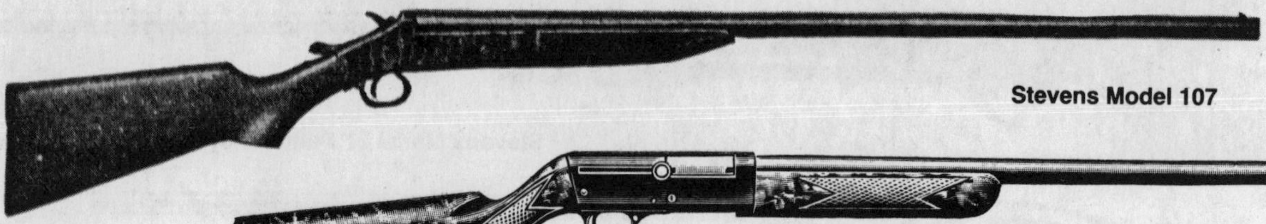

Stevens Model 107

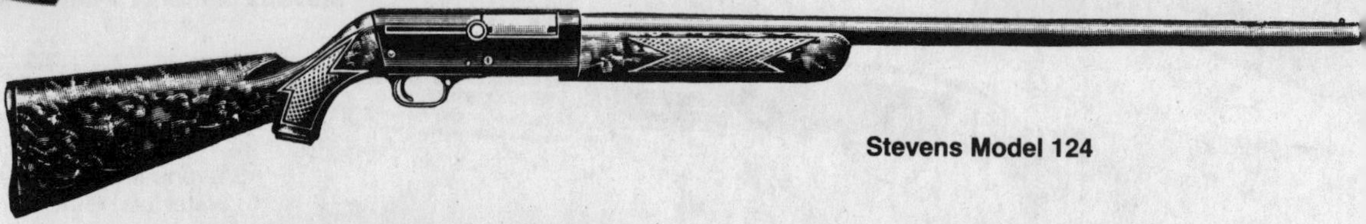

Stevens Model 124

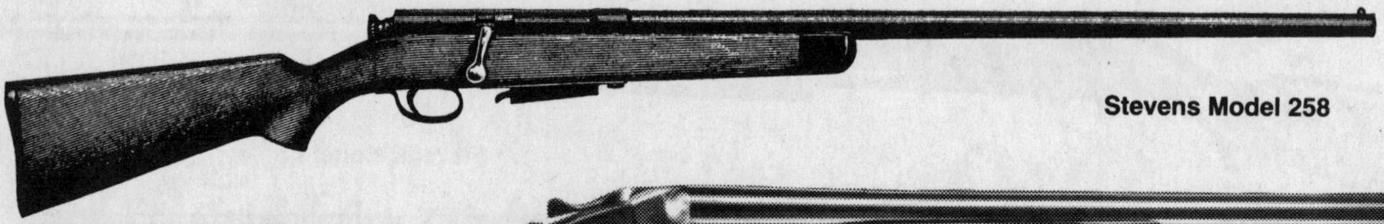

Stevens Model 258

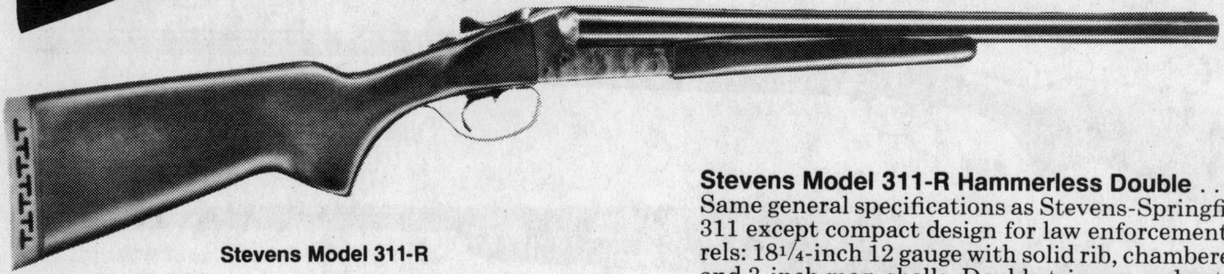

Stevens Model 311-R

Stevens Model 107 Single Barrel Hammer Shotgun **$65**
Takedown. Auto ejector. Gauges: 12, 16, 20, .410. Barrel lengths: 28- and 30-inch (12 and 16 ga.), 28-inch (20 ga.), 26-inch (.410); full choke only. Weight: about 6 pounds, 12 bore ga. Plain pistol-grip stock and forearm. Made about 1937 to 1953.

Stevens Model 124 Cross Bolt Repeater **$125**
Hammerless. Solid frame. 12 gauge only. 2-shot tubular magazine. 28-inch barrel; improved cylinder, modified or full choke. Weight: about 7 pounds. Tenite stock and forearm. Made from 1947 to 1952.

Stevens Model 240 Over-and-Under Shotgun . . . **$325**
Visible hammer. Takedown. Double triggers. .410 gauge. 26-inch barrels, full choke. Weight: about 6 pounds. Tenite (plastic) pistol-grip stock and forearm. Made 1940 to 1949.

Stevens Model 258 Bolt Action Repeater **$70**
Takedown. 20-gauge. 2-shell detachable box magazine. 26-inch barrel, full choke. Weight: about 6¼ pounds. Plain one-piece pistol-grip stock. Made 1937 to 1965.

Stevens Model 311-R Hammerless Double **$155**
Same general specifications as Stevens-Springfield Model 311 except compact design for law enforcement use. Barrels: 18¼-inch 12 gauge with solid rib, chambered for 2¾- and 3-inch mag. shells. Double triggers and auto top tang safety. Walnut finished hardwood stock with recoil pad and semibeavertail forend. Weight: about 6¾ pounds. Made 1982 to date.

Stevens Model 530 Hammerless Double **$175**
Box lock. Double triggers. Gauges: 12, 16, 20, .410. Barrel lengths: 26- to 32-inch; choked modified/full, cylinder/modified, full/full. Weight: 6 to 7½ pounds depending upon gauge and barrel length. Checkered pistol-grip stock and forearm; some early models with recoil pad. Made 1936 to 1954.

Stevens Model 530M **$140**
Same as Model 530, except has Tenite (plastic) stock and forearm. Discontinued about 1947.

Stevens Model 530ST Double Gun **$195**
Same as Model 530, except has non-selective single trigger. Discontinued.

Stevens Model 620 Hammerless Slide Action Repeating Shotgun **$160**
Takedown. Gauges: 12, 16, 20. 5-shell tubular magazine. Barrel lengths: 26-, 28-, 30-, 32-inch; choked full, modified, improved cylinder, cylinder. Weight: about 7¾ lbs., 12 ga.; 7¼ lbs., 16 ga.; 6 lbs., 20 ga. Checkered pistol-grip stock and slide handle. Made 1927 to 1953.

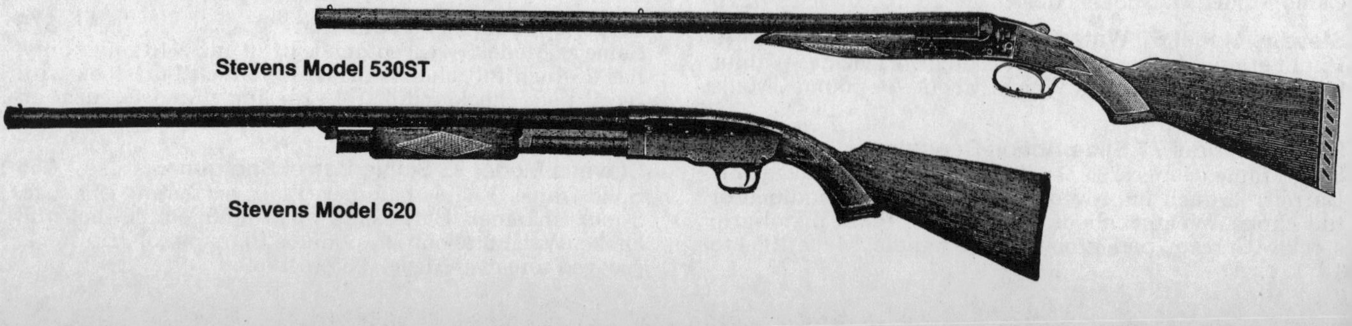

Stevens Model 530ST

Stevens Model 620

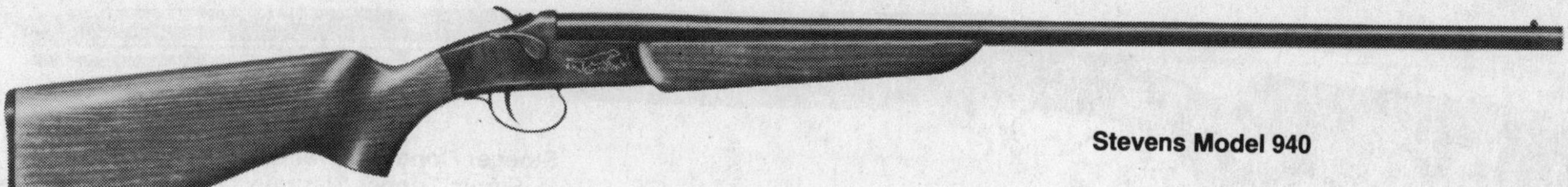
Stevens Model 940

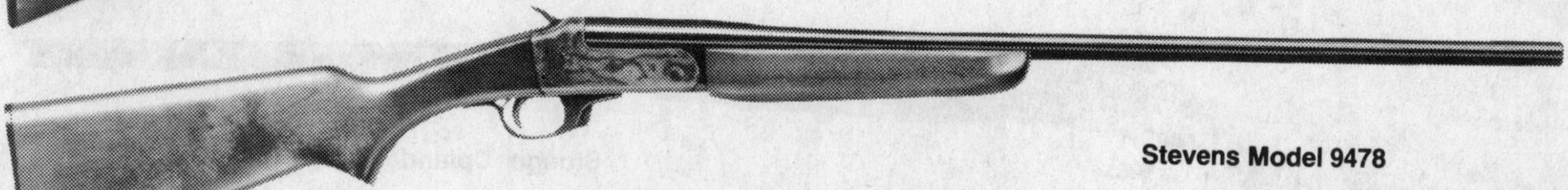
Stevens Model 9478

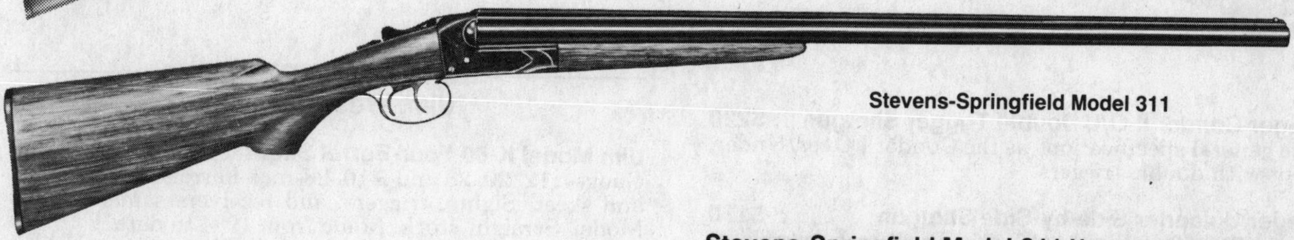
Stevens-Springfield Model 311

Stevens Model 621 . . . . **$195**
Same as Model 620, except has raised solid matted-rib barrel. Discontinued.

Stevens Model 820 Hammerless Slide Action Repeating Shotgun **$145**
Solid frame. 12 gauge only. 5-shell tubular magazine. 28-inch barrel; improved cylinder, modified or full choke. Weight: about 7½ pounds. Plain pistol-grip stock, grooved slide handle. Made 1949 to 1954.

Stevens Model 820-SC **$150**
Same as Model 820, except has Savage Super Choke.

Stevens Model 940 Single Barrel Shotgun **$75**
Same general specifications as Model 94, except has side lever opening instead of top lever. Made 1961 to 1970.

Stevens Model 940Y Youth Gun **$80**
Same general specifications as Model 94Y, except has side lever opening instead of top lever. Made 1961 to 1970.

Stevens Model 9478 . . . . **$85**
Takedown. Visible hammer. Automatic ejector. Gauges: 12, 20, .410. Barrels: 26-, 28-, 30-, 36-inch; full choke. Weight: average 6 pounds depending upon gauge and barrel. Plain pistol-grip stock and forearm. Made 1978 to 1985.

Stevens-Springfield Model 311 Hammerless Double
Same general specifications as Stevens Model 530, except earlier production has plain stock and forearm; checkered on current guns. Originally produced as a "Springfield" gun, this model became a part of the "Stevens" line in 1948 when the "Springfield" brand name was discontinued. Made 1931 to date.

Pre-WWII **$190**
Post-WWII **160**

STOEGER SHOTGUNS
So. Hackensack, New Jersey

Formerly IGA Shotguns.

Stoeger Coach Gun **$170**
Gauge: 12 or 20. 20-inch side-by-side barrels of chrome-molybdenum steel. Chokes: imp. cyl./mod. 3-inch chambers. Weight: 6½ pounds. Double triggers. Automatic safety. Hand-rubbed, oil-finish pistol grip hardwood stock and forend with hand-checkering. Made from 1983 to date.

Stoeger Condor I O/U Single Trigger Shotgun . . **$255**
Gauge: 12 or 20. 26- or 28-inch barrels of chrome-molybdenum steel. Chokes: mod./full or imp. cyl./mod. 3-inch chambers. Weight: 6¾ to 7 pounds. Sighting rib with anti-glare surface. Hand-checkered, hardwood pistol grip stock and forend. Made from 1983 to date.

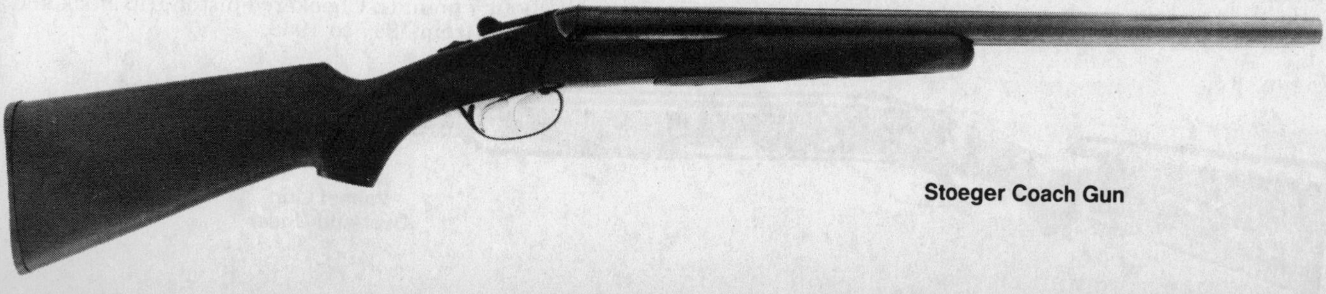
Stoeger Coach Gun

Stoeger Condor I Over/Under Single Trigger Shotgun

Stoeger Uplander Side-by-Side

Stoeger Condor II O/U Double Trigger Shotgun . $220
Same general specifications as the Condor I Over/Under, except with double triggers.

Stoeger Uplander Side-by-Side Shotgun $170
Gauges: 12, 20, 28 and .410. 26- or 28-inch barrels of chrome-molybdenum steel. Various choke combinations. 2¾-inch chambers (3-inch in .410 caliber). Weight: 6¾ to 7 pounds. Double triggers. Automatic safety. Matte-finished solid sighting rib. Hand-rubbed, oil-finish pistol grip stock and forend with hand-checkering. Made from 1983 to date.

TIKKA SHOTGUNS
Tikkakoski, Finland

Tikka M 07 Shotgun/Rifle Combination $795
Gauge/caliber: 12/222 Rem. Shotgun barrel: about 25 inches; rifle barrel: about 22¾ inches. 40⅔ inches overall. Weight: about 7 pounds. Dovetailed for telescopic sight. Single trigger with selector between the barrels. Ventilated rib. Monte-Carlo-style walnut stock with checkered pistol grip and forend. Made from 1965 to 1987.

Tikka M 77 Over/Under Shotgun $995
Gauge: 12. 27-inch vent-rib barrels. Approx. 44 inches overall. Weight: about 7¼ pounds. Barrel selector. Ejectors. Monte Carlo-style walnut stock with checkered pistol grip and forend; rollover cheekpiece. Made 1977 to 1987.

Tikka M 77K Shotgun/Rifle Combination $1050
Gauge: 12/70. Calibers: 222 Rem., 5.6×52r5, 6.5×55, 7×57r5, 7×65r5, 308 Win. Vent-rib barrels: about 25 inches (shotgun); almost 23 inches (rifle). 42.3 inches overall. Weight: about 7½ pounds. Double triggers. Monte Carlo-style walnut stock with checkered pistol grip and forend; rollover cheekpiece. Made from 1977 to 1986.

SHOTGUNS OF ULM
Ulm, West Germany

Ulm Model K-80 Four-Barrel Skeet $5360
Gauges: 12, 20, 28 and .410. 28-inch barrels. Chokes: tula and skeet. Sights, triggers, and receivers same as Trap Model. Straight stock. Made from 1984 to date.

Ulm Model K-80 Live Pigeon $2621
Gauge: 12. Barrels: 28-, 29- or 30-inch. Chokes: IM/SF. Sights, triggers, and receivers same as Trap Model. Straight stock. Made from 1984 to date.

Ulm Model K-80 Over/Under Trap $2530
Gauge: 12. 30- or 32-inch barrels. Chokes: IM/F+Full. Metal front sight with insert and metal center bead. Triggers: wide profile, single selective, position adjustable. Receivers: hard satin-nickel finish. Hand-checkered, oil-finished select walnut forearm and Monte Carlo stock. Made from 1984 to date.

U.S. REPEATING ARMS CO.
New Haven, Connecticut
See Winchester Shotgun listings.

VALMET OY
Helsinki, Finland

See also Savage Models 330, 333T, 333 and 2400, which are Valmet guns.

Valmet Lion Over-and-Under Shotgun $440
Box lock. Selective single trigger. Plain extractors. 12 gauge only. Barrels: 26-inch improved cylinder/modified; 28-inch modified/full; 30-inch modified full, full/full. Weight: about 7 pounds. Checkered pistol-grip stock and forearm. Made from 1947 to 1968.

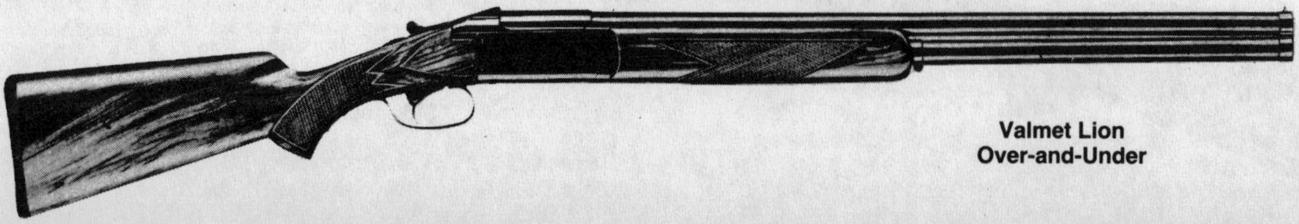

Valmet Lion Over-and-Under

Valmet Model 412 K
Combination Shotgun/Rifle

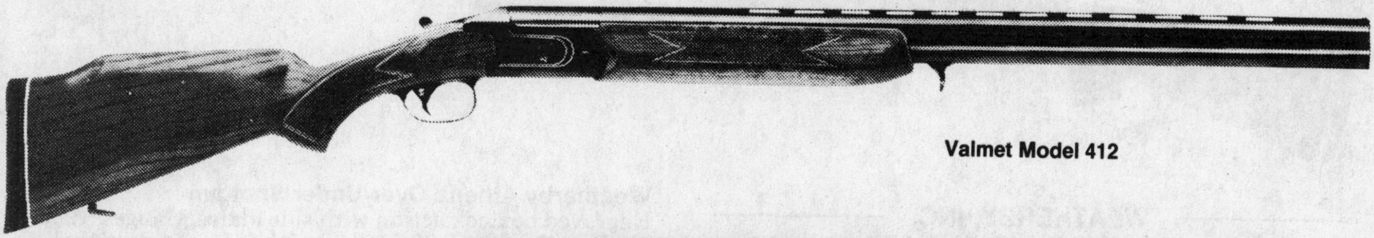

Valmet Model 412

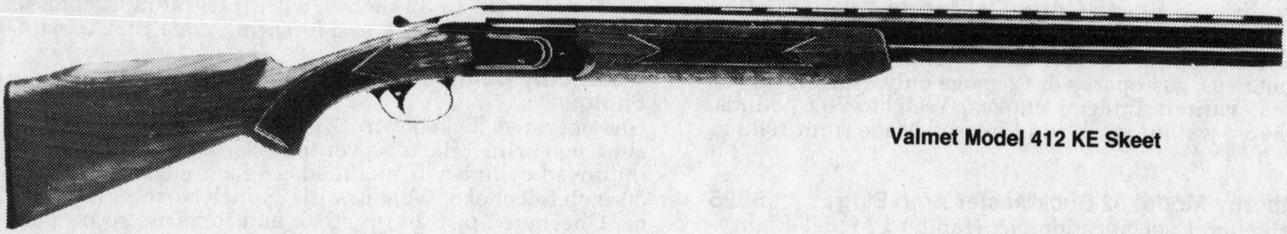

Valmet Model 412 KE Skeet

Valmet Model 412 K Combination Shotgun/Rifle . . $590
Similar to Model 412 K, except bottom barrel chambered for either 222 Rem., 223 Rem., 243 Win., 308 Win. or 30-06. 12-gauge shotgun barrel with improved modified choke. Monte Carlo American walnut stock, recoil pad.

Valmet Model 412 K Over/Under Field Shotgun . . $525
Hammerless. 12-gauge, 3-inch chamber. 36-inch barrel, full/full chokes. American walnut Monte Carlo stock. Made from 1982 to date.

Valmet Model 412 KE Over/Under Field Shotgun . $510
12-gauge chambered for 2¾-inch shells; 26-inch barrel, IC/M chokes; 28-inch barrel, M/F chokes; 12-gauge chambered for 3-inch shells, 30-inch barrel, M/F chokes. 20-gauge chambered for 3-inch shells; 26-inch barrel IC/M chokes; 28-inch barrel, M/F chokes. American walnut Monte Carlo stock.

Valmet Model 412 KE Skeet $615
Similar to Model 412 K, except Skeet stock and chokes. 12 and 20 gauges.

Valmet Model 412 KE Trap $620
Similar to Model 412 K Field, except trap stock, recoil pad. 30-inch barrels, improved mod./full chokes.

Valmet 3-Band Set $1595

MONTGOMERY WARD
Chicago, Illinois
Western Field and Hercules Models

Although they do not correspond to specific models below, the names Western Field and Hercules have been used to designate various Montgomery Ward shotguns at various times.

Wards Model 25 Slide Action Repeater $125
Solid frame. 12 gauge only. 5-shot tubular magazine. 28-inch barrel, various chokes. Weight: about 7½ pounds. Plain pistol-grip stock, grooved slide handle.

Wards Model 40 Over-and-Under Shotgun $500
Hammerless. Box lock. Double triggers. Gauges: 12, 16, 20, .410. Barrels: plain; 26- to 30-inch, various chokes. Checkered pistol-grip stock and forearm.

Wards Model 40N Slide Action Repeater $125
Same general specifications as Model 25.

Wards Model 172 Bolt Action Shotgun $75
Takedown. 2-shot detachable clip magazine. 12 gauge. 28-inch barrel with variable choke. Weight: about 7½ pounds. Monte Carlo stock with recoil pad.

Wards Model 550A Slide Action Repeater $190
Takedown. Gauges: 12, 16, 20, .410. 5-shot tubular magazine. Barrels: plain, 26- to 30-inch, various chokes. Weight: 6 to 8 pounds. Plain pistol-grip stock and grooved slide handle.

Wards Model SB300 Double Barrel Shotgun $150
Same general specifications as Model SD52A.

Wards Model SB312 Double Barrel Shotgun $200
Box lock. Double triggers. Plain extractors. Gauges: 12, 16, 20, .410. Barrels: 24- to 30-inch. Various chokes. Weight, about 7½ pounds in 12 gauge. Checkered pistol-grip stock and forearm.

Wards Model SD52A Double Barrel Shotgun . . . $150
Box lock. Double triggers. Gauges: 12, 16, 20, .410. Barrels: 26- to 32-inch, various chokes. Weight: 6 to 7½ pounds.

Weatherby Model 82 Automatic

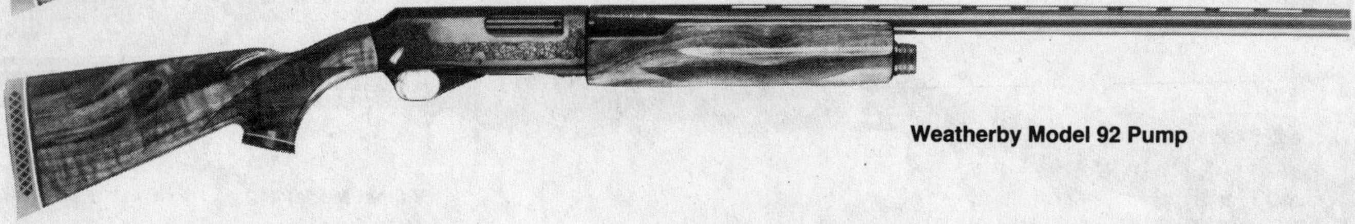

Weatherby Model 92 Pump

WEATHERBY, INC.
South Gate, California

Weatherby Model 82 Autoloading Shotgun $365
Hammerless, gas-operated. 12 gauge only. Barrels: 22- to 30-inch, various integral chokes. Weight: $7\frac{1}{2}$ pounds. Checkered walnut stock and forearm. Made from 1982 to date.

Weatherby Model 82 BuckMaster Auto Slug $395
Same general specifications as standard Model Eighty-Two, except has rifle sights. Made from 1986 to date.

Weatherby Model 92 Slide Action Shotgun $350
Hammerless, short-stroke action. 12 gauge; 3-inch chamber. Tubular magazine. Barrels: 22-, 26-, 28-, 30-inch with fixed choke or IMC choke tubes; ventilated rib or plain with rifle sights. Weight: $7\frac{1}{2}$ pounds. Engraved, matte black receiver and blued barrel. Checkered high-gloss buttstock and forend. Imported from Japan since 1982.

Weatherby Model 92 BuckMaster Pump Slug . . . $345
Same general specifications as standard Model Ninety-Two, except has rifle sights. Made from 1986 to date.

Weatherby Athena Over/Under Shotgun $1050
Engraved boxlock action with side plates. Gauges: 12 and 20. Barrels: 26- to 32-inches, with integral multichokes. Checkered walnut stock and forearm. Made 1982 to date.

Weatherby Centurion Field Grade Automatic Shotgun $325
Gas-operated. Takedown. 12 gauge. $2\frac{3}{4}$-inch chamber. 3-shot magazine. Barrels: ventilated ribs; 26-inch skeet, improved cylinder or modified; 28-inch modified or full; 30-inch full choke. Weight: with 28-inch barrel, 7 lbs. $10\frac{1}{2}$ oz. Checkered pistol-grip stock and forearm, recoil pad. Made in Japan 1972 to 1981.

Weatherby Centurion Trap Gun $330
Same as Centurion Field Grade, except has 30-inch full choke barrel only, trap-style stock. Weight: 7 lbs. $11\frac{3}{4}$ oz. Made in Japan 1972 to 1981.

Weatherby Centurion Deluxe $350
Same as Centurion Field Grade, except has etched receiver, fancy grade wood. Made in Japan from 1972 to date.

Weatherby Ducks Unlimited Shotgun $1000

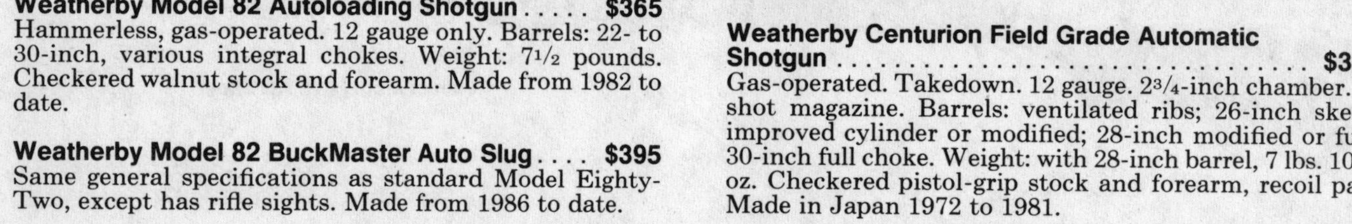

Weatherby Athena

Weatherby Centurion Deluxe

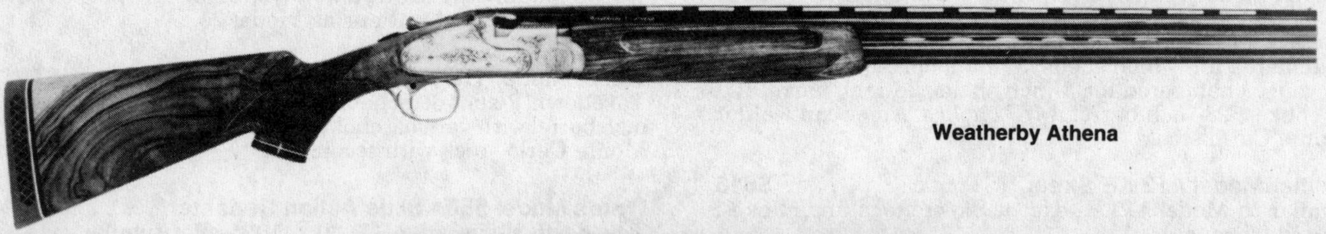

Weatherby Centurion Field Grade

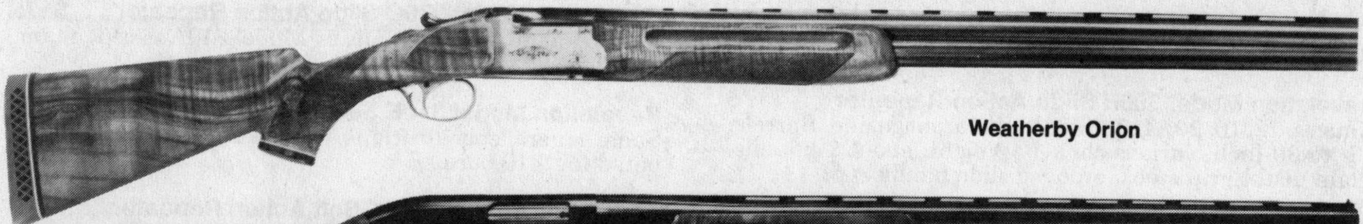

Weatherby Orion

Weatherby Patrician Field Grade

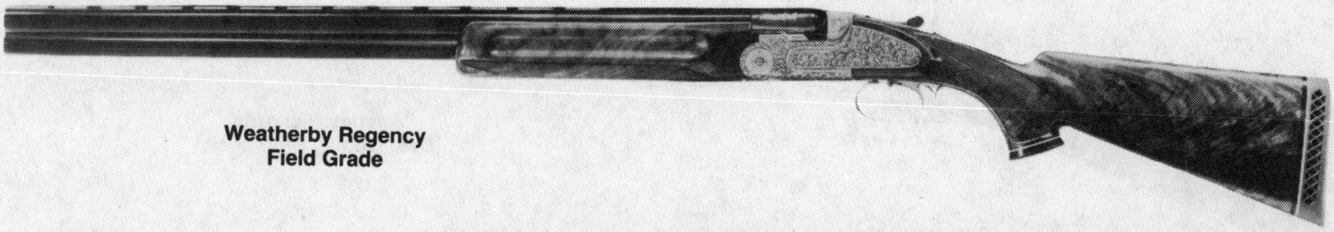

Weatherby Regency Field Grade

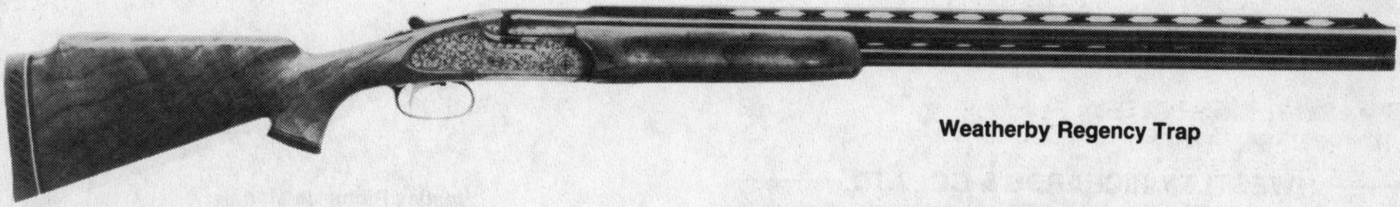

Weatherby Regency Trap

Weatherby Orion Over/Under Shotgun $695
Box lock. Gauges: 12 and 20. Barrels: 26- to 32-inch, with integral multichokes. Weight: 6½ to 8 pounds. Checkered walnut stock and forearm. Made from 1982 to 1986.

Weatherby Patrician Deluxe $400
Same as Patrician Field Grade, except has etched receiver, fancy grade wood. Made in Japan from 1972 to 1982.

Weatherby Patrician Field Grade Slide Action Shotgun $310
Hammerless. Takedown. 12 gauge. 2¾-inch chamber. 4 shot tubular magazine. Barrels: vent rib; 26-inch, skeet, improved cylinder, modified; 28-inch, modified, full; 30-inch, full choke. Weight: with 28-inch barrel, 7 lbs. 7 oz. Checkered pistol-grip stock and slide handle, recoil pad. Made in Japan from 1972 to 1982.

Weatherby Patrician Trap Gun $335
Same as Patrician Field Grade, except has 30-inch full choke barrel only, trap-style stock. Weight: 7 lbs. 9 oz. Made in Japan from 1972 to 1982.

Weatherby Regency Field Grade O/U Shotgun . . $1100
Box lock with side plates, elaborately engraved. Auto ejectors. Selective single trigger. Gauges: 12, 20. 2¾-inch chamber in 12 gauge, 3-inch in 20 gauge. Barrels: vent rib; 26-inch skeet, improved cylinder/modified, modified/full (20 ga. only); 28-inch skeet, improved cylinder/modified, modified/full; 30-inch modified/full (12 ga. only). Weight with 28-inch barrels: 7 lbs. 6 oz., 12 ga.; 6 lbs. 14 oz., 20 ga. Checkered pistol-grip stock and forearm of fancy walnut. Made in Italy from 1965 to 1982.

Weatherby Regency Trap Gun $995
Similar to Regency Field Grade, except has trap-style stock with straight or Monte Carlo comb. Barrels have vent side ribs and high, wide vent top rib; 30- or 32-inch, modified/full, improved modified/full or both full choke. Weight: with 32-inch barrels, 8 pounds. Made in Italy from 1965 to 1982.

WESTERN ARMS CORP.
Ithaca, New York
Division of Ithaca Gun Company

Western Long Range

Western Long Range Hammerless Double
Box lock. Plain extractors. Single or double triggers. Gauges: 12, 16, 20, .410. Barrels: 26- to 32-inch, modified and full choke standard. Weight: 7½ pounds, 12 ga. Plain pistol-grip stock and forend. Made from 1929 to 1946.
With double triggers **$175**
With single trigger **200**

SHOTGUNS

WESTERN AUTO SHOTGUNS
Kansas City, Missouri

Revelation Model 300H Slide Action Repeater . . $175
Gauges: 12, 16, 20, .410. 4-shot tubular magazine. Barrels: 26- to 30-inch, various chokes. Weight: about 7 pounds. Plain pistol-grip stock, grooved slide handle.

Revelation Model 310A Slide Action Repeater . . $175
Takedown. 12 gauge. 5-shot tubular magazine. Barrels: 28- and 30-inch. Weight: about 7½ pounds. Plain pistol-grip stock.

Revelation Model 310B Slide Action Repeater . . $155
Same general specifications as Model 310A except chambered for 16 gauge.

Revelation Model 310C Slide Action Repeater . . $175
Same general specifications as Model 310A except chambered for 20 gauge.

Revelation Model 310E Slide Action Repeater . . $195
Same general specifications as Model 310A except chambered for .410 bore.

Revelation Model 325BK Bolt Action Repeater . . . $70
Takedown. 2-shot detachable clip magazine. 20 gauge. 26-inch barrel with variable choke. Weight: 6¼ pounds.

WESTERN FIELD SHOTGUNS
See "W" for listings under Montgomery Ward.

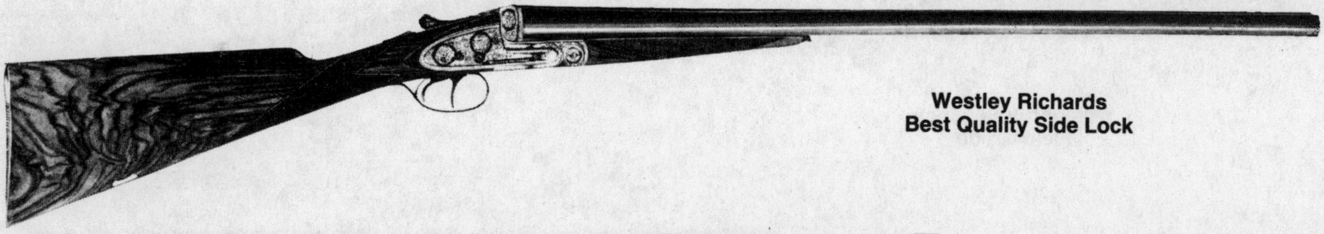

Westley Richards
Best Quality Side Lock

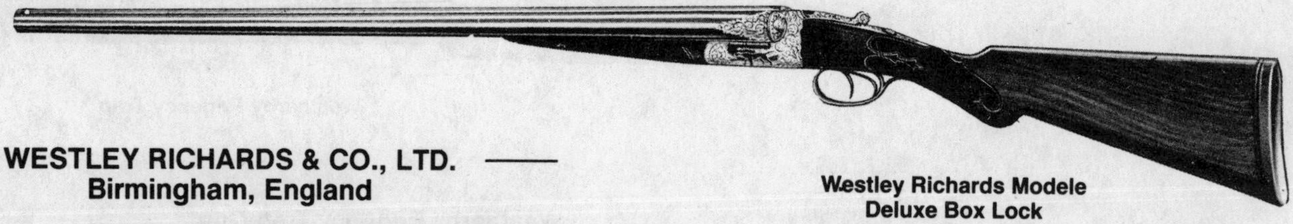

Westley Richards Modele
Deluxe Box Lock

WESTLEY RICHARDS & CO., LTD.
Birmingham, England

The Pigeon and Wildfowl Gun, available in all of the Westley Richards models except the Ovundo, has the same general specifications as the corresponding standard field gun, except has magnum action of extra strength and treble bolting; chambered for 12 gauge only (2¾- or 3-inch); 30-inch full choke barrels standard. Weight: about 8 pounds. The manufacturer warns that 12 gauge magnum shells should not be used in their standard weight double barrel shotguns.

Westley Richards Best Quality Box Lock Hammerless Double Barrel Shotgun
Box lock. Hand-detachable locks and hinged cover plate. Selective ejectors. Double triggers or selective single trigger. Gauges: 12, 16, 20. Barrel lengths and boring to order. Weight: 5½ to 6¼ pounds depending upon gauge and barrel length. Checkered stock and forend, straight or half-pistol grip. Also supplied in Pigeon and Wildfowl Model with same values. Currently manufactured. Produced since 1899.
With double triggers **$7000**
With selective single trigger **7500**

Westley Richards Best Quality Side Lock Hammerless Double Barrel Shotgun
Hand-detachable side locks. Selective ejectors. Double triggers or selective single trigger. Gauges: 12, 16, 20, 28, .410. Barrel lengths and boring to order. Weight: 4¾ to 6¾ pounds depending upon gauge and barrel length. Checkered stock and forend, straight or half-pistol grip. Also supplied in Pigeon and Wildfowl Model with same values. Currently manufactured.
With double triggers **$12,000**
With selective single trigger **13,000**

Westley Richards Modele Deluxe Box Lock Hammerless Double Barrel Shotgun
Same general specifications as standard Best Quality gun, except higher quality throughout. Has Westley Richards top-projection and treble-bite lever-work, hand-detachable locks. Also supplied in Pigeon and Wildfowl Model with same values. Currently manufactured.
With double triggers **$7500**
With selective single trigger **8200**

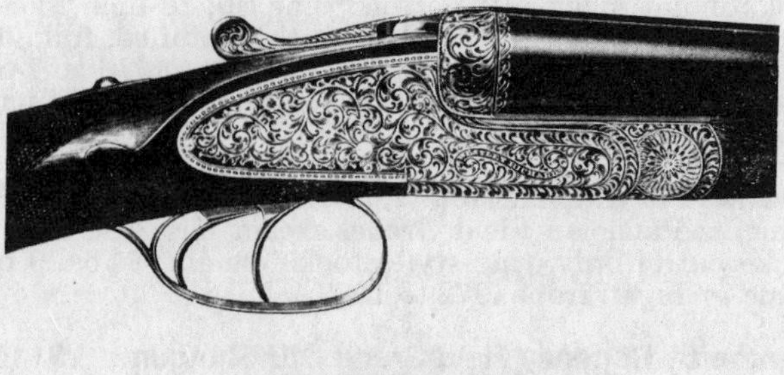

Westley Richards Modele
Deluxe Side Lock

Westley Richards Modele Deluxe Side Lock
Same as Best Quality Side Lock, except higher grade engraving and wood. Currently manufactured.
With double triggers **$16,000**
With single trigger **20,000**

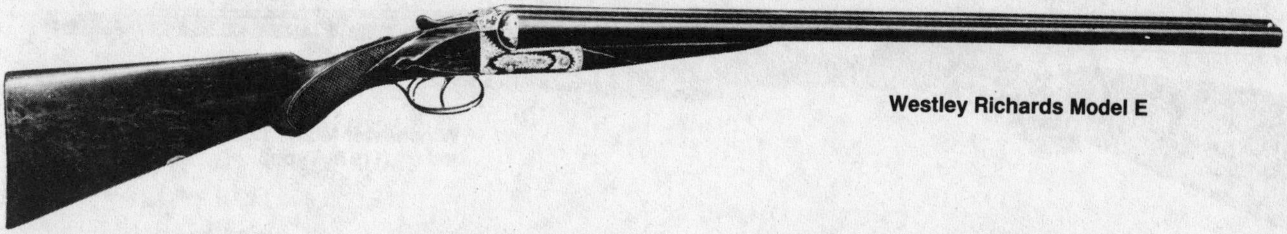

Westley Richards Model E

Westley Richards Model E Hammerless Double
Anson & Deeley-type boxlock action. Selective ejector or non-ejector. Double triggers. Gauges: 12, 16, 20. Barrel lengths and boring to order. Weight: 5½ to 7¼ pounds depending upon type, gauge and barrel length. Checkered stock and forend, straight or half-pistol grip. Also supplied in Pigeon and Wildfowl Model with same values. Currently manufactured.
Ejector model **$3500**
Non-ejector model **3000**

Westley Richards Ovundo (Over/Under) $14,000
Hammerless. Box lock. Hand-detachable locks. Dummy side plates. Selective ejectors. Selective single trigger. 12 gauge. Barrel lengths and boring to order. Checkered stock and forend, straight or half-pistol grip. Mfd. prior to World War II.

TED WILLIAMS SHOTGUNS

See Sears shotguns.

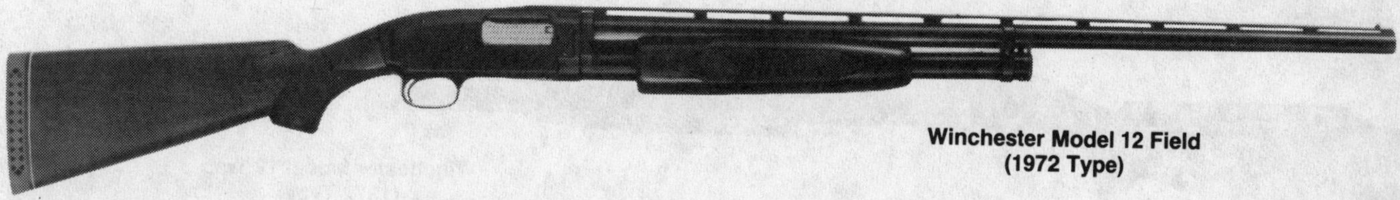

Winchester Model 12 Field
(1972 Type)

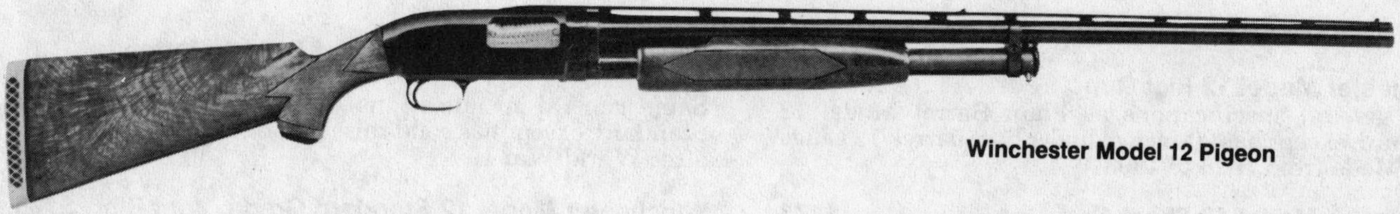

Winchester Model 12 Pigeon

WINCHESTER SHOTGUNS
New Haven, Connecticut

Formerly Winchester Repeating Arms Co. Now mfd. by Winchester-Western Div., Olin Corp., and by U.S. Repeating Arms Co.

Winchester Model 12 Featherweight $595
Same as Plain Barrel Model 12 Standard, except has alloy guard, modified takedown. 12 gauge only. Barrels: 26-inch improved cylinder; 28-inch modified or full; 30-inch full choke. Weight: about 6¾ pounds. Made from 1959 to 1962.

Winchester Model 12 Field Gun, 1972 Type $650
Same general specifications as Standard Model 12. 12 gauge only. 26-, 28- or 30-inch vent-rib barrel, standard chokes. Engine-turned bolt and carrier. Hand-checkered stock and slide handle of semi-fancy walnut. Made from 1972 to 1975.

Winchester Model 12 Heavy Duck Gun $750
12 gauge only, chambered for 3-inch shells. Same general specifications as Standard Grade, except 30- or 32-inch

Winchester Model 12 Heavy Duck Gun (cont.)
plain full choke barrel only, 3-shot magazine, recoil pad. Weight: about 8¾ pounds. Discont. 1964.

Winchester Model 12 Heavy Duck Gun, Matt Rib $795
Same as Plain Barrel Model 12 Heavy Duck Gun, except has solid raised matted rib. Discont. 1959.

Winchester Model 12 Pigeon Grade
Deluxe versions of the regular Model 12 Standard or Field Gun, Duck Gun, Skeet Gun and Trap Gun made on special order. This grade has finer finish throughout, hand-smoothed action, engine-turned breech bolt and carrier, stock and extension slide handle of high grade walnut, fancy checkering, stock dimensions to individual specifications. Engraving and carving available at extra cost ranging from about $35 to over $200. Discont. 1965.
Field Gun, plain barrel . . . . **$ 1100**
Field Gun, ventilated rib **1300**
Skeet Gun, matted rib **1400**
Skeet Gun, ventilated rib **1495**
Skeet Gun, Cutts Compensator **995**
Trap Gun, matted rib **1295**
Trap Gun, ventilated rib **1395**

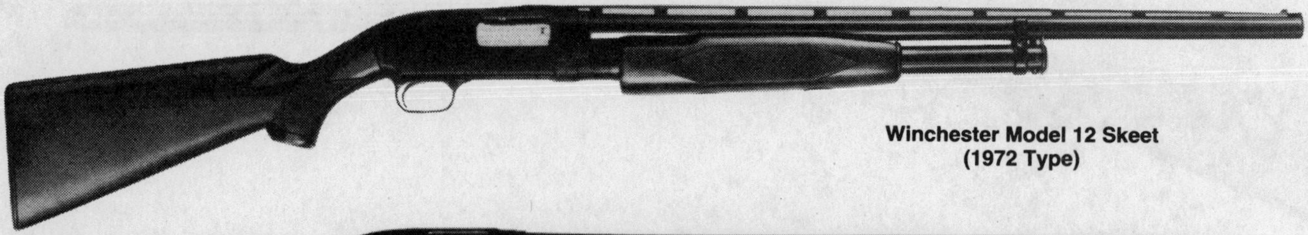

Winchester Model 12 Skeet (1972 Type)

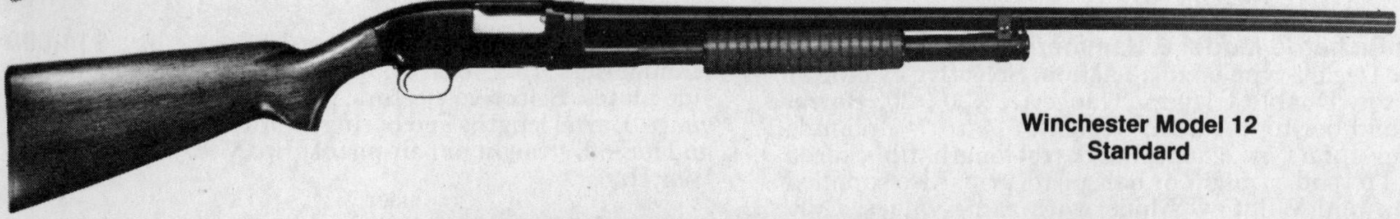

Winchester Model 12 Standard

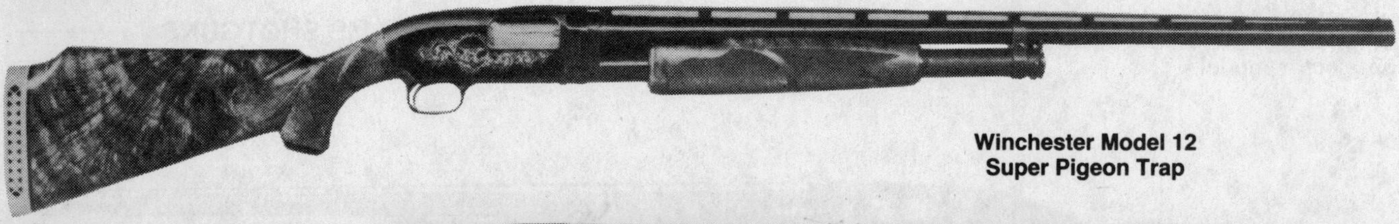

Winchester Model 12 Super Pigeon Trap

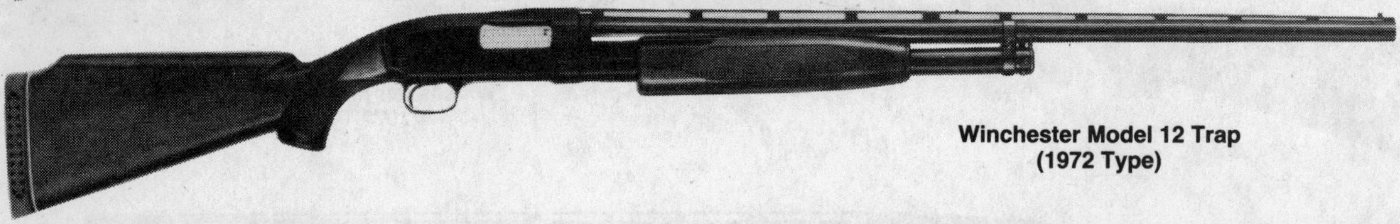

Winchester Model 12 Trap (1972 Type)

Winchester Model 12 Riot Gun $495
Same general specifications as Plain Barrel Model 12 Standard, except has 20-inch cylinder bore barrel, 12 gauge only. Made from 1918 to 1963.

Winchester Model 12 Skeet Gun $875
Gauges: 12, 16, 20, 28. 5-shot tubular magazine. 26-inch matted rib barrel, skeet choke. Weight: about $7\frac{3}{4}$ pounds, 12 ga.; $6\frac{3}{4}$ pounds in other gauges. Bradley red or ivory bead front sight. Winchester 94B middle sight. Checkered pistol-grip stock and extension slide handle. Discont. after World War II.

Winchester Model 12 Skeet Gun, Cutts Compensator $775
Same general specifications as standard Model 12 Skeet Gun, except has plain barrel fitted with Cutts Compensator, 26 inches overall. Discont. 1954.

Winchester Model 12 Skeet Gun, Plain Barrel . . $725
Same general specifications as standard Model 12 Skeet Gun, except has plain barrel. Made from 1937 to 1947.

Winchester Model 12 Skeet Gun, Vent Rib $995
Same general specifications as standard Model 12 Skeet Gun, except has 26-inch barrel with vent rib, 12 and 20 gauge. Discontinued in 1965.

Winchester Model 12 Skeet Gun, 1972 Type . . . $700
Same general specifications as Standard Model 12. 12 gauge only. 26-inch vent-rib barrel, skeet choke. Engine-turned bolt and carrier. Hand-checkered skeet-style stock and slide handle of choice walnut, recoil pad. Made 1972 to 1975.

Winchester Model 12 Standard Grade, Matted Rib $695
Same general specifications as Plain Barrel Model 12 Standard, except has solid raised matted rib. Discontinued after World War II.

Winchester Model 12 Standard Grade, Vent Rib . $795
Same general specifications as Plain Barrel Model 12 Standard, except has ventilated rib. $26\frac{3}{4}$- or 30-inch barrel, 12 gauge only. Discont. after World War II.

Winchester Model 12 Standard Slide Action Repeater
Hammerless. Takedown. Gauges: 12, 16, 20, 28. 6-shell tubular magazine. Plain barrel. Lengths: 26- to 32-inches; choked full to cylinder. Weight: about $7\frac{1}{2}$ pounds, 12 ga. 30-inch; $6\frac{1}{2}$ pounds in other gauges with 28-inch barrel. Plain pistol-grip stock, grooved slide handle. Made from 1912 to 1964.
28 gauge **$1995**
12 ga., 28-inch barrel (full) **595**
Other gauges, etc. **550**

Winchester Model 12 Super Pigeon Grade $1995
Custom version of Model 12 with same general specifications as standard models. 12 gauge only. 26-, 28- or 30-inch vent-rib barrel, any standard choke. Engraved receiver. Hand-smoothed and fitted action. Full fancy walnut stock and forearm made to individual order. Made from 1965 to 1972.

Winchester Model 12 Trap Gun $825
Same general specifications as standard Model 12, except has straighter stock, checkered pistol grip and extension slide handle, recoil pad, 30-inch matted-rib barrel, full choke, 12 gauge only. Discont. after World War II.

Winchester Model 20

Winchester Model 21 Field

Winchester Model 21 Grand American

Winchester Model 21 Pigeon

Winchester Model 12 Trap Gun, Ventilated Rib
Same as standard Model 12 Trap Gun, except has ventilated rib. Discontinued in 1965.
With straight stock **$950**
With Monte Carlo stock **995**

Winchester Model 12 Trap Gun, 1972 Type $795
Same general specifications as Standard Model 12. 12 gauge only. 30-inch ventilated-rib barrel, full choke. Engine-turned bolt and carrier. Hand-checkered trap-style stock (straight or Monte Carlo comb) and slide handle of select walnut, recoil pad. Intro. in 1972. Discont.

Winchester Model 20 Single Shot Hammer Gun. . . $235
Takedown. .410 bore. 2½-inch chamber. 26-inch barrel, full choke. Checkered pistol-grip stock and forearm. Weight: about 6 pounds. Made from 1919 to 1924.

Winchester Model 21 Custom, Pigeon, Grand American
Since 1959, the Model 21 has been offered only in deluxe models: Custom, Pigeon, Grand American—on special order. General specifications same as for Model 21 standard models, except these custom guns have full fancy American walnut stock and forearm with fancy checkering, finely polished and hand-smoothed working parts, etc.; engraving inlays, carved stocks and other extras are available at additional cost. Made from 1960 to date.
Custom Grade . . . . **$ 6,000**
Pigeon Grade **8,000**
Grand American **12,500**

Winchester Model 21 Double Barrel Field Gun
Hammerless. Box lock. Automatic safety. Double triggers or selective single trigger, selective or non-selective ejection (all postwar Model 21 shotguns have selective single trigger and selective ejection). Gauges: 12, 16, 20. Barrels: raised matted rib or vent rib; 26-, 28-, 30-, 32-inch, the latter in 12 gauge only; full choke, improved modified, modified, improved cylinder, skeet chokes. Weight: 7½ pounds, 12 ga. w/30-inch barrel; about 6½ pounds, 16 or 20 ga. w/28-inch barrel. Pistol- or straight-grip stock, regular or beavertail forend, both checkered. Made 1930 to 1958.
With double trigger, non-selective ejection **$2140**
With double trigger, selective ejection **2350**
With selective single trigger, non-selective ejection **2500**
With selective single trigger, selective ejection . . . **2695**
Extra for ventilated rib **500**

Winchester Model 21 Duck Gun
Same general specifications as Model 21 Field Gun, except chambered for 12 gauge 3-inch shells, 30- or 32-inch barrels only, full choke, selective single trigger, selective ejection, pistol-grip stock with recoil pad, beavertail forearm, both checkered. Discont. 1958.
With matted-rib barrels **$2950**
With ventilated-rib barrels **3200**

Winchester Model 21 Skeet Gun
Same general specifications as Model 21 Standard, except has 26- or 28-inch barrels only, skeet chokes No. 1 and 2, Bradley red bead front sight, selective single trigger, selective ejection, nonauto safety, checkered pistol- or straight-grip stock without buttplate or pad (wood butt checkered), checkered beavertail forearm. Discont. 1958.
With matted-rib barrels **$3225**
With ventilated-rib barrels **4200**

Winchester Model 24

Winchester Model 25

Winchester Model 21 Trap Gun
Same general specifications as Model 21 Standard, except has 30- or 32-inch barrels only, full choke, selective single trigger, selective ejection, nonauto safety, checkered pistol- or straight-grip stock with recoil pad, checkered beavertail forearm. Discont. 1958.

With matted-rib barrels	$3575
With ventilated-rib barrels	4200

Winchester Model 23 Side-by-Side Shotgun
Box lock. Single trigger. Automatic safety. Gauges: 12, 20, 28, .410. Barrels: 25½-, 26-, 28-inch with fixed chokes or Winchoke tubes. Weight: 5⅞ to 7 pounds. Checkered American walnut buttstock and forend. Made from 1979 to date for Olin at its Olin-Kodensha facility, Japan.

Classic 23—Gold inlay, Engraved	$1500
Custom 23—Plain receiver, Winchoke system	1275
Heavy Duck 23—Standard	1240
Lightweight 23—Classic Style	1215
Light Duck 23—Standard	1215
Light Duck 23—12 ga. Golden Quail	1500
Light Duck 23—.410 Golden Quail	1650
Custom Set 23—20 & 28 gauge	3560

Winchester Model 24 Hammerless Double $345
Box lock. Double triggers. Plain extractors. Auto safety. Gauges: 12, 16, 20. Barrels: 26-inch improved cylinder/modified; 28-inch modified/full (also improved cylinder/modified in 12 ga. only); 30-inch modified and full in 12 ga. only. Weight: about 7½ pounds, 12 ga. Metal bead front sight. Plain pistol-grip stock, semibeavertail forearm. Made from 1939 to 1957.

Winchester Model 25 Riot Gun $325
Same as Model 25 Standard, except has 20-inch cylinder bore barrel, 12 gauge only. Made from 1949 to 1955.

Winchester Model 25 Slide Action Repeater $325
Hammerless. Solid frame. 12 gauge only. 4-shell tubular magazine. 28-inch plain barrel; improved cylinder, modified or full choke. Weight: about 7½ pounds. Metal bead front sight. Plain pistol-grip stock, grooved slide handle. Made from 1949 to 1955.

Winchester Model 36 Single Shot Bolt Action ... $250
Takedown. Uses 9mm Short or Long shot or ball cartridges interchangeably. 18-inch barrel. Plain stock. Weight: about 3 pounds. Made from 1920 to 1927.

Winchester Model 37 Single Barrel Shotgun
Semi-hammerless. Auto ejection. Takedown. Gauges: 12, 16, 20, 28, .410. Barrel lengths: 28-, 30-, 32-inch in all gauges except .410; 26- or 28-inch in .410; all barrels plain with full choke. Weight: about 6½ pounds, 12 ga. Made from 1937 to 1963.

12 Gauge	$225
28 Gauge	695
Other Gauges	150

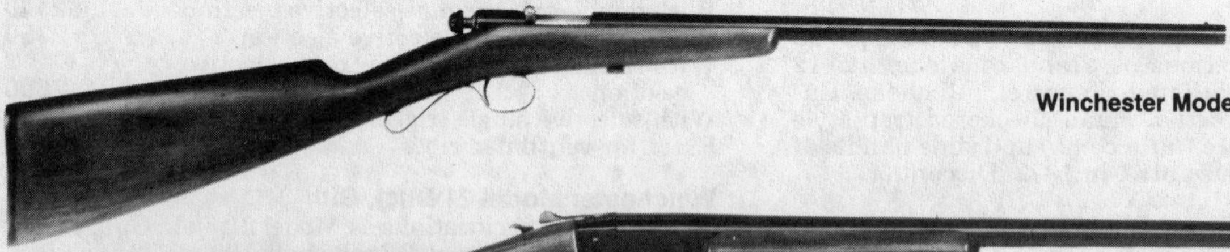

Winchester Model 36

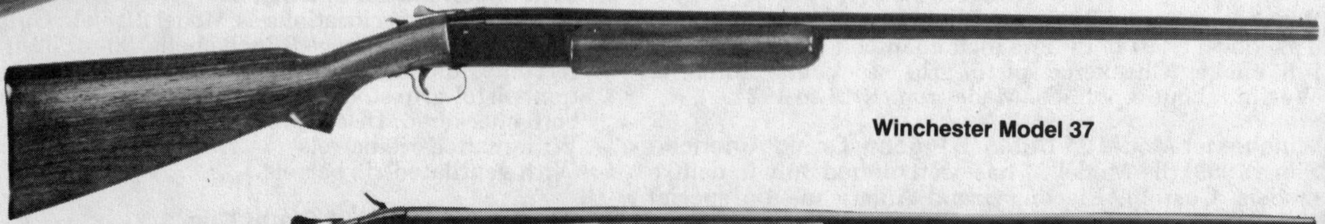

Winchester Model 37

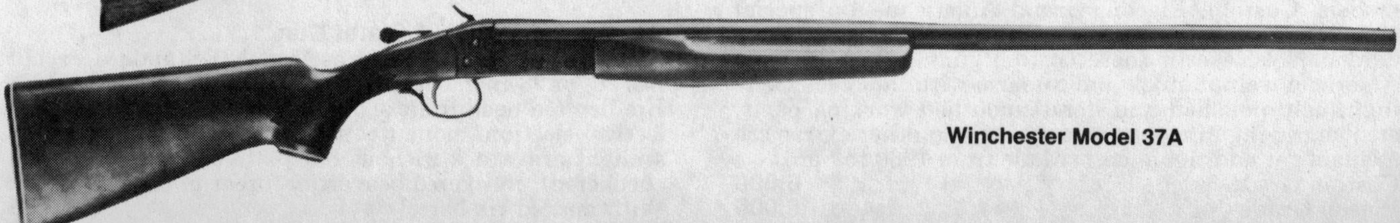

Winchester Model 37A

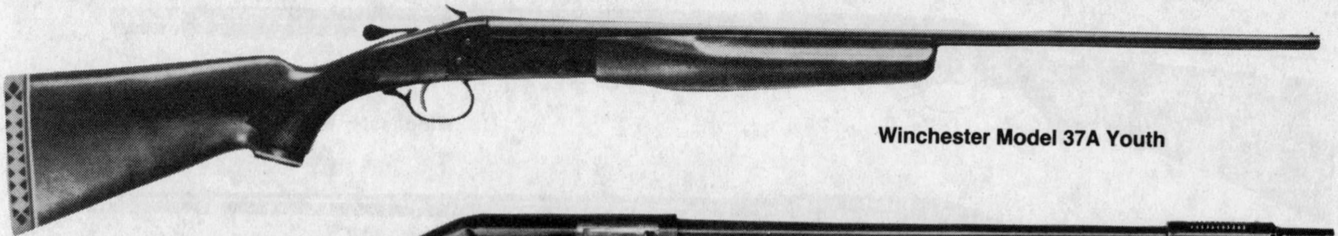

Winchester Model 37A Youth

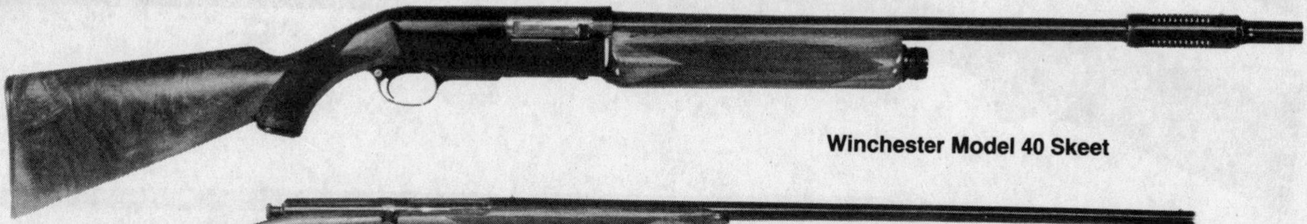

Winchester Model 40 Skeet

Winchester Model 41

Winchester Model 42 Standard Slide Action Repeater

Winchester Model 37A Single Barrel Shotgun . . . $75
Similar to Model 370, except has engraved receiver and gold trigger, checkered pistol-grip stock, fluted forearm; 16 gauge available with 30-inch barrel only. Made from 1973 to 1980.

Winchester Model 37A Youth $90
Similar to Model 370 Youth, except has engraved receiver and gold trigger, checkered pistol-grip stock, fluted forearm. Made from 1973 to 1980.

Winchester Model 40 Skeet Gun $625
Same general specifications as Model 40 Standard, except has 24-inch plain barrel with Cutts Compensator, checkered forearm and pistol grip, grip cap. Made from 1940-41.

Winchester Model 40 Standard Autoloader $500
Streamlined receiver. Hammerless. Takedown. 12 gauge only. 4-shell tubular magazine. 28- or 30-inch barrel; modified or full choke. Weight: about 8 pounds. Bead sight on ramp. Plain pistol-grip stock, semibeavertail forearm. Made 1940-41.

Winchester Model 41 Single Shot Bolt Action . . . $260
Takedown. .410 bore. 2½-inch chamber (chambered for 3-inch shells after 1932). 24-inch barrel, full choke. Plain straight stock standard. Made from 1920 to 1934.

Winchester Model 42 Deluxe $1400
Same general specifications as the Model 42 Standard, except has vent rib, finer finish throughout, hand-smoothed action, engine-turned breech bolt and carrier, stock and extension slide handle of high grade walnut, fancy checkering, stock dimensions to individual specifications. Engraving and carving were offered at extra cost. Made from 1933 to 1963.

Winchester Model 42 Skeet Gun $1495
Same general specifications as Model 42 Standard, except has checkered straight or pistol-grip stock and extension slide handle, 26- or 28-inch matted-rib barrel, skeet choke. *Note:* Some Model 42 Skeet Guns are chambered for 2½-inch shells only. Discont. 1963.

Winchester Model 42 Standard Grade, Matt Rib $1295
Same general specifications as Plain Barrel Model 42, except has solid raised matted rib. Discont. 1963.

Winchester Model 42 Standard Slide Action Repeating Shotgun $640
Hammerless. Takedown. .410 bore (3- or 2½-inch shell). Tubular magazine holds five 3-inch or six 2½-inch shells. 26- or 28-inch plain barrel; cylinder bore, modified or full choke. Weight: about 6 pounds. Plain pistol-grip stock; grooved slide handle. Made from 1933 to 1963.

Winchester Model 50 Field Gun, Vent Rib $375
Same as Model 50 Standard, except has ventilated rib.

Winchester Model 50 Skeet Gun $415
Same as Model 50 Standard, except has 26-inch vent-rib barrel with skeet choke, skeet-style stock of selected walnut.

Winchester Model 50 Standard Grade Autoloader $300
Non-recoiling barrel and independent chamber. Gauges: 12 and 20. 2-shot tubular magazine. Barrels: 12 ga.—26-, 28-, 30-inch; 20 ga.—26-, 28-inch; improved cylinder, skeet, modified, full choke. Checkered pistol-grip stock and forearm. Weight: about 7¾ pounds. Made from 1954 to 1961.

Winchester Model 50 Skeet

Winchester Model 59

Winchester Model 97
Visible Hammer

Winchester Model 50 Trap Gun $525
Same as Model 50 Standard, except 12 gauge only, has 30-inch vent-rib barrel with full choke, Monte Carlo stock of selected walnut.

Winchester Model 59 Autoloading Shotgun $375
12 gauge. Magazine holds two shells. Alloy receiver. Win-Lite steel and fiberglass barrel: 26-inch improved cylinder, 28-inch modified or full choke, 30-inch full choke; also furnished with 26-inch barrel with Versalite choke (interchangeable full, modified, improved cylinder tubes; one supplied with gun). Weight: about 6½ pounds. Checkered pistol-grip stock and forearm. Made from 1959 to 1965.

Winchester Model 97 Riot Gun............... $580
Takedown or solid frame. Same general specifications as standard Model 97, except 12 gauge only, 20-inch cylinder bore barrel. Made from 1897 to 1957.

Winchester Model 97 Trap, Tournament and Pigeon Grade Guns
These higher grade models differ from the standard grade in type and forearm and higher general quality. Discont. 1939.

Trap Gun	**$710**
Tournament Grade	**825**
Pigeon Grade	**995**

Winchester Model 97 Trench Gun $695
Solid frame. Same as Model 97 Riot Gun, except has handguard and is equipped with a bayonet. World War I government issue, 1917—-1918.

Winchester Model 97 Visible Hammer Slide Action Repeating Shotgun $495
Standard Grade. Takedown or solid frame. Gauges: 12 and 16. 5-shell tubular magazine. Barrel: plain; 26 to 32 inches, the latter in 12 ga. only; choked full to cylinder. Weight: about 7¾ pounds (12 ga. with 28-inch barrel). Plain pistol-grip stock, grooved slide handle. Made from 1897 to 1957.

Note: All Winchester Model 101's are mfd. for Olin Corp. at its Olin-Kodensha facility in Tochigi, Japan.

Winchester Model 101 Diamond Grade Target .. $1200
Similar to Model 101 Standard except silvered frame and Winchoke interchangeable choke tubes. Made from 1981 to date.

Winchester Model 101 Field Gun Over/Under
Box lock. Engraved receiver. Auto ejectors. Single selective trigger. Combination barrel selector and safety. Gauges: 12 and 28, 2¾-inch chambers; 20 and .410, 3-inch chambers. Vent-rib barrels: 30- (12 ga. only) and 26½-inch, improved cylinder and modified. Weight: 6¼ to 7¾ pounds depending upon gauge and barrel length. Hand-checkered French walnut stock and forearm. Made 1963 to 1981; gauges other than 12 intro. 1966.

12 and 20 gauge	**$630**
28 and .410 gauge	**700**

Winchester Model 101 Grand European $1200
Similar to Model 101 Pigeon Grade except silvered frame and Winchoke interchangeable choke tubes. Made from 1981 to date.

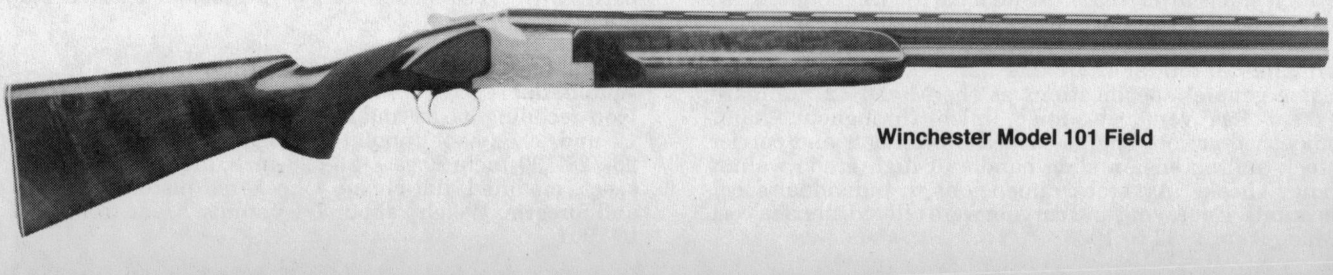

Winchester Model 101 Field

Winchester Model 101 Pigeon Trap Monte Carlo Stock

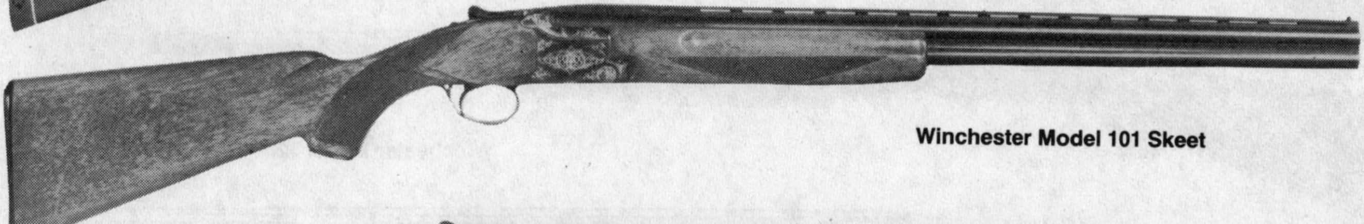

Winchester Model 101 Skeet

Winchester Model 370

Winchester Model 101 Magnum Field Gun $695
Same as Model 101 Field Gun, except chambered for 12 or 20 ga. 3-inch magnum shells only, 30-inch barrels (full/full or modified/full), recoil pad. Made from 1966 to 1981.

Winchester Model 101 Pigeon Grade
Same general specifications as standard Model 101 Field and Skeet, except higher grade with more elaborately engraved satin gray steel receiver, fancier wood and finer checkering. 12 and 20 gauge only. Made 1974 to 1981.
Field Gun **$875**
Skeet Gun **995**
Trap Gun with straight stock **995**
Trap Gun with Monte Carlo stock **1000**

Winchester Model 101 Skeet Gun
Same as Model 101 Field Gun, except skeet-style stock and forearm. Barrels: 12 ga., 26-inch; 20 ga., 26½-inch; 28 and .410 ga., 28-inch; all skeet choked. Made 1966 to 1981.
12 and 20 gauge **$560**
28 and .410 gauge **650**

Winchester Model 101 Waterfowl $895
Similar to Model 101 Magnum Field, except silvered frame and Winchoke interchangeable choke tubes. Made from 1981 to date.

Winchester Model 370 Single Barrel Shotgun $75
Visible hammer. Auto ejector. Takedown. Gauges: 12, 16, 20, 28, .410. 2¾-inch chambers in 16 and 28 gauge, 3-inch in other gauges. Barrels: 12 ga., 30-, 32- or 36-inch; 16 ga., 30- or 32-inch; 20 and 28 ga., 28-inch; .410 bore, 26-inch; all full choke. Weight: 5½ to 6¼ pounds depending upon gauge and barrel. Plain pistol-grip stock and forearm. Made from 1968 to 1973.

Winchester Model 370 Youth $80
Same as standard Model 370, except has 26-inch barrel and 12½-inch stock with recoil pad; 20 gauge with improved modified choke, .410 bore with full choke. Made from 1968 to 1973.

Winchester Model 1200 Deer Gun $160
Same as standard Model 1200, except has special 22-inch barrel with rifle-type sights, for rifled slug or buckshot; 12 gauge only. Weight: 6½ pounds. Made 1965 to 1974.

Winchester Model 1200 Defender Slide Action Security Shotgun $155
Hammerless. 12 and 20 gauge (3-inch chambers). 18-inch barrel. 8-shot capacity. Low-glare blued finish. Weight: 6¾ pounds. Made from 1984 to date by U. S. Repeating Arms.

Winchester Model 1200 Field Gun—Magnum
Same as standard Model 1200, except chambered for 3-inch 12 and 20 gauge magnum shells; plain or vent-rib

SHOTGUNS

Winchester Model 1200 Defender

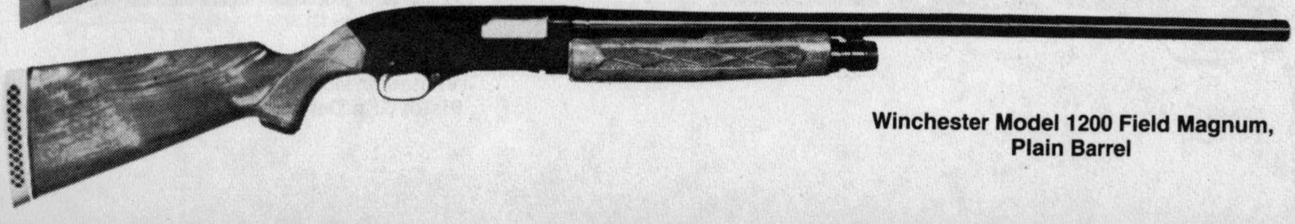

Winchester Model 1200 Field Magnum, Plain Barrel

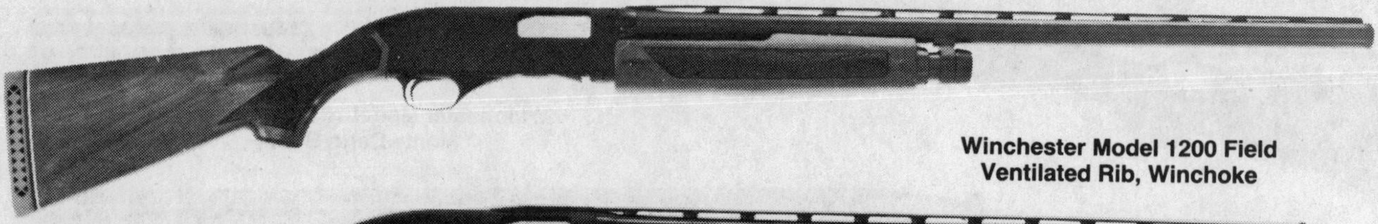

Winchester Model 1200 Field Ventilated Rib, Winchoke

Winchester Model 1200 Skeet

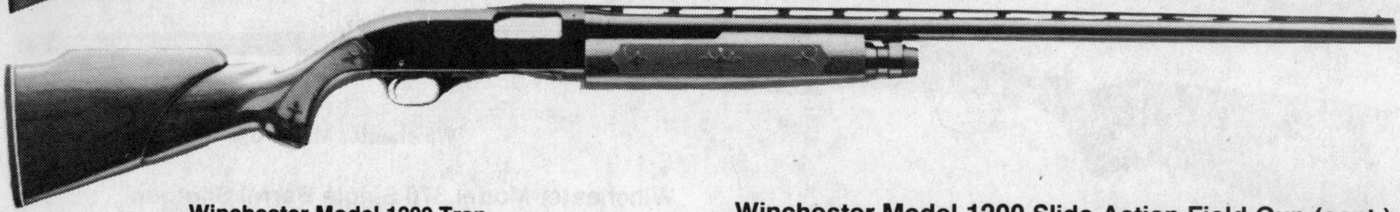

Winchester Model 1200 Trap With Recoil Reduction System

Winchester Model 1200 Field Magnum (cont.)
barrel, 28- or 30-inch, full choke. Weight: 7³/₈ to 7⁷/₈ pounds. Made 1964 to 1983.
With plain barrel **$165**
With ventilated-rib barrel **175**
Add for Winchester Recoil Reduction System **50**

Winchester Model 1200 Pistol Grip Defender ... $155
Same general specifications as standard Model 1200, except has 18-inch barrel, 7-shot magazine and pistol grip. Mfd. by U. S. Repeating Arms.

Winchester Model 1200 Police $175
Same general specifications as 1200 Defender, except has rifle-type front and rear sights. Stainless-steel barrel and satin chrome finish on all external metal parts.

Winchester Model 1200 Skeet Gun $175
Same as standard Model 1200, except 12 and 20 gauge only; has 2-shot magazine, specially tuned trigger, 26-inch vent-rib barrel skeet choke, semi-fancy walnut stock and forearm. Weight: 7¹/₄ to 7¹/₂ pounds. Made 1965 to 1973. Also avail. 1966-70 with Winchester Recoil Reduction System (add $50 to value).

Winchester Model 1200 Slide Action Field Gun
Front-locking rotary bolt. Takedown. 4-shot magazine. Gauges: 12, 16, 20 (2³/₄-inch chamber). Barrel: plain or vent rib; 26-, 28-, 30-inch; improved cylinder, modified,

Winchester Model 1200 Slide Action Field Gun (cont.)
full choke, or with Winchoke (interchangeable tubes IC-M-F). Weight: 6¹/₂ to 7¹/₄ pounds. Checkered pistol-grip stock and forearm (slide handle), recoil pad; also available 1966-70 with Winchester Recoil Reduction System (Cycolac stock). Made 1964 to 1983.
With plain barrel **$175**
With ventilated-rib barrel **200**
Add for Winchester Recoil Reduction System **50**
Add for Winchoke **25**

Winchester Model 1200 Stainless $260
Same as standard Model 1200 Defender, except has stainless-steel barrel and special bright chrome finish on external metal parts.

Winchester Model 1200 Trap Gun
Same as standard Model 1200, except 12 gauge only. Has 2-shot magazine, 30-inch vent-rib barrel, full choke or 28-inch with Winchoke. Semi-fancy walnut stock, straight or Monte Carlo trap style. Weight: about 8¹/₄ pounds. Made 1965 to 1973. Also available 1966-70 with Winchester Recoil Reduction System.
With straight-trap stock **$275**
With Monte Carlo stock **325**
Add for Winchester Recoil Reduction System **50**
Add for Winchoke **25**

Winchester Model 1300 CamoPack $325
Gauge: 12. 3-inch Magnum. 5-shot magazine. Barrels: 30- and 22-inch with Winchoke system. Weight: 7 pounds. Laminated stock with Win-Cam camouflage green, cut checkering, recoil pad, swivels and sling. Made from 1987.

Winchester Model 1200 Pistol Grip Defender

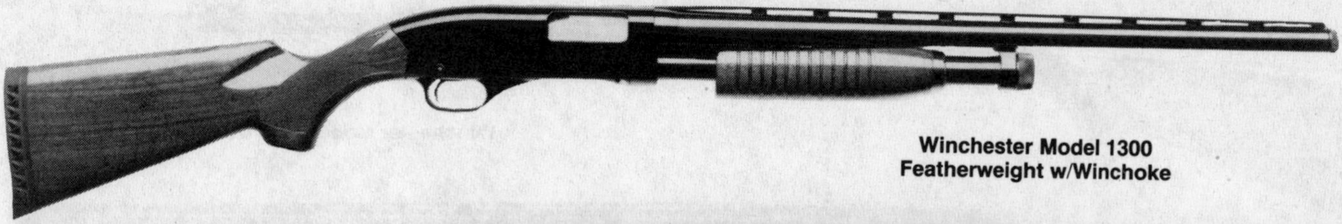

Winchester Model 1300
Featherweight w/Winchoke

Winchester Model 1300 Turkey
Win-Cam Shotgun

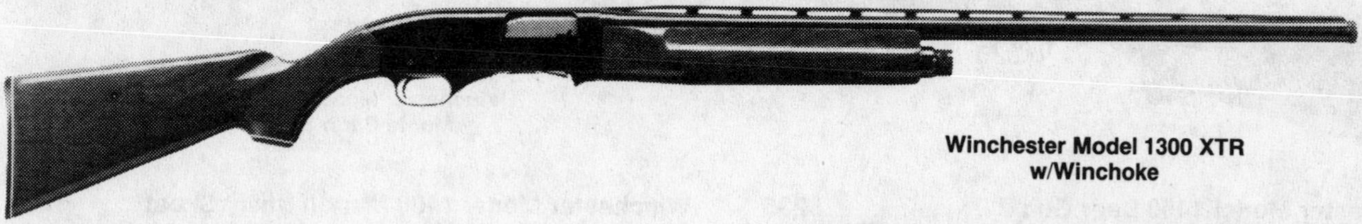

Winchester Model 1300 XTR
w/Winchoke

Winchester Model 1300 Deer Gun **$225**
Same as standard Model 1300, except has special $24\frac{1}{8}$-inch barrel with rifle-type sights, for rifled slug or buckshot; 12 gauge only. Weight: $6\frac{1}{2}$ pounds.

Winchester Model 1300 Featherweight Slide Action Shotgun **$275**
Hammerless. Takedown. 4-shot magazine. Gauges: 12 and 20 (3-inch chambers). Barrel: 22-inch vent rib. Weight: $6\frac{3}{8}$ pounds. Checkered walnut buttstock, rib slide handled. Made from 1985 to date.

Winchester Model 1300 Turkey Slide Action Shotgun **$245**
Same general specifications as Model 1300 Featherweight, except low-luster finish on walnut stock and forearm; non-glare matte finish on receiver, barrel and exterior metal surfaces.

Winchester Model 1300 Turkey Win-Cam **$295**
Same as Model 1300 CamoPack, except has only one 22-inch barrel. Made from 1987 to date.

Winchester Model 1300 Waterfowl Slide Action Shotgun **$275**
Same general specifications as Model 1300 Featherweight, except 30-inch barrel. Weight: 7 pounds. Made from 1985 to date.

Winchester Model 1300 XTR Slide Action **$295**
Hammerless. Takedown. 4-shot magazine. Gauges: 12 and 20 (3-inch chambers). Barrel: plain or vent rib; 28-inch barrels; Winchoke (interchangeable tubes IC-M-F). Weight: about 7 pounds.

> *Note:* Model 1400 shotguns were available in left-hand versions (ejection port and safety on left side), with values the same as for right-hand models.
> In 1968, Model 1400 was replaced by Model 1400 Mark II, which is the same gun with an improved action release and restyled checkering on stock and forearm. Winchester dropped the "Mark II" designation in 1972; however, to distinguish between the two types, it has been retained in the following listings. Until 1973, the Mark II shotguns were available in left-hand versions (ejection port and safety on left side), with values the same as for right-hand models.

Winchester Model 1400 Automatic Field Gun
Gas-operated. Front-locking rotary bolt. Takedown. 2-shot magazine. Gauges: 12, 16, 20 ($2\frac{3}{4}$-inch chamber). Barrel: plain or vent rib; 26-, 28-, 30-inch; improved cylinder, modified, full choke, or with Winchoke (interchangeable tubes IC-M-F). Weight: $6\frac{1}{2}$ to $7\frac{1}{4}$ pounds. Checkered pistol-grip stock and forearm, recoil pad; also available with Winchester Recoil Reduction System (Cycolac stock). Made 1964 to 1968.
With plain barrel **$225**
With ventilated-rib barrel **245**
Add for Winchester Recoil Reduction System **50**
Add for Winchoke **25**

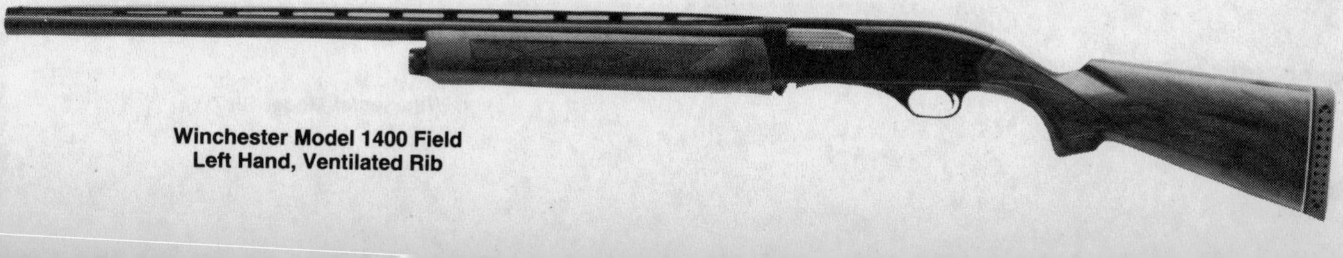

Winchester Model 1400 Field
Left Hand, Ventilated Rib

Winchester Model 1400 Deer Gun

Winchester Model 1400 Mark II
Ventilated Rib, Winchoke

Winchester Model 1400 Trap
Monte Carlo Stock

Winchester Model 1400 Deer Gun $235
Same as standard Model 1400, except has special 22-inch barrel with rifle-type sights, for rifle slug or buckshot; 12 gauge only. Weight: 6½ pounds. Made 1965 to 1968.

Winchester Model 1400 Mark II Deer Gun $265
Same general specifications as Model 1400 Deer Gun. Made from 1968 to 1973.

Winchester Model 1400 Mark II Field Gun
Same general specifications as Model 1400 Field Gun, except not chambered for 16 gauge; Winchester Recoil Reduction System not available after 1970; only 28-inch barrels with Winchoke furnished after 1973. Made from 1968 to 1978.
With plain barrel $225
With plain barrel and Winchoke 245
With ventilated-rib barrel 255
With ventilated-rib barrel and Winchoke 275
Add for Winchester Recoil Reduction System 50

Winchester Model 1400 Mark II Skeet Gun $330
Same general specifications as Model 1400 Skeet Gun. Made from 1968 to 1973.

Winchester Model 1400 Mark II Trap Gun
Same general specifications as Model 1400 Trap Gun, except also furnished with 28-inch barrel and Winchoke. Winchester Recoil Reduction System not available after 1970. Made from 1968 to 1973.
With straight stock $330
With Monte Carlo stock 350
Add for Winchester Recoil Reduction System 50
Add for Winchoke 25

Winchester Model 1400 Mark II Utility Skeet $225
Same general specifications as Model 1400 Mark II Skeet Gun, except has stock and forearm of field grade walnut. Made from 1970 to 1973.

Winchester Model 1400 Mark II Utility Trap $250
Same as Model 1400 Mark II Trap Gun, except has Monte Carlo stock and forearm of field grade walnut. Made from 1970 to 1973.

Winchester Model 1400 Skeet Gun $250
Same as standard Model 1400, except 12 and 20 gauge only, 26-inch vent-rib barrel, skeet choke, semi-fancy walnut stock and forearm. Weight: 7¼ to 7½ pounds. Made from 1965 to 1968. Also available with Winchester Recoil Reduction System (add $50 to value).

Winchester Model 1400 Trap Gun
Same as standard Model 1400, except 12 gauge only with 30-inch vent-rib barrel, full choke. Semi-fancy walnut stock, straight or Monte Carlo trap style. Also available with Winchester Recoil Reduction System. Weight: about 8¼ pounds. Made 1965 to 1968.
With straight stock $325
With Monte Carlo stock 360
Add for Winchester Recoil Reduction System 50

Winchester Model 1500 XTR Semiautomatic . . . $295
Gas-operated. Gauges: 12 and 20 (2¾-inch chambers). Barrel: plain or vent rib; 28-inch; Winchoke (interchangeable tubes IC-M-F). American walnut stock and forend; checkered grip and forend. Weight: 7¼ pounds.

Winchester Model 1887

Winchester Model 1901

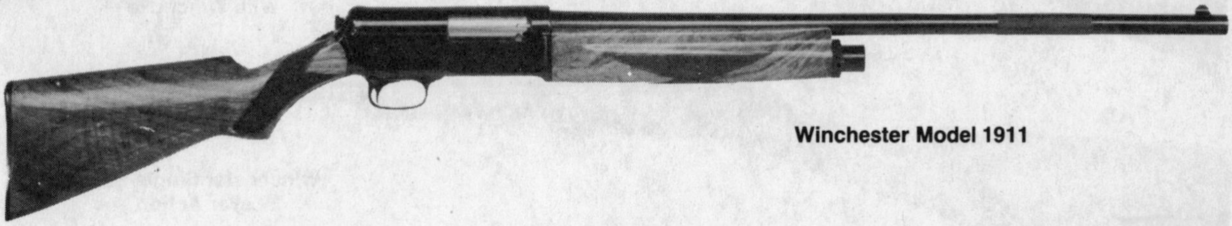

Winchester Model 1911

Winchester Model 1887 Lever Action Repeater $600
Solid frame. Gauges: 10 and 12; 4-shot tubular magazine. Plain barrel; 30- and 32-inch, full choke. Plain pistol-grip stock and forend. Weight: 9 pounds, 10 ga.; 8 pounds, 12 ga. (*Note:* This model was also offered in Deluxe Grade with Damascus barrel, checkered stock and forend.) Made from 1887 to 1901.

Winchester Model 1901 Lever Action Repeater $750
Same general specifications as Model 1887 of which this is a redesigned version. 10 gauge only. Made 1901 to 1920.

Winchester Model 1911 Autoloading Shotgun . . $375
Hammerless. Takedown. 12 gauge only. 4-shell tubular magazine. Barrels: plain, 26- to 32-inch, standard borings. Weight: about 8½ pounds. Plain or checkered pistol-grip stock and forearm. Made from 1911 to 1925.

Winchester Pistol Grip Stainless Marine $175
Same general specifications as standard Model 1200, except has 18-inch barrel, 6-shot magazine and pistol grip. Mfd. by U. S. Repeating Arms.

Winchester Pistol Grip Stainless Police $175
Same general specifications as standard Model 1200, except has 18-inch barrel, 6-shot magazine and pistol grip. Mfd. by U. S. Repeating Arms.

Winchester Quail Special O/U Small Frame . . . $1650
Same Specifications as small-frame Model 101, except in 28 and .410 ga. with 3-inch chambers. 25½-inch barrels with choke tubes (28 ga.) or mod./full chokes (.410). Imported from Japan in 1987.

Winchester Ranger Combination Shotgun $210
Same as Ranger Deer Combination, except has one 28-inch vent-rib barrel with modified choke and one 18-inch Police cylinder bore. Made from 1987 to date.

Winchester Ranger Deer Combination $210
Gauge: 12; 3-inch Magnum. 3-shot magazine. Barrels: 24-inch cylinder bore deer barrel and 28-inch ventilated rib barrel with Winchoke system. Weight: 7¼ pounds. Made from 1987 to date.

Winchester Ranger Semiautomatic $195
Gauges: 12, 20. 2-shot magazine. 28-inch vent-rib barrel with full choke. Overall length: 48⅝ inches. Weight: 7 to 7¼ pounds. Walnut finish, hardwood stock and forearm with cut checkering. Made from 1984 to date by U. S. Repeating Arms.

Winchester Ranger Semiauto Deer Shotgun $195
Same general specifications as Ranger Semiautomatic, except 24⅛-inch plain barrel with rifle sights. Mfd. by U. S. Repeating Arms.

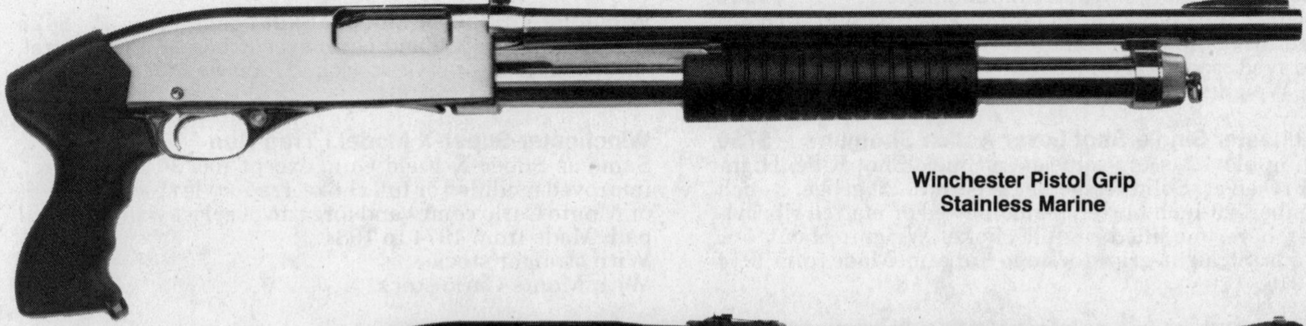

Winchester Pistol Grip Stainless Marine

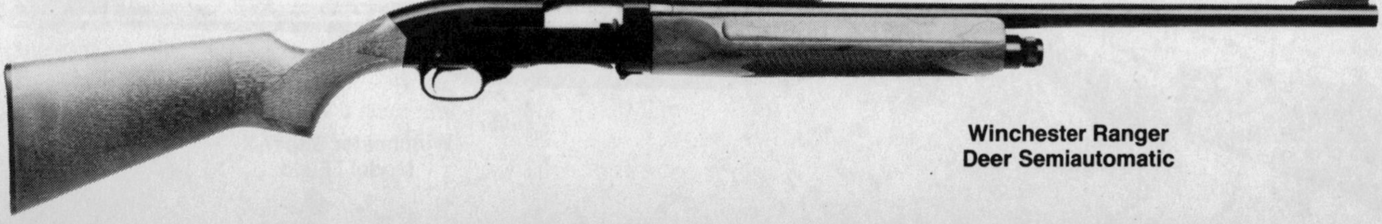

Winchester Ranger Deer Semiautomatic

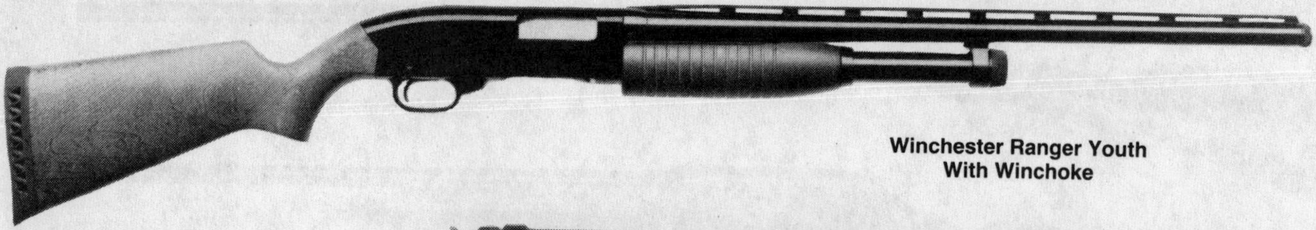

Winchester Ranger Youth With Winchoke

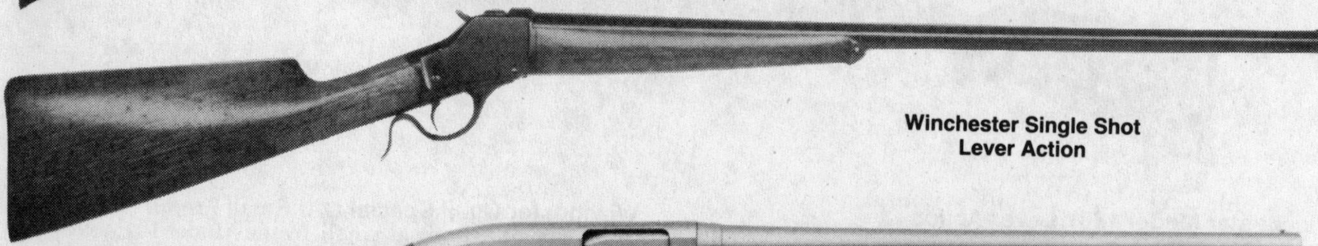

Winchester Single Shot Lever Action

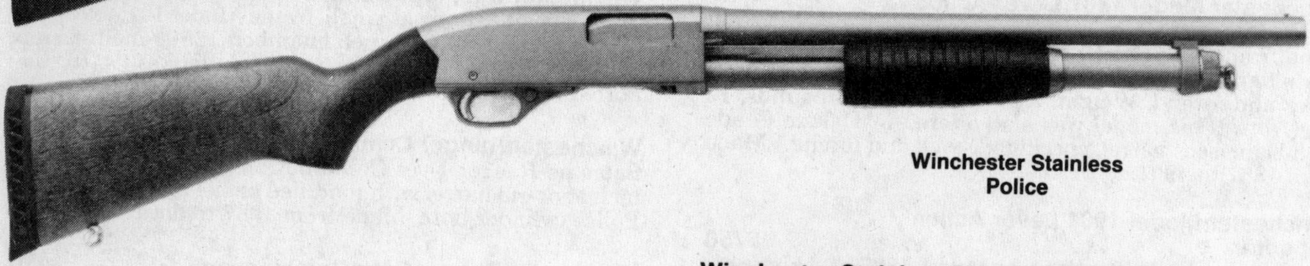

Winchester Stainless Police

Winchester Ranger Slide Action Shotgun $170
Hammerless. 12 and 20 gauge; 3-inch chambers. Walnut finished hardwood stock, ribbed forearm. 28-inch ventilated-rib barrel; Winchoke system. Weight: 7¼ pounds. Made from 1982 to date by U. S. Repeating Arms.

Winchester Ranger Youth Slide Action $160
Same general specifications as standard Ranger Slide Action except chambered for 20 gauge only, has 4-shot magazine, recoil pad on buttstock and weighs 6½ pounds. Mfd. by U. S. Repeating Arms.

Winchester Shotgun/Rifle Combination $1550
12-gauge Winchoke barrel on top and rifle barrel chambered for 30-06 on bottom (over/under). 25-inch barrels. Engraved receiver. Hand checkered walnut stock and forend. Weight: 8½ pounds. Mfd. for Olin Corp. in Japan.

Winchester Single Shot Lever Action Shotgun .. $750
Falling-block action, same as in Single Shot Rifle. Highwall receiver. Solid frame or takedown. 20 gauge. 3-inch chamber. 26-inch barrel; plain, matted or matted rib; cylinder bore, modified or full choke. Weight: about 5½ pounds. Straight-grip stock and forearm. Made from 1914 to 1916.

Winchester Stainless Marine Slide Action Security Shotgun $260
Hammerless. 12 gauge only. 18-inch barrel of ordnance stainless steel. 7-shot capacity. Weight: 7 pounds. Made from 1984 to date by U. S. Repeating Arms.

Winchester Stainless Police Slide Action Security Shotgun $260
Hammerless. 12 gauge only. 18-inch ordnance stainless steel barrel accommodates gas launchers. Rifle-type front and rear sights. Made from 1984 to date by U. S. Repeating Arms.

Winchester Super-X Model I Auto Field Gun $360
Gas-operated. Takedown. 12 gauge. 2¾-inch chamber. 4-shot magazine. Barrels: vent rib; 26-inch improved cylinder; 28-inch modified or full; 30-inch full choke. Weight: about 7 pounds. Checkered pistol-grip stock and forearm. Made from 1974 to 1984.

Winchester Super-X Model I Skeet Gun $425
Same as Super-X Field Gun, except has 26-inch barrel, skeet choke, skeet-style stock and forearm of select walnut. Made from 1974 to 1984.

Winchester Super-X Model I Trap Gun
Same as Super-X Field Gun, except has 30-inch barrel, improved modified or full choke, trap-style stock (straight or Monte Carlo comb) and forearm of select walnut, recoil pad. Made from 1974 to 1984.
With straight stock **$360**
With Monte Carlo stock **425**

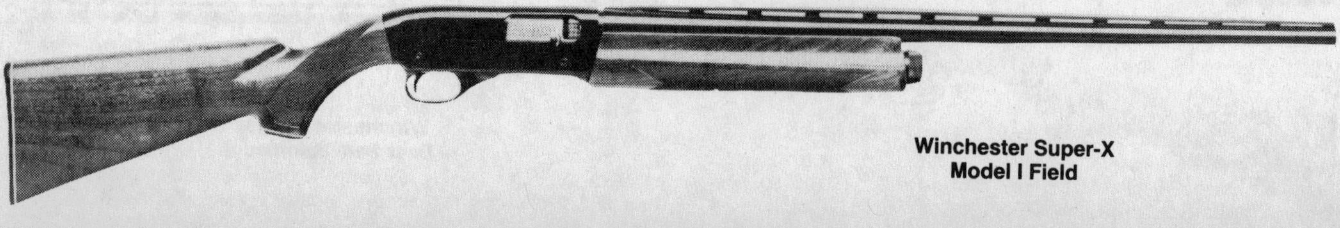

Winchester Super-X Model I Field

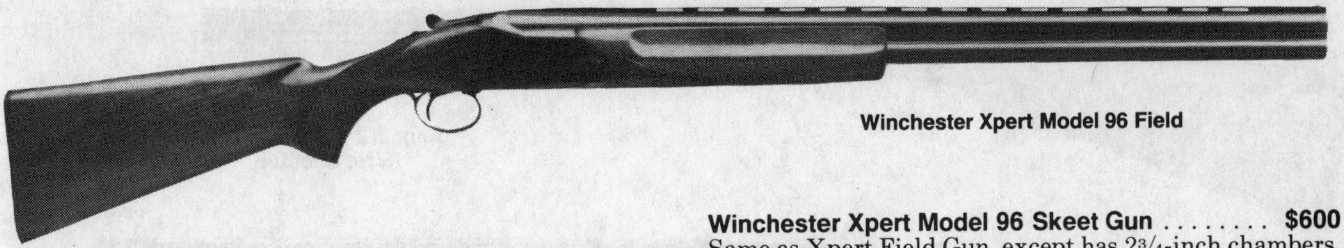

Winchester Xpert Model 96 Field

Winchester Xpert Model 96 O/U Field Gun $575
Boxlock action similar to Model 101. Plain receiver. Auto ejectors. Selective single trigger. Gauges: 12, 20. 3-inch chambers. Barrels: vent rib; 26-inch improved cylinder/modified; 28-inch modified/full; 30-inch both full choke (12 ga. only). Weight: $6\frac{1}{4}$ to $8\frac{1}{4}$ pounds depending upon gauge and barrels. Checkered pistol-grip stock and forearm. Made 1976 to 1981 for Olin Corp. at its Olin-Kodensha facility in Japan.

Winchester Xpert Model 96 Skeet Gun $600
Same as Xpert Field Gun, except has $2\frac{3}{4}$-inch chambers, 27-inch barrels, skeet choke, skeet-style stock and forearm. Made 1976 to 1981.

Winchester Xpert Model 96 Trap Gun
Same as Xpert Field Gun, except 12 gauge only, $2\frac{3}{4}$-inch chambers, has 30-inch barrels, improved modified/full or both full choke, trap-style stock (straight or Monte Carlo comb) with recoil pad. Made 1976 to 1981.
With straight stock **$580**
With Monte Carlo stock **595**

Woodward Single Barrel Trap

Woodward Under-and-Over
Special Trap Grade

Woodward Best Quality
Under-and-Over

JAMES WOODWARD & SONS
London, England

The business of this firm was acquired by James Purdey & Sons after World War II.

Woodward Best Quality Hammerless Double
Side lock. Automatic ejectors. Double triggers or single trigger. Built to order in all standard gauges, barrel lengths, boring and other specifications; made as a field gun, pigeon and wildfowl gun, skeet gun or trap gun. Manufactured prior to World War II.
With double triggers **$18,000**
With single trigger **19,000**

Woodward Best Quality Single Barrel Trap ... $14,000
Side lock. Mechanical features of the Under and Over Gun. Ventilated-rib barrel. 12 gauge only. Built to customers' specifications. Made prior to World War II.

Woodward Best Quality Under-and-Over Shotgun
Side lock. Automatic ejectors. Double triggers or single trigger. Built to order in all standard gauges, barrel lengths, boring and other specifications, including Special Trap Grade with ventilated rib. Woodward introduced this type of gun in 1908. Made until World War II. See listing of Purdey Over-and-Under Gun.
With double triggers **$24,500**
Single trigger, extra **1000**

ANGELO ZOLI
Mississauga, Ontario, Canada

Angelo Zoli Alley Cleaner S/S Shotgun $495
Gauges: 12 and 20. 20-inch barrel. $26\frac{1}{2}$ inches overall. Weight: 7 pounds average. Chokes: full/mod., full, imp. mod., mod., imp. cyl., skeet. Chrome-lined barrels. Walnut stock and engraved action. Made from 1986 to 1987.

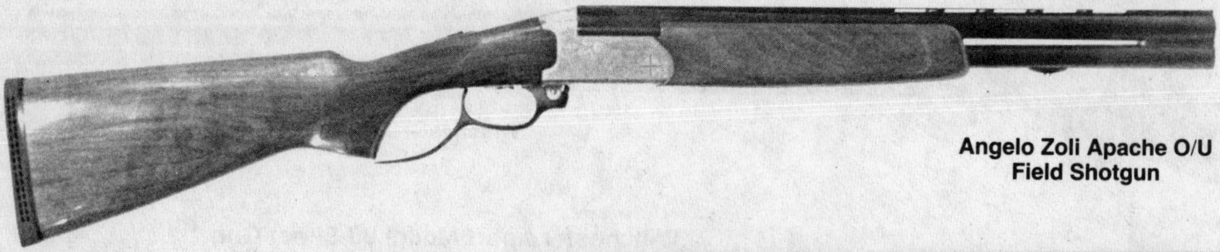

Angelo Zoli Apache O/U Field Shotgun

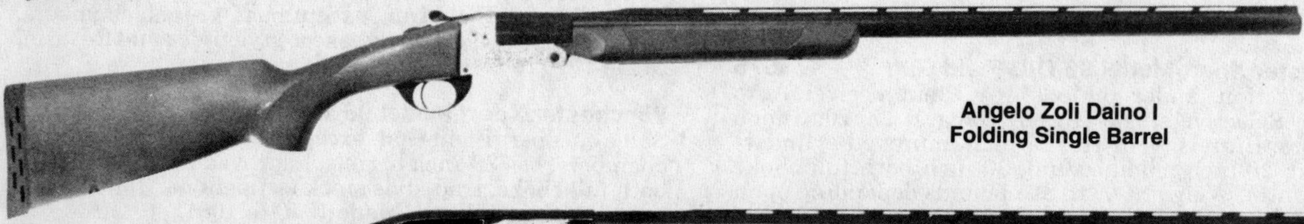

Angelo Zoli Daino I Folding Single Barrel

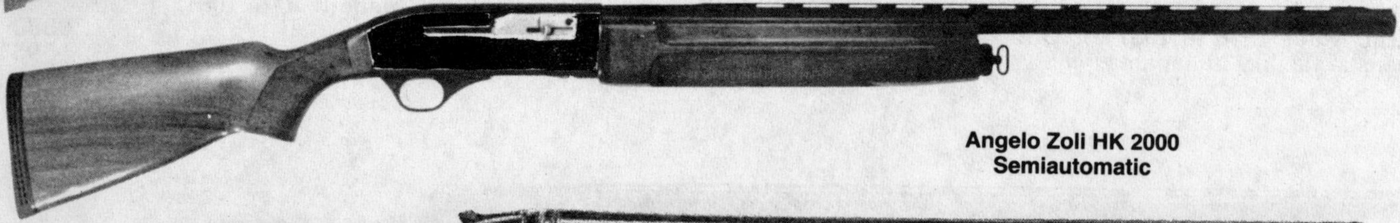

Angelo Zoli HK 2000 Semiautomatic

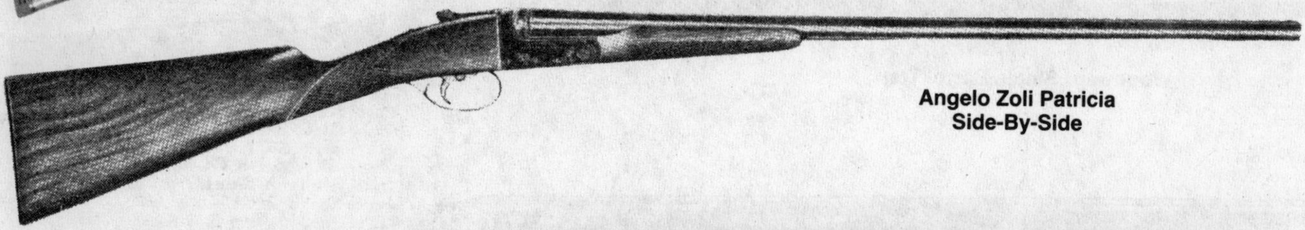

Angelo Zoli Patricia Side-By-Side

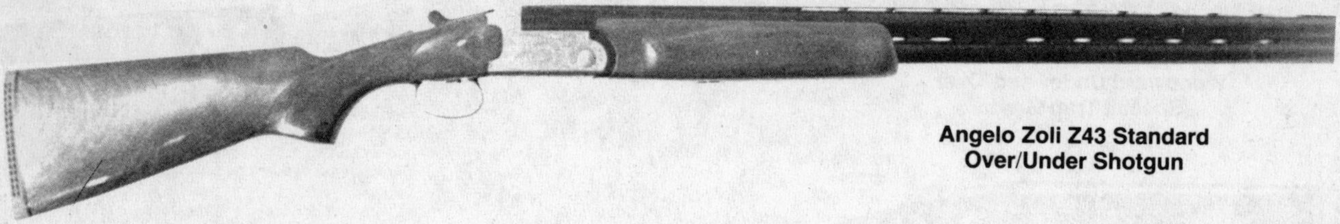

Angelo Zoli Z43 Standard Over/Under Shotgun

Angelo Zoli Apache O/U Field Shotgun $395
Gauge: 12. Chokes: full/mod., full, imp. mod., mod., imp. cyl., skeet. 20-inch barrel. Short ventilated rib. Weight: 7½ pounds. Checkered walnut stock and forearm. Lever action. Pistol grip. Made from 1986 to 1988.

Angelo Zoli Daino I Folding Single Barrel $95
Gauges: 12, 20 and .410. 28- or 30-inch barrel. Weight: 6 pounds average. Choke: full. Chrome-lined barrel, ventilated rib. Walnut stock with pistol grip. Engraved action. Made from 1986 to 1988.

Angelo Zoli HK 2000 Semiautomatic Shotgun . . . $410
Gauge: 12. 5-shot capacity. Barrels: 24-, 26-, 28- and 30-inch. Weight: 6½ to 7½ pounds. Ventilated rib. Checkered walnut stock and forearm. Glossy finish. Pistol grip. Engraved receiver. Made 1988.

Angelo Zoli Patricia Side-by-Side Shotguns . . . $1008
Gauge: .410 only. 28-inch barrel. Choke: full/mod. Weight: 5½ lbs. Automatic ejectors; Zoli single selective trigger,

Angelo Zoli Patricia Side-by-Side Shotguns (cont.)
box lock. Hand-checkered walnut stock with English straight grip, splinter forearm. Made from 1986 to 1988.

Angelo Zoli Saint George O/U Competition Trap Combo $770
Gauge: 12. 30- and 32-inch barrels. Weight: 8 pounds. Ventilated rib, single selective trigger. Oil-finished, pistol grip walnut stock. Made from 1986 to 1988.

Angelo Zoli Silver Snipe Over/Under Shotgun . . $600
Purdey-type box lock with crossbolt. Selective single trigger. Gauges: 12, 20; 3-inch chambers. Barrels: 26-, 28- or 30-inch with a variety of choke combinations. Weight: 5¾ to 6¾ pounds. Checkered European walnut buttstock and forend. Made in Italy.

Angelo Zoli Z43 Standard O/U Shotgun $395
Gauge: 12 or 20. 26-, 28- or 30-inch barrels. Chokes: full/mod., mod./imp. cyl. Weight: 6¾ to 8 pounds. Ventilated lateral ribs, standard extractors,, single non-selective trigger. Glossy-finished walnut stock and forearm. Automatic safety. Made from 1986 to 1988.

INDEX